The Invention of the White Race

The Invention
of the White Race

The Origin of Racial Oppression

THEODORE W. ALLEN

VERSO
London • New York

This one-volume edition published by Verso 2021
Introduction to the 2021 edition © Jeffrey B. Perry 2021

Volume One: Racial Oppression and Social Control
Second edition published by Verso 2012
First published by Verso 1994
© Theodore W. Allen 1994
Introduction to the second edition and appendices M and N
© Jeffrey B. Perry 2012

Volume Two: The Origin of Racial Oppression in Anglo-America
Second edition published by Verso 2012
First published by Verso 1997
© Theodore W. Allen 1997
Introduction to the second edition and appendices G and H
© Jeffrey B. Perry 2012

1 3 5 7 9 10 8 6 4 2

Verso
UK: 6 Meard Street, London W1F 0EG
US: 20 Jay Street, Suite 1010, Brooklyn, NY 11201
versobooks.com

Verso is the imprint of New Left Books

ISBN-13: 978-1-83976-392-2
ISBN-13: 978-1-83976-393-9 (UK EBK)
ISBN-13: 978-1-83976-394-6 (US EBK)

British Library Cataloguing in Publication Data
A catalogue record for this book is available from the British Library

Library of Congress Cataloging-in-Publication Data
A catalog record for this book is available from the Library of Congress

Typeset in Times New Roman
Printed and bound by CPI Group (UK) Ltd, Croydon CR0 4YY

Contents

Volume One: Racial Oppression and Social Control

Acknowledgements   vii
Introduction to the 2021 Edition   ix
Introduction to the Second Edition   xv
Introduction   1

1. The Anatomy of Racial Oppression   27
2. Social Control and the Intermediate Strata: Ireland   52
3. Protestant Ascendancy and White Supremacy   71
4. Social Control: From Racial to National Oppression   91
5. Ulster   115
6. Anglo-America: Ulster Writ Large   136
7. The Sea-change   159
8. How the Sea-change was Wrought   177

Appendices   201
Chronological Finding Aid   263
Notes   265
Index   334

Volume Two: The Origin of Racial Oppression in Anglo-America

Lists of Figures and Tables and a Note on Dates   i
Introduction to the Second Edition   ii

Part One. Labor Problems of the European Colonizing Powers

1. The Labor Supply Problem: England a Special Case   3
2. English Background, with Angle-American Variations Noted   14
3. Euro-Indian Relation and the Problem of Social Control   30

Part Two. The Plantation of Bondage

4. The Fateful Addiction to "Present Profit"   49
5. The Massacre of the Tenantry   75
6. Bricks without Straw: Bondage, but No Intermediate Stratum   97

Part Three. Road to Rebellion

  7. Bond-labor: Enduring …   119

  8. … and Resisting   148

  9. The Insubstantiality of the Intermediate Stratum   163

10. The Status of African-Americans   177

Part Four. Rebellion to Reaction

11. Rebellion – and Its Aftermath   203

12. The Abortion of the "White Race" Social Control System in
      the Anglo-Caribbean   223

13. The Invention of the White Race – and the Ordeal of America   239

Appendices   261

Notes   298

Index   388

Acknowledgements

This work began as a spark of intuition in the charged ambience of the civil rights struggles of the 1960s. I am therefore above all inspired by that movement and its ongoing forms, and spurred on by the reminders of the "dream deferred" that I see every day in the generations of my Brooklyn neighbors.

Many individuals and institutions have assisted me during the decades spent working on this book. Space allows specific mention of only a few.

First, I acknowledge my obligation to two fellow proletarian intellectuals, Charles Johnson and William Carlotti, who cleared away ideological barnacles left from my previous moorings, and taught me to say, as Carlotti did, "I am not 'white'."

Jeffrey Babcock Perry – himself a historian and the biographer of Hubert Henry Harrison – has throughout been the individual most intimately acquainted with the development of the book's argument. He has been as ready to offer helpful criticism as the work progressed, as to defend its basic themes in the forum. As personal friend he has stood by me through the vicissitudes of my reckless domestic economy, as well as in my bouts with not always user-friendly computers. If this work had brought me nothing more, to have made such a friend would be reward enough.

It is to the hospitality of my beloved friend Dr. Edward Harden Peeples, of Richmond, veteran civil rights battler, that I am forever indebted for the opportunity to conduct my months of research of the Virginia records of the seventeenth and early eighteenth centuries.

I have been the beneficiary of the kind disinterested assistance of a legion of library-staff persons, including, but not limited to those of the following institutions: Alderman Library, University of Virginia; Cornell University Olin Library; the New York Historical Society; New York Public Library, Research Libraries; New York University Bobst Library and Law Library; and the Virginia State Library, Archives Division. I take this opportunity to express my gratitude to, and my affection for, the Brooklyn Public Library, my resource of first resort. I am obliged to BPL, not only for the regular services it provides, despite a decade and more of budget cuts, but for convenient access to the great store of individual titles, serials, periodicals, and microfilms, which it maintains from acquisitions of more prosperous times.

Though I have not been a part of the academic scene, a number of historians and others in that world have taken the time to offer me their criticisms at various stages of the work. I am grateful to them all, and particularly to Peter Bohmer, Michael Farrell, Gwen Midlo Hall, Noel Ignatiev, David Slavin, John W. Smit, James Turner, and, especially to Peter H. Wood for his detailed early-stage commentary. On their behalf, I enter a disclaimer of responsibility for the faults of the work, for which I alone am accountable.

My thanks go to Michael Sprinker for his initiative in promoting my book as a publishing prospect, and for his support and suggestions as the writing progressed. I cannot adequately express my appreciation to Pat Harper, the Verso copy-editor to whom the manuscript for the first volume of this work was assigned. By her patience and perseverance, and her willingness to shoulder a burden beyond that for which she would normally be obligated, Pat caused important clarifications to be made at various points of the manuscript.

Two generous grants – from the Rabinowitz Foundation and from Charles Knight, respectively – buoyed me up at critical moments as I paddled my way toward completion of the work. I hope the grantors will find their confidence in me justified at last.

Finally, I thank the Vidinha-Rothenhausen group who sustained me with unreflecting love.

Introduction to the 2021 Edition

Theodore W. Allen's *The Invention of the White Race* was first published by Verso Books in two volumes subtitled *Racial Oppression and Social Control* (1994) and *The Origin of Racial Oppression in Anglo-America* (1997). These volumes were succeeded by their expanded editions, which I oversaw and contributed Notes and Introductions to in 2012. Since then, interest in Allen's work has continued to grow, and in 2018 his papers were placed with the Special Collections and University Archives at the University of Massachusetts Amherst Libraries, where they are available to the public, and a portion are online.[1]

This 2021 consolidated edition combines both volumes in a single book with the pagination of each previous volume maintained. It also contains corrections, a consolidated table of contents, and this new Introduction. I am extremely pleased that Verso Books, through the efforts of editor Ben Mabie, has agreed to this new edition.

In the near decade since the publication of the last edition of *Invention*, struggles against white supremacy have surged to the forefront of national political life. The concepts that Allen labored on – such as "white skin privilege," the origin of racial oppression, and the histories of capitalism, class struggle, and racial slavery – are increasingly important today. His work is an indispensable resource for making sense of our present situation. The significance of combining both volumes in one book should not be underestimated.

A careful reader will immediately detect some striking differences between Allen's use of certain keywords and the language of many contemporary scholars and activists. Based on feedback I have received from people who have read *Invention* and/or heard one or more of my over one hundred presentations on Allen, I offer the following comments to readers of this new composite edition.

1. "White Identity" and the "White Race" as a Ruling Class Social Control Formation

Allen stresses that "the logic of 'race as a social construct' must be tightened and the focus sharpened" and "the 'white race' must be understood, not simply as a social construct [rather than a genetic phenomenon], but as a *ruling class social control formation*."[2] He also points out that "laboring-class European-Americans in the continental plantation colonies showed little interest in 'white identity' before the institution of the system of 'race' privileges at the end of the seventeenth century."[3]

2. The Use of "Origin" of "Racial Oppression" in Allen's Titles and Analysis

These terms are particularly prominent in the subtitles of Volume One, *Racial Oppression and Social Control*, and Volume Two, *The Origin of Racial Oppression in Anglo-America*. Allen tried to be precise with his wording, and this was especially the case for the subtitle of Volume Two. He chose the word "Origin" (singular), not "Origins," and "Racial Oppression," not "Racism," in that subtitle. He did this because he understood the invention of the "white" race and the origin of racial oppression in the late seventeenth- and early eighteenth-century Anglo-American plantation colonies, most particularly in the pattern-setting Virginia colony, to be crucial to U.S. history and to have their origin in class struggle.

He also explained, "My book is not about, and does not pretend to be about 'racism.' It is about the white race, – the true 'peculiar institution' – its origin and its modus operandi, as the more general form of class collaboration in continental Anglo-America during both its colonial and its regenerate United States form." To this he added, "I generally avoid the use of the self-standing word, 'racism,' on account of the ruinous ambiguity [that] white supremacists have managed to give it."[4]

3. "Whiteness" and "Race"

Allen's volumes offer a detailed historical materialist interpretation of "the invention of the white race" and of "racial oppression." His books are not about "whiteness" or the misleading term "race." He places "whiteness" in quotes because he shied away from the term. As he explained, "It's an abstract noun, it's an abstraction, it's an attribute of some people, it's not the role they play."[5]

He also writes:

By considering "racial oppression" in terms of the substantive, the operative element, namely "oppression," it is possible to avoid the contradictions and howling absurdities that result from attempts to splice genetics and sociology. By examining "racial oppression" as a particular system of oppression – like gender oppression or class oppression or national oppression – we find firmer footing for analyzing racial slavery and the invention and peculiar function of the "white race," and for confronting the theory that racial oppression can be explained in terms of "phenotype" [physical appearance] – "the old ace-in-the hole of racist apologetics."[6]

4. Capitalist (Not Racial Capitalist) Relations of Production in the Virginia Colony in 1618

Allen describes capitalist relations of production in Jamestown in the period before Africans arrived in the pattern-setting Virginia colony and before the establishment (later in the century) of a system of racial oppression and "the invention of the white race." He writes that "at the close of the 1610–1618 period … It was to be a capitalist farming system in Virginia."[7]

This point is important because, if we understand the Virginia plantations as agricultural capitalism, and the plantation owners as capitalists, then we are better able to understand enslaved Black laborers as proletarians (as both Hubert Harrison and W. E. B. Du Bois would later do). This enables us to tear the covers off "white" labor's betrayals of Black labor; to learn many important lessons of "labor history;" and to understand the origin of the invention of the "white race" – all of which have great importance for today.

5. The 1619 Controversy

In his "Notes for an interview on the Tom Pope Show," Allen writes:

> When the first Africans arrived in Virginia in 1619, there were no "white" people there. Others living in the colony at that time were English; they had been English when they left England, and naturally they and their Virginia-born children were English, they were not "white."[8]

Regarding 1619, Allen emphasizes:

> Historians are cautioned to avoid the vice of "presentism," that is, the assignment of motivations for behavior to suit current vogues without proof that those motivations actually figured in the needs and feelings of the people in the historic period under consideration. One common example of this error is that of casually classing Negroes in colonial Anglo-America as "slaves" from the first mention in 1619 on, decades before there is any justification in the record for such a generalization.[9]

6. "White Indentured Servants and Negro Slaves"

This phrase does not describe the laborers of Virginia before Bacon's Rebellion. Allen describes conditions in pre–Bacon's Rebellion (1676–77) as ones in which Europeans were not "white," the great majority of European laborers had not signed "indentures" (chattelization was imposed upon them), and Africans were not "slaves" (the system of lifetime, hereditary, chattel bond-servitude, or racial slavery, in Virginia was imposed later).

7. These European and African Chattel Bond-Laborers, Who Could Be Bought and Sold, Were Not "Settler Colonialists."

Allen writes:

> In all, some 92,000 European immigrants were bought to Virginia and Maryland between 1607 and 1682, the great majority being sent to Virginia. More than three-quarters of them were chattel bond-laborers, the great majority of them English. In 1676, it was [Virginia] Governor [William] Berkeley's estimate that about 1,500 European chattel bond-laborers were then arriving in Virginia yearly, "the majority English, with a few Scots and fewer Irish."[10]

He later adds, "Of the 30,000 Europeans who came to the Chesapeake region between 1680 and 1699, we may assume that 24,000 were bond-laborers. In a roughly equivalent period, 1674–1700, around 6,000 African bond-laborers were imported."[11]

It is important to understand that these European and African chattel bond-laborers, who could be bought and sold, were not "settler colonialists."

8. "White Privilege"

The term "white privilege" is a concept that Allen had pioneered and deployed long before writing this book. Already in the mid-1960s, Allen emphasized that these privileges were a "poison bait" and they "do not permit" the masses of European American workers nor their children "to escape" from that class. "It is not that the ordinary white worker gets more than he must have to support himself," but "the black worker gets less than the white worker." By thus "inducing, reinforcing and perpetuating racist attitudes on the part of the white workers, the present-day power masters get the political support of the rank-and-file of the white workers in critical situations, and without having to share with them their super profits in the slightest measure."[12]

As one example, to support his position he would provide statistics showing that in the South where race privilege "has always been most emphasized ... the white workers have fared worse than the white workers in the rest of the country."[13]

Probing more deeply, Allen explained why these race privileges are conferred by the ruling class. He pointed out that "the ideology of white racism" is "not appropriate to the white workers" because it is "contrary to their class interests." Because of this "the bourgeoisie could not long have maintained this ideological influence over the white proletarians by mere racist ideology." Under these circumstances white supremacist thought is "given a material basis in the form of the deliberately contrived system of race privileges for white workers."[14]

Allen added, "The white supremacist system that had originally been designed in around 1700 by the plantation bourgeoisie to protect the base, the chattel bond labor relation of production" also served "as a part of the 'legal and political' superstructure of the United States government that, until the Civil War, was dominated by the slaveholders with the complicity of the majority of the European-American workers." Then, after emancipation, "the industrial and financial bourgeoisie found that it could be serviceable to their program of social control, anachronistic as it was, and incorporated it into their own 'legal and political' superstructure."[15]

He felt that two essential points must be kept in mind: First, "the race-privilege policy is deliberate bourgeois class policy." Second, "the race-privilege policy is, contrary to surface appearance, contrary to the interests, short range as well as long range interests of not only the Black workers but of the white workers as well." He repeatedly emphasized that "the day-to-day real interests" of the European American worker "is not the white skin privileges, but in the development of an ever-expanding union of class-conscious workers."[16]

Throughout his work Allen emphasizes "that the initiator and the ultimate guarantor of the white skin privileges of the white worker is not the white worker, but the white worker's masters," and the masters do this because it is "an indispensable necessity for their continued class rule."[17] He describes how

an all-pervasive system of racial privileges was conferred on laboring-class European-Americans, rural and urban, *exploited and insecure though they themselves were*. Its threads, woven into the fabric of every aspect of daily life, of family, church, and state, have constituted the main historical guarantee of the rule of the "Titans," damping down anti-capitalist pressures, by making "race, and not class, the distinction in social life." That, more than any other factor, has shaped the contours of American history – from the Constitutional Convention of 1787 to the Civil War, to the overthrow of Reconstruction, to the Populist Revolt of the 1890s, to the Great Depression, to the civil rights struggle and 'white backlash' of our own day.[18]

Based on his research Allen wrote, "History has shown that the white-skin privilege does not serve the real interests of the white workers, it also shows that the concomitant racist ideology has blinded them to that fact." He emphasized, "'Solidarity forever!' means 'Privileges never!'"[19]

Jeffrey B. Perry
Summer 2021

Notes

1 On the Theodore W. Allen Papers see http://scua.library.umass.edu/umarmot/allen-theodore-w-1919-2005.

2 See Volume One of this work, p. 235.

3 Ibid., p. 240.

4 Theodore W. Allen, "Ted Allen's reply to Judith Levine's VLS (September 1994) review of the Invention of the White Race, Volume One," Theodore W. Allen Papers (hereafter, TWAP), September 6, 1994, Box 10: 70.

5 See Theodore W. Allen, interview by Chad Pearson, Part 1, May 13, 2004, minutes 30:14–31:22, http://www.albany.edu/talkinghistory/arch2004jan-june.html; and Volume One of this work, p. 332 n. 18.

6 Volume One of this work, p. 28.

7 Volume Two of this work, p. 60.

8 September 8, 2000, TWAP, Box 11: 102.

9 Volume One of this work, p. 9.

10 Volume Two of this work, p. 119.

11 Ibid., p. 218.

12 Theodore W. Allen, "The Kernel and Meaning: A Critique of Labor Historiography," TWAP, ca. 2000–2005, Box 9: 32; and Ted (Theodore W.) Allen, "Can White ~~Workers~~ Radicals Be Radicalized?," in Noel Ignatin (Ignatiev) and Ted (Theodore W.) Allen, *"White Blindspot" and "Can White ~~Workers~~ Radicals Be Radicalized?"* (Detroit: Radical Education Project and New York: NYC Revolutionary Youth Movement, 1969), p. 15.

13 Allen, "Can White ~~Workers~~ Radicals Be Radicalized?" p. 15.

14 Theodore W. Allen, "The Most Vulnerable Point" (paper presented at the Conference of Eastern and Midwestern Shop and Community Organizers, Loveland, OH, October 20, 1972), pp. 3–4, Special Collections and University Archives, University of Massachusetts Amherst Libraries, https://credo.library.umass.edu/view/pageturn/mums1021-s02-i013/#page/1/mode/1up.

15 Theodore W. Allen, "Commentary on István Mészáros's *Beyond Capital*," *Cultural Logic*, 12 (2005), n. 19, at https://ojs.library.ubc.ca/index.php/clogic/issue/view/182859.

16 Allen, "The Most Vulnerable Point," p. 4; and Allen, "Can White ~~Workers~~ Radicals Be Radicalized?," p. 15.

17 Allen, "Can White ~~Workers~~ Radicals Be Radicalized?," p. 16.

18 Allen, "Summary of the Argument of *The Invention of the White Race, Cultural Logic*, Vol. 2 (1998), p. 17 at https://ojs.library.ubc.ca/index.php/clogic/issue/view/182876.

19 Allen, "Can White ~~Workers~~ Radicals Be Radicalized?," p. 18.

Introduction
to the Second Edition

Theodore W. Allen's *The Invention of the White Race,* with its focus on racial oppression and social control, is one of the twentieth century's major contributions to historical understanding. This two-volume classic, first published in 1994 and 1997, presents a full-scale challenge to what Allen refers to as "The Great White Assumption" – "the unquestioning, indeed unthinking acceptance of the 'white' identity of European-Americans of all classes as a natural attribute rather than a social construct." Its thesis on the origin and nature of the "white race" contains the root of a new and radical approach to U.S. history, one that challenges master narratives taught in the media and in schools, colleges, and universities. With its equalitarian motif and emphasis on class struggle, it speaks to people today who strive for change worldwide. Its influence on our understanding of American, African-American, and labor history will continue to grow in the twenty-first century.

Readers of the first edition of *The Invention of the White Race* were startled by Allen's bold assertion on the back cover: "When the first Africans arrived in Virginia in 1619, there were no 'white' people there; nor, according to the colonial records, would there be for another sixty years." That statement, based on twenty-plus years of research in Virginia's colonial records, reflected the fact that Allen found "no instance of the official use of the word 'white' as a token of social status" prior to its appearance in a Virginia law passed in 1691. As he later explained, "Others living in the colony at that time were English; they had been English when they left England, and naturally they and their Virginia-born children were English, they were not 'white.' White identity had to be carefully taught, and it would be only after the passage of some six crucial decades" that the word "would appear as a synonym for European-American."

Allen was not merely speaking of word usage, however. His probing research led him to conclude – based on the commonality of experience and demonstrated solidarity between African-American and European-American laboring people; the lack of a substantial intermediate buffer social-control stratum; and the indeterminate status of African-Americans – that the "white race" was not, and could not have been, functioning in early Virginia.

It is in the context of such findings that he offers his major thesis – the "white race" was invented as a ruling-class social-control formation in response to labor solidarity as manifested in the later, civil-war stages of Bacon's Rebellion (1676–77). To this he adds two important corollaries: 1) the ruling elite, in its own class interest, deliberately instituted a system of racial privileges to define and maintain the "white race"; and 2) the consequences were not only ruinous to the interests of African-Americans, they were also "disastrous" for European-American workers, whose class interests differed fundamentally from those of the ruling elite.

In developing these theses Allen challenges the two main ideological props of white supremacy – the notion that "racism" is innate, and it is therefore useless to struggle against it, and the argument that European-American workers benefit from "white race" privileges and that it is in their interest not to oppose them and not to oppose white supremacy.

His challenge to these convictions is both historical and theoretical. Allen offers the meticulous use of sources, a probing analysis of " 'Racial Oppression and Social Control" (the subtitle of this volume), and an important comparative study that includes analogies, parallels, and contrasts between the Anglo-American plantation colonies, Ireland, and the Anglo-Caribbean colonies. He chooses these examples, all subjected to domination by ruling Anglo elites, in order to show that racial oppression is "not dependent upon differences of 'phenotype'" (skin color, etc.) and that social-control factors impact how racial oppression begins, is maintained, and can be transformed.

The Invention of the White Race is Allen's magnum opus – he worked on it for over twenty years. Its second volume, subtitled *The Origin of Racial Oppression in Anglo-America*, rigorously details the invention of the "white race" and the development of racial slavery, a particular form of racial oppression, in late seventeenth- and early eighteenth-century Virginia. He claimed, with justification, that the second volume "contains the best of me."

A major purpose for his writing Volume I was to lay the conceptual groundwork for Volume II, free of what he refers to as the "White Blindspot" – the hindered vision caused by the "historically omnipresent factor of white supremacism in United States history" that W. E. B. Du Bois "warned us about in *Black Reconstruction*." To work free of that blind spot, Allen uses the approach in Volume I of "looking into an Irish mirror for insights into the nature of racial oppression and its implication for ruling-class social control in the United States."

Allen begins his wide-ranging first volume by offering a critical examination of the two main historiographical positions on the slavery and racism debate. He addresses and strongly criticizes the psycho-cultural approach, and he seeks to free the socio-economic approach from certain weaknesses. He then proceeds, using that "mirror of Irish history," to develop a definition of racial oppression in terms of social control; a definition that is "free of the howling absurdities of 'phenotype,' or classification by complexion." In the process, Allen offers compelling analogies between the oppression of the Irish in Ireland (under Anglo-Norman rule and under "Protestant Ascendancy") and white supremacist oppression of African-Americans and Indians. He also shows the relativity of race by examining the sea-change in which Irish haters of racial oppression in Ireland were transformed into "white American" defenders of racial slavery and racial oppression in the US.

In the course of his treatment Allen emphasizes that maximizing profit and maintaining social control are two priorities of the ruling class. He also offers a comparison of the different outcomes of "Catholic Emancipation" (outside of Ulster) in Ireland and "Negro Emancipation" in America. The difference centers upon what group is the key component incorporated into the ruling class's intermediate social-control stratum to serve its interests. In Ireland (outside of Ulster) it was the Catholic bourgeoisie; in the United States it was the "white race," composed primarily of laboring people who were not promoted out of their class. The first outcome, in which members of the oppressed group are incorporated into the social-control stratum, he describes as national oppression. The second outcome, in which members of the oppressed group are excluded from the social-control stratum and denied normal class mobility, he describes as racial oppression.

In discussing the topics of this volume's subtitle, *Racial Oppression and Social Control*, Allen emphasizes that racial oppression is one form of ruling-class response to the problem of social control; national oppression is another. He describes the hallmark of racial oppression as "the reduction of all members of the oppressed group to one undifferentiated social status, beneath that of any member of the oppressor group." He identifies its four common defining characteristics as: a) declassing legislation, directed at property-holding members of the oppressed group; b) the deprivation of civil rights; c) the outlawing of literacy; and d) the displacement of family rights and authorities.

With stunning international and domestic examples, Allen shows how racial oppression (particularly in the form of religio-racial oppression) was developed and maintained by the phenotypically similar British against the Irish Catholics in Ireland; how the phenotypically similar Anglo bourgeoisie established national oppression in the Anglo-Caribbean and racial oppression in the continental Anglo-American plantation colonies; how racial oppression was transformed into national oppression due to ruling-class social control needs in Ireland (while racial oppression was maintained in Ulster); how the same people who were victims of racial oppression in Ireland became "white American" defenders of racial oppression; and how in America racial oppression took the form of racial slavery, yet when racial slavery ended racial oppression remained and was reconstituted in a new form.

The Invention of the White Race is a compelling work that re-examines centuries of history. It also offers Allen's glimpse of "the future in the distance."

When he completed Volume II fifteen years ago, he ended by describing "unmistakable signs of maturing social conflict" between the "common people" and the "Titans." He suggested that "Perhaps, in the impending ... struggle," influenced by the "indelible stamp of the African-American civil rights struggle of the 1960s," the "white-skin privileges may finally come to be seen and rejected by laboring-class European-Americans as the incubus that for three centuries has paralyzed their will in defense of their class interests *vis-à-vis* those of the ruling class." It was with that prospect in mind, that Theodore W. Allen wrote *The Invention of the White Race*.

In an effort to assist readers and to encourage meaningful engagement with Allen's work, I offer a few contributions in this new edition of *The Invention of the White Race* Vol. I: *Racial Oppression and Social Control*. First, minor corrections based mostly on Allen's notes have been incorporated. Second, two new appendices have been added: Appendix M: "A Brief Biography of Theodore W. Allen" (p. 231); and Appendix N: "Notes to Encourage Engagement with *The Invention of the White Race*, Volume I" (p. 239), which can be used for classes, study groups, and individual readings. Finally, a new and expanded index is provided at the end of this volume.

Jeffrey B. Perry
2012

Introduction

In this Introduction I criticize freely both "friend and foe", even as I have drawn upon their research and insights to a great and obvious extent. I have tried to remain aware that any unfairness could only weaken my own argument. I ask indulgence for only one assumption, namely, that while some people may desire to be masters, all persons are born equally unwilling and unsuited to be slaves.

In the broad division of historians into "psycho-cultural" and "socio-economic" groups as I have defined them, I, of course, belong with the socio-economic category – with them, but not altogether of them. I have tried to show that one cannot rest content with the socio-economic case as it now stands, because of serious compromising ambiguities and inconsistencies in it. This book is intended as a contribution toward freeing the socio-economic thesis of such weaknesses.

The doing of it, however, has led me to cast the argument in a new conceptual mold. I approach racial slavery as a particular form of *racial oppression*, and racial oppression as a sociogenic – rather than a phylogenic – phenomenon, homologous with gender and class oppression. Second, in considering the phenomenon of racial slavery I focus primarily not on *why* the bourgeoisie in continental Anglo-America had recourse to that anachronistic form of labor, slavery, but rather on *how* they could establish and maintain for such a long historical period that degree of *social control* without which no motive of profit or prejudice could have had effect.

I believe that the thesis here presented – of the origin and nature of the so-called "white race," the quintessential "Peculiar Institution"[1] – contains the root (from the seed planted by W.E.B. DuBois's *Black Reconstruction*) of a general theory of United States history, more consistent than others that have been advanced. Only by understanding what was peculiar about the Peculiar Institution can one know what is exceptionable about American Exceptionalism; know how, in normal times, the ruling class has been able to operate without "laborite" disguises; and know how, in critical times, democratic new departures have been frustrated by *re*inventions of the "white race".

1

The Search for Beginnings

The liberating impulses set loose by World War Two, and the impact of the United States civil rights movement in particular brought official society for the first time in American history to acknowledge racism to be an evil in itself. Addressing itself to the problem of the nation's social policy, the presidential commission appointed in the wake of a number of insurrectionary anti-white-supremacy urban outbreaks of recent years concluded:

> Few appreciate how central the problem of the Negro has been to our social policy. Fewer still understand that today's problems can be solved only if white Americans comprehend the rigid social, economic, and educational barriers that have prevented Negroes from participating in the mainstream of American life.[2]

It was in this context that racial slavery became the central preoccupation not only of African-American historians, but of American historians in general. It had long been a truism of our social sciences that the historical roots of racism were traceable to the slave system. But that was a proposition that quickly deteriorated into a pointless tautology: European-Americans deny equal place to African-Americans today because European-Americans denied equal place to African-Americans in slavery times. This tautology could no longer be reconciled with a national consciousness in what some have ventured to call the Second Reconstruction.[3] If racism was an evil, historians were impelled to question the tautology, to examine the basis on which it rested, to understand not only that racism and slavery were connected, but to study the nature of that connection more deeply than before. What were the roots of the tautology, how did the imposition of lifetime hereditary bond-servitude, the quintessential denial of equal place to African-Americans, begin?

Striking parallels were to be seen between patterns of history and its interpretation. Just as consideration of the injustices imposed on African-Americans had for half a century been confined within the constitutional lines of the "equal-but-separate" doctrine, so European-American historians generally dealt with the subject of African-American bond-labor on the basis of an unchallenged assumption of a natural instinct for "racial" domination.[4] Just as the constitutional principle of racial segregation was challenged by Oliver Brown of Topeka and by Rosa Parks of Montgomery, the African-Caribbean historian Eric Williams challenged his profession with the proposition that "Slavery was not born of racism; rather racism was the consequence of slavery."[5] Just as Brown and Parks sent shock waves deep into the foundations of United States society, so did the Williams idea evoke a convulsive controversy in the field of American historiography.[6] Just as the forces of racism rallied on the "white-man's-country" premises of the United States constitution to produce the Wallace movement, self-servingly called a "white backlash," so from the ranks of American historians there emerged a cohort of defenders of the basic validity of the old assumption of "natural" racism. Like the slaveholders who absolved themselves by putting the blame on evil British ancestors, or like those who today excuse their own defense of white-race privileges by noting that their ancestors never owned slaves, this avowedly "anti-liberal" contingent revels in condemning as "racism" every reference to "anti-blackness" that antedates the founding of Jamestown, the first permanent English settlement in America, in 1607, and then concludes on that ground that regrettably there is little, if anything, they or anyone else can do to change it. And just as in time the political scene came to be dominated by those who celebrate the battles won but forget that the war is just begun, so some historians claimed to rediscover a symbiosis of democratic freedoms and racial slavery.

The Origins Debate

In 1950, in an article published in the *William and Mary Quarterly*, Oscar and Mary Handlin planted the Williams banner most appropriately on continental Anglo-American soil, particularly that of seventeenth-century Virginia and Maryland. The Handlins argued that African-American laborers during the first four decades after their arrival, that is, up until 1660, were not lifetime hereditary bondmen and bondwomen; rather, their status was essentially the same as that of European-American bond-laborers, namely limited-term bond-servitude. Furthermore, the Handlins maintained, when a difference in the treatment of African-American and European-American laborers did emerge, it was by deliberately contrived ruling-class policy, rather than as the outcome of some inborn or preconditioned "race consciousness." The Handlins also briefly noted that in England's Caribbean island colonies, in contrast to those on the continent, the pattern of "race" privileges for "white" laborers, free or bond, did not develop. The root of this difference, they said, was the scarcity of land on which a free, or prospectively free, person of even modest means might subsist.[7]

The basic historical fact upon which the Handlins rested their thesis – the non-slave status of African-Americans in early Virginia – had long been established in the opinion of a number of the most eminent scholars in that field.[8] And at least one, John H. Russell, in 1913, charged that to contend otherwise was to make apology for the slave system.[9]

The Handlins therefore were renewing an old debate, but one whose time had come. Its implications for the rising anti-racism cause were of the utmost significance. If racism was historically prior and the oppression of the African-American was derivative, then the shadow of "natural racism" was cast over the prospect. On the other hand, if racism was derivative of ill-treatment of African-Americans in the form of slavery, then the hope was encouraged that

racism could be eliminated from present-day American society by establishing
equality for African-Americans. As Winthrop D. Jordan, who would emerge as
one of the two foremost opponents of the Handlin thesis, put it: "If whites and
Negroes could share the same status of half freedom for forty years in the
seventeenth century, why could they not share full freedom in the twentieth?"[10]

The Psycho-cultural Argument

The issue began its evolution into a major controversy with the appearance in
1959 of an article by Carl N. Degler, "Slavery and the Genesis of American
Race Prejudice," and a published exchange of letters with the Handlins in the
following year.[11] In 1971 Degler elaborated his views in a book comparing
social attitudes toward race and prejudice in Brazil and in the United States of
America.[12] In 1962 Winthrop Jordan took his stand with Degler in "Modern
Tensions and the Origins of American Slavery." In a series of subsequent
journal articles, Jordan defended and developed the anti-Handlin argument.
Then, in 1968, his main work appeared under the title *White over Black:
American Attitudes Toward the Negro, 1550–1812.*[13]

Although Degler and Jordan deeply wished it otherwise, they were
convinced all along that there was practically no possibility that "whites and
Negroes could share full freedom in the twentieth" or any other century. "It is
my conviction," said Degler, "that blacks will be ... discriminated against
whenever nonblacks have the power and incentive to do so ... [because] it is
human nature to have prejudice against those who are different."[14] Jordan
understood the concept of race in exclusively genetic terms. He argued that
"races are incipient species," but that the prevalence of interbreeding makes
the full development of different race-species "very unlikely." Even so, he was
convinced, and his study of "historical experience" confirmed his belief, that
the white man's "blackness within" constitutes an insuperable barrier to
finding "a way out of [racist] degradation."[15]

From the time of the first Degler article, the argument over the origin of
slavery has been enriched by the contributions of scores of scholars
representing the two fundamental lines of analysis: the Williams–Handlin
socio-economic approach and the Degler–Jordan psycho-cultural approach.

Whether they avowed or merely tacitly accepted the gloomy Degler and
Jordan premises, historians on the psycho-cultural side of the issue quite
logically emphasized those aspects of the record that might serve to indicate
that prior to 1660 African-Americans in Virginia and Maryland were held in
a bondage and contempt worse even than that inflicted on the European-
American bond-laborers. They also drew support from the works of pre-
controversy historians who had tended to the opinion that in continental

Anglo-America the status of African-Americans was not significantly different in 1619 from what it was in 1719 or 1819.

Holding that the Handlins had erred by assuming that the subordination of African-American laborers could not have occurred until it was done by positive legislation, the psycho-cultural school easily found sufficient evidence in the records to demonstrate that the matter was at least more complicated than the Handlins had suggested. On the other hand, there was much evidence that in those early decades "Negro" was not simply another word for "slave."[16] Jordan himself was forced to concede that until at least 1640, "There simply is not enough evidence to indicate with any certainty whether Negroes were treated like white servants or not."[17] Small matter; the strategy of the psycho-cultural school would depend not upon direct frontal assault, but upon encirclement and inferential attack from the rear.

If racial discrimination were the consequence of slavery, said Carl Degler, then how could one account for the differences in the treatment of free African-Americans and of free African-Brazilians? Since both emerged from an initial condition of slavery, why was there a racist rejection in one case, and an assimilationist and positive attitude in the other? Why did Brazil provide an "escape hatch" of social mobility for the free African-Brazilian, while in America the African-American was systematically denied such opportunities? Or, from another perspective, if racism was a function of slavery, he asked, why was the free Negro in the USA obliged to cope with the same cruel racist exclusionism in the non-slave states as in the slave states?[18]

This contradiction could be avoided, said Degler, "only if we reverse our assumption as to which came first, slavery or discrimination ... and work on the assumption that discrimination preceded slavery and thereby conditioned it." Degler accordingly projected three theses: (1) "American race prejudice originated in the discriminatory social atmosphere of the early seventeenth century"; (2) "slavery in the English colonies was the institutionalization of [pre-existent] race prejudice"; and (3) "from the outset, as far as the evidence tells us, the Negro was treated as inferior to the white man, servant or free."[19]

Determined though he was to block the Handlins' passage, Degler stood on a slippery sill. His evidence was too little, and that little tendentiously selected. As evidence of the predominance of anti-Negro attitudes in England before the founding of the first Anglo-American colony, Degler cited the depiction of two Moorish characters in Shakespeare plays, Aaron in *Titus Andronicus* and the title character of *Othello*.[20] But if one proceeds consistently with this exegesis, it is possible to find implications quite contrary to those inferred by Degler. Shakespeare's Aaron is black and villainous; Othello is black and noble. Since Othello appeared ten years after Aaron, might we not, by Degler's logic, infer that this indicated a growth of respect and a reduction of contempt in the English attitude toward Africans? It seems pertinent, if we develop the subject along this line, to point out the transformation undergone by the character of the Moor in Shakespeare's hands. In the original Italian play, the Moor is simply a weak-minded cowardly murderer, uncomplicated by any redeeming quality. Othello, on the contrary, was made a tragic hero, said to be modelled on the real-life Earl of Essex, and in literary power and pathos ranking with Lear.[21] Othello's flaw was not his color but his male ego, made to pass for some part of "honor" and surely calculated to evoke universal sympathy from the English male audience. It may be worth noting that Degler's sense of audience appreciation of Othello is not one the American slaveholders would have shared. An English traveler to Charleston, South Carolina about 1807 found that there "*Othello* and other plays where a black man is the hero of the piece are not allowed to be performed."[22]

Or again, were contrary opinions and attitudes with respect to Negroes, as expressed by some of Shakespeare's contemporaries, to be ignored for want of iambic pentameter? Take Sir Francis Drake. At least three times in the 1560s, Drake (under the command of his kinsman John Hawkins) participated in the premature first English interloper venture in the African trade to the Americas, selling captive Africans into bondage in the Caribbean and on the Spanish Main.[23] A few years later, in 1572–73, this time under his own command, Drake returned to the Spanish Main to conduct a campaign of privateering raids. After an initial setback, the English decided on a basic strategy of alliance with the Maroons (or Cimarrons) of Panama, self-liberated former African slaves and their freeborn descendants, some three thousand in all, living in a number of independent settlements, "growne to a nation, under two Kings of their owne."[24] The English and the African-Panamanians, in mutual sympathy for the particular aims of each in the common anti-Spanish cause, worked, suffered, rejoiced and fought side by side and, according to Drake, "These Symerons during all the time that wee were with them, did us continually good service . . . and they would shew themselves no lesse valiant then [than] industrious and of good judgement." On parting there were exchanges of gifts, including silks and linens, from the English in token of friendship and appreciation; the English also burned their small ships in order to leave the precious ironwork, nails etcetera, for the Maroons (iron was worth more to the Maroons than the gold and silver so eagerly sought by the English and other Europeans).[25] Richard Hakluyt, the English visionary of exploration and colonization, generalized from Drake's Panamanian experience and proposed that the Straits of Magellan at the tip of South America be made an English stronghold against the Spanish, defended by a colony of Cimarrons.[26] Edmund S. Morgan, in his *American Slavery, American Freedom*, cited this record in order to argue that the defeat of such antecedent English attitudes was a necessary precondition for the eventual establishment of racial slavery in Virginia.[27] Certainly these facts do not conform to Degler's facile thesis that the origin of racial slavery is in part to be found in an English precedent of racial prejudice against non-Europeans.

One more example. When ship captain Richard Jobson in 1620 and 1621 made a trading voyage to Africa, he refused to engage in slave-trading because the English "were a people who did not deal in any such commodities, neither did we buy or sell one another or any that had our own shapes."[28] When the local dealer insisted that it was the custom there to sell Africans "to white men," Jobson answered that "They," that is, "white men," "were another kinde of people from us ..." Jobson's account was alluded to by Basil Davidson in *The African Slave Trade*, in which he argued that "European attitudes toward Africans in those early times displayed a wide range of contrast ... [but] they supposed no natural inferiority in Africans."[29]

For those who feel that a generalization about "the English attitude toward the Negro" must be attempted, it might be safer to see in the contrasting "Moors," Othello and Aaron, a reflection of a common ambiguity expressed by another Shakespeare contemporary and poet, Sir John Davies of Hereford:

Southward men are cruel, moody, mad
Hot, black, lean leapers, lustful, used to vaunt [boast]
Yet wise in action, sober, fearful, sad
If good, most good, if bad, exceeding bad.[30]

Even such a "balanced" view cannot be made to conform with the assumptions on which Degler chose to rest his case.

Finally, if ingrained English prejudices, institutionally evolved, predetermined the reduction of African-Americans to slavery, why should Degler not at least have indicated why equally apparent contemporary English anti-Irish and anti-Jewish biases did not eventuate in the enslavement of Irish and Jews?[31] The anthropologist Marvin Harris challenged Degler specifically on this question. "Ethnocentrism," Harris said, "is a universal feature of inter-group relations, and obviously both the English and the Iberians were prejudiced against foreigners, white and black." Proceeding from this generalization, Harris directly controverted Degler. In the Anglo-American colonies, said Harris, "the Negroes were not enslaved because the British colonists specifically despised dark-skinned people and regarded them alone as properly suited to slavery." Two historians who have devoted a great deal of study to the attitudes of early English colonialists, Nicholas P. Canny and P. E. H. Hair, have explicitly challenged Jordan on this question. Canny maintains that early colonial records of the fellowship between Anglo-American and African-American laborers in Virginia "greatly modify the opinions on seventeenth-century Englishmen's antipathy for people with black pigmentation advanced in W. D. Jordan, *White over Black*." Professor Hair, writing on the basis of sixteenth-century documents, argues that, "English opinions about Africans ... were more varied than has been suggested in works which set out to show that Anglo-African contacts in Elizabethan times were dominated by 'racialist' considerations." He too specifically mentions Jordan's *White over Black* as tending to this error.[32]

As I have noted, Degler recognized the fundamental significance of the contrast between the racist exclusionism faced by all African-Americans, free or bond, on the one hand, and the assimilationist policy with regard to African-Brazilians. This difference he ascribed to the difference between the cultural backgrounds of Iberia and England.[33] But no such cultural variation could be invoked to explain the difference in the positions of the free Negro in the British West Indies and in continental Anglo-America. Despite the explosive implications of this historic fact, Degler ignored it completely. The omission was especially deplorable since the Handlin article, which originally drew Degler to battle, had directed attention to differences between the Anglo-Caribbean and continental Anglo-America.

Worse still, Degler attempted to support his thesis by citations from the record of the short-lived (1630–41) English colony on Providence Island, located in the western Caribbean about 350 miles northwest of Panama. In the very record he cited, he completely neglected the dispute among the English colonizers of Providence Island over the legal and moral permissibility of attempting to hold Africans in lifetime servitude. In the end the colony had to be abandoned because of mutiny by the Negro laborers and the external pressure of the Spanish.[34]

Having insisted on the assumption that the origin of slavery depended upon the English colonists having come to the Americas with already indelible prejudices against "black men," Degler proceeded with a most explicit self-contradiction by asserting that slavery-producing prejudice "did not depend" on an imported mind-set but rather was fostered by the sight of Africans "as the cargo of the international slave trade ... those wretches newly spilled out of the slave ships!"[35] If the prejudices "originated long before slavery became legal" (and therefore long before the arrival in the Chesapeake of "slave ships" directly from Africa),[36] why intrude "fostering" (without a pretense of documentation) and, incidentally, hold the Africans responsible for it? Instead of racial prejudice causing slavery, here Degler was making slavery the cause of racial prejudice. In seeking to support his argument with both the *a priori* belt and the *post facto* suspenders, Degler instead rendered untenable the "reversal of assumptions" upon which his thesis depended.

Most regrettable of all, Degler was oblivious of the transcendental fact that, *whatever the state of English prejudices at that time*, any attempt to hold African laborers in lifetime hereditary bond-servitude was doomed by the African "prejudice" against it, as expressed by flight and rebellion.

Jordan scornfully distanced himself from "liberals on the race question ... uninterested in tired questions of historical evidence ... [who] could not easily assume a natural prejudice in the white man ... [because it] would violate their basic assumptions concerning the dominance of culture."[37] He took up the gauntlet of his own design: "If prejudice was natural there would be little one could do to wipe it out"; and his book, naturally called *White over Black*, was written to say a defiant "Amen."

With regard to the crucial question of the origin of racial slavery, Jordan believed he had found a way to save the psycho-cultural case from the "which-came-first" dilemma on which Degler had impaled himself.[38]

> Rather than slavery causing "prejudice" or vice versa, they seem rather to have generated each other. Both were ... twin aspects of a general debasement of the Negro. Slavery and "prejudice" may have been equally cause and effect, continuously reacting upon each other ...: a mutually interactive growth of slavery and unfavorable assessment, with no cause for either which did not cause the other.[39]

In thus conflating cause and effect, Jordan disposed of the dilemma by evoking a parthenogenetic unicorn called "the general debasement of the Negro." If, in the process, he abandoned the principle of chronological order by which the historian is bound to live, Jordan found a *cause* outside of time (at least, time as measured by the rhythms of recorded history) in instinct (or, at most, the unconscious). There, in an atavistic domain of aversion to black, of guilt as blackness, of blackward projection of guilt; there, in the pits of identity crisis, in the realm of dreams and symbols, Jordan said, was prefigured time out of mind the "unthinking decision" that produced racial slavery in Anglo-America.[40] So it was that Jordan contributed a book on the history of thought, the crux of which was an *un*thought choice.

As a corollary to the asserted instinctive drive to "debase the Negro," Jordan posited a psychological compulsion: "the need of transplanted Englishmen to know who it was they were." And what they were, he said, was "white": "white men had to know who they were if they were to survive."[41] This notion, Jordan avowed, was the thread that bound his study together. It was the old "germ theory" of American history decked out in up-to-date psychological trappings: before the Mayflower Compact, before the Petition of Right, before the Magna Charta, before the German-Saxon Hundred, there was the Word: White over Black, innate, ineradicable – a Calvinism of the genes, a Manifest Destiny of the White Soul.[42]

Historians are cautioned to avoid the vice of "presentism," that is, the assignment of motivations for behavior to suit current vogues without proof that those motivations actually figured in the needs and feelings of the people of the historic period under consideration. One common example of this error is that of casually classing Negroes in colonial Anglo-America as "slaves" from the first mention in 1619 on, decades before there is any justification in the record for such a generalization. On account of the inevitable deficiencies of the record, the tendency to this kind of error has to be guarded against, even when the subject is the objective, material world of actual places, persons, and events. But when, as in Jordan's book, the subject is the thoughts, reflections, attitudes of the observers of actual places, people and events, the danger is of a higher order of magnitude, because it involves the interpretation of interpretations.

As a citizen of the twentieth century, Jordan could look forward from his spaceship-in-time and see that the war to abolish slavery would be led by anti-abolitionists; that the war fought to strike the chains of slavery from the African-American would sow the seeds of a "white" imperialism; that even on the bank of the river of martyrs' blood the promise of equality would be repudiated after the Civil War, by a white-supremacist exclusion of Africans,[43] Asian-Americans, Mexicans, Indians and African-Americans. But the "transplanted Englishmen" in the new republic where Jordan left them – perched on the Atlantic slope of a continent inhabited in its vastness by a non-European majority, and further opposed by a rival European power's ancient claim to much of that territory – they could not know what the future would hold with regard to "the Negro question," or "the Indian question," or "the Spanish-Mexican question." For all they knew, Spain would maintain its claim to Texas and the West, and the "Indians" would continue (perhaps with outside help) to preside over most of the rest of the continent.[44] At the same time, they were increasingly convinced that slavery would have to end, and that, whatever some of the literate, record-leaving "whites" might wish, schemes for colonization of African-Americans outside the United States offered no answer to the "race" question.[45]

In this situation, might not the imminent freedom of the African-American lead to a peopling of the United States by a primarily African-European blend?[46] The Spanish and the Portuguese had blended with "not-whites" in their areas of American settlement without losing their Spanish or Portuguese identity. Among the population of the British West Indies the descendants of Englishmen were overwhelmingly persons of African descent, whose very struggle for equal rights was largely predicated upon their British identity.[47]

Jordan ascribes the West Indies blending to "race" and sex ratios such as were unachievable in the continental colonies.[48] But the "attitudes of ["white"] Americans", which is his proclaimed concern, did not show much of Jordan's faith in the demographic ratios as the controlling factor. The belief that such a blending with African-Americans was sure to happen was the major argument of the advocates of forced shipping of freed Negroes to the West Indies, Latin America, Africa or the periphery of the United States.[49]

They had known "who they were" in the seventeenth century and during most of the eighteenth century: they were Englishmen. But then something happened to their "need to know" that they were Englishmen, and they found a new identity, as "white" Americans. Might not the same obsolescence swallow up the "need to know" they were "white", just as their previous "need to know" that they were "Englishmen" had been superseded? They had been Englishmen far longer than they had been "white". Might they not have experienced "a new birth of freedom", and a new identity, American still, but simply human instead of "white"?

But there is more here than a mere lapse of professionalism. Jordan takes as his subject "attitudes ... thoughts and feelings (as opposed to actions)," regarding them as "discrete entities susceptible of historical analysis." He proclaims his philosophic adherence to the ultimate primacy of "attitudes" in delimiting "the categories of possibilities within which for the time being we are born to live."[50] Was it possible that because of his personal conviction that nothing much can be done by remedial social action to end the curse of racism, Jordan was far from careful about the extent to which this attitude might lower his guard against his own "white" bias in his presentation of the picture of American society up to 1812?[51] Bad as this was in itself, it caused Jordan's analysis of "attitudes" to parody more than it explained of the "actions", the causal course of events, to which they stand opposed.[52]

As the root of "white attitudes" toward the African-American, Jordan staked all on what he saw as the ineluctable need of the English psycho-cultural heritage to preserve its identity in the New World. But how could the same heritage produce the "social accommodation of mixed offspring" in the British West Indies and the contrasting refusal to allow for any such special status for "mulattos" in the continental plantation colonies? Faced by this problem (which the Handlins had suggested and Degler had ignored), Jordan was compelled to acknowledge that the variance could not derive from "the English cultural heritage."[53] But in so doing Jordan punctured his basic assumption. He was saying that the gene-pool factor, the "need to know they were 'white'", etcetera were not, after all, timeless absolutes in the English psyche; rather, they were only relative, alterable by sudden circumstance.

Jordan began his repair work with a sly reference to "the push and pull of an irreconcilable conflict between desire and aversion for interracial sexual union," with desire proving the stronger in the British West Indies.[54] "No one thought intermixture [of African and Anglo] was a good thing," Jordan asserted.[55] But it is just as true to say that no one in England thought that the "intermixture" by seduction and rape of poor women by propertied men was "a good thing", and the law and the pulpit were as productive of the appropriate expressions of disapproval there as they were in the corresponding case in the Anglo-American plantation colonies. Jordan's belief in "aversion" as a special operative factor in "biracial" America is unsupported by contrasting evidence involving dependent-class women in England and Ireland. (J. H. Plumb makes a similar criticism in his review of Jordan's book.) It seems doubtful that Jordan fairly conveys the feelings of English colonists in Jamaica in this regard. They disdained to account for their "interracial liaisons" as a result of a scarcity of European women. Quite the contrary; they proclaimed the moral superiority of their conduct as compared with that of the master class in England, contrasting the "relatively permanent" relationships in Jamaican society with the "prostitution, infanticide and unnatural neglect of illegitimate children in England."[56]

As for the Caribbean versus continental differences, since the push of desire under continental elms is no less fundamental than it is under insular palms,[57] Jordan turned a metaphor of his own: "The West Indian planters were lost . . . in a sea of blacks."[58] That men of the owning leisure classes impose their desires on women of the non-owning laboring classes is as old and as general as the division of society into such classes, although those men are never thought of as being "lost in a sea of laborers."

Still, demographic facts are appropriate to demographic studies. In colonial Anglo-America, the higher the proportion of African-American laboring women among the non-owning classes in an area, the higher we could expect to be the incidence of sexual unions of Anglo men with African-American women. The varying degrees of "acceptance" of the relationship among Anglos in the plantation colonies was basically a function of its practice, with a tendency to vary toward "desire" rather than "aversion." If we can accept the testimony of two of the most cited chroniclers of Jamaican affairs prior to emancipation, we must conclude that the proportion of English men there involved in child-producing unions with non-European women was greater than might be expected from the demographic ratios.[59] That fact testifies to the racist operation of ruling-class male domination, but not to the "aversion" thesis posited by Jordan. Discounting the differences in opportunity as determined by demographic variations, the sexual exploitation of African-American women by European-American men (the main, though not the only social form of "interracial" sex) does not appear to have been less practiced on the continent than in the British West Indies.[60]

The difference in the status won by the Anglo-African in the West Indies, on the one hand, and in the continental plantation colonies, on the other, was, Jordan said, due to differences of "self-identification" by the fathers in the two different settings.[61] And how the Anglo fathers identified themselves was determined by demographics, the "race" and sex ratios. Whereas the Caribbean Anglos, he argued, were "lost in a sea of blacks," the continental colonist felt "the weight of the Negroes on his community heavy enough to be a burden, yet not so heavy as to make him abandon all hope of maintaining his own identity."[62] This conclusion is tautological since the maintenance of "white" identity was equivalent to rejection of the "mulatto."

We turn now to what Jordan calls the "single exception" to the pattern of non-acceptance of "mulatto" status in the Anglo-American continental colonies. Georgia colony originated in 1732 as a buffer against Spanish Florida. It was set up especially to stop African-American bond-laborers from fleeing to freedom in Florida, either to the Spanish or to friendly Indians. For this reason, the new colony was founded on the exclusion of "Negroes," in order to seal South Carolina against the outflow of fugitive bond-laborers. But in less than twenty years the expansive power of the South Carolina plantation bourgeoisie made hash of the no-slavery principle and quickly brought Georgia into the system.

The consequent rise in the proportion of African-American bond-laborers in the total population of the new colony largely negated the territorial buffer function, despite the English takeover of Florida in 1763 at the end of the Seven Years War. Faced with this crisis, the Georgia authorities acted to erect a new *social* buffer to reinforce, restore, replace the territorial one. In 1765, the Georgia Commons House of Assembly enacted that free "mulatto" immigrants be "naturalized" and accorded "all the Rights, Priviledges, Powers and Immunities whatsoever which [belong to] any person born of British parents."[63]

In the shadow world of "attitudes," this Georgia law may seem merely an exception to the general policy of rejection of the "mulatto" as it was practiced in the continental Anglo-American colonies. But, in its own person it appears not as an exception, but as a perfectly consistent element of a general policy of social control, a *sine qua non* of all government, at all times, in all places. The Georgia case was exceptional only in the brevity of its duration. Every plantation colony faced the same social control problem; each required a buffer social control stratum to stand between the mass of slaves and the numerically tiny class of slaveholders. In the Americas there was no such historically developed middle stratum, and therefore it had to be invented.

The records richly attest to the deliberate pursuit of this fundamental principle of colonial policy in the English colonies. Repeatedly, the theory and the practice of promoting the "free colored" to an intermediate social status in the British West Indies was proposed in order that they "would ... attach themselves to the White race ... and so become a barrier against the designs of the Black."[64] This essential social control function was operative in Jamaica in the 1730s. The European militia there was found altogether inadequate to the task of combating the African-Jamaican runaway maroons, who from mountain bases encouraged plantation workers to join them. In 1739, when a military campaign was waged against the maroons, the British forces were composed of two hundred British sailors and two hundred Moskito Indians, free Negroes and "mulattoes."[65] In Barbados, in order to control the bond-laborers the plantation bourgeoisie "created" and promoted the "mulatto" group, which then "functioned as 'whites' *vis à vis* the slaves."[66] In Georgia the 1765 "mulatto" policy was designed, as Jordan himself put it, "to attract men who might be *counted as white* and who would thereby strengthen the colony's defenses against her foreign and domestic enemies," the powerful Indian tribes on its frontiers and the rising proportion of Negro bond-laborers.[67] Whatever reasons Jordan had for ignoring the obvious parallel of the Georgia case, a fair inference is that he found it incompatible with his approach to the question of the origin and function of racial slavery. The parallel argues that everywhere in Anglo-America, not just in Georgia, the "white attitude" was, in the final analysis, shaped by the exigencies of the relationship of contending social forces. In the dynamic tension of ideas and experience, ideas were the bowstring, experience was the bow. The "mulatto" distinction was a functional one; being necessarily and above all concerned with maintaining their ascendancy, members of the plantation bourgeoisie sometimes made accommodations in their thinking in the interest of having a "mulatto" buffer between themselves and the plantation bond-laborers.[68]

Sometimes, but not always. Why was this not the practice, except to the possible extent of the Georgia case, in continental Anglo-America, in either its colonial or its regenerate United States form? Jordan, from other premisses, argues that unlike the English in the Caribbean, "lost in a sea of blacks," those on the continent were able to beat back the challenge to their ancestral "white" identity.[69] But as Jordan himself points out, the continental slaveholders no less than those in the West Indies were constantly concerned with dealing with the various forms of resistance on the part of those whom they held in bondage.[70] The Georgia case shows that they were prepared, in certain circumstances, to resort to the "mulatto" option. If the "mulatto" on the continent were not generally, however, to be accorded the West Indies style social promotion, nevertheless for the slaveholders – outnumbered sometimes twenty or more times by their African-American bond-laborers – the "mulatto" *function* was as necessary as it was in the West Indies. If, there, "mulattos" could "function as whites," then on the continent laboring-class, largely propertyless and poor European-Americans could function as "mulattos". In the West Indies the "mulatto" was compensated by emancipation and promotion to some sort of petit bourgeois status.[71] Since the poor European-Americans were or, after a term of servitude, would be free, and since they typically had already lost upward social mobility, they were promoted to the "white race" and endowed with unprecedented civil and social privileges *vis-à-vis* the African-American, privileges that, furthermore, were made to appear to be conditional on keeping "not-whites" down and out. This entailed the exclusion of "free Negroes" from participation in the buffer role in the continental colonies, because their inclusion would have undermined the racial privileges upon which depended the loyalty of the laboring-class "whites" to the plantation bourgeoisie.[72] Whatever might have been the case with literate members of the ruling class, the record indicates that laboring-class European-Americans in the continental plantation colonies showed little interest in "white identity" before the institution of the system of "race" privileges at the end of the seventeenth century.[73]

The Socio-economic Argument

Despite the more or less obvious inadequacies and fallacies of the Jordan–Degler psycho-cultural analysis, efforts by the opposition to emphasize the primacy of socio-economic causes have often betrayed a critical ambiguity toward the origin of anti-Negro prejudice. In other cases an "economic" thesis was weakened by oversimplification. In still others, economic facts were tendentiously attenuated to the point where they could not bear the weight of their argument. In one instance, the embryo of a complete and consistent socio-economic interpretation was formulated, but remained undeveloped.

Although the Handlins were aware of the uncongenial inferences they were inviting, they nevertheless explained the rise of anti-Negro discrimination as "simply the reaction of [English and other European] immigrants ... isolated in an immense wilderness ... [who] longed in the strangeness for the company of those who were most like themselves."[74] This was pure intuition on the part of the Handlins, devoid of any reference to the colonial records. They had thus adopted so much of the Degler natural racism principle, that Degler could say, "Actually our two positions are not as far apart as the Handlins would lead one to believe."[75]

Eric Williams, at the very outset of post-1945 discussion of the origin of Anglo-American slavery, provided a corrective for a fundamental historiographical blindspot. Referring specifically to the political crisis in Britain that more than a century earlier had led to the emancipation of bond-laborers in the West Indies, he made a point of fundamental importance not only for the Anglo-Caribbean but for the Americas generally, including the Anglo-American continental plantation colonies:

> Contrary to popular and even learned belief, ... the most dynamic and powerful social force in the colonies was the slave himself. This aspect of the ... problem has been studiously ignored. ... The planter looked upon slavery as eternal, ordained by God. ... There was no reason [however] why the slave should think the same.[76]

The bond-laborer accordingly made the counter-argument of resistance by "indolence, sabotage and revolt."

After Williams made this point, European-American historians showed a greater awareness of the need to include the African-American bond-laborers as self-activating participants in historic events. But generally they continued the old tendency of ignoring an equally crucial matter, namely, the question of social control. Unfortunately Williams, by an oversimplification of the particular reason for the employment of Africans as plantation bond-laborers, may have contributed to a perpetuation of this problem.

In the course of his refutation of the various "racial" explanations for the unique enslavement of the African (climatic adaptability, skin color, race prejudice, etcetera), Williams argued from "a simple economic fact: that the colonies needed labor and resorted to Negro labor because it was cheapest and best."[77] There is no evidence, however, to show that the cost of the acquisition and delivery of African laborers to Anglo-America, even the Caribbean, was lower than the corresponding costs for laborers brought from England, Scotland and Ireland.[78] The significant relationship between cheapness and enslavement was this: the African laborers were cheaper because they were enslaved, before they were enslaved because they were cheaper. To assume the cheapness is to assume the enslavement. That is an error against which, as has been noted above, Williams himself argued most forcefully, in pointing out that the desire of the plantation bourgeoisie for cheap labor was matched by the African laborer's desire not to be enslaved. Clearly, then, their enslavement was not simply the result of the plantation bourgeoisie's perception of an economic advantage to be gained by it. Such a perception meant nothing without its other half, the successful construction of a system of social control whereby the normal process of peaceful day-to-day exploitation of bond-labor could be conducted.[79]

A number of other historians seeking an economic interpretation of the origin of racial slavery in continental Anglo-America have leaned heavily on the "cheaper labor" rationale.[80] They have then proceeded as if the ability of the plantation bourgeoisie to control the African-American bond-laborer could be taken for granted. That assumption is especially harmful for the study of the continental colonies, because it was there that the operation of social control was obscured by its "white race" form.

Edmund S. Morgan authored several journal articles in 1971 and 1972 bearing on the establishment of racial slavery in colonial Virginia. The publication in 1975 of his full 500-page treatment of the subject, *American Slavery/American Freedom: The Ordeal of Colonial Virginia*, provided the most substantial contribution so far to a socio-economic interpretation of the origin of racial slavery. Morgan was recognized by reviewers as the socio-economic party's counterpoise to Jordan.[81]

Making use of the Virginia Colony and County Records (to an extent exceeded only by Philip Alexander Bruce more than seventy-five years earlier) Morgan drew a picture of seventeenth-century Virginia as "the Volatile Society," in which the ruling elite was faced with critical problems of social control. Racism was not a significant factor. African-American bond-laborers were increasing in number, but they still made up only one-fourth or one-fifth of the bond-labor force until the 1690s. The threat to social order, Morgan said, came from propertyless, discontented, poverty-ridden European-Americans, mainly former limited-term bond-laborers.

Social order was achieved, according to Morgan, through two policies. First, motivated by simple profit considerations, the plantation bourgeoisie gained, incidentally and unconsciously, a more docile laboring class by shifting its primary reliance from limited-term to lifetime bond-labor. "Slaves," Morgan said, "[were] less dangerous than free or semi-free [limited-term-bond-] laborers," because slaves "had none of the rising expectations that have so often prompted rebellion in human history."[82] Morgan dismissed the frequently encountered ruling-class fears of servile rebellion as unfounded in reality. In explaining why only Africans were enslaved, Morgan differed sharply with the Jordan–Degler thesis. Morgan showed that the bourgeoisie was quite willing to consider proposals for the enslavement of Englishmen and Scots. But whereas the Africans arrived already enslaved, Morgan argued, "the transformation of free men [from England, for example] into slaves would have been a tricky business."[83] Welcome as his rejection of the "innate racism" explanation of racial slavery may be, Morgan's "non-rebellious slave" belongs with the mythical "friendly master" in the analysis of the dynamics of slavery in the Americas.[84] If the extent of rebellion by African-American bond-laborers in continental Anglo-America did not reach the levels witnessed in such countries as Santo Domingo, Jamaica, Guiana and Brazil, it was not because of any difference in their status upon their arrival in America.

The second policy was deliberately calculated as a social control measure. It was in this connection that Morgan made his most valuable contribution to the socio-economic analysis of the origin of racial slavery. The plantation bourgeoisie did not hold Morgan's low opinion of the bond-laborers as potential rebels; their ultimate fear was that "freemen with disappointed hopes should make common cause with slaves of desperate hope ..." and jointly re-enact their part in Bacon's Rebellion of 1676, in which African-American and Anglo bond-laborers together had demanded an end to bond-servitude.[85] Against this danger, "the answer ... obvious if unspoken and only gradually recognized, was racism, to separate free whites from dangerous slave blacks by a screen of racial contempt."[86] Morgan then proceeded to catalogue and analyze "a series of acts" passed by the Virginia Assembly over a period of some thirty-five years, culminating with the revisal of the laws in 1705, whereby "the assembly deliberately did what it could to foster the contempt of whites for blacks and Indians."[87] He argued that European-Americans of the laboring classes, since they were not slaveowners, did not derive any "direct economic benefits" from the establishment of slavery. But, according to Morgan, the "small men," the old rebellious types, "were ... allowed to prosper" and were accorded "social, psychological, and political advantages." The deliberately calculated result was to turn "the thrust of exploitation" away from the European-American petty bourgeoisie and "[align] them on the side of the exploiters," that is, the slaveholders.[88] Morgan also noted that, as "Christian whites," even the unpropertied European-Americans (including bond-laborers) were offered a number of benefits previously denied them, in order to alienate them from their African-American fellow bondmen and bondwomen.[89]

Thus Morgan carried the argument against the "unthinking decision" explanation of racial slavery to its logical conclusion: deliberate ruling-class choice. The resort of the plantation bourgeoisie to slave labor might have been a matter of mere profit-seeking instinct, he said, but racial slavery and racism were a calculated form, designed to cope with problems of social control.[90]

Bold and cogent, and full of promise as it was at the start, Morgan's argument involved false premises that would vitiate its full development. With the turn to African and African-American lifetime bond-labor as the basis of the economy, coupled with the simultaneous expansion of opportunities for European-American freedmen, the social control problem, according to Morgan, evaporated in a cloud of upward mobility until "the remaining free laborers and tenant farmers were too few in number to be a serious threat."[91]

Morgan had documented most convincingly the non-racist character of the volatile society of seventeenth-century Virginia, and the deliberateness of the development of the racist policy of social control. But now (without, however, his customarily scrupulous documentation), he presented a denouement that not only rendered redundant the theme of "racism as the answer" to social discontent, but spared the life of the "innate racism" idea that he had so trenchantly attacked as an explanation of racial slavery.

In proceeding on the assumption that there were now "too few free poor on hand to matter,"[92] Morgan was wrong on the facts and wrong on the theory. The proportion of landless European-Americans did not shrink to insignificance as a social category in the plantation colonies in the century between Bacon's Rebellion and the American Revolution. In 1676, the overwhelming proportion of the population of Virginia was in the Tidewater region. Of its economically active (tithable) European-American population, half were bond-laborers and another one-eighth were propertyless freemen.[93] A century later this proletarian proportion of the European-American population of that same area was still more than 40 per cent. This marked the limit of proletarian promotion to the owning classes. Furthermore, relative to the conditions prevailing in the northern, non-plantation colonies, those of the European-Americans were worse in general in the plantation colonies.[94]

Consider now the theory of it. If the European-American laboring classes "aligned themselves with the exploiters" because they, the "white" poor, benefited indirectly in the slave-labor-based monocultural plantation economy by becoming property-holders during the so-called golden age of the Chesapeake (that is, the colonies of Virginia and Maryland bordering the Chesapeake Bay) in the middle quarters of the eighteenth century, then why did that collaboration not diminish as the contrary tendency set in, as it evidently did, and "racial" competition for employment became one of the well-known features of American society? Or again, if the operation of slave economics was such as to make free people generally into property-holders, why were the free African-Americans excluded from a fair share of the bounty? Would not their participation have strengthened the front against the threat of slave revolt, which strengthening, as we well know, was calculated to be the effect elsewhere in the plantation Americas? The exclusion of the free African-American from such participation is prima facie proof that the mass of the "whites" was not composed of property-owners but of proletarians and semi-proletarians, whose social status thus depended not upon their property but upon their "race."[95]

In contrast with the British West Indies, the social control problem in the continental plantation colonies was not that there were too few European-American laborers, but that there were too many. It was this circumstance that accounted for the decisive role of "race" which came to characterize the system of social control in the continental colonies. Primary emphasis upon "race" became the pattern only where the bourgeoisie could not form its social control apparatus without the inclusion of propertyless European-Americans. If, in the plantation colonies, there had really been "too few free poor to matter", as Morgan argued, then those few would have been relegated to social irrelevance, as indeed happened in the West Indies, and the "white race" would never have become the essence of the social control policy of the Anglo-American continental plantation bourgeoisie. By conceptually erasing the European-American proletarian, Morgan was inviting back the psycho-cultural theory of the origin of racism, the theory he had done so much to refute by his scholarly study of seventeenth-century Virginia. Propertied classes do not need special motivation to unite around their interests *vis-à-vis* the propertyless and exploited. Racism among the propertied classes alone would be evidence for the psycho-cultural belief in "natural" racism. But Morgan's theory that practically all European-Americans benefited, directly or indirectly, from keeping African-Americans out and down has more specific and dire implications favorable to the psycho-cultural view with respect to "modern tensions." For, whether racism be "natural-born" in European-Americans, or whether it be the function of actual (as against illusory) benefits for all "whites" as a result of racial oppression, the implications for ridding our society of the curse of racism are equally unfavorable.

In seeking to understand this trend of Morgan's argument, it may be helpful to note that he shares with Jordan the "paradox" theory of American history.[96] "In committing themselves to a slavery whose logic rested, in the final analysis, on racial differences," Jordan wrote, "the colonists may in fact have enhanced the fluidity of the American social structure above the racial line."[97] A paraphrase of Jordan accurately expresses Morgan: in committing them-selves to a political order whose logic rested, in the final analysis, on racial distinctions, Virginians such as Jefferson and Madison had assured equality and justice for all "above the racial line." There is no place in this scenario for a growth of proletarian misery on the "white" side of the line. But even in Jefferson's time, the ugly fact was evident.[98]

Plowing furrows through the records side by side with Morgan, Timothy H.

Breen produced strong reinforcement for the socio-economic explanation of
the emergence of racial slavery in colonial Virginia. In his 1973 article "A
Changing Labor Force and Race Relations in Virginia 1660–1710,"[99] Breen
drew attention to the extent and significance of actual rebellion involving
African-American and European-American bond-laborers, and poor freedmen.
Breen, furthermore, regarded the African-American bond-laborers as a
constant potential for rebellion against the plantocracy.[100]

On the other hand, in this article, and as co-author with Stephen Innes of a
book published in 1980,[101] Breen ascribes the cancellation of laboring-class
solidarity by the counterfeit of "white race" identification to exclusively
objective factors. Of these, said Breen, "none was more important than the rise
of tobacco prices after 1684 ... [which] raised white laborers out of
poverty."[102] But there does not seem to have been any significant rise in
tobacco prices and production in the critical period chosen by Breen. Allan
Kulikoff in a later study found that, "From 1680 to 1715, except for a short
boom between 1697 and 1702, the real [tobacco] price level was almost always
low or declining." Although the status of poor whites was elevated relative to
African-Americans by the new system of racial privileges, they faced a decline
of opportunity for social mobility in the decades after 1680.[103] According to
economic historian Jacob M. Price, "It was precisely in the 1680s and 1690s
that slaves were first introduced into the Chesapeake in large numbers, yet we
can observe no effect on production before the 1720s."[104]

The second of the factors listed by Breen was the increasing proportion of
laborers arriving in Virginia direct from Africa, lacking previous Christian
"seasoning." "No white servant," said Breen, "... could identify with these
frightened Africans."[105] The concomitant "language barrier," he added, further
inhibited the development of labor solidarity. On this point, in the absence of
documentation Breen resorted to intuition, as first Degler and then others on
both sides of the aisle had taken to doing. He made no attempt, however, to
learn by a comparison with the at least somewhat parallel situation elsewhere
in the Americas, where new laborers were constantly arriving direct from
Africa in far larger proportions, and where language differences not only
occurred naturally, but were deliberately manipulated by the capitalist
employers hoping thereby to frustrate bond-labor solidarity. To reject out of
hand, or not even think of, such a possible light on the question seems
justifiable only on the assumption of the existence in the European-American
bond-laborers of an overriding sense of "white" identity with their owners,
contrary to the tenor of the well-documented presentation that Breen had made
up to that point.

Finally, among these objective factors Breen included improved wage scales
for a relatively diminished number of free laborers, and improved opportunities for freedmen to become landholders (a point whose limited importance
has been indicated above in connection with Morgan, and which is further to

be inferred from Breen's comment that "If landless freemen could not afford acreage in Virginia, they could move to Carolina or Pennsylvania ..."[106]) Whatever those expanded opportunities, and whatever the increase in the number of African-American bond-laborers might be, such objective factors could not explain the exclusion of the free African-American from their benefits.

Despite the obvious limitations of such mechanical reliance upon objective factors to explain white racism among European-Americans of the laboring classes, Breen gives no scope at all to deliberate ruling-class policy in the displacement of European-American proletarian class consciousness by the incubus of a "white" identity with the employing classes, which has presided over our history for three centuries.

Of all the historians of the "social" side of the question, only the African-American historian Lerone Bennett Jr. succeeds in placing the argument on the three essential bearing points from which it cannot be toppled. First, that racial slavery constituted a ruling-class response to a problem of labor solidarity. Second, that a system of racial privileges for the propertyless "whites" was deliberately instituted in order to align them on the side of the plantation bourgeoisie against the African-American bond-laborers. Third, that the consequence was not only ruinous to the interests of the African-Americans, but was "disastrous" for the propertyless "whites" as well.[107]

Bennett's aim was to look at three and a half centuries of African-American history. Understandably, he was limited in the scope he could give in his book to his treatment of the origin of racial slavery, a development of the first century of that history. Whether or not he might otherwise have devoted attention to Bacon's Rebellion and compared the various systems of social control in the colonial period we do not know. In any case, when primary attention is directed to the origin of racial slavery, these matters need to be taken into consideration.

On the Misleading Term "Race"

In an avowed attempt to make clear the meaning of the terms "race" and "racial" as he used them in *White over Black*, Winthrop D. Jordan appended a "Note on the Concept of Race," which he had composed as editor of an earlier book. He also devoted a section of his "Essay on Sources" to works by anthropologists and biologists, particularly geneticists, which he had consulted on the question of "race."

Two geneticists whose works obviously influenced the formulation of that note were Stanley M. Garn and Theodosius Dobzhansky.[108] Garn's book *Human Races* was said by Jordan to be "the best single book on race." Of Dobzhansky's well-known writings, Jordan particularly mentioned *Mankind*

Evolving as "an absorbing treatment" of the subject. But a study of these two sources does not help one understand why Jordan thought that their concept of "race" was important to him as a historian.

Garn concludes his discussion of "The Contemporary Approach to Race" by explicitly separating genetics from the social sciences with regard to "race" and "racism." His book, he says:

> has nothing to do with racism, which is simply the attempt to deny some people deserved opportunities simply because of their origin, or to accord other people certain undeserved opportunities, only because of their origins. The history of our species is far too long (and periods of national glory far too short) to direct attention away from race as an evolutionary phenomenon to futile arguments about superiority, inferiority, or moral supremacy, which become two-edged and detrimental to all who wield them. (pp. v–vi)

In *Mankind Evolving*, Dobzhansky insists on the cultural significance of "race differences," but condemns any and all attempts to find in the human genetic make-up any justification for racism; there is no gene for a "white" attitude. "The mighty vision of human equality," he says, "belongs to the realm of ethics and politics, not to that of biology" (p. 13).

Jordan's search among arcana of genetic evolution to better understand "white men's attitudes," was, at best, an exercise in irrelevancy. For when an emigrant population from "multiracial" Europe goes to North America or South Africa and there, by constitutional fiat, incorporates itself as the "white race," that is no part of genetic evolution. It is rather a political act: the invention of "the white race." It lies within the proper sphere of study of social scientists, and it is an appropriate objective for alteration by social activists. Leave genetics to the geneticists; as Garn and Dobzhansky say, genetics has nothing but disclaimers to contribute to the study of racism as a historical phenomenon.

The Irish Mirror

Just as instruments of observation operating above the earth's enveloping atmosphere reveal significant meteorological phenomena with a clarity unachievable from the earth's lowly surface, so does the reflector of Irish history afford insights into American racial oppression and white supremacy – the overriding jetstream that has governed the flow of United States history down to this very day – free of the "White Blindspot" that Dr DuBois warned us about in *Black Reconstruction*.[109] Irish history presents a case of *racial oppression without reference to alleged skin color or, as the jargon goes, "phenotype."*

That is why *Racial Oppression and Social Control*, Volume One of this study of the origin of the paramount issue in American history, begins with a long look into an Irish mirror.

From that vantage point I will: (1) substantiate a definition of racial slavery as a sociogenic rather than a phylogenic phenomenon; (2) show racial oppression introduced as a deliberate ruling-class policy where it was not originally intended; (3) present an example of the casting-off of racial oppression to be superseded by "non-racial," natural human affinity (though in the contexts of a normally class-differentiated society); (4) show how, at a critical moment, when racial oppression might have been displaced, it was renewed by deliberate ruling-class decision; (5) demonstrate historically that racial oppression can be maintained only by a military establishment, except where the oppressor group is in a majority; (6) show how, even after centuries of racial oppression, where the oppressed group is the majority a ruling class can be forced to abandon racial oppression (or face civil war), even though, as in the Irish case, racial oppression may be replaced by national oppression under the same ruling class; (7) supply, incidentally, a definition of the difference between national and racial oppression, in terms of the recruitment of the intermediate buffer social control stratum; (8) show by examples how propertyless classes are recruited into the intermediate stratum, through anomalous "racial" privileges not involving escape from propertylessness; (9) present analogies, relating to the question of racial oppression, between features of continental Anglo-American and United States history and the history of Ireland; and, finally, (10) show the relativity of race by describing how persons, actually the same individuals, or at least persons of the same "gene pool," were first transformed from Irish haters of racial oppression into white-supremacists in America.

The Invention of the White Race

With the conceptual groundwork laid, free of the "White Blindspot," *The Invention of the White Race* turns its attention in Volume Two to the plantation colonies of Anglo-America during the period from the founding of Jamestown in 1607 to the cancellation of the original ban on slavery in the colony of Georgia in 1750. The pivotal events are seen to be Bacon's Rebellion in 1676 and the 1705 revision of the Virginia laws, in particular, the "Act concerning Servants and Slaves." Topics to be considered in Volume Two include: the English background, the origin and peculiarities of England's original colonial labor supply and their implications for the evolution of the bond-labor system in Anglo-America; why the Spanish example could not be followed in regard to the labor force; the consequence of the economic addiction to tobacco – the plantation system, foreclosing the emergence of an intermediate buffer social control stratum; the chattelization of labor; the oppression and resistance of the bond-laborers – African-Americans and Euro-Americans – together; the growing interest on the part of the Anglo-American continental plantation bourgeoisie in reducing African-Americans to lifetime hereditary bond-servitude; the divided mind of the English law on the enslavability of Christians; the sharpening class struggle – in the absence of a system of racial oppression – between the plantation elite on the one hand and on the other the debt-burdened small planters and the majority of the economically productive population, the bond-laborers, three-fourths Anglo-, one-fourth African-American; the dispute over "Indian policy" between "frontier" planters and the ruling elite; the eruption of the social contradictions in Bacon's Rebellion, in which the main rebel force came to be made up of Anglo- and African-American bond-laborers together demanding an end to bond-servitude; the defeat of the rebels, followed by a period of continued instability of social control; apprehension of a recurrence of rebellion; the social control problem in attempting to exploit the newly gained African source of labor by reducing African-Americans to lifetime hereditary bondage, especially considering the refuge available for escaping bond-laborers in the mountains at the back of the colonies, and in a continent beyond; the problem of social control reconsidered; the invention of the "white race" – the truly Peculiar Institution – as the solution to the problem of social control, its failure in the West Indies, its establishment in the continental plantation colonies, signaled by the enactment of the "Act concerning Servants and Slaves," which formally instituted the system of privileges for European-Americans, of even the lowest social status, vis-à-vis any person of any degree of African ancestry, not only bond-laborers but free Negroes as well, however possessed of property they might be; the remolding of male supremacy as white male supremacy, the peculiar American form of male supremacy, as an essential element of the system of white-skin privileges; the creation of white male privileges with regard to African-American women – white male supremacy. Volume Two will take note of the fact that the revision of the laws in Virginia to codify racial oppression coincided with the codification of racial oppression in Ireland by the enactment of the Penal Laws. It will also contain my observations on how the "Ordeal of Colonial Virginia" gave birth to the Ordeal of America.

VOLUME ONE
Racial Oppression and Social Control

1

The Anatomy of Racial Oppression

However one may choose to define the term "racial", it concerns the historian only as it relates to a pattern of oppression (subordination, subjugation, exploitation) of one set of human beings by another. Orlando Patterson, in his *Slavery and Social Death*, takes "the racial factor to mean the assumption of innate differences based on real or imagined physical or other differences."[1] But, as I have pointed out in the Introduction, such an assumption does not an oppressor make; presumably the objects of racial oppression (however the term is defined) are capable of the same sorts of assumptions. David Brion Davis, explaining slavery in the United States, says, "racial dissimilarity [was] offered as an excuse" for it.[2] That is true enough and consistent with Patterson's definition of "the racial factor." But again, excuses are not an automatic promotion to oppressor; before racial oppression is excused, it must first be imposed and sustained. That is what needs to be explained.

Unfortunately, "racial dissimilarity" in the conventional phenotypical sense proves to be more banana peel than stepping stone. Historically, "racial dissimilarities" have not only been artificially used, they are themselves artificial. In colonial Hispanic America, it was possible for a person, regardless of phenotype (physical appearance), to become "white" by purchasing a royal certificate of "whiteness."[3] With less formality, but equal success, one may move from one "racial category" to another in today's Brazil where, it is said, "money whitens."[4] On the other hand, in the United States the organizing principle of society is that no such "whitening" be recognized – whether "whitening" by genetic variation or by simple wealth. In 1890, a Portuguese emigrant settling in Guyana (British Guiana) would learn that he/she was not "white." But a sibling of that same person arriving in the United States in that same year would learn that by a sea-change he/she had become "white."[5] In the last Spanish census of Cuba, Mexican Indians and Chinese were classified as "white", but in 1907 the first United States census there classed these groups as "colored."[6] According to Virginia law in 1860, a person with but three "white" grandparents was a Negro; in 1907, having no more than fifteen out of sixteen "white" great-great-grandparents entitled one to the same classification; in 1910, the limit was

asymptotic: "every person in whom there is ascertainable any Negro blood ...
[was to] be deemed a colored person."[7] As of 1983, the National Center for
Health Statistics was effectively following the 1910 Virginia principle by
classifying any person as black if either of the parents was black. At the same
time, in Texas the "race" classification was determined by the "race" of the
father.[8] Prior to 1970, a set of Louisiana court decisions dating back to the late
1700s had upheld the legal concept that "any traceable amount" of African
ancestry defined a "Negro." In 1970, "racial" classification became the subject of
hard bargaining in the Louisiana state legislature. The Conservatives held out for
1/64, but the "more enlightened" opposition forced a compromise at 1/32 as the
requisite proportion of Negro forebears, a principle that was upheld by the state's
Supreme Court in 1974.[9]

By considering the notion of "racial oppression" in terms of the substantive,
the operative element, namely "oppression," it is possible to avoid the
contradictions and howling absurdities that result from attempts to splice
genetics and sociology.[10] By examining racial oppression as a particular
system of oppression – like gender oppression or class oppression or national
oppression – we find firmer footing for analyzing racial slavery and the
invention and peculiar function of the "white race," and for confronting the
theory that racial oppression can be explained in terms of "phenotype" – the
old ace-in-the-hole of racist apologetics. This approach also preserves the basis
for a consistent theory of the organic interconnection of racial, class, national,
and gender oppression.[11]

The Irish Analogy

To our conditioned minds, the attitude and behavior of Anglo-Americans
toward African-Americans and American Indians have the readily recognizable character of racial oppression. But when racial oppression is defined in
terms of its operational principles, the exclusion of the Irish case is seen to be
wholly arbitrary. The exclusion is especially deplorable when practiced by
European-American scholars, because it ignores a case where "white"
consciousness on the part of the observer is least likely to affect the drawing
of conclusions. A "need to know they were white"[12] cannot possibly serve to
explain the attitude of the English toward the Irish. The history of English rule
in Ireland, and of the Irish in America, presents instructive parallels and
divergences for the understanding of "race" as a sociogenic rather than a
phylogenic category; and of racial slavery as a system of social control.

Historians and the Analogy

Even as the nineteenth-century imperialist "scramble for Africa" was unfolding, resonances of English abolitionism and Chartism, and of the great Civil War and Emancipation in America, still thrilled somewhere in the collective consciousness of historians toiling to interpret the past to the present. One such, the distinguished English historian and abolitionist Henry Hallam (1777–1859), pointed out the racist affinity of the Spanish genocide of the Christian Moors and the English oppression of the Irish.[13]

The pre-eminent Anglo-Irish historian William Edward Hartpole Lecky (1838–1903) noted how the people of the English Pale in Ireland came to "look upon the Irish as later colonists looked upon the Red Indians."[14] Or consider the remarkable insight of W. K. Sullivan, Irish historian and President of Queen's College, Cork, who analogized the social role of the non-gentry Protestants in Ireland and the "poor whites" in America.[15] Karl Marx applied the analogy in pursuit of the unity of working people of all countries:

> The ordinary English worker hates the Irish worker ... [and] in relation to the Irish worker he feels himself a member of the *ruling* nation.... His attitude is much the same as that of the "poor whites" to the "niggers".[16]

The most depraved derivation of the analogy was voiced by the English historian Edward A. Freeman (1823–92) during a visit to America in 1881. The United States, he said, "would be a grand land if only every Irishman would kill a negro, and be hanged for it."[17]

World War Two had an obvious effect on consciousness of the analogy among historians concerned with the problem of slavery and racism. They have devoted considerable attention to the attitudes of the English in the Tudor and Stuart periods toward the Irish, as homologues of the general European attitude toward the Indians of the Americas.[18] In his richly documented exposition of the close relation of the images of the Irish and the American Indians and Africans, David Beers Quinn claims that this closeness revealed "what some Englishmen thought about some Irishmen and about Irish society."[19] Historians such as Quinn, Jones, Canny and Muldoon argue effectively that racism among Europeans is not limited to their relations with non-Europeans, but that it can exist in the most extreme form between one European nation, such as England, and another, such as Ireland. To that extent they make a worthy contribution to the analysis of the societies based on lifetime bond-labor in the Americas, and of the Anglo-American continental plantation colonies in particular.

Since their studies center mainly on Elizabethan times, they give no particular attention to the white-supremacism directed particularly against African-Americans that is of central importance for the study of American history. The same circumstance forecloses any close examination and analysis of the parallels between white supremacy in Anglo-America and the religio-racial oppression of the Irish resulting from the Cromwellian English conquest in 1652 and the Penal Laws of the eighteenth-century Protestant Ascendancy. Finally, this limitation of perspective leaves unconsidered the case of the Irish immigrant who, however poor, Catholic and racially oppressed he/she might have been in Ireland, could emerge in Anglo-America as an ordained member of the "white race" along with Anglo- and other European-Americans, with all the privileges, rights and immunities appertaining thereto. This peculiar social transition is instructive in the principle of the relativity of "race." It certainly was a thing not dreamt of in the philosophy of the English planters of Munster.

Some historians accept the parallels so far as the American Indians are concerned, but do so in such a way as to deny their relevance to the white-supremacist oppression of African-Americans. They cite the opinion of certain seventeenth-century Englishmen to the effect that Indians are born "white" and only become "tawny" by prolonged exposure to the elements.[20] Muldoon, for example, taking note of the English way of lumping the Irish and the Indians together as "savages", asserts, "Crucial to this comparison was the belief that Indians were white men …"[21]

George M. Frederickson defines "racism" in such a way as to exclude extension of the parallel between Irish and Indians to the African-American. While noting that the English justified their genocidal treatment of the Irish and the American Indians by classing them as "savages," he maintains that this did not involve "a 'racial' concept in the modern sense" because it was "not yet associated with pigmentation."[22]

Nicholas P. Canny, developing the lead provided by David Beers Quinn, documented and analyzed significant parallels in the attitudes taken by the Elizabethan English ruling classes toward the Irish and the American Indians. It was his specific aim "to show how the justification for colonization influenced or reflected English attitudes toward the Gaelic Irish and, by extension, toward the imported slave and the indigenous populations in North America."[23] While Canny does not undertake a treatment of the parallel between the Irish and African-Americans, it is not because he considers it irrelevant. Quite the contrary; he writes: "We find the same indictments being brought against the Indians, and later the blacks, in the New World that had been brought against the Irish."[24]

Michael Hechter makes a special contribution by explicitly challenging, in the context of the same parallel, the dominance of the "phenotype" fixation.

Anglo-Saxons and Celts cannot be differentiated by *color*. Despite this, however, racism came to flower [in Ireland] as well. I think that Americans have come to realize how this is possible by following the recent events in Northern Ireland.[25]

The Analogy as Practice

The chronology of English colonial exploits being what it was, Professor Quinn found that the Irish became the "standard of savage or outlandish" social behavior for interpreting African and American Indian societies.[26] In its sameness with respect to the Irish and to American Indians and African-Americans, this ideology and practice was not concerned with "phenotype," color, etcetera, but rather with the "uncivilized ways" of the victims.[27] Once categorized as "uncivilized," they were regarded by the ruling class as doubtful prospects, at best, for admittance to the "Christian" establishment. Resistance to conquest and the ways of colonial exploitation was interpreted in terms of an incapacity for civilization, and this exclusion from "Christian civilization" served to excuse further oppression.[28]

Walter Devereux (1541–76), the first Earl of Essex, who unsuccessfully attempted to plant an English colony in Ulster in 1573, envisaged Ireland as England's Indies, and he predicted that the English government would soon be forced to restrict emigration to Ireland just as the Spanish imposed restraints "for going to the Indies."[29] Another early English conquistador was Robert Dudley (1532–88), first Earl of Leicester. The Irish were "a barbarous people," said Leicester, and the English should deal with them as other Christian colonizers did with barbarians elsewhere in the world.[30] This theme, repeated with variations, supplied a continuing rationale for English oppression of the Irish.

At the time of the plantation of Ulster launched in 1609, the English appealed to Christian fellowship in urging the Spanish government not to give aid and comfort to the Irish resistance. Addressing the Spanish Lords of Council in Madrid, the English ambassador, Sir Charles Cornwallis, asserted that the Irish were "so savage a people" that they long ago deserved the same treatment "used by the Kings of Spain in the Indies, or those employed with the Moors … scattering them in other parts."[31]

Nearly two centuries later Dublin-born Edmund Burke, then the pre-eminent British statesman, observed that the English Protestant Ascendancy regarded the Irish "as enemies to God and Man, and indeed, as a race of savages who were a disgrace to human nature."[32]

English practice in Ireland included elements that are counterposed in the experiences of the Indians and of the African-Americans: namely the expropriation of the lands of the former, and the super-exploitation of the labor and the incorporation-without-integration of the latter. In the one case, "Irish land might be confiscated without much more scruple than the land over which the Red Indian roves."[33] In the other, "The poor people of Ireland [in the eighteenth century] are used worse than negroes by their lords and masters, and their deputies of deputies of deputies."[34]

In 1814, the great Irish leader Daniel O'Connell, himself a staunch abolitionist, wishing to express his disappointment with his English Whig friends for lapsing into chauvinism toward the Irish people, chose to base his comment on the same analogy. "I did imagine," he said, "we [Catholic Irish] had ceased to be whitewashed negroes, and had thrown off for them [the Whigs] all traces of the colour of servitude."[35]

The Whig baron Henry Brougham, for all of his avowed abolitionism, found reason to protest in the House of Lords when Robert Tyler and then his father, United States President John Tyler of Virginia, spoke out in favor of repeal of the Union of Britain and Ireland. It was, Brougham said:

> ... as if the Queen of this country, like the President, were to say she had her heart and soul in the cause of the Carolina and Virginia negroes, and that she hoped ere long to see a white republic in the north, and a black republic in the south.[36]

The Hallmark of Racial Oppression

The assault upon the tribal affinities, customs, laws and institutions of the Africans, the American Indians and the Irish by English/British and Anglo-American colonialism reduced all members of the oppressed group to one undifferentiated social status, a status beneath that of any member of any social class within the colonizing population. *This is the hallmark of racial oppression* in its colonial origins, and as it has persisted in subsequent historical contexts.

The African-Americans

Of the bond-laborers who escaped to become leaders of maroon settlements before 1700, four had been kings in Africa. Toussaint L'Ouverture was the son of an African chieftain, as was his general, Henri Christophe, a subsequent ruler of Haiti, who died in 1820.[37] It is notable that the names of these representatives of African chieftaincy have endured only because they successfully revolted and threw off the social death of racial oppression that the European colonizers intended for them. One "Moorish chief," Abdul Rahamah, was sold into bondage in Mississippi early in the nineteenth century.[38] Abou Bekir Sadliki endured thirty years of bondage in Jamaica before being freed from post-Emancipation "apprenticeship" in Jamaica. The daughter of an "Ebo" (Ibo?) king and her daughter Christiana Gibbons were living in Philadelphia in 1833, having been freed from chattel bondage some time earlier by their Georgia mistress.[39] We can never know how many more Africans were stripped of all vestiges of the social distinction they had known in their homelands by a social order predicated upon "the subordination of the servile class to every free white person," however base.[40]

In taking note of the plight of Africans shipped as bond-laborers to Anglo-American plantations and deprived of their very names, Adam Smith in 1759 touched the essence of the matter of racial oppression. "Fortune never exerted more cruelly her empire over mankind," he wrote, "than when she subjected those nations of heroes to the refuse of Europe."[41] A century later the United States Supreme Court affirmed the constitutional principle that any "white" man, however degraded, was the social superior of any African-American, however cultured and independent in means.[42]

This hallmark of racial oppression in the United States was no less tragically apparent even after the abolition of chattel bond-servitude. In 1867, the newly freed African-Americans bespoke the tragic indignation of generations yet to come: "The virtuous aspirations of our children must be continually checked by the knowledge that no matter how upright their conduct, they will be looked upon as less worthy of respect than the lowest wretch on earth who wears a white skin."[43]

The American Indians

In 1831 a delegation of the Cherokee nation went to Washington to appeal first to the Supreme Court and then to President Andrew Jackson to halt the treaty-breaking "Indian Removal" policy, designed to drive them from their ancestral homes. The delegation included men who were not only chosen chiefs of their tribe but had succeeded in farming and commerce to become "Cherokee planter-merchants."[44] Their appeals were rebuffed; President Jackson was well pleased with the decision of the Supreme Court denying the Cherokees legitimacy as an independent tribal entity in relation to the United States.[45]

This was a culmination, as well as a beginning. Proposals made over a period of two decades by church groups and by the Secretary of War for the assimilation of the Indians by intermarriage had been rejected.[46] At the same time, the independent tribal rights of the Indians were challenged by United States "frontier" aggression. As a consequence of this rejection on the one hand and the disallowance of tribal self-existence on the other, the individual American Indian, of whatever degree of social distinction, was increasingly exposed to personal degradation by any "white" person. In 1823, the Cherokee leader John Ridge (son of Major Ridge), a man of considerable wealth, supplied out of his own experience this scornful definition of racial oppression of the Indian:

An Indian ... is frowned upon by the meanest peasant, and the scum of the earth are considered sacred in comparison to the son of nature. If an Indian is educated in the sciences, has a good knowledge of the classics, astronomy, mathematics, moral and natural philosophy, and his conduct equally modest and polite, yet he is an Indian, and the most stupid and illiterate white man will disdain and triumph over this worthy individual. It is disgusting to enter the house of a white man and be stared at full face in inquisitive ignorance.[47]

The Irish

From early in the thirteenth century until their power entered a two-and-a-half-century eclipse in 1315,[48] the English dealt with the contradictions between English law and Irish tribal Brehon law by refusing to recognize the latter, at the same time denying the Irish admittance to the writs and rights of English law.[49]

In 1277, high Irish churchmen, having secured support among powerful tribal chieftains, submitted a petition to the English king Edward I, offering to pay him 8,000 marks in gold over a five-year period for the general enfranchisement of free Irishmen under English law. The king was not himself unwilling to make this grant of English law. But he thought he ought to get more money for it, and so the Irish three years later raised the offer to 10,000 marks.[50]

What was being asked was not the revolutionary reconstitution of society but merely the abandonment of a "racial" distinction among freemen ruled by English law in Ireland. In the end the king left the decision to the Anglo-Norman magnates of Ireland, and they declined to give their assent. Referring to a replay of this issue which occurred some years later, Sir John Davies concluded, "The great [English] Lordes of Ireland had informed the king that the Irishry might not be naturalized, without damage and prejudice either to themselves, or to the Crowne."[51]

Irish resentment and anger found full voice in the wake of the Scots invasion effected in 1315 at the invitation of some Irish tribes. In 1317, Irish chieftains led by Donal O'Neill, king of Tyrone, joined in a Remonstrance to John XXII, Pope to both English and Irish. In that manifesto the Irish charged that the kings of England and the Anglo-Norman "middle nation" had practiced genocide against the Irish, "enacting for the extermination of our race most pernicious laws."[52] The manifesto presented a four-count indictment: (1) Any Englishman could bring an Irishman into court on complaint or charge, but "every Irishman, except prelates, is refused all recourse to the law by the very fact [of being Irish]"; (2) "When ... some Englishman kills an Irishman ... no punishment or correction is inflicted;" (3) Irish widows of English men were denied their proper portion of inheritance; and (4) Irish men were denied the right to bequeath property.

Whatever exactly the remonstrants meant by their word "race," their grievances, like those of the African-Americans and the American Indians I

have cited, bore the hallmark of racial oppression. From the Petition of 1277
to the Remonstrance of 1317, it was specifically the legal status of the free Irish
men, rather than the unfree, which was at issue.

> The really peculiar feature about the situation in Ireland is that the free Irishman
> who had not been admitted to English law was, as far as the royal courts were
> concerned, in much the same position as the betagh [the Irish laborer bound to the
> land].[53]

From Analogy to Analysis: Colony versus Tribe

In each of these historical instances, a society organized on the basis of the
segmentation of land and other natural resources under private, heritable
individual titles, and having a corresponding set of laws and customs, acting
under the direction of its ruling class brings under its colonial authority people
of societies organized on principles of collective, tribal tenure of land and other
natural resources, and having their respective corresponding sets of laws and
customs.[54] In each of these confrontations of incompatible principles, the
colonizing power institutes a system of rule of a special character: designed to
deny, disregard and delegitimate the hierarchical social – tribal, kinship –
distinctions previously existing among the people brought under colonial rule.
The members of the subjugated group, stripped of their tribal and kinship
identity, are rendered institutionally naked to their enemies, completely
deprived of the shield of social identity and the corresponding self-protective
forms of the tribal and kinship associations that were formerly theirs. Although
not all are to be made slaves of the colonizing power, the object is social death
for the subjugated group as a whole, whether individually and in groups they
are forcibly torn from their home country to serve abroad among strangers, or
they are made strangers in their own native land.[55] They are "desocialized by
the brutal rupture of the relations which characterize the social person," the
tribal, kinship and even the unit family relationships that constituted their
social identity. They are to be allowed only one social tie, that which
"attache[s] them unilaterally to" the colonizing power.[56]

Once the conquest is complete, the "clash of cultures" takes on the flesh-
and-blood form of a host of colonists with newly acquired property claims.[57]
These interests, and their concomitant social and legal attributes, once more
bar the subject people from admittance to the common law of the colonizing
power, although tribal and kinship-group law and custom have been overthrown.

The social death of the subjugated people is followed by social resurrection
in new forms from which they take up the task of overthrowing racial
oppression. In some cases, the ruling power is able to maintain its dominance

only by co-opting a stratum of the subject population into the system of social control. In thus officially establishing a social distinction among the oppressed, the colonial power transforms its system of social control from racial oppression to national oppression. In the nineteenth century, the Haitian Revolution represented the failure of this colonial policy of co-optation; British policy in the West Indies, and the policy of Union with Britain and Catholic Emancipation in Ireland, represented its success. On the other hand, in continental Anglo-America and in the Union of South Africa, the colonial power succeeded in stabilizing its rule on the foundation of racial oppression.

The assault on tribal relations among Africans

The English and other Europeans, and in time European-Americans, first came to Africa as traders and raiders, not as colonists. The colonial option was not theirs, since the people of subequatorial Africa, universally organized as tribal societies made up of kinship groups, were then too strong and independent to allow the seaborne Europeans any other course.[58] For that reason the inherent contradiction of the tribal relations of the African peoples and the European relations based on individual ownership of land and other natural resources remained a latent factor offering no serious obstacle to the development of the enterprises characteristic of that period of the history of that region.[59]

But upon those millions, mainly from West Africa and Angola, who were transported as captive bondmen and bondwomen to the plantation Americas, the clash of cultures was visited with the abruptness of a thunderclap, undiminished by time, and with the harsh and stifling cruelty of exile in chains. In America the colonial employers made "detribalization" a deliberate part of the "seasoning" process undergone by all newly arriving bond-laborers.[60] Colonial authorities made it a matter of policy to frustrate bond-labor rebelliousness by segregating laborers of the same language or other affinity groups from each other. The Coromantees and the Ashanti were particularly feared, it was said.[61]

The acquisition of African bond-laborers for American plantation colonies was made exclusively by capture and abduction. The consequent destruction of their family ties was unaccompanied by the gloss of Christian preachments on the "heathenism" of kinship group and marriage customs, such as were directed at the Irish and the American Indians.

The assault on American Indian tribal relationships

Whilst United States policy very early showed a disregard for the rights of Indian tribes, the avowed determination to destroy Indian tribal relations did not become the dominant theme until after the Civil War. Prior to that time, "Indian policy" moved in a three-phase cycle – massive treaty-breaking incursions by Americans on Indian lands; war; and then another "treaty" involving "cessions" of Indian lands – systematically repeated, until finally the Indians had been "ceded" into the confines of "reservations."[62]

The direct assault on tribal relations had been anticipated by half a century; in 1830 the Georgia state legislature nullified Indian tribal laws within the state's boundaries. This legislation was condemned by its critics as an attack against "the entire social existence of the [Cherokee] tribe." The exiling of thousands of the Cherokee people over the Trail of Tears in 1838 was justified on the grounds that "Common property and civilization cannot coexist."[63] In 1854 (the year of the passage of the Kansas–Nebraska "squatter sovereignty" law) the Omaha Indians "ceded" 10,000,000 acres of land to the United States in a "treaty" which, for the first time, provided for the breaking up of the tribe's remaining lands into individual allotments.[64] The treaty was hailed as giving hope that soon all Indian lands would be "thrown open to the Anglo-Saxon plough."[65]

To the extent that they were consulted in the matter, the Indians overwhelmingly rejected the "severalty" (individual ownership) option for cancelling tribal land rights. If, in the end, their wishes were ignored, it was not because the Indian point of view was not understood. As the ethnologist J. W. Powell of the Smithsonian Institution informed the United States Congress:

> In Indian tribes individual or personal rights and clan rights are very carefully differentiated. The right to the soil, with many other rights, inheres in the clan. Indian morality consists chiefly in the recognition of clan rights; and crime in Indian society chiefly consists in the violation of these clan rights. In Indian society the greatest crime is the claim of an individual to land, and it is also a heinous sin against religion.[66]

"Citizenship," he concluded, "is incompatible with kinship society."

By 1859, a general assault on tribal ownership of land was under way, which would become the central feature of United States "Indian policy" and its "civilizing mission." The legislative culmination of that assault came with Congressional passage in 1887 of the Dawes General Allotment Act. Its purpose and rationale were articulated with drumfire consistency and remarkable clarity. In his 1859 annual report to Congress, US Indian Affairs Commissioner Charles E. Mix advocated converting reservation lands to individual allotments. Indian "possession of large bodies of land in common" was the root of what Mix saw as "habits of indolence and profligacy."[67] A Congressman cited Mix's report in arguing that "the first step to be taken" in the execution of Indian policy was in "uprooting the community of property system [and] . . . extinguishing or modifying the tribal relation."[68] In the course of the 1866 debate on relations with the Sioux, Representative Burleigh of Dakota recalled that, as United States Indian Agent there in 1862, he "did advocate the removal of the [Sioux] women and children with a view to wiping out the tribe."[69]

While the Paris Commune was yet within living memory, in the era of Haymarket and the robber barons,[70] the destruction of tribal relations was polemically associated with the threat of socialism and communism. In the year the Second Socialist International was formed, Indian Commissioner T. J. Morgan showed, more than most socialists did, an instinctual grasp of the vital link between white supremacy and anti-socialism. "The Indians," Morgan said, "must conform to 'the white man's ways,' peaceably if they will, forcibly if they must. The tribal relations should be broken up, socialism destroyed and the family and the autonomy of the individual substituted." The year before, Commissioner Oberly had pointed out the great moral gulf fixed between the two societies. He condemned "the degrading communism" of Indian tribal ownership, where "neither can say of all the acres of the tribe, 'This is mine.'" With the allotment to individuals of Indian tribal lands, he theorized, the Indian would be able to emulate "the exalting egotism of American civilization, so that he will say 'I' instead of 'We,' and 'This is mine,' instead of 'This is ours.'" If the Indians rejected this tutelage, he concluded, it should be forced on them, as it were, for their own good.[71]

The assault on Irish tribal relationships

The conflict between colonizing powers, on the one hand, and African and American Indian societies, on the other, is a familiar story (however distorted); indeed, it is still not completely played out. Not so with Irish tribal society, which was finally and completely destroyed even as the first English settlers were setting foot outside Europe. For that reason, and because everything that is "white" in our historiography instinctively rejects the notion of an affinity of non-European and Irish tribal societies, it seems necessary to treat the Irish case in somewhat greater detail.[72]

In ancient Ireland, that is, up to the invasion of the Norsemen in the middle of the ninth century, "The legal and political unit ... was the *tuath*, ruled by the tribal king," writes D. A. Binchy, "and though the number of tribes tended to vary with the vicissitudes of Irish and political history, it never fell below one hundred."[73] The *tuath*, though tribal,[74] that is, a kinship society, was characterized by a highly developed class differentiation, originating perhaps in the differential disposition of spoils from inter-tribal raids and wars, and in adventitious turns of fortune. However class differentiation began, it represented a contradiction within tribal society. The general evolutionary course of Irish tribal life, as it was at the time of the Anglo-Norman invasion in 1169, appears to have been shaped by this internal contradiction along the following lines: (1) there was a predominant tendency toward downward social mobility;[75] (2) although only a small proportion of the land was held as private property by generations of individual chieftain families,[76] a much larger proportion of the cattle, the main form of wealth, was owned by these nobles (*flaiths*) and by cattle-lords (*boaires*);[77] (3) these chiefs were able to "leverage" (as we might say today) certain factors, such as relative over-population[78] and the recruitment of laborers and tenants (*fuidirs*) from "kin-wrecked" remnants of broken tribes, in a way that enhanced the social power of the chieftain class relative to the generality of tribe members;[79] (4) increasing numbers of tribe members, from the lower category of tenant and share-herder (the *daer-chele*) on down were very poor and dependent,[80] and increasingly reduced to the serflike status of the *sen-cleithe*, who made up the common labor class known to the Anglo-Normans as the *betagh*.[81]

This process of class differentiation took place within the matrix of tribal kinship relationships, the basic social unit of which was the *fine*, more particularly the *derbfine*.[82] Each *derbfine* was made up of all the males patrilineally descended from the same great-grandfather. The *derbfine* was the most basic form of the *fine*; although the latter term is given a wide-ranging application, it always signifies "kinship group." The *fine*, more particularly the *derbfine*, was the radial center of the obligations and loyalties of the individual tribe members, and the sanctuary of that member's rights.

Each *derbfine* occupied its land by assignment from the tribal authority. Upon the death of the great-grandfather there would be, let us say, four surviving grandfathers (his sons). Each of these, then, would be the peak of a new *derbfine*, and usually its chosen chief. Or, at the other extreme, the appearance of a new generation, being a fresh set of great-grandsons, would create, let us say, four new or immanent *derbfines*. Consequently, at regular intervals a redistribution of the lands of the old *fine* was necessary, according to the prescribed schedule of apportionment. (The same schedule governed the distribution of the *derbfine*'s share of booty from cattle raids, and of the lands and property of any deceased member of the *derbfine*.)

The tribal form circumscribed and inhibited the process of class differentiation. For instance, since the *derbfine* was collectively responsible for default by any of its members, no member could become a "free" client of a lord belonging to another *derbfine*, without the collective consent of the *derbfine* as a whole. Likewise, the chief of the *derbfine* could not enter into any external contract without the consent of the entire *derbfine*. Or again, in the exceptional case of the individual acquisition of land by means other than through *derbfine* distribution, the land could not be sold by its acquirer without the consent of the full membership of the *derbfine* – an unlikely prospect. Nor could an individual member of the *derbfine* dispose of his inherited land without the consent of the full membership of the *derbfine*. In general, to the maximum possible extent trade or contract relations were to be entered into only with fellow *derbfine* members. In a society in which the members of the noble (chieftain) class derived their main support from the contracted services of share-herders, such tribal principles obviously would present barriers to class differentiation.[83]

A small proportion of the land was possessed and passed down from generation to generation by chieftains and by certain professional families (families of historians, poets, judges, artisans, physicians). But the vast majority of the land belonged to the tribe as a whole, and not to any individual.

Out of the tribal lands, arable land was assigned by the tribal council to the respective kinship groups as their own, to be used and periodically redistributed among their members as described above. The largest part of the land (which later appeared in the records as "waste, woods, bog, and mountain land") was common land, open without artificial or legal barrier for the free use of all members of the tribe, according to established practices, for grazing cattle, finding fuel, hunting, and whatever other advantages it might offer.[84]

The general tendency of the development of the contradiction between the tribal principles and class differentiation, along the lines noted above, culminated in the emergence of a handful of chieftains, who not only dominated their respective *tuaths* but also subordinated weaker tribes simply by *force majeure*. The eleventh and twelfth centuries, up to the coming of the Anglo-Normans, were consumed by this internecine struggle of these over-kings, some of whom aspired to the eminence of high king (*ard-ri*) over all Ireland.

To what extent – if any – did the emergence of provincial tribal powers and their struggles for dominance affect the basic tribal constitution of Irish society? Was history working its purpose out and "a race evolving its monarchy" so far toward a European-style Irish feudal order that "[t]ribes had ceased to exist ... the Brehon law did not check kings; the tribal control had ceased; old rules and customs were inapplicable to the new order of things"?[85] Was this century and a half of ceaseless war and destruction preparing Ireland to "join Europe" under Anglo-Norman and papal sponsorship?[86] Or did "The structure of [Irish] society ... [retain] a recognizable identity throughout the first half of Irish history, up to the coming of the Normans,"[87] despite this bloody epoch of "centralization" by battle-axe? Was Otway-Ruthren's verdict still correct?

> ... the structure of Celtic society differed far more widely from the general continental pattern than had that of Anglo-Saxon England [at the time of the Norman Conquest], while by the later twelfth century the new Anglo-Norman society was setting on lines which had been so marked a feature of the Norman conquest of Wales and Italy.[88]

If we are to grant political economy its dominion, at the root of the question lies the fact that whereas the English economy was based mainly on land cultivation, the Irish economy was primarily based on cattle-herding.

England's Domesday Book, compiled about 1086 to estimate the national wealth for royal tax purposes, was essentially a survey of cultivable landholdings and resources for their cultivation. A century later in Gaelic Ireland, hides, wool and meat were still the essentials of commerce, and animals and animal products supplied the staples of everyday existence.[89] The main demands of the English Peasant Revolt of 1381 were for an end to the serf's bondage to the land, and for the limiting of rent to four pence per acre. (See Volume Two.) The main problem of the Irish tenant (client) family (along with just surviving the perils of the depopulating random wars) was that of keeping up with the annual rent on the cattle advanced on loan by the chief, which was to be paid back out of the increase and produce of their cattle.[90]

The difference between herding and tillage produced a corresponding variation in the manner of holding and distributing land. Herds vary in extent within very elastic limits, according to their rate of natural increase. They are not fixed in one place, except by the daily care of the herders. Otherwise they rove over the land, no respecters of plot markers, guided by their own feeding and sheltering instincts, their scope limited only by seasonal changes, natural variations of terrain, and grass yield. The net product is measured in terms of the natural increase and produce of the herd. Land, by contrast, is a limited, specific, fixed portion of the earth's surface. For cultivation purposes, it lends itself to parcelling on virtually permanent lines, and to the exclusive use of the parcels by individual production units, where some enforceable advantage is seen in it, according to the differential rent – the marginal yield per unit of labor per measured unit of land.

In Gaelic Ireland, whatever the form of landholding, an individual could not own a large tract of land "in the same sense that he might own a knife or a spade ... [L]ordship of the land belonged to the political rather than the economic order of ideas. It implied authority rather than ownership."[91] Under English (Anglo-Norman) law every inch of land was either held directly by the king or held in fee from the king by private individuals.[92] The colonizers coming from England

> ... believed that they were acquiring a rigid, complete and perpetual ownership of the "land" from the zenith to the uttermost depths – an ownership more complete than that of any chattel – an ownership which they imagined to be self-existing even when the person in whom it should be "vested" was unknown or unascertained. They called this sort of ownership an "estate," i.e., a status, something that stood of its own virtue.[93]

Out of this basic divergence arose a set of superstructural dissonances with regard to principles of marriage and family, post-mortem reversion of property, succession as chief or king, and the conduct of war, to say nothing of other lifestyle and cultural values.[94] There were two conflicting rules of inheritance: gavelkind (an English word adapted for a much different Irish custom) and English primogeniture; two laws of succession: the Irish "tanistry" and the English royal primogeniture; two marriage forms: polygyny for men of the Irish noble classes, and the formally strict but strictly formal monogamy of the English man; two concepts of criminal justice: the adjudication of compensatory liability for particular individual damages, as determined by Irish judges, known as Brehons; and the English public law of offenses against "the king's peace"; and two styles of war: Irish cattle-raiding and tribal political alliances, but non-interference in internal affairs,[95] in contrast to the English territorial conquest and possession under new, presumably permanent sovereignty and land title.

Under the custom of Irish gavelkind, a deceased man's partible wealth – most notably his cattle and assigned cultivable land – was distributed among the surviving men of his particular kinship group, numbering perhaps four to the fourth power,[96] according to a prescribed order of apportionment up and down the generation ladder. Brotherless daughters had restricted rights of inheritance.[97] By English feudal, and later bourgeois, law, the firstborn son was the sole heir, and in the case of "a failure in the male line" the inheritance belonged to the widow, or to the daughters equally. Upon the subsequent marriage of such a female heir, her "estate" became the husband's.

Upon the death of an Irish king or tribal chief, his wealth was disposed of by gavelkind in the same way as that of any other man so summoned. His successor in office was chosen from the ranks of the most influential kinship group, by election of all the enfranchised members of the tribe. This man also succeeded to the perquisites of office, including free entertainment as he travelled the territory, and the use of mesne land cultivated by "base clients" or bond-laborers. In England, at least from the thirteenth century onward, whenever succession to the throne was orderly it was by the rule of primogeniture, and carried with it, of course, private ownership of royal property.

A man of an Irish tribe typically sought to have a large number of sons to add to the strength of his *fine* as a part of his tribe.[98] To that end, the man of sufficient wealth might have a plurality of wives. "Irish law, even in the Christian period," Binchy writes, "extends a limited recognition to other types of union [other than the one with the *cetmuinter*, the "head wife"] of varying degrees of social standing (*lanamnas*), which are neither permanent nor monogamous."[99] The sons of each wife enjoyed equal social standing. The exception was the son of a slave woman, who was barred from inheriting not because the union was any less legitimate than any other, but because the slave was not a member of the kinship group.[100]

The feudal order that the Anglo-Normans brought to Ireland was conceived of as a pyramid of authority and obligation radiating from the king down through various grades of lordship and vassalage, and based on the principle that every rood of ground was privately owned, whether the owner be the king himself or a holder "in fee" from the king. Great lords then let out their lands to lesser lords, and ultimately to the laboring people of various degrees. Given this pyramid of power, the benefits (then as now) were apt to be greater as one rose in the scale of power. Under the terms of the "fee," the land was held "in perpetuity," to be passed undiminished from generation to generation and, more particularly, from eldest son to eldest son. This principle was intended to promote and preserve the stability of the pyramid of authority, which it was thought would be weakened by the division of the land among several heirs. And when a father or other male guardian was negotiating an alliance by the marriage of a prospective heir, a son or a brotherless daughter, there was advantage in brokering for a whole inheritance rather than by fractions of it. Thus entrenched, the principle of primogeniture produced by logical extension the extreme feudal cult of bridal virginity, the chastity-belt mentality, and the illegitimizing of "bastards" in order to assure the integrity of the inheritance.

The contrasting English and Irish laws of inheritance appear to be at the root of one of the most remarkable of the ineluctable contradictions between the two social systems. Under English law, children of wealthy fathers were hostages to their inheritances.[101] The eldest son was the heir; a younger son might move into that position by the death of an elder brother; daughters were to be assigned "marriage portions." Orphan children of the wealthy classes were assigned as "wards" of male "guardians" who exercised the legal authority of parents over them, including the privilege of disposing in marriage of the orphans along with their inheritances or "portions." Where estates of the greatest extent were involved, the marriage engagement of orphans became a source of enrichment for monarchs, at first, and then of the members of a Court of Wards. Whatever the circumstance, it was an essential principle of estate management to preserve a male heir and the virginity of daughters. Consequently, the closest supervision over the children was enforced by the father or the guardian who had the disposal of the estate and the marriage portions. It would have been unthinkable for an English lord to give complete custody of his children to another lord, to be reared and educated from the age of seven until the girls reached the age of fourteen and the boys seventeen.

But in Ireland just such a system of fosterage (called by the English "gossipred") was practiced.[102] For all its formal resemblance to hostage-giving,[103] it was something quite different; it bound rich families to each other in strong fraternal relations. The foster children were cared for with such affection and concern that the foster family ties became as close as those within their own respective families. But whatever might by accident befall the foster child, the disposition of the inheritance among the father's kinship group would not otherwise be affected.

Except for high political offenses such as treason, crimes under the laws of Celtic Ireland were treated as private, personal grievances, indeed like civil suits. The aim was to provide satisfaction for the aggrieved party, and thereby to prevent resort to vengeance. What was denied to the victims, the state did not arrogate to itself. There was, therefore, no capital punishment,[104] no jail, no sheriff, no special instrument of punishment touching life or limb. Complaints originated exclusively with the suit of the aggrieved party, who if successful was awarded reparations assessed by the Brehon. If the guilty party defaulted, his kinship group was liable. English law, by contrast, was aimed at maintaining "the king's peace." Crimes against individuals were breaches of that peace, and subject to public prosecution under public law. Having assumed the role of aggrieved party, the English state, "the crown," substituted public vengeance for private vengeance, and imposed it by means of chains, stocks and prisons, but most commonly the gibbet. In appropriate cases the estate of the guilty party was also subject to heavy fines or escheat to the crown.

Four and a half centuries of coexistence of Gaels with the foreigners, from Henry II to Henry VIII, added force to the transforming effect on the tribal system of the internal contradiction of developing class differentiation. Yet there remained at the end a residue of deep-rooted conflicts between the constitutional principles of the Gaelic and English systems: (1) corporate ownership of land by agnatic descent groups (the *derbfines*) as against individual ownership with testamentary rights; (2) tanistry and election against primogeniture in choosing kings; (3) crimes as torts, and collective liability, in contrast to private liability, the concept of "crown" against the individual for breach of "the king's peace"; (4) inheritance by gavelkind as against primogeniture.

There can be no doubt that the constitutional differences of the Celtic Irish and the English social orders were regarded by the English as a fundamental barrier to colonization. The need for English colonialism to destroy Irish tribal forms and ways was analyzed by Sir John Davies (1569–1626) in his *A Discovery of the True Causes why Ireland was never entirely Subdued ...*, written in 1612.[105] Davies's career uniquely qualified him to observe the course of English interests in Ireland, as he had already served King James I there as Solicitor-General for three years (1603–1606), and then as Attorney-General. He made a thorough research of the records of all reigns from the Anglo-Norman invasion of Ireland in 1169 to the Plantation of Ulster in 1609. In the course of his study he presented the case against the laws and customs of the Irish tribes, which in the English fashion he called "septs."

Tribal customs, Davies said, necessarily tended to cause the Irish to be "Rebelles to all good Government," to "destroy the commonwealth wherein they live, and bring Barbarisme and desolation upon the richest and most fruitfull Land of the world."[106] Unlike "well-governed Kingdomes and Commonweals," Ireland lacked the death penalty, and consequently the strong might freely prey upon the weak.[107] Tanistry made for unstable government because chieftaincy was not a hereditary estate, and election was to the "strong hand."[108] Gavelkind, made more ruinous by the equal standing of "bastards," was the root cause of the "barbarous and desolate" condition of the country. It fragmented estates and made titles transitory, impoverishing the nobility, who nevertheless would not engage in trade or mechanical arts.[109] It was all of a piece with the Irish family form, with its "common repudiation of their wives," the "promiscuous generation of children," and the "neglect of lawful matrimony."[110] The solidarity of the kinship groups, doubly reinforced by the close-as-blood affinities of fosterage, had made it impossible, Davies said, for English authorities to prosecute Irish malefactors.[111]

But as experience in Scotland and Wales would show, and as Davies himself pointed out, such a clash of systems did not make racial oppression the only option. The papal assignment of "lordship" over Ireland to the English in about 1155 did not envisage any such a socio-political monstrosity as racial oppression, but merely the imposition of conformity in Christian practices.[112] For their part, the Anglo-Normans under kings Henry II and John were prepared to proceed in Ireland as they had in Scotland. There they had supplanted tribal organization with feudal power vested in the Scottish chieftains Malcolm Canmore and David I in the late eleventh and the early twelfth centuries.[113] In such proceedings, intermarriage linking families of the respective upper classes was a normal, indeed essential, part of the process. So it began in Ireland. The first of the Anglo-Norman arrivers, Richard Fitzgilbert (Strongbow) de Clare, agreed in 1169 to assist an Irish king, Diarmuit Macmurchada, to regain the domains from which he had been driven by rival Irish chieftains, but only on condition that Strongbow take Macmurchada's daughter in marriage. In 1180 Hugh de Lacy, then chief bearer of King Henry's authority in Ireland, married the daughter of another Irish king, Ruaidri Ua Conchobair. In both cases King Henry reacted with suspicion, sensing a threat to his authority in Strongbow and de Lacy thus independently becoming heirs to Irish lands.[114] Both the marriages and the king's suspicions were rooted in recognition of the legitimacy, in Anglo-Norman terms, of class distinctions among the Gaelic Irish. For the first fifty years of the Anglo-Norman incursion, the English government under three successive kings held to this policy of "assimilating [Gaelic] Irish local government to the system prevailing in England," even though, as I have suggested, it seemed to be learning that this clash of social orders was perhaps more profound than that which the Normans had faced when they invaded England a century before.[115]

Why then was the tested Scottish policy of overlordship abandoned in favor of an attempt to rule in Ireland by racial oppression? Sir John Davies, looking back, ascribed the decision to power jealousy on the part of the Anglo-Norman lords toward any rivalry for royal favor that might evolve among native Irish.[116] A recent study suggests a more particular, that is, economic, basis for the case against the Anglo-Norman lords, along the following lines.[117]

The change of policy began with the death of the English king, John, in 1216, followed by the installation of the Anglo-Norman triumvirate – William Marshal, Geoffrey de Marisco and Archbishop Henry "of London" – in charge of Irish affairs. By that time European grain prices had been rising sharply for fifty years to a level which remained high throughout the thirteenth century.[118] The merchant-connected palatinate Anglo-Norman lords, headed by the aggressive triumvirate, reacted to the prospects for profit to be made by a change from herding to tillage by becoming impatient with the slow-moving, more civil policy of converting the Irish to European ways. William Marshal himself was one of those who profited by switching the land he seized from herding to tillage, and his labor supply from Irish herders to English tillers.[119] We may well believe that such motives were a sharp spur to the abandonment of the policy of assimilation and to the turn to the abortive but historically instructive first attempt to impose racial oppression in Ireland.

How well, if at all, this economic determinist thesis will stand the test of focused research must be left to Irish scholars to decide. That the change was being made with regard to priests was evident by 1220. In June of that year, Pope Honorius III replaced his papal legate in Ireland, Henry of London, for complicity in an English decree "that no Irish cleric, no matter how educated or reputable, is to be admitted to any ecclesiastical dignity."[120] Whatever the explanation – Anglo-Norman power jealousy or high grain prices or a combination of these, and/or possibly still other factors – a pope is our witness that this turn to racial oppression was made by deliberate ruling-class decree, rather than by compulsive fulfillment of some gene-ordained "need to know they were English."

Compelling Parallels

Given the common constitutional principles of the three cases – the Irish, the American Indian, and the African-American – the abundant parallels they present are more than suggestive; they constitute a compelling argument for the sociogenic theory of racial oppression.[121]

If from the beginning of the eighteenth century in Anglo-America the term "negro" meant slave, except when explicitly modified by the word "free,"[122] so under English law the term "hibernicus," Latin for "Irishman," was the legal term for "unfree."[123] If African-Americans were obliged to guard closely any document they might have attesting their freedom, so in Ireland, at the beginning of the fourteenth century, letters patent, attesting to a person's Englishness, were cherished by those who might fall under suspicion of trying to "pass."[124] If under Anglo-American slavery "the rape of a female slave was not a crime, but a mere trespass on the master's property,"[125] so in 1278 two Anglo-Normans brought into court and charged with raping Margaret O'Rorke were found not guilty because "the said Margaret is an Irishwoman."[126] If a law enacted in Virginia in 1723 provided that "manslaughter of a slave is not punishable,"[127] so under Anglo-Norman law it sufficed for acquittal to show that the victim in a killing was Irish.[128] Anglo-Norman priests granted absolution on the grounds that it was "no more sin to kill an Irishman than a dog or any other brute."[129] If the Georgia Supreme Court ruled in 1851 that "the killing of a negro" was not a felony, but upheld an award of damages to the owner of an African-American bond-laborer murdered by another "white" man,[130] so an English court freed Robert Walsh, an Anglo-Norman charged with killing John Mac Gilmore, because the victim was "a mere Irishman and not of free blood," it being stipulated that "when the master of the said John shall ask damages for the slaying, he [Walsh] will be ready to answer him as the law may require."[131] If in 1884 the United States Supreme Court, citing much precedent authority, including the Dred Scott decision, declared that Indians were legally like immigrants, and therefore not citizens except by process of individual naturalization,[132] so for more than four centuries, until 1613, the Irish were regarded by English law as foreigners in their own land. If the testimony of even free African-Americans was inadmissible,[133] so in Anglo-Norman Ireland native Irish of the free classes were deprived of legal defense against English abuse because they were not "admitted to English law," and hence had no rights that an Englishman was bound to respect.

A minor proportion of the Irish were enfranchised in that two-thirds to three-fourths of Ireland where English law prevailed at the height of the Anglo-Norman era.[134] Members of five noble Irish families were granted procedural standing in English courts. Designated the "Five Bloods," they were the O'Neills of Ulster, the O'Connors of Connaught, the O'Melaglins of Meath, the O'Briens of Munster and the M'Murroughs of Leinster.[135] The inclusion of the M'Murroughs and the O'Connors in this list suggests that these exceptions were made, in part at least, to protect land titles and ancillary rights deriving from some of the previously mentioned early intermarriages between Irish and English. Just as in Jamaica centuries later individual free "persons of color" might be enfranchised by "private bills" approved by the colonial authorities, just as prospering individuals of African or Indian descent in colonial Spanish-America could buy royal certificates of "whiteness,"[136] so in the thirteenth century individual free Irishmen might occasionally purchase admission to English law. However, in the three years when this form of enfranchisement was most used, only twenty-six Irish were enrolled. Whilst the number enfranchised is said to have been greater than the number formally enrolled in that status, the generality of the free Irish remained outside its protection.[137] However, unlike the Jamaica and Spanish-America instances, events in Ireland aborted the initial possibility of the emergence of an Irish buffer social control stratum for the English.

The Persistence of Racial Oppression – by Policy Decision

The renewal of English efforts to reduce Ireland to its control in the latter part of the sixteenth century coincided with the full and final commitment of England to the Reformation.[138] Since the twelfth century the English had operated in Ireland under papal authorization; now that benign relationship came quickly to an end, emphasized by continual English Crown expropriations of Church property in Ireland. Not only was Ireland made the object of a more aggressive English colonial expansionism, it became a particular focus of the rivalry between Protestant England and Catholic Spain, then England's chief colonial competitor. In this historical context the Protestant Reformation worked its purpose out by recasting anti-Irish racism in a deeper and more enduring mold. What had fed primarily on simple xenophobia now, as religio-racism, drank at eternal springs of private feelings about "man and God." The historian and member of the British House of Commons Thomas Babington Macaulay would say that the Reformation "brought new divisions to embitter the old ... a new line of demarcation was drawn; theological antipathies were added to the previous differences, and revived the dying animosities of race."[139]

For more than two centuries, Anglo-Irish and native Irish over almost all of Ireland had coexisted in a "nonracial" symbiosis. But now increasing English colonial expansionism and desperate Irish resistance culminated in the nine-year Tyrone War, 1594–1603, over the issue of the very existence of Celtic society. The spiral of history had come full circle. "The issue in the Nine Years War," writes Sean O'Domhnaill, "was knit as never before in any war in Ireland since the days of Edward Bruce." It was not merely a matter of the English "breaking the great lords"; in so doing they had "to subjugate the Irish people."[140] "Neither the Irish nobles nor their followers," writes O'Domhnaill, "wanted innovations in religion, or laws which were not of their own making, or a centralised system of government based on a kingship which had its origin and being in another country."[141] This supreme historic effort of Celtic Ireland by its forces alone to throw off English colonialism ended in defeat.

Before, Irish chieftains had retained sufficient initiative to strengthen their tribal authority by the opportune exploitation of relationships with the English (or with the Spanish). But their social base remained the tribe, with its basic principles of landholding, inheritance and succession.[142] In the decades of "the king's peace" that followed the Tyrone War, however, the English social order in Ireland demonstrated the advantages it held for economic survival and advancement in the context of the emergent modern capitalist commodity production system. The English landlord system was more profitable for the exploitation of Irish tenants and laborers than the Irish tribal system. It was a period of economic undermining of the Celtic system, marked by steady English pressure in the form of "plantation" projects, and by a degree of assimilation of the Irish chieftains into the English system through leasing and mortgaging.[143] It would seem that such erosive factors account in part for the fact that when Irish rebellion was renewed in 1641, rather than being an independent Gaelic struggle it became a subordinate component of the Royalist side in the War of the Three Kingdoms, which grew out of the English Civil War of Crown and Parliament.

Besides the Celtic Catholic Irish, there were the "Old English" Catholics, descended mainly from pre-seventeenth-century settlers. Although they used Gaelic extensively, rather than English, as their everyday language, they sought to assure Protestant English authorities of their loyalty to the mother country and their abhorrence of the ways of the native Irish.[144] Even so, they were stigmatized and penalized as "recusants" for refusing to abandon the faith of their fathers. In 1628 Charles I, hard pressed by the sea of troubles that would eventually topple his throne, sought to raise money by selling certain concessions, called Graces, to the Catholic Anglo-Irish. These dispensations were to include: security of the land titles of Catholics in possession for sixty years or more; permission for Catholic lawyers to represent clients before the courts; and an easing of the pressure to conform to Protestant forms of worship. In return, Anglo-Irish Catholics fulfilled an undertaking to provide the king with £120,000 sterling in three annual installments. But within a few years the king, having spent the money, lost all interest in giving the Graces the promised force of law.

The royal repudiation of the Graces was the culmination of a long train of slights, disabilities and confiscations endured by the Catholic Old English under Protestant English monarchs and the Church of England. Yet despite Charles's bad faith, when the choice was to be made between an Anglican king and Establishment and various kinds of no-bishop Puritans, the Catholic Anglo-Irish became involved for some period and to some extent on the losing royal side in alliance with the native Irish.

The Irish phase of the War of the Three Kingdoms ended in 1652 with complete English Parliamentary victory and conquest. The terms of the English Act of Settlement of 1652 and the Act of Satisfaction of the following year[145] resounded in Celtic Ireland like clods on a coffin lid. Irish rebellion having become fatally involved in the English Civil War, the complete extirpation of Celtic society was made an integral part of the settlement imposed by the Parliamentary Party even though its members might engage in the most bitter polemics over aspects of its implementation. In 1655 a pamphlet by Vincent Gookin, a Cromwellian adviser and functionary in Ireland, called for a tempering of the wholesale uprooting of the Irish under the English "transplantation" policy as set down in the 1652 Act of Settlement.[146] Colonel Richard Lawrence, a member of the parliamentary commission charged with carrying out the transplantation policy, was a Cromwellian settler in Ireland and a leading spokesman for the military party in regard to Irish affairs. Apparently offended by what he considered Gookin's unwarranted interference with his execution of his duties, Lawrence charged Gookin with launching "poisoned arrows against authority ... intended to wound and weaken the English government [in Ireland]."[147] But on the matter of completing the destruction of the Irish tribes, he and Gookin were as one. The Irish, Gookin said, must above all be prevented from "knitting again like

Worms, their divided septs and amities." Lawrence declared that the first
requirement of a successful Irish policy was to:

> break or (at le[a]st) much weaken and limit that great spreading interest of the Irish,
> (viz.) their spreading Septs, which have been hetherto the very seed spots and
> nurseries of all factions and Rebellions, and (withal) the preservers of all their old
> Heathenish, wicked Customs and Habits, which are like the Humane, Jewish and
> Popish Traditions (though generally of a more wicked nature and tendentie)
> recommended from father to son, and so rivited into them by the reputation of
> Antiquity that there is little hope of reclaiming them while those Septs continue.[148]

Not only were previous social distinctions among the Irish to be ignored by
English colonial law; now the English proceeded unrelentingly to decimate the
Irish tribal lords by exile. Within a space of some twenty-four months, 35,000 to
40,000 Irish men – that is to say, one out of every six men over the age of about
twenty-five – were sold in groups to serve as soldiers in foreign armies, chiefly
the Spanish.[149] Vincent Gookin noted with satisfaction that "the chiefest and
eminentest of the nobility and many of the Gentry" had been driven into exile.[150]
As for those that remained, one colonial administrator was overheard to say, they
"must . . . turn into common peasants or die if they don't."[151]

A Classic Case of Racial Oppression

Before the outbreak of the rebellion in 1641, the Celtic, "native" Irish Catholics,
the Old English Catholics and the Protestant "New English" shared possession of
Irish lands in roughly equal proportions.[152] Under the Act of Settlement all
persons, except such as could prove they had maintained "constant good
affection" toward the English Parliamentary government between 1642 and
1652, were to be totally expropriated and evicted from their holdings. Such of the
"ill-affected" as were not under sentence of death or banishment, were
nevertheless also to be expropriated of their lands. They, however, were to be
assigned some fractional equivalent of their original acreage in Connaught and
County Clare. Catholics, according to their degree of "guilt," were to receive
from one-half to one-third portions. "Ill-affected" Protestants were to forfeit
only one-fifth of their estates, and were allowed to relocate outside of
Connaught.[153] More than half the land in Ireland fell under this attainder; of
Catholic landlords, only twenty-six out of a total of around ten thousand were
excepted.[154] As for the native Irish, whatever distribution of their lands might
subsequently be made, it would be done according to English law. This
expropriation meant, therefore, the destruction of Celtic tribal landholding, and
of Celtic society, even in its last stronghold west of the Shannon. Except for the
Royalist Protestants,[155] those of the attainted class who were not hanged or
exiled or otherwise debarred were – much like American Indians of the

nineteenth century – assigned to live on some fractional equivalent of their former holdings in Connaught and in Clare where they found "not wood enough to hang a man, water enough to drown him, nor earth enough to bury him."[156] Of the ten thousand Catholic landholders of 1641, no more than four thousand qualified for any such land assignment at all; only one in five of the original ten thousand was actually assigned land west of the Shannon; and of these about six hundred were in possession twenty years later.[157]

About five out of every eight acres of profitable land were held by Catholics in 1641; by 1654 that share was reduced to one out of twelve.[158] The restoration of Charles II to the English throne in 1660 was followed by some restitution of Catholic lands, to a total of two out of every nine acres.[159] The defeat of Ireland's last great trial at arms, 1689–91, under the banner of the deposed English Catholic king, James II,[160] was made the occasion for the final swamping wave of expropriations, until in 1703 Catholics, who were fifteen out of every twenty in the population, held no more than one acre in nine of the profitable land; within another fifty years the Penal Laws operated to reduce the share to one out of every sixteen acres.[161] Four centuries before, the Anglo-Normans had refused to share English law with the Irish; now the English refused to share Irish land with the Irish. There was to be no new ascendance of assimilation and equality such as the amities of the fourteenth and fifteenth centuries might have promised. From 1652 onward, racial oppression, written into every new title deed, was anchored in the very bedrock of the Irish colonial economy. It was "The Act [of Settlement] by which most of us hold our Estates," said Chancellor John Fitzgibbon with painful candor. ". . . [E]very acre of land which pays quitrent to the Crown is held by title derived under the Act of Settlement."[162]

The native or, as they were termed, the "mere" Irish had been "admitted to" English law in 1613 (11 James I c. 5 [Irish Statutes]), only to be outlawed as "Papists," the common English epithet for Roman Catholics, in 1641. In December of that year the English Parliament in a joint declaration of both Houses had vowed unalterable determination to prevent the practice of the "Popish" religion in Ireland.[163] Now, in the aftermath of the rebellion, the Catholic Anglo-Irish landlords – no less "Popish" than the native Irish – were to suffer under the same religio-racist interdictions as did the Irish chiefs and lords, tenants and laborers.[164] The ancient amities of Anglo-Irish and native Irish survived only in the common fate of Catholics.

When the historian W. F. T. Butler concluded that "A common misfortune had welded all these [Catholics – Old English and native Irish] into one race,"[165] he was not referring to a genetic "merger" of Old English and Irish Catholics, nor to the appearance of some new Irish phenotype. He was affirming, rather, that that which in Ireland took the form of anti-Popery, and in time would be officially known as the Protestant Ascendancy, was a classic system of racial oppression.

2

Social Control and the Intermediate Strata: Ireland

From the standpoint of the ruling classes generally, the imposition on a colony of racial oppression afforded a dual advantage. It relieved the colonial regime of encumbering social forms unsuited to its purposes. Free of such impediments, it could exploit the wealth and the labor of the country with a minimum of interference or embarrassment. The employer could resort to compulsion, by corporal "correction" of a bond-laborer in one case or the threat of eviction of a tenant-at-will in another, in order to secure greater exertion from the laborer, who was denied protection of the law.[1] Normally protected rights or customs could be disregarded in the case of the racially oppressed. A married woman could be denied "coverture," that is, exemption from service to any except her own personal "lord and master," thus affording the master class the opportunity to exploit her labor directly.[2] Labor costs could be reduced by the disregard of religious customs. In Ireland Catholic holidays were disallowed, being not only "heretical" but, more important from a profit-and-loss perspective, more numerous than those provided in the Protestant calendar.[3] American Indian religious observances, such as the Sun Dance, the Ghost Dance and the Messiah phenomenon, were suppressed by United States military force at the end of the nineteenth century in pursuit of white America's "Manifest Destiny" and the capitalist exploitation of the "public" lands and their natural resources.[4]

On the other hand, racial oppression produced an extreme degree of alienation of the laboring people of the oppressed group, and at the same time deprived the colonial ruling class of the services of an indigenous intermediate social control stratum as an instrument for profitable operations.[5] It was a system that limited the possibilities of resort to the normal bourgeois methods for raising of the rate of return by exploitation of labor. In Anglo-America large plantations worked under the system of racial slavery had a higher rate of labor productivity than smaller farms engaged in the same lines of production employing free labor.[6] But the chief means of raising the productivity of plantation labor (given the same input of constant capital on land of the same natural fertility) was the intensification of labor, which necessitated increased supervisory investment, and was absolutely limited by the physical constitution of the laborers.[7] The alternative method, the chief one under "normal" capitalist operations, the revolutionizing of the instruments of production, was inhibited under racial slavery by the employers' reluctance "to trust delicate and costly implements to the carelessness of slaves,"[8] for whom they promised nothing but an intensification of labor. In Ireland under the eighteenth-century Penal Laws, the ban on the Catholic acquisition of land, even on long-term leases – a ban which lay at the very core of British rule there – foreclosed all possibility of significantly raising the productivity of labor by resort to incentives for the Catholics of the laboring classes. In Ireland and in the continental Anglo-American plantation colonies, the criminalization of literacy among the laboring classes made impossible the achievement of even that minimum degree of general elementary literacy required for the use of increasingly complex implements and techniques of production.

The successful conduct of colonial policy required that neither of the negative tendencies reach its fullest development. Exploitation without check led to the genocidal destruction of labor resources; unrelieved alienation led to the revolutionary overthrow of the colonial regime. The history of Hispaniola at the beginning of the sixteenth century and again at the end of the eighteenth century presents examples of both these extreme denouements.[9] Where the option was for racial oppression, the art and science of colonial rule lay in seeking the golden mean to maximize the return on capital investment from a social order based on racial oppression, while assuring its perpetuation through an efficient system of social control.

The history of England in Ireland for more than four centuries from early in the thirteenth century to the initiation of the plantation of Ulster in 1609 is a history of the failure of three strategies of social control: the Anglo-Norman "middle nation"; the policy of "surrender-and-regrant"; and the policy of "plantation".

The First Strategy – the Anglo-Norman "Middle Nation"

The English (Anglo-Norman) invaders found it impossible to establish an adequate social base in Ireland by the permanent settlement of English tenants and laborers, whose situations would be dependent on keeping the natives down and out. "Above all," writes the Irish historian J. C. Beckett, "the number of settlers was too small ... there was no solid body of English or Anglo-Norman middle-class population."[10] This fact was destined to be perpetuated as the historic Achilles heel of English social control policy in Ireland.[11]

On the other hand, the English would not broaden their base of power by admitting the Irish free classes to English law, and for this they lost the power to rule Ireland.[12] Such was the considered judgment of Sir John Davies:

> For as long as they [the Irish] were out of the protection of the Lawe; so as every English-man might oppress, spoyle, and kill them without controulment, Howe was it possible they should bee other than Out-lawes? .. In a word … the English would neither in peace govern them by the Lawe nor could in war root them out by the sword … and so the Conquest [could] never be brought to completion.'

It was the Scots invasion in 1315–18, under Edward and Robert Bruce, in support of an Irish resistance already begun, that sounded the knell of the medieval English attempt to rule Ireland through an intermediate stratum of colonial settlers.[14] The Scots went home, but in the decades that followed Irish resistance proved stronger than the English conquest and y 1400, "English lordship in Ireland in any real sense [had] ceased to exist."[15] Thereafter, the range of actual English control in Ireland was reduced to a few towns and shires; before the end of the fifteenth century it had dwindled to an even smaller area around Dublin, called the English Pale. Elsewhere in Ireland, English control was only nominal at best, being represented by the formal acknowledgement of English suzerainty by the Anglo-Irish feudal lords, and when opportune by occasional native Irish chieftains.

The initial, thirteenth-century attempt to impose racial oppression on the Irish had thus contributed decisively to the defeat of its perpetrators. Speaking specifically of the Anglo-Norman feudal lords, to whom the Anglicization of Ireland had been entrusted, Orpen concludes: "above all, their lack of sympathy with the Irish, whom they regarded as an inferior race, prevented them from establishing their power on the firm basis of a contented people."[16]

While in absolute terms the overall strength of the English side became weaker *vis-à-vis* the native Irish, the strength of the Anglo-Irish[74] *vis-à-vis* the English became greater. It became a matter of concern to the Anglo-Irish lords to make accommodation with the native Irish chieftains. Concomitantly, the old fears of a dilution of their authority with the Crown as a result of the enfranchisement of the native Irish free classes became doubly inappropriate. First, the authority of the Crown itself was reduced nearly to vanishing point in Ireland; second, the English had lost the power to arbitrate Irish rights. Before, the sharing of power with "an inferior race" had seemed impossible. Now it had suddenly become possible, so that "a Gaelic and Norman aristocracy divided the land."[18] Basic questions of landholding and inheritance, formerly so insoluble, were seen in a new light. As previously noted, the Celtic rules of inheritance found favor among the resident Anglo-Irish concerned with the difficulties attendant upon the growth of absentee ownership. And, in a longer process, the Gaelic chieftains came to see possible advantages in the transition from tribal to individual, hereditary forms of landholding, succession and revenue-raising.[19]

More remarkable still, perhaps, the "inferior race" now became the object of the sincerest form of Anglo-Irish flattery. The Anglo-Irish, who had given a social definition to a nationality by synonymizing "hibernicus" with "unfree," now saw the value of themselves becoming "hibernicized." Normal tendencies of social assimilation derived added force from the attraction exerted on the Anglo-Irish by the Gaelic society, its language, family forms and general social customs; and by the native interpreters of the country's culture, its poets, bards, storytellers, and singers.[20]

The English government was understandably alarmed. As Edmund Curtis has noted, "Without the consent and aid of this [Anglo-Irish] 'middle nation' Ireland could not be reconquered. But ... this great class, the race of 'the first Conquest,' which held a third of Ireland, was becoming with every generation more and more Irish in habit, speech, custom, and sympathy."[21] In 1367, the English government convoked an Anglo-Irish Parliament at Kilkenny to cope with the "degenerate English" phenomenon, which was described in the following terms:

> ... now many of the English of the said land, forsaking the English language, fashion, mode of riding, laws and usages, live and govern themselves according to the manners, fashion and language of the Irish enemies, and have also made divers marriages and alliances between themselves and the Irish enemies aforesaid; whereby the said land and the liege people thereof, the English language, and the allegiance due to our lord the King, and the English laws there, are put in subjection and decayed.[22]

One of the most deplored forms of "alliance" was the custom of "fostering," or "gossipred," the giving over of the child of one family into the care and rearing of another, as a way of strengthening class ties (see page 43). The Statute of Kilkenny enacted by this Anglo-Irish Parliament established harsh penalties aimed at stamping out such practices. Any Englishman who thereafter entered into the relationship of "fostering" with any native Irish family, or who married any Irish person, was to be judged guilty of treason and made subject to the full penalty thereof. Other provisions forbade any Englishman to assume an Irish name, use the Irish language or adopt the Irish mode of dress or riding, under penalty of forfeiture of all his lands and tenements.[23]

Seeking to emphasize the distinction to be enforced between all English (native-born or Ireland-born) on the one hand and the native Irish ("the Irish enemy") on the other, the Statute of Kilkenny prohibited Irish tenants, laborers, and tradespeople from speaking their own language while engaged in their occupations within English-held territory. The ban against the Irish grazing their herds within lands claimed by the English suggests a level of economic interpenetration of borderline Gaelic and Anglo-Norman sectors. Members of the Gaelic upper classes were barred from becoming priests or lawyers. All "minstrels, tympanours, pipers, story-tellers, rimers, and harpers" were forbidden to come among the English, on pain of fine or imprisonment and forfeiture of their pipes, percussive instruments, harps, and other weapons.[24]

All in vain. Before it ended in 1534, this phase of Irish history had produced the "all-but-kingship" of Gerald Fitzgerald, the Anglo-Irish eighth Earl of Kildare (1477–1513).[25] Known by the Gaelic name of Garret More (the Great Earl), Kildare formally professed allegiance to the English Crown while presiding, after his fashion, over a grand cohabitation of Anglo-Irish lords and Irish chieftains that was much fortified by intermarriage and fostering, or gossipred, and much disturbed by a constant round of warring over cattle, land, and power.[26]

The political economy of this transformation seems to have brought a net gain for Ireland. The basic factor was the relative weakness of the English colony, the most dramatic demonstration of which was the regular payment of "black rents," or protection money, by the English colonists to the Irish tribes, from the early fourteenth to the early sixteenth century. Viewed macro-economically, as we might say today, these assessments are seen as a form of redistribution of wealth. Following the death of King Edward III in 1377, an Irish Parliament called by the Viceroy was interrupted by Irish, come to demand their "black rent." The Irish agreed to settle for 100 marks, but there were only nine in the exchequer. The balance was made up by individual donations. The O'Connors of Offaly at the end of the fifteenth century "were paid a black rent of £40 a year from the exchequer." By that time, the historians tell us, the English king, Henry VII, had learned that the cheapest way to protect the border of the Pale against the Irish was by payment of "black rents" to the O'Conchobhairs and the O'Neills. Payments were made almost routinely by towns and by counties – Clonmel, Carlow, Wexford, Cork, Waterford. When the English Lord Deputy in Ireland, Richard Nugent Lord Delvin decided not to continue the payments to O'Neill and O'Conchobhair, he was seized and held hostage until the arrangements were made for resumption of the payments.[27] At the same time the disruption of former ruling-class arrangements, coupled with the direct and indirect effects of the plague, tended to improve the conditions of those laborers who survived and for whose services landlords and cattle-lords were forced into extraordinary competition.[28] Although English control of Ireland was eclipsed and the racist mode of rule was supplanted by the workings of "hibernization," ruling-class control in both colonial and Gaelic Ireland remained effective. The Irish laboring classes had probably benefited from the Peasant Revolt in England which, by increasing labor income in England, reduced the incentive for emigrating to or staying in Ireland. But there was to be no replay of that social upheaval in Ireland.

The English identity of the Anglo-Normans proved to be no serious barrier to the emergence of the intimate partnership of the "degenerate English" with the Irish chieftains in ruling Ireland from the fourteenth to the sixteenth century. This fact of medieval Irish history refutes the most fundamental assumption of the Jordan/Degler thesis, namely that, given a choice, persons of a given "gene pool" will naturally choose to maintain that "identity."

The Second Strategy – Surrender-and-Regrant

What the Anglo-Irish palatinate lords could not or would not do, Henry VIII, having taken direct charge of Irish affairs in 1534, would attempt by a strategy of coopting Irish tribal chieftains through a policy of surrender-and-regrant.[29] Under this plan, Gaelic chiefs who surrendered their land claims and pledged their allegiance to the English Crown were in turn regranted English titles to the lands that they already held. (The plan was also designed to cover the cases of "degenerate English" whose land titles might have emerged tainted in the wake of the War of the Roses.)[30] To facilitate and regularize matters, Henry caused the Anglo-Irish Parliament to enact two laws, in 1536 and 1541 respectively. The first (28 Henry VIII, c. 5, *Irish Statutes*) proclaimed Henry VIII to be the spiritual head of the Church of Ireland and obliged all government officers to swear an oath of support of that Church (the Oath of Supremacy); non-compliance was to be punished as treason. The second (33 Henry VIII, c. 2, *Irish Statutes*) established that any king of England was, *ex officio*, king of Ireland.

To the English government the arrangement implied the displacement of Gaelic tribal and customary law regarding landholding, inheritance, marriage and family, and civil and criminal justice generally, and its replacement with English statutory and common law, together with its corresponding administrative forms. For the Irish chieftains, there was a definite appeal in the prospect that – in the Scottish and Welsh way – they might, by a mere formality, secure personal hereditary title to authority and wealth, in place of the Celtic-style elected leadership and tribal ownership. The attitude of the O'Neills of Ulster was typical. "They were not unwilling to be English earls, provided they might retain their sovereignty as O'Neills."[31]

But the Irish chieftains were not disposed to trade Irish land and power for mere English parchment and wax. By way of emphasizing the point, and bringing home to the English government a proper sense of reality, the Irish continued occasionally to collect "black rents" – from English landlords in Ireland. In short, surrender-and-regrant bespoke a parity of weakness in which momentary advantage was decisive. The English government, for its part, was unable or unwilling to pay the cost of a decisive military conquest and occupation of Ireland, and the quartering of troops on the Anglo-Irish proved often more burdensome than the terms that the Anglo-Irish could arrange with the Gaelic lords. The Irish chieftains, on the other hand, could not or would not achieve sufficient unity of will to remove the English thorn from their country's side. In the main, only on those limited occasions when the English could, with their improved military technical means, obtain the advantage was the surrender-and-regrant ritual performed. In sum, for the English, land was "easier won than kept ... if it be gotten one day it [was] lost the next."[32] As for the Anglo-Irish, the complaint of "degeneracy" raised at Kilkenny was being heard a hundred and fifty years later: except in the walled towns, they were still adherents "of Irish habits, [and] of Irish language."[33]

If the Irish chieftains might sometimes be tempted, the tribes of which they were the elected leaders were not; they rejected surrender-and-regrant as a recipe for Celtic suicide. They took their stand on constitutional principles: a tribal chief "had no more than a lifetime tenure of the territory to be ruled and ... in accepting feudal tenure of the territory he was disposing of what did not belong to him."[34] In 1585, the English-educated Hugh O'Neill asked to be given the title Earl of Tyrone, which his grandfather had borne, and agreed to forswear the title "the O'Neill." Elizabeth and her councillors eagerly granted the request, believing that in the greatest Ulster chieftain they had found, as Hill puts it, "an apostle worthy of his great mission, to wit, the introduction of English manners and customs – and even costumes – in Ulster." But, he continues, "they had evidently calculated 'without their host,' or at least had overlooked the fact that, even were the earl thoroughly disposed to carry out his friends' ideas, he had not the power to impress this new policy, at least not very promptly, on the native population."[35]

Such promptness was not to be expected, however, for the completion of a process in Ireland such as had required a century (mid-eleventh to mid-twelfth) in Scotland and, after nearly four centuries, was completed in Wales only in 1534. Furthermore, events in Ireland were overtaken by rapid developments on the wider stage of European history that doomed this second social control strategy after a trial period of less than twenty-five years.

The Third Strategy – Protestant Plantation

The failure of the surrender-and-regrant policy became apparent at the very time the split with Rome resulting from the English Protestant Reformation was bringing new complications and greater urgency to the "Irish problem." Here began the redefinition of the struggle between England and Ireland as one of Protestant against Catholic, a process which took more than a century to reach its fullest development. Encouraged by Rome and Spain, Irish Catholics, Anglo and Gaelic, began to show occasional readiness to unite not just for a change of English government, but for the end of English rule in Ireland.

In the face of this challenge, the English had recourse to a third plan, that of "plantation," begun, interestingly, during the last two years of the Catholic

Mary Tudor's reign (1553–58).[36] Just as the eclipse of the feudal barons and the rise of the bourgeois monarchy in England had necessitated the development of a new buffer social control group of gentry and yeomen (see Chapter 2 of Volume Two), so now with the "removal of the Old English as a buffer" in Ireland "a colonizing gentry and yeomanry were desired instead."[37]

Under this new plan the English capitalists were to finance the settlement of English tenants in Ireland in numbers sufficient to provide a self-supporting militia to guarantee the eventual subjugation of the entire country. Title to the lands to be settled would be transferred from Gaelic Irish and Old English to New English, by confiscation of Church lands, by challenge to defective titles, and especially by the escheat of lands of Irish and Anglo-Irish resisters. The English tenants would supplant Irish tenants for the most part, although laborers were to be mainly native Irish; for the rest, the Irish would to some considerable degree be displaced and transplanted beyond the advancing areas of English settlement. Under the rules laid down for the ill-starred first Ulster plantation (1572–73), for instance, no member of the Celtic Irish owning or learned classes was to be admitted. Within the plantation boundaries, to be Irish was to be a "churl," a laborer "that will plow the ground and bear no kind of weapon."[38] It was even proposed by some of these early English colonialists that the Irish be enslaved *en masse*.[39] In any case, it was ordered that, "no Irishman, born of Irish race and brought up Irish, shall purchase land, beare office, be chosen of any jury or admitted witness in any real or personal action, nor be bound apprentice to any science or art that may damage the Queen's Majesty's subjects."[40]

Designed as a "specific response to rebellion,"[41] plantations were undertaken with varying degrees of success in Leix and Offaly (1556), Ulster (first attempt 1572) and Munster (1585).[42] Yet, none of the basic barriers to the establishment of an English peace in Ireland was cleared away. Gaelic resistance proved incurably resilient, and the ambivalent Catholic Anglo-Irish (the English by "blood") were increasingly put on the defensive and alienated by the government-fostered Protestant New English (the English by "birth"). The effort continued to be hampered throughout the period by the fiscal priorities and limitations of an English exchequer burdened with the charges incident to England's increased role in world affairs, while military and administrative costs in Ireland generally exceeded Irish Crown revenues.[43]

As a program for establishing social control, the plantation concept was a negation of surrender-and-regrant. The latter presumed the cooptation of the Irish chieftains as the social buffer; "plantation" was based on their degradation and exclusion. That did not, however, prevent a cynical use of the vestige of surrender-and-regrant as a mask for a two-step expropriation of tribal lands into the hands of Protestant English "planters." In such instances, the English first went through the form of granting a chieftain title as owner of the tribal lands. Then charges were trumped up against him, he was tried by a corrupt and/or coerced jury, and executed. The chieftain having been convicted of a crime against English law, "his" – that is, the tribe's – lands were escheated by the English crown for distribution to English planters, often the same officials who had themselves managed the matter.[44]

The anger, revulsion and trepidation that the Irish chiefs and tribes felt on witnessing such a treacherous assault on Celtic rights precipitated the most dramatic demonstration of the ineffectualness of the plantation policy, the great Celtic war of liberation, the Tyrone War, 1594–1603. Hugh O'Neill and Red Hugh O'Donnell had been "ennobled" as the earls of Tyrone and Tyrconnell respectively under the surrender-and-regrant arrangement. Under their leadership, the Irish defeated the English forces in a series of field engagements in the north, climaxed by the great victory at Yellow Ford (called "the defeat of Blackwater" by the English) on 14 August 1598.[45] The contagion of the rebellion swept southward and "shaked the English government in this kingdom [of Ireland], till it tottered, and wanted little of fatal ruine." By November the Irish had obliterated the Plantation of Munster, which the English had boasted was theirs by right of fire, sword, and famine. "Neither did these gentle Undertakers make any resistance to the Rebels," wrote an English chronicler, "but left their dwellings and fled to walled Townes,"[46] and thereby supplied the epitaph for three failed English strategies for establishing an intermediate social control stratum in Ireland.

Within the walls of the port city of Cork, Edmund Spenser, the promised Sheriff of Cork, "mused full sadly in his sullen mind"[47] upon the ruin of the English plantation, and of his own personal estate there.[48] As poet, Spenser had written his masterpiece *The Faerie Queene* with Queen Elizabeth as his model. Now, "out of the desolation and wastedness of this ... wretched Realm of Ireland," Spenser addressed to her "A Breife Note of Ireland." The policy of conquest by piecemeal plantation was a demonstrated failure, he told her, nor would England ever win the submission of the Irish by negotiated terms. He proffered his judgment that only by complete conquest with overwhelming force, and by a strategy of famine, could a lasting English peace be achieved in Ireland.[49]

Celtic Ireland in a New World Context

To equate "the king's peace" in Ireland with the complete conquest of the entire island was by no means a timeless truism. The Anglo-Normans, even at the height of their power at the beginning of the fourteenth century, were reconciled to the fact that one-fourth to one-third of Ireland was outside the range of English authority.[50] From that time, English power in Ireland waned and wasted for more than two centuries, during which English policy did not equate "the king's peace" with complete conquest, but merely with the defense and control of the area of the English Pale. While the English government condemned the "Irish enemy" in extreme terms, its operational object for "conquest" was not the "wild Irish" but the "degenerate English" throughout most of the island. Even as the tide was beginning to turn in England's favor, England felt obliged at least to pretend that the surrender-and-regrant policy was intended only as a formal rather than as a substantive alteration of the power equation in Ireland.

As late as 1600, the English position in relation to Ireland was much like that of the European powers as it was and would remain until well into the nineteenth century with respect to sub-Saharan Africa. In neither case could the invaders accomplish the first essential step in colonization, the establishment of their commanding authority over the prospective colonial territory.[51] "If the Europeans were masters on the water," writes Basil Davidson, "the Africans were masters on the land; and they made sure they remained so."[52] Consequently, instead of conquering and occupying African territory as they were able to do in the nineteenth and twentieth centuries, the Europeans, as Kenneth G. Davies puts it, could only be "drawn into quarrels which they had not sufficient force to conclude."[53] In a review of Irish history made in 1800, Lord Clare, the Chancellor of Ireland, commented on the parallel. "The first English settlements here," he said, "[were] ... such as has [sic] been made by the different nations of Europe on the coast of Asia, Africa, or America."[54]

The frustration of the English was all the more galling as they watched the Iberians establish successful colonies on newly discovered territories, not merely to raid or trade, but to exploit directly the labor of the native peoples and transported Africans. The ruin of the English plantation of Munster lent emphasis to Sir Edwin Sandy's comment on the apparent inability of "Northern people" to compete with Iberia in the matter of "durable and grounded settlement."[55]

A turning point came, however, with the close of the sixteenth century. On a surging tide of economic development, and of a corresponding social and political transformation, England emerged as an aggressive competitor in the new-fledged world market that had been opened up by the Portuguese as navigators and colonists and the Spanish as colonialists and gold-grabbing conquistadors. In this new role England entered into an historic confrontation with Spain (with whom Portugal was united in a single kingdom from 1580 to 1640). This challenge was signalled most dramatically by Sir Francis Drake's 1577–80 circumnavigation of the globe, from which he returned to England laden with Spanish treasure worth half a million English pounds sterling,[56] and by the defeat of the Spanish Armada in the English Channel eight years later. In addition to its simple exploitative colonialist ambitions regarding Ireland, the English government was preoccupied with the potential Spanish threat from that quarter. If the proximity of Ireland to England was an advantage for the purposes of English expansionism, that very proximity made it a potentially deadly staging point for the invasion of England. It was already an "old Prophesie" in 1600, that "He that will England winne / Must with Ireland first beginne."[57] Now England was poised at the threshold of its career as a world colonial power, with Ireland as its first objective. Such was the wider context out of which, at the very moment marked by the ruin of the Munster plantation, England's new "complete conquest" perspective arose.[58]

Conquest by Famine

For nearly a year and a half after the Battle of Yellow Ford, the cause of Irish independence remained in the ascendant. The largest English army ever assembled in Ireland until that time, twenty thousand men under Robert Devereux, second Earl of Essex, marched and counter-marched, dwindled, and (some said) dawdled through the spring and summer of 1599, but to no other end than an empty truce with O'Neill. The English were fain to acknowledge that "Tyrone [is] now master of the field."[59] But under Queen Elizabeth's Great Warrant of Ireland of January 1600, the English created a new military establishment in Ireland of twelve thousand foot and three hundred horse, which was increased to sixteen thousand foot and twelve hundred horse by November 1601.[60] The newly constituted army was commanded by a new Lord Deputy, Charles Blount, Lord Mountjoy.[61] In the four and a half years between the Battle of Yellow Ford and Tyrone's submission on 31 March 1603, the English government expended 1.3 million pounds sterling for the conduct of the war in Ireland, not counting charges for munitions, employment of spies, bribe money and military construction, or the costs of transporting personnel, equipment, and supplies.[62]

England's "early industrial revolution" (with assistance, of course, from piratical depredations like Drake's) provided the money capital needed to support massive military expenditures in Ireland; it made particular technological contributions vital to English victory in the Tyrone War. By this period English cast iron cannon were of such excellent quality and yet so low in price that they were being exported to countries throughout Europe.[63] It is not surprising, then, that the English made telling use of their artillery advantage in Ireland.[64] Thanks to England's rapidly expanding cloth industry, the English army's appeals for warm clothing were on the whole adequately met. Of the total charges of 283,674 pounds sterling for the English army in Ireland for the fiscal year 1601–2, almost one-fourth went for soldiers' apparel made in England.[65]

The new and rapidly expanding gunpowder mills in England gave the English army in Ireland a very substantial advantage.[66] Moryson explained the disparity in the respective numbers of battle casualties of the English and the Irish thus:

"... we had plentie of powder, and sparing not to shoot at random, might well kill many more of them, than they ill furnished of powder, and commanded to spare it, could kill of ours."[67] The advantage was limited by the fact that fewer than six out of every ten of the English foot soldiers were armed with muskets. The bulk of the remainder were pikemen,[68] a category in which the Irish were a match for the English.

Although Spain's rate of industrial progress was by now slower than England's, Spanish industrial production, except in the output of cheap cloth, was at that time on the whole equal to the English.[69] Still, aside from whatever merit there was in Irish complaints regarding Spain's commitment to the Irish cause, the Spanish unquestionably were at a disadvantage by virtue of the fact that men and materials sent to Ireland from Spain had to travel six times as far as those sent from England.

Great as England's resources were with respect to Ireland's, and more favorable as was its geographic position than Spain's for purposes of intervention in Irish affairs, the advantages were not all on the English side. The Irish were fighting on their own ground for their own way of life; and they were leagued with Rome. When it came to enduring the rigors of campaigning, especially in cold weather, the English believed that the Irish soldiers were "harder" than the English.[70] England's enormous war expenditures could not be sustained indefinitely, draining one-third more every year than was invested in joint stock overseas ventures. This problem increasingly preoccupied the English government, as the correspondence of Queen Elizabeth and Robert Cecil with Mountjoy reveals. Lord Cecil, a chief minister, wrote to Mountjoy about the end of June 1602 to say that the army could not continue to be maintained at its present size, "without extreme prejudice to [the English] state." For that reason he was, he said, trying to persuade the queen to propose terms to the Irish for ending the war, for "in short time the sword cannot end the warre, and long time the State of England cannot wel indure it." Four months later the queen expressed her alarm that the cost of the war "consumes Our treasure, which is the sinewes of our Crowne."[71] The English had to win clearly and decisively; the Irish had only not to lose.

Edmund Spenser in his "Breife Note" to the queen had coined an English maxim: "Until Ireland can be famished, it cannot be subdued."[72] As secretary to the Lord Deputy of Ireland, Spenser had seen this method practiced during the second Desmond War (1578–83).[73] Although Essex had been unable to carry his mission through to success, he had based his early hopes on "burning and spoiling the Country in all places ... [thus to] starve the Rebell." When Mountjoy arrived, he resolved unhesitatingly to base his strategy on that same principle, the war being "no way so likely to be brought to an end, as by general famine."[74] The denial of all sense of human fellowship, even to the most eminent Irish chieftain,[75] implicit in this policy was given a gloss of Christian religiosity and English patriotism. At one point, as he surveyed the death and desolation he had brought to Tyrone's country, Mountjoy confessed a feeling of "humane commiseration," especially because the souls of the dead starved Irish had "never had the meanes to know God," nor to acknowledge a divinely anointed sovereign like England's, but only a tribal Irish chieftain.[76]

Under Mountjoy, the starvation strategy was prosecuted without remission for three and a half years throughout three-fourths of the country, most significantly in Ulster, the main stronghold of Celtic tribal power. The strategy was pressed in harvest and in seedtime; by winter warfare, driving the Irish naked into the woods; and in all seasons cutting down crops in the field, preventing planting, and confiscating stored grain.[77]

In Ulster, it appears, the English strategy involved not merely reducing the natives to submission, but at the same time clearing the territory for English plantation. Writing to the government in August of 1601, Mountjoy said, "We doe not omit anything of our purposes, but ... every day cut downe his [Tyrone's] Woods or his Corne." Mountjoy went on to express the hope that before the end of the winter he could depopulate Tyrone's country and thus prepare the way "to make Ulster one of the most quiet, assured, and profitable Provinces."[78] Although he was unable to keep to his original schedule, Mountjoy remained firm in his resolve. In September he directed Sir Arthur Chichester to proceed with "clearing the Country of Tyrone of all inhabitants, and to spoil all the Corne which he could not preserve for the Garrisons."[79]

None the less, it seems likely that the English might again have failed of complete conquest if they had not been able to procure the collaboration of a number of the native chieftain class by promises of support in securing tribal leadership.[80]

Throughout the war the English recruited surrendering Irish units who pledged their allegiance to the queen. At times more than half of the English fighting force was made up of such recruits, and Mountjoy was provided with a special allowance of 1,000 pounds sterling per month for their employment.[81] Whatever expedient arrangements were made with members of the Irish chieftain class, however, the English government did not find it appropriate to make any promises of future favor for the rank-and-file Irish soldier. Indeed, a deliberate policy was followed most likely to foreclose his future altogether. While such Irish units remained in English service, Mountjoy was resolved to "so employ them ... as they shall not be idle, but shall be exposed to endure the brunt of service upon all occasions." These Irish submitters, Mountjoy said, "were kept in pay, rather to prevent their fighting against us, than for confidence in their fighting for us."[82] In the same cynical vein, Moryson wrote: "the death of these peaceable swordsmen, though falling on our [English] side, was yet [regarded as] rather a gain than a loss."[83] Clearly, such new-won Irish adherents were not looked upon as harbingers of a peacetime reconciliation in a "king's peace" of fraternal English subjects all;

they were not presumed to be prototypes of an emergent Irish middle class.[84]

Plantation – Once More

In the wake of Mountjoy's victory over the Irish, the English Solicitor-General for Ireland, Sir John Davies, was duly sanguine about English colonial prospects in Ireland under the "happier reign" of his new sovereign, James I, whose succession to the throne of England upon Elizabeth's death near the end of March 1603 coincided with the formal surrender of the Celtic forces. By Davies's own definition, however, the English were still a long way from having achieved an English peace in Ireland. "For, though the Prince both beare the Title of Soveraigne Lord of an entire Country," said Davies, the conquest cannot be regarded as complete "if the jurisdiction of his ordinary Courts of justice doth not extend" to all parts of the territory, and if "he cannot punish Treasons, Murders, or Thefts, unlesse he send an Army to do it."[85]

For nearly a decade the English had warred against O'Neill, invariably termed by them "the arch traitor." But instead of rooting him out and hanging him (as they had done with many lesser "rebels"), they granted him personally generous terms. O'Neill was to retain the title Earl of Tyrone and was allowed to keep the greater part of his lands, long since legally transmuted from tribal to individual chieftain property by surrender-and-regrant. Indeed the title was allowed as a specific quid pro quo for O'Neill's disavowal of the tribal title of "the O'Neill."[86]

Celtic Ireland was defeated but not uprooted; its Ulster bastion was overthrown, but tribal affinities remained strong in Connaught, and in refugee bogs and woods in Ulster and other parts of the country. English armies had dispersed the Irish military forces, but in Connaught and most of the rest of Ireland "the jurisdiction of ... ordinary courts of justice" did not prevail. At the same time, for urgent state reasons, financial and otherwise, the English army in Ireland had to be reduced from over twelve thousand to nine thousand by April 1604.[87] Despite the devastation and conquest that Mountjoy had achieved, Moryson said, "Yet hee left this great worke unperfect."[88] Indeed it was the ancient imperfection: the lack of a system of social control "without sending an army to do it"; and the essence of that problem was still the lack of an intermediate social control stratum.

Opting for Racial Oppression

So long as the English colonialists had lacked the force to impose and stabilize their commanding authority in Ireland, all schemes for English social control had been foredoomed. English victory in the Tyrone War, however, presented a realistic prospect for reducing Ireland to an English colony. At that point the English might have opted for the establishment of social control by the cooptation method, as Portugal and Spain did in appropriate circumstances, or along the lines that the English themselves had employed with respect to Scotland and Wales. But the very process that produced English military dominance over Ireland had made Ireland a major focus of the struggle between Catholic Spain and Protestant England. As a consequence, just when cooptation of the Irish upper classes might have supplied a basis for a viable system of social control in the Irish colony, the option was foreclosed by a redefinition of racial oppression in Ireland as *religio-racial* oppression. For the same reason, the English ruling class could not recruit an intermediate stratum by promotion of a portion of the Irish laboring classes to the yeoman status, on the English model. Such being the limitations, there was no alternative for the English colonialists but a return to the policy of plantation, in the hope that Mountjoy had finally cleared the way for the installation of a Protestant middle-class buffer and social control stratum throughout Ireland.

But military conquest, however complete, could not free English policy from the fundamental contradiction inherent in its option for racial oppression in Ireland. The heart of the matter was that the fundamental purpose was to accumulate capital at the highest possible annual rate by the exploitation of labor, primarily, at the time, the labor of high-rent-paying Irish tenants-at-will. As Sir John Davies said in his *Discovery of the True Causes why Ireland was never Entirely Subdued*, considered from the standpoint of the colonial bourgeoisie as a whole, this objective required for its most profitable development the establishment of a "civil" regime, free of heavy deductions necessary for military occupation. But he had already concluded, as English Attorney-General in Ireland, that a civil regime could not be achieved until the majority of the population were settlers, not native Irish. Since this result could not be accomplished by converting the Irish to Protestantism nor by genocidal depopulation, a massive infusion of Protestant settlers was needed. Aside from the Scots and Ulster, and the "Ulster custom", which will be discussed in Chapter 5, this meant almost complete reliance on bringing in English tenants. But as noted in Chapter 3, and more fully in Chapter 5, the English tenant's prospects in Ireland were unattractive because the rents that the Irish were required to pay to the landlords were so much higher than they were at home in England that it would not pay the English tenant to emigrate to Ireland. For their part, the English landlords throughout plantation Ireland had long since proclaimed their preference for Irish tenants on account of the high rents they paid. The English Privy Council, at the beginning of the seventeenth century, laid down rules against employing the natives in the new Plantation of Ulster, on the premiss that: "As long as the British undertakers may receive their rents from the natives, they will never remove them."[89]

"Here," concluded historian George Hill, "was the grand dilemma . . . for the undertakers [the capitalist landlord investors] ... naturally held out their hands for help to those who could most readily and efficiently render it. In fact they actually clung to the Irish ... although to do so was risking more or less the overthrow of the whole [plantation] movement."[90]

Because the English were unable to escape that dilemma, plantation as a strategy of social control would fail finally and forever in three-fourths of the country. Ulster was of course the exception. There, plantation did ultimately achieve an historic success, due to special circumstances that made it possible to avoid the paralysis of the grand dilemma. The Ulster plantation is reserved for a later point of our discussion (see Chapter 5).

It is to be noted in proceeding to the implementation of the plantation policy, the first step toward "the king's peace" was invariably a military one: the mass exiling of tens of thousands of Irish men – in the wake of the Tyrone War; again, after the peace of 1652; and at the end of the Jacobite war of 1689–91.

In 1634, after thirty years of "complete conquest," England's Irish Council was fain to confess to King Charles I that dependence upon the treasury-draining, "rebel"-infested (that is, made up mainly of native Irish Catholics) army was "of absolute necessity" as "the great Preserver of public Peace, and the most effectual Minister in the Execution of your Majesty's Justice amongst us."[91] Between 1616 and 1641, plantation was tried in Longford, Leitrim, Wexford, southern Offaly and Galway. Despite some limited success, the effort ultimately ground to a halt, its basic purpose as unrealized as ever.[92] Thus, eighty years and nine plantations after that strategy was first undertaken, the Gaelic Irish still held one-third of all the profitable land in Ireland, the same proportion that they had held at the beginning.[93] The greatest of all Irish wars of resistance was in the offing.

The exiling of the defeated Irish soldiers by the victorious English under the terms of the Cromwellian Act of Settlement of 1652 did improve the prospects for reducing the English government's prohibitively high military costs in Ireland. By January 1653, thirteen thousand Irish soldiers had gone to "foreign parts," and some time later that year the English army of occupation was reduced by ten thousand to a level of twenty-four thousand. By the spring of 1654, the remaining twenty-some thousand Irish soldiers had been sold away. In August of the following year, the English forces were reduced again, to nineteen thousand on a budget of £336,000 per year. Officials in England were trying to convince those in Ireland that the number should be still further reduced to fifteen thousand.[94] Yet in 1658, annual military expenditure was still £246,000, far exceeding total English revenue from the colony.[95] Nevertheless, Lord Deputy Henry Cromwell had already concluded that no further reductions should be made "until an efficient Protestant militia could be provided."[96]

The first specific aim of the Cromwellian expropriation policy provided for in the Act of Settlement and the Act of Satisfaction was to reward the capitalists (called "Adventurers") who had lent the Parliament war money, and to pay off the veteran officers and soldiers who had served in Ireland. But it was to be done in a form designed to provide Ireland with enough yeomen and resident gentry to make a self-sustaining, well-officered, horse-and-foot, Protestant English settler militia.

As a capital fund for discharging English government obligations and pledges,[97] Irish land served its purpose. By May 1656 all soldier claims had been settled.[98] But settling claims against the English government was one thing; settling Protestant English on Irish soil was another. By 1670, 7,500 disbanded English soldiers out of 35,000, and 500 out of 15,000 Adventurers, had received confirmed titles to Irish land.[99] Yet, of those, only a fraction actually settled there, far too few to provide the hoped-for militia. In 1662, Sir William Petty expressed the opinion that even if every last one of the 50,000 Adventurers and soldiers settled in Ireland, military government would still be necessary. "Government [in Ireland] can never be safe without chargeable Armies," said Petty, "until the major part of the Inhabitants be English."[100] He was thus stating a general principle of social control by regimes based on racial oppression.

Added emphasis was lent to the impossibility of achieving any such requisite proportions of English emigration when the flow of migration was actually reversed during the brief reign of the Catholic James II (1685–88). Protestant settlers fled Ireland in large numbers, and almost no Protestants remained in the nominally English army there, all as a result of the pressure of the Irish Catholic cause, reinvigorated by the expectation of imminent repeal of the Act of Settlement.[101] At that point, in the summer of 1687, Petty was led to propose a final solution to the Irish question, one intended to eliminate the need to develop an intermediate social control stratum, and at the same time to reduce the requisite military administration there to fiscally manageable proportions.

Displaying his professional penchant for quantification, Petty estimated the adult Catholic population of Ireland at somewhat over 1,200,000. The maintenance of social control by military administration, he said, required somewhat more than one English soldier to every ten Irish men.[102] At such a ratio, the English would need to maintain an Irish military establishment of more than 60,000 men, a fiscal impossibility.

Citing supposed historic precedents, Petty proposed a way out: a mass transplantation to end all transplantations, to be achieved not by force but by the appeal of universal benefit to be derived by English and Irish, Protestant and Catholic.[103] Protestants and Catholics in proportional numbers would be transplanted to England, reducing the total population of Ireland from 1,300,000 to 300,000,[104] eight-ninths Catholic, one-ninth Protestant. Though the Irish Catholics to be transplanted to England would number nearly 900,000, they could, he argued, be safely controlled by the Protestant majority there only slightly diluted from its existing eight-to-one majority. The 300,000 Catholics remaining in Ireland would be kept exclusively to animal husbandry, half as "herdsmen" and half as "dairy women" (a division of labor by gender). According to Petty, this arrangement would prosper both England and Ireland.[105] In this way the problem of social control in the colony was to be reduced to manageable proportions. The proper one-to-ten ratio of military forces to subject population could be maintained, the 150,000 Irish herdsmen being matched by 15,000 English foot soldiers. Some 2,000 horse soldiers and 4,000 men at sea would make assurance doubly secure.[106]

Petty's proposal, though courteously received by the king, did not get lengthy consideration because at that moment the Jacobite–Catholic cause was riding high. However wildly implausible this plan may seem in retrospect, we should not believe it was so regarded by Petty's English contemporaries.[107] But no practical implementation of the idea was ever attempted; within a couple of years, James II was defeated and deposed, Petty had died, and the plan became no more than a footnote.

Fantastic and unrealizable as it was, nevertheless it is a very illuminating footnote for the subject of social control. For it proceeded with flawless logic from the ineluctable problem of the establishment of a civil regime in Ireland.

Ireland and General Principles of Colonial Social Control

The English efforts to establish social control in Ireland that are noted in this chapter present a variation on the general principles of the social control problems and policies of colonizing powers, and their relationship to the option for racial oppression. After first establishing commanding authority, colonizers pursued one of two general lines of policy according to circumstances as they found them.[108] Where they found a developed and well-defined hierarchical system of classes, the new rulers sought to adapt the pre-existing social structure to their own needs, coopting amenable elements of the old order into their colonial administration as a buffer and social control stratum over and against the masses of the superexploited wealth-producing laboring classes. Such was the case of the Spanish in Peru and Mexico;[109] of the Portuguese in India[110] and the East Indies; of the English in India; and of the Dutch in the East Indies.

Where, on the other hand, the conquerors encountered a society with no previously developed significant class differentiation, and therefore with no available social handle to serve their rule, they employed a policy tending to the complete elimination of the indigenous population by slaughter and expulsion. The Spanish in the Caribbean, the Portuguese in Brazil, the English in St Vincent, and the English and Anglo-Americans in North America demonstrated this approach. In such cases, the colonizers found themselves obliged to seek foreign supplies of commodity-producing labor,[111] and were obliged to invent and establish an intermediate social control stratum for each colony by promoting elements of the imported laboring class.

With regard to the extermination option, English military and economic policies from the sixteenth to the eighteenth century produced in Ireland episodes of mass extermination, as we have noted, which in absolute numerical terms and ferocity were possibly a match for those chronicled by Las Casas in the West Indies. But it would have been impossible for the English to have perpetrated such complete extermination of the Irish people as that executed upon the Caribs and Arawaks by the Spanish in the Caribbean in the sixteenth century. Unlike the situation of the Spanish in the Caribbean, there was in Ireland a much more substantial general English hostage population subject to retaliation for any such attempt. Although the English achieved an over-whelming military advantage over the Irish, still they at no time enjoyed the degree of practical invulnerability possessed by the Spanish *vis-à-vis* the indigenous peoples of the Americas. Moreover, but one Las Casas arose to deplore genocide in the Caribbean, and then only after the deed was done. But the Catholic Irish and Anglo-Irish had as allies popes, potentates and powers, sworn antagonists all of the English Protestant "heretics." In the struggle against their English rivals, the hopes of these powers depended, militarily and morally, on the preservation of the Irish resistance to the English, though not necessarily upon Irish independence. Finally, even if the English colonialists could have safely undertaken a Caribbean-style extermination of the Irish, it would have been detrimental to their own interest. Unlike the Spanish, the English were sixty years away from sure access to African sources of labor. And England could not supply English agricultural laborers for Ireland at a cost matching that of Irish labor already in place.[112]

On the other hand, the English option for religio-racial oppression in Ireland at the end of the sixteenth century eliminated the possibility of recruiting an indigenous intermediate social control stratum. This would remain the central problem of British rule in Ireland for more than two centuries. To the partial extent, namely in Ulster, that they succeeded in establishing an intermediate stratum, they were able to maintain racial oppression "without sending an army to do it." Outside Ulster, they would in time be forced to abandon rule by racial oppression. These developments and their Anglo-American parallels will be the subject of other chapters.

3

Protestant Ascendancy and
White Supremacy

Following the defeat of the Irish–Jacobite cause in the brief war of 1689–91, the Protestant Parliament of Ireland embarked on a seventy-year program of Penal Law enactments to rivet the Protestant Ascendancy in place.[1] In due historical course, Edmund Burke analyzed and arraigned Protestant Ascendancy as a "contrivance," an invention unexcelled in the history of statecraft "for the oppression, impoverishment, and degradation of a people." But it is the less frequently cited analytical portion of his argument that exposes the hallmark of racial oppression characteristic of Protestant Ascendancy, and which is equally applicable to white supremacy. Burke compared various forms of the normal principles of social hierarchy characteristic of class societies, as exampled by the Venetian oligarchy, on the one hand, and the British constitutional combination of aristocracy and democracy, on the other. In the former, the members of the subject population are excluded from all participation in "the State." But they are "indemnified" by the untrammeled freedom to find places in the "subordinate employments," according to their individual competitiveness and their mutual accommodation. "The nobles" in such a society, said Burke, "have the monopoly of honor; the plebeians a monopoly of all the means of acquiring wealth." The British state, on the other hand, has a plebeian component; yet the aristocrats and plebeians do not compete with each other, and social rank among the non-aristocrats is arranged, again, by the normal process of free competition. But, "A plebeian aristocracy is a monster," said Burke, and such was the system of Protestant Ascendancy in Ireland. There, he said, Roman Catholics are obliged to submit to "[Protestant] plebeians like themselves, and many of them tradesmen, servants, and otherwise inferior to some of them [yet] ... exercising upon them, daily and hourly, an insulting and vexatious superiority."[2]

A full century of Irish history – between the overshadowing English Glorious Revolution of 1688 and the French Revolution of 1789 – was entirely dominated by the Protestant Ascendancy and its Penal Laws. Down to the present day, the spirit of Protestant Ascendancy has continued to inform British rule in Ireland.[3] Students of Irish history have therefore necessarily devoted

71

much attention to the nature and operation of the Ascendancy and the Penal Laws. Students of American history, however, have almost completely neglected this field of investigation for insights into the system of racial oppression which, more than any other force or factor, has controlled the flow of United States history.[4]

This neglect is due, no doubt, to the fact that they mistake the chattel form of labor, along with perceived variations in physical appearance, for the essential substance of racial oppression. This shallow view has remained an unchallenged assumption. But if asked to defend the exclusion of the Protestant Ascendancy from the category of racial oppression, our historians might seek to rest their case on two arguments. First, they might say, however relentlessly destructive the intentions of the English ruling class might have been, they did not try to impose a system of chattel bond-servitude on the Irish in Ireland, as they did on African-Americans. They might further argue that the Irish could escape from the penalties of the Penal Laws simply by becoming Protestant, whereas the African-Americans had no such simple way out of their bondage. A fairly long digression is required here to confront these two issues. Readers who wish to avoid the detour may go directly to the subheading, "Penal Laws and 'Race' Laws" (page 81).

Why Not Chattel Bond-servitude?

If the English conquistadors did not formally enslave the Irish, it was not because they were economically and militarily weaker in relation to the Irish than they were *vis-à-vis* the chattel bond-laborers in the distant American plantations. In 1654 Ireland's armies had been defeated and exiled; the only horses to be seen bore English soldiery. To the English ruling class Ireland was a *tabula rasa* on which it could inscribe what it would.[5]

Nor was it because the slavery idea was unthinkable among the British ruling classes. In the period 1571–75 the English government sponsored two unsuccessful private enterprise efforts to colonize Ulster, the northern province of Ireland. At least some of the organizers of these projects proposed to reduce the natives of the area to slavery, as their role models had done in "the Indies."[6] In 1662 Sir William Petty proposed that slavery be instituted in England itself for "insolvent Thieves," as a profitable alternative to the customary hanging. "As slaves," he said, "they may be forced to as much labour and as cheap fare as nature will endure."[7]

Indeed, in Scotland, whence so many Presbyterian lowlanders came to Ireland as junior partners in the English colonization, that very prescription had been established practice since the sixteenth century.[8] Then, in 1606, not only thieves and vagrants but free coalminers and salt-pan workers were made bond-slaves by law. Out of consideration of the "great prejudice" to the owners of coal and salt enterprises resulting from workers leaving their jobs "upon hope of greater gain" in some other employment, the Privy Council legally bound those workers to their masters, for life, unless they were sold along with the mine or saltworks, or were otherwise disposed of by their owners.[9] Their servitude was not only perpetual but in practice hereditary. This chattel slavery lasted until after it had ceased to be economically advantageous to the employers at the end of the eighteenth century.[10] In the second half of the seventeenth century, the expansion of Anglo-American colonial enterprises opened a wider field for employment of "vagrants" and convicts as chattel bond-laborers, although for terms somewhat shorter than those commonly imposed in Scotland. Bond-laborers, said the *Edinburgh Review*, "were a leading export of the country, and it was the regular custom, when a ship was sailing for the plantations, for the master, or owner, or charterer to petition the Privy Council for a certain number of vagrants."[11] These unfortunates would then be provided as if they were so many bushels of oats, or tubs of coal. In the period between the Restoration and the Act of Union of England and Scotland in 1707, when the English Trade and Navigation Laws were effective in reducing Scottish trade with the colonies, "a cargo of Scottish servants ... was probably the most profitable cargo a merchant could take to the colonies."[12]

In Ireland, the resumption of the bond-labor trade after a lapse of some five hundred years began as an English – primarily political – policy. The English embarked on the plantation of Ulster in 1609, aiming to establish a colony of English and Scots in six counties[13] in the north of Ireland, the land there having been expropriated from Irish "rebels" defeated in the Tyrone War.[14] There were in Ulster still four thousand "idle men ... who have neither house, lands, trade nor other means,"[15] and whose heads were full of "treasonous" designs against the English occupiers of their lands. At this point the English found a way of promoting the colony's tranquility and improving the balance of trade at the same time. In the autumn of 1610, one thousand Irish men, nine hundred of them from Ulster, were shipped under a contract of sale to the King of Sweden to serve his royal Protestant will, presumably as soldiers. An English officer was to go along and look after the exporters' interests in the completion of the transaction.[16]

After the victory over the Irish in the 1641–52 rebellion and war, the English renewed this policy on a scale which proved to have fateful historic consequences. As mentioned on page 249, note 149, some 35,000 to 40,000 defeated Irish soldiers were sold to foreign states,[17] again presumably to serve as soldiers, although some number, thought to have been less than a thousand, were shipped to the West Indies as plantation laborers.[18] At some point in the process, these Irish soldiers would fall into the power of "drovers and sellers ... who now find the miserable Irishman to be the best commodity in trade."[19] Petty says that six thousand priests, women and boys were shipped along with the soldiers, although it does not appear that they were separately entered in the accounts.[20] In this case, the primary concern of the English was again political; so much so that when the Spanish Crown or some other customer was slow in paying, the English government would underwrite the process.[21] But for those alert to opportunity and favorably situated socially, it offered a profitable field of private enterprise.[22]

In the forced transportation of Irish women, children and men to bond-servitude in the Anglo-American colonies between 1652 and 1657, mercenary motives were predominant. On 20 April 1652, the English House of Commons empowered the Council of State "to give away to the Transporting out of Ireland, into foreign parts such of the Irish as they shall think fit, for the Advantage of the Commonwealth."[23] Upon application to the English authorities, merchants were issued licenses to take cargoes of Irish to America for sale as bond-laborers. The terms were such as to assure the merchant's profit. At first, it seems, the licenses were issued upon application to the English Council of State. In a period of less than one year, April 1653 to January 1654, six merchants were thus authorized to take nearly 2,000 Irish, including 400 children and 310 women, to be sold as bond-laborers in Anglo-America. Among the transport ships to be used under these licenses were two specifically designed for this beginning of "the Irish slave trade," a character-ization made by contemporary observers and adopted by a number of Irish historians.[24] Subsequently the common practice was direct negotiation between the slave trader and the magistrates, jail-keepers and overseers of the poor in specific Irish localities. The procedure was conducted under color of the English vagrancy act of 1597 (39 Eliz. c. 4), an English domestic law transposed unceremoniously to another country for a purpose for which it had never been contemplated. It was a legal fiction, of course. The people taken up were not, for the most part, "rogues, vagabonds or sturdy beggars," as defined in the English Poor Law of 1601 (43 Eliz. I c. 2). Furthermore, these measures were taken under color of an English statute; it had never been enacted by the Irish Parliament. Nevertheless, it served just as well for capturing, selling and transporting non-vagrants, as actual vagrants. There ensued, says Abbot E. Smith, "a period of licensed kidnapping on a large scale, with the magistrates and officers of the law actively conniving at it under some pretense of statutory sanction."[25] When this slave trade was ended in 1657, the Council of State, all in seeming innocence, declared that "for the money's sake" the system had "enticed and forced women from their children and husbands, and children from their parents, who maintained them at school."[26] The execution of this policy, writes Prendergast, "must have exhibited scenes in every part like the slave hunts in Africa."[27] Again, following the defeat of the Irish–Jacobite struggle of 1689–91, Irish soldiers were shipped by the thousands into perpetual exile, mainly to France.[28]

If the English did not establish their regime in Ireland on a system of chattel bond-labor as they did in the plantation colonies in America, it was simply a matter of relative "cost/benefit" ratios. A comparative study of the living standards of laborers in Ireland and bond-laborers in continental Anglo-America is yet to be made. But there is much evidence to suggest that the cost of labor per unit of output in Ireland would not have been reduced by the substitution of chattel bond-labor for the common Irish condition of tenancy-at-will.[29]

In 1652, at the end of eleven years of war, the land of Ireland was "void as a wilderness," so that, as the records found by Prendergast told, people were driven by desperate hunger to eat carrion and even human flesh.[30] Over the next two decades, a remarkable economic recovery occurred, but only the merchants and landlords benefited by it; six-sevenths of the population of Ireland were still living at mere subsistence level.[31] It was during that period that William Petty wrote his *Political Anatomy of Ireland* for the edification of the restored Stuart monarch, Charles II, in the course of which he estimated the financial losses suffered in Ireland as a result of the 1641–52 war. The cost of the population loss he put at £10,355,000 sterling, on the assumption that "you value the people who have been destroyed in Ireland as Slaves and Negroes are usually rated, viz., at about £15 one with another; Men being sold for £25 and Children £5 each."[32]

During the eighteenth century, normal economic conditions prevailed generally in Ireland. Yet despite the fame of Irish livestock products, Ireland's tenants were obliged to "live on potatoes and buttermilk, and yield all other profitable produce as rent."[33]

A weekly newspaper in 1721 described the cottiers of Ireland (a category closely corresponding to the United States sharecropper of the post-Reconstruction period, except that the cottiers were share-laborers, paying their rent by laboring on the landlord's land) as "Poor wretches who think themselves blessed if they can obtain a hut worse than the squire's dog kennel, and an acre of ground for potato plantation, on condition of being as very slaves as any in America."[34] An Englishman who traveled in Ireland in 1764 observed that their condition was "little better than slavery." That same year Lord Chesterfield, who had served as Lord Lieutenant of Ireland twenty years before, declared: "The poor people of Ireland are used worse than the negroes."[35] Yet according to Lecky the unemployed agricultural laborers, without a "cabbin and garden" were even worse off than the cottiers. The mass of the Irish laboring people were cottiers, he says, "because in most parts of Ireland it was impossible to gain a livelihood as agricultural labourers or in mechanical pursuits."[36] The great majority of the Irish Catholic cottier families were forced to eke out a subsistence on plots of less than an English acre.[37] Yet they were by law forbidden to surrender less than two-thirds of the crop yield to the landlord, or less than one-tenth to the Anglican Church of Ireland.[38] An indication of how much the Irish laborer's conditions had deteriorated may perhaps be inferred from the fact that in 1589 English landlords in Ireland preferred Irish to English as tenants because, it was said, Irish tenants, paying one-fourth the yield as rent, were a much more profitable labor force.[39]

Being too impoverished to put by any store, the people were famished when crops failed. Untold thousands of people died in famines between 1721 and 1741.[40] At such times the cost of labor might sink beneath the absolute limit required to sustain it. During one such dearth, in 1729, a keen observer of Irish life estimated that only 15 percent of "breeding couples" in the country were able to maintain their own children. The workers were generally unemployed, but their deprivation was such, he said, that "if at any time they are accidentally hired to common labour, they have not strength to perform it."[41] During the worst of these eighteenth-century famines, in 1740–41, a country gentleman in Munster wrote of its horror in a letter to Primate Boulter:

> I have seen the labourer endeavouring to work at his spade, but fainting for want of food, and forced to quit it. I have seen the aged father eating grass like a beast and in the anguish of his soul wishing for his dissolution. I have seen the helpless orphan exposed on the dunghill, and none to take him in for fear of infection; and I have seen the hungry infant sucking at the breast of the already expired parent.[42]

In that famine, according to one historian, nearly 400,000 people died,[43] nearly one out of every five of the total population. Then might people driven to beggary seek a competitive edge by blinding their children, to make them more appealing objects for charity.[44]

In the non-famine year of 1787, the Attorney-General of Ireland declared in a speech to the Irish House of Commons:

> It was impossible for the peasantry of Munster any longer to exist in the extreme wretchedness, under which they laboured. A poor man was to pay £6 for an acre of potato ground, which £6 he was obliged to work out with his landlord at 5d. per day.[45]

The impossibility of the peasant's position was a mathematical certainty. At 5d. a day, in order to pay the rent for his potato ground the peasant would have to devote 288 days a year exclusively to working for the landlord.

If the eighteenth-century Anglo-Irish Establishment ever wondered whether, from the standpoint of political economy, they had chosen wisely in the matter of labor relations, they could have found comfort in the following fact. Taking English and American current money wage rates as the respective bases, the relative cost differential between English and Irish common labor was more than two and a half times the cost differential between wage-labor and bond-labor in continental Anglo-America. In real terms, the England/Ireland differential was still greater than the American free/bond differential.[46]

Why not Conversion to Protestantism?

The consensus of authorities is that the population of Ireland doubled, rising from around 2 million to 4 million over the course of the eighteenth century,[47] of whom between 75 and 80 percent were Catholics.[48] Beginning in 1703 an official record was kept of all Irish Catholics converted to Protestantism; by the end of 1800, about 5,800 names had been enrolled.[49] Let it be assumed for purposes of statistical convenience that the incidence of conversion was constant from year to year, and remained so for the entire eighteenth century, and that the rate of natural increase among the convert population was the same as it was for the general population.[50] The indicated convert population at the end of the century would then be less than 8,000, representing a ratio of less than three converts to 1,000 nonconverts.

Since conversion was the only road to emancipation for the Irish Catholics ground down by the Penal Laws, it is interesting to compare these Irish statistics with those regarding the achievement of emancipation from the slave laws in the Americas by persons of African descent. In the African-American population at the end of the eighteenth century, the ratio of free to bond persons appears to have been not less than ten times the convert-to-nonconvert ratio in Ireland. In the United States the overall proportion of free African-Americans to those in bondage was thirty-five times the corresponding Irish ratio.[51]

Where conversion did take place, it occurred mainly among the propertied and professional strata (and with varying degrees of religious conviction).[52] By becoming Protestants – and only by becoming Protestants – they were enabled to enjoy social recognition and the privileges normal and essential to members of their class: the rights to purchase land, hold office, serve on grand juries, hold army commissions, have their sons educated in schools and universities, bear arms, exercise the rights of patriarchy (including that of bequeathing their property), etcetera.

For the rank-and-file of Catholic laboring people there was little prospect of bourgeois enrichment; yet even for them, as Butler puts it, "there was always the possibility of escape from all disabilities, and of a rise into the dominant caste provided only that they embraced the dominant religion."[53] Within that "dominant caste," even those of the laboring classes had their Protestant privileges: the right to long-term leases and security against eviction; the right to become trades apprentices, and to that end to be taught to read and write; the right to marry without the landlord's permission, and exemption from systematized degradation at the hands of the Protestant landlords, "middle-men," etcetera. "A Protestant boy," writes J. C. Beckett, "however humble his origin, might hope to rise, by some combination of ability, good luck and patronage, to a position of influence from which a Roman Catholic, however well-born or wealthy, would be utterly excluded."[54]

Why then was the Protestant harvest of souls so meagre? There was certainly an aversion to surrendering this last main institutional vestige of Celtic Irish selfhood, an aversion daily reinforced by the indefatigable labors of a thousand Catholic priests, working illegally, and the equally energetic efforts of the Protestant tithe-proctors. But, if there had been not one Catholic priest in Ireland, if the Irish people could have amnestied the Protestant conquistadors and their descendants for their arrogant rapacity, if 997 out of 1,000 of the Catholic Irish had signified a desire to become "born-again" as Anglican Protestants, it is doubtful whether so much as a page would thereby have been added to the roll of converts.

The reason is not hard to see. Ireland, as a British colonial enterprise, was founded on the original expropriation of Catholic-owned lands and the continuing exclusion of Catholics from acquiring new land titles or even long-term leases. From this flowed the disfranchisement of Irish people of the entrepreneurial and professional classes, as well as the superexploitation of the laboring people, mainly tenants-at-will.[55] Speaking of the motives for the enactment of the Penal Laws, Lecky writes:

> ... behind all this lay the great fact that most of the land of the country was held by the title of recent confiscation, and that the old possessors or their children were still living, still remembered, still honoured by the people. It was the dread of a change of property springing from this fact that was the real cause of most of the enactments of the penal code.... It was this which gave the landlord class most of their arrogance.... It was this above all that made them implacably hostile to every project for ameliorating the condition of the Catholics. In 1709, the [Irish] House of Commons presented an address to the Queen [reminding her that] "the titles of more than half the estates now belonging to Protestants depend on the forfeitures in the two last rebellions."[56]

To impede and frustrate the efforts of Catholics to get legal redress for the loss of lands and rights in the wake of the 1689–91 war, the Irish Parliament enacted a law, effective 1 March 1698, barring any Catholic from acting as "solicitor, agent, or manager in any cause or sute ... in this kingdom [Ireland]."[57] When, in time, conforming former Catholics began to enter law practice, the Protestant Ascendancy, instead of rejoicing at the growth of their flock and the betokened defeat of the "Papist enemy," slammed the gate against further entry. A law was enacted requiring conformists to undergo years of closely supervised probation of the sincerity of their conversion. Only when, after that period, they merited the Protestant seal of approval, might they practice their profession.[58] Between 1703 and 1760 a dozen laws were enacted "To prevent the growth of Popery," but not even one "To promote the growth of Protestantism."

"There are too many amongst us," said Archbishop Synge, "who had rather keep the Papists in an almost slavish subjection, than have them made Protestants, and thereby entitled to the same liberties and privileges with the rest of their fellow-subjects."[59] The historian W. K. Sullivan concurred. "If the whole body of the Catholics had become Protestant," he wrote, "the Ascendancy would lose their advantages." The unwillingness of the Protestant Ascendancy to promote the conversion of Catholics to Protestantism was, he declared, "one of the great central facts of Irish history."[60] The findings of the late Maureen Wall led her to concur with those opinions, and to advert to an analogy: "The religious bar operated to exclude the Catholic majority from all positions of importance . . . in the same way as the colour bar has operated to ensure white ascendancy in African countries."[61]

There was another set of reasons for the ruling-class opposition to conversion, reasons having to do with the problem of social control. Although the ruling party was the Anglican Church of Ireland Establishment, two-thirds of the Protestants were Dissenters, primarily the Presbyterian Scots-Irish of Ulster. From the very first year of his assumption of the role of manager of Irish affairs in 1724, Primate Hugh Boulter understood that the maintenance of British rule in Ireland required the prevention of any tendency toward coalescence of a potential opposition majority.[62] Above all, that meant preventing the aggrieved middle-class yeomanry-type Presbyterian and other Dissenters from making common "nationalist" cause with the mass of the peasantry. The time-tested key to that strategy was the inveterate prejudice of the Dissenters against the Catholic peasantry. In 1798, the rebellion of the United Irishmen was defeated, and with it the last best hope (until 1922) for a republican and independent Ireland. In the aftermath of that defeat, John Beresford, one of the most powerful figures in the Anglo-Irish establishment, pointed to this anti-Catholic prejudice as the key to the government's victorious policy:

> The lower order of Roman Catholics of this country are totally inimical to the English Government. . . . Again, the Dissenters are another set of enemies to British Government. They are greatly under the influence of their clergy also, and are taught from their cradles to be republicans; but their religion, which is as fierce as their politics, forbids them to unite with the Catholics; and to that, in a great measure, is owing that we were not all destroyed in this rebellion.[63]

Obviously, any serious effort to convert Irish Catholics to Protestantism would have been potentially ruinous for Anglo-Irish statecraft. On both primary and secondary grounds, therefore, if the English colonial system of racial oppression in Ireland was to be perpetuated, it was essential that the people not be converted, but remain Catholic.[64]

Anglo-America: Parallels and Divergence

In Anglo-America, no less than in Ireland, spiritual rebirth by conversion to Protestant Christianity presented a contradiction to social death by racial oppression. It had been received doctrine in England, at least since before the publication of Thomas Smith's *De Republica Anglorum* in 1583, that Christians could not hold Christians in bondage.[65]

In the early 1630s, the directors in England of the ill-fated English colony on Providence Island rebuked the resident official, Samuel Rishworth, in this regard. Rishworth, they said, had been in error in saying that African laborers who had not yet been converted to Christianity, could not legally be held in bondage.[66] The Englishman Richard Ligon lived in Barbados from 1647 to 1650. In those years the island was beginning its transition from a primarily tobacco-based economy to one of sugar planting, with the help of fellow Protestant Dutch sugar planters retreating from Brazil.[67] At that time the majority of the workers were English, Irish and Scots limited-term bond-laborers, although African workers, serving unlimited terms, were present in an increasing proportion; by 1655, they would outnumber the Europeans in the labor force.[68] At one plantation an African-Barbadian asked Ligon to help him become a convert to the English religion. Ligon promised "to do my best endeavours," it being understood that the worker's owner had the final say. But when approached, the owner rejected the suggestion as bad business practice. "The people of that Island were governed by the Lawes of England," he said, "and by those Lawes, we could not make a Christian a slave." Ligon then advanced the argument which, half a century later, would be the staple of plantation missionaries. He was not requesting that a Christian be made a slave, said Ligon, but merely that a slave be made a Christian. The owner rejected this as mere prevarication. Once the man was converted to the English religion, he said, "he could no more account him a slave," and "all the planters in the Island would curse him" for having opened "such a gap" whereby these laborers could escape from their bondage.[69]

In Virginia in 1656, an African-American woman successfully sued for her freedom, citing among other grounds the fact that she was a Christian.[70] The implications of the decision in this case caused considerable concern among Virginia employers of bond-labor. In 1667, the Virginia Assembly cut the knot wherein freedom was tangled with conversion; they enacted a law providing that "the conferring of baptisme doth not alter the condition of the person as to his bondage or freedome."[71] Thus the Anglo-American plantation bourgeoisie had found a way to have the best of both the sacred and the profane spheres. The best of the sacred was gained in a new gospel that reconciled "English liberties" to slavery; the best of the profane by insuring against legal challenges made on religious grounds against holding lifetime hereditary bond-laborers.

Despite the assurance of this Virginia precedent, South Carolina owners were still wary of the conversion of Africans and African-Americans to the English religion. By 1710, the Society for the Propagation of the Gospel, whose business was converting "heathens," had learned that it was "to do nothing without the Master's good testimony" as to the reliability of the prospective convert.[72]

The very language of conversion became an issue both in Ireland and in the English beginnings in the West Indies. In the first flush of Reformationism, the Anglo-Irish Parliament excluded the use of Gaelic in the conduct of church services.[73] Despite an Elizabethan mood swing on the matter of Gaelic, and despite occasional evangelical gambits, official policy continued to be guided by the warning that Edmund Spenser took from history and taught to his fellow English colonizers: "The speech being Irish, the heart must need be."[74]

In Anglo-America, plantation owners at first viewed the diversity of languages among the bond-laborers as a major factor in effective social control. In 1680 the Gentlemen Planters of Barbados in London argued that they had "no greater security than the diversity of our negroe's languages [,] which would be destroyed by conversion, in that it would be necessary to teach them in English."[75] For reasons already discussed, avoidance of conversion of the Irish to the English religion was essential to the system of religio-racial oppression. On the other hand, the Anglo-American plantation bourgeoisie, whose land claims and social control did not rest on religious distinctions, learned – with the help of the new exegesis – to reconcile their class interests with the conversion of Africans to the English religion.

Penal Laws and "Race" Laws

The parallels to be noted here are the more forceful, perhaps, because they originate in contemporary aspects of British colonialism.[76] At the threshold of the eighteenth century, it was Virginia that led the way among Anglo-American continental colonies in codifying the concept that, "race, not class ... [is] the great distinction in society."[77] It was then, too, that the Protestant Ascendancy instituted its system of Penal Laws, designed to "put an end to all other distinctions in Ireland, but that of Protestant and Papist."[78]

Professor Maureen Wall extended the parallel with racial oppression. The Penal Laws, she wrote:

> operated to exclude the Catholic majority from all positions of importance in the country – from the professions, from parliament, and from the ownership of property – in the same way as the colour bar has operated to ensure white ascendancy in African countries in recent times.[79]

The essential elements of discrimination against the Irish in Ireland, and

against the African-Americans, which gave these respective regimes the
character of racial oppression, were those that destroyed the original forms
of social identity, and then excluded the oppressed groups from admittance
into the forms of social identity normal to the colonizing power. Take away
these elements, and racial oppression would cease to exist. The codification of
this system in the Penal Laws of the Protestant Ascendancy in Ireland and in
the slave codes of white supremacy in continental Anglo-America have been
frequently abstracted and analyzed in the works cited here. The discussion that
follows considers them according to the defining characteristics of racial
oppression: (1) declassing legislation, directed at property-holding members of
the oppressed group; (2) deprivation of civil rights; (3) illegalization of
literacy; and (4) displacement of family rights and authorities.

Declassing legislation

The English had destroyed the Celtic tribal form of individual social identity.
With the Penal Laws they proceeded to bar the Irish from the system of social
class identification normal to the bourgeois social order. The process began
with laws designed to declass the members of the Catholic Irish freehold
classes of all degrees from life tenants upward. The aim was, as Sigerson put
it, "to thrust them down into the slough of despond with the racked under-
tenantry."[80] This non-recognition of social distinction among the oppressed
population was made explicit by the highest judicial authorities in Ireland, the
Chancellor and Chief Justice, who laid down the principle that except for
repression and punishment "the law does not suppose any such person to exist
as an Irish Roman Catholic."[81]

Even in the wake of the last great sweeping confiscations, there were still
a few Catholic landholders in Ireland with undisputed titles to their estates.
Normally, though reduced in means these freeholders, gentry and noblemen,
would enter into the fortune-building activities appropriate to persons of their
economic status. But the Anglo-Irish government proceeded with speedy
deliberation to frustrate such hopes.[82] Though garbed as a holy war against
popery, this policy was governed mainly by considerations of capital
accumulation.[83]

The cornerstone of the legislative prisonhouse that was the Penal Law
system was "The Act to Prevent the Growth of Popery," passed in 1704
(2 Anne c. 6).[84] Under this law, as amended in 1709 (8 Anne c. 3), and enforced
by confiscatorial penalties:

1. Catholic tenants could not acquire land from a Protestant, neither by
purchase, gift or inheritance, or have benefit of annuities on any land held by
a Protestant.

2.   Catholic tenants could not lease land for more than thirty-one years. They were thus barred from becoming freeholders and, as such, voters. Social class degradation was made especially effective by the requirement that they pay rent of not less than two-thirds of the yield on the land they rented. In this respect all Catholic Irish tenants were reduced to the status of the lowest-ranking tenant of ancient Celtic custom, that of the marginal free *fuidir* class, reserved for the wandering stranger. (The likeness to the free *fuidir* was soon made more complete as the workings of the Penal Laws reduced the overwhelming majority of the Irish to one-year tenants-at-will.)[85]

3.   A Catholic landholder was deprived of all rights of testament over his estate. Here, the gavelkind principle, which the British had once so abominated, was put to use as a deliberate means to fragment Catholic landholdings (2 Anne c. 6). An amendment provided that any Protestant, regardless of social rank, had standing to "discover" Catholic evasions of the land restriction laws, the title to the land to be awarded to the discoverer (8 Anne 27).

4.   Catholic men were barred from acquiring property from Protestants by dowry, under terms of a law of 1697 (9 Will. III c. 3) forbidding the marriage of a Catholic to a Protestant. The language of the law's preamble seems worth sampling: "Many protestant maidens and women," it says, ". . . have been seduced . . . to take to husband, papists or popish persons . . . [thus] corrupting and perverting such protestants . . . [as they] become papists to the great dishonour of Almighty God".

In order to compete in the world of the colonial bourgeoisie in Ireland, or in Anglo-America, two things were necessary: land and labor. In Ireland, Catholics who might have succeeded in bourgeois terms had ready access to labor, but they were by law forbidden to acquire land (except as short-term tenants). In Virginia (the pattern-setting colony), the African-Americans who might have succeeded in bourgeois terms could, by virtue of the headright system, have had access to land, but by a law enacted in 1670 they were forbidden to acquire any bond-laborers except those of African ancestry.[86] Being necessarily persons of small means, African-Americans were thus put at an almost insurmountable competitive disadvantage, since the capital outlay for each African or African-American bond-laborer was about two or three times as high as that required for each bond-laborer from Europe.[87] After 1691, African-Americans who sought to enter the competitive struggle as newly emancipated persons were not (except by express official leave) allowed to remain in Virginia. And, like the Catholic Irish by law forbidden to marry Protestants, the African-Americans were by a 1691 law barred from acquiring property by marriage with Europeans or European-Americans.[88] Unlike the Catholic Irish, however, African-American property-holders seem to have retained their testamentary rights intact.[89]

Deprivation of civil rights

In trying to defend such property as did remain to them, or in any effort at social mobility, the Catholic Irish labored under the burden of a general denial of civil rights. A series of a dozen laws forbade "Papists" to possess arms or gunpowder; or practice law, publicly or privately; or serve on grand juries; or hold any position of authority or trust above subordinate constable; or have the freedom of cities and towns corporate; or serve in the army or navy; or own a horse worth more than £5; or serve in Parliament; or vote in any election for public office.[90]

All the disabilities imposed on the Catholic Irish in Ireland in regard to civil rights were sooner or later imposed against African-Americans. In Ireland, the Protestant Ascendancy and the Penal Laws were based on the legal fiction that, as Scully put it, "All the effective inhabitants of Ireland are presumed to be Protestants – and therefore . . . the Catholics . . . are not to be supposed to exist – save for reprehension and penalty."[91] That would be a fair representation, *mutatis mutandis*, of the situation of the African-American in Anglo-America, as Chief Justice Taney characterized it in the Dred Scott decision, saying, "there are no rights which negroes have that white men are bound to respect."[92]

The kinship of spirit between the Protestant Ascendancy and white supremacy was put on record at the outset of the "white race" era in a 1705 Virginia law reconstituting the Virginia Court system: "popish recusants convict, negroes, mulattoes and Indian servants, and others not being christians, shall be deemed and taken to be persons incapable in law, to be witnesses in any case whatsoever."[93] Under the slave codes in continental Anglo-America, beginning with a Virginia law of 1705, African-American bond-laborers were excluded from the right to trial by jury; and in 1832, in the wake of Nat Turner's Rebellion,[94] even free African-Americans were denied jury trials, except in capital cases.[95] In Ireland the jury form of trial was not canceled, but the jury could be limited to Protestants only in any case in which the defendant was a Catholic.[96]

The absolute disfranchisement of the Catholic Irish in Ireland and the disfranchisement of African-Americans in Virginia occurred about the same time. In 1727 an act passed by the Irish Parliament provided that "[n]o papist, though not convict, shall be entitled or admitted to vote at the election of any member to serve in Parliament as knight, citizen, or burgess, or at the election of any magistrate for any city or other town-corporate."[97]

Prior to 1723, all freeholders in Virginia, African-American and European-American, were permitted to vote, with the exception of women, persons under twenty-one years of age, and non-conforming Catholics. These categories had been excluded from the franchise by laws passed in 1699 and again in 1705.[98] But in 1723, an act concerned with "the better government of Negroes,

Mulattos, and Indians, bond or free," for the first time deprived African-Americans of the vote.[99]

The illegalization of literacy

A more general barrier to maintaining or achieving propertied status was the illegalization of literacy. Even before the formal inauguration of the Penal Laws system, a 1692 law (4 W & M c. 2) made it a crime for a Catholic to go abroad to be educated. Then the first of the Penal Laws (7 Will. III c. 4, *Irish Statutes*), passed in 1695, made it a criminal offense for any person (except within one's immediate family) to teach "Papists" to read or write, or otherwise school them. "No person whatsoever of the popish religion," it said, "shall publickly or in private houses teach school or instruct youth in learning within this realm." In its final version (8 Anne c. 3 [1709]), the penalty for Catholics who ventured to teach the youth was increased, from three months in jail and a £20 fine, to perpetual imprisonment and complete forfeiture of property, that being the punishment prescribed for unlicensed Catholic clergy.[100] Protestants who employed Catholics as even assistant teachers were subject to a £10 fine for each offense.

In like spirit, Catholics were by law strictly excluded from some apprenticeships (7 Will. III c. 4, sec. 8); even Catholic masters were discriminated against as to the number and terms of the apprentices they could employ (8 Anne c. 3, sec. 37).[101] The most prevalent form of discrimination was by local custom and regulation. "At present," said an observer writing in 1724, "there is not one freeman or master of any corporation ... of the Roman Catholic religion in all the kingdom [Ireland]."[102] Lecky adds the comment, "In the most Catholic parts of Ireland many of the most lucrative trades were long a strict monopoly of the Protestants, who refused to admit any Catholic as an apprentice."[103] In the last quarter of the eighteenth century, Arthur Young found the Catholic Irish "under such discouragements that they cannot engage in any trade which requires both capital and industry. ... [E]very means is taken to reduce and keep them in a state of poverty."[104]

Sooner or later laws were enacted in the Anglo-American South to forbid the teaching of reading and writing to African-American bond-laborers,[105] on the grounds that it unsuited them for slavery.[106] In Virginia in 1832, after Nat Turner's Rebellion, it was made a crime to teach a free African-American to read and write.[107] The same law forbade the return to Virginia of African-Americans who went north to be educated. The Protestant Ascendancy had acted in a similar vein in Ireland by passing a law taking away all civil rights from any Catholic Irish person who went abroad for an education (7 Will. III c. 4 [1695]).

With regard to the trades, African-Americans were confronted with the same sort of exclusion by law and customary discrimination as was faced by the

Catholics in Ireland. In the 1690s Protestant porters in Dublin and "white" porters in New York City were petitioning the authorities against allowing the employment of "Papists" and "Negroes" respectively in that trade.[108] Under the heading "Concerted Action by White Workmen Against Negro Artisans," Professor Morris cited from the record of the eighteenth and early nineteenth centuries more than a dozen such instances involving white racist appeals for legislative prohibitions against free or bond African-American workers in non-agricultural labor.[109] A study made in Philadelphia in 1821 found that on account of racial discrimination, free African-Americans were "excluded from most of the respectable and profitable employments of life, confined to the humblest and least gainful occupations."[110] Frederick Douglass relates his personal experience with this sort of "white" exclusionism both as a bondman in Baltimore and as a free person in New Bedford.[111]

Assault on the family

The Protestant Ascendancy being a system of racial oppression, even the family was no refuge of social identity for the Irish Catholics under the Penal Laws. In the social displacement of the Irish propertied classes, the prerogatives of the husband and father were set aside. As already noted, a Catholic Irish male could not add to his estate by marrying a Protestant. If he married a Catholic woman who subsequently became a Protestant, the very basis of his status of lord and master over her was drastically impaired, unless he too became a Protestant. Ordinarily, a widow was not entitled to any share of her deceased husband's real estate (lands, houses, etcetera), unless under the terms of her marriage contract some particular and explicit contrary provision were required to be included in the husband's last will and testament. Under the Penal Laws (8 Anne 3, sections 14 and 15 [1709]), a wife who became a convert to Protestantism was automatically entitled to inherit one-third of her husband's lands, as well as retaining her right to the customary one-third "widow's portion" of his personal estate (silver, money, movables, etcetera).

The Catholic father's authority over his children was similarly undermined if they chose to desert the faith of their fathers by becoming Protestants (2 Anne 6, section 3). The father, regardless of his own wishes, could be compelled to provide for such convert children "fitting maintenance" and to guarantee "future provision" for them appropriate to his material means. If that convert happened to be the eldest son, the father was automatically rendered a mere tenant-for-life; the son became the landlord with all the vested rights of that title, as if the father were dead. Given the cunning pressure thus exerted on propertied Catholics, more than a few of them understandably became at least formally Protestants.

In all this disallowance of the legitimacy of the Catholic Irish family, of course, nothing was intended against the patriarchy or male supremacy as such. It was another variation of the attack on Catholic property-holding, and another way of delegitimating whatever degree of social eminence that the Catholic property-holder might still retain. It was at the same time the continuation of expropriation by other means. But as far as male privileges were concerned, the modifications were limited and specific, and by no means represented any equalitarian impulse.

With regard to the propertyless masses, the tenants-at-will, the male privileges of the Protestant landlord had precedence over those of the tenant with respect to the women members of the tenant's family. More than one landlord boasted to Arthur Young that "Many of their cotters would think themselves honoured by having their wives and daughters sent for to the bed of their masters."[112] A peasant might not appreciate such lordly condescension, but he knew that he "would have his bones broken if he offered to raise his hand" against the landlord. The custom, says Young, was "a mark of slavery." If the cottier appealed to the Justice of the Peace for redress, the Justice would not even venture to issue a summons to the landlord for fear of affronting the landlord's honor. Incredible as it is, Sigerson assures us that even in the early nineteenth century there were cases in which this ultimate form of negation of the Catholic Irish family was stipulated in the lease as a privilege of the landlord.[113]

The Protestant Ascendancy gave special attention to breaking the tie of parent to child in Catholic Irish families of the poorer classes. In so doing the Ascendancy produced a living irony to match that of Jonathan Swift's *Modest Proposal*. Swift's essay provides the most widely known testimony regarding the devastation of the Irish family by the effects of the recurring "dearths" and famines in eighteenth-century Ireland. Writing in 1729, a third successive year of famine, Swift noted that on every hand one found hungry Irish mothers begging for food, accompanied by their starving children. Swift's proposal to make food *of* the children, rather than *for* them, remains the classic of English literary irony.

The same starving time that inspired Swift's essay gave rise to the notion of a system of schools "to teach the children of the papists ... the principles of the Christian religion," as Primate Boulter put it. (Boulter had despaired of making headway with the adults.)[114] That proposal took on material form as the "Charter Society of Protestant Schools" in 1733.[115] Just as Swift's *Modest Proposal* included aspects designed to appeal to the interests of Irish parents, the Charter Schools administration promised to care for and educate young children. It was supposed to make the boys apprentices in farming, and to train the girls in housekeeping duties, and provide them with a small marriage portion when the time should arrive.[116]

It was here that the racist refusal to recognize the legitimacy of the Irish family took on its cruelest – and most ironic – aspect.[117] Under the Charter Schools scheme, in the name of religion children were taken from their families. To prevent risk of their further exposure to "papist idolatry," all further contact between parents and children was forbidden. Driven by hunger, parents were obliged to accept this condition. But it was found that as soon as their circumstances had sufficiently mended, the parents would take their children back again. The law countered by requiring that, once lodged in one of the institutions, the inmates were never to be released from Protestant custody while they remained children. By way of guaranteeing the effect of this rule, the children "were transplanted to the districts most remote from their parents." There, "they were brought up in profound ignorance of their names, situation and very existence."[118] Enrollment lagged and was supplemented by facilities for taking in foundlings. At the same time, the Charter Schools were given the authority to take into their permanent custody, with or without parental consent, any child between the ages of five and twelve who might be found begging.[119]

The families paid the price, willingly or not, but in return their children were cheated of the most elementary instruction in literacy, and instead were exploited as field laborers for the profit of their masters. In 1788 the Irish Inspector-General and the prison reformer John Howard reported to the Irish House of Commons that the inmates of the Charter Schools "generally speaking, are unhealthy; half starved; in rags; *totally uneducated*; too much worked; and, in all respects, shamefully neglected."[120]

An alternative educational track was established by a law passed in 1716 directing "That the Parsons and churchwardens in every parish should together with a Justice of the Peace, bind any child found begging, or any other child (with consent of the Parent) to a Protestant master, until his age of 21, or to a Protestant tradesman until his age of 24 years."[121] Again, it is to be noted that parental consent was not necessary in the case of children found begging. A child who fled such bondage was subject to punishment by being put in the stocks and ten days' hard-labor imprisonment. Any person, even his own parent, who sheltered the runaway was subject to a crushing penalty of £40, payable to the master.

Corporations were established, first in Dublin and then in Cork, whose business it was to take up all children of five years of age or older found begging and keep them in their service until the children were sixteen, and then apprentice them to serve Protestant masters, the boys until they were twenty-four, the girls until twenty-one. When it was found that "Popish" mothers were clandestinely securing employment as parish nurses in order to be near their own kidnapped children, arrangements were made to exchange the inmate populations between the two cities, the 170-mile separation being calculated to foil such connivance.[122]

Nothing so became the Charter Schools as their general failure. They represented the one major concerted effort to convert Catholics to Protestants, and yet their average "enrollment" for the entire country averaged less than

2,000. It was the regretful judgment of John Howard, after his investigation of the Charter Schools, that they were "so deplorable as to disgrace Protestantism and to encourage Popery in Ireland, rather than the contrary."[123] Lecky probed more harshly, calling them "a system which in the supposed interests of religion, made it a first object to break the tie of affection between the parent and the child."[124] What then was this but an assault upon the family as a form of social identification for members of the racially oppressed population?

A few years before Arthur Young recorded the Protestant landlords' boasts of their sexual privileges with regard to women of "their" cottier families, the Maryland Provincial Court proclaimed similar white-male privileges as constitutional Anglo-American law. Lifetime hereditary bond-laborers "are incapable of marriage," the court said; therefore, it continued, "we do not consider them as objects of such laws as relate to the commerce between the sexes. A slave [has no legal recourse], against the violator of his bed."[125] As far as the law was concerned, the most intimate and sacred attachments could be unceremoniously broken at any time by any of a number of forms of intrusion by the "white race," including separation by purchase and sale. As for the normal course of everyday life: "The slave woman was first a full-time worker for her owner . . . she was not usually nurse to her husband or children during illness . . . children soon learned that their parents were . . . [not] the seat of authority. . . . The husband was not the head of the family."[126]

Even free African-Americans were restricted in regard to the civil right of marriage. In 1691, Virginia law for the first time instituted penalties for marriages between European-Americans on the one hand and African-Americans and Indians, bond or free.[127] The pattern became general: free African-Americans might marry, but only if the spouse was not a European-American. In Ireland the bar to the intermarriage of English and Irish had precedent as far back as the fourteenth century. The Anglo-Irish Parliament, as I have noted, re-enacted that principle in law as a part of the Penal Laws in 1697.[128] In Virginia the cry was "abominable mixture"; in Ireland it was "corruption and perversion" and "dishonour to Almighty God."

Mention has been made earlier in this work of the United States Indian Agent in the Dakotas who forcefully removed Sioux women and children in order to "wipe out" that tribe.[129] In the general effort made by the United States government to break up Indian tribal society, the program of individuation of Indian land ownership involved a conscious challenge to the Indian family. Just as the Anglo-Irish Penal Laws presented the irony of resort to "gavelkind" in order to reduce the size of Catholic Irish landholdings, so the United States attempted to make use of empowerment of the husband as the "head of the family" as a part of the destruction of the power of the tribe. The process of expropriating the Indian lands did not, however, depend upon this legal fiction. As late as 1905, the United States Supreme Court decided a case in favor of an Indian woman, "the head of a family, consisting of herself, her husband, and children," even when (as in this particular case) her husband was a "white" man.[130]

The difference of these two American cases is not that the Indians were any less the object of racial oppression, but that the form of the Indian family was not a decisive obstacle to the expropriation of their lands and the extirpation of their people, while the African-American family represented a fundamental barrier to the system of chattel bondage. A Maryland Provincial Court decision made the point in 1767:

> No one has ever imagined that the property of the master can be affected by the contract of a slave, whether of marriage, or any other occasion, utility being the parent of right and justice.[131]

4

Social Control: From Racial to National Oppression

The English Parliament in 1689 established as a constitutional principle that no standing army be maintained in that country in time of peace; for the future, when England was at peace the militia was to guarantee the safety of the country.[1] But in Ireland, where a funereal conqueror's peace would descend for a century following the Jacobite War of 1689–90, the English military establishment was to be maintained at an "invariable 12,000."[2] Some historians believe that keeping such a large regular army in Ireland was more of an English convenience than an Irish necessity. They point out that the cost was borne altogether by exactions on the people in Ireland, even though the forces were from time to time drawn upon for duty elsewhere. The fact remains, however, that English rule in Ireland continued to be dependent on regular military forces for ordinary police duty.[3] The military role was supplemented by that of Protestant civil officers, magistrates, sheriffs, and constables, and Protestant petit juries and grand juries. There were places, such as parts of Ulster and some cities and towns, where the Protestant proportion of the population was kept large enough to make possible some normal degree of local civil administration, but the garrisons were there anyway. For the greater part of Ireland, however, the Catholic Irish so far outnumbered the Protestant English – sometimes by more than thirty to one – that there the writ of Protestant civil law could not run.[4]

But before the end of the eighteenth century a cloud of doubt formed over even the traditional resort to the military option – the tradition of Mountjoy and Cromwell – for maintaining racial oppression in Ireland.

Two centuries before, Ireland had been drawn, thrust, dragged into the context of international colonial power rivalry. Now that new world context erupted in a storm of revolution: Anglo-American continental colonies, 1776 to 1782; France, 1789 to 1794; Haiti (St Domingue), 1791 to 1804; and the English government's military forces were everywhere engaged in counter-revolution. In Ireland, Protestant nationalists raised their sails to catch the winds for independence from English trade restrictions, and for a time looked favorably on the connection of independence with the cause of Catholic "emancipation". At the same time, a large part of the Irish military establishment was being shipped for war in America, in St Domingue, Guadeloupe, Martinique, and other eastern Caribbean islands;[5] and around the world against the Napoleonic genie loosed by the French Revolution, a round of wars that would last for forty years, 1775–1815. In 1798 the armed revolt of the United Irishmen broke out, on such a scale that a military force of 76,000 was needed to suppress it,[6] and the politicization of the Catholic masses had just begun.

The crisis of British rule in Ireland – with its threat of revolution and French invasion – brought to maturation a process of rapprochement between the British king, Parliament and the Protestant Ascendancy, on the one hand, and the emergent Catholic bourgeoisie, on the other. "The professed object [of the Penal Laws]," said Edmund Burke, had been "to deprive the few [Catholic] men who, in spite of those laws, might hold or retain any property amongst them, of all sort of influence or authority over the rest."[7] That was a luxury that the British ruling class could no longer afford. *The resolution of the crisis, therefore, would mean nothing less, and nothing more, than a change in the system of British colonial rule in Ireland from racial oppression to national oppression, by the incorporation of the Irish bourgeoisie into the intermediate buffer social control stratum.* The process – from the first exchange of glances to the disestablishment of the Church of Ireland in 1869 – occupied a century of vicissitudes. But by 1793 the decision was irrevocable, by 1829 it was affirmed in law, and by 1843 it was defined in practice.

Facing a heavy demand for cannon-fodder in the Seven Years War (1757–63) for colonial empire against France, the British government had decided to abandon the Penal Law against recruiting Irish Catholics for military service.[8] This decision meant that a vital interest of the British empire was made dependent upon the Irish Catholic clergy, without whose assent Irishmen – however needy their families might be – would not join the British army. From then on, Thomas Bartlett writes, "war would mean opportunity rather than danger for Irish Catholics . . . [and therefore it] was no coincidence that the major catholic relief acts of the late eighteenth century were put through in time of war."[9]

Penal Laws that effectively denied Catholics the right to acquire or retain land ownership had been inspired by the ghost of confiscations past.[10] The first and most comprehensive of these, the "Act to Prevent the Growth of Popery," passed in 1704, set a limit of thirty-one acres on the amount of land a Catholic might lease, and allowed that much only on the condition that the rent be no less than two-thirds of the net yield.[11] But after half a dozen generations had been buried, and with them prospects for a restoration of those confiscated lands to Catholic claimants, other motives came to bear upon policy decisions of the English and Anglo-Irish Establishment.[12] As revolutionary sentiment for an independent republican Ireland began to grow, inspired by events in France and America, the prospect of such a change of policy in respect to the propertied Irish Catholics appeared increasingly opportune for the British colonialists.

The Protestant Irish Parliament itself proclaimed the strategic reorientation. The anti-Popery laws of 1704 and 1709, which had made "Roman Catholics of Ireland ... subject to several disabilities and incapacities," they said, had become obsolete and indeed counter-productive. Finding that the Catholics had exhibited "uniform peaceable behavior for a long series of years," Parliament declared that it was:

> reasonable and expedient to relax the [laws], and [that] it must tend not only to the cultivation and improvement of this kingdom, but to the prosperity and strength of all his Majesty's dominions, that his subjects of all denominations should enjoy the blessings of our free constitution, and should be bound by mutual interest and mutual affection.[13]

Parliament accordingly began to enact substantial land reforms. In 1772, the law was amended in order to encourage the reclamation of bogland and other wastelands for agriculture and, at the same time, to promote the detente with the Catholic hierarchy and bourgeoisie that was sprouting between the cracks of Protestant Ascendancy.[14] The new law provided that Catholics were to be permitted to take leases on such worthless lands tax free for seven years, although a Catholic tenant still could lease no more than fifty acres, and that much for not more than sixty-one years. In 1778, Parliament eliminated all the formal legal disabilities of Catholics with respect to leasing; finally, in 1782, the ban on Catholic purchase and inheritance of lands was ended.[15] After a century and more of enforced tenancy-at-will, such reforms could have little effect on the proportion of land held by the Catholic rank and file. What good was the right to own land, or even to sustain the entry fees on long-term leases, for rack-rented, tithe-extorted tenants-at-will, or for laborers living in semi-beggary?[16] But for the emergent Catholic bourgeoisie, with access to capital or credit, the leasehold reforms proved to be of substantial significance.[17]

America and France, and the Spectre of Republicanism

In 1778, when the regular garrisons had been depleted for service in America, there arose in Ireland the (overwhelmingly Protestant) Volunteers movement, ostensibly to defend the country from foreign invasion. Soon the Volunteers began to alarm the government by their obvious republican and independentist tendency and, above all, by their declarations of support for equal rights for Catholics. In December 1791, the British government proposed that the Irish Parliament allow the elective franchise to sufficiently propertied Catholics.[18] The calculated effect was that the Catholics of "the most consequence and property" would become "sharers in" the system of social control.[19] Within little over a year, the government and the authoritative negotiating team, known as the Catholic Committee, reached an agreement that in effect ended Catholic collaboration with the Volunteers in exchange for the passage of a law in 1793 (33 Geo. III, c. 21 [*Irish Statutes*]), giving Catholic forty-shilling freeholders the right to vote in elections of members of the exclusively Protestant Irish Parliament.[20] A companion act (33 Geo. III, c. 22 [*Irish Statutes*]) established an Irish militia of about fifteen thousand (increased to nearly twenty-two thousand two years later) which, although officered by Protestants, had a predominantly Catholic rank and file.[21]

Thrown on the political defensive by the cumulative effect of this shift in the strategic orientation of the British government, the forces of Protestant Ascendancy rallied behind the racist tradition symbolized by the Dutch William of Orange (of "glorious . . . and immortal memory") who, as King William III of England, had defeated the Irish and Catholic cause in 1689 and ushered in the long night of the Penal Laws.

The first to rally were laboring-class Protestants in 1795, who sensed a creeping Catholic Emancipationism threatening their racial privileges – such as their preferential tenant status and the right to keep and bear arms.[22] The surge of Protestant bigotry took organized form with the establishment of the Orange Order, following an armed clash between Protestant and Catholic tenants in County Armagh in September 1795. This event was immediately followed by a terror campaign which drove hundreds of Catholic families from their Ulster homes into stony Connaught.[23] Viewed at first with a considerable degree of upper-class suspicion for its lowly origins, Orangeism gained in respectability, especially among the diehard Protestant Ascendancy elements of the ruling class who had not yet got the message that it was time for a change. In the Rebellion of 1798, the Orange Order, now formally constituted in Ireland and Britain, played a key role in splitting Protestants from the equalitarian stand of the United Irishmen, and in the form of the armed and mounted yeomanry units served also as auxiliaries in the repressive operations of the military.[24]

The Act of Union – a Role for the Catholic Bourgeoisie

Faced with this formidable Orangeist opposition on the one hand and the ominous implications of the 1793 voting rights and militia acts in a country with an overwhelmingly Catholic population on the other,[25] and with the French threat undiminished, the British government, headed by William Pitt, resorted to the tactic of legislative union of Great Britain and Ireland. It was a sort of symbolic adaptation of the notion that William Petty had suggested to James II in 1672 (see pages 68–69). The majority principle would be preserved, but in a 658-member Parliament in which only 100 members would be from Ireland. In this setting, any Irish Home Rule or less radical nationalist minority could be easily controlled. It was a prototype of the pattern to be followed by the British colonialists of embedding a hook in each concession as an essential component at every juncture of the process, to ensure that the transition to a new system of social control in Ireland would not get out of hand. In this case, the newly enfranchised Irish forty-shilling freeholders were safely "landed" by the dilution of their representation in the British Parliament.

The opponents to union expressed a variety of political interests, even directly contradictory ones; they included republican independentist United Irishmen (and the young Daniel O'Connell, destined to be the dominant leader of the Irish national liberation struggle), and on the other hand some Protestant Ascendancy types fearful that the new United Kingdom Parliament would be heavily infiltrated with liberals and abolitionists soft on Catholicism. In addition, there was the resistance of the placemen in the Irish church and state Establishment, worried about their careers, which were dependent upon the maintenance of the separate kingdom.

In the political pulling and hauling on the issue, the "support of the catholic hierarchy was decisive".[26] It was not to be expected that the Irish Catholics, riding a tide of "great and sanguine expectations," would go quietly into parliamentary union, with a Parliament from which not merely were Catholics excluded, but in which the Irish were to be in a permanent minority.[27] In January 1799, Pitt and the Irish Catholic hierarchy (four archbishops and six of the bishops) came to an agreement in which the hierarchy agreed to support the Union Bill and to grant British Protestant monarchs a veto over the naming of Catholic bishops in Ireland. In return the British government was to pay the salaries of Catholic priests.[28] The government further led the Catholics to expect favorable consideration of "reform" of the tithe system (the compulsory exaction of payments for the support of the Church of Ireland), and a "catholic relief" bill, removing the ban on Catholic membership in Parliament.[29] Pitt's immediate purpose was achieved: the Act of Union was passed in 1800. But in Ireland and England the Orange and Tory forces of Protestant Ascendancy, staunchly backed by three successive British monarchs, were able to postpone the consummation of the bargain for thirty years.

From a far-sighted post-Union British ruling-class point of view, this Ascendancy element in Ireland might conceivably have been seen as a historical anachronism, like the pre-European peoples of Canada or Australia, where the parliaments would represent the invested colonist-descended majority. But Ireland was different.[30] In Ireland the British Protestants were a minority, yet strategically a very significant minority, the historic trustee of English rule and now anchor of the Empire, the embodiment of Protestant Ascendancy, socially dominant throughout Ireland. It was a very substantial,

deep-rooted interest, as it had demonstrated in frustrating the promise of
Catholic Emancipation in the understanding reached between Pitt and the Catholic episcopate on parliamentary union. Most significant of all in the present
context, it was constituted in the main of members of the laboring classes. In
order to carry through the transition to Union national oppression, not only the
Protestant exploiting classes but the laboring-class Protestants as well had to
be given reassurances on their privileges *vis-à-vis* laboring-class Catholics, at
least in Ulster, the main stronghold of Protestant Ascendancy.[31] Historians and
others agree that Catholic Emancipation – the admission of Catholics to civil
rights, to membership in Parliament, to the professions and to positions of
public trust, military or civilian – was an historical inevitability.[32] In the British
Parliament "the Catholics could count on the general support of the whole
body of the English Whigs, of a considerable section of the English Tories,
including ... most of the rising men of ability, and also of a large and perhaps
preponderating section of the English press."[33] But, for twenty-five of the
twenty-eight years from Union to Emancipation, the House of Commons was
controlled by the Tory Party, the main political bastion of Protestant
Ascendancy. The Ascendancy was even more strongly entrenched in the House
of Lords, and, as noted, the Hanoverian English kings of the time were last-
ditch, hard-loser Ascendancy men.

Here was a new version of the Grand Dilemma: how could the Catholic
bourgeoisie be incorporated into the colonial buffer social control stratum
without sparking a movement for Irish national independence, or, alternatively,
alienating the Irish Protestants by threats to their dominance in ownership, and
preference in tenancy and employment, thereby risking the re-emergence of
the United Irishmen phenomenon, republican and independentist? This
dilemma would govern the course of Irish history from 1801 (the Union as
law), to 1843 (the Union as settled fact).

Defining Issues

In the second half of that period the overlapping issues of "Catholic
Emancipation" so-called,[34] agrarian grievances, and repeal of the Union
erupted in three acute crises of British social control in Ireland, in 1828–29,
1832–35 and 1843.

For the Catholic bourgeoisie the strategic issues were Catholic Emancipation
and repeal of the Union. Within limits, each reinforced the other, yet they were
fundamentally contradictory. Catholic Emancipation meant the ending of the
Penal Law exclusion of propertied Catholics from Parliament and other offices,
jobs, emoluments and perquisites, as well as entry into trades and professions on
an equal basis with non-Catholics of those classes; in short, the formal
admittance of propertied Catholics, although on a necessarily subordinate basis,

into the buffer social control stratum.[35] As William Grenville, one of the principal advocates of Catholic Emancipation, put it to the House of Lords, what concerned the Irish Catholic propertied classes was "not their situation as subjects, but their claim to political power." The idea was clearly stated by the Irish Catholic aristocracy and gentry themselves, in their emancipation petition to Parliament in 1805. The trouble with Protestant Ascendancy, they said, was that "it detach[ed] from property its proportion of political power under a [British] constitution whose vital principle is the union of one with the other . . . the best constitution that has ever been established."[36] It was the same demand that the free classes of Ireland had made in 1277 for admittance to English law, but with the difference wrought by nearly six hundred years of invasion, resistance, conquest and racial oppression. In the thirteenth century the Gaelic tribal chieftains, in undislodgeable control of at least one-third of the island, were confronting a tentative and insecure invader. Modern Emancipationism, on the other hand, was conditioned on the acknowledgement of the indefeasibility of British Protestant landlordism, of the British domination of the Irish national economy, and of the permanent subordination of Ireland to the authority of a British Parliament, in which Catholics were forever a minority. In short, what was called Catholic Emancipation involved the acceptance of the national subordination of Ireland to Britain.[37]

Repeal of the Union, on the other hand, was a demand for national independence: not necessarily separation, as in the case of the United States, but nothing less than a proto-dominion status, like that granted to Canada in 1840, and practiced in Australia in its various parts. But, again, Ireland was not Australia or Canada. The demand for repeal of the Union not only went far beyond Catholic Emancipation; its proposed independent Irish Parliament was a dagger pointed at British Protestant landlordism, at the automatic priority of British economic interests, and at the whole legacy of two centuries of preferential treatment of Protestants.[38] It was seen as a threat to the British Empire as a whole.[39] Repeal of the Union promised to remove the very question of British social control in Ireland from history's agenda.

For the British colonial bourgeoisie, the categorical imperative was maintenance of the legislative union. If forced to it, they would be ready to abandon rule by religio-racial oppression in favor of admitting the Irish Catholic bourgeoisie into a role in the system of social control. But the British government made manifest its resolve to go to war to prevent the establishment of a separate Irish parliament, whether of an independent country or of a British dominion. For the Irish Catholic bourgeoisie the categorical imperative was that there must be no return to the Penal Laws regime with its denial of their class status. If forced to it, they (including O'Connell) were ready to accept the role of being the major component in the system of British colonial control in Ireland; in short, to content themselves with the transition from racial oppression to national oppression, instead of Irish self-rule.[40]

Enter the Irish Peasant

In the end it was neither the British nor the Irish bourgeoisie that drove the issue to crisis and resolution, but rather the laboring classes of the countryside with *their* strategic joint issue of tithes and tenant rights. The poor tenants and laborers who made up the great majority of the Irish population had little practical interest in either Emancipation or repeal.[41] They were more particularly concerned with the oppressive landlord system, the fall of agricultural prices after the defeat of Napoleon, the ravages of famine in a number of these years, and the predations of the tithe proctor, who was empowered to seize the crops and stock of those delinquent in their payments for the support of the Protestant Church of Ireland.[42] They were not going to run for Parliament, few laboring people were even voters,[43] and tradition's chains bound those few to vote for the landlord's candidate, or face retribution. Nor were they going to be candidates for admittance to trades or professions. They, "the poverty of the country," as O'Connell called them, were more disposed to translate Emancipation and repeal in their own terms. They expected the Catholic "'rent' to be used for the purchase of arms, and that after emancipation ... the land would be redivided."[44] Maintaining a direct-action tradition that had begun in the 1760s with the White Boys, they organized as Threshers, as White Feet, and as Ribbon Men to prosecute their grievances by various means. They maimed cattle, prevented foreclosure sales and forcible tithe collections; they intimidated Catholic or Protestant landlords and their witnesses, and fought with what arms they had against law-enforcing police and yeomanry;[45] and they enforced "exclusive dealing," a practice later to be eponymously known as "boycotting." From 1815 until the Great Famine struck in 1845, agrarian unrest was a constant reminder of the unresolved state of the social control problem. As evidence for this we have the successive pronouncements of one of the dominant figures in British politics throughout this period, the Irish-born arch-Tory Duke of Wellington (1769–1852). In December 1828, as the campaign for Catholic Emancipation was approaching culmination, Wellington, then Prime Minister, declared that the situation in Ireland could not be worse, short of actual civil war. During the tithe war of the early 1830s, Wellington, then in the parliamentary Opposition, was uncontradicted when he told the House of Lords that all former "disturbances in Ireland ... were trifling compared to the scenes" currently to be witnessed in that country. In 1843, when the struggle for repeal of the Union approached its climax and he was once more a member of the government, Wellington's cold eye judged Ireland to be "in truth no longer in a civil state."[46] In each case, it was the involvement of the masses of the peasantry and rural proletariat that made the situation critical.

The leaders of the Catholic bourgeoisie could not have ignored the surging agrarian unrest if they had wanted to do so. By class instinct they were mistrustful of spontaneity and independence among the laboring classes; they were painfully aware of the sentiments current among the rural poor majority favoring revolutionary land redistribution. At the same time, the tithe system was a grievance that the Catholic bourgeoisie shared with their co-religionists of other classes.[47] It was symbol and substance of the very exclusion from "official society" for which they were seeking remedy in Emancipation and repeal; and, of more practical importance, it was the ideal link to the power of agrarian anger. In moving to exploit the power of laboring-class discontent, the Catholic Irish bourgeoisie was following standard operating procedure for the national bourgeoisie, wherever that class was still aspiring to power or to a share in it.[48]

The Campaign for Catholic Emancipation

The quest for empowerment began with the campaign for Catholic Emancipation, so-called, organized by the Catholic Association, formed in 1823 by Daniel O'Connell (The Great Emancipator), Richard Lalor Sheil (who would emerge as O'Connell's co-leader) and Thomas Wyse.[49] Under the leadership of O'Connell and his co-workers, starting with only forty-seven members the association produced a non-revolutionary liberationist movement of a scope and depth probably unmatched except by that led by Gandhi in another English colony a century later. The key to their success lay in enlisting the priesthood as "lashers up" of the rural masses, as dues collection supervisors, and as grassroots agitators and mobilizers.[50] The chief tactic of the movement consisted of mass mobilizations, peaceful indeed in the assemblies but, more than that, disciplined in coming and going in mass contingents.[51] On 13 January 1828, Emancipation rallies were held in some 1,600 of Ireland's 2,500 parishes.[52] Besides the meetings, there were the "processions," marches done in military form but without arms. In the summer and fall of 1828 – on local initiative, rather than by central direction – processions of two or three thousand men drilled and marched in the southwest of Ireland wearing green insignia of various sorts, and organized "like regular troops."[53]

Since 1792, the British had become practiced in responding to threats in the Irish quarter with both repression and concessions. In part this reflected differences of policy within the British ruling class, but perhaps more often it merely represented dual aspects of a single strategy.[54] Habeas corpus, the most fundamental British constitutional right, was suspended in Ireland during twelve of the twenty-five years from the passage of the Act of Union to the founding of the Catholic Association in 1823.[55] As the campaign for Catholic Emancipation approached its peak of intensity, overwhelming military force was arrayed against it. Between 1823 and 1828, the British garrison in Ireland was increased from 28,000 to 35,000, when five out of every six members of the regular infantry were either in Ireland or on the west coast of England ready to go there.[56]

The use of concessions to maintain control began with the granting of the forty-shilling freehold franchise in 1793. Although the passage of the Act of Union of 1800 was not accompanied by the promised "Catholic relief," there were always those, aside from the "Catholic sympathizers," in the British Parliament who advocated Catholic Emancipation as a means of tying the Catholic bourgeoisie to the cause of the Empire.[57] The British government had established an Irish Catholic seminary at Maynooth in 1795 to provide training for Irish students for the priesthood without their having to risk contamination with republican ideas by the traditional sojourn in France.[58] In 1807, Parliament raised the annual grant to Maynooth from £8,000 to £9,200.[59] The idea of state payment of Catholic clergy salaries, linked to one form or another of the royal veto on nominations of Irish Catholic bishops (see note 29), gained support in Parliament until Catholic lay opposition in Ireland forced the Irish Catholic hierarchy to repudiate the proposal in 1808, and forced its temporary abandonment in Parliament.[60] Slowly, and with many checks and challenges, the conviction grew that conciliation of the Irish Catholics was not merely (if at all) a matter of justice, nor of countering the threat of foreign invasion (after the battle of Trafalgar in 1805), but rather a requirement for keeping "the king's peace" in the face of the democratic force of the Catholic liberation movement. The conciliationist tendency was expressed in ongoing contacts with the Vatican, and in the Tory proposal of the "two-wings" bill in 1825, coupling state payment of priests' salaries with repeal of the franchise of the forty-shilling freeholders.[61] But by the end of 1826 the initiative had passed to the Irish national liberation movement.[62]

Finally, even the Tory Wellington government with Peel as Home Secretary (1828–30) adopted the Emancipation Bill as its own, convinced as it was that the only alternative was a war of incalculable financial, military, diplomatic, and political costs.[63] Even as the Tories swallowed hard, the concession was fashioned with the invariable hook or, as Peel phrased it, "the securities and restrictions by which it is fitting that this measure of relief should be accompanied." In this case, it was the cancellation of the franchise of the forty-shilling freeholder. In this way, Peel argued, as "the avenues to honour, and power, and distinction" were being opened to the Irish Catholic upper crust, the "disfranchisement of poverty and ignorance" would "restore the Protestants to [their] just weight in the [Parliamentary] representation;" it was to be hoped that finally "a respectable [English-style] class of yeomanry would be created."[64] Still, for all the long reluctance in coming to it, the passage of what was known as the Catholic Emancipation Act on 13 April 1829 was the crossing of the Rubicon from the era of racial oppression: "the State was no longer committed to Protestant Ascendancy."[65]

Although passage of the Emancipation Act did make it possible for

O'Connell and a number of other Catholic Irishmen to enter upon the "honour, and power, and distinction" of membership in the British Parliament,[66] it was too little and too late to pacify the country. First of all, the Catholic bourgeoisie had surrendered the forty-shilling freehold vote – the very ram that had forced open the doors of Parliament to them – and thus seriously impaired their electoral range of action.[67] By raising the property-yield requirement for voting from forty shillings to ten pounds (200 shillings), Parliament had succeeded in its intention to "limit the practical implications of the admission of Catholics to full civil rights."[68] The higher property qualification reduced the electoral rolls in Ireland from a hundred thousand to sixteen thousand.[69] As far as the small tenant was concerned, this meant not only a loss of political rights; it deprived him of that degree of protection from eviction, or access to perquisites, that being a landlord's constituent might provide. The Tory government had said "A" by passing Catholic Emancipation, but from congenital defect appeared incapable of saying "B"; they were resistant to clearing away the debris of the old regime of social control, still highly operative in Ireland in the form of the Orange Order, composed of tens of thousands of armed and militant Protestants,[70] and the official local agencies of social control, the Orange magistrates and yeomanry. This obsolescent Establishment in effect denied the Catholic bourgeoisie the *normal* access to their proper political base, the Catholic masses. Accordingly, the "avenues to honour, and power, and distinction" that Peel had promised to the Catholic propertied, professional and commercial classes were still closed. Above all, the begrudged Emancipation was too late because the movement had been lastingly imbued with a passion for relief from Protestant tithes, for agrarian reform, and for repeal of the Union.

The Tithe War of the Irish Peasantry

The mass organized protest of the angry and impoverished peasants against payment of the tithe to the Church of Ireland began in November 1830, at Graiguenamanach in County Carlow, when an attempt was made to seize cattle belonging to a Catholic priest.[71] The scope and intensity of the protest were unprecedented in Irish history.[72] It went on for more than five years, and even after that the substantive issue continued unresolved so far as leaseholders were concerned. Besides the Catholics, the Dissenters, mainly Ulster Presbyterians, being peasants, also resisted payment of tithes to the Established Church of Ireland, even though as anti-Catholics they were wary of the predominant anti-Protestant tone of the campaign as a whole.

According to official claims, in the year 1832 nine thousand crimes, including 196 homicides, were attributable to the tithe protesters. The peasants and laborers were charged with "agrarian outrages;" but when the police and the yeomanry killed thirteen unarmed protesters and wounded twenty others at Newtonbarry or carried off a poor widow's cow for tithes at Rathcormack, that was a matter of keeping "the king's peace." At any rate, the attempt to collect the tithes arrears was a failure; after spending £15,000 in the effort, the authorities had collected only £12,000 of the £104,000 owed for the year 1831.[73]

In 1833, Parliament enacted a Coercion Bill (3 & 4 William IV c. 4), providing that any county in Ireland could be placed under martial law, with a sun-down to sun-up curfew, violators to be transported to penal colonies in Australia.[74] Nevertheless, the government was fought to a standstill in the tithe war, and was forced to resort to concessions and political maneuvers. The government itself undertook to compensate the Church of Ireland for uncollected tithes due for 1831 and 1832, in effect admitting defeat in the effort to collect them by the use of magistrates, constables and yeomanry; attempts to collect the arrears for 1832, 1833, and 1834 were abandoned. Legislatively, the matter was concluded in August 1838 with passage of 1 & 2 Victoria c. 109. All tithes arrears for 1834 through 1837 were written off. The great mass of the peasantry, the tenants-at-will, were exempted from the tithe. For all other tenants, the tithe was folded into the rent, the landlords being allowed a 25 percent rebate for making the collection. Parliament was convinced that the landlord, wielding his powers of eviction, was a more reliable agent than the tithe proctor.[75]

The Repeal Campaign – Bidding for a Form of Independence

As O'Connell and others had warned, by turning landlords into tithe proctors the commutation of tithes into rents for leaseholders had the simultaneous effect of merging the struggle against tithes into the general agrarian struggle directed against rents and, indeed, "property rights" in general.[76] O'Connell moved to turn this dreaded result to advantage. Intending to replicate the Emancipation victory of 1829, he sought to direct the wrath of the peasants into a revival of the repeal campaign, organized under the Loyal National Repeal Association (the name it took a year after its founding in 1840). The association proclaimed 1843 Repeal Year. Again, and despite ever-stronger rescripts from the Vatican, which was fearful of imperiling its increasingly promising negotiations with the British government, the priesthood with a few high-ranked exceptions supported quite strongly the repeal campaign.[77] The government was guided by its own police reports, which called the priesthood "the very spring and essence" of the campaign.[78] When the Irish administration dismissed seven Catholic magistrates who had attended repeal meetings, the effect was to bring wider bourgeois support to the movement, particularly among persons in the legal profession. The masses who rallied to the cause, however, continued to be the peasants and proletarians,[79] as is self-evident from the estimates (even discounted for friendly exaggeration) of the attendance at the "monster meetings." These mass mobilizations were the main tactic of the repeal movement, as they had been in the Emancipation campaign. Beginning at Carrickmacross, in Ulster, on the first Sunday after Easter with 150,000 in attendance, in the months until the first day of October, a score of "monster meetings" were held, attended by an estimated average of over 300,000 persons,[80] including 150,000 people at Donnybrook, 300,000 at Tuam, half a million at Cork in May and 1 million at Tara in August,[81] despite the intimidating deployment of 35,000 British troops.[82] Before the campaign was over, almost the entire adult population of Ireland (outside of Ulster) had been in attendance at repeal meetings, on the parish or some grander scale.[83]

The Decommissioning of the Protestant Yeomanry

The decision of the British government in about 1835 to abandon attempts at forcible collection of tithes was a defining moment in the fundamental change being made in the system of social control in Ireland. The controversy within the British ruling class between the defenders of the Protestant Ascendancy status quo and those who favored conciliation of the Catholics was to be seen in ambivalence toward the Protestant yeomanry. From its origin as an opposition to the republican and pro-Emancipation United Irishmen, and its notoriously cruel participation in the suppression of the rebellion of 1798, the yeomanry remained for twenty-five years the principal instrument for policing the Catholic peasantry. At that time it had come to number nearly twenty-five thousand, more indeed than the total combined yeomanry of England, Scotland, and Wales.[84] Its main base of strength was in the Protestant areas of Ulster, but its local units were the staple of law and order throughout the country.[85] Obviously, the yeomanry's "croppy-lie-down" credo was fundamentally contradictory to the trend toward conciliation of the Catholic bourgeoisie. The yeomanry was supplanted in 1822 as the primary police force by an all-Ireland constabulary, composed roughly half and half of Catholics and Protestants, and thus guarded against domination by Protestant bigotry.[86] Nevertheless, Protestant response to the intensifying conflict increased the yeomanry to some thirty thousand men by the time of the tithe war.[87] The British government re-equipped them in 1830 with modern weapons, on the recommendation of the Whig Prime Minister who privately avowed that, in a pinch, "there is no body in Ireland like the Protestant yeomanry in the North."[88] The "croppies," however, were less and less disposed to "lie down"; instead, in the struggle against the Protestant tithes, they were openly defying the yeomanry with a fierce determination and on a scale that alarmed not only the British ruling class but also the Irish bourgeoisie, fearful of the logic: tithes today, rents tomorrow.[89] Rather suddenly, the English ruling class, heeding arguments of the Irish bourgeoisie, found that there was more risk than security to be found in resort to the yeomanry. The Orange Order, which was the directing force of the yeomanry, was dissolved in 1836, and a new all-Ireland, "professionalized," non-sectarian police force was established.[90] The new police force, which superseded the county and peace preservation forces (except in Dublin, Belfast and Derry), was distinguished, writes historian Oliver MacDonagh, by "their complete centralisation and coordination, their professionalism and mobility, and their quasi-military organisation and discipline." It was "integrated," and by the time it took the name Royal Irish Constabulary in 1867, its ranks were in great majority Catholic. All in all, it represented a great change from the regime of the yeomanry, and represented an essential aspect of the change in the system of social control from one of racial oppression to one of national oppression. Outside Ulster, the last hurrah of the yeomanry was a lament for the Protestant intermediate social control stratum.[91]

Nor could the problem any longer be solved by resort to the British army. The reason was not simply fiscal, as it had been in the days of Sir John Davies or Sir William Petty – nor, indeed, as it was in the view of Sir Robert Peel in 1829, when he said, "reliance can be placed on the army," though he, in his historic turn, doubted that the British people would be willing to "bear the enormous expense" of such an effort. Now he said, "We cannot replace the Roman Catholics in the position in which we found them, when the system of relaxation and indulgence began."[92] By 1845 Peel would publicly admit, referring to the Irish independence movement, "you can not break it up by force."[93] *Outside Ulster, therefore, the British had abandoned rule by racial oppression, that is, rule by Protestant Ascendancy, in return for the Catholic bourgeoisie's abandonment of national independence and land reform.* In terms of social control this meant that, outside Ulster, the Catholic bourgeoisie, in its new capacity of intermediate buffer social control stratum, would be the first guarantor of "the king's peace."

The Apprenticeship of the Catholic Bourgeoisie

The British concession-cum-hook strategy for dividing and/or appeasing the Irish Catholic bourgeoisie would not have succeeded unless the latter had actually been able to prove its ability to function as a buffer social control stratum *vis-à-vis* the Irish peasantry. Time and again the British were in a state of great anxiety concerning the need for the O'Connellite leaders to play along with peasant militancy in order to control it; time and again, the government expected the buffer would not hold. For their part, O'Connell and his party were fully aware of the role they were playing; indeed, at times they reveled in it for the leverage it gave them in winning concessions from the British colonial bourgeoisie without violence.[94]

In December 1824, British Home Secretary Robert Peel regarded the situation in Ireland as so turbulent and the role of the Catholic Association as so critical that only "the prudence and discretion" of the leadership of the association stood between the government and imminent rebellion in Ireland.[95] Indeed, in the next five years the situation at times became touch and go.[96] Would the Catholic Association be able to turn the peasant movement aside before it became a general assault on rents and tithes? Priests trying to rein in the movement were spurned by their congregations. The Association leadership, most notably O'Connell and Sheil, threw all their energies into the effort to keep the masses quiet. O'Connell issued an address to the peasants of Munster commanding them to stop their meetings; hundreds of posters were distributed bearing the same urgent appeal. Even within the Association, O'Connell had to exert himself to stop an endorsement of the resort to "exclusive dealing," which was already being practiced widely by the peasants against their enemies and all who trafficked with them. Within the Protestant establishment, private letters and official reports expressed a general apprehension that some slight incident might set off a general rebellion. O'Connell and Sheil were determined to keep the lid on "predial agitation," that is, land agitation, even as they were turning up the rhetorical fires of "political agitation" to secure their more narrow goal of achieving the legitimacy of their class in the British system.[97] Indeed, they were successful, although not by repudiating agrarian demands but rather by persuading the peasants that Catholic so-called Emancipation was the way to go. Expressing a sense of gratitude to the British government for Emancipation, the Catholic bishops of Ireland on 9 February 1830 aimed a blow at the solar plexus of the Irish national liberation movement by directing all priests to avoid political controversy.[98]

By these efforts, the Catholic bourgeoisie gave the first great demonstration of its fitness for the buffer social control function. Its members' acquiescence in the disfranchisement of the forty-shilling freeholders was an earnest of their acceptance of the status of subordinates to an alien upper class.[99] In passing the Catholic Emancipation Act of 1829 the British Parliament certified the end of religio-racial oppression of Ireland, and the inauguration of the Catholic Irish bourgeoisie in its new role in the British system of social control in Ireland.

Out of the experience of this Emancipation crisis, O'Connell propounded a general theoretical proposition regarding social control for Ireland in those times: "The fact is," he said, "that political agitation is calculated to stop predial agitation."[100] He made the point in the course of an eloquent but vain effort to dissuade the British Parliament from enacting the Coercion Bill of 1833 (3 William IV c. 4), directed at suppressing the tithe war of the early

1830s. The danger to the social order posed by the tithe war, he argued, would be more wisely handled by working with the Irish Catholic bourgeois leadership than by adding another hateful round of military repression and penal transportation to the shameful history of British rule in Ireland.

In their dismay over the increasingly militant development of the tithe war, the O'Connellites were motivated by general bourgeois class interests, British and Irish, Protestant and Catholic, as well as by the new role of the Irish bourgeoisie in the British system. In 1833, the Catholic clergy withdrew support from the anti-tithe movement, and a year later the bishops secretly ordered priests to abstain from political activity and forbade the further use of chapels for political meetings. In these pronouncements, the bishops were expressing the attitude of O'Connell and the Catholic bourgeoisie in general, who had "abandoned full-scale opposition to the tithe."[101] In January, at the height of the tithe war, O'Connell, in Dublin, wrote to British Lord Chancellor Duncannon, "the only person connected with power" to whom he felt he could write who might "appreciate the exact state of this country." There was in Ireland at that moment, he said, "so general a disposition for ... insurrectionary outrage" as he had never seen before. O'Connell warned, however, against any attempt to use the hated Protestant yeomanry against the Catholic peasants; they would "prove to be weakness not strength." Military repression should be left to the British army, he thought, and "the more troops sent over here the better." For his part, he promised, "I will use all my influence to stop the career of those who are engaged in urging on the people."[102] The earnestness of that pledge is to be read in the public warning to the rebellious peasantry that was posted in market towns of O'Connell's home county, Kerry, over the name of one of his close friends: "Unless you desist," it said, "I denounce you as traitors to the cause of the liberty of Ireland.... I leave you to the Government and the fire and bayonet of the military. Your blood be upon your own souls."[103]

James Warren Doyle (1796–1834), Catholic Bishop of Kildare and Leighlin, having made a record for "repressing all disorders" in his diocese before becoming the first bishop to join the Repeal Association, was the pre-eminent spokesman among the Catholic hierarchy with respect to political questions. Doctor Doyle regretted the British resort to the 1833 Coercion Bill, but, when the chips were down he put his trust in – gentlemen. "If we are to be subjected to a despotism," he said, "let it be the despotism of gentlemen ... not of the brutal *canaille* composing the Trades Union and Black Feet confederacies."[104] Doyle's comment captured the essence of the choice the Irish Catholic bourgeoisie was making in order to enter upon its new role in the governing of Ireland.

The same class affinity governed the repeal campaign when it reached its most critical juncture. Historians have all pointed out the ambiguity of the term "repeal" as O'Connell defined it in his public and his private pronouncements.

This ambiguity would in time take the objective form of a split between the O'Connellite old guard and the nationalist Young Ireland tendency. But "repeal" meant at least a dominion status like that of Canada, or, like Jamaica, a colony under the authority of the "home" country government, but with a legislature with authority in insular matters.[105] However, even so limited a degree of Irish legislative autonomy carried unacceptable risks to real British economic interests, and to the real or fancied geopolitical interests of empire.[106] The government of Robert Peel therefore threw down the gauntlet in the form of a decree banning the climactic "monster meeting" planned for 8 October 1843 at Clontarf. The challenge could hardly have been more flagrant, as the order was promulgated in Dublin less than twenty-four hours before the time set for the meeting. O'Connell capitulated. The Repeal Association looked at the alternatives – rule by a Parliament forever dominated by their ancient English enemy, or the specter of the French Revolution being re-embodied in an Irish *jacquerie* – and chose the first.[107] The desperate haste with which the Repeal Association reacted to the government's ultimatum was nothing less than a caricature of itself as a buffer social control agency. O'Connell immediately proclaimed the cancellation of the Clontarf meeting, saw to the dismantling of the speakers' platform, and sent swift riders out in all directions to intercept people already *en route* to Clontarf and turn them back. Although it proved to be an act of political self-immolation for O'Connell personally, it was the ultimate proof of the readiness of the Catholic Irish bourgeoisie for its indispensable role in the British national domination of Ireland.

The decade and a half following the passage of the Catholic Emancipation Act of 1829 witnessed the maturation of a process begun in 1793 with the enfranchisement of the Catholic forty-shilling freeholder in exchange for the disavowal by the Catholic bourgeoisie of the Volunteer movement and the cause of Irish national independence. True to its congenital nature, the phenomenon in its full development presents itself to history in a dual aspect.[108] The Catholic bourgeoisie, which under the Penal Laws system of racial oppression had been denied recognition as a class, effectively exploited the opportunity presented by the exigencies of British government policy to achieve social legitimacy, with officially sanctioned hegemony over the Catholic population, in exchange for its enlistment as the main buffer social control stratum in the British system of rule in Catholic Ireland.

Historian Oliver MacDonagh speaks of this fifteen-year period as one of "very substantial change in approach to the government of Ireland," which set a new and long-enduring "pattern for Anglo-Irish relations."[109] The essentials of this change were three: (1) the ending of reliance on Protestant Ascendancy for social control in Ireland, and simultaneous "moves toward religious parity"; (2) a greater degree of parity between Catholics and Protestants with respect to courts, political patronage and favors, government employment, etcetera; (3) integration of Catholics in the British parliamentary and party system.

The most dramatic demonstration of the inauguration of the O'Connellite contingent into the British parliamentary and party system was the so-called Lichfield House Compact, an agreement arrived at in a series of meetings of Parliamentary Whigs, O'Connellites, and English Radicals in February, March and April 1835.[110] The technical parliamentary basis of the arrangement was that the Irish Repealers and Liberals as well as the English Radicals preferred the more liberal Whigs to Robert Peel, Wellington and the Tories; second, the elections of December–January 1834–35 had so reduced the Whig fraction in Parliament that the party could form a government only with the support of O'Connell and the "Irish Party."[111] The fundamental socio-economic basis for the O'Connellite–Whig alliance was, first, agrarian rebellion as manifested in the struggle against the tithes and, second, the fact that since the final repeal of the Penal Law prohibitions against Catholic landholding in 1782, the proportion of Irish land owned by Catholics had increased, according to a contemporary estimate, from around 5 percent to around 20 percent. Nearly half the land in Ireland was held on long-term lease by Catholics.[112]

Just two years before, in 1833, the Whig government had secured the passage of the Coercion Bill to put down peasant resistance to the tithes. Now an altered Whig Party made a number of concessions to support the efforts of its O'Connellite partners to defuse the explosive situation in the Irish countryside.[113] But the relationship became a general one, in which the O'Connellites soft-pedaled repeal and worked as an auxiliary of the Whig government in exchange for the promise of the Whigs "to do something for" Ireland.[114] The representatives of the Catholic Irish bourgeoisie in Parliament did not hesitate long over the alternative policy of greater independence from the Whigs and closer alliance with the English Radicals and Chartists. The English Radicals and Chartists were generally supportive of equal rights of Catholics in Ireland within the Union. When the Radicals and Chartists pressed their demand that Parliament go beyond the mere abolition of rotten boroughs and the extremely limited extension of the suffrage in the Whig Reform Bill of 1832, and instead enact "universal" (male) suffrage, the Irish Party took the side of the Whig party leaders. The O'Connell party likewise opposed the Ten-hour Day Bill that was being demanded by the English workers but was opposed by the English bourgeoisie.[115]

In the execution of this bore-from-within tactic, O'Connell did not always succeed in placing his choices in government posts in Ireland, but he did have a veto on appointments he opposed.[116] The social promotion of the Catholic bourgeoisie as a class was personified in the careers of Catholic Irishmen – repealers, Liberals and others. Of the original thirty-nine members of the Repeal Party in the House of Commons in 1832, twenty-six were Catholics; of the Catholics, nine were given offices, places or titles; they included junior cabinet ministers, one of whom was made an hereditary baronet; another of the group was knighted.[117] Richard Lalor Sheil became Commissioner of

Greenwich Hospital and progressed to ever more exalted office; he was Master of the Mint (1846–50) before ending his career as British Minister at the Court of Tuscany.

The Whig three-member executive put in place in Ireland, especially Thomas Drummond (British Under-Secretary for Ireland, 1835–40), aggressively promoted a policy of fairness to Catholics and opposition to Orangeism in the appointment of judges, magistrates, commissioners and army officers, and in the reorganization of the police force.[118] At a time when a "liberal" Protestant was one who opposed Orangeism and favored an end to anti-Catholic discrimination, half the judges, salaried magistrates and police inspectors appointed in Ireland were Protestant liberals and half were Catholics.[119] Simultaneously, a traditional phalanx of Protestant Ascendancy, the unpaid squireen magistracy, was purged of one-third of its members. But the most important single blow to the Protestant Ascendancy was the establishment of a centralized professional police force, recruited and organized with an unprecedented degree of religious impartiality.[120]

This Whig government was voted down in 1841, despite O'Connell's loyalty. Basically, its demise resulted not from its differences with the Conservative (Tory) opposition, but rather because it shared the same fundamental class interests. Thus limited, it fell, a victim of the intractability of the agrarian-rooted "Irish Question," Conservative obstructionism in the House of Commons, constant badgering by the Tory-dominated House of Lords, and attrition at the polls, deliberately exacerbated by Conservative appeals to British "no popery" sentiments.

But the eventual course taken by Peel's new Conservative government would show that the new departure with regard to the Catholic Irish bourgeoisie was not merely a coalition-building Whig maneuver; a shift of the political center of gravity had occurred within the British ruling class.[121] Having said "A" by passage of Catholic Emancipation in 1829, the British bourgeoisie as a whole was finally ready to say "B," to accept the practical consequences of the fact that it could not govern Ireland without the enlistment of the Catholic bourgeoisie in the system of social control. Peel was determined to adhere to the ancient principle of English statecraft of withholding necessary concessions until a point is reached at which the concessions can appear as royal largesse rather than as a surrender to popular pressure.[122] It was obvious that the course of excessive delay followed by panicky surrender to popular clamor for Catholic Emancipation in 1829 had weakened the government's authority rather than strengthening it. It was therefore only after he had successfully challenged the "monster meeting" strategy and the plan to make 1843 the "Repeal Year" that Peel found it opportune to advance reforms that he had for some time understood would be necessary. He then proceeded, guided by two general principles: first, "sever the clergy from the agitators and the agitation must cease";[123] second, open up patronage for Catholics.

Under the Penal Laws, as I have noted, priests had been outlaws, to be run down by bounty-hunters. The British government now resolved on a course aimed at making the Catholic clergy independent of Irish democracy and dependent upon the British Exchequer, on an equal legal basis with the Protestant clergy, and thus installing them as the most pervasive agency of social control in Catholic Ireland. This matter would not be fully settled until the disestablishment of the Protestant Church of Ireland by the passage of the Irish Church Act (32 & 33 Vict. c. 42) in 1869. But the course was irrevocably set by laws enacted in 1844 and 1845.[124] A major source of funds, blocked under the Penal Laws, was opened to the Catholic Church and its institutions by passage of the Charitable Donations and Bequests Act (7 & 8 Vict. c. 97). The administrative board of thirteen established under this act included five Catholics. The following year, Maynooth College was given a capital grant of £30,000, and its annual grant was tripled and made permanent (8 & 9 Vict. c. 25). More significant in terms of a direct social control function was the inclusion of priests as ex-officio members of the government's famine relief committees in 1846, as priests in general were "increasingly accepted as a legitimate part of local power and influence."[125]

Although the British government attached great importance to measures designed to detach the bourgeois Irish Catholic priesthood from democratic movements, that policy would have been utterly ineffective except for measures taken to detach the Catholic bourgeoisie from the discontents of the masses of the Irish peasants, cottiers and laborers.[126] Without that, the priesthood as an instrument of social control would have broken in the government's hands, a fact clearly implicit in the experience with both the Emancipation and the Repeal struggles.

Affirmative Action to Implement the New Arrangement

The social promotion of the Irish Catholic bourgeoisie made necessary an historic program of affirmative action to install Catholics in posts and fields of activity previously reserved for Protestants. "We must look out for respectable Roman Catholics for office," Peel told his Home Secretary, stressing the necessity to reject as a "specious principle" the idea that "if Protestants are better qualified for appointments that fall vacant, Protestants ought [therefore] to be preferred to Catholics." Peel urged Earl De Grey, the Lord Lieutenant in Ireland, to get on with the promotion to office of a certain well-regarded Catholic barrister. When De Grey argued that he did "not feel that it is either wise or expedient to appoint an unfit man to an office merely because he is a Catholic," Peel patiently explained the alphabetical logic of their situation: "What motive can we hold out to the well-affected Roman Catholic to abjure agitation ... if the avenue to ... legitimate distinction be in point of fact closed to him ..." It was folly, he continued, to open up for the Catholic bourgeoisie access to "popular favour" by passage of the Catholic Emancipation Act, while at the same time, "every avenue to Royal favour be closed" to them. To combine Emancipation with such persistent anti-Catholic exclusionism, he concluded, would simply have been to "organize a force of mischievous demagogues" to pour oil on the fire of Irish insurrectionism.[127] In 1845 a number of senior offices in the Irish government were given to Catholics, while a county deputy lieutenant and a magistrate were dismissed from office for participation in protests against what they called the government's "surrender to popery."[128]

Under the racial oppression of the Penal Laws period, Catholic tradesmen, before they could practice their trades, were made to pay extortionate fees every quarter to the "masters" of their respective trades, the alternative being to swear an oath abjuring the Catholic religion; and in the 1776–80 period, Arthur Young found that Irish Catholics were effectively barred from trades requiring capital.[129] From 1835 onward, despite reflexive Orangeist obstructionism and partisan jockeying by the Conservative Party when it was the parliamentary opposition, there occurred an historic degree of "progressive dismantling of Protestant privilege."[130]

The transformation was made the basis for urging the elevation of Archbishop Paul Cullen to the College of Cardinals as a manifestation of the enhanced status of the Irish Catholic bourgeoisie in general. "We are ... a population growing every day in wealth and social importance," wrote one advocate of the archbishop's elevation. "Out of *three* Chief Justices of the Supreme Counts the Catholics have *two*. Of nine Judges of the same Courts we have *three* – with minor judgeships too numerous to reckon." The writer also asserted: "*Commercially* we have almost one half of the administrative power in all the great undertakings," of which he specifically mentions banks and railways. Though Protestants still outnumbered Catholics in the higher levels of public office, increasing numbers of Catholics were appointed in the 1850s and 1860s, whilst the prospects were increasingly favorable for lower-order positions, for which qualification was by competitive examination.[131] These appointees were not mere window-dressing, tokens to ward off evil social spirits for a season; they gained position by virtue of their base, which was made up not only of the peasants and farm laborers who were the majority of the total population, but also of the Catholic half or more of the skilled and semi-skilled workers in trades and industries and public service employees in such key social control sectors as the police (70 percent Catholics), school-teachers (61 percent), and civil servants (50 percent).[132]

At the same time the national subordination of Ireland to Britain was apparent in the gross under-representation of Catholics in the professions, notably medicine and the law. It was most substantial in the major field of economic activity, agriculture. Of the total number of landowners, 38 percent were Catholics, but they received only 15 percent of the land rent; this probably reflected their share of the total agricultural land area.[133] The peasants of Catholic Ireland, reduced in number by famine and emigration, and still mainly dependants of Protestant landlords, were still fighting to win the tenant rights that the Protestant peasants in Ulster had enjoyed for two and a half centuries.

Making the Besiegers Part of the Garrison

Sir John Davies could finally rest in peace: the English sovereign could at last govern Ireland through "Ordinary Lawes and Magistrates" without the necessity of "sending an army to do it." By 1850, Ireland had a police force of 14,000, half of them Catholics, a force equal to one policeman for every 425 people (as compared to a ratio of only one to about 1,060 in Scotland, and one to about 840 in England and Wales).[134] At the same time, the continued presence of a standing British army of twenty to thirty thousand in Ireland was the most blatant symbol of the country's national oppression. However, since the British constitution forbade a standing army in the home country, the military establishment in Ireland provided a ready reserve for both empire and home country service. It was the proud boast of O'Connell and his English Whig colleagues that the social control services of the Catholic bourgeoisie had enabled the government to supply from its Irish garrisons one force to put down the English workers fighting for the right to vote, and another to fight the French Catholic and English rebels in Canada in 1837.[135]

A realist ahead of his time, the famous Whig politician Charles James Fox had said in 1805: "The Protestant Ascendancy has been compared to a garrison in Ireland; it is not in our power to add to the strength of this garrison, but I would make the besiegers themselves part of the garrison."[136]

The "garrison," an intermediate buffer social control stratum adequate to the needs of British rule in Ireland, could not be had without scrapping racial oppression; the "besiegers," the Catholic bourgeoisie lay and clerical, would now be the main part of the garrison of a system of national oppression.

Of Divergence and Parallels

In Ireland, the British ruling class found it necessary to draw the Irish Catholic bourgeoisie into the intermediate social control stratum and thus to end racial oppression, except in Ulster. Whilst the history of the United States presents no parallel of this phenomenon, a parallel is seen in the history of the British West Indies. Both the British West Indies and Ireland demonstrate the general principle of "relativity of race" as a function of ruling-class social control. In

both cases the colonial ruling power, faced with a combination of insurrectionary pressures and external threats, over a period of time (much the same
period of time, indeed) resolved the situation by the decision to recruit
elements of the oppressed group – Catholics in one case and persons of African
descent in the other – into the intermediate buffer social control stratum. (The
British West Indies parallel will be further considered in Volume Two of the
present study. See p. 144 for the brief United States parallel.)

Aside from whatever light this fact has for the study of West Indies history,
it helps us to understand better the testimony and studies regarding the
integration of West Indian immigrants into United States society as African-
Americans. Such works serve to underscore the contrast in the systems of
bourgeois social control – national oppression in the West Indies, racial
oppression in the United States.

These immigrants experienced the "cultural shock" of the transition from the
class-based "tri-partite social order"[137] with its African-Caribbean "colored"
intermediate stratum,[138] to the white-supremacist social order in the United
States that subordinates class distinction to an all-pervading "race" distinction.
In the West Indies these immigrants had "had access to all skilled trades and
professions," but in the United States they were barred from the trades by "white"
unions and employers, and from participation in the "mainstream" of professional life. Marcus Garvey, leader of the United Negro Improvement
Association, was trained in the printing trade by his godfather in Jamaica, but he
came to "acknowledge the difference";[139] in the United States he would have
been barred from the "whites"-only union of his trade. In Danish St Croix in the
Virgin Islands the free "colored" were a middle-class category – in 1834, thirteen
years before the abolition of slavery was decreed there.[140] The "culture shock" in
this instance was brought to the island from the United States, in the form of the
regime instituted there under the administration of the United States navy after
the United States purchase of the island in 1917. The official policy of disregard
of class distinctions among persons of African ancestry was combined with the
strict racial segregation policies of the United States. The new white-supremacist
order, such as had never been known on St Croix, was "violently thrust upon the
islanders," according to Hubert H. Harrison, a Crucian immigrant in the United
States who kept in close touch with his homeland.[141]

Writing of the period between 1900 and 1937, scholar Ira De A. Reid said
the West Indian immigrant did not understand "the synonymous use of 'Negro'
and 'colored' in the United States" – a distinction which was critical in the
tripartite social order in the West Indies, but which was to be strictly ignored
in the racial oppression system in the United States. Reid observed: "Many
Negro immigrants had to go into a mental reverse to accept such stratification."[142] For that same reason, says Wilfred Samuels, African-Caribbean
immigrants resisted "being cast in the same mold as their Afro-American
kinsmen."[143] Perhaps we should find that the experience of these West Indian

immigrants to the United States was like that of landless and unemployed Catholic Irish migrating to Belfast. The difference was, of course, that the starved-out Irish peasant and weaver could escape submission to racial oppression by emigrating and becoming a part of the system of "white" supremacy in the United States, where being Catholic was a forgivable offense, but being not-"white" was not.

5

Ulster

Catholic Emancipation in 1829 led within a decade and a half to the replacement of racial oppression by national oppression as the main form of British colonial rule in Ireland, and to the concomitant incorporation of the Catholic Irish bourgeoisie into the British system of social control over that country. "Negro Emancipation," proclaimed in 1863, did not lead to the end of racial oppression in the United States, nor to any fundamental change in the system of bourgeois social control. Why the difference?[1] Within the context of this study of racial oppression, social control and the invention of the white race, the Ulster analogy, to which the next two chapters are devoted, best illuminates that problem of United States history and its ongoing development.[2]

The Plantation of Ulster

When the plantation of Ulster was launched in 1609 – two years after the founding of Jamestown – King James's Lord Deputy for Ireland, Sir Arthur Chichester, did not envision it as a more successful Munster or Leinster. Rather, he said, it was "as if His Majesty were to begin a new plantation in America, from which it does not greatly differ."[3] There was, sadly, more prophecy in his remark than he could know. Thus far, however, he could see: it would begin with the extirpation of the native social order, and a massive displacement of the native population by laboring-class immigrant settlers.

Victory in the Tyrone War (1594–1603) had convinced the British colonialists that the conditions were finally ripe for the success of the plantation policy, provided the lessons of past experience were kept in mind. They had learned that a civil regime of racial oppression would be destroyed by rebelling Irish or by the "degeneracy" of the English colonists "within a few years, if the number of civil persons who are planted do not exceed the number of the natives."[4] But in those days Ulster was the most Irish of the four Irish provinces. "The entire mass of the population was Irish,"

115

.

said Sir John Davies, "following Irish customs and obeying only Irish law."[5]

The English began by taking advantage of the opportunity provided by the Flight of the Earls in 1607 and the defeat of O'Doherty's revolt in 1608, events famous to Irish history. In order to bring to an end the prohibitively expensive war in Ireland, in 1603 the English government had granted O'Neill and O'Donnell generous terms of submission, pardoning them and restoring their lands and titles as English earls, of Tyrone and Tyrconnell respectively.[6] It soon became apparent, however, that this was merely a tactical maneuver, designed to gain time for the putting into place of the administrative and legal apparatus for dismantling the old Gaelic social order completely. By portentous land surveys, by legal challenges to the chieftains' land titles and authority, and by deliberate insults, this prospect was borne in upon O'Neill and O'Donnell, with adumbrations of a tragic fate by English treachery. Finally, in fear for their very lives, or of perpetual imprisonment, Tyrone and Tyrconnell fled into exile, sailing secretly out of Lough Swilly at midnight on 4 September 1607.[7]

Cahir O'Doherty, on the other hand, had been an ally of the English. Upon failing to win election to succeed his father as head of his tribe, he had deserted to the English side at a critical moment of the Tyrone War. The arrangement involved an English pledge to support Sir Cahir in gaining the chieftaincy, and the grant of the O'Doherty tribal lands and fisheries of Inishowen to Sir Cahir as his private estate.[8] But when the war was won, the English conveniently displaced the commander, Sir Henry Docwra, who had made the wartime agreement. Even though O'Doherty had served as the foreman of the jury that had indicted O'Neill and O'Donnell for treason,[9] the English government proceeded piecemeal to cancel their promise to O'Doherty, all the while adding the meanest sort of personal insult to the injury they were doing him. In May 1608, provoked beyond endurance by the faithless English for whom he had been faithless to the Irish cause, O'Doherty rose in a brief but fiery revolt, which ended with his death in battle in the following July. Two years later O'Doherty's vast domain in Inishowen was granted to the Lord Deputy, Sir Arthur Chichester.[10] Before the outbreak of the rebellion, King James had sent an order to make O'Doherty whole, but it was fatally "delayed in transmission," according to its addressee, Chichester. But, in a historical sense, it was already too late when it was written.[11]

Under color of "punishing" these three "rebels," the English government confiscated ("escheated") six entire northern Irish counties, the lands of Irish tribes from time immemorial.[12] In seeking the economic, political and social degradation of its conquered enemies, the government was merely honoring a long tradition in English statecraft: reward your friends and punish your enemies. But in Ulster it was to be punish your enemies and punish your friends. Few if any British civil or military servitors in Ireland had contributed more to the English cause than did such Irish of the chieftain class as O'Doherty, Nial Garve O'Donnell, Ballagh O'Cahan, Mulmorie Og O'Reilly,

Oghie O'Hanlon and Connor Roe Maguire ("the English Maguire"). These friends of the English had made possible the opening of the second front on the northern shore of Ireland, whereby Mountjoy was at last able to overwhelm Ulster, the bastion of Celtic power. For their treachery each of these Irish chieftains was promised possession of vast tribal lands. And, for their part, these chieftains were ready, even eager, to be integrated into the English-style social order, as the Scots and the Welsh chieftains had been in an earlier time.[13]

But the option for racial oppression left no room in the ranks of the colonial upper class for Catholic Irish chieftains, for all that some of them might wear the title "Sir." The English therefore proceeded systematically with the repudiation of their promises to their Irish wartime allies.[14] Whether they had been enemies (like O'Neill and O'Donnell) or allies (like O'Doherty) in the Tyrone War, whether they flew to arms or merely protested at court, the Irish of chieftain class were to be demoted socially to the status of no more than small landlords, politically excluded from posts of authority, and placed socially beyond the pale of British respectability. Tanistry and gavelkind, the Celtic forms of succession and inheritance, were outlawed.[15] Irish chieftains might be expropriated and put to death for making an appeal based on Celtic law, and the practice of the Catholic religion was outlawed. "Britons" were forbidden to acquire land from "Britons," that is, English or Scots;[16] they were to get it from the Irish. In the six escheated Ulster counties, only a score of the "deserving Irish" were allowed to keep as much as one thousand acres of land.[17] Some 280 others were granted an average of 180 acres each.[18] "Few of the favored Irish received grants of land which they actually occupied"; writes Aidan Clarke, "none received as much as they believed themselves entitled to."[19] Whatever their former standing or their service to the English, the natives, being Celts and Catholics, were to be excluded from any role in the English colonial social control system. Throughout the six escheated counties, they were to be beset by social and legal disabilities that steadily eroded their economic status.[20]

Nor was this wholesale demotion of the native chieftain class to be balanced by a Tudor-style social promotion of select members of the lower orders to the yeoman farmer and small gentry classes. The great majority of the Ulster natives were to be left to find places as they might as tenants-at-will of British settlers, or were forced to take up a more precarious existence on wastelands.[21]

Many of these displaced natives formed themselves into bands of "wood-kernes" who "stood upon their keeping," living off the land in the fastnesses of woods and mountains, issuing forth on occasion to impose upon the British settlers the payment of the equivalent of the old "black rents." By official estimates, in October 1609, there were 12,000 of these "loose and idle swordsmen" in Ireland, one-third of them in Ulster.[22]

The English authorities decided to round up these men and sell them to the Protestant King of Sweden as soldiers.[23] The only actual mass shipment of which there is a record occurred in the autumn of 1610. The treacherous deceit with which the authorities conducted the round-up, and the frenzied resistance of the intended victims are reminiscent of accounts of the capture and shipment of Africans into bond-servitude in the Americas.[24] Precaution was taken to keep the Irish unaware of the fact that they were destined for sale "into a country so remote, and of no good fame" as far as the Irish were concerned. In order to prevent an explosive reaction when the men intended for shipment should suddenly "perceive that an alteration of their state and course of life [was] intended," Lord Deputy Chichester ordered that they not be assembled until all was in order for prompt embarkation. Even so, the shock of recognition of the fate intended for them set off a revolt among the intended transportees. Three shiploads sailed from Derry. But the men on the fourth ship, at Carlingford, rose in mutiny, with the intention of beaching the vessel a short way from its mooring and thus escaping into the countryside. Unfortunately, a contrary wind fatally delayed them, and after twenty-four hours they were subdued by English forces, although a number of them did manage to escape. The Lord Deputy ordered "exemplary punishment of three, four, five, or six" of the leaders of the mutiny; the rest were finally shipped.[25] Although perils of the sea forced all four of the vessels into harbors in England, most of the original transportees were ultimately delivered in Sweden.[26]

Despite such draconian measures, the discontent of the majority of the native population, who had received nothing, became merged with the alarm of remnants of the old Irish chieftain class, to generate a hostility that endangered the success of the British colonial project. In 1615 the colony was in a state of high tension because of a revolt conspiracy led by declassed and persecuted members of the native chieftain class.[27] The conspirators were undone by disdaining to conceal their aims. But a quarter of a century later in Ulster a like-purposed revolt would begin the War of the Three Kingdoms.

The first social control measure proposed for the plantation of Ulster was aimed at establishing a special category of planters, composed of veterans of military service in Ireland and accordingly called "servitors." The intention was to reward past service, but to do so in such a way as to recruit a corps of men qualified in repressing Irish resistance. This being the main consideration, most of the servitors were not expected to supply significant investment capital. With the exception of a few high officials of the colony, servitors were in the main to be "captains and officers who have served in those parts, and are yet so poor as not to be able to manure [that is, work] any great quantity of land."[28] So critical was their role conceived to be for keeping the Irish natives under control that in May 1609 the bishop of Armagh successfully urged that installation of the other category of planters, the "undertakers" (so called because they undertook to supply the investment capital for the plantation) be delayed until a sufficient complement of servitors could be installed. "Except the servitors defend the borders and fastnesses and suppress the Irishry," the bishop said, "the new planters who neither know the country nor the wars nor the qualities of that people can never prosper."[29] Besides those posted to protect against the woodkernes at the borders of settlement, other servitors were to be posted to keep watch over such of the native Irish as were allowed grants within the area of plantation.[30]

Special inducements were provided to attract servitors. Whilst those who had managed to prosper by their years of military duty had the most promising prospects, others, being men "of least ability of purse," were to be assigned the most perilous locations. These latter were to be encouraged by allowances of military perquisites sufficient to enable them to "help themselves" to succeed and possibly to move up to the undertaker rank.[31]

Although the prospects of such social mobility were limited, servitors were accorded certain unique privileges. For example, they did not have to build and maintain two-story fortifications at their own expense, as undertakers were obliged to do. The most substantial of their privileges, however, concerned the terms of engagement of tenants. Whereas undertakers were to be permitted to let their land only to non-Irish settler tenants, and only on long-term leases, the servitors were allowed the option of retaining tenants-at-will from the ranks of the great mass of displaced natives. Although the servitors had to pay a 50 percent premium in quit-rent to the Crown for the privilege, the benefit of the higher rents obtainable from the hard-pressed native Irish made this a very profitable option.[32]

The servitors embodied the essential characteristics of a system of racial oppression: their social status was predicated upon the exclusion of Catholics from social mobility, and, second, their civic function was to maintain and enforce that exclusion. The number of servitor planters was so limited, however (fewer than sixty in 1610, fewer than seventy in 1618),[33] that they could be no more than a small-gentry embryo of an artificial middle-class implant adequate to the social control needs of the Ulster plantation. The requisite adequate body of substantial Protestant yeomanry was yet to be formed.

The Scottish Factor

With the succession of James VI of Scotland as James I of England in 1603, two sixteenth-century developments of Scottish national life suddenly assumed a historical relevance for English policy in Ireland.[34] The first of these was the triumph of Protestantism, although in the unepiscopal Presbyterian form. The other was the mass impoverishment that resulted from the reduction of the mass of the agricultural population from the effective status of "kindly tenants" to that of tenants-at-will.[35]

The turn to Protestantism brought Scotland and England into basic anti-Catholic alignment. National doctrinal differences between the Scottish Kirk and the Anglican Church (including its eventual Anglo-Irish Church of Ireland form) were the occasion for major political conflicts that lasted in Britain until the Glorious Revolution, and in Ireland a century longer.[36] If the British occupiers treated the Catholic Irish like aliens in their own country, it was also true that the Scots-Irish junior partners of the English were slighted as second-class citizens for their nonconformist Presbyterian, "Dissenter," religious beliefs. Nevertheless, when put to the test the anti-Catholic accord between Presbyterians and Anglicans has so far proved stronger than their sectarian differences.[37]

The second factor, mass impoverishment, reduced the laboring people of Scotland to an even more extreme condition of destitution than was visited upon the English peasantry by the Agrarian Revolution. In the Lowlands of Scotland, "life was generally harder and rougher than in England," wrote the late Professor Moody. The Scots migrant was therefore more likely to persevere as an Ulster "pioneer" than many of the English colonists, who were so disappointed by Ulster conditions that "they sold out and returned home."[38] The land was less fertile and the tenant was in a less favorable relationship to the landlord in Scotland than in England.[39]

At the end of the sixteenth century, when Scotland's population was less than 1 million,[40] every tenth person was a vagrant.[41] Scotland had no Early Industrial Revolution such as that which to a degree had afforded alternative opportunities for the displaced peasantry in England; nor did Scotland experience in the seventeenth century the overall economic expansion such as developed in England following the beginning of the English Revolution in 1640.[42] At the end of the seventeenth century, when the Scots numbered somewhat over 1 million,[43] there were among them 200,000 vagrants, according to Andrew Fletcher of Saltoun. While noting that a recent run of bad harvests had swollen the ranks of the homeless, Fletcher asserted that even in good times they numbered one hundred thousand.[44]

Fletcher ascribed this impoverishment mainly to exorbitant rents, which made "the tenant poorer even than his servant whose wages he cannot pay."[45] It was these "surplussed" Scots tenants and cottagers who chiefly supplied the migration to Ulster.[46] To the extent that this displacement was the product of the workings of the expansion of commodity production and a money economy, the pool of potential emigrants was supplied mainly from the more anglicized Lowland Presbyterian areas.[47] To the degree that the emigrants had delayed their evictions by credit, they were debtors on the run. To the extent that they were forced into vagrancy but proved unsuited to the competition of beggary, they were thieves. In so far as the ruling class saw no hope for their reabsorption into normal economic life, they were a surplus population of which Scotland was "constrained to disburthen herself."[48]

A Scottish minister, the Reverend Andrew Stewart, who settled in the port town of Donaghadee in County Down, would achieve a kind of immortality by his ever-quoted description of the Ulster immigrants passing by his door:

> From Scotland came many, and from England not a few, yet all of them generally the scum of both nations, who, for debts, or breaking and fleeing from justice, or seeking shelter, came hither, hoping to be without fear of man's justice in a land where there was nothing or but little, as yet, of the fear of God.... Going for Ireland was looked upon as the miserable mark of a deplorable person.[49]

It was such as these who were to make up the majority of Scots immigrant leaseholders and cottagers in Ulster.[50] They were to be the main bulwark of social control over the dispossessed native Irish chiefs and lords and their tribes. These Scots, writes Perceval-Maxwell, "were ideal material for populating a frontier." He cites a settlement scheme for County Monaghan put forward in 1622, in which it was recommended that Scots be planted in the northern part of that county, bordering Tyrone and Armagh, where English tenants could not be readily induced to settle. In this way, it was said, "the difficulties of the plantation [would be] ended[,] for the English then wilt gladly sitt down upon the other when *the Scots shall be as a walt [wall] betwixt them and the Irish* [emphasis added]".[51]

The Ulster Custom

Whatever their station in life may have been in Scotland, Scots emigrated to Ulster as a way to a substantial improvement of their lot. Early emigrants of the gentry class could double their wealth as capitalist planters in Ireland, and most of them became richer than the nobility in Scotland. As much money could be made in trade in Ulster in four years as could be made in England in ten. In the building trades, wages in Ulster were 20 percent above the level at which they were set in Scotland. The great hopeful expectation was increased wealth, and for a chance at a rise in social status.[52]

If the mass of Protestants who were to make up the "wall between" were to be expected to emigrate from their native lands, to serve in the posts of greatest danger, to bear the day-to-day burden of controlling the Ulster natives, and to cultivate the land and make it fruitful, they would obviously have to be assured a status other than that of tenants-at-will, even though they too would sweat at the plow and ache from their labors even as the natives did.

The solution was to be the establishment of a system of Protestant privilege specifically designed for the laboring-class British (mainly Scots) immigrants and their descendants. No promise was made or could be made that they would become "gentlemen"; the colony depended upon their remaining productive laborers. This privilege system did not, strictly speaking, mean automatic social mobility out of the laboring class; but it was a leg up, and a scrambling chance. And most important of all, it was made conditional upon the guarantee of preferential consideration *vis-à-vis* all Catholics under all circumstances.

These laboring-class settlers received guarantees of most favorable treatment in the beginning not only because they were Protestants, but also because Protestants were scarce. In effect, the Scots majority of them regained in Ulster the status of "kindly tenants" of which they had been divested in Scotland.[53] This was the beginning of the "Ulster custom," although it came to be known by that name only in the early eighteenth century, when it was tested by the emergence of a relative surplus of tenants and consequently significant antagonisms between landlords and tenants.[54]

The core of the Ulster Custom, the Protestant "tenant-right," was the privilege of heritable leases (leases "for lives") and of a full equity claim for any and all improvements made by the tenant. Appearing before the Devon Commission in 1844, the land agent to Lord Lurgan, a magistrate of the counties of Armagh and Down, gave a description of the Ulster Custom, the tenant-right, which deserves quotation at length for its combination of historical, economic and sociological aspects.

> Tenant right ... [is] the claim of the tenant and his heirs to continue in undisturbed possession of the farm, so long as the rent is paid; and in case of an ejectment, or in the event of a change of occupancy, whether at the wish of the landlord or the tenant, it is the sum of money which the new occupier must pay to the old one, for the peaceable enjoyment of his holding. It is a system which has more or less prevailed since the settlement of Ulster by James I when the ancestors of many of the present landlords got grants, on condition of bringing over a certain number of sturdy yeomen and their families as settlers. . . . [T]he early settlers built their own houses, and made their improvements at their own expense, contrary to English practice. This, together with the fact of their being Protestants, with arms in their hands, gave them strong claims on their landlord and leader, and it is probable . . . the tenant-right may have first originated . . . [by] the Protestant settler obtaining it in this way.[55]

There were never any restrictions on the time for which a Protestant tenant could take a leasehold. But by a royal decree promulgated in 1628, the longest term for a Catholic tenant's lease was twenty-one years or "three lives" (meaning as long as the tenant, his wife, or his oldest son lived). But even this right was rendered practically meaningless by the requirement that the tenant's children be brought up in the Protestant religion. It was still further limited by the provision that the total area leased to Catholics not exceed one-fourth of the landlord's leased land. The remaining three-fourths had to be reserved for Protestants.[56] The plantation scheme called for the physical removal of natives from lands allotted to the undertakers, who were to be allowed to take only Scots or English tenants (non-"papists," of course). But, since the dispossessed

Irish were available at the lowest cost of all, the undertakers often evaded these restrictions, preferring to engage as tenants-at-will the natives who were willing to accept that social degradation in order to wait for fairer times on their ancestral ground.[57] As already noted, the servitors were legally permitted to engage native Irish as tenants. Servitor Thomas Dutton, for example, "wisely let his lands to Irish tenants who could be cleared off at very short notice, but who, whilst permitted to remain, paid higher rents than British settlers would consent to pay."[58] Whether employed legally by individual servitors or illegally by individual undertakers, the Irish tenant was excluded from the tenant-right; the whole point of the tenant-right was that it be maintained as a Protestant privilege of laboring-class British immigrants.

The Protestant tenant's long-term lease privilege came to carry with it certain ancillary aspects which further exalted the Protestant tenants' social standing over the Catholic natives. Since Catholic tenants were limited generally to the status of tenant-at-will, any improvements made by them could be claimed by the landlord as his own property. This early discrimination marked the system of racial oppression that would come to be called Protestant Ascendancy. By making doubly certain that the Catholic tenants could not accumulate savings wherewith to expand their enterprises it implemented the cardinal feature of racial oppression, the refusal to acknowledge the legitimacy of class differentiation and normal social mobility within and by members of the oppressed group.[59] If in rare cases the natives did manage, by whatever means, to secure a store of capital, they were by law forbidden to purchase land from any Protestant, and their testamentary rights were hedged about with legal disqualifications, noted in Chapter 2.[60] Protestant laboring-class tenants, on the other hand, by virtue of their long hereditary leases were able to secure a vested interest in any improvements they made to the land, its buildings, fencing, ditching hedges, orchards, etcetera. Upon expiry of the lease the Protestant tenant had the right to renew it. If he was unwilling or unable to pay the rent demanded for renewal of the lease, he was practically immovable unless he received full satisfaction for the improvements that the family had made over a period of perhaps decades. And, being Protestant, whatever he died possessed of, including his lease rights, was inherited by his surviving family in accordance with English law.[61]

The effective range of this immigration scheme for providing a "potential army at practically no cost"[62] would be limited to Ulster. In Ireland's other three provinces – Leinster, Munster, and Connaught – English land claims had priority, whether they stemmed from ancient Old English desmesnes, or from New English post-Reformation encroachments, or from bounties to Cromwellian adventurers and English officers and soldiers, or from gifts to royal favorites in the wake of the Williamite confiscations. The prospect for laboring-class Presbyterian Scots settling in those remote quarters under a Dutch-English king and exclusively English landlords at the end of the seventeenth century was far less promising than that presented to those who settled in Ulster at the start of the century under a Scots-English king where, by legal quota, half the undertakers were Scots.[63]

Eighty years and several immigrant surges after the plantation of Ulster was begun, the full and final establishment of this Protestant social control force was celebrated on the walls of Derry and the banks of the Boyne.[64] Then, between 1689 and 1698, a great wave of some 50,000 to 80,000 Scots settled in Ireland, chiefly in Ulster.[65]

The irrepressible rebelliousness of the Catholic peasant revolt that made possible the repeal crisis of 1840–43 (see Chapter 4), forced British official society to take a critical look at the land tenure system in Ireland. The Devon Commission, which Parliament established for that purpose, observed that the Ulster Custom was "a most striking peculiarity." It was, they said, indeed "anomalous ... if considered with reference to all ordinary notions of property." Yet the commission "foresaw some danger to the just rights of property" in any attempt to legislate it for Catholics (the commission's words were "unlimited allowance of this 'tenant-right'").[66] The British government would rely on the Catholic lay and clerical bourgeoisie, newly installed in the social control system, to maintain the understanding that had been established with the cancellation of the monster meeting at Clontarf. (Concern along that line was soon to be greatly eased by the demoralizing effect of the massive depopulation of Catholic Ireland by the Great Famine of 1845–49, and the consequent mass emigration.) On the other hand, the commission was "sure that evils more immediate, and of still greater magnitude, would result from any hasty or general disallowance of it." In other words, the interests of the British ruling class in Ireland required that the Protestant privilege of tenant-right, the Ulster Custom, for all its "anomaly" and contravention of "the just rights" of the landlords of Protestant tenants, must not be interfered with. For the employing class, it afforded the optimal settlement of the competing claims of security and maximum profit. Individual landlords and employers might risk the penalties for disregarding the principle in the interest of private profit. But it was generally understood that – whatever the inconveniences and expense – the privileges of the Protestant laboring classes could not be disregarded without endangering the entire structure of social control upon which all operations depended.[67]

Intramural Tensions in Protestant Ulster

Despite the class collaboration that was the political heart of Protestant Ascendancy,[68] the arrangement was subject to strain and stress resulting from the vicissitudes of capitalist economy and from episcopal establishmentarianism. Furthermore, intramural conflicts were inevitably affected by pressure from the Irish Catholic struggle against racial oppression, by occasional devastating crop failures, by unfavorable turns in the terms of trade with Britain and the rest of Europe, and ultimately by the nationalist and republican influence of the American and the French revolutions. At the same time, the Protestant tenants' position was being undermined both by the subdivision of holdings generation after generation and by the consequent development of a new and potentially unsettling class differentiation between the over-tenant and his sub-tenants, the latter reduced, at least formally, to tenants-at-will.[69]

Ensconced in their indefeasible tenant-right, Protestant laboring-class tenant families during the greater part of the eighteenth century were able to earn additional income by the sale of linen cloth woven on their three or four looms, from yarn they spun from flax they grew.[70] A time would come when tenants' income from the sale of cloth exceeded their income from primary agricultural products. The typical small-plot, single-loom sub-tenants were dependent on weaving to pay their rent.[71]

The Ulster Scots, the Scots-Irish, were second-class citizens in Ireland as "dissenters" from the doctrines of the established Anglican state church. True, they were not subject to the economic exclusionism enforced against Catholics; indeed, the Presbyterian Kirk in Ulster was allotted an annual stipend for its support under Charles II, which was later increased under William of Orange. But from the Act of Uniformity of 1666 (17 & 18 Chas. II c. 6) until the Toleration Act of 1719 (6 Geo. I c. 2, 5), Dissenters were required to attend Anglican church services. Unlike their brethren in Scotland in the eighteenth century, the Presbyterian clergy in Ulster were even denied legitimacy in their normal pastoral functions. Marriages performed by them, for example, were not legal, and children of such marriages were "illegitimate." Presbyterian ministers were forbidden to conduct schools. Although Dissenters were eligible to be elected to the Irish Parliament, this right was hedged about by the Religious Test Oath (2 Anne c. 6, sec. 17), which barred them from holding any salaried office, civil or military, and which was not repealed until 1780 (19 & 20 Geo. III c. 6).

The Anglo-Irish bourgeoisie itself had grievances against British domination. Until 1782, the Anglo-Irish Parliament was denied the power to enact laws for Ireland unless and until those laws were first proposed by the English government.[72] At the same time, the development of trade was subject to such restrictions as the English Parliament was disposed to enact. A 1663 law (15 Chas II c. 7) banned Irish exports, except chattel bond-laborers, horses and provisions. Four years later, a ban that would last ninety-two years was imposed on the import of Irish cattle into England (18 Chas II c. 2). For a period of ten years beginning in 1671, Ireland was forbidden to import directly from the colonies. The ban was reinstituted in 1685 (1 Jas II c. 17), and remained in effect until 1731. In 1699 import duties that would last for nearly half a century were imposed on English imports of Irish woollens (10 Will. III

c. 5); in the same year the export of Irish woollens to any country but England was forbidden (10 & 11 Will. III c. 10).[73]

Protestant revolutionaries versus the Orange strategy

Large-scale emigration served as a safety valve for relieving social tensions in Protestant Ulster. Between 1715 and 1775, America alone was the destination of some quarter-million Ulster emigrants. The emigration came in waves, each from three to five years' duration, corresponding to periods of severe economic difficulty in Ulster.[74] But the worsening lot of the tenant weavers gave rise to secret direct-action societies of Protestant peasants in Ulster (Oakboys and Hearts of Steel) to resist the general weakening of their position vis-à-vis the landlords, just as the Catholic Whiteboys in the other provinces had first resisted capitalist-landlord exploitation intensified by racial oppression.

Among the Anglo-Irish bourgeoisie, a faction emerged favoring some form of national independence and Catholic Emancipation. The examples of the American Revolution and the French Revolution had an irresistible appeal. "In those years," writes A. T. Q. Stewart, referring to the last quarter of the eighteenth century, "the Protestant north produced the most ambitious attempt yet made in Ireland to separate religion from politics, and to unite all Irishmen in a purpose at once liberal and patriotic."[75] Rebellion, when it came in 1798, was plotted and launched by members of this bourgeoisie, first organized as United Irishmen in 1791, with Ulster Protestants in the front rank. Their 1794 Parliamentary Reform manifesto was like a combined Declaration of Independence and Emancipation Proclamation. "We have no National Government," they declared, "we are ruled by Englishmen and the Servants of Englishmen." There was revolutionary republicanism in their demand for "equal representation of all the People," as "the Great measure essential to the Prosperity and Freedom of Ireland." Most important of all, they understood and avowed "That no Reform is practicable, efficacious or just, which shall not include Irishmen of every religious Persuasion."[76]

This bold bid for Irish independence, or at least coequal dominion status within the British empire, which came within the context of the developing tendency toward a new entente between the British colonial power and the Irish Catholic bourgeoisie, was countered, as we have seen, by what modern-day apologists of racial oppression might call a Protestant backlash. It was formally established as the Orange Order in 1795, but Orangeism had emerged in Ulster a decade before as an anti-Catholic movement dedicated to preserving the racial privileges of the laboring-class Protestant tenants. Anger at increasing rents for ever-smaller holdings[77] was translated in anti-popery terms against Protestant landlords, in those parts of the province between the respectively Protestant and Catholic majority areas, who let their lands to Catholic tenants. But the movement reserved its greatest fury for Catholic tenants, burning their homes, driving them out and searching for violators of the Penal Laws that forbade Catholics to keep arms.

"The fate of Ulster," writes Liam de Paor, "now turned on the decisions . . . of Protestant democrats and radicals, whether to opt for orange or green."[78] By way of influencing that decision, the government brought to bear its legal and extralegal forces to intimidate and suppress the United Irishmen, by the use of informants, arrests, destruction of printing facilities, martial law and the disarming of United Irishmen. British success depended ultimately, however, on the support of the Orange rank-and-file, laboring-class Protestants, on their choosing to regard equality with Catholics as the equivalent of treason, that is, as an attack on the privileges they were accorded by the system of racial oppression. The concept was explained in the frequently cited report of a British general at Dungannon in County Tyrone:

> I have arranged . . . to increase the animosity between the Orange men and the United Irish. Upon that animosity depends the safety of the centre counties of the North. Were the orangemen disarmed or put down, or were they coalesced with the other party, the whole of Ulster would be as bad as Antrim and Down.[79]

What to the British military commanders at Dungannon was a local tactic would become an essential of British overall political strategy in Ireland. In coming to grips with the problem of social control, the British colonial bourgeoisie was opting for the admission of the Catholic bourgeoisie into the intermediate buffer social control stratum. But if social control was to be maintained in the Catholic provinces of Leinster, Munster and Connaught by the abandonment of the system of racial oppression, it was equally imperative that racial oppression – Protestant Ascendancy – remain in place in Ulster. Anything other than that would invite a resurrection of the equalitarian notions of the United Irishmen, with all their uncongenial implications for the British bourgeoisie. The maintenance of the racial privileges of the Protestant tenants in Ulster therefore was the necessary complement of the strategic admission of the Catholic lay and clerical bourgeoisie in the rest of Ireland into the system of social control.

Industrialization Governed by Ascendancy Principles

So far as British capital was concerned, industrialization when it came to Ireland was to be cast in the mold of Protestant Ascendancy. In 1825 James Cropper, Esquire, Liverpool merchant, abolitionist and supporter of Catholic Emancipation, testified before the Parliamentary Inquiry on the State of Ireland. Cropper had personally toured almost a dozen Irish cities and towns to investigate the prospects for profitable investment in industrial enterprise. If "political and moral" factors were the same in Ireland as they were in

England, he said, flax, cotton, woolen, and silk manufacture would thrive in Catholic Ireland. The great obstacle, he asserted, lay in the "feelings that are generated by the Catholic question, by the disabilities of the Catholics." He expressed his full agreement with the proposition stated by the presider over the inquiry: ". . . so long as the statute law of the country treats four-fifths of the country as persons who are dangerous to the State . . . there will exist a distrust on the part of English capitalists which will keep them from investing in the country."[80] Four years after this hearing, the Catholic Emancipation Bill became law; but the policy of "red-lining" (to use a modern American term describing discriminatory lending by banks in favour of "whites" and "white" areas) continued in effect to bar British investment in industrializing the Catholic provinces.

In the post-Emancipation period, considerations of social control continued to produce a pro-Protestant policy with respect to industrial investment. The emergence of Belfast, and Belfast alone of Irish towns and cities, as a major industrial center was based on the Protestants' heritage of two centuries of racial privileges. *The Formation of the Irish Economy*, edited by the eminent Irish economic historian L. M. Cullen (Cork, 1969), presents a number of articles, including the concluding article by the editor himself, "Irish Economic History: Fact and Myth," which argue "that Irish economic development is more independent of non-economic factors than has been generally believed" (p. 113). According to this view, "The real determinants of Irish economic retardation, although political resentment obscured the issue . . . were the technological and organizational advances of the Industrial Revolution and the radical improvement in transport wrought by the railroads . . . [and] the growth of the population" (p. 114). Cullen contends that after a fairly prosperous eighteenth century, Ireland went into decline in the nineteenth century. He rejects earlier writers, such as Hely Hutchinson (member of the Irish Parliament and author in 1779 of *The commercial restraints on Ireland*) and W. E. H. Lecky, who attributed Ireland's difficulties to the British mode of rule, trade restriction, and Penal Laws against Catholics. Those arguments, says Cullen, have merely served to fuel "nationalist" obfuscation of economic questions. He concludes that "this [eighteenth–nineteenth-century] decline was inevitable." The explanation is not easy, he says, but, "Lack of capital was not a cause" (p. 123). Contributor Michael Drake ("Population Growth and the Irish Economy") believes that "even with a much more favourable political and social climate" the Industrial Revolution was an impossible dream for Ireland because it lacked coal and iron resources (p. 74). Another writer, J. M. Goldstrom, deals specifically with "The Industrialisation of the North-East." The key to Ulster's prosperity, he claims, "was its dependence on foreign markets." He notes, without further comment, that Belfast was able to rely on coal imports from Britain. The reason that Ulster's prosperity did not spread to the rest of Ireland was the lack of "a thriving agricultural sector," he suggests (p. 110), as if that were just a fact of life, unrelated to the heritage of religio-racial oppression.[81]

The reader will see by my footnotes that I have relied on authorities who effectively resist the anti-nationalist revision of Irish economic history represented by the Cullen school. I am led to do so by a desire to see objective economic circumstances in the context of the great all-pervasive effect of the racial oppression wrought in the name of Protestant Ascendancy; Cullen et al. seem to dismiss the latter as irrelevant. I have been more influenced, therefore, by such historians as Joel Mokyr, author of *Why Ireland Starved: A Quantitative and Analytical History of the Irish Economy, 1800–1850* (1983), and R. F. Foster, whose *Modern Ireland, 1600–1972* was first published in 1988. The Ulster Custom, a Protestant privilege, made possible the accumulation of capital in the hands of successful tenants, capital that was readily moved into the linen industry in that northern province.[82] By 1820, it was said that Protestants owned nearly forty times as much of Belfast's merchant and industrial capital as did Catholics.[83] One "objective" factor did favor Belfast; being only a hundred miles from the Scottish shipyards on the Clyde, Belfast shipbuilding got its start as a convenient extension of those Scottish enterprises. It was the infusion of large amounts of British capital, however, that was decisive. The Belfast Harbour Commission was established and subsidized by Parliament to encourage British investment. Under its supervision extensive improvements were undertaken, including the making of the Belfast docks accessible to ships in low tide. This cleared the way for Belfast to become a major shipbuilding and ship repair center.[84] Except for the policy of deliberate exclusion of Catholic Munster, Leinster and Connaught from investment of industrial capital, there is no reason to believe that centers of industry would not have appeared in those areas just as Belfast did in Ulster.[85]

The Ulster Custom preserved as a proletarian privilege

Protestant tenants had rallied successfully against the extension of Catholic Emancipation to Ulster. At the same time, however, their most precious racial privilege, the Ulster tenant-right, was being drained of much of its material substance by normal processes of capital accumulation. When the lease expired, the tenant who had profited by sub-tenants lost the tenant-right with respect to those sublet portions of his holding. The sub-tenants, for their part, were glad to be promoted to direct lessees of the landlord. Soon, however, they would find themselves reduced to tenants-at-will, as a result of the refusal of the landlords to grant leases on the ever-smaller subdivisions of their lands, whereon the sole economically significant activity was weaving,[86] and which were too small to provide a forty-shilling freeholder voter for the landlord's candidate at election time. Still, even the smallest of these cottier-weavers invoked the Ulster Custom to maintain his right of tenure. The Ulster tenant-at-will was thus brought within political hailing distance of the Catholic peasant, so that far-sighted reformers could hope for an all-Ireland tenant movement that would guarantee the Ulster Custom to Catholics as well as Protestants. A number of Protestant leaders, including Presbyterian clergymen, took the initiative, organizing the Tenant Right Association in 1847. Within three years they joined with southern Catholics to form the League of North and South, and a "cross-cultural" exchange was practiced, with Catholic priests invited to address Ulster Protestant tenants, and Presbyterian ministers responding to similar invitations to Catholic parishes in the other provinces.[87] But in the end, the bogey of "Catholic domination" and Irish nationalism worked to prevent Protestant tenants in Ulster from consummating the engagement.[88]

The very basis of the issue facing the hard-pressed Protestant cottier-weavers – to accept or reject common cause with Catholic cottier-weavers – was washed away by the Industrial Revolution, which spelled the doom of cottage weaving in Ireland as it did in Britain. The process would take place over some four decades, beginning with spinning about 1825. Weaving, while still done in the individual tenant's home, underwent some dislocation because of the weavers' dependence upon proximity to the factory-supplied yarn. As a result, the incomes of the weavers were severely undermined by the re-entry of surplussed spinners into the labor market as weavers. Twenty-five years later, hand-weaving quickly lost out to the textile mill.

, Tenant families by the thousands abandoned the unequal struggle against the machine and flocked into Belfast, looking for work in the last city of the Industrial Revolution.[89] The process was speeded by the Famine, 1845–49, although predominantly Protestant Ulster counties were among the areas least affected by that scourge of nature and British policy.[90] After 1850 came a period of rapid development not only in textiles, where weaving as well as spinning was now done by machine, but in shipbuilding and civil and mechanical engineering, until the typical Ulster laboring-class Protestant was socially transmuted from smallholder rural tenant to slum-dwelling proletarian.[91]

In Daniel O'Connell's judgment, the Protestants of Ireland were only "political protestants, that is, Protestants by reason of their participation in political power"; once they were put on an equal plane with Catholics, he thought, the bigotry represented by Orangeism would wither away.[92] As a result of the economic changes that have been described, the Protestant tenant-right, which for more than two hundred years had been the main social bulwark of British rule in Ireland, was now deprived of that significance.

Laboring-class Catholics emigrated from Ireland by the millions in the nineteenth century. In the single decade that began with the famine year of 1846, the United States alone received nearly 1,300,000 Irish émigrés, the overwhelming majority being laboring-class Catholics. Others took the road, within their own country, to Belfast, where the Catholic proportion of the population grew from less than 10 percent in a town of 20,000 in 1800, to more than one-third in a city of more than 120,000 in 1861.[93] Would sectarian conflict be dissolved in the pool of "abstract labour" to be replaced by "the strongest bond of human sympathy, outside of the family relation ... one uniting laboring people of all nations, and tongues, and kindreds"?[94] Would, then, racial oppression finally be left behind, even in Protestant-majority Ulster? Would "Protestant politics" die out with the eclipse of the Protestant tenantry and be superseded by working-class solidarity, under the "pressure of a common exploitation"?[95]

Just as it had been arranged in the case of the tenants three hundred years before, again it was arranged by the British ruling class, with all necessary deliberation, that the "pressure of exploitation" of Protestant and Catholic workers would not be a "common" one. In doing so, the British ruling class was able to draw upon the superstructural elements – "anti-popery," the habituation to Protestant preferment, the "croppies lie down" arrogance – anchored in a history of more than two centuries of religio-racial oppression. "The widespread practice of keeping jobs for one's own co-religionists"[96] in a situation in which almost all the industrial jobs were in the keeping of Protestant employers defined the most elemental form of Protestant racial privilege. The Catholic workers came, but found that "networks of family and friends reinforced the hold which the protestant community had obtained over the engineering trades," and barred Catholics from apprenticeships, the only path to skilled jobs. Catholic workers were obliged to serve as laborers, making less than half the wage of the Protestant tradesmen under whom they worked; in general, they worked longer hours under the pressure of a high rate of unemployment.[97] Workers in general would have to live in slums, but if there was an extra room, if there was running water, the Protestant worker customarily had the preference in housing. By the 1860s, housing in Belfast was almost completely segregated, a factor that facilitates racial discrimination in housing conditions,[98] as it has in Anglo-America ever since the institution of separate "quarters" for African-Americans in the late seventeenth century. Still, the Catholic workers came; more women than men. Though forced to submit to the gender discrimination that barred all women from apprentice-ships and thus doubly excluded them from the better-paid jobs, Catholic women in large numbers found work, mainly in textile mills in classifications reserved for women. By 1901, at a time when the divorce rate was practically zero, one-third of all Catholic households in Belfast were headed by women, as compared with one-fourth of Protestant households. The statistical difference was in the figures for "single heads, unmarried."[99]

In short, in place of the tenant-right system, the religio-racial privileges of the Ulster Protestants were translated into a proletarian mode.[100] Although the wages of the Protestant workers of Belfast were not especially high as compared with workers in the same trades in Britain, the differential between skilled and unskilled workers was far greater in Belfast than it was in any area in Britain.[101] The British skilled tradesmen would have had to receive more than a 40 percent wage increase to achieve the same wage position relative to that of the unskilled British laborer as that enjoyed by the skilled Protestant worker in Belfast vis-à-vis the Catholic laborer. This is characteristic of systems of racial oppression, where workers of the oppressed group are generally confined to the lowest-paid occupations, as in the United States and South Africa.[102]

If the Protestant privilege of job preference replaced tenant-right as the economic link between the Protestant worker and the British ruling class, the oppressive role of the Protestant yeomen was taken up by Protestant workers; eventually, in a perversion of class struggle, the role was cast in the form of an "Orange" labor movement.[103] Rallying to the slogan "Home Rule is Rome Rule," these workers became champions of union with Britain, which they saw clearly as the ultimate guarantee of their Protestant privileges. Arrogance was the customary bearing of the Protestant worker toward Catholics. This supremacist behavior led to deadly full-scale riots in 1857, 1864, 1872, 1886 and 1893.[104] The Protestants appear to have been even less inhibited than usual about escalating the violence on these occasions. A presumably Protestant justice of the peace, testifying before the commission investigating the Belfast riot(s) of 1886, denied that Catholics had provoked the riot; "The endurance and patience of the Roman Catholics was, in my opinion, simply wonderful," he said.[105] "Patience" was a term not found in testimony with regard to the general conduct of Protestants in such situations. The advantages were with them – the mayor and town council were all Protestants, as were the employers (who could punish absenteeism), the police were Protestants, and, if matters got to that stage, verdicts would be made by Protestant-majority juries, in Protestant magistrates' courts. The outbreaks were often set off by provocative marches celebrating Protestant victories of nearly two hundred summers before. The riot or, more accurately, series of riots during June, July and August 1886 was one of the worst, if not the worst, in terms of injuries, fatal or otherwise, and destruction of dwellings and other structures.[106] It began when Protestant shipyard workers took the occasion of a fight between a Catholic and a Protestant at work on a nearby dock to launch a general assault on Catholic workers, in the true yeoman tradition. A constant element in all these outbreaks was the driving of Catholic men from the workplace. The largest single employer in Belfast was the Harland and Wolff shipyard, which employed 3,000 workers at the time. Sir Edward Harland, senior partner in the firm and also Lord Mayor of Belfast, testified before the commission investigating the riots. "Are these men of mixed religion?" he was asked. "Mixed," said Harland, "but they are almost all, or chiefly Protestants," and he gave the figures. There had been about 225 Catholic workers employed by his firm before the riot; 190 were driven off the job, of whom 77 returned after the situation had calmed down.[107] It was the hateful pressure to which Catholic men were subjected, reaching its most flagrant forms in the riots, that mainly accounts for the fact that Catholics, who were more than one in three of the population in Belfast in 1861, were fewer than one in four in 1901.[108]

Partition – the Salvation of Racial Oppression

The preservation of the Ulster Protestant bastion proved to be an overriding principle of British ruling-class policy, despite Catholic Emancipation. The British were not prepared to grant Ireland separate nationhood or, as events would prove, even Home Rule. The Liberal Party, faced with a Conservative-backed threat of armed insurrection by Ulster Protestants, opted to "compromise" its way to defeat on the issue.[109] There were also Empire interests: Ireland must be kept from any involvement in foreign affairs that might be inimical to British overseas interests. There were also the traditional links between the militaristic English Conservatives and Protestant Ascendancy in Ireland, which were the prevailing interest in the veto-holding (until 1911) House of Lords. The abandonment of Protestant racial domination in Ulster would render irresistible the demand for Irish national independence (in one form or another). The Ireland that would emerge, "a nation once again," containing a population one-fourth Protestant, could never be a sectarian state, giving a special place and special influence to the Catholic Church; the social control function of the clerical section of the Irish bourgeoisie (which the British had worked so earnestly to put in place) would be rendered ineffective. It would mean the second coming of the United Irishmen, with dreadful democratic implications for Britain itself. Consider the comments made by George Bernard Shaw, writing as a "Protestant Irishman" his "Preface for Politicians" for his 1904 play *John Bull's Other Island*. "[T]he Irish coast is for the invasion-scaremongerer the heel of Achilles," he said, and that fixation was made to justify the denial of Irish Home Rule. But that belief could not justify rule by the "Protestant 'Loyalist' garrison." The sectarian conflict between Catholics and Protestants, in which that fear was rooted, would be resolved if England would only "take its thumb away" and grant Ireland Home Rule, for then "the unnaturally combined elements in Irish politics would fly asunder and recombine, according to their proper nature with results entirely satisfactory to real Protestantism ... [and] the Catholic laity will make as short work of sacerdotal tyranny in Ireland as it has done in France and Italy."[110] In the play, Father Keegan, chief exponent for this Shavian concept of a better Ireland, is made to call it "the dream of a madman."[111] Prime Minister Balfour is said to have been so delighted by the play that he went to see it four times. At the command performance King Edward laughed so hard that his exertions broke the chair beneath him.[112]

On General Principles

With "perfectly devilish ingenuity," as James Connolly put it in 1913, "the master class" had contrived to turn the Protestant Ulster workers into allies not of the Catholic workers, but of the exploiting class itself. He sadly concluded that the obligatory Marxist optimism with which three years before he had ended his *Labour in Irish History* – that common proletarian experience could "make enthusiastic rebels out of a Protestant working class" – had "missed the mark by several million miles." He seemed to say that the Protestant workers had been corrupted beyond socialist and nationalist redemption by "having been reared up among a people whose conditions of servitude were more slavish than their own."[113] Liam de Paor's work *Divided Ulster*, which has been much relied upon in the writing of this chapter, was published in 1970. Twenty years later, he published further reflections in his *Unfinished Business*. As Connolly seemed to despair of the Protestant worker, de Paor seems to have finally despaired of a united Ireland, placing his hopes on "a large section of the Catholic population and a large section of the Protestant population in which there is a desire for mutual agreement to make a new Northern Ireland work." Success, he stresses, would require "ensuring equality under law ... [and] personal and civil rights of all citizens."[114] It is not for this foreigner to attempt to make a judgment on de Paor's new thesis. But for the analogy of Protestant Ascendancy and white supremacy, one comment seems in order. Just as Connolly saw the religio-racial privileges of the Protestant workers as the ultimate frustration of Irish socialism and nationalism, de Paor's solution, however widely different from that first envisaged by Connolly, still requires confronting the issue of Protestant racial privileges.

This episodic review of Ulster history provides positive evidence[115] of four essential operative principles of social control in a stable civil society constituted on the basis of racial oppression:

1.   The oppressor group must be in the majority. This might be called the Sir William Petty principle, after the person who first formulated it. This principle may incidentally serve to give racial oppression a "democratic" gloss.

2.   From this "majority principle," and from the pyramidal structure of class society, it follows that the majority of the oppressor group is necessarily composed not of members of the exploiting classes, but of an intermediate social control stratum of laboring classes, non-capitalist tenants, and wage-laborers.

3.   These laboring-class members of the oppressor group are to be shielded against the competition of the members of the oppressed group by the establishment of economically artificial, "anomalous" privileges – artificial because they subordinate short-term private individual profits to considerations of social control.

4.   Just as the system of capitalist production presents cyclical crises and regeneration, so the system of racial privileges of the laboring classes of the oppressor group is adapted and preserved, come what may of economic crisis, impoverishment, famine, intramural conflict, natural calamity or war, in order to maintain the function of the intermediate buffer social control stratum.

6

Anglo-America: Ulster Writ Large

In continental Anglo-America the most fundamental obstacle facing the English colonizers was that the undifferentiated social structure typical of the Indian tribes in North America did not present a serviceable indigenous ruling class that could be co-opted as supplier and controller of a labor force. Indeed, it would be some time before the English would achieve sufficient relative strength *vis-à-vis* the native peoples even to be able to think in terms of social control over them.[1] Well before that time, the English in continental Anglo-America had chosen the course of plantation monoculture and the combination of racial oppression with the chattel labor form, both of which ruled out the use of Indian labor (although thousands of Indian "war captives" were shipped to perpetual bond-servitude in the Caribbean before the end of the seventeenth century). The fateful option for tobacco monoculture required the continual expansion of the "frontier" and the displacement of the Indians from their ancestral lands, a fact not calculated to promote mutual goodwill and peaceful cohabitation. The option for chattel bond-servitude rendered counter-productive the enslavement of Indians, which would have deprived Anglo-American employers of essential assistance in combating the problem of runaway bond-laborers.[2]

The Extirpation of the Native Social Order

Every aspect of the Ulster Plantation policy aimed at destroying the tribal leadership and dispersing the tribe is matched by typical examples from Anglo-American colonial and United States policy toward the indigenous population, the "American Indians" – a policy we clearly recognize as racial oppression of "the red man." In the Creek War of 1813–14 of the United States against the Red Stick Creek Indians, White Stick Creeks and Cherokees fought on the victorious "American" side under the command of General Andrew Jackson. In the decisive battle of that war forty-nine of Jackson's men were killed; of these, twenty-three were Indians, eighteen Cherokees and five Creeks.[3] Under

the terms of the peace treaty subsequently dictated by Jackson,[4] two-thirds of
the Creek territories were confiscated by the United States at one stroke, aimed
at allies no less than enemies: White Sticks and the Red Sticks, all were driven
from their tribal lands.[5] Might not the White Sticks have felt a kindred fury to
that which drove O'Doherty in 1608 into revolt against the English false-
promisers for whom he and his kin had risked and sacrificed so much?

Note has been made of the Cherokee tribal leaders who successfully adapted
to Anglo-American ways of commercial agriculture and were prepared to
relate to the settlers on that basis, just as some of the Ulster Irish chieftains
appeared prepared, even eager, to do in 1609. As one of the Cherokee leaders,
John Ridge, pleaded so eloquently before a New York City rally against
President Jackson's Indian Removal policy in 1832:

> You asked us to throw off the hunter and the warrior state: We did so – you asked
> us to form a republican government: We did so – adopting your own as a model.
> You asked us to cultivate the earth, and learn the mechanic arts: We did so. You
> asked us to learn to read: We did so. You asked us to cast away our idols, and
> worship your God: We did so.[6]

Yet like the thousands of Irish woodkernes whom Lord Deputy Chichester
shipped by force to Sweden, at a stroke thousands of Cherokee families were
uprooted in 1837 and 1838 from their ancestral lands in northern Georgia and
Alabama, western North Carolina and eastern Tennessee, and force-marched
over the Trail of Tears[7] a thousand miles to a country that was, as Sweden to
the Irish, "remote and of no good fame to them." The protesting Cherokees
invoked United States government treaty promises; but as it had been with the
king's mislaid reassurance to O'Doherty, it was "already too late," gold having
been discovered within Cherokee lands in northern Georgia ten years before.[8]

The Social Control "Anomalies" in America

As in Ulster, the ruling class saw that it was necessary to support the privileges
of the laboring class of the oppressor group as an investment in social control
made at the expense of immediate profits.[9] Ulrich Bonnell Phillips, an eminent
white historian of American slavery, concluded, "In the divergence of
economic interest and social needs it became increasingly clear that social
needs were paramount."[10] The records are replete with precept and example
showing the general prevalence of this principle of governance in Anglo-
American plantation colonies.[11] It was expressed, for example, in "deficiency
laws" to provide quotas, as they might be termed today, according to which the
plantation owners were required, under penalty of the law, to employ at least
one "white" male for every so many "Negroes," the proportion varying from
colony to colony and time to time, from one-to-twenty (Nevis, 1701) to

one-to-four (Georgia, 1750).[12] While the Nevis "white" quota law stressed the importance of measures "for the Importation of white Servants," it specified "the Irish Papist excepted." This provision was related to actual incidents of liberationist solidarity of Irish and African bond-laborers and the widely expressed official fears on this score.[13] Just as the Penal Laws excluded Catholics generally from apprenticeships to trades, Anglo-American plantation colonies (Barbados, 1670; South Carolina, 1742; Georgia, 1750) were urged to exclude Negroes from trades in order to preserve the trades for "white" artisans.[14] Tenancy did not take on the great significance in the Anglo-America plantation colonies that it did in Ireland, but its relation to social control was not completely ignored. Just as promises of restored fortune were used to entice laboring-class Scots to Ulster to serve as "the wall betwixt" the landlords and the Irish natives, so were "Swiss" immigrants solicited for the American Piedmont with promises of prosperous tenancies and a ten-year exemption from taxes, on the assumption that they would prevent runaway African-Americans from passing through to establish maroon settlements in the mountains beyond, like those in Jamaica.[15] On a grander scale, at the same time, the exclusively Protestant Anglo-American colony of Georgia was being founded as a buffer to prevent African-American bond-laborers from escaping to freedom in Spanish Florida.[16]

The Ulster custom found its most complete parallel in the United States homestead right, which reached its perfected form in the Homestead Act of 1862, after decades of controversial evolution. The heart of the policy was to make land available in small parcels at little or very modest cost to European-American laboring-class settlers (160 acres free, according to the 1862 act). The land to be distributed was "public land," the Indians' rights thereto having been punctiliously "extinguished." The mass campaign for this policy took the form of Free Soil – first the movement and then the party. Its rallying standard was the Wilmot Proviso which, in the words of its author, Representative David Wilmot of Pennsylvania, was intended to "preserve to free white labor a fair country, a rich inheritance, where the sons of toil of my own race and own color can live without the disgrace which association with Negro slavery brings upon free labor."[17] Accordingly, the 1854 Graduation Act, designed to make unsold "public" lands available to "squatters" and others at prices graduated from $1.25 to as low as $12\frac{1}{2}$ cents an acre, limited its benefits to "white" persons.[18]

Six years earlier the historic Women's Rights Convention, held in Seneca Falls, New York, included in its resolutions the demand for the right of women to own property.[19] It was gratifying for the supporters of equal rights for women, therefore, that the Graduation Act of 1854 did make women eligible to be homesteaders "in their own right."[20] But African-Americans of either sex, including strong advocates of equal rights for women such as Sojourner Truth and Frederick Douglass, himself an active participant in the Seneca Falls meeting, were denied the right to become homesteaders.

In the same year in which Congress passed the Graduation Act, it also passed the "squatter sovereignty" Kansas–Nebraska Act, leaving it to the citizens of these territories to decide whether their respective states-to-be should be "free" or "slave." As far as Kansas was concerned, the issue would in the end be merged with the greater struggle to determine whether any state could exclude slavery.[21] Before that time a tense, prolonged and sometimes deadly struggle in that territory between the supporters of Free Soil and the pro-slavery "Missouri ruffians" earned it the name of "Bleeding Kansas." Early in the struggle, Frederick Douglass proposed a "Plan for Making Kansas a Free State," which called for the settling of a thousand free Negroes on homesteads in that territory as a means of greatly strengthening the hand of those who wanted to keep Kansas out of the grasp of the slave power.[22] The outcome of the struggle in Kansas, which was critical for the cause of Free Soil, hung in the balance; indeed for a time the territory had a dual government. Such a reinforcement as Douglass was suggesting would have decisively strengthened the Free Soil cause. But the Free Soil "Free State" convention held in Topeka in the fall of 1855 proposed a constitution that would have barred African-Americans altogether from the proposed state, preferring to risk everything in order to keep the homestead right as a "race" privilege.

The historic Homestead Act of 1862 maintained the exclusion, by limiting the homestead right to citizens or those immigrants who intended to become citizens of the United States, a status which the' Constitution denied to African-Americans.

Reconstruction: Racial Oppression Challenged and Defended

Racial slavery, the Fugitive Slave Laws, and Taney's notorious phrase (see Chapter 1, note 132) were smashed by the Union armies and navies, whose ranks included more than 200,000 African-Americans and at least 48,000 European-Americans, representing every state of the Confederacy, among them a full brigade of Irish laborers from Louisiana.[23] Among the European-Americans of the defeated Confederate states, there were manifestations of a readiness to share with the freedmen in the confiscation and redistribution of plantation lands.[24] Such factors, and the general implications of their victory, confronted the victorious Northern bourgeoisie with a fundamental question of social control: whether to continue the system of racial oppression or to undertake to institute a new system of social control – as the British ruling class had been obliged to do in respect to Ireland a few decades before.

Just as in Ulster there were urban bourgeois republican-minded Protestants who favored equal rights for Catholics, there were in the United States in the 1860s elements – and, for a time, very powerful elements – of the industrial bourgeoisie who believed in fulfilling the logic of Emancipation by the redistribution of land in the South, transforming the economy there into one of small independent farmers in place of an economy dominated by large plantations and plantation owners. Senator Charles Sumner of Massachusetts, for instance, became convinced of the correctness of this path.

> We must see that the freedmen are established on the soil, and that they may become proprietors.... The great plantations, which have been so many nurseries of rebellion, must be broken up, and the freedmen must have the pieces.[25]

His colleague Thaddeus Stevens of Pennsylvania proposed a detailed plan for implementing this revolutionary confiscation and redistribution of the lands of the former slaveholders. Stevens's proposal called for the giving to every male former bond-laborer of forty acres of this land, and for further opportunity for other African-Americans – discharged Union soldiers, and the more prosperous of the 400,000 African-Americans who were already free at the time of Emancipation – who might have sufficient money or credit to join the bidding for moderate-sized plots at ten dollars per acre.[26]

Finding the opposition to confiscation of plantation lands insurmountable, the Radical Republicans succeeded in passing the Southern Homestead Law in June 1866, providing for 47 million acres of public lands to be opened for eighty-acre homesteading. But the author of the bill, Representative George W. Julian of Indiana, understood that it "could only prove a very partial measure without an enactment reaching the fee of the slaveholders."[27] Nevertheless, land historian Paul Wallace Gates writes that, "between 1867 and 1876, there was more homesteading in [the South] in proportion to the land available than there was elsewhere in the public land states."[28] Some 40,000 original entries were made under this act, although an indeterminate large number of them were "dummy" claims managed by land and timber companies.[29] Within sixteen months of its enactment 2,012 homesteads, totaling 168,960 acres, were taken up.[30] Even this token measure was repealed in 1876, as part of the repudiation of Reconstruction, most specifically because "Southerners wanted to have all restrictions upon [access to timber and mineral lands] removed so that extensive areas could be acquired by capitalist groups which might utilize their resources."[31]

The momentous significance of the program for redistribution of plantation lands was that it meant the abandonment of the principle that made slavery in the United States a special form of a general racial oppression and likewise made Protestant Ascendancy and the Penal Laws system racial oppression in Ireland: the refusal to give legitimacy to social class differentiation among the oppressed group. The creation of a class of one million African-American freeholders by decree of the national legislature was necessarily predicated upon the presumption that African-Americans were to be accorded social status according to the norms of any society based on capitalist commodity production.

Still, despite the fact that the class to be expropriated had been responsible for a war that cost one million lives for the right to buy and sell babies by the pound,[32] the Sumner and Stevens proposals failed to be enacted because of their unacceptable implications for the capitalist class in general.[33] "Expropriate the expropriators" had, since 1848, become a slogan intended for general application, and the United States bourgeoisie was ready to perceive "the specter of communism" in the expropriation of the plantation lands. But the implications for the American system of social control were more immediate and critical. The entire United States, not just a sector of it, was a society wherein the heedless, heartless, headlong, pell-mell push for capital accumulation could proceed with "the consent of the governed" only by virtue of the "white" racial privileges of the European-American laboring-class population. That population, particularly in the cities, was increasingly wretched[34] and, at the same time, was constitutionally guaranteed the citizen's right to bear arms. Yet the social control system worked, *mutatis mutandis*, as it did in Ulster where the Protestant worker "however wretched he might be, could still be persuaded" to tolerate it all, "so long as he could keep his Catholic neighbour in a still more wretched state."[35]

Working-class European-Americans were well aware that they had the homestead right as a "white" racial privilege, although in fact few of them had any real prospects of actualizing it.[36] Now it was proposed to extend a variation of that right to African-Americans, but on the very land they had worked as bond-laborers. The transcendent significance of the proposal was that it necessarily implied the end of racial oppression, of social control by means of racial privileges for laboring-class "whites"; it posed "a new birth of freedom" versus "a white man's country."

Just as the Ulster Protestants had had a choice between Green and Orange, between the United Irishmen and the Protestant Ascendancy in 1798, the European-Americans of the wage-laboring class faced a fateful choice in the late 1860s. For at least several decades, the "white labor" rationale for opposing the abolition of slavery was the competition argument, namely, that Negroes, if freed, would become part of the wage-labor supply and would lower wages and reduce opportunities for "white" workers. This same basic argument, as we have noted, was made more respectable by the Free Soilers preachments against competition between "free" and slave labor. But now the land distribution program of the Radical Republicans presented an historically unique practical opportunity to reduce the impoverishing effect of the competition of an oversupply of wage labor.

The land question in the United States at that time presented itself in two aspects, the Western, "free land" aspect and the Southern, rebel land aspect. In actual practice, the former was primarily the interest of the petty bourgeoisie, and not of the masses of wage workers (which is not to deny that the emigration of petit bourgeois families to the West may have made the over-supply of labor less than it would have become if they had stayed on the Atlantic seaboard where they first landed). The most realistic hope that ever existed for proletarians, European-American and African-American, to become successful homesteaders lay in the appropriation of the rebel plantations, along the lines put forward by the Radical Republicans.

By deed, as well as in words, the African-American freedmen expressed their dedication to that proposition. Before the guns of war were still, African-American families were making crops as independent farmers on lands where they had been chattel slaves on the Sea Islands and other South Carolina, Georgia and Florida lands set aside for them under General Sherman's Field Order No. 15 of 16 January 1865.[37] In the face of fierce opposition from the old plantation owners and ambivalence within the government, South Carolina freedmen demanded that "no impediments be put in the way of our acquiring homesteads."[38] In the South as a whole, 800,000 acres of confiscated rebel land were worked by freedmen families as renters under the administration of the Freedmen's Bureau of the federal government. After the issues of the franchise and public education, which were addressed by the Reconstruction Conventions of the various states, "none was more critical than the question of the land," writes John Hope Franklin.[39] In Alabama they spoke of confiscation of land "forfeited by the treason of its owners."[40] The Negro National Labor Union at its first convention in Washington, DC, in 1869, speaking of the dreadful dimensions of the problem of oversupply of wage labor in the Southern states, urged the United States Congress to understand that, "The true and immediate practicable remedy lies in making a fair proportion of the laborers themselves land-owners."[41]

Meanwhile, the white National Labor Union (NLU) at its founding convention in 1866 put the land question first in its "Address to the Workingmen of the United States" but limited it to consideration of "the Public Lands."[42] The following year, citing the jobs lost in New England mills because of a shortage of cotton, the NLU called for "the speedy restoration of the Southern states" to the Union, meaning a speedy end to Reconstruction with its promise of expropriation of rebels' plantations for distribution to the landless.[43] William H. Sylvis, the most famous of the leaders of the NLU, speaking as its president in 1868, stridently denounced Reconstruction. Instead of financing the Freedmen's Bureau, he said, "it would have been much better to loan the planters a few millions of dollars."[44] In an attack on the "Land Monopoly" in the United States, Sylvis pointed to Ireland where the land was economically and politically dominated by large plantation owners. He regarded the Irish case as an instructive parallel for the United States, and urged the English government to "divide the land equitably."[45] He chose to ignore the fact that such a reform in Ireland involved taking land not from the "public domain" but from plantation owners – the very policy which he and the NLU refused to support in the United States.

By making freedom a *human right*, Negro Emancipation had destroyed it as *racial privilege*, and thereby threatened to dissolve on the instant the mortar holding together the system of bourgeois social control, the system of "white"-labor privileges based on the presumption of African-American chattel bond-servitude. Writing to President Lincoln on behalf of the International Working-men's Association, Karl Marx was hopeful:

> While the working men, the true political power of the North, allowed slavery to defile their own republic, while before the Negro, mastered and sold without his concurrence, they boasted it the highest prerogative of the white-skinned labourer to sell himself and choose his own master, they were unable to attain the true freedom of labour ... but this barrier to progress has been swept off by the red sea of civil war.

Emancipation, said Marx, therefore heralded "a new era ... of ascendancy of the working classes."[46] Radical Republican congressman William Darrah Kelley of Pennsylvania was a vigorous promoter of American industrial capitalism. He appreciated the opportunities for the development of natural resources in the South with the aid of Northern capital, but under Republican leadership based on the suffrage of, and equal rights and opportunity for, African-Americans. At about the time that Marx's letter was being delivered to Lincoln, Kelley was making his point in a speech in the House of Representatives.

> Shall he [the Negro], though black as ebony his skin, who by patient industry, obedience to the laws, and unvarying good habits, has accumulated property on which he cheerfully pays taxes be denied the right of a choice in the government ... while the idle reckless, thriftless men of fairer complexion shall vote away his earnings and trifle with his life or interests as a juror?[47]

Kelley regarded it as intolerable that the African-American soldier who had endured the perils of battle in defense of the Constitution should be denied its protection, while "traitors in the conquest of whom he assisted enjoy those rights, and use them as instruments for his oppression and degradation."

Today it is apparent that Marx's vision was falsely heralded; but the record left by bourgeois Radical Republicans like William D. Kelley reminds us that it was not an impossible dream for the United States to have ended the curse of racial oppression; given that, all else might have been added unto us. With more proper detachment, a modern historian writes: "... the race question [as it stood at the end of the Civil War] raised new problems for the South. Slavery was gone.... The status of both white and colored men remained to be defined."[48]

In the end, the status question was resolved when the bourgeoisie as a whole,[49] drawing upon practices that had ante-bellum roots, opted for what we may term White Reconstruction, that is, the re-establishment of the social control system of racial oppression, based on racial privileges for laboring-class "whites" with regard to "free" land, immigration, and industrial employment. In that process, the Negro Exodus of 1879 and the Cotton Mill Campaign, dated from the following year, were to be defining moments.

The Material Basis for the Abandonment of Reconstruction

Just as the British ruling class had come to accept the necessity of involving the Catholic bourgeoisie in Ireland in the maintenance of social control, so the Northern bourgeoisie, though only for a limited period of time as it turned out, "made him [the Negro] a part of the state," as the investigative journalist Charles Nordhoff wrote. "If the North had not given the negroes suffrage," a Southern Democrat confided to him, "it would have had to hold our states under an exclusively military government for ten years."[50] John Pool, a Republican Senator from North Carolina, said he "accepted the necessity of Negro suffrage only reluctantly," as the only means by which the country could be "nationalized."[51] The country was in fact in a material sense "nationalized" by other agencies. In 1867 Abilene, Kansas, became the railroad loading point for cattle driven up the Chisholm Trail from Texas, intended for northern and eastern markets. Two years later, the Union Pacific and the Central Pacific railroads met at Promontory Point in Utah, completing the transcontinental steel spine of United States industrial capitalism. Thus were doomed the hopes of the slave bourgeoisie beyond all appeals to ink or blood. The Northern bourgeoisie, its hegemony in national affairs thus undergirded, signified its acceptance of post-Emancipation racial oppression by abandoning Reconstruction. The subsequent white-supremacist system in the South was established not by civil means, but by nightrider terror and one-sided "riots" in order to deprive African-Americans of their constitutional rights,[52] reducing them again, by debt peonage and prisoner-leasing, to a status that was slavery in all but name.[53]

That still left the basic problem, however – the problem that concerned Sir John Davies and Sir William Petty in Ireland – how to achieve stability and civil order in a system based on racial oppression. Even from the ruling-class point of view, there is a limit to profitability in the maintenance of social control by unconstitutional methods ("sending an army to do it"); that manifests a deficiency in the intermediate, buffer social control stratum, a situation that discourages venture capital.[54]

The Negro Exodus of 1879

A hundred thousand laboring-class African-Americans in the South had a different sense of the limits, and they determined to make a withdrawal of variable capital, that is, their own labor power, from the plantation system. They ventured for the dream deferred, of homes and homesteads, by making an exodus like that of ancient example.[55] They persevered, despite objections voiced by Frederick Douglass and some other leaders, local as well as national, who argued that the tide could still be reversed in the South, and that the Exodus was a sort of desertion of the cause.[56] The best-known leaders of the Exodus, such as Benjamin "Pap" Singleton of Tennessee and Henry Adams of Louisiana, were former bond-laborers. Singleton had escaped to points north, and Adams had served as a sergeant in the Union army.[57] They were not likely to be deterred by advice belied by their experience.

Groundwork, and underground work, had been under way for some years before. Indeed over the decade many African-Americans had gone into Kansas from Tennessee, Kentucky and Missouri. In Texas, Louisiana, Mississippi and Alabama, the organizers of the Exodus had since 1874 enrolled 98,000 persons for the enterprise.[58] The destination was "free ground";[59] for some that meant Indiana or Ohio, but the most favored place was Kansas – the Kansas of old John Brown – and thousands got there. Between 1870 and 1880, the number of African-Americans living in Kansas but not born there increased by more than two and a half times, from about 12,000 to about 33,000; a major contribution was made by the arrival of around 6,000 from Louisiana, Mississippi and Texas in that dramatic spring of 1879. Thousands more arrived at the transfer point of Saint Louis, who migrated then to other states.[60] Most of the migrants had little or no financial resources; sympathizers, locally and throughout the country ("a few incurable fanatics," as a spiteful New York journal called them),[61] organized to defend the right of migration, to assist the Exodusters in finding gainful employment, and in general to help them surmount their difficulties.[62] Only a handful of the Exodusters gave up and returned to the South; most of the others, with or without further assistance, found places for themselves in the local economy, although they were not financially able to start out as homesteaders.[63] Many of those from Texas, however, three or four thousand of whom arrived between November 1879 and March 1880, came in their own wagons with their own furniture and were financially able to fend for themselves from the beginning.[64]

One fairly prominent Republican, Benjamin H. Bristow of Kentucky, was optimistic; he saw the Exodus as "Perhaps ... the final settlement of the 'Negro question.'"[65] Whatever the particulars as Bristow conceived them, there is no doubt that the migration of African-Americans from the South had profound implications for the course of United States history. If African-Americans had become completely free to escape from the South, the white-supremacists would have been unable to institute and maintain the white reign of terror by which they overthrew Reconstruction. Then, paradoxically, those who stayed might indeed have prospered in freedom in the South, in the way that Douglass envisioned.

But just as Home Rule for Ireland proved to be unacceptable to the British ruling class as a whole because of its threatening democratic implications for England itself, so the United States ruling class in the end rejected this, or any, "settlement of the Negro question," sensing the potential emergence of an unwelcome array of popular forces against the course of unchecked capitalist greed, an array freed of the paralyzing incubus of "white" racial privileges. Just as the British played the Orange card against Home Rule,[66] so did the bourgeoisie in the United States play the "White card" to destroy the Exodus. Before the Exodusters could even set foot on the Exodus Road, they were subjected to threats and violence by whites for expressing the intention of leaving. "[Y]ou will get your head shot away," a Louisiana landlord told one of his black tenants who said he wanted to leave the state. A white mob hanged a woman, although she was in an advanced stage of pregnancy, for intending to go to Kansas to join her husband; her child was born as she was being murdered.[67] There was the threatening publication by a white-owned Mississippi newspaper of the names of those active in enrolling people for the Exodus. A group of white men "killed [a Mississippi man] because he wanted to go to Kansas," one Exoduster testified. Most common was the threatened or actual imprisonment of would-be Exodusters on the charge of attempting to escape the systemic indebtedness to the landlord.[68]

The main strategy was directed at the most vulnerable point, the Mississippi river landings. The river being the lifeline of escape, the effort to stop it centered on depriving the migrants of riverboat transportation. Armed and mounted gangs of white men, known as "bulldozers," ranged both sides of the river, not only to intimidate the Exodusters but also to prevent boats from even stopping where Exodusters were congregated. Direct terrorism was supplemented by non-terroristic measures, such as the pressure brought by St Louis businessmen to force ship operators to raise ticket prices to levels that would be prohibitive for the Exodusters.[69]

The strategy proved effective.[70] Many hundreds of Exodusters were actually stranded at the landings; others, who had not yet reached the river, were likely to be deterred by the prospect. They had the money (about four dollars) for the fare on the riverboat, but only if their embarkation was prompt and if the price of the tickets was not raised. But they were not prepared to withstand the pressures entailed by delay. If they spent their money for food, their ticket money was gone. If, as it often happened, white merchants refused to sell to them, hunger forced them to stop where they were and hire themselves out locally. They were subjected to constant efforts to get them to turn back, an activity in which some African-Americans engaged as agents of the plantation owners. The Exodusters were strong in spirit and faith, but the movement was structurally weak. What the bulldozers and the ship companies were doing was eventually stopped by threats of court action and of providing alternative shipping facilities. But by that time the back of the Exodus had been broken.[71]

The Exodus and the white immigration privilege

Some Kansas whites reacted negatively to the spectacular proportions of the Exodus. At Leavenworth, white authorities refused to allow boats carrying Exodusters to land. Others saw in the Exodus a threat of tax-draining pauperism. In one area aspiring to countyhood, it was suggested that only "whites" be counted toward the minimum population requirement. On the outskirts of Topeka, a gang of whites destroyed a temporary shelter provided by friends of the Exodusters.[72] By contrast, the increasing hundreds of North Carolina whites migrating to the West at that time seem not to have been bulldozed or otherwise intimidated into returning to the plantation country, nor driven away by residents of the states of their destination.[73]

The rationale that whites were being crowded out by an excessive influx of black people should scarcely have satisfied even those disposed to think in such bigoted terms. The decennial census figures indicate that the rate of influx of white people was slightly greater than that of black people. For every 10 African-Americans in Kansas in 1870, there were 204 Euro-Americans; in 1880 there were 210.[74] The white-skin privilege of immigration was apparent in the fact that for every 10 African-Americans in Kansas at the end of that decade who were not born in Kansas, there were 14 foreign-born persons. Yet there is no record of boats being interfered with for bringing the foreigners to Kansas; they, of course, had been baptized "white" when they first set foot in the country, and thus endowed with the inalienable right of immigration. Some of these came by riverboat from New Orleans, a fact that will be further noted below (pp. 155–7).

A Mutual Understanding Regarding Social Control

"Northern commercial interests," writes Hirshson, "espousing views which they consistently advocated since 1877, strongly opposed the exodus." A typical instance was given by the New York *Commercial Bulletin*: "Can the South or the North be benefited by encouraging the migration of that labor upon which our chief commercial crop is dependent?" it asked. Another business organ, the New York *Journal of Commerce*, was eager to "assure the Southerners, once for all, that . . . the people of the North feel no desire to break up the Southern labor system."[75]

The African-Americans were not objecting to making cotton – that was a specialty of many of them. All they asked was put simply by John Solomon Lewis of Tensas parish, Louisiana: to be allowed "to make headway like white workingmen,"[76] and not to be terrorized out of the constitutional rights that they had fought for in the Union army, cheated of their pay, or forced into peonage; and that a black woman not have to live in fear of being made the victim of sexual molestation by any white man who encountered her.[77] That was "the Southern labor system" to those who did the labor. When the dominant sections of the bourgeoisie called for its preservation, they were opting for the post-Emancipation reinstitution of racial oppression. And again, as in the days of the Fugitive Slave Laws, the preservation of "the southern labor system" required the maintenance of the system of racial privileges of laboring-class Euro-Americans, the "whites," *vis-à-vis* African-Americans not just in the South, but throughout the country. On this a mutual North–South bourgeois understanding was attained, as can be gleaned from a US senator's questioning of a typical representative of the plantation bourgeoisie, John C. Calhoun, grandson and namesake of the South Carolina statesman. The testimony, given in September 1883 before the Senate Education and Labor Committee on the Relations between Labor and Capital,[78] seems the more interesting since it was the elder Calhoun who first defied the authority of the United States over his own state in the famous Nullification controversy in the 1830s.

The grandson left South Carolina at the height of Reconstruction in 1869, for reasons which we may in part infer were not altogether limited to matters of soil exhaustion, to take up a large plantation on the Arkansas side of the Mississippi river.[79] In 1879, some one hundred and fifty of his African-American laborers and/or tenants set out on the Exodus to Kansas, a move he claimed to have had some success in discouraging by intercepting them at the banks of the Mississippi.[80] Times had changed since his grandfather's day, and the South, Calhoun told the committee, was now "strongly for the Union," for which he gave the following reason:

> ... the negro population of the South, compared with the white population of the South, might be a dangerous element, but the negro population, compared with the whole white population of the United States as an integral body, sinks into insignificance.

Calhoun endorsed the view expressed by committee chairman Senator Blair of New Hampshire, who was questioning him, that it was to the advantage of "the South" that

> ... the negro should be dealt with by the forty or fifty millions of whites, that the races should be balanced in that proportion rather than in the proportion that exists between them and the white population of the South.[81]

Sir William Petty would have been pleased by this grand realization of the principle of his proposal to James II for a merger of the Irish and English populations to achieve the proportions necessary for social control in a society based on racial oppression.

Calhoun felt that in the light of all that had happened, "There is really very little conflict between labor and capital. The conflict in my section, if any should come in the future, will not assume the form of labor against capital, but of race against race."[82]

The Organized White Workers

But did the motivations and plans of the white workers, especially as organized in the National Labor Union between 1866 and 1872, justify such ruling-class self-assurance as that voiced by Calhoun? The NLU had entered into fraternal relations with the International Workingmen's Association, which had high expectations of labor in the United States as the trailblazer toward "the ascendancy of the working class." The record of the NLU's deliberations on "negro labor," and of its relations with the Black National Labor Union, needs to be studied closely, with the heightened consciousness that is one legacy of the civil rights struggles of the 1960s. It is too extensive for treatment in the present context, but the tone of it, beneath occasional rhetorical flourishes, seems more likely to anticipate Calhoun's expectations than to affirm those of the First International.

At its inaugural convention in Baltimore in 1866, the NLU urged the inculcation of the idea that:

> ... the interests of labor are one; that there should be no distinction of race or nationality; no classification of Jew or Gentile, Christian or Infidel; that there is but one dividing line – that which separates mankind into two great classes, the class that labors and the class that lives by others' labor.[83]

But then and thereafter, as the documents show, the NLU was determined to interpret that idea in the same narrow "white labor" sense as before the war, namely, the desire to avoid competition by black workers. Obviously, the International had not sent the NLU a copy of Marx's letter to Lincoln, with its injunction to throw off the incubus of "white" labor's privileges over black labor. I have already noted the disparagement of Black Reconstruction by the NLU and its President William Sylvis. The NLU went out of existence after 1872, but the "white labor" principles by which it was bound unfortunately did not. Solidarity with the Exodusters was left to the remnants of Radical Republicanism; there is no record of a labor component in it.

It is to the credit of Frederick A. Sorge, Marx's friend and correspondent and NLU activist, that he came later to understand this much about his adopted country: "The race prejudice of the Caucasians against the Negro prevents the rise of labor organizations in many southern states, and the beginning of a healthy labor movement."[84] By way of remedy, however, Sorge merely offered the suggestion that the mass of black workers on the cotton and sugar plantations of the South "will arise by their own strength and must put an end to the misery under which they suffer." He was silent on what to do about the white workers' "prejudice," and put his faith in the "rise of industry in the New South," which he believed would "pull the Negro population into the movement – [and] ... revolutionize *them*"[85] (emphasis added). But what was to revolutionize the Euro-American workers by ridding them of "race" prejudice? The absurdity of putting faith in "objective" factors such as the industrialization of the South will appear in the discussion of the Cotton Mill Campaign below.

At the very moment, in December 1879, when thousands of Exodusters were making their way overland from Texas to Kansas, the Socialist Labor Party, of which Sorge was a chief founder, held its national convention in Pittsburgh, Pennsylvania. Albert Parsons, himself a Texan driven out for his equalitarian views, introduced a resolution "concerning land grants." The whole country by that time was aware of the Exodus, but the records do not show whether Parsons made any mention of it in his talk and resolution. In any case, the convention as a whole ignored it; the resolution was referred to the Committee on Platforms and is not heard of again.[86]

The South Revisits the Problem of Social Control

I have noted how the Protestant tenants, their exclusive Ulster Custom tenant-right eroded by structural economic changes and drained by reduction of the size of their holdings, indicated for a brief period a readiness to make common cause with the Catholic peasants to secure the legal enactment of a tenant-right law for all Ireland. Radical Reconstruction had likewise shown that there were some Southern whites who were ready to make common cause with the black population to establish a society there based on racial equality of constitutional rights.[87]

They dared, and some died as John Brown had done, struggling side by side with African-American freedom fighters for their common cause, the end of racial oppression. They are not so well known as they should be; here is a selected list of ten of them:

- A. P. Dostie, described by one historian as "animated by a fanatical ambition to subdue rebels and elevate slaves" (Shugg, *Class Struggle in Louisiana*, p. 217), killed in a mob attack on the New Orleans Black and White Convention in July 1866; his dying words: "Let the good fight go on!" (*Proceedings of the Southern Loyalist Convention*, September 1866, printed in the *Reporter*, no. 33, Washington, DC, 17 September 1866).

- Calvin Pepper of Virginia, the only white person on the delegation which Frederick Douglass led to present a petition to the President on behalf of Negro suffrage (Black, *Home-made Yankees*, p. 189. John Richard Dennett, *The South As It Is, 1865–1866* [New York, 1866], pp. 6–7).

- James W. Hunnicutt of Virginia, who "campaigned vigorously against the vagrancy laws, for racial equality, and against voting and office-holding by 'rebels'" (Black, p. 250, citing Union League Club of New York, *Aid for Virginia* [New York, 1867]).

- George W. Ashburn of Georgia, murdered "for consorting with Negroes" (Black, p. 30).

- J. W. Smith, of Texas, killed for "organizing Negroes" (ibid.).

- Thomas J. Mackey of South Carolina, "one of the few white men to attend the state labor convention in Columbia in 1869" (ibid., p. 34).

- William Wallace Chisolm and John P. Gilmer, killed in Mississippi in 1877 in order that "confidence [be] restored between the races" (James D. Lynch, *Kemper County Vindicated: A Peep at Radical Rule in Mississippi* [New York, 1879], p. 319).

- Alexander Boyd, murdered in Eutaw, Alabama, "for too earnest inquiries into outrages committed against freedmen" (Black, pp. 47–8, citing the Greensboro, North Carolina *Republican*, 28 April 1870).

- John Walter Stephens of North Carolina, poor farmer, uncompromising activist in the struggle against white supremacy, whose lynching and the manner of it are described in Chapter 30 of Albion W. Tourgée's novel *A Fool's Errand* (1879; New York, 1961).

The ruling class strangled Reconstruction by sheer terror, but they could not forget the time when the impossible happened and a part of the European-American population arrayed itself against white supremacy. The consensus is that the proportion of this defection from the white-race function was insignificant. If it was so insignificant why the reign of terror against it? Was the terror not simply a new edition of the gag rules, the tar and feathers, and the interdiction of abolitionist mail that had been produced by the fears of abolitionism in the South in the pre-war decades?[88] And, in the end, had not those forebodings proved valid? Given the decision to continue the system of racial oppression, given the self-limiting advantages of rule by mere terrorism, given the dilemma-dictated reliance on African-American labor, given the constitutional leverage, actual or potential, now in the hands of the African-Americans – the matter of the intermediate stratum remained in urgent need of attention.

The immigrant labor supply fantasy

At some point on the road to the Hayes–Tilden deal, the plantation bourgeoisie was seized with the fantasy of recruiting Chinese laborers in numbers sufficient even to threaten the Negroes with marginalization.[89] The main problem with regard to the Chinese was that the Southern planters could not/ would not pay as much as those workers were earning building railroads in the West.[90] A few were procured for Louisiana plantations, but they ran away to work as fishermen or truck farmers around New Orleans. A number of Southern states established agencies to recruit laborers from Europe, especially Ireland and Germany. "There is one answer – *and one only* – WHITE IMMIGRATION," declared an Alabama editor.[91] Many Irish and German immigrants had come to New Orleans before the war. Perhaps, it was thought, the same sources would go a long way toward supplying the needed intermediate stratum.[92] The trouble in this case was that Germans and Irish would not be coming to work as field hands, but would have to be offered homesteads, and those homesteads would have to be cut out of the holdings of the plantation owners themselves. When that realization struck home, the whole idea lost its appeal. Indeed, the bourgeoisie did want "a wall betwixt" themselves and the laboring-class African-Americans; and, like the planters of Ulster, they were perfectly willing to provide some land for settlers when it could be taken from the native population. But to cut up their own land for giveaway freeholds would be to lose sight altogether of their lives' basic purpose.[93] Balancing social needs against economic interests, it seemed, would require exploration of other possibilities for shoring up the buffer middle stratum in the face of problems presented by Emancipation. The Irish and the Germans meantime paddleboated up the Mississippi in search of homestead prospects brighter than any they could expect in the South,[94] perhaps passing stranded Exodusters as they went. In the Exodus decade, 1870–79, in Kansas the foreign-born became the fastest-growing segment of the population (as compared with the native-born, African-American and European-American segments), while in Louisiana the foreign-born proportion of the population continued to decline.[95]

Homesteaders pay the price of Free Soil

White labor had, by accepting the white-skin privilege principle of Free Soil and the Homestead Act of 1862, rendered itself powerless to shape land policy; then, by turning its back on black labor's dream for land and loans for the freedmen, it had endorsed capitalist land monopoly in the South. The result was to foredoom opposition to land monopoly in the West. The industrial bourgeoisie, having consolidated its power by the Hayes–Tilden deal that perpetuated the system of racial oppression, proceeded unchecked to dispose of the "public lands" for railroad building enterprises and for other forms of direct and indirect exploitation of the land and its resources by large capitalist enterprises. By 1890, four times as much land had been given to the railroad capitalists as the total acreage of homestead entries made since 1862.[96]

Yet upon those tillers of the soil who did succeed in perfecting their homestead claims, the pressure of capitalist exploiters took a devastating toll. The homesteaders were always in debt; by 1890, in the five Plains states (Kansas, Nebraska, North Dakota, South Dakota and Minnesota) there was a ratio of more than one mortgage per family.[97] Then came an epidemic of foreclosures. Worst hit was Kansas, where between 1889 and 1893 eleven thousand farms were foreclosed; in some counties "as much as ninety per cent of the farm lands passed into the ownership of the loan companies," writes historian John D. Hicks. But the other Plains states were also heavily hit.[98]

By 1890, of the 8.4 million people engaged in agriculture in the United States, more than 35 percent were hired laborers, and another 18 percent were laboring-class tenants.[99] Land historian Fred A. Shannon comments thus:

> Equally certain as that railroad companies, private speculators, and loan companies profited most from the government's land policy, is the fact that the labor surplus became a constantly increasing factor in the national life after 1864. . . . The years of agricultural distress in the 1870s and 1880s were accompanied by an ever-increasing roll of unemployed in the cities. Even the pioneers on the homesteads, baffled by fortune and beaten by nature, edged their way back, more often than not, to the ancestral farms and from there to the factory and, too frequently, to the bread line.[100]

By shaping the homestead policy as a white-skin privilege, the ruling class had secured the acquiescence of laboring-class whites in the overthrow of black Reconstruction. Now it was time for the bourgeoisie to reveal the other side of its policy on the land question: the power of capital to expropriate a great proportion of the white farmers and cast them – racial privileges and all – into the ranks of the proletariat. But precisely because the white-skin privileges were sedulously preserved, history would present the farce of Populism as the sequel to the tragedy of Reconstruction.

As a general principle of social control the interests of the intermediate stratum conflict at points with those of the ruling class. This poses the possibility that the middle stratum, or a decisive part of it, might defect to the side of the oppressed masses. To insure against this possibility, certain inviolable spheres of development are apportioned to people of the middle stratum, which afford them an appropriate degree of independence and security. Typical are the Ulster Custom, the Homestead Law, and hereditary apprenticeship opportunities.

What had distinguished the ante-bellum South in this regard was the total absence of such guarantees from the ruling plantation-owning class to the non-owners of bond-labor, who made up three-fourths of the European-American population.[101] Scholars are agreed. The plantation social order "walled them up and locked them in ... blocked them off from escape or any considerable economic and social advance ... left them virtually out of account ... [and the ruling class] concerned itself but little if at all about making use of them as economic auxiliaries."[102] The better-off of them, the "yeoman," so-called, had little if any vital economic connection with the larger plantation society. He "might have devoted a few acres to one of the staples for a 'cash crop', but he directed most of his land and time to food crops for the subsistence of his own family."[103] In Louisiana in 1850, three out of five whites owned no land, and "white labor ... was excluded from the plantation economy." Before the advancing tide of plantations, "Yeomen had no choice but to move westward, or to retreat to ... the woods ... swamps or bayous."[104] They were "left out of the scheme of things ... on the fringe of civilization and in most respects were just tolerated ... [with] no place provided for them by those in social control."[105]

Unlike the Protestant tenant in Ulster, or the homesteader in the West, or the skilled craftsman in industry, the intermediate status of the poor whites hung by a single thread: the enslavement of the Negro and the concomitant fact of their own non-slave status. That did, of course, carry the privileges of keeping weapons, marrying, moving about freely in the public domain, becoming literate if they could, voting at elections, and the male white privilege of assuming familiarity with Negro females; but that all meant nothing in the way of property status or economic security. As one eastern Virginia plantation owner, "Civis", wrote of most of the poor whites in his area of the country, they had "little but their complexion to console them for being born into a higher caste."[106] Yet that one tie bound them to the plantation owners like hoops of steel, and made them "always ready to respond to any call of race prejudice, [so that they] voted with the planter, though the economic interests of the two parties of white men were as separate as the poles."[107]

Because of this about one million Southern poor whites marched off to a war from which more than one out of four would not return.[108] Those who did return found that the very foundation of their social status had been blasted away: the Negro was free, too. Adding to that were the effects of the war's desolation. For the planters there was a silver lining. The price of cotton in 1866 was more than two and a half times its level in the high-price half-decade before the war. Though it declined after 1866, it did not reach the pre-war level until 1875.[109] High prices made it attractive to raise cotton on the less fertile land in poor-white country. Poor whites became for the first time totally committed to cotton farming, and in fairly short order they were enmeshed in the credit system, reduced to tenants, on shares, less self-sufficient and as poor if not poorer than before it all began.[110] Most significant of all, they were on the same economic plane with freedmen tenants who were also striving to succeed as cotton farmers.

The prospect of the poor whites being put on a footing of equality with the African-American tenant and sharecropper, as would be pointed out by W. J. Cash, carried implications that "filled [the plantation bourgeoisie] with terror." For who could doubt that "intimate competition with the Negro would lead to social equality," and to the breakdown of "the convention of white super-iority."[111]

> Who did not see again, that, despairing of their racial status ... these whites would eventually be swept fully into the bitterest class consciousness: that this slow impulse which the master class was at least aware of from the beginning [since Bacon's Rebellion?], would develop a power no barrier and no argument could hold back? Who could not see, in a word, that here was chaos?[112]

The Cotton Mill Campaign – the "way out"[113]

I have noted how the Industrial Revolution came to Ireland in the mold of Protestant Ascendancy. Industrialization was limited to Ulster while poten-tially profitable opportunities were ignored in the Catholic south and west on political grounds. The point was given emphasis by the deliberate decision of the British government to let the Famine run its course, with the resulting loss of one-fourth of the labor power of Ireland through death and emigration. Similarly, when the Industrial Revolution came to the United States South, it was cast in the mold of white supremacy in the most explicit way:

> The Poor Whites under slavery had been excluded, while slaves were cherished. Now the disinherited were read into the will. They had been unnecessary, now they were all-important. The bond of sympathy between whites of both classes was cemented against the common enemy, the Negro.[114]

In its "determination to find a way out for the South,"[115] meaning the continuation of racial oppression of the Negro in the United States, the bourgeoisie now wove the third strand into the post-Emancipation system of privileges of white workers – preference in industrial employment – by means of the Cotton Mill Campaign. It was not merely an investment strategy to take advantage of the poverty-level wages prevailing in the South, and to reduce the cost of cotton at the mill, although it was that, too. Capital investment in cotton manufacture in the South, which had grown at a rate of about $3 million per decade from 1840 to 1880, to a level of $17 million, rose to a total of $124.4 million between 1880 and 1900.[116] It was to be the foundation of a reconstructed system of social control.

From before the Civil War on up through the Reconstruction period, Southern mills generally employed African-American workers, often together with white workers.[117] In the 1850s Saluda mill, near Columbia, South Carolina, had a labor force of 128, including children, all African-Americans.[118] Supervisors who came from the North overcame their early prejudices upon finding that African-American bond-laborers worked "with equal efficiency and even superiority in many respects as compared with whites." The authoritative all-South journal *De Bow's Review*, based in New Orleans, at that time found the possibilities of "African labor" so promising for factory employment that an end should be put to schemes for its "emigration to other countries," an apparent reference to various proposals for "colonization" of Negroes outside the country.[119] A study done by De Bow in 1852–53 endorsed the use of African-American bond-laborers in textile manufacture throughout the South, basing the recommendation on favorable past experience.[120] After the war the "familiar practice" of employing African-Americans in cotton mills was continued.[121] Even as late as 1880, of the 100 workers at the Saluda mill, 25 were Negroes.[122]

The explosion of capital investment in the last two decades of the century was accompanied by a sixfold increase in the number of cotton mill operatives in the South, from 16,741 in 1880 to 97,559 in 1900. This was a period when cotton prices were falling; in the mid-1890s the price stood at about a nickel a pound, far less than half what it had been in 1880. A typical small tenant farm family might earn, say, $525 in a year's work. By going into the cotton mill, where again the entire family would be employed, the family income would be increased to $900.[123] It was a perfectly normal response when debt-ridden tenants "industrious and lazy alike flocked to the mill communities."[124]

What was not normal from the standpoint of lowering operating costs was to refuse to hire Negroes as cotton mill operatives, even though the mill owners believed that African-American laborers were perfectly capable of doing the work,[125] and possibly at lower cost (given the augmented labor pool, and assuming non-union conditions). It was altogether rational, however, in terms of the maintenance of bourgeois social control, one more instance of balancing the economic and the social aspects of rulership. The mill owners as a class had "recognized the fact that the mill life is the only avenue open ... to our poor whites, and we have with earnestness and practically without exception kept that avenue open to the white man alone."[126] The aim, said D. A. Tompkins, prominent cotton mill entrepreneur, had to be "to reestablish as quickly as possible respectability for white labor."[127] Prospective Cotton Mill investors were urged to rise above "purely mercenary considerations," and think of the thousands of jobs they would be providing for unemployed "white" women. Mitchell "explains": "whites, particularly women, could not compete with negroes in certain occupations, and in 'servile' ones would not."[128] At the conclusion of its investigation of the cotton mill industry, the United States Industrial Commission noted uncritically "[t]he finding ... that the white mill workers ought to be saved from negro competition; that this field ought to be reserved for white labor."[129] I leave aside here the frequent self-serving white-supremacist allusion to "social equality," except to note that the discrimination in employment was related to the white male privilege aspect of the system of social control peculiar to the United States, which it seems was regarded as certain to be undermined by white women and black men working together, especially in the same room! Undoubtedly, W. J. Cash was faithfully interpreting the mind of the South's mill owners in saying, "... we shall create a sanctuary for the falling common whites and place thousands of them in employment which by common agreement shall be closed to the Negro."[130] In earnest whereof, the mill owners had awarded the poor white an annual income differential *vis-à-vis* the African-American equal to the difference between the share-tenant's $525 and the mill worker's $900.

For some time now, official society has fled from the concept of affirmative action as a measure of fairness and equality for African-Americans and other not-"whites." Some opportunists have preeningly repudiated affirmative action. A chorus of white pundits have sung a steady dirge about "preferential treatment." One of them denounces affirmative action as "an ethnic spoils system."[131] One can only imagine how indignant they all would have been if they had been alive to witness the workings of the Cotton Mill Campaign!

White-skin Privilege as a Depressor of Wage Levels

The effects of the development of this discrimination in employment were ramified not only across the South, but throughout the United States. Cotton goods manufacture was the one factory industry in the South; it was necessarily a family affair, not like mining or logging, or other extractive industries. More than 90 percent of all African-Americans lived in the South; escape to the west and north, as we have seen in the story of the Exodus of 1879, was effectively cut off for all but the most hardy and lucky of them. Outside the South, industrial employers understood that the white-skin privilege employment policy, when combined with a corresponding racist immigration policy, was on the whole perfectly compatible with profitable operations, and that it served their long-range class interests as a preventive against class-consciousness in the North and in the West, no less than in the South. It had another very tangible effect outside the South: the gradual decline of the importance of the New England textile mills, due largely to the low wages paid in the South. Taking the combined number of active spindles in the two regions as an index, New England's share declined from 94 percent in 1880 to 75 percent in 1890; the decline continued until New England was destroyed as a textile region, along with its relatively higher wage scale.[132]

Textile mill wages in the South were not only low relative to those of New England, but absolutely low with reference to their own daily needs. Mitchell quotes mill owners as saying that the North–South cotton mill wage differential was about 25 percent.[133] But Vann Woodward cites a variety of more disinterested authorities who found that the wages of Southern mill hands were much lower than those given by Mitchell as a basis for comparison with New England wages. Instead of three to four dollars a week, the workers in North Carolina received from ten cents a day, for children, to fifty cents a day for men. In Alabama in 1885, male spinners got $2.53 a week and women $2.76. The work week was seventy hours.[134] The condition was self-perpetuating. Ordinarily the wages of operatives living in cotton mill towns were so low "that all available members of a family had to work in the mill, and the companies refuse[d] to let houses except to families which [could] furnish two, three or sometimes even four workers to a family."[135]

This historic persistence of low wages was not due, however, to the conditions of rural poverty of those tenant farmers and sharecroppers alone, or to the lack of opportunities for other industrial employment. It was bound to perpetuity because of the paralyzing effect of white-supremacism, *a barrier that could not be overcome without a facing of the issue*. That seems to be the clear conclusion to which the brothers Mitchell were led by their extensive studies in the field. They said: "Managements have encouraged the maxim that the cotton manufacture is a white man's industry; the implied danger of Negro invasion is supposed to render the operatives glad to hold what they have, rather than reach out for more."[136]

Of Parallels and Intertwining

It is a century now since the Populist Revolt and the Cotton Mill Campaign, a century that has merely underscored the judgment rendered by DuBois in 1935 that Reconstruction had "presented the greatest opportunity" we were likely to see for "many decades"[137] for breaking the mold the slaveholders made. Except for the consciousness-raising civil rights movement in the United States and in Ulster, dating from the Montgomery bus boycott, little of significance has been added to or subtracted from the message of the parallels drawn in these six chapters, to contribute to an understanding of the essential principles of racial oppression and their organic relationship to the problems of ruling-class social control.

These histories present not only parallels, however, but an intertwining which is no less valuable for its illumination of the social process of recruitment of Euro-Americans into the "white race" social control formation, and the resistance to that process, in the period between 1820 and 1860.

The Sea-change

I have been looking into an Irish mirror for insights into the nature of racial oppression and its implication for ruling-class social control in the United States. I conclude this volume with a look at a unique historical phenomenon associated with the massive Irish immigration into the arena of the ante-bellum struggle between racial slavery and freedom in the United States. The image passes through the looking-glass to become American reality; but as if governed by the mirror metaphor, it reappears as the opposite of its original self. Subjects of a history of racial oppression as Irish Catholics are sea-changed into "white Americans," into opponents both of the abolition of racial slavery and of equal rights of African-Americans in general.

Between 1820 and 1860 Ireland and America became interlinked by two historic developments: first, the maturation of the struggle that culminated in the overthrow of racial slavery; and, second, massive emigration from Ireland to the United States.

The Struggle over Racial Slavery

The issue of racial slavery versus freedom was undermining "compromises" three decades before William Seward named it "the irrepressible conflict."[1] The United States Constitution itself was the first "compromise": the Southern slaveholding states were given enhanced representation in Congress, based on the number of their bond-laborers, and a fugitive slave law, in exchange for the Northwest Ordinance barring slavery from the territory north and west of the Ohio River and the decision to end by 1808 the importation of African-American bond-laborers. Next the Missouri Compromise of 1820, seventeen years after the Louisiana Purchase and five years after the end of the War of 1812, admitted Missouri as a slave state but stipulated that thereafter the southern boundary of that state was to be the limiting latitude (36 degrees 30 minutes) of slave territory. The third was the Compromise of 1850 passed in the wake of the Mexican War. It revoked the 36 degrees 30 minutes limit on the extension of slaveholding and instead introduced "squatter sovereignty" whereby in new states African-Americans were to be enslaved or free according to the majority vote of European-Americans in the territory. Its second most significant provision was a drastic strengthening of the Fugitive Slave Law.

In the beginning, however, the Emancipationist mood had been in the ascendant; slavery was such a shameful thing that the Founders resorted to elaborate circumlocution to avoid the use of the word "slave" in the Constitution.[2] There was a sense that both lifetime and limited-term bond-servitude would die a natural economic death with the development of the reserve army of unemployed labor normal to the capitalist social system.[3] In earnest of that belief, they enacted a ban on the "importation" of African bond-laborers after 1807. Events, however, took a turn as tragic as it was unexpected.

The cotton gin

Never has a truism borne the test of scholarship more successfully than that of the epochal impact of the invention of the cotton gin by Eli Whitney in 1793. That simple device for separating seed from lint increased labor productivity tenfold when driven by foot treadle, or fiftyfold when driven by animal power,[4] and thereby suddenly presented the plantation bourgeoisie with a field of profitable capital investment of an unprecedented scale. Within ten years, by 1803, raw cotton production in the United States increased twelvefold, and by 1820 it was triple what it had been in 1803.[5] The price of bond-laborers rose sixfold relative to the price of cotton between 1805 and 1860.[6] Profits were sufficient to increase the demand for plantation bond-labor twentyfold between 1810 and 1860.[7] In 1860, the pro-slavery writer Thomas Prentice Kettell observed that the "civilized world [was] pressing on the small force of blacks" so sorely that "every straggler is turned into the fields, to add ten more bales to the annual crop." The same program of impressment was directed at bond-laborers engaged in "the non-productive employments of the cities" of the South, and their places were taken by wage workers brought from Ireland and Germany.[8] Since the rate of profit per bond-laborer varied but without a long-term trend,[9] while the price of bond-laborers rose relative to the price of cotton and no post-gin technical revolutions occurred in the plantation economy, it is clear that the maintenance of the rate of profit resulted from the intensification of the labor of the bond-laborers.[10] This intensification was achieved by physical compulsion, work-gang discipline, close supervision, and the fact that slavery was a form of racial oppression imposed on free, as well as bound, African-Americans.[11] This increased exploitation of African-American laborers, carried out on a vastly expanding scale, brought a new intensity and scope to the struggle between freedom and slavery, and made it indeed "the irrepressible conflict."

Events in the Caribbean added further heat and pressure to the unfolding issue in the United States. In 1804, after a thirteen-year struggle, the revolutionary abolition of slavery was finally and forever an established fact in Haiti. Thirty years later the bond-laborers of the British West Indies – with the support of the British abolitionists and the Irish Emancipation movement led by Daniel O'Connell – won Emancipation.[12] "Abolition agitation," said the Governor of South Carolina in 1845, made it necessary "to draw the reins tighter and tighter day by day," for fear that bond-laborers would "cut our throats."[13]

The pro-slavery phalanx

A pro-slavery political phalanx emerged on the national scene, comprising three chief elements. First of all, of course, there was the plantation bourgeoisie itself, which was as one in its adamant opposition to abolition, but which was divided on tactical assumptions.[14] There were those, typically from the Deep South, like John C. Calhoun of South Carolina who, with the traditional support of the majority of the racially privileged non-slaveholders, scorned time-buying apologetics and instead justified slavery as "a positive good."[15] There were others, typically from the border South, most notably represented by Henry Clay of Kentucky, whose asserted abhorrence of slavery was exceeded by their absolute rejection of the possibility of coexistence with African-Americans *except* under a condition of racial slavery. For them, the end of slavery was inconceivable without the "colonization" of all African-Americans outside the United States[16]: a concept more monstrous in scope than that of the Cromwellian "transplantation" of Catholics to "Hell or Connaught" in 1652.

The second rank was supplied by elements of the bourgeoisie of the North who shared with the slaveholders a general class prejudice against abolitionism on the ground of "property rights." But their position was most particularly based on their business relationships with the plantation bourgeoisie. A major center of such connections was New York,[17] where banks profited greatly as suppliers of the bills of credit that were indispensable for financing the production and export of the annual cotton crop. In the five years immediately before the Civil War, the value of cotton exports amounted to nearly $750 million, constituting more than half the value of all United States exports;[18] of this total, it was said that 10 to 15 percent became part of disposable income in the state of New York.[19] It was the boast of *De Bow's Review*, the South's main business organ, that New York was so dependent on slavery that without it the great metropolis would become a mere historical artifact.[20] The sale of manufactures and processed commodities provided another major basis for political sympathies with the slaveholders. At a time when textiles accounted for one-third of the value of all United States imports, New York merchants, enjoying a practical monopoly of the field, were able to exploit that advantage as the suppliers of textiles to the slaveholding states.[21] A wide variety of other goods, from boots to butter, from hardware to hard liquor, helped to raise to more than $130 million by 1859 the value of commodities supplied to the slave states by "the same men who financed their crops and carried them to England."[22] It was claimed that annual Northern profits from all transactions with the South on the eve of the Civil War reached the level of $231,500,000.[23]

There was an even more intimate and direct connection between New York business interests and the slaveholders. Various shipowners, shipbuilders, merchants and other entrepreneurs – operating with the general approval of the pro-slavery elements in official society – conducted a large-scale trade supplying African bond-laborers to Cuba and to the slaveholders of the southern United States. The volume of this increasing commerce is indicated by the fact that in just three months at the end of 1860, US naval cruisers operating on the high seas took more than three thousand Africans from these New York-based ships. Although this trade had been illegal since 1808, the profits were deemed worth the risk of capture, confiscation and prosecution. Late in September 1860, seven hundred Africans were taken from one of these slave ships by a US cruiser off the coast of Africa. The owner was arrested and returned to New York for prosecution, but he was allowed to escape with the patent though unpunished connivance of the Federal Marshal.[24]

Eighteen days after South Carolina seceded from the Union rather than stay in it under the elected Republican administration of Abraham Lincoln, Mayor Fernando Wood, in his annual message to the New York City Common Council, expressed his endorsement of the secessionist course. Noting that the New Yorkers for whom he claimed to speak had a "common sympathy" with "our aggrieved brethren of the Slave States," Wood proposed that New York City too "disrupt the bands which bind her to a venal and corrupt master" by seceding from the United States and becoming "a Free City" open for business with all comers.[25] This was no mere political demagoguery. Many New York merchants and Southern leaders shared a common commitment to free trade and white supremacy, Iver Bernstein writes in his recent thoroughly researched study of the New York City Draft Riots.[26] At a meeting of these New York merchant capitalists in December 1860, called to consider their course of action with regard to secession, one of the leaders asserted that their unity with the South was first and foremost a matter of "race," and that "the city of New York will stand by their brethren, the white race."[27]

In order to maintain their dominant position in the national government[28] in the face of the threat of the faster-growing wage-labor industrial system in the North and West, and the consequent dilution of the Southern presence in Congress, the slaveholders increasingly depended on their links to the laboring-class European-Americans. This was to be the third rank of the pro-slavery phalanx.

Early on in the sharpening controversy, during the discussion of the Missouri Compromise of 1820, John Randolph of Virginia hurled defiance at the Northern proponents of restricting the spread of slavery, boasting, "We do not govern them [the free states] by our black slaves, but by their own white slaves."[29] Randolph's challenge differed from the appeal to capitalist class solidarity which the plantation bourgeoisie regularly addressed to the Northern bourgeoisie. Rather, it represented the strategic extension of an old Southern custom of social control, dating from the end of the seventeenth century,[30] to forestall the emergence of a proletarian front in favor of abolition. The critical element of this political strategy was the defense of the "white" racial privileges of laboring-class European-Americans against the "threat" of equalitarianism implicit in abolition. Its basic "theoretical" principle was an intolerance of the presence of African-Americans as free persons.

This grossly manipulative strategy was adapted and articulated for the consumption of Northern white laborers in ways derived from both the "positive good" and the "colonization" variations on the anti-abolition theme. The "positive good" school argued that wage workers in the Northern United States were worse off (or, at least, no better off) than the Southern bond-laborers, thus establishing a rationale for European-American workers to ignore (or indeed to be hostile toward) the plight of the African-American workers held in chattel bondage and those who were fleeing from it. Governor and Senator J. H. Hammond of South Carolina and pro-slavery ideologue George Fitzhugh of Virginia were among those who sought to compare the lot of the slave favorably to that of the free wage worker of the North.[31]

Addressing his Northern colleagues in the United States Senate in March 1858, James H. Hammond contrasted the pitiable insecurity and starvation wages of the Northern white worker with the position of the African-American "slaves [who] are hired for life and well compensated." He crowned his argument by reproachfully pointing out, "Your slaves are white, of your own race – you are brothers of one blood."[32]

George Fitzhugh produced such "sociological" insights as this:

> The employers of free labor ... try to get the most out of them for the least hire. ... No slaveholder was ever so brutal as to boast of the low wages he paid his slaves, to pride himself on feeding and clothing them badly – neglecting the young, the aged, the sick and the infirm; such a man would be hooted from society as a monster. ... But disguise the process a little, and it is a popular virtue to oppress the free white people.[33]

Fitzhugh linked an incitation against "free negroes" with an argument designed to appeal to the white workingman's other claim to social status. When he cited the fact that, "We subject wives to the dominion of their husbands,"[34] Fitzhugh apparently thought it self-evident that both "free Negro" and "free wife" were subversive concepts.

These ideas were translated in the name of Northern "workingmen."[35] By the 1830s, the organized and unorganized protests of the Northern artisans and wage workers against the ferocity of the capitalist juggernaut that was consuming them alive[36] were almost always couched in terms of the conventional anti-abolitionist rationale, according to which the lot of the Negro plantation bond-laborer was on the whole better than theirs, or according to which racial slavery was at most a secondary matter which should not be allowed to interfere with the interests of "[white] workingmen."[37] One of the most prominent and typical of this tendency was George Henry Evans, in 1844 editor of *Working Man's Advocate*. "I was formerly ... a very warm advocate of the abolition of slavery," he wrote. "This was before I saw that there was white slavery."[38] His newspaper said that only free distribution of public lands could abolish all slavery: wage slavery and chattel slavery. Without that, it said, the African-American slave would be "the loser" if freed to become a wage worker like the European-American workers in the North.[39] This pretense of concern for all laborers, slave and waged, was apt to be belied by the coupling of references to the "pride and delicacy of the Caucasian," with the most hateful white-supremacist references to African-Americans.[40] Brother Basil Leo Lee, in his study of the social and political atmosphere prevailing in New York during the Civil War, paraphrased the "proletarian" form of this "well-off-slave-worse-off-wage-worker" propaganda thus: "Why worry about the wrongs of the negro when you have evils in your own cities;" the New England capitalist abolitionist, he alleged, merely "sought to draw attention to the negro so that he might oppress his wage slaves without notice."[41]

Although the very enormity of the proposed "colonization" of freed African-American bond-laborers outside the United States meant that it could never be more than a "white race" fantasy, the insistent agitation on the subject was calculated to serve as ideological reinforcement against the spread of abolitionism among laboring-class European-Americans. The "colonization" school proceeded from the premise that the free white workers were *better off* than the African-American bond-laborers, and that all their hopes depended upon their being protected from competition with African-Americans, whether slave or free. Henry Clay of Kentucky, Whig statesman and party leader, who was perhaps the foremost advocate of "colonization," pretended that it would, among other things, "elevate the social conditions of the white laborer."[42] Then as now, however, the motivational emphasis was less on future vistas than on alleged present perils. He used all his prestige as Whig leader in the effort to present freedom for the African-American as a deadly threat to the "white" worker. "To make the black man free," he said in the summer of 1842, "it would virtually enslave the white man."[43] A year later, as he was preparing to make his great bid for the Presidency, in 1844, Clay gave instructions for the writing of a pamphlet to be used in his campaign.

[T]he great aim ... should be to arouse the ["white"] laboring classes in the free States against abolition. Depict the consequences to them of immediate abolition; they [emancipated African-Americans] being free would enter into competition with the free laborer; with the American, the Irish, the German; reduce his wages; be confounded with him, and affect his moral and social standing. And as the ultras go for abolition and amalgamation, show that their object is to unite, in marriage, the laboring white man, and the laboring black man, and to reduce the white laboring man to the despised and degraded condition of the black man.[44]

It is to be noted that by his reference to "marriage" Clay was invoking subliminally the "racial" and gender privileges of the "white" male proletarian.

Again, there was the "proletarian" echo. The typical arguments were summarized in resolutions adopted in the name of "workingmen" in January 1861, in that pregnant pause between the election of Lincoln in November and the firing on Fort Sumter in April. They linked a defense of the slaveholders with condemnation of the Republican government for intending "to reduce white men to a forbidden level with negroes."[45]

The Developing Front against Slavery

The anti-slavery front too comprised a number of elements. African-American bond-laborers fled north, to the Free States or to Canada, at the rate of a thousand a year, with the organized support of three thousand or more personnel of the Underground Railroad, the system established by abolitionists to aid escaping slaves.[46] Some resolved to fight where they were, as did Denmark Vesey of Charleston, South Carolina, in 1822, and as did Nat Turner in Southampton County, Virginia, nine years later. Some, 135 in number, shipped from Norfolk, Virginia, on 30 October 1841 bound for New Orleans on board the coastal slave-trade ship the *Creole*, rose in revolt on 7 November, took over the ship, and arrived as free people two days later in the British West Indies.[47] Other African-Americans – Shields Green, Osborne Perry Anderson, Dangerfield Newby, John A. Copeland, Lewis Sherrard Leary, and John Anderson – together with ten or so European-American comrades, under the leadership of John Brown made the daring raid on the federal arsenal at Harper's Ferry in 1859.[48] Others – born free, emancipated, self-bought or free by defiant flight, but still forced to contend with racial oppression even in "free" states – began what would eventually become the abolitionist movement as early as the closing years of the eighteenth century. When the *Liberator* was first founded by William Lloyd Garrison in 1831, its main subscriber base was made up of Northern African-Americans.[49] This is not the place even to attempt to call the roll of these African-American abolitionists; the widely available and forever valuable resource *Documentary History of the Negro*

People of the United States, edited by Herbert Aptheker, presents their story. Two of them, Charles L. Remond and Frederick Douglass, figure particularly in our discussion below of Ireland and Irish-Americans. Nor is this a place to try to list the European-American abolitionists whose equalitarian convictions and instincts, rooted in religious principles and/or in the democratic side of political tradition, led them into battle against racial slavery. Many of them also are found in Aptheker's *Documentary History*. Perhaps the richest sources are abolitionist journals, including the *Liberator*, the *National Anti-slavery Standard*, and the *North Star* (later called *Frederick Douglass' Paper*). What can and must be said about the abolitionists generally is that they were widely persecuted, even lynched, but they never stopped their agitation. In our present context there are two aspects of the abolitionist movement that should be especially noted.

First, the abolitionist movement articulated a far better understanding of the "class question" than the "white" labor apologists did of the "race question." Frederick Douglass saw through the false "proletarian" pretensions of "white" labor movements that excluded African-American workers and yet took offense when Negro workers could not respond to their notions of "labor solidarity."[50] At the same time, more than any "white" workers' organization the abolitionist movement, in a resolution adopted in 1849 by the Massachusetts Anti-slavery Society, articulated the essential principle of true solidarity in the United States, two decades before Karl Marx said, "Labour cannot emancipate itself in the white skin where in the black it is branded."[51]

> Whereas, the rights of the laborer at the North are identified with those of the Southern slave, and cannot be obtained as long as chattel slavery rears its hydra head in our land; and whereas, the same arguments which apply to the situation of the crushed slave, are also in force in reference to the condition of the Northern laborer – although in a less degree, therefore
>
> Resolved, That it is equally incumbent upon the working-man of the North to espouse the cause of the emancipation of the slave and upon Abolitionists to advocate the claims of the free laborer.[52]

Second, the American abolitionist movement – African-Americans and European-Americans together – faithfully supported the struggle of the Irish people, led by Daniel O'Connell, for repeal of the Union with England.

The Free Soil component

The abolitionists never succeeded in winning over a majority of the people of the North to their principles; they could never have brought about the end of racial slavery themselves. The end of slavery came because the abolitionists were moving with the tide of history, and thus became allies with others who were anti-abolitionist but who were opposed to the expansion of slavery.

In 1848, the Free Soil Party came into being with the limited aim of preventing the expansion of slavery, while leaving it undisturbed where it already existed. Its politically strategic significance was that it replaced the illusion of "colonization" of the African-American with a more practical-sounding illusion of "colonization" of the laboring-class European-American homesteaders in "whites-only" Western territories.[53]

This idea of solving the "slavery question" without abolishing slavery paradoxically made possible the formation in 1856 of the Republican Party, which six years later would lead the nation into the abolition of slavery. Despite its original disavowals of abolitionist intentions, the new party was rooted in the reality of the "irrepressible conflict" between two modes of capitalist production, one employing wage labor and the other employing bond labor.

The Slaveholders' Strategic Assessment

The slaveholders were only too aware that the reign of King Cotton was being eclipsed by the rapidly growing industrial system of the North. They perceived the prospective victory of the Republican Party as a death warrant for their system, and they were prepared to resist it by armed rebellion. But they were confident that the North would be impaled on a dilemma. If the Northern bourgeoisie declined to adopt the abolitionist course, the plantation bourgeoisie would ultimately win, if only by attrition, by exploiting politically, diplomatically and economically the essential moral parity of North and South, and by reliance on the African-American bond-labor force for maintaining production of the principal crops for export, and domestic food supplies. If, on the other hand, the Northern bourgeoisie did opt for abolition, the plantation bourgeoisie maintained the confidence of John Randolph that the Northern white worker would refuse to support such a course, and would instead defend the cause of the slaveholders.[54]

The Irish-American Immigrants

Three particular characteristics of the Irish immigration into the United States during the period 1820 to 1860 have a special significance for our treatment of the subject: (1) its massive volume, combined with the pattern of concentrated settlement which it produced; (2) the shared historic background of these immigrants in struggle against racial oppression in Ireland; and (3) its status as being a Catholic minority in a strongly Protestant society characterized by widespread anti-Catholic bigotry.

Extraordinary economic hardships in Ireland associated with the ending of the Napoleonic Wars, the destruction of cottage-weaving by a tardy Industrial Revolution (in Ulster), and above all the Great Famine of 1845–50, led to the emigration of more than 3 million people, accounting in considerable part for the decline of Ireland's population by over 1 million in the forty-year period to 1860.[55]

Among the Irish who made their exodus across the Atlantic, Catholics predominated to an extent greater than in Ireland itself; the disproportion was even more pronounced among those who came to the United States, since most of those who settled in Canada were Protestants.[56] By 1860, the number of Irish-born residents of the United States was 1.2 million, equal to one-fifth of the total population of Ireland itself.[57] In 1860, the population of New York City numbered nearly 814,000; nearly half, 47 percent, were foreign-born, and of these more than half were Irish.[58] For reasons I shall consider later, although these Irish immigrants were almost all from rural parts of Ireland, they, more than other immigrant groups, congregated where they landed, and settled into urban life rather than moving to the West or to agrarian regions nearer by.[59]

No immigrants ever came to the United States better prepared by tradition and experience to empathize with the African-Americans than were these Irish who were emerging directly from the historic struggle against racial oppression in their own country. If there was any people who had demonstrated a sense of the cruel injustices of such a system, it was the Catholic Irish, such as those who came to the United States in this period.

One of their number, an Irish laborer named John Hughes, expressed this kinship in a poem he wrote under the name "Leander" in 1825. He had brought memories of mistreatment and humiliations imposed on his father and himself at the hands of good ol' Protestant boys in Ulster, where, as his father saw it, "a Catholic farmer ranked below a Protestant beggar" in the social scale. He recalled that when his sister died, the priest was forbidden to enter the

Table 1 (A) The percentages, by country of nativity, of immigrants disembarked at New York between 5 May 1847 and 31 December 1860; (B) The percentages, by country of nativity, of the foreign-born population of New York City in 1860; and (C) The indicated dispersal index (A/B)[60]

	A	B	C
Ireland	41.4	53.1	0.78
Germany	36.7	31.3	1.17
England and Scotland	14.5	9.5	1.53
France	2.2	2.1	1.05
Switzerland	1.6	0.5	3.20
Scandinavia	1.0	0.4	2.50
Others	2.6	3.1	0.84

graveyard to conduct the graveside ceremony.[61] Hughes had been in the United States some seven or eight years when he wrote his poem, titled simply "The Slave."[62]

The Irish-American poet observes the African-American bond-laborer in the field working beneath the broiling sun, while the author and others, more "fair" of color, are allowed a respite in the shade. The observer dwells on the life of unremitting, unrewarded toil of the slave, under the brutal whip-wielding overseer. In an apostrophe to Columbia, as poets then were wont to call the United States, Leander pleads:

> Wipe from thy code, Columbia, wipe the stain;
> Be free as air, but yet be kind as free,
> And chase foul bondage from thy Southern plain:
> If such the right of man, by heaven's decree,
> Oh, then let Afric's sons feel what it is – to be.

There is sad irony, however, in the comment made by Hughes's biographer that soon after the writing of "The Slave," "poetry was driven out of [Hughes's] mind by more important matters" connected with his entrance upon his clerical career.[63] Thereafter, Hughes became an "organization man" in a double sense: for the Church and for the "white race."

In Ireland the spirit of Leander lived in the abolition and repeal movements.[64] It lived in the kind reception given to African-Americans who toured Ireland campaigning for abolition. It lived, above all, in O'Connell, called by William Lloyd Garrison "that fearless eloquent champion of liberty" and by slaveholders "the greatest abolitionist in the world";[65] the person whose leadership of the struggle to end racial oppression and for Irish independence earned him the name "The Liberator" in his own country.

We have met O'Connell as the peerless leader of the fight against racial oppression in his own country, but still a conventional bourgeois revolutionary, so mistrustful of the masses that in the end he drew back from the logic of the movement he had created. Yet, though he cancelled at Clontarf the threat he had made at Mallow,[66] the fight that overthrew the system of Protestant Ascendancy in non-Ulster Ireland was led by O'Connell with courage, audacity and skill anchored in his inveterate hatred for racial oppression. Africans had never been held in bondage in Ireland and, O'Connell declared, "Ireland and Irishmen should therefore be forward in seeking to effect the emancipation of mankind."[67] He was proud that "the Irish nation almost unanimously" supported the abolition of slavery, and cited the fact that though the Irish delegation within the British Parliament was "divided on other points ... there is not a man of them ... of any sect, party or denomination, whose voice has been raised but to cry down negro slavery."[68] Saying "there is something Irish at my heart, which makes me sympathize with all those who are suffering under oppression," he promised to put his prestige at the service of "the abolition of slavery all over the world."[69]

And he did so without regard to the consequences. Drawing an image from the psalm, he said, "may my right hand forget its cunning, and my tongue cleave to the roof of my mouth, if, to save Ireland, – even Ireland, I forget the Negro one single hour!"[70] This was no mere rhetorical flourish of a fledgling member of the British Parliament, but a direct and explicit rebuff of the West Indies planters' offer of their parliamentary support of the program of the Irish Party in 1830 if O'Connell would abandon the abolitionist cause. Far from abandoning the abolitionist cause, he regarded the victory over slavery in the West Indies in 1833 as a lever to be used for overturning slavery in the United States.[71]

He accordingly continued the struggle, directing the most powerful and trenchant attacks at the American slaveholders and the entire system of white supremacism. He arraigned them with his matchless oratorical powers on the full range of abolitionist indictments: the plot to annex Texas and thus reduce it again to slavery, which had been abolished in the territory by Mexico in 1830; the treacherous treatment of Osceola, the Seminole chief, in the same pro-slavery expansionist cause; the refusal to abolish slavery even in the Federal District of Columbia; the terrorizing of abolitionists; the criminalization of Negro literacy; and, ever and again, the very notion of the constitutionality of "property in man," with all its train of human degradation, suffering and destruction of family life. He would not visit such a country. He would not welcome slaveholders in his country. He would not shake the hand of an American until he was assured it was not the hand of a slaveholder.

O'Connell was bent on ending not only slavery, but racial oppression in general. He continually contrasted the theory of the Declaration of Independence with the denial of the presumption of liberty to free African-Americans, with the denial of their equal rights in voting, in public transportation, and other accommodations; and with the denial of their civil rights in general. He recognized as well as Burke before him had done in the letter to Langrishe (see p. 71) the monstrous absurdity of "plebeian aristocracy," characteristic of a social order based on racial oppression. The worst of all aristocracies, he said, "is that which prevails in America – an aristocracy of the human skin."[72] When the American notion of "colonization" came to his attention, he ripped it to shreds with scorn and derision. He likened it to proposals made to rid England of surplus peasantry by shipping them to Canada. The only difference in principle, he said, was that the Colonization Society was motivated by no other reason than "color" prejudice.

The barbs stuck and stung, and the United States ruling plantation bourgeoisie reacted. They roundly condemned O'Connell for "interference in American affairs," and in the South some voices were raised against Irish immigration, fearful of contamination with abolitionist ideas. The most specific counter-blow, however, was the refusal to give financial support to the cause of Repeal unless O'Connell desisted from his abolitionist ways. As he had done in the West Indies case, O'Connell scornfully spurned all such threats.

It is doubtful whether the withholding of slaveholders' support by itself could have brought down the repeal movement in the United States; every month, low-earning Irish-Americans were sending tens of thousands of dollars back to Ireland to help the people left behind.[73] Half a tithe of that amount would have made a sizable "Repeal Rent" from America. It was up to the repeal movement to win its portion. The threat, however, was buttressed with aspersions – supported by the Catholic press – against O'Connell's Protestant allies and, by association, the women's rights movement.[74] In the political arena, narrowly conceived, the Democratic Party sought to identify O'Connell's position with British (and by inference anti-Irish) policy, especially after the abolition of slavery in the British West Indies in 1833.

O'Connell did not seek to avoid such questions, but dealt with them directly, promptly and frankly. He acknowledged the doctrinal differences between himself, as a Catholic, and Dissenters. But he was not put off by the fact that it had been the Wesleyan Methodists who had taken the initiative in the abolitionist cause in Britain and Ireland. "It is to their honor," said the Catholic Liberator, "and not to their reproach that they have been persecuted. It is my wish to imitate them."[75]

He met head on the issue of women's rights as it arose within the abolition movement itself, even though doing so required self-criticism of his male ego. After the World Anti-slavery Convention held in London in 1840 voted to exclude women delegates, the American abolitionist and women's rights leader Lucretia Mott, one of those excluded, wrote to O'Connell criticizing his stand on the matter. He promptly re-examined his position, admitted his error and, not sparing his male ego, said he "easily perceived" that his vote to exclude the women delegates was based on fear of "the ridicule it [his support of their inclusion] might excite." This, he said, "was an unworthy, and indeed a cowardly motive." He accordingly reversed his opinion and, however belatedly, adopted Mott's point of view.[76]

As for whether British government policy was informed by an abolitionist disposition after 1833, to any extent that that may have been so it was the by-product of the long abolitionist struggle in which O'Connell played a part, which he could not have desired to repudiate.

The abolitionists' strategy to win the Irish-Americans

The American abolitionists were well aware of the dimensions and the significance of the almost universal anti-abolitionist stand of the leadership and the rank and file of the Irish-American population. Catholic Irish-Americans were almost totally tied into the Democratic Party, the openly avowed party of slavery.[77] Furthermore, by the early 1840s there was "fairly unanimous agreement" among the Catholic clergy and press in the United States that "the principles and methods of Garrisonian abolitionism were not only a threat to the safety of the country but also in conflict with Catholic ethics and ideals."[78] It was at this juncture, as the repeal campaign was mobilizing in Ireland, as the World Anti-slavery Convention was pressing forward, heartened by the victory over slavery in the British West Indies, that the abolitionist movement conceived a strategy for winning Irish-Americans away from the pro-slavery front. The attack was to be directed at the most vulnerable spot at which a decisive blow could be struck against the power of the slaveholders, namely the anomalous seam between Irish-America and the slaveholders. A choice was to be posed between O'Connell and Hughes; between Pope Gregory XVI's denunciation of slavery and the apologetics for it put forward by Bishop England of Charleston; and, within the "Irish-American heart," between the reverence for O'Connell, Catholic Liberator, embattled leader of the historic struggle for repeal of the Union, and the blandishments of white supremacy.

The implement chosen was conceived and shaped in Ireland by two American abolitionists, the African-American Charles Lenox Remond and the European-American John Anderson Collins, together with members of the Hibernian Anti-Slavery Society.[79] It was a simple device – an "Address from the People of Ireland to Their Countrymen and Countrywomen in America." For some four months, the Irish abolitionists and repealers organized and supported a campaign to collect signatures to the Address. In addition to O'Connell, signers included two other figures revered among Irish-American Catholics: the Capuchin father Theobald Mathew, of Tipperary and Cork, the leader of the campaign against alcohol addiction, and the historian of the rebellion of 1798, Richard Robert Madden.[80]

Remond was the tireless featured speaker at meetings throughout most of Ireland. Starting in Dublin, he enthralled and enthused audiences in Cork, Waterford, Wexford, Limerick, Belfast and elsewhere. Night after night, this descendant of American Revolutionary War forebears poured out testimony and logic and historical example against the chattel-bondage in which African-Americans were held in the South, and no less against the humiliation of the petty and gross racial discrimination to which African-Americans were systematically subjected in the "free" states of the North. Understandably given to bitterness, he was nevertheless energized by the warmth of his reception by the Irish people, and by the sympathetic coverage of his appearance in the Irish press. During Remond's tour, sixty thousand people subscribed their names to the Address, and in the following year another ten thousand did so. As Remond embarked for America at the end of his tour in mid-December, he said, "Never were my hopes higher, my expectations stronger, or my zeal more ardent, than at present. Since my travels in Ireland . . ."[81]

Those high hopes, expectations and zeal were shared by the Boston abolitionists. Garrison said: "The Irish Address, I trust, is to be the means of breaking up a stupendous conspiracy, which I believe is going on between the leading Irish demagogues, the leading pseudo-Democrats and the Southern slaveholders."[82] Within days of Remond's return to America with the precious scroll, it was formally presented at a meeting of five thousand people, "a third of them Irishmen,"[83] at historic Faneuil Hall in Boston. The enthusiastic audience was addressed by Garrison, Wendell Phillips and George Bradburn, the "half-Irish" leader of the Massachusetts Anti-slavery Society. Thus began a campaign that would last for four years,[84] a strategy well conceived but one that failed in its purpose.

Indeed its only effect was an unintended one, the production of a terminal crisis in the American Repeal Association, which attempted to combine repeal with cordiality to the slaveholders. The American repealers were instructed by the National Loyal Repeal Association in Ireland that no anti-abolition conditions were to be attached to financial or political support for repeal. The American repealers held two national conventions, one in Philadelphia in February 1842 and the other in New York in September of the following year. Overriding the objections of a tiny number of courageous supporters of the anti-slavery Address, the conventions rejected O'Connell's attacks on American slaveholders. To emphasize the point, the second gathering chose as its presiding officer Robert Tyler, son of the slaveholding and slavery-upholding President John Tyler.[85] Thus, at the very moment the Repeal movement was confronting the British government with the most serious crisis it had ever faced in Ireland, the Irish-American repeal organizations were assailing O'Connell for his opposition to racial oppression. One copiously annotated study summarizes the outcome as follows: "O'Connell's repeated denunciations of American Negro slavery alienated segments of Irish American opinion ... [therefore] almost all Irish-American Repeal Associations, as well as Bishop John Hughes of New York ... repudiated O'Connell's statements, and some Repeal societies actually dissolved."[86] The delegates to the National Repeal Convention in Philadelphia in 1842 unanimously rejected "the connection of the two subjects," namely repeal and abolition. The chief debate was whether simply not to be diverted by O'Connell's abolitionism, while continuing to revere him as "the Liberator"; or explicitly to repudiate O'Connell on that issue regardless of "whatever the Irish may think." Irish-Americans were said to be "too grateful ... to the land of their adoption" to follow the Irish abolitionist lead.[87] O'Connell found a metaphor in the course taken by the head of the Philadelphia repeal organization who abandoned repeal work upon becoming married to a slaveowner.[88]

O'Connell and the Cincinnati Repeal Association

The controversy intensified between the American repealers and O'Connell even as the issue of repeal was reaching its climax in Ireland. Through it all – through a tiff with Garrison, through the catastrophe of Clontarf, through the rising challenge of the Young Irelanders, who questioned the priority given to abolition – through it all O'Connell continued to strike out against racial oppression and its corrupting influence on Irish-Americans. The matter was brought to a head by a letter from the Cincinnati Repeal Association, dated 28 August 1843. The Cincinnati repealers were blunt, speaking the language of the slaveholders without apology: the Negro was of a lower natural order than "whites", they said, slavery was his proper social condition, and, they asserted, "the two races cannot exist on equal terms under our government and institutions." The cause of repeal could not survive in America unless it repudiated O'Connell and the Address.

O'Connell delivered an impromptu oral refutation of the Cincinnati letter when it was read at a meeting of the Repeal Association in Dublin; a few weeks later, commissioned by the association, he sent a written reply.[89] The synopsis attempted here hardly suggests the perspicacity and passion of the statement; yet it may give an inkling perhaps of the oratorical power that could engage a throng of hundreds of thousands in rapt attention, although, with one exception, it omits the humorous sallies often displayed on those occasions. Even in synopsis it suggests the need for a more critical examination of the facile justifications put forth for the rejection of the Irish abolitionist Address, since those justifications are all there in the points made by the Cincinnati pro-slavery repealers, which O'Connell so effectively refutes. Moreover, taken in its context, it remains to this day an inspirational indictment of racial oppression.

"*How*, then, can you have become so depraved?" O'Connell asks the Cincinnati repealers. Their entire letter, he charged, was "an advocacy of human bondage." Was it true that their feelings had been "made so obtuse by the air of America"? It was astounding that they, who were non-slaveholders living in a free state and thus having no "pecuniary interest" in slavery, would take the side of the slaveholders against the African-Americans; the mass of Irish-Americans, "who have not even that futile excuse, and yet justify slavery, are indefensible."

I have chosen to present the exchange in the form of a series of the Cincinnati Repealers' "Allegations" and O'Connell "Rebuttals."

Allegation 1: The abolitionists have caused the treatment of the Negro to become more harsh. *Rebuttal 1*: Not true. But if it were true, it would add to the indictment of the slaveholder, who would punish an innocent person for the offense of a third party. *Allegation 2*: The great majority, in a country where the majority rules, favors slavery. *Rebuttal 2*: If public opinion rules then, as

"Irishmen ought to do," they should work to influence the public mind in favor of the oppressed!" instead of lauding "the master as generous and humane." *Allegation 3*: The aristocrats in England would more readily accept laborers as "sheet fellows," than would "whites" of any social class in the United States consent to accept Negroes "on terms of equality." "[H]owever much humanity may lament it, we make no rash declaration when we say that the two races cannot exist on equal terms under our government and our institutions." The Negro is naturally inferior to the "white." *Rebuttal 3*: How, where it is a crime to teach even a free Negro to read, can one presume a "natural inferiority" of those so deprived? Finally, on this point, there are Negro Catholic priests in Brazil, and in Rome, and one of their number delivered a sermon before Louis Philippe, King of France. "To judge properly of the negro you must see him as educated, and treated with the respect due to a fellow-creature, uninsulted, by the filthy aristocracy of skin." *Allegation 4*: "Black and white cannot live on equal terms under the United States Constitution." *Rebuttal 4*: That argument has been disproved in Jamaica by the post-Emancipation peaceful relations between blacks and whites. Perhaps, by the way, that fact reveals a superiority of Negroes in moral qualities considering the magnanimity they have shown toward their former masters, who are compensated while the Negroes, the injured party, are not. *Allegation 5*: The abolitionists are the cause of the slaves' restlessness, and even abet the crime of horse-stealing by escaping slaves. *Rebuttal 5*: As if the Negro would not otherwise know of the miseries of slavery. Even though his, O'Connell's, knowledge of casuistry was too deficient to decide whether that would be an excusable act or not, "we are of this … quite certain, that not one of you … if he were under similar circumstances, that is, having no other means of escaping perpetual slavery, would not make free with your neighbour's horse to effectuate your just and reasonable purpose." *Allegation 6*: The happiness of 15 million white Americans depends upon the slave economy. *Rebuttal 6*: The Benthamite principle of promoting the greatest good for the greatest number is valid, and counting the African-American population the balance would come down on the anti-slavery side. *Allegation 7*: There is no reproach due to the concept of "property in men." *Rebuttal 7*: It is as if "you were speaking of beasts of the field … that makes us disclaim you as countrymen." *Allegation 8*: Many clergymen, especially Catholic clergymen, are ranged on the side of the slaveholders. *Rebuttal 8*: That is hard to believe; but in any case, "every Catholic knows how distinctly slave-holding, and especially slave-trading, is condemned by the Catholic church," as was emphasized by the recent pronouncement of Pope Gregory XVI. That condemnation of the slave trade certainly applies to the inter-state sale of slaves and most of all to "the diabolical raising of slaves for sale."

O'Connell urged the Cincinnati repealers, and by implication Irish-Americans in general, not to come out of America but to "come out of the councils of the iniquitous, and out of the congregation of the wicked;" assist the "free persons of colour," promote educational opportunities for them, avoid selfishness based on race with regard to the free African-Americans, and support their efforts to secure equal rights and to resist the Fugitive Slave Law. Work for the abolition of slavery. Repudiate by action the reputation of "being the worst enemies of the men of colour," in order that it "shall be atoned for, and blotted out and effaced forever."

How the Sea-change was Wrought

In 1842, Irish-American abolitionist James Canning Fuller sadly observed:

> ... however true to liberty an Irishman's heart is, when it beats on his own native soil, ... on his emigration to America, circumstances and influences by which he becomes surrounded, in too many cases warp his judgment, and bias his heart.[1]

Why? That is the question. How was wrought this sea-change in so many immigrant Irish-Americans? What were those fateful "circumstances and influences"?

Before proceeding, it must be emphasized that there *was* a change. Make due allowance for O'Connell's affiliations with the English Whigs. Make due allowance for the incident of O'Connell's "disavowal" of Garrison's brand of abolitionism, prompted by reports of anti-Catholic religious slights. Make due allowance for the Young Irelanders' criticism of O'Connell for, as they saw it, not giving the proper priority to the struggle for repeal over the cause of abolition. Make due allowance, finally, for the subsequent American "white backlash" that produced its effect to some degree in Ireland at the time of the Civil War in the United States.[2] Indisputable facts remain.

O'Connell's never-failing advocacy of abolition, while he lived, probably reached as many people in Ireland and Britain as did abolitionists in the United States. The Loyal National Repeal Association, the official repeal organization in Ireland, actively associated itself with the work of the Hibernian Anti-Slavery Society, the chief organized form of the abolitionist movement in Ireland. The Repeal Association published a collection of numerous of its denunciations of "the hideous system" of American slavery.[3] In the United States, on the other hand, as we have noted, the Repeal Associations overwhelmingly repudiated the call to stand with the abolitionists.

The majority of the signers of the Irish Address urging Irish-Americans to stand by the abolitionists were Catholics.[4] One collector claimed to have obtained the signatures of one Catholic bishop and seventy-two Catholic priests.[5] The "first inquiries" of a Catholic priest in Ireland to an American woman evangelist "were concerning American slavery. Its principles and practices he abhorred, and he could not comprehend its existence in a republican country."[6] But in the United States authoritative Irish-Americans, in the clergy, in the press and in the legal profession, maintained an unrelenting attack against abolitionists, coupling it with a "patriotic" defense of the "institution" of slavery on constitutional grounds.

Perhaps the most graphic illustration of the contrast is to be noted in the treatment of African-American abolitionists such as Charles Lenox Remond in 1841, and Frederick Douglass four years later. I have noted Remond's buoyant reaction to his four-month campaign as the guest of the Irish abolitionists. Douglass, at the end of his four-month lecture tour of Ireland, wrote to Garrison that he had spent "some of the happiest moments of [his] life since landing in this country." He went on to mention "the warm and generous cooperation . . . the glorious enthusiasm with which thousands have flocked to hear [his message] . . . the kind hospitality constantly proffered me by persons of the highest rank in society . . . and the entire absence of every thing that looked like prejudice against me, on account of the color of my skin."[7] At a repeal meeting at Conciliation Hall in Dublin, Daniel O'Connell introduced Douglass as "the Black O'Connell of the United States."[8] But in their own homeland these men were not only subjected to the white-supremacist indignities that were the common lot of free African-Americans, but as African-American lecturers they were time and again subjected to special harassment, sometimes life-threatening.

These contrasts need to be stressed because the prevailing historiographical consensus takes note of O'Connell's abolitionism and the Irish "Address . . . to Fellow Countrymen and Countrywomen in America" only to minimize their significance. Historians have apparently felt justified in this neglect by the mere fact that the anti-slavery appeals from Ireland were repudiated by Irish-Americans. Their explanation of the sea-change, therefore, tends to be little more than an uncritical acceptance of the self-justifying rationale advanced by the original repudiators themselves.

The Two-front Attack on Abolitionism among Irish-Americans

The Irish abolitionist Address was met by a two-pronged campaign, directed, as it were, against the "Catholic-Irish" front and the "white worker" front respectively. The main burden of the attack on the "Irish" front was carried by what may be called the Irish-American establishment, the Catholic hierarchy, led by John Hughes, bishop and archbishop, together with the official and the unofficial Irish Catholic press.[9] Reinforcement was supplied by certain Young Irelanders exiled following the defeat of the brief rising of 1848. Their role was circumscribed, however, as a result of the censure to which they were soon subjected by the Irish-American establishment for their "red republicanism."

John Mitchel and Thomas Francis Meagher were the most notable figures in this Irish nationalist contingent.[10] On the "white worker" front the counter-attack was carried mainly by the Jacksonian Democratic Party nationally, and its local New York form, Tammany Hall. The Democratic Party was the preferred party of the plantation bourgeoisie who, as we have noted, had benefited from almost unbroken ascendancy in the United States federal government from the beginning.

Attacking Abolitionism on the "Catholic-Irish" Front

Archbishop Hughes was a single-minded American organizer of Roman Catholicism, which in the interest of combining central authority with all-nation inclusiveness followed a strict policy of avoiding conflicts with authority, wherever the Church found acceptance of its own authority, under a commodious Caesar-and-God tent.[11] This was the root of a pandemic political conservatism, a tradition to which the American Catholic Church was determined to adhere. "The spirit of the Catholic Church is eminently conservative," said one typical pastoral letter, justifying the refusal to "take sides" on the slavery question on the grounds of preserving "the unity of spirit" of the Church.[12] John Kelly, the only Catholic member of the United States Congress, speaking in the House of Representatives in 1857 pledged that "the Catholics of the United States," responding to "a higher power which has commanded them to 'give unto Caesar the things that are Caesar's,'" would avoid the councils of the "Abolitionists" and "fanatics."[13] The New York Catholic newspaper *Freeman's Journal* thought that by rights *Uncle Tom's Cabin* ought to be put on the Vatican's index of forbidden books since its abolitionism was just an American version of "Red Republicanism."[14]

The proclivity to worship authority was no less fundamental to Protestants, but for them, with generally more homogeneous constituencies, centralist organiza-tional authority was not the critical problem that it was for Catholicism. The Protestant tradition was one of a succession of hivings-off of dissenters from a previous church authority. Such schisms were much harder to accommodate in Catholicism, tolerated by constitutional guarantees but nevertheless beset by the erosive proselytizing efforts of the Protestant majority,[15] and by "anti-popery" fulminations on a local scale. Hughes met the situation by strict repression of even potential schismatic tendencies. In 1856, for instance, Hughes, by then Archbishop of New York and "the most prominent American Catholic prelate,"[16] advised Catholic periodicals "that they shall not presume to draw odious comparisons, and publish them, between the [Catholic] clergy of one section of the country and those of another."[17]

But the big problem was the abolition issue in a country whose government was traditionally dominated by slaveholders. Hughes could see that abolition-ism, often with ministers themselves as its protagonists, was putting a divisive pressure on Protestant congregations of various denominations.[18] The New Orleans *Catholic Mirror* was proud that the Catholic Church in America had avoided the pitfalls of "Protestant moral theology . . . [that] varies with degrees of latitude."[19]

But American Catholic Church authorities found it politic to deny or ignore the degrees of *longitude* that increasingly separated them from the pronouncements of Church authorities in continental Europe, beginning with Pope Gregory XVI's Apostolic Letter of 1839 and followed by statements of national Church leaders. In the name of Christ, the Pope "vehemently admonish[ed] and adjure[ed]" Christians not

> to molest Indians, negroes, or other men of this sort; or to spoil them of their goods, or to reduce them to slavery; or to extend help or favor to others who perpetrate such things against them; or to exercise that inhuman trade by which negroes, as if they were not men, but mere animals, howsoever reduced to slavery, are . . . bought, sold, and doomed sometimes to the most severe and exhausting labors.[20]

Bishop England of Charleston, South Carolina, wrote a series of long letters to John Forsyth of Georgia, Secretary of State under both Jackson and Van Buren, which soon were edited for "our fellow citizens of Irish origin" in refutation of the abolitionism of Daniel O'Connell. England, like Hughes Irish-born, argued that the Pope was merely condemning the international slave trade, and meant nothing hostile to "domestic slavery,"[21] as if "chattels" would be other than objects of sale and purchase, when he knew well that capitalist commodity production based on slave labor could not possibly exist without "slave trading" such as regularly occurred virtually on his own doorstep. In sharp contrast, Madeleine Rice documents the fact that "Catholic opinion abroad was coming more and more to outright condemnation of slavery."[22]

If the Union itself were to be split into two nations over the deep-running moral issue of racial slavery, the American Catholic Church would be presented with a painful dilemma. Either the essential unity of the Church would be destroyed over a moral issue or, in either the South or the North, it would stand in minority opposition to the civil authority.[23]

And so it came to pass, at some point in his post-Leander career, that Hughes found it advisable to be an organization man in a second sense, in relating to the predominately Protestant American, slaveholder-dominated society in general, that is, the "white race." Leader and authority that he was, he became a most influential foe of abolition and defender of white-race privileges.

A dramatic encounter between Hughes and O'Connell occurred in 1840. The bishop secured an introduction to O'Connell in London, "with a determination," as Hughes later recorded, "to have a struggle" with O'Connell on the issue of his abolitionism.[24] The account, slightly abridged here, is as biographer Hassard found it set down by Hughes himself.

"[W]hile you have many friends in America," [said Hughes] "you have some who are much displeased with certain of your public remarks."

And he asked, "Which?"

"Well," I replied, ". . . [T]hey think you are too severe upon . . . slavery."

[O'Connell] paused, and said: "It would be strange, indeed, if I should not be the friend of the slave throughout the world – I, who was born a slave myself."

"He silenced me," Hughes wrote, "although he did not convince me."[25] Regrettably, this repression of his views did not last.

As archbishop, Hughes presented his view of the position of the Catholic Church in the United States (more especially the New York diocese) and his own role in it in a letter he submitted to the Vatican in 1858.

... *my* lot was cast in the great metropolis. Catholics were surrounded by inducements to diverge from the unity of the Church.... [Therefore I] found it expedient to stand up among them, as their ... chief; to warn them ... to repel the spirit of faction.... [and] to convince their judgment ... in regard to public questions.... [But due to my influence] New York acquired a certain kind of general predominancy in the minds of Catholics. What was done at New York, or said by me, was taken to be true for every place else as well as this. And thus, through the medium of the newspapers, rather than from any direct instruction or guidance on the part of the local ecclesiastical authority, a certain tone and feeling became prevalent among the Catholics.[26]

Hughes regarded the Irish immigrant as the "mainstay" of the Church in the United States.[27] He associated this belief with the fact that, "It is only when he has the consolation of his religion within his reach that he feels comparatively happy in his new position."[28] It was his assessment of the special importance of "the metropolis," and of the Irish as the basic membership of the diocese, that, it is generally believed, led him to disapprove sternly of proposals for the establishment of Catholic colonies[29] for the relief of the congested living conditions of the misplaced Irish peasants in New York.[30]

Though Hughes opposed the dispersal of New York Catholics by westward migration, he at the same time enjoined his Irish-American flock to "merge socially and politically with the American people." That he did mean white people was clear from the inveterate opposition he expressed toward abolitionists, and his "determination to struggle" with O'Connell on the question of slavery. As was the fashion among American Catholic prelates, Hughes would generally make a formal obeisance in the direction of Gregory XVI's anti-slavery edict by saying he was not an advocate of slavery. But the substance of his actions and of his frequent denunciations of abolitionism were not calculated to "convince the judgment" of Irish Catholics to oppose the bondage of the African-American; quite the contrary.

After visits to the Spanish sugar slave colony of Cuba and the American

South in 1853, and several other Southern visits during which he was a sometime plantation guest, Hughes defended the international slave trade in classical slaveholder terms.[31] In May 1854, Hughes delivered a sermon at St Patrick's Cathedral in which he spoke of his 1853 trip. Taking as his text John 10:11–16, he discussed slavery in terms of the slaveholder's endowment by God to be a shepherd over his flock of slaves. "Is not the father of the family invested with the power of god that he is a sovereign, commanding and expecting to be obeyed, as he should?" he analogized. All God demanded was that the shepherd exert a good Christian influence on the slaves. Hughes was convinced that the lot of the Africans was improved by being kidnapped and enslaved in America. He was reinforced in this opinion by the fact that when he had asked plantation slaves whether they would prefer to stay as they were in America or to go back to Africa, they had unanimously told him that they much preferred being slaves in America. He apparently did not ask them whether they would prefer freedom to bondage.[32] From the beginning of the Civil War, Hughes condemned the very idea that the abolition of slavery might be a war aim, saying Irish-Americans would not fight for such a cause, adding that if Lincoln had such an intention, he ought to resign the presidency.[33] Hughes denounced the Emancipation Proclamation before the ink was dry.[34] And he blamed the New York Draft Riots of the summer of 1863 on the belief that the government intended to make Negroes equal to white men.[35]

The Irish-American establishment was determined to prevent the spread of the influence of abolitionism through the Irish abolitionist Address. They first sought to asperse the authenticity of O'Connell's signature, and to impute fraud to the African-American bringer of the news and his fellow American abolitionists. They surely knew from Bishop Hughes's encounter with O'Connell in 1840 that this pretense could not be maintained. In any case, they quickly shifted to more substantive questions.

They demanded that Irish-Americans repudiate the Irish abolitionist Address on two general grounds, namely, loyalty to the United States and loyalty to the anti-Protestant interest. The Irish-Americans were to disregard the appeal to be brethren to the racially oppressed African-Americans because it was an unwarranted interference in American affairs, involvement in which would bring heavy censure upon Irish-Americans for being "un-American." At best this was advice to silently "pass by on the other side"[36] from where the Negro lay in chains. But among those who were not silent on the issue, there was almost unanimity in identifying American "patriotism" with support of the slavery-sanctifying United States Constitution.

The abolitionist cause was to be sternly resisted as a hive of anti-Catholicism, since many of the abolitionists, African-American and European-American, also held strong Protestant convictions. As noted above, O'Connell had no difficulty in dealing with the issue, and Pope Gregory XVI felt no need to bring the subject up. It was true, of course, that the relative strengths of the contending branches of Christianity in the United States were the opposite of what they had been in Ireland, where the Protestant evangelists were few and where the Protestant Ascendancy, the Church of Ireland and the yeomanry were not really interested in Protestantizing the Catholic masses. In the United States the Catholics were not only in a permanent minority, they were beset by the Know-Nothing movement and generally subjected to the prejudices of the general Protestant majority. Views hostile to the Catholic Church were evident among abolitionists.[37] O'Connell, in the course of his reply to the Cincinnati repealers, noted that "there are amongst the abolitionists, many wicked and calumniating enemies of Catholicity and the Irish, especially in that most intolerant class, the Wesleyan Methodists."[38] But it is fair to note that the abolitionists were no less severe with pro-slavery attitudes in Protestant churches. The New England Anti-slavery Society in 1841 made no Protestant exception in declaring that "the church and clergy of the United States, as a whole, constitute a gross brotherhood of thieves, inasmuch as they countenance the highest kind of theft, i.e., man-stealing."[39] Abolitionists were not interested in winning Catholics to Protestantism; they were busy trying to "convert" the whole population to the anti-slavery cause. On the other hand, most of the slaveholders and the political leaders were Protestant, even as the abolitionist leaders were. Evangelism may not have in all cases been the slaveholders' style, but when the Irish Address was first broached in the United States, some slaveholders even reacted by advocating an end to immigration from Ireland.[40] How then did the Irish-American mistrust of Protestantism come to be translated by the Irish-American establishment into fervent support of Protestant slaveholders? The apparent inconsistency is seen to be explained by the principle of "merger" with the "white" people. By this light, the Protestantism of the abolitionists was the threat to be stressed, rather than the Protestantism of the defenders of slavery.

Within the United States Catholic Church there was no desire to promote a revolutionary overthrow of British rule in Ireland, but when the time came it would support Vatican policy favoring encouragement of the United States as a counterweight to perfidious Albion.[41] To that extent they shared with some Young Ireland exiles the strategic principle that "the enemy of my enemy is my friend." Even though the Church anathematized the Young Irelanders as "red republicans," Young Irelanders in the United States reinforced the establishment's position; they condemned O'Connell's abolitionism for antagonizing the United States, from whom they expected to get direct or indirect support in throwing the British out of Ireland.[42] This was an open avowal of alliance with the slaveholders.

Some of the Young Irelander exiles in the United States entered into that spirit with a vengeance. John Mitchel, who considered O'Connell, "next to the British Government, the worst enemy that Ireland ever had, or rather the most fatal friend,"[43] was the most extreme example. He published a stridently anti-Negro weekly newspaper, the *Citizen*, in which he delivered himself of these sentiments:

> We deny that it is a crime, or a wrong, or even a peccadillo, to hold slaves, to buy slaves, to keep slaves to their work by flogging or other needful coercion.... we, for our part, wish we had a good plantation, well-stocked with healthy negroes.[44]

Another well-known post-1848 Irish exile, Francis Meagher, was a typical anti-Negro Democrat up to the time of the Civil War. He published the *Irish News* wherein he charged the abolitionists with "hostility to our republican form of government by their assaults on the domestic institutions of the South."[45]

The notable lack of success of this approach to Irish liberation by way of Anglo-American antagonism would seem to refute it as a strategy for overthrowing British rule in Ireland.[46] The anti-British angle served most significantly as an excuse for the pro-slavery stand among Irish-Americans, rather than as a cause of it. Most of the political exiles found "more practical and profitable ways to use their nationalism," says Kerby Miller. "Many former Young Irelanders drifted into Democratic politics, using their talents and reputations to cement emigrant loyalties to the party of Jackson."[47]

The Attack on the "White Worker" Front

The desire of the Protestant slaveholders to turn Catholic Irish-Americans against the abolitionism of the Catholic Liberator, O'Connell, has been noted. But that negative stimulus of withholding support for repeal was too little and too remote to account for the emergence of the predominant pro-slavery Irish-American politics of the ante-bellum and Civil War periods.

The America to which these Irish immigrants came was already constructed on the principle of racial oppression, including the white-skin privileges of laboring-class European-Americans. If Irish-Americans rejected the heritage represented by O'Connell and the Address, and if they were frequently identified with the most hostile actions against Negroes in the Northern cities, it was basically because they – like immigrants from Germany, France, England, Scotland and Scandinavia – accepted their place in the white-race system of social control and claimed the racial privileges entailed by it. Before the Civil War, the main basic white-skin privileges were: (1) the presumption of liberty; (2) the right of immigration and naturalization; and (3) the right to vote.[48] The first two of these were in place before the Jacksonian phenomenon, the third was crafted by it.

The presumption of liberty distinguished the poorest of European-Americans from the free African-American. Under the white-race system of social control, even the most destitute of European-Americans were expected to exercise this racial prerogative by supporting the enforcement of the Fugitive Slave Law.

The United States Constitution implicity made immigration a white-skin privilege, when in Article I, Section 9, Europeans were classed as migrants whilst Africans were classed as imports. Naturalization statutes enacted, amended and re-enacted before the Civil War repeated the phraseology of the original "Act to establish an uniform Rule of Naturalization" signed into law on 26 March 1790, providing that "any alien, being a free white person ... may be admitted to become a citizen" of the United States.[49] Seen in historical context, this "whites"-only immigration policy was a corollary of another constitutional provision which was the basis of the Fugitive Slave Laws that effectively restricted the presumption of liberty to European-Americans, by providing that any "person held to service in one State ... escaping into another ... shall be delivered up" to the owner (Article 4, Section 2, paragraph 2).

This privilege of immigration carried with it a status entirely new to the newcomers; the moment they set foot on United States soil, however lowly their social status might otherwise be they were endowed with all the immunities, rights and privileges of "American whites." By the same token they were implicitly enrolled in the system of racial oppression of all African-Americans, which the ruling slaveowning plantation bourgeoisie first imposed during the country's colonial pre-history in order to maintain effective social control.

From "Irish" to "white American"

The Jacksonians made politics "practical" by means of the "spoils system," the egregious exploitation of political jobbery and systematic patronage. Jackson, the founder of the system, construed his obligation to the country in strictly partisan terms: "I can have no other view," he said, "but to administer the government in such a way as will strengthen the democratic party."[50] This practice was essential in launching the big-city machine politics in the United States.

Political scientists have long since identified Jacksonianism with the spoils system. But no one acquainted with the history of the Irish Protestant Parliament in the eighteenth century, or the open vote-buying and pocket boroughs that characterized English politics before the assertion of the Chartist influence in the nineteenth century, could be especially horrified by the corruption of Jackson's program for establishing the same sort of principle on a national scale in the United States. Indeed, Arthur M. Schlesinger Jr, author of the most popular history of the era, defends the practice as essential to Jackson's program, which Schlesinger views favorably as bringing about a "democratic" social transformation of United States politics.[51]

Regrettably, critics and defenders alike generally seem to ignore the most historically significant fact about the spoils system, namely that it was first of all a "white-race" spoils system. At the outset, it was given this character by the "manhood suffrage" laws (ending the property qualification for voting), adopted mostly between 1820 and 1830, which recognized only "whites" as "men." Either African-Americans were explicitly excluded from voting rights under this "sweeping democratic reform," or they were subject to special property qualification designed to have the same practical effect, even in states where they had historically exercised that right.[52] This policy was of key importance for recruiting a labor base in the North for slaveholder dominance of the United States government in general, and for assuring active or passive support in the enforcement of the Fugitive Slave Law as a constitutional principle.

In regard to "white" privileges in general, the Irish-American position did not differ from that of other European-Americans. The special significance of the Irish-American case was that: (1) they were the largest immigrant group in the ante-bellum period; (2) they explicitly rejected their own national heritage to become part of the system of "white" racial oppression of African-Americans; and (3) by virtue of their concentration in Northern cities – above all, New York, the locale of the most important Northern links with the plantation bourgeoisie – they became a key factor in national politics.

In the early 1820s, a discredited aristocratic pro-slavery leadership of Tammany Hall was replaced by a prototypical Jacksonian leadership: mass-oriented, "democratic," but again, aligned with the plantation bourgeoisie. Thenceforward, "Throughout the slavery agitation up to the firing on Fort Sumter," wrote historian Gustavus Myers, "the South had no firmer supporter than Tammany."[53]

This new departure at Tammany Hall coincided with the beginning of a sharp rise in Catholic Irish immigration and the granting of "white" manhood suffrage. The number of Irish immigrants nearly doubled on an average every half-decade from 1821 to 1850,[54] and they settled in New York in inordinate proportions. They came from an Ireland where Catholics had a long history of being aliens in their own land or, after 1829, only second-class citizens. But Catholics entered the United States eligible, under the general provisions of the naturalization laws, to receive the full and unlimited rights of citizenship, on an equal legal footing with Protestants. They came from an Ireland where, as a part of Catholic Emancipation, the voting rights of forty-shilling freeholders were taken away in 1829, after a period of thirty-six years, and a much more restricted franchise was imposed.[55] In the United States they were entering they would, on becoming citizens, be able to vote, without property qualifications.

"White" suffrage and African-American disfranchisement

Though barred from the militia many New York Negroes served as volunteers in the War of 1812 against Britain. They were among the African-American one-fourth of the American forces in Perry's command at the Battle of Lake Erie, 10 April 1813, under the famous pennant-borne resolve "Don't give up the ship!" For forty years African-Americans had been voting on the same basis as other men who paid taxes or owned fifty dollars' worth of real estate or paid an annual rent of five dollars. As voters, they gave their allegiance to the Federalist Party because of its stand in favor of ending slavery and for equal rights for free African-Americans. In more than one election (in 1810 in Brooklyn, and in 1813 in New York, for instance) the outcome was decided by the margin provided by African-American voters.[56] The 1821 New York State Constitutional Convention effectively disfranchised African-Americans by requiring them (and only them) to be freeholders worth $250.[57]

Resistance to this disfranchisement of African-Americans continued to play a central part in New York politics for a quarter of a century.[58] Attempts to restore those rights were made in constitutional conventions in 1826 and 1846, only to be defeated each time primarily by the exertions of Tammany Democrats. It would take a great civil war to repeal that discriminatory law, which was formally done in 1870, though still, however, against Tammany opposition.[59] Fox, the historian of the subject, notes two facts especially relevant to my thesis. The "white" laborers, he writes, "prized the luxury of feeling themselves better than the Negro." Second, the New York City wards in which "the anti-Negro vote was strongest, were the sixth and fourteenth, which had the largest number of immigrant citizens,"[60] and most of the new voters were Irish-Americans. This was certainly so in the Sixth Ward[61] which, in 1848, "gave the largest anti-Negro vote ... [and] was the very citadel of Tammany."[62]

The historical affinity of the generality of Irish-Americans and Tammany Hall[63] was thus from the beginning conditioned on denial of the rights of African-Americans, and on a concomitant attachment to the national program of the slaveholders. The Tammany machine did its part in a number of ways. It facilitated naturalization of Irish immigrants, with careless regard for the letter of the law, in order to hasten the inauguration of the Irish immigrants into slaveholder electoral service.[64] Graft-rich government contracts afforded benefits to Irish-American ward heelers, who had important local appointive powers, including appointment of the police in each ward.[65] The merest Irish voter was encouraged in his loyalty by little favors, especially at election time, such as early or temporary release from prison,[66] or by payments in money or in kind at the ward heeler's saloon.[67] (This chance to market his franchise was just what many an immigrant had lost as insurance against eviction in the wake of Catholic Emancipation.) The whitening effect in due course became manifest. Though the poor Irish-Catholics were not immediately delivered from their low-caste status in Protestant Anglo-America, these perquisites and privileges were intended and defended – not as Irish-American rights, but as "white men's" rights. Along the way, the sense of white-race identity was regularly reinforced by pro-slavery lectures sponsored by Tammany. Among the guests at celebrations of the slavery-extending Mexican War were such eminent Southerners as President James Polk and Sam Houston of Texas, along with Generals Henry Martin Foote and Leslie Combs, enthusiastic veterans of that invasion.[68]

Irish-American Voters and the Annexation of Texas

The counter-attack against the abolitionist appeals from Ireland, especially through the "white" spoils system, proved to be a key factor in one history-shaping political victory of the slaveholders, the presidential election of 1844, in which the leading question was whether or not the United States should annex Texas.[69]

American abolitionist opposition to annexation had the support of Daniel O'Connell who, despite opposition from Young Irelanders,[70] denounced the slaveholders' designs on Mexican territory as the scheme of a "gang of land pirates" which, among other ills, would increase the political base of the slaveholders in national affairs. He recommended that the Mexican government "form a colony of free persons of colour ... [which] would be a refuge for free men of colour of the United States who are naturally enough disgusted with the paltry injustice of being called 'free' while they are deprived of all the practical rights of freedom," to oppose the incursions of the "white monsters."[71]

The Democratic Party candidate, James K. Polk, was aggressively committed to annexation. The Democrats' hand was strengthened among Irish-Americans not only by their "white" spoils system, but specifically by success in linking anti-abolitionism with the anti-British cause, by playing up British support for the establishment of an independent Texas on abolitionist principles. The Whig Party candidate, Henry Clay, had forfeited the Northern anti-slavery vote by being (as historian Freehling calls him) "a Whig for all regions"[72] in his two-faced behavior regarding annexation. But, as noted above,[73] he was determined to compete with the Democrats for the vote of the "white workers," including explicitly the Irish and the Germans, by promising to protect their white-skin privileges *vis-à-vis* African-Americans.

The New York vote was expected to be crucial, and it proved to be so. Polk won with an electoral college vote of 170 to Clay's 105, the thirty-six New York votes supplying the margin of victory. Polk won in New York by a margin of only 5,016 out of a total popular vote of 470,000, of which

15,012 were cast for the abolitionist Liberty Party candidate, James G. Birney. In view of the calculated risk taken with regard to the anti-slavery voters, it is fair to say that New York's Irish-Americans, who (far more than German-Americans) voted solidly for the Democrats, decided the outcome of the national election. That conclusion is supported by the lament of Clay's vice-presidential running mate, Theodore Frehlinghuysen of New York, five days after the election.

> [T]he foreign vote was tremendous. More than three thousand, it is confidently said, have been naturalized in this city, alone, since the first of October. It is an alarming fact that this foreign vote has decided the great question of American policy.[74]

The Irish-American voters of New York had not only opted for the "filthy aristocracy of skin," but had become a key factor in national politics, all in fulfillment of the strategic plan of the slaveholders as formulated by John Randolph a quarter of a century before (see page 163).

Acting as "Whites"

Charles Spencer of Mississippi, spying out the North some five weeks after Lincoln's election in November 1860, reported that the slaveholders could "safely rely on" the Irish of New York because "they hate the [African-American] as they do the devil."[75] The die was cast for war, which began with secession of Southern states from the Union, followed by the rebel attack on the Federal Fort Sumter in April 1861. In effective coordination with the slaveholder Confederacy, pro-slavery, anti-Negro elements in the North intensified agitation on the "Catholic-Irish" and the "white worker" fronts. A major role in that effort was taken by the publications directed mainly at a Catholic Irish-American readership in New York, such as the *New York Freeman's Journal* (later *Freeman's Journal and Catholic Register*), *Irish-American*, *Irish News*, and *Citizen* (later *Caucasian*).[76]

The campaign produced a combination of white-supremacist rallies, anti-abolitionist exhortations, pronouncements aimed at undermining the anti-Confederate cause, physical assaults on African-Americans, a "dress rehearsal" riot in south Brooklyn in August 1862 and the culminating Draft Riot/"white" pogrom of July 1863.[77] The following selected chronology may serve to indicate the unrelenting intensity of the campaign.

7 January 1861 – The Democrat Mayor Fernando Wood, expressing the "common sympathy" felt for the slaveholders by the people he represents, proposes the secession of New York City from the United States.[78]

15 January 1861 – A mass meeting, "well attended", at Brooks Hall, is largely officered by "Irish personnel" and "engineered" by the infamous Democratic leader Isaiah Rynders, who is implicated as US Marshal in the escape of a convicted New York slave-trader; and by R. G. Horton, co-conspirator in the frustrated Confederate coup in New York of November 1864. The meeting denounces "the black Republican Party" for attempting to overthrow the Constitution in order "to reduce white men to a forbidden level with Negroes." Its manifesto opens with the call, "Workingmen Arouse!"[79]

7 May 1861 – Twenty-five days after the attack on Fort Sumter, and twenty-two days after Lincoln's call for 75,000 volunteers to fight the insurrection, Archbishop Hughes, writing to a Southern bishop, takes a stand of "non-interference" in the war; he neither encourages "Catholics to take part in it," nor advises them "not to do so."[80]

18 May 1861 – Archbishop John Hughes declares that any effort by the government to abolish slavery would be a violation of the United States Constitution, and that if such be the intention, President Lincoln should forthwith resign from office.[81]

16 June 1861 – The Democratic Party newspaper, the *Leader*, upon hearing that an African-American has been hired at the New York United States Custom Office in the place of a "white" man, threatens that if the report proves true, "it would take more than honied words to quiet . . . the entire race of white men [who] would rise in vindictive rebellion against it."[82]

October 1861 – Archbishop Hughes writes to Secretary of War Simon Cameron that if "the purpose of the war is the abolition of slavery in the South," then "among a certain class [read, Irish Catholics], it would make the business of recruiting slack indeed."[83]

12 October 1861 – The *Metropolitan Record*, Archbishop Hughes's "official organ," in an editorial personally written by Hughes declares that Catholics will fight for the Union, but not for ending slavery, that slavery exists by "Divine permission of God's providence;" Hughes even defends the international slave trade, failing to see any "crime . . . or moral transgression of the law of God" in such a transaction; rather, indeed, it is in the end a good way "for humane masters to . . . take care of these unfortunate people." Although it is perhaps sad that the slavery should be transmitted to the children, that is no worse than the Divine command to eat bread in the sweat of the brow borne by "men who are living now who had no part in the commission of original sin."[84]

27 November 1861 – The Democratic Mayor of New York Fernando Wood denounces the federal government as having provoked the war.[85]

18 January 1862 – The *Metropolitan Record* declares that, for the "mechanics and labourers of our country," abolition of slavery, "would be the worst evil that could befall them," because "the influx of negro labour on the Northern market would reduce them to a condition worse than that of the pauperized operatives of Europe."[86]

4 July 1862 – The Grand Sachem, or highest officer, of Tammany Hall, Nelson J. Waterbury, declares that the fighting spirit of the Union soldiers requires that the President "set his foot firmly on abolitionism and crush it to pieces."[87]

26 July 1862 – The *Caucasian* warns "white" workers that free Negroes are taking "their" jobs, and publishes a letter on the subject, demanding: "White Men! mechanics and workingmen of New York! how long is this state of things to exist? If you are asleep, awake! If awake, arouse! When aroused from your slumbers, act!"[88]

4 August 1862 – Acting as "whites," a mob of from two to three thousand from an Irish-American Brooklyn neighborhood force two local tobacco factories to end the employment of African-Americans. The owners of Lorillard's, where for years 250 "colored and white ... worked harmoniously side by side," surrender to the demand, discharge the Negro workers, and agree never to hire African-Americans again. Watson's, the other factory, employing 50 persons, all Negroes, is attacked by the mob, who try to burn the building down. The workers retreat to the second floor and successfully defy the attackers until police arrive. But shortly thereafter the factory is shut down.[89]

9 October 1862 – The prominent Irish-American lawyer Richard O'Gorman, speaking before the Democratic Union Association, declares that constitutionally the federal government has no more authority to "alter the relation" of slaveholder and slave than it has to alter that between parent and child or husband and wife.[90]

12 October 1862 – The *Caucasian*, under the heading, "Archbishop Hughes's Thunderbolt Against the Abolitionists," publishes from the *Metropolitan Record* of the week before Hughes's long editorial condemning the Emancipation Proclamation (announced by Lincoln about three weeks before). Hughes equates Emancipation with highway robbery, arguing that to say that slavery is the cause of the war is like saying, "that a man's carrying money on his person is the cause of his being robbed on the highway."[91]

December 1862 – Presumably without violating the confidence of the confessional, Archbishop Hughes advises Secretary of State William H. Seward that "there are men ... who say rather that *their* fighting is to be done in the streets of this city."[92]

18 July 1863 – After four days of continuous rioting and lynching of African-

Americans, by mobs composed mainly of Irish-Americans, Archbishop Hughes, at the request of the Governor, speaks to an audience numbering three or four thousand whom he has invited to congregate by his residence. Identifying with them as a Catholic and an Irishman, he urges that the rioting cease. He is in a frail condition due to an illness from which he will die within a year, and does not make any reply to anti-Negro cries from the audience.[93]

18 or 19 July 1863 – Archbishop Hughes writes to Secretary of State Seward that the real cause of the riots was not the draft, but the prospect that powerful influences were at work, disposed "to make black labor equal to white labor," and that "black labor shall have local patronage over the toil of the white man."[94]

The "Labor Competition" Rationale Re-examined

The archbishop's comment was not adding anything new to the Secretary of State's knowledge. It had been the most common justification relied upon by the perpetrators of the white-supremacism in that period. A number of historians, even as they have made valuable contributions to the study of anti-Negro attitudes and behavior on the part of Irish-American workers in the antebellum and Civil War periods, have made the assumptions characteristic of the "labor competition" rationale, accompanied almost invariably by palliative allusions to "Negro strikebreakers."[95] The remainder of this chapter is chiefly intended to offer a more critical examination than is usually given to the "labor competition" thesis.

Competition among individuals for employment is a necessary condition of the wage-labor system. Moreover, groupings, unintentionally formed by family extension, language, or locality, are commonly projected into labor-pool groupings. Even within the ranks of Catholic Irish-Americans, job competition took the form of "many a bloody brawl" between men from Cork and men from Connaught, or, again, from Ulster.[96]

In the 1800s competition occurred between groups, formed with some degree of deliberation, as "native-born" and immigrants, when Irish immigrants "sought such occupations as offered; [and] they underbid labor."[97] The nativist movement sought restrictions on immigration and naturalization because, it was said, the influx of immigrants was driving wages down.[98] Nativism, drawing on the heritage of British and Ulster Protestant Ascendancy, was mainly directed against the Catholic Irish. The movement peaked about 1845,[99] having had only a limited effect on job competition; it never reduced the inflow of immigrants.

The "labor competition" commonly alluded to in reference to the anti-Negro attitude of Irish-American "white" laborers also involved a deliberate choice, but one profoundly more significant than that which produced conflicts between native-born and immigrant, even in their most violent Protestant-versus-Catholic form.

The latter was a quarrel between factions of the "white race," which did not threaten the fundamental Constitution of the country. The former was a fight for the system of white supremacy, on which the government was founded. The Catholic *St Louis Leader* defined the difference in essentially the same way. The ascendancy of Know-Nothingism, the paper said, would bring only "temporary and local" difficulties; but a victory of the "anti-slavery Republicans" would be a forerunner of the "general and final catastrophe."[100]

New York City's foreign-born population grew steadily; in 1855, the foreign-born actually made up more than half of the city's inhabitants. The number of foreign-born rose by over 57,000 in the next five years, to nearly 384,000, of whom over 53 percent were from Ireland.[101] Fifteen thousand people a year were settling in the city,[102] more than the *total* African-American resident population. Such a rate of immigration would, of course, tend to increase "labor competition." But why should it have been "racial"?

Leaving aside workers born in the United States, Table 2 shows that the number of foreign-born "white" competitors with the Irish for employment was greater in every category than the number of African-American competitors. The overall figures for the occupations covered by the table show a 5 to 1 ratio of foreign-born "whites" to African-Americans competing with the Irish immigrants for jobs. In the most critical socio-political category, laborers, there were four times as many non-Irish foreign-born "whites," European-

Table 2 The numbers of Irish and other workers in the occupations in which Irish workers were most numerous in New York City in 1855[103]

	Foreign-born European-Americans			African-Americans
	Total	*Irish*	*Non-Irish*	
Domestic servants*	29,470	23,386	6,084	1,025
Laborers	19,783	17,426	2,357	536
Dressmakers and seamstresses	6,606	4,559	2,047	111
Waiters	2,006	1,491	515	499
Coachmen	972	805	167	102
Total	*58,837*	*47,667*	*11,170*	*2,273*

*The notice "No Irish need apply" has been more effective in discrediting anti-Irish bigotry than it was in reducing the entry of Irish workers into domestic service employment.

Americans, in the labor market as there were African-Americans. If information showing the number of native-born workers in these categories were included, the ratios of non-Irish "whites" to African-Americans would be yet higher.

The "fear of Negro job competition," so much favored as an explanation of the concentration of Irish-American workers' hostility on the African-American minority of their non-Irish competitors thus had no basis in actual fact.[104] These Irish-American workers may have been led to believe that their interest depended above all upon the exclusion of the African-American workers. But that "fear" was no more justified than the exaggerated allegations of Jesse Helms's 1990 campaign concerning the horrific consequences to be feared by "white" workers from affirmative action employment programs; nor did the existence of such fears qualify a "white" pogrom against Negro men, women and children in July 1863 as a "working-class movement."

It does not help the "labor competition" case to speak of "Negro strikebreakers" when no special mention is made of "German strikebreakers," such as those who took the jobs of Irish workers striking for higher pay and shorter hours at the Atlantic Dock in Brooklyn in 1846,[105] or other European-American strikebreakers on the Erie Railroad docks in January 1863, or the Hudson River Railroad docks two months later.[106] Both African-American and European-American strikebreakers were employed at various times, but the murderous wrath of the strikers was reserved for those of "dark skin," who were pursued by the mob crying, "Drive off the damn niggers," and "Kill the niggers."[107]

Possible alternatives to that entire historically evolved scenario were suggested in two separate events, one of which became the rule, and one of which remained an exception. Naturalized European-American workers complained of being shut out by native Americans as if the former were no more than "foreigners." "If you don't include us to get better wages," said one of their number in a letter to a labor paper of the 1850s, "you needn't expect our help." In response the labor movement "aided the immigrants and in turn sought their cooperation."[108] African-Americans in the waiters' trade in New York in 1853 demanded and won an advance in wages which put them four dollars a month ahead of the wage paid to white waiters. A meeting was held at which the white workers considered measures to secure parity. A "Negro delegate" to the meeting encouraged the white workers in their campaign.[109]

If the opportunistic use of the label "strikebreaker" is to be so selectively applied in order to excuse the adherence by Irish-American or other European-American workers to what O'Connell called "the filthy aristocracy of skin," then there should be a name for the process that drove thousands of African-Americans from jobs and from the city of New York altogether in the age of Jackson and the *ante-bellum* period.

Labor competitions given an abnormal "racial" form

Prior to 1840, a wide range of industrial employments (from longshoring to coachman), service occupations (from stableman to table-waiting), as well as domestic service in New York were "almost wholly in the hands of" African-Americans. Their wages were good relative to those of other workers. The Irish, driven into exile by famine, competed for those jobs by taking lower wages, and by the early 1850s they had made extensive inroads into those fields of employment.[110] To *assume* that it was in the nature of the case that Irish would seek to drive Negroes out, off the job, and do so on the basis of an Irish claim to a "white" identity, is to assume the Jordan–Degler assumption, that "white over black" is a memory of the blood. But that is precisely the notion that the Irish Address denied, denounced and refuted. The Leanders of Ireland remembered what racial oppression meant: the Penal Laws which reduced them to aliens in their own country, the assaults on their families, the denial of education and apprenticeships, the daily humiliations at the hands of Protestants, however lowly in the social scale. If they appealed to their countrymen and countrywomen in America to be brethren to the Negro, and to enter the struggle for abolition, it was not out of ignorance of "race" as a social motive. To the extent that Irish-Americans rejected that appeal and opted instead to stand by the slaveholders on the grounds of fear of job competition from African-Americans, the cause was not actual "job competition." Rather, the problem of job competition was cast in the mold of white supremacy as an integral part of the social control system instituted by the American slaveholders in the days of William of Orange and Queen Anne and the opening of the Penal Laws era in Ireland.

Although there was widespread discrimination in public services against African-Americans, private employers in the ante-bellum North tended, by contrast, to act as straightforward buyers of labor-power, indifferent to "racial" considerations. It was only after the Civil War that the Northern employers adopted as their own the general principle of racial discrimination in industrial employment.[111] Nevertheless, there were powerful countervailing influences: constitutional guarantees, the "white" manhood suffrage laws, and the pervasive power of the Democratic spoils system, which served to encourage the extensions of the principle of "racial" preference in employment to the North. Special mention is due to the Custom House as a bell-wether in the effort to establish the principle of "racial" preference in hiring in the North.

Control of hiring at the United States Custom House was in the hands of the national government, and consequently most of the time in the hands of the Democrats. It was "the largest single federal office in the country and was the greatest source of patronage." The Collector "had at his disposal hundreds of relatively well-paying jobs which he could distribute to the advantage of the political party or faction he represented," and "[i]t was at the Custom House that the spoils system reached its highest form of development."[112] The Custom House therefore offered an opportunity not only to build up the pro-slavery political machine; by strictly keeping employment at this government facility as a white-skin privilege, it effectively was a Northern bastion of the principle that the Negro had no job rights that a "white" person was bound to respect.

When, in the first few months of Lincoln's administration, an African-American man, Robert Vosburgh, was hired at the New York United States Custom House, the editor of the Tammany paper, the *Leader*, erupted with vituperation. His editorial, titled "A [Negro] Appointed in the Custom House," began thus: "A startling rumor has reached us, which we can scarcely credit … a *negro* has been appointed" to a job in the Custom House.[113] Since, according to long-established Democratic principles, Custom House jobs were for "whites" only, the editorial could only see Vosburgh's employment as a displacement of the "white" William O'Brien. By the fall of 1862, a number of other Negro workers had found jobs at the Custom House. A month after the issuance of the Emancipation Proclamation and ten days before the gubernatorial and congressional elections, Tammany's *Leader* thought it seasonable to charge that the continued employment of Negroes in the Custom House was a plot against the Democratic Party.[114] As we have noted, this incident was used by the Democrat press to call for "White" men to rise in "vindictive rebellion."

From true competition to "white" racial preference

In the context of the "white" spoils system, what began as a form of normally occurring wage labor competition soon developed on the Irish-American side into an assertion of the right of "white" preference. It will be noted that the Cincinnati Repeal Association spoke as "white" men in attacking O'Connell in 1843 for his denunciations of slavery; he, on the other hand, repeatedly called upon them as Irishmen to make the cause of the Negro their own. John Mitchel's *Citizen* declared in 1856, "He would be a bad Irishman who voted for the ascendancy of principles which proscribed himself, and which jeopardized the present system of a nation of white men."[115] In January 1860, the New York paper the *Irish American*, taking note of a Massachusetts cotton mill disaster which took the lives of scores of young Irish women, voiced their grievance in terms of an abuse of "white" workers.[116] A mass meeting made up mainly of Irish-American workers in New York in January 1861 declared labor to be the natural ally of the slaveholders, in opposition to any and all efforts "to reduce white men to a forbidden level with negroes."[117]

In the riots in Brooklyn and in New York to which I have referred, the mobs made up primarily of Irish-Americans did not express their demands and aims in terms of Irishness, but in the name of "white workingmen."

By 1863, "[a]lmost all longshoremen in New York City were Irish;" they were organized in the Longshoremen's Association, and resolved that dock work would be limited to "such white laborers as they see fit to permit upon the premises."[118] African-Americans were driven from the trade in which they had predominated twenty years before, not in the normal course of economic competition, but by Irish-Americans operating under the immunities of "whiteness." The African-American population had declined perhaps 16 percent between 1840 and 1860, "owing to the aroused hostility to Negroes," as one historian put it.[119] Then, between 1860 and 1865, it fell by another one-fourth, to less than ten thousand. It is sadly ironic that the Catholic proportion of the population of Belfast was reduced as a result of similar pogrom-like attacks by Protestant workers, as noted in Chapter 5.

Labor competition – the reality

It was said at the time, and has been stressed by historians, that the "white" workers were motivated mainly by a fear of the prospect of freed African-Americans coming to the North looking for work in such large numbers that the oversupply of labor would result in lower wages.[120] This explanation ignores the fact that more than two million European immigrants came into the United States in the decade before the Civil War, and two and three-quarters million in the ten years after the war,[121] of whom several hundred thousand remained in New York City. Yet no European immigrants were lynched, no "white" orphanages were burned, for fear of "competition" in the labor market. Second, to come North to escape slavery made sense, but to come North to escape freedom would not. To the extent that the Irish-American and the other "whites" were worried on this account, therefore, they should have supported the struggle of the African-American people and the abolitionists for an end to bond-servitude. This precise point was made at the time by the *New York Tribune*. The Irish-born Brigadier-General Richard Busteed directed the same argument at his fellow Irish-Americans in a speech in City Hall Park in August 1862.[122] General David Hunter, Union commander at Port Royal, South Carolina, offered free passes North for freedmen, but so few took up the offer that Hunter concluded that the idea of mass migration of freedmen was a "carefully fostered illusion." A special official investigation of the matter found that there was no basis for believing that freed Negroes were eager to leave the South.[123]

In short, strike off the chains of the African-American bond-laborers, apply the principle of "land to the tiller" with a land redistribution program in the South, and the main incentive to go North would dissolve. The story of the Negro Exodus of 1879 would in time bear out this judgment.[124] Only a protracted white-supremacist terroristic campaign intended to reimpose virtual bondage could convince African-Americans of the South to undertake a concerted effort to escape; and, then, the destination was not the Northern cities, but the farm lands of Kansas.

There was indeed a real competition between African-American bond-labor and Irish-American (and other "white") workers, that if understood would have provided a basis for a joint struggle against slavery. As DuBois put it, "[T]he black man enslaved was an even more formidable and fatal competitor than the black man free."[125] It was in the interest of the slave-labor system to maintain the white-skin privilege differential in favor of the European-American workers. At the same time, however, it was equally in the interest of the employers of wage-labor, as well as of bond-labor, that the differential be kept to no more than the minimum necessary for the purpose of keeping the European-American workers in the "white race" corral. To increase the differential beyond that degree would entail an unnecessary deduction from capitalist profits, which would be distributed by the workings of the average rate over the employers of bond-labor as well as employers of wage-labor. Furthermore, it would tend to increase the traffic on the Underground Railroad. The chains that bound the African-American thus also held down the living standards of the Irish-American slum-dweller and canal-digger as well. This underlying reality also gave a basis to the connection that the Catholic press, with hostile intent, alleged to exist between Free Soil and abolitionism. The "competition" for Western lands was between the bond-labor system and the wage-labor system. It was no coincidence that it was in 1862 that both the Homestead Act and the Emancipation Proclamation were promulgated in the interest of a war to abolish slavery.

The Pre-existing Logic

In 1864, the year that Archbishop Hughes died, Thomas Francis Meagher, with the fervor of the wartime convert to Lincoln's cause, pronounced a bitter judgment on his fellow Irish-Americans and, so it would seem, on his own former self:

> To their own discredit and degradation, they have suffered themselves to be bamboozled into being obstinate herds in the political field, contracting inveterate instincts, following with gross stupidity and the stoniest blindness certain worn out old path-ways described for them by their drivers, but never doing anything worthy of the intellectual and chivalrous reputation of their race.[126]

It was not the rank and file of Irish immigrants, however, who framed the issues in pro-slavery terms; Leander himself had proved that with his youthful poem. The white-supremacist and pro-slavery attitudes and behavior among Irish-Americans of "the metropolis," as universally recorded by historians of the ante-bellum and Civil War periods, were driven first by the Democratic Party's Tammany Hall, and then by the naturally conservative, "merger"-minded, Hughes-led American Catholic establishment – in the interest of the plantation bourgeoisie. It was chiefly they who brought about the rejection of the appeal by O'Connell and seventy thousand of their countrymen, in the Address, to "stand with the Abolitionists," and "treat the coloured people as your equals, as brethren." That is why a historian must move beyond the uncritical repetition of the catalog of self justifications – "job competition" etcetera – as if that were an adequate explanation of the question.

But there is more involved here than merely setting the record straight. If the rationale was valid for the ante-bellum Irish-Americans and, *mutatis mutandis*, for European-Americans in general in that day, it is no less valid in its familiar modern-day forms: "preservation of property values" in "ethnic" neighborhoods, "quota" phobia, the denunciation of affirmative action, etcetera.

Irish-Americans were not the originators of white supremacy; they adapted to and were adopted into an already "white" American social order. A modern Irish historian puts it in terms of later-arriving Catholic Irish imitating the example of earlier-arriving Ulster Protestants. The Catholic Irish who chose to follow the "pre-existing presbyterian logic in seeking "popular rights," were met by the slaveholders' Jacksonian Democratic Party that "had to promote outsiders and small men."127 Those "popular rights" of Irish-Americans were given the form of white-skin privileges, the token of their membership in the American "white race."

Then who were the originators, from whom the Jacksonians came; who were the first "bamboozlers"; who were the "drivers"; why did they have to "promote the small men"; why did they "promote" them to the "white race"? I turn to that subject in Volume Two.

Appendix A

(see Introduction, note 46)

In the 1816 edition of the memoirs of his tour of duty, with the British military expedition to the West Indies in 1795–96, physician George Pinckard advocated the gradual emancipation of slaves and the social promotion of freedmen. Thus by an intermingling of "all shades," he believed, "the colored inhabitants would be made fellow-citizens with the whites and they would aspire to be Englishmen!" (George Pinckard, *Notes on the West Indies*, 2nd edn, 3 vols [London, 1816]; reprinted by Negro Universities Press, Westport, 1970, pp. 2:531–2.)

In 1787 the French Marquis de Chastellux, who had traveled extensively in the United States, proposed a way of blending Anglo- and African-American populations through a plan combining racist exile with sexual oppression. According to this idea, African-American women were to be taken to wife by Anglo-American men, while "a great number" of African-American males were to be "exported" (Marquis de Chastellux, *Travels in North America in the Years 1780, 1781, and 1782*, 2 vols, second edition [London, 1787; New York, 1968], pp. 199–200). Other French writers also suggested intermarriage as a general solution to the United States "race question" (cited in Winthrop D. Jordan, *White over Black* [Chapel Hill, 1968] p. 554 n. 17).

A modern monograph on relations between the French and the Canadian Indians in the sixteenth and seventeenth centuries reports that in 1666 Colbert, Louis XIV's chief minister, "recommended that the French and the Indians should be made one people by means of intermarriage." The author declares that, "Physical differences then were not ... a barrier of major importance to the miscegenation of the two races.... In Acadia the French had been encouraged to intermarry freely with the Micomac by the home government in order that the new land might be peopled without draining France of its inhabitants.... Miscegenation was general in settlement and hinterland ..." (Alfred Goldsworthy Bailey, *The Conflict of European and Algonkian Cultures, 1504–1700; a Study in Canadian Civilization* [Sackville, New

Brunswick, 1937], pp. 107, 110, 112, 113).

An English Royal Instruction was issued in 1719 providing for the grant of fifty acres of land, with a ten-year tax exemption, to any "white" Protestant British subject – woman or man – in Nova Scotia who would marry an Indian native of that province. This order was amended in 1749 to say "British" instead of "Protestant," probably out of consideration for Scots Dissenters; the tax exemption period was increased to twenty years; and a bonus of £10 sterling was added (Leonard Woods Labaree, collator and editor, *Royal Instructions to British Colonial Governors, 1670–1776*, 2 vols [New York and London, 1935], p. 2:470). Jordan takes note of these facts merely to stress what he sees as a difference in the English attitudes toward sexual union with African-Americans and with American Indians. Intermarriage with Indians might have been advocated, he says, but "never with Negroes" (p. 550 n. 61).

In 1815, William H. Crawford, then serving as Secretary of War in James Madison's cabinet, proposed a policy of merger by intermarriage of European-Americans and American Indians (Ulrich Bonnell Phillips, in Eugene D. Genovese, ed., *The Slave Economy of the Old South* [Baton Rouge, 1968], p. 24). Crawford had been a member of the United States Senate and, beginning in 1816, served as Secretary of Treasury for Madison and then eight years under Monroe. He was a nationally prominent figure as leader of the anti-Federalist party and candidate for President in 1816 and 1824.

In connection with their support of the Cherokees' resistance to expulsion from their southern lands, first the Methodist Church and then the Moravian, Baptist, Congregationalist and Presbyterian churches jointly expressed themselves in favor of intermarriage "as a force for improvement" (Thurman Wilkins, *Cherokee Tragedy: The Story of the Ridge Family and the Decimation of a People* [New York, 1970], p. 219, citing the *Cherokee Phoenix*, a Cherokee-language newspaper, 18 February 1832, quoting the New York *Commercial Advertiser*).

Appendix B

(see Introduction, note 80)

In the mid-seventeenth century, Sir William Petty found the profitability of agricultural enterprise to be dependent upon the proportion of the number of laboring people to the amount of cultivable land, what might have been called the labor/land ratio. Because he believed bond labor, provided it could be secured, was cheaper than wage labor, Petty advocated slavery, and not only for thieves, vagabonds, etcetera, in England and Ireland ("A Treatise of Taxes and Contributions" [1652], in *The Economic Writings of Sir William Petty*, 2 vols, edited by C. H. Russell [1899; New York, 1967], 1:34 and 1:68).

By the early nineteenth century, at a time when slavery had been forced on the defensive, a reversal of the terms of the ratio provided a much-needed apology, which would in time come to be known as the land/labor ratio. Instead of the emphasis on "cheap labor," with its connotation of greed, the emphasis was placed on the other end, "cheap land." In this way the existence of slavery might be removed beyond questions of moral responsibility to the realm of topography, and made to appear not as a matter of choice, but of national necessity. At the same time it provided a parallel theme in "economic law" for the "paradox thesis" of United States democracy, according to which American liberties were necessarily predicated upon the slavery imposed on African-Americans. "Cheap land" was a good, whose potential could only be realized by resort to the evil of slavery.

The author of the land/labor ratio theory (although he did not give it that name) was Edward Gibbon Wakefield (1796–1862). Wakefield elaborated his idea in two books, *England and America, a Comparison of the Social and Political State of Both Nations* (New York, 1834; 1967), especially pp. 202, 206–8, and 212, and *A View of the Art of Colonization in Present Reference to the British Empire, in Letters Between a Statesman and a Colonist* (1849; New York, 1969), see especially pp. 322–9. "Superabundance of land," he argued, "has never led to great prosperity without some kind of slavery" (*England and America*, p. 212). He believed that "[slavery] happens wherever population is scanty in proportion to land" (*Art of Colonization*, p. 304). "The operation of superabundance of land in causing a scarcity of free labour and a desire for slaves" was, for Wakefield, an economic law (ibid., p. 326).

Eminent American historians writing in the late nineteenth and early twentieth centuries also ascribed the establishment of slavery to economic laws. Philip Alexander Bruce stated categorically, "The Institution of slavery sprang up [in Virginia] under the operation of an irresistible economic law" (Bruce, *Economic History of Virginia in the Seventeenth Century*, 2 vols [New York, 1895; 1935], 2:57). Ulrich Bonnell Phillips was in accord with Wakefield: "Land [in the plantation colonies] was plentiful and free," he said, "and men would not work as voluntary wage earners…. Finally the negroes were discovered to be cheap and useful laborers" ("Economics of the Plantation", *South Atlantic Quarterly*, Vol. 2, pp. 231–6 [July 1903]; reprinted in Eugene D. Genovese, *The Slave Economy of the Old South* [Baton Rouge, 1968], p. 118). Thomas J. Wertenbaker used a metaphor derived from natural laws: "the Black Tide," which, he asserted, brought such low labor costs that the free laboring person could not sustain the competitive struggle (*The Planters of Colonial Virginia* [Princeton, 1922], pp. 123–7 and 139–44).

Winthrop D. Jordan asserts that "there were social and economic necessities which called for some sort of bound, controlled labor" (*White over Black* [Chapel Hill, 1968], p. 61). And Edmund S. Morgan argues that the land/labor ratio hypothesis "would seem to be borne out by the developments under way in seventeenth-century Virginia" (*American Slavery/American Freedom* [New York, 1975], pp. 218 n. 11, 296).

Evsey D. Domar, in his 1970 article "The Causes of Slavery or Serfdom: A Hypothesis" (*Journal of Economic History*, Vol. 30, No. 1 [March 1970], pp. 18–32), found that land/labor ratio theorem ideally consistent with the history of bond-labor in Russia, Poland–Lithuania, western Europe and the United States. But when he came to consider the situation in plague-depopulated England in the latter half of the fourteenth century, he confessed with good-humored self-criticism, "my hypothesis is of little value," and he had no good alternate hypothesis to fit that situation (p. 28). The answer is, of course, that the old system of social control had broken down. The English villeins and wage workers of that period took hold of the "land/labor ratio" by the other end and used it to destroy serfdom in England, by walking away from their old obligations and by rebelling under Wat Tyler and John Ball. Contrary to the presumed economic laws and irresistible necessities upon which the land/labor thesis is based, it turned out that English cultivation continued to thrive through the fourteenth century, on the basis of leasehold and copyhold tenantry. (See Volume Two.)

Domar credits his own hypothesis particularly to the very substantial work on the land/labor theory of bond-servitude as presented in Herman J. Nieboer's *Slavery as an Industrial System* (1900; revised edition, The Hague, 1910). It is interesting to note that Nieboer (at least in the 1910 edition), did take into account the nullifying effect of laboring-class rebelliousness on the operation of the land/labor ratio (pp. 410–18).

Appendix C

(see Chapter 1, note 58 and Chapter 2, note 51)

The Portuguese in 1490 were the first to learn this fact of life. They were "disappointed in their hope of penetrating the interior by the way of the great [Congo] river for the states of the Congo resolutely barred their way" (Basil Davidson, *The African Slave Trade* [Boston, 1961], p. 150). Their efforts to penetrate adjacent Angola for purposes of establishing a plantation economy were likewise fruitless, because "their direct control of the country ... seldom extended more than a few miles from the coast" (ibid., p. 152). The Portuguese did establish a sugar plantation colony two hundred miles off the coast of West Africa on the island of São Tomé in 1506. But the bond-laborers were imported from the African continent (supplemented by two thousand Jewish children taken from their parents in Portugal). Despite the natural advantage typically devolving upon a sea-power ruling class in an insular colony, a massive slave revolt occurred in 1586 on São Tomé, which drove out many of the Portuguese owners and marked the beginning of the decline of the plantation economy there (Luis Ivens Ferraz, "The Creole of São Tomé," *African Studies*, 37 [1978]:3–68, cited in Orlando Patterson, *Slavery and Social Death* [New York, 1990], p. 465 nn. 51, 52, and 53).

In 1675 the British launched a crown colony, to be called Senegambia, on the west coast of Africa between the Gambia and Senegal rivers. The project was abandoned in 1783. (J. D. Fage, *A History of West Africa: An Introductory Survey* [Cambridge, 1969], pp. 77–8; Basil Davidson, *Africa in History* [New York, 1974], p. 202 and 202n.)

Since they were not powerful enough to occupy African territory, the Europeans established forts and "factories" (trading posts and detention pens for laborers purchased or otherwise procured). Although Africans entered into trading arrangements with the Europeans, the Africans would attack these alien enclaves with little or no hesitation, whenever they felt policy required it. On numerous occasions – at Kommenda in 1687, Sekondi in 1694, and Anomabu in 1701, for example – European forts fell to such attacks (W. E. F. Ward,

A History of the Gold Coast [London, 1935], p. 87; John and Awsham Churchill, comp., *Churchill's Voyages and Travels ...*, 6 vols [London, 1732], p. 5:446; Davies, *The Royal African Company* [London, 1957], pp. 263 and 267).

The Dutch (specifically the Dutch East India Company) colony established at the Cape of Good Hope in 1652 represents a partial, technical exception, but one that proves the rule. The Dutch were not intending to establish a plantation colony there, but only a victualing station for ships in the Far East trade. Until the discovery of gold and diamonds in the second half of the nineteenth century, South Africa (the British takeover was begun in 1795 and completed in 1806) was primarily engaged in cattle-raising, an activity not typical of plantation economies, and one poorly suited for slavery, especially on continental territory. Holland in the seventeenth century did not have an exportable labor supply. (See Volume Two, Chapter 2 of this study.) In the first fifty-five years of the colony's existence only some 2,500 European immigrants arrived, and only half of that number were Dutch. Yet they were not able to enslave the Khoisan people native to the territory. The Dutch found that, "It would be impossible to obtain slaves here, for they will not for anything in the world dispose of their children or any of their relatives, having an outstanding love and regard for one another" (*The Early Cape Hottentots described in the writings of Olfert Dapper [1668], William Ten Rhyne [1686], and Johannes Gulielmus de Grevenbroek [1695]*, original text, with translation into English by I. Schapera and B. Farrington [Cape Town, 1933], p. 197, and n. 27). Although there were African slaves in the colony as early as 1658, they, as well as those later recruited, were brought in from the outside, from Angola, Madagascar and Mozambique. And of these early arrivals at least, a goodly portion were destined for transshipment to the Dutch colonies in the East Indies (*Journal of Jan Van Riebeeck*, edited by H. B. Thom, 3 vols [Cape Town and Amsterdam, 1952–58], pp. 2:267–8). European immigration was suspended in 1707, a ban that lasted till the British takeover nearly a century later. And, although a deliberate decision was made in 1717 to use African bond-laborers instead of Europeans, the colony grew very slowly so that in 1795 there were only 17,000 slaves and 16,000 free Europeans in the colony. By contrast, the population of the English colonies on the mainland of North America had grown to 50,000 within less than thirty-five years of the founding of Jamestown; the Anglo-American colony of South Carolina grew from a population of fewer than 400 in 1672 to a quarter of a million in 1790, of whom 107,000 were African-American bond-laborers (Theodore K. Rabb, *Enterprise and Empire: Merchant and Gentry Investment in the Expansion of England, 1575–1630* [Cambridge, Massachusetts, 1967], p. 99; Lewis C. Gray, assisted by Esther Katherine Thompson, *History of Agriculture in the Southern United States to 1860*, 2 vols [Washington, DC, 1932], p. 2:1025).

The Dutch were able to defeat the Khoisan peoples, thousands of whom succumbed to European diseases. Some simply retreated before the Dutch advance, but others were incorporated, though not assimilated, into the colony, generally on a peon-like basis, as low-wage herdsmen and laborers, and as militiamen. Thus the nature and the rate of growth of the colony were such that the decisive battles – with the Xosa and the Zulu peoples – for territory were not fought until late in the nineteenth century, well after the legal abolition of slavery in all British colonies.

Appendix D

(see Chapter 2, notes 42 and 73)

Technical military advantage having swung to the English side through improved organization and increased employment of cannon and firearms, the "plantation" campaigns became the occasion for English war by starvation, exile, extermination and terror against the resisting Irish. Certain events of the Munster campaign, familiar to students of Irish history, clearly indicate that no sense of "white Christian" affinity operated to moderate the cruelty of English racial oppression of the Irish.

The plantation of Munster was prepared by the repression of two (Desmond) rebellions. The first began in 1569, the year that Queen Elizabeth was excommunicated by the Catholic Church; it was ended in 1574. The second began in 1578 and lasted until 1583. In these wars Anglo-Irish and native Irish joined to oppose the English. During the first of these rebellions Humphrey Gilbert, the English commander, made it his aim not merely to subdue his Irish enemies, but to employ such terror in the process as would ever after deter the very thought of resistance to English rule; to spare neither sex nor age among his Irish foes, so that thenceforward the very name of "Englishman" should be more feared than the actual presence of a hundred Englishmen had been before. (Here I am following Professor Nicholas P. Canny's account [*The Elizabethan Conquest of Ireland* (New York, 1978), pp. 121–2]. Canny cites Great Britain Public Record Office, State Papers Office, n.s., *State Papers, Ireland, Elizabeth to George III*, 1:79, 1558–1580, p. 63/29/70.)

To this end, Gilbert instituted the following practice: at the close of each day's work, the severed heads of the Irish slain were arranged in two inward-facing rows to form a lane leading to the tent where Gilbert sat to receive the abject surrender of his enemies. In passing, the Irish were thus forced to see "the heads of their dead fathers, brothers, children, kinsfolke and friends lie on the ground before their faces." (From the eyewitness account of Thomas Churchyard, an English correspondent, in *Churchyard's Choise, a General Rehearsal of Warres* [London, 1578], cited by Canny, pp. 121–2; the quotation as given here modernizes the spelling.) In recognition of his services, Gilbert was shortly thereafter knighted by Queen Elizabeth and made Governor of Munster.

Following the second Desmond War, the man who served as secretary to the Lord Deputy propounded a historical theory of colonial war in Ireland: "Great force must be the instrument," he wrote, "but famine must be the meane [the principal element] for till Ireland can be famished it can not be subdued" (*A Breife Note of Ireland* [1598–99], in *The Works of Edmund Spenser, a Variorum Edition* [Baltimore, 1949], 10 vols Vol. 9 [special editor Rudolf Gottfried], p. 244).

Indeed, fire and sword were employed with such ferocity that, as the chronicles tell, "From Dingle [on the Kerry coast] to the Rock of Cashel [in Tipperary, a hundred miles distant], not the lowing of a cow was that year to be heard" (from the Gaelic Irish account in *The Annals of the Four Masters*, cited in William Edward Hartpole Lecky, *A History of Ireland in the Eighteenth Century*, 5 vols [London, 1893], 1:7). In just one year of such warfare, 1582, in that one Irish province of Munster more than 30,000 men, women, and children starved to death (*Pacata Hibernia* [1820 edition], p. 645, cited in Lecky, 1:7; Robert Dunlop, "The Plantation of Munster, 1584–89," *English Historical Review*, 3:269).

Appendix E

(see Chapter 2, note 58)

Domestically the basis had been laid by the expropriation of the copyhold peasantry (see Volume Two) By the early seventeenth century, English agriculture had been transformed from primarily an activity of independent peasantry to that of wage labor and capital. Even the loss of the trans-Channel markets for raw English wool, a result of the Spanish occupation of the Netherlands, was turned to advantage. With the help of Protestant refugee craftsmen from Flanders, England became an exporter of wool cloth, finished as well as unfinished, rather than raw wool. English cloth production was a capitalist operation from the outset, with cottage weavers working up yarn and thread supplied by capitalist "clothiers" (John Ulrich Nef, *The Conquest of the Material World* [Chicago, 1964], pp. 96–9). "The history of the change from medieval to modern England," writes Trevelyan, "might well be written in the form of a social history of the cloth trade" (G. M. Trevelyan, *A Shortened History of England* [Harmondsworth, 1942], p. 206).

The essential element in this social transformation was the accumulation of capital: primitive accumulation by expropriation, followed by normal reproductive accumulation. Implicit in the process were the principles of free trade in commodities and the free flow of capital according to the prospective rate of profit. Under the stimulus of these principles, England by the end of the sixteenth century was well advanced in what Nef has called the "Early Industrial Revolution" (Nef: see particularly the two essays: "The Progress of Technology and Growth of Large-scale Industry in Great Britain, 1540–1640," pp. 121–43, and "A Comparison of Industrial Growth in France and England from 1540 to 1640," pp. 144–212; Nef defines "Early Industrial Revolution" at pp. 220–21). Of England Nef observes:

> During the last sixty years of the sixteenth century the first paper and gunpowder mills, the first cannon foundries, the first alum and copperas factories, the first sugar refineries, and the first considerable saltpetre works were all introduced into the

country from abroad. The discovery of calamine, the ore of zinc, in Somerset and elsewhere, together with the first really effective attempts to mine copper ore, made possible the establishment of brassmaking and battery works for hammering brass and copper ingots into plates. (ibid., pp. 123–4)

(At this point Professor Nef supplies the names of two bibliographies, and lists a dozen particular indispensable works for the study of this early industrialization. To these must be added Nef's own *Rise of the British Coal Industry*.)

In addition to the advances in cloth-finishing, there were significant improvements in deep-mining of coal, iron-making, and shipbuilding, and in the production of glass, brass, salt, gunpowder, alum, saltpetre, dyes, and printed materials. New industries using water-powered machinery in factories began to turn out paper, saltpetre, and refined sugar. (Nef, *Conquest of the Material World*; see the particular items listed under "England" in the index.) England had been "something of a backwater" before 1540; but thereafter it forged rapidly to the fore (ibid., pp. 142–3).

Sir Francis Bacon, vaunting the united productive potential of England and Scotland as the promise of enrichment of the kingdom, made reference to an ancient saying: "Iron commands gold" (letter to Sir George Villiers – later Duke of Buckingham – 5 July 1616, in Spedding, ed., *The Letters and Life of Francis Bacon*, 7:175).

The link between the mundane and the legendary in all this, between the tradesmen and the crew of the *Golden Hind*, between the clothiers and the victors in the Channel, was supplied by the emergence in England of the joint-stock company for mobilizing capital for overseas commercial ventures and for colonization in Ireland and America. Commerce led the way, if for no other reason than that it promised quicker and more certain profits (Theodore K. Rabb, *Enterprise and Empire* [Cambridge, Mass., 1967], p. 38).

Appendix F

(see Chapter 2, note 77)

Moryson's *Itinerary* details more than a score of particular instances of the ruthless application of this starvation strategy.

In August of 1600, Mountjoy confiscated cattle, horses and sheep in Leix. With the example of their officers before them, initially hesitant soldiers proceeded to "cut downe with their swords all the Rebels corne to the value of ten thousand pounds and upward [about 80,000 bushels], the onely meanes by which they were to live." Sir Oliver Lambert took 1,000 cows, 500 horses, and "great store of sheep." Sir Arthur Savage "spoiled the Countrey and took great prey" (Fynes Moryson, *An Itinerary, Containing His Ten Yeeres Travell through the Twelve Dominions of Germany, Bohmerland, Sweitzerland, Netherland, Denmarke and Ireland*, 4 vols [London, 1617; Glasgow, 1907], 2:329–30). The English marveled that the land was so well cultivated and orderly fenced by such "barbarous inhabitants."

For a month, beginning at Christmas 1600, Mountjoy spoiled and ransacked what came to be County Wicklow, "swept away the most part of their cattle and goods, burnt all their Corne, and almost all their Houses, leaving little or nothing to relieve them" (ibid., 2:250). In February, Mountjoy crossed and recrossed the counties of Meath and Westmeath; before he moved on, "the greatest part lay waste." He devoted attention not only to planted fields, but sent his men into the woods "to fetch out the rebels corne, and to burn the houses, and such things for their reliefe." On 17 March, St Patrick's Day, Moryson says, "we burnt the houses and spoiled the goods of the inhabitants" in the northern part of County Meath (ibid., 2:355–6, 2:358).

In orders issued to the commander of the northern wing of a north–south pincers invasion of Tyrone, the Ulster stronghold, Mountjoy said "he should burn all the dwellings, and destroy the corne on the ground, which might be done by incamping upon it, and cutting it downe with swords, and other waies, [Mountjoy] holding it best they should spoile all the corne, except that which he could gather." Mountjoy made it a particular point that they should not be

213

dissuaded from this course by the importunings of those of the Irish who submitted to the English (ibid., 2:399).

In a letter written on 19 July 1601, Mountjoy informed the English government that "he had destroied the rebels Corne about Armagh (whereof he found great abundance), and would destroy the rest, this course causing famine, being the only way to reduce or root out the Rebels." On the next day his forces "cut a field of Corne lying on the skirt of the Woods" near the site of the rebuilding of a fort on the Blackwater river. The next day after that, they "cut all the Corne by the Bogge and Wood side near our Fort, except that which our men had power to reape." Then, on 23 July, they marched "two little miles" out and "camped and cut downe the Corne on every side." Four days later three regiments from the same base cut down the corn, not only in open fields but in the woods as well, "burning many houses in the skirts of the woods," as they went. Six days later, Sir Henry Davers, "with three hundred foote, and fortie horse, was sent into a Fastnesse to burne some twentie faire timber houses" (ibid., 2:412, 2:413–14, 2:415–16).

So effectively was their work done that the English army itself was in short supply when victuals were slow to arrive from England. Already in June 1601, Mountjoy foresaw the danger. "Our only way to ruine the rebels," he said to the lords in England, "must be to make all possible wast[e] of the meanes for life," and therefore it was vital that for the future the shipments of victuals arrive in due time. By December he was reporting that they could not even feed their horses, and he requested the prompt shipment of 2,000 quarters of oats, without which the horses would starve. Three weeks later Mountjoy renewed his appeal, noting that "the whole Countrie is so harried and wasted, that it cannot yielde any reliefe." In May 1602, Mountjoy combined his report of wasting the countryside in Wicklow and Meath with the reminder that the English army could find themselves neither "victuals or any other necessary provision, but what we bring with us." In September a promised supply of victuals was more than a month past due, although the northern garrisons for whom they were intended were dependent upon them, particularly for bread and salt (ibid., 2:394; 3:67, 3:85, 3:157–8, 3:210–11).

Fynes Moryson was well situated to observe this Operation Starvation (as it would be called today). Moryson was Mountjoy's chief secretary and he had a brother, Sir Richard, who was a colonel in the field with the English forces. A decade after the event, drawing upon the eyewitness accounts provided by his brother, and Sir Arthur Chichester, as well as a number of other English commanders and officers; and the testimony of "many honest [English] Gentlemen" who were colonists in Ireland, Moryson described at length the "unspeakable extremities" to which Irish victims of the English war by famine had been driven in order to survive. But, he wrote,

[N]o spectacle was more frequent in the Ditches of Townes, and especially in the wasted Countries, than to see multitudes of these poore people dead with their mouthes all coloured greene by eating nettles, docks, and all things they could rend up above ground. (Ibid., 3: 281–3)

Appendix G

(see Chapter 2, note 108)

Professor J. A. Barnes, of Australia National University, has provided an illuminating analysis of the social control policies of the Western colonizing powers ("Indigenous Politics and Colonial Administration with Special Reference to Australia," *Comparative Studies in Society and History*, 2:133–49 [January 1960]). Centering his study on British colonial administration in Africa, Australia and Australian New Guinea, Barnes discerns a pattern of essential principles employed for effecting social control of conquered tribal peoples. "The distribution of authority characteristic of statelessness," he writes, "is incompatible with the hierarchical administration and judicial system" required by the colonizing power (p. 145). Therefore, in stateless societies, the colonizers more or less arbitrarily bring into being an intermediate stratum, since "no system of administration seems to be able to operate entirely without this buffer of local employees" (p. 143). Alternately, he says, some of the indigenous people of stateless societies are incorporated (without being assimilated) directly into the colony as "peons." Still others flee, "so long as the deserts are large enough and contain some wildlife and water, or the jungles are deep enough [so that] the old way of life can be continued" (p. 138).

On the other hand, Professor Barnes says, "where indigenous peoples live in a well ordered state with powerful centralized authority, it is economical for the conqueror to govern through the native rule." Barnes quotes a letter written from Uganda by an English colonial administrator in 1887, explaining this policy of indirect rule. Barnes notes, however, that this principle for ruling countries with pre-existing state systems did not originate with the English, but "goes back to the Romans, or even earlier". (p. 140 see also Roland Oliver and J. D. Fage, *A Short History of Africa* [New York, 1963], p.117, on the failure of the conquering Moroccans to establish a system of social control in tribal Songhai).

Barnes's passing references to the European colonizers in the Americas conform to his general thesis. Although he makes no mention of the English colonization of Ireland, his general principles seem no less applicable to that case.

In Brazil, where the Portuguese encountered a stateless society, the course of relations was quite different. Due to a combination of resistance, including rebellion, by the indigenous population and their decimation by European diseases, early attempts to enslave them for plantation labor failed, and the Portuguese began to turn to African labor supplies. The Indians for the most part found safe refuge by retreat to the jungles of the interior (Charles R. Boxer, *The Portuguese Seaborne Empire* [New York, 1969], p. 88; Charles Edward Chapman, *Colonial Hispanic America: A History* [New York, 1933], pp. 77–80; Barnes, pp. 77–80; Marvin Harris, *Patterns of Race in the Americas* [New York, 1964], pp. 12–13).

E. G. Bourne traces statistically the extinction of the stateless Carib population of Hispaniola, from 300,000 in 1492 (when, as Columbus recorded it, the Spanish explorers were courteously greeted by the people there), to 60,000 in 1508, to 14,000 in 1514, and finally to 500, virtual extinction, in 1548 (E. G. Bourne, *Spain in America: 1450–1580* [New York, 1904], pp. 211–14).

"In the newly annexed Island of St Vincent," writes the English military historian Fortescue, "there was a fierce race of men known as the Black Caribs, indigenous to the Archipelago, and of negro slaves who had escaped, or, as tradition goes, had been wrecked on the coast and had taken refuge in the forest. . . . They claimed two-thirds of the best and richest land in the island . . . and were a great obstacle to settlement" (W. J. Fortescue, *A History of the British Army* [London, 1899–1930], 3:41–2). The Black Caribs rose in revolt against the British in 1795, but were defeated in 1796. Considered intractable for British social control purposes, the majority of the Black Caribs were deported from their homeland.

In an instance that was not a part of the Western colonizing activity, the Incas of pre-Columbian times were able to extend their empire over a territory two thousand miles long by the conquest of other state-organized societies. But they failed when they attempted to take over the stateless peoples in the Amazon basin (Harris, pp. 9–10).

Appendix H

(see Chapter 3, notes 8 and 9)

The subject of Scottish slavery is generally ignored by historians of the Anglo-American colonies, although it is a phenomenon contemporaneous with colonial bond-servitude and closely kin in form. Abbot E. Smith does not allude to it in his *Colonists in Bondage* (Chapel Hill, 1947; New York, 1971). Winthrop D. Jordan, in his *White over Black* (Chapel Hill, 1968), mentions the relatively favored situation of Scots bond-laborers in the continental colonies, but he ignores the contrasting situation of bondmen in Scotland, and its possible implications for his thesis regarding the origin of racial slavery.

The Scots Poor Law was amended in 1597 to make vagrants and their children – together comprising one-tenth of the population of Scotland – subject to court sentence to lifetime servitude to private employers. In 1605, any member of the employing class was legally authorized to take such vagrant persons before the authorities, have them officially declared vagrants, and "set his burning iron upon thame and retaene thame as slaves"; this slavery was for life. The following year, the Scottish Parliament by law forbade any coal miner or salt-pan worker to leave his or her job without written consent of the employer. The same law authorized the owners of coal mines and salt works themselves to seize unemployed men, whether vagrants or not, and, without further legal formality, to force them to work for the owner as slaves, In 1607, owners of metal ore mines were granted the same powers. In 1617, children of poor parents – whether they were orphans or not – were made subject to serve masters until they were thirty years of age. It was the practical effect of this law that made the slavery of the coal miners not only perpetual, but hereditary. The law provided perpetual servitude for the adult miner after he or she had served the master for one year. The children of miners were customarily, and practically inescapably, bound to service by their parents through the acceptance from the master of a payment of "earnest money," or "arle," as it was sometimes called, usually at the christening of the child. The period of service being thirty years, the young miners, male and female, could not escape the system, since their common-law option to leave during their twenty-first year was superseded by the original thirty-year term into which their parents had sold them.

In 1649 Scottish law gave any British subject of Charles II the right to capture a vagrant and sell him or use him in servitude of unlimited duration, the subject's only obligation being to provide the slave with food and clothing. "It is impossible," says the author of the *Edinburgh Review* account, "to read this law in any other sense than as establishing a slave trade in Scotch vagrants, and throwing it open to the male inhabitants of the empire" ("Slavery in Modern Scotland," p. 131). In 1661 the Scottish Parliament extended slavery to workers around the mines, not just the miners themselves. In 1685 the Edinburgh authorities decreed lifetime servitude in manufacturing work for vagrants and unemployed persons over the age of five years. Scotland's criminals were at the beginning of the eighteenth century subject to be sentenced to slavery for life. There were various forms of the status of slavery in Scotland. Temporary slavery might mean eleven, fifteen or twenty-five years, but "slavery for life [was] commonest of all" (ibid., p. 140).

In 1698, the influential Scottish statesman Andrew Fletcher of Saltoun (1655–1716) criticized the notion that Christians could not be enslaved, and proposed that two hundred thousand Scottish beggars be made slaves for life to men of means (A. Fletcher, *The Political Works of Andrew Fletcher, Esq., of Saltoun* [Glasgow, 1749], "Second Discourse Concerning the Affairs of Scotland," [1698], pp. 87–8, 100). Whether or not Fletcher's advocacy of slavery as a cure for vagrancy, etcetera, received the "obloquy and disdain" that he anticipated, it seems not to have been given its due as a counter-argument to the land/labor-ratio theory of slavery as propounded by Wakefield and his disciples (see Appendix B).

The Scottish Habeas Corpus Act of 1701 expressly excluded coal-bearers and salters from its protection. Their slavery was reconfirmed in law by the Scottish Parliament in 1747, forty years after the union with England. This was "the last legal sanction given in the United Kingdom to the slavery of native Britons" ("Slavery in Modern Scotland," p. 142).

The last of the Scottish colliery slaves was finally freed in 1799, under the gradual emancipation act passed by the British Parliament in 1775 (*Statutes at Large from the thirteenth year of the Reign of King George the Third, to the Sixteenth Year of the Reign of George the Third* [London, 1776], 12:296–8 [15 Geo. III c. 28]). Although the preamble of this act deplored the immorality of holding "Colliers and Coal-bearers and Salters ... in a state of Slavery," the fact is that, as the *Edinburgh Review* put it, "They were emancipated in the same great cause they were enslaved in – the cause of low wages" ("Slavery in Modern Scotland," p. 144). With the coming of the Industrial Revolution, opportunities in free-labor jobs were opening up. As a result, in the words of the act, "many new-discovered Coals remain unwrought, and many not sufficiently wrought, nor are there a sufficient number of Salters for the Salt-works, to the great loss of the Owners and Disadvantage to the Publick" (15 Geo c. 28).

The moral factor derived strength, however, from the relation between the opposition to the slavery of Scottish people and the slavery of laborers of African descent in the British colonies. In 1769 a Scotsman named Steuart returned to Scotland from Virginia. He brought with him the African-American James Somerset, whom he claimed as his property. In 1771, Somerset emancipated himself by removing himself from Steuart's control. However, after a lapse of about two months, Steuart was able to seize Somerset and put him captive on board a ship, intending to take him to Jamaica to be sold as a slave. Somerset sued in court for a writ of habeas corpus, maintaining that he could not legally be held a slave under English law. The Chief Justice of the King's bench, Lord Mansfield, heard the case and rendered his historic decision:

> The state of slavery is of such a nature, that it is incapable of being introduced on any reasons, moral or political, but only by positive law.... It is so odious, that nothing can be suffered to support it but positive law. (Barnett Hollander, *Slavery in America* [New York, 1964], p. 2; A. Leon Higginbotham, *In the Matter of Color, Race and the American Legal Process, the Colonial Period* [New York, 1978], pp. 333, 353)

Somerset was freed, and in consequence of the same decision, the 14,000 to 15,000 Anglo-Africans then held as slaves in England won the right to be free. English abolitionists had been instrumental in carrying this case through to victory. Immediately thereafter the English abolitionist leader Granville Sharp (1735–1815) "was approached on the subject of a public agitation for the abolition of collier slavery in Scotland, and he would have probably undertaken the task had not some of the coalmasters themselves engaged to bring about the emancipation of their labourers" ("Slavery in Modern Scotland," p. 144). It is interesting to note that while Scottish colliers and salters were still enslaved, the Glasgow Court of Sessions in 1775 granted freedom to Joseph Knight, who had been brought from the West Indies by his owner, John Weddeburn, Esq. For all that he might have been a slave in the West Indies, said the Court, he had become a free man by the mere fact of being in Scotland (Chambers, 3:453–4).

It thus seems that the campaign for the liberation of persons of African ancestry in America and England supplied much of the moral force for the ending of the ancient slavery of the Scots colliers and salt-pan workers.

Appendix I

(see Chapter 3, note 46)

The English money wage for common labor in 1776 was about 18*d*. per day, on an average, winter and summer. The corresponding wage in Ireland was 6½*d*., but the cost of necessaries was about half what it was in England (Arthur Young, *Tour in Ireland* [London, 1780], book 2, p. 28; W. E. H. Lecky, *History of England in the Eighteenth Century*, 8 vols [New York, 1878–90], 2:323, n. 3). In nominal money terms, therefore, the employers could hire Irish workers for 64 percent less than they paid English workers. However, in seeking the lowest possible limit of costs, the employers would have had to take into account the real wage level, which was only 28 percent less in Ireland than in England.

In continental Anglo-America near the end of the eighteenth century, the labor of lifetime bond-laborers hired out by the year cost £8 to £12, which was 80 percent of the annual outlay for wage labor (£10 to £15) doing the same sort of work (Lewis C. Gray, *History of Agriculture in the Southern United States to 1860*, 2 vols [Washington 1932; 1956], 1:468–9). Thus the employer's cost was reduced by 20 percent by hiring bond-labor instead of wage-labor. This was still less than the England/Ireland real wage differential. The fact that in continental Anglo-America in the eighteenth century real wages ranged from 30 percent to 100 percent above those in England (Richard B. Morris, *Encyclopedia of American History* [New York, 1982], p. 760) further strengthens the implication that labor costs in Ireland were at a level such that bond-labor would not have reduced.

Information provided by Arthur Young, however, shows that the actual annual money cost of most Irish common agricultural labor was only about half that which would have been represented by a wage of 6½*d*. per day (Young, Vol. 2, p. 28; in the remainder of this appendix I have relied on the same work, mainly Vol. 2, pp. 19–23).

At the conclusion of four years (1776–80) of observing Irish agricultural economics and social life, Young made certain generalizations concerning

"The Labouring Poor," particularly the cottiers, who constituted the majority of the Irish laboring people. The cottier, with a wife and typically five children, lived mainly by renting a plot of ground, usually, but not always, provided with a single-room shack ("cabbin and garden"); and by wages earned by working for the landlord. Rental on the land was £5 10s. 2d. per Irish acre (equal to about 1.6 English acres). The average cottier paid £1 13s. 10d. ground rent, the indicated average holding thus being less than one-third of an Irish acre, less than half an English acre. For the graze of one cow, the cottier paid £1 11s. 3d., the total thus costing the cottier £3 5s. 1d.

Working for the landlord 250 days a year at $6\frac{1}{2}d.$, the cottier could earn £6 7s. 1d. per year. The staple diet of the cottier family was the potatoes they raised in the family's plot (the man being able to work at it less than one day a week [County Derry; Young, Vol. 1, p. 364]). These, together with the buttermilk left after the butter-fat products had been reserved for paying the landlord his rent, and a bit of oatmeal when the potatoes were gone, was their food.

Such a family needed sixty 280-pound barrels of potatoes per year. The average output of potatoes on one acre was 82 barrels per year (one barrel containing four English bushels). Obviously, one-third of an acre could provide less than half the potato requirement of the cottier family.

Wages were paid every six months, in some cases, and at the end of the year in others. The £3 2s. difference between what the landlord collected from the cottier in rent and the wages he paid to the cottier represents the annual labor cost per cottier. At 2s. 8d. per barrel, the difference between the price of sixty 280-pound barrels of potatoes and the 28-barrel yield of the cottier's $\frac{1}{3}$-acre "garden," amounting to £4 5s. 4d., was supplied perhaps by wages earned by other members of the family at fractional rates, by keeping another cow, a pig, some poultry, and by going hungry to the point of starvation in bad crop years. (With regard to the calculated function of beggary, see Lecky, 2:251, n. 1.)

Even worse off were the *spalpeens*, the landless laborers, living on casual cash-wage employment, at annual wages of £3 to £4 for men, and £1 2s. for "maids" (the *spalpeen* figures were those for the Castle Lloyd locality).

Appendix J

(see Chapter 4, note 107)

For reasons more than just that I am a foreigner, I am deterred from expressing a personal judgment about Daniel O'Connell's views regarding revolutionary violence in Ireland. When he sought to apply to Ireland the principle that "[N]o human revolution is worth the effusion of one single drop of human blood" (W. E. H. Lecky, *Leaders of Public Opinion in Ireland*, 2 vols [London, 1903], pp. 263–4), he was expressing the attitude of the Irish bourgeoisie, lay and clerical, in general. O'Connell was a uniquely powerful leader; perhaps no other individual could have brought matters to such a climax as that of Clontarf. But if there had been another leader of the bourgeois class, it is certain that their decision would have been the same. The behavior of the Irish bourgeoisie in this situation was typical of that of their class confronted with similar crises in the nineteenth century. We, as citizens of the twentieth century, cannot easily dismiss O'Connell's assertion that "Human blood is no cement for the temple of human liberty" (ibid.). So much has been done in the twentieth century in the name of proletarian liberation that has only gone to show that we are still unprepared for the role that Marx prescribed, that we cannot disregard O'Connell's dictum as if it were a self-evident fallacy.

Still, there are questions that an American student may ask. If he had lived so long, would O'Connell, the unwavering enemy of African-American slavery, have rejected the stand ultimately taken by Lincoln that a righteous God could hold that "every drop of blood drawn with the lash, shall be paid by another drawn with the sword" (Second Inaugural Address, 4 March 1865)? To follow Lincoln a bit further: O'Connell's aversion to embracing an armed Irish peasantry was no greater than was Lincoln's aversion in 1860 to freeing, arming, and enlisting African-American bond-laborers to fight the white rebels. He could have had a peace that would have saved hundreds of thousands of lives. If Lincoln had done so, would he have received the same approbation that many historians have bestowed upon O'Connell for his Clontarf decision, even though chattel bond-servitude would thereby have been prolonged indefinitely?

We can ask, as others have before us, was it in a pacifist spirit that O'Connell sent his own son Morgan to fight under Bolívar in South America? Was it, then, aversion to bloodshed, or rather the imminent involvement of the propertyless masses that he in the end could not embrace? (This despite his repeated oratorical invocations of Byron: "Hereditary bondsmen! know ye not,/ Who would be free, themselves must strike the blow" [*Childe Harold*, canto 2, stanza 76].) Was he tacitly distinguishing a war between Spanish colonists and the Spanish government, over issues in which the mass of the super-exploited Indios were not involved, from the situation in Ireland in which the laboring classes would have been involved as the main force in any revolution? When, speaking at a "monster meeting" at Mallow on 11 June 1843, O'Connell said, "The time is come when we must be doing ... you may soon have the alternative to live as slaves or die as freemen," did he think only to create a propitious attitude in Westminster, and not to suggest that the thousands of his listening fellow countrymen suit actions to the words? (The text of O'Connell's Mallow speech as reported in the Young Ireland *Nation* [Dublin] 17 June 1843, cited in Kevin P. Nolan, *The Politics of Repeal* [London, 1965], p. 48).

Historians seem to believe that the alternative was a bloody civil war which the British would have won quickly and decisively by slaughtering tens of thousands of poorly armed and untrained Irish peasants and laborers. However awkward and however politically damaging to O'Connell, it is said, surrender was the only sensible course in the face of the British government's monstrous provocation (see, for example, R. F. Foster, *Modern Ireland* [New York, 1989], p. 313). Of course, the Young Irelanders rejected this rationale, and split with O'Connell over the issue, a stand not generally supported.

Yet, even if the criticism of Young Ireland is correct in this regard, there is another aspect of the matter that seems to deserve more consideration than it has had. Two years after Clontarf, the Great Famine began. Within five years the population of Ireland had been reduced by one-fourth; of that two million gone, *one million had died of starvation* or starvation-induced disease. This catastrophe must be attributed not only to the history of English landlordism in Ireland, but to the British government's response to the Famine by deliberate malign neglect more destructive of life than even Mountjoy's strategy of conquest by famine in the closing years of the Tyrone War. If the British government had got its war and won it in 1843, might it not thereby have so seriously damaged its moral position in the world that it could not, as it actually did, sacrifice *hundreds* of thousands of Irish men, women and children on the altar of *laissez-faire*, or as it is said today, "free market forces" operating without "government interference"? If so, would the self-sacrifice of *tens of* thousands fighting for equality have been in vain? Is such quantification of quick and dead unspeakable? Did not O'Connell himself set the example?

"A living friend," he estimated, "is worth a churchyard full of dead ones" (Robert Dunlop, *Daniel O'Connell* [New York, 1900], p. 353; O'Connell was riposting the Horatian slogan, "Sweet it is to die for one's country"). O'Connell died during the Famine, in 1847. Did he at the end ever speculate along such lines? May not we ourselves do so, without forgetting lessons our own century has taught us?

Appendix K

(see Chapter 7, note 62)

The Slave

by Leander (John Hughes)

Hard is the lot of him who's doomed to toil,
Without one slender hope to soothe his pain,
Whose sweat and labor are a master's spoil,
Whose sad reward a master's proud disdain.
Wipe from thy code, Columbia, wipe the stain;
Be free as air, but yet be kind as free,
And chase foul bondage from thy Southern plain:
If such the right of man, by heaven's decree,
Oh, then let Afric's sons feel what it is – to be.

In hot meridian day of late, I hied
To court the covert of a spreading oak;
I sat beneath – and thence in pity eyed
The negro moiling at his daily yoke.
And still he plied the dull, desponding stroke,
Beneath the scorching of the noon-tide sun,
Sullen and silent, or if words he spoke,
I could not hear; but ever and anon
I heard the lash – which even brutes are fain to shun.

The ruthless driver soon was forced to yield:
Though strong of sinew, still he could not bear

The tyrant labors of the parching field,
But sought the shade to breathe a cooler air;
Whilst, less inhuman, but alas! less fair,
The drudging slave began to pour his song
Upon the heedless wind, and breathe despair.
He sung the negroes' foul, unpitied wrong,
Sad and ironical – late he felt the thong.

"Hail Columbia, happy land!
Where freedom waves her golden wand,
    Where equal justice reigns
But ah! Columbia great and free
Has not a boon for mine and me,
    But slavery and chains.
Oh! once I had a soothing joy,
    The hope of other years,
That free Columbia would destroy
    The source of these my tears.
        But pining, declining,
    I still drag to the grave,
        Doomed to sigh till I die,
    Free Columbia's slave.

"Hail Columbia, happy land!
Whose sons, a free, a heaven-born band,
    Will free us soon with blows.
If freeman's freest blood were shed,
Could it be purer or more red
    Than this of mine that flows?
'Twas freeman's whip that brought this gore
    That trickles down my breast;
But soon my bleeding will be o'er,
    My grave will yield me rest.
        I will, then, until then
    Abide my hard and hopeless lot;
        But there's room in the tomb
    For freemen too to rot.

"Hail Columbia, happy land!
Where those who show a fairer hand
    Enjoy sweet liberty.
But from the moment of my birth,
I slave along Columbia's earth,

Nor freedom smiles on me.
Long have I pined through years of woe
   Adown life's bleeding track,
And still my tears, my blood must flow,
   Because my hand is black.
    Still boiling, still toiling,
   Beneath the burning heats of noon,
    I, poor slave, court the grave;
   O Columbia, grant the boon!

"Hail, Columbia, hap–"

He ceased the song, and heaved another sigh
In silent, cheerless mood – for ah! the while
The driver's hated steps were drawing nigh;
Nor song of woe, nor words dare then beguile
The goaded sorrows of a thing so vile.
Yet such the plaintive song that caught my ear,
That cold humanity may blush to smile,
When dove-eyed mercy softly leans to hear,
And Pity turns aside to shed another tear.

Appendix L

(see Chapter 7, note 80)

Address from the people of Ireland to their Countrymen and Countrywomen in America[1]

You are at a great distance from your native land! A wide expanse of water separates you from the beloved country of your birth – from us and from the kindred whom you love, and who love you, and pray for your happiness and prosperity in the land of your adoption.

We regard America with feelings of admiration; we do not look upon her as a strange land, nor upon her people as aliens from our affections. The power of steam has brought us nearer together; it will increase the intercourse between us, so that the character of the Irish people and of the American people must in future be acted upon by the feelings and disposition of each.

The object of this address is to call your attention to the subject of slavery in America – that foul blot upon the noble institutions and the fair fame of your adopted country. But for this one stain, America would, indeed, be a land worthy your adoption; but she will never be the glorious country that her free constitution designed her to be, so long as her soil is polluted by the footprint of a single slave.

Slavery is the most tremendous invasion of the natural, inalienable rights of man, and of some of the noblest gifts of God, "life, liberty, and the pursuit of happiness." What a spectacle does America present to the people of the earth! A land of professing christian republicans, uniting their energies for the oppression and degradation of three millions of innocent human beings, the children of one common Father, who suffer the most grievous wrongs and the utmost degradation for no crime of their ancestors or of their own!

---

1. The Address as published in the *Liberator*, 25 March 1842.

Slavery is a sin against God and man. All who are not for it, must be against it. None can be neutral! We entreat you to take the part of justice, religion and liberty.

It is in vain that American citizens attempt to conceal their own and their country's degradation under this withering curse. America is cursed by slavery! We call upon you to unite with the abolitionists, and never to cease your efforts, until perfect liberty be granted to every one of her inhabitants, the black man as well as the white man. We are all children of the same gracious God; all equally entitled to life, liberty, and the pursuit of happiness.

We are told that you possess great power, both moral and political, in America. We entreat you to exercise that power and that influence for the sake of humanity.

You will not witness the horrors of slavery in all the states of America. Thirteen of them are free, and thirteen are slave states. But in all, the pro-slavery feeling, though rapidly decreasing, is still strong. Do not unite with it: on the contrary, oppose it with all the peaceful means in your power. Join with the abolitionists everywhere. They are the only consistent advocates of liberty. Tell every man, that you do not understand liberty for the white man, and slavery for the black man: that you are for liberty for all, of every color, creed, and country.

The American citizen proudly points to the national declaration of independence, which declares that "All mankind are born free and equal, and are alike entitled to life, liberty, and the pursuit of happiness." Aid him to carry out this noble declaration, by obtaining freedom for the slave.

Irishmen and Irishwomen! treat the colored people as your equals, as brethren. By all your memories of Ireland, continue to love liberty – hate slavery – cling by the abolitionists – and in America, *you will do honor to the name of Ireland.*

Editor's Appendix M
A Brief Biography of Theodore W. Allen

Theodore W. Allen (1919–2005) was an anti–white supremacist, working-class intellectual and activist born in Indiana to a family "proletarianized by the Great Depression." He grew up in Huntington, West Virginia, and at the age of seventeen joined the Communist Party and his first union, Local 362 of the American Federation of Musicians. He subsequently served as a delegate to the Huntington Central Labor Union, AFL, worked as a coal miner in West Virginia, and was a member of three different United Mine Workers' locals, including Local 6206 (Gary), where he was an organizer and local president and co-organized a trade union organizing program for the Marion County West Virginia Industrial Union Council, CIO. After moving to New York City in the late 1940s, Allen conducted industrial economic research at the Labor Research Association, taught economics at the Communist Party's Jefferson School, and taught math at the Crown Heights Yeshiva in Brooklyn and the Grace Church School in New York. He left the Communist Party in the late 1950s, and, over the next forty-plus years, while living on the edge of poverty in the Crown Heights section of Brooklyn, he worked as a factory worker, retail clerk, mechanical design draftsmen, undergraduate instructor, postal worker (and member of Local 300 of the National Postal Mail Handlers Union), librarian, and independent scholar.[1]

Beginning in the 1960s, Allen began a forty-year-long study of white supremacy, racial oppression, and class struggle in American history. He was informed by the civil rights, anti-colonial, and national liberation struggles; by his prior experience as a Communist, a labor activist, and a student of history; and by close readings of Marxian political economics and W.E.B. Du Bois's *Black Reconstruction*.[2]

Allen pioneered the "white-skin privilege" analysis in 1965,[3] co-authored *White Blindspot* in 1967 and authored the accompanying "Can White ~~Workers~~ Radicals Be Radicalized?" (1969),[4] wrote the ground-breaking "'... They would have destroyed me': Slavery and the Origins of Racism" and *Class Struggle and the Origin of Racial Slavery: The Invention of the White Race* in 1974–75,[5] authored the seminal two-volume *The Invention of the White Race* in 1994 and 1997,[6] and wrote a number of extremely important published and unpublished pieces including "The Kernel and the Meaning ..." (1972), "White Supremacy in U.S. History" (1973), "The Peculiar Seed: The Plantation of Bondage" (1974), "Summary of the Argument of *The Invention of the White Race*" in two parts (1998), "In Defense of Affirmative Action in Employment Policy" (1998), " 'Race' and 'Ethnicity': History and the 2000 Census" (1999), and "Toward a Revolution in Labor History" (2004). He also wrote extremely important critical reviews of Edmund S. Morgan's *American Slavery, American Freedom* in 1978 and David Roediger's *The Wages of Whiteness: Race and the Making of the American Working Class* in 2001 and did a number of insightful interviews related to *The Invention of the White Race*.[7]

Allen was specifically inspired by Du Bois's insight that the South after the Civil War "presented the greatest opportunity for a real national labor movement which the nation ever saw" and that the organized labor movement failed to recognize "in black slavery and Reconstruction" "the kernel and meaning of the labor movement in the United States."[8] Drawing from these insights, Allen initially conceived of the idea of writing a historical study of three crises in United States history in which there were general confrontations "between capital and urban and rural laboring classes." The crises were those of the Civil War and Reconstruction, the Populist Revolt of the 1890s, and the Great Depression of the 1930s. In analyzing those confrontations, Allen found that "the key to the defeat of the forces of democracy, labor and socialism was in each case achieved by ruling-class appeals to white supremacism, basically by fostering white-skin privileges of laboring-class European-Americans." Drawing again on Du Bois and his notion of the "Blindspot in the eyes of America," which Allen paraphrased as "the white blindspot," he went on to describe the role of the theory and practice of white supremacy in shaping the outcomes of those three great crises.[9]

In his historical research, Allen was addressing the recurring question of "Why No Socialism in the United States?" His historical findings led him to challenge what he described as the prevailing consensus among left and labor historians that attributed the low level of class consciousness among American workers to such factors as the early development of civil liberties, the heterogeneity of the work force, the safety valve of homesteading opportunities in the west, the ease of social mobility, the relative shortage of labor, and the early development of "pure and simple trade unionism." He argued that the "classical consensus on the subject" was the product of the efforts of such writers as Frederick Engels, "co-founder with Karl Marx of the very theory of proletarian revolution"; Frederick A. Sorge, "main correspondent of Marx and Engels in the United States" and a socialist and labor activist for almost sixty years; Frederick Jackson Turner, giant of U.S. history; Richard T. Ely, Christian Socialist and author of "the first attempt at a labor history in the United States"; Morris Hillquit, founder and leading figure of the Socialist Party for almost two decades; John R. Commons, who with his associates authored the first comprehensive history of the U.S. labor movement; Selig Perlman, a Commons associate who later authored *A Theory of the Labor Movement*; Mary Beard and Charles A. Beard, labor and general historians; and William Z. Foster, a major figure in the history of U.S. communism with "his analyses of 'American exceptionalism.'" Allen challenged this "old consensus" as being "seriously flawed ... by erroneous assumptions, one-sidedness, exaggeration, and above all, by white-blindness." He offered an alternate theory, which maintained that white supremacism, reinforced among European-Americans by "white-skin privilege," was the main retardant of working-class consciousness in the U.S. He further argued that proponents of radical social change should direct principle efforts at challenging the system of white supremacy and "white-skin privilege."[10]

Allen's theoretical contributions were based on a lifetime of study and participation in the class struggle. His work influenced Students for a Democratic Society and sectors of the "New Left" and paved the way for the academic study of "white privilege" and "race as social construct." Despite the influence of his ideas, his own writings were largely ignored, misunderstood, or mischaracterized, and when used, they were often omitted from sources or not properly cited. Such practices did not encourage, and at times discouraged, the reading of his original writings and the sources he so meticulously cited.[11]

In the course of his work on the three great social crises, in the midst of the ruling-class-led and state-supported white supremacist counter-offensive to the 1960s, and as wide attention was being given to Winthrop D. Jordan's National Book Award–winning *White Over Black: American Attitudes Toward the Negro, 1550–1812*, Allen shifted his historical focus. He decided that the problems of white supremacy couldn't be resolved without a history of the continental Anglo-American plantation colonies of the seventeenth and eighteenth centuries. His reasoning was clear: more than a century after the abolition of slavery, white supremacy still ruled in the United States, and this phenomenon needed to be explained. The "racism-is-natural" argument associated with Jordan would not do. Allen felt "there was no way of getting around the challenge posed by Jordan's book." If white supremacy was natural, as Jordan suggested, then the prospects for a successful struggle against it were not encouraging. It was at that point that Allen "joined the ranks of historians searching for the origin of racial slavery" (see his introduction to this volume for a discussion of the historical debate). He turned "to the seventeenth-century Chesapeake and to the study of Bacon's Rebellion" to find an essential structural principle of the social order based on enslaved labor in the continental plantation colonies that was still essential to late twentieth-century America's social order based on wage labor.[12]

The first products of Allen's colonial research included a talk he delivered at a Union of Radical Political Economists (URPE) Conference at Yale

University in 1974, an unpublished paper entitled "The Peculiar Seed: The Plantation of Bondage" (1974) that grew into a lengthy manuscript of the same name by 1976, and an outline entitled "Toward an Integral Theory of Early Colonial History (Ten Theses)" that he used for a course he taught at Essex County Community College in Newark, New Jersey, in the fall of 1974. In 1975, he published "'... They would have destroyed me': Slavery and the Origins of Racism" in *Radical America*, which was later published, with more complete notes, as *Class Struggle and the Origin of Racial Slavery: The Invention of the White Race* by the Hoboken Education Project. The core theses that he put forth and later developed can be described as follows:

1. The "white race" was invented as a ruling-class social control formation in response to labor solidarity and heightened class struggle as manifested in the later, civil-war stages of Bacon's Rebellion (1676–77).
2. A system of racial privileges was deliberately instituted as a conscious ruling-class social control policy in order to define, establish, and maintain the "white race."
3. The consequences were not only ruinous to the interests of African-Americans, they were also "disastrous" for the European-American workers.[13]

In this period, Allen was also particularly insightful in his treatment of the reduction of European laborers and tenants to chattel bond-servants in Virginia in the 1620s. He describes how that reduction was not a feudal carryover, but rather a qualitative break from English law as codified in the Statute of Artificers of 1563 and represented an essential step toward racial slavery. It was imposed under capitalism and involved "conscious decision-making on the part of the London and Virginia capitalist 'adventurers.'" He also describes how into the 1670s, three-fourths of Virginia's chattel bond-servants were European-Americans, how there was a similarity of conditions for laboring-class and bond-servant European-Americans and African-Americans, and how, in the period from "the 1663 Servants' Plot for an insurrectionary march to freedom, to the tobacco riots of 1682, there were no fewer than ten popular and servile revolts and revolt plots in Virginia." In addition Allen documents how solidarity among the laboring classes reached a peak during the later, civil-war stage of Bacon's Rebellion when the capital, Jamestown, was burned; two thousand rebels forced the governor to flee across the Chesapeake Bay and "foure hundred English and Negroes in Arms" demanded their freedom from bondage.[14]

It took almost twenty years for Allen to complete Volume I of *The Invention of the White Race*, which was first published by Verso in 1994. On the back cover, Allen wrote that "there were no 'white' people" in Virginia in 1619 when the first African-Americans arrived. In two decades of meticulous research into Virginia's colonial records, he found "no instance of the official use of the word 'white' as a token of social status" prior to 1691. This was not merely a matter of semantics; he found that the "white race" was not and could not have been functioning in early Virginia.[15]

Allen's writings played a major, though often unacknowledged role in influencing the work of other historians and social theorists. However, much of the work that followed his was not quite along the lines he desired. Thus, in 1997, Stanford University professor George M. Fredrickson asserted in the *New York Review of Books* that "the proposition that race is 'a social and cultural construction' has become an academic cliché."[16] But, as Allen explained, "Just as it is unhelpful ... to euphemize racial slavery in continental Anglo-America as 'the Peculiar Institution,' instead of identifying the 'white race,' itself, as the truly peculiar institution governing the life of the country after emancipation as it did in slavery times; just as it is not 'race' in general, that must be understood, but the 'white race,' in particular."[17]

According to Allen, viewing "race as a social and cultural construction" has value in "objectifying 'whiteness,' as a historical rather than a biological category," but it is "an insufficient basis for refutation of white-supremacist apologetics."[18] He stressed that "the logic of 'race as a social construct' must be tightened and the focus sharpened" and "the 'white race' must be understood, not simply as a social construct [rather than a genetic phenomenon], but as a *ruling class social control formation*."[19]

This position is consistent with Allen's repeated efforts to challenge what he considered to be the two main arguments that undermine and disarm the struggle against white supremacy in the working class: 1) the argument that white supremacism is innate, and 2) the argument that European-American workers benefit from "white race" privileges and white supremacism, that the privileges are in their class interest. These two arguments, opposed by Allen, are related to two master historical narratives rooted in writings on the colonial period. The first argument is associated with the "unthinking decision" explanation for the development of racial slavery offered by historian Winthrop D. Jordan in his influential, National Book Award–winning work *White Over Black*. The second argument is associated with historian Edmund S. Morgan's similarly influential *American Slavery, American Freedom*, which maintains that, as racial slavery developed, "there were too few free poor [European-Americans] on hand to matter." Allen's work directly challenged both Jordan's theory of the "unthinking decision" and Morgan's theory of "too few free poor."[20]

The work of historian David Roediger, especially his book *The Wages of Whiteness*, also drew Allen's criticism and, although he thought Roediger had "contributed to the objectivation of whiteness" and the struggle against white supremacy, he saw "flaws, errors, and distortions of historical interpretation" in his work. He thought that it offered "an insufficient basis for refutation of white-supremacist apologetics, and for advancing 'the abolition of whiteness.'"[21] Allen emphasized that there was a "fundamental difference between Roediger's analysis of the etiology of the historical curse of white supremacism among laboring-class European-Americans" and his own view, and he felt the difference was important because "understanding the cause [of white supremacism] is essential for knowing the cure."[22] He then explained:

> The main difference, as I see it, is this: I fix responsibility on the bourgeoisie for the invention and nurture of the "white race," *as a social control formation*, as the most general form of class collaboration in Anglo-America in its colonial and its regenerated United States form, whereby the "white" workers are incorporated in the intermediate buffer social control stratum.

Roediger, on the other hand, "claiming to be influenced [by] the writings of those whom he calls 'neo-Marxists' Herbert Gutman and E. P. Thompson … denies that 'racism simply trickles down the class structure'" and "goes on to disparage the 'conspiratorial views' of those who believe that the bourgeoisie invented the white race, and guarantees it preservation as a means of social control."[23]

Allen continued, "No serious student of history nor any critical observer of the workaday world thinks that ruling-class intentions and preferences regarding social control 'simply trickle down' to mindless proles programmed to comply with prescribed roles and rules of social behavior." He thought that Roediger had created "a polemical straw man." Allen also concluded that it was "not reassuring to find Roediger flattering Winthrop D. Jordan, author of *White Over Black*, for the 'full and eloquent' way Jordan 'trace[d] the roots of racism.'"[24]

Allen emphasized that "it was Jordan, along with Carl N. Degler, who played the role of 'point man' in the historiographical 'white backlash' against the revival of equalitarianism that accompanied the rise of the African-American civil rights movement in the post–World War II period." According to Jordan, wrote Allen, "European-Americans were indeed pre-programmed by their gene-pool for white supremacism, that ordained the 'need of transplanted Englishmen to know … they were … white.'"[25] In Allen's estimation, Jordan was saying that white supremacism among European-American workers "was merely an expression of the natural affinity of European-Americans in general, an ingrained characteristic older and more deeply rooted than even the division of society into labor and capital." Allen wondered "why Roediger, after dispatching the 'trickle-down' straw man so handily" could "ignore the very real and fundamental challenge posed by Jordan, namely, the belief that the white supremacism is natural in European-Americans and that therefore 'there [is] little one [can] do to wipe it out.'"[26]

Jordan's argument had to be addressed. Allen explained, "Unless we are ready to face the Jordan challenge, how can we persuade others of the possibility of moving this country, in Roediger's phrase, 'towards the abolition of whiteness'? Simply ignoring Jordan's argument will not do, there needs to be a counter to Jordan's simple genetic 'need to know they were white.'"[27]

Allen then reached the crux of the matter. "If racial oppression ... is a bad thing and there are people who are determined to do something about it, then 'two basic strategic questions must be weighed and decided.'" First, "Is white supremacism ... a natural, genetically determined characteristic (or ... a trait ineradicably ingrained in them by an immemorial heritage) of European-Americans; or is it a learned behavior that can be unlearned?" Second, "Does ... white supremacism ... correspond to and express the interests of European-Americans?" Allen reasoned,

> If white supremacism is a *natural* attribute of European-Americans, then there are two alternatives: either to resort to moral appeals to human decency, which in the nature of the case, would be directed primarily to the wealthy and socially power-ful elements of the European-American population; *or*, rebellion by the oppressed.

Regarding laboring-class European-Americans, Allen makes the very impor-tant point that "if white supremacism is an inborn characteristic, there is no need for the ruling-class to divert what would otherwise add to capitalist profits in order to grant them special 'racial' privileges to guarantee their support in keeping the African-Americans down and out." If, however, "white suprema-cism is a *learned* behavior, there must be a possibility that it can be unlearned by sufficient sectors of the European-American population to render the 'white race' defunct, and bring an end to the system of racial oppression in the United States."[28]

That led Allen to the second strategic question: "Does ... white suprema-cism ... correspond to and express the interests of European-Americans?" The answer was clearly yes "for the European-American ruling class" who "have consistently ... confirmed the system of racial oppression as representing their best class interests." In contrast, "the rank-and-file European-Americans have no part in the basic policy decisions regarding the economic and politi-cal course of national affairs, provided that their racial privileges vis-à-vis the African-Americans do not appear to be threatened." To Allen, this was "the essence of the historic American class-collaboration compact, the true Peculiar Institution, the 'white race.'" Allen then asked, "Does this policy correspond to the interests of the European-American dependent classes that live by their wage and salary income?" If so, he answered, "there is basically no hope for a successful laboring-class 'black-and-white-unite-and-fight' policy; and the racially oppressed are forced to face the prospect ... of either appealing to the rich and powerful, or rebellion (with whatever support others may give them out of equalitarian principles)." On the other hand, he asks, "If white supremacism does not correspond to the interests of the laboring-class European-Americans, what induces them to give it their active or passive support?"[29]

To Allen, Roediger "saw 'whiteness' and white supremacy as creations, in part, of the white working class itself." He writes that for Roediger, it "was a way in which white workers responded to a fear of dependency on wage labor and to the necessities of capitalist work discipline." But, asks Allen, "*why* did these workers 'respond' to capitalist expropriation, exploitation and regimentation *in that particular way*, and not by supporting Abolition, as did Frederick Douglass, Solomon Northrup, and conventions of African-Americans in New England, Ohio, and Connecticut?" And why did they not support Abolition like the Chartists in England did?[30]

For Allen, Roediger's statement that the white workers were only "in part" the creators of white supremacism "leaves the inference that others elements in the society made up the other part." But "he does not tell his readers who these others were, nor why they favored white supremacism and how they created it," though, as Allen points out, drawing from Marx, "the ruling ideas of any society are the ideas of the ruling class." "In the period between the American Revolution and the Civil War the ruling ideas were those of the bourgeoisie." These ideas included: "the defeat of the proposal to stop the slave trade in the beginning of the new country"; "the establishment of a quota system that gave a bonus such that two 'white' persons in the main slaveholding states counted as much as three 'whites' in other states in the allotment of electoral votes for President and Vice President and for members of the House of Representatives"; "the nullification of the slavery-limitation of the Northwest Ordinance"; and "a succession of 'compromises,' and ever harsher fugitive slave laws, capped by the Dred Scott decision." In each of these cases, points out Allen, "it was the plantation bourgeoisie who ruled."[31]

Writing less than two years before his death, the 83-year-old Allen urged "those of us who hope to learn from history in order to prepare for future confrontations, large and small, between capital and anti-capital, between 'the people and the Titans'" to "take up – behaviorally and forensically" four challenges on the ideological front in order to refute "white supremacist apologetics":

> First, show that white supremacism is not an inherited attribute of the European-American personality
>
> Second, demonstrate that swallowing the white-supremacist bait has not been in the best interests of laboring-class European-Americans
>
> Third, account for the prevalence of white supremacism within the ranks of laboring-class European-Americans
>
> Fourth, by the light of history, consider ways whereby European-American laboring people may cast off the stifling incubus of "white" identity[32]

These are the challenges that Allen addresses in *The Invention of the White Race*.

Editor's Appendix N
Notes to Encourage Engagement
with Volume I

Theodore W. Allen's *The Invention of the White Race* is an extremely important and complex work. He believed that his thesis on "the origin and nature of the so-called 'white race'" contain the "root ... of a general theory of United States history, more consistent than others that have been advanced" (p. 1). The work moves between historical, theoretical, and statistical presentations; covers materials from four continents and from medieval times to the present; presents new theoretical concepts and definitions; and poses, in a very principled way, formidable challenges to much assumed history.

In his 1998 "Summary of the Argument of *The Invention of the White Race*," Allen explains that the two volumes offer a historical treatment of a few precisely defined concepts including: 1) "the essential nature of the social control structure of class societies"; 2) "racial oppression without reference to 'phenotype' factors"; 3) "racial slavery in continental Anglo-America as a particular form of racial oppression"; and 4) "the 'white race' – an all-class association of European-Americans held together by 'racial' privileges conferred on laboring-class European-Americans relative to African-Americans – as the principal historic guarantor of ruling-class domination of national life."

Allen's "Summary," which is over one hundred pages long, was written one year after the publication of the second volume in an effort to introduce new readers to the subject matter of *Invention*. It is a well thought out, well written, and highly recommended read.[1]

The Invention of the White Race Volume I: *Racial Oppression and Social Control* was published in 1994. The first volume was written, according to Allen, to create a "conceptual groundwork" free of the "White Blindspot." In his way, he hoped the reader would more clearly understand the "invention of the white race" at the end of the seventeenth century – a history that he thoroughly details in Volume II and briefly outlines on pp. 23–4 of this volume.

In the "Introduction" to Volume I, Allen begins by reviewing the historical debate on the relationship of slavery and racism. At its core, the debate centered on whether "racism was historically prior and the oppression of the African-American was derivative" (the "natural racism" argument) or whether "racism was derivative of ill-treatment of African-Americans in the form of slavery." The "implications" of this debate for the "rising anti-racism cause" are profound (pp. 1–3).

Allen proceeds to divide historians writing on slavery and racism in the seventeenth century into two broad groups, "psycho-cultural" and "socio-economic." His main critique is directed toward the "psycho-culturals," since he places himself in, but not totally of, the "socio-economic" group. Due to "serious compromising ambiguities and inconsistencies" in their work, he sees the need to free the socio-economic thesis of certain critical weaknesses. He then casts the argument "in a new conceptual mold" by approaching "racial slavery as a particular form of *racial oppression*, and racial oppression as a sociogenic – rather than a phylogenic – phenomenon." His focus is "primarily, not on *why* the bourgeoisie … had recourse to … slavery, but rather on *how* they could establish … that degree of *social control*" necessary to maintain such a system (p. 1).

Allen's discussion of the psycho-cultural historians focuses primarily on the work of Winthrop D. Jordan, who describes the advent of racial slavery as "an unthinking decision." It also addresses the work of Carl Degler, who, according to Allen, offers "the facile thesis that the origin of racial slavery is to be found in an English precedent of racial prejudice against non-Europeans." In countering these historians, Allen offers historical facts that contradict their positions, paying particular attention to the treatment of "mulattos" in the West Indies as compared to those in the continental Anglo-American plantation colonies, and emphasizes that "the record indicates that laboring-class European-Americans in the continental plantation colonies showed little interest in 'white identity' before the institution of the system of 'race' privileges at the end of the seventeenth century" (pp. 6, 9, 14).

In reviewing proponents of "the socio-economic argument," Allen discusses the strengths and weaknesses of the work of Oscar and Mary Handlin, Eric Williams, Edmund S. Morgan, and Timothy Breen. He points out that:

1. The Handlins correctly emphasized the similarity of conditions for Anglo-American and African-American bond-laborers in early Virginia and the difference of treatment of "white" laborers in Anglo-America and in the Anglo-Caribbean, but they were close to Degler in assuming a "natural racism"-type explanation for the development of racial discrimination (pp. 3, 15);
2. Williams correctly pointed out the self-activating role of bond-laborers but offered an oversimplified economic explanation regarding the employment of Africans as bond-laborers which ignored social control issues (pp. 15–16); and
3. Breen correctly emphasized the role of African-American bond-laborers in struggle, including struggles alongside European-American bond-laborers and poor freedmen, but "in his reliance on objective factors to explain white racism among European-Americans of the laboring class," he gave "no scope at all

to deliberate ruling-class policy in the displacement of European-American proletarian class consciousness by the incubus of a 'white' identity with the employing classes" (pp. 19–21).

Allen's major treatment of a socio-economic interpretation is that of Morgan's *American Slavery, American Freedom*. Though the work "provided the most substantial contribution so far to a socio-economic interpretation of the origin of racial slavery" (p. 16), Allen maintains that Morgan was, nevertheless, "wrong on the facts and wrong on the theory" when he wrote that there were "too few free poor [whites] on hand to matter" in colonial Virginia (p. 18).

Following his analysis of Morgan, Allen turns his attention to the work of historian Lerone Bennett, Jr. He believes that Bennett places the argument "on the three essential bearing-points from which it cannot be toppled":

> First, that racial slavery constituted a ruling-class response to a problem of labor solidarity. Second, that a system of racial privileges for the propertyless "whites" was deliberately instituted in order to align them on the side of the plantation bour-geoisie against the African-American bond-laborers. Third, the consequence was not only ruinous to the interests of the African-Americans, but was "disastrous" for the propertyless "whites" as well. (p. 21)

After reviewing the historiography of the debate, Allen offers brief comments on "The Misleading Term 'Race.'" He emphasizes that "when an emigrant population from 'multiracial' Europe goes to North America ... [and] by constitutional fiat incorporates itself as 'the white race,' that is no part of genetic evolution. It is rather a political act: the invention of 'the white race.' It lies within the proper sphere of study of social scientists, and it is an appropriate objective for alteration by social activists" (p. 22).

Allen concludes his introduction by describing how "the reflector of Irish history" affords "insights into American racial oppression and white supremacy" and "presents a case of racial oppression *without reference to 'skin color' or, as the jargon goes, 'phenotype'* " (p. 22).

On pages 22–3, Allen offers an instructive ten-point outline of the first volume and on pages 231–2 he offers a brief chronology of Irish history.

In Chapter 1, on "The Anatomy of Racial Oppression," Allen explains that by considering racial oppression "in terms of the substantive, the operative element, i.e., 'oppression,'" it is possible to avoid "contradictions and howling absurdities that result from attempts to splice genetics and sociology." In addition, by examining it as a particular system of oppression – like oppression based on gender, class, or nationality – there is "firmer footing for analyzing racial slavery, and the invention and peculiar function of the 'white race,' and for confronting the theory that racial oppression can be explained in terms of 'phenotype.'" He considers the "phenotype" argument to be "the old ace-in-the hole of racist apologetics" (p. 28).

His core argument in this regard, as he later summarized it, is that "a comparative study of Anglo-Norman rule and 'Protestant Ascendancy' in Ireland, and 'white supremacy' in continental Anglo-America (in both its colonial and regenerate United States forms) demonstrates that racial oppression is not dependent upon differences of 'phenotype,' i.e., of physical appearances of the oppressor and the oppressed."[2] Further, as he explains in Chapter 1, "The history of English rule in Ireland, and of the Irish in America, presents instructive parallels and divergences for the understanding of 'race' as a sociogenic, rather than a phylogenic category; and of racial slavery as a system of social control" (p. 28).

In a summary of his argument, Allen writes, "Racial oppression, gender oppression, and national oppression, all present basic lines of social distinction other than economic ones," and, though "inherently contradictory to class distinctions, these forms of social oppression, nevertheless, under normal conditions, serve to reinforce the ascendancy of the ruling class." He describes the informing principle of racial oppression, in its colonial origins and as it has persisted in subsequent historical contexts, as *the reduction of all members of the oppressed group to one undifferentiated social status, beneath that of any member of the oppressor group.*"[3]

Allen describes several examples of racial oppression throughout history, including African-Americans in the United States both pre- and post-emancipation (pp. 32–3), American Indians in the nineteenth century (pp. 33–4), and the Irish in the early 1300s and then again after 1652 (pp. 34–5), particularly under the Protestant Ascendancy (p. 51). He points out that in each of these instances, "a society, organized on the basis of the segmentation of land and other natural resources under private, heritable individual titles, and having a corresponding set of laws and customs, acting under the direction of its ruling class … institutes a system of rule … designed to deny, disregard and delegitimize the … distinctions previously existing among the people brought under colonial rule." After being subjected to "social death," the members of the subjugated group take up new forms of resistance with the task of overthrowing racial oppression. In some cases, "the ruling power is able to maintain its dominance only by co-opting a stratum of the subject population into the system of social control." In such a case, by "officially establishing a social distinction among the oppressed, the colonial power transforms its system of social control from racial oppression to national oppression" (pp. 35–6).

For Allen, the Haitian Revolution represented "failure of this colonial policy of cooptation." "British policy in the West Indies, and the policy of British Union and Catholic Emancipation in Ireland, represented its success." In contrast, "the colonial power in continental Anglo-America, and in the Union of South Africa, succeeded in stabilizing its rule on the foundation of racial oppression" (p. 36).

Allen moves from analogy to analysis as he describes the assault on tribal relations of African-Americans and American Indians, contradictory Irish and English social structures, and the assault on Irish tribal relationships. He concludes that "given the common constitutional principles of the three cases – the Irish, the American Indian, and the African-American – the abundant parallels they present … constitute a compelling argument for the sociogenic theory of racial oppression" (p. 46). In Ireland, from the 1652 Act of Settlement onward, racial oppression "was written into every new title deed and anchored in the bedrock of the colonial economy" and "'The Protestant Ascendancy,' was a classic system of racial oppression" (p. 51).

In Chapter 2, on "Social Control and the Intermediate Strata: Ireland," Allen demonstrates his understanding of the ruling class's efforts to try to address two priority tasks – maximizing profit and maintaining social control. He begins with an analysis of how "the imposition of racial oppression" enables the colonial regime to "exploit the wealth and the labor of the country with a minimum of interference." On the other hand, it produces "an extreme degree of alienation of the laboring people of the oppressed group" and deprives "the colonial ruling class … of an indigenous intermediate social control stratum as an instrumentality for a profitable operation." In so doing, it limits "normal bourgeois methods for raising of the rate of return by exploitation of labor" (p. 52).

Thus, in Anglo-America, the primary method of raising plantation-labor productivity was "the intensification of labor, which necessitated increased supervisory investment, and was absolutely limited by the physical constitution of the laborers." The alternative, capitalist, method was "the revolutionizing of the instruments of production," and it "was inhibited under racial slavery by the employers' reluctance 'to trust delicate and costly implements to the … slaves.'" In Ireland, the eighteenth-century Penal Laws that banned Catholic acquisition of land similarly "foreclosed all possibility of significantly raising productivity of labor by resorting to incentives for the Catholics of the laboring classes." In addition, in both Ireland and the continental Anglo-American plantation colonies, "the illegalization of literacy of the laboring classes made impossible … the use of increasingly complex implements and techniques of production" (pp. 52–3).

Allen writes, "Where the option was for racial oppression," a "successful" policy was one that could "maximize the return on capital investment … while assuring its perpetuation through an efficient system of social control." With that understanding, he discusses how the history of England in Ireland from the Anglo-Norman invasion of 1169 through the Plantation of Ulster in 1609 was "a history of the failure of three strategies of social control: 1) the Anglo-Norman 'middle nation'; 2) the policy of 'surrender-and-regrant' [of land claims]; and 3) the policy of 'plantation'" (p. 53).

In the case of the English (Anglo-Norman) "middle nation," he contends that "human affinity" prevailed over "racist exclusionism" and the initial, thirteenth-century attempt "to impose racial oppression on the Irish …

contributed decisively to the defeat of its perpetrators." The English side became weaker and the Anglo-Irish side became stronger as they sought "to make accommodation with the native Irish chieftains" (p. 54). The "English 'identity' of the Anglo-Normans proved to be no serious barrier" to partnership with the Irish chieftains in ruling Ireland from the fourteenth to the sixteenth century. This feature of Irish history, Allen argues, "refutes the most fundamental assumption of the Jordan/Degler thesis, namely, that, given a choice, persons of a given 'gene pool,' will naturally choose to maintain that 'identity' " (pp. 55–6).

Under the "surrender-and-regrant" policy, Gaelic chieftains who surrendered their land claims and pledged allegiance to the English Crown were regranted English titles to the lands. This policy lasted only twenty-five years and was soon "overtaken" by European political developments. The bourgeois monarchy in England then sought to develop a new buffer social-control group along the lines of a gentry and yeomanry (pp. 57–9).

Under this new plan of "Protestant Plantation," English capitalists first financed the settlement of English tenants in Ireland in order "to provide a self-supporting militia to guarantee the eventual subjugation of the entire country." Land titles were transferred from Gaelic Irish and Old English to New English. English tenants would generally supplant Irish tenants, and laborers were to be mainly native Irish. The displaced Irish would be transplanted beyond the areas of English settlement. Under the rules for the first Ulster Plantation (1572–73), no member of the Celtic Irish owning or learned classes was to be admitted. Within the Plantation boundaries, "to be Irish was to be a 'churl,' a laborer," and it was ordered that "no Irishman … shall purchase land, beare office, be chosen of any jury," etc. Designed as a "response to rebellion," plantations were also undertaken in Leix and Offaly (1556) and Munster (1585). However, Gaelic resistance persisted, and the Catholic Anglo-Irish "were increasingly … alienated by the government-fostered Protestant New English" (p. 59).

As a program for establishing social control, "plantation" was a negation of "surrender-and-regrant," which "presumed the cooptation of the Irish chieftains as the social buffer." "Plantation was based on the degradation and exclusion of the chieftains" and led to further resistance from the Irish chiefs and tribes culminating in the Tyrone War of 1594–1603, the great Celtic war of liberation. Under the leadership of Hugh O'Neill and Red Hugh O'Donnell, the Irish defeated the English in a series of battles that climaxed in the great victory at Yellow Ford on August 14, 1598 (pp. 59–60).

Allen makes the very important point that "as late as 1600, the English position in relation to Ireland was much like that of the European powers as it was and would remain until well into the nineteenth century with respect to sub-Saharan Africa. In neither case could the invaders accomplish the first essential step in colonization, i.e., the establishment of their commanding authority over the prospective colonial territory." While the Europeans controlled the seas, as historian Basil Davidson explains, "the Africans were masters on the land; and they made sure they remained so." Consequently, "conquering and occupying African territory" would absorb European attention in the nineteenth and twentieth centuries (p. 61 and Appendix C, pp. 206–8).

In Ireland, conditions were complicated by proximity to England and European politics. Economic development and "a corresponding social and political transformation" enabled England to emerge "as an aggressive competitor in the new-fledged world market." In addition to its exploitative colonialist ambitions regarding Ireland, England engaged in a historic confrontation with Spain and was increasingly concerned about the Spanish threat as well as with potential ties between Catholic Spain and Catholic Ireland (p. 61).

With the cause of Irish independence gaining support, Queen Elizabeth issued her "Great Warrant of Ireland" in January 1600, which created a military establishment in Ireland of over 12,000 personnel. By November 1601, the military presence had increased to over 17,000. This force, commanded by Lord Mountjoy, waged a vicious war involving a "starvation strategy" across three-fourths of Ireland, including Ulster. This approach, which included clearing territory for English "plantations," led to Irish submission in 1603 (pp. 62–4).

The option for racial oppression was "sustainable in three of Ireland's four provinces only by the continual presence of large British military garrisons." In this context, Ireland became "a major focus" of the struggle between Catholic Spain and Protestant England and, as a consequence, there was "a redefinition of racial oppression in Ireland as *religio-racial* oppression." For that reason, "the English ruling class could not recruit an intermediate stratum by promotion of a portion of the Irish laboring classes to the yeoman status, on the English model" and the English colonialists returned anew to the policy of "plantation" (p. 66).

The "fundamental contradiction" inherent in England's option for racial oppression in Ireland was that between "the economic aim of the most rapid accumulation of capital by the super-exploitation of the racially oppressed Irish tenants and laborers" and the need to develop a stable "civil regime" free of "heavy deductions necessary for military occupation." "Plantation" as a strategy of social control failed in three-fourths of the country. Ulster was the exception, "due to special circumstances" (pp. 65–6).

After reviewing this history, Allen suggests some "general principles of social control problems and policies of colonizing powers, and their relationship to the option for racial oppression" (pp. 69–70):

> After first establishing commanding authority, the colonizers pursued one of two general lines of policy, according to circumstances ... Where they found a developed and well-defined hierarchical system of classes, the new rulers sought to adapt the pre-existing social structure to their own needs, co-opting amenable elements

of the old order into their colonial administration, as a buffer and social control stratum over and against the masses of the super-exploited wealth-producing laboring classes. Such was the case of the Spanish in Peru and Mexico; of the Portuguese in India and the East Indies; of the English in India; and the Dutch in the East Indies.

Where, on the other hand, they encountered a society with no previously developed significant class differentiation, ... the conquerors employed a policy tending to the complete elimination of the indigenous population by slaughter and expulsion. The Spanish in the Caribbean, the Portuguese in Brazil, the English in St. Vincent, and the English and Anglo-Americans in North America, demonstrated this approach. In such cases, the colonizers found themselves obliged to seek foreign supplies of commodity-producing labor, and were obliged to "invent" and establish an intermediate social control stratum for each colony by promoting elements of the imported laboring class. (pp. 69–70)

Allen explains in regard to the extermination option that "it would have been impossible for the English [from the sixteenth to the eighteenth century] to have perpetrated such complete extermination of the Irish people as that executed upon the Caribs and Arawaks by the Spanish in the Caribbean in the sixteenth century" because there was in Ireland "a much more substantial general English hostage population subject to retaliation." In addition, the Catholic Irish and Anglo-Irish had allies including "popes, potentates, and powers." On the other hand, the English option for religio-racial oppression in Ireland at the end of the sixteenth century "eliminated the possibility of recruiting an indigenous intermediate social control stratum" and this "would remain the central problem of British rule in Ireland for over two more centuries." The result was that, in Ulster, "they succeeded in establishing an intermediate stratum" and maintained racial oppression "without sending an army," while outside of Ulster, "they would in time be forced to abandon rule by racial oppression" (pp. 69–70).

In Chapter 3, on "Protestant Ascendancy and Racial Oppression," Allen explains that after the defeat of the Irish-Jacobite cause in the war of 1689–91, the Protestant Parliament of Ireland began "a seventy-year program of Penal Law enactments to rivet the Protestant Ascendancy in place." Protestant Ascendancy then dominated Ireland for the next hundred years. Allen points out that though Protestant Ascendancy offers many insights into understanding racial oppression, students of American history have neglected this field of investigation because "they mistake the chattel *form* of labor, along with perceived variations in physical *appearance,* for the essential substance of racial oppression" (pp. 71–2).

Aware that the comparison between Protestant Ascendancy and racial oppression may raise questions, Allen first addresses why the English Protestant ruling class "did not try to impose a system of chattel bond-servitude on the Irish in Ireland, as they did on Afro-Americans." As a counter to a "phenotype"-like argument, he notes the existence of "white" on "white" slavery in Scotland, the shipment of Irish men to Sweden in 1610, and the "Irish Slave Trade" of the 1650s. He maintains that the principal reason there was no chattel bond-servitude in Ireland had to do with "cost-benefit ratios" (pp. 71–5, 218–20).

Next, Allen addresses why the Irish could not become Protestant, which would seem to be a simple way out of their bondage. He focuses on the issue of "social control." He points out that although the ruling party was the Anglican Church of Ireland Establishment, some two-thirds of the Protestants were Dissenters, primarily Presbyterian Scots-Irish of Ulster. British rule in Ireland required preventing any coalescence of a potential opposition majority and this meant "above all" that it was necessary to prevent "the aggrieved middle-class yeomanry-type Presbyterian and other Dissenters from making common 'nationalist' cause with the mass of the peasantry." The key to that strategy was maintaining the "prejudice of the Dissenters against the Catholic peasantry," and it was thus essential that the Irish "not be converted, but remain Catholic" (p. 79).

Allen then writes, "*The essential elements of discrimination against the Irish in Ireland, and against the Afro-Americans, which gave these respective regimes the character of racial oppression, were those that destroyed the original forms of social identity, and then excluded the oppressed groups from admittance into the forms of social identity normal to the colonizing power.*" In support of this analysis, he offers instructive comparisons between Protestant Ascendancy in Ireland and white supremacy in continental Anglo-America according to "the defining characteristics of racial oppression: 1) declassing legislation, directed at property-holding members of the oppressed group; 2) deprivation of civil rights; 3) illegalization of literacy; and 4) displacement of family rights and authorities" (pp. 81–9, esp. 82–3).

In Chapter 4, on "Social Control: From Racial to National Oppression," Allen examines that a key distinction between national oppression and racial oppression—the source from which the buffer social-control stratum is recruited. In doing so he demonstrates that under a system of racial oppression "social control depends upon the denial of the legitimacy of social distinctions within the oppressed group" while under national oppression "social control depends upon the acceptance and fostering of social distinctions within the oppressed group" (p. 273n11).

In 1689, the English Parliament established that there would be no standing army in that country. However, in the greater part of Ireland, the Catholic Irish outnumbered the Protestant English by over thirty to one and "Protestant civil law simply could not run." The English Parliament therefore decreed that the English military establishment in Ireland was to be an "invariable 12,000." Continued English rule, writes Allen, was "to be dependent on regular military forces for ordinary police duty" (p. 91).

Before the end of the eighteenth century, there was new pressure from external developments. There was a "storm of revolution" in the Anglo-American continental colonies, France, and Haiti (St. Domingue). In Ireland, Protestant nationalists spoke of independence and, for a time, favored Catholic Emancipation. At the same time, a significant part of the Irish military was deployed for war in America and elsewhere in the world. When the 1798 revolt of the United Irishmen broke out, 76,000 soldiers were needed to suppress it (pp. 91–2).

Allen describes how the crisis of British rule in Ireland, including threats of revolution and French invasion, "brought to maturation a process of rapprochement between the British king and parliament and Protestant Ascendancy, on the one hand; and the emergent Catholic bourgeoisie, on the other." The resolution of this crisis led to *a change in the system of British colonial rule in Ireland from racial oppression to national oppression, by the incorporation of the Irish bourgeoisie into the intermediate buffer social control stratum.*" By 1843, this process was defined in practice (pp. 91–2).

Allen then discusses both the Catholic Emancipation and the Repeal movements. Catholic Emancipation implied civil rights for propertied Catholics as well as membership in Parliament and the professions, in short, admittance "on a necessarily subordinate basis, into the buffer social control stratum." Repeal of the Union was aimed at the Acts of Union of 1800 that formed the United Kingdom of Great Britain and Ireland and "was a demand for national independence; not necessarily separation." The demand for repeal went far beyond Catholic Emancipation, and its proposed independent Irish Parliament "was a dagger pointed at British Protestant landlordism, at the automatic priority of British economic interests and the whole legacy of two centuries of preferential treatment of Protestants." As such, "it was seen as a threat to the British Empire as a whole" (pp. 96–7, 102–3).

The British colonial bourgeoisie's "Grand Dilemma" was how to incorporate the Catholic bourgeoisie "into the colonial buffer social-control stratum" without "sparking a movement for Irish national independence, or, alternately, alienating the Irish Protestants." It was determined they would maintain the Union and, "if forced to, would be ready to abandon rule by religio-racial oppression in favor of admitting the Irish Catholic bourgeoisie into a role in the system of social control." However, they would "go to war to prevent the establishment of a separate Irish parliament." The Irish Catholic bourgeoisie, while determined not to return to the Penal Law regime, was willing "to accept assignment as the major component in the system of British colonial control in Ireland" and to "content themselves with the transition from racial oppression to national oppression, instead of Irish self-rule" (pp. 96–7).

What is key, Allen points out, is that "In Ireland, the British ruling class found it necessary to draw the Irish Catholic bourgeoisie into the intermediate social control stratum, and thus to end racial oppression, except in Ulster." There was "no parallel of this phenomenon" in the U.S., but there was a parallel in the history of the British West Indies. Thus both "the British West Indies and Ireland demonstrate the general principle of 'relativity of race,' as a function of ruling-class social control." In both cases, "the colonial ruling power, faced with a combination of insurrectionary pressures, combined with external threats, over a period of time ... resolved the situation by the decision to recruit elements of the oppressed group – Catholics in one case and persons of African descent, in the other – into the intermediate buffer social control stratum" (pp. 112–3).

For Allen, the mechanisms of this transition from racial to national oppression help to better understand statements regarding West Indian immigrant integration in the U.S. It also serves "to underscore the contrast in the systems of bourgeois social control – national oppression in the West Indies, racial oppression in the United States." He quotes from Marcus Garvey and from Hubert Harrison, who experienced the "cultural shock" of the transition from what Allen describes as the "class-based 'tri-partite social order' with its Afro-Caribbean 'colored' intermediate stratum, to the white-supremacist social order in the United States" (pp. 112–3).

In Chapter 5, on "Ulster," Allen opens by discussing the transition from racial oppression to national oppression outside of Ulster. "Catholic Emancipation in 1829 led within a decade and a half to the replacement of racial oppression by national oppression as the main form of British colonial rule in Ireland, and to the concomitant incorporation of the Catholic Irish bourgeoisie into the British system of social control over that country." He contrasts this with the U.S., where African-American Emancipation in 1863 "did not lead to the end of racial oppression" or "to any fundamental change in the system of bourgeois social control." He asks, "Why the difference?" (p. 115).

To answer that question, he shows how the first social control measure proposed after the Plantation of Ulster was launched in 1609 was aimed at establishing "servitors," or planters, who were veterans of military service in Ireland. The servitors "embodied the essential character of a system of racial oppression: their social status was predicated upon the exclusion of Catholics from social mobility, and ... their civic function was to maintain and enforce that exclusion." However, their numbers were very small, and they never adequately met the social control needs of the Ulster plantation (p. 119).

These laboring-class settlers received guarantees of favorable treatment in what later came to be known as "the Ulster custom." The core of this custom, the "Protestant 'tenant right,' included the privilege of heritable leases and a full equity claim for improvements made by the tenant." This "Protestant social control force" was cemented in the period from 1689 to 1698 when fifty to eighty thousand Scots settled in Ireland, primarily in Ulster (pp. 122–4).

The interests of the British ruling class in Ireland, writes Allen, required that "the Protestant privilege of tenant-right, the Ulster Custom, ... not be interfered with." For the employing class, it was "the optimal settlement of ...

security and maximum profit," and it was generally understood that "the privileges of the Protestant laboring classes could not be disregarded without endangering the entire structure of social control" (p. 124).

Allen makes the important point that if social control was to be maintained in the Catholic provinces by the abandonment of the system of racial oppression, it was "imperative that racial oppression – Protestant Ascendancy – remain in place in Ulster." To do otherwise would invite "the equalitarian notions of the United Irishmen." Thus, "maintenance of the racial privileges" of Protestant tenants in Ulster "was the necessary complement" of the strategic admission of the Catholic bourgeoisie into the system of social control in the rest of Ireland (p. 127).

Allen also describes how in the nineteenth century "the religio-racial privileges of the Ulster Protestants were translated into a proletarian mode." He stresses that though the wages of the Protestant workers of Belfast were not especially high when compared with wages in Great Britain, "the differential between the skilled and the unskilled workers was far greater in Belfast than … in Britain." Allen comments that this "is characteristic of systems of racial oppression." Thus, preservation of the Ulster Protestant bastion was "an overriding principle of British ruling class policy, despite 'Catholic Emancipation.'" With "perfectly devilish ingenuity," as the Irish republican and socialist leader James Connolly would explain in 1913, "the master class," had contrived to turn the Protestant Ulster workers into allies, not of Catholic workers, but of the exploiting class (pp. 131–4).

Allen maintains that Ulster history provides evidence of four key principles of social control "in a stable civil society constituted on the basis of racial oppression," which can be summarized as follows (pp. 134–5):

1) The oppressor group must be in the majority;
2) The oppressor group is necessarily composed of an intermediate social control stratum of laboring classes, non-capitalist tenants, and wage-laborers;
3) These laboring-class members of the oppressor group are to be shielded against the competition of the members of the oppressed group, by the establishment of privileges; and
4) The system of racial privileges of the laboring classes of the oppressor group are adapted and preserved, in order to maintain the function of the intermediate buffer social-control stratum.

In Chapter 6, on "Anglo-America: Ulster Writ Large," Allen begins by offering important insights on the relations between the English and American Indians in the continental plantation colonies. He makes the key point that "the most fundamental obstacle facing the English colonizers was that the undifferentiated structure typical of the Indian tribes in North America did not present a serviceable indigenous ruling class that could be co-opted as supplier and controller of a labor force." He further explains that "it would be some time" before the English "would achieve sufficient relative strength vis-à-vis the native peoples even to ... think in terms of 'social control' over them" and well before then, they "had chosen the course of plantation monoculture and the combination of racial oppression with the chattel-labor form, both of which ruled out the use of Indian labor." Tobacco monoculture "required the continual expansion of the 'frontier' and the displacement of the Indians" and "chattel bond-servitude rendered counter-productive the enslavement of Indians, which would have deprived Anglo-American employers of essential assistance in combating the problem of runaway bond-laborers." Allen adds that "every aspect of the Ulster Plantation policy aimed at destroying the tribal leadership and dispersing the tribe" was "matched" in the nineteenth century by U.S. policy toward the American Indians. This, he adds, was "a policy we clearly recognize as racial oppression" (p. 136).

After this opening, Allen goes on to explain, "As in Ulster, the ruling class saw that it was necessary to support the privileges of the laboring class of the oppressor group as an investment in social control made at the expense of immediate profits." In this sense, Anglo-America was "Ulster Writ Large." He cites as examples the Penal Laws that excluded Catholics from apprenticeships to trades in Ireland and policies "to exclude Negroes from trades in order to preserve those places for 'white' artisans" in the Anglo-American plantation colonies of Barbados, South Carolina, and Georgia (pp. 137–8).

For Allen, the "most complete parallel" to the Ulster Custom was the "Homestead Right," exemplified in the Homestead Act of 1862, which sought to make land available in small parcels at no cost to European-American laboring-class settlers. The land would be "public land" taken from the Indians, and the campaign for it was led by the "Free Soil" movement. The 1854 Graduation Act had made "public" lands available to "white" "squatters" at low prices and the Homestead Act maintained the exclusion by limiting its provision "to 'citizens' or those immigrants who intended to become citizens of the United States" (pp. 138–9).

After winning the Civil War, the Northern bourgeoisie faced a funda-mental question of social control, "whether to continue the system of racial oppression, or to undertake to institute a new system of social control as the British ruling class had done in Ireland." For a time, powerful elements of the industrial bourgeoisie believed in land redistribution in the South and trans-forming that economy from one dominated by plantation owners to one of small independent farmers. In that spirit, in June of 1866, radicals in Congress passed the Southern Homestead Law, which opened up forty-seven million acres for eighty-acre homesteading. Congressman Thaddeus Stevens and Senator Charles Sumner put forth proposals for confiscation and redistribution of the lands of former slaveholders. Such a program, explains Allen, "meant the abandonment of the principle that made slavery in this country a special form of a general racial oppression … the refusal to give legitimacy to social class differentiation among the oppressed group." The creation "of a class of a million African-American freeholders by decree of the national legislature" would mean "African-Americans were to be accorded social status according to the norms of any society based on capitalist commodity production." The Sumner and Stevens proposals were not enacted, however, "because of their unacceptable implications for the capitalist class in general" (pp. 139–41).

Just as the Protestants had a choice between the United Irishmen and the Protestant Ascendancy in 1798, the European-Americans of the wage-laboring class "faced a fateful choice also in the late 1860s." That choice was whether or not to support "appropriation of the rebel plantations along the lines put forward by the Radical Republicans." For at least several decades, "the 'white labor' rationale for opposing the abolition of slavery was the 'competition' argument," which held "that Negroes, if freed, would become part of the wage-labor supply and would lower wages and reduce opportunities for 'white' workers." The Radical Republicans' land distribution program presented a historically unique opportunity "for reducing the impoverishing effect of the competition of an oversupply of wage-labor" (p. 141).

The land question had two important aspects, "the Western, 'free land' aspect, and the Southern rebel land aspect." Allen judges that "the former was primarily the interest of the petty bourgeoisie." In contrast, the latter offered the "most realistic hope that ever existed for proletarians, European-Americans, and African-Americans to become successful homesteaders" if rebel plantations were appropriated "along the lines put forward by the Radical Republicans" (pp. 141–2).

African-American freedmen in the South did work 800,000 acres of confiscated rebel land as renters under the administration of the Freedmen's Bureau. At its first convention in 1869, the Negro National Labor Union addressed the problem of oversupply of wage-labor in the southern states by urging Congress to understand that the "true and immediate practicable remedy lies in making a fair proportion of the laborers themselves land-owners." In contrast, the "white" National Labor Union, at its own founding convention in 1866, limited its consideration to "the Public Lands." The following year, citing jobs lost in New England mills because of a cotton shortage, the NLU called for "the speedy restoration of the Southern states" to the Union, meaning "a speedy end to Reconstruction with its promise of expropriation of rebels' plantations for distribution to the landless." In 1868, NLU leader William H. Sylvis "stridently denounced Reconstruction," and the NLU refused to support taking land from owners for distribution. Allen adds, "The NLU went out of existence after 1872, but the 'white labor' principles by which it was bound unfortunately did not" (pp. 142, 149).

Allen contends that when "Negro Emancipation" made "freedom a *human right*" it "destroyed it as *racial privilege*, and thereby threatened to dissolve …

the mortar holding together the system of bourgeois social control, the system of 'white'-labor privileges, based on the presumption of African-American chattel bond-servitude." He quotes Karl Marx in his 1864 letter to Abraham Lincoln, in which he writes that the Emancipation heralded "a new era ... of ascendancy of the working classes," and Allen adds that though Marx's comment was "falsely heralded," the record left by bourgeois Radical Republicans makes clear "that it was not an impossible dream for the United States to have ended the curse of racial oppression" (pp. 143, 150–1).

The Northern bourgeoisie indicated "its acceptance of post-Emancipation racial oppression by abandoning Reconstruction." The subsequent white-supremacist system in the South was established "by night-rider terror and one-sided 'riots' in order to deprive African-Americans of their Constitutional rights, reducing them again, by debt peonage and prisoner-leasing to a status that was slavery in all but name." The bourgeoisie, however, still faced the basic problem of "how to achieve civil order in a system based on racial oppression." From "the ruling-class point of view," there is "a limit of profitability in the maintenance of social control by ... sending an army," which indicates "a deficiency in the intermediate, buffer social-control stratum" and "discourages venture capital."

In that setting, writes Allen, the "bourgeoisie as a whole, drawing upon practices that had ante-bellum roots," opted for "White Reconstruction." It supported "reestablishment of the social control system of racial oppression, based on racial privileges for laboring-class 'whites' with regard to 'free' land, immigration, and industrial employment." The Negro Exodus of 1879 and the Cotton Mill Campaign from 1880 were "defining moments" of this movement (p. 144).

Regarding the Exodus of 1879, Allen describes how 100,000 "laboring-class African-Americans in the South" were "determined to make a withdrawal of variable capital, i.e., their own labor-power, from the plantation system." However, just as Home Rule for Ireland was unacceptable to the British ruling class "because of its threatening democratic implications," so did the U.S. ruling class reject "this, or any, 'settlement of the Negro question,'" that might lead to "an unwelcome array of popular forces against the course of unchecked capitalist greed," an array "freed of the paralyzing incubus of 'white' racial privileges." Allen describes how the ruling class turned to terror and contends that the bourgeoisie in the U.S. "play[ed] 'the White card' to destroy the Exodus" as the British "played 'the Orange card,' against Home Rule." Northern commercial interests opposed the Exodus and supported the existing Southern labor system, and, Allen emphasizes, the "preservation of 'the southern labor system' required the maintenance of the system of racial privileges of laboring-class Euro-Americans ... not just in the South but throughout the country" (pp. 145–7).

Allen then describes how "white labor rendered itself powerless to shape land policy by accepting the white-skin privilege principle of Free Soil and the Homestead Act of 1862" and how "by turning its back on Black labor's dream for land and loans for the freedmen, it had endorsed capitalist land monopoly in the South." Then, the industrial bourgeoisie, having consolidated its power, proceeded "to dispose of the 'public lands' for railroad building enterprises, and for other forms of direct and indirect exploitation ... by large capitalist enterprises." By 1890, four times as much land had been given to railroad capitalists as had been given to homesteaders since 1862, and for those homesteaders who got land, "the pressure of capitalist exploiters took a devastating toll." Of the 8.4 million people engaged in agriculture in the U.S. in 1890, over 35 percent were hired laborers and another 18 percent were laboring-class tenants (pp. 152–3).

Allen emphasizes – "by shaping the homestead policy as a white-skin privilege, the ruling class had secured the acquiescence of laboring-class whites in the overthrow of Black Reconstruction." This was followed by "the other side of its policy on the land question – the power of Capital to expropriate a great proportion of the white farmers and cast them – racial privileges and all – into the ranks of the proletariat" (p. 153).

In addition to white-skin-privilege land policy, the bourgeoisie also implemented preference in industrial employment and immigration policy. The Cotton Mill Campaign was a prime example of white-skin-privilege employment, and it would exert major downward pressure of wage levels. "Outside the South," explains Allen, "industrial employers understood that the whiteskin-privilege employment policy, when combined with a corresponding racist immigration policy, was on the whole perfectly compatible with profitable operations, and that it served their long-range class interests as a preventive against class consciousness in the North and in the West, no less than in the South." One "very tangible effect" of that policy was the gradual decline of the New England textile mills, "due largely to the low level of wages paid in the South." That decline continued until New England "was destroyed as a textile region." Thus, the "historic persistence of low wages ... was bound to perpetuity because of the paralyzing effect of white supremacism, *a barrier that could not be overcome without a facing of the issue*" (pp. 155, 157–8).

Allen concludes the chapter by reaffirming the judgment rendered by Du Bois in 1935 that Reconstruction had "presented the greatest opportunity" we were likely to see for "many decades" for breaking what Allen calls "the mold the slaveholders made" (p. 158).

In Chapter 7, on "The Sea-change," Allen looks at "an absolutely unique historical phenomenon associated with the massive Irish immigration into the antebellum struggle between racial slavery and freedom in the United States." He is referring to the process by which "subjects of a history of racial oppression as Irish Catholics, are sea-changed into 'white Americans,' and opponents of both the abolition of racial slavery and of equal rights of African-Americans in general" (p. 159).

He begins by offering a brief review of aspects of the struggle over racial slavery beginning with the U.S. Constitution's "compromise" and moving on to the Missouri Compromise of 1820 and the Compromise of 1850. He then details the significance of the cotton gin (which increased productivity, profit, and the intensification of labor for bond-laborers) and events in the Caribbean, including "the revolutionary abolition of slavery" in Haiti and emancipation in the British West Indies (pp. 159–61).

In that context, he discusses three chief elements of the pro-slavery phalanx. First, there was the plantation bourgeoisie, which included those from the Deep South, like John C. Calhoun of South Carolina, who justified slavery as "a positive good" and those from the Border South, like Henry Clay of Kentucky, "whose asserted abhorrence of slavery was exceeded by ... absolute rejection of the possibility of coexistence with African-Americans *except* under a condition of racial slavery." For the latter group, "the end of slavery was inconceivable without the 'colonization,' of all African-Americans outside the United States" (p. 161).

The second element was the Northern bourgeoisie, who opposed abolitionism on the ground of "property rights" and whose position was "most particularly based on their business relationships with the plantation bourgeoisie." This group also included those involved in the international trade of supplying Africans as bond-laborers and people like New York City Mayor Fernando Wood, who endorsed secession and proposed that New York City become "a Free City," open for business with all (pp. 161–2).

The slaveholders "increasingly depended" on a third element – laboring-class European-Americans. They sought what Allen describes as "the strategic extension of an old Southern custom of social control" and the political strategy they used was "defense of the 'white' racial privileges of laboring-class European-Americans against the 'threat' of equalitarianism." This "grossly manipulative plan was adapted ... for the consumption of Northern white laborers" in ways "derived from both the 'positive good' and the 'colonization' variations on the anti-abolition theme" (pp. 162–3).

The "positive good" adherents "argued that wage workers in the Northern United States were *worse off* (or, at least, no better off) than the Southern bond-laborers, thus establishing a rationale for European-American workers to ignore (or indeed be hostile toward) the plight of the African-American workers held in chattel bondage and those who were fleeing from it." These ideas were put forth "in the name of Northern 'workingmen,'" and Allen explains that by the 1830s, "protests of the Northern artisans and wage-workers against the ferocity of the capitalist juggernaut ... were almost always couched in terms of the conventional anti-abolitionist rationale, according to which the lot of the Negro plantation bond-laborer was on the whole better than theirs, or that racial slavery was at most a secondary matter which should not be allowed to interfere with the interests of '[white] workingmen.'" A prominent example of this tendency was George Henry Evans, editor of *Working Man's Advocate* in 1844, who explained he "was formerly ... a very warm advocate of the abolition of slavery," until he "saw that there was *white* slavery." Allen adds that this "pretense of concern for all laborers, slave and waged, was apt to be belied by coupling references to the 'pride and delicacy of the Caucasian'" with "the most hateful white-supremacist references to African-Americans" (pp. 163–4).

The colonization argument served as an additional "ideological reinforcement against the spread of abolitionism among laboring-class European-Americans." The Whig statesman and colonization proponent Henry Clay "pretended that [colonization] would ... 'elevate the social conditions of the white laborer.'" In 1844, as he was preparing to run for the presidency, Clay gave instructions for a campaign pamphlet explaining that "the great aim ... should be to arouse the ['white'] laboring classes in the free States against abolition," to depict "the consequences to them of immediate abolition" and how "they [emancipated African-Americans] being free would enter into competition with the free laborer" and "reduce the white laboring man to the despised and degraded condition of the black man" (pp. 164–5).

The developing anti-slavery movement stood in opposition to the adherents of the "positive good" and "colonization" arguments, and it included African-American bond-laborers who fled north, other African-Americans and European-American comrades, and the abolitionist movement. Allen calls attention to two important aspects of the abolitionist movement. First, it "articulated a far better understanding of the 'class question' than the 'white' labor apologists did of the 'race question.'" He points in particular to the resolution, adopted in 1849 by the Massachusetts Anti-Slavery Society, that articulated the essential principle of true solidarity in the U.S. two decades before Karl Marx wrote, "Labour cannot emancipate itself in the white skin where in the black it is branded." Second, the American abolitionist movement "faithfully supported the struggle of the Irish people, led by Daniel O'Connell, for Repeal of the Union with England" (pp. 165–6).

Allen explains that slavery ended because the abolitionists "were moving with the tide of history, and thus became allies with others who were anti-abolitionist but who were opposed to expansion of slavery." This included the Free Soil Party, founded in 1848 "with the limited aim of preventing the expansion of slavery, while leaving it undisturbed where it already existed." To Allen, Free Soil "replaced the illusion of 'colonization' of the African-American, with a more practical-sounding illusion of 'colonization' of the laboring-class European-American homesteaders in 'whites-only' Western territories." This idea "of solving the 'slavery question' without abolishing slavery" led to the formation of the Republican Party (pp. 166–7).

The slaveholders, aware that they were being eclipsed by the rapidly growing industrial system of the North and prepared to resist by armed rebellion, were confident that the Northern bourgeoisie would either not support abolition and lose by attrition or opt for abolition and see that "the Northern white worker would ... defend the cause of the slaveholders" (p. 167).

In discussing Irish immigration into the U.S. from 1820 to 1860, Allen focuses on three characteristics: its "massive volume" and "concentrated settlement"; the immigrants' "shared historic background ... in struggle against racial oppression in Ireland"; and "its status of being a Catholic minority in a strongly Protestant society characterized by widespread anti-Catholic bigotry." He judges that "No immigrants ever came to the United States better prepared by tradition and experience to empathize with the African-Americans than were these Irish who were emerging directly from the historic struggle against racial oppression in their own country" (pp. 167–8).

In America, however, these immigrants confronted "an already 'white' American social order." John Hughes, a laborer, then priest, then bishop and archbishop, went from being a supporter of abolition to being an "organization man" for both "the Church and for the 'white race'" and an anti-abolitionist. In addition, the ruling plantation bourgeoisie "roundly condemned [Daniel] O'Connell for "interference in American affairs" and refused to financially support Repeal "unless O'Connell, known in Ireland as 'The Liberator,' desisted from his abolitionist ways." To his credit, O'Connell, "as he had done in the West Indies case ... scornfully spurned all such threats" (pp. 169–71, 199).

The American abolitionists were aware of the anti-abolitionist position of the leadership and rank-and-file of the Irish-American population and knew that Catholic Irish-Americans were "almost totally tied into the Democratic Party, the openly avowed party of slavery." Furthermore, by the early 1840s, there was agreement among the Catholic clergy and press in the U.S. that "the principles and methods of Garrisonian abolitionism" threatened the country and were "in conflict with Catholic ethics and ideals." In this context, the abolitionist movement devised a plan for winning Irish-Americans by directly attacking "the most vulnerable spot at which a decisive blow could be struck against the power of the slaveholders," namely, "the anomalous seam between Irish-America and the slaveholders." To accomplish this, they developed an "Address from the people of Ireland to their Countrymen and Countrywomen in America." Allen reviews the "Address" in detail and recounts how it prompted a crisis in the American Repeal Association and a heated controversy with O'Connell (pp. 171–6, 229–30).

In Chapter 8, on "How The Sea-change Was Wrought," Allen examines how "Irish haters of racial oppression" were "transformed into white supremacists in America." He begins by explaining how the Irish abolitionist Address and abolitionism among Irish-Americans were met by "a two-pronged campaign, directed ... against the Catholic-Irish front and the 'white' worker front."

The attack on the Catholic-Irish front was "carried by the Irish-American Establishment and the Catholic hierarchy, led by John Hughes" and demanded that Irish-Americans repudiate the Irish abolitionist Address on two grounds, "loyalty to the United States and loyalty to the anti-Protestant interest." On the "white worker" front, the counterattack "was carried mainly by the Jacksonian Democratic Party, nationally," and by "Tammany Hall" in New York (pp. 23, 177–9, 182, 184).

Allen gives special attention to the attack on the "white worker" front when he writes:

> The America to which these Irish immigrants came was already constructed on the principle of racial oppression, including the white-skin privileges of laboring-class European-Americans. If Irish-Americans rejected the heritage represented by O'Connell and the Address, and if they were frequently identified with the most hostile actions against Negroes in the Northern cities, it was basically because they – like immigrants from Germany, France, England, Scotland, and Scandinavia – accepted their place in the white-race system of social control and claimed the racial privileges entailed by it. Before the Civil War, the main basic white-skin privileges were 1) the presumption of liberty, 2) the right of immigration and naturalization, and 3) the right to vote. The first two of these were in place before the Jacksonian phenomenon, the third was crafted by it. (p. 184)

He describes how the "presumption of liberty distinguished the poorest of European-Americans from the free African-American" and how, under the "white race" system of social control, "even the most destitute of European-Americans were expected to exercise this racial prerogative by supporting the enforcement of the Fugitive Slave Law." The U.S. Constitution "implicitly made immigration a white-skin privilege, when … Europeans were classed as migrants while Africans were classed as imports." Subsequent naturalization statutes repeated phraseology from the 1790 "Act to establish an uniform Rule of Naturalization," which provided that "any alien, being a free white person … may be admitted to become a citizen." As Allen emphasizes, the "privilege of immigration" carried with it a status, entirely new to the immigrants; "the moment they set foot on United States soil, … they were endowed with all the immunities, rights, and privileges of 'American whites' " (pp. 184–5).

In comparing the Irish to other immigrant groups, Allen points out that they were the largest immigrant group in the antebellum period, they "rejected explicitly their own national heritage to become part of the system of 'white' racial oppression of African-Americans," and, by virtue of their concentration in Northern cities, particularly New York, "they became a key factor in national politics" (p. 186).

The situation for African-Americans in New York was different. They had served as volunteers in the War of 1812 against Great Britain, had been voting for years, and supported the Federalist Party because of its opposition to slavery and its support for equal rights for free African-Americans. In the 1810 election in Brooklyn and the 1813 New York City election, the outcome was decided by their votes. Then, in 1821, the New York Constitutional Convention "effectively disfranchised African-Americans by requiring them, (and only them) to be freeholders worth $250" (p. 187).

The plantation bourgeoisie "had no firmer supporter" than Tammany Hall in New York, whose "historic affinity" with Irish-Americans was "from the beginning conditioned on denial of the rights of African-Americans, and a concomitant attachment to the national program of the slaveholders." Tammany facilitated naturalization of Irish immigrants and extended "graft-rich government contracts to Irish-American ward-heelers." The "whitening" effect became manifest and "privileges were intended and defended – not as Irish-American rights, but as 'white men's' rights." Along the way, the sense of "white race" identity was "regularly reinforced by pro-slavery lectures sponsored by Tammany" (pp. 186–8).

The counter-attack against abolitionist appeals from Ireland, "especially through the 'white' Spoils System," was a key factor in political victory of the slaveholders in the 1844 presidential election, during which attention focused on whether or not the U.S. should annex Texas. Abolitionists and O'Connell opposed annexation, while the Democratic Party candidate, James K. Polk, was pro-"annexation" and drew support among Irish-Americans by calling attention to British opposition to annexation. Polk won, and Allen describes how New York Irish-Americans "decided the outcome" (pp. 186, 188–9).

Following the election of Lincoln in 1860, "the die was cast." The "pressure on the 'Catholic-Irish' and the 'white-worker' fronts were linked up and intensified" through "white supremacist rallies, anti-abolitionist exhortations, quiet undermining of the anti-Confederate cause, murderous physical assaults on African-Americans, a … riot in South Brooklyn in August 1862 and the climactic Draft Riot/'white' pogrom of July 1863" (p. 189).

In the discussion of this period, Allen pays special attention to the "labor competition" rationale. He notes that "a number of historians … have made the assumptions characteristic of the 'labor competition' rationale, accompanied almost invariably by palliative allusions to 'Negro strikebreakers.'" To counter those assumptions, he begins by explaining that "competition among individuals for employment is a necessary condition of the wage-labor system"; that "Naturally occurring social groupings of family, religion, nationality, etc., are commonly projected into labor-pool groupings"; and that even within the ranks of Catholic Irish-Americans, job competition at times took the form of brawls "between men from Cork, with men from Connaught, or, … Ulster." He also points out that "labor competition between 'native Americans' and immigrants was a fact of early nineteenth-century life in America" and the nativist movement sought restrictions on immigration and naturalization "because, it was said, the influx of immigrants was driving wages down."

Such nativism drew "on the heritage of British-Ulster Protestant Ascendancy" and "was mainly directed against the Catholic Irish." It "did not," however, "threaten the fundamental Constitution of the country." The " 'labor competition,' commonly alluded to in reference to the anti-Negro attitude of Irish-American 'white' laborers" was of a different order, however, because it "was a fight for the system of white supremacy, on which the government was founded" (p. 193).

By 1855, over half of the population of New York was foreign-born, and in that period, an average of fifteen thousand immigrants were settling in New York each year, more than the total African-American resident population. Allen comments, "such a rate of immigration would ... tend to increase 'labor competition.'" He also points out that "the number of foreign-born 'white' competitors with the Irish for employment was greater in every category than the number of African-American competitors," and he produces figures showing "a five-to-one ratio of foreign-born 'whites' to African-Americans competing with the Irish immigrants" in major job categories (pp. 193–4).

He then concludes that "the 'fear of Negro job competition,' so much favored as an explanation of the concentration of Irish-American workers' hostility on the African-American minority of their non-Irish competitors ... had no basis in actual fact." While "these Irish-American workers may have been led to believe that their interest depended above all upon the exclusion of the African-American workers," that "fear" was not "justified" and it certainly was no basis for describing the " 'white' pogrom against Negro men, women and children in July of 1863 as a 'working-class movement.'" In a similar vein, Allen points out, "it does not help ... to speak of 'Negro strikebreakers,' when no special mention is made of 'German strikebreakers, such as those who took the jobs of Irish workers striking ... at the Atlantic Dock in Brooklyn in 1846, or other European-American strikebreakers on the Erie Railroad docks in January 1863, or the Hudson River Railroad docks two months later" (p. 194).

Allen shows how labor competitions were given the abnormal "racial" form. He notes that "prior to 1840, a wide range of industrial employments ... in New York were 'almost wholly in the hands of' African-Americans." Then, the Irish, "driven into exile by famine, competed for those jobs by taking lower wages." He writes, "To *assume* that it was in the nature of the case that Irish would seek to drive Negroes out, off the job, and do so on the basis of an Irish claim to a 'white' identity, is to assume the Jordan-Degler assumption, that 'white over black' is a memory of the blood." Rather, argues Allen, "the problem of job competition was cast in the mold of white supremacy as an integral part of the social control system instituted by the American slaveholders" (p. 195).

Allen describes how after the Civil War "the Northern employers adopted as their own the general principle of racial discrimination in industrial employment." He again points to "powerful ... influences – Constitutional guarantees, the 'white' manhood suffrage laws, and the pervasive power of the Democratic Spoils system, which served to encourage the extensions of principle of 'racial' preference in employment to the North." In this context, he pays special attention to the Custom House "as a bell-wether in the effort to establish the principle of 'racial' preference in hiring in the North." The U.S. Custom House was in the hands of the national government, which was led by Democrats most of the time. It was the largest federal office in the country, and it was where "the spoils system reached its highest form." Allen emphasizes, by "keeping employment at this Government facility as a white-skin privilege," it served as "a Northern bastion of the principle that the Negro had no job rights that a 'white' person was bound to respect" (pp. 195–6).

In the context of the " 'white' spoils system," Allen shows that "what began as a form of naturally occurring group labor competition, soon developed on the Irish-American side into an assertion of the right of 'white' preference." The mobs "made up primarily of Irish-Americans" in the Brooklyn and New York riots "did not express their demands and aims in terms of Irishness, but in the name of 'white workingmen.'" In the case of New York City longshoremen, almost all were Irish by 1863, and the Longshoremen's Association resolved that dock work would be limited to "white laborers." African-Americans "were driven from the trade in which they had predominated twenty years before, not in the normal course of economic competition, but by Irish-Americans operating under the immunities of 'whiteness.'" African-Americans were not only driven from the docks, they were also driven from Manhattan, where the African-American population "declined perhaps 16 percent between 1840 and 1860" and then fell by another one-fourth to less than 10,000 by 1865 (pp. 196–7).

Allen concludes that the reality of labor competition was far different from how it was perceived at the time and what has been perpetuated by historians, namely "that the 'white' workers were motivated mainly by a fear of the prospect of freed African-Americans coming to the North looking for work in such large numbers that the oversupply of labor would result in lower wages." That explanation "ignores the fact that more than two million European immigrants came into the United States in the decade before the Civil War, and two-and-three-quarters million in the ten years after the War, of whom several hundred thousand remained in New York City." Yet, he points out, "no European immigrants were lynched, no 'white' orphanages burned, for fear of their 'competition in the labor market" (p. 197).

Allen also stresses the importance of workers' support for abolition in this period. For African-Americans "to come North to escape slavery made sense, but to come North to escape freedom would not." In addition, by striking "off the chains of the African-American bond-laborers" and applying the "principle of 'land to the tiller' with a land redistribution program in the South" the "main incentive to go North would dissolve." Thus, "to the extent that

the Irish-American and the other 'whites' were worried on this account, ...
they should have supported the struggle of the African-American people"
(p. 197).

As Allen explains:

> There was indeed a real competition between African-American bond-labor and
> Irish-American (and other "white") workers, that if understood would have pro-
> vided a basis for a joint struggle against slavery. As Du Bois put it, "[T]he black
> man enslaved was an even more formidable and fatal competitor than the black
> man free." It was in the interest of the slave-labor system to maintain the white-skin
> privilege differential in favor of the European-American workers. At the same time,
> however, it was equally in the interest of the employers of wage-labor, as well as
> of bond-labor, that the differential be kept to no more than the minimum necessary
> for the purposes of keeping the European-American workers in the "white race"
> corral. To increase the differential beyond that degree would entail an unnecessary
> deduction from capitalist profits, which would be distributed by the workings of the
> average rate over the employers of bond-labor as well as employers of wage-labor.
> Furthermore, it would tend to increase the traffic on the Underground Railroad. The
> chains that bound the African-American thus also held down the living standards of
> the Irish-American. (p. 198)

Allen strongly believes that the "historian must move beyond the uncritical
repetition of the catalog of self-justification – 'job competition' etcetera."
There is "more involved ... than merely setting the record straight." "If the
rationale was valid for the ante-bellum Irish-Americans," he reasons, "it is no
less valid in its familiar modern-day white-supremacist forms: 'preservation
of property values' in 'ethnic' neighborhoods, 'quota' phobia, the denunciation
of affirmative action, etc." He writes, "Irish-Americans were not the originators of white supremacy; they adapted to and were adopted into an already
'white' American social order." The "'popular rights' of Irish-Americans were
given the form of white-skin privileges, the token of their membership in the
American 'white race'" (p. 199).

In Volume II, *The Invention of the White Race: The Origin of Racial
Oppression in Anglo-America*, Allen details the origin and the originators
of that white supremacist social order in late-seventeenth/early-eighteenth-
century Virginia.

Chronological Finding Aid
for Users of this Volume

Below are listed the main Irish historical periods as defined by the Irish Royal Academy, together with sub-periods as noted and characterized in this work.

Medieval Ireland (1169–1534)

1169–ca. 1216   Papal-sponsored English "overlordship"
ca. 1217–1315   English option for racial oppression
ca. 1315–1534   Scots invasion; defeat of racial oppression; eclipse of English power

Early Modern Ireland (1534–1691)

1534–1603   Breaking of tribal power; English opt for religio-racial oppression
1594–1603   Tyrone War
1603–1641   English encroachment by plantation, most notably in Ulster
1641–1652   Irish are involved in the War of the Three Kingdoms, climaxed by the Cromwellian conquest
1652–1656   Irish Catholics are subjected to mass exile, expropriation and "transplantation"
1660–1689   Stuart Restoration; Irish hopes are revived
1689–1691   Jacobite War; defeat of the Irish Catholic cause by Protestant Dutch-English King William III

Eighteenth-century Ireland (1691–1800)

1691–1700   Williamite expropriations of Catholic lands
1704–1829   Penal Law system of religio-racial oppression of the Catholic Irish
  ca. 1760   Mitigation of the Penal Law system is begun
1782–1798   Anglo-Irish Protestant independence movement; United Irishmen rebellion is defeated
1792–1800   British overtures to Irish Catholics to counter Anglo-Irish radicalism

Ireland Under the Union (I) (1801–1870)

          1801   Union of Great Britain and Ireland Act
ca. 1811–1829   Catholic Emancipation struggle
   1829–1845   Catholic Emancipation permits Catholics in the British Parliament, but restricts suffrage. A period of adjustment: tithe war; defeat of Repeal; Catholic bourgeoisie is incorporated into the British colonial social control system, racial oppression is replaced by national oppression (except in Ulster)
   1845–1850   The Great Famine; depopulation by starvation, disease, and mass emigration
          1870   First fruits of the War for the Land, Gladstone's first Land Reform Bill

Notes

Introduction

1. The term "Peculiar Institution" was a euphemism for the socio-economic system based on the lifetime, hereditary, chattel bond-servitude of African-Americans, which existed in the continental Anglo-American colonies and in the United States until the ratification of the Thirteenth Amendment to the Constitution in 1865, mainly in the Southern plantation region.

2. *Report of the National Advisory Commission on Civil Disorders* (New York, 1968), pp. 206–7. Pronouncements made by Presidents Kennedy and Johnson reflected the spirit of the time. According to Kennedy, "[Negroes] are not fully free ... [therefore] this nation ... is not fully free...." "[V]ictory for the American Negro," Johnson asserted, "is a victory for the ... nation" (Civil Rights Address by Kennedy and Johnson's speech on passage of the Civil Rights Act of 1965, respectively, *New York Times*, 12 June 1963 and 7 August 1965).

3. Peter H. Wood, "'I Did the Best I Could for My Day': The Study of Early Black History during the Second Reconstruction, 1960–76," *William and Mary Quarterly*, 3rd series, 35:185–225 (April 1978), p. 189.

4. Regarding "the origins of slavery ... contemporary attitudes have affected the positions historians have taken on the subject" (Raymond Starr, "Historians and the Origins of British North American Slavery," *Historian*, 36:1–19 [1973–4], p. 16).

5. Eric Williams, *Capitalism and Slavery* (Chapel Hill, 1944), p. 7.

The "equal-but-separate" doctrine was promulgated in an 1896 decision by the United States Supreme Court in the case of *Plessy v. Ferguson*, holding that "racial" segregation could not be interfered with provided only that the accommodations offered were of equal quality. Under a Louisiana state law, Homer Plessy, an American of African ancestry, had been forced from a "white" railroad coach under provisions of Louisiana state law, because he was not "white." Plessy sought relief from the courts for deprivation of civil rights protected by the post-Civil War Fourteenth Amendment of the United States Constitution. The *Plessy* decision remained the ruling precedent until it was overturned in 1954 by the Supreme Court in the case brought by Oliver Brown against the Board of Education in Topeka, Kansas, against school segregation. The *Brown v. Board of Education* decision held that racial segregation is in itself a denial of equal rights. The historic United States civil rights crusade originated a year later, on 1 December 1955 when Mrs Parks, an African-American worker, refused to give up her seat to a white fellow bus passenger, and was arrested for that violation of a Montgomery city law. The incident led to the historic year-long Montgomery bus boycott by African-Americans, which ended with another Supreme Court order based on the principle of the *Brown* decision.

6. Recognition among historians of the signal significance of Williams's contribution is represented in Barbara Lewis Solow and Stanley L. Engerman, eds, *British Capitalism and Caribbean Slavery: The Legacy of Eric Williams* (New York, 1987). The editors' preface cites as the first of four Williams themes that "slavery was an economic phenomenon; and thus racism was a consequence, not the cause, of slavery."

Two helpful bibliographies of this controversy are: Joseph Boskin, *Into Slavery, Racial Decisions in the Virginia Colony* (Philadelphia, 1976), pp. 101–12; and James M. McPherson, Laurence B. Holland, James M. Banner, Jr, Nancy J. Weiss and Michael D. Bell, eds, *Blacks in*

America: Bibliographical Essays (Garden City, New York, 1971), especially pp. 26–8 and 39–44. See also: Alden T. Vaughan, "The Origins Debate: Slavery and Racism in Seventeenth-Century Virginia," *Virginia Magazine of History and Biography*, 97:311–54 (July 1989), for a more recent, avowedly partisan, analysis of the state of the discussion; and Raymond Starr's earlier review of the discussion, cited in n. 4.

7. Oscar and Mary F. Handlin, "Origins of the Southern Labor System," *William and Mary Quarterly*, 3rd series, No. 7 (1950), pp. 214 and 220–21.

8. See, for example: James Curtis Ballagh, *A History of Slavery in Virginia* (Baltimore, 1902), especially pp. 28–32; Ulrich Bonnell Phillips, *American Negro Slavery* (New York, 1933), pp. 74–7, and "Racial Problems, Adjustments and Disturbances," in *The South in the Building of the Nation*, 13 vols (Richmond, 1909–13), VI:194–241, reprinted in Eugene D. Genovese, ed., *The Slave Economy of the Old South: Selected Essays in Economic and Social History by Ulrich Bonnell Phillips* (Baton Rouge, 1968), pp. 23–64, also pp. 26–7; and John H. Russell, *The Free Negro in Virginia, 1619–1865* (Baltimore, 1913), Chapter 2, "The Origin of the Free Negro Class."

9. Russell, pp. 16–17.

10. Winthrop D. Jordan, "Modern Tensions and the Origins of American Slavery," *Journal of Southern History*, 28:18–30 (February 1962), p. 20.

11. The most recent general review of the state of the discussion is Vaughan. He refers to and makes comments on some forty works published since 1976, the year following the date of Boskin's bibliography, also cited in n. 6. Vaughan's review, however, is in the form of an essay wherein the author "takes a stand" on the general Jordan–Degler psycho-cultural side of the issue, namely that pre-colonial anti-black prejudice in England predetermined the enslavement of African-Americans in Anglo-America. He summarizes what he sees as three points upon which consensus has been reached: (1) the numbers of African-Americans in Virginia and Maryland in the seventeenth century; (2) the ambiguity of the legal status of these African-Americans; and (3) the tightening of restrictions on African-Americans late in the seventeenth century; and four points of remaining fundamental disagreement: (1) the status of most African-Americans before the 1660s; (2) the amount of anti-Negro discrimination before the 1660s; (3) the reasons the African-Americans were enslaved, and (4) the point at which ethnocentrism became racism directed at the African-Americans. The reader will be able to infer quite clearly from the present work points at which I disagree with, agree with, or have reservations about Vaughan's presentation. In the main the differences derive from my particular approach to the entire question of the origin of racial slavery, indicated in the third paragraph of this Introduction.

Just one note: Vaughan mentions my *Class Struggle and the Origin of Racial Slavery* (1975) and says that my argument, along with those of Edmund S. Morgan (1972 and later) and Timothy Breen (1972 and later), quickly "succumbed" to "a withering fire" by economic, labor-supply, and skilled/unskilled labor-differentiation theses put forward by Russell Menard (1977) and David W. Galenson (1981). Speaking for myself, while my interpretation of the political and social significance of economic facts presented by Menard and Galenson may vary from theirs in some, even important, respects, the reader will judge whether it has "succumbed."

12. Carl N. Degler, "Slavery and the Genesis of American Race Prejudice," *Comparative Studies in Society and History*, Vol. II, No. 1 (October, 1959), pp. 49–66; and No. 4 (July 1960), pp. 488–95. *Neither Black Nor White: Slavery and Race Relations in Brazil and the United States* (New York, 1971).

13. Winthrop D. Jordan, *White over Black: American Attitudes Toward the Negro, 1550–1812* (Chapel Hill, 1968).

14. Degler, *Neither Black Nor White*, pp. 287 and 290. Degler's conviction on this point finds expression in the title of his latest book, *In Search of Human Nature: The Decline and Revival of Darwinianism in American Social Thought* (New York, 1991), a thesis in defense of socio-biology, that is, the search for biological explanations of social behavior. To the extent that that is intended to "explain racism," it would seem to merit the mistrust expressed by Doctor Ross (Dorothy Ross, *American Historical Review*, April 1992, pp. 608–9).

15. Jordan, *White over Black*, pp. 582 and 584.

16. As will be further noted in Volume Two, the fact that the term "free Negro" does not appear in court record references to African-American non-bond-laborers in the early decades (with one exception in which a deponent so describes himself) would tend to show that

African-Americans at that time shared the presumption of liberty with European-Americans. With the one exception, the first use found was in a record of hog marks dated 29 April 1699 ("Cattle and Hog Marks, 1665–1707," pages which somehow got inserted at the back of *Northampton County Records, 1651–54*, Virginia State Archives, Richmond).

17. Jordan, *White over Black*, p. 75. Here Jordan seems to disregard his own express caution against "reading the past backwards," (p. ix), and thus falls into a common error of historians on both sides of this argument. That is the error of casually fixing the label "white," on people who never identified themselves as such. Furthermore, he would seem to have less excuse than some others, since he himself tells us that the term "white" was not current in Virginia before 1680 (p. 95). In this seemingly insignificant detail is revealed the key to the whole puzzle of the origin of racial slavery.

18. Degler, "Slavery," p. 49; *Out of Our Past, The Forces that Shaped Modern America* (New York, 1959), pp. 27–30 and 36–8; and *Neither Black Nor White*, which in its entirety is a development of this point.

19. Degler, *Out of Our Past*, pp. 30 and 38; and "Slavery," p. 52. Some time later Degler sought to emphasize the perhaps subtle point of his case. He did not intend to say that prejudice caused slavery, but simply that it caused slavery to be racial (Degler, letter to *New York Review of Books*, 22 January 1976).

20. Degler, *Out of Our Past*, pp. 30–31.

21. Oscar James Campbell and Edward G. Quinn, The *Reader's Encyclopedia of Shakespeare* (New York, 1966), particularly "Othello – sources." John Gassner, Masters of the Drama, 3rd edition (New York, 1951), p. 232.

22. John Lambert, *Travels through Canada, and the US*, 2:138, cited in Jordan, *White over Black*, p. 405.

23. Irene A. Wright, Documents *Concerning English Voyages to the Caribbean, 1527–1568*, Works Issued by the Hakluyt Society, 2nd series, LXII (London, 1928), pp. 7, 14, 18–19.

24. Irene A. Wright, ed., *Documents Concerning English Voyages to the Spanish Main, 1569–1580*, Works Issued by the Hakluyt Society, 2nd series, LXXI (London, 1932), pp. xxxvii–xxxix, 72, 258–9 and 279.

25. Ibid., pp. 21, 24, 170, 324 and 310.

26. E. G. R. Taylor, ed., *The Original Writing and Correspondence of the Two Richard Hakluyts*, Works Issued by the Hakluyt Society, 2nd series, LXXVI and LXXVII (London, 1935), pp. 17, 142–3, and 318. English policy, said Hakluyt, should be to "use the naturall people there [on the Spanish Main in America] with all humanitie, curtesie, and freedome … [so that] with the Symerons a few hundrethes of this nation [England under Elizabeth] may bring greate things to passe" (p, 318).

27. Edmund S. Morgan, American Slavery, *American Freedom: The Ordeal of Colonial Virginia* (New York, 1975), pp. 10–17.

28. Richard Jobson, *The Golden Trade or a Discovery of the River Gambra, and The Golden Trade of the Aethiopians* (London, 1623; Teignmouth, 1904).

29. Basil Davidson, *The African Slave Trade: Precolonial History, 1450–1850* (Boston, 1961), p. 5.

30. Sir John Davies, "Microcosmos," (spelling modernized) in a two-volume collection of Davies's writings made by Alexander Balloch Grosart in 1878. This John Davies (1565?–1618) is not to be confused with the better-known John Davies (1569–1626), who served James I as English solicitor-general and attorney-general in Ireland, and is referred to later in this work, who was also a poet collected by Grosart.

31. Since Degler brought Shakespeare into it, he might have tipped his hat to Shylock (whose name was the English transliteration of the Hebrew word for "cormorant," a symbol in Christendom of the "pervert" usurer) and to a century-by-century anti-Jewish lineage from the folktale of poor murdered Christian Hugh of Lincoln to Chaucer's Prioress, and to Marlowe's *Jew of Malta*. He might have mentioned how the Irishman Macmorris in *Henry V* (Act 3, Scene 2) is had to repeat the characterization of his own nation as "villain and a bastard, a knave and a rascal." And Degler might have put this remark in the context of the English attitude toward the Irish as expressed, say, from the fourteenth-century Statute of Kilkenny to the eighteenth-century Penal Laws, which I shall have further occasion to note in Chapter 3. Any discussion of this point would have benefited by reference to James O. Bartley's analysis of stereotypical presentations of the Irish, Welsh and Scots in English

plays (James O. Bartley, *Teague, Shenkin and Sawney, Being an Historical Study of the Earliest Irish, Welsh and Scottish Characters in English Plays* [Cork, 1954]).

32. Marvin Harris, *Patterns of Race in the Americas* (New York, 1964), pp. 69–70. P. E. H. Hair, "Protestants as Pirates, Slavers and Proto-Missionaries: Sierra Leone 1568 and 1582," *Journal of Ecclesiastical History*, 21:203–24.Canny was equally specific in his criticism of Jordan in this regard. See his "The Permissive Frontier: The Problem of Social Control in English Settlements in Ireland and Virginia, 1550–1650," in K. R. Andrews, N. P. Canny and P. E. H. Hair, *The Westward Enterprise: English Activities in Ireland, the Atlantic and America, 1480–1650* (Detroit, 1979), p. 35.

33. This well-known thesis is identified with the names of social anthropologists Frank Tannenbaum, author of *Slave and Citizen* (New York, 1947), and Gilberto Freyre, author of *The Masters and the Slaves* (New York, 1956).

34. See Great Britain Public Record Office, *Calendar of State Papers, Colonial*, Vol. I, pp. 123, 152–3, 168, 201–3, 247–9 and 277–8. Unfortunately, historians on both sides of the issue commonly fail to grasp the significance of this central aspect of the history of Providence Island. Jordan mentions it in a footnote, but for the purpose of emphasizing the enslavability of heathens, rather than the non-enslavability of Christians (*White over Black*, p. 92, n. 112).

35. Degler, *Out of Our Past*, p. 31,

36. Philip Alexander Bruce, *Economic History of Virginia in the Seventeenth Century: An Inquiry into the material condition of the people, based on original and contemporaneous records*, 2 vols (New York, 1895), 2:74–7. It was not until after the Treaty of Breda in 1667, ending the Second Anglo-Dutch War, that the English had direct access to the African labor-supply coast. It was only in mid–1680s that the direct Africa-to-Virginia bond-labor trade began in ships exclusively used for that purpose (Bruce, 2:84).

37. Jordan, "Modern Tensions," p. 21.

38. Jordan expressed his dissatisfaction with all previous attempts to deal with the origin of racial slavery. He specifically mentioned the "virtually opposite" views of the Handlins and Degler on the relation of "slavery and prejudice" (*White over Black*, p. 599), and claimed to hold "a still different view." But he differed differently from those respectively polar positions. His difference with the Handlins was substantial; his difference with Degler was technical, designed to make more effective historiography's service to the proposition that white racism could never be eliminated by purposive social action.

39. Jordan, *White over Black*, p. 80. It is interesting that throughout his book, Jordan puts "prejudice" in quotation marks (other instances are found at pp. 276, 281, 565, 568 and 569). Perhaps he felt that this was merely being consistent with his thesis that "white over black" is not a matter of judgment, or prejudgment, but of instinct.

40. Jordan titled Chapter 2 of *White over Black* "Unthinking Decision: Enslavement of Negroes in America to 1700." Although he did not use the term "unthinking decision" in the 1962 article "Modern Tensions," the explication there is nearly verbatim that in the book.

41. Jordan, *White over Black*, p.xiv.

42. In the epilogue to his book, Jordan concludes: "… the most profound continuities ran through the centuries of change. Particularly there were the tightly harnessed energies of a reckless, trafficking, migrating people emerging from death and darkness into plenty and enlightenment. These were a people of the Word, adventuring into a New World; they sought to retain their identity – their identity as a peculiar people" (*White over Black*, p. 574).

43. African immigrants were barred from the United States. By contrast, in the decade following the abolition of slavery in British Guiana, some eleven thousand African workers came there as wage-workers (Walter Rodney, *A History of the Guyanese Working People, 1881–1905* [Baltimore, 1981], pp. 33, 97 and 241).

44. "The western states," said George Washington in 1784 "(I speak now from my own observation) stand as it were on a pivot. A touch of a feather would turn them either way" (letter to Governor Harrison of Virginia, 10 October 1784, cited in Benjamin Horace Hibbard, *A History of Public Land Policies* [New York, 1924: republished by University of Wisconsin Press, 1965], p. 34).

45. Jordan, *White over Black*, Chapter XV, "Toward a White Man's Country," especially pp. 542 and 569.

46. See Appendix A.

47. Eric Williams wrote that persons of joint European-African ancestry in the Caribbean, "In training and in outlook … retain little or no trace of their African origin, except the color of their skin…. When they go 'home' every four years to enjoy a well earned holiday … they imply by 'home' not Africa, but England, France, even Spain" (Eric E. Williams, *The Negro in the Caribbean* [New York, 1942], p. 60).

In Jamaica in the immediate post-emancipation period, "The people of color were very conscious of their European heritage and extremely proud of it," according to Philip D. Curtin (*Two Jamaicas: The Role of Ideas in Tropical Society, 1830–65* [Cambridge, Massachusetts, 1955], p. 45). Curtin cites three nineteenth-century sources, including "A Protest of the [Jamaica] House of Assembly," dated June 1838.

See also: Douglas Hall, "Jamaica," pp. 199–200; and Jerome S. Handler and Arnold A. Sio, "Barbados," pp. 236–8, and 256–7, in David W. Cohen and Jack P. Greene, eds, *Neither Slave Nor Free* (Baltimore, 1972). See also: Elsa V. Goveia, *Slave Society in the British Leeward Islands at the End of the Eighteenth Century* (New Haven, 1965), pp. 223 and 232; and Jerome S. Handler, *The Unappropriated People, Freedmen in the Slave Society of Barbados* (Baltimore, 1974), pp. 75–6, 91–2, 94–5, 109, 216–17.

48. Jordan, *White over Black*, pp. 141 and 175.

49. Ibid., Chapter 15, passim.

50. Ibid., pp. viii–ix. As is made more explicit at the other end of his book (p. 582), Jordan intended an epitaph to aspirations for the achievement of equal rights of, by and for African-Americans in the United States.

51. Jordan does say that his book "is not about Negroes" (ibid., p. viii). But he does not say explicitly that it is not a book for Negroes. It would seem that elementary sensitivity, if no other consideration, should have led him to distance himself more consistently than he does from some of the racist "attitudes" he dug up in the course of his research ("The Negro's admittedly unattractive characteristics", which were supposedly an embarrassment to opponents of slavery [p. 305]; "No wonder Linnaeus backed away" from the conclusion that the Negro was a different species [p. 236]; "[C]ertain superficial physical characteristics in the West African Negro helped sustain (and perhaps helped initiate) the popular connection with the ape" [p. 237]; "During the seventeenth century there had been little progress on the scientific problem of the Negro's blackness" [p. 242]). Perhaps Jordan's failure to do so validates his own observation that "an historian's relationship with the raw materials of history is a profoundly reciprocal one" (ibid., p. vii). In choosing his subtitle, "The American Attitude Toward the Negro," Jordan, consciously or not, was in tune with the sentiment expressed by Thomas Dixon Jr, whose book *The Clansman* was made into the movie *Birth of a Nation*. "[W]ho thinks of a Negro when he says American?" said Dixon (*Saturday Evening Post*, 19 August 1905, pp. 1–2, cited in Stanley Feldstein, ed., *The Poisoned Tongue: A Documentary History of American Racism and Prejudice* [New York, 1972], p. 200).

52. Reviewers were typically kind, though some of them expressed serious reservations. Richard D. Browne saw "intuitive generalizations … not sustained by the evidence" (*New England Quarterly*, 41:447–9 [September 1968]). The evidence occasionally fails to carry the burden, wrote David H. Fowler (*Journal of American History*, 56:344–5 [September 1969]). Challenging a number of Jordan's themes, including his assumption of an immemorial "revulsionfor-blackness," J. H. Plumb counterposed the proposition. that "Racism does not cause slavery. It is an excuse for it" (*New York Review of Books*, 12:3 [13 March 1969]).

53. In his "Essay on Sources," Jordan avowed his deliberate avoidance of comparisons between English and other European colonies in the Americas. Displaying unusual acerbity, Jordan dismissed as worthless the body of scholarly work accumulated in the period after World War Two that attempted to shed light on racism and slavery in North America by comparison with non-English colonies. "Virtually all such studies," Jordan said, were done by people who were "ignorant" of their subjects. In such hands, he said, "the comparative approach proved to be extremely dangerous" (*White over Black*, pp. 604–5). It seems all the more regrettable therefore that Jordan was not able to set a better example of the comparative approach in its application to English colonies in the Caribbean, as an illuminator of the nature of racial slavery in the continental colonies and the United States.

54. Jordan, *White over Black*, Chapter 4, "Fruits of Passion," *passim*; especially sub-chapters I and 6. The quoted phrase is at p. 137.

55. Ibid.

56. Philip D. Curtin, *Two Jamaicas*, p. 45.

57. The human sexual drive, Jordan says by way of explication, overrides not only the "sense of difference between two groups of human beings [but also that] … between themselves and animals" (*White over Black*, p. 138). One wonders at Jordan's seeming gradation of English lapses from the libidinal norm: "interracial" sex, then interspecies sex.

58. Ibid., p. 141.

59. Donald L. Horowitz, "Color Differentiation in the American System of Slavery," *Journal of Interdisciplinary History*, vol. 3, no. 3 (Winter 1973), pp. 509–41; p. 528, citing: James Stewart, *View of the Past and Present State of the Island of Jamaica* (Edinburgh, 1823), p. 333; and Edward Long, *The History of Jamaica or, General Survey of the Ancient and Modern State of That Island*, 3 vols (London, 1774), Vol. II, Book 2, p. 328.

60. A convenient brief account of the prevalence of "interracial" sex in the Southern slave states is presented in Kenneth Stampp's *The Peculiar Institution: Slavery in the Ante-bellum South* (New York, 1956), pp. 350–61. Jordan's desire-versus-aversion-in-a-sea-of-blacks scenario seems a relic of the nineteenth-century thesis that "going native" bore the seed of the fall of the British Empire.

61. Jordan, *White over Black*, p. 167.

62. Ibid., pp. 175 and 177.

63. Allen D. Candler, comp., *The Colonial Records of Georgia*, 26 vols (Atlanta, 1904–16), Vol. 18, Statutes of the Royal Legislature, p. 659.

64. James Ramsay, *An Essay on the Treatment and Conversion of African Slaves in the British Sugar Colonies* (London, 1784), pp. 288–9.

65. Alan Burns, *History of the West Indies* (London, 1954), pp. 446–7.

66. Sidney Greenfield, *English Rustics in Black Skins: A Study of Modern Family Forms in a Pre-Industrial Society* (New Haven, 1966), pp. 42 and 46.

67. Jordan, *White over Black*, p. 169 (emphasis added).

68. Long, *History of Jamaica*, Vol. 2, Book 2, pp. 270, 327, 332–7.

69. Jordan, *White over Black*, p. 177.

70. Ibid.

71. "In many areas one of the major concerns of responsible men was the effective control of masses of slaves" (Ibid., p. 102).

72. Horowitz, "Color Differentiation," pp. 529–30.

73. Jordan notes in passing: "The only rebellions by white servants in the continental colonies came before the firm entrenchment of slavery" (*White over Black*).

74. Oscar and Mary F. Handlin, "Origins of the Southern Labor System," p. 208.

75. From Degler's final letter in the exchange with the Handlins, published in *Comparative Studies in History and Society*, Vol. 2 (1959–60), No. 4 (July 1960), p. 495.

76. Williams, *Capitalism and Slavery*, pp. 201–2. The crisis, according to Williams, began in 1823 when the home government sought to impose limitations on the harshness and brutality of treatment of bond-laborers in the British West Indies. The sugar bourgeoisie resisted, even threatening secession from the Empire. The tide was turned by the numerous insurrectionary actions of the bond-laborers themselves (inspired by the Santo Domingo example of 1804), climaxing in revolts in Antigua and in the biggest sugar colony, Jamaica, in 1831. Their intervention transformed the question from that of abating the owners' cruelties to ending the ownership itself. Faced with the alternatives of "emancipation from above, or emancipation from below" (Williams, p. 208), the British Parliament resolved the crisis in 1833 by decreeing the end of slavery in the West Indies.

77. Ibid., pp. 19–20.

78. The cost of transporting a cargo of African bond-laborers from São Tomé to Barbados in 1693–94 was ten pounds ten shillings per laborer ("A Journal of a Voyage in the Hannibal of London, Ann. 1693, 1694 from England to Africa and so Forward to Barbadoes, by Thomas Phillips, Commander of the said Ship," in John and Awsham Churchill, comp., *A Collection of Voyages and Travels* [Churchill's Voyages], 6 vols [London, 1704–32], 6:171–239, p. 236). "Never during the colonial period did it cost more than five or six pounds sterling to transport a servant to the plantations" (Abbott Emerson Smith, *Colonists in Bondage: White Servitude and Convict Labor in America, 1607–1776* [Chapel Hill, 1947; New York, 1971], p. 35). See also Bruce, 1:629–30.

79. "Will the manager with the two or three bookkeepers he has to assist him attempt ... to enforce the obedience of 200 or 300 negroes?" (Viscount Hamrick speech, 14 May 1833, in United Kingdom, *Hansard Parliamentary Debates*, 3d series (1830–91), vol. 18, cols 1231–59; 1255.)

80. See Appendix B.

81. Interestingly, Morgan did not present his work as a contribution to the controversy over the origin of racial slavery. His aim, rather, was to explore the symbiosis of racial slavery and the Jeffersonian freedom doctrines. Nevertheless, most reviewers tended to consider *American Slavery/American Freedom* (New York, 1975) in the context of the controversy, believing that Morgan's account of the emergence of racial slavery was the strongest part of his book. See for instance: J. H. Plumb (*New York Review of Books*, 27 November 1975); Peter H. Wood (*New York Times Book Review*, 21 December 1975); Rhys Isaac (*Reviews in American History*, Vol. 4, No. 1 (March 1976); and Theodore William Allen (*Monthly Review*, March, 1978). Carl N. Degler, in a letter commenting on Plumb's review, limited his criticism to what he called Morgan's "flawed" argument regarding the rise of racism (*New York Review of Books*, 22 January 1976).

82. Morgan, p. 309. For a telling criticism of Morgan in this negation of the African-American bond-laborer, see Peter Wood's review, cited in n. 81.

83. Morgan, pp. 296–7.

84. "The Myth of the Friendly Master" is a chapter title in Harris's *Patterns of Race*.

85. Morgan, p. 328.

86. Ibid.

87. Ibid., p. 331.

88. Ibid., p. 344.

89. Ibid., pp. 331–3 and 344.

90. Ibid., pp. 330–31.

91. Ibid., p. 380.

92. Ibid., p. 386.

93. Letter of Thomas Ludwell and Robert Smith to Charles II, 18 June 1676, Henry Coventry Papers at the Bath Estate at Longleat, Vol. 77, f. 128 (American Council of Learned Societies British Manuscripts Project, microfilm reel no. 63, Library of Congress).

94. Jackson T. Main, "The Distribution of Property in Post-Revolutionary Virginia," *Mississippi Valley Historical Review*, 1954–55, 41:241–58, p. 248, n. 21; Jackson T. Main, *The Social Structure of Revolutionary America* (Princeton, 1965), especially pp. 42, 47, 54–57, and 61; D. Alan Williams, "The Small Farmer in Eighteenth-century Politics," *Agricultural History*, 43:91–101 (January 1969); Gloria L. Main, "Inequality in Early America: The Evidence from Probate Records of Massachusetts and Maryland," *Journal of Interdisciplinary History*, 7:559–81 (Spring 1977). Although Morgan cites some of these sources he apparently does not see them in the light intended here.

95. "Strange is the situation of our community in Eastern Virginia, where more than one-half the population is born to absolute slavery, and fully half the other with little but their complexion to console them for being born in a higher caste" ("Civis," writing in the *Richmond Enquirer*, 4 May 1832).

96. In addition to the early-nineteenth-century English traveller Sir Augustus John Foster, cited by Morgan (p. 380), other notable antecedent expressions of fondness for this "paradox" are found in the commentaries of Edmund Burke, Thomas R. Dew, Lyon G. Tyler and Henry A. Wise (see Theodore William Allen, "Slavery, Racism and Democracy," review of Morgan's *American Slavery/American Freedom*, in *Monthly Review*, March 1978).

97. Jordan, *White over Black*, p. 134.

98. We have the familiar testimony of Chastellux, who traveled in America in the early 1780s, concerning "the state of poverty, in which a great number of white people live in Virginia ... [where] I saw poor persons [in America] for the first time ... [and where] miserable huts are often to be met with, inhabited by whites, whose wan looks and ragged garments bespeak poverty" (François Jean, Marquis de Chastellux, *Travels in North America in the Years 1780, 1781, and 1782*, trans. and ed. Howard C. Rice Jr [Chapel Hill, 1963], 2:190). The historian John B. MacMaster's research led him to conclude that between 1810 and 1820, "Although the population of the seaboard had grown but slowly, the pauper, dependent, and petty criminal class had multiplied with what seemed alarming rapidity ... [and, in 1817] one-seventh of the population [of New York] were actually living on charity" (John B. McMaster, *History of the People of the*

United States from the Revolution to the Civil War, selected and edited by Louis B. Filler [New York: Farrar, Straus and Company, 1964], pp. 211 and 214).

99. Timothy H. Breen, "A Changing Labor Force and Race Relations in Virginia 1660–1710," *Journal of Social History*, Fall 1973, pp. 3–25.

100. Ibid., pp. 10–12 and 17.

101. Timothy H. Breen and Stephen Innes, *"Myne Owne Ground", Race and Freedom on Virginia's Eastern Shore, 1640–1676* (New York, 1980).

102. Breen, "Changing Labor Force," pp. 13–14.

103. Allan Kulikoff, *Tobacco and Slaves: The Development of Southern Cultures in the Chesapeake, 1680–1800* (Chapel Hill and London, 1986), pp. 4–5, 79.

104. Jacob M. Price, "The Economic Growth of the Chesapeake and the European Market, 1697–1775," *Journal of Economic History*, 24(1964):496–516, p. 498.

105. Breen, "Changing Labor Force," p. 16.

106. Breen, "Changing Labor Force," pp. 15–16.

107. Lerone Bennett Jr., *The Shaping of Black America* (Chicago, 1975), pp. 76–8.

108. See Stanley Garn, *Human Races*, rev. 2nd printing (Springfield, Illinois, 1962), and Theodosius Dobzhansky, *Mankind Evolving: The Evolution of the Human Species* (New Haven and London, 1962).

109. W. E. B. DuBois, *Black Reconstruction* (New York, 1935), p. 577.

1 The Anatomy of Racial Oppression

1. "A great deal, of course, depends on what one means by race. I take the racial factor to mean the assumption of innate differences based on real or imagined physical or other characteristics" (O. Patterson, *Slavery and Social Death* [New York, 1990], p. 176). What other, "non-physical," characteristics are meant, Patterson does not say at this point (pp. 176–8) in his discussion. Elsewhere his presentation may justify the inference that he had in mind considerations of presumed mental, temperamental, or moral attributes.

2. David Brion Davis, *The Problem of Slavery in Western Culture* (Ithaca, 1966), pp. 23–4. Davis makes this comment in the context of a critical examination of the views of George Bancroft as expressed in his *History of the United States, from the Discovery of the American Continent*, 10 vols, 14th edn (Boston, 1850–74). Davis cites from 1:159–61, 2:451. Bancroft (1800–91), a fervent Jacksonian and US expansionist, served as Secretary of the Navy, 1845–46, and was Ambassador to Britain from 1846 to 1849.

3. Charles Edward Chapman, *Colonial Hispanic America: A History* (New York, 1933), p. 118.

4. Marvin Harris, *Patterns of Race in the Americas* (New York, 1964), p. 59.

5. US Department of Commerce, Bureau of the Census, *Historical Statistics of the United States, 1789–1945* (Washington, DC, 1975), Series B 40–47 and n. 1. Walter Rodney, *A History of the Guyanese Working People, 1881–1905* (Baltimore, 1981), p. 143.

6. Franklin W. Knight, "Cuba", in David W. Cohen and Jack P. Greene, *Neither Slave Nor Free* (Baltimore, 1972), p. 280, n. 8.

7. Cited in June Purcell Guild, *Black Laws of Virginia* (1936; Negro Universities Press reprint, 1969), from the Virginia Statutes for the given years.

8. "What Makes You Black?", *Ebony*, 38:115–16 (January 1983).

9. *Boston Globe*, 17 September 1983. In an apparent misprint, the *Globe* says the Conservatives took their stand on "1/164," which I have taken the liberty of inferring to have intended "1/64." I do so not out of any pro-Conservative bias, but simply because of the fact that 164 is not a power of two. See also the *New York Times*, 6 July 1983.

10. In Louisiana in 1970 a lawyer went down to the Legislature to lobby for a definition of "Negro" sufficiently limited to leave a client of his on the "white" side of the line. "I got into a hassle with some of them," he later said; "... they started off at one one-hundred-and-twenty-eighth, and just to have some bargaining power I started off with ... an eighth. We finally struck the bargain at one thirty-second, and it sailed through" (*New York Times*, 30 September 1982).

11. The essential difference between racial and national oppression is the following. In the system of racial oppression, social control depends upon the denial of the legitimacy of social distinctions within the oppressed group. In the system of national oppression, social control depends upon the acceptance and fostering of social distinctions within the oppressed group.

12. See my discussion of Winthrop D. Jordan's view in the Introduction.

13. Henry Hallam, *Constitutional History of England from Henry VII to George II* (London, 1827), 3:401.

14. William Edward Hartpole Lecky, *A History of England in the Eighteenth Century*, 8 vols (New York and London, 1878–90), 2(1882):103.

15. W. K. Sullivan, *Two Centuries of Irish History, 1691–1870*, Part I, *From the Treaty of Limerick to the Establishment of Legislative Independence, 1691–1782*, edited by James Bryce (London, 1888), pp. 39–40.

16. Letter from Marx (London, 9 April 1870) to S. Meyer and A. Vogt, revolutionary German exiles in the United States (*Karl Marx and Friedrich Engels on Britain* [Moscow, 1962], pp. 551–2); emphasis in original.

17. Lewis P. Curtis, *Anglo-Saxons and Celts* (Bridgeport, Connecticut, 1968), p. 81, citing W. R. W. Stephens, *The Life and Letters of Edward A. Freeman*, 2 vols (London, 1895), 2:242.

18. Notable contributions to this field of study include: David Beers Quinn, "Sir Thomas Smith and the Beginning of English Colonial Theory," *Proceedings of the American Philosophical Society*, 89:543–60 (1945); David Beers Quinn, "Ireland and Sixteenth-century European Expansionism," in T. Desmond Williams, ed., *Historical Studies*, 1:20–32 (Papers Read before the Second Irish Conference of Historians, London, 1958); David Beers Quinn, *The Elizabethans and the Irish* (Ithaca, 1966); Howard Mumford Jones, "The Origins of the Colonial Idea in England," *Proceedings of the American Philosophical Society* (1949); Howard Mumford Jones, *O Strange New World: American Culture, the Formative Years* (New York, 1964); Nicholas P. Canny, "The Ideology of English Colonization: from Ireland to America," *William and Mary Quarterly*, 3rd series, 30:575–98; Nicholas P. Canny, *The Elizabethan Conquest of Ireland: A Pattern Established, 1565–76* (New York, 1978); and James Muldoon, "The Indian as Irishman," *Essex Institute Historical Collections*, 3:267–89 (October 1975).

19. Quinn, *Elizabethans and the Irish*, p. vii. See particularly pp. 20–27 for an example of Quinn's presentation of this point.

20. Wesley Frank Craven, *White, Red, and Black: The Seventeenth-century Virginian* (Charlottesville, 1971; New York, W. W. Norton reprint, 1977), pp. 39–40.

21. Muldoon, p. 270.

22. George M. Frederickson, *White Supremacy: A Comparative Study in American and South African History* (London University Press, 1981), p. 15.

23. Canny, "Ideology of English Colonization," p. 596 (repeated almost verbatim in his *Elizabethan Conquest of Ireland*, pp. 160, 576).

24. Canny, "Ideology of English Colonization," p. 596.

25. Michael Hechter, *Internal Colonialism: The Celtic Fringe in British National Development, 1536–1966* (Berkeley, 1975), pp. xvi–xvii. Cf. Raymond Crotty, *Ireland in Crisis: A Study in Capitalist Colonial Undevelopment* (Dover, New Hampshire, 1986), p. 38.

Sociologist Richard Williams makes a signal contribution along this line by bringing a study of history to a trenchant critique of misleading American sociological categories, which he believes impede the struggle for equality. He starts with the proposition that "race and ethnicity are social designations rather than natural categories" (Richard Williams, *Hierarchical Structures and Social Value: The Creation of Black and Irish Identities in the United States* [New York, 1990], p. ix).

26. Quinn, *Elizabethans and the Irish*, p. 26.

27. In 1978, Alden Vaughan questioned the validity of the Irish parallels, but he found no satisfactory alternative rationale for the contempt shown by Elizabethan Englishmen toward the American Indians. But whatever it may have been, he is convinced that it was not a matter of color prejudice, "for Englishmen believed the Virginia Indians to be approximately as white as themselves" (Alden T. Vaughan, "'Expulsion of the Savages': English Policy and the Virginia Massacre of 1622," *William and Mary Quarterly*, 3rd series, 35:57–84 [January 1978], p. 59, n. 3). Might it not have been that the earliest Anglo-Americans "believed the Virginia Indians to be as white as themselves" for the simple reason that they had not yet identified themselves as

"whites"? Later, Vaughan returned to the subject, and noted a shift in the English color perception of Indians beginning in the late seventeenth century, corresponding to the beginning of the usage "white" to distinguish Europeans and European-Americans from Indians; but he excludes African-Americans in making this observation, implying that where European-Americans and African-Americans were involved the former were immemorially designated "whites" (Alden T. Vaughan, "From White Man to Redskin: Changing Anglo-American Perceptions of the American Indian," *American Historical Journal*, 87:917–53 [October 1982]. For his exclusions of African-Americans from his generalization, see p. 931.) Instances in which the seventeenth-century Virginia court records seem to contradict him in this regard will be considered in Volume Two of this study. It is encouraging to note that by 1989 Vaughan had come to believe in the germaneness of "possible parallels and contrasts between English–African and English–Irish relations" (Alden T. Vaughan, "The Origins Debate," *Virginia Magazine of History and Biography* 97:311–54 [July 1989], p. 353, n. 129).

28. Canny, "Ideology of English Colonization," pp. 575–6, 588–92.

29. Canny, *Elizabethan Conquest of Ireland*, pp. 133–4, citing Essex to Privy Council, Additional Manuscripts 48015, fols 305–14.

30. Canny, *Elizabethan Conquest of Ireland*, p. 134, citing a letter of Leicester to (Sir William?) Fitzwilliam, 24 August 1572. Canny also cites another Elizabethan as likening Sidney's mission in Ireland to that of the Spanish in America, as one of "brideling the barbarous and wicked."

31. Cornwallis to the Spanish Council, 16 October 1609. Great Britain Public Record Office, *Calendar of State Papers relating to Ireland of the Reign of James I*, vol. 3 (1608–10) (London and Edinburgh, 1874), edited by C. W. Russell and John P. Prendergast, 3:83. When it had suited their Reformationist purposes a quarter of a century earlier, however, the English ruling class published the writings of Bartolomeo de las Casas exposing and condemning the usages of the Christian conquistadors in the Americas (Bartholomew de Las Casas, *The Spanish Colonie, Or Briefe Chronicle of the Acts and gestes of the Spaniards in the West Indies, called the newe World for the space of xl yeeres* [London, 1583; Readers Microprint Corporation, 1966; see the Foreword for the history of the appearance of this English edition of writings of Las Casas]. See, for instance, sigs A, A2, B2, B3.)

32. In a letter to Hercules Langrishe, 3 January 1792, *The Works of the Right Honorable Edmund Burke*, 6th edition (Boston, 1880), 12 vols, 6:305.

33. Lecky, *History of England*, 2:280.

34. Philip Dormer Stanhope, Fourth Earl of Chesterfield (1694–1773), who had served as Lord Lieutenant of Ireland (1745–46), writing to the Bishop of Waterford on 1 October 1764 (cited in Philip Henry Lord Mahon, *History of England from the Peace of Utrecht to the Peace of Versailles*, 7 vols [London, 1858], 5:123).

35. From a speech given at a meeting of the Catholic Board, Shakespeare Gallery, Exchequer Street, Dublin, 8 January 1814 (*Select Speeches of Daniel O'Connell, M. P.*, edited with historical sections by his son John O'Connell, Esq., 2 vols [Dublin, 1865], 1:408).

36. *Hansard's Parliamentary Debates*, 3rd series, 71:391 (8 August 1843). Brougham, an English abolitionist but an opponent of Irish independence, knew that the slaveholding Tyler family was playing politics with the repeal issue in the United States (see Chapter 8).

37. Richard Price, ed., *Maroon Societies: Rebel Slave Communities in the Americas* (Garden City, New York, 1973), p. 20; C. L. R. James, *The Black Jacobins: Toussaint L'Ouverture and the San Domingo Revolution* (revised edition, New York, 1963), pp. 17, 19.

38. Alfred H. Stone, "The Mulatto Factor in the Race Problem," *Atlantic Monthly*, 91:658–62 (1903), p. 660. Stone pegged his thesis on a distinction between "mulattoes" and "negroes." However, his awareness of social distinctions among Africans who were to be declassed in plantation America is worth noting. Terry Alford's *Prince Among Slaves: The True Story of an African Prince Sold into Slavery* (New York, 1977) is the history of Ibrahim, who is identified (p. 61) as "Rahahma" in a context which makes it apparent that he is the same person to whom Alfred H. Stone referred as "Rahamah." Stone also mentions "Otman dan Fodio, the poet chief of the Fulahs" as among distinguished Africans brought as slaves to plantation America.

39. E. S. Abdy, *Journal of a Residence and Tour in the United States of North America, from April 1833 to October 1834*, 3 vols (London, 1835), 3:346–8.

40. H. M. Henry, *Police Control of the Slave in South Carolina* (Emory, 1914), p. 11, citing

Nott and McCord (Law): *Witsell v. Parker*; and 2 Strobhart (Law), 43: ex parte Boylston.

41. Adam Smith, *Theory of Moral Sentiments*, 6th edition, 2 vols (London, 1790), 2:37.

42. US Supreme Court decision in *Dred Scott v. Sanford*, March 1857.

43. *Address of the Colored Convention to the People of Alabama*, published in the *Daily State Sentinel*, 21 May 1867 (James S. Allen, *Reconstruction: The Battle for Democracy [1865–1876]* [New York, 1937], pp. 237–8).

44. Major Ridge, who was not the richest man in the Cherokee nation, and who was not on the delegation, had an estate at this time of $22,000, not counting his thirty African-American bond-laborers and his interest in a trading post business (Thurman Wilkins, *Cherokee Tragedy: The Story of the Ridge Family and the Decimation of a People* [New York, 1970], pp. 183–4). An official census in 1835 found that of the population of the Cherokee nation (in contiguous areas of Georgia, North Carolina, Alabama and Tennessee) numbering 17,000, 1,600 were African-American bond-laborers (Samuel Carter III, *Cherokee Sunset, A Nation Betrayed: A Narrative of Travail and Triumph, Persecution and Exile* [Garden City, 1976], p. 22). The phrase "Cherokee planter-merchant" is Carter's (p. 23).

45. Opinion of Chief Justice John Marshall in *Cherokee Nation v. State of Georgia*, 30 US (1831), in Wilcomb E. Washburn, *The American Indian and the United States: A Documentary History*, 4 vols (New York, 1973), p. 2558. On Jackson's attitude, see ibid., pp. 2352–3, 2461–2, 2554, 2603; and Carter, pp. 216–17.

46. The Methodists having first taken the lead, the Moravians, Baptists, Congregationalists and Presbyterians, in concert, denounced the "white" incursions against Cherokee tribal lands and individual rights, attacks that became especially aggressive after the discovery of gold on Cherokee land in 1828. These Christian missionary workers "attached value to intermarriage as a force for improvement" (Wilkins, pp. 35, n. 58, 202–3, 219).

In 1815, William H. Crawford of Georgia, Secretary of War in Madison's cabinet, proposed a policy of merger by intermarriage of European-Americans and American Indians (see Introduction, n. 54). See Wilkins, p. 145, citing *Christian Herald*, Vol. 10, p. 468 (20 December 1823).

47. Wilkins, p. 145, citing *Christian Herald*, Vol. 10, p. 468 (20 December 1823).

48. "The [Scots] invasion [of Ireland] by Edward Bruce in 1315 has been recognized as the turning point of English influence in medieval Ireland" (G. H. Orpen, *Ireland Under the Normans*, 4 vols [Oxford, 1911–20], 4:160).

49. In a Gaelic-language article, a modern Franciscan historian, Canice Mooney (Cainneach O Maonaigh) finds in this Anglo-Norman policy a "racist" precedent of what occurred "yesterday in Birmingham, Alabama, or earlier in Sharpeville, South Africa" ("Racialism and nationalism in the Irish church, 1169–1534," *Galvia*, 10:4–17 [1954]). I am indebted to Brother Quinn of Iona College for translating this article for me. F. X. Martin characterizes Mooney's article as an "Irish nationalist interpretation" ("John, Lord of Ireland, 1185–1216," in *A New History*, 2:147, n. 3). The abbreviation *A New History* is used throughout this work to refer to *A New History of Ireland, under the auspices of the Royal Irish Academy*, planned and established by the late T. W. Moody, 10 vols (Oxford, 1976–), of which all but vols 1, 6, and 7 were published as of 1992. The volumes, composed by a select group of Irish scholars, are variously edited thus far by Art Cosgrove, T. W. Moody, F. X. Martin, F. J. Byrne, W. E. Vaughan. The citations will note the name of the contributor and the contribution, with locations cited by volume number and page number.

50. Jocelyn Otway-Ruthven, "The Request of the Irish for English Law, 1277–80," *Irish Historical Studies*, 6:261–70 (1948–49), pp. 264–5; Jocelyn Otway-Ruthven, "The Native Irish and English Law in Medieval Ireland," *Irish Historical Studies*, 7:1–16 (1950–51), pp. 14–15.

51. Sir John Davies, *A Discovery of the True Causes why Ireland was never Entirely Subdued ...* (London, 1612; 1969) p. 116. Orpen noted that Davies's comment was even more applicable to the earlier rejection of the Irish petition for enfranchisement (*Orpen*, 4:23, n. 3).

52. Edmund Curtis and R. B. McDowell, eds, "Remonstrance of the Irish Princes to Pope John XXII, 1317," in *Irish Historical Documents* (London, 1943), p. 41.

53. Otway-Ruthven, "Native Irish and English Law," p. 6. The complaint of the Irish "free" classes of the thirteenth century was despairingly echoed five centuries and three conquests later, during the early years of the Penal Laws era, by a Gaelic poet raging against a trinity of oppressions: the poverty from which escape was forbidden; the systemic frustration of all hope of social recognition; and, above all, "the contempt that follows it, for which there is no cure" (cited and translated in T. W. Moody and J. C. Beckett, *Ulster Since 1800, second series, a social*

survey [London, 1957], p. 171).

Daniel O'Connell, looking back in about 1815, reminisced: "It was easy to tell a Catholic in the streets by his subdued demeanour and crouching walk. So deeply had the iron of oppression entered into their souls" (a paraphrase given by Robert Dunlop, *Daniel O'Connell* [New York, 1908], p. 45).

54. Speaking of kinship societies in general, Orlando Patterson says, "Land was corporately owned" (Patterson, *Slavery and Social Death*, p. 241). A fairly recent comprehensive bibliography makes it manifest that the central problem of "land reform" in colonial, neo-colonial and post-colonial Africa is the conversion from tribal land ownership to individual (corporate or personal) title (*Land Tenure and Agrarian Reform in Africa and the Near East: an Annotated Bibliography*, compiled by the staff of the Land Tenure Center Library, Madison, Wisconsin, under the direction of Teresa Anderson, Librarian [Boston, 1976]). For the view of an early Pan-Africanist and pioneer of "African socialism," see J. E. Casely-Hayford (African name, Ekra Agiman), *The Truth about the West African Land Question* (London, 1971), with an Introduction by E. U. Essien-Udom, Department of Political Science, University of Ibadan. Casely-Hayford (Ekra Agiman) was " a member of the Anona clan, Ghana." "He was not opposed to modernization as such, but he wanted it to take place within the framework of 'African humanism'" (Professor Essien-Udom's Introduction). See also the Senate testimony of Major J. W. Powell of the American Bureau of Ethnology, Smithsonian Institution, at hearings on the Allotment Act of 1881 (Washburn, pp. 1751–2). The Irish case is discussed at length below.

55. The term and concept "social death," credit for which is given to Michel Izard, was used in a seminar on slavery in pre-colonial Africa held in Paris in 1971 under the auspices of the Institut international africain. Orlando Patterson found it appropriate to his general critique of slavery, to which he gave the title *Slavery and Social Death*. See Claude Meillassoux, ed., *L'Esclavage en Afrique précoloniale* (Paris, 1975), pp. 21–2.

56. The quoted phrases are in Meillassoux, p. 21.

57. "... colonists soon enough develop a sense of their own interests" (Liam de Paor, *Divided Ulster* [Harmondsworth, 1970], p. 24).

58. See Appendix C.

59. "By the sixteenth century, for example, much of the land of Europe was in the private possession of a landowning class. In West Africa, even today, most of the land is not so divided" (Basil Davidson with F. K. Bush and the advice of Ade Adayi, *A History of West Africa to the Nineteenth Century* [New York, 1966], p. 176).

See also Williams, *Hierarchical Structures and Social Value*, pp. 55–6.

60. Orlando Patterson, "Slavery and Slave Revolts: A Sociological Analysis of the First Maroon War, 1665–1740," in Richard Price, ed., *Maroon Societies*, p. 283. Patterson's article was originally published in *Social and Economic Studies*, 19:289–325 (1970).

In contrasting the situation of the African captives and the American Indians in the Anglo-American colonies, Phillips notes that the former were more vulnerable because "they were completely broken from their tribal stems" (Ulrich Bonnell Phillips, *Life and Labor in the Old South* [Boston: Little, Brown and Company, 1929], p. 160).

61. "The chief circumstance upon which the planters based their hope of security was the diversity of language and race among the negroes" (Vincent T. Harlow, *A History of Barbados, 1625–1685* [Oxford, 1926], p. 325). See Patterson, "Slavery and Slave Revolts," pp. 256, 261, 263, 282–3.

62. After the war against the Powder River Sioux in 1866, General John Pope testified on the basis of his own personal participation in this cynical program of spoliation of the Indian: "... the peace commissioners promise the Indians, in the first place, that the whites shall not go into the Indian country, knowing well that it is impossible to fulfill any promise of the sort; the parties who make these treaties know they must be broken; I have broken them, and I have known for twelve months that war would come out of it" (Washburn, *American Indian and the United States*, pp. 1508, 1522).

63. Ibid., pp. 1134, 1158. In December 1827 the Georgia legislature nullified the treaty-based land rights of the Cherokees and declared them tenants-at-will subject to dispossession by the colonists (Wilkins, *Cherokee Tragedy*, p. 196). This reduction of natives to colonial tenants-at-will was a re-enactment of the treatment of the native Irish under the Plantation of Ulster (see Chapter 5). Ulster Protestant settlers were numerous in the original Cherokee territory, but whatever record

there may be of contemporary references to this parallel has escaped this author.

64. Washburn, p. 2484.

65. Ibid., quoting an editorial in the St Louis *Republican*.

66. Ibid., p. 1752.

67. Ibid., p. 68.

68. Ibid., p. 1230.

69. Ibid., p. 1429.

70. Haymarket Square in Chicago was the scene of a rally on 4 May 1886, held in support of the eight-hour-day campaign and specifically to protest the police brutality against an assembly of strikers on the previous day. A large contingent of armed police came to stop the meeting. A bomb went off, resulting in the death of eight of the police. Eight anarchist leaders were convicted, who became known to labor history as the "Haymarket martyrs." Of the eight, four were hanged, and one died in jail, a suicide it was said. In 1893, the remaining three were freed from prison by Illinois Governor Peter Altgeld, who declared that they had been tried unfairly.

In the United States the term "robber barons" is applied to capitalist entrepreneurs who, in the latter part of the nineteenth century, accumulated (and occasionally lost) vast fortunes by unabashed fraud, bribery and force, including the brutal repression of working-class resistance. There were railroad barons, timber barons and cattle barons, who were licensed by a corrupt Congress and state legislatures to privatize (as today's Conservatives would say) public lands taken by force and fraud from Indian tribes, and to loot the public treasury. They enacted a reversion to the primitive accumulation period of the English enclosures of the sixteenth century and the plunder of Aztec and Inca treasures by the conquistadors. The reader is referred to the old but still champion history of this United States phenomenon, Gustavus Myers, *History of the Great American Fortunes* (New York, 1907, republished 1937). See also Matthew Josephson, *The Robber Barons: The Great American Capitalists, 1861–1901* (New York, 1934).

71. Washburn, 1:422. Morgan's views can be found in ibid., pp. 1:424–5.

72. Graven in my consciousness is the caution offered by Professor Eoin MacNeill regarding "the sort of fallacy common enough when the history of a nation or description of its customs is undertaken by foreigners" (Eoin MacNeill, *Celtic Ireland* [Dublin, 1921], p. 116). I am a student of Irish history, but not a scholar in it as those whose works I cite are. I have tried to stay clear of controversies in this field. In some instances, where it appears that I am involved willy-nilly, I have sought to present the contrary views fairly, and to defend my own. My focus here is always on the nature and extent of the structural differences between the Anglo-Norman social order and the Gaelic–Celtic social order as they confronted each other in Ireland – and their significance for an understanding of racial oppression.

73. D. A. Binchy, "Ancient Irish Law," *Irish Jurist*, new series, 1:85–92 (1966), p. 89. Estimates of the number of *tuaths* for later periods may reflect a demise of weaker tribes, as cattle raids concentrated wealth in the hands of the strong tribes (Kenneth Nicholls, "Gaelic Society and Economy in the High Middle Ages," in *A New History*, 2:414–15.

74. Professor Eoin MacNeill, who made some of the most important investigations of the records of ancient Ireland, argued that the term "tribe" should not be applied to early Irish society because he thought it invidiously suggested a comparison with the societies found among the "Australian or Central African aborigines" in the modern day (Eoin MacNeill, *Phases of Irish History* [Dublin, 1919], pp. 288–9; Eoin MacNeill, *Early Irish Laws and Institutions* [Dublin, 1935], pp. 24–5). MacNeill categorized the ancient Irish as "European white men" (*Celtic Ireland*, Preface). P. W. Joyce regularly used the term "tribe," although he made reference only to "Aryan" parallels (*A Social History of Ancient Ireland* [1913], 1:167). Kenneth Nicholls, however, points a footnote at an African parallel ("Gaelic Society and Economy in the High Middle Ages," p. 425). Students of early Irish history will recognize the validity of the parallels with Africa apparent in *Land Tenure and Agrarian Reform in Africa and the Near East*, the bibliography cited in n. 54.

Other Irish historians, before and after MacNeill, who have found the terms "tribe" and "tribal" appropriate include: D. A. Binchy, cited above, n. 73; W. K. Sullivan ("permission of the tribe council"), cited by his contemporary George Sigerson at p. 8 of *History of the Land Tenures and Land Classes of Ireland with an account of the Various Secret Agrarian Confederacies* (London, 1871), a work recommended highly by MacNeill; Sigerson himself, ("another tribe" [ibid., p. 9]); Alexander George Richey, ed., *Ancient Laws of Ireland* (Dublin and London, 1879), Vol. VI, Glossary (*fine* = "tribe"; "it is probably impossible to use any word in translation that will not be liable to a misconception; the translator renders it mostly by tribe, but also by family"); ibid., Vol. IV, *Brehon Law Tracts*, p. cxvii ("a system of tribe law"); Standish O'Grady, in "The Last Kings of Ireland," *English Historical Review*, 4:286–303 (1899), uses "tribe," "tribal," "clan"; Irish Texts Society, *A Smaller Irish–English Dictionary for the Use of Schools* (1932) (*fine* = "tribe; family"); and *A New History*, 8:11 (*tuath* = "people, tribe, tribal kingdom ...").

75. Gearoid Mac Niocaill, *Ireland Before the Vikings* (Dublin, 1972), p. 67; Nicholls, pp. 397–8.

76. In Gaelic Ireland in the sixteenth century, the chiefs exercised their privileges in the matter of the customary land redistribution in ways that "tended to concentrate land ownership" in their own hands. Furthermore, the conveyance of land rights, by inheritance or otherwise, was subject to such heavy assessments by the chiefs that the land in question often passed into the hands of the chief. Most common of all was the takeover of lands that the landholder had mortgaged to a chief (lord) for stock. If the charges were not met, the client (tenant) lost his holding. Whilst the tenant had a theoretical right to pay up and reclaim his land, "the conditions for redemption were ... often virtually impossible of fulfillment" (D. B. Quinn and K. W. Nicholls, "Ireland in 1534," in *A New History*, 2:34–5). See also: Joyce, 1:186–7; and George Sigerson, pp. 6–7.

77. Joyce, 1:156–60, 1:194–5.

78. Mac Niocaill, pp. 68–9.

79. Joyce, 1:163–4.

80. Ibid., 1:193, 1:195. Mac Niocaill, pp. 63, 65.

81. For all its Gaelic appearance, the term *betagh* does not seem to have appeared until it was used by the Anglo-Norman settlers to describe the native Irish of the laboring classes, who like the English villein (serf) were *adscriptus glebae*, that is, not free tenants for a term of years or at-will, but bound hereditarily to the land of their lord.

82. This section on the *derbfine* is based on (1) Mac Niocaill, pp. 49–53; (2) MacNeill, *Celtic Ireland*, p. 151; (3) MacNeill, *Phases of Irish History*, pp. 296–7; and (4) Sigerson, pp. 8–11.

83. "This constitution of the clans was one of the evils of ancient Ireland. It weakened the power of the kings or supreme chieftains" (James Henthorne Todd, ed., *The War of the Gaedhil with the Gaill; or the Invasion of Ireland by the Danes and other Norsemen* [originally a twelfth-century work], in *Chronicles and Memorials of Great Britain and Ireland during the Middle Ages* [London, 1867], vol. 48, p. cxviii).

84. See Joyce, 1:187–8, 2:282–4, for a discussion of the practical arrangements for sharing the use of common lands.

85. Standish O'Grady, "The Last Kings of Ireland," pp. 287, 291. This view is supported by Brian Cuiv in *The Course of Irish History* (Cork, 1967), pp. 120–22; and by F. J. Byrne, "The Trembling Sod," in *A New History*, 2:4–5.

86. In 1155, or within a few years thereafter, Pope Adrian, the only Englishman ever elected pope, in an act that came to be known as the Donation of Adrian granted Ireland to Henry II and commanded the Irish to submit to the English king. Rome was particularly interested in rooting out unacceptable practices by the Celtic clergy, such as rejection of celibacy, and the hereditary succession to office. In parallel with the temporal authorities, this pope intended to secure "the abandonment of features of Gaelic society going back to pre-Christian times" (F. X. Martin, "Diarmait Mac Murchada and the Coming of the Anglo-Normans," in *A New History*, p. 56).

87. Kathleen Hughes, Introduction to Jocelyn Otway-Ruthven, *A History of Medieval Ireland* (New York, 1986), p. 14.

88. Otway-Ruthven, *History of Medieval Ireland*, p. 102. It is interesting to note that during the Norse occupations of parts of Ireland, from the end of the eighth century to the middle of the eleventh, though many were the battles between the "Gaedhil" and the "Gaill," the Irish and the foreigners, land tenure principles were not at issue. Possibly that was in part due to the fact that the Scandinavians were primarily raiders and traders rather than cultivators. But it would seem equally due to the fact that "The Norse system [of land tenure] resembled the Irish in a marked manner" (Sigerson, p. 12).

The French views of land tenure certainly differed from those of the Algonkian people inhabiting Canada in the two centuries after the French made their first appearance on that coast in 1504. But since the French were soon primarily concerned first with fishing and then with the fur trade, their relations with the Algonkians were little troubled by land tenure issues (Gary B. Nash, *Red, White, and Black: The Peoples of Early America* [Englewood Cliffs, NJ, 1974], pp. 107–8). See also Alfred G. Bailey, *The Conflict of European and Algonkian Cultures, 1504–1800* (St John, New Brunswick, 1937); and William Eccles, *The Canadian Frontier, 1534–1670* (New York, 1969).

89. R. E. Glasscock, "Land and People, c. 1300," in *A New History*, 2:226.

90. Mac Niocaill cites an instance of annual rent on twenty-four milk cows; it included: one cow, three calves, a pig, a sheep, cream and butter, a flitch of salt pork, lard, suet, and three handfuls of candles (*Ireland Before the Vikings*, p. 64). P. W. Joyce noted a later record which showed the tenant paying an annual rent of one animal for every seven (*Social History of Ancient Ireland*, 1:188–9).

91. MacNeill, *Celtic Ireland*, p. 169.

92. "In Anglo-Norman society ... all land was held of someone, of the king in chief, or of someone on a ladder leading to the king." (The major exception – Church land – was to disappear under Henry VIII.) The settlers "had no interest in the theoretical basis of Irish land-tenure, and were fully aware of having overthrown the Irish order." The quotations are from Mac Niocaill, *Irish Jurist*, new series, 1:293 (1966).

93. MacNeill, *Celtic Ireland*, p. 170.

94. See Hughes, pp. 4–14.

95. Speaking of warring by cattle raids, O'Grady writes, "ownership of land divested of cattle or other exchangeable property meant subjugation; permanent military occupation of such territory was not necessary" (O'Grady, p. 300.) So it remained three centuries later, and these wars involved "rent and tribute ... [but] little interference in the internal affairs of the tributary" (O'Domhnaill, "Warfare in Sixteenth-century Ireland," *Irish Historical Studies*, 5 [1946–47]: 29–54, p. 29). See also Mac Niocaill, pp. 53, 54. MacNeill, *Celtic Ireland*, p. 122.

96. Mac Niocaill, p. 54.

97. Early Brehon Law provided that orphan brotherless "daughters should obtain all the land with obligation to perform service of attack and defence, or the half of it, without obligation to perform service of attack and defence; and there is a power over them to compel them to restore the land after their time" (Alexander George Richey, ed., *Ancient Laws of Ireland*, vol. IV, *Brehon Law Tracts* [Dublin, 1879], p. 41): Under this law, the woman would seem to have had no heirs, so that, upon her death, her land "fell back into the common fund of land out of which it had been taken" (Richey's Introduction, p. cxix). Mac Niocaill, referring to a later period (the latter half of the seventh century), suggests that this return to the common fund was made by way of the woman's son or sons, if she had any, or otherwise the "nearest male member" of the kinship group (*Ireland Before the Vikings*, p. 52).

98. Ibid., p. 58.

99. D. A. Binchy, *Crith Gablach* (Dublin, 1941), pp. 80–81. Noting that when women married they "passed to their husband's *fine* for the duration of the marriage," Mac Niocaill adds parenthetically, "some marriages were merely temporary arrangements" (*Ireland Before the Vikings*, p. 51).

100. Ibid., pp. 55, 58.

101. For this characterization of English family custom, I have relied on Lawrence Stone, *The Crisis of the Aristocracy, 1558–1641* (London, 1967), pp. 594–605. See also John P. Prendergast, *The Cromwellian Settlement of Ireland* (New York, 1868), pp. 17–18.

102. Mac Niocaill, pp. 58–9. Etymological note: "gossipred" is derived from "god-sib," godchild.

103. The practice of the stronger party demanding and holding hostages of the weaker one was regular in these times, Ireland being no exception. See O'Grady, "The Last Kings of Ireland," pp. 292, 294, 297, 301. Ordinary captives were a source of wealth, according to O'Grady, "for war captives were then [in the 12th century] sold into slavery" (p. 302).

104. G. J. Hand, *English Law in Ireland, 1290–1324* (Cambridge, 1967), p. 202.

105. Sir John Davies, *A Discovery of the True Causes why Ireland was never entirely Subdued, nor brought under Obedience of the Crowne of England, Untill the Beginning of his Majesties happie Raigne* (London, 1612).

Despite his anti-Irish bias, Davies brought to his task experience as a lawmaker and colonial administrator, a good literary style, a legal concern for precision, and a reverence for history. This work of some three hundred pages ranks in these respects with Francis Bacon's *History of the Reign of King Henry VII*.

106. *Discovery of the True Causes* . . . , p. 167.

107. Ibid., pp. 167–8.

108. Ibid., p. 169.

109. Ibid., pp. 170–73.

110. Ibid., p. 182.

111. Ibid., pp. 174, 179.

112. F. X. Martin, "Diarmait Macmurchada," pp. 57–9.

113. F. X. Martin, "Overlord Becomes Feudal Lord, 1172–85," in *A New History*; 2:111; F. X. Martin, "John, Lord of Ireland, 1185–1216", in *A New History*, 2:128.

114. Martin, "Diurmait Macmurchada," pp. 64, 65; Martin, "Overlord," p. 117.

115. Otway-Ruthven, *History of Medieval Ireland*, p. 102. As is often noted, the chronicle of Giraldus Cambrensis (Gerald of Wales – who accompanied King John to Ireland in 1185) both recorded and concurred with the supercilious and disdainful Anglo-Norman references to the Irish and their way of life. But that cannot explain the English resort to racial oppression in Ireland; sooner or later, the same chauvinistic attitude was directed by the English at the Welsh and the Scots, in whose countries a fundamentally different system of English domination was instituted.

116. Davies, p. 116.

117. See Martin, "John, Lord of Ireland," pp. 147, 150–53.

118. Immanuel Wallerstein, *The Modern World-System: Capitalist Agriculture and the Origins of the European World-Economy in the Sixteenth Century* (New York, 1974), pp. 68–9.

119. Martin, "John, Lord of Ireland," pp. 150–51.

120. Ibid., p. 153.

121. In insisting on the relevance of the parallel between incidents so widely separated in time, I appeal to the example of the Irish historian James C. Beckett. Speaking of the resentment felt by the Anglo-Irish toward English "newcomers," Beckett argues: "This parallel between the fourteenth century and the eighteenth is not merely adventitious. It indicates a real continuity of tradition. . . . The constitutional programme of the Anglo-Irish patriots in the reign of George III was consciously derived from precedents set by the 'English in Ireland' three or four hundred years earlier" (J. C. Beckett, *The Anglo-Irish Tradition* [Ithaca, 1976], p. 25).

122. See Introduction, n. 16.

123. Hand, p. 194.

124. Ibid., p. 188.

125. Phillips, *Life and Labor in the Old South*, p. 162.

126. John P. Prendergast, *The Cromwellian Settlement of Ireland*, second, enlarged edition (Dublin, 1875), p. 21, n. 2.

127. 4 Hening 132–3 (1723).

128. Hand, pp. 201–2.

129. "Remonstrance of the Irish Princes to Pope John XXII," 1317, p. 43.

130. *Neale v. Farmer* in *Reports of Cases in Law and Equity Argued and Determined in the Supreme Court of the State of Georgia from August 1850–May 1851*, Thomas R. Cobb, reporter, Vol. IX (Athens, Georgia, 1851), pp. 555–84. The court, far from considering this fact a loophole in the law, held it an indispensable principle because, "If [the Common Law] protects the life of the slave, why not his liberty? and if it protects his liberty, then it breaks down at once the *status* of the slave" (p. 579). The same principle had been written into law in colonial Virginia in 1723 (4 Hening 133).

131. Prendergast, p. 2, n. 1, citing Sir John Davies, *Discovery of the True Causes* . . .

132. Washburn, *The American Indian and the United States*, pp. 2669–70, 2676. The Dred Scott decision rendered by the United States Supreme Court in 1857 held that Negroes were not citizens of the United States, and in the words of Chief Justice Roger B. Taney, had "no rights which a white man is bound to respect" (Richard D. Heffner, *A Documentary History of the United States, An Expanded Edition* [New York, 1956], p. 131).

133. 4 Hening 326–7 (1732).

134. J. C. Beckett, *A Short History of Ireland* (New York, 1968), p. 22; Orpen, *Ireland Under the Normans*, 4:259–60; Otway-Ruthven, " Native Irish and English Law," p. 3; Otway-Ruthven, "Anglo-Irish Shire Government in the Thirteenth Century," *Irish Historical Studies*, 5:1–7 (1946).

135. Otway-Ruthven, "Native Irish and English Law," p. 6.

136. Douglas Hall, "Jamaica," in Cohen and Greene, eds, *Neither Slave Nor Free*, p. 201;

Charles Edward Chapman, *Colonial Hispanic America*, pp. 118–19.

137. Hand, p. 207. Compare Otway-Ruthven, "Native Irish and English Law," pp. 6–7.

138. The eclipse of English power in Ireland in the fourteenth and fifteenth centuries, touched only in passing in this chapter, is dealt with in Chapter 2.

139. *Hansard Parliamentary Debates*, 2d series, vol. 72 (1844), 1172. The subject was "The State of Ireland."

140. Sean O'Domhnaill, "Warfare in Sixteenth-century Ireland," p. 46.

141. Ibid., p. 30.

142. Sigerson, *History of Land Tenures*, pp. 24–5.

143. Aidan Clarke, "The Irish Economy, 1600–60," in *A New History*, 3:169–70. The word "plantation," as found in this work, has two meanings, derived from two kinds of "planting": the planting of colonies of settlers, and the planting of agricultural crops. The British Board of Trade was for a time called, in the first sense, the "Lords of Trade and Plantations." In the Anglo-American context the term acquired its second meaning. There, at first, the term "plantation colonies" had the same colonial connotation as it did with regard to the plantation of Ulster. In time, the terms "plantation" and "plantation system" came to refer to a system of agricultural operations producing staple crops on large tracts of privately owned land.

144. J. C. Beckett, *The Anglo-Irish Tradition*, p. 131.

145. The "Act for the Settling of Ireland," commonly called the Act of Settlement, was passed on 12 August 1652 (*Statutes and Ordinances of the Interregnum, 1642–1660*, collected and edited by C. H. Firth and R. S. Raitt, 2 vols [London, 1911], 2:598–603).

The full title of the Act of Satisfaction is informative: "An Act for the speedy and effectual Satisfaction of the Adventurers [London merchants and other capitalists backers of the English war effort] for Lands in Ireland, and of the [English] Soldiers there, and of other Publique Debts, and for the Encouragement of Protestants to plant and inhabit Ireland" (ibid., 2:722).

146. Vincent Gookin, *The Great Case of Transplantation in Ireland Discussed; or Certain Considerations, wherein the many great inconveniences in the transplanting the Natives of Ireland generally out of the three provinces of Leinster, Ulster, and Munster, into the Province of Connaught, are shewn* (London, 1655), p. 26.

147. Richard Lawrence, *The Interest of England in the Irish Transplantation, Stated . . . Being chiefly intended as An Answer to a scandalous seditious Pamphlet, intituled, The great case of Transplantation, discussed* (Dublin, 1655), p. 12.

148. Ibid., p. 25.

149. According to William Petty, the native Irish population of about 850,000 was reduced to around 700,000 in the course of the war. Gardiner estimates that some 180,000 were males twenty-five years of age or older. According to Petty, 35,000–40,000 Irish soldiers, that is, approximately one-sixth of the adult male population, were sold abroad to serve in the armies of Spain, France, Flanders, etcetera (William Petty, *The Political Anatomy of Ireland* [1672] in Charles Henry Hull, ed., *The Economic Writings of Sir William Petty*, 2 vols [1899; New York, 1963], p. 150; Samuel Rawson Gardiner, "The Transplantation to Connaught," *English Historical Review*, 14:700–734 [October 1899], p. 703; Gookin, *The Great Case of Transplantation*, p. 22). Spain was probably the chief first destination of these transported men under conduct of their officers. Many were abandoned there among a hostile population. Of those enrolled in actual Spanish units, thousands deserted to France because of neglect and ill-treatment suffered under the Spanish. Some were shipped to be sold as plantation bond-laborers in Barbados, St Christopher and elsewhere, possibly Virginia in Anglo-America (Richard Bagwell, *Ireland under the Stuarts and during the Interregnum* 3 vols, [London, 1909], pp. 2:303–4, 2:310; A. E. Smith, *Colonists in Bondage: White Servitude and Convict Labor in America, 1607–1776* [Chapel Hill, 1947; New York, 1971], pp. 163–5; *The Petty Papers: Some Unpublished Writings of Sir William Petty*, edited from the Bowood Papers by the Marquis of Lansdowne, 2 vols in 1 [London, 1927; New York, 1967], p. 2:229; Philip Alexander Bruce, *Economic History of Virginia in the Seventeenth Century, An Inquiry into the Material Conditions of the People based upon Original and Contemporaneous Records*, 2 vols [New York, 1895; reprinted 1935], pp. 1:608–9).

Rather than be the primary financier of the process, the Parliamentary government worked through intermediaries, former Irish officers, English officers willing to invest in it as a business proposition, or enterprising Spanish officers, but with the King of Spain as the main ultimate payer (Robert Dunlop, ed., *Ireland under the Commonwealth, Being a Selection of Documents Relating to the Government of Ireland from 1651 to 1659* [Manchester, 1913], 2 vols; 1:177, 1:238, 2:310, 2:430; Bagwell, 2:303; Day's Proceedings, Council of State, 10 December 1652 and 9 April 1653, Great Britain Public Record Office, *Calendar of State Papers, Domestic, 1652–53*). So eager was the English government to dispose of these Irish fighters that when the Spanish Crown, or some other customer or merchant, failed to make prompt payment, the government would underwrite the process to keep it moving (Dunlop, 2:310, 2:370). During the war launched by Cromwell against Spain for the West Indies in 1655, no Irish could be sent to Spain, but, by that time the process had been completed to the general satisfaction of the English government. In August 1657, Oliver Cromwell himself, writing to the Lord Deputy and Council in Ireland, appears to be concerned only with seeing to it that proper financial settlements be made with those shippers and contractors who were unpaid as a result of the war "between us and the Spaniard" (ibid., 2:669–70). The following year, after Oliver's death, his son and successor Richard Cromwell, in the course of discussing the same subject of unresolved debts, speaks of the advantage that had been gained by "transporting into Spain very great numbers of Irish soldiers, pestering our good people of Ireland and endangering the peace of that nation" (Richard Cromwell to the Lord Deputy and Council [in Ireland], 9 November 1658, ibid., 2:689–90).

150. Gookin, pp. 22, 26.

151. Prendergast, *Cromwellian Settlement of Ireland*, p. 98. "The object was to de-grade the evicted upper-tenant or landlord to a lower condition . . . of cultivators" (Sigerson, *History of Land Tenures*, p. 80).

152. Aidan Clarke, *The Old English in Ireland, 1625–1642* (London, 1966), pp. 26, 236; Aidan Clarke, "Irish Economy, 1600–60," p. 169; Karl S. Bottigheimer, *English Money and Irish Land: The "Adventurers" in the Cromwellian Settlement of Ireland* (Oxford, 1971), p. 5, n. 1.

153. For the provisions of the Act of Settlement, see Firth and Raitt; and Gardiner, "Transplantation to Connaught."

154. W. F. T. Butler, *Confiscation in Irish History* (London, 1918), pp. 132, 156. Butler (p. 156) says that in 1641 Catholic landowners numbered at least eight thousand, or even twelve thousand. Clarke, on the other hand, says that the total of all "proprietors" could not have been more than six thousand, of whom about four thousand were Old English or Irish, presumably Catholics (Clarke, "Irish Economy, 1600–60," p. 170). A possible clue to the discrepancy may be supplied by Butler (p. 198, n. 59). Speaking of two thousand Catholics who were assigned Connaught land, he said that, "possibly many of these had only been tenants or leaseholders in 1641." Perhaps Clarke's "freeholders" do not include tenants. While in England and in Ireland most English were "freeholders" having hereditary leases, Catholic tenants generally did not have hereditary leases; they were tenants, but not freeholders. Perhaps the Butler and the Clarke figures can be reconciled on this basis. I have chosen to use Butler's in this instance, but a picture of mass expropriation is indicated in either case, and is corroborated by all historians of the period. J. G. Simms's criticisms of Butler's estimates, whatever their validity, do not impair the argument being made here as to the significance of the massive expropriation of Catholic lands (J. G. Simms, "Land Owned by Catholics in Ireland in 1688," *Irish Historical Studies*, 7:180–90 [1950–51]).

155. As a further concession to their religio-racial status, Protestants were later allowed to pay money fines instead of forfeiting lands. But they combined to spurn even that condition, and in the end the English government simply left them alone (Dunlop, 1:cxlix–cl.)

156. Dunlop, 1:cxlvi. The history of the continuous transplantation of the American Indians by the United States government, which began with the Indian Removal Act of 1832, was in many respects a virtual re-enactment of the transplantation to Connaught.

157. Butler, pp. 157–8. "The number of transplantees who finally held land west of the Shannon . . . [was] above 580" (ibid., pp. 198–9).

158. The data for Catholic-held land presented in this paragraph are drawn from Butler, especially p. 162; and Simms, especially pp. 180, 182, 189–90. Of the total land, about seven out of every ten acres (71 per cent) were profitable (Simms, p. 180, citing William Petty). About five out of every eight acres of profitable land belonged to Catholics in 1641 (Butler, p. 162; Simms, pp. 180, 189).

159. Simms, pp. 182, 189.

160. The Irish historian and revolutionary martyr of 1916 James Connolly declared that Ireland lost this struggle because the Irish leaders refused "to raise the standard of the Irish nation instead of an English faction" (James Connolly, *Labour in Irish History* [New York, 1919], pp. 20–21).

161. Simms, pp. 189–90. After losing 615,000 (Irish) acres in the Williamite confiscations, the Catholics owned 1,086,000 acres. Simms says the Penal Law toll amounted to as much as the Williamite confiscations, indicating that by the middle of the eighteenth century only 471,000 of some 7.5 million acres of profitable land was still Catholic-owned. Butler, *Confiscation in Irish History*, says that the Williamite confiscations had already reduced the Catholic share to no more than one out of every twenty acres (p. 237). It is commonly accepted that Catholics owned only 5 per cent of the land at the close of the eighteenth century. Catholics made up four-fifths of the population of Ireland at the beginning of the eighteenth century (see p. 77).

162. Speech in the Irish Parliament in 1789. By this reminder, Fitzgibbon was warning his independence-minded fellow members of the Irish Parliament to reflect on the possible consequences of withdrawing from British authority (Quoted in E. M. Johnston, *Ireland in the Eighteenth Century* [Dublin, 1974], p. 161).

163. Prendergast, *Cromwellian Settlement*, pp. 180–81.

164. John Locke (1632–1704), son of a Cromwellian soldier, member of the Board of Trade and Plantations, and philosophic patron saint of the American and French Revolutions, endorsed the rationale of this anti-Catholic persecution. In the first of four famous *Letters on Toleration*, he excluded Roman Catholics from the right of toleration on the ground that they "deliver themselves up to the protection of a foreign prince . . . and [are] soldiers against the government."

165. Butler, p. 237.

2 Social Control and the Intermediate Strata: Ireland

1. For Anglo-American examples, see: 3 Hening 459; and A. Leon Higginbotham Jr, *In the Matter of Color: Race and the American Legal Process, the Colonial Period*, pp. 194–96 (South Carolina, 1740), and p. 254 (Georgia, 1755). For the insecurity and lack of legal defense of the Catholic tenant-at-will in Ireland, see Chapter 3.

2. See 2 Hening 267. Literally, *coverture* means "concealment"; the male-supremacist legal lexicography uses this term to class married women with minors as lacking independent legal standing.

3. W. K. Sullivan, *Two Centuries of Irish History, 1691–1870* (London, 1888), part I, pp. 20–21.

4. See John Collier's moving account *Indians of the Americas* (New York, 1948), pp. 104–5, 135–7. For documentary materials see the annual reports of the United States Commissioners of Indian Affairs for 1891 and 1901. Wilcomb E. Washburn, *The American Indian and the United States: A Documentary History*, 4 vols (New York, 1973), especially 1:560–69, 1:712–14.

5. As did the anti-Catholic Penal Laws in Ireland under which Catholic merchants and other middle-class elements suffered "[e]xclusion from local politics and from formal civic life" (David J. Dickson, "Catholics and Trade in Eighteenth-century Ireland: An Old Debate Renewed," in T. P. Power and Kevin Whelan, eds, *Endurance and Emergence: Catholics in Ireland in the Eighteenth Century* [Dublin, 1990], p. 91). Archbishop William King wrote to the Archbishop of Canterbury in April 1719 expressing anxiety about the possible risks to the security of his Protestants in this exclusion. "How will the protestants secure themselves," he said, "when all the commonalty are all papists?" (Thomas Bartlett, "The Origins of the Catholic Question in Ireland, 1690–1800," in Power and Whelan, p. 3).

6. Lewis C. Gray, assisted by Esther Thompson, *History of Agriculture in the Southern United States to 1860*, 2 vols (Washington DC, 1932; Peter Smith reprint, 1958), 1:478–80; Robert William Fogel and Stanley L. Engerman, *Time on the Cross: The Economics of American Negro Slavery* (Boston: Little, Brown, 1974), pp. 192–4; Robert William Fogel, *Without Consent or Contract: The Rise and Fall of American Slavery* (New York: W. W. Norton, 1989), pp. 72–80.

7. Fogel, pp. 78–9. In regard to the "overseer problem" as seen from the plantation owner's point of view, see Ulrich Bonnell Phillips, "The Origin and Growth of the Southern Black Belts," *American Historical Review*, 11:798–816 (July 1906); 11:808, n. 13.

8. Gray, 2:794, citing agricultural journals of the 1840s.

9. Bartholomew de Las Casas, *The Spanish Colonie, Or Briefe Chronicle of the Acts and*

gestes of the Spaniards in the West Indies, called the newe World for the space of xl yeeres (London, 1583; Readers Microprint Corporation, 1966 – see the Foreword for the history of the appearance of this English edition of writings of Las Casas), sigs A, A2, B2, B3; E. G. Bourne, *Spain in America: 1450–1580* (New York, 1904), pp. 211–14; C. L. R. James, *Black Jacobins: Toussaint L'Ouverture and the San Domingo Revolution*, 2nd revised edition (New York, 1973), pp. 9–24, 36–42.

10. J. C. Beckett, *A Short History of Ireland*, 6th edition (London, 1973), p. 24.

11. In one of a number of studies which he did on English plantation projects in Ireland, Robert Dunlop found that the failure to induce English tenant farmers and laborers to migrate to Ireland was "the weakest point of the whole scheme" ("The Plantation of Munster, 1584–89," *English Historical Review*, 3:250–69, p. 269).

12. Sir John Davies, *A Discovery of the True Causes why Ireland was never entirely Subdued, nor brought under Obedience of the Crowne of England, Untill the Beginning of his Majesties happie Raigne* (London, 1612), pp. 118–20. Compare G. H. Orpen, *Ireland Under the Normans*, 4 vols (Oxford, 1911–20), 2:332–4.

13. Davies, pp. 119–20.

14. The invasion of Ireland by Edward Bruce in the year 1315 marks a major turn in the story of English influence in medieval Ireland (James Lydon, "The Impact of the Bruce Invasion, 1315–27," in *A New History*, pp. 296–302; Orpen, 4:160).

15. Edmund Curtis, *A History of Medieval Ireland from 1086 to 1513* (London, 1938; reprinted 1968), p. 277. See also Richard Bagwell, *Ireland Under the Tudors, with a Succinct Account of the Earlier History*, 3 vols (London, 1885–90), 1:65, 1:80; and J. C. Beckett, *The Making of Modern Ireland 1603–1923* (New York, 1966), p. 15.

16. Orpen, 4:161.

17. The term "Anglo-Irish" is, strictly speaking, anachronistic here, as it was not in use until the nineteenth century (see Beckett, *Short History* p. 15, n. 1). But already in the course of the medieval era the Norman character was superseded by the English, as the definition of the distinct interest of the English colonists emerged.

18. Curtis, p. 277.

19. Ibid., pp. 203, 219, 372.

20. Richard Bagwell, 1:70–71; Beckett, *Short History*, p. 15; Curtis, pp. 219, 255, 299; Davies, p. 211; Seamus MacManus, *The Story of the Irish Race: A Popular History of Ireland* (New York, 1944), pp. 337–9.

21. Curtis, p. 255.

22. *Statutes and Ordinances and acts of the parliament of Ireland, King John to Henry V*, edited by H. F. Berry (Dublin, 1907), pp. 431–69, excerpted in Edmund Curtis and R. B. McDowell, eds, *Irish Historical Documents* (London, 1943), p. 52.

23. Curtis and McDowell, eds, pp. 52–6. The proscribed Irish mode of riding was the bareback style.

24. Ibid.

25. Bagwell, 1:123. In conceding the situation, King Henry VII said that since Ireland could not rule Kildare, then Kildare must rule Ireland (Curtis, p. 338).

26. George Hill, *An historical account of the Plantation in Ulster at the commencement of the seventeenth century, 1608–1620* (Belfast, 1877; reprinted Shannon: Irish University Press, 1970), pp. 21–2, n. 21. Hill cites the preface to the *Calendar of Patent Rolls*, Elizabeth [I], p. xvii.

". . . Mr Allen, Master of the Rolls, reported to the King [Henry VIII], that his laws were not obeyed twenty miles from the capital" (John Fitzgibbon, Earl of Clare, Lord Chancellor of Ireland, addressing the Irish House of Lords, 10 February 1800, in support of the Union of Great Britain and Ireland; pamphlet in the collection at New York Public Library Research Libraries, p. 5).

27. Bagwell, 1:84; D. B. Quinn, "'Irish' Ireland and 'English' Ireland," in *A New History*, 2: 633; D. B. Quinn, "The Hegemony of the Earls of Kildare," in *A New History*, 2:647; J. A. Watt, "The Anglo-Irish Colony under Strain, 1327–1399," in *A New History*, 2:369–70; D. B. Quinn, "The Re-emergence of English Policy as a Major Factor in Irish Affairs," in *A New History*, p. 675.

28. Kenneth W. Nicholls, "Gaelic Society and Economy in the High Middle Ages," in *A New History*, 2:408–9; Art Cosgrove, "The Emergence of the Pale, 1399–1447," in *A New History*, 2:552–3; Curtis, *A History of Medieval Ireland* (1923 edition), pp. 202, 417.

29. Bagwell, 1:134–5, citing *State Papers, Henry VIII*, 12, 14, 18. (The letter of instruction on this subject sent by Henry VIII to Lord Deputy Sir Anthony St Leger was dated 23 September 1541.) G. A. Hayes-McCoy, "The Ecclesiastical Revolution, 1534–47," in *A New History*, 5:48.

30. It is to be noted that the terms of tenure attendant upon these regrants to the Irish and the Catholic Old English were more burdensome than those allowed to Protestant New English colonists (Karl S. Bottigheimer, *English Money and Irish Land: The "Adventurers" in the Cromwellian Settlement of Ireland* [Oxford, 1971], p. 11, n. 1).

31. Gerard Anthony Hayes-McCoy, "Conciliation, coercion, and the protestant reformation, 1547–71," in *A New History*, 3:79. For a highly interesting and well-documented account of the workings of the surrender-and-regrant policy told vicariously from the point of view of the participating chieftain class, see N. C. Macnamara, *The Story of an Irish Sept, their Character & Struggle to Maintain their Lands in Clare, by a Member of the Sept* (London, 1896), pp. 148–71.

32. Robert Dunlop, "The Plantation of Leix and Offaly," *English Historical Review*, 6:61, citing Commissioner Anthony St Leger to Thomas Cromwell (1537), in Great Britain Public Record Office, State Paper Office, *State Papers, Henry VIII*, 2:526.

33. Macnamara, p. 148, citing *Calendar of State Papers, Henry VIII*, 1520.

34. Eoin MacNeill, *Phases of Irish History* (Dublin, 1919), 298–9.

35. George Hill, *An historical account of the Plantation in Ulster at the commencement of the seventeenth century, 1608–1620* (Dublin 1877; 1970), p. 30.

36. Though the Irish were firmly supportive of Mary Tudor for her promotion of Catholicism, they regarded her administration of affairs, particularly her failure to restore confiscated lands to Catholic owners, as injurious to Ireland (Francis Peter Plowden, *An Historical Review of the State of Ireland from the Invasion of that Country under Henry II to its Union with Great Britain on the first of January 1801*, 5 vols [Philadelphia, 1805], 1:63).

37. Karl S. Bottigheimer, "Kingdom and Colony: Ireland," in K. R. Andrews, N. P. Canny, and P. E. H. Hair, eds, *The Westward Enterprise: Essays in Tribute to David Beers Quinn* (Detroit, 1979), p. 51. Karl S. Bottigheimer, *English Money and Irish Land*, p. 11.

38. D. B. Quinn, *The Elizabethans and the Irish* (Ithaca, 1966), p. 108.

39. G. A. Hayes-McCoy, "The Completion of the Tudor Conquest and the Advance of the Counter-reformation, 1571–1603," in *A New History*, 3:96–7.

40. Quinn, *The Elizabethans and the Irish*, p. 108, citing Historical Manuscripts Commission, De l'isle and Dudley MSS., II, 12–15.

41. Bottigheimer, *English Money and Irish Land*, p. 26.

42. See Appendix D.

43. Hayes-McCoy, "Completion of the Tudor Conquest," pp. 102–3.

44. Hill, pp. 42 n. 45, 48–50, 62.

45. G. A. Hayes-McCoy, *Irish Battles* (London: Longman Green, 1969), chapter entitled "The Yellow Ford," especially pp. 118–28; P. W. Joyce, *A Concise History of Ireland from the Earliest Times to 1837*, 6th edition (Dublin, 1897), pp. 162–8.

"The English from their first arrivall in that Kingdome, never had received so great an overthrow" (Fynes Moryson, *An Itinerary, Containing His Ten Yeeres Travell through the Twelve Dominions of Germany, Bohmerland, Sweitzerland, Netherland, Denmarke and Ireland*, 4 vols (London, 1617; Glasgow, 1907), 2:217. Moryson (1566–1629) served as chief secretary to the English Lord Deputy Mountjoy in Ireland from November 1600 until he returned with his employer to England in 1603. His *Itinerary* devotes 650 pages to "The Rebellion in Ireland."

46. Moryson, pp. 218–20, 273–4.

47. As did his despairing Red Cross Knight in *The Faerie Queene*, Book I, Canto ix, Stanza 35, line 111.

48. Queen Elizabeth's recommendation of Spenser to be Sheriff was overtaken by events, and the poet never actually served in that post. His "Breife note" to the queen was composed in Cork, where he had taken refuge with other English colonists (Pauline Henley, *Spenser in Ireland* [Cork, 1928; reissued New York, 1969], pp. 144, 153–6, 165).

49. "A Breife Note of Ireland," in Greenlaw et al., eds, *The Works of Edmund Spenser*, 10 vols (Baltimore, 1949), 9:236, 9:244.

50. F. X. Martin, "Medieval Ireland," in *A New History*, 2:lx; R. E. Glasscock, "Land and People, c. 1300," *A New History*, 2:225.

51. See Appendix C.

52. Basil Davidson with F. K. Bush and the advice of Ade Adayi, *A History of West Africa to the Nineteenth Century* (New York, 1966), p. 213.

53. Kenneth G. Davies, *The Royal African Company* (London, 1957), p. 284.

54. *John Fitzgibbon Lord Clare speech to the Irish House of Lords in support of the Act of Union of Great Britain and Ireland, 10 February 1800*, p. 4 (pamphlet in the New York Public Library Research Libraries).

55. Theodore K. Rabb, *Enterprise and Empire, Merchant and Gentry Investment in the Expansion of England, 1575–1630* (Cambridge, Massachusetts, 1967), p. 40.

56. A. L. Rowse, *The Elizabethans and America* (New York, 1959), p. 24.

57. Moryson, 2:170. Did Karl Marx know of this old prophecy? "If England is the bulwark of landlordism and European capitalism," he wrote in 1869, "the only point where one can hit official England really hard is *Ireland*" (Resolution of the International Workingmen's Association, 1 January 1870, *The General Council of the First International, 1868–70 – Minutes* [Moscow, n. d.], pp. 399–405; 403).

58. See Appendix E.

59. Moryson, 2:229, 2:277.

60. Ibid.

61. Mountjoy (1536–1606) was made Earl of Devonshire in 1603 in recognition of his services in Ireland. He was an instance of the one in fifty of the gentry and nobility in England between 1575 and 1630 who invested in joint stock companies for overseas ventures (Rabb, pp. 26–7, 248).

62. Moryson, Vol. 2, pp. 222–4, 276, 360, 369–72; Vol. 3, 36, and (for summary figures) 341–2.

63. John Ulrich Nef, *The Conquest of the Material World* (Chicago, 1964), p. 127. See also p. 181.

64. Moryson, 2:407–8, 3:53–4, 3:61, 3:72–5. See also 2:456, 3:110, 3:256.

65. Moryson, 3:143. Since the soldiers had to pay for their food and clothing, or have the costs docked from their pay, the actual costs to the exchequer were much less.

66. Nef, pp. 126–7, 195–7.

67. Moryson, 2:410.

68. "Muster of the Army at Dundalk" (ibid., 2:334–6). Compare the illustration of the siege of Kinsale (17 October 1601 to 9 January 1602) in which the pikemen appear in a far greater proportion than they do in the muster at Dundalk (ibid., 3:96–7, foldout).

69. Nef, p. 114, n. 109. Spanish tools and arms that came into the hands of the English during the siege of Kinsale were so much superior to those of the English that Moryson complained, ". . . the sight of them would have put her Majesties Ministers of the Ordinance to shame, who for private gaine sent sale ware to us, unfit to be used" (*Itinerary*, 3:55).

70. Moryson, 2:241–2 (Essex to Queen Elizabeth I, 25 June 1599), 3:152 (Mountjoy to Privy Council, 5 May 1602). Mountjoy suggested Scots be sent as reinforcements because they "would in all likelihood better endure the winters hardnesse . . . than such new men as come usually from England" (ibid., 2:210, Mountjoy to Privy Council, 12 September 1602).

71. Ibid., 2:172–3, 2:174, 2:228. For a summary of expenditures, see ibid., 3:341–2. For joint stock investment figures, see Rabb, Table 5, p. 66 and the concluding paragraph of n. 96.

72. "Breife Note of Ireland," p. 244.

73. See Appendix D.

74. Moryson, 2:241, 2:311. "Rebels," was the official English designation for the Irish fighters against English colonization.

75. In the five-point indictment that had started the Earl of Essex toward the executioner's block, it was charged that he had dishonored the English Queen by conferring "in equal sort" with O'Neill, "a bush Kerne, and base [bastard] sonne of a Blacksmith" (Moryson, 2:313–14). For Moryson's version of the relevant O'Neill genealogy, see ibid., 2:176–8.

76. Ibid., 3:208–9 (Mountjoy to the Lords in England, 10 September 1602).

77. Ibid., 2:270–71. See Appendix F.

78. Ibid., 2:423, 2:424. "To add to Ulster's attractiveness, war had decimated the population. The whole of Ireland had suffered during Elizabeth's wars . . . the reduction in population encouraged the idea of plantation" (M. Perceval-Maxwell, *The Scottish Migration to Ulster in the Reign of James I* [London and New York, 1973], p. 17).

79. Moryson, 3:200, 3:207.

80. "The English succeeded, principally by playing off one of a family or sept against another, and holding out bright prospects to their Irish adherents" (Hill, *Plantation in Ulster*, p. 56).

The list of their Irish adherents, in which the great Ulster family names were represented, included: Mulmorie O'Reilly, who died fighting for the English at Yellow Ford; Connor Roe Maguire, O'Neill's son-in-law, who sought the chieftaincy of the Maguires of Fermanagh; Sir Arthur O'Neill, his brother Tirlogh and Henry Og O'Neill (of a rival branch of the O'Neills). Sir Donnell Ballagh O'Cahan, (another son-in-law of the Irish leader Hugh O'Neill, Earl of Tyrone) and Neil Garve O'Donnell (aggrieved at having been passed over in his tribe's choice of chief) rendered indispensable service to the launching of the English second front on Ulster's northern coast. Sir Cahir O'Doherty, angry at not being elected to succeed his father as chieftain, helped the English conquer Donegal in return for a promise that he would be given that territory at the end of the war (ibid., pp. 60–63, 96 n. 3, 318 n. 221; Moryson, 2:308–9, 332–3, 352, 357, 379; 3:179–80, 206, 302).

81. Moryson, 2:309, 2:421, 2:425.

82. Ibid., 3:259 (Mountjoy to the Lords in England, 9 January 1603).

83. Ibid., 2:410.

84. Indeed, when the war was over, English officials looked upon Irish veterans with undiminished hostility and suspicion. When the plantation of Ulster was begun in 1609, plans were made and executed to round up many of these men and sell them to Sweden. See Chapter 5.

85. Davies, *Discovery of the True Causes*, pp. 6–7.

86. Moryson, 3:292–3 (Mountjoy to Cecil, 25 March 1603); 3:300 (O'Neill's oath of submission, 31 March 1603); 3:302 (the Mountjoy grant to the Earl of Tyrone, same day). Hugh's grandfather Conn, the first Earl of Tyrone, had likewise foresworn the title and name of "the O'Neill," under a surrender-and-regrant pact with Henry VIII in 1541 (Hayes-McCoy, "Completion of the Tudor Conquest," p. 50).

Similar terms were allowed to Rory O'Donnell, who had succeeded to the chieftaincy after the death of his brother Red Hugh in Spain in 1602 (Moryson, 3:232, 3:328).

87. Ibid., 3:341–2.

88. Ibid., 3:337.

89. On Sir John Davies's views see p. 65, and Great Britain Public Records Office, *Calendar of State Papers relating to Ireland of the reign of James I*, Vol. 3, *1608–10*, edited by C. W. Russell and John P. Prendergast (London and Edinburgh, 1874), 3:17. See also pp. 115–16. On the attitudes of English landlords, see p. 76 and Chapter 3, n. 39. On the Privy Council, see Hill, *Plantation in Ulster*, p. 408.

90. As noted above (p. 53 and n. 11) the studies of two other eminent scholars, Beckett and Dunlop, arrive at the same conclusion as Hill (ibid., p. 407, n. 56).

91. William Knowlson, *The Earl of Strafford's Letters and Dispatches, with an Essay towards his Life, by Sir George Radcliff, from the Originals in the Possession of his Great Grandson, the Right Honourable Thomas, Earl of Malton, Knight of the Bath*, 2 vols (London, 1739), 1:264.

92. Hugh F. Kearney, *Strafford in Ireland, 1633–41: A Short Study in Absolutism* (Manchester, 1959), pp. 100–101. In 1639 Wentworth conveyed his mistrust of native Irish soldiers as "children of habituated rebels" (Wentworth to Secretary of State Windebank, cited in Richard Bagwell, *Ireland Under the Stuarts and During the Interregnum* (London, 1909), 1:287).

93. Another one-third was held by the Catholic Anglo-Irish (Aidan Clarke, *The Old English in Ireland, 1625–1642* [London, 1966], pp. 26 and 236; Bottigheimer, *English Money and Irish Land*, p. 5, n. 1).

94. Robert Dunlop, ed., *Ireland under the Commonwealth, Being a Selection of Documents relating to the Government of Ireland from 1651 to 1659*, 2 vols (Manchester, 1913), 1:cxxxiv, cliv–clv; Bagwell, *Ireland Under the Stuarts*, 2:347.

95. Beckett, *Making of Modern Ireland*, p. 1109.

96. *A Collection of State Papers of John Thurloe, containing authentic materials of the English affairs from the year 1638 to the Restoration of King Charles II*, 7 vols (London, 1742); 5:558, t70–71, correspondence of Henry Cromwell and Colonel Moore, November 1656 (cited in Bagwell, *Ireland Under the Stuarts*, 2:351).

97. "Ireland was the great capital out of which all debts were paid, all services rewarded, and all bounties performed" (Edward Hyde, 1st Earl of Clarendon, *The Life of Edward, Earl of*

Clarendon ... [and the] Continuation of the History [1672; London, 1759], p. 116 [cited in Bagwell, *Ireland Under the Stuarts*, 2:338]).

98. Dunlop, *Ireland under the Commonwealth*, 1:clvi, 1:clx.

99. Bottigheimer, *English Money and Irish Land*, pp. 135, 140.

100. "A Treatise of Taxes," in C. H. Hull, ed., *The Economic Writings of Sir William Petty*, 2 vols (1899; reprinted 1963), 1:1–97; p. 6. By chargeable armies, Petty appears to have meant armies whose costs could be paid out of revenues generated in the occupied country.

101. Bagwell, *Ireland Under the Stuarts*, 3:179; *A New History*, 8:249–50.

102. Sir William Petty, "A Treatise of Taxes," in Hull, ed., *The Economic Writings of Sir William Petty*, 2:545–621; p. 559.

103. Petty, "Treatise of Taxes," p. 561.

104. Ibid., pp. 551, 555.

105. Ibid., pp. 555, 557, 558, 560–61, 563–5.

106. Ibid., p. 559.

107. "Petty's transplantation scheme (within limits) would not have appeared to his contemporaries quite so fantastic as it does to us. ... Cromwell's Settlement, though never carried out in its entirety, was founded on a general transplantation of the Irish to Connaught and a 'plantation' of English soldiers in their stead" (*The Petty Papers: Some Unpublished Writings of Sir William Petty*, edited from the Bowood Papers by the Marquis of Lansdowne [London, 1927], Editor's Note, 1:47).

108. See Appendix G.

109. For an authoritative treatment of the Mexican case, see Charles Gibson, "The Aztec Aristocracy in Colonial Mexico," *Comparative Studies in Society and History*, 1:169–96 (January 1960). See also John K. Chance, *Race and Class in Colonial Oaxaca* (Stanford: Stanford University Press, 1978).

110. *The Commentaries of the Great Afonso Dalboquerque, Second Viceroy of India*, translated and edited by Walter deGray Birch, 4 vols (London: Hakluyt Society, 1875–84), 4:204, 4:206; Marguerite Eyer Wilbur, *The East India Company and the British Empire in the Far East* (New York, 1945), p. 56. E. E. Rich and C. H. Wilson, editors of *The Economy of Expanding Europe in the Sixteenth and Seventeenth Centuries* (Cambridge, 1967), vol. 4 of *The Cambridge Economic History of Europe*, note, pp. 309, 328–9, but with undisguised bias, the same unique Portuguese attitude. See Basil Davidson, *The African Slave Trade: Precolonial History, 1450–1850* (Boston, 1961), pp. 22–3. Davidson makes clear in his Chapter 4, however, that this policy did not prevent the Portuguese from being just as unprincipled as other European colonizers in their dealings in Africa.

111. Most of the Africans taken as laborers to the Americas came from West Africa. Two-thirds of those taken by British traders came from West Africa (Davidson, *African Slave Trade*, p. 104; J. D. Fage, *A History of West Africa*, 3rd edition [Cambridge, 1969], p. 79).

112. Sigerson, *History of the Land Tenures and Land Classes of Ireland with an account of the Various Secret Agrarian Confederacies* (London, 1871), p. 35.

3 Protestant Ascendancy and White Supremacy

1. *The Statutes at Large, Passed in the Parliaments held in Ireland from the Third year of Edward the Second, AD, 1310 to the Twenty Sixth year of George the Third, AD 1786 inclusive with Marginal Notes, and a Compleat Index to the Whole*, continued through the fortieth year of George Third, 1800, 20 vols. Published in 20 volumes (Dublin 1765–1800), hereinafter noted as *Irish Statutes*. The list of the religio-racist Penal Laws includes principally the following enactments, reenactments, and amended acts: 7 Will III c. 4, c. 5, c. 17; 9 Will III c. 1, c. 3; 10 Will III c. 13; 2 Anne c. 3, c. 6, c. 7; 6 Anne c. 13; 8 Anne c. 3; 2 Geo I c. 10; 4 Geo I c. 9; 6 Geo I c. 6; 12 Geo I c. 3; 1 Geo II c. 2, c. 12, c. 20; 7 Geo 2 c. 4, c. 6; 15 Geo II c. 4; 17 Geo II c. 9; 19 Geo II c. 7, c. 13; 23 Geo II c. 7, c. 10; 25 Geo II c. 7; 29 Geo II c. 2; 31 Geo II c. 4; 33 Geo II c. 3; and 1 Geo III c. 4, c. 12.

W. K. Sullivan says that with the passage of 8 Anne c. 3 (1709), "the Penal Code was now practically complete" (*Two Centuries of Irish History, 1691–1870* [London, 1888], Part I, p. 39). Edmund Curtis (*A History of Ireland,* 6th edition [London, 1950], p. 277) says that it was completed in 1727 (1 Geo II). Beginning about 1760, certain modifying amendments were enacted, but the body of the Penal Laws was repealed by act of the British Parliament only in 1829.

2. Burke, letter to Hercules Langrishe, 3 January 1792, in *The Works of the Right Honorable Edmund Burke,* 6th edition (Boston, 1880), 4:241–306, 4:249–52, 4:305.

3. See Chapter 5.

4. Recent welcome exceptions include: Michael Hechter, *Internal Colonialism: The Celtic Fringe in British National Development, 1536–1966* (Berkeley, 1975); and Richard Ned Lebow, *White Britain and Black Ireland: the Influence of Stereotypes on Colonial Policy* (Philadelphia, 1976).

5. Curtis, *History of Ireland,* p. 251; James Anthony Froude, *The English in Ireland in the Eighteenth Century,* 3 vols (London, 1881), 1:130.

6. Gerard Anthony Hayes-McCoy, "The Completion of the Tudor Conquest, and the Advance of the Counter-reformation, 1571–1603," in *A New History,* 3:96–7.

7. Petty, *A Treatise of Taxes and Contributions* (1662), in Charles Henry Hull, ed., *The Economic Writings of Sir William Petty,* 2 vols (1899; New York, 1963), 1:68–9.

8. "Slavery in Modern Scotland," *Edinburgh Review,* 189:119–48 (January 1899). John Ulrich Nef called that essay, "the most important treatment of the subject" (*The Rise of the British Coal Industry,* 2 vols [London, 1932], 2:157). In the following comments I have relied principally upon that *Edinburgh Review* article, and secondarily upon the following works: Robert Chambers, *Domestic Annals of Scotland,* 3 vols (London and Edinburgh, 1861); Henry Grey Graham, *Social Life of Scotland in the Eighteenth Century* (1899; London, 1950); Henry Hamilton, *An Economic History of Scotland in the Eighteenth Century* (Oxford, 1963). See Appendix H to this volume.

9. Scotland, Privy Council, *Registry of the Privy Council of Scotland,* 14 vols, edited by John Hill Burton (vols 1 and 2) and David Masson (vols 3–14) (Edinburgh, 1877–98), 7:434 (July 1606).

10. Chambers himself personally knew Scotsmen who had been slaves in their youth. He also relates an anecdote told to him by a mining engineer concerning old Moss Nook who "had been a slave, and was exchanged for a pony" (Chambers, *Domestic Annals,* 3:250).

According to Hamilton, the wife and her children, along with the collier himself, "were listed in colliery inventories, like machinery, stocks, or gin horses. Wives, and often sons and daughters, acted as bearers and carried coal in baskets on their heads from the coal face to the surface. At Dunmore colliery there were 28 colliers, 23 bearing wives, 17 bearing sons, 29 bearing daughters" (Hamilton, p. 369). A nimble climber would carry $1\frac{1}{2}$ tons of coal per day up from the working face to the surface (ibid.).

11. "Slavery in Modern Scotland," p. 132.

12. A. E. Smith, *Colonists in Bondage: White Servitude and Convict Labor in America, 1607–1776* (Chapel Hill, 1947; New York, 1971), p. 146.

13. Armagh, Derry, Fermanagh, Tyrone, Cavan and Donegal. See Chapter 5.

14. The plantation of Ulster will be further discussed in Chapter 5.

15. Sir Robert Jacob [King James' Solicitor] to Lord Salisbury, Dublin, October 1609, *Calendar of State Papers relating to Ireland of the Reign of James I,* vol. 3, 1608–10 (London and Edinburgh, 1874), edited by C. W. Russell and John P. Prendergast, 3:299. (For subsequent notes this series will be abbreviated to: *Cal. S. P., Ireland, James I, [date] [vol. no.]*).

16. Sir John Davies, then Attorney-General of Ireland, suggested the English settlement at Jamestown in Virginia as a possible exile for these Irish "swordsmen" (*Cal. S. P., Ireland, James I, 1608–10, vol. 3,* p. 416, answer to queries from the Privy Council [?], 14 March 1610). See Chapter 5.

17. Petty, *The Political Anatomy of Ireland,* in Hull, 1:151. *The Petty Papers: Some Unpublished Writings of Sir William Petty,* edited from the Bowood papers by the Marquis of Lansdowne (London 1927; 1967), 2:229. Vincent Gookin, *The Great Case of Transplantation in Ireland Discussed; or Certain Considerations, wherein the many great inconveniencies in the transplanting the Natives of Ireland generally out of the three provinces of Leinster, Ulster, and Munster, into the Province of Connaught, are shewn* (London, 1655), p. 22. Richard Bagwell, *Ireland under the Stuarts and during the Interregnum* (London, 1909), 3 vols, 2:304–5. Samuel

Rawson Gardiner, "The Transplantation to Connaught," *English Historical Review*, 14:700–734 (October 1899), p. 703. Commenting on a problem raised by Gardiner (ibid. pp. 708–9), Robert Dunlop suggests that an additional 80,000 Irish persons liable to be hanged, under terms of the Act of Settlement, were instead sent into exile (*Ireland under the Commonwealth, Being a Selection of Documents Relating to the Government of Ireland from 1651 to 1659*, 2 vols (Manchester, 1913), 1:cxxxiii, n. 1).

18. A. E. Smith, *Colonists in Bondage*, p. 165. Aubrey Gwynne presents extensive documentation of the social control problems in the English colonies that arose from the presence of transported Irish. Three of his Barbados documents, dated 1655–57, suggest that the Irish mentioned might be exiled soldiers (Aubrey Gwynne, sr, *Analecta Hibernia*, Irish Manuscripts Commission [Dublin: Stationery Office], No. 4 [October 1932], pp. 234–8).

19. Letter written from Spain, 4 March 1653, cited in Bagwell, 2:301, n. 1.

20. Petty, *The Political Economy of Ireland*, in Hull, 1:151.

21. Dunlop, 2:310, 2:370; John Patrick Prendergast, *Ireland from the Restoration to the Revolution* (Dublin, 1887), pp. 11–13.

22. Great Britain Public Record Office, *Calendar of State Papers, Domestic, 1652–53*, pp. 21, 270 (Day's Proceedings, Council of State, 10 December 1652 and 9 April 1653). Dunlop, 1:177, 1:240. Bagwell, 2:303.

23. *Journals of the House of Commons*, vol. 7 (15 August 1651–16 March 1959), p. 123.

24. Smith, p. 166. With regard to the propriety of applying the term "slave trade" to this dealing in Irish laborers, see: John P. Prendergast, *The Cromwellian Settlement of Ireland*, 2nd edition (Dublin, 1875); and Patrick Francis Moran, *Historical Sketch of the Persecutions Suffered by the Catholics of Ireland Under the Rule of Cromwell and the Puritans* (Dublin, 1884). Moran's Chapter 7, "Irish Exported as Slaves," cites a number of references to the Irish victims of this English policy as "slaves." Moran, writing in Australia, made the point of saying "white Slaves" (p. 332). But it is to be noted that Smith distances himself from the idea by putting the phrase "Irish slave trade" in quotation marks and insisting that "there was never any such thing as perpetual slavery for any white man in any English colony" (*Colonists in Bondage*, pp. 163, 171). My copy of *A Smaller Irish English Dictionary* (compiled and edited by Patrick S. Dineen) translates *sclabha* as "slave"; and *sclabhuide* as "slave; labourer; peasant." These are of course cognates, Latin-derived. What then would the Irish have called their life of plantation servitude but *sclabhaideacht*, "slavery"? It seems, furthermore, that they would not have felt it necessary to distinguish their servitude from any other plantation servitude. It is only a "white" habit of mind that reserves "slave" for the African-American and boggles at the term "Irish slave trade."

25. Smith, p. 167.

26. Dunlop, 2:655–6.

27. Prendergast, p. 238.

28. "… mercenaries without a fatherland in the armies of kings in whose quarrels they had no interest …" (Sullivan, 1:16). As to the numbers of such exiles, see Robert Dunlop, *Ireland from the Earliest Times* (Oxford, 1922), p. 129; and William Edward Hartpole Lecky, History of England in the Eighteenth Century, 8 vols (New York, 1878–90), 2(1882):286.

29. In the United States in the period after the Civil War, employers of agricultural labor in the South were able to institute what was a tenancy-at-will system, called "contract labor," later transmuted to a system of sharecropping peonage, under which the African-American laborers saw no more of cash wages than they and their forebears had seen before under chattel bondage (Charles Wesley, *Negro Labor in the United States* [New York, 1927], pp. 126–7, 130–35).

30. Prendergast, pp. 307–8.

31. J. C. Beckett, *The Making of Modern Ireland: 1603–1923* (New York, 1966), pp. 132, 135.

32. Petty, *The Political Economy of Ireland*, in Hull, 1:152.

33. Sigerson, *History of the Land Tenures and Land Classes of Ireland with an account of the Various Secret Agrarian Confederacies* (London, 1871), p. 132.

34. *Mist's Weekly Journal*, 30 September 1721. Cited in Herbert Davis, ed., *Major British Writers*, enlarged edition, 2 vols (New York: Harcourt Brace, 1954), 1:642, n. 13. The view was confirmed by R. C. Dallas who had observed West Indies life first-hand. Speaking of the plantation bond-laborers' housing, he declared, "In structure and comfort, these cottages certainly surpass the cabins of the Irish peasants" (R. C. Dallas, *History of the Maroons*, 2 vols [London, 1803], 1:cviii).

35. Lecky, 2:317; Philip Henry Lord Mahon, *History of England from the Peace of Utrecht to the Peace of Versailles*, 7 vols (London, 1858), 5:123.

36. Lecky, 2:265.

37. Ibid., 2:198. A study made in County Tyrone in 1802 found that in general the cottier was allowed half an acre for oats, one-eighth to one-fourth of an acre for potatoes, one-eighth of an acre for flax, graze for a cow, turf for fuel, and "sometimes" a small garden. The rent amounted to £5 to 5 guineas, which the cottier paid by work in the landlord's fields, the time of payment being scheduled to fall in the busiest seasons of the year (John M'Evoy, *A Statistical Survey of the County of Tyrone, with Observations on the Means of Improvement, Drawn upon the Years 1801, and 1802, for the Consideration, and Under the Direction of The Dublin Society* [Dublin, 1802], pp. 99–100). This was the condition of the typical Catholic tenant-at-will, not of the Protestant Scots-Irish leaseholder (see Edward Wakefield [père], *An Account of Ireland, Statistical and Political*, 2 vols [London, 1812], 2:589–90, 2:730, 2:744).

38. Ibid., 2:241–2.

39. Sigerson, p. 35, citing *A Briefe Description of Ireland; made in this yeare 1589, by Robert Paine, unto xxv of his Partners [in England], for whom he is undertaker there [in Ireland]*, in Irish Archaeological Society, *Tracts Relating to Ireland*.

40. Sullivan, *Two Centuries of Irish History*, 1:47.

41. Jonathan Swift, *A Modest Proposal for preventing the children of poor people in Ireland, from being a burden to their parents; and for making them beneficial to the public* (Dublin, 1729).

42. Lecky, 2:239.

43. Sullivan, 1:47.

44. Lecky, 2:274.

45. Francis Lewis Plowden, *History of Ireland from the invasion of Ireland during the reign of Henry II to the Union of England and Ireland/An Historical Review of the State of Ireland from the Invasion of that Country under Henry II to its Union with Great Britain on the first of January 1801*, 5 vols (Philadelphia, 1805), 3:146.

46. See Appendix I.

47. *A New History*, Ancillary Volume II, *Irish Historical Statistics: Population, 1821–71* (Dublin, 1978), edited by W. E. Vaughan and A. J. Fitzpatrick, cites the gamut of estimates of the population of Ireland in the eighteenth century.

48. W. E. H. Lecky, *History of Ireland in the Eighteenth Century*, 5 vols (London, 1893), 2:198–200; 2:221 n. 1, 2:255. J. C. Beckett, *The Anglo-Irish Tradition* (Ithaca, 1976), p. 64. Hugh Boulter, *Letters Written by His Excellency Hugh Boulter, D. D., Lord Primate of All Ireland, &c., Containing An Account of the Most Interesting Transactions which passed in Ireland from 1724 to 1738*, 2 vols, edited by "G.F." (George Faulkner?), (1770; Oxford: Clarendon Press, 1969–70), 2:10. Arthur Young, *A Tour in Ireland* (1780), vol. 2, book 2, p. 33.

49. T. P. Power and Kevin Whelan, eds, *Endurance and Emergence: Catholics in the Eighteenth Century* (Dublin: Irish Academic Press, 1990), p. 102; Lecky, *History of Ireland*, 2:315–16.

50. The most rapid rate of population increase occurred during the last quarter of the century, while a statistically offsetting conversion bulge occurred in the third quarter of the century (T. P. Power, "Converts," in Power and Whelan) after a quarter-century marked by severe famine conditions (J. L. McCracken, "The Social Structure and Social Life, 1714–1760," in *A New History*, 4:34). A doubling of the population in the century, which is the assumption made for this calculation, represents a compound annual rate of increase of 0.7 percent.

51. For comparative figures in regard to the Americas, see David W. Cohn and Jack B. Greene, eds, *Neither Slave Nor Free: The Freedman of African Descent in the Slave Societies of the New World* (Baltimore, 1972), Appendix. Even in the Lower South (principally South Carolina, Georgia, Alabama, Mississippi, Louisiana and Texas, the chief areas for the production of cotton by bond-labor) where free African-Americans were in an especially precarious position, the emancipation ratio was eight times what it was in Ireland (ibid.). Patterson provides a similar set of tables, citing the Cohn and Greene appendix among other sources (Orlando Patterson, *Slavery and Social Death* [New York, 1990] Appendix C, and Tables for Notes to Appendix C).

52. "Apostasy was the first step in the path of ambition" (Lecky, *History of England*, 2:315–16). "Of the upper classes a fairly large number adopted Protestantism, and so became identified with the ruling caste, while preserving a certain amount of sympathy with their Catholic kindred" (W. F. T. Butler, *Confiscation in Irish History* [London, 1918], p. 246). See also: J. G.

Simms, "The Establishment of Protestant Ascendancy, 1691–1714," in *A New History*, 4:19; and Power and Whelan, p. 124.

Because they were by law forbidden to purchase land, or to take long leases, Catholic entrepreneurs were most often merchants and graziers, and prospered there more than in other lines of endeavor (Lecky, *History of England*, 2:245. See also Sullivan, 1:43–4.) See also p. 93.

53. Butler, p. 246.

54. Beckett, *Anglo-Irish Tradition*, p. 65.

55. The exploitation of Irish labor was so relatively intense that landlords in Ireland were able to "make as much or more of their estates than any in the three kingdoms [England, Scotland and Ireland] while the [Irish] lands, for equal goodness, produced the least" (Lecky, *History of England*, 2:264, citing Bush, *Hibernia Curiosa*, p. 33).

56. Lecky, *History of England*, 2:311–12, citing the Irish *Commons Journal*, 20 June 1709. A quarter-century later, says Lecky, the sentiment was repeated (Irish *Commons Journal*, 17 December 1735):

57. 10 Will c. 13 (*Irish Statutes*).

58. 1 Geo II c. 20 (1728) (*Irish Statutes*).

59. Lecky, *History of England*, 2:311.

60. Sullivan, 1:36.

61. Maureen Wall, *The Penal Laws, 1691–1760* (Dundalk, 1961), p. 9.

62. Boulter favored the abandonment of the highly questionable "Wood's halfpence" monetary reform proposal precisely because the widespread opposition to the measure had been the occasion for "intimacies between Papists and Jacobites [Scots-Irish Presbyterians] and Whigs [the Anglo-Irish opposition party]" (Boulter to the Duke of Newcastle, 19 January, 1724/5, in Ambrose Phillips, ed., *Letters Written by His Excellency Hugh Boulter, D.D., Lord Primate of All Ireland &c. to Several Ministers of State in England, and some others containing an account of the most interesting transactions which passed in Ireland from 1724 to 1731 (to 1738)*, 2 vols in one [Dublin, 1770], 1:7). Sullivan cites this letter as an illustration of "one of the chief maxims of British rule in Ireland, and one which [Boulter] carefully followed – keep the different sections and parties of the nation asunder" (Sullivan, 1:45).

63. Lord John Beresford to William Eden Lord Auckland, 9 August 1798 (W. Beresford, ed., *Correspondence of the Right Honourable John Beresford*, 2 vols [London, 1854], 2:169–70). Beresford (1738–1805), an Anglo-Irish member of the English Privy Council, enjoyed such influence in the Irish Parliament that he was called "king of Ireland." He displayed his power in securing the dismissal of William Fitzwilliam as Lord Lieutenant of Ireland in 1795, on the grounds that Fitzwilliam was soft on Catholics (Dunlop, *Ireland from the Earliest Times*, p. 151).

64. This apparent absurdity – private encouragement of a tendency publicly anathematized – has its present-day manifestation. The Catholic establishment in Ireland prefers the continuation of Protestant Ascendancy in Northern Ireland rather than accept the disestablishment of religion in the rebirth of a united Ireland.

65. Thomas Smith, *De Republica Anglorum, a Discourse on the Commonwealth of England* (1583; New York, 1906), p. 139 (bk 3, ch. 9).

For a greater appreciation of the importance attached to this issue in the social and economic development of plantation Anglo-America, see: Patterson, pp. 70–76; David Brion Davis, *The Problem of Slavery in Western Culture* (Ithaca, 1966), pp. 13–24, 85–90, 165–73, 222 and 294; and Winthrop D. Jordan, White Over Black (Chapel Hill, 1969), pp. 190–215.

66. *Calendar of State Papers*, Colonial, 1:202.

67. Richard Ligon, *A True and Exact History of the Island of Barbadoes* (London, 1673), p. 85; Vincent T. Harlow, *A History of Barbados, 1625–1685* (Oxford, 1926; New York, 1969), p. 84; E. E. Rich and C. H. Wilson, eds, *The Cambridge Economic History of Europe*, vol. IV, *The Economy of Expanding Europe in the Sixteenth and Seventeenth Centuries* (Cambridge, 1967), pp. 334, 338, 344 and 347.

68. Harlow, pp. 338–9.

69. Ligon, p. 50.

70. Virginia County Records, *Northumberland County Record Book, 1652–58*, p. 85 (21 July 1656); *Northumberland County Order Book*, pp. 80 (20 January 1655/6) and 97 (?) (21 July 1656). For a discussion and documentation of this case see "The Elizabeth Key Case," in Volume Two of this work.

71. 2 Hening 26, 170, 260.

72. Peter H. Wood, *Black Majority: Negroes in Colonial South Carolina from 1670 through the Stono Rebellion* (New York: Norton Library, 1975), p. 137.

73. 28 Henry VIII, c. 15, sec., 15. *The Statutes at Large, passed in the Parliaments held in Ireland from the Third Year of Edward the Second, AD 1310, to the First Year of George the Third, AD 1786 inclusive with Marginal Notes, and a Compleat Index to the Whole*, 20 vols (Dublin, 1765–1800). Richard Mant, *History of the Church of Ireland from the Reformation to the union of the Churches of England and Ireland, January 1, 1801*, 2 vols (London, 1840), 1:292–3.

74. Edmund Spenser, *A View of the State of Ireland* [1596], in Edwin Greenlaw, Charles Grosvenor Osgood, and Frederick Morgan Paddelford, eds, *The Works of Edmund Spenser, a Variorum Edition*, 10 vols (Baltimore: Johns Hopkins University Press, 1966), 9:119.

75. *Calendar of State Papers, Colonial*, 10:611 (8 October 1680).

76. The first use in a Virginia statute of the term "white" to designate European-Americans as a social category occurred in 1691 (see 3 Hening 87). The Irish Penal Laws were inaugurated with two acts passed by the Irish Parliament in 1695 (7 Will III c. 4 and c. 5).

77. Lyon G. Tyler, reviewing Philip Alexander Bruce, *Social Life of Virginia in the Seventeenth Century*, in *William and Mary Quarterly*, series 1, 16(1907–8):145–7. Other book reviews, earlier and later, made the same point almost verbatim (*William and Mary Quarterly*, series 1, 6[1897–98:202–3]; 25[1916–17]:145–6).

78. Plowden, *History of Ireland*, 1:199.

79. Wall, *Penal Laws*, p. 9.

80. Sigerson, *History of Land Tenures*, p. 117.

81. Denys Scully, *A Statement of the Penal Laws, which Aggrieve the Catholics of Ireland: With Commentaries* (Dublin, 1812), p. 334. Sullivan (*Two Centuries of Irish History*, pp. 59–60) cites a mid-eighteenth-century case in which the judge decided against a Catholic by precisely the legal formula quoted.

82. Despite the racist restrictions of the Penal Laws and the general spirit of the Protestant Ascendancy, Catholics, by evasion or taking advantage of loopholes in the system, did find some success in trade and leasehold farming and livestock. As the detente between the Catholic bourgeoisie and the British government matured in the closing decades of the eighteenth century, a Catholic middle class was able to make some economic headway. See: Maureen Wall, "The Rise of a Catholic Middle Class in Eighteenth-century Ireland," *Irish Historical Studies*, vol. 11, no. 42 (September 1958); Louis M. Cullen, "Catholic Social Classes Under the Penal Laws," in Powers and Whelan, pp. 58–63. A number of historians have sought to redress the neglect of "the presence of a significant number of propertied catholics who not only survived but prospered and increased in number even before 1782" (Cullen, p. 62). The "Catholic relief act of 1782" allowed Catholics to acquire land.

83. "The penal code, as it was actually carried out, was inspired much less by fanaticism than by rapacity" (Lecky, *History of Ireland*, 1:312).

84. All the Penal Laws relating to Ireland cited in this section are, of course, to be found in *Irish Statutes*.

85. Sigerson, p. 118.

86. 2 Hening 280–81. In time there were African-American owners of bondmen and bondwomen throughout the South, except in Delaware and Arkansas, where that practice was legally barred to African-Americans on "race" principles (Kenneth M. Stampp, *The Peculiar Institution* [New York, 1956], pp. 194–5, citing Carter G. Woodson, *Free Negro Owners of Slaves in the United States in 1830* [Washington, DC, 1924]; and Helen Tunncliff Catterall, ed., *Judicial Cases Concerning American Slavery and the Negro*, 5 vols [Washington: Carnegie Institution, 1926–37; Octagon Books reprint, 1968], 4:215 and 5:257). In 1832 Virginia also made it illegal for an African-American to acquire bond-laborers (except through inheritance), other than the purchaser's own wife or husband, parent or descendant (Luther Porter Jackson, *Free Negro Labor and Property Holding in Virginia, 1830–1860* [New York, 1942], p. 23).

87. Philip Alexander Bruce, *Economic History of Virginia in the Seventeenth Century* (New York, 1895), 2:51–2, 89–90. Not all African-American bond-laborers were bound for life; as limited-term bond-laborers they were priced comparably with European-American bond-laborers (ibid., 2:51–3).

88. 2 Hening 86–7; 3 W & M Act 16 (Virginia).

89. In 1670 the 750 acres left by Anthony Johnson in Accomack County were escheated on the grounds that he was "a Negroe and by consequence an alien" (*Virginia Miscellany, Foreign Business and Inquisitions, 1665–1676*, Library of Congress Manuscript Collection. Photocopy at Virginia State Library, Archives Division. Access number: 22388). I am indebted to Robert Clay of the Virginia State Library Archives for bringing this item to my attention, and to Fred Dornan who exhumed it from the Jefferson Manuscripts at the Library of Congress. Whether this became a precedent and, if so, for what period of time, this writer cannot say. It had ceased to be Virginia law sometime before 1830 (see Jackson). The Mississippi Black Code, a short-lived attempt to nullify the Thirteenth Amendment, in 1866 forbade Negroes to acquire farm land (John Hope Franklin, *Reconstruction After the Civil War* [Chicago, 1961], p. 50).

90. *Irish Statutes*: 7 Will III c. 5; 10 Will III c. 8, 13; 2 Anne c. 6; 8 Anne c. 3; 2 Geo I c. 10; 6 Geo I c. 10; 1 Geo II c. 9; 9 Geo II c. 3; 17 & 18 Geo II c. 2; 15 Geo III c. 21. One English statute, 3 W & M c. 2, belongs in this list. The citations of laws passed by English (or, after 1700, British) Parliaments refer to (1) *The Statutes at Large from Magna Charta* ... to 1807, 46 vols in 52 (London 1762–1807), the title to be abbreviated *English Statutes*; and (2) *The Statutes of the United Kingdom*, 46 volumes in 52 (London, 1807–69). Citations are by reign and chapter.

91. Scully, p. 333.

92. From the decision of Chief Justice Roger B. Taney for the Supreme Court in 1857, and cited here from Richard D. Heffner, ed., *A Documentary History of the United States* (New York, 1956), p. 131.

93. 3 Hening 298 (4 Anne c. 19, sec. 31 [Virginia]). Catholics were by law required to abandon allegiance to the Church of Rome, to accept the authority of the Anglican Protestant church, and regularly to attend its services. Offenders were "recusants." A "recusant convict" was any person officially declared guilty of the offense.

94. In August 1831 three score African-American bond-laborers in Southampton County, Virginia, rose in rebellion under the leadership of Nat Turner. Around sixty "whites" were killed by the rebels. Twice that number of African-Americans were killed in the repression of the rebellion, mostly randomly and summarily. Nat Turner and sixteen others, including three free Negroes, were executed after trial. However, the rebellion brought the issue of abolition to a level of attention that it had not held before in the United States, and thus may be said to mark the beginning of the pre-Civil War period (see: Herbert Aptheker, *Documentary History of the Negro People of the United States*, [New York, 1951], pp. 119–25; John Hope Franklin, *From Slavery to Freedom: A History of Negro Americans*, 6th edition [New York, 1988], pp. 133–5; William Freehling, *The Road to Disunion*, vol. I, *Secessionists at Bay* [New York, 1990], especially pp. 178–81; William Loren Katz: *Eyewitness: The Negro in American History: A Living Documentary of the Afro-American Contribution to US History* [New York, 1967], 120–22).

95. 3 Hening 102 (4 W & M Act 3 [Virginia]); Stampp, pp. 224–8; Jackson, p. 22.

96. Sullivan, 1:37.

97. 1 Geo II c. 6, sec. 7 (Ireland).

98. 3 Hening 172, 238 (11 Will III, Act 2, and 4 Anne c. 2, sec. 3 [Virginia]).

99. 4 Hening 133–34 (9 Geo I c. 4, sec. 3 [Virginia]).

100. 8 Anne c. 3, sec. 16. The name of the offense was "praemunire," that is, following an authority other than that of the queen. Catholic priests were assumed to be guilty of praemunire simply by virtue of their affiliation with Rome. Hedgerow schools were indeed taught by Catholic priests illegally. This law simply treated Catholic Irish teachers as if they were all in fact priests.

101. David J. Dixon ("Catholics and Trade in Eighteenth-century Ireland: An Old Debate Revisited," in Powers and Whelan, *Endurance and Emergence*, pp. 85–100) believes that the apprenticeship restrictions were little more than a nuisance to Catholic tradespeople, and that it was the ban on urban leasing by Catholics that was the most serious handicap to the urban Catholic bourgeois's aspirations (p. 91).

102. Lecky, *History of England*, 2:309, citing *The case of the Roman Catholics of Ireland*, drawn up by the Reverend Doctor Nary in 1724.

103. Lecky, *History of England*, 2:309–10.

104. Young, *Tour in Ireland*, bk 2, p. 34.

105. "No person, not even the master, was to teach a slave to read or write, employ him in setting type in a printing office, or given him books or pamphlets" (Stampp, p. 208).

106. Frederick Douglass, *Life and Times of Frederick Douglass, Written by Himself, His Early*

Life as a Slave, His escape from Bondage, and his complete History, revised edition (1892; New York: Collier Books, 1962), p. 79.

107. Jackson, pp. 19–21.

108. Lecky, *History of Ireland*, 1:308, n. 1; Richard B. Morris, *Government and Labor in Early America* (New York, 1946), p. 183, citing New York Common Council Records.

109. Morris, pp. 182–8.

110. Leon F. Litwak, *North of Slavery: The Negro in the Free States, 1790–1860* (Chicago, 1961), p. 17.

111. Douglass, pp. 179–85, 210–11. An irony to which I shall return is to be found in the identical nature of the treatment suffered by Douglass in these instances at the hands of "white" workers, including Irish immigrant workers in the United States, and the hostility often directed against Irish (and not just Catholic Irish) immigrant laborers in England and Scotland. (See J. H. Treble, "Irish Navvies in the North of England 1830–50," *Transport History*, 6:227–47 [1973], especially, p. 239, for an incident reminiscent of Douglass's experience in the Baltimore shipyard.)

112. Young, bk 2, p. 29.

113. Sigerson, p. 130. Sigerson draws this inference from a list of eight "Particular Clauses of Leases," in M'Evoy, *Statistical Survey of the County of Tyrone*, pp. 102–3. See also Robert Dunlop, *Daniel O'Connell* (New York, 1900), pp. 45–6. Compare Louis M. Cullen, "Economic Development, 1750–1800," in *A New History*, 4:171–2.

114. Boulter, letters to the Bishop of London, the Archbishop of Canterbury and the Duke of Newcastle, an English secretary of state, in May 1730 (in his *Letters*, 2:9–12).

115. So termed by Primate Boulter (*Letters*, 2:103).

116. Lecky, *History of England*, 2:219. I have relied much on Lecky's work, pp. 218–23.

117. Writing in 1888, Sullivan remembered how "Charter School kidnappers [served] as a bogey for wayward children" (*Two Centuries of Irish History*, 1:53).

118. Denys Scully, *A Statement of the Penal Laws, which aggrieve the Catholics of Ireland: with Commentaries*, 2nd enlarged edition (Dublin, 1802), p. 267.

119. Lecky, *History of England*, 2:219.

120. *Commons Journal* (1788), cited in Scully, pp. 268–9.

121. 2 Geo I, c. 17, sec. 11 (*Irish Statutes*).

122. Lecky, *History of England*, 2:276–7.

123. Ibid., pp. 221, 222. The English imperial historian J. A. Froude had not the slightest objection to the racial oppression aspect of the Charter School system. He seems to suggest that a stricter enforcement of the Penal Laws would have made it possible for the Charter Schools to succeed. But as it was, he said, they were "choked in Irish society, as wholesome vegetables are choked in a garden when the weeds are allowed scope to spring." The reader is left to apply the weed-and-vegetable metaphor to the following intelligence, added by Froude in a footnote: "The industrial training, so excellent in conception, degenerated by negligence into a system in which the children became the slaves of the masters and grew up in rags and starvation" (*The English in Ireland in the Eighteenth Century*, 4 vols [London, 1871–74]; 2:12 n. 1).

124. Lecky, *History of England*, 2:223. What the Protestant Ascendancy produced by way of the Charter Schools was emulated by American white supremacy in many respects through the United States Indian education program initiated about 1879. See John Collier, *Indians of the Americas* (New York, 1948), p. 134; and Wilcomb E. Washburn, *The American Indian and the United States: A Documentary History*, 4 vols (New York, 1973), under the index entries, "Education, Indian: outing system; purposes of; and schools." See especially, 1:430, 1:433–4.

125. Thomas Harris Jr and John McHenry, *Maryland Reports, being a Series of the Most Important Law Cases argued and determined in the Provincial Court and Court of Appeals of the then Province of Maryland from the Year 1700 down to the American Revolution* (New York, 1809), Vol. 1, p. 563; henceforth referred to as Harris and McHenry.

126. Stampp, *Peculiar Institution*, p. 343. The African-American family resisted with determination, courage and historical persistence. Stampp related the details of several such instances. But for a fuller treatment of the generations of African-American family tradition see Herbert Gutman, *The Black Family in Slavery and Freedom, 1750–1925* (New York: Vintage Books, 1977). For some interesting citations of Irish/Negro parallels drawn by nineteenth-century commentators, see particularly pp. 199–301 in that work. For Gutman's critique of the writings of other historians

(including Stampp, Elkins and Genovese) regarding the struggles of the African-American under bondage, see pp. 304–19.

127. 3 Hening 86–87 (3 W & M Act 16 [Virginia]).

128. Royal Instructions to the Governor of Nova Scotia in 1719 offered a grant of fifty acres, to be exempt from quit-rent for ten years, to "every white man . . . and every white woman" who married a native "Indian." This order was reissued in 1749, raising the inducement to intermarriage to a payment of £10 sterling and exemption from quit-rent for twenty years. Genetic imperatives upon which Winthrop Jordan relies to explain racial exclusionism, and blinding sexual passion by which he accounts for "interracial" mating, seem not to have entered into consideration in the framing of these instructions. The orders were officially said to be intended as "a further mark of [the Royal] good will towards the said Indian nations." This order remained in effect until 1773 (Leonard Woods Labaree, collator and editor, *Royal Instructions to British Colonial Governors, 1670–1776*, 2 vols [New York and London, 1935], p. 470). Jordan refers to these orders in a footnote, emphasizing that the scope of the orders was limited to Nova Scotia, and that they did not mention African-Americans (*White over Black*, p. 163 n. 61).

129. Washburn, 2:1429.

130. Ibid., 4:2723–4.

131. Judge Dulany, Maryland Provincial Court, 1767 (1 Harris and McHenry, p. 562.)

4 Social Control: From Racial to National Oppression

1. 1 W. & M. c. 2. John William Fortescue, *A History of the British Army*, 13 vols (London, 1899–1930), 3:11.

2. Fortescue, 3:10, 3:40. In 1779, Henry Burg, a member of the Protestant Anglo-Irish Parliament, said, "Ireland is not at peace; it is a smothered war" (P. W. Joyce, *A Concise History of Ireland from the Earliest Times to 1837*, 6th edition [Dublin, 1897], pp. 253–4).

3. In the 1780s, the cost of the military forces required to collect the hearth tax and the tax on "private distilleries" by special "still-hunting" detachments of the cavalry was as much as the amount of the taxes collected. "Throughout the eighteenth century the army played a crucial role in the internal peace of Ireland" (Kevin Boyle, "Police in Ireland before the Union," *Irish Jurist*, 7[1972]:115–37; pp. 125, 134).

When faced with the threat of a French invasion of Ireland in 1796, the British commander in Ireland sent an urgent request for reinforcements, because "his troops were so much dispersed on police-duty" (Fortescue, 4:518).

4. Maureen Wall, *The Penal Laws, 1691–1760, Church and State from the Treaty of Limerick to the Accession of George III* (Dundalk: Dundalgan Press, 1961), pp. 26–8. Lecky, *History of England in the Eighteenth Century*, 8 vols (New York, 1878–90), 2(1882):370. Of the 14,000 inhabitants of Galway in 1762, only 350 were Protestants (Maureen Wall, "Catholics in Economic Life," in L. C. Cullen, ed., *The Formation of the Irish Economy* (Cork, 1969), p. 47.

5. See Robin Blackburn, *The Overthrow of Colonial Slavery, 1776–1848* (London and New York: Verso, 1988), pp. 220–51. Blackburn's book is an excellent comprehensive treatment of the title subject.

6. R. B. McDowell, "The Age of the United Irishmen: Revolution and the Union, 1794–1800," in *A New History*, 4:357. Although in the absence of source citations it is not possible to reconcile differences in the numbers given for the size of the repressive force (Bottigheimer says 40,000 yeomanry, plus 25,000 Irish militia, and only 7,000 regular troops were employed), McDowell's conclusion is consonant with Bottigheimer's: "How viable was a state so palpably dependent upon the 'foreign' power of Britain to preserve it from the ravages of its own unruly population?" (Karl S. Bottigheimer, *Ireland and the Irish: A Short History* [New York, 1982], p. 157).

7. Burke to Langrishe, 3 January 1792, in *The Works of The Right Honorable Edmund Burke*, 6th edition (Boston, 1880), 4:265.

8. Thomas Bartlett, "The Origin and Progress of the Catholic Question in Ireland," in T. P. Powers and Kevin Whelan, eds, *Endurance and Emergence: Catholics in Ireland in the Eighteenth Century* (Dublin: Irish Academic Press, 1990), p. 8.

9. Ibid.

10. See Chapter 2. Two voices were still being raised in the British Parliament in May 1805 warning that Irish Catholic families secretly kept maps showing their ancestral lands in anticipation of regaining them upon Emancipation (cited by Connolly, in "Aftermath and Adjustment," in *A New History*, 5:29–30). Keeping to the safe side, indeed, the eventual Catholic Emancipation Act of 1829 required each Member of Parliament to swear an oath to "defend to the utmost of my Power the Settlement of Property within this Realm, as established by the Laws" (10 Geo. IV, c. 7, sec. 2).

11. 2 Anne c. 6., sec. 5.

12. Bartlett, p. 6.

13. Preamble to 17 & 18 Geo. III, c. 21 (1777–78), c. 49 (*Irish Statutes*), "An act for the relief of his Majesty's subjects of this kingdom professing the popish religion."

14. L. M. Cullen, "Catholic Social Classes under the Penal Laws," in Powers and Whelan, pp. 58–63. The law, 11 & 12 Geo. III (*Irish Statutes*), was called the "Bogland Act."

15. The first of these new laws, 17 & 18 Geo. III, c. 6, allowed to Catholics the right to be accepted for 999-year leases, a right hitherto reserved for Protestants. The second, 21 & 22 Geo. III, c. 24, permitted Catholics to acquire land, except in parliamentary boroughs. This last formal restriction was repealed only with Catholic Emancipation in 1829.

16. "The mass of the people lived on the borders of penury and starvation, [as] tenants at will ..." (Boyle, p. 127). Forty years after the Union, twelve years after Catholic Emancipation, still the census of Ireland showed that 76 percent of employed males were poor peasants (17.6 percent) or laborers (58.8 percent), with an average holding of less than two acres, comprising only one-eighth of the total acreage. Landlords, capitalist farmers and "comfortable farmers" had average holdings of 350 acres, 80 acres and 50 acres respectively, and their shares of the country's total acreage were 17.5 percent, 20 percent, and 25 percent (Cormac O'Grada, "Poverty, Population, and Agriculture, 1801–45," in *A New History*, 5:114).

17. L. M. Cullen, "Catholic Social Classes," p. 58; L. M. Cullen, "Economic Development, 1691–1750," in *A New History*, 4:128.

18. "The concessions to catholics in 1792 and 1793 were a product of fear rather than philanthropy" (Bartlett, p. 14).

19. Cited by R. B. McDowell, 4:307–8. Home Secretary Henry Dundas's exact words, as cited, were "sharers in the general predilection with which moderate men are accustomed to contemplate the existing government."

20. Patrick Rogers, *The Irish Volunteers and Catholic Emancipation, 1778–1793* (London, 1934), pp. 306–7, 312. Bartlett's assertion "The catholics were bought off" ("Origin and Progress," p. 14) might seem too harsh. But we have the corroborating testimony of Daniel O'Connell himself on the subject. Speaking of the critical years 1792 and 1793, O'Connell recalled "the spirit of republican phrensy" that was spreading throughout Ireland. He continued: "had not England wisely and prudently bought all the Catholic nobility and gentry, and the far greater part of the Catholic people out of the market of republicanism, that which was but a rebellion, would most assuredly have been a revolution. The Presbyterians and the Catholics would have united" (*The Select Speeches of Daniel O'Connell, MP, edited with historical sections Etc., by his son, John O'Connell, Esq.*, two vols [Dublin, 1865], 1:198 [15 June 1815]).

21. Hereward Senior, *Orangeism in Ireland and Britain, 1795–1836* (London: Routledge & Kegan Paul, 1966), p. 13.

22. Ibid.

23. Ibid., pp. 16–18, 29–30, 48.

24. Ibid., pp. 83, 88, 97–8, 102, 104.

25. "A restoration of the Irish parliament as it had been before 1801 was one thing; the creation of an independent parliament in the wake of catholic emancipation and a possible reform of the electoral system was quite another" (S. J. Connolly, "Aftermath and Adjustment," 5:22).

26. Bartlett, p. 17.

27. It was "a strange kind of arithmetical comfort" whereby the Irish Catholics "might be told that though they went to bed a majority, yet by the magic of a piece of parchment they awoke in a minority." So argued the Whig member Hobhouse in the House of Commons, adding that it would "provoke the indignation" of its presumed beneficiaries (*Cobbett's Parliamentary History of England ... 1066 to 1803*, 36 vols [London, 1806–20], 34:471 [14 February 1799]).

28. "... [G]iving stipends to the Roman Catholic priesthood, from the public funds ... was the measure contemplated by Mr Pitt in 1801." The speech of Home Secretary Robert Peel, on 5 March 1829, introducing the government's Measure for the Removal of Roman Catholic Disabilities (which came to be known as the Catholic Emancipation Act upon its enactment on 13 April 1829) took four hours to deliver; it required over fifty columns to print (*Hansard Parliamentary Debates*, 2d series, 20:727–80). In subsequent references, it will be called Peel's "Emancipation" speech.

29. The Irish Catholic prelacy "thankfully accepted" the proposal of the "Government of an independent provision for the Roman Catholic clergy of Ireland ... [in return for which the Irish Catholics agreed that] ... in the appointment of prelates of the Roman Catholic religion[, if] Government have any proper objection against such candidates" for bishop, then the Irish Catholics were to proceed "to the election of another candidate." The resolution was signed by all four of the archbishops and thirteen of the nineteen bishops. It was endorsed in quick succession by the other bishops and the generality of the priesthood (T. Dunbar Ingram, *A History of the Legislative Union of Great Britain and Ireland* [Dublin, 1887], pp. 146–58). The text of the resolution, with the names of the signers, is reprinted at pages 148–9. This proposition was consistently supported by the Vatican, even after most Irish Catholics had repudiated it.

It was Lord Grenville (1759–1834) who, referring back to the tacit pledges made to secure the support of the Irish Catholic hierarchy, said that the churchmen had been "justified in entertaining great and sanguine expectations that the measure would lead to the consequences anxiously desired" (*Cobbett's Parliamentary Debates 1803–12*, 22 vols [London, 1804–12], 4:659–60 [10 May 1805]).

30. "The people of Ireland are unable to understand why one system of government should be adopted in Canada, and another of a totally opposite character should, greatly to their disadvantage, be applied to Ireland" (William Smith O'Brien, Irish Protestant Liberal and nationalist Member of Parliament, speaking in a debate on "The State of Ireland," 4 July 1843 [*Hansard Parliamentary Debates*, 3d series, 70:669]).

Oliver Macdonagh (in his Introduction to Volume 5 of *A New History*: 5:lii–liii) makes a comment which seems relevant to the "relativity of race" theme in the present work. "Ireland in 1801–70 was dwindling into a colonial condition," he says. But noting the failure of Ireland to attain responsible government and the fact of its representation in the British Parliament, he concludes that Ireland "differed from the British colonies of white settlement." Translation: the Protestant ("white") sector of the colony was too small to function as the intermediate social control stratum, except in a gerrymandered Ulster; there, from 1922 to 1972, the Protestants ("whites") did have a separate parliament, and a "responsible government" in which their dominance was guaranteed, à la Canada and Australia.

31. Edward Wakefield, *père* (1774–1854) was of the opinion that one of the customs that legal reforms would not eradicate was the practice among "country gentlemen" of "making 'pets' of protestant yeomen, or in common language giving them the preference in every occurrence of life" (Edward Wakefield, *An Account of Ireland, Statistical and Political*, 2 vols [London, 1812], 2:589–90).

32. For example, W. E. H. Lecky, *Leaders of Public Opinion in Ireland*, 2 vols "new edition" (London, 1903), 2:70, 2:97. James Reynolds, *The Catholic Emancipation Crisis in Ireland, 1823–29* (Westport, Connecticut, 1954), p. 164.

33. Lecky, *Leaders of Public Opinion*, 2:101.

34. In its most common usage, "Catholic Emancipation" is understood to mean the passage of the Roman Catholic Relief Act (10 Geo IV, c. 7) in 1829, removing the religious test oaths which under the Penal Laws barred Catholics from Parliament and from trades and professions. The reader will notice that the qualification "so-called" given here to this historic term is here put in ironic quotation marks. The reason is that, while what was eventually accomplished under this heading was historically quite significant – the overthrow of racial oppression outside of Ulster – yet that still left Catholic Ireland under British domination as an oppressed nation, a point most tragically demonstrated in the conduct of the British government during the Great Irish Famine, which began in 1845. Moreover, it still left religio-racial oppression intact in Ulster. And it still left the masses of Irish Catholic peasants without the tenant-right of Protestant Ulster.

35. See especially Sections II, V, XIV, XXII, and XXIII of the Catholic Emancipation Act (10 Geo. IV, c. 7). "Emancipation was essentially the demand of a rising Catholic middle class,

of gentry owning or holding land, lawyers and journalists, merchants, shopkeepers, small and large tenant farmers, a broad and growing class which demanded a full share in local and central government and of which O'Connell himself ... was a perfectly representative member" (Angus Macintyre, *The Liberator: Daniel O'Connell and the Irish Party, 1830–1847* [New York, 1965], p. 12).

36. *Cobbett's Parliamentary Debates*, 4:659–60 (10 May 1805), and 4:101–2 (25 March 1805).

37. "[T]he moment we have resolved on the admission of the Roman Catholics to Parliament," said Peel in his "Emancipation" speech (5 March 1829), "[t]he eligibility of the Roman Catholic for civil office, becomes a 'security' for the Protestant establishments" (*Hansard Parliamentary Debates*, 2d series, 20:762).

38. "We must have the Irish rent spent in Ireland. We must have no foreign landlords. Let those who will not live in Ireland sell their Irish estates. The rents of Ireland *must* be spent in Ireland! Irish affairs must be managed by Irishmen; and, indeed, they *certainly* will be so soon as hope becomes extinct in the Orange leaders" (letter from Daniel O'Connell to P. V. FitzPatrick, 17 September 1833, emphasis in original; in Maurice R. O'Connell, ed., *The Correspondence of Daniel O'Connell*, 8 vols [Dublin: Irish University Press, 1973–80]).

39. To Prime Minister Robert Peel, repeal of the Union involved "not merely the repeal of an act of Parliament, but the dismemberment of this great empire," and he said he was prepared to launch a civil war to prevent it (*Hansard Parliamentary Debates*, 3d series, 4:24–5 (9 May 1843]).

40. See Daniel O'Connell's letter to John Campbell, then Irish Lord Chancellor, 9 September 1843, at the height of the Repeal campaign, in which O'Connell urged Campbell, a Whig, to promote a series of British reform measures for "conciliating the Irish nation and strengthening the British empire" (W. J. Fitzpatrick, ed., *The Correspondence of Daniel O'Connell, The Liberator*, 2 vols [London, 1888] 2:290–91). See also Campbell's letter of 16 September to his brother George Campbell, acquainting him with the contents of O'Connell's letter, and saying it showed that O'Connell would be "glad of a pretext for relaxing from Repeal agitation" (*Life of Lord Campbell, Lord High Chancellor of Great Britain, consisting of his autobiography, diary and letters*, by his daughter, Mrs Hardcastle, 2 vols [London, 1881], 1:179–80).

41. Robert Dunlop, *Daniel O'Connell* (New York, 1900), pp. 16–17. "[The Irish peasantry] favour Repeal in the hope of change" from "the poverty of the tenantry, and of the exactions of landlords and their agents" (letter of Home Secretary Sir James Graham to Prime Minister Robert Peel, 17 October 1843, in Charles Stuart Parker, ed., *Sir Robert Peel, from his Private Papers*, 3 vols [London, 1899], 3:64).

42. Gustave de Beaumont, the liberal-minded contemporary and fellow countryman of Alexis de Tocqueville, traveled extensively in America before visiting Ireland. In his Irish account he devoted an entire chapter to the poverty he encountered there. He wrote that he had thought that the condition of the driven-out American Indians and the enchained African-Americans must represent the ultimate in human deprivation, until he saw "the lot of poor Ireland" (Gustave de Beaumont, *L'Irelande sociale, politique et religieuse*, 2 vols [Paris, 1839], 1:204).

43. According to Daniel O'Connell, probably not one of the agrarian rebels was a qualified voter (O'Connell to Lord Duncannon, 14 January 1833, in O'Connell, ed., *Correspondence of Daniel O'Connell*, vol. 5, item 1949).

44. S. J. Connolly, "Mass Politics and Sectarian Conflict, 1823–30," in *A New History*, 5:92–3. Following the passage of the Catholic Emancipation Act, "the prevailing feeling of the ... masses in Ireland was undoubtedly that the victory they had achieved was only the forerunner of armed rebellion which was to break down English dominion in Ireland" (Lecky, *Leaders of Public Opinion*, 2:98).

45. James Connolly, *Labour in Irish History* (New York, 1919), p. 87; Brian O'Neill, *The War for the Land in Ireland* (London, 1933), pp. 37–8.

46. Reynolds, *Catholic Emancipation Crisis*, p. 155; *Hansard Parliamentary Debates*, 3d series, 13:1206 (2 July 1832); Robert Kee, *The Green Flag* (London, 1972), p. 205.

47. Angus Macintyre, *The Liberator*, pp. 180–81. "O'Connell ... fully justified the conspiracy to refuse ... payment [of the tithe]" (Lecky, *Leaders of Public Opinion*, 2:128). However, he and the other Catholic politicians and clergy were uncompromisingly opposed to the peasants' resorting to violence; they worried that the tithe war would get out of hand and become involved in anti-landlordism.

48. Historian S. J. Connolly's judgment regarding the O'Connell party and the development of the Catholic Emancipation campaign applies generally to the entire twenty-year period from the founding of the Catholic Association in 1823 to the miscarried Repeal Year of 1843: "[T]he catholic leaders took up the characteristic stance of bourgeois politicians throughout early nineteenth-century Europe, seeking to use popular discontent to further their own political aims, while at the same time holding back from the point at which that discontent would erupt into uncontrollable violence" (S. J. Connolly, "Mass Politics and Sectarian Conflict," 5:94).

49. Ibid., 5:84. A convenient source for brief biographical notes on many of the Irish figures of the seventeenth and eighteenth centuries is R. F. Foster, *Modern Ireland, 1600–1972* (New York, 1989), whose index italicizes the page numbers to show where the note is to be found, e.g., Sheil, p. *307*; Wyse, p. *297*. For more extensive notes on Sheil and Wyse and other Irish figures mentioned in this study see Alfred Webb, ed., *A Compendium of Irish Biography* (Dublin, 1878); Henry Boylan, ed., *Dictionary of Irish Biography* (New York: Barnes and Noble, 1978). See also Lecky, *Leaders of Public Opinion*, 2:57–8, and his sketch of Sheil, ibid., 2:58–9. Both Sheil and Wyse would eventually part with O'Connell on the issue of repeal of the Union. O'Connell, writing to Sheil at that time, referred to himself as having been "once your co-leader" (W. J. Fitzpatrick, ed., *Correspondence of Daniel O'Connell, The Liberator*, 2 vols [London, 1888], 2:323 [Richmond Bridewell prison, 19 June 1844]).

50. Fergus O'Ferrall, "'The only lever ...': The Catholic Priest in Irish Politics," *Studies* (Dublin), 70(1981), pp. 313, 317, and 322 n. 37.

51. Peel said: "We were watching the movement of tens of thousands of disciplined fanatics, abstaining from every excess and indulgence, and concentrating every passion and feeling on one single object" (Reynolds, p.158 n. 111).

52. Ibid., p. 149.

53. Ibid., pp. 149–50; 150 n. 75.

54. "... either restraints in Ireland unknown in the ordinary practice of the constitution, or concession in some form or other ..." (Duke of Wellington, as Prime Minister, to Robert Peel, Home Secretary, 12 December 1828, cited in Reynolds, p. 164).

55. Lecky, *Leaders of Public Opinion*, 2:99.

56. Even so, the government was apprehensive concerning the high percentage of Catholics among the troops (Reynolds, pp. 146, 149). See also Lecky, *Leaders of Public Opinion*, 2:83.

57. S. J. Connolly, "The Catholic Question, 1801–12," in *A New History*, 5:39.

58. J. G. Simms, "The Irish on the Continent," in *A New History*, 4:650. O'Ferrall, p. 314. Testifying in favor of the subsidy for Maynooth in 1825, Daniel O'Connell saw Maynooth as a way "to take away the temptation and necessity of foreign education, which I take to be dangerous in the event of the continuance of the existing order of things" (*The Evidence taken before the Select Committees of the Houses of Lords and Commons appointed in the Sessions of 1824 and 1825 to inquire into The State of Ireland* [London, 1825], p. 547).

59. S. J. Connolly, "Catholic Question," 5: 31–2, 5:36. Despite Ascendentist obstructionism, the commitment to the support of Maynooth remained an essential element of British policy (Oliver MacDonagh, "Politics, 1830–45," in *A New History*, 5:186; W. E. Vaughan, "Ireland, c. 1870," in *A New History*, 5:726). The hook in the Maynooth grants was always in "giving the State at once a control over the education and a hold upon the affection or the interests of the Roman Catholic priesthood" (Lord Edward Stanley to Sir Robert Peel, 21 October 1843 [Parker, 3:66]).

60. S. J. Connolly, "Catholic Question," 5:37.

61. Reynolds, pp. 161–2. S. J. Connolly, "Mass Politics and Sectarian Conflict," 5:95, 5:101. The "two-wings" bill was defeated in the House of Lords by a vote of 178–130 (*A New History*, 8:306–7).

62. The change was signaled by the defeat of two Protestant lords seeking parliamentary seats from Waterford and Louth, respectively, when forty-shilling freeholders defied custom by refusing to vote for their landlords' candidates (S. J. Connolly, "Mass Politics and Sectarian Conflict," 5:97–100; Lecky, *Leaders of Public Opinion*, 2:72–5).

63. Reynolds, p. 165; S. J. Connolly, "Mass Politics and Sectarian Conflict," 5:106.

64. Peel's "Emancipation" speech, *Hansard Parliamentary Debates*, 2d series, 20:769, 20:772.

65. Senior, *Orangeism*, p. 281.

66. Irish representation in the British Parliament was increased from 100 to 105 in 1832 (2 &

3 Will. IV, c. 88), and the Irish delegation elected that December included about forty repealers. Although Ireland contained 30 percent of the population of the United Kingdom, only 16 percent of the seats in the Reformed Parliament were allotted to Ireland.

67. "The limited Irish £10 franchise was an obstacle, for it gave the advantage to [O'Connell's] opponents" (Kevin B. Nowlan, *The Politics of Repeal: A Study in the Relations between Great Britain and Ireland, 1841–50* [London, 1965], p. 23).

68. S. J. Connolly, "Mass Politics and Sectarian Conflict," 5:106.

69. Reynolds, p. 168.

70. James O'Connor, *The History of Ireland, 1798–1924*, 2 vols (London, 1925), 1:229.

71. Report of the Select [Parliamentary] Commission on Tithes (1831–32), 21:294, 327, 381, cited in Macintyre, *The Liberator*, p. 176.

72. Oliver MacDonagh, "The Economy and Society, 1830–45," in *A New History*, 5:222–3. MacDonagh's comment is completely consonant with Wellington's characterization of the tithe war (see p. 98). See also Macintyre, pp. 175–6. For a contemporary account of the inception of the anti-tithe movement, see the speech of Mr Stanley in the House of Commons, 13 March 1832 (*Hansard Parliamentary Debates*, 3d series, 11:135–42).

73. Ibid. Lecky, *Leaders of Public Opinion*, 2:130.

74. Lecky, *Leaders of Public Opinion*, 2:131–2. For an account of the unspeakably inhuman conditions to which the transportees were subjected, and the related impact on the original population of the country, see Robert Hughes, *The Fatal Shore* (New York: Alfred A. Knopf, 1986).

75. MacDonagh, "Economy and Society, 1830–45," 5:223–4. An intermediate step toward turning the collection over to landlords was taken in 1832 with "tithe composition" legislation (2 William IV, c. 119). See Macintyre, p. 198.

76. MacDonagh, "Economy and Society, 1830–45," 5:225. Assign this role to the landlords, said O'Connell, "and the spirit which had continued the present agitation for seventy years, would be applied to rent" (*Hansard Parliamentary Debates*, 3d series, 21:596, 20 February 1834; cited in Macintyre, p. 190).

77. See Father John F. Broderick, sj, *The Holy See and the Irish Movement for the Repeal of the Union with England, 1829–47* (*Analecta Gregoriana*, Cura Pontificiae Universitatis Gregoriana edita, Vol. IV, monograph Series Facultatis Historiae Ecclesiastiae, Rome, 1951). See also Donal A. Kerr, *Peel, Priests and Politics* (Oxford, 1982), Chapter 2, "The Irish Clergy and Politics," especially pp. 75–85.

78. Kerr, p. 85.

79. L. A. McCaffrey, *Daniel O'Connell and the Repeal Year* (Lexington, 1966) pp. 62–3.

80. Broderick, pp. 125–54.

81. Ibid.; Lecky, *Leaders of Public Opinion*, 2:239; Kee, pp. 204–5. Such estimates might be exaggerated where made by Repeal partisans, but whatever the actual numbers, they were sufficient to move the government to desperate countermeasures.

82. Lecky, *Leaders of Public Opinion*, 2:253.

83. Ibid., 2:239. For a concise, flavorful, and well-documented account of the Repeal campaign, see McCaffrey, *Daniel O'Connell and the Repeal Year*, especially Chapter 2.

84. Reynolds, *Catholic Emancipation Crisis*, p. 146 n. 53.

85. Senior, *Orangeism*, p. 279.

86. Ibid., pp. 200, 217, 279; S. J. Connolly, "Union Government, 1812–23," in *A New History*, 5:71.

87. Reynolds, p. 146. Two years before the death of William IV, an Orange plot was discovered aimed at awarding the succession to Ernst Augustus, Duke of Cumberland (1771–1851) King of Hanover (Germany), fifth son of George III. The Duke himself was a militant anti-Catholic spokesman in the House of Lords, and titular head of the Orange Order. In 1835 the Radical Joseph Hume, head of an investigating committee of the House of Commons, charged that there were two hundred thousand armed Orangemen in Ireland, who met in armies numbering in the tens of thousands (see Senior, pp. 266–71; and O'Connor, *History of Ireland*, 1:229).

88. Senior, p. 245.

89. MacDonagh, "Economy and Society, 1830–45," 5:224.

90. MacDonagh, "Ideas and Institutions, 1830–45", in *A New History*, 5:213–14; Vaughan, "Ireland c. 1870," 5:741.

91. In the wake of the tithe war, the constabulary and magistracy were deliberately reconstituted, "federalized" and "professionalized," to be free of the domination of Ascendancy types (MacDonagh, "Politics, 1830–45," and "Ideas and Institutions," in *A New History*, 5:180, and 5:214).

Within the highest levels of British authority, the last hurrah fittingly came from the Iron Duke, Wellington. In the summer of 1843, he asked for the formation of an armed yeomanry under crown-commissioned officers to confront the Repeal campaign. The British government rejected the proposal because it believed such a step would inevitably unleash a religious war (Kevin B. Nowlan, *Politics of Repeal*, p. 52).

92. Peel's "Emancipation" speech, *Hansard Parliamentary Debates*, 2d series, 20:746 (emphasis added).

93. Ibid., 3d series, 74:1026 (18 April 1845). Privately, Peel had even earlier conceded that in Ireland, "mere force ... will do nothing as a permanent remedy for the social evils" (Peel Papers. British Museum, Additional Manuscripts, 40449, ff. 105–6 [19 October 1843], cited in Kerr, *Peel, Priests and Politics*, p. 121).

94. When it came to the question of armed struggle, for O'Connell South America was one thing, Ireland another. He cheered on the independence campaign of Bolivar in South America, and sent off his son Morgan to fight in that war. There the conflict was not likely to get out of hand, but would remain a quarrel between Spain and the Spanish colonists; the masses of the superexploited "Indios" would not be dealt a hand in the game. But in Ireland the impoverished peasantry had dealt themselves in.

95. Kee, *The Green Flag*, p. 185.

96. The remainder of this paragraph is conveniently based on Reynolds, *Catholic Emancipation Crisis*, pp. 151–4.

97. "While rebellion was no part of their program, they had to keep popular passions at a fever pitch in order to intimidate and extort" (ibid., p. 153).

98. *A New History*, 8:309. This and similar orders subsequently issued were often overborne by the force of the movement and by the power of O'Connell's argument that the best hope for Catholicism lay in the liberation struggle (see Kerr, Chapter 2).

99. "O'Connell and his colleagues ... never broke with the notion of accepting emancipation as a boon from an upper-class legislature rather than as a right won by the people" (ibid., p. 169).

100. *Hansard Parliamentary Debates*, 3d series, 16:264 (5 March 1833). O'Connell documented his case with statistics showing a decline in "agrarian crime" in Ireland between 1823 and 1829, as proof of "the effect of establishing the Catholic Association."

101. MacDonagh, "Economy and Society, 1830–45," 5:224; *A New History*, 8:313.

102. Maurice R. O'Connell, ed., *Correspondence of Daniel O'Connell*, vol. 5, letter no. 1949 (14 January 1833).

103. Cited in James Connolly, *Labour in Irish History*, p. 85.

104. Lecky, *Leaders of Public Opinion*, 2:133, citing, *Life of Dr Doyle*, 2:452. "Blackfeet" was one of the names under which the secret peasant societies operated. My veiled allusion is, of course, to Psalms, 146:3: "Put not your trust in princes ..." For a sketch of Bishop Doyle's life, see *Compendium of Irish Biography*, compiled by Alfred Webb (Dublin, 1878), pp. 155–6.

In the House of Commons in 1838, O'Connell too declared his opposition to trade unionism, saying that there was "no tyranny equal to that which was exercised by the trade unionists in Dublin over their fellow labourers" (cited in James Connolly, *Labour in Irish History*, p. 101).

105. At a time when he was Solicitor-General in the British government, the Whig John Campbell told of an exchange he had had with O'Connell. O'Connell, he said, indicated his readiness to accept Campbell's insincerely proffered notion that O'Connell could get a separate Irish Parliament if "he were to agree that it should be subordinate to our [British] Parliament ... like the House of Assembly in Jamaica" (letter to Campbell's brother George, 23 March 1833, cited in Mrs Hardcastle, ed., *Life of John Lord Campbell*, p. 34).

106. James S. Donnelly, Jr., "A Famine in Irish Politics," in *A New History*, 5:357.

107. See Appendix J.

108. The generalizations made in this regard do not, of course, apply to the Protestant-majority area of Ulster, which will be treated in Chapter 5.

109. Oliver MacDonagh, "The Age of O'Connell, 1830–45," in *A New History*, 5:158–9. In recapitulating MacDonagh's thesis, I have combined his point four (the ending of "total

reliance on protestant ascendancy") with point one ("broadening the base of loyalism").

110. See Macintyre, *The Liberator*, pp. 142, 144, 145.

111. Ibid., pp. 152, 154. The "Irish Party" was not a formal party but an informal coalition of the Irish Parliamentary fraction, some repealers, some not (see ibid., pp. xiii–xvi).

112. Ibid., p. 104, citing Wellesley Papers, Additional MSS, 37307, pp. 217–20. Compare Vaughan, "Ireland c. 1870," 5:741–2.

113. "... the old Whig regime in Ireland was not to be resurrected" (Macintyre, p. 146).

114. Ibid., pp. 154, 163. "To do something for Ireland" seems to have been a common phrase at that time. For an abbreviated use of it by O'Connell, see *Hansard Parliamentary Debates*, 3d series, 50:201.

115. Macintyre, pp. 145, 165.

116. Ibid., p. 147; MacDonagh, "Politics, 1830–45," 5:178.

117. Macintyre, p. 161.

118. Macintyre, p. 158; MacDonagh, "Politics, 1830–45," 5:175, 5:180.

119. Oliver MacDonagh, ibid. 5:179.

120. Oliver MacDonagh, "Ideas and Institutions, 1830–45," in *A New History*, 5:212–14.

121. "Both in Parliament and outside of it, the necessity of reform for Ireland was now [February 1844] generally admitted" (Kerr, *Peel, Priests and Politics*, p. 116).

122. For a reference to examples of this ruling-class policy in regard to peasant uprisings in England in 1549 and 1607, see "A Consideration of the Cause in Question before the Lords touching Depopulation" (5 July 1607). If concessions were not to be avoided, the Lords concluded, they should be delayed for a couple of years, if possible, "lest encouragement move the people to seek redress by like outrages" (Eric Kerridge, *Agrarian Problems in the Sixteenth Century and After* [London: Allen and Unwin, 1969], pp. 200–203; Kerridge cites British Museum Cottonian Manuscripts, Titus F. iv, ff 322–3).

123. Kerr, p. 108.

124. MacDonagh, "Politics, 1830–45," 5:186–7.

125. Kerr, pp. 11–12.

126. In November 1843, a parliamentary commission (the Devon Commission) was appointed to look into the conditions of the peasantry and the possibility of agrarian reform. Its work, of course, was to be of no help to the Irish laboring classes in the holocaust of famine that loomed just ahead. Limited as the commission was in its purpose and outlook, its report, when made in 1845, gave legitimacy to the issue of landlordism in Ireland.

Speaking of the Irish priesthood of the nineteenth century, S. J. Connolly states: "the great majority of Maynooth priests, like those trained elsewhere in Ireland or abroad, were the sons of substantial tenant farmers or of the lower middle and middle classes of the towns and cities" (S. J. Connolly, *Religion and Society in Nineteenth-Century Ireland* [Dundalk, 1985], p. 40).

127. Parker, ed., *Sir Robert Peel, from his Private Papers*, 3:53–7: Peel to James Graham, 16 July 1843 (emphasis in original); Peel to De Grey, 24 July 1843; De Grey to Peel, 18 August 1843; Peel to De Grey, 22 August 1843. In due course, Peel's persuasion took effect and De Grey did make the recommended appointment (ibid., p. 60).

128. MacDonagh, "Age of O'Connell," 5:189.

129. Arthur Young, *A Tour in Ireland (1780)*, book 2, p. 34; Lecky, *History of England*, 2:261.

130. S. J. Connolly, *Religion and Society*, p. 30.

131. R. V. Comerford, "Ireland 1850–70: Post-Famine and Mid-Victorian," in *A New History*, 5:388–9. For the letter quoted above, see Emmet Larkin, *The Making of the Catholic Church in Ireland, 1850–1860* (Chapel Hill, 1980), pp. 445, 447. Larkin says that the letter gives a "thoughtful and accurate measure of what Cullen had achieved."

132. Vaughan, "Ireland c. 1870," 5:741.

133. Ibid., 5:740–2.

134. By the mid-Victorian period, Ireland witnessed "the enforcement throughout the land of order based on the rule of law and publicly administered in the courts" (Comerford, 5:390). The police-to-population ratios are given by Comerford, or derived from his presentation (ibid., 5:389).

135. O'Connell said his party's collaboration with the Whig government had made possible "... having troops [from Ireland] to spare for [rebelling] Canada, and for putting down the disturbances in England." Lord John Russell, Whig leader in the House of Commons and future

Prime Minister, praised O'Connell's steadfast support of the British government in these two crises. T. B. Macaulay expressed appreciation for the fact that "the Catholics of Ireland had remained true in all things to the general Government of the Empire," so that troops could be spared from Ireland to suppress the insurrections in England and in Canada (*Hansard Parliamentary Debates*, 50:201-2 [O'Connell, 12 August 1839]; 72:707 [Russell, 13 February 1844]; and 72:1178-9 [Macaulay, 19 February 1844]).

Ireland would serve as an "excuse of the English Government for maintaining *a big standing army*, which in case of need they send against the English workers, as has happened after the army became turned into praetorians in Ireland" (Karl Marx, Resolution adopted by the General Council of the International Workingmen's Association, 1 January 1870, in *The General Council of the First International, Minutes*, 4 vols [Moscow, n.d.], vol. 2 [1868-70], p. 404; emphasis in original).

136. Quoted by Lord John Russell from a speech made by Fox, 14 May 1805 (*Hansard Parliamentary Debates*, 3d series, 70:109, 11 July 1843).

137. W. Burghardt Turner and Joyce Moore Turner, eds, *Richard B. Moore, Caribbean Militant in Harlem: Collected Writings 1920-1972* (Bloomington, Indiana, 1988), p. 29.

138. Wilfred D. Samuels, *Five Afro-Caribbean Voices in American Culture, 1917-1929* (Bloomington, Indiana, 1977), p. 3.

139. Robert A. Hill, *The Marcus Garvey and Universal Negro Improvement Association Papers* (Berkeley, California, 1983), 1:xxxvii-xxxviii. Garvey thought that the American Negroes were better for the "[r]acial caste oppression" to which they were subjected in the United States, according to editor Hill; on that account, Garvey said, the Americans were blessed with a "race consciousness" that the West Indians lacked (ibid.). Ira De A. Reid, looking at the matter somewhat differently, believed, "The Negro immigrant is beyond doubt more radical than the native" (Ira De A. Reid, *The Negro Immigrant: His Background, Characteristics and Social Adjustment, 1899-1937* [New York, 1939], p. 221).

140. Norwell Harrigan and Pearl I. Varlack, "The US Virgin Islands and the Black Experience," *Journal of Black Studies*, 7:387-410 (June 1977), 389-91.

141. Hubert H. Harrison, "The Virgin Islands," pp. 5-6, 12-13. Cited by Jeffrey Babcock Perry in his forthcoming (Louisiana State University Press) biography of Harrison.

142. Reid, pp. 216, 226.

143. Wilfred D. Samuels, *Five Afro-Caribbean Voices in American Culture, 1917-1929* (Boulder, 1977), p. 22.

5 Ulster

1. This question lies beyond the scope of the present work. The essence of the matter, however, was presented nearly sixty years ago by W. E. B. DuBois in his *Black Reconstruction*, most particularly in Chapter 2, "The White Worker."

2. Irish writers and social activists for more than thirty years now have been pointing out the pertinence of the United States/Ulster analogy to the struggle for equal rights. See, for example, the forceful statement of the general parallel of the Ulster and the United States situations today in Liam de Paor, *Divided Ulster* (Harmondsworth, England, 1970), p. 13. Recollect the Irish civil rights marchers of 1969 going into battle singing "We Shall Overcome."

3. Instructions by Arthur Chichester, Lord Deputy in Ireland, to Sir James Ley and Sir John Davys [Davies], 14 October 1608 (Great Britain Public Record Office, *Calendar of State Papers, relating to Ireland of the reign of James I*, vol. 3, *1608-10*, edited by C. W. Russell and John P. Prendergast [London and Edinburgh, 1874], 3:54-65; p. 64). (In subsequent notes this series will be abbreviated to *Cal. S. P., Ireland, James I, [date] [vol. no.].)*

More than half of the investors in Irish plantations in this period were also stockholders in the Virginia Company (Theodore K. Rabb, *Enterprise and Empire: Merchant and Gentry Investment in the Expansion of England, 1575-1630* [Cambridge, Massachusetts, 1967], p. 108).

4. *Cal. S. P., James I*, 3:17.

5. Ibid., 3:xiv.

6. Fynes Moryson, *An Itinerary, Containing His Ten Yeeres Travell through the Twelve Dominions of Germany, Bohmerland, Sweitzerland, Netherland, Denmarke and Ireland,* 4 vols (London, 1617; Glasgow, 1907), 3:302, 328.

7. George Hill, *An historical account of the Plantation in Ulster at the commencement of the seventeenth century, 1608–1620* (Belfast, 1877; republished [with an introduction by John G. Barry] Shannon: Irish University Press, 1977), pp. 58–9.

8. Ibid., p. 61; Aidan Clarke with Dudley Edwards, "Pacification, Plantation, and the Catholic Question, 1603–23," in *A New History,* 3:196.

9. Hill, p. 61.

10. Ibid. Clarke with Edwards, 3:199 n. 5a.

11. Hill, p. 57.

12. Geographically Ulster included nine counties: Antrim, Down, Coleraine (Derry), Donegal, Tyrone, Fermanagh, Cavan, Armagh and Monaghan. Neither Antrim, Down nor Monaghan was included in the escheated lands of the "rebel" earls O'Neill and O'Donnell. By 1609, however, parts of Antrim and Down were already rather heavily settled by Scots, ancient settlers, as well as by the newcomers lodged on lands granted to James's fellow countrymen James Hamilton and Hugh Montgomery. Antrim and Down were to remain the main base of Protestant Ulster from that day to this.

13. In his *Confiscation in Irish History* (London, 1918), W. F. T. Butler speculates that the Irish chiefs would have been no less grasping than their Scottish counterparts, who had "reduced all their clansmen to the condition of tenants at will." He implies that English government sincerely wanted to draw the Irish chiefs into the English-style social structure as the Scottish chiefs had been drawn into it. At that point, however, Butler cuts short his "speculation as to what might have been." But the general tenor of Butler's study would seem to cast doubt on the depth of the sincerity of the British government toward such a reconciliation with the Irish chieftains.

14. Hill, pp. 60–64; 97; 109–10 nn. 79, 82; 112; 229; 300 n. 166; 347; 360; 411 n. 61. Moryson, 2:348–9. *Cal. S. P., Ireland, James I, 1608–1610,* 3:364. Aidan Clarke, "Plantation and the Catholic Question, 1603–23," in *A New History,* 3:199 n. 6(e).

15. When, in time, the chieftain class had been disposed of as a social force, the English found gavelkind serviceable for dispersing such Catholic landholding as remained. In 1704 it was made mandatory that such inheritance was "to be by the rule of gavelkind" (6 Anne c. 6, sec. 10).

16. Hill, pp. 37, 42, 49, 83, 318 n. 221. Moryson, 3:311–33. Clarke with Edwards, "Pacification, Plantation, and the Catholic Question, 1603–23," in *A New History,* 3:206–8.

The use of the term "Briton" in these early-seventeenth-century documents anticipates by a century the Act of Union of 1707, uniting England and Scotland in one state, Great Britain.

17. For deserting to the English side in 1598, Sir Tirlough McHenry O'Neill (half-brother of the leader of the Irish rebellion, Hugh O'Neill, Earl of Tyrone) and Sir Henry Oge O'Neill (Tyrone's son-in-law) were granted English land titles that were exceptional in two ways. The grants were exceptionally large, Sir Tirlough receiving 9,900 acres and Sir Henry Oge 4,900 acres. Second, while other native grantees were obliged to move to other lands in order to get their allotted acreage, Sir Tirlough and Sir Henry Oge were allowed to have the lands they had always occupied. Sir Henry died in battle against O'Doherty's revolt in 1608, and his lands were distributed to his wife and six sons (an opportune English show of regard for the rule of gavelkind, whereby the few exceptionally large family landholdings that still existed could be broken up) (Hill, pp. ii n. 1, 115, 318–19).

18. W. F. T. Butler gives their number as 280, but notes that "the numbers differ in the various lists" (*Confiscation in Irish History,* p. 50). Aidan Clarke says that no more than fifty natives in each of the six counties were allotted any land (Clarke with Edwards, 3:202). A perusal of the documents relating to grants and grantees for the year 1610, as reprinted by Hill, shows 231 "native grants" in the five counties (not including Coleraine/Derry) (*Plantation in Ulster,* pp. 309–48). The estimated total adult population of Ulster at this time was between 25,000 and 40,000 (M. Perceval-Maxwell, *The Scottish Migration to Ulster in the Reign of James I* [London, 1973], p. 17). Obviously, however large one estimates the size of the families to have been, the overwhelming majority of them were left landless.

19. Clarke, with Edwards, 3:202.

20. Patrick J. Corish, "The Rising of 1641 and the Catholic Confederacy, 1641–45," in *A New History,* 3:289. See also Hill, pp. 348–9, for a number of specific instances of the pressured

passing of land titles from Irish to British hands.

21. T. W. Moody, *The Ulster Question, 1603–1973* (Dublin and Cork, 1974), p. 5.

22. Hill, p. iii n. 2. *Cal. S. P., Ireland, James I*, 3:299 (Sir Robert Jacob to Lord Salisbury, 18 October 1609). Compare Hill, p. 205 n. 40.

23. *Cal. S. P., Ireland, James I*, 3:299 (Sir Robert Jacob, King James's Solicitor, to Lord Salisbury, October 1609); 3:287 (Lord Deputy Chichester to Lord Salisbury, 18 September 1609); 3:304–5 (Chichester to the Privy Council, 31 October 1609); 3:458–60 (Privy Council to Chichester, 8 June 1610; and 3:496 (Chichester to Privy Council, 23 September 1610). For a recurrence in 1619 of this proposed solution of the "woodkerne" problem, see Hill, p. iii n. 2 (citing MS *State Papers*, vol. 35, No. 60).

24. For African references see: Letter of John Lyle to Secretary of State Joseph Williamson, 16 September 1667, Great Britain *Cal. S. P., Dom., 1667, Charles II*; Narcissus Luttrell, diary entry 5 March 1701/2, cited in George M. Trevelyan, *England under Queen Anne*, 3 vols (London, 1934), 2:149; John and Awsham Churchill, compilers, *A Collection of Voyages and Travels . . .*, 6 vols (London, 1704–32), 6:219.

25. *Cal. S. P., Ireland, James I*, 3:287, 3:458–60, 3:496; T. W. Moody, "Sir Thomas Phillips of Limavady, Servitor," *Irish Historical Studies*, 1:251–72 (1938–39), pp. 256–8.

26. Moody, "Sir Thomas Phillips," p. 257; Hill, p. 189; John J. Silke, "The Irish Abroad, 1534–1691," in *A New History*, 3:593. (Moody's transcription from the Cecil Manuscripts varies in some details from the version printed in *The Cecil Papers*, published by the Great Britain Public Record Office. But the discrepancies, mainly relating to the daily allowance for maintenance of the transportees, do not seem important.)

27. T. W. Moody, "Sir Thomas Phillips," 1:260–61.

28. Lord Deputy Sir Arthur Chichester, Instructions to Lord Chief Justice Sir James Ley and Sir John Davys [Davies], 14 October 1608 (*Cal. S. P., Ireland, James I*, 3:63).

In the contemporaneous fledgling colony of Virginia, such settlers were called "officers." Like the Ulster servitors, they were recruited from surplus veterans, who were "truly bred in that nursery of Warre, the Lowe countries" and, indeed, in some cases in Ireland itself (John Rolfe, *Relation of Virginia* [1616], reprinted in part in Alexander Brown, *The First Republic in America* [Boston, 1898], p. 227; Alexander Brown, *The Genesis of the United States*, 2 vols [Boston, 1890], 2:1065; and ibid., appended "Brief Biographies". See also Volume Two of this study.

29. *Cal. S. P., Ireland, James I*, 3:211–12.

30. Ibid., 3:68 (Lord Deputy to Privy Council, 14 October 1608); 3:41 ("A Brief of the Proceedings of the Commissioners for the Plantation of Ulster . . .," 19 March 1610).

31. Ibid., 3:63.

32. The quit-rent rates payable to the Crown per 1,000 acres were to be as follows: undertakers (barred from engaging native tenants or laborers), £5 6s. 8d.; servitors, if engaging only English or Scots tenants or laborers, the same as undertakers, but 50 percent more if engaging natives as tenants or laborers, i.e., £8 and native landholders, twice the undertaker rate, namely, £10 13s. 4d. (*Cal. S. P., Ireland, James I*, 3:490.)

33. Hill, *Plantation in Ulster*, pp. 310–48, 445–590.

34. "Without the succession of King James VI to the throne of England, it is unlikely that Scots would have been able to colonize any significant districts of Ireland" (W. H. Crawford, "Ulster as a Mirror of Two Societies," paper delivered at the Social Science Research Council of Great Britain Conference on Irish–Scottish Development, Strathclyde University, 16–18 September 1981, in T. M. Devine and David Dickson, eds, *Ireland and Scotland, 1600–1850, Parallels and Contrasts in Economic and Social Development* [Edinburgh, 1982(?)], p. 61). "The Ulster problem, it will be generally agreed, begins with the Plantation of Ulster in the early seventeenth century" (A. T. Q. Stewart, "The Mind of Protestant Ulster," in David Watt, ed., *The Constitution of Northern Ireland, Problems and Prospects* [London, 1981], p. 32).

35. For a discussion of the Scots "kindly tenant" status, and its disappearance as money rent superseded rent in kind, and of the emergence of "feu-farming" and the consequent prevalence of tenancy-at-will, see I. F. Grant, *The Social and Economic Development of Scotland before 1603* (Edinburgh, 1930; 1971). Section II, Chapter I, Parts VIII and IX; and Chapters IV and V. "Feuing was primarily undertaken as a method of increasing revenue. The cash nexus was predominant" (ibid., p. 279).

36. J. D. Mackie, *A History of Scotland* (Harmondsworth, England, 1964), Chapters 12 through

16; Curtis, *A History of Ireland*, 6th edn (London, 1950) pp. 288, 293, 310.

37. Curtis, pp. 397–8.

38. Moody, *Ulster Question*, p. 7. Perceval-Maxwell, *Scottish Migration*, p. 33.

39. Perceval-Maxwell, p. 33.

40. Ibid., p. 26.

41. *Edinburgh Review*, 159 (1899):126.

42. For the eighteenth-century contrast in Scotland, see Mackie, *A History of Scotland*, pp. 285 ff. For the English case, see: Eleanora Carus-Wilson, ed., *Essays in Economic History* (New York: St Martin's Press, 1966), 2:268–9; Leslie A. Clarkson, *The Pre-industrial Economy in England, 1500–1750* (New York, 1972), pp. 114–16; W. E. Lunt, *History of England*, 4th edition (New York, Evanston and London, 1957), pp. 485–8; and George M. Trevelyan, *English Social History: A Survey of Six Centuries, Chaucer to Queen Victoria* (London, 1942), pp. 141, 284–9.

43. *Encyclopedia Britannica*, "Scotland. – Population."

44. Andrew Fletcher, "Second Discourse concerning the affairs of Scotland" (1698) in *Andrew Fletcher of Saltoun, Selected Political Writings and Speeches*, edited by David Daiches (Edinburgh, 1979), p. 55.

45. Ibid., p. 58.

46. "The Scottish colonists ... should be regarded as displaced people superfluous to the economic and social needs of the colonizing society" (Crawford, p. 61). See Perceval-Maxwell, pp. 26–7.

47. A. T. Q. Stewart, p. 35; Moody, *Ulster Question*, p. 7; Perceval-Maxwell, pp. 25–6.

48. Perceval-Maxwell, p. 27.

49. A. T. Q. Stewart, Reader in Irish History at Queen's University, Belfast, and a defender of partition, says that the Revd Stewart's comment is "sometimes maliciously quoted" ("The Mind of Protestant Ulster," p. 35). Since Stewart is seeking to make the point that the English and Scots did not seize "the richest and most fertile of the Ulster lands from the Gaels," he includes in his citation a sentence which is often omitted, and which speaks of the Scots immigrants planting lands which were previously unoccupied, or at least uncultivated. That some did so may well be true, but all the documents concerning the plantation make it clear that the official purpose was precisely to displace the native population, not to coexist with them. The fact that this "ethnic cleansing," as it might be called today, was not fully accomplished is another matter.

50. Perceval-Maxwell, p. 277.

51. Ibid., p. 278.

52. Ibid.

53. Ibid., pp. 31–3. Impoverished Scots immigrants "received farms at low rents in order to colonize Ulster" (Curtis, p. 287).

54. "The seventeenth century was to elapse before there were sufficient British farmers in Ulster to generate significant competition for land" (Crawford, p. 61).

55. Great Britain, *Parliamentary Papers*, vols 19–22 (1845), "Reports from Her Majesty's Commissioners of Inquiry into the State of the Law and Practice in Relation to the Occupation of Land in Ireland" (the Devon Commission Report) (Dublin, 1845) 19:545/483. (There are two sets of page numbers, a confusion that I did not resolve.) Testimony of John Hancock, Esq., land agent to the Right Hon. Lord Lurgan, a magistrate of the Counties of Armagh, Down and Antrim, 23 March 1844.

56. Hill, *Plantation in Ulster*, pp. 447–8 n. 2. The measure failed of its basic purpose of displacing the native population because it was so widely disregarded. Instead, it served only to provide grounds a decade later for still other self-aggrandizing British landgrabbers to challenge the titles of earlier British occupiers (ibid.). The three-fourths Protestant quota served to emphasize the government's early awareness of the paradox that too much conversion would threaten Protestant rule, by diluting the privileges of the laboring-class Protestants.

57. "... the Irish were too hard to displace, the colonists too glad to find tenants on the spot.... But the plantation none the less meant a social revolution in Ulster, a clean sweep of all the traditional property-rights of the occupying Irish. The great mass of Ulster Irish remained on their former lands, but degraded to the status of tenants-at-will" (Moody, *Ulster Question*, p. 5). See also: Hill, p. 454 n. 13; Butler, *Confiscation in Irish History*, pp. 45–6; de Paor, *Divided Ulster*, p. 21.

58. Hill, p. 501 nn. 144 and 145. See also ibid., p. 447 n. 2; and Butler, p. 47.

59. "The tenant-right of Ulster, when considered economically, is only ... the right of the tenant to the fair profit of the capital vested by him by purchase or expenditure ... or to the inherited profit arising from such improvements made by some of his ancestors" (William Nelson Hancock, Esq., [brother of John Hancock, Esq., quoted in n. 55] barrister-at-law, *The Tenant Right of Ulster considered economically, being an essay read before the Dublin University Philosophical Society* [Dublin, 1845], pp. 33–4).

60. Hill, pp. 447–8 n. 2.

61. For a comprehensive discussion of the evolution of the Ulster tenant-right, presented in relation to its detailed historical context, see W. H. Crawford, "Landlord–Tenant Relations in Ulster, 1609–1820," in *Irish Economic and Social History*, 2:5–21 (1975).

62. Hill, p. 311.

63. Perceval-Maxwell, pp. 274, 284, 314–15. J. H. Andrews, "Land and People, c. 1685," in *A New History*, 3:459, 3:461.

Even within Ulster, sufficient as this Protestant implantation was in normal times for keeping watch over and repressing the hostile and excluded natives, it could not prevent the northern province from being the first to rise in rebellion in 1641. Then the British position was restored not by local militia but by a regular army of Scots under General Munro. "The situation [of the British settlers in Ulster for most of the seventeenth century] has often been compared to that of the early colonists in North America, whose little settlements lived under the threat of Indian attack ... [like] white farmers in Kenya watching their Kikuyu workers and thinking of the midnight advent of the Mau-Mau" (de Paor, pp. 21, 23).

64. The siege of Protestant Derry by the forces of the Catholic James II was lifted in 1689. British Protestant units from Ulster distinguished themselves in the defeat of the Catholic forces at the Battle of the Boyne in 1690 (John Gerald Simms, "The War of the Two Kings, 1685–91," in *A New History*, 3:492–3, 3:497–8).

Ulster Protestant tradition, we are told, holds that the defenders of Derry found strength in "pride of race" as well as anti-Catholicism (Simms, 3:492).

65. John Patrick Prendergast, *Ireland from the Restoration to the Revolution* (London, 1873), p. 98. W. Macafee and V. Morgan, "Population in Ulster, 1660–1760," in Peter Roebuck ed., *Essays in Ulster History in honour of J. L. McCracken* (Belfast, 1981), pp. 47, 58.

66. Devon Commission Report, 19:14–15. The Devon Commission asked a John Andrews of County Down, land agent of the Marquess of Londonderry, if the "curtailment of the tenant-right [could] be carried without danger to the country." Andrews replied that the Protestant tenants of Down would resist such a curtailment as violently as the Catholics of Tipperary were wont to resist their landlords: "You would have a Tipperary in Down if it was attempted to be carried out" (ibid., 19:608/546, 27 March 1844).

67. Ibid.

68. "In Ulster ... [there] was this bond between [the Presbyterian Scot] and his landlord that each was an intruder and knew he was looked upon as such. ... [They] were Protestants, belonging to the conquering race" (James O'Connor, *History of Ireland*, 2 vols [London, 1924], 2:27–8).

69. Crawford, "Landlord–Tenant Relations," 2:13–16.

70. Crawford, "Ulster as a Mirror," pp. 62–4.

71. Ibid. See also Crawford's "Landlord–Tenant Relations," 2:16.

72. Such were the terms of Poyning's Law, enacted in 1494. It was of course no coincidence that, after 287 years, the 1782 law (21 & 22 Geo. III c. 47) was approved by the British government within nine months after the British surrender at Yorktown, ending the military phase of the American Revolution.

73. The cited laws are acts of the English Parliament.

74. James G. Leyburn, *The Scotch-Irish, A Social History* (Chapel Hill, 1962), pp. 157, 168–9.

75. A. T. Q. Stewart, *The Ulster Crisis* (London, 1967), p. 29.

76. From the United Irishmen's plan for parliamentary reform, 15 February 1794 (*Journals of the House of Commons of the Kingdom of Ireland* [Dublin, 1753–1800], vol. 17, p. 888; reprinted in Charles Carlton, *Bigotry and Blood: Documents on the Ulster Troubles* [Chicago, 1977], pp. 45–6).

77. Crawford, "Landlord–Tenant Relations." See especially Table I, p. 13.

78. De Paor, *Divided Ulster*, p. 43.

79. National Library of Ireland, Lake MSS 56, quoted in Hereward Senior, *Orangeism in*

Ireland, 1795–1836 (London, 1866), p. 67.

80. Great Britain, *Parliamentary Papers*, 1825, vol. VIII, *State of Ireland, with Four Reports of the Evidence taken in the Present Session*, pp. 688–9 (18 May 1825). See also: Kenneth Charlton, "The State of Ireland in the 1820s: James Cropper's Plan," *Irish Historical Studies*, 17:320–39 (March 1971); and R. F. Foster, *Modern Ireland, 1600–1972* (London, 1988), pp. 321–2.

81. L. C. Cullen, ed., *The Formation of the Irish Economy* (Cork, 1969).

82. Raymond Crotty, *Ireland in Crisis: A Study in Capitalist Colonial Development* (Dover, New Hampshire, 1986), p. 52; George O'Brien, *The Economic History of Ireland from the Union to the Famine* (London, 1921), p. 444.

83. T. M. Devine and David Dickson, "In Pursuit of Comparative Aspects of Irish and Scottish Development: A Review of the Symposium," in their *Ireland and Scotland*, p. 271.

84. Cullen, p. 105; T. A. Jackson, *Ireland Her Own* (New York, 1947), p. 188.

85. See Roy Foster's discussion of the question Why did Ireland, outside Ulster, fail to industrialize? (*Modern Ireland*), p. 321–2.

86. Crawford, "Landlord–Tenant Relations," 2:12–18.

87. De Paor, pp. 63–4.

88. Ibid., p. 66. See also: Stewart, *Ulster Crisis*, p. 30; O'Connor, *History of Ireland*, 2:28; Moody, *Ulster Question*, p. 17.

89. J. C. Beckett et al., *Belfast: The Making of the City* (Belfast, 1983), pp. 153–4, 159–60.

90. "... in Ulster alone was landlord help sufficiently widespread to reduce mortality in a poor county to a figure similar to that obtaining in the wealthier counties of eastern Ireland.... Only in Ulster were excess mortality rates below 7.5%" (S. H. Cousens, "The Regional Variations in Mortality During the Great Irish Famine," *Proceedings of the Royal Irish Academy*, Vol. 63, Section C [1963], p. 146). See also, Cousens, "Regional Death Rates in Ireland During the Great Famine from 1846 to 1851," *Population Studies*, Vol. 14, No. 1 (July 1960), pp. 55–7. With regard to the deliberateness of England's genocidal policy as rationalized by a government infatuated by laissez-faire economics and population theories, as first laid down by Adam Smith and Malthus, and elaborated and applied by such social theorists as Nassau Senior and Spencer, see: Thomas P. O'Neill, "The Organization and Administration of Relief, 1845–52," in R. Dudley Edwards and T. Desmond Williams, *The Great Famine* (New York, 1957), pp. 209–63; and Joel Mokyr, *Why Ireland Starved: A Quantitative and Analytical History of the Irish Economy, 1800–1850* (London, 1983), especially, pp. 290–92.

91. Beckett, pp. 44–7.

92. O'Connell to Revd Dr Paul Cullen, Rector of Irish College, Rome, 9 May 1842, in Maurice R. O'Connell, ed., *Correspondence of Daniel O'Connell*, 7:157.

93. A. C. Hepburn and B. Collins, "Industrial Society: The Structure of Belfast, 1901," in Peter Roebuck, ed., *Plantation to Partition*, p. 211; Leslie Clarkson, "The City and the Country," in Beckett, p. 153; D. J. Cowan, *History of Belfast* as quoted by Constantine Fitzgibbon, *Red Hand: The Ulster Colony* (London, 1971), p. 340.

94. "Abstract labour" is of course Marx's phrase, used to distinguish labor as value-creating as against labor as productive of particular items of use, "concrete labour." It also implies labor in general, regardless of the particular national, religious, or other characteristics of the laborers (see *Capital*, Vol. I, Chapter 1, Section 2, "The twofold character of the labour embodied in commodities"). The second quotation is from Abraham Lincoln's "Reply to the New York Workingmen's Democratic Republican Association," 21 March 1864 (Mario M. Cuomo and Harold Holzer, eds, *Lincoln on Democracy: His Own Words with Essays by America's Foremost Historians* [New York, 1990], p. 315).

95. These words are taken from the concluding sentence of James Connolly's *Labour in Irish History*, which was first published as a book in Dublin in 1910, having previously appeared in serial form in the Edinburgh *Socialist* and the New York *Harp* (*A New History*, 8:383). The cited passage appears on p. 137 of the 1919 New York printing.

96. Beckett, p. 136.

97. Ibid., pp. 174–7. A century later, concerned scholars in Northern Ireland note that the still-prevailing practice of hiring workers on the informal recommendation of friends and family of the employee "tend[s] to reproduce the existing patterns of job distributions both in terms of religion and geographical area." They urge adoption of the principle that "The company should not recruit new

employees on the recommendations of existing employees" (R. J. Cormack and R. D. Osborne, eds, *Religion, Education and Employment: Aspects of Equal Opportunity in Northern Ireland* [Belfast, 1983], pp. 160, 218). Although Catholics make up only one-third of the economically active population of Northern Ireland, they are the majority of the unemployed (ibid., p. 40).

98. Beckett et al., pp. 173–4. The authors were here referring to the 1901 census data. In 1974 one commentator, taking note of the prevalence of sectarian conflict in Belfast, offered the opinion that "Residential segregation may thus be viewed as a necessary, if unpleasant, way to preserve civic peace" (M. A. Busteed, *Northern Ireland*, in the series Problem Regions of Europe, General Editor D. I. Scargill [New York, 1974], p. 101). No thought was given apparently to whether the systematic segregation of Protestants in better housing might contribute to civic unrest.

99. A. C. Hepburn and B. Collins, "Industrial Society: The Structure of Belfast, 1901," in Roebuck, *Plantation to Partition*, p. 217. Was there not some anti-Catholic Moynihan type, as yet unknown to the present author, who felt obliged to address the social problems of Northern Ireland with a treatise on "The Breakdown of the Catholic Family Leading to Increased Dependency on the Dole," and "The Pathology of Matriarchy"? See Daniel Patrick Moynihan, *The Negro Family: The Case for National Action* (Washington: Office of Policy Planning and Research, United States Department of Labor, 1965), reprinted in Lee Rainwater and William L. Yancey, eds, *The Moynihan Report and the Politics of Controversy* (Cambridge, MIT Press, 1967).

100. Geoffrey Bell illustrates the point with selected official statistics, covering the period from 1871 to 1971, regarding wages and wage differentials, job classification, unemployment and housing conditions (*The Protestants of Ulster* [London: Pluto Press, 1976], pp. 18–30).

101. Ibid., pp. 18–19. Bell cites: *British Parliamentary Papers*: 1893, Vol. 83, Pt 2; 1897, Vol. 84; and 1899, Vol. 70.

102. South Africa is the extreme case, where the differential between "white" and African earnings is of such proportions as could not be supported even in the United States (see Robert H. Davies, *Capital, State and White Labour in South Africa, 1900–1960, An Historical Materialist Analysis of Class Formation and Class Relations* [New York: Humanities Press, 1979], p. 352). In the United States, historically, wages in the skilled trades (from which African-Americans have been excluded) have been lower in the South, where African-American workers have mostly lived and been most systematically kept down. Yet the wage differential between skilled workers and laborers has been greater there than in other regions of the country.

103. Beckett, pp. 147–9. See Henry Patterson, "Independent Orangeism and Class Conflict in Edwardian Belfast: A Reinterpretation," *Proceedings of the Royal Irish Academy*, Vol. 80c, pp. 1–27 (1980).

104. See Ian Budge and Cornelius O'Leary, *Belfast: Approach to Crisis, a Study of Belfast Politics, 1613–1970* (London, 1973), pp. 89–95; de Paor, *Divided Ulster*, pp. 49, 61; Hepburn and Collins, p. 211.

105. Great Britain, *Parliamentary Papers*, 1887, Vol. 18, "Report of the Belfast Riots Commission ...," p. 321. Historian A. T. Q. Stewart, however, states flatly that the cause of the riots was "the influx of a considerable Catholic and nationalist population into Belfast ... and the topography of their settlement ..." ("Mind of Protestant Ulster," p. 42).

106. See *British Parliamentary Papers*, 1887, Vol. 18, "Report of the Belfast Riots Commission. ..."

107. *British Parliamentary Papers*, 1887, Vol. 18, p. 267.

108. Hepburn and Collins, p. 211. The Catholic population of Belfast increased in absolute numbers by some 42,000 in this period. This, however, represented only a 1.7 percent annual increase, possibly no more than the natural increase, as contrasted with an approximate 5.1 percent annual increase during the first six decades of the century. (This calculation applies the percentage figures given by Hepburn and Collins to the population figures given by D. J. Cowan [*History of Belfast*] for 1861 and 1901, together with the figure for the year 1800, given at p. 131, above.) Historian Brenda Collins notes that rural Ulster Catholics in this period chose to emigrate rather than go to Belfast. "This attitude," she writes, "was scarcely surprising in view of the repeated demonstrations of anti-catholic feeling at intervals during the nineteenth century, which often resulted in rioting" ("The Edwardian City," in Beckett, p. 173).

109. Roy Jenkins, *Asquith, Portrait of a Man and an Era* (New York, 1964), pp. 315–23.

110. George Bernard Shaw, *John Bull's Other Island and Major Barbara* (New York, 1926), pp. xxi, xxv, xxx.

111. Keegan's last speech.

112. R. F. Rattray, *Bernard Shaw: A Chronicle* (London, 1951), pp. 158–9.

113. *Labour in Irish History*, concluding paragraph. "North East Ulster," *Forward* 2 August 1913; reprinted in P. Berresford Ellis, ed., *James Connolly; Selected Writings* (New York: Monthly Review Press, 1973), pp. 264, 265.

114. Liam de Paor, *Unfinished Business: Ireland Today and Tomorrow* (London: Hutchinson Radius, 1990), pp. 147, 150.

115. The histories of the other provinces, where social control required the sending of an army to do it, provide the negative confirmation.

6 Anglo-America: Ulster Writ Large

1. The French did not have to face this problem on the North American continent because they were primarily hunters and trappers in the fur trade, which did not involve any attempt to displace the Indian population, but rather led to the development of a cooperative relationship with the Indian tribes.

2. See Volume Two.

3. Jackson, report to Tennessee Governor Blount, 31 March 1814, *Correspondence of Andrew Jackson*, Carnegie Institution of Washington Publication 371, edited by John Spencer Bassett, 7 vols, 1926–1935; 1:492.

4. Jackson's parents were Ulster Scots who emigrated to America in 1765, it is said. Whether or to what extent this circumstance may hold some special significance, the version of "democracy" prevalent in the Protestant-majority Ulster Protestant Ascendancy seems to lose nothing in Jacksonian translation in America. "Jackson, race-obsessed authoritarian, believed upper-class control must end at the color line," writes a modern historian. "[He] aimed at institutionalizing classic herrenvolk democracy: both the complete equality of white men and the absolute superiority of whites over non-whites" (William W. Freehling, *Road to Disunion*, 2 vols; Vol. 1, *Secessionists at Bay, 1776–1854* [New York: Oxford University Press, 1990], p. 262).

5. Michael D. Green, *The Politics of Indian Removal: Creek Government and Society in Crisis* (Lincoln: Nebraska University Press, 1982), pp. 42–3; Angie Debo, *A History of the Indians of the United States* (Norman, Oklahoma, 1970), p. 112; Samuel Carter III, *Cherokee Sunset: A Narrative of Travail and Triumph, Persecution and Exile* (New York: Doubleday, 1976), pp. 2–3.

6. Thurman Wilkins, *Cherokee Tragedy: The Story of the Ridge Family and the Decimation of a People* (New York, 1970), p. 227. The report of the meeting was originally published in the New York *Commercial Advertiser* (date not given) and was reprinted in the Cherokee newspaper *Cherokee Phoenix*, 18 February 1832. See also Debo, p. 113.

7. See Carter, chapters 17, 18 and 19.

8. Wilkins, pp. 202–3.

9. Rather than risk the social instability of ruling without an intermediate stratum, the English ruling classes in the early sixteenth century deliberately chose to accept the economic cost of preserving a yeoman section of the laboring peasantry from expropriation to serve as a buffer social control group (see Volume Two). The option for racial oppression in Ireland and in continental Anglo-America, however, meant that the social control solution could not be achieved simply by the act of preserving a middle class.

10. Ulrich Bonnell Phillips, "The Slave Labor Problem in the Charleston [South Carolina] District," *Political Science Quarterly*, 22:416–39 (September 1907), 422.

11. See further details and discussion in Volume Two.

12. *Acts of Assembly Passed in the Island of Nevis, from 1664 to 1739, inclusive*, printed by Order of the Lords Commissioners of Trade and Plantations (1740), p. 37. *The Colonial Records of the State of Georgia*, edited by Alan D. Candler, 26 vols (Atlanta, 1904–16), 1:58.

13. See Volume Two.

14. For the Irish case, see pp. 81–2, 85–6. For further mention and discussion of cases in the Anglo-American colonies see Phillips, p. 423; Great Britain Public Record Office, *Calendar of*

State Papers, Colonial, 7:141 (14 December 1670); and *Colonial Records of the State of Georgia,* 1:58.

15. Letter of William Byrd, II, of Westover to Mr Ochs, "about 1735," *Virginia Magazine of History and Biography,* 9:22–6 (January 1902); 4 Hening 78 (1720).

16. Letter of William Byrd, II, of Westover to Lord Egmont, president of the trustees of Georgia, 12 July 1736, in *American Historical Review,* 1:88–90, Kenneth W. Porter, "Negroes on the Southern Frontier, 1670–1763," *Journal of Negro History,* 33:53–78 (1948); pp. 58–9, 60, 67, 76, 77–8. *Journal of the Earl of Egmont, Abstract of the Trustees Proceedings for Establishing the Colony of Georgia, 1732–1738,* edited by Robert G. McPherson (Atlanta, 1962), p. 83 (entry for 23 April 1735), approval of a law "prohibiting the use of negroes" in the Georgia colony.

17. *Congressional Globe,* 29th Congress, 2nd Session, Appendix, p. 317.

18. Benjamin Horace Hibbard, *A History of the Public Land Policies* (Madison: University of Wisconsin Press, 1965), pp. 300, 354.

19. Elizabeth Cady Stanton, Susan B. Anthony and Matilde Joselyn Gage, eds, *History of Woman Suffrage,* 2nd edition, 3 vols (Rochester, 1889), Vol. 1, pp. 69, 71, 74, 115–17.

20. Hibbard, p.354.

21. Kansas was admitted to the Union as a free state on 29 January 1861, sixty-six days before the outbreak of the Civil War.

22. *Frederick Douglass' Paper,* 15 September 1854. See Philip S. Foner, *The Life and Writings of Frederick Douglass* (New York, 1950), 4 vols; 2:311–15.

23. Benjamin Quarles, *The Negro in the Civil War* (Boston, 1953), p. xii. The late Isabella Black generously allowed me to draw upon her scrupulously researched manuscript, as yet not accepted for publication, which she titled "Home-made Yankees, a South-side View of the War for the Union, 1860–1877." The data on the number of European-Americans from the slaveholding states who enlisted in the Union armies are summarized in that work at pp. 128–9.

24. South Carolina, Constitutional Convention, 1868: *Proceedings of the Constitutional Convention* ... (Charleston, 1868), pp. 105–7 (cited by Black, pp. 240–41). *Official Proceedings of the Convention for Framing a Constitution for the State of Louisiana* (New Orleans, 1867–68), pp. 110, 266–7, 306 (cited by Roger W. Shugg, *Origins of Class Struggle in Louisiana: A Social History of White Farmers and Laborers during Slavery and After, 1840–1875* [Baton Rouge: Louisiana State Press, 1966], p. 243 n. 40). Clara M. Thompson, *Reconstruction in Georgia, Economic, Social, Political, 1805–72* (New York, 1915), p. 204. B. F. Perry, who had served as Provisional Governor of South Carolina during the brief period of Presidential Reconstruction, expressed the fear that the poor whites of that state would "unite with the Negro in parceling out the lands of the State" (letter to the Columbia [SC] Phoenix, reprinted in the Charleston *Courier,* 4 May 1967; quoted in Paul Lewinson, *Race, Class and Party: A History of Negro Suffrage and White Politics in the South* [New York: Russell and Russell, 1924; reissued, 1969], p. 39).

25. Charles Sumner to John Bright, 13 March 1869, in Edward L. Pierce, ed., *Memoir and Letters of Charles Sumner,* 4 vols (Boston, 1893), 4:229.

26. Stevens made this proposal in a speech in his home town, Lancaster, Pennsylvania, on 7 September 1865. It was published in the New York Herald Supplement, 13 December 1865 (cited by Ralph Korngold, *Thaddeus Stevens, a Being Darkly Wise and Rudely Great* [New York, 1955], pp. 282–3).

27. George W. Julian, *Political Recollections, 1840–1872* (Chicago, 1884), p. 240.

28. Paul Wallace Gates, "Federal Land Policy in the South," *Journal of Southern History,* 6:303–30 (August, 1940), pp. 309–10.

29. Ibid.

30. Charles H. Wesley, Negro *Labor in the United States, 1850–1925, a Study in American Economic History* (New York, 1927), p. 138. Wesley cites Report of Hon. T. D. Eliot to the House of Representatives, 10 March 1868 (House Report, No. 121, 41st Congress, 1st Session, p. 486).

31. Gates, p. 310.

32. "In 1859 infants were valued at from $7 to $10 a pound" (Lewis C. Gray, *History of Agriculture in the Southern United States to 1860* [Washington, 1932; Peter Smith reprint, 1958], 2 vols; 2:664).

33. *De Bow's Review,* 4:587–8 (December 1867) (cited in Shugg, p. 243). Lewinson, p. 39 n.

34. Robert William Fogel, *Without Consent or Contract: The Rise and Fall of American Slavery* (New York: W. W. Norton, 1989), pp. 307–10. John Francis Maguire, *The Irish in America*

(London, 1868; Arno Press reprint, 1969), Chapter XI. Jurgen Kuczynski, *A Short History of Labor Conditions under Industrial Capitalism*, 4 vols (in 6); Vol. 2, *The United States of America, 1789 to the Present Day* (New York, 1943), p. 57. John B. MacMaster, *History of the People of the United States from the Revolution to the Civil War*, selected and edited by Louis B. Filler (New York: Farrar, Strauss, 1964), pp. 211, 214. Matthew Carey, *The Public Charities of Philadelphia* (cited by Gustavas Myers, *History of the Great American Fortunes* [New York, 1907; 1937], p. 81). Matthew Carey, *Appeal to the Wealthy of the Land* (3rd edition), pp. 3–5, 33 (cited in Arthur Schlesinger Jr, *The Age of Jackson* [Boston, 1945], pp. 132–3). Matthew Carey, *Letters on the Condition of the Poor* (2nd edition), pp. 16–17 (cited by Schlesinger, pp. 132–3).

35. Liam de Paor, *Divided Ulster*, p. 49.

36. Clarence H. Danhof, "Farm-making Costs and the 'Safety-valve,' 1850–1860," *Journal of Political Economy*, Vol. 49 (1941), pp. 317–59, reprinted in Vernon C. Carstensen, ed., *The Public Lands, Studies on the History of the Public Domain* (Madison, 1968), pp. 253–96; see particularly pp. 269–70.

37. Willie Lee Rose, *Rehearsal for Reconstruction: The Port Royal Experiment* (New York: Vintage Books, 1967), p. 331.

38. Address of the Colored People's Convention of the State of South Carolina held in Charleston, 20–25 November 1865, to the people of South Carolina, *Congressional Globe*, 41st Congress, Session 2, *Senate Miscellaneous Documents*, No. 8.

39. John Hope Franklin, *Reconstruction: After the Civil War* (Chicago, 1961), p. 114.

40. Address of the Colored Convention to the People of Alabama, published in the *Daily State Sentinel*, 21 May 1867; in James S. Allen, *Reconstruction, Battle for Democracy* (New York, 1937), p. 240.

41. "To the honorable the Senate and House of Representatives of the United States of America," 6 December 1869 (Senate Miscellaneous Document No. 8, 41st Congress, 2nd Session). The convention was attended by more than two hundred elected representatives of African-American workers in twenty-three states (Wesley, *Negro Labor in the United States*, pp. 179–80).

42. John R. Commons and Associates, *Documentary History of American Industrial Society*, 10 vols (1910), 9:160–64. The convention was held in Baltimore in August 1866.

43. Ibid., pp. 190–91.

44. Address delivered at Sunbury, Pennsylvania, 16 September 1868 (in *The Life, Speeches, Labors and Essays of William H. Sylvis*, edited by James C. Sylvis [1872; 1968], pp. 231–49, 235–6).

45. Letter to the editor of the Philadelphia *Evening Advocate*, 17 January 1868 (ibid., p. 313).

46. "To Abraham Lincoln, President of the United States of America," *Documents of the First International*, 4 vols (Moscow, 1964); 1:53. The document was approved at the meeting of the Council of the Association on 29 November 1864; it was published in the *Beehive* newspaper, 7 January 1865.

47. *Congressional Globe*, 38th Congress, 2nd Session, p. 286 (16 January 1865). Kelley was perhaps the most explicit of all governmental figures in his advocacy of complete racial equality and in his scorn for white supremacism. He liked to advert (as he did in the speech cited here) to the imposition of white male privileges against Negro women, in denunciation of the white racist scare words concerning "miscegenation." In a later speech, he championed voting rights of African-American "laboring people and republican soldiers," among whom were "descendants of the kings of Dahomey and of American Congressmen, Senators, Presidents, and Cabinet ministers" (*Congressional Globe*, 39th Congress, 1st Session, p. 183 [10 January 1866]). It was only much later in his career that Congressman Kelley was tagged with the unexpungeable soubriquet "Pig Iron Kelley," as a result of his strong advocacy of tariff protection for American manufacturers. Those interested in learning about Kelley as a foe of white supremacism would do well to start with Ira V. Brown, "William D. Kelley and Radical Reconstruction," *Pennsylvania Magazine of History and Biography*, 85:316–29 (July 1961).

48. Stanley P. Hirschson, *Farewell to the Bloody Shirt: Northern Republicans and the Southern Negro, 1877–1893* (Bloomington, 1962), p. 21.

49. Of course, the bourgeoisie was not a monolith: the defeat of Reconstruction did not silence all bourgeois advocates of Negro rights; the subject of Negro rights became intermixed with factional and partisan concerns; the reversion to rule by the Democratic Party in the South, aided

by open terrorism against African-Americans, was mediated by proto-populist Southern "Independents" and their Northern counterpart, the Mugwumps.

But the will of the ruling class as a whole was made unmistakable by such signal events as the following: (1) the repeal of the Southern Homestead Act in 1876, it having been vitiated from the start by a lack of financial assistance to the freedmen; (2) the Hayes–Tilden deal of 1877 when, after negotiations at the highest level of the government, Hayes (who had received 250,000 fewer votes than Tilden [the Democrat]) was allowed to be president for one term in return for (a) agreeing to withdraw federal troops from the South (leaving the African-Americans there completely at the mercy of organized white terrorism), (b) extending substantial financial aid (such as was never granted to aid the freedmen to realize on the promise of "forty acres and a mule") to the overthrowers of Reconstruction to finance "internal improvements," (c) promising of public and private aid for the construction of a railroad from the South to the Pacific, and (d) appointing a Southern Democrat as Postmaster-General, dispenser of many patronage jobs and contracts; (3) a series of Supreme Court decisions rendered between 1873 and 1883, striking down constitutional and statute protections of civil rights (for a convenient notation on these decisions see Robert Cruden, *The Negro in Reconstruction* [Englewood Cliffs, 1969] pp. 140–41.)

50. Charles Nordhoff, *The Cotton States in the Spring and Summer of 1875* (New York, 1876), p. 19.

51. John Pool, *Address to the People of North Carolina* (Raleigh, 1867), p. 4, cited in Black, "Home-made Yankees," pp. 186–7. Black points out that it was not uncommon for Southern Republicans to vote for Negro suffrage for this reason, while at the same time refusing to support the right of Negroes to testify in court or to serve on juries.

52. In 1876 President Grant submitted to Congress a list of four thousand cases of murder, maiming and whipping committed by white terrorists since 1868. William Murrell, an African-American former member of the Louisiana state legislature, testified that 2,115 Negroes had been killed in the course of the white-supremacist repression of the Reconstruction regime in Louisiana between 1866 and 1875 (John G. Van Deusen, "The Exodus of 1879," *Journal of Negro History*, Vol. 21, No. 2 [April 1936], pp. 112–13).

53. For principal primary sources, see the following Congressional reports: 42nd Congress, 2nd Session (1871–72), *Testimony Taken by the Joint Committee to Enquire into the Condition of Affairs in the Late Insurrectionary States*, Vol. 2 (13 parts); 43rd Congress, 2nd Session (1874–75), *House Reports 101; 261 (Testimony) Condition of Affairs in the South (Louisiana)*; and, *Testimony 262 (Alabama)*; 44th Congress, 1st Session (1875–76), *Senate Report 527 (Mississippi)*; 44th Congress, 2nd Session (1876–77), *House Miscellaneous Document 31: Recent Election in South Carolina*; 44th Congress, 2nd Session, *Senate Miscellaneous Document 48 (South Carolina)*, 3 vols.

54. "Capitalists up to this time have been afraid to go to the South, owing to the disturbed condition of affairs politically and this very race question. A man does not want to carry his money down there and put it in a country that might be involved in riots or disturbances." (From the testimony of John Caldwell Calhoun, 13 September 1883. See Senate Committee on Education and Labor Committee *Report upon the Relations between Labor and Capital*, 5 vols, [Washington, 1885], 2:169.)

55. The principal primary source for information about the Negro Exodus of 1879 is the three-part Senate Report 693, 46th Congress, 2nd Session (1879–80), *Report and Testimony of the Select Committee of the US Senate to Investigate the Causes of the Removal of the Negroes from the Southern States to the Northern States*, henceforth referred to as *Exodus Hearings*. The chief secondary source is Nell Irvin Painter, *Exodusters: Black Migration to Kansas after Reconstruction* (New York, 1977). Especially valuable for putting the Exodus in a national political context is Hirshson, *Farewell to the Bloody Shirt*. See also Van Deusen.

56. See Douglass, "Address before the Convention of the American Social Science Association" (Saratoga Springs, New York, 12 September 1879). The address is reprinted in Foner, *Life and Writings of Frederick Douglass*, 4:324–42.

57. Painter, pp. 75, 109. Professor Painter, who presents the most exhaustive study of the Exodus, stresses that black migration from the Southern and border states to Kansas totaled much more than the number who migrated there in the "Kansas Fever Exodus of 1879." But the Exodus of 1879, concentrated in the period of a few months, was "the most remarkable migration in the

United States after the Civil War" (pp. 147, 184).

58. Ibid., p. 87. Van Deusen, pp. 119–20.

59. "I asked my wife did she know the ground she stands on. She said, 'No.' I said it is free ground; and she cried like a child for joy" (John Solomon Lewis, Leavenworth, Kansas, cited in Painter, p. 4).

60. The reference to John Brown is in Painter, p. 159. Painter seems to have made the most particular investigation of the numbers: see pp. 146–7, 158, 184, 184 n. 1, 185, 201. Compare Hirshson, p. 282; Van Deusen, p. 122.

61. Quoted in Hirshson, p. 70, from the *Journal of Commerce*.

62. For particulars regarding these supportive efforts, see Hirshson, pp. 64–5, 68; and Van Deusen, pp. 125–7.

63. Painter, p. 152.

64. Painter, pp. 200–201. Van Deusen, pp. 123–4.

65. Bristow to John Murray Forbes, New York, 1 October 1879 (Forbes Papers, Massachusetts Historical Society, quoted by Hirshson, p. 71). Bristow served for two years as Secretary of the Treasury in President Grant's first administration.

66. "I decided some time ago that if the GOM [Grand Old Man, Prime Minister William Gladstone] went for Home Rule, the Orange card would be the one to play" (letter of the Conservative leader Randolph Churchill to the Irish Lord Chief Justice Fitzgibbon, February 1885 [cited in Winston Spencer Churchill, *Lord Randolph Churchill*, 2 vols (New York, 1906), 2:59]). This resolve of Churchill *père* is, of course, only too familiar to students of Irish history.

67. Painter, p. 3; Hirshson, pp. 66–7.

68. Painter, pp. 155, 196, 197.

69. Hirshson, pp. 68–71.

70. Hirshson, pp. 68–9.

71. Painter, pp. 185–6, 197–200.

72. Van Deusen, p. 125. Among those who were diverted from Kansas was a group that ended up in Greencastle, Indiana. A white mob drove them from the town and burned the house they had lived in (testimony of the Sheriff of Putnam County, Indiana, M. T. Lewman, *Exodus Hearings*, 1:176–8).

73. Broadus Mitchell, *The Rise of the Cotton Mills in the South*, Johns Hopkins University Studies in Historical and Political Science, xxxix, No. 2 (Baltimore, 1921; Peter Smith reprint, 1966), p. 178.

74. US Department of Commerce, Bureau of the Census, *Statistics of the Population at the Tenth Census* (Washington, DC, 1883).

75. Hirshson, pp. 70–71.

76. Hirshson, p. 3.

77. For instances of terroristic imposition of white male privilege, see the testimonies of Henry Adams and Benjamin Singleton, in Part II, pp. 177–8, and Part III, pp. 382–3, respectively, of Senate Report 693, 46th Congress, 2nd session.

78. US Senate Education and Labor Committee, *Report upon the Relations Between Labor and Capital*, 2:157–88, henceforth referred to as the "Calhoun testimony."

79. Calhoun testimony, 2:157. In March 1869 in South Carolina, where black voters outnumbered white voters by 30,000, a State Land Commission was established to purchase land and sell it in parcels of from 25 to 100 acres to freedmen and poor whites. In Arkansas, African-Americans constituted only about 25 percent of the population; and in 1869 no Republican, not even the governor, felt safe from assassination by white-supremacists (Richard Nelson Current, *Those Terrible Carpetbaggers* [New York, 1988], pp. 140, 142, 222–3).

80. Calhoun testimony, pp. 178–9. "Once, I suppose there were 150 negroes, perhaps more, on the bank of the [Mississippi] river. . . . We notified all the boats coming up the river not to land at this point" (p. 179).

81. Calhoun testimony, p. 169.

82. Ibid., p. 160.

83. Commons, *Documentary History of American Industrial Society*, 9:158–9.

84. This observation occurs in one of a series of articles by Sorge published in the German Social Democratic organ *Neue Zeit* during the years 1890–96, under the general title of *Die Arbeiterbewegung in den Vereinigten Staaten*. The quotation here is from *Neue Zeit*, 2:243 (1891–92).

85. Ibid., 2:244.

86. See *Socialist Labor Party of America Records*, microfilm edition, State Historical Society of Wisconsin, 1970.

87. The great value of the late Isabella Black's work "Home-made Yankees" is its collection of the stories of these whites who risked their lives, fortunes and sacred honor to join hands with the African-Americans in the Reconstruction cause. Black's work is the product of years of exhaustive research, which took her to state archives throughout the South. It is enriched by reference to secondary works, mainly biographical, long practically forgotten. In just one chapter, Chapter Seven, "The Year of Jubilo," this reader encountered some degree of record of the actions and points of view of some forty-five such individuals, representing every one of the states that had been in rebellion.

88. Freehling, *Secessionists at Bay*, pp. 103, 308–36.

89. Charles H. Wesley, *Negro Labor in the United States*, pp. 196–7; Shugg, *Class Struggle in Louisiana*, pp. 254–60.

"... even if it forced them to retire like the Indians to unwanted land," said the *Opelousas Courier* of Louisiana, 21 August 1869 (cited in Shugg, p. 254). "The desire to weaken the negro by increasing the white population, was one of the considerations in seeking mill operatives [from] outside the South" (Mitchell, *Rise of the Cotton Mills*, p. 200).

90. Shugg, p. 255. The pay in California was said to be ninety cents to $1.50 per day; in the South they would get only twenty dollars a month (Wesley, p. 197). Calhoun, in the testimony cited above, said wages for field hands in his section were ten to twenty dollars a month, or seventy-five cents to one dollar by the day.

91. Mobile *Register*, 19 July 1873. Cited in Allen Johnston Going, *Bourbon Democracy in Alabama, 1874–1898* (Tuscaloosa, 1951), p. 122.

92. The South Carolina Immigration Office wanted "to get rid of the negro and bring in whites to take his place." The most famous effort was made in 1906, but, as Mitchell puts it, "the newcomers were not so well content as to form a satisfied nucleus which would automatically attract relatives in future years" (*Rise of the Cotton Mills*, pp. 206–7, nn. 91, 92).

93. Shugg, pp. 255–61.

94. Ibid., pp. 256–8.

95. Ibid., p. 258, citing census reports.

96. Fred A. Shannon, "The Homestead Act and the Labor Surplus," in Carstensen, *The Public Lands*, p. 298.

97. John D. Hicks, *The Populist Revolt: A History of the Farmers' Alliance and the People's Party* (University of Nebraska Press, 1961), pp. 23–4.

98. Ibid., pp. 82–5.

99. Shannon, p. 307.

100. Ibid., pp. 307–8.

101. Kenneth M. Stampp, *The Peculiar Institution: Slavery in the Ante-bellum South* (New York, 1956), p. 30.

102. W. J. Cash, *The Mind of the South* (New York, 1941), p. 23.

103. Stampp, p. 29.

104. Shugg, pp. 33, 85, 86, 92, 95.

105. Broadus Mitchell and George Sinclair Mitchell, *The Industrial Revolution in the South* (Baltimore, 1930), pp. 241, 242.

106. *Richmond Enquirer*, 4 May 1832.

107. Mitchell and Mitchell, p. 244 (paraphrasing Walter Hines Page, of North Carolina, editor and US diplomat). A small minority of the poor whites were known to favor abolition of slavery; they ranged in opinion from violent white-supremacism to thoroughgoing and militant equalitarianism. Hinton Rowan Helper's opposition to slavery was coextensive with his hatred of the Negro, and he expressed this point of view as author of a number of books, including *The Negroes in Negroland; the Negroes in America; and Negroes Generally. Also the Several Races of White Men, Considered as the Involuntary and Predestined Supplanters of the Black Race* (New York, 1868). The equalitarian abolitionists were outstandingly represented by John Fairfield of Virginia, a "conductor" on the Underground Railroad, the system established to aid escaping slaves, for more than twenty years, who died while taking part in a slave insurrection in 1861 in Tennessee (Fernando G. Cartland, *Southern Heroes: The Friends in War-time* [Cambridge, Massachusetts,

1895], p. 86, cited in Black, "Home-made Yankees," p. 11).

108. James M. McPherson, *Battle Cry of Freedom: The Civil War Era* (New York, 1988), pp. 306–7 n. 41, 854.

109. Ben F. Lemert, *The Cotton Textile Industry of the Southern Appalachian Piedmont* (Chapel Hill, 1933), p. 27.

110. Cash, pp. 149–52, 160–61; Mitchell, *Rise of the Cotton Mills*, pp. 174–6.

111. Cash, pp. 175, 176.

112. Ibid., pp. 176–7.

113. The still standard monograph on the Cotton Mill Campaign is Broadus Mitchell, *The Rise of the Cotton Mills in the South*, Johns Hopkins University Studies in Historical and Political Science, xxxix, No. 2 (Baltimore, 1921; Peter Smith reprint, 1966). See also: Broadus Mitchell and George Sinclair Mitchell, *The Industrial Revolution in the South* (Baltimore, 1930); August Kohn, *The Cotton Mills of the South*, letters written to the Charleston *News and Courier*, October December 1907; *United States Industrial Commission on the Relations and Conditions of Capital and Labor Employed in Manufactures and General Business, Reports*, (Washington, DC, 1901) Vol. xiv, "Review of the Evidence", p. lii. See also the treatments of the subject by: W. J. Cash, *The Mind of the South* (New York, 1941); C. Vann Woodward, *Origins of the New South, 1877–1913* (Baton Rouge, 1952); and William M. Brewer, "Poor Whites and Negroes in the South Since the Civil War," *Journal of Negro History*, 15:26–37 (January 1930).

114. Mitchell and Mitchell, p. 148.

115. Cash, p. 195.

116. Mitchell, p. 232, citing US Census of Manufactures, 1900. The rate of increase was rising before 1880; half the increase between 1840 and 1880 occurred in the final decade.

117. Mitchell, pp. 25, 210, 211, 212 n. 100, 213.

118. Ibid., p. 211.

119. Ibid., p. 211 n. 100.

120. Ibid.

121. Ibid., p. 213.

122. Ibid., p. 214.

123. Kohn, pp. 27–8.

124. Mitchell, p. 174.

125. Testimony of Lewis W. Parker at hearings held by the House of Representatives Judiciary Committee, 29 April 1902, pp. 11f. Cited in Mitchell, pp. 136–7.

126. Ibid. To say that the cotton mill investors were motivated by political considerations, the shoring up of white supremacism, is not to imply that by employing poor whites they were acting altruistically, a theme given much currency by Mitchell and his authorities. Mitchell himself cites the fact that "upon the whole, the return upon investment in Southern cotton mills has exceeded that upon factories in the North" (*Rise of the Cotton Mills*, p. 152 n. 214, citing *US Census of Manufactures, 1990*, "Cotton Manufacture," by Edward Stanwood, pp. 28–9; Mitchell provides many instances at pp. 261–5). Vann Woodward objects to the emphasis on the altruism of the cotton mill entrepreneurs (*Origins of the New South*, p. 133).

127. D. A. Tompkins, "Cotton Mill, Commercial Features," in *The South in the Building of the Nation*, 2:109–10. Cited in Mitchell, pp. 27–8 n. 40.

128. Mitchell, p. 134 n.162.

129. *Reports of the US Industrial Commission (1901)*, Vol. XIV, *Review of the Evidence*, p. LII (52). Just as the British Protestant investors in the Industrial Revolution in Belfast followed the practice of "keeping jobs for one's own co-religionists" (J. C. Beckett, *Belfast – the Making of the City* [New York, 1966], p. 136) the Cotton Mill Campaigners similarly shored up the poor whites' racial privileges by excluding Negroes from jobs as mill operatives.

130. Cash, p. 179.

131. George Will, New York *Daily News*, 19 December 1989.

132. William Hayes Simpson, *Some Aspects of America's Textile Industry* (Columbia, South Carolina, 1966), pp. 8–12.

133. Mitchell, p. 224.

134. Woodward, pp. 224–5.

135. Mitchell and Mitchell, p. 136.

136. Ibid., p. 143. After Mrs Rosa Parks had held her place on the Montgomery bus, after the

passage of the Civil Rights Act of 1964, with its provisions concerning government contracts, and about the time James Baldwin was asking, "Tell Me How Long the Train's Been Gone?," Mrs Mamie Chance was hired as an operative, and James Douglas got a job as a fork-lift operator at the Erwin Mills in North Carolina. They were parts of a change that raised the proportion of African-Americans among textile mill production workers from 3.3 per cent in 1960 to 11.6 percent by 1969. David Griffin, Euro-American President of the Textile Workers Local 250, points out the importance of facing the issue of white supremacy: "Whites hate to organize. They want to 'get along' with management. But Negroes *know* it's not on *their* side. They've known that sort of thing way back to slavery times" (Reese Cleghorn, "The Mill: A Giant Step for the Southern Negro," *New York Times Magazine*, 9 November 1969). Perhaps President Griffin also mentioned why – the white-skin privilege – but if so, the author did not report it.

137. "The South after the war presented the greatest opportunity for a real national labor movement which the nation ever saw or is likely to see for many decades" (W. E. B. DuBois, *Black Reconstruction. An Essay toward a History of the Part which Black Folk Played in the Attempt to Reconstruct Democracy in America, 1860–1880* [New York, 1935], p. 353).

7 The Sea-change

1. This famous phrase is credited to a speech made by Senator William H. Seward of New York in 1858: "An irrepressible conflict between opposing and enduring forces . . ."

2. The term adopted was "persons bound to service" (Article I, Section 9.1). James Madison opposed the use of "slave" and "slavery" because he "thought it wrong to admit in the Constitution the idea that there could be property in men" (*The Debates in the Federal Convention of 1787 which Framed the Constitution of the United States of America, reported by James Madison, a Delegate from the State of Virginia*, 2 vols, edited by Gaillard Hunt and James Brown Scott [1908, Prometheus Books reprint], 2:469).

3. "As population increases poor laborers will be so plenty as to render slaves useless," said Oliver Ellsworth of Connecticut. Charles Pinkney of South Carolina, however, still secured the postponement of the importation of African bond-laborers until 1808 (ibid., pp. 2:444, 2:467).

4. Jeannette Mirsky and Allan Nevins, *The World of Eli Whitney* (New York, 1952), p. 66; Roger Burlingame, *Machines That Built America* (New York, 1953), pp. 44–6.

5. Lewis C. Gray, *History of Agriculture in the Southern United States to 1860*, 2 vols (Washington, 1932; 1956), 2:1026.

6. Robert William Fogel and Stanley L. Engerman, *Time on the Cross: The Economics of Negro Slavery* (Boston, 1974), p. 61.

7. Ibid., pp. 68–70; Robert William Fogel, *Without Consent or Contract: The Rise and Fall of American Slavery* (New York, 1989), p. 64.

8. Thomas Prentice Kettell, *Southern Wealth and Northern Profits* (New York, 1860; Alabama, 1965), pp. 159–60. For all the partisanship of Kettell's point of view, the passages quoted here are confirmed by Fogel (p. 71). Kettell's work was intended as a riposte to Hinton Rowan Helper's *The Impending Crisis of the South*, first published three years earlier, aimed at contrasting the sluggish Southern economy with that of the bustling free-labor North (Hinton Rowan Helper, *The Impending Crisis of the South* [New York, 1857; 1963]).

9. Fogel and Engerman, p. 70.

10. Kettel gives an index of the increase in labor productivity that, despite its obvious inexactitude, indicates a steady rise in the intensity of plantation labor. There were 9 African-American bond-laborers for every 10 bales of cotton produced in 1860, whereas in 1800 the ratio was 240 for every 10 bales (*Southern Wealth and Northern Profits*, p. 159). Lewis Gray seems to suggest that the overall increase in cotton productivity was largely due to the extension of cultivation to new lands in the Lower South, along with some minor improvements in production technique and fertilization (Gray, 2:708–10). The undisputed relative scarcity of bond-labor and the extraordinary efforts made to scrape up supplementary labor for the cottonfields from other spheres of activity leaves no room for doubt that there was an intensification of exploitation of plantation labor.

11. Fogel and Engerman offer a quantification of this super-exploitation of plantation bond-labor, under the heading of "non-pecuniary disadvantages" (pp. 235–45).

12. See Eric Williams, *Capitalism and Slavery* (Chapel Hill, 1944), pp. 200–207.

13. *The Pro-slavery argument, as maintained by the most distinguished writers of the Southern States* (Philadelphia, 1852; 1968), pp. 124, 127.

14. See William W. Freehling's analytical summary of the geography of the intramural politi-cal divergencies among the politicians of the slave states (William W. Freehling, *The Road to Disunion*, 2 vols (Vol. II forthcoming), Vol. I, *Secessionists at Bay, 1776–1854* (New York, 1990), pp. 17–18.

15. "I hold that … the relation now existing in the slaveholding States between the two [i.e., the Euro-Americans and the African-Americans], is, instead of an evil, a good-a positive good" (John C. Calhoun, speech in the United States Senate, 6 February 1837 [*Register of Debates*, 24th Cong., 2nd sess., cols 2184–8]). "It is impossible to place labor and capital in harmonious or friendly relations, except by the means of slavery, which identifies their interests" (George Fitzhugh, *Cannibals All! or Slaves Without Masters* [1857], in Harvey Wish, ed., *Ante-bellum Writings of George Fitzhugh and Hinton Rowan Helper on Slavery* [New York, 1960], p. 125). "Our new Government['s] … foundations are laid, its cornerstone rests, upon the great truth, that the negro is not equal to the white man; that slavery – subordination to the superior race – his natural and normal condition…. This, our new Government, is the first in the history of the world based upon this great physical, philosophical, and moral truth" (Alexander H. Stephens, Vice-President of the slaveholder Confederacy, speaking at Savannah, Georgia, 21 March 1861, quoted in Michael P. Johnson, *Toward a Patriarchal Republic: The Secession of Georgia* [Baton Rouge, 1977], p. 135).

16. See Henry Clay to Richard Pindell, 17 February 1849, in *Candidate, Compromiser, Elder Statesman, January 1, 1844 June 29, 1852*, edited by Melba Porter Hay and Carol Reardon (Lexington, Kentucky, 1991), Vol. 10 of *The Papers of Henry Clay*, 10:574–81. For the fullest statement made by Clay on the subject of abolition and "colonization," see his speech in the Senate on 7 February 1839 (*Works of Henry Clay*, edited by Calvin Colton, 6 vols [New York, 1897], 6:140–59).

17. The reader will notice that of all United States cities only New York is given particular attention here. By way of apology, I offer the following considerations: New York was the largest city, and the main center of finance and commerce; New York was the most important single city in the North politically, because of its size and because of its distinction as perfecter of machine politics, in service to the slaveholders through the Tammany Hall-National Democrat axis; New York City contained the largest concentration of Irish-Americans and, for various reasons, as a whole they served as the most important political base of the Democratic Party, the main national organization of the slaveholders.

18. Richard B. Morris, ed., *Encyclopedia of American History*, 6th edn (New York, 1982), p. 488.

19. Gray, 2:931.

20. Philip S. Foner, *Business and Slavery: The New York Merchants and the Irrepressible Conflict* (Chapel Hill, 1941), pp. 1–5.

21. The volume of Southern imports was insufficient to make economical use of the ships returning from delivering bulky cotton cargoes to England. It was cheaper to pay the Northern middleman whose import volume sufficed to fill the returning ships.

22. Amy Bridges, *A City in the Republic: Antebellum New York and the Origins of Machine Politics* (New York, 1984), p. 44.

23. Kettell, p. 127. In tabulating the North-South balance of trade, included in this total are customs duties entering the Northern economy, professional services, and tourism, totaling about $100,000,000. Kettell, a former editor of the Jacksonian *Democratic Review* and a devout believer in chattel bondage, was seeking to counter the effect of Hinton Rowan Helper's *The Impending Crisis of the South*, which argued a contrast between an economically sluggish Southern economy and the productive vigor of the free-labor North.

24. Brother Basil Leo Lee, *Discontent in New York City, 1861–1865* (Washington, DC, 1943), pp. 131–5.

25. Message of Mayor Fernando Wood, Annual Report to the Common Council, 7 January 1861, in *Proceedings of the Board of Aldermen of the City of New York*, Vol. 81 (New York, 1861), pp. 12, 24–6.

26. Iver Bernstein, *The New York City Draft Riots: Their Significance for American Society and Politics in the Age of the Civil War* (New York, 1990), p. 143.

27. Ibid.

28. "[N]o man acquainted with the history of the country can deny, that the general lead in the politics of the country, for three-fourths of the period that has elapsed since the adoption of the Constitution, has been a southern lead," said Daniel Webster (*Congressional Globe*, 31st Cong., 1st sess. [7 March 1850], p. 478). "The South, so far from having become an abject minority ... has controlled the Government ... for 60 out of the 72 [years] of our national existence" (Alexander H. Stephens, shortly before his election to the post of Vice-President of the Confederate [slave] States of America; cited by Rudloph von Abele, *Alexander H. Stephens: A Biography* [New York, 1971], p. 186).

29. *Congressional Globe*, 29th Cong., 2nd sess., Appendix (8 February 1847), p. 316. This is part of a direct quotation from one of Randolph's speeches against the Missouri Compromise. It was cited by David Wilmot at the time of the controversy over the inclusion or exclusion of slavery from California, where under the Mexican government slavery had been abolished a quarter of a century earlier.

30. See Theodore William Allen, *Class Struggle and the Origin of Racial Slavery, the Invention of the White Race*, a pamphlet (Hoboken, 1975; originally published, with abridgement of footnotes, in *Radical America*, 9:40–63 [May–June 1975]. See Volume Two of the present work for a full treatment of the subject.

31. See also William J. Grayson, "The Hireling and the Slave," in *The Hireling and the Slave, Chicora, and Other Poems* (Charleston, 1856).

32. *Congressional Globe*, 35th Cong., 1st sess., Appendix, pp. 68–71 (4 March 1858).

33. George Fitzhugh, *Sociology for the South, or The Failure of Free Society* (1854; 1960 reprint).

34. Ibid., p. 263.

35. The translation was always cleansed, however, of the less sympathetic second half of the generalizations voiced by Calhoun, Hammond, et al. It would obviously have been inappropriate for involving the laboring-class Americans on the side of the slaveholders to have them dwell on the political economy preached by Calhoun, namely that "the non-producing classes" would always appropriate the larger share of the social product whether produced by bond labor or wage labor: as it was in the beginning, was then, and ever should be (*Register of Debates*, 24th Cong., 2nd sess., cols 2184–8; 2186 [6 February 1837]). Discretion likewise would omit Hammond's thesis that wage labor and bond labor were merely variations in form of the "mudsills of society," necessary to "all social systems ... to do the menial duties, to perform the drudgery of life" (Hammond, *Congressional Globe*, 35th Cong., 1st sess., Appendix, p. 77 [4 May 1858]). Virginia lawmaker Benjamin Watkins Leigh in the same vein declared that while a "racial" distinction had to be observed, nevertheless, however "white" they might be, the "peasantry," dependent on "their daily labor for their subsistence," could never be admitted into "political affairs" (*Proceedings of the Virginia State Convention of 1829–1830* [Richmond, 1830], p. 158, cited by Freehling, p. 173).

36. "[T]he progress of machinery is so fast diminishing the profits of hand-labor as to render ... escape ... necessary to our existence." From an editorial addressed to Feargus O'Connor, Irish leader in the Irish liberation struggle and in the British Chartist movement, who had urged Americans to support the abolition cause. The letter was signed by "A Member of the NY Society for the Abolition of ALL Slavery" (*Working Man's Advocate*, 22 June 1844).

37. Ibid. See also Arthur M. Schlesinger Jr, *The Age of Jackson* (Boston, 1945), pp. 425–6.

38. Open letter from George Henry Evans to Gerrit Smith, a wealthy abolitionist (*Working Man's Advocate*, 6 July 1844; emphasis in original).

39. Ibid. For other examples of this tendency see Herman Schlueter, *Lincoln, Labor and Slavery* (New York, 1913), pp. 60–67, 72–3. Schlueter has the dubious distinction of founding the "Marxist" white-apologist school of American labor historiography. Schlueter interprets the growing "white labor" hostility toward abolitionism as a manifestation of "awakening class

consciousness" on the part of the increasingly "organized" European-American workers (pp. 46–7).

40. Open letter from George Henry Evans to Gerrit Smith, *Working Man's Advocate*, 6 July 1844.

41. Lee, *Discontent in New York City, 1861–1865*, pp. 143–4. Lee cites the president of the Painters Union, who scorned abolitionism because "the slaves in the South, where he had lived, were fed and clothed better than many thousands of white mechanics in New York City."

42. Henry Clay to Richard Pindell, 17 February 1849, in *Papers of Henry Clay*; 10:580.

43. Letter to Jacob Gibson, 25 July 1842, in *Works of Henry Clay*, 4:464.

44. Henry Clay to Calvin Colton, 2 September 1843, in *Works of Henry Clay*, 4:476–7.

45. Florence E. Gibson, *The Attitude of the New York Irish Toward State and National Affairs, 1848–1892* (New York, 1951), pp. 116–17. Two years after the Emancipation Proclamation, a Fourth of July "Address to the Workingmen of the United States," issued by the Workingmen's United Political Association of New York, espoused the slaveholder interest as the ally of the European-American worker, whose war-intensified miseries, it said, stemmed from the abolitionist effort to put Negro workers on an equal plane with white workers (Lee, pp. 142–3).

46. Wilbur H. Siebert, *The Underground Railroad from Slavery to Freedom*, with an Introduction by Albert Bushnell Hart (New York, 1899), pp. 341–2; Morris, *Encyclopedia of American History*, p. 758.

47. W. P. Garrison and F. J. Garrison, *William Lloyd Garrison, 1805–1879: The Story of his Life as Told by his Children*, 4 vols (New York, 1889), 3:51 n. 1. This footnote of the Garrisons is rich in detail and references.

48. W. E. Burghardt DuBois, *John Brown*, centennial edition (New York, 1962), pp. 280–86.

49. Aptheker cites William Lloyd Garrison as saying that 400 out of the *Liberator*'s 450 first-year subscribers were African-Americans, and that three years later, in 1834, African-Americans still accounted for three-fourths of the paper's 2,300 subscribers (Herbert Aptheker, ed., *A Documentary History of the Negro People in the United States* [New York, 1951], p. 108).

50. *Frederick Douglass' Paper*, 2 and 16 February 1855 (cited by Leon F. Litwak, *North of Slavery* [Chicago, 1961], pp. 160–61).

51. Karl Marx, *Capital: A Critique of Political Economy*, Vol. I, *The Process of Capitalist Production*, translated from the third edition by Samuel Moore and Edward Aveling (Chicago, 1906), Chapter VII, Section 7.

52. "Seventeenth Annual Meeting of the Massachusetts A. Slavery Society," *Liberator*, 1 February 1849. This resolution was offered by Charles Stearns, who "supported it in some very earnest remarks respecting the suffering of many of the laboring people of the North." Despite one tangential comment, tending to blame the workers' suffering on excessive drinking, especially among the Irish, the motion was passed without dissent. The record shows that resolutions were not routinely passed, as exampled by those on Free Soil and the religious connection.

53. See p. 138.

54. "I hear many expressions of sympathy for us in this City, and in case of an attempt to coerce us, I believe we can safely rely on much material aid from here, and especially from the Irish" (from a letter by Charles C. Spencer of Mississippi, *New York Times*, 14 December 1860: Spencer was in New York expressly to assess support for Southern secession from the United States; three days later an anonymous Irish-American disputed Spencer on the Irish and the Union, though not on the question of "Slavery or the wrongs [done to] the South" [*New York Times*, 17 December 1860]).

55. Despite the fact that pre-twentieth-century Irish emigration statistics are considered "notoriously unreliable". (R. F. Foster, *Modern Ireland, 1600–1972* [New York: Viking, 1988; Penguin Books, 1989], p. 345), especially for the period before 1840, emigration looms so large in Ireland's story that commentators are obliged to attempt to quantify it. In the period 1841 to 1861, emigration was more than 2.6 million, of whom two-thirds, 1.7 million, went to the United States. (This does not include the secondary migration of those whose first stop was Canada.) Irish emigration and United States immigration statistics seem comparable. (Total population and emigration figures are given in *A New History*, Ancillary Volume II, *Population, 1821–1971*, edited by W. E. Vaughan and A. J. Fitzpatrick [Dublin, 1978], Tables 13, 53 and 54). The total number of Irish immigrants entering the United States between 1820 and 1860 was just under 2

million, of whom $1\frac{3}{4}$ million arrived between 1841 and 1860 (United States Department of Commerce, Bureau of the Census, *Historical Statistics of the United States, Colonial Times to 1970* [Washington, DC, 1975], p. 106, Series C-92. Compare Foster, pp. 345, 354–5; Cormac O Grada, "A Note on Nineteenth Century Emigration Statistics," *Population Studies*, 29:143–9 [March 1975].)

56. Cecil J. Houston, *Irish Emigration and Canadian Settlement* (Toronto, 1990), p. 77. In 1861, Catholics made up 78 per cent of the 5.8 million total population of Ireland (*A New History*, Ancillary Volume II, Table 13).

57. *Historical Statistics of the United States*, p. 118. *A New History*, Ancillary Volume II, Table 3.

58. Eighth Census of the United States, 1860, "Population," p. 609, in Robert Ernst, *Immigrant Life in New York City, 1825–1863* (New York, 1949), p. 198. In 1855 more than half the city's population was foreign-born. See also Bridges, *City in the Republic*, p. 41.

59. David Noel Doyle ("The Irish in North America, 1776–1845," in *A New History*, 5:720–21) without attempting to document his argument, appears to challenge the traditional belief implied in the low dispersal ratio of Irish-Americans shown here. Doyle states flatly that "there was no over-concentration in seaboard slums." However, he makes exceptions for "the famine decade and its aftermath," which would include the period from 1845 to 1860, and for the protracted period of economic stagnation, 1837–43. Those periods together cover the majority of the period with which the present chapter is concerned. (Compare Carl Wittke, *The Irish in America* [Baton Rouge, 1956], pp. 24–6; and John Francis Maguire, *The Irish in America*, [London, 1868, New York, 1968], pp. 214–35].)

60. The percentages in columns A and B are based on *Annual Reports of the Commissioners of Immigration of the State of New York, from the Organization of the Commission 5 May 1847 to 1860 Inclusive* . . . (New York, 1861), Appendix, p. 288; and Eighth Census of the United States, 1860, "Population," p. 609, in Ernst, pp. 188, 198.

61. John R. G. Hassard, *Life of the Most Reverend John Hughes, DD, First Archbishop of New York, with Extracts from his Private Correspondence* (New York, 1866), p. 17. The poem was published in the Gettysburg, Pennsylvania, *Centinel*.

62. Ibid. pp. 42–4. See Appendix K for the full text of the poem.

63. Ibid., p. 45. Shortly after entering upon his new career, Hughes heard from French refugees accounts of the Haitian Revolution that left him with "an exaggerated fear of Negro insurrection." It would be wrong to simplify the matter; still it is not to be ignored that thirty years later, in the middle of the Civil War, in arguing against Negro emancipation Hughes sought to reason from his encounters "as a young priest with refugees from the Dominican massacres" (Madeleine Hook Rice, *American Catholic Opinion in the Slavery Controversy* [New York, 1944], p. 120; Rice cites Hughes to the editor of the *Journal des Débats* in *Metropolitan Record*, 1 March 1862).

64. In an article written in 1976, Douglas C. Riach pointed to half a dozen issues regarding internal Irish affairs that had a negative impact on the development of the abolitionist front in Ireland ("Daniel O'Connell and American Anti-slavery," *Irish Historical Studies*, 20:3–25 [March 1976]). Of particular importance was the difference over the attitude to be taken toward offers of assistance by American slaveholders. Young Irelander critics, said Riach, "insisted that O'Connell, in pursuing an abolitionist course, was damaging Ireland's interest." In a subsequent article, Riach found that the issue of American slavery became "an important source of discord within the Repeal Association" (Douglas C. Riach, "O'Connell and Slavery," in Donal McCartney, ed., *The World of Daniel O'Connell* [Dublin and Cork, 1980], p. 184). More recently another Irish historian, Maurice O'Connell, contributed an informative treatment of the subject, including a review of discussions in the Repeal Association, in the columns of *Nation*, the organ of the Young Irelanders, and in the Irish Confederation, the Young Ireland breakaway organization formed in January 1847 (Maurice R. O'Connell, *Daniel O'Connell, the Man and His Politics* [Dublin, 1990]). The Young Irelanders saw the Irish cause as dependent upon working the Anglo-American contradiction in such a way that the American slaveholders would somehow create an opportunity to free Ireland from British rule (see Chapter 8 n. 42, for John Mitchel's defense of this strategy in *Nation*). Therefore, they argued, it was at least folly to antagonize the slaveholders.

The findings of Riach, O'Connell, and other Irish historians, leave no room for doubt that in the wake of Clontarf, the opposition to O'Connell's leadership became more definite and articulate, and that much of it took the form of criticism of O'Connell's abolitionism as a sacrifice of the interests of repeal. Yet, after all is said and done, the contrast in the relative strengths of abolitionism among the Irish in Ireland and among the Irish-Americans seems unmistakable. Riach's generalization ("O'Connell and Slavery," p. 185) regarding the state of Irish opinion on abolitionism – that "many" in Ireland objected to it – could hardly serve to describe the prevalence of anti-abolitionism among Irish-Americans. Nor would the Young Irelanders in the United States have felt as Young Irelanders in Ireland did, that "Had they neglected to condemn slavery they would have handed O'Connell an important debating point" (Maurice R. O'Connell, *Daniel O'Connell*, p. 130). To note the Young Irelanders' challenge at home to O'Connell's abolitionism does not negate the fact of the "sea-change" effect, the explanation of which is the concern of this study.

65. *Liberator*, 3:179. Charleston, South Carolina *Courier* article reprinted in the "Refuge of Oppression" column in the *Liberator*, 11: 41.

66. In a speech to a "monster meeting" of 400,000 at Mallow, near Cork, on 11 June 1843, a speech that came to be called "The Mallow Defiance," O'Connell declared that "Irishmen would soon have to choose between living as slaves and dying as freemen" (L. A. McCaffrey, *Daniel O'Connell and the Repeal Year* [Lexington, 1966], p. 82).

67. Except as otherwise noted, the citations of O'Connell's pronouncements are taken from a collection of excerpts of his speeches published in the *Liberator*, the organ of the Massachusetts Anti-slavery Society, 25 March 1842.

68. Speech before the London Anti-slavery Society, 12 May 1832. Riach cites a single exception, having to do with the parliamentary debate over the terms and time allowed for the "transition" from slavery to full emancipation in the British West Indies ("Daniel O'Connell and American Anti-slavery," pp. 4–5).

69. In two London speeches: at the British India Society on 6 July 1839, and at the anniversary of the British and Foreign Anti-slavery Society on 24 June 1840.

70. Oscar Sherwin, *Prophet of Liberty: The Life and Times of Wendell Phillips* (New York, 1958), pp. 631–2. O'Connell's allusion was to Psalm 137, verses 5 and 6. The citation is from Phillips's 6 August 1875 oration on the occasion of a celebration of the centennial of O'Connell's birth (Wendell Phillips, *Speeches, Lectures, and Letters*, 2 vols [Boston, 1894], 2:406–9).

71. London Anti-slavery Society speech, 24 June 1840.

72. Speech before the Glasgow Emancipation Society, September 1835.

73. In 1847, the remittances to Ireland from the United States amounted to £200,000 (about a million dollars); over the next seventeen years, the remittances averaged over £380,000 per year. Most of the money sent at Christmas and Easter "came from Irish laborers and servant girls" (Wittke, *The Irish in America*, p. 51).

74. Rice, pp. 79, 100. Rice cites a Boston *Pilot* editor, who drew no fine distinctions between abolitionism and Free Soilism, warning its predominantly Irish readership in 1851: "wherever you find a free-soiler, you find . . . a woman's rights man" (p. 100).

75. Speech to the British Anti-slavery Society General Meeting, 23 April 1831; excerpted in the *Liberator*, 25 March 1842.

76. Garrison and Garrison, *William Lloyd Garrison*, 1:373, 379. The exclusionary vote had been taken on 12 June. O'Connell replied to Mott's letter of criticism on 20 June.

77. William Lloyd Garrison, letter to G. W. Benson, 22 March 1842, in Garrison and Garrison, 3:50.

78. Rice, p. 85.

79. Gilbert Osofsky, "Abolitionists, Irish Immigrants, and the Dilemmas of Romantic Nationalism," *American Historical Review*, 80:889–912 (October 1975), p. 897.

80. Madden (1798–1886) had struggled against the obstructionism of the plantation owners when he served as a magistrate overseeing the dismantlement of the slavery system in Jamaica under the terms of the Emancipation Law passed by the British Parliament in 1833 (Henry Boylan, ed., *Dictionary of Irish Biography* [New York, 1978]). He became best known perhaps for a history of the Irish rebellion of 1798, *The United Irishmen: Their Lives and Times*, the first two volumes of which were published in 1842. See Appendix L for the text of the Address.

81. *Liberator*, 18 December 1841 (Osofsky, pp. 895–8).

82. William Lloyd Garrison to Benson, 22 March 1842, in Garrison and Garrison, 3:50.

83. Letter dated 1 February 1842 from Maria Weston Chapman (The *Liberator*, 1 April 1842).

84. Osofsky, p. 903. Osofsky refers specifically to the campaign against "the pro-slavery position of the Repeal Associations" in the United States.

85. Ibid., pp. 904–5; Doyle, "The Irish in North America, 1776–1845."

86. Robert Francis Hueston, *The Catholic Press and Nativism, 1840–1860* (New York, 1976), p. 30.

87. *Report of the Proceedings of the National Repeal Convention of the Friends of Ireland in the United States of America held in Philadelphia, February 22nd and 23d, 1842* (Philadelphia, 1842), pp. 9–11.

88. O'Connell at the weekly meeting of the Loyal National Repeal Association, Dublin, around 1 October 1843 (*Liberator*, 10 November 1843).

89. I am indebted to the kindness of Professor Maurice O'Connell, now living in retirement in Dublin, for my copy of the Cincinnati repealers' letter. See Dublin *Pilot*, 12 April 1844, British Museum Library, Newspaper Library, Colindale, London.

O'Connell's written reply was published in the *British and Foreign Anti-slavery Reporter*, 15 November 1843. The manuscript, dated 11 October 1843, is at University College Library, Dublin (McCaffrey, p. 74 n. 39).

8 How the Sea-change was Wrought

1. *Liberator*, 8 April 1842.

2. See: Joseph M. Hernon, "Irish Sympathy for the Southern Confederacy," *Eire–Ireland*, vol. 2, no. 3, pp. 72–85; and Joseph M. Hernon Jr, "Irish Religious Opinion on the American Civil War," *Catholic Historical Review*, 4:508–23 (January 1964). "The clergy in Ireland adopted the temporizing tactics of the Catholic clergy in the United States on the slavery issue", *Irish Religious Opinion*, p. 511. "Confederate agents in Ireland played upon the religious sensitivity of Irish Catholics in order to influence public opinion" (ibid., p. 515).

3. John O'Connell, letter to James Haughton of the Hibernian Anti-slavery Society, 27 January 1842 (*Liberator*, 25 March 1842).

4. According to James Canning Fuller (*Liberator*, 8 April 1842).

5. Letter dated 17 October 1841 (*Liberator*, 18 March 1842).

6. Asenath Nicholson, *Ireland's welcome to a stranger*, cited in George Potter, *To the Golden Door: The Story of the Irish in Ireland and America* (Boston and Toronto, 1960), p. 21.

7. Douglass, writing from Belfast to Garrison in America, 1 January 1846 (*Liberator*, 30 January 1846).

8. Frederick Douglass, *Life and Times of Frederick Douglass, Written by Himself: His Early Life as a Slave, His Escape from Bondage, and his Complete History*, revised edition (1892; New York and Toronto, 1962), p. 237. Ten years before, the year before Douglass escaped from slavery, O'Connell (apologizing for his conceit) had expressed the hope that in the United States "some Black O'Connell might arise among his fellow slaves, who would cry, 'Agitate, Agitate' till the two millions and a half of his fellow-sufferers learned the secret of their strength" (speech to the Glasgow Emancipation Society, September 1835; excerpted in the *Liberator*, 25 March 1842).

9. "Nearly all the Irish journals were strongly political, and each was a stalwart supporter of the Democratic party.... Influenced by the authoritarian traditionalism of Irish Catholicism, the papers rejected all schemes for the reformation of society.... Above all, the Celtic journals gave vent to the ... hatred of abolitionists" (Robert Ernst, *Immigrant Life in New York City, 1825–1863* [New York, 1949], pp. 150–53). See also: Robert Francis Hueston, *The Catholic Press and Nativism, 1840–1860* (New York, 1976); Florence E. Gibson, *The Attitude of the New York Irish Toward State and National Affairs, 1848–1892* (New York, 1951).

10. These Young Irelander publications (such as the *Nation*, the *Citizen*, and the *Irish News*) were extremely white-supremacist in their policies, and therefore they were objectively auxiliaries of the avowedly Catholic press in respect to the slavery question. They are refracted by Ernst as "left-wing"!

All the more honor is due, then, to those Irish-Americans who kept faith with O'Connell and

Irish abolitionism. The present writer has encountered their names only incidentally in the research for this work. Perhaps some other student – even some priest or heroic nun, such as those who have stood up for the peasants and workers even when not fully supported by their Church, or who marched or were Freedom Riders in the 1960s, or who stand up for women's rights to reproductive choice and to their right of ordination; or independent scholars, their consciousness raised by the Ulster civil rights demonstrators marching and singing "We Shall Overcome"; or some doctoral candidate – will search them out in the newspaper archives, letters preserved, forgotten memoirs, etc., and dedicate a volume to their memory and their message for today. If they do, they will surely give consideration (warts and all) to such immigrants as James Canning Fuller, the Garrisonian; Michael Sheehy, staunch abolitionist made to suffer privation on that account; Judge Doran, Philadelphia anti-slavery repealer, praised by O'Connell; lecturer Mason Jones (was he a resident or only a visitor?), booed from the stage for glorifying the "Universal Emancipation" principle. Perhaps room will be found for Confederate General Patrick Cleburne who in 1864 advocated arming African-American bond-laborers and giving them freedom.

11. See, for example, Hughes's lecture at St Patrick's Institute in Pittsburgh, 27 June 1856, on "the relationship between the civil and religious duties of the Catholic clergy" (*Complete Works of the Most Reverend John Hughes*, edited by Lawrence Kehoe, 2 vols [New York, 1866], 2:144–8].

12. Third Pastoral of the Province of Cincinnati, May 1861; cited, along with a number of others to the same effect, in Madeleine Hook Rice, *American Catholic Opinion in the Slavery Controversy* (New York, 1944), p. 94, and n. 32.

13. Rice, p. 96, citing *Speech delivered in the House of Representatives on Tuesday, Feb. 10, 1857*, p. 19.

14. *Freeman's Journal*, 4 June 1853, cited in Hueston, p. 212 n. 45.

15. Speaking in Baltimore in 1856, Archbishop Hughes stated that Catholics were being converted to Protestantism in America at more than three times the rate of conversion of Protestants to Catholicism (lecture on "The Present Condition of the Catholic Church in the United States," delivered at a meeting of the Catholic Friend's Society, in *Complete Works ... of John Hughes*, 2:128).

16. David J. Alvarez, "The Papacy in the American Civil War," *Catholic Historical Review*, 69:227–48 (April 1983), p. 231.

17. John R. G. Hassard, *Life of the Most Reverend John Hughes, D.D., First Archbishop of New York, with Extracts from his Private Correspondence* (New York, 1866), p. 384.

18. For a discussion of the schismatic pressures arising within Protestantism, see John R. McKivigan, *The War against Proslavery Religion: Abolitionism and the Northern Churches, 1830–1865* (Ithaca, 1984), pp. 82–90.

19. *Catholic Mirror*, 25 January 1850; cited in Rice, p. 101.

20. *Letters of the late Bishop [John] England to Hon. John Forsyth on the Subject of Domestic Slavery, to which are prefixed copies, in Latin and English, of the Pope's Apostolic Letter, concerning the African Slave Trade, with some Introductory Remarks, etc.* (Baltimore, 1844).

21. Ibid., p. iii.

22. Rice, pp. 108–9.

23. Indeed, during the Civil War, especially after the Emancipation Proclamation was issued, differences over abolition did surface within the United States hierarchy (ibid.).

24. Hassard, pp. 215–16. Hughes's description of his attitude on this occasion seems consistent with his practice at home, where he is quoted as saying, "I will suffer no man in my diocese that I cannot control. I will either put him down, or he shall put me down" (Henry J. Browne, "Archbishop Hughes and Western Colonization," *Catholic Historical Review*, 36:257–85 [October 1950], p. 284).

25. Hassard, p. 216. Hassard's understated observation was that, "[T]he bishop's sentiments on the slavery question had undergone some change since Leander wrote verses for the Gettysburg *Centinel.*" Incidentally, apparently during this same trip, Hughes heard O'Connell's Repeal address at a Donnybrook "monster meeting" which he estimated at "not less than two hundred thousand" (ibid).

26. The letter, with accompanying documents, dated New York, 30 March 1858, was sent to a friend in Rome for translation and eventual submission to Vatican officials (Hassard, pp. 389–90, emphasis in original).

27. Ibid., p. 351.

28. Ibid., p. 212.

29. Ibid., pp. 392–3. Richard J. Purcell says, "In no way was Hughes more mistaken than in his opposition to the Irish movement westward in the [eighteen] fifties" (*Dictionary of American Biography*: "Hughes, John Joseph"). See Browne, p. 283. Browne makes allowance for Hughes's eing purely the expression of a concern for protecting the flock from malign influences (p. 284).

30. John Francis Maguire, upon returning to Ireland after a visit to the United States, was moved to write: "… it is not within the power of language to describe adequately, much less exaggerate, the evil consequences of this unhappy tendency of the Irish to congregate in the large towns of America," which tendency he calls a "fatal blunder" (John Francis Maguire, *The Irish in America* [London, 1868; New York, 19681, pp. 214, 218. Maguire devotes a full chapter to documentation of the abominable conditions under which the Irish of the laboring class were condemned to live in New York).

31. Hassard, pp. 435–6. Historian Lee Benson observes that about 1854 "Catholic leaders reversed the policy of nonalignment" with any particular party (Lee Benson, *The Concept of Jacksonian Democracy: New York as a Test Case* [Princeton, 1961], p. 191).

32. *Complete Works of … John Hughes*, 2:220–22.

33. Brother Basil Leo Lee, *Discontent in New York City, 1861–1865* (Washington, DC, 1943) p. 156.

34. *Caucasian*, 12 October 1862.

35. Lee, p. 142.

36. See the story of the Good Samaritan in Luke 10:30–34. Horace Greeley, editor of the *New York Tribune*, used this allusion to make the same charge against Archbishop Hughes just four days before the beginning of the 1863 anti-draft riots (*New York Tribune*, 9 July 1863, cited in Albon P. Man, "The Church and the New York Draft Riots of 1863," *Records of the American Catholic Historical Society of Philadelphia*, 62: 33–50 [March 1951], p. 46).

37. For a modern historian's criticism of Elijah P. Lovejoy on this ground, see the unsigned article, "Elijah P. Lovejoy as an Anti-Catholic," *Records of the American Catholic Historical Society of Philadelphia*, 62:172–80 (September 1951).

38. "Reply of the Repeal Association to the Address from Cincinnati," *British and Foreign Anti-slavery Reporter*, London, 15 November 1843. The way to "disarm" such anti-Catholics, he said, was "not by giving up to them the side of humanity," but by taking "a superior station of Christian virtue" as fighters "for the freedom of all mankind."

39. Massachusetts Anti-slavery Society, *Tenth Annual Report*, 1842, Appendix 8, cited in Oscar Sherwin, *Prophet of Liberty: The Life and Times of Wendell Phillips* (New York, 1958), p. 154. See also Aileen S. Kraditor's account of the Protestant in-fighting (*Means and Ends in American Abolitionism: Garrison and His Critics on Strategy and Tactics, 1834–1850* [New York, 1967; Vintage books edition, 1970], Chapter 4, "Religion and the Good Society").

40. William Darrell Overdyke, *The Know-Nothing Party in the South* (Baton Rouge: Louisiana State Press, 1950), pp. 198–9.

41. Alvarez, "Papacy in the American Civil War," pp. 234, 239.

42. Douglas C. Riach, "Daniel O'Connell and American Anti-slavery," *Irish Historical Studies*, 20:3–25 (March 1976) pp. 18–20. John Mitchel, writing in the Young Irelanders' *Nation* saw the "opportunity" for Irish independence in "a war between England and the United States." He defended this strategy against those who thought it cowardly to expect others to deliver the main blow (*Nation*, 6 and 13 December 1841, cited in William Dillon, *Life of John Mitchel*, 2 vols in 1 [London, 1888], 1:102).

43. Dillon 1:115.

44. Ibid., 2:43–4.

45. Quoted in Robert G. Athearn, *Thomas Francis Meagher: An Irish Revolutionary in America* (Boulder, 1949), p. 17. During the Civil War, Meagher switched affiliations, served as an officer in the Union Army, and made scathing attacks on the pro-slavery politics of those whose views he had formerly shared (see p. 198).

46. This strategic approach to Irish independence was taken up by the Irish Republican Brotherhood, or Fenians, as they were more commonly known, when they were organized in 1858. In 1866 and again in 1870, the American Fenians launched quixotic "invasions" of Canada. On

the first occasion, a few hundred Irish-Americans crossed the Niagara River and bravely fought an engagement with the local militia, but were forced to flee back to United States territory. The 1870 attempt was likewise defeated, and the US Marshal in Vermont arrested those who returned across the border.

47. Kerby A. Miller, *Emigrants and Exiles: Ireland and the Irish Exodus to North America* (New York, 1985), p. 335.

48. See p. 143 ff for the main lines on which the white-skin privilege system was reinstituted after the Civil War.

49. *Statutes at Large of the United States of America, 1789–1873* (17 vols, Washington, DC, 1850–73), 1 Stat. 103. The volume and page citations, and date of final passage of subsequent pre-Civil War immigration and naturalization laws are as follows: 1 Stat. 414 (29 January 1795); 2 Stat. 153 (14 April 1802); 2 Stat. 292 (26 March 1804); 3 Stat. 258 (22 March 1816); 4 Stat. 69 (26 May 1824); 4 Stat. 310 (24 May 1828).

In 1870, after passage of the Fifteenth Amendment, "the naturalization laws [were] ... extended to aliens of African nativity and to persons of African descent." Thereafter, until at least 1924, the law still bore its phraseological birthmark in the curious formulation giving the right of immigration to "... aliens being free white persons, and to aliens of African nativity and to persons of African descent" (United States Department of Justice, *Administrative Decisions under Immigration and Nationality Laws*, Vol. II [January 1944–August 1947], [Washington, 1948], p. 254). On 6 May 1882 the so-called Oriental Exclusion Law was enacted barring entry to the United States by any Chinese, except diplomats and individuals bearing special Chinese government certificates (22 Stat. 58). By a series of extensions this bar to Chinese entry remained in effect until 1943, when the first Chinese quota was established permitting the entry of 105 persons per year. Similar white-supremacist immigration bars were put into effect against Japanese, as being persons "ineligible to citizenship."

In 1922, the Supreme Court denied the appeal of a Hindu who argued that by anthropological classification he was a "Caucasian." The Supreme Court held that, although the book definition of "Caucasian" included Hindus, "the statutory words, 'white persons' ... [were] 'words of common speech, to be interpreted in accordance with the understanding of the common man ...'" Hindus were therefore to be excluded under that interpretation, because "Hindus could not merge into the mass of our population ... so as to [be] recognized as white" (*Administrative Decisions under Immigration and Nationality Laws*, Vol. II, pp. 254–5; the case citation is *United States vs. Thind*, 261 U.S. 206 [1923]).

50. Jackson, letter to his Vice-President-elect Martin Van Buren in November 1832, regarding a number of persons under consideration for appointment to office (*Correspondence of Andrew Jackson*, edited by John Spencer Bassett, 7 vols [Washington, 1926–35], 4:489).

51. Arthur M. Schlesinger Jr, *The Age of Jackson* (New York, 1945), pp. 45–7.

52. Leon F. Litwak, *North of Slavery* (Chicago, 1961), pp. 74–6.

53. Gustavus Myers, *A History of Tammany Hall*, 2nd edn (New York, 1917), p. 143.

54. United States Department of Commerce, Bureau of the Census, *Historical Statistics of the United States, Colonial Times to 1970* (Washington, DC, 1975), p. 106.

55. See p. 101.

56. Dixon Ryan Fox, "The Negro Vote in Old New York," *Political Science Quarterly*, 32:252–75 (1917), pp. 255–7.

57. The last of the restrictions on poor-white suffrage were removed by the New York Constitutional Convention of 1826 (Fox, p. 263).

58. The distinction attempted in this thesis between simple slavery and *racial* slavery, a *form* of racial oppression, is highlighted by the attitude of Federalist Philip Hone, who was an anti-abolitionist and yet a vigorous champion of equal voting rights for free African-Americans (see Fox, p. 265). What the slaveholders understood better than Hone did was that slavery in the United States could be maintained only as *racial* slavery, as a form of racial oppression of African-Americans, free as well as bond.

59. Fox, pp. 262 n. 5, 263–71.

60. Ibid., p. 274.

61. Amy Bridges, *A City in the Republic: Antebellum New York and the Origins of Machine Politics* (New York, 1984), p. 43.

62. Fox, pp. 273–4.

63. See Potter, *To the Golden Door*, Chapter 6, "The Irish as 'Ready Made' Democrats."

64. Myers, pp. 128–9; Man, "Church and the New York Draft Riots of 1863," p. 96.

65. Ernst, pp. 163–4; Myers, p. 132.

66. Myers, pp. 129, 133, 135.

67. Ernst, *Immigrant Life in New York City*, p. 163.

68. Myers, p. 141; Albon P. Man Jr, "Labor Competition and the New York Draft Riots of 1863," *Journal of Negro History*, 36:375–405 (October 1951), p. 378.

69. The purpose of annexation was to counter the limitations imposed by the Northwest Ordinance and the Missouri Compromise of 1820, by extending slavery to a vast territory, of 249 million acres, equal to more than one-sixth of the total area of the United States prior to that time.

70. Riach, "Daniel O'Connell and American Anti-slavery," pp. 18–19.

71. Letter to the London *Morning Chronicle*, 1838, reprinted in the *Liberator*, 25 March 1842.

72. William W. Freehling, *The Road to Disunion*, 2 vols (Vol. II forthcoming) Vol. I, *Secessionists at Bay, 1776–1854* (New York, 1990), p. 359.

73. See pp. 164–5.

74. *Works of Henry Clay*, edited by Calvin Colton, 6 vols (New York, 1897), 4:495 (letter of Frelinghuysen to Clay, 9 November 1844). See also Ambrose Spence to Clay, 21 November 1844 (p. 501), and Adam Beatty to Clay, 24 December 1848 (p. 517).

75. Letter dated New York, 6 December 1860, published in the Charleston (South Carolina) *Mercury*, and republished in the *New York Times*, 14 December 1860.

76. "Far more vehement than the clergy on the slavery question, especially after the issuance of the Emancipation Proclamation, were the newspapers conducted by Catholics. In fact, the editors of the Catholic *Metropolitan Record* and the *Freeman's Journal and Catholic Register* played leading parts in the movement to encourage violent resistance to the draft" (Man, "Church and the New York Draft Riots," pp. 49–50). Man adds, however, that "when the agitation bore fruit in the draft riots, the clergy of New York, headed by Archbishop Hughes, worked to restrain the mobs."

James McMasters, editor of the *Freeman's Journal*, was the chief representative of the New York forces who plotted with Confederate agents to exploit the discontent with the draft to seize New York City on election day in 1864 (John W. Headley, *Confederate Operations in Canada and New York* [New York and Washington, 1906], pp. 222–3, 265, 270). See also Gibson, *Attitudes of the New York Irish*, pp. 170–71.

77. The Union forces having sustained heavy battle losses, and the terms of volunteer enlistment expiring for many soldiers, on 1 March 1863 the Federal Congress passed a Conscription Act. "White" men between the ages of twenty and forty-five were subject to conscription, selection to be by lottery. Any man whose "number was up" who had the means could escape by paying $300 or by furnishing a substitute enlistee for himself. It was, of course, a raw assertion of bourgeois class privilege, and tended to give the war itself, at the heart of which was the abolition of chattel bond-servitude, the image of "a rich man's war and a poor man's fight." The draft lottery in New York City, set for mid-July, was taken as an opportunity by the anti-abolition forces to strike a mortal blow at the possibility of a Union victory. That blow took the form of the Draft Riot (sometimes described as a succession of riots) which lasted five days, during which eleven African-Americans were lynched in an atmosphere of bloodthirsty white-supremacism. The rioting was finally ended by Federal troops. (See: Adrian Cook, *The Armies of the Street; the New York City Draft Riots of 1863* [Lexington, Kentucky, 1974]; Iver Bernstein, *The New York City Draft Riots: Their Significance for American Society and Politics in the Age of the Civil War* [New York, 1990].)

78. *Proceedings of the Board of Aldermen of the City of New York*, Vol. 81 (New York, 1861), pp. 25–6.

79. Gibson, *Attitudes of the New York Irish*, pp. 116–17, 170.

80. Hassard, *Life of . . . John Hughes*, p. 439.

81. Lee, *Discontent in New York City*, p. 156.

82. *Leader*, 15 June 1861.

83. Theodore Maynard, *The Story of American Catholicism* (New York, 1941), p. 354; Rice, *American Catholic Opinion in the Slavery Controversy*, p. 123; Hassard, p. 437.

84. Hassard, p. 436. Rice, pp. 120–21.

85. Myers, *History of Tammany Hall*, p. 196.

86. Rice, pp. 124–5.

87. Myers, p. 196.

88. Quoted from the *Caucasian* in Lee, p. 138. Lee suggests that the event listed next in this chronology was "Perhaps the desired response ..."

89. Man, "Labor Competition and the New York Draft Riots," pp. 389–90; Lee, pp. 139–40. Their citations are from the New York *Tribune*, 5, 6, 8 and 24 August 1862, and 24 January 1863.

90. Lee, p. 157.

91. *Caucasian*, 12 October 1862.

92. Lee, p. 102.

93. Man, "Church and the New York Draft Riots," p. 47; Thomas F. Meehan, "Archbishop Hughes and the Draft Riots," *United States Catholic Historical Society Records (1899–1900)*, 1:171–90. In this impromptu speech, there was none of the sternness he had employed against the promoters of western colonization, or the Protestant New York School Board. When the crowd cried, "Let the nigger stay South," Hughes gave no apparent direct reply; he merely continued, "I am not a legislator. Everything is in the hands of the supreme people of the United States, and the majority of them, whether they make a blunder or not, must govern" (Meehan, p. 182).

94. Man, "Church and the New York Draft Riots," p. 47. Lee, p. 142.

95. See for example: Man, "Labour Competition and the New York Draft Riots," pp. 404–5; Man, "Church and the New York Draft Riots," p. 47; Gilbert Osofsky, "Abolitionists, Irish Immigrants, and the Dilemmas of Romantic Nationalism," *American Historical Review*, 80:889–912 (October 1975), p. 900; Rice, p. 84; Carl Wittke, *The Irish in America* (Baton Rouge, 1956), pp. 125–6.

96. Ernst, *Immigrant Life in New York City*, p. 105.

97. Philip Bagenal, *The American Irish and Their Influence on Irish Politics* (Boston, 1882), p. 73, cited in Florence E. Gibson, *Attitudes of the New York Irish*, p. 16.

98. Natives feared the added competition would drive wages down from $1.50 a day to a shilling or twenty cents (Myers, *History of Tammany Hall*, p. 134).

99. William Forbes Adams, *Ireland and Irish Emigration to the New World, from 1815 to the Famine* (New Haven, 1932), p. 379. Adams attributes the decline of the nativist movement to the massive immigration of Irish Catholics coupled with the political power available to them through "manhood suffrage."

100. *St Louis Leader*, 10 November 1855, cited in Rice, p. 101.

101. Bridges, *City in the Republic*, p. 41. Ernst, p. 199.

102. Ernst, p. 61.

103. Figures as presented by Ernst, pp. 214–15. Native-born European-Americans certainly added to the competition for jobs, but they are excluded here because, according to Ernst, comparative data are not available for them.

104. The Belfast parallel is again most striking. The Irish political scientists Budge and O'Leary comment upon the chronology of the anti-Catholic riots in Belfast in the period 1813 to 1912: "It is easy to postulate economic factors as the underlying cause," they observe, but they note that these outbreaks correlate not with economic cycles, but with political, for example electoral, cycles. "Moreover," they add, "the general facts in respect of the years when major riots occurred do not support an interpretation in terms of job-competition" (Ian Budge and Cornelius O'Leary, *Belfast: Approach to Crisis, a Study of Belfast Politics* [London, 1973], pp. 89, 91–2).

105. Ernst, p. 107.

106. Man, "Labor Competition and the New York Draft Riots," pp. 397–8.

107. Ibid., citing the *New York Tribune*, 13, 14, and 16 April 1863.

108. Ernst, pp. 107–8.

109. Ibid., pp. 104–5.

110. Man, "Labor Competition and the New York Draft Riots," pp. 376–7.

111. The Lorillard and Watson tobacco factories referred to above are cases in point. Negroes were well-entrenched in laborer and service occupations "before the spurt in immigration in the decades of the [eighteen] forties and fifties" (ibid., p. 376).

112. William Hartman, "The New York Custom House: Seat of Spoils Politics," *New York History*, 34:149–63 (April 1953), 34:149–50.

113. *Leader*, 15 June 1861 (emphasis in original).

114. *Leader*, 25 August 1862.

115. Gibson, *Attitudes of the New York Irish*, p. 90.

116. Albon P. Man Jr, "The Irish in New York in the Early Eighteen-sixties," *Irish Historical Studies*, 7:87–108 (1950–51), p. 100.

117. Gibson, pp. 116–17.

118. Man, "Labor Competition and the New York City Draft Riots," p. 401.

119. George Edmund Haynes, *The Negro at Work in New York City* (New York, 1912), pp. 46–7; cited in Ernst, *Immigrant Life in New York City*, pp. 230 n. 60, and 235 n. 37. Haynes shows a decline from 18,600 to 15,000 in 1860. The African-American population of Brooklyn, however, increased from 2,000 in 1840 to 5,000 in 1860. If Haynes's 1860 number is for Manhattan only, it is considerably higher than that given by Ernst himself at p. 199 and by Bernstein (*New York City Draft Riots*, p. 267), both of which cite the US Census to show that the number for 1860 was about 12,500.

120. It is ironic that Ernst, whose work provides such valuable materials for the study of the myth of "labor competition," seems to have remained a captive of it. To a reference to "a possible fear that Irish labor would be overwhelmed by the competition of emancipated Negroes," Ernst appended a note saying, "I have no evidence of the fear of possible competition from colored workers, but this is a reasonable assumption" (Ernst, *Immigrant Life in New York*, pp. 153, 279 n. 4).

121. *Historical Statistics of the United States*, p. 106.

122. Lee, p. 140, citing *Tribune*, 16 April 1863 and New York *World*, 28 August 1862.

123. Man, "Labor Competition and the New York Draft Riots," p. 387, citing the New York *Tribune*, 4 August and 7 November 1862.

124. See Chapter 6.

125. W. E. B. Du Bois, *Black Reconstruction, An Essay toward a History of the Part which Black Folk Played in the Attempt to Reconstruct Democracy in America, 1860–1880* (New York, 1935), p. 20.

126. Athearn, *Thomas Francis Meagher*, p. 134.

127. Doyle, "The Irish in North America, 1776–1845," in *A New History*, 5:687.

Appendix M

1. This section is drawn from Jeffrey B. Perry, "The Developing Conjuncture and Some Insights From Hubert Harrison and Theodore W. Allen On the Centrality of the Fight Against White Supremacy," *Cultural Logic* (2010) at http://clogic.eserver.org/2010/Perry.pdf. See also Jeffrey B. Perry, "In Memoriam: Theodore W. Allen," *Cultural Logic*, Vol. 8 (2005), at http://clogic.eserver.org/2005/perry.html and Jeffrey B. Perry, "Introduction," in Theodore W. Allen, *Class Struggle and the Origin of Racial Slavery: The Invention of the White Race* (The Center for the Study of Working Class Life, SUNY, Stony Brook, 2006) and in *Cultural Logic*, Vol. 9 (2006) at http://clogic.eserver.org/2006/allen.html.

2. Perry, "The Developing Conjuncture ..." and W. E. B. Du Bois, *Black Reconstruction, An Essay Toward a History of the Part Which Black Folk Played in the Attempt to Reconstruct Democracy in America, 1860–1880* (New York: Athenaeum, 1971 [1935]).

3. Allen, "A Call ... John Brown Memorial Pilgrimage ... December 4, 1965," John Brown Commemoration Committee, 1965, in the Theodore W. Allen Papers, in possession of the author (hereafter TWAP).

4. J. H. Kagin (pseudonym for Theodore W. Allen and Noel Ignatiev), *White Blindspot* (Osawatomie Associates, 1967) reprinted along with Allen, "Can White ~~Workers~~ Radicals Be Radicalized?" (c. 1968–69) as Noel Ignatin (Ignatiev) and Ted Allen, *White Blindspot & Can White ~~Workers~~ Radicals Be Radicalized?* (Detroit: The Radical Education Project, and New York: NYC Revolutionary Youth Movement, 1969).

5. Allen's thesis on the invention of the "white race" was first articulated in a February 23, 1974, talk he delivered at Yale University at a Union of Radical Political Economists meeting in New Haven. Versions of the text of that talk include: "Toward an Integral Theory of Early Colonial History (Ten Theses)" (TWAP, 1974); "'... They would have destroyed me': Slavery and

the Origins of Racism," *Radical America*, Vol. 9, No. 3 (May-June 1975), pp. 40–63, republished in *White Supremacy: A Collection* (Chicago: Sojourner Truth Organization, 1976); and *Class Struggle and the Origin of Racial Slavery: The Invention of the White Race* (Hoboken: Hoboken Education Project, 1975), republished in 2006 with an introduction by Jeffrey B. Perry for The Center for the Study of Working Class Life, SUNY, Stony Brook and by *Cultural Logic* at http:// clogic.eserver.org/2006/allen.html.

6. Allen, *The Invention of the White Race*, Vol. I: *Racial Oppression and Social Control* (New York: Verso, 1994) and Vol. II: *The Origin of Racial Oppression in Anglo-America* (New York: Verso, 1997).

7. Allen, " 'The Kernel and the Meaning' … : A Contribution to a Proletarian Critique of United States History" Part One – Civil War and Reconstruction: Crisis and Resolution" (TWAP, 1972); "White Supremacy in U.S. History," a speech delivered at a *Guardian* forum on the national question, April 28, 1973, reprinted in *White Supremacy: A Collection* (Chicago: Sojourner Truth Organization, 1976)*;* "The Peculiar Seed: The Plantation of Bondage" (TWAP, 1974); "Summary of the Argument of *The Invention of the White Race*," *Cultural Logic*, Vol. 1, No. 2 (Spring 1998); "In Defense of Affirmative Action in Employment Policy," *Cultural Logic*, Vol. 1, No. 2 (Spring 1998); " 'Race' and 'Ethnicity': History and the 2000 Census," *Cultural Logic*, Vol. 3, No. 1 (Fall 1999); "Introduction to 'The Kernel and the Meaning': A Critique of Labor Historiography" (TWAP, May 8, 2003); "Toward a Revolution in Labor History: book outline," (TWAP, January 5, 2004); "Slavery, Racism, and Democracy," *Monthly Review*, Vol. 29, No. 10 (March 1978), pp. 57–63; and "On Roediger's *Wages of Whiteness* (Revised Edition)," *Cultural Logic*, Vol. 4, No. 2 (Spring 2001). Among the interviews, see in particular "An Interview with Theodore W. Allen," by Jonathan Scott and Gregory Meyerson, *Cultural Logic*, Vol. 1, No. 2 (Spring 1998) and Theodore W. Allen, interview by Chad Pearson (in two parts) May 13 and 20, 2004, at http://www.albany. edu/talkinghistory/arch2004jan-june.html.

8. Allen, "Can White ~~Workers~~ Radicals Be Radicalized?," p. 12 and Du Bois, *Black Reconstruction*, p. 353.

9. Ted (Theodore W.) Allen and Esther Kusic, "A Letter of Support," March 23, 1967, in Noel Ignatin (Ignatiev) and Ted (Theodore W.) Allen, *White Blindspot* (n.p., 1967) reprinted as Noel Ignatin (Ignatiev) and Ted (Theodore W.) Allen, *"White Blindspot" & "Can White ~~Workers~~ Radicals Be Radicalized?"* (1969), p. 10. See also Du Bois, *Black Reconstruction*, p. 577; Allen, "Introduction to 'The Kernel and the Meaning'" (TWAP, May 8, 2003); and Allen, Letter to Louis M. Rabinowitz Foundation (TWAP, February 15, 1976).

10. Allen, "The Kernel and the Meaning," pp. 1, 41; and Allen, "Can White ~~Workers~~ Radicals Be Radicalized?" pp. 12–14. As he further developed his analysis, Allen would later emphasize that the "white race," through its all-class form, conceals the operation of the ruling-class social-control system by providing it with a majoritarian "democratic" façade and that "the main barrier to class consciousness" among European-American workers was "the incubus of 'white' identity." Allen, "The Historical Roots of 'American Exceptionalism': The 'Race-not-class' Principle" (TWAP, Draft for a Presentation on Radio Station WBAI in New York, February 15, 1996, p. 40), and Allen, "Toward a Revolution in Labor History" (TWAP, January 5, 2004).

11. See Perry, "The Developing Conjuncture …," p. 10; Perry, "Introduction," in Allen, *Class Struggle*, pp. i–xii; Allen, "Summary of the Argument of *The Invention of the White Race*," Part 1, No. 8; Allen, "On Roediger's *Wages of Whiteness*" (Revised Edition), # 66; and Allen, interview by Chad Pearson, Part 1, May 13, 2004, min. 28.

12. Allen, "History of My Book" (TWAP, July 3, 2001); Allen, "Development of the Labor Movement, Part 1: 1607–1750 (outline of the course) (TWAP, Fall 1974, p. 1); and Winthrop D. Jordan, *White Over Black: American Attitudes Toward the Negro, 1550–1812* (Chapel Hill: University of North Carolina Press, 1968). Volume II of *The Invention of the White Race* was largely written in the 1970s and 1980s, before Volume I.

13. Allen, "Prospectus of the Presentation to be made by Ted Allen at the URPE Conference in New Haven (TWAP, February 23–4, 1974); "Toward an Integral Theory of Early Colonial History (Ten Theses)"; " '… They would have destroyed me'"; and *Class Struggle and the Origin of Racial Slavery: The Invention of the White Race.*

14. Allen, *Class Struggle,* pp. viii–ix, 3–5, 19n12, 19n63; Letter to Rabinowitz Foundation; "Summary of the Argument of *The Invention of the White Race*," Part 1; and "The 'White Race' as 'The Peculiar Institution': Ten Theses" (TWAP, September 25, 1997). Allen points out that chattel

bond-servitude was often recorded as "the custom of the country" in colonial records and that the majority of European-American bond-servants had not signed indentures in their home country.

15. Allen, *The Invention of the White Race*, Volume I. Allen writes, "During my own study of page after page of Virginia county records, reel after reel of microfilm prepared by the Virginia Colonial Records Project, and other seventeenth-century sources, I have found no instance of the official use of the word 'white' as a token of social status before its appearance in a Virginia law passed in 1691, referring to 'English or other white women.'" See Allen, "Summary of the Argument of *The Invention of the White Race*," Part 1.

16. George M. Fredrickson, "America's Caste System: Will it Change?" *New York Review of Books* (October 23, 1997), p. 68.

17. Allen, "Summary of the Argument of *The Invention of the White Race*," Part 1, No. 7 and 8.

18. Allen, "Summary of the Argument of *The Invention of the White Race*," Part 1, No. 7. Allen puts "whiteness" in quotes because, he explained, "it's an abstract noun, it's an abstraction, it's an attribute of some people, it's not the role they play. And the white race is an actual objective thing. It's not anthropologic, it's a historically developed identity of European Americans and Anglo-Americans and so it has to be dealt with. It functions … in this history of ours and it has to be recognized as such … to slough it off under the heading of 'whiteness,' to me seems to get away from the basic white race identity trauma." See Allen, interview with Chad Pearson, May 13, 2004.

In later years, Allen similarly shied away from use of "the self-standing word 'racism.'" As he explained in a letter in response to a review of *The Invention of the White Race*: "First, my book is not about, and does not pretend to be about 'racism.' It is about the white race, – the true 'peculiar institution' – its origin and its modus operandi, as the more general form of class collaboration in continental Anglo-America during both its colonial and its regenerate United States form. (Indeed, I generally avoid the use of the self-standing word 'racism,' on account of the ruinous ambiguity [that] white supremacists have managed to give it. However, I think it can be appropriate in the defining form, 'white racism.')" Allen, "Reply to Judith Levine (TWAP, September 6, 1994).

19. Allen, "Summary of the Argument of *The Invention of the White Race*," Part 1, No. 8.

20. Allen, *The Invention of the White Race*, Vol. I, pp. 4–21; "Summary of the Argument of *The Invention of the White Race*," Part 1, No. 7 and 8 and Part 2, No. 125, 129 and n197; "Slavery, Racism, and Democracy," *Monthly Review*, pp. 57–63; Jordan, *White Over Black*, Chapter 2, "Unthinking Decision: Enslavement of Negroes in America to 1700," pp. 44–98; Edmund S. Morgan, *American Slavery, American Freedom: The Ordeal of Colonial Virginia* (New York: W. W. Norton, 1975), pp. 380, 386; and Allen, Letter to Rabinowitz Foundation.

21. Allen, "On Roediger's *Wages of Whiteness*" and Allen, Email to David Siar, Gregory Meyerson, and Jeffrey B. Perry, "Roediger essay" (TWAP, February 2, 2002).

22. Allen, "Comments on Roediger," p. 6.

23. Allen, "Comments on Roediger," p. 6, and Roediger, *Wages of Whiteness*, pp. 9–10.

24. Allen, "Comments on Roediger," p. 6, and Roediger, *Wages of Whiteness*, p. 23.

25. Allen, "Comments on Roediger," p. 7, and Jordan, *White Over Black*, p. xiv.

26. Allen, "Comments on Roediger" p. 6, and Winthrop Jordan, "Modern Tensions and the Origins of American Slavery," *Journal of Southern History*, 28:19–30 (1962), p. 21.

27. Allen, "Comments on Roediger," p. 7. See Roediger, *Towards the Abolition of Whiteness: Essays on Race, Politics, and Working Class History* (New York: Verso, 1994).

28. Allen, "Comments on Roediger," pp. 7–8.

29. Allen, "Comments on Roediger," p. 9.

30. Allen, "Comments on Roediger," p. 15, and Roediger, *Wages of Whiteness*, pp. 9, 13. Allen cites Frederick Douglass, *Life and Times of Frederick Douglass* (1892) and Herbert Aptheker, *Documentary History of the Negro People in the United States* (1951). On the Chartists, see Allen, "From the War of Independence to the Civil War," draft for "Toward a Revolution in Labor History" (TWAP, December 2003).

31. Allen, "Comments on Roediger," p. 16, which cites Karl Marx and Frederick Engels, *The German Ideology* (1846), Part 1, where they write, "The ideas of the ruling class, are in every epoch the ruling ideas, i.e., the class which is the ruling material force of society, is at the same time its ruling intellectual force." Allen quotes Senator Daniel Webster of Massachusetts in his famous March 7, 1850, Oration on the Missouri Compromise that "the general lead in the politics of the country, for three-fourths of the period that has elapsed since the adoption of the Constitution,

has been a southern lead." Allen also quotes the January 1861 boast of Alexander Stephens, the future Vice President of the Confederacy: "We [the southern slaveholder states] have always had control of it [the Federal government] … we have had a majority of the Presidents chosen from the South, as well as the control and management of most of those chosen from the north. We have had sixty years of southern presidents, to their 24, thus controlling the executive department. So of the judges of the Supreme Court, we have had 18 from the south, and but 11 from the north; although nearly four-fifths of the judicial business has arisen from the free states, yet a majority of this court have always been from the south. *This we have required, so as to guard against any interpretation of the Constitution unfavorable to us.* In like manner, we have been equally watchful to guard our interests in the legislative branch of government. In choosing the presiding presidents (pro tempore of the Senate) we have had 24 to their 11. Speaker of the House, we have had 23 and they 12. While the majority of the Representatives, from their greater population, have always been from the North, yet we have so generally secured the Speaker because he, to a great extent, shapes and controls the legislation of the country … Nor have we had less control of every other department of the general government." See also Roediger, *Wages of Whiteness*, p. 9.

32. Allen, "Introduction to 'The Kernel and the Meaning,'" alternate introduction (TWAP, May 8, 2003).

Appendix N

1. Theodore W. Allen, "Summary of the Argument of *The Invention of the White Race*," *Cultural Logic*, Vol. 1, No. 2 (Spring 1998).
2. "Summary," Part 1, No. 15.
3. "Summary," Part 1, No. 13–14. See also Chapter 1, p. 32.

Index

abolitionist movement: African-Americans in 165–6; and British West Indies 161, 171–2; Clay on 319n16; differences within 10, 325n23; Free Soil and 167, 323n74; Hughes foe of 180; Liberty Party and 189; persecution of 150, 166; strategy to win Irish-Americans 171–6; southern whites who favor 150–1, 316n87, 316n107; supports struggle of Irish 126; in U.S. 165–7; "white labor" apologists on 166, 320–1n39

Act concerning Servants and Slaves (1705) 23–4

Act "directing the trial of Slaves . . . and for the better government of Negroes, Mulattos, and Indians bond or free" (1723) 84–5

Act to Prevent the Growth of Popery (1704) 78, 82, 92

Act of Settlement (1652) and Act of Satisfaction (1653) 49–51, 67–8, 281n145, 250n10, 2578n17

Act of Union of England and Scotland (1707) 73, 305n16

Act of Union of Great Britain and Ireland (1801) 36, 94–7, 99, 297n27, 298n29

Adams, Henry 145, 315n77

"Address from the People of Ireland to Their Countrymen and Countrywomen in America" 172, 174–8, 182–4, 195, 199: text of 229–30

"Address to the Workingmen of the United States" 142, 321n45

Adventurers 67–8, 281n145

"affirmative action" 110–12, 157, 309n97

Africa: Cape Colony 207–8; clash with European social system 36, 38; colonial social control policies 216; Europeans unable to establish commanding authority in 36, 61, 206–8; Irish analogies 31, 61, 74, 275n49; landholding 276n54, 276n59; South Africa 36, 310n102; supplier of plantation labor 36, 70, 80, 161–2, 268n36, 288n111; tribal vs. individual ownership in 276n54; West Africa 36, 276n59, 288n111

African bond-laborers: ban on "importation" of 160, 318n3; Cape colony 207–8; capture and abduction 36; labor transportation costs 15–6, 270n78

"African humanism" 276n54

Africans: assault on and racial oppression of 32–6, 274n38; attack on European forts 206–7; conjectures on "white" bias against 6–8, 15, 20–21; flight and rebellion of 8; immigrants allowed in British Guiana barred from U.S. 268n43; language diversity of 276n61; as masters of African land 61; opposition to lifetime hereditary bond-servitude of 8; Williams's refutation of racial explanations about 15–16

African-American bond-laborers: cost of labor of 75–6, 221; former 165; and historians 2, 8, 12–21; Hughes on 169; intensification of exploitation of 160, 318n10; Irish parallels 75–6, 85–6, 221–2; lifetime and limited term 293n87; and marriage 89; and plantation bourgeoisie 167; and "positive good" rationale 163; productivity 318n10; rebelliousness of 17, 20, 23–4; and religion 80–81; ruling class policy to treat differently 3, 17–18; sexual exploitation of women by European-American men 12, 46; in Southern mills 155–6; status similar to European-American bond-laborers in seventeenth century 3; supply of 162; "white" exclusionism in employment 85–6

African-Americans: African-Brazilian contrasts 4–5, 8, 17; African-Caribbean contrasts 112–13; in anti-slavery front 165–6; barred from acquiring property 83; and citizenship 139, 185–6; in colonial period 80–81, 84, 89, 138;

disfranchisement of 187–88; and family 86–90, 295n126; free (pre-Emancipation) 163–6, 170, 187, 191–5, 197–8; freed (post-Emancipation) 83, 140, 197; Jordan's epitaph for equal rights of 269n50; men to be "exported" 201; in New York 187–8, 197, 330n119; non-slave status in early America 3; as owners of bond-laborers 293n86; parallels with American Indians 30, 46–7; parallels with Irish 30–32, 72–7, 83–90, 118, 329n104; parallels with Irish Catholics in Ulster 81–90, 136–9; parallels with Irish and Indians 34–5, 46–7, 273–4n27; post-Emancipation 140, 142, 144–8, 157, 191–2, 314n51; prohibitions against reading and writing 85; prohibitions on ownership of bond-laborers 83, 293n86; racial classifications of 27–8; racial slavery as racial oppression of free as well as bonded 327n58; reduced by debt peonage and prisoner-leasing to "slavery in all but name" 144; sexual exploitation of women by European-American men 12, 148, 201, 313n47; status of 266n11; and struggle over racial slavery 159–160; Vaughan on 266n11
African-Brazilians 4–5, 8, 17
African-Caribbeans 2, 113, 269n47: "cultural shock" of 113
African-descended liberation and slavery in Scotland 220
African-Panamanians and English against Spanish 6
Alabama 145, 151
Allen, Theodore W.: assumption 1; racial oppression, social control, and the white race 115
American Exceptionalism 1
American Repeal Association 173
American Revolution 126, 308n72
Americas 13, 15, 53, 69–70
anarchists 277n70
Anglo-American continental colonies 36: contrasts with West Indies 3, 8, 10–14, 19; "Indian policy" 24, 84, 89–90; monoculture and bond-servitude 136; non-plantation colonies 18; plantation colonies 12–14, 24; policy parallels with Ireland 131, 136–7; racial oppression in 311n9; revolution in 91; shaped by racial slavery 52–3; social control principles 69–70
Anglo-Caribbeans 8, 12, 15
Anglo-Irish 49, 51, 57–9, 70, 287n93: bourgeoisie 125–6; establishment 76, 78–9; fourteenth- and eighteenth-century parallels 280n121; "non-racial" symbiosis with native Irish 48; term 284n17

Anglo-Normans (in Ireland): assault on Irish tribal relationships 38–46; assimilation with natives 54–6; invasion (1169) 38, 40, 45, 278n86; "Middle Nation" social control strategy 34, 53–7; option for racial oppression of 45–6; refutation of Jordan/Degler thesis 56–7
Angola 36, 206–7
Anomabu 206
"another kind of people" (Jobson) 7
anti-slavery front 165–7
Antigua bond-laborer insurrection 270n76
apprenticeship: of Catholic bourgeoisie 104–110; Catholics excluded from 85, 131, 138, 294n101; and Charter schools 87; hereditary 153; Irish excluded from 59; to Protestant masters 88; as Protestant privilege 77
Aptheker, Herbert 166, 321n49
Arkansas 148, 315n79
Asian-Americans, exclusion of 10
Australia 95, 97, 102, 216, 298n30

Bacon, Sir Francis 212, 279n105
Bacon's Rebellion (1676) 17–18, 21, 23–4, 155
Ball, John 204
Baptists 202
Baptism 80
Barbados: Afro-Barbadian request to convert to English religion 80; bourgeoisie promotes mulattoes who function as "whites" in 13
Barnes, J. A. 216–17
De Beaumont, Gustave 299n42
Beckett, James C. 77, 280n121, 287n90
Belfast 127–33, 309n97, 310n98, 310n108, 329n104: pogrom-like attacks by Protestants in 197; women in 131
benefits for all "whites" theory, unfavorable implications of 19
Bennett, Lerone, Jr., essential points 21
betagh 35, 278n81
Birney, James G. 189
Black, Isabella 312n23, 314n51, 316n87
Black Reconstruction 149, 153
Black Reconstruction (Du Bois) 1, 22, 158, 318n137
"black rents" 56–7, 117
Bolívar, Símon 224, 302n94
bond-laborers: British West Indies emancipation of 161, 270n73; European-American and African-American class solidarity 15, 17, 20–21, 23–4; former 165; number of 24; resistance of 23, 270n73; in São Tomé 206; super-exploitation of 319n11; competition with wage-labor

system 198; transportation costs 16, 270n78; "were cheaper because they were enslaved" 16. *See also* African bond-laborers; African-American bond-laborers; chattel bond-servitude; European-American bond-laborers; labor, chattel form

bondsmen 3, 17, 24

Boulter, Hugh 76, 79, 87

bourgeois social control system: national oppression in West Indies and racial oppression in U.S. 113; from racial to national oppression in Ireland 92

bourgeoisie, Anglo-American plantation: and brief Georgia exception 12–13; colonial 1, 16, 24, 80–81, 311n9; deliberate separation of European-Americans for social control 17–18; extends race privileges in Cotton Mills 155; headright land claims 83; and invention of the "white race" 23–4; non-acceptance of "mulatto" social control policy 12–14; and reduction of African-Americans to lifetime hereditary bond-servitude 16–17, 24

bourgeoisie, Anglo-Caribbean plantation: and creation and promotion of "mulatto" in Barbados 12–13; social control policy 12–14, 17–19, 20–21, 137–8

bourgeoisie: British, 124, 131–2; British colonists in Ireland and social control 92, 113, 127

bourgeoisie, Irish Catholic: abandonment of national independence 104; Act of Union 94–9; apprenticeship of 104–10; Catholic Emancipation and 99–101; and end of religio-racial oppression 105; follows procedure for national bourgeoisie 99; incorporated into buffer social control stratum 92, 105; and renewal of religio-racial social control 30, 47–8, 66; social promotion of 108–9

bourgeoisie, U.S., national: maintains system of racial privileges of laboring class "whites" 148; opposes redistribution of plantation lands 141; opts for White Reconstruction 143–4; plays "white card" to destroy Exodus 146; will expressed in signal events 313–4n49

bourgeoisie, U.S., northern: abandons Reconstruction and accepts post-Emancipation racial oppression 144; in pro-slavery phalanx 161–2; shapes homestead policy as white-skin privilege 153; and slave trade 162; victorious, confronts question of social control 139; white privilege industrial employment policy 155

Boyne, Battle of the (1690) 124, 308n64

Brazil: difference in treatment of African-Americans and African-Brazilians 4–5; indigenous resistance and social control 217; "money whitens" 27; Negro Catholic priests 175; Portuguese policy 69; Protestant Dutch sugar planters 80; rebellion 17

Breen, Timothy H. 19–21

British Empire: and Africa 206–7; interests 133; Ireland and 95, 112, 126; reforms 299n40; standing army in Ireland 99, 303–4n135; and storm of revolution 91–2

British government "Irish policy": Catholic Emancipation 96, 99–100; dismantling of Protestant privilege 111; from racial to national oppression 92, 104; social promotion of Catholic bourgeoisie 107–9; towards yeomanry 102–4; and Union 95–6, 97

British West Indies: bond-laborer housing 290n34; bond-laborers' emancipation 161, 170, 172, 270n76, 323n80; contrast with continent 3, 8, 10–14, 17; decision to promote "free colored" in 13–4, 113; insurrections by bond-laborers in 270n76; Irish shipped to 73; from racial to national oppression in 36; social control system in 13–4, 24, 81, 112–4; too few European laborers in 19; "tripartite social order" 113

Brooklyn 187, 330n119

Brown, John 145, 150, 165, 315n60

Brown v. Board of Education 2, 265n5

Bruce, Edward 48, 54, 275n48, 284n14

Burke, Edmund 31, 71, 92, 271n96

Butler, W. F. T. 282n154, 305n13, 305n18

Calhoun, John C. (U.S. Vice President) 148, 161, 319n15, 320n35

Calhoun, John C. (grandson) 148–9, 314n54, 315nn79–80, 316n55

Canada 95, 107, 168, 201–2, 298n30, 303–4n135, 326–7n46

Canny, Nicholas P. 29–30

capital accumulation: in England by end of sixteenth century 211–12; in U.S. by virtue of "white" racial privileges of European-American laboring class 141

capitalism 143–4: reserve army of unemployed normal to 160

capitalist class: opposes expropriation and redistribution of Southern plantations 141; and the South 314n54

Casely-Hayford, J. E. 276n54

Cash, W. J. 155, 157

Catholic Association, the 99, 105, 302n100

Catholic clergy, Ireland: abolitionist sentiment among 172, 177–8, 324n2; banned and exiled 73, 78; in Catholic emancipation campaign 99; post-1829 role in social control 107, 110, 300n59; pre-1829 collaboration with British 92–5, 100, 110, 298nn28–9, 300n5

Catholic clergy, U.S. 179–81, 324n2, 324n9

Catholic Committee 94, 297n18, 297n20

"Catholic Emancipation": as campaign, and class struggle 97, 99–100, 299n44, 300n48, 300n51; as historical issue 91–2, 94, 96–7, 100, 298n35; Peel's strategy toward 109; and religio-racial and then national oppression 96, 105, 115, 298n34; Roman Catholic Relief Act (1829) 100–101, 107, 297n10; and voting rights 186–7

Catholic Irish-Americans: leaders reverse "nonalignment" policy 326n31; racially oppressed in Ireland emerge as members of "white race" in U.S. 30

Catholic press and clergy (in U.S.): abolitionist strategy toward 171–2; drive white-supremacist pro-slavery attitudes 189, 198; journals' support Democratic Party and hatred of abolitionists 324n9; vehemence on slavery question 328n76; white supremacist Young Irelander publications 324n10

Catholics in Ireland 29, 32, 48–51, 282n154, 283n164

Caucasian (formerly *Citizen*) 188–9, 191, 324n10

Charter Schools 87–9, 123–4, 295n117: emulated by white supremacy and racial oppression in Indian education 295nn123–4

Chartist movement 320n36

Chastellux, Francois Jean, Marquis de 201, 271n98

chattel bond-servitude 118, 136, 141, 312n32: "cheap land" apology for 203–4; defended as "a positive good" 10, 163, 320n35; expected to die out 160; not profitable option in Ireland 74–6; and super-exploitation 319n11; "white" labor on 164–5; why not in Ireland 72–6

"cheaper labor" rationale 15–16, 203–4

Chichester, Arthur, 64, 115–6, 118, 137, 214

children 38–9, 45, 125, 287n92: African-American under racial oppression 33; and Charter Schools 87–8; chattel bond-servants 73–6, 206, 289n10; cotton mill workers 156, 158; illegitimate in England 12; and inheritance 43; of Irish tenants brought up Protestant 122

Chinese: exclusion and quotas 327n49; workers 152; as "white" in Cuba 27

Christianity: Anglican standards for Irish 87; colonialist standards 29, 31, 36; in Ireland, avoidance of conversion 80–81; for the Irish 278n86; as grounds for "Indians" rights 70, 274n31, 275n46; in Virginia does not alter condition of bond-laborer 80–81

Christians: English common law divided on enslavability of 23–4; forbidden to enslave Christians 80–81, 84

Christophe, Henri 32

Church of Ireland (Anglican): disestablishment 92; establishment of 57; Irish like aliens 120; payment of tithes to 75, 98, 101–2; and Presbyterians 79, 120

Cincinnati Repeal Association 174–6

Citizen (later *Caucasian*) 184, 189, 324n10

citizenship: and African-Americans 139, 185–6; and Indians 47; and kinship society 37; and Ulster Scots 125; as "white race" privilege 139, 185–6

civil rights, issues and movement 2, 134, 149, 265n2, 304n2, 317–8n136: in U.S. and Ulster 158

Civil War: African-Americans in 139; and ending of disfranchisement in New York 187; English 48–9, 118; labor movement's "greatest opportunity" after (Du Bois) 318n137; and new problems for the South 143; and New York political atmosphere 162, 164; U.S. 10, 143, 161–2, 164; and "white-skinned labourer" prerogative (Marx) 143

"Civis" 271n95

Clare (County) 50, 285n31

class collaboration, political heart of Protestant Ascendancy 124

class consciousness (proletarian): displacement of by "white" identity 21; subordinated to "race" distinction in U.S. 113; white skin privilege as preventive against 157

class differentiation: and colonizing strategy 69–70; in Irish tribal society 38–40; among Ulster tenantry 123, 125

Clay, Henry 161, 164–5, 188–9, 319n16

Clontarf 107, 124, 169, 174, 224

Coercion Bill 102, 105–6, 108, 192, 195

Collins, John Anderson 172

colonial power: and Anglo-Hispanic rivalry 61–3; social control problems of 1–2, 52–4, 67–9

colonialists: British and Ireland 65–6, 70, 93, 95; some propose that Irish be enslaved *en masse* 59; Spanish 61; varied English opinions on Africans 7

"colonization" of free African-Americans:

Clay on 319n16; in Ireland 212; schemes
for 10, 161, 163–4, 167, 170; as "white
race" fantasy 164
colony versus tribe 35–46
"colored" people: classification 27–8; free,
middle-class intermediate stratum in West
Indies not understood as synonym to
"Negro" as in U.S. 113; orphanage burned
197
Colored People's Conventions 142, 313n38,
313n40
"Compromises" on slavery (1787, 1820, 1850)
159–60
Congo 206
Congregationalist Church 202
Congress of the U.S. 37, 139, 314n52
Connaught (Province): 127, "transplantation"
to 50, 282n154, 282n156, 288n107; tribal
affinities in 65; Ulster Protestants drive
Catholics into 94
Connolly, James 134, 282n160, 309n95
Connolly, S. J. 300n48, 303n126
Conscription Act (1863) 328n77
constitutional barriers to English colonization
in Ireland 44–5
cottage weaving 125, 130, 168
cottiers (cotters) 75, 87, 291n37: housing of
Irish compared to bond-labor housing in
West Indies 290n34; Irish, compared to
U.S. sharecroppers 139
cotton gin 160–61
Cotton Mill Campaign and industry 142,
144, 155–8, 317n113, 317n126, 317n129,
318n136
coverture: defined 52, 283n2; denied under
racial oppression 52
Crawford, William H. 202
Creole (ship) 165
Cromwell, Henry 67
Cromwell, Oliver 281–2n149: Cromwellian
conquest 49–50, 91, results in religio-racial
oppression 30; transplantation of Catholics
161
"croppy-lie-down" (war cry of Protestant
yeomanry) 103
Cuba 27, 162, 181
cultural variation: doesn't explain different
treatment of Africans in British West Indies
and Anglo-America 8
Custom House patronage 190, 195–6

Davidson, Basil 7, 61
Davies, Sir John (1565?–1618) 7, 267n30
Davies, Sir John (1569–1626) 267n30,
279n105: ambiguity "toward the Negro"
7; on Ireland 44–5, 54,115–16; and social
control in 65–6, 112, 144; suggests

Virginia exile 289n16
Davis, David Brion 27
Dawes General Allotment Act 37
De Clare, Richard Fitzgilbert (Strongbow) 45
De Lacy, Hugh 45
De Marisco, Geoffrey 45
De Paor, Liam 127, 134, 303n2
De Bow's Review 156, 161
"deficiency laws" 137–8; "Irish Papists" not
suitable as "whites" in Nevis (1701) 138
"degenerate English" 61
Degler, Carl N.: defense of socio-biology
266n14; Harris challenge to 7; and psycho-
cultural argument 4–9, 11, 15, 266n11
Democratic Party: attack on "white worker"
front 184–8; calls for "White" "vindictive
rebellion" 196; Irish Americans and 171–3;
main national organization of slaveholders
and plantation bourgeoisie 179, 319n17;
New York 319n17; opposes African-
Americans at Custom Office 190, 195; and
spoils system 188, 195; and Texas 188
Derry 118, 124, 308n64
Desmond War, second 63, 210
Devereux, Robert 62, 286n75
Devon Commission 122, 124, 303n126,
308n66
Dew, Thomas Roderick 271n96
Dissenters 79, 120, 125, 300n62
District of Columbia 170
Dixon, Thomas, Jr. 269n51
Dobzhansky, Theodosius 21–2
Douglass, Frederick 86, 138–9, 145, 151,
166, 178, 295n111, 324n8; on false
"proletarian" pretensions of "white" labor
movement 166
Down (County) 121–2, 127, 305n12, 308n66
Draft Riot "white" pogrom 162, 182,
326n36, 328n77: Catholic Press's role in
328n76; chronology of white-supremacist
preparation 189–92; mobs as "white
workingmen" 197; not a "working-class
movement" 194
Drake, Sir Francis 6, 61–2
Dred Scott decision 33, 47, 280n142; and Irish
Catholic parallel 84
Du Bois, W.E.B.: and "Blindspot" 22; enslaved
Black worker more of a labor competitor
than free 198; "greatest opportunity" 158,
318n137; seed of general theory of U.S.
history 1; and "white worker" 304n1
Dublin 54, 86, 88, 172, 174
Dunlop, Robert 284n11, 287n90, 289–90n17
Dutch: in Brazil 80; East India Company
207–8; in East Indies 69

emancipation: in British West Indies 161; rate

of African-American and Irish 291n51
Emancipation Proclamation 198, 321n45, 325n23
England: agricultural activity of wage labor and capital 211; and bond-labor transport costs 16, 270n78; colonial rivalry with Spain 48, 58, 61, 63, 66; colonial social control strategy 69–70; commitment to Reformation 47–8; Conservative (Tory) Party 109, 111, 133; divided mind on enslavability of Christians 23–4; economy based on land cultivation 40; fear of Ireland-based invasion 61, 133, 286n57; industry in 21–2; joint stock company emergence 212; laws contradict Irish tribal Brehon law 34–5; peculiarities of colonial labor supply and implications for development of bond-labor system in Anglo-America 23; Petty proposes slavery in 72; Poor Law (1601) 73; "population" theory versus famine relief 309n90; ruling class policy in regard to peasant uprisings 303n122; and Scotland, economic contrasts 120; slavery of Christians barred 80; vagrancy act (1597) 73; wage differential between English and Irish and between wage- and bond-labor in continental Anglo-America 76, 221–2
England, John, Bishop of Charleston 172, 180
English people: find new identity as "white" 10–11; historians on racism of some toward another European nation (Ireland) 29–31; notion of bias greatly modified by early colonial records 5–7; opinions of African-Americans varied and lack antipathy 7
English monarchs: Henry II (1154–89) 44–6; John (1199–1216) 45; Edward I (1272–1307) 34; Edward III (1312–77) 56; Henry VII (1485–1509) 56, 284n25; Henry VIII (1509–47) 44, 57, 279n92, 284n29, 287n86; Mary I (Mary Tudor) 58–9, 275n36; Elizabeth I (1558–1603) 60, 62–3, 65, 81, 285n48, 286n75, excommunicated 209; James I (VI of Scotland) (1603–25) 44, 65, 115, 119, 122, 305n12, 306n34; Charles I (1625–49) 49, 67; Charles II (1660–85) 51, 75, 125, 219; James II (1685–89) 51, 68–9, 94, 308n64; William III (William of Orange) (1689–1702) 94; William IV (1765–1837) 301n87
English Pale 29, 54, 56, 61
Ernst, Robert 298n119: on "labor competition" 298n120
ethnocentrism 7
European-American bond-laborers: half of (tithable) European-American population

in 1676 Tidewater region of Virginia 18; limited-term African-Americans priced similarly to 293n87; majority of bond-laborers in 1650 Barbados 80; "only rebellions by white servants in the continental colonies came before firm entrenchment of slavery" (Jordan) 270n73; resistance of 23–4. See also bond-laborers
European-American laborers: different treatment of European-Americans and African-Americans deliberate ruling class policy 3, 17–18; laboring class component of pro-slavery phalanx 162; "showed little interest in 'white identity'" before system of "race" privileges conferred on at end of seventeenth century 14
European-American Southerners who fought racial oppression 50–51, 316n87, 316n107: bourgeoisie fears of masses doing likewise 154–5, 312n24
European-Americans 2, 4, 14–17, 19–21, 162–6: adapted to and adopted into "white race" 30, 199; immigrants confront America constructed on racial oppression and white-skin privileges 184
Europeans: historians of Irish history comment on racism of Europeans toward non-Europeans and between one European nation and another 29; "supposed no natural inferiority in Africans" 7
Evans, George Henry 164, 320n38
"exclusive dealing" ("boycotting") 98
expropriation 50–51, 282nn154–5, 161, 251: "expropriate the expropriators" 141
extirpation of native social order: and displacement by laboring-class immigrants 115: of Irish and Indians 136–7; and racial oppression of "red man" 136

family: African-American, fundamental barrier to system of chattel bondage 90; Indian, not a decisive obstacle to expropriation of land and extirpation of 90; ties assaulted by racial oppression 35–8, 86–90, 295n124
famine: as English weapon of war 209–10; families flocked to Belfast 130; the Great Famine (1845–50) 98, 224, 298n34, 303n126; in Ireland 60, 62–5, 73, 78, 98; led to mass emigration 112, 124, 168; priests' role in relief of 110; in Ulster 309n90
Federalist Party 187, 327n58
feudal order 42–3, eclipse of 59
Fitzgibbon, John (Lord Clare) 51, 61
Fitzhugh, George 163
Fletcher, Andrew 219

Flight of the Earls 116
Florida 12–13, 138, 142
forty-shilling freeholders 91, 94–5, 100–101,
    107, 300n62: disfranchisement of 105
Fox, Charles James 112
Fox, George 269n52
France 91–2, 100
Franklin, John Hope 142
Frederickson, George M. 30
free African-Americans: contrast with free
    African-Brazilians 4–5, 8; excluded from
    buffer social control stratum 14, 18, 21;
    exclusions against, evidence that mass of
    "whites" were proletarians and semi-
    proletarians 19; as proportion of total
    African-Americans 77, 291n51
"free Negro" 163, 266–7n16: in British West
    Indies 3, 8, 10–14
Free Soil movement and Party 138–9, 166–7,
    321n52: opposed to competition between
    "free" and slave labor 141; "white labor"
    accepts white-skin privilege of, renders
    itself powerless to shape land policy 152–3
freedmen/freedwomen 140, 142, 151–2, 155,
    315n79
Freehling, William W. 188, 311n4, 319n14
freeholders 81, 84, 186, 282n154: African-
    American 140
Freeman's Journal (later *Freeman's Journal
    and Catholic Register*) 179, 189, 328n76
French people: intermarriage 201; in North
    America 201–2, 311n1
French Revolution 92
Fugitive Slave Law 139, 148, 159–60, 176,
    186: destitute European-Americans
    expected to support 185
Fuller, James Canning 177, 324–5n10

Gaelic Irish language and culture 54–6, 59:
    land redistribution and ownership 278n76
Galway (County) 67, 296n4
Garn, Stanley M. 21–2
Garrison, William Lloyd 165, 169, 172–4,
    177, 321n49
garrisons 93, 112
Garvey, Marcus 113, 304n139
Gates, Paul Wallace 140
gavelkind inheritance 41–2, 44, 117: used to
    reduce Catholic landholding 83, 89, 305n15
gender oppression: Irish tribal and English
    feudal/capitalist variations 41–3;
    organically related to class, race, and
    national oppression 28. *See also* coverture;
    male supremacy; women
genocide: Anglo-Norman "middle nation"
    against Irish 34; Spanish against Christian
    Moors 29

gentry 59
Georgia 142, 151: brief extending of rights
    to mulatto as social control policy 12–14;
    cancels ban on slavery 23; deficiency law
    137–8; "killing of a negro" not a felony
    47, 280n130; nullification of tribal laws
    and land rights, "Trail of Tears," and racial
    oppression of Cherokees 33, 37, 137,
    276–7n63; originates as no-slavery buffer
    against flight to Spanish Florida or friendly
    Indians 12–13; South Carolina plantation
    bourgeoisie ends no-slavery period 13;
    Ulster Protestants in 276n63
"germ theory" of American history 9
German immigrant workers 15, 152, 184, 189:
    "German strikebreakers" 194
Gilbert, Humphrey: displays heads of Irish
    209; knighted 210
Gladstone, William 315n66
Glorious Revolution 71, 120
gossipred (fosterage) 43, 45, 55, 279n102
Graduation Act (1854) 138
grain prices 45–6
"Grand Dilemma" 66–7, 94, 96
Guadeloupe 92
Guiana Guyana (British Guiana) 17, 27,
    268n43

Haiti (Hispaniola, St Domingue): abolition of
    slavery 161; Haitian Revolution 36, 91,
    322n63; sons of African chieftains in 32
Hakluyt, Richard 6, 267n26
Hammond, Senator J. H. 163, 317n35
Handlin, Oscar and Mary 3–5, 8, 11, 15,
    295n3
Harper's Ferry 165
Harris, Marvin 7
Harrison, Hubert 113
Hassard, John R. G. 180, 325n24, 325n25
Hayes-Tilden deal (1876) 152, 314n49
Haymarket Affair 38, 277n70
Hechter, Michael 30–32
Helper, Hinton Rowan 316n107, 318n8,
    319n15, 319n23
Henry "of London" (Archbishop) 45–6
herding vs. cultivation economies 35, 41–2,
    45–6, 278n88, 279n90
Hibernian Anti-Slavery Society 172, 177
Hill, George 66–67, 287n90
Hindus, "Caucasians" not "recognized as
    white" 327n49
Hispanic America 27, 47
Holland, lack of exportable labor 207
"Home Rule" 94, 132–3, 146, 315n66
Homestead Act (1862) 138–9, 152–3, 198
homestead right: as African-American demand
    139–42, 149; and free soil 138; parallel to

Ulster custom 138; as "white" privilege 138–41, 149, 153–4
homesteads: in Plains states 153; in South 140; in West 152
House of Commons 73
Houston, Sam 188
Hughes, Archbishop John 190–92, 326n36: calls for Lincoln to resign 190; on Catholic and Protestant conversion rates 325n15; changes on slavery question 325n25; "chief" of American Catholics 169, 179–81, 183, 198, 325n11, 325n24; defender of white-race privileges 180; Draft Riots 182; encounter with O'Connell 181; foe of abolition 178, 180; on Irish movement westward 326n29; as "Leander" 168–9, 180, 226–8, 325n25; no reply to anti-Negro cries 93, 329n93; "non-interference" stand on war 190; opposes equality for free African-Americans 182, 190–92; rejects Emancipation as war aim 182, 190–91; seeks to restrain mobs 328n76; and slaveholders 172–3, 180–82, 192, 198–9, 322n63

immigrants 13, 15, 138–9, 168, 268n43: a fantasy as plantation labor supply 152, 154, 157, 184–5
immigration as "white" privilege 144, 152–4, 184–5, 327n49: and "labor competition" 194; and Negro Exodus 147; preventive against class consciousness 157
imperialism, "white" 10
incubus: of "race" privileges 146; of "white" identity 21; of "white" labor's privileges over black labor 149
India 69
Indians (of the Americas) 28–30, 216–17; African-American parallels 31–2, 34, 46–7, 276n6; Algonkians 278n88; Anglo-American "white race" laws and 84, 90; Arawaks 70; assault on tribal collective ownership becomes dominant theme after Civil War 36–8; Black Caribs 217; "Blackfeet" 302n104; Canadian 201; Caribs 70, 217; in Central and South America 302n94; certificates of "whiteness" and Irish equivalent 47; and continental plantation bond-servitude 136; colonial powers policy toward 69–70; Cherokees 33, 37, 136–7, 275nn44–6, 276–7n63; Creek, U.S. war against (1813–14) 136–7; education programs emulate Charter schools 88–9, 295n124; English lack sufficient relative strength over 136; family relationships 89–90, 295n124; Incas 217; "Indian policy"

dispute 24; "Indian Removal," "Trail of Tears" 33, 37, 137; "Indios" 302n94; Irish parallels 28–31, 34, 276n62, 282n156, 299n42; Mexican Indians as "white" in Cuba 27; Micomac 201; Moskito used against Maroons 13; in North America 29, 31, 33–4, 273n27, 282n56; Omaha 37; perceived as white by Englishmen 273–4n27; plantation monoculture and racial oppression of African-Americans rules out use of Indian labor 136; racial oppression of 90; Seminoles 170; some time before English thought of social control over 136; Sioux (Dakota) 37–8, 89, 276n62; treaties broken 36–7, 276nn62–3; treatment by Spanish like English treatment of Irish 31, 274n30; undifferentiated social structure 136; war captives shipped to Caribbean as bond-laborers 136; "white" receives incentive for marriage to 202, 296n128; white supremacist exclusion of 10
industrial employment: "almost wholly" African-American in New York City 195; Cotton Mill Campaign 155–7; Northern employers adopt principle of racial discrimination in 195; and religio-racial privilege in Belfast 131–5; as "white" privilege 141, 155, 195
Industrial Revolution 128, 130, 168: "early" (England, sixteenth century) 62, 120, 211–12; in Ireland in mold of Protestant Ascendancy 155; in U.S. South in mold of white supremacy 155
inheritance 279n97. See also gavelkind
Innes, Stephen 20, 272n101
intermarriage 201–2: churches support 202
intermediate buffer social control stratum: foreclosed by plantation system 23; as "garrison" 112; general principle, interests conflict at points with ruling class and inviolable spheres apportioned to prevent defection to side of masses 153; recruitment of 23
International Workingmen's Association 149
"interracial" mating 11–12, 83, 89: Jordan on 201–2n57, 270n60, 201–2; Stampp on 270n60
invention: of middle stratum 13; as a political act 22; Protestant Ascendancy as 71; of the "white race" 22–4
Ireland (ancient and medieval): attempt to impose racial oppression fails (c. 1317–c. 1534) 54–6, 231; bid for English legal rights (1277) denied 34–5; Brehons (judges) 34, 40, 42–3, 329n97; central problem of British rule 70; clash of Irish

and English social systems 34, 40–44, 277n72, 278n76, 278n88, 279n92, 95, 97, 99; economy based mainly on land cultivation 40; Gaelic and English constitutional conflicts 44–5; hereditary bondage to land 278n81; kinship society 35–44, 276n54; land ownership 278n76; laws of succession 42; noble families "Not admitted to English law" 47; political economy (late medieval) 56; population 281n149, 310n108; pre-Christian 278n88; racial oppression in first period 34–5, 46, 231, 280n115; "Remonstrance" to Pope John XXII (1317) 35; Scots (Bruce) invasion (1315–18) 54, 284n14; superstructural dissonance of Gaelic Ireland under English (Anglo-Norman) rule 41–6; tribal social system 38–43

Ireland (after 1534): agrarian unrest 96, 101, 104, 106, 109; and ante-bellum America 159–60, 166–8, 177–8; chronological finding aid 231–2; emigration from, famine related 124; as safety valve for Ulster discontents 126; English play off one sept against another 287n80; exile from 50, 67, 73–4, 116, 281–2n149, 289nn16–18; expropriation of lands 282n154, 287n97; gentry and yeomanry sought for social control 59; habeas corpus suspended 99; history 277n72; "Irish slave trade" (post 1600) 74, 290n24; land in, as capital fund for English government 68, 287n97; land reform, Ireland 49, 93, 104, 303n126; leasing disabilities on Catholics ended 93, 297n15; military and 91–2, 94, 112, 296n3, 296n6, 308n63; national subordination to Britain 111; in new world context 60–62; parallels 107, 112–14, 302n106, 280n121, 329n104; Parliamentary/Cromwellian 50–1, 67–8, 282n154, 287n97; refutes fundamental assumption of Jordan/Degler thesis 57; Spanish Caribbean extermination policy differs 70; textile manufacture 130–31; threat of French invasion 296n1; tribal lands, confiscated 116; tribal social system 47–50, 54–9, 64–5; Williamite 51, 282–3n160, 283n161. *See also* racial oppression (Ireland); social control (Ireland)

Irish: British treat Irish as standard of "savage or outlandish social behavior" 31; Catholic men barred from acquiring property from Protestants by dowry 83; chieftains class 117–18, 121, 305n15; collaborators with British 84, 287n80; Connolly on defeat of 282n160; forced transportation to bond-servitude in Anglo-American colonies 73–4; forced to view severed heads of kinsfolk 209; free classes, complaint of 275–6n53; free in position similar to betagh 35; landholders, Catholic 83, 297n16; oppression of by English compared to Spanish genocide of Christian Moors 29; revolutionary American and French influences on 91–2, 107, 125–6, 297n20; "slave trade" 74; sold to serve as soldiers in foreign armies 50, 67, 73, 281–2n149; voting rights 47, 94, 299n43, 301n67

Irish Abolitionist Address to Irish Americans (1842) 177: opposition from Irish-American establishment 182–4

Irish-American Establishment: and "Catholic-Irish" front 178–84, 189, 196, 324n9, 328n76; frame issues in pro-slavery terms 198

Irish-Americans: and abolitionists 171–3; acting as "whites" 189–92; adapted to and adopted into "white" American social order 199; in America constructed on racial oppression and white-skin privileges 184; apprenticeship, bans on 85, 294n101; background in struggle against racial oppression in Ireland 167, 186, 195; Catholic minority in strongly Protestant society 167–9; conditions in New York 326n30; dispersal of 322n59, 326n30; emerge as members of "white race" 30, 185–6; employment 195–8; immigrant parallels and divergences with West Indian immigrants of African descent to U.S. 114; immigrant workers 167–8, 193–4; immigrants 167–76; "labor competition" rationale 192–8; massive volume 167–8, 186, 321–2n55; in nation 186; in New York 319n17; not originators of white supremacy 199; O'Connell and the Cincinnati Repeal Association 174–6; opposition to draft 328n77; popular rights as "white-skin privileges" and token of "white race" membership 199; press 189, 322–3n64, 324n10; reject own national heritage to become part of system of "white" racial oppression 186; remittances to Ireland 323n74; sea-change of 159, 177, 199; solidarity with African-Americans 324–5n10; and the Southern prospect 152; and Texas annexation 188–9; two-front campaign 178–81, 183–9; "white worker" front 178–81, 183–8; white-supremacist attitudes driven by Tammany Hall and Catholic Establishment in interest of plantation bourgeoisie 198–9

Irish analogies and parallels: African-Americans 23, 28–33, 85, 138, 141; American Indians 29–31, 34–6, 273n27, 274n62, 282n156; as argument for sociogenic theory of racial oppression 46–7; British West Indies 112–14; deliberate ruling class turns to racial oppression 46; English express similar chauvinism toward Scots and Welsh with different results 280n115; uprooting of Cherokee 137. *See also* United States, analogies

Irish (Catholic) bourgeoisie 294n101, 300n48: and 1798 Rebellion 94, 297n52; and agrarian unrest 94; bought off 297n20; clerical section 133; economic situation of 92–3, 291–2n52; on Emancipation and Repeal 96–7; hibernicus 46, 55; integration into British social control system 92, 104, 109–12, 115, 127; large number adopted Protestantism 291–2n52; as national bourgeoisie 99; outside Ulster as intermediate buffer social control stratum 104–5, 107, 112; racial oppression of 30, 92; rapprochement with British bourgeoisie 92–4, 126, 303n135; regarded by English law as foreigners in own land 47; and social control 105

Irish (Catholic) peasantry 98–9, 103, 105–6, 110, 113: landless and poor predominate among 98; poor compared to African-Americans and Indians 297n20; as tenants-at-will 123; tithe war of 101–2; translate "Emancipation" and Repeal in own terms 98, 105; view repeal as forerunner of attack on landlordism 299n42

Irish (Catholic) workers: abuse of, and difference in treatment as "white" in America 295n111; cottier-weavers 130; intense exploitation of 292n55; proletarians and non-capitalist tenants 123, 130; restrictions against right to work in trades 96, 111

Irish mirror 22–3: for insights into racial oppression and ruling class social control in the U.S. 159; metaphor, subjects of racial oppression are sea-changed into "white Americans" and opponents of abolition and equal rights 159

"Irish Party" 303n111

Irish (Protestant) laborers 122–3, 125, 127, 130, 275: Protestant Ascendancy and privilege in employment 129–33, 155

"Irish Republican Brotherhood" (Fenians) 327–8n46

Irish women: in Belfast (1860s) 131; rape of 46; sold into exile 74; status of tribal 42–3, 279n99

"irrepressible conflict" 159, 318n1

Italy 40

Jackson, Andrew 33, 136–7, 185–6, 311n4

Jacksonian Democratic Party 179

Jacksonian Democracy: "equality of white men" and "absolute superiority" over non-whites 311n4; right to vote as white-skin privilege 184

Jacksonians and spoils system 185

Jacobite War (1689–91) 71, 74

Jacobites 292n62

Jamaica: colonists defend "interracial liaisons" 11–12; dismantling of slavery in 323n80; Garvey on "difference" from white supremacist social order of U.S. 113; individual Negroes enfranchised 148; insurrection by bond-laborers (1831) 270n76; Irish parallel 107, 302n106; magnanimity of freed persons 175; maroons 12; people of European and African ancestry in 269n47; resistance and social control 13, 15, 138, 270n76

Jamestown, Virginia 3, 23, 115, 207, 289n16

Japanese, bars against immigration of 327n49

Jefferson, Thomas 19

Jewish children 206

Jobson, Richard 7

Johnson, Anthony 294n89

Johnson, Lyndon Baines 2

Jordan, Winthrop D.: avoidance of comparisons between English and other European colonies in the Americas 269n53; book subtitle 269n51; fixes label of "white" on people who never so identified 267n17; on genetic imperatives, racial exclusionism, and Nova Scotia case 296n128; on "Georgia exception" 12–14; and "germ theory" 9; epitaph for equal rights by African-Americans 269n50; on human sexual drive and "interracial" and interspecies sex 270n57; on "incipient species" 4; on intermarriage 202; "lost in a sea of blacks" 12; not distanced from his book's presentation of racist attitudes 269n51; and origin of racial slavery debate 268n39; and "paradox" theory 19; "people of the Word, adventuring into a New World" 268n42; "presentism" 9; and "psycho-cultural" argument 4–14; on "race" 21–2; reviewers of 269n52; "social and economic necessities ... called for ... bound, controlled labor" 204; on sex ratios 10; "unthinking decision" explanation

9, 268n40; views of 8–11, 268nn38–9, 268n41; and West Indies/continental differences 11–12, 269n53
Jordan/Degler thesis 4, 195, 266n11: Irish history refutes fundamental assumption of 57
Julian, George W. 140, 312n27

Kansas 139, 144–7, 150, 197, 312n21: foreclosures in 153; foreign-born fastest growing population in 152
Kelley, William Darrah 143: as foe of white supremacism 313n47
Kennedy, John F. 265n2
Kentucky 145
Kenya 308n63
Kettel, Thomas Prentice 318n8, 10, 319n23
Key, Elizabeth 80, 292n70
Khoisan people 207–8
killing, of Negro and Irish, parallels 47, 280n130, 329n104
"kindly tenants" 119, 122, 306n35
"king's peace" 42–4, 48
King, Archbishop William 283n5
Kinsale, Siege of 286nn68–9
kinship society 35–44, 276n54
Kommenda 206

labor: "abstract labour" (Marx) 131, 309n94; chattel form 72, 23; "contract" 290n29; intensification of, natural limits 52, 75–6, 283n7; productivity of 160, 318n10, 319n11; relative costs of 74–6; South after Civil War presented "greatest opportunity for a real national labor movement" (Du Bois) 318n137; "two-fold character of" 309n94. See also deficiency laws; racial privileges; "white labor"
"labor competition": as a "white-labor" issue, "fear of Negro job competition" had no basis in fact 194, 197; between bond and free 198; in context of "white" spoils system develops into assertion of right of "white" preference 196; countered by solidarity 194; Ernst on 330n120; Free Soil opposition to competition between "free" and slave labor 141; given abnormal "racial" form 18, 195–6; group competition, historical 192, 194; Hughes on Draft Riot's cause as 192; "native-born" and immigrant 192; normal under wage-labor system 192; number of foreign-born "white" competitors greater than number of African-Americans 193–4; and palliative allusions to "negro strikebreakers" 192; popular rights given form of "white-skin privileges" 199;

rationale 192–99; and strikebreaking 192, 194
laborers: African-Americans and sharecropping peonage 290n29; different treatment of European- and African-Americans due to deliberate ruling-class policy 3, 17–18; European-American adapted to and adopted into "white" American social order 199; exclusion from skilled trades 113, 138; status of African-American and European-American essentially same in much of seventeenth century 3; fellowship between 7. See also African bond-laborers; African-American bond-laborers; bond-laborers; chattel bond-servitude; European-American bond-laborers; National Labor Union ("white"); Negro National Labor Union; Workingmen's United Political Association
"Labour cannot emancipate itself in the white skin where in the black it is branded" (Marx) 166
Land/labor ratio theory 203–5
landownership: in Europe and West Africa 276n59
land question, United States 138–43, 149, 152–3, 198: "free land" aspect 131; in interest of petty bourgeoisie 141–2; Southern land aspect and proletarians 142; as "white" racial privilege 141
land tenure principles: Anglo-Norman 279n92; collective ownership 35, 38, 276n54; Franco-Algonkian relations 278n88; Irish-Norse relations 278n88; private segmentation 35; Ulster Custom 121–4
Las Casas, Bartolomé de 70, 274n31
laws: contrasting English and Irish 41–44; disfranchisement of African-Americans 187, 327n58; Fugitive Slave Law 185; immigration 185, 327n49; naturalization 186–7; New York State "white" manhood suffrage 187–8, 195, 327n57
"Leander." See Hughes, John
Lecky, William Edward Hartpole 85, 128, 293n83
Leinster (Province) 120, 127, 129
Lewis, John Solomon 148, 315n59
Liberator, The 166, 169, 323n67: African-American readership 321n49
liberty, presumption of: African-Americans shared 266–7n16; a white-skin privilege 184–5
Liberty Party 189
Lichfield House 108
Ligon, Richard 80
Lincoln, Abraham 164, 182, 189–91, 223, 309n94: Marx to 143, 149

Locke, John 283n164
Longshoremen's Association 196–7
Lorillard tobacco factory 191, 329n111
Louisiana 28, 139, 145, 154, 159: definition
   of "Negro" 272n10; African-Americans
   killed by white-supremacist repression
   (1866–75) 314n52
Loyal National Repeal Association 102,
   106–7, 177
lynching: of African-Americans 192, 328n77;
   not of European immigrants 197

Mac Murchada, Diarmait 45
Macaulay, Thomas Babington 48, 303–4n135
MacNeill, Eoin 277n72: objects to term
   "tribe" 277n74
Madagascar 207
Madden, Richard Robert 172, 323n80
Madison, James 19, 202: opposition to use of
   "slave" and "slavery" in U.S. Constitution
   318n2
Maguire, Conor Roe 117, 287n80
male privileges 140, 154, 157, 313n47,
   315n77
male supremacy: patriarchy 24, 42–3, 86–7,
   283n2; white 24
Mallow Defiance 169, 224, 323n66
Malthus, Thomas Robert 309n90
Mansfield, Lord 220
maroons 6, 13
marriage 33, 41–5, 55–6, 82–3, 275n46:
   incentives for "white" Protestant to marry
   "Indian" 202, 296n128; "race" laws
   against intermarriage of Protestants to
   Catholics 83, 89; "whites" to Indians or
   Negroes 83, 89. See also coverture
Martinique 92
Marx, Karl 149, 223: on "abstract labour"
   and "two-fold character of the labour
   embodied in commodities" 309n94; "the
   highest prerogative of the white-skinned
   labourer" 143; Ireland as England's excuse
   for "big standing army" 303–4n135;
   Ireland's strategic importance to England
   286n57; "Labour cannot emancipate itself
   in the white skin where in the black it is
   branded" 166; "ordinary English worker
   hates the Irish" like "poor whites" hate
   African-Americans 29
"'Marxist' white apologist school of American
   labor historiography" 320–1n39
Maryland Provincial Supreme Court
   89–90
mass mobilizations. See "monster meetings"
Massachusetts Anti-Slavery Society 166, 173,
   321n52, 323n67
Mathew, Theobold 172

Mau-Mau 308n63
Maynooth (Royal College of St. Patrick) 100,
   110, 300nn58–9, 303n126
Meagher, Thomas Francis 178, 184, 198,
   326n45
Methodists 202, 275n46
Mexicans: Indians as "white" in Cuba 27;
   white supremacist exclusion of 10
Mexico 60, 69, 159, 170, 188
"Middle Nation," Anglo-Norman, English
   social control strategy 53–7
middle stratum: in America had to be invented
   13; England (sixteenth century) preserved
   yeoman section to serve as 311n9; in
   Ireland and British West Indies 113;
   option for racial oppression in Ireland and
   continental Anglo-America could not be
   achieved by simply preserving a middle
   class 311n9
migrants 21, 145–6, 284n11
militia 13, 91, 94, 296n6, 308n63
Minnesota 153
Mississippi Black Code 294n89
Missouri Compromise (1820) 159, 163,
   328n69,
Mitchel, John 179, 183, 196, 326n42
Mitchell, Broadus 317n113, 317n126
"A Modest Proposal" (Swift) 87
Monaghan (County) 121, 305n12
"money whitens" 27
"monster meeting(s)" 99, 323n66, 326n25:
   Donnybrook 325n25; "Emancipation"
   and Repeal strategy 102–3, 106–7, 109,
   301n81. See also Clontarf, Mallow
   Defiance
Mooney, Canice 275n49
Moors: Spanish genocide of Christian 29
Moravians 202
Morgan, Edmund S. 6, 16–20: aims "to
   explore the symbiosis of racial slavery and
   Jeffersonian freedom doctrine" 271n81;
   criticisms of 18–19, 271n81, 271n82; land/
   labor ratio hypothesis 204; "non-rebellious
   slave" 17; racial slavery and racism due to
   deliberate ruling-class choice to cope with
   social control problem17–18; "too few free
   poor on hand to matter" 18
Moryson, Fynes 62, 213–15, 285n45, 286n57,
   286n69
most vulnerable point: for decisive blow
   against slaveholders 172; to attack
   Exodusters 146
Mott, Lucretia 171
Mountjoy, Charles Blount 62–3, 91, 117,
   286n61, 286n70: famine strategy 64,
   213–15; task remains "unperfect" 65
Mozambique 207

"mulatto" (intermediate social stratum): maintenance of "white identity" equivalent to rejection of 12; promoted to petit bourgeois status in West Indies 14; plantation bourgeoisie created and promoted in Barbados where functioned as "whites" 13–14

Munster plantation 115: preparation for 209–10; ruin of 61–2; as "specific response to rebellion" 59; racial oppression and 127–9

Munster province 76, 123

Murrell, William 314n52

Nat Turner Rebellion 84, 165, 294n94

National Anti-slavery Standard 166

National independence, as an Irish purpose 96, 104, 107, 126, 133

National Labor Union ("white") 142–3, 149

national oppression: British change in Ireland from racial to 92, 96–7, 107; British West Indies parallel 112–14; Catholic Emancipation led to replacement of racial oppression by 115; colonial power establishes social distinction among oppressed and transforms system from racial oppression to 36–7; essential difference from racial oppression 23, 273n11; Irish garrison as symbol of 112, 303n135; as a particular system of oppression 28; replaces racial oppression as ruling-class social control system 23, 36, 92, 96–7, 112–15; social control system in West Indies 113

National Repeal Convention of the Friends of Ireland (1842–43) 173

nativism, "Know-Nothing" anti-Catholic bigotry: Catholic Americans beset by 183; draws on Ulster heritage 192; decline explained 329n99; considered less threatening than Abolitionism 193

"natural racism" assumption 3

naturalization 184–6, 192: defines "any alien" as "a free white person" 185; extended "to persons of African descent" 327n49

Nebraska 153

Nef, John Ulrich 211–12

"Negro" classification 27–8

"Negro Emancipation" did not lead to end of racial oppression in U.S. or to any fundamental change in bourgeois social control 115

Negro Exodus (of 1879) 144–8, 150–52, 157, 197, 314–5n57, 315n59: aims of 148; as withdrawal of variable capital 145

Negro National Labor Union 142, 149, 313n41

"Negro strikebreakers" 192: no mention of "German strikebreakers" 194

Netherlands 211

New Orleans Black and White Convention 150

New York City: African-American population in 330n119; commercial ties with "Slave States" 161–2, 319n21; and the 1913 election 187; political importance of 161–2, 319n17; plot between New York forces and Confederate agents to seize City on election day (1864) 328n76

New York State Constitution Convention (1813) 187

Norman Conquest of England (1066) 40

Norsemen 38, 278n88

North Dakota 153

North Star (later *Frederick Douglass' Paper*) 166

Northwest Ordinance 159, 328n69

"not-whites" 10

Nova Scotia 202, 296n128

O'Connell, Daniel "The Liberator" 275–6n53, 301n76: abolitionist leader 32, 161, 169–73, 177, 180–83, 322–3n64; ambivalence toward peasantry 98, 100, 102–6, 299n47, 302n97; aversion to embracing armed Irish peasantry 223; bourgeois dread of revolution 100, 105, 297n20, 302n94, 302n106; and "Catholic Emancipation" 99–101, 298–9n35, 302n98; denounces slaveholders' designs on Mexico and opposes annexation of Texas 188; on disarming anti-Catholics 326n38; encounter with Hughes 181; enemy of African-American slavery 223; on exclusion of women at World Anti-Slavery Convention 171; expresses ideas of Irish bourgeoisie 223–5; on "the filthy aristocracy of skin" 194; foe of racial oppression and white supremacy 169–70, 174–6, 178, 199; on lack of voting rights among agrarian rebels 299n43; as leader 166, 324n88; opposition to trade unionism 302n104; national liberation struggle leader 95; Parliamentary politician 100, 108–9, 112, 299n40, 302n105, 303n135; on "political protestants" 130; recommends Mexican government "for a colony of free persons of color" to oppose incursions of the "white monster" 188; and Repeal of the Union 97, 102–3, 105–6, 299n38, 299n40, 300nn48–9, 300n58; on revolutionary violence 223, 302n94; views victory over slavery in West Indies as lever for overturning slavery in U.S. 170

O'Connell, Maurice 322–3n64, 324n89
O'Connell, Morgan 224, 302n94
O'Connor, Feargus 320n36
O'Doherty, Sir Cahir, Revolt led by (1608) 116, 305n17
O'Donnell, Neil Garve 116, 287n80
O'Donnell, Red Hugh 60, 62, 65, 116, 287n86
O'Donnell, Rory, Earl of Tyrconnell 116–17, 287n86
O'Neill, Donal (king of Tyrone) 34
O'Reilly, Mulmorie Og 116, 287n80
Orangeism and the Orange order 101, 103–4, 126–7, 299n38, 301n87: rally to defend Protestant privileges 94, 126; key to British victory in 1798 127; succeed in delaying "Catholic Emancipation" 95
"Ordeal of Colonial Virginia" as "Ordeal of America" 24
"Oriental Exclusion," immigration laws 327n49
Osceola 170
Othello 5–7

Painter, Nell Irvin 314–5n57, 315n60
paradox thesis 19, 203, 271n96
Paris Commune 38
Parks, Rosa 2, 317–8n136
Parliament, Anglo-Irish 297n25: authorized to legislate independently of British Parliament 57, 84, 93–6, 125, 308n72; enacts land reforms 93; Irish delegation within 169; rapprochement with British King, Protestant Ascendancy, and Catholic bourgeoisie 92
Parliament, English (British after Union with Scotland in 1707) 94–6, 101–2, 105–9, 124, 129: and Emancipation law 323n80; establishment of different forms of government 298n30; Irish representation in 300–301n66
Parsons, Albert 150
"particular plantations" partition preserves racial oppression 133
Patterson, Orlando 27, 276n55
"peculiar institution" 1, 265n1: failure in the West Indies 24; "white race" as 24
"a peculiar people" (Jordan) 268n42
Peel, Sir Robert: on Catholic Emancipation 100–101, 110, 298n28, 299n37, 299n39; on force and social evils in Ireland 104–5, 302n93; and repeal of the Union 107–10
Penal Laws 275–6n53, 283n5: and African-American parallels 86–90; and Anglo-Saxon "Race" Laws 81–90; and assault on family 86–90; bar Catholics from legal profession 78; Burke on 92; cause lack of intermediate social control

stratum 284n5; coincide with Virginia laws to codify racial oppression 24; declassing 82–3; and deprivation of civil rights 84–5; dominate century of Irish history 71–2; easing of 92–3, 293n83; economic impact disputed 128–9; enumerated 288–9n1; and exclusion from trades 85–6, 137–8; further reduce Catholic landholding 51, 78, 283n161; and illegalization of literacy 85–6; inaugurated with two laws (1695) 293n76; Irish could not acquire land due to 82, 293n87; Lecky on 293n83; loopholes in, and Catholic middle class 293n82; operate to prevent increased productivity of labor 53; priests as outlaws under 110; racial oppression principle of refusal to legitimate class differentiation among oppressed 140; repeal of 288–9n1; rivet white supremacy in place 71
Perry, B. F. 312n24
Perry, Oliver Hazard 187
"persons bound to service" 318n2
Peru 69
Petty, Sir William 94, 104: advocates slavery in England 72, 202; on cost of war in Ireland 75; on exiling and selling of Irish 281–2n149; land/labor ratio 202; proposes mass transplantation 68–9, 288n107; social control doctrine 68–9, 134, 148–9, 288n100; states general principle of social control based on racial oppression 68, 134
phenotype 22, 27–8, 30–31: explanation as "ace-in-the-hole" of racist apologetics 28
Phillips, Ulrich Bonnell 137, 204, 276n60
Phillips, Wendell 173
phylogenic phenomenon: racial oppression/ racial slavery as sociogenic rather than 1, 23, 28
Pinckard, George 201
Pitt, William 94–5
plantation colonies: cost of transporting bond-laborers to Anglo-America 15–16, 270n78; Caribbean colonies 12–16, 69–70, European and African ancestry in 269n47; Irish men and women shipped as bond-laborers to 74
Plantation of Ulster: accession of James I key factor in 306n34; advanced by sale of Irish swordsmen to Sweden 118, 287n84; attempted (1571–5) 73; escheat (confiscation) of six counties 116, 305n12; displaces native population 117, 305n18, 307n49; extirpates native social order 117; higher wages factor in 121; most investors also Virginia Company investors 303n3; originated (1609) 31, 44, 53, 73, 115; Scots poverty and Protestantism as factors

120–21; "servitors" role in 118–19; start of "the Ulster problem" 306n34, 307n53; status of native Irish in 117, 123; treatment under 276n63; "undertakers" (capitalist investors) 118–19, 122–3, 306n32

plantations, Irish 83: campaigns against Irish and 209–10; lands, confiscation, and redistribution of 139–40; Protestant Plantation as social control strategy 58–60, 65–7; as rejection of "surrender-and-regrant" 59; two meanings of 281n143. *See also* Munster Plantation; Plantation of Ulster

"plebeian aristocracy" 71, 170

Plessy v. Ferguson 265n5

Polk, James 188

Poor Law, England (1601) 74, Scotland (1597) 218

Pope, General John 276n62

Popes: Adrian IV (1154–9) 278n86; Honorius III (1216–27) 46; John XXII (1316–34) 34; Gregory XVI (1831–46) 172, 175, 180–82

population: African-American in Brooklyn and Manhattan 330n119; in Cape Colony, Jamestown, and South Carolina 207–8

Portuguese 10: cooptation of buffer social control stratum in India and East Indies, 69; emigrants 27; navigators and colonizers 61, 66, 69, 288n110; policy of elimination of indigenous population and use of foreign labor in Brazil 69–70; in São Tomé 206

Poyning's Law 308n72

praemunire 294n100

Presbyterians 46, 72, 79, 101, 119–20, 125, 130, 202, 292n62

primogeniture 41–42, 44

privileges: "anomalous," of laboring-class of oppressor group subordinate short-term profits to social control under system of racial oppression in stable civil society 134–35; bourgeois class privilege of Conscription Act 328n77; "deficiency laws" as 137–8; and Irish Americans 30; race privileges for "whites" did not develop in Anglo-Caribbean 3; system of racial privileges must be preserved to maintain intermediate buffer social control stratum 135. *See also* Protestant racial privileges; religio-racial privileges; "white race" privileges; white-skin privileges

Privy Council 66, 72

pro-slavery phalanx, three chief elements of 161–5, 319n15

proletarians: majority of Virginia's economically active European-American population 18–19; twentieth-century actions in the name of revolution by 223

Protestant Ascendancy 51, 95, 97, 141: analogy with white supremacy 23, 81, 134, 295n124; British abandon 104; characteristics similar to white supremacy in U.S. 71–2, 73–90 *passim*; and Charter Schools 295n124; as class collaboration 124, 308n68; contrivance for "oppression, impoverishment, and degradation of a people" (Burke) 71; "democracy" of 311n4; emulated by American white supremacy in Indian education program 295n124; the "ending of all other distinctions" 81; industrial policy molded to 127–8; and Irish economic history 128–9; laboring classes and 96; link with British Conservatives 133; mold to industrialization 127–33; Nativism draws on heritage of 192; neglect by students of American history 72; present-day manifestation of 292n64; Protestant tenant-rights basic to 123; as racial oppression 86, 123, 127, 140; rapprochement with British King, Parliament, and Catholic bourgeoisie 92; red-lining 128; and shipbuilding 129–30; upper-class Irish and 77, 291n52. *See also* Protestant racial privileges; Ulster Custom; United States, analogies

Protestant "New English" 59, 285n30: nationalists 91–2

Protestant Plantation social control strategy in Ireland 58–60, 65–7

Protestant racial privileges: anomaly of 124; Belfast's rise as industrial center based on 128; Catholic Emancipation threatens 94; "country gentlemen" giving 298n31; dismantling of 111; and preferential hiring 131; established 121; family connections perpetuate 131, 309–10n97; frustrates Irish socialism and nationalism 134; heritable lease, at core 122; industrial Belfast's adaptation of 127, 131–2, 309n97, 310n98; of bourgeois and professional classes 77–8, 86–7, 291n52; of laboring classes 71, 77–9, 81–3, 96, 121–4, 137, 317n129; maintenance of necessary in Ulster if Catholic bourgeoisie to be admitted into social control system 127; Orange Order's dedication to 94, 101, 111, 126; preserved in post-"Emancipation" Ulster 100, 112, 128; remains the issue 134; of servitors 119; substance of draining away 129; tenant-right and ancillary aspects 123; Ulster Custom as 122; Union with Britain as guarantee of 132. *See also* Ulster Custom

Protestant Reformation 47–8, 58, 81
Protestantism: conversion to 77–81, 86–7; threat to English colonial system in Ireland 77–9
Protestants: analogy to poor "whites" 29; as anchor of the Empire 95; if "white," receive tax incentive in Nova Scotia for marrying Indian 202; in Ireland 281n145; James Connolly on 134; laboring-class, oppose concessions to Catholics 94; O'Connell on 130; as Royalists, Cromwellian concessions to 50, 282n155; Shaw on 133; in Ulster face choice between United Irishmen and Protestant Ascendancy 141; in the U.S. and the slavery issue 179, 183, 325n18; yeomanry 91, 94, 101–4, 106, 302n91
Providence Island 80, 268n34: dispute over holding Africans in lifetime servitude 8
psycho-cultural arguments 1, 4–14, 268n38

Quinn, David Beers 29–31
quotas 122, 199, 307n56, 327n49. *See also* deficiency laws

"race": concept of 21–2; definitions of 27–8, 272n1, 273n25; distinction, all-pervading, over class distinction in U.S. 113; "howling absurdities" 28, 272n10; "inferior race" in Ireland becomes object of sincerest form of Anglo-Irish flattery refuting Jordan/Degler thesis 54–7; Irish remonstrants use word 34, "pride of" (in Derry) 308n64; "relativity of" 23, 27–8, 30, 112–13, 298n30. *See also* "white race"
"race consciousness" 3, 304n139
racial oppression: advantages and disadvantages to ruling class of 52–3; analogous to gender, class, and national oppression 28, 36; Anglo-American/Ulster parallels 136–8, 273–4n27; and assault on the family 86–90, Irish parallels 86–9, 329n104; casting off 23; civil rights movement challenges 158; class struggle sharpens in absence of 24; and colonial rule in general 69–70; considered in terms of oppression 28; defining practices of 81–90; deliberate ruling-class policy of 23, 46; deprivation of civil rights through 84–5; differs from national oppression in recruitment of intermediate buffer social control stratum 23, 36, 273n11; divergence from in Ireland and British West Indies 112–14; excludes oppressed from normal forms of social identity 81–2; and extreme skilled/unskilled wage differentials 131–2; and general social control principles 68, 134–5; Irish example mistakenly neglected on grounds of no chattel form and no perceived skin color variations 72; immigrants implicitly enrolled in system 185; hallmark of 32–3, 35, 71; and illegalization of literacy 85–6, 170, 294n105; Irish mirror for insights into 22–3, 159; laboring classes of oppressor group receive privileges that subordinate short-term private profits to ruling class social control needs 135; laws against reading and writing 85, 294n105; maintained by military except where oppressor is majority 23; majority of oppressor group is intermediate social control stratum composed of laboring classes, non-capitalist tenants, and wage-laborers 134; and maximizing return on capital investment while maintaining social control 52–4; not a phylogenic phenomenon 23; provides "democratic" gloss 134; racial slavery a form of 327n58; renewal of 23; racial oppression in U.S. and national oppression in West Indies 113; sociogenic theory of 1, 46; in stable civil society oppressor group must be in the majority 134; system of racial privileges to maintain intermediate buffer social control stratum 135; without reference to alleged skin color or "phenotype" 22; women denied "coverture" 52
racial oppression (Anglo-America and the United States): advantages and limitations of, as ruling-class policy 52–3; of African-Americans 32–3, 90; America constructed on principle of, and white-skin privileges of laboring class European-Americans 184; of American Indians 32–4, 90, 136; chauvinist attitude doesn't explain resort to 280n115; controlled flow of U.S. history 72; conversion to Christianity in Virginia does not alter condition of bond-laborer 80–81; declassing legislation 82–3; English opt for plantation monoculture and racial oppression ruling out use of Indian labor before thinking in terms of social control over Indians 136; formalized in Hayes-Tilden Deal (1876) 152–3, 313–4n49; imperiled by emergence of a million African-American freeholders 140–44; issue revisited in U.S. (1866) as in Ireland (1829) 139; mirror metaphor as Irish subjects of, in Ireland, are sea-changed into "white Americans" 159; "Negro Emancipation" in U.S. did not lead to any change in bourgeois social control based

on 115; option period for racial oppression in Ireland and continental Anglo-America meant social control could not be achieved by preserving a middle class 311n9; racial slavery as one form of, imposed on free as well as bound African-Americans 160, 327n58; redistribution of confiscated plantation lands to African-Americans implied end of 141; re-established after Reconstruction abandoned based on racial privileges for laboring class "whites" regarding "free" land, immigration, and industrial employment 144; and refusal to legitimate class differentiation among oppressed 140; renewal of 23; ruling-class rededication to 148, 313–4n49; transformation of Irish haters of, to white supremacists in America 23; victorious Northern bourgeoisie confronts question of continuing social control system based on 139. *See also* social control (Anglo-America and the United States)

racial oppression (Ireland) 280n115, 311n9: aborted thirteenth-century attempt 34–5, 45–6, 54–6; aspect in Charter Schools 295n123; British bourgeoisie replace religion-racial oppression with national oppression outside Ulster and maintain racial oppression by Protestant Ascendancy in Ulster 23, 92, 96–97, 104–5, 107, 112–15,127, 131; Catholic Emancipation led to national oppression and replacement of 115, while leaving intact in Ulster 298n34; classic case of 50–51; conversion to Christianity avoided in Ireland as threat to religio-racial oppression 80–81; co-optation option foreclosed, English ruling class opts for redefinition of racial oppression as religio-racial oppression 30, 65–6, 231; cruelty of 209; defining characteristics of 32, 82–6; a deliberate turn to 46; denies Catholic social mobility 119; eclipse of 56–8; and the "Grand Dilemma" 66–7; Irish Catholic struggle against 124–5; Irish chieftains denied status 117; maintained by military establishment or by oppressor group majority 23, 66; military enforcement doubted 91, 104; mirror of Irish history offers insights into 22–3, 159; option left no room for Catholic upper class Irish chieftains 117; in Penal Laws 81–2, 107, 110–11, 295n123; persistence of by policy decisions 47–50; Petty states general principle of social control based on 68–9; preserved by partition 133; Protestant Ascendancy as 51–2, 86, 123, 127; servitor

functions 119; social structure difference between Anglo-Norman and Gaelic-Celtic social orders and 277n72; a variation on general principles 69; without reference to skin color 22

racial prejudice, facts that do not conform to an English precedent of 6–7

racial privileges. *See* privileges

racial slavery: a form of racial oppression of African-Americans, imposed on freemen as well as bond-laborers 160, 327n58; as deliberate ruling-class decision 3, 17–18, 20–21, 23; distinct from slavery 327n58; dual advantage by imposing on a colony 52; facts that do not conform to an English precedent of racial prejudice as cause of 6–7; and "innate racism" position 4, 8, 18–19; key to puzzle of origin of 267n17; "origins" debate regarding 2–5, 15–18, 265n4, 265–6n6, 266n11, 267n38; racial slavery versus freedom struggle 159; ruling class, response to problem of labor solidarity 21; slavery in U.S. could be maintained only as 291n58; smashed by Union armies and navies 139; as sociogenic rather than phylogenic phenomenon 23, 28; as system of social control 28

racism: an evil 2; Jordan's conviction that social action can't end 11; as "natural born" theory, unfavorable implications of 19; religio-racial 48; or slavery, which came first debate 2–21

Rahamah (Ibrahim), Abdul 32, 274n38

Randolph, John 163, 167, 320n29

Rebellion of 1798. *See* United Irishmen

Reconstruction: "greatest opportunity" likely to see for "many decades" 158, 318n137; overthrown by terror and violence 144–5; racial oppression challenged and defended 139–46; Radical 150, 313n47; repudiation by Northern bourgeoisie 144; ruling-class response to 313–4n49; white supremacist repression in Louisiana 314n52; whites who joined in solidarity with African-Americans 150–51, 316n87

"recusants" 49, 84, 294n93

Reid, Ira D.A. 304n139

religio-racial oppression. *See* racial oppression (in Ireland)

religio-racial privileges. *See* privileges

Remond, Charles Lenox 166, 172–3, 178

Remonstrance to John XXII 34

Repeal of the Union: British government rejects 107; as critical issue in crises of British social control in Ireland 96; historical issue of 97, 108–10; implies

Irish national independence 97

Repeal movement (and class struggle): Irish bourgeoisie's critical retreat from 107; laboring people interpret in anti-landlord terms 98; mortal threat to Protestant landlordism 97; mass campaign for, linked to tithe war 101–2; Party 108; plantation bourgeoisie withhold support for because of O'Connell's abolitionism 171; soft-pedaled by O'Connellites allied with British Whigs 108, 177; supports U.S. Abolition movement 172; in the U.S. 170–71, 173, 184

Republican Party: condemned for intending to "reduce white men to a forbidden level with Negro" 165, 190; Radical Republicans 140–43, 149

Republicanism 93–4

Riach, Douglas C. 322n64, 323n68

Ridge, John 33, 137

Ridge, Major 33, 275n44

Rishworth, Samuel 80

robber barons 277n70

Romans and social control 216

ruling class policy 3, 31, 303n122, 313–4n49

Russell, John H. 3

St. Croix (Danish) 113

St. Domingue 91–2. *See also* Haiti

St. Louis 145: *Leader* 192

St. Vincent 69, 217

Samuels, Wilfred 223

Santo Domingo, 1804 insurrection by bond-laborers 270n76

São Tomé 206

Schlessinger, Arthur M., Jr. 185

Schleuter, Herman 320–1n39

Scotland: clan chieftains 305n13; cost of laborers from 16; and England, anti-Catholic alignment and economic contrasts 120; English cooptation of tribal chieftains 57; holds appeal for Irish chieftains 57–8; and Ireland, relative proportions of yeomanry and police 103, 112; impoverishment of laboring people 120; insecurity of tenants in 120, 122, 306n35; king of, made king of England (1603) 119; option for social control through cooptation foreclosed 66; slavery in coal mines and salt-works 72–3, 218–20, 218–20, 289n8, 289n10; slavery for life in 219; surplus laboring population 120, 307n46; tribal organizations supplanted with feudal power 45

Scots: English chauvinism toward similar to that against Irish, but different system of domination instituted 280n115; invasion of

Ireland (1315) 34, 275n48; main bulwark of social control over Irish in Ulster 121; Poor Law 218; stereotypes of in English plays 267–8n31; as wall "betwixt" English and Irish 121, 136, 138

Scots-Irish, the Ulster Scots as second-class citizens in Ireland 125

Sea Islands 142

sea-change 27, 159–76, 322–3n64: how wrought 177–99; Irish subjects of racial oppression, into "white Americans" and opponents of abolition and equal rights 159, 177–8

Sekondi 206

Senegambia 206

Senior, Nassau William 309n90

"septs" 44, 49–50, 287n80

servitors 116, 118–19, 123, 306n28, 306n32

Seven Years' War (1757–63) 92

Seward, William Henry 159, 191–2, 318n1

Shakespeare, William 5–7, 267–8n31

Shannon, Fred A. 153

Sharp, Granville 220

Shaw, George Bernard 133

Sheil, Richard Lalor 99–105, 108–9, 300n49

Singleton, Benjamin "Pap" 145, 315n77

"The Slave" (Hughes) 169, 226–8

slave trade 6–7, 74

slaveholders: in America who blame English ancestors 3, 5; concerned with bond-laborer resistance 14; deliberately calculated act to have European-American bond-laborers side with 17; demand Irish Repealers abandon Abolitionism 170–71; most vulnerable political point for decisive blow against power of 172; numerically tiny class 13; Reconstruction as greatest opportunity to break the mold made by 158; Stevens's plan for confiscation and redistribution of lands of former 140; strategic assessment by 167; tighten reins on plantation labor 161; understood slavery in U.S. could be maintained only as racial slavery, 327n58

slavery 4, 6–7, 27, 280n130: as "a positive good" (Calhoun) 319n15; campaign for liberation of persons of African ancestry moral force for ending ancient slavery in Scotland 220; Catholic Press vehemence on 328n76; in coal mines and salt-works of Scotland 72–3, 218–20, 289n8, 289n10; for life in Scotland 219; historians seeking economic explanation and cheaper land and labor theories for 16, 203–5, take for granted plantation bourgeoisie's ability to control African-Americans 204; how, not why, this anachronistic form of labor established and maintained 1; or racism, which came first debate 2–21; racial slavery, a form of racial oppression distinct from 327n58; in U.S., could be maintained only as racial slavery 327n58; "slavery in all but name" 144. *See also* chattel bond-servitude; racial slavery

"slaves": "presentism" in "casually classing Negroes in colonial Anglo-America as" 9

Smith, Abbot Emerson 218, 290n24

Smith, Adam 33, 309n90

Smith, Gerrit 320n38

Smith, Thomas 80

social control: art and science of 53; and buffer intermediate stratum 13–14; and "cheaper labor" rationale 15–16; in civil racial-oppression societies 115, 134–5; continental vs. insular factor 8; contrast between Anglo-America and British West Indies 18–19; cooptation of buffer stratum strategy 66, 69; English ruling classes deliberately choose to preserve yeoman as buffer 311n9; elimination of indigenous population and use of foreign labor supplies strategy 69–70; essential principles for, of conquered tribal peoples 216–17; existing class structure and 69–70; option for racial oppression in Ireland and continental Anglo-America meant middle class would not maintain 311n9; general principles of 1, 23, 52; in colonial society 69–70, 216–17; in stable civil society based on racial oppression 134–5; general problem, need for buffer social control stratum 13, 16; interests of intermediate stratum conflict with ruling class 153; land/labor ratio theory of little value regarding plague-depopulated England with broken system of 204; plantation system forecloses emergence of intermediate buffer stratum for 23

social control (Anglo-America and the United States): "anomalies" in 137–9; and Bacon's Rebellion 24; insights from Irish mirror 159; invention of the "white race" as solution to problem of 23–4; lack of, discourages venture capital 144; "Negro Emancipation" did not lead to any fundamental change in 115; Northern bourgeoisie for limited time involves "Negro" in 144; not to be supplied by European immigration to South 151, 316n92; problem in attempt to exploit newly gained African source of labor by lifetime hereditary bondage on a continent 24; proportion of defection from white race and the intermediate social control

stratum 151; in Reconstruction buffer-intermediate social control stratum in urgent need of ruling-class attention 151; redistribution of confiscated plantation lands to African-Americans implied end of racial oppression and racial privileges system of 141; re-established system of, by racial oppression based on privileges for laboring class "whites" regarding "free" land, immigration, and industrial employment 144; in settlement of Georgia 138; and underlying contempt of "white" laborers 320n35; victorious Northern bourgeoisie confronts question of continuing or instituting new system of 139; white male privilege aspect of 157. *See also* racial oppression (Anglo-America and the United States)

social control (British West Indies): decision to recruit persons of African descent into intermediate stratum 112–14; failure to develop system based on "white race" 24; national oppression social control system in 113; theory and practice of promoting "free colored" and the "mulatto" function 13–14; problems in English colonies from presence of Irish 290n18

social control (Ireland): as Achilles heel of English policy 53; British bourgeoisie find it necessary to draw Irish Catholic bourgeoisie into intermediate social control stratum, replace religion-racial oppression with national oppression outside Ulster and maintain racial oppression by Protestant Ascendancy in Ulster 92, 97, 104–5, 107, 112–5, 127; central problem for English was recruiting indigenous intermediate social control stratum 70; co-optation option foreclosed by redefinition of racial oppression in Ireland as religio-racial oppression 30, 47–8, 66, 70; crises of British social control in 92, 96; English lacked force to impose and stabilize their commanding authority 65; general principles of colonial social control 69–70; general principles of social control in stable civil society based on racial oppression 134–5, 311n115; general problem of 43, 65, 70; "a history of the failure of three strategies" 53, 56, 58, 60; impossible for British to use extermination option 70; inclusion of priests in 110; initial thirteenth-century attempt to impose racial oppression 54; language difference as a factor in 81; Orangeism in the service of 94, 127; Petty states general principle of, based on racial oppression 68; Protestant Ascendancy, ending of reliance on 107; and Protestant laboring-class privileges 131–2, 307n56; Protestant plantation strategy of 59; Scots as main bulwark of, over Irish in Ulster 121; servitors as Plantation of Ulster's first measure of 118

social death 27, 32, 35–6, 80, 276n55

socio-biology, Degler's thesis in defense of 266n14

socio-economic arguments 1, 15–16, 18, 21, 271n81: and ignoring of social control 15

sociogenic phenomenon, and theory of racial oppression 1, 28, 46

Somerset, James 220

Sorge, Frederic A. 149, 315n84

the South: "after the Civil War presented the greatest opportunity for a real labor movement" (Du Bois) 318n137; "general lead in the politics of the country" (Webster) 320n28; "has controlled the government" (Stephens) 320n28; Hughes's visit 182; and social control 150–51; whites in, who made common cause with black population 150–52

South Africa 22, 39, 206–8, 310n102

South America 224

South Carolina 148, 151, 161, 163: African-Americans as independent farmers in 142; ex-governor fears "interracial" labor unity 312n24; Georgia as a buffer for 12; government seeks "white" immigrants 316n92; "Othello" prohibited in 6; population of 207; Reconstruction land law 315n79; Saluda, cotton mill 156; trades preserved for "whites" 138

South Dakota 153

Southern Homestead Law (1866, repealed 1876): meant abandoning racial oppression 140, 313–4n49

Spain: in the Americas 10; colonial and social control options of 66, 69–70; colonial example of, not followed 23; cooptation of buffer social control stratum in Peru and Mexico by 69; England sells Irish as soldiers to 50, 73–4, 281–2n149; England's rival, Ireland's ally 48, 58, 61–3; English ambassador's comments on Irish, Moors, and those "in the Indies" urging action by 31; and independence campaign in South America 302n94: occupation of Netherlands 211; racist affinity of treatment of Irish by England and treatment of Christian Moors by 29; superiority of tools and arms of 286n69

Spanish Armada 61

Spanish Florida 12

Spanish Main 6

Spenser, Edmund 60, 63, 81, 209–10, 285n48

spoils system: Jackson and 185; a "white race" spoils system 186, 196–7; and "whites only" manhood suffrage 186; strengthens Democratic hand among Irish-Americans 185, 188

"squatter sovereignty" 160

standing army 91, 303–4n135

starvation 62–5, 87, 222, 297n16: strategy 213–15

Statute of Kilkenny 55

Stearns, Charles 321n52

Stephens, Alexander H. 319n15, 320n28

Stevens, Thaddeus 140–41, 312n26

Sumner, Charles 140–41

Supreme Court of the U.S.: Dred Scott decision 33, 47, 280n132; "Indian Removal" decision 33; Indians-not-citizens decision 47; and the overthrow of Reconstruction 313–4n49

"surrender-and-regrant" 65, 285n30, 285n31, 287n86: English social control strategy in Ireland 53, 57–60

Sweden 73, 118

Swift, Jonathan 87

Swiss immigrants as wall "betwixt" African-Americans and maroon settlements in Piedmont mountains 137

Sylvis, William H. 142–3, 149

Synge, Edward, Archbishop 78

Tammany Hall, New York Democratic Party 190–91: attack on abolition 179; aligned with plantation bourgeoisie and pro-slavery 186, 319n17; driver of white supremacist and pro-slavery attitudes of Irish 198; opposes employment of African-Americans in Custom House 196; "white" suffrage and African-American disfranchisement 187–8

Taney, Roger B. 84, 139

Tenant Right Association 130

tenant-right. See Ulster Custom

tenants, Catholic 82–3, 282n154: sub-tenants 125, 129

tenants-at-will: eighteenth-century Protestant sub-tenants reduced to 125, 129; condition of Irish Catholic 291n37; Georgia Cherokee classed as 276n63; majority of Irish reduced to 78, 83; masses of, exempted from tithe (1838) 102; Plantation of Ulster (1609) reduces natives to 117, 307n57; eighteenth-century Scots "kindly tenants" reduced to, in Scotland 119, 306n35 but restored in Ulster (seventeenth century) 122; servitors as 119; tithe-extorted enforced status 93; in U.S., as "contract labor" and later sharecropping peonage 290n29. *See also* "kindly tenants"

Tennessee 145, 148

terror: against abolitionists 170; against Catholics in Ulster 94; and establishment of white-supremacist system in the South 144; in Munster campaign 209–10; against Negro Exodus of 1879 146–8; against Reconstruction 151; and white male privilege 315n77; white-supremacist in Louisiana 314n52

Texas 10, 28, 144–5, 151, 159: annexation as election issue 188–9, to counter Northwest Ordinance and Missouri Compromise by extending slavery 170, 328n69

Textile Workers Union 317–8n136

tithe war 98, 101–6, 108, 300n48, 302n91

tithes 93, 95, 98, 103, 301n75

tobacco monoculture 20, 23

"too few free poor on hand to matter" (Morgan) 18: criticism of 18–21; in British West Indies not in continental plantation colonies 19

Tories: Tory Party (later named Conservatives) 95–6, 100–101, 109

Toussaint L'Ouverture 32

"Trail of Tears" 37, 137

"transplantation" to Connaught 49, 282n154, 282n156

Treaty of Breda (1667) 268n36

Trevelyan, G.M. 211

tribal (kinship) societal relations: colonialist assault upon: African 36, 276n60, North American Indian 36–8, 89–90, 276n60, Irish 44, 49–50, 82; general principles 31, 35, 276n54

"tribe": colony vs. 35–46 *passim*; "detribalization" 36; the term 277–8n74

Truth, Sojourner 138

tuath 38–9

Tudor England (1485–1603) 59, 285n36, 287n91

Turner, Nat, rebellion of 84–5, 165, 294n94

Tyler, John 32, 173, 274n36

Tyrone (County) 121, 127, 213, 291n37

Tyrone War (1594–1603) 48: British victory in, and plantation policy of 73; English conquest-by-famine strategy 62–5, 213–5, 224; English costs of unsustainable 63; English's Irish adherents 287n80; supreme historic effort of Celtic Ireland to throw off British colonialism 115

Ulster: British colonial bourgeoisie draw Irish Catholic bourgeoisie into intermediate stratum, abandon social control by racial oppression outside Ulster, and maintain racial oppression and Protestant Ascendancy in Ulster 70, 104, 127, 142; British industrial investment policy 127–9, 155; Celtic bastion overthrown 65; chieftains of, in British service 116–17; civil rights movement in 158, 324–5n10; escheated counties 116–17, 305n12; geographically nine counties (post-Partition Northern Ireland) 305n12; living under threat in 308n63; "most Irish" province (1609) 115; O'Neills of 47; opting for orange or green (1798) 127; revolt in, starts War of Three Kingdoms (1641) 118, 308n63; "servitors" as first social control measure proposed for the Plantation of 118; tardy industrial revolution 168. *See also* Plantation of Ulster; Ulster/America analogies

Ulster/America analogies: Catholic and African-American "Emancipations" 115, 291n51, 304n2; Catholics and African-Americans involved "in the state" 144; disallowance of class differentiation 140; exiling of Irish and Cherokees 137; "Home Rule" and "settlement of the Negro question" 146, 315n66; housing segregation and discrimination 131, 310n98; "land monopoly" 142; making common cause 150; privilege of Protestants and "whites" 141; privileges as ruling-class investment in social control 115; Protestant Ascendant/white supremacist capital investment policy 155–6; racial oppression 23; the tenant wall "betwixt" (between) 121, 136, 138; treatment of Irish and Indian chieftains 137; Ulster analogy best illuminates problem of United States history and its ongoing development 115; "Ulster Custom" and Homestead right 138. *See also* United States, analogies

Ulster Custom (the tenant-right): erosion and draining of and brief period of readiness to make common cause with the Catholic peasants 150; economic description 308n59, 308n61; parallel in United States homestead right 138; as Protestant privilege 121–4; as inviolable sphere of the middle stratum 153; marked Protestant Ascendancy system of racial oppression 123; Protestants' most precious racial privilege 129; translated into a proletarian mode of religion-racial privileges 131

"uncivilized ways" of victims of colonial exploitation not phenotype concern of

English ruling class 31
Underground Railroad 165, 198
"Undertakers" (Plantation capital investors) 118, 306n32
Union Armies 139
United Irishmen 95, 126–7, 133, 141, 296n6: equalitarian manifesto 126; Rebellion of 1798 79, 92, 94, 103. *See also* Rebellion of 1798
United States, analogies: Ireland 115, 195; South Africa 310n102; Ulster 304n2, 136–8, 139–49; uprooting of Cherokee and Irish 137. *See also* Irish analogies and parallels; Protestant Ascendancy, analogy with white supremacy; Protestants, analogy to poor whites; Ulster/America analogies
United States Congress 159, 162
United States Constitution 159–60, 175, 327n49: attempt to nullify Thirteenth Amendment in Mississippi Black Code 294n89; circumlocution to avoid use of the word "slave" 160, 318n2; classed Europeans as migrants and Africans as imports 185; enhanced representation of Southern slave-holding state 159; Fifteenth Amendment 327n49; made immigration a white-skin privilege 185; U.S. "Indian policy" 35–6, 89–90, 295n124
"unthinking decision" explanation 9, 268n40
uprooting of Cherokee and Irish 137

vagrancy 74, 210
Vatican 58, 63, 100, 102, 298n29
Vaughan, Alden T. 265–6n6, 266n11, 273–n27
Vesey, Denmark 165
Virginia: African-Americans and shared presumption of liberty in 266–7n16; African-Americans' status in seventeenth century 3–6, 9; Assembly acts to deliberately foster contempt for blacks and Indians 17; "Civis" on "poor whites" in 154; Colony and Council Records 16; Company 304n3; Davies suggests sending exiled Irish to 289n16; European-Americans against white supremacy in 151; differences in treatment of European- and African-Americans due to ruling class policy 3; and the invention of the "white race" 23–4; limited term African-American bond-laborers priced similarly to European-Americans 293n87; and Nat Turner rebellion 294n94; "officers" 306n28; social control and racial privileges in 18–21; Vaughan on status of African-Americans in seventeenth century 266n11
villein 278n81

Volunteers movement 93–4
Vosburgh, Robert 196
voting rights: and citizenship for Irish immigrants 186; disfranchisement of Catholics in Ireland and African-Americans 78, 84; Irish-American voters and annexation of Texas 188–9; Jamaica free "persons of color" might be enfranchised 47; law (1793) gives Catholic forty-shilling freeholders right to vote 94, right taken away in 1829 after 36 years 186; limited Irish franchise 301n67; "Negro suffrage" in Reconstruction era 144; O'Connell doubts any agrarian rebels were qualified voters 299n43; and "whites only" manhood suffrage 185; as a white-skin privilege 184; "white" suffrage and African-American disfranchisement 187–8, 195, 327n58

wage differential: between English and Irish common labor far greater than that between wage- and bond-labor in continental Anglo-America 76, 221–2; in employers' interest to keep differential at no more than is necessary to keep European-American workers in "white race" corral 198; South Africa as extreme case 310n102; in U.S. is greater in South where skilled wages are lower 310n102
wage-labor system, competition with bond-labor system 198
wages 141, 155, 157–8, 316n90, 221–2: historic persistence in America of low 158; low money cost of Irish labor 221–2
Wakefield, Edward, *père* 202, 219, 298n31
Wales 40, 45, 57, 61, 280n115: and Ireland, relative proportions of yeomanry and police 103, 112
"a wall betwixt" 121, 136–7, 138, 152
Wallace, George C. 2
War of the Three Kingdoms (1639–51) 48–9, 118
War of 1812 159, 187
Wat Tyler's Rebellion (1381) 41, 56, 204
Watson tobacco factory 191, 329n111
Webster, Daniel 320n28
Wellington, Arthur Wellesley 98, 108, 300n54, 301n72, 302n91: sees civil war threats in Ireland 98; conceded "Catholic Emancipation" to avert war 100; proposal to use yeomanry to crush Repeal movement is rejected by government 302n92
Wesleyan Methodists 171
West Africa 276n59, 288n111
West Indian immigrant of African descent to

U.S. 304n139: parallels and divergences with Irish Catholic migrant to Belfast 114

West Indies 30, 36, 70, 73

Wexford 67, 172

Whigs, Whig Party (Britain) 108–9: early supporters of Catholic Emancipation 96; strengthen yeomanry to counter agrarian unrest 103; Reform Bill of 1832 108; in U.S. 188

"white": American, from Irish to 185–6; attitude 11, 14, 22; "backlash" 2l; "Blindspot" 15, 22–3; card 146; Chinese in Cuba as 27; Christians as 17; defined in Virginia 27–8; first use of, to designate social status in Virginia statute (1691) 293n76; habit of mind 290n24; Hindus, excludable "Caucasians" because not "recognized as white" 327n49; identity 10, 12, 14, 195; incubus of 21; and displacement of European-American proletarian class consciousness 21; immigration 152; imperialism 10; incentives for marriage to Indian 202, 296n128; Irish Americans adapted to and adopted into white American social order 183, 195, 199; Jordan's casually fixing label of, on people who never identified as such 267n17; Jordan's "need to know they were" 9–11; laborers 3, 86, 187, think "themselves better than the Negro" (Fox) 187; "laboring-class European-Americans in continental plantation colonies showed little interest in "white identity before institution of system of 'race' privileges at end of the seventeenth century" 14; male supremacy 24; man judged superior to African-American by Supreme Court 33; "manhood" suffrage 186–7, 195, 329n90; "man's country" 2; "men," "another kinde of people from us" (Jobson) 7; Mexican Indians in Cuba as 27; "monster" (O'Connell) 188; "only rebellions by white servants in the continental colonies" 270n73; "over black" 268n39; poor 18–19, 29, 154–7, 271n95, 312n24, 315n79, 316–7n107; "racism" 2–3, 18; Republicans condemned for intending to "reduce white men to a forbidden level with Negro" 165, 190; "slavery" 164; Southern whites who made common cause with black population for society based on racial equality 150–52; supremacy 2, 10, 22, 34, 144, 157–8, 170, 319n14; analogy with Protestant Ascendancy 71, 84, 134, 295n124; the term 267n17, 293n77; unions; 113; "'white' Christian" affinity absent in cruelty of English treatment of

Irish in Munster campaign 209

"white labor": accepts white-skin privilege of Free Soil and Homestead Act and endorses capitalist monopoly 152–3; apologists 166, 320–1n39; competition argument as rationale for opposing abolition of slavery 141; positions that Abolitionism a "capitalist" plot 164, that bond-laborers better off than wage-laborers 164–5, that "Negroes, if freed, . . .would lower wages and reduce opportunities for 'white' workers" 141; and "white race" fantasy of colonization 164

"white race": "corral" 198; counterfeit identity cancels laboring class solidarity 19–20; "free colored" promoted in West Indies to attach themselves to 13; function 13–14; intrusion by any member of 89; invention of 22–4, 28; Irish-Americans and European-Americans emerge as members of in America 30; poor European-Americans without social mobility promoted to 14; origin of 1; proportion of defections from, and the intermediate stratum 151; for purpose of ruling class social control 3, 14, 21, 137, 141; "quintessential 'Peculiar Institution'" 1; recruitment of Euro-Americans into the, social control formation 158; reinventions of 1

"white race" privileges 24, 141, 146–8, 153–4, 184, 317n129: of "American whites" for immigrants 185; as bar "to the true freedom of labor" 143–4; Belfast Protestant privilege parallel to Cotton Mill campaign 317n129; capital accumulation in U.S. proceeded by virtue of "white" racial privileges of European-American laboring class 141; as class-consciousness preventive 157; conferred by ruling class on laboring-class European-Americans 14; consequence of system of, ruinous to interest of African-Americans and disastrous for propertyless "whites" 21; counterfeit identity of 20; defense of, against threat of egalitarianism implicit in abolition 163; creation of "white" male race privileges 24, 157, 315n77; deliberately instituted in order to align propertyless "whites" with plantation bourgeoisie against African-American bond-laborers 21; entailed exclusion of "free Negroes" 14; as facilitator of lower labor costs 156–8; "free land" homesteads 138–41; imperiled by land for freedmen 139; homesteaders pay the price for 152–3; and gender oppression 24, 154, 313n47,

315n77; in industrial employment (after Emancipation) 144, 155, 157–8; Irish-American position on, not different from other European-Americans 186; as key to "consent of the governed" ("whites") 141; laboring-class European-Americans receive privileges that subordinate short-term private profits to ruling class social control needs 137; laboring-class European-Americans "showed little interest in 'white identity'" before system of "race" privileges at end of seventeenth century 14; and male supremacy 89–90, 163, 165; as mortar binding bourgeois system of social control 143; Negro Emancipation formally destroys freedom as 143; at outset of "white race" era in 1705 law 84; pattern did not develop in Anglo-Caribbean 3; in political patronage 186, 195–6; the presumption of liberty 184–5; redistribution of plantation lands to African-Americans implied end of racial oppression and social control by means of racial privileges for laboring-class "whites" 141; re-established social control system of racial oppression based on racial privileges for laboring class "whites" with regard to "free" land, immigration, and industrial employment 144; as requisite of "the Southern labor system" 148; "right" of immigration and migration 144, 147, 152, 157, 184–5, 327n49; system formally instituted 24; system of, relative to African-Americans led to decline in social mobility of poor whites 20; in the trades 138, 155; white male privileges 313n47; "white manhood" suffrage 186, 195

"White Reconstruction": bourgeoisie as a whole opted for, re-established social control system of racial oppression 144

white-skin privileges 24, 147, 153–4, 180, 317–8n136: America constructed on principle of racial oppression and, of laboring class European-Americans 184; employment and immigration policies based on, profitable to bourgeoisie and preventive against class-consciousness of laborers 157; as depressor of wages 157–8; of Free Soil and Homestead Act accepted by "white labor" which endorses capitalist monopoly 152–3; Hughes as defender of 180; immigration, naturalization, and voting rights as 184; popular rights of Irish-Americans given form of, as token of membership in the "white race" 199; presumption of liberty 184; white farmers with, cast into proletariat 153

white supremacy: "deliberate choice" for 192–3; in Draft Riots 328n77; in exclusion of Asian-Americans, Mexicans, Indians, and African-Americans 10; importance of facing issue of 317–8n136; in Indian education program 295n124; Irish-Americans not originators of 199; paralyzing effect of, thought 158; part of European-American population against 151; and publications of Young Irelanders 324n10; in series of acts passed to deliberately foster contempt for blacks and Indians 17; in social order in the U.S. 113; system in south 144; "violently thrust upon" (Harrison) St. Croix 113

"white worker," organized 149–50: and the cause of slaveholders 167. *See also* Democratic Party

"whiteness," certificates of in colonial Hispanic/Spanish America 27, 47

"whites": acting as 189–92; "Christians" as 17; labor leader describes how hate to organize, get along with management, and not on side of Negroes 317–8n136; mob of, forces factories to end employment of African-Americans 191; propertyless 14, 21; should have supported struggle for end to bond-servitude 197; in West Indies "mulattoes" could "function as" 14; and "whites only" manhood suffrage 186

Williams, Eric E. 2–3, 265n5, 265n6, 269n47, 270n76; "cheaper labor" rationale 15–16

Williams, Richard 273n25

Wilmot, David 138, 320n29

women: Christian woman sues for freedom 80; denied "coverture" under racial oppression 52; denied the vote 84; grant of homestead right to "white" (1854) 138; oppression of 138; plan for taking African-American women by Anglo-American men 201; poor, in England 11; rape of Irish and African-American 46; rights of, and the Abolitionist movement and O'Connell on 171; sexual exploitation of African-American women by European-American men 12, 89, 148, 201, 313n47; in Southern textile industry 157–8, 318n136; status of English-feudal 42–3; Women's Rights Convention (1848) 138–9. *See also* coverture; Irish women; male privileges; male supremacy

Wood, Fernando 162: denounces federal government for provoking war 190; expresses "common sympathy" for slaveholders, proposes secession from U.S. 189

Wood, Peter H. 271nn81–2

Woodward, C. Vann 158
Working Man's Advocate 164
Workingmen's United Political Association
    321n45
World Anti-Slavery Convention 171–2
Wyse, Thomas 99, 300n49

Xosa people 208

Yellow Ford, Battle of (1598) 60, 62,
    286–7n80
yeomanry: as armed repressive force 94, 98,
    102–4, 106, 296n6; eclipse of feudalism
    and rise of bourgeois monarchy in England
    necessitated development of new buffer
    social control group of gentry and 59; in
    Louisiana 154; preferences for Protestant
    298n31; religio-racial oppression meant
    English ruling class could not recruit
    portion of the Irish Catholic laboring class
    to yeomanry status 66; as social control
    stratum 6, 100, 119, 122, 131–3
Young, Arthur 85, 87, 89, 221–2
Young Irelanders 107, 174, 177, 178–9,
    183–4, 224: extreme white supremacism of
    324n10; folly to antagonize slaveholders
    and opposition to O'Connell's abolitionism
    322–3n64

Zulu people 208

List of Figures

1   Map of the Chesapeake region, *circa* 1700   110

2   List of governors of Colonial Virginia   112

3   Virginia counties, and dates of their formation   114

List of Tables

4.1   Shipments of persons to Virginia by the Virginia Company and by separate planters, 1619–21   71

4.2   Comparative day wages in Virginia, January 1622, and in Rutland County, England, in 1610–34   73

5.1   Approximate number of English emigrants to Virginia and the death rate among them in the Company period   76

9.1   Increase in concentration of landholdings in Virginia, 1626–1704   167

10.1   African-American and European-American landholding in the entire state of Virginia in 1860 and in Northampton County in 1666   185

A Note on Dates

Prior to 1750, the legal year began on 25 March. Therefore, dates from 1 January through 24 March are often rendered with a double-year notation. For example, 24 March 1749 would be written as 24 March 1748/9, but the next day would be given as 25 March 1749. But a year later the dates for those March days would be, in the normal modern way, 24 March 1750 and 25 March 1750. Where one year only is indicated, it is to be understood to accord with the modern calendar.

i

Introduction to the Second Edition

"When the first Africans arrived in Virginia in 1619, there were no 'white' people there; nor, according to the colonial records, would there be for another sixty years." That arresting statement, printed on the back cover of the first volume of *The Invention of the White Race* by Theodore W. Allen, first published in 1994, reflected the fact that, after twenty-plus years of studying Virginia's colonial records, he found no instance of the official use of the word "white" as a symbol of social status prior to its appearance in a 1691 law. As he explained, "Others living in the colony at that time were English; they had been English when they left England, and naturally they and their Virginia-born children were English, they were not 'white.'" White identity had to be taught, and it would be another six decades until the word "would appear as a synonym for European-American."

In this second volume of *The Invention of the White Race*, Allen elaborates on his findings in order to develop the groundbreaking thesis that the ruling class invented the "white race" as a social-control mechanism in response to the labor solidarity manifested in the later, civil-war stages of Bacon's Rebellion (1676–77). To this he adds two important corollaries: 1) the ruling elite deliberately instituted a system of racial privileges in order to define and establish the "white race"; and 2) the consequences were not only ruinous to the interests of African-Americans, they were also "disastrous" for European-American workers, whose class interests differed fundamentally from those of the ruling elite.

In Volume I, subtitled *Racial Oppression and Social Control*, Allen prepared the conceptual groundwork for Volume II to be free of what he calls the "White Blindspot." He offered a critical examination of the two main historiographical positions on the slavery and racism debate: the psycho-cultural approach, which he strongly criticized, and the socioeconomic approach, which he sought to free from certain theoretical weaknesses. He then proceeded, using the mirror of Irish history, to develop a definition of racial oppression in terms of social control, a definition free of the absurdities of "phenotype," or classification by complexion. The volume offered compelling analogies between the oppression of the Irish in Ireland (under Anglo-Norman rule and under "Protestant Ascendancy") and white supremacist oppression of

African-Americans and Indians. Allen showed the relativity of race by exam-ining how Irish opponents of racial oppression in Ireland were transformed into "white American" defenders of racial oppression. He also examined the difference between national and racial oppression through a comparison of "Catholic Emancipation" outside of Ulster and "Negro Emancipation" in America.

In this volume, *The Origin of Racial Oppression in Anglo-America*, Allen tells the story of the invention of the "white race" in the late seventeenth- and early eighteenth-century Anglo-American plantation colonies. His primary focus lies with the pattern-setting Virginia colony, and he pays special atten-tion to how the majority-English labor force was reduced from tenants and wage-laborers to chattel bond-servants in the 1620s. In this qualitative break from long-established English labor laws, Allen finds an essential precondition for the emergence of the lifetime hereditary chattel bond-servitude imposed upon African-American laborers under the system of white supremacy and racial slavery. He also documents many significant instances of labor soli-darity and unrest, especially during the 1660s and 1670s, most spectacularly during the civil-war stage of Bacon's Rebellion, when "foure hundred English and Negroes in Arms" fought together to secure freedom from bondage.

It was in the period after Bacon's Rebellion that the "white race" was invented as a ruling-class social-control formation. Allen describes systematic ruling-class policies that conferred privileges on European-American labor-ers and bond-servants while blocking normal class mobility and imposing or extending harsh disabilities on African-Americans. Eventually, these policies culminated in a system of racial slavery, a form of racial oppression that also imposed severe proscriptions on free African-Americans. Allen emphasizes that, in 1735, when African-Americans in Virginia were deprived of their long-held right to vote – with the aim, in the words of Governor William Gooch, "to fix a perpetual Brand upon Free Negros & Mulattos" – it was not an "unthinking decision." Rather, it was a deliberate step in the process of establishing a system of racial oppression by the plantation bourgeoisie, even though it entailed repealing a law that had existed in Virginia for more than a century.

The key to understanding racial oppression, Allen argues, can be found in the formation of the intermediate social-control buffer stratum, which serves the interests of the ruling class. In the case of racial oppression in Virginia, any persons of discernible non-European ancestry after Bacon's Rebellion were denied a role in the social-control buffer group, the bulk of which was made up of laboring-class "whites." In the Anglo-Caribbean, by contrast, under a similar Anglo ruling elite, "mulattos" were included in the social-control group and often promoted to middle-class status. For Allen, this was the key to understanding the difference between Virginia's ruling-class policy of fixing "a perpetual Brand" on African-Americans and the West Indian planters' policy of formally recognizing the middle-class status of "colored" descendants who earned special merit through their service to the regime.

Here, the difference between racial oppression and national oppression can be explained by the fact that in the West Indies there were "too few" poor and laboring-class Europeans to create an adequate petit bourgeoisie, while in the continental colonies there were "too many" laborers to extend social mobility to all of them.

The references to an "unthinking decision" and "too few" poor and laboring class Europeans are consistent with Allen's repeated efforts to challenge what he considered to be the two main arguments that undermine and disarm the struggle against white supremacy in the working class: 1) white supremacism is innate, and it is therefore useless to challenge it, and 2) European-American workers benefit from "white race" privileges. These two arguments, opposed by Allen, are related to two master historical narratives rooted in writings on the colonial period. The first argument is associated with the "unthinking decision" explanation for the development of racial slavery offered by historian Winthrop D. Jordan in his influential work *White Over Black*. The second argument is associated with historian Edmund S. Morgan's similarly influential *American Slavery, American Freedom*, which maintains that, as racial slavery developed, "there were too few free poor [European-Americans] on hand to matter." Allen's work directly challenges both Jordan's theory of the "unthinking decision" and Morgan's theory of "too few free poor."

Allen convincingly argues that the racial privileges conferred by the ruling class upon European-American workers not only work against the interests of the direct victims of white supremacy, they also work against the workers' interests. He further argues that these "white-skin privileges" are "the incubus that for three centuries has paralyzed" the will of European-Americans "in defense of their class interests *vis-à-vis* those of the ruling class."

With its meticulous primary research, its equalitarian motif, its emphasis on the dimension of class struggle in history, and its groundbreaking analysis, Allen's *The Invention of the White Race* is now widely recognized as a scholarly classic. It has profound implications for American history, African-American history, labor history, American studies, and "whiteness" studies, as well as important insights in the areas of Caribbean history, Irish history, and African Diaspora studies. Its influence will only continue to grow in the twenty-first century.

In an effort to assist readers and encourage meaningful engagement with Allen's work, this new edition of Volume II of *The Invention of the White Race: The Origin of Racial Oppression in Anglo-America* includes a few minor corrections, many based on Allen's notes. There are also two new appendices, "A Guide to *The Invention of the White Race*, Volume II" (drawn in part from Allen's unpublished "Synoptic Table of Contents") and a select bibliography. In addition, you will find a new, expanded index at the end of this volume.

Jeffrey B. Perry

PART ONE
Labor Problems of the European Colonizing Powers

The Labor Supply Problem:
England a Special Case

In 1497, within half a decade of Columbus's first return to Spain from America, the Anglo-Italian Giovanni Caboto, or John Cabot as he was known in his adopted country, made a discovery of North America, and claimed it for King Henry VII, the first Tudor monarch of England. The English westering impulse, after then lying dormant for half a century, gradually revived in a variety of projects, schemes and false starts. By the first decade of the seventeenth century, an interval of peace with Spain having arrived with the accession of James I to the throne, English colonization was an idea whose time had come.[1] In 1607 the first permanent English settlement in America was founded at Jamestown, Virginia. By the end of the first third of the century four more permanent Anglo-American colonies had been established: Somers Islands (the Bermudas), 1612; Plymouth (Massachusetts), 1620; Barbados, 1627; and Maryland, 1634.[2]

The English were confronted with the common twofold problem crucial to success in the Americas: (1) how to secure an adequate supply of labor; and (2) how to establish and maintain the degree of social control necessary to assure the rapid and continuous expansion of their capital by the exploitation of that labor. In each of these respects, however, the English case differed from those of other European colonizing powers in the Americas, in ways that have a decisive bearing on the origin of the "peculiar institution" – white racial oppression, most particularly racial slavery – in continental Anglo-America.

European Continental Powers and the Colonial Labor Supply

The continental European colonizing powers, for economic, military and political reasons, and in some cases because of access to external sources, did not employ Europeans as basic plantation laborers.

Spain and Portugal

The accession in 1516 of Francis I of France and in 1517 of Charles I of Spain, and the installation of the latter as Charles V, Emperor of the Holy Roman

Empire, in 1519, set off a round of warring that would involve almost every country in Europe, from Sweden to Portugal, from the Low Countries to Hungary, for a century and a quarter. The Spanish-headed Holy Roman Empire was at the same time heavily engaged in war with the Ottoman Turks until after the defeat of the latter in the Mediterranean naval battle of Lepanto in 1571. Portugal, with a population of fewer than 1.4 million,[3] was involved in protecting its world-circling empire against opposition from both Christian and Moslem rivals. France was Spain's main adversary in the struggle over Italy, the Netherlands and smaller European principalities.

These wars imposed great manpower demands on every one of the continental governments seeking at the same time to establish colonial ventures. Belligerents who could afford them sought to hire soldiers from other countries. The bulk of Spain's armies, for example, were made up of foreign mercenaries.[4] Portugal, however, lacking Spain's access to American silver and gold to maintain armies of foreign mercenaries, had to rely on its own resources.[5] So critical was the resulting manpower situation in 1648 that Antonio Vieira, the chief adviser to King John IV, felt obliged to advocate the temporary surrender of Brazil to Protestant Holland as the best way out of the sea of troubles besetting the Portuguese interest in Africa, Asia, America, and, indeed, vis-à-vis Portugal's Iberian neighbor. Portugal was so depleted of men for defense, he said, that "every alarm" took "laborers from the plough."[6] Even if, despite this circumstance, a ploughman did manage to get to Brazil, he was not to be expected to do any manual labor there: "the Portuguese who emigrated to Brazil, even if they were peasants from the tail of the plough, had no intention of doing any manual work."[7]

Bartolomé de Las Casas, concerned with the genocidal exploitation of the native population by the Christian colonizers in the West Indies, suggested that, "If necessary, white and black slaves be brought from Castile [Spain] to keep herds, build sugar mills, wash gold," and otherwise be of service to the colonists. In 1518, Las Casas briefly secured favorable consideration from King Carlos for a detailed proposal designed to recruit "quiet peasants" in Spain for emigration to the West Indies. The emigrants were to be transported free of charge from their Spanish homes to the colonies. Once there, they were to be "provided with land, animals, and farming tools, and also granted a year's supply of food from the royal granaries." But, again, these emigrant peasants were not expected to do much labor. Rather they were to be provided with slaves from Spain. It was specified that any emigrant who offered to build a sugar mill in the Indies was to be licensed to take twenty Negro slaves with him. With his assistants, Las Casas toured Spain on behalf of the plan and received a favorable response from the peasants he wanted to recruit for the project. But as a result mainly of the opposition of great landowners who feared the loss of their tenants in such a venture, the plan was quickly defeated.[8] Thus was defined official emigration policy; it assured that Spaniards going to the American colonies were not to be laborers, but such as lawyers and clerks, and men (women emigrants were extremely few) of the nobility or knighthood, who were "forbidden by force of custom even to think of industry or commerce."[9] A few Spanish and Portuguese convicts, presumably of satisfactory Christian ancestry, were transported to the colonies early on, but they were not intended and themselves did not intend to serve in the basic colonial labor force.[10]

The single instance in which basic plantation labor needs were supplied from the Iberian population occurred in 1493. In that year, two thousand Jewish children, eight years old and younger, were taken from their parents, baptized as Christians, and shipped to the newly founded Portuguese island sugar colony of São Tomé, where fewer than one-third were to be counted thirteen years later.[11]

In Spain, seven years of plague and famine from 1596 to 1602, followed by the expulsion of 275,000 Christianized Moors in a six-year period beginning in 1602,[12] reduced the population by 600,000 or 700,000, one-tenth of all the inhabitants.[13] Thus began a course of absolute population decline that lasted throughout the seventeenth century.[14] As it had been with the Jews before, the expelled *moriscos* were officially ineligible for emigration to the Americas, since émigrés were required to prove several generations of Catholic ancestry.[15]

Holland

For the better part of a century up to the 1660s, Holland, in the process of winning her independence from Spain in the Eighty Years' War (1568–1648), was the leading commercial and trading country of Europe. Holland's 10,000 ships exceeded the total number held by the rest of northern Europe combined.[16] On this basis the new Dutch Republic developed a thriving and expanding internal economy. Large areas were diked and drained to increase the amount of cultivable land.[17] Up until 1622, Dutch cities grew, some at a phenomenal rate; in that year, half of Holland's population lived in cities of more than 10,000 inhabitants.[18] The population of Amsterdam alone had grown to 105,000, three and a half times its size in 1585.[19] These cities were expanding not from an influx of displaced Dutch peasants, but because urban needs were growing faster than those of rural areas,[20] and because Holland's "obvious prosperity ... acted as a lodestar to the unemployed and the under-employed of neighboring countries."[21]

Although the casual laborer in Holland was frequently out of work, "unemployment ... was never sufficiently severe to induce industrial and agricultural workers to emigrate on an adequate scale to the overseas possessions of the Dutch East and West India Companies."[22] Those who did decide to emigrate to find work "preferred to seek their fortune in countries nearer home."[23] Plans for enlisting Dutch peasant families for colonizing purposes came to little, outside of the small settlement at the Cape of Good Hope, which in the seventeenth century was mainly a way station for ships passing to and from the Dutch East Indies.[24] As far as the East Indies were concerned, it was never contemplated "that the European peasant should cultivate the soil himself." Rather, he would supervise the labor of others.[25]

France

In seventeenth-century France the great majority of the peasants were holders of small plots scarcely large enough to provide the minimum essentials for survival. The almost interminable religious wars that culminated in the Thirty Years' War (1618–48) had ravaged much of the country, and epidemic disease had greatly reduced the population.[26] But while French poor peasants groaned under the burden of feudal exactions, they were still bound by feudal ties to the land;[27] they had not been "surplussed" by sheep, as many peasants had been in Spain and England.

The first successful French colonization efforts were undertaken on the Bay of Fundy (1604) and at Quebec (1608). The laborers for the colony's upbuilding and development were to be wage workers, transported at the expense of the French government or other sponsoring entity, and employed under three to five year contracts. But New France was not destined to become a plantation colony, indeed not even a primarily agricultural colony.[28] A century after these first Canadian settlements were established, their population was only ten thousand, including a few persons representing a soon-abandoned notion of supplying the labor needs of Canadian colonies from African sources.[29] Some time before the end of the seventeenth century, the French government turned to the idea of Christianizing and Gallicizing the Indians as a means of peopling New France and developing a labor force for it; that plan also failed, however, because the Indians did not perceive sufficient advantage in such a change in their way of living,[30] and they had the resources and abilities to be able to fend off French pressure on the tribal order. Indeed, until the establishment of the Louisiana colony early in the eighteenth century, the entire question of supplying labor for French agricultural undertakings became irrelevant for North America.

French participation in the development of plantation colonies was to occur in the West Indies and, as mentioned, in Louisiana. Having begun with Martinique and Guadeloupe in 1635, in 1697 the French capped a series of Caribbean acquisitions by taking control from Spain of the previously French-invested western half of Hispaniola under the terms of the Treaty of Ryswick.[31] In the beginning, wage laborers called *engagés*, hired under three-year contracts at rates four or five times those prevailing in France, were shipped to serve the labor needs of these colonies.[32] The supply of labor in this form seems to have reached its peak, however, well before 1697. Although the total number of *engagés* is not known, some 5,200 were shipped from La Rochelle, the chief embarkation point, in the period 1660–1710, a rate of around one hundred per year.[33] This was numerically miniscule compared to the total number of imported laborers, which was running at a rate of 25,000 to 30,000 per year in the latter half of this period.

The reasons for the relegation of *engagé* labor to economic insignificance were both economic and political.[34] The mortality rate among plantation laborers on St Domingue, whatever their nativity, was such that most did not survive three years.[35] However, the obligation to pay relatively high wages to the *engagés*, be their numbers large or small, coupled with the fact that the French colonies had ready access to African labor supplies, first through the Dutch and later from French businessmen, made *engagé* labor relatively less profitable, provided that the costs of social control of the laboring population drawn from African sources could be kept satisfactorily low.[36]

Moreover, the need to recruit large French armies for the wars first with Spain and then with England, and the drain on revenues entailed in their support, rendered politically inappropriate the export of *engagés* to the French West Indies. Louis XIV finally forbade even the forcible transportation of indigent persons to the American colonies. His chief minister from 1661 to 1683, Jean Baptiste Colbert, declared that he had no intention of depopulating France in order to populate the colonies.[37]

Other sources of labor

The Spanish and the Portuguese first looked to the native populations to solve their colonial labor problem. The Spanish did so with such spirit that, in the course of a century and a half from 1503 to 1660, they tripled Europe's silver resources and added one-fifth to Europe's supply of gold.[38] In the process, the fire-armed and steel-bladed Conquistadors almost completely destroyed the indigenous population by introducing exotic diseases, and by the merciless imposition of forced labor in gold mining and in the fields. The native population of Hispaniola was thus reduced from 1 million in 1492 to around twenty-six thousand in 1514, and to virtual extinction by the end of the sixteenth century.[39] The same genocidal labor regime in mines and fields simultaneously destroyed the native population of Cuba at a comparable rate.[40]

Epidemic European diseases – smallpox, measles, and typhus – and forced labor under a system of *encomienda* and *repartimiento*[41] reduced the population of central Mexico from 13.9 million in 1492 to 1.1 million in 1605.[42] The impact of disease and of the *mita*,[43] the equivalent of the Mexican *repartimiento*, was equally devastating to the Indian population of Peru, which was reduced from 9 million to 670,000 in 1620.[44]

In Brazil, the Portuguese (and the Dutch as well, during the life of the New Holland colony, 1630–54) also sought to recruit their labor force from the native population. However, they found that, while the people "were prepared to work intermittently for such tools and trinkets as they fancied," they were unwilling to work for them as long-term agricultural laborers, or as bound-servants.[45] In the test of wills that lasted until late in the seventeenth century, the indigenous population was largely successful in avoiding reduction to slavery.[46]

Thus for two opposite reasons – the accessibility of a native labor force that eventually led to its destruction, and the inaccessibility due to resistance by the native population ensconced in dense continental forests – the Iberians turned to Africa as a source of labor for colonial America. This was a labor reserve with which they, as part of medieval Europe and as colonizers of Atlantic islands, were already somewhat familiar.[47] Medieval Europe secured its slaves by trade with southern Russia, Turkey, the Levant and the eastern coast of the Adriatic Sea (the ethnic name Slav is the root of the various Western European variations of the word "slave"), as well as by purchasing Negroes supplied by North African Arab merchants.[48] Spain enslaved Moslem "Moors" in border regions during the "reconquista" wars against the Arab regime on the Iberian peninsula.[49] In the middle of the fifteenth century, the Portuguese established direct access to African labor sources by successfully executing a maritime end run around the North African Arabs.[50] By the end of that century Portuguese enterprise, with papal blessing,[51] had supplied twenty-five thousand Africans as unpaid laborers to Europe, plus one thousand to São Tomé, and seven and a half thousand to islands in the Atlantic.[52] In the sixteenth century the African proportion of the slave population increased in Portugal and Spain. In Lisbon, a city of 100,000 people in 1551, there were 9,950 slaves, most of them Africans. In Seville (1565), Cadiz (1616), and Madrid (up to about 1660), the slave population included Turks and Moors, but the largest number were Africans.[53] During the very early days of American colonization, a number of American Indians were shipped to be sold at a profit in Spain.[54]

In 1518, King Charles I of Spain, acting with papal sanction, authorized the supply to Spanish America of four thousand Africans as bond-laborers, for which project he awarded the contract to a favorite of his.[55] This was the origin of the infamous *Asiento de negros* (or simply *Asiento*, as it came generally to be called), a license giving the holder the exclusive right to supply African laborers to Spanish colonies in the Americas (and to Portuguese Brazil as well during the sixty years, 1580–1640, when Portugal was united with Spain in a single kingdom). At various times it was directly awarded by the Spanish crown to individuals or to governments by state treaty. The *Asiento* was the object of fierce competition among European powers, especially in the last half of the seventeenth century. Allowing for brief periods of suspension, it was held successively by Portugal, Holland, and France, and passed finally to Britain as a part of the spoils of the War of Spanish Succession (1702–14).[56] The *Asiento* was finally ransomed from Britain for £100,000 in 1750.[57]

Scholars' estimates of the total number of Africans shipped for bond-servitude in the Americas under the *Asiento* and otherwise range from 11 to 15 million.[58] Of the 2,966,000 who disembarked in Anglo-America, 2,443,000 went to the British West Indies and 523,000 to continental Anglo-America (including the United States).[59] Two other aspects of the matter seem to have been slighted in previous scholarship: first, the significance of this movement of labor in the "peopling" of the Americas; and, second, the implications to be found in the story of this massive transplantation of laborers for the history of class struggle and social control in general in the Americas.

I am not qualified to treat these subjects in any comprehensive way, but I venture to comment briefly, prompted by an observation made by James A. Rawley, whose work I have cited a number of times:

> The Atlantic slave trade was a great migration long ignored by historians. Euro-centered, historians have lavished attention upon the transplanting of Europeans. Every European ethnic group has had an abundance of historians investigating its roots and manner of migration. The transplanting of Africans is another matter ... [that] belongs to the future.[60]

As to the first of the questions – the African migration and the "peopling" of the Americas – it is to be hoped that among subjects that belong to the future historiography invoked by Rawley, emphasis may be given to the degree to which the migration (forced though it was) of 10 or 11 million Africans shaped the demographics of the Americas as a whole. It is certain that more Africans than Europeans came to the Americas between 1500 and 1800.[61] It would seem that such a demographic assessment might add strength to arguments that place the African-American and the "Indian" in the center of the economic history of the hemisphere, and in so doing sustain and promote the cause of the dignity of labor in general. Such a demographic assessment might be of service in responding to the cry for justice for the Indians from Chiapas (from Las Casas to Subcómmandante Marcos), or to an African-American demand for reparations for unpaid bond-servitude; or in assessing the claim of the "Unknown Proletarian," in a possibly wider sense than even he intended:

> We have fed you all for a thousand years –
> For that was our doom you know,
> From the days when you chained us in your fields
> To the strike of a week ago
> You have taken our lives, and our babies and wives,
> And we're told it's your legal share;
> But if blood be the price of your lawful wealth,
> Good God! We have bought it fair.[62]

Second, with regard to the class struggle and social control in general in the Americas, attention will need to be given to the resistance and rebellion practiced by the African bond-laborers and their descendants, from the moment of embarkation from the shores of Africa[63] to the years of maroon defiance in the mountains and forests of America;[64] from the quarry's first start of alarm[65] to the merger of the emancipation struggle with movements for national independence and democracy four hundred years later.[66]

Historically most significant of all was the Haitian Revolution – an abolition and a national liberation rolled into one: it was the destruction of French rule in Haiti that convinced Emperor Napoleon to see and cede the Louisiana territory (encompassing roughly all the territory between the Mississippi River and the Rocky Mountains) to the United States, without which there would have been no United States west of the Mississippi. By defeating Napoleon's plan to keep St Domingue in sugar plantation slavery, the Haitian Revolution ushered in an era of emancipation that in eighty-five years broke forever the chains of chattel bondage in the Western Hemisphere – from the British West Indies (1833–48), to the United States (1865), to Cuba (1868–78), to Brazil (1871–78). It was in Haiti that the Great Liberator, Simón Bolívar, twice found refuge and assistance when he had been driven from Venezuela. Pledging to the Haitian president, Pétion, that he would fight to abolish slavery, Bolívar sailed from Haiti at the end of 1816 to break the colonial rule of Spain in Latin America.[67]

England and the Colonial Labor Supply

English colonialists were to share the motives and aspirations felt by their counterparts looking westward from the European continent: the search for uncontested access to the fabled treasures of the East; the hope of finding rich gold and silver mines; an eagerness to find alternate sources of more mundane products such as hides, timber, fish and salt; and the furtherance of strategic interests *vis-à-vis* rival military and commercial powers in the development of this new field of activity.[68] Much would be said and proposed also in the name of the defense of one Christian faith (of the Protestant variety in the English case of course). But all endeavors, holy and profane, were to be held in orbit by the gravitational field of capital accumulation.[69]

In regard to the problem of a colonial labor supply, however, the situation of the English bourgeoisie was unique; this was as a result of developments that are so familiar to students of English history that a brief summary will suffice in the present context. With the end of the Wars of the Roses (1450–85), a convergence of circumstances – some old, some new – launched the cloth-making industry into its historic role as the transformer of English economic life to the capitalist basis.[70] Principal among these circumstances were: (1) the emergence of a strong monarchy; (2) England's relative isolation, compared to the countries of continental Europe;[71] (3) improved means of navigation, especially benefiting the coastal shipping so well suited to the needs of an island nation; (4) improved and extended use of water power for cloth-fulling mills, and for other industrial purposes; and (5) the rural setting of the cloth industry, outside the range of the regulations of the urban-centred guilds.

The price of wool rose faster than the price of grain, and the rent on pasture rose to several times the rent on crop land.[72] The owners increased the proportion of pasture at the expense of arable land. One shepherd and flock occupied as much land as a dozen or score of peasants could cultivate with the plough. Ploughmen were therefore replaced by sheep and hired shepherds; peasants were deprived of their copyhold and common-land rights, while laborers on the lords' demesne lands found their services in reduced demand. Rack-rents and impoverishing leasehold entry fees were imposed with increasing severity on laboring peasants competing with sheep for land. At the beginning of the sixteenth century, somewhere between one sixth and one third of all the land in England belonged to abbeys, monasteries, nunneries and other church enterprises. In the process of the dissolution of the monasteries, most of the estimated 44,000 religious and lay persons attached to these institutions were cast adrift among the growing unemployed, homeless population.[73] As these lands were expropriated, under Henry VIII the process of conversion to pasture was promoted more vigorously than it had been by their former owners.[74] Henry VIII's return of 48,000 English soldiers in 1546 from a two-year turn in Boulogne tended further to the creation of a surplus proletariat.[75] The effect was only partially offset by the participation of regular and volunteer English soldiers in the Dutch war for the independence of Holland from Spain later in the century, and by the Tyrone War in Ireland.[76] Generally speaking, the sixteenth century was relatively free of war and plague.[77] The population of England is estimated to have grown by 1.3 million in the last six decades of the sixteenth century, to 4.1 million, but by only another 0.9 million in the entire seventeenth century.[78] Occurring at a time when employment in cultivation was being reduced more rapidly than it was being increased in sheep raising and industry, this demographic factor added substantially to the swelling surplus of the semi-proletarian and vagrant population.[79] During the early decades of the seventeenth century, the oppressive effects of this catastrophic general tendency to increasing unemployment and vagrancy were exacerbated by purely political and cyclical factors, and by market disruptions occasioned by continental wars. In 1614–17, James I – enticed by Alderman Cockayne's scheme whereby the Crown coffers were to be enriched by five shillings on each of 36,000 pieces of finished and dyed cloth to be exported annually – imposed extremely strict limitations on the export of unfinished cloth.[80] The effect was a serious dislocation of trade, and mass unemployment in the cloth industry. English cloth exports fell until in 1620 they were only half the pre-1614 level.[81]

The man who had been serving for some time as treasurer and chief officer of the Virginia Company, Edwin Sandys, urged the colony's cause by pointing out that in Britain, "Looms are laid down. Every loom maintains forty persons. The farmer is not able to pay his rent. The fairs and markets stand still . . ."[82] Recovery was slow. In 1624, an investigating committee of the House of Commons reported that there were still twelve thousand unemployed cloth workers.[83] A modern scholar has concluded that the next decade did not mark much improvement, noting that the proportion of the people receiving poor relief was greater in the 1631–40 period than at any other time before or since.[84] East Anglia, the native region of most of the emigrants to Anglo-America in those years, was at that time especially hard hit by a depression in the cloth trade.[85]

The English case for colonization came thus to be distinguished from those of Spain, Portugal, France, and Holland in its advocacy of colonization as a means of "venting" the nation's surplus of "necessitous people" into New World plantations.[86] Francis Bacon (1561–1626) favored colonization as a way to "disburthen the land of such inhabitants as may well be spared." Just who those were who could be spared had been identified some time before by the premier advocate of overseas exploration and settlement, Richard Hakluyt (1552?–1616): it was the surplus proletarians who should be sent. Contrasting England with the continental countries interminably devouring their man-power in wars and their train of disease and pestilence, Hakluyt pointed out that "[t]hrough our long peace and seldom sickness wee are growen more populous ... (and) there are of every arte and science so many, that they can hardly lyve by one another." Richard Johnson, in his promotional pamphlet *Nova Britannia*, noted that England abounded "with swarmes of idle persons ... having no meanes of labour to releeve their misery." He went on to prescribe that there be provided "some waies for their forreine employment" as English colonists in America.[87] Commenting on the peasant uprising in the English Midlands in 1607, the House of Lords expressed the belief that unless war or colonization "vent" the daily increase of the population, "there must break out yearly tumours and impostures as did of late."[88]

The English Variation and the "Peculiar Institution"

The conjunction of the matured colonizing impulse, the momentarily favorable geopolitical constellation of powers, the English surplus of unemployed and underemployed labor, coupled with the particular native demographic and social factors as the English found them in Virginia, and the lack of direct English access to African labor sources, produced that most portentous and distinctive factor of English colonialism: of all the European colonizing powers in the Americas, only England used European workers as basic plantation workers. This truly "unthinking decision,"[89] or, more properly, historical accident, was of incidental importance in the ultimate deliberate Anglo-American ruling class option for racial oppression. Except for this peculiarity, racial slavery as it was finally and fully established in continental America, with all of its tragic historical consequences, would never have been brought into being.

Essential as this variation in the English plantation labor supply proved to be for the emergence of the Anglo-American system of racial slavery, however, it was not the cause of racial oppression in Anglo-America. The peculiarity of the "peculiar institution" did not derive from the fact that the labor needs of Anglo-American plantation colonies came to the colonies in the chattel-labor form. Nor did it inhere in the fact that the supply of lifetime, hereditary bond-laborers was made up of non-Europeans exclusively. These were common characteristics throughout the plantation Americas.

The peculiarity of the "peculiar institution" derived, rather, from the *control* aspect; yet not merely in its reliance upon the support of the free non-owners of bond-labor, as buffer and enforcer against the unfree proletariat; for that again was a general characteristic of plantation societies in America.

The peculiarity of the system of social control which came to be established in continental Anglo-America lay in the following two characteristics: (1) all persons of any degree of non-European ancestry were excluded from the buffer social control stratum; and (2) a major, indispensable, and decisive factor of the buffer social control stratum maintained against the unfree proletarians was that it was itself made up of free proletarians and semi-proletarians.

How did this monstrous social mutation begin, evolve, survive and finally prevail in continental Anglo-America? That is the question to be examined in the chapters that follow.

2

English Background, with Anglo-American Variations Noted

The same economic, social, and technological developments in sixteenth-century England that supplied the material means for the final overthrow of Celtic Ireland in the Tyrone War (1594–1603) provided the impetus that launched England on its career as a world colonial power. The capitalist overthrow of the English peasantry in the first half of the sixteenth century was the forerunner of the destruction of the Celtic tribal system in the seventeenth. The expropriated and uprooted sixteenth-century English copy-holders had their counterparts in the "kin-wrecked" remnants of broken Irish tribes reduced to tenantry-at-will and made aliens in their own country.

But while the adventitious factor of the English Protestant Reformation in the sixteenth century was a decisive condition for the seventeenth-century English option for racial oppression in Ireland, it was not the force that shaped the events that culminated in the establishment of racial oppression in continental Anglo-America.[1]

Rather, the system of class relations and social control that emerged in the colonies in the seventeenth century rested on the rejection in fundamental respects of the pattern established in England in the sixteenth century. With few exceptions, historians of the origin of racial slavery have generally ignored, or inferentially denied, the significance of this oceanic disjunction in social patterns.[2] The "social control" approach which the present work takes to the origin and nature of "the peculiar institution" makes it necessary to revisit the epoch of English history that produced the founders of Jamestown.

On the Matter of "Transitions"

Many economic historians, taking the long view, have agreed with Adam Smith that the transition to capitalist agriculture in England in the sixteenth century was "a revolution of the greatest importance to public happiness."[3] At the threshold of the sixteenth century, however, the English copyholder, plowing the same land that his grandfather had plowed with the same plow,[4] had little feeling for "transitions." If it had been given to him to speak in such terms, he might well have made his case on historical grounds. It was the laboring people – the copyholders, freeholders, serfs, artisans and wage earners – and not the bourgeoisie, who had swept away the feudal system. Out of the workings of the general fall in agricultural prices in the period between the third quarters of the fourteenth and fifteenth centuries as a result of which landlords preferred to get cash rents rather than rents in produce; out of the shortage of labor induced by the worst-ever onset of plague in England, which, within a space of sixteen months in 1349–50 carried off from one-fifth to one-half of the population;[5] out of the constant round of bloody and treacherous baronial wars for state hegemony (ended only with the Wars of the Roses, 1450–85), and the desultory Hundred Years' War with France, 1336–1453; and, above all, out of the Peasant Revolt of 1381, Wat Tyler's Rebellion,[6] which drew a line in the ancient soil beyond which feudal claims would never be reasserted – thus had been wrought the end of the feudal order in England. And so occurred the English peasant's Golden Age,[7] wherein the self-employed laboring peasant, as freeholder, leaseholder, or copyholder, held ascendancy in English agriculture.[8]

Our copyholder might then go on to say that now the bourgeoisie, burgesses, landlords, merchants and such were apparently attempting to destroy the peasantry; and if that was what was meant by transition to capitalism, the price was too high.[9] And he would conclude with a reminder and a warning: he – his kith and kin – had fought once, and would fight again, to maintain their place on the land and in it.[10]

Fight they did. Between 1500 and 1650, "hardly a generation ... elapsed without a peasant uprising." In local fence-destroying escapades, in large riots, and in rebellions of armed forces of thousands which "at intervals between 1530 and 1560 set half the counties of England in a blaze,"[11] the English "commons" fought. In some cases they were allies of the anti-Reformation, sensing the connection between the Reformation and the agrarian changes that threatened the majority of the peasantry. Even then, the peasants still forwarded their own demands regarding land ownership and use, enclosures, rack-rents, etc. Years that their revolts have made memorable include 1536, 1549, 1554, 1569 and 1607.

In these struggles the peasants made clear their sense of the great heart of the matter; in the words of Tawney:

> Reduced to its elements their complaint is a very simple one, very ancient and very modern. It is that ... their property is being taken away from them ... [and] to them it seems that all the trouble arises because the rich have been stealing the property of the poor.[12]

For this they fought in the northern rebellion of 1536, known as the Pilgrimage of Grace.[13] This revolt, set off by Henry VIII's suppression of monasteries, confronted that king with the greatest crisis of his reign.[14] Although ecclesiastical issues united the movement, "the first demands of the peasants were social and not religious"; for them it was a class struggle "of the poor against the rich," and their demands "against raised rents and enclosures" were included in the program of the movement.[15]

The peasants fought again in 1549, climaxing a three-year period of "the greatest popular outcry against enclosing."[16] In that year, peasant revolts spread to more than half the counties of England. Led by Robert Ket, himself a landowner, a rebel army of sixteen thousand peasants captured Norwich, England's second-largest city. They set up their "court" on Mousehold Heath outside the city, where they maintained their cause for six weeks.[17] They demanded that "lords, knights, esquires, and gentlemen" be stopped from commercial stock-raising, and rent-gouging, and from privatizing common lands. We can agree with Bindoff that this was "a radical programme, indeed, which would have clipped the wings of rural capitalism."[18]

The peasants fought also in 1607, the very year of the founding of Jamestown. These were the peasants of the Midland counties. Thousands, armed with bows and arrows, with pikes and bills, and with stones, sought justice by their own direct action. The later use of the term "Levellers," though more figurative, still was socially congruent with the literal sense in which these Midland rebels applied it to themselves as "levellers" of fences and hedges set up by the landlords to bar peasants from their ancient rights of common land. To the royal demand that they disperse, they defiantly replied that they would do so only if the king "wolde promis to reforme those abuses."[19]

The peasants fought, but in the end they could not stop the "rich . . . stealing the property of the poor." Small landholders constituted the majority of the laboring population in English agriculture at the end of the fifteenth century,[20] but by the end of the seventeenth century more than four-fifths of the land was held by capitalist employers of wage-labor.[21] Well before that time, the majority of the English people were no longer self-employed peasants but laborers dependent upon wages.[22]

Not only were they to be dependent upon wages, making crops and cloth that they would never own, but at wages lower than they had ever been. In the course of the sixteenth century the real wages of English laborers fell into an abyss from which they would not emerge until the end of the nineteenth century.[23] As a typical peasant, "Day labourer was now [his or her] full description . . . and the poor cottager[s] could expect only seasonal employment at a wage fixed by the justice of the peace."[24] One-fourth of the people of England in the 1640s were but "housed beggars," the term used by Francis Bacon to distinguish them from wandering roadside mendicants.[25]

"Why No Upheaval?"

"Why did it not cause an upheaval?" That is a logically compelling question which some historians have posed in light of their findings regarding the general deterioration wrought upon the lives of the laboring population during the "long" sixteenth century, 1500–1640.[26] The same question, but in a form more particularly suited to this present study, is, "How did the English bourgeoisie maintain social control?"

In establishing its dominance over the pillaged and outraged peasantry, the English bourgeoisie did, of course, meet rebellion with armed repression (generally after deceitful "negotiations" designed to divide the opposition and to buy time for the mobilization of government military forces). Having traditionally no standing army, the government employed German and Italian mercenaries on some occasions, along with men recruited from the personal retinues of the nobility. But foreign mercenaries, however important they might have been in certain critical moments, for fiscal and political reasons could not supply the basic control functions on a regular basis. And the very economic transformation that brought the laboring masses of the countryside to revolt was simultaneously reducing the ranks of the retainers whom the nobility might profitably maintain for such ongoing repressive services.

Saving a portion of the yeomanry

The solution was found by deliberately fostering a lower-middle-class stratum. It was in the nature of the capitalist Agrarian Revolution that non-aristocrats rose out of the ranks of the bourgeoisie into the highest councils and organs of power, to serve side by side with the increasingly bourgeoisified old-line aristocrats. Likewise, lower and local functions at the shire level were filled by men from the ranks of the lesser bourgeois country gentlemen and exceptionally upwardly mobile peasants turned capitalist farmers, who might buy into a knighthood. But yet another layer was needed, which would be of sufficient number to stand steadfast between the gentry and the peasants and laborers.

But the juggernaut of the Agrarian Revolution threatened the land titles of the laboring peasants of all categories, from those with hereditary freeholds through all the gradations of tenants to the "customary" tenant-at-will.[27] The state therefore made a political decision to preserve a sufficient proportion of peasants – preference going naturally, but not exclusively, to hereditary freehold tenants – as a petit bourgeois yeomanry (typified by the classic "forty-shilling freeholder"[28]) to serve in militia and police functions.[29]

The case has not been better understood or stated than it was by Francis Bacon, looking back at close range in 1625 to write his *History of the Reign of King Henry VII* (1485–1509):

> Another statute was made for the ... soldiery and militar[y] forces of the realm.... That all houses of husbandry, that were used with twenty acres of ground and upwards, should be maintained and kept up for ever; together with a competent proportion of land to be used and occupied by them; and in no wise severed from them (as by another statute in his successor's [Henry VIII's] time was more fully declared).... This did wonderfully concern the might and mannerhood of the kingdom, to have farms of a standard, sufficient to maintain an able body out of penury, and did in effect amortise a great part of the lands of the kingdom unto the

hold and occupation of the yeomanry or middle people, of a condition between gentlemen and cottagers or peasants. . . . For to make good infantry, it requireth men bred not in a servile or indigent fashion, but in some free and plentiful manner. Therefore if a state run most to noblemen and gentlemen, and that the husbandmen and ploughmen be but as their work folks and labourers, or else mere cottagers (which are but housed beggars), you may have a good cavalry, but never good stable bands of foot [soldiers]. . . . Thus did the King secretly sow Hydra's teeth whereupon (according to the poet's fiction) should rise up armed men for the service of this kingdom.[30]

Bacon likened the process of expropriation of the peasants to the necessary thinning of a stand of timber, whereby all but a few trees are cleared away to allow sound growth of the rest for future needs. By this policy, he said, England would escape certain ills besetting the governments of other countries such as France and Italy

[w]here in effect all is noblesse or peasantry (I speak of people out of towns), and therefore no middle people; and therefore no good forces of foot; in so much as they are enforced to employ mercenary bands of Switzers and the like for their foot [soldiers].[31]

Here was the recognition of the curbs that policy must sometimes impose on blind economic forces, restraining "the invisible hand" in order to avoid promoting "an end which was no part of [the] intention" of the ruling class.[32] It was in the nature of the transformation powered by the capitalist Agrarian Revolution that the non-aristocratic bourgeois gentry should move increasingly into the control of affairs. On the other hand, the deliberate preservation of a portion of economically independent self-employed and laboring small property-owners was not an economic necessity but rather a first derivative of the economic necessities, a political necessity for the maintenance of bourgeois social control, upon which the conduct of the normal process of capitalist accumulation depended. (Even so, it was not a total loss economically, since the yeoman was a self-provider and a principal source of tax revenue.)[33]

The inner conflicts of the bourgeoisie, the conflicts with self in its own various parts – now the governors of a strife-torn nation among striving nations; and, again, as land-grabbing, rack-renting landlords, gentry, merchants, squires, and occasional interloping peasant upstarts, "like tame hawks for their master, and like wild hawks for themselves," as Bacon put it[34] – caused this basic policy to evolve by vicissitudes. But the center held: the same guiding principle obtained when Bacon wrote his history of Henry VII's reign that been in force more than a century before.

The successful day-to-day operation of the social order of the newly ascendant bourgeoisie depended upon the supervisory and enforcement functions performed at the parish level by yeoman constables, church wardens, Overseers of the Poor, jailers, directors of houses of correction, etc.[35] They were charged with serving legal orders and enforcing warrants issued by magistrates or higher courts. They arrested vagrants, administered the prescribed whippings on these vagrants' naked backs, and conveyed them to the boundary of the next parish, enforcing their return to their home parishes. As Overseers of the Poor, they ordered unemployed men and women to the workhouses and apprenticed poor children without their parents' leave. Trial juries were generally composed of yeomen, and they largely constituted the foot soldiery of the militia, the so-called "trained bands." They discharged most of these unpaid obligations unenthusiastically, but with a sense of duty appropriate to their social station.[36] Nevertheless, prior to the Great Rebellion and Civil War of the mid-seventeenth century, yeomen militiamen showed themselves less than reliable for major armed clashes with peasants. In Ket's Rebellion they were left behind when the final assault was made by the king's forces of cavalry and one thousand foreign mercenaries.[37] And, on account of the "great backwardness in the trained bands," the king's commanders were constrained to rely exclusively on the gentlemen cavalry and their own personal employees in the battle against one thousand peasant rebels at Newton in the Midlands in 1607.[38]

Yeomen did enjoy certain special privileges. For one, they were entitled to vote for their shire's member of Parliament. Of far more substantial import-ance was their right to apprentice their sons to lucrative trades and commerce, and to send their sons to schools and universities.[39] But like the civic duties to which they were assigned, these privileges were theirs because, and only because, of their property status. It never occurred to the ruling classes of England that they could enlist such a cheap yet effective social control force from the ranks of the propertyless classes, the housed beggars, laborers and cottagers, or the vagabonds. That notion would await the coming of the Anglo-American continental colonies.

The "Labor Question": Conflict and Resolution

The ruling class effected the same balance of class policy and the blind instinctual drive for maximum immediate profits by its individual parts in regard to the costs of employment of propertyless laborers.[40]

In the century and a half, 1350–1500, following the great plague, it had been seen that no amount of legislation could keep down labor costs where labor was in short supply. Laws designed to prevent laborers from moving about in search of higher wages, and laws fixing penalties for paying or receiving wages in excess of statutory maximums, were equally ineffective in restraining wages. Half a dozen such laws were passed in that period,[41] but by its end the laborer's real wage was nearly thrice what it had been at its beginning.[42] The objective might have been accomplished if it had been possible to reimpose serfdom, but the landlord class no longer had the power to do so.[43]

But the emergence of a massive labor surplus in the early decades of the sixteenth century presented the employing classes with an opportunity which they were quick to exploit for regulating labor costs. At a certain point it occurred to the government to redress the imbalance by instituting slave labor. Parliament accordingly in 1547 enacted a law, 1 Edw. VI 3, which would have had the effect of creating a marginal, yet substantial, body of unpaid bond-labor, to serve as an anchor on the costs of paid labor. Refusing to recognize the legitimacy of the offspring of their own agrarian revolution, the ruling class presumed that every unemployed person was merely another "vagabond," willfully refusing to work and thus frustrating the proper establishment of fair wages. The 1547 law sought remedy along the following lines:

> who so ever ... man or woman [being able-bodied and not provided with the prescribed property income exemption] shall either like a serving man wanting [lacking] a maister or lyke a Begger or after anny other such sorte be lurking in anny howse or howses or loytringe or Idelye wander[ing] by the high waies syde or in stretes, not applying them self to soem honnest and allowed art, Scyence, service or Labour, and so do contynew by the space of three dayes or more to gither and offer them self to Labour with anny that will take them according to their facultie, And yf no man otherwise will take them, doe not offer themself to work for meate and drynk ... shall be taken for a Vagabonde ...[44]

Any person found to be transgressing the provisions of the law, upon information provided to a magistrate by any man, was upon conviction to be formally declared a "vagabond," branded with a *V*, and made a slave for a period of two years to the informant. The slave was to be fed only bread and water and, at the owner's discretion, such scraps as the owner might choose to throw to the slave. The law specified that the slave was to be driven to work by beating, and held to the task by chaining, no matter how vile the work assignment might be. Such a two-year slave who failed in a runaway attempt was to be branded with an *S* and made a slave for life to the same owner from whom he or she had tried to escape. A second unsuccessful attempt to escape was to be punished by death.

This was not just one of the many anti-vagabond laws enacted by the English Parliament in the sixteenth century;[45] it was distinguished from others by three features: (1) the definition of "vagrancy" was extended to cover any unemployed worker refusing to work for mere board; (2) the beneficiary of the penalty was not the state in any of its parts, but private individual owners of those who were enslaved; (3) the enslaved persons were reduced to chattels of the owners, like cattle or sheep, and as such they could be bought, sold, rented, given away, and inherited ("as any other movable goodes or Catelles").[46] With this 1547 law, the quest for wage control had passed its limits in a double sense, by going to zero wages, and by exceeding the limits of practicability. In 1550, Parliament repealed the law, citing as a reason the fact that "the good and wholesome laws of the realm have not been put in execution because of the extremity of some of them."[47]

Many contemporary observers perceived the causal connection of the officially deplored depopulating enclosures of arable land and the growth of vagrancy, and they viewed the case of the displaced peasants and laborers with sympathy. "Whither shall they go?" asked one anguished commentary. "Forth from shire to shire, and to be scattered thus abroad ... and for lack of masters, by compulsion driven, some of them to beg and to steal."[48] During the life of the slave law, bold, honest preacher Bernard Gilpin made the point in a sermon in the presence of Edward VI himself: "Thousands in England beg now from door to door who have kept honest houses."[49]

There were those who considered such facts a justification for slavery as a means of saving these victims of expropriation from running further risks to their very souls, by the sin of idleness. But a widespread reluctance to attempt slavery as the answer seems to have had much to do with the paralysis of the will that kept the law from being "put in execution."[50]

The interval between the passage and the repeal of this slave law was also the period of "the greatest popular outcry against enclosing,"[51] which, as we have noted, took the form of mass peasant revolts, culminating in Ket's Rebellion. John Cheke, scholar, member of Parliament and former tutor of Edward VI, lectured the Norfolk rebels on "The Hurt of Sedition," linking their contumacy with the spirit of lawless vagabondage plaguing the country.[52] Certainly the rebels were as aware as anyone else of the connection between the threat they were facing, that of depopulating enclosures, and the rise of vagrancy. But there seem to be no reports as to the attitude, if any, that the rebels may have held towards vagrancy in general, or toward the slave law of 1547 in particular. Perhaps we may agree with Davies in seeing this fact as evidence that the law was effectively defunct in 1549.[53] In any case, the Ket rebels evinced no disposition to clear their skirts of the splatters of John Cheke's vagabond-baiting.

What they did say, touching bondage, was this: "We pray that all bondmen may be made free, for God hath made all free with his precious bloodshedding."[54] There has been some conjecture about the significance of the inclusion of this demand in the program issued from Mousehold Heath.[55] Whatever scholars may finally conclude on the point, it was a demand that sounded in sharp dissonance to the cruel clanking of chains in the 1547 slave law. The rebels were, furthermore, voicing the main moral scruple which contributed so much to the nullification of the law: namely that it was wrong "to have any Christen man bound to another."[56]

"Doubtless, moral scruples could have been overcome," Davies says, "if slavery had been practical and profitable."[57] He explains that "dealing with a single slave or a small number ... slavery would have been utterly uneconomic; the constant driving, the continuous need to check into the work done, the ease of flight, the difficulty of recapture, easily outweigh any advantage which might have accrued from 'cheap labor.'" He then takes note of a fact that is of particular relevance for the understanding of racial slavery and social control. He contrasts the situation as it would have obtained under the 1547 law in England and the slavery system in continental Anglo-America, which was operable only because "half the population of the South [was] employed in seeing that the other half do their work."[58] The maintenance of such a system of social control was neither an economically valid option nor a necessary resort of bourgeois social control in sixteenth-century England. In this attempt to turn "anti-vagabondism" into a paying proposition by enslaving laborers, the bourgeoisie found that its reach exceeded its grasp. When in 1558–59 diehards proposed that the old slave law be reinstated, even with amendments to lessen its "extremity," the idea failed of adoption.[59]

Wages had to be paid, low though they were

The slave-law experiment had revealed to the English employing classes a limit beyond which they could not go, but they were not disposed to miss the opportunity to validate their prerogative to control labor costs by state intervention.[60] The result was the Statute of Artificers,[61] which was made law on 10 April 1563.[62] Whether the aim of controlling labor costs was achieved by this act, and, if so to what degree, is a subject beyond the concern of this present work.[63] What is significant is that it remained the basic English master–servant law for more than two and a half centuries until its repeal in 1813.[64] It represented the achievement of an historic equilibrium – after two centuries of class struggle, blow and counter-blow – between high wages and unpaid bondage, between freedom and compulsion, in the disposition of alienable labor power.[65]

English historians of the liberal, labor and socialist tendencies have correctly emphasized the compulsion aspect of the Statute of Artificers.[66] This emphasis would seem to be altogether appropriate for the study of the continuum of English national development. But when one comes to consider Anglo-American history, particularly during the crucial seventeenth century, special concern needs to be directed to the limits of compulsion under the Statute of Artificers, to that counter-balancing residue of freedom of labor which experience had shown to be necessary for the maintenance of social control in England in order that the process of normal capitalist accumulation might go forward. Consider briefly the relevant provisions of the Statute of Artificers in terms of a compulsion-versus-freedom analysis.

Any unpropertied, unemployed, unapprenticed man between the ages of twelve and sixty was obliged to work at farm labor by the year in his locality for any farmer requiring his services. But he had to be paid the established wages. Equally significant, recalling the law of 1547, the 1563 Statute of Artificers put the onus on the employers to offer employment, rather than on the workers to find employment, before the penalties of vagrancy could be imposed upon the worker.

Workers who entered into contract to perform specific works were compelled to continue in them, without leaving to seek other employment, until that job was finished, on penalty of a month in jail and, in some cases, being liable to a suit (in "Action of Debt") by the employer for damages amounting to five pounds sterling. But the punishment entailed no extension of service to the private employer, and the employer had no further recourse than the debt action.[67]

Workers bound to serve by the year were subject to a penalty of thirty days in jail for leaving their employers' service before the completion of their terms. But they could terminate their employment legally by giving three months' notice prior to the scheduled completion of their terms. If a person wished to go outside his own parish or town to take a job, he had first to secure from the authorities a formal written testimonial from the town authorities. If such a worker failed to present such a testimonial when taking a job outside his own town or parish, he was to be given twenty-one days to obtain the needed testimonial, being held in jail the while. Upon failure to secure the testimonial within that time, he was "to be whipped and used as a Vagabond."[68]

Male youths were indentured as apprentices to employers, usually for seven years, but sometimes for longer periods. No person might, without prohibitive penalty, practice any trade without having completed the appropriate apprenticeship. Therefore, the more lucrative the prospective trade, the greater was the incentive and the less the compulsion involved in the recruitment of apprentices. In the more remunerative occupations, apprenticeship was restricted to sons of men already in the trade, or to owners of property yielding an annual revenue of two or three pounds. For more common trades, there were no property or family qualifications, but the number of apprentices might be limited to a quota of one apprentice to one journeyman, after an initial quota of three to one. For "Apprenticeship to Husbandry [farming]," however, there were no restrictions except as to age, and it had generally more the aspect of impressment than selection of a career. Under a policy conceived "for the better Advancement of Husbandry and Tillage," any male between the ages of ten and eighteen and "fit" for such employment was obliged to enter into an "indenture" to serve as a "husbandry apprentice" to any farmer who required him for that purpose, for a term lasting until the youth reached twenty-one years of age at least, and possibly until he was twenty-four, depending upon the terms of the individual arrangement.

Refusal to serve as an apprentice was punishable by commitment to jail until the culprit was placed under bond to assure compliance. An apprentice was forbidden to marry without the employer's consent. He was a member of the employer's household and was obliged to obey the employer in any legal command.

It would seem therefore that, observing the limits of the law of 1547, the English bourgeoisie had decided – as far as male workers were concerned – to venture no further in that direction than the terms prescribed for Apprenticeship to Husbandry. Whatever the apprentice's infractions of the terms of the apprenticeship, his punishment for them entailed no extension of his time of service. If the proper authorities approved, in special circumstances and if the apprentice consented, he might be assigned to another master.[69] The apprentice could be freed from his service before the end of his term upon a validated complaint made to the authorities (magistrates, mayors, etc.) of ill-treatment or of misuse, including failure to provide instruction in the trade as agreed upon in the indenture.

Finally, any woman of the laboring class, between the ages of twelve and forty, being unmarried and "forth of work" (unemployed) was compellable to serve by the year, week, or day in any "reasonable" sort of work and at such wage rates as any two magistrates or aldermen, or the mayor, having local jurisdiction might assign for her. Upon refusal so to serve, the woman was to be held in jail "until she shall be bounded to serve." Even if impressed for labor, she was to be paid wages. At least as far as this law was concerned, there was no impediment to her marrying and chancing thereby whatever better escape such a course might afford.

The oppressive intent of the Statute of Artificers was obvious on the face of it. In a situation made especially difficult by the oversupply of labor, workers were compelled to work for whatever the employing class, through the magistrates, chose to offer, and to forgo any improvement through individual or collective bargaining. By both its general and its apprenticeship provisions, the statute consigned the generality of the wage-earning population to agricultural labor. Women workers were excluded from apprenticeship and made to serve in the lowest-paid drudgery. The severest censures of the anti-vagabond laws were threatened against the worker who sought to move from one place to another to improve his lot, unless he bore the magistrate's certificate of permission. Yet oppressive as that law was, neither its contrivers nor its victims would have believed that within several short generations, in a "New Albion,"[70] English workers would be worked as unpaid chattel bondmen and bondwomen, bought and sold from hand to hand for long terms of years, subject, for infraction, to extensions of that servitude for private owners; denied the right to marry, their children "bastards" by definition – and that such would be the common lot (not a real apprentice in a hundred) under "the custom of the country!"

The Poor Law as Social Control

A third major problem of social control – after the peasant revolts and labor relations – arose out of the mass pauperization wrought by the Agrarian Revolution. The presence of a set of persons having no fixed abode was not a new phenomenon in England. But prior to the sixteenth century it was more likely to be associated with a shortage of labor, leading laborers to slip their villein bonds to take better offers from new employers. The vagrancy problem of the sixteenth century, by contrast, was associated with a protracted general decline of wages, and with a stubborn struggle by laboring people to maintain their rights to stay on their land.

The extent of this "structural unemployment," as it would be called today, is not statistically verifiable,[71] but it cannot be doubted that its appearance presented the state with serious difficulties. It was fundamental; a by-product of the vitality of ascendant capitalism. It was intimately linked with the resistance of the copyholders to expropriation of their lands. In the words of Queen Elizabeth's chief adviser, Lord Burghley, the problem arose from "the depopulating of whole towns ... and keeping of a shepherd only, whereby many subjects are turned without habitation and fill the country with rogues and idle persons."[72]

The repeal of the 1547 slave law (1 Edw. VI 3), after three years of ineffectualness, marked the first glimmer of official acknowledgement that unemployment was not synonymous with willful idleness, vagabondage and roguery. A series of laws still sought to draw a significant distinction between the "impotent poor," who were to be relieved, and the "sturdy beggars."[73] The former were to be certified and provided for by propertied persons of their parishes. But the "sturdy beggars" were still to be subject to whipping, to transportation to their home parishes, and, in some cases, to exile or hanging as felons.

But the threat to the orderly transaction of affairs continued. "All parts of this realm of England and Wales," said Parliament in 1572, "be presently with rogues, vagabonds, and sturdy beggars exceedingly pestered ... to the great annoyance of the common weal."[74] They had become so emboldened by their desperate plight that in 1580 they even pressed their clamor upon the Queen personally "one evening as she was riding abroad to take the air."[75]

"Many thousands of idle persons are within this realm," warned Hakluyt in 1584, "which, haveing no way to be sett on worke, be either mutinous and seeke alteration in the state, or at least [are] very burthensome to the commonwealthe."[76] Two years later, another observer expressed fear that a surfeit of paupers must lead to "divers kinds of wrongs, mutinies, sedition, commotion, & rebellion."[77]

A royal decree of 1593 demanded stricter enforcement of the laws against the multitudes of rootless people who were wandering the highways, begging and extorting relief from the more prosperous persons they encountered. It was said that many of the predators were military and naval veterans "exacting money on pretense of service in the wars."[78]

In time the government came to see, as Nicholls, the pre-eminent student of the Poor Law, puts it, that "severe punishment loses its terrors in the presence of actual want – that a man will beg, or steal, or resort to violence rather than starve;" and that it was not wise to force the unemployed into that hard choice.[79] In 1601 Parliament accordingly made the law (43 Eliz. 2) that was to govern English poor relief for more than three centuries.[80] It provided for a system of guaranteed work to be maintained under the supervision of the Overseers of the Poor of each parish, comprised of the church wardens and from two to four other property owners. In central locations, called work-houses, or in their own abodes, the otherwise unemployed persons were to be set to work on materials such as hemp, wool, iron and thread. The proceeds from their products were to defray the costs incurred and to provide for payment for the workers "according to the desert of their work." Refusal to work on such terms was a legal offense, punishable by a term in the house of correction or common jail. Funds needed for furtherance of work and relief programs were to be raised by the Poor Rate, a regular tax periodically assessed against the property holders of each parish.[81]

In practice this formal relief was supplemented by illegal or semi-legal resort by the pauperized population to unauthorized infiltration into supposedly guild-protected trades, or by "squatting" on wastelands to eke out enough of an existence to escape the ministrations of the Overseers of the Poor.[82] But to the extent that such diversions were attempted, they were but supplementary to the workings of 43 Eliz. 2, the Poor Law, the ultimate monumental "attempt on the part of the powerful Tudor state to prevent the social disorder caused by economic changes, which in spite of its efforts it had not been strong enough to control."[83]

Notorious as the operation of the English system of Poor Relief was ever to be for its parsimony and sanctimony, the right of workers to be paid wages for the work done under its program, and the right to leave that employment if and when a turn of fortune – a legacy, a good apprenticeship opportunity, a decent job, or, for a woman, a marriage prospect – occurred, were matters never questioned by those who first established the system in 1601. Yet within a few decades, irreducible rights and privileges of the most condemned ward of the parish were to be denied to the general run of English workers performing the most essential labor in Anglo-America. To those contrivers of the Poor Rate, it would have seemed unthinkable that the support of the poor might, even in the slightest degree, be derived from impositions on other propertyless laborers.[84]

Oppression of Women

The social transformation wrought by the Agrarian Revolution and the rise of capitalism in England was indeed great. But the class coming to power found no need to amend common or statute law with regard to the subordination of women; it found male domination to be no less congenial to the functioning of the new order than it had been to the old.[85]

Given the absence of a women's rights movement – the first concerted cries for justice would not be heard for another two centuries; and, given the quick bourgeois appetite for wealth accumulation, making their historical ruling-class antecedents dilettantes by comparison – the brutal treatment of women in the new era proceeded unchecked.

As it was in man's record of the beginning, and had since been, the non-person civil status of women should ever be, so far as the bourgeoisie of England was concerned.[86] Classed with children in matters of civil rights, women continued to be classed with heretics when punishment for treason was prescribed; only women were to be burned at the stake for that offense.[87] And, like servants who killed their masters, women who killed their husbands were guilty of petty treason. By law, persons convicted of a felony were subject to the death penalty. But priests so convicted could be pardoned for the first offense by claiming "benefit of clergy," a relic of a former time when cleric felons were dealt with by ecclesiastical courts. (Persons granted this privilege were to be branded in the meat of the thumb to prevent their claiming that right a second time.) From the eve of the sixteenth century onwards, increasing categories of non-clerical men were admitted to this privilege. But women, barred by gender from being priests, were excluded from this mercy. They were granted full access to the benefit-of-clergy plea only in 1692.

The men of the ruling classes had immemorially exercised sex–class privileges at the expense of the women of the laboring classes. In feudal times in England the custom said to have been most hated by the serfs was that of "merchet," which required payment in kind or in money by the serf to the lord when the serf's daughter was to be married.[88] This was considered the most degrading and certain mark of servile status, since it forced the serfs to acknowledge possessory claims of one degree or another by the lord to every female virgin among his "family" of "dependants." The same theme was evident in the fact that a woman serf who married a free man and was later divorced by him again became a serf of her former lord. On the other hand, a woman who had originally been free but who married a serf herself, fell to the status of serfdom, which she could not escape by being divorced; instead she remained a serf, at least during the lifetime of her husband. The widow of a serf was designated by the special term "widewe," meaning the lord's widow.[89] She was obliged to guarantee production sufficient to meet the lord's due. Failing in that, a woman was required to surrender her holding, or else to make arrangements (with the lord's sanction) for the proper performance of her duties, as the ward of some man.

In the new order, women of the propertied classes continued to be hostages to the property to which they were linked through inheritance laws. As before, the cult of female chastity, with all its concomitant social and legal repression and sanctions imposed on women, remained an essential of the process of fortune-building through inheritances and marriage portions.[90] When the most important decisions were to be made concerning a woman's life, her personal interests or preferences carried less weight than the property and power interests of the men with whom her life was involved.[91] As of old, but with possibly greater cynicism, fatherless under-age daughters were, as "wards," dealt about like commodities. A man well regarded by the Court of Wards stood to gain when such a girl or woman was made his ward, for that brought him control of her property with all the opportunity for self-advancement it might make possible for him.[92]

There was to be for women no reformation in the Reformation. The notorious 1547 slave law, even in its general extremity, found a special disability to impose on the woman. If a man slave, by coming into an inheritance or otherwise, secured a "convenient living" he was to be freed. If, for instance, such a possibility presented itself in the form of marriage, a male slave had the unimpeded right to free himself by that course. But the female slave, if she were under twenty years of age, could avail herself of such an opportunity only if she could secure the permission of her owner to do so.[93] And, as we have seen, the Statute of Artificers of 1563 assigned unmarried, unpropertied women to the lowest labor status. If they were unemployed and between the ages of twelve and forty, they could be compelled to serve in any employment to which the magistrates might assign them. Furthermore, their wages were set at only about half of those paid to men doing comparable services.[94]

Above all, there were the reasons of state. The "ancient rights and liberties" of the small-propertied and propertyless classes were, as noted, subject to heavy assault in the sixteenth century. But the new order brought no threat to their rights and liberties as English men *vis-à-vis* English women.

Sir Francis Bacon voiced official sanction of this limitation on interference with traditional ways, saying that male domination and patriarchy were "natural and more ancient than the law." Addressing "The Lord Chancellor and all the Judges of England" in his capacity as Solicitor-General in 1608, Bacon set forth the premise that monarchy was the best form of rule because its authority was first of all based on the "platform" of male domination and patriarchy.

> The first [platform], he submitted, "is that of a father or chief of a family; who governing over his wife by prerogative of sex, over his children by prerogative of age, and because he is author to them of being, and over his servants by prerogative of virtue and providence (for he that is able of body and improvident of mind is *natura servus*), is the very model of a king.[95]

But before the king is every man, every man must be a king.[96] In feudal England, in the exercise of male domination over the wife, the serf's claims had priority over those of the feudal lord. The wife was a "feme covert," against whom the lord had no process of claim except through the husband. And in the new day, after the repression of the Pilgrimage of Grace, Henry VIII did not venture to pursue vengeance against the persons of a number of women who had been active rebels. The definitive work on this event explains that royal discretion as follows:

> Henry knew that in the excited state of public opinion it would be dangerous to meddle with them. His reign was not by any means the age of chivalry, but there still remained a good deal of the old tribal feeling about women, that they were the most valuable possessions of the clan, and that if any stranger, even the King, touched them all the men were disgraced.[97]

In the "new age", a man's home was still to be his castle and, if the matter were forced to an issue, a woman's prison. Men could divorce women; women could not divorce men. Some time late in the sixteenth century, Joan Wynstone ran away from her husband John, a man of humble station.[98] Taken up as a vagrant, she was sentenced under the law to work as a servant of the husband she had fled. Finding that life intolerable, Joan again escaped, but she was again recaptured. For this second offense she was hanged on the gallows.

The poor and laboring people of England might not prevail over their kings, or their queens, or their lords and masters, but the man of these classes could be king and lord and master to his wife. Male domination in this way served as a link between the beaten-down peasants and proletarians and the very authority that was beating them down. As such it operated as another instrument of ruling-class social control, disguised as the natural outcome of the sexual differentiation occurring in the population.

No English man of that day, from Lord Chancellor Francis Bacon to lowly John Wynstone, would have imagined that propertyless, yet non-apprenticed, English men would ever be so degraded (as they would have considered it) that under the law they might not have their own "castles" and the male privileges appertaining to their gender status.[99] Nor would Bacon or Wynstone have thought to find in "nature" an apology for the assertion of a general sexual privilege by one set of men – propertied and unpropertied – over all women of another set of the propertyless population. Yet the first of these inconceivable ideas would not only be thought of, it would become an essential operating principle of the Anglo-American plantation economy.[100] And, more amazing, the second, thought of and instituted, would become an indispensable element in the maintenance of bourgeois social control in continental plantation Anglo-America.[101]

3

Euro-Indian Relations and the Problem of Social Control

For all the talk of using colonies as vents for proletarian discontent, the first group of English to arrive in Virginia in 1607 included a disproportionate number of aristocrats and gentlemen, and their personal attendants, for whom productive labor was as unthinkable as it was for any Spanish *hidalgo* bound for New Spain.[1] Like Cortés, they were prepared to find ready access to gold and silver rather than to start cultivation of the soil.[2] By 1622,[3] however, the Virginia Company investors, realizing that Virginia was to be no El Dorado, rationalized their abandonment of dreams of emulating the treasure hunts of the Spanish in Mexico and Peru. "[T]o thinke that Gold and Silver mynes in a Country [Virginia] (otherwise most rich and fruitful) the greatest wealth of a Plantation is but popular error," wrote Edward Waterhouse in a long letter of advice to fellow members of the Virginia Company. He now saw the Spanish case in a different light. The law of diminishing returns had set in for silver and gold mining in Spanish America, he said, and Spain had turned to agricultural products, such as sugar, cotton, indigo, and brazil wood, to offset the decline of mining output.[4] He left no doubt that, in his opinion, the future prosperity of the Virginia plantation likewise lay in exploiting the country's natural potential for commodity production.

Why, he thought, could not the English do as the Spanish had done and recruit a labor force from the native population for that purpose? True, the colony was intended as a vent for the "troublesome poor" of England, but why should they not serve in the English plantation as an intermediate stratum, as overseers and tradesmen, such as had been formed by a certain portion of Spanish immigrants and Spanish creoles in Mexico and Peru?[5] Why should not the Virginia Indians be

> compelled to servitude and drudgery, and supply the roome of men that labour, whereby even the meanest [Englishmen] of the Plantation may imploy themselves more entirely in their Arts and Occupations, which are more generous, whilest Savages performe their inferior workes of digging in mynes and the like, of whom also some may be sent for the service of the Sommer Ilands [Bermuda Islands].[6]

Old planter John Martin likewise suggested that the Indians be "brought into subjection," they being "apter for worke then yet our English are ... and fitt to rowe in Gallies & friggetts and many other pregnant uses."[7] Captain John Smith (1580–1631), the most famous leader of the early Jamestown settlers, retrospectively regretted that the English had not from the beginning done as the Spanish had done, namely "forced the ... [Indians] to do all manner of drudgery worke and slavery for them, themselves [the Spanish] living like Souldiers upon the fruit of their [the Indians'] labours."[8] The Spanish option was not to be dismissed out of hand. Indeed Captain John Smith reasoned that, *vis-à-vis* the respective native populations, the English in Virginia and New England were better situated than the Spanish had been in the West Indies. The Spanish, outnumbered by the West Indies Indians by fifty or more to one, had "no other remedy" but mass extermination of the natives. "Ours," said Smith, referring possessively to Virginia and New England Indians, were "such a few, and so dispersed, it were nothing in a short time to bring them to labour and obedience."[9]

If the English had subdued and forced "their" Indians into "drudgery and slavery," they would have had to confront, as the Iberians had had to do, the problem of establishing a system of social control over the native population that would be, as the phrase is nowadays, "cost-effective."

Social Control: Haiti (Hispaniola), Cuba and Puerto Rico

When European colonization of the so-called New World began in Hispaniola in 1492, the population density of that island was about the same as that of Portugal (around 33 and 38 inhabitants per square mile, respectively), but the society of the island was not highly stratified.[10] Speaking of the Indians of the West Indies, Las Casas said, "They are very poor folk, which possess little ... they are accustomed to have no more store than they ordinarily have need of and that such as they get with little travail [labor]." He elaborated with notations of the people's diet, apparel, and shelter.[11] There was no distinct native social stratum that could act as a buffer between the laboring people and the Spanish conquerors in the administration of a normal, orderly, colony. Hence the *encomienda* system, whereby the King of Spain "commended" the natives to "the care" of individual Spanish colonists as laborers,[12] was conducted "in an irregular, uncontrolled, and highly exploitative form.... Spaniards raided Indian communities, took captives, and, in order to prevent escape or to ensure the full measure of work, practiced large-scale enslavement."[13]

The native population did not willingly submit to such brutal administration. In Hispaniola the Maguana people rose in revolt after the treacherous Spanish killing of the captive Maguana chief Canaobo.[14] In 1511 in Puerto Rico, the Borinqueños under the leadership of a *cacique* named Guaybana mounted a major rebellion against the imposition of the Spanish system of forced labor. A second Borinquen uprising was led by another *cacique*, Humacao, four years later.[15] Other Borinqueños, possibly one-third of the population, sought refuge in remote mountainous areas, or fled by boat to other islands.[16] But in

Haiti (Hispaniola/Santo Domingo) and Cuba, the Spanish advantage of overwhelming military strength exerted without restraint, in the context of the even more devastating toll of epidemic European diseases, resulted in almost complete extermination of the native population. There it was a mathematical certainty that without an intermediate social stratum, "social control" by mere unbridled military force would be self-defeating because it exceeded the limits that had to be observed to preserve an exploitable labor force.

Social Control: Mexico and Peru

At the time of the Spanish invasion in 1519, the population of central Mexico,[17] an area of about 200,000 square miles, was an estimated 13.9 million,[18] representing a density of almost 70 people per square mile. Of this population, 2.5 million, concentrated more than 350 per square mile, lived in the 8,000-square-mile area in and near the Basin of Mexico.[19] Tenochitlan (Mexico City), in the heart of this area, had a population of 300,000.

The invaders found already in place "an elaborate system of levy providing products of all kinds, slaves, and services for the three capitals of the so-called Aztec Empire," and a similar system in other large states outside the Aztec territory. In each case it was organized to support its central government ruling group.[20] Originally a three-layered stratum,[21] the ruling group came to be designated by the Spanish under the general name of *caciques*.[22]

The Spanish were able to adapt this pre-existing form of social organization to extort labor and tribute from the Indians, even in the most rapacious manner,[23] using "Indian office-holders ... at the subordinate levels of the hierarchy for the enforcement of Spanish rules."[24] In the opinion of the well-known historian of colonial Mexico Charles Gibson, it was "[t]he power and prestige of the pre-Spanish states, and their continuing traditions of popular subservience, [that] made it possible for the Spaniards to exact labor and tribute with little opposition." Summarizing, Gibson writes that in both Mexico and Peru, "Spaniards took charge of an established society, substituting themselves for the rulers they had deposed or killed."[25]

But such a displacement at the top would not have been effective in gaining the Spaniards' purposes without the preservation of a buffer social control function for the socially demoted *caciques*.

The ease with which the first Spaniards manipulated huge numbers of native peoples, even the ease with which the first missionaries induced huge numbers of conversions, depended upon the intermediate position of the caciques. ... Caciques were in the vanguard in the adoption of Spanish dress, foods, language, and styles of house construction. They were excused from tribute and labor exactions and given special privileges, such as permission to ride horses and carry arms. ... Indian caciques and Spanish *corregidores* [Spanish officers in charge of local districts] joined forces to extract from the mass of the Indian population whatever wealth it possessed over and above the subsistence level of its economy.[26]

Considered in terms of social control and resistance, the story of the Spanish defeat of and rule over the Inca civilization of Peru in the sixteenth century closely corresponds to the pattern set in Mexico. The Inca word for chiefs, *kurakas*, was by Spanish decree in 1572 changed to *cacique*,[27] appropriately enough it would seem, since the buffer social control function of that office in Peru was identical with its function in Mexico. The hereditary Peruvian *caciques* were exempt from paying tribute or labor service. They were the collectors of tribute to be paid to the Spanish by Indians between the ages of eighteen and fifty. They were responsible also for furnishing the *mita* laborers for service to Spanish masters in industries, in farming and, worst of all, in the silver and mercury mines of Potosi and Huancavelica.[28]

In Peru, the *caciques* "exercised considerable power over Indians, even within the borders of Spanish towns."[29] In 1558, supreme Inca chief Sayri Tupac struck a sort of surrender-and-regrant "bargain" with the Spanish – as O'Neill and other Irish chieftains had done a few year earlier in Ireland (see Volume One).[30]

For at least a century and a half, the *caciques* of Mexico and Peru served as the principal buffer social control stratum in the Spanish system of social control in those domains.[31] But in Mexico, the relatively class-undifferentiated Chichimecs drew a line, and long maintained it, beyond which the Spanish *encomienda* could not be established.[32] In Peru, the Incas defended the remnants of their independent state in two open rebellions. In 1536, Inca Manco and his uncle Titu Yupanqui, taking advantage of a momentary political and military division among the Spanish, rose in revolt to end the desecration of their lands and temples. Manco led a five-month siege of Cuzco, and Titu headed a large army in an assault on Lima.[33] Thirty-five years later, Tupac Amaru, youngest son of Inca Sayri Tupac, served as a rallying symbol for a last great uprising to throw off the Spanish yoke.[34]

The Social Control Problem in Brazil

Brazil, like Hispaniola, presented no previously established social stratum adaptable to the colonizing power's social control purposes, and Catholic religious orders, most notably the Jesuits and Franciscans, largely succeeded in substituting themselves in that function. It was the Dominican friar Bartolomé de Las Casas, however, who first raised the standard of battle for "protection of the Indians" of the West Indies in the sixteenth century, but his pleas were brushed aside by the gold-crazed colonists. A basic factor in the genocide of the native peoples of the West Indies in the early sixteenth century was the difficulty of their making a mass flight by sea. The Indians of Brazil, on the other hand, would serve to establish a general principle of social control in European colonies in the Americas: dominance was less easily established and maintained over continental colonies than over insular colonies.[35]

In the continental expanse of Brazil, there was space, and therefore time, for development of an effective class struggle of the Indian laborers and the Portuguese plantation bourgeoisie (the *moradores*). The Indians, as we have noted, were successful in making the point in the sixteenth century that they had no desire to become long-term sugar plantation bond-laborers (see page 7). Indeed, in the sixteenth century a number of projected areas of Portuguese settlement had to be abandoned in the face of Indian attacks.[36] More generally, the Indians resisted plantation servitude by removing themselves to the continental interior.[37] The Portuguese plantation owners countered by conducting armed expeditions (*entradas*) into the interior in order to "entice or force" Indians into Portuguese-controlled villages (*aldeias*),[38] which were located to provide easy access to a supply of Indian plantation laborers, to be used under conditions that were, for all practical purposes, mere slavery.[39] Just as elsewhere in the plantation Americas, super-exploitation of labor and the spread of epidemic European diseases took a heavy toll on the indigenous labor supply in Brazil.[40] In any case, since Indians, having the continental advantage, "deserted their *aldeias* in large numbers,"[41] the colonists were unable to solve the labor-supply problem by resort to raw force through the *entradas*.

It was in the Amazon region of Brazil during the seventeenth century that the Franciscans and then the Jesuits, led most prominently by António Vieira, after a campaign lasting from 1624 to 1686, were able to win a royal decree outlawing enslavement of Indians and bestowing custody of the *aldeia* Indians on the religious orders. These Indians were then to be assigned by the religious authorities as free laborers to plantation owners for a limited part of each year.[42] In terms of social control, the religious orders were filling in relation to a class-undifferentiated native population a role similar to that performed by the *caciques* in relation to the native class-differentiated societies of Mexico and Peru.[43]

In the Amazon region, Portuguese plantation owners rebelled against the idea of non-enslavability of Indians as government interference with free enterprise; they insisted that the free play of market forces required slave labor. Vieira met the objection by proposing the extension to the Amazon region of the practice that had been in operation in more southern coastal regions of Brazil since the middle of the sixteenth century, namely, by the enslavement of Angolans "of both sexes to assure their propagation." The principle was to be "The Negroes to the colonists, the Indians to the Jesuits." A suitable religious exegetical rationale was contrived. The Angolans, by being baptized Christians, were afforded an opportunity to escape the everlasting torment to which they had been certainly doomed as "pagans." Their souls were to be redeemed by the Calvary-like suffering of lifetime hereditary servitude in the sugar industry. The Indians, having been made wards of a Christian order, could not be consigned to slavery.[44] For an indication of the widespread failure of Afro-Brazilian bond-laborers to find comfort in this thesis, see the note on the Palmares *guilombo* in Appendix II-A.

The Powhatans of Virginia

Of all the Ibero-American cases, Brazil was the one that most resembled Anglo-American Virginia with respect to the problem of establishing that degree of social control essential for basing the colonial economy on the forced labor of the indigenous population. Like Brazil, Virginia was a continental colony, not an insular one. Like the indigenous society of Brazil,[45] Powhatan society exhibited little significant stratification, lacking a strong rulership[46] and concomitant intermediate stratum[47] adaptable to the social control purposes of the conquerors. Storage facilities were insufficient to permit long-term accumulation in the hands of the ruling element of products upon which the people were dependent. There was no wealth in the form of domesticated animals, nor did wealth exist in any other form such as to permit accumulations adequate for the support of a permanent leisure class or a non-productive politico-military bureaucracy. The people derived three-fourths of their living from hunting, fishing and gathering, one-fourth from cultivation. With a population density of only one or two persons per square mile,[48] the Powhatan Indians for most of the year were on the whole well-provisioned, so that they could even share with the starving English colonists on occasion.[49]

There was a degree of social stratification; a chief (Powhatan, the person himself, when the English first arrived) lived on the tribute assessed on the people and had privileged access to the best hunting grounds. He received labor tribute by having his fields planted for him, and tended by a multiplicity of women bound to him. But social distinction was insufficient to produce a permanent category "intermediate between rulers and ruled,"[50] or any politico-military bureaucracy. Powhatan had authority to make alliances and war, and to control trade with other tribes and the English. But he was not always able to enforce his will on all his subjects, nor was he always able to enforce it upon the supposedly tributary tribes. The result was to limit the intensity of the exploitation of the laborers; indeed, the chief himself did productive labor at "men's work" such as hunting and hand crafts.

Any attempt by the English plantation bourgeoisie to subjugate the Indians to "drudgery and slavery" would have to face the "Brazilian" problem, but without the agency of the Catholic religious orders; they had been banned in the sixteenth-century English Reformation.[51] More immediately to the point, at the time that Smith and others were fantasizing about emulating the Spanish Conquistadors, the English simply did not have the preponderance of military force such as that which the Spanish unleashed against the indigenous peoples upon whom they made war.[52] The weakness of the English colony in the early period was such that in the three years 1620–22 the colony was dependent upon *trade* with neighboring Indians to save itself from "absolute starvation."[53]

In these respects, the Powhatan social order was essentially the same as those found among the Pequots, Narragansetts, Wampanoags, and other peoples in New England, and the Yamassees, Creeks, Tuscororas, Cherokees, Choctaws, Chickasaws, and other peoples confronting the colonists of the southernmost region, the Carolinas. With regard to establishing social control, the Anglo-American continental bourgeoisie faced the "Brazilian" problem: a continental people without a *cacique* class.

Despite their early difficulties, the English from the beginning had a fundamental potential advantage over the Indians due to the discrepancy in the development of productive forces and productivity of labor. This advantage was enhanced by the fact that the Indians could not possibly have known what the appearance of the first handfuls of settlers portended for the land.[54] Yet, even if they had foreseen from Powhatan to Powder River, and had been able to mobilize a united resistance to the taking of the Trail of Tears, the Indians probably could not have prevented eventual European colonization in North America,[55] although by such a united effort they might have given American history a more humane course than the one it took.

English Buying and Selling of Indian Captives

The actual strength of the English colony in relation to the Virginia Indians changed markedly to the disadvantage of the latter in the period between 1622 and 1644, the dates of two concerted Indian attacks on the colony. By 1644, the relative superiority of the forces at the disposal of the colony was well established, and all Indian hope of ousting the settlers from the Chesapeake region was lost. The treaty of 1646[56] that ended the Indian war begun by Opechancanough, Chief Powhatan's brother and successor, marked the beginning of Anglo-American "Indian policy." At first that policy contemplated only the displacement of the Indian tribes obstructing the advance of the Anglo-American "frontier," but ultimately it would challenge the legitimacy of Indian tribal society itself.[57] In the context of this chapter, consideration is limited to the relationship of that policy to the general labor supply and social control problem faced by the continental colonial bourgeoisie. The basic considerations that shaped the policy, the optimizing of the combination of the rate of capital accumulation and social control,[58] were essentially the same in Virginia as elsewhere, although in one respect, namely the commerce in Indian chattel bond-laborers, the grossest development occurred in South Carolina and secondarily in New England.

Fourteen years after the 1646 treaty, the Virginia General Assembly declared that if the Indians of Northumberland County failed to pay the damages to be assessed by the court of that county for damages done by the Indians to a colonist there, then "soe many off them as the court shall determine shall be apprehended and sold into a forraigne country to satisfie the award."[59] Although in that particular instance no legal justification was cited, it appears to have been under the principle of *lex talionis*, simple retaliation. In general, however, the Anglo-Americans throughout the continental colonies drew on the ancient principle that victors in "just" wars who spared the lives of "heathen" captives thereby gained the right to hold them as slaves, which Europeans used to justify the forced transportation of Africans to perpetual servitude in the Americas. The Virginia Assembly gave this principle the force of law regarding Indians during Bacon's Rebellion in 1676. It was reasserted in 1677 following the defeat of Bacon's Rebellion, and subsequently in 1679, 1682, 1711 and 1722.[60] Enslavement of Indian captives – children and women as well as men – was general in Massachusetts following the Pequot War of 1636–37, and again after King Philip's War of 1675–76.[61] In Carolina province (both before and after its division into South and North Carolina, first called Albemarle, in 1691), the Anglo-Americans made direct war on Indians and enslaved the captives.

But the chief means of securing Indian bond-laborers was by trade with Indian tribes, in the course of which captives of intertribal warfare, along with deer skins and beaver pelts, were exchanged for English commodities such as firearms and ammunition, metal tools and containers, woven fabrics and garments, mirrors and rum.[62] It was English policy to foment "just wars" between tribes for the particular purpose of securing Indian captives as chattel bond-laborers.[63] As tribes became increasingly dependent upon the English for trade goods, some, out of narrow considerations of tribal interests, made war on other tribes in order to maintain their trade with the English.[64] Nash states for a certainty that "the number [of Indians] enslaved reached into the tens of thousands in the half-century after Carolina was settled by Europeans."[65]

The Abandonment of the Native Sources of Plantation Bond-labor

Yet the fantasy of an Anglo-America based on Indian drudgery and slavery was not to be realized. Why not? The standard reference work in the field is still Almon Wheeler Lauber's *Indian Slavery in Colonial Times within the Present Limits of the United States*, published more than eighty years ago.[66] Lauber presents four theses to explain "the decline of Indian slavery." First, depopulation caused by a combination of European diseases, a declining Indian birth rate, and internecine wars in considerable degree fomented by the English interested in trading for the captives whom they would then use in commercial transactions, principally with other English colonies, most often those in the West Indies. Second, Indians "disappeared" as a result of "the amalgamation of red and black slaves." Third, Indians were "unfitted for servitude," being "unable to endure sustained labor," incapable of developing to a "civilized" social level, and bred and reared to be "opposed to all restraint ... by an exterior force." Fourth, if kept in the capturing colony, Indian bond-laborers were possibly even more likely than other bond-laborers to run away, because of the Indians' hope of "returning to their own people."[67]

It is argued here, from a somewhat different perspective, that the failure of the European power to establish a plantation system based on the bond-labor of the native population in the Anglo-American continental colonies was analogous to that of the Portuguese colonizers in Brazil. The decisive factors in each case were two: each colonization was enacted on a continental land mass, as distinct from insular areas such as those in the West Indies; and, second, the indigenous society was not stratified, in any case not stratified enough to produce a separate and distinct social class of *caciques*, accustomed to command and adaptable for colonialist social control purposes, particularly as mobilizers of forced labor for the European capitalist investors.

From those premises I venture a criticism of Lauber's first and third theses about "the decline of Indian slavery."[68] I take them in reverse order because the third directly confronts the one assumption for which I crave indulgence in the first paragraph of the Introduction to the first volume of this work.

The "unfitness" sour-grapes rationale

Some historians whose approach to the subject is informed with the spirit of the civil rights movement, and whose citations of Lauber have been quite appropriate, have perhaps thought it redundant to take note of the white-supremacist assumptions encountered in a work conceived in what Rayford W. Logan called the "nadir" of the struggle for civil rights in the United States. One latter-day scholar even endorses the Lauber view of this issue, "despite the racist implications of arguments about the relative adaptability of one people over another to tropical labor."[69]

In my view, if being "constitutionally unfitted" for servitude could explain the "decline of slavery," then it should have led to the extinction of bond-servitude in such places as the following:

- Virginia, where for four or five early decades, not one in five of the English chattel laborers survived the period of "indenture." (Governor William Berkeley in reply to queries of the Lords of Trade and Plantations, in 1671 [Hening 2:511.])

- St Domingue, where the average French *engagé* or African bond-laborer survived only three years. See note 35 of Chapter 1.

- Barbados, where in 1680 an annual supply of five thousand African laborers was required to maintain a Negro population of forty thousand (Vincent T. Harlow, *A History of Barbados, 1625–1685* [1926; Negro Universities reprint, 1969], pp. 323–4); where from 1680 to 1800 hundreds of thousands of African bond-laborers arrived, but the population increased by less than ten thousand. (David Lowenthal, "The Population of Barbados," *Social and Economic Studies*, 6:445–501.)

- The British West Indies as a whole which, between 1700 and 1780, absorbed about 850,000 African bond-laborers, yet the Negro population increased only 350,000. (Gary B. Nash, *Red, White, and Black* [Englewood Cliffs, New Jersey, 1974] p. 178.)

• Mexico and Peru, where in the first centuries after the beginning of Spanish rule, the *repartimiento* and *mita* recruitment by the *caciques* contributed so heavily to the reduction of the Mexican and Peruvian native populations. (See page 7.)

Why were the Spanish so slow to learn what the Portuguese capitalists, with whom they shared a common realm for much of the time, had learned: "the unfitness" of Indians for sustained labor? Was it perhaps because they were laughing so hard all the way to the counting house in Seville? Or could it have been that they felt satisfied that the total value of the gold and silver produced by the Indians of Mexico and Peru was probably as great as, if not greater than, that of the sugar produced by Angolans in colonial Brazil?

Did forced labor itself exact a greater toll among Indians than it did among Africans and their descendants? Despite pious protestations in religious quarters and in occasional formal governmental expressions of sympathy, neither the *encomenderos* of Mexico and Peru, nor the *moradores* of Brazil, nor the "planters" of Anglo-America cared a fig about the unfitness of the labor as long as they could be assured of an affordable functioning supply. Time and again in the seventeenth century the Portuguese *moradores* in northern Brazil rebelled against royal and religious authority in order to keep the Indians enslaved, driving out the religious troublemakers, who themselves were forced to admit that "without the Indians the inhabitants [meaning the Portuguese settlers] would die."[70] In South Carolina, for fifty years, the English colonists ridiculed and evaded the strictures of the London proprietors against trading in captive Indian laborers, the profits of which went to the locals rather than to London.[71]

On the other hand, as the record shows, laborers throughout the Americas considered forced labor "unfit" for *themselves*, and resisted servitude as well as they could. In the *cacique*-habituated countries of Mexico and Peru they could not prevail. But the tribal Indians in continental situations did resist enslavement successfully, and in the process provided the frustrated colonialists with the sour-grapes argument about the "unfitness" of Indians for plantation labor.

It would seem that little time needs be spent in this post–World War Two era on Lauber's notion that the North American Indians were not enslavable because of their inability to become "civilized." Are we to believe that, to paraphrase Chairman Mao, "civilization grows out of the barrel of a gun"? Without that one advantage, the work of the Anglo-American "blessings-of-civilization trust," as Mark Twain called it, would surely have been brought to an end before it ever got to South Carolina. In reacting to Lauber's doubt about the "capacity of the Indian for civilization," because "the dominant idea of Indian life was the love of liberty," one can only ask, "What price civilization?" Looking at the figures on the depopulation of the indigenous Americas, one might better ask: If "civilization" is assumed to correlate with increased well-being, did the age of colonization of the Americas demonstrate a "capacity for civilization"? Finally, how was it that Lauber could ignore that precisely the opposite premise was the mainstay of slaveholder ideology, namely that slavery was the only possible normal basis for "civilized" people like themselves to relate to the "uncivilized"?[72]

Enslavement of Indian labor not a problem of supply, but of social control

Lauber's first thesis, namely that European colonization had a devastating depopulating effect through infections of smallpox, tuberculosis, and other exotic diseases, is undoubtedly true. So also did the intensification of warfare, both against the English and between Indian tribes. These general conditions, coupled with the English policy of trading away a disproportionate number of male captives, would certainly tend to lower the birth rate among the Indians. Before South Carolina came to be chiefly a producer of rice and cotton early in the eighteenth century, the colony was primarily dependent upon commerce with the Indian tribes. It was in that colony's trading sphere, therefore, that the depopulating effect of enslavement was most in evidence. In 1708, the Spanish governor of Florida charged that some 10,000 to 12,000 Florida Indians, chiefly Apalachee people, had been taken as slaves by Creek and Yamassee Indians, directed by English Carolinians; only 300 Florida Indians survived, by finding refuge in St Augustine.[73] The extension of slave-trading into the interior in that same year was justified by South Carolina businessmen on the ground that "it serves to lessen their [the Indians'] number before the French can arm them."[74] The shipment of Indian captives from Carolina to bond-servitude in other English colonies, particularly those in the West Indies,[75] was, while it lasted, a major cause of Indian depopulation. The practice was also a factor in New England in the wake of the defeat of the forces commanded by the Wampanoag chieftain Metacom (called King Philip by the English) in 1675–76. An undetermined number of the captives were sent as bond-laborers "to various parts," namely the Spanish West Indies, Spain, Portugal, Bermuda, Virginia, and the Azores.[76] The Virginia colony Indian trade was primarily for beaver pelts and deer skins in the seventeenth century;[77] the labor supply was mainly English, together with a number of other European bond-laborers, and, to an increasing extent at the end of the seventeenth century, Afro-Caribbean and African.[78] Consequently, in Virginia the employment of and trade in Indian labor was comparatively limited.[79] But whatever the degree of involvement of the respective colonies, it is certain that depopulating wars were, paradoxically, the necessary condition for the beginning and continuation of Indian slavery, while it lasted, in the continental Anglo-American colonies. I know of no study, however, which concludes that the ending of enslavement of Indians within the capturing colony, or for trading abroad, was the result of the depopulating effect of that practice.[80] It was not the "supply' aspect, but rather the "control" aspect that was decisive in ending the labor policy of Indian enslavement in continental Anglo-America.

It was the common rule that enslaved Indian war captives, most particularly the men, be shipped out of the colony, sometimes to other continental colonies, even to England or Spain, but most commonly to England's West Indian sugar plantation colonies.[81] The proportion of Indian bond-laborers was by far the highest in South Carolina. There it peaked in about 1708, when 1,400 Indians (500 men, 600 women and 300 children) constituted one-fourth of the total lifetime hereditary bond-labor force.[82] Yet "only a small proportion of the whole number of Indians enslaved were kept in the [South Carolina] colony."[83] The total numbers of Indians enslaved in the Massachusetts and Plymouth colonies was far less, but it was policy to send male captives "outside the colonies."[84] Shipping value-producing Indian labor out of the colony was not what policy advisers to the Virginia Company had in mind in the early 1620s. Why was it, then, that the great majority were transported by sea to other colonies or countries?[85]

It was not that Indian laborers were unemployable in plantation labor; after all, that is why they were wanted in the West Indies. Nor was it that those colonies were oversupplied with plantation laborers; indeed, the Indians shipped to the West Indies were traded for Afro-Caribbean plantation laborers to be employed in the continental colonies.[86] It was not that Indians could not learn trades; actual instances of Indian craftsmen working within the colonies showed that they could, even as chattel bondmen.[87] Rather, the reasons were rooted in three intractable problems of "white race" social control: (1) resistance by the Indian bond-laborers, principally by running away, which merged sometimes with the same form of resistance of African and European bond-laborers; (2) the necessity to maintain nearby friendly, or "treaty," Indians in the buffer role,[88] in the first instance between the Anglo-American colonies and the more remote "hostile," or foreign-allied, tribes; and then against the escape of African-American bond-laborers beyond the Anglo-American "frontier"; and (3) with the institution of the "white race" system of social control, the key necessity of preserving "white skin" privileges of laboring-class European-Americans *vis-à-vis* all non-European-Americans.

Indian resistance to being reduced to plantation bond-labor

In the absence of a *cacique* class[89] that from positions of traditional upper-class authority could be co-opted as recruiters of plantation bond-labor, the Anglo-American bourgeoisie adapted the phenomenon of inter-tribal rivalries for their purposes. This was a basic element of the colonialist "Indian policy," and it was made to dovetail with the strategy according to which Indian "allies" were to serve as a protective buffer for the colony against the generally more remote tribes.

But if the English colonizers had the advantage of firearms and the buffer of dependent tribes, the victim tribes had a continental space at their backs.[90] This "continental factor" made possible Indian resistance by migration. When the Savannah Indians of South Carolina migrated north in 1707, "[t]he Iroquois themselves received [them] as brothers and the Delaware called them grandsons."[91] Sometimes migration would enable a tribe largely to avoid the enslaving onslaught;[92] sometimes victim tribes retained sufficient cohesion to be able to maintain their identity even as they migrated; and in other cases broken remnants found refuge with other tribes into which they were adopted.[93]

Unlike the African bond-laborers displaced from home by thousands of ocean miles into an utterly strange land, those relatively few Indian captives retained in a given colony were not so "completely broken from their tribal stems,"[94] and were still in at least somewhat familiar terrain, facing a familiar enemy whom they had already met in open battle. South Carolina Provincial policy was focused on the constant danger of Indian bond-laborers escaping into the woods, or conspiring with enemy tribes, or mounting insurrections, such as the one suspected in 1700.[95]

Colonialist concern was heightened by fears of Indians joining with African-Americans in resistance to their common bondage. In 1729, the French governor of Louisiana expressed his concern that "Indian slaves being mixed with our negroes may induce them to desert."[96] That same year he abandoned a mission of revenge against one Indian tribe, the Nabanez (Natchez?), lest Choctaws and Negroes seize the opportunity to attack New Orleans "to free themselves from slavery."[97] In South Carolina, precautions were advised to prevent "intimacy" between Indians and Negroes, "any Intercourse between Indians and Negroes" being seen as a threat to the colony.[98] In his signal study of the relationship of the Indians and African-Americans in the southeastern Anglo-American colonies, William S. Willis found that "[t]he determination [on the part of the English colonial authorities] to prevent Indian–Negro contacts within the White settlements was a main cause for curtailing the enslavement of Indians."[99]

The threat was made more acute by the constant efforts of the Spanish in Florida and the French in Louisiana to encourage resistance to and flight from the English colonies.[100] In 1716 and for some years thereafter, Yamassees and some Creeks, as well as numbers of Negroes, deserted English Carolina for Spanish Florida; from there Yamassees and Negroes carried on raids against the English colony, spreading the word to the South Carolina Indians and Negroes that freedom was theirs for the having in Florida.[101] When the English commanded by General Oglethorpe invaded Spanish Florida in 1740–42, they were opposed there by joint forces of Indians, Negroes, and Spanish.[102]

As time went on, Indian peoples grew less inclined to engage in internecine wars simply to provide slaves for the trade and exploitation of English "planters" who were intruding on villages of "friendly" and "hostile" Indians alike.[103] This trend matured in the great Indian revolt in 1715, called the

Yamassee War (see page 44), which marked the beginning of the irreversible discontinuation of enslavement of Indians in South Carolina, the province where it had been most extensively practiced.[104]

The inherent ambivalence of the "buffer" role

The buffer tribes had a dual role in the English colonial system of social control.[105] They served as a shield for the English against hostile tribes, including those linked to French and Spanish colonial rivals. Prior to 1715, South Carolina colonial policy "sought to consolidate a double bulwark of Indian allies in the zone of the Savannah and Altamaha Rivers" (present-day east–central Georgia). In the northwestern region, it was the mountain-dwelling Overhill Cherokee who long "bore the brunt of the French Indians." In 1723 the South Carolina Assembly solemnly affirmed, "The safety of this Province does, under God, depend on the friendship of the Cherokees."[106] In England the Commissioners of Trade and Plantations communicated to the King their concern that this dependence had even wider ramifications: if the Cherokees were to desert "your Majesty's interest," then "not only Carolina, but Virginia likewise would be exposed to their excursions."[107]

The buffer tribes were also a buffer between the runaway African-American bond-laborer and refuge beyond the boundaries of the Anglo-American colony.[108] This function was a regular provision in every treaty or memorandum of understanding between the colonies and their "tributary," "friendly," or newly "subject" tribes. Nash notes the "persistent inclusion in Indian treaties of a clause providing for the return of escaped slaves."[109] "Most treaties," Willis writes of the southeastern region in the eighteenth century, "stipulated that Indians surrender all Negroes and return all future runaways at an agreed price."[110] But the pattern had been set more than half a century earlier in the 1646 treaty between the Virginia colony and "Necotowance, King of the Indians."[111] Under the terms of the treaty made in 1700 between the Maryland colonial government and the chief of the Piscataway Indians, "[i]n case any servants or slaves runaway from their masters" to any Piscataway town, "the Indians shall be bound to apprehend them and bring them to the next English Plantation," or be subject to the penalties of Maryland law for the harborers of fugitives.[112]

By definition, "buffer" tribes were those located nearer to,[113] more accessible to, and, above all, economically more dependent upon the English colonists than were other tribes. But by the same token they were therefore more vulnerable to the predations of colonists who were ready to risk, to some degree, the buffer's protective function. It was precisely this sort of undermining of the buffer understanding that led to the Westo War of 1708. For the same reason, in the 1701–8 period the Savannah Indians acted out their resentment by emigrating northward out of South Carolina, "much to the annoyance of the white government, which found them useful as a bulwark against other tribes, and what was probably more important, as slave raiders."[114] As mentioned above, the aggravation of Indian grievances culminated in the Yamassee War (1715–17). The fate of southeast Anglo-America hung by a single thread, namely the loyalty of the Cherokees to the English, and that linkage was itself gravely weakened. But the tie held, and as a result the rebellion was defeated.[115] But it was, nevertheless, a historic victory over Indian enslavement, which immediately went into decline. "Justice to the Indians," Crane writes, "and, in particular the suppression of the traffic in Indian slavery, these were injunctions to successive [South Carolina Provincial] governors and councils," from 1680 to 1715.[116] In the wake of the Yamassee War, the issue could no longer be avoided. South Carolina was becoming a rice, cotton and indigo plantation enterprise for which were wanted African bond-laborers, such as many of the colony elite had been exploiting in the Barbadian sugar plantations. In 1690 the Lords Proprietors had sent an urgent instruction to the Carolina authorities:

> We hear that Indians are still being shipped away underhand. . . . You will do your best to prevent this. . . . [W]ithout them you cannot recover runaway Negroes.[117]

Twenty-five years later, the logic of their lordships' warning finally struck home. That logic was fundamentally dictated by the "continental factor" – providing the vast area for bond-labor escape that no army could patrol, and no navy could surround – and by the absence of an Indian *cacique* class.

Indian Labor and the Invention of the White Race

If not by compulsion, if not as "drudges" for the English colonists of every class, what were the possibilities of voluntary enlistment by Indians in the work of the colony, alongside the "surplus" English men and women who were brought to Anglo-America? In the period ending in 1622, there were instances of Indians who did work voluntarily within the Virginia colony.[118] In 1709 Robin, an Indian shoemaker, was granted leave to practice his trade among the English colonists "wherever he shall find encouragement."[119] But in general the Indians found their tribal life more comfortable and better supplied than the life offered by the English community so sore beset with starvation and disease. The English laboring people after 1622 worked as bond-laborers for terms which most of them did not survive, for debts they should not have had to owe for the trip to America. The Indians, as natives of the country, could not be bound by any such "transportation charges." It was hardly to be expected that Indians would submit voluntarily to the oppressive life endured by the English bond-laborers. Nor would the English employers be willing to spend more for Indian laborers than they had to spend for English laborers in such plentiful supply.

Was there another way? Despite the general inaccessibility of Indians as plantation laborers and the continual displacement of the tribal settlements, could they not, as groups or individuals, still have abandoned the Indian way of life for the English way? Although by far the greater number of the European immigrants arriving in the southern colonies came as bond-laborers, there were some who were able to make the trip from Europe at their own expense, and who began their lives in Anglo-America as independent farmers or artisans. Why might not Indians have opted for the same sort of enterprise within the colony? The English homeland itself was mainly a nation of immigrants, Saxons, Angles, Danes, Normans, Flemings, consolidating with the ancient Angles, Celts and Scots. True, the Indians' tribal lands were being taken away, but might not the inducements for individual Indians entering into the Anglo-American common economic life well have outweighed the disinclining factors, just as it did for some Scots-Irish, for example? Such inducements included credit from capitalist land speculators and freedom from taxes for as much as ten years.[120] With access to English-made iron implements and utensils, and other manufactured goods and supplies, the prospects might well have persuaded enterprising Indians to take up the life of the free yeoman farmer or artisan. Evidence of the appeal of Anglo-American commodity culture would become woefully evident in its ability to dissolve Indian society. Why should not at least a few individual Indians be successful in that culture as members of the colony?

This avenue to use of the labor of the Indian was never taken. The policy of special inducements to independent farmers referred to above was not developed until the early eighteenth century. The immigrants to whom this opportunity was opened were counted upon to provide a barrier against external dangers from French and hostile Indian attacks, and against the establishment of maroon centers of freedom and resistance by African-American bond-laborers in the Allegheny Mountains.[121] By that time, by a historical transformation which is the central concern of this volume, the bourgeoisie had drawn the color line between freedom and slavery, and established white supremacy as article one of the Anglo-American constitution. Only European-Americans, as "whites," were thereafter to be entitled to the full rights of the free citizen, Indians being by definition not "white."[122] The presence within the colony of free independent Indian farmers or tenants would have been a constitutionally intolerable anomaly.

The fate of the Indians under the principle of racial slavery and white supremacy was thus in the end controlled by twin parameters: nonenslavability and nonassimilability. These parameters would eventually govern Anglo-American "Indian policy" throughout the continental colonies.

PART TWO
The Plantation of Bondage

4

The Fateful Addiction to "Present Profit"

The years 1607–24 are known as "the Company period" of Virginia history, when the affairs of the colony were conducted under the aegis of the Virginia Company of London, chartered by James I in 1606, successively re-chartered in 1609 and 1612, and reformed in 1618 under Sir Edwin Sandys. Historians have long noted that the development of the Virginia colony during the Company period falls naturally into three time phases.[1] (1) 1607 to 1610: Virginia as an experimental colony, 24 May 1607 to the granting of a new charter in May 1609 through the "starving time" in the winter of 1609–10. (2) 1610 to 1618: the expansion of the royal territorial grant to the Virginia Company; the establishment of a special royal council for the Virginia Company; the beginning of tobacco cultivation and export, with the widening of the Company's charter in 1612 to cover the Bermuda (Somers) Islands, and authorization of a local Colony Council to function as a legislative body. (3) 1619 to 1624: the installation of George Yeardley as Governor of Virginia under the Sandys instructions (which the colony elite called the "Great Charter"), authorizing the establishment of an elected General Assembly "for the happy guiding and governing of the people there inhabiting;"[2] the growth of independent, non-Company, plantations; the bankruptcy of the Virginia Company; the devastating Indian attack on the colony in March 1622; the revocation of its charter, and the reversion of custody of Virginia affairs to a royal commission in June 1624.[3]

Most historians treat the Company period primarily in terms of the rise of the Virginia Company, its internal and external struggles, and its eventual dissolution, rather than in terms of the counter-revolution in labor relations that it brought. Some among them see in those events a confirmation of their particular strain of the "germ" theory of American history. This theory is summarized by Alexander Brown in his *First Republic* as follows:[4]

[T]his nation was not brought forth in a day.... The evolution had been going on ever since the free air of America inspired the first petitions against a royal form of government in 1608, to the present day [1898]. The germ is still unfolding and so long as it remains true to the seed it will continue to put forth to the glory of the nation and for the betterment of mankind.... The seedling, after being fostered in England under the advanced statesmen of that transition period, continued to grow in the political system of the new nation . . .

Works of this genre interpret the history of the 1606–24 period in Virginia as an aspect of the struggle of the English bourgeoisie in general against the absolutist tendencies of the bourgeois monarchy, which culminated in the English Civil War in the middle of the seventeenth century. This, for example, is the approach taken to consideration of the successive Virginia Company charters of 1609 and 1612; to the instructions to the newly designated colony governor, Francis Yeardley, in 1618, the so-called "Great Charter"; and to the internal factional disputes of the Virginia Company.

Since such scholars find no differences between the contending policy-setting English parties with respect to the status to be imposed on the laboring people, they find it unnecessary to inquire into the anomalous character of labor relations that evolved in the Company period. Nor do they perceive the causal link between that transformation and the later institution of lifetime chattel bond-servitude as the basis of the continental plantation colonies' economy, which the final victory of the Parliamentary bourgeoisie at home "brought forth."[5]

For the present work on the origin of racial slavery as a particular form of racial oppression of African-Americans, the Company period of Virginia history is of crucial significance, even though only a very small number of Africans or African-Americans were then living in Virginia. The findings of historians of seventeenth-century economic development in Virginia, the plantation system, and racial slavery offer a firm foundation for this approach. A century ago, Philip A. Bruce concluded thus:

But for the introduction of the indented servant into the Colony upon the threshold of settlement . . . . [t]he unique social conditions established at a later period would never have existed, or, indeed, if such had been the case, only in a modified form.[6]

James C. Ballagh made the point more explicitly:

Servitude not only preceded slavery in the logical development of the principle of subjection, standing midway between freedom and absolute subjection, but it was the historic base upon which slavery, by the expansion and addition of incidents, was constructed.[7]

Eric Williams, though centering his attention on Caribbean history, included colonial Virginia in the generalization that "[w]hite servitude was the historic base upon which slavery was constructed."[8] Lerone Bennett Jr, looking at colonial Virginia, found:

[W]hite servitude was the proving ground. . . . The plantation pass system, the slave trade, the sexual exploitation of servant women, the whipping-post and slave chain and branding iron, the overseer, the house servant, the Uncle Tom: all these mechanisms were tried out and perfected on white men and women. . . . [I]t is plain that nothing substantial can be said about the mechanisms of black bondage in

America except against the background and within the perspective of white bondage in America.[9]

Of English "Liberties, Franchises and Immunities"

As profound as the implication of this general premise is, it has never been confuted, although it has been ignored and implicitly rejected by many,[10] and expressly challenged by two.[11]

But when it is accepted, attention is immediately drawn to a basic constitutional principle that informed all of these charters and instructions as first stated in the 1606 charter and reaffirmed in the 1609 charter, establishing the Royal intent that all colonists

> shall have and enjoy all liberties, franchises and immunities of free denizens and natural subjects, ... to all intents and purposes as if they had been abiding and born within this our Realm of England, or any other of our said Domains.[12]

Before the social demotion of the laboring people to chattel bond-servitude could form the basis for the subsequent lifetime hereditary chattel bondage of African-Americans, those "liberties, franchises and immunities" established in England had to be overthrown insofar as they concerned the relations between employer and employee established in the Statute of Artificers of 1563. The parity of colonists' rights with those prevailing in England was stated again in the 1612 charter that established a Virginia Colony Council, with authority to legislate for the colony, provided that the law and ordinances "be not contrary to the laws and statutes of this our realm of England."[13] So how then was it that the plantation bourgeoisie was able to overthrow basic English constitutional principles and reduce the laboring-class in colonial Virginia to a general condition of chattel bond-servitude? Following the lead of Edmund S. Morgan, I will examine this question by emphasizing the transformation of the relations of production, the relations between laborer and employer.

The 1607–1610 Years

The conditions of life were unimaginably difficult for the English colonists during much of the 1607–1610 period. One statistic will suffice: nine out of ten of the emigrants who came in that period died, an annual death rate of almost 50 percent.[14] The winter of 1609–10, the "starving time," reduced the population of the colony "from 500 to about sixty as a result of disease, sickness, Indian arrows, and malnutrition."[15] In June 1610, Governor Thomas Gates ordered the abandonment of the premises by a demoralized remnant of colonists, and on 17 June the entire company embarked for England. Much to the dismay of the abandoners, they were intercepted by newcomers under the command of Governor de la Warre, at whose order the old settlers returned to Jamestown.[16]

The records of the sufferings of these earliest of Virginia colonists have been extensively reprinted and discussed in the sources noted. I wish, however, to direct special attention to two aspects of the story that are of special relevance for the thesis I am presenting.

First, however appalling the situation was in other regards, the labor, whatever it was, conformed to the traditional English system; none of the laboring people was a chattel bond-servant. In 1607, the Virginia Colony Council complained of English sailors diverting colony laborers from their proper work to pursue a sideline in the sassafras trade. Referring to these men, the council said, "they be all our waged men."[17] It has been questioned whether this use of the term "waged men" should be understood in the modern sense.[18] But the Colony Council was composed of persons who were familiar with the wages system of labor, and who had no experience at all with chattel bond-servitude of English workers. Furthermore, in later years, when the chattel-labor relation of production was established for English workers in Virginia, those workers were never referred to as "waged" workers. Finally, in 1624 when his advice was sought, the famous Captain John Smith, who was a member of the Colony council from 1608 to 1610 and its president for most of that time, firmly believed English workers in Virginia should be "hyred good labourers and mechanical men." He explicitly denounced the buying and selling of workers as an un-English practice.[19]

Second, the sex ratio in this first period was extremely high. The total number of women in the colony was raised to two on the arrival of the second supply ship on about 1 October 1608. Some one hundred women were among the four or five hundred passengers who arrived in Virginia in the nine ships of the so-called Great Supply in 1609. But the death toll of the following winter's "starving time" canceled the sex ratio as a meaningful statistic. English women continued to arrive; still, in the middle of the 1610–1618 period, women and children together constituted less than a one-fifth of the 351-member colony.[20] Whether the scarcity of women contributed to the demoralizing death toll that led to the aborted decision to abandon the colony is speculative. Some of the men were veterans of European armies, accustomed to the ready services of women camp followers. Perhaps even then complaints were heard like one made a decade later, that men were dying for the lack of women to tend them in their sickness.[21] This attention to the sex ratio could perhaps be omitted, if it were not for the fact that it was not a transitory phenomenon soon to be eroded as a result of the normal process of natural reproduction. (See pp. 69–70, below.)

The Middle Years, 1610–1618

The middle period, 1610–1618, began under the new charter of 1609.[22] It was the interlude between the fade-out of the "gold fever" and the beginning of the "tobacco fever"; between the factional president-and-council conduct of the colony's affairs and the establishment of the Virginia Assembly under the "Great Charter" of 1618. It was a period of military dictatorship in the colony headed by a succession of veteran officers of the wars in Ireland and the Netherlands;[23] it saw the creation of the privately organized, separate plantations and the beginning of increasing difficulties for the Company. It ended with the frustration of the social control efforts of the military regime, whose attempts to enforce the progam for balanced economic development wilted in the heat of the "tobacco fever."[24]

The author of the standard study of the Virginia Company regards this 1610–1618 period as primarily an ebb tide in the life of the colony.[25] Nevertheless, it was a time of great significance with regard to the development of the status of labor. The English had, as noted, realized that the Indians were not going to labor for them; therefore,

[a]fter 1609 the chief attention of all concerned was concentrated on the task of sending a sufficient labor supply to produce in Virginia the commodities that would find a ready and profitable market at home.[26]

Under the new administration, production relations were to be those of a producer's cooperative type of enterprise. The projected arrangement was outlined in the pamphlet *Nova Britannia*, published in 1609:

All charges [expenses] of settling and maintaining the plantation, and of making supplies shall be borne in a joint stock of the adventurers [stockholders], for seven yeares after the date of our new enlargement [1609]: during which time there shall be no adventure, nor goods returned in private from thence, neyther by Master [ship's captain], Marriner, Planter, nor Passenger, they shall be restrained by bond and search, that as we supplie from hence to the Planters at our own charge all necessaries for food and apparel, for fortifying and building of houses in a joynt stock, so they are to returne from thence the encrease and fruits of their labours, for the use and advancement of the same joynt stocke, till the end of seven years.[27]

The joint stock was made up of shares purchased by investors, the minimum cost of one share being £12 10*d*. A distinction was made between those who invested money but stayed in England, and those who went to Virginia as colonists. The former were called "Adventurers," the latter were called "Planters." Among the colonists, the power-structure personnel, "the extraordinarie men [as distinguished from the 'ordinary man or woman'], Divines, Governors, Ministers of State and Justice, Knights, Gentlemen, Physitions, and such as be men of worth for special services," were not required to labor, but were still counted as Planters and were "to be maintained out of the common store." At the end of seven years a dividend was to be declared which, it was anticipated, would amount to "five hundred acres, at least," for each stockholder. These Adventurers and Planters would then be free and independent Virginia landowners.

In a further quest for settlers, the Company turned its attention to the destitute proletarians of London, charitably described as "a swarme of unnecessary inmates . . . a continual cause of dearth and famine, and the very originall cause of all the Plagues that happen in this Kingdome." In 1609, the Virginia Company, in a letter to the bourgeoisie corporate of London, "The Lord Mayor, Aldermen and Companies," sought to stress the value of ridding "the city and suburbs" of the surplus poor by shipping them to Virginia.[28] The Company proposed that the London bourgeoisie, individually or in organized forms, should purchase shares of Virginia Company stock. For every share thus purchased, the Company would offer to transport one poor London "inmate" to Virginia. Since it was a fundamental right of English men and women that, except by explicit order of the Crown, they might not be sent out of the kingdom without their own consent, the Company suggested persuasive arguments whereby the city fathers might get that consent:

> And if the inmate called before you and enjoined to remove shall alleadge that he hath not place to remove unto, but must lye in the streets; and being offered to go this Journey, shall demaund what may be theire present mayntenance, what maye be their future hopes? it may please you to let them Knowe that for the present they shall have meate, drinke and clothing, and with an howse, orchard and garden, for the meanest [poorest] family, and a possession of lands to them and their posterity, one hundred acres for every man's person that hath a trade, or a body able to endure day labour, as much for his wife, as much for his child, that are of yeres to do service to the Colony, with further particular reward according to theire particular meritts and industry.

The exact terms on which these people were to "have possession" of the allotted land was not stated; as tenants, apparently,[29] with future prospects of becoming independent landowners. They certainly were not to be chattel proletarians.

In 1614, Acting Governor Thomas Dale sought to rouse the labor force of the colony to a more consistent effort. Among the measures he instituted was the allotment of three acres each to a large number of the colonists. These persons were referred to as "farmers," that is, tenants. Their relation to production was described at the time as follows:

> They are not called into any service or labor belonging to the Colony, more than one month in the year, which shall neither be in seed time, or in harvest, for which, doing no other duty to the Colony, they are yearly to pay into the store two barrels and a half of corn.[30]

The rest of the workforce were to be Company laborers. It is not known how the selection of tenants was made, but it is a reasonable conjecture that the expatriated proletarians were found more frequently among the Colony laborers than among tenants. These workers were required to labor eleven months a year for the Company in exchange for supplies and were additionally allowed to work one month's time for their own private accounts. Among this number some were also given a day a week, from May to harvest time, to tend their own crops.[31] The laborers were, like other colonists, subject to the severities of "*Lawes Divine, Morall, and Martiall.*" Offenses against the code could bring down on a worker the harsh cruelty of the military camp, such as pillorying, cutting off of ears, boring through of the tongue, whipping of offenders through the town tied to a cart, banishment from the colony to the wilderness, and inducement of the premature birth and death of an infant by the whipping of a pregnant woman, for offenses such as speaking ill of a master or official, stealing food from a master's store, and failure to complete a work task.[32]

By way of summary of the production relationships as they existed in the period July 1614 to March 1616, we have John Rolfe's account:

> The general mayne body of the planters are divided into ... Officers; Laborers, and Farmors
>
> (1) the officers [soldiers, guards, etc.] have the charge and care as well over the farmors as laborers generallie – that they watch and ward for their preservation, etc.
>
> (2) The Laborers are of two sorts – lst those employed only in the generall works, who are fed and clothed out of the store. 2nd others, specially artificers, as smiths, carpenters, shoemakers, taylors, tanners, etc. do work in their professions for the colony, and maintayne themselves with food and apparrell, having time permitted them to till and manure their ground.
>
> (3) The Farmors live at most ease – yet by their good endeavors bring yearlie much plentie to the plantation. They are bound by covenant, both for themselves and servants, to maintaine your Majestie's right and title in that Kingdom, against all foreign and domestic enemies. To watch and ward in the townes where they are resident. To do thirty one days service for the colony, when they shall be called thereunto – yet not at all times, but when their own business can best spare them. To maintayne themselves and families with food and rayment – and every farmor to pay yearlie into the magazine, for himself and every man servant, wheat [corn], which amounteth to twelve bushells and a halfe of English measure.[33]

There is not one laboring person in this catalogue whose status is that of chattel bond-servant.[34] Even the least favored member of this labor force was working under a bilateral, mutually binding contract which could not legally be dissolved except by common consent of the laborer and the employer. The laborer was not a chattel; the employer, whether it were the Virginia Company or an independent farmer, could not dispose of the laborer as he could of property. Furthermore, these laborers were assured at least a degree of propertied status at the completion of the terms of their contracts.

A prominent English colonist and member of the Virginia Company returned in 1610 from a trip to the colony and published his "Newes from Virginia," enthusiastically setting forth the prospects of the new land. He described the relations of production in verse:

> To such as to Virginia
> Do purpose to repaire;

And when that they shall hither come
   Each man shall have his share,
Day wages for the laborer,
   And for his more content,
A house and garden plot shall have.[35]

In March of 1616 there were, by Colony Secretary John Rolfe's account, 81 tenants and some 140 laborers working for the Company in Virginia, out of a total population of 351.[36] Later that same spring, the servants belonging to the group favored with extra time for tending their own private crops were granted complete freedom from servant status; this was in accordance with the agreement made between them and the Company three years before in England, prior to their signing on for service in Virginia.[37] They now became tenants like those previously mentioned or, possibly, they joined others in the classification of artisans, or they became agricultural laborers for farmers. A year later, in 1617, at the time of Captain Samuel Argall's assumption of his duties as Governor in Virginia, the number of laborers employed by the Company was reduced to only fifty-four.[38] Perhaps 20 percent of the total population of the colony (after making allowance for the death rate) was thus shifted in one year from the status of contract wage-laborer for the Company – not to chattel bond-servitude but upward to a status preferable and more profitable for them.[39]

It was during the latter part of this middle period that the English first cultivated tobacco in Virginia.[40] The discovery of tobacco was "by far the most momentous fact in the history of Virginia in the seventeenth century," writes Bruce, declaring that it shaped the fate of the people of Virginia absolutely.[41] The high profits that the crop soon began to yield drew the labor of the colony like a magnet. The Company and colony authorities offered special inducements and prescribed penalties to stem the tendency, but to no avail. By the spring of 1618, the former food surplus had become a scarcity:

> The lack of corn became so great in consequence of the exclusive attention paid to the culture of tobacco, that there would have been ground for anticipating a severe famine if two hundred quarters of meal had not been imported into the magazine.[42]

Governor Argall at first attempted to enforce limitations on tobacco planting, and to encourage needed attention to food production.[43] But he had come just at the time when separate private plantations outside the Company were beginning to operate, making the task of enforcing controls on production practically impossible by the efforts of colony officials alone. In 1616, the operation of the supply magazine was farmed out to a separate company of merchants.[44] In that same year, the Virginia Company, having no other means of paying the seven-year dividend that was due to its stockholders, awarded land titles to the original investors.[45]

The initial effort at imposing minimum corn cultivation while limiting the planting of tobacco was soon allowed to lapse.[46] In June 1617, the newly arrived Governor, Samuel Argall, proclaimed a fixed price of three shillings per pound of tobacco. In order to secure compliance with this regulation, he decreed a scale of penalties which serve to throw light on the question of production relations. Violators of the price decree were subject to a "penalty [of] 3 years slavery to the colony."[47] To protect the colonists against profiteering by the newly privatized magazine, the same penalty was to be exacted on those who bought tobacco at less than three shillings. Though Argall's interest in controlling tobacco planting diminished sharply, his belief in slavery as punishment for malefactors remained constant. The following year, desiring to encourage piety among the colonists, Argall ordered that persons failing to attend church on Sundays and holidays should suffer corporal punishment, "and be a slave the week following – 2nd offense a month – 3rd, a year and a day."[48]

What did Argall mean here by "slavery"? And what does it tell us of the nature of the production relationships at that time prevailing? Since this slavery was intended as a punishment, it could not have been the normal condition of labor as it then existed in the colony. The culprit under punishment would be unpaid, but would receive maintenance. It can be inferred, therefore, that workers were normally entitled to recompense other than mere maintenance. This penalty-servitude was imposed without regard to the will or consent of the person subject to it. On the other hand, the laborer under this sentence was not a chattel, subject to purchase and sale. It appears that what Argall meant by "slavery" in this instance was a status between that of the "waged man," the colony laborer working for pay under contract, and that of limited-term unpaid servitude.

Further evidence that the typical laborer at this time was a hired wage worker, and not one employed for "meat and drink only," is to be seen in the following two items. In June 1618, Argall complained that he had personally had to pay "sundry debts of the Company,"[49] including "wages ... payde" for Company laborers.[50] The Company denied knowledge of any such debts, but did not deny the possibility of them. Furthermore, Article XIV of the Virginia Charter of 1612 was specifically aimed at checking the practice of workers who, "having received wages etc. [in England] from the company, and agreed to serve the colony, have afterwards refused to go thither," or who, having gone to Virginia, returned before their contracts expired.[51]

Argall occupied a dual position; he was the Governor of the colony, appointed to serve by and for the Company, and he was also the holder of a 400-acre land patent,[52] being therefore a private planter. As time went on, it was said, he showed an increasing tendency to resolve any conflict of interest in favor of his private-planter side rather than his Company-official side. In August 1618, the Company in London addressed a letter to Argall charging him with peculation and other violations of trust, and notifying him that he was to stand trial before the Company Court in England upon his return to that country. Argall, it was alleged, had used the Company's ships and crews for trading for his own private profit; he had forbidden any other person from trading with the Indians for furs, in order that he, Argall, might have the monopoly of that profitable commerce; he had appropriated Company-owned corn for his own private plantation use; and he had disposed of the Company's livestock to private planters, including himself, in violation of explicit orders from the Company.[53] One of the Company's accusations is particularly relevant to the question of the status of the laboring classes in the colony:

> that you take the ancient Planters which ought to be free and likewise those [colony servants] from the common garden to sett them upon your corne to feed your own men as if the Plantacon were onely intended to serve your turne.[54]

Here is the first alleged instance of a worker being treated like a chattel, in that the worker is transferred without his prior consent from one employer (in this instance, the Company) to another (Argall, the private planter). Lastly, and equally significant, these alleged acts were officially condemned as violations of the rights of the laborers under the Virginia charter, for which the violator would have to render account before English authorities.

In the end, Argall was able to avoid trial. His guilt or innocence is of no particular importance today, except for historical scholars.[55] What is of lasting significance is that these charges against Argall anticipated in detail the known course of self-aggrandizement followed by colony governors, and by other strategically advantaged officers, who succeeded Argall, conduct that was to have historical consequences.

Finally, in this listing of innovations in property and production relations in the 1610–1618 period, we come to the establishment of what would in time come to be called the "headright" principle. As has been mentioned, the investors of 1609 were given their dividend in 1616 in the form of land titles, this being the only form in which the financially embarrassed Virginia Company could meet its obligations. Having struck on this device, the Company decided to use it for raising capital.[56]

This new procedure was distinguished from the old in the provisions it contained for facilitating the free flow of capital. These features betokened not only the difficulties facing the Company in securing capital, but also the impending break-up of the Company's monopoly of colonial enterprise. Under the new Company policy, the investor, or group of investors jointly, though remaining in England, could receive immediate title and possession of Virginia land, at the rate of fifty acres for every £12½ sterling paid to the Company; this clearly was a more attractive arrangement than the previous one of having to leave the investment in the parlous environment of the Company treasury for seven years, with dubious prospects of profitable returns, before getting any land title. Or, alternatively, these private investors could get land by means of the headright,[57] which allowed the investors the same portion of fifty acres for each person whose emigration expenses were paid by the investors. No less significant for our present focus, it was specified that this new opening to capitalist investment in Virginia land was to be used for "sending families to manure [work] it for yearely rent, or for halfe the clear profits as many others doe."[58] These enterprises were called "particular plantations." The perspective here being put forward was that of a capitalist agriculture of the English style, with landlord, tenants and wage laborers, distinguished only by the fact that the landlord was an absentee.[59]

Under this provision, by 1618 six such separate companies had been granted patents for land in Virginia,[60] some of really vast extent, including one for 200,000 acres and another for 80,000 acres.[61] These independent capitalists were given, along with the land, beginning in February 1619, legal jurisdiction over the control of their tenants and laborers; in the words of the Company's order: "to make Orders, Ordinances and Constitutions for the better ordering and dyrectinge of their servants." Yet, significantly, they added the stipulation, "provided they be not repugnant to the Lawes of England."[62]

The new departure represented by the issuance of the Virginia charter of 1609 reflected a change in perspective for the colony; the gold fever was abated, and attention was directed toward the establishment and development of agriculture and of extractive enterprises of sea and stream, of forest and mine, as well as to the trade with the Indians for beaver skins. Virginia, under the new direction, was expected to become a supplier of a wide variety of products, supporting and supplementing the profit-making processes of the home country. The author of "Newes from Virginia" had rhapsodized on the prospects foreshadowed in his mind by two ships he had recently seen coming into England from the colony:

> Well fraught, and in the Same
> Two ships, are these commodities
> Furres, sturgeon, caviare,
> Black-walnut-tree, and some deal boards
> With such they laden are;
> Some pearl, some wainscot and clap boards,
> With some sasafras wood,
> And iron promis't for 'tis true
> Their mynes are very good.[63]

As our account has indicated, these hopes were not, in the main, to be realized. On the other hand, the colony's success in achieving self-sufficiency in food production and in developing commerce with the Indians no doubt explains in large part the lowering of the annual death rate in the 1610–1618 period to less than 9 percent, compared with the rate of just under 50 percent in the 1607–1610 period.[64] In 1616, John Rolfe, his term as Secretary of the Colony having ended, returned temporarily to England with his wife, the Indian princess Pocahontas, and their infant son;[65] there he wrote an account of the colony, now at peace with its neighbors. He said:

The great blessings of God have followed this peace, and it next under him, hath bredd our plentie – every man sitting under his fig tree in safety, gathering and reaping the fruits of their labors with much joy and comfort.[66]

But now, at the close of the 1610–1618 period, the system of allocation of land by head-right, and the opportunity for a freer flow of and quicker turnover of capital had cast a shadow over the peace, the land and the laborer. It was to be a capitalist farming system in Virginia.[67] But what kind of capitalist farming – the English type, or some peculiar system? That was the question to which the next and final phase of the Company period would give an answer.

The Final Phase, 1619–24: The Tobacco Price Problem

The 1619–24 period begins with the installation of Sir Edwin Sandys as Treasurer and chief executive of the Virginia Company, and the entrance of George Yeardley upon his duty as the Company's governor in Virginia, in the spring of 1619. Basic lines of policy, however, had been worked out in the latter part of 1618, in discussions that sought to draw lessons from the experiences of the past, and of the Argall regime in particular.[68]

The program that emerged was fashioned along three main lines: (1) the reclamation of Company lands and stock, and the revitalization and extension of various Company enterprises, all to be financed initially by the sale of patents for separate plantations to be organized by individual and group capitalists outside the Company; (2) the promotion of a generalized economy, and avoidance of reliance upon tobacco as the mainstay; (3) the definition and systemization of land tenure in the colony, and the encouragement of emigration of laboring hands to the colony.[69] Integrally and separately, from the beginning the three points of this program bore within themselves latent contradictions which quickly matured.

As a capitalist operation, the Virginia Company was a failure in 1619. For twelve years of effort and the outlay of £75,000 sterling of investors' money and credit, the Company had nothing in Virginia to show for it but – six goats!:

> [The] wholl State of the publique [Company property in the Colony] was gone and consumed, there beinge not lefte att that time to the Company either the land ... or any Tennant, Servant, Rent or trybute corne [from the Indians], cowe or salte-worke and but six Goates onely.[70]

Paradoxically, however, the colony was beginning to throb under the first stimulus of "America's first Boom," as Professor Morgan has called it.[71] It was the tobacco boom, of course, and it drew into itself an increasing share of the colony's labor. The shipment of tobacco from Virginia to England in 1615 amounted to less than one-third of a pound for every person in the colony. By 1619, the figure was twenty pounds per person, and by 1622 it had reached forty-eight pounds.[72] The number of separate non-Company plantations showed a parallel growth. Between 1616 and 1619, six patents were issued to separate capitalist plantation groups. Between 1619 and 1623, forty-four such patents were granted by the Company.[73]

Conceived as a means of financing the development of a generalized economy under Company leadership in the colony, the policy of selling land for separate plantations produced the opposite effect. The directors of these new enterprises emerged increasingly as the vital force in the direction of the economic and political affairs of the colony, and in the ever-increasing reliance upon tobacco cultivation.[74] Although they made some gestures toward developing non-tobacco enterprises, they were not interested in risking very far along a path that had proved so costly to the Company. Their eyes were fixed on tobacco, with its quick turnover and profits. From 1619 on, writes Craven, "the chief interest of the Virginia planter was devoted to his tobacco crop."[75]

A competition developed between the Company and the separate plantations for the supplies of labor and capital. In 1619 and 1620, separate planters were already accounting for the transport of 30 percent of the emigrants; after that, the majority were supplied by the separate planters.[76] This competition took its most dramatic and sharpest form in the Argall-like practice of colony officers diverting Company tenants from Company service to these officers' own private exploitation. In its instructions to the new Governor Yeardley, the Company had endowed the colony officers with lands to be cultivated for their support by tenants supplied by the Company. Leading the list was an allotment of 3,000 acres to be attached to the office of the governor. In addition to this substantial perquisite of office, Yeardley was granted outright a personal plantation of 2,200 acres.[77] Yeardley was an especially arrant offender among the colony officers who appropriated tenants for "their own private Lands, not upon land belongeth to their office," and wasted the time of many others by requiring personal services of them.[78] When he surrendered his office at the end of his three-year term, Yeardley kept for himself all but forty-six of his Company complement of one hundred tenants.[79] The Company officers also betrayed their trust and advantaged themselves by hiring out Company-supplied tenants to private non-Company employers.[80]

In the competition for investment capital, the Virginia Company was also being outdone. In 1620 and 1621, the Company was forced on this account to rely mainly on its public lottery as its capital funds source.[81] By the summer of 1621, the par £12½ sterling Virginia Company shares were selling in London at from £2 to £2½.[82]

The definition and systemization of land tenure was elaborated in the instructions for Yeardley, adopted by the Company Court in London in November 1618, prior to Yeardley's coming to Virginia.[83] These instructions represented a further development of the trend to large-capitalist agriculture and a freer flow of capital, both of which were established principles informing the 1616 policy.[84] The tenants who had been brought to Virginia prior to mid-1616 were, upon completion of their term of service, to receive one hundred acres "to be held by them, their Heirs and assigns for ever," paying only two shillings annual rent. But persons transported at Company expense since mid-1616 had a less attractive option. They could remain as tenants for the Company at the completion of their seven-year term, or be "free to move where they will," but with no land guarantee.[85]

Obviously the prospective creation of a permanent class of tenants would be designed to encourage capital investment, as would the reduction of the growth in numbers of self-employed freehold farmers, through the accretion of landless ex-tenants. On the other hand, this was a policy that would increase class differentiations by reducing social mobility from tenant to landowner, and sharpen class contradictions. The same effects were to be expected from the expansion of the headright principle to provide a grant of fifty acres to any investor who would pay for the transportation of "persons . . . which shall go into Virginia with intent there to inhabit, if they continue there three years or dye after they are shipped."[86]

Under Sandys's leadership the Company launched a number of projects – iron mining, processing wood for potash and pitch, timbering, fishing, glass making and fur trading – designed to promote a generalization of the Virginia economy, as a market for and a supplier to England, and in the interest of the strength and stability of the colony itself. Lacking capital of its own, the Company farmed out a number of these efforts to subsidiary joint-stock companies. Although one of these projects – shipping women to be sold for wives among the more prosperous men – was profitable, most of the other endeavors were less remunerative for the investors.[87] By the summer of 1621, writes Craven: "The company was for all practical purposes bankrupt."[88]

Crisis of overproduction of tobacco

Most disastrous, however, was the outbreak of a characteristic capitalist crisis of overproduction:

> [T]he Company had not reckoned with the effect of the rapidly expanded supply of Virginia tobacco, nor with the increasing competition from the new British settlements in Barbados and St Christopher. Consequently, during 1620 and 1621, the adventurers who had underwritten the purchase of the product had been compelled to sell much of it at less than they had paid in Virginia.[89]

In the hope of riding out the storm, the Sandys administration joined, indeed put itself at the head of, the tobacco party.[90] Succumbing to what one of Sandys's opponents called the "straunge dream"[91] of salvation through tobacco, the Company decided to stake all on an application for a royal grant of the monopoly of the English tobacco import trade. They got the contract, but the terms dictated by King James were so onerous that it was guaranteed to fail so far as the Company's interests were concerned.[92] Although the insupportable conditions of the contract led the Company to surrender it within a year, it was of momentous historic significance. It expressed the choice of the Anglo-American plantation bourgeoisie as a whole to base the development of Virginia Colony on a monocultural, rather than on a diversified economy. From the time of the forlornly ambitious projects for non-tobacco products plotted by the Virginia Company, the records of seventeenth-century Virginia are filled with instructions, advice, appeals, exhortations and injunctions aimed at diversifying the economy and avoiding dependence upon tobacco.[93] With even greater consistency the colony was fashioned at every turn in the opposite image. In the end it was a victory of blind instinct over articulate wisdom. But not instinct in general: Indian society had mastered the uses of tobacco without letting tobacco master Indian society. It was, rather, the victory of the specifically bourgeois class instinct for their annual rate of profit and quick turnover of capital.

The "Adventurers" Seek Ways to Support the Tobacco Addiction

The drop in tobacco prices fell upon the just and the unjust, the "publique" and the separate private plantation owners, alike. The Virginia Company passed into history in 1624, but the price of tobacco continued a general course of decline; by 1630 it was less than a penny a pound in Virginia.[94] By the middle of the seventeenth century, Barbados and St Christopher had been transformed into sugar plantation colonies in the interest of a higher rate of profit, but the price of Virginia tobacco never again rose to even one-third of what it had been in the day of the "straunge dream." If the losses sustained on other enterprises had dried up the source of capital flowing into the Virginia Company, the decline in the price of tobacco implied a similar effect, if it were not somehow to be averted, upon the flow of English capital into Virginia tobacco cultivation, whether that cultivation were conducted by a royally chartered company or by separate entrepreneurs operating on their own account.

The capitalists would have to find a way to counteract the market-driven tendency of the rate of profit to fall. As we have noted, the Company and the Virginia Assembly in 1619 had indicated their idea of a fair profit, stipulating a limit of 25 percent mark-up on English goods brought for sale in Virginia. Faced with falling tobacco prices in England, the merchants accordingly discounted the tobacco with which the Virginia people paid for English goods. From a contentious exchange of letters between the Virginia Company of London and the Virginia Colony Council in Jamestown in 1623, we learn that a bushel of meal delivered in Virginia and worth thirteen shillings was exchanged for nine or ten pounds of tobacco, officially rated at three shillings the pound, a discount of 55 percent.[95]

Conceivably this deterioration of the Virginia tobacco-seller's position could have been countered by administrative measures. This was not a practical possibility, however, as more than a century of subsequent efforts at "stinting" tobacco, pegging prices, destroying surplus stocks, etcetera, would prove.[96]

Almost the entire cost of production in Virginia was in payment for labor power, and since these payments were made in tobacco, the capitalists' cost of production declined proportionately to the decline in the price of tobacco.[97] Therefore, although the capitalists' profit was being reduced, the decline was not caused by a rise in the absolute or relative wages of the laboring people, but by the fall of tobacco prices. This built-in elasticity of laborer and tenant costs served to reduce the impact of the lowered price of tobacco upon the interests of the capitalists, in Virginia or in England or in both places. However, it did not protect the capitalists against a reduction of their equity or profit rate in terms of their pound-sterling investment. If the adventurer or planter invested one hundred pounds sterling in Virginia tobacco and the price of tobacco declined by half, the rate of profit on the investment would be cut in half. The plantation bourgeoisie accordingly sought ways to raise its share of the net product by an attack on "entitlements," as they would be called by today's "Conservatives," namely the tenants' "moiety" and the laborers' free-market wage levels.

Intermediate Bond-Servitude Forms: Convicts, Apprentices and "Maids-for-wives"

For some time before 1622, the adventurers and planters had taken measures to secure supplies of non-tenant laborers on conditions more favorable than those provided under the Virginia wage scale. For this purpose they turned their attention to those segments of the English population most vulnerable to such superexploitation, namely prisoners, impoverished youth, and women of the laboring classes.

In the spring of 1617, the Privy Council issued a warrant for the transport of a number of "malefactors" then being held in custody; the king specified that they be sent to Virginia and nowhere else.[98] In October 1619, the king supplied the Company with another one hundred "divers dissolute persons," who were to be transported as "servants" to Virginia. The exact terms on which they were to serve in the colony were not specified, but it was anticipated that the conditions would not be agreeable to the prisoners. This feeling was, it has been said, all the stronger on account of the fact that the group of prisoners included a number of Irish persons captured in their own country in the course of the brutal English plantation of Ulster.[99] Their disaffection caused some delay in the execution of the order for their transportation, as Edwin Sandys explained in speaking of the intended shipment of the first fifty of these persons:

> [T]hey could not goe in lesse than fower Shipps, for feare they beinge many together may drawe more unto them and so muteny and carry away the Ship, which would stand [cost] the Company fowre thousand pounds.[100]

The records of the Privy Council proceedings are sprinkled with orders for the surrender of imprisoned convicts to Company authorities for transportation to Virginia as "servants," on the condition that "they retourne not again into England," on pain of death.[101] For instance:

- 13 July 1617: Chris Potley, Roger Powell, Sapcott Molineux and Thomas Chrouchley, prisoners at Oxford jail; and George Harrison, convicted of stealing a horse, prisoner at Hartford jail.

- March and November 1618: William Lambe and James Stringer, respectively, prisoners at Newgate prison.

- May 1622: Daniell Frank,[102] William Beare and John Ireland, prisoners at White Lion jail in Southwark.

- Also in 1622: James Wharton, convicted of picking pockets, in Norfolk; and John Carter of London, convicted of horse-stealing, but for whom injustice was tempered with mercy since it was doubtful "whether the horse was stolen or not."

Still, as Sandys had warned in 1619, there was a critical mass where further congregation of such deportees meant mutiny. Therefore, whilst they might supplement the labor supply, they were not to be the main source of it, and thus were not the means of achieving a general reduction of labor costs in the colony.

The "Duty boys"

In the 1618–22 period, considerable effort was made to recruit "vagrant" children – mainly, but not exclusively, in London – to work in Virginia. In autumn 1618, the London Common Council and the Virginia Company agreed upon the "taking up" of one hundred homeless boys and girls, aged eight to sixteen, for shipment to Virginia.[103] A year later the Company congratulated itself and the city fathers on the successful delivery of the full one hundred, minus "such as dyed on the waie."[104] The Company then proposed a renewal of the collaboration, with the object of sending another one hundred youths, but this time they were to be "twelve years old and upward."[105]

The program encountered opposition on the part of the youth who were its objects. Two months after the second plan was proposed, it was discovered "that among that number there are divers unwilling to be carryed thither [to Virginia]." Special care was taken that the "troublemakers" who sought to obstruct the program were included among those selected for transport, but they were to be taken to jail for punishment before their departure.[106]

Fifty such young persons were delivered in Virginia in May of 1620 on board the ship *Duty*; thereafter, apprentices brought on the same sort of program were called "Duty boys."[107]

From the standpoint of labor costs, the apprentice role for which these "Duty boys" were destined had obvious advantages for the plantation bourgeoisie. Apprentices were bound to serve seven years, the common apprentice term in England. The cost of getting them to Virginia was "Three pounds a peece for the Transportation and forty shillings a peece for their apparrell."[108] In addition to this outlay, the expenditure for their equipment and food for the first year of the term was not likely to amount to more than another £5 sterling, since their own labor provided their own food and most of their other necessities, except clothing, bedding, metal products and other manufactured goods supplied from England. The cost of maintaining the apprentice declined to practically nothing in subsequent years of the term.[109] The apprentice received no wages except his board and keep; thus the cost of the apprentice's labor, assuming the worker survived for the full term, came to less than thirty shillings per year.

The annual output of the apprentice in the period 1619–23 averaged 712 pounds of tobacco,[110] which would yield £44 10s., at 15d.,[111] in Virginia and £106 16s., at 36d.,[112] in London. The Virginia "planter" would thus get for his tobacco in one year thirty times its annualized labor cost. The use of apprentice youth as a labor supply, however, involved certain negative features. The planters expressed a preference for men "such as have been brought up to labor & those between 20 & 30 yeres of age"[113] rather than inexperienced and less muscular teenagers such as the apprentices mostly were.[114]

Yet each of these drawbacks carried its own partial offset. If the youthful apprentice was not so strong as a mature adult, he was perhaps more tractable for that reason. If the apprentice died before the end of his term, then at least he would not be around to raise the cost of labor by becoming first a tenant-at-halves and then a free farm owner.

There remained one unmitigated handicap in the apprentice arrangement, so far as the needs of the capitalist plantation development in Virginia was concerned. Under English custom and law, even the parish or country apprentice was bound to one particular employer in a one-to-one relationship. It was a relationship equally binding on each party and the apprentice could not be sold to or bought from another employer.[115]

A new opportunity for venture capital: "maids-for-wives"

A third direct and indirect source of labor power that was unpaid was sought by the importation of women. As early as 1618, enterprising men were specializing in this labor supply service. This was revealed in two arrests made in the fall of that year. One man, Owen Evans,[116] who was a messenger for the king, ranged over three counties of southeastern England "pressing maidens" for "His Majesty's service for the Bermudas and Virginia." Paying four shillings to one man, five to another, twelve pence to third, and threatening them with hanging for refusal to comply (so they testified), Evans ordered women to be taken up in the king's name and delivered to him at Sherborne in Dorset. He bore a badge of authority from the King's Chamber which, it was later said, was validly his, but which he used illegally in this business. As many as forty women were said to have fled the one parish of Ottery in Devon to escape this frightful form of class and sex oppression. They must have had to flee to points far distant, because young women from adjoining parishes were also taking flight in terror. Jacob Crystie of Ottery sold his daughter to Evans for twelve pence. A member of the local establishment paid Evans ten shillings to dissuade him from further oppression of the Ottery parish. Evans was finally arrested and sent back to London, being treated in due course with the deference reserved for personal agents of the king. What if anything in the way of punishment was given to Evans for this crime, our historians do not tell us.

Another man, named Robinson, forged a commission for himself and used it "to take up rich Yeomen's daughters to serve his majesty for breeders in Virginia" unless they were ransomed by their parents and friends. He was apprehended, tried, hanged, drawn and quartered for counterfeiting the Great Seal.[117]

Subsequently, bourgeois gentlemen and aristocrats made the trade respectable and profitable: respectable, on the ground of "making of the men feel at home in Virginia";[118] and profitable, by operating it as a Virginia Company monopoly. Of 650 persons sent by the Company to Virginia between August 1619 and April 1620 (see Table 4.1 on page 71), ninety were "Young maids to make wives for so many of the former tenants."[119] This item is included in a "Noate of Shipping, Men and Provisions Sent to Virginia"; women, it seems, were counted as "provisions." The Company in June 1620 projected a plan for sending one hundred more "maids-for-wives," in a total of eight hundred emigrants.[120] On 20 December 1621, the *Warwick* arrived in Virginia with a cargo that the Company's accompanying letter advertized as "an extraordinary choice lot of thirty-eight maids for wives."[121] Investors were apparently encouraged by this bright aspect of an otherwise not very promising general business outlook. In November 1621, a subsidiary joint stock for trading in "maids-for-wives" to Virginia was established in the amount of £800 sterling. Virginia Company leaders Edwin Sandys and the Earl of Southampton patriotically headed the list of investors with subscriptions of £200 each. [122]

The shipment of "one widow and eleven maids for wives" on board the *George* in the late summer of 1621 was accompanied by a Company letter to the Colony Council regarding the disposal of the cargo.[123] That letter, when considered together with other records of the time, helps to outline the economic aspects of this branch of business, as well as to suggest inferences regarding the life of the women traded. The *George* women were to be sold at "120 lb waight of the best leafe Tobacco." The price of the *Warwick* women who arrived in Virginia a month later was increased to 150 pounds of tobacco, partially on the grounds of the declining price of tobacco in England.[124] It was provided that the total payment on the *George*'s twelve would have to be equal to 12 times 120 pounds of tobacco, and that, therefore, "if any of them dye (before sale was made) that proportion must be advanced to make it uppon those that survive."[125] Some of the business had to be done on credit, judging by an order of the Virginia General Court of 2 May 1625 requiring "Debtors for Maids" to pay up or face punitive action by the Court.[126]

Such problems arose despite the effort made to limit the purchasing rights to men of substance. While allowing love its dominion, the Company authorities directed that it operate within the limits of sound business practice. Accordingly, the Company kept one eye on the improvement of prospects; it promised the women that they would not be married off to poor men, "for we would have their condition so much better as multitudes will be allured thereby to come unto you."[127] Therefore, a line was drawn on eligible men for wiving: the Company would "not have those maides deterred and married to servants but only to such freemen or tenants as have meanes to maintain them."[128]

There is evidence of resentment on the part of poor men on account of the deprivation they had to endure because of this pounds-shillings-and-pence approach to the woman question. Thomas Niccolls expressed indignation at this discrimination in a letter he sent to England.[129] Women were so "well sold," he said, that a poor man could never get possession of one. Poor tenants, he wrote, desperately needed wives, for "they depart this world in their own dung for want of help in their sickness." Furthermore, Niccolls could not see why women should not

> be bound to serve the Company for a certain number of years whether they married or not, [since] all the multitude of women [do is] nothing but to devour the food of the land without doing any day's deed whereby any benefit [may] arise wither to the company or the Country.

To speed the turnover of their capital, the stockholders offered a special inducement to prospective customers: "you may assure such men as marry those women that the first servants sent over by the Company shall be consigned to them."[130]

Niccolls's comment and Company promises to the contrary notwithstanding, these women were not absolutely insured against becoming "servants." In its instructions, the Company said that they might "be servants ... in case of extremetie." Extremity of what exact sort is left to our own inferences. Several years later, a case came before the Virginia General Court concerning a woman who had been brought over to the colony to serve as a wife. But the marriage plan had aborted "because of some dislike between them," and "it was agreed" that the woman was to be a servant to her former fiancé for two years.[131] The Virginia census of 1624–25 showed that of the 222 English women in the colony, forty-six were propertyless workers. How many of this unmarried group had originally come to be sold as wives, and how many came as girl apprentices, or by some other particular arrangement, is not known.[132]

The same census showed that there were 107 Virginia-born English children in Virginia. This statistic points up the special contribution to be had from the importation of women in connection with the reduction of labor costs, but Virginia births were not to furnish the quick solution sought by the tobacco plantation bourgeoisie. In fact, there was a contradiction between the woman's role as child-bearer and as laborer. Her pregnancy, child-bearing and childcare responsibilities entailed an uncompensated expense and loss of labor time for the employer. The child would not reach working age during the mother's term of service, and in any case the child was born free and not under any contractual obligation to the mother's employer. For that reason, severe penalties were imposed upon servant women who became pregnant, or who risked becoming pregnant, and upon men (except the particular employer) who were thus involved with servant women.[133] On the other hand, if a landholder wanted to establish an ongoing estate, male heirs must be produced of undoubted paternity. In those cases, one particular woman in the capacity of wife and mother was indispensable, in spite of the added expense at a time of rising labor costs, it being understood that this particular woman would not be available for common labor as a general rule.

A man could buy a wife, but he could not sell her. Once the investment was made, it dropped forever out of the sphere of circulation of capital, by the law of coverture. The investment could not be restored to its original money form by a return to the market; nor could it be used to settle outstanding debts or as collateral to meet needs for credit. This form of "property," whatever the benefits to its possessor, clearly inhibited the free flow of capital. For these several reasons, therefore, the importation of women was not a means for reducing the general cost of labor to any degree commensurate with the fall in tobacco prices, which by 1622 was already a critical problem.

Sex Ratio and Economic Base: Virginia and New England

The maids-for-wives program may have contributed to a reduction of the sex ratio, but in the colony census of 1624–25 the sex ratio among adults was still nearly four men to one woman.[134] Although it is not surprising to learn that the ratio of men to women in the earliest colonial settlements was high, the ratio in Virginia was significantly higher than it was in New England. In the four-year period 1620 to 1623, 212 persons left England for New England. Among the 203 identified by sex, the sex ratio was just over two to one.[135] Among the adults on the first of these ships, the *Mayflower*, there were 56 men, 26 women, and 19 children.[136]

The contrast would prove to be more than momentary. In the years 1634 and 1635, among passengers embarking for Virginia, males outnumbered females by more than six to one. A similarly derived index for English emigrants going to New England in the years 1620 to 1638 indicated a rough ratio of 150, 60 men to 40 women.[137] A tabulation by Russell R. Menard of eleven selected quantifying items, yields a weighted sex ratio of 338 for European immigrants to Maryland and Virginia for the period 1634 to 1707.[138]

This contrast with New England was a function of the differing relations of production in the two regions. Of the 5,190 bond-laborers shipped for continental Anglo-America from the port of Bristol between 1654 and 1686, New England took only 165, while Virginia took 4,924. The relatively insignificant proportion of bond-labor in New England reflected the fact that there the relations of production originally developed in the matrix of the family kinship group.[139] In Virginia, where bond-servitude was the status of the great majority of European immigrants, family formation was inhibited because the laborers, being chattels, were legally barred from marrying. The retarding effect on family formation due to the bond-labor system is seen in the fact that in seventeenth-century Chesapeake the average age of female European immigrants, who were mainly bond-laborers, was 24.9 years at the time of the first marriage; the corresponding figure for native-born European-American women was 16.8 years.[140]

Tenantry, Wage Labor and Captain Nuce's Plan

The laboring people in Virginia in the beginning of 1622 were predominately tenants, not convicts, wives, or apprentice youth. This is a fact of obvious importance in any effort to investigate the beginnings of the system of chattel bond-servitude as the basic form of labor in the Anglo-American plantation colonies. Since it deserves greater attention than most historians of the period have given to it, the matter merits some documentation here.[141]

Prior to 1622, most emigrants to Virginia were transported by the Virginia Company.[142] The proportion of tenants among those sent by the Virginia Company in the 1619–21 period, and for whom we have a categorization in the records, was about 60 percent, that is, 860 out of 1,450 (see Table 4.1 on page 71). If the 190 "maids for wives" are left out of the account, or if they are counted in the category into which they were inducted by marriage, the tenant proportion among these Company emigrants would amount to around 70 percent.

There is much evidence in the records to indicate that in this period the proportion of tenants was as high, or possibly higher, among emigrants dispatched from England by separate, non-Company, enterprisers. The best and most complete, if not the only, substantial record of a non-Company plantation which has come down from that time is that of Berkeley Hundred, in the form of the papers of John Smyth of Nibley, one of the four incorporators of that enterprise.[143] These documents present a picture of the employment relation of those engaged for service in Berkeley Hundred. The terms of employment are written, specific for each individual (or family), and they are formalized before the emigrant leaves England. The contracted arrangement is mutually binding on both parties; the person employed is bound to service to this employer only; his or her contract is not "assignable" to another employer.

The list includes thirty-four men sent to Berkeley Hundred in September 1619 to serve under plantation manager John Woodleefe, apparently as tenants, excepting two men sent apparently to serve only in their trade of joiner.[144] Beside each tenant's name is the term to be served, in years. The shortest term is three years; all of the "assistants" to Woodleefe are in that category, and that term is most common (nine cases) among the other twenty-

Table 4.1 Shipments of persons to Virginia by the Virginia Company
and by separate planters, 1619–21

	Total	Tenants	Servants[a]	Apprentices	Maids
Sent by Company	1,450[b]				
for own use	1,060	860	100	–	100
for former tenants	390	–	100	200	90
for separate plantations	221[c]				
Sent by separate planters (estimate)	750[d]				

Source: *Records of the Virginia Company of London* (4 vols. edited by Susan Myra Kingsbury [Washington, DC, 1906–35]), 3: 313.

a. The Company records distinguish between tenants and servants among those shipped by the Company, but not in the case of those shipped for the separate plantations.
b. The Company figures include some persons who were to have gone, but did not; and others who died en route. Yet a comparison with Alexander Brown's figures (*The First Republic in America* [Boston and New York, 1898], pp. 299, 345, 363, 364) shows the proportion sent by the Company and by the separate planters to have been as presented in this table.
c. In the 1619–20 period, of the 611 sent to private plantations 221 were transported by the Company.
d. The ratio of privately shipped to Company-shipped persons remained constant at about 45 per cent during this period. (See Wesley Frank Craven, *The Dissolution of the Virginia Company* [New York, 1932], p. 301.) For the 800 shipped by the Company in 1620–21, 360 thus would have been shipped for private planters. This number plus the 390 sent by separate planters in 1619–20 equals 750.

eight tenants. There was one serving the longest term, of eight years. Four of Woodleefe's five assistants were assigned 50 acres each; the fifth, one of the two non-tenants, was a skilled artisan (one of the two joiners), who was to receive a percentage of the business. Of the twenty-eight rank-and-file tenants, eighteen were assigned 30 acres each, two were assigned 40 acres each, and the single smallest allotment was 15 acres. Five of these persons were put on a supplemental wage (in some cases paid in whole or part in advance, in England), apparently in consideration of special expected services in trades such as sawyer, cooper, gunsmith, etcetera. Thirteen of these men, including five who were tradesmen, were paid individual earnest money and promised family maintenance money before leaving England. They were engaged as tenants for from three to seven years, and were assigned land, most commonly 30 acres.[145]

A year later, in September 1620, seven persons entered into a contract to go to Berkeley Hundred as tenants.[146] This agreement is remarkable in that there is no time set for the expiration of the agreement; indeed, reference is made to a continued arrangement of the "heires" on both sides. Still, two things are clear: (1) these tenants are to have two-thirds of the corn and wheat they raise, and half of everything else they produce; and (2) there is no provision for a "setting over," "assigning," or "selling" of the tenants to another employer.

These papers show the employers as paying the cost of the transportation of the employees; the laboring emigrants are not obligated to "pay back" this expenditure by servitude or otherwise. The contract agreed to by Robert Coopy, a smith, carpenter and turner, in September 1619 is seen by A. E. Smith as the "first genuine servant's indenture."[147] But Coopy's arrangement was obviously quite different from that of the "indentured servant" that was to be. Although the only recompense appears to have been "to maintayne him with convenient [appropriate] diet and apparell meet for such a servant," it is equally provided that, at the end of his three-year term, he is to be given 30 acres of land, and is "to enjoy all the freedomes and privileges of a free man"; that is to say, within three years Coopy would be a self-employed owner of a 30-acre farm.[148] More fundamental, Coopy was not a chattel, alienable to any person to whom his employer might "assign" him; and his right to a land grant was written into the contract.[149]

The significant aspect of the Robert Coopy document is that it is the earliest evidence in the record that rationalizes transferring the burden of a transatlantic transportation costs from the employer to the laborer. It is perhaps also worth noting that Robert Coopy did not actually come to Virginia, but stayed in England.[150] Whether or not he reneged on the arrangement on account of the obnoxious uniqueness of its wageless feature is not revealed in the record.

While the documentation presented here is not exhaustive, there is nothing in the record, or in the argumentation based on it, to negate its clear implication. The typical form of labor in Virginia at the beginning of 1622 was that of the tenant, "the planters being," as Alderman Johnson said in reviewing the period 1619–22, "most of them Tenants at halves."[151]

A new proposal for getting "hands at Cheaper rates"

The relationship of tenant-at-halves interposed limits to the recoupment of profits by the reduction of labor costs. The tenant relationship also involved a relatively important and less reducible cost of the initial installation in Virginia. Tenants transported by the Virginia Company, for instance, were to be provided with "Apparell, Victuall, Armes, Tooles and Household Implements," the cost of which, delivered with the tenants in Virginia, came to a total of £20 sterling, of which only £6 sterling represented the cost of the transportation of the person, the remainder being for the purchase and freight of the equipment and supplies.[152]

A wage worker, on the other hand, was provided only with transportation, a cost amounting, as in the case of the person of the tenant, to £6 sterling.[153] But once in Virginia, the wage worker was entitled to wages set by the Colony Council several times as great as those of England (see Table 4.2). Even as the Colony Council was establishing that schedule of wages, in January 1621/2, it was telling London that the advancement of the work was hindered by a lack of "hands at so Cheape a rate as cannot yett possibly bee."[154] Although Captain Thomas Nuce was one of the council members who signed their names to the proclamation of wages that January, four months later he was

Table 4.2 Comparative day wages in Virginia, January 1622,
and in Rutland County, England, in 1610–1634

	with meals		without meals	
	Virginia	England[a]	Virginia	England
Master carpenter	3s.[b]	8d.	4s.	14d.
Helper[c]	2s. 3d.[d]	4d.	3s.	6d.
Master bricklayer	3s.	5d.	4s.	9d.
Helper	2s. 3d.	3d.	3s.	7d.
Master sawyer	3s.	6d.	4s.	12d.
Helper	2s. 3d.	–	3s.	–
Master mason	3s.	8d.	4s.	12d.
Helper	2s. 3d.	–	3s.	–
Master joiner	4s.	6d.	5s.	12d.
Helper	3s.	4d.	3s. 9d.	8d.
Master tailor	2s.	4d.	3s.	8d.
Helper	1s. 6d.	–	2s. 9d.	–
Farm laborer	2s.	[40s./year]	3s.	8 d.

a. English wages are for spring and summer; fall and winter wages were one-fourth to one-third less.

b. 1s. equals 12d.

c. "Helper" is intended here as a generic for "apprentice" (England) and "labourer in husbandry" (Virginia).

d. The Virginia helper's wage was set at one-fourth less than that of the respective master tradesman.

Sources: For England: James E. Thorold Rogers, *History of Agriculture and Prices in England*, 7 vols. in 8 (London, 1886–1902), 6:691–3. For Virginia: Virginia Colony Council, Settlement of the Wages of Tradesmen in Virginia, 14 January, 1621/22, (*Records of the Virginia Company of London* [4 vols. edited by Susan Myra Kingsbury, Washington, DC, 1906–35], 3: 589–90). See also wages of farm laborers paid by the year, in G. E. Russell, ed., *Robert Loder's Farm Accounts, 1610–1620*, Camden Society Publications, 3rd ser., vol. 53 (London, 1936), pp. xxviii–xxix.

moving for a reconsideration.[155] He had been sent to the colony to superintend the revival of the Company's enterprises, but he found the prevailing wage rates an obstacle. With patriotic discretion, Nuce chose for illustrative contrast not the wage scale of the Mother Country, but that of Catholic lands. Virginia, he said, where "wee pay iii s [three shillings] a day for the labor of a man who hath no other waie but to digg and dealve," must not be confused with "Italie, Spain, or ffraunce: countries plentiful and prosperous: where are thousands of women and children and such ydle people to be hyred for i d [a penny] or ii d [two pence] a day."

Two things were obvious: first, the decisive element in the cost of labor in the colony at that time was the tenant. Second, given the irrevocability of the bourgeois commitment to the tobacco plantation monoculture in the situation of everlastingly low tobacco prices, wage labor was not to be the alternative to the tenant.

In the course of discussions within the Virginia Assembly on the problem of how "yett" to get "hands at so Cheape a rate" as would satisfy the employers,

Captain Thomas Nuce, having these two above-mentioned imperatives in mind, advanced a plan that received enthusiastic endorsement. In January, 1622, the Governor and Council forwarded that proposal to London:

> Wee have heerin closed sent you a project of Capt newces which if you shalbe pleased to take likinge of, it is thought here will yeelde you, a more certain proffitt then [than] your Tenantes to halfes, which beinge proposed to the generall Assemblie, was by them well approved of.[156]

In reply the Company promised to give careful consideration to the "project of Capt Newce concerning the altering of the Condicons with our Tenants," especially because it was recommended by the Virginia Assembly.[157] A few months later the Company returned to the subject, and assured the colony officials that the Company was more than prepared to send Virginia employers "servants instead of tenants" and to do so "in a manner very advantageable to you."[158] A year after the Virginia Governor and Council had initiated the proposal in the interest of "a more certain profitt," the Virginia Council urged the question again:[159]

> Wee conceave that if you would be pleased to Chaunge the Conditione of Tenants into servants for future Supplies, . . . your revenues might be greatly improved.

In the spring of 1623 Alderman Johnson declared that the Colony officers had all desired to reduce their tenants to servants.[160]

5

The Massacre of the Tenantry

English historical experience had shown that the reduction of non-proletarian laboring people to proletarians, and the creation of a large surplus of labor were the conditions necessary for bringing about a general lowering of labor costs. The essence of the matter was shown to be the placing of the laborers in a position of great and growing dependency upon capitalist employment under conditions in which many workers compete for relatively few jobs. The English bourgeoisie had accomplished both these steps in one operation, the enclosures, during the late fifteenth and early sixteenth centuries. In Virginia in the 1620s the starting point was to be the destruction of tenancy. But whereas the enclosures involved the replacement of one hundred peasant tillers of the soil with one shepherd, the mere transformation of tenants into non-tenants did not involve any increase in labor productivity. Therefore, the Anglo-American plantation bourgeoisie, unable to create a labor surplus above labor demand, sought by other means to achieve a condition of extreme dependency of the laboring people.

The first requisite for the successful completion of the general offensive against the rights of the laboring classes that reduced them to chattels in Virginia was the maintenance of social control. The Anglo-American bourgeoisie did not need to be told that they were dealing with people who were not to be taken for granted in such a matter. The rebellious resistance of the English freehold and copyhold tenants in the sixteenth century had produced a large peasant revolt in the Midlands in the very year Jamestown was founded. Fresher in the minds of the rulers was the meltdown of the regime of *Lawes Divine, Morall and Martiall* in the face of colonists determined to defy attempts to restrict the planting of tobacco.[1]

Open military dictatorship was over; the colony was now governed by the newly created General Assembly, the Colony Council and General Court. Reliance would still be placed on English mercenary veterans of wars in Ireland and the Netherlands, not only to command in warfare against the native population but also for the maintenance of social control in the interest of the tobacco bourgeoisie. The fulfillment of this social control function was favored by four special conditions prevailing in the colony at this time.

Four Special Conditions

First of these was the appalling death rate. The record is filled with testimony of the dying, the doomed and the fearful, about the insufficiency of food, clothing and housing; and about the perils of the period of "seasoning," the first year of acclimatization. Half of the six hundred colonists living in Virginia at the beginning of 1619 were still living in March 1625. But only one out of every six of the new immigrants who came during that period was alive at the end of it. An influx of nearly five thousand persons increased the population by less than five hundred (see Table 5.1). By modern standards, the death rate in England in these years was very high, being about 2.7 percent per year;[2] but it was not such as to interfere with the continuity of the social pattern, as happened at the time of the great plague of the fourteenth century. In the Virginia colony, however, the death rate in this period was seven times that of England. In such a small, far-distant colony, the sheer physical annihilation of property owners implicit in these figures inevitably overwhelmed the orderly procedures of property transfers and afforded exceptional opportunities for illegal expropriations, including the "expropriation" of laboring people.[3] From the standpoint of social control, mere survival in these circumstances became the overriding concern for many of the working people, and the question of rebellion or social rights came to be of lesser concern for the moment.

The second special condition affecting the bourgeoisie's ability to maintain

Table 5.1 Approximate number of English emigrants to Virginia
and the death rate among them in the Company period
(omitting May 1618 to November 1619)

	1607–10[a]	1610–18[b]	1619–24[c]
Shipped from England	640	1,125	5,009
Survivors in Virginia		65	900
Total in Virginia, start of period		1,191	5,909
Alive at end of period	65	600	1,218
Dead *en route* or in Virginia	575	591	4,691
Death toll	90%	45%	80%
Annual death rate	49.5%	8.2%	26.4%
Death rate in England	2.5%	2.6%	2.1%

Sources: Alexander Brown, *The First Republic in America* (Boston and New York, 1898). pp. 129, 285, 612; Charles E. Hatch, *The First Seventeen Years: Virginia, 1607–1624* (Williamsburg, 1957), pp. 3, 7, 5; Irene W. D. Hecht, 'The Virginia Muster of 1624/5 as a Source for Demographic History,' *William and Mary Quarterly* 30:65–92 (1973), p. 70; E. A. Wrigley and R. S. Schofield, *The Population History of England, 1541–1871*, (Cambridge, MA, 1981), p.532. Cf. Evarts B. Greene and Virginia D. Harrington, *American Population Before the Federal Census of 1790* (New York, 1932), pp. 134–6.

a. December 1606 to prior to May 23, 1610, 3.42 years.
b. May 1610 to May 1618, 8 years.
c. November 1619 to February 1624/25, 5.17 years.

social control was the external contradiction represented by the Indians' resistance to massive, rapid and aggressive English encroachment upon the land. On the one hand, this contradiction made ruling-class social control more difficult, since it presented the laboring people of the colony with a means of frustrating the bourgeois pressure on their living standards and social rights, by abandoning the colony and joining one or the other of the nearby Indian communities. This was more than an abstract possibility. Instances of English colonists fleeing to the Indians are found throughout the records of the early colonial period. They went despite the fact that recapture could mean death "by hanginge, shootinge and breakinge uppon the wheele."[4] The death penalty was not always imposed, however, as the following entries in the record for 20 October 1617 seem to show:

> Geo White pardoned [by Governor Argall] for running away to the Indians with his arms & ammunition which facts deserve death according to the express articles & laws of this colony in that case provided and established and for which offenses he stands liable to censure of a marchalls Court.[5]

> Henry Potter for Stealing a Calf & running to Indians death [blank space in manuscript].

On the other hand, the increase of immigration worked to the advantage of the plantation bourgeoisie in dealing with the flight of laborers. Expansion of the colony permitted the development of an English institutional superstructure as an inhibitor to self-banishment in a strange country. A second factor was more immediate. While the Indians had been able to absorb a score or so of English left at Roanoke in 1587, the level of development of the productive forces among the Indians, and the need to avoid the strange epidemic diseases of the English, set rather close limits on the numbers of English defectors who could be absorbed into the Indian settlements. English national consciousness aside, the great inpouring of colonists made impossible a general resort to escape from bourgeois oppression by going to the Indians.

Third among these special conditions facilitating the attack by the Anglo-American plantation bourgeoisie against the social status of the laboring people in the colony was the intensified economic pressure on the laboring people in England that occurred just at this time, and that might be assumed to predispose more workers to consider emigration than would have been the case at other times. As I have previously noted,[6] in England real wages had pursued a generally downward course since the close of the fifteenth century. The situation became particularlay acute with the onset of the severe depression in England's chief industry, cloth making, in the period 1620–25. In 1624 there were still twelve thousand cloth workers out of work in England.[7]

Finally, there was the fact of the complete and utter dependence of the colony upon England for supplies, especially of clothing and metal products but also, to a considerable extent, of food and beverages. Not a nail, let alone a plow or a saw, but had to be brought a long sea voyage from England. Not a requested ball of yarn, let alone a coat, a shirt, or a bit of bedding, not a hoe, axe or pail, but must be waited for for six months at least to come from England. This was a major factor in the maintenance of social control, even when the greatest provocation to revolt was being brought to bear on the working people. If they were to succeed, the situation would not be as in England, where there were means of production to be taken over in the form of manufacturing facilities. This dependence upon English supplies enhanced the power of the bourgeoisie, the governor and Colony Council members, the plantation owners, the Cape Merchant in charge of the Company's "magazine," and free-trading ship captains relative to the "dependent classes."

The Emergent Colony Elite

The basis for the rise of an elite of rich Virginia planters was laid at the very outset of the Edwin Sandys regime, in 1619; it is seen outlined in the famous "Instructions" issued to George Yeardley upon his appointment as Governor of Virginia that April.[8] For every £12½ share of Virginia stock, "separate planter" capitalists were granted free title to one hundred acres of land, and when that land was "sufficiently peopled," an additional amount was to be given to the stockholder equal to the original amount. The term "sufficiently peopled" is not defined. The four incorporators of Berkeley Hundred, for example, jointly purchased forty-five shares and were given a patent for 4,500 acres of Virginia land, the price being equivalent to 2½ shillings per acre.[9] Furthermore, the separate planters were to benefit from the "headright" principle under which they were to be compensated for transporting laboring people to Virginia at the rate of fifty acres per "head." Later, when the next sections of land were surveyed, the planters were to receive an equal additional amount, provided they had sufficiently peopled the first grant. The capitalist was entitled to the headright land even if the person whose passage he had paid died before the ship ever reached Virginia, or starved or died of disease in Virginia, as most of them did before their three-year term was completed. Such a provision would seem designed to exacerbate the shortage of food and other supplies in the colony. Six pounds sterling invested in supplies and the freight for them to be used by laborers in Virginia could yield a return only if the laborers lived and produced commodities for the capitalist, which were then sold at a profit. But the same amount invested in getting a laborer on board a ship bound for Virginia brought the capitalist a patent on fifty acres of Virginia land. Of course, land needed laborers, and laborers needed provisions, and there was a point beyond which a stinting of supplies would prove counterproductive. But the "headright" privilege tended to push the contradiction to the limit in terms of maximum profit for the capitalist and minimum provisions for the laboring people.

The new governor, Yeardley, who had served as Acting Governor in 1616–17 and was already, before his appointment, the owner of two hundred acres by virtue of his two Company shares, was granted two thousand more acres in appreciation of his "long and faithful service." Those lands were to be held by him, his heirs and assigns forever. Three thousand acres, to be called "the Governor's Land," were set aside "in the best and most convenient place," and one-fourth of the produce of them was to belong to the Governor in his official capacity. A similar one-fourth share of the output on twelve thousand acres, called "Company lands," was to be apportioned among four or five other colony officers,[10] such as the Treasurer, the Secretary, and the Vice-Admiral, and for payments to lesser functionaries. One-twentieth of the total product of the Company lands was to be provided for the services of overseers of the Company tenants and other laboring people, and for compensating those who were responsible for dividing the product according to the proper shares.

While concentration of land ownership at this time was less than it would become by the end of the seventeenth century,[11] it was still significant. The land patent rolls for the year 1626 in Virginia show that 20 percent of the patents, comprising those of two hundred acres and more, accounted for 50 percent of the patented acreage. More than half the patents were for one hundred acres or less, but they accounted for only one-fourth of the total acreage.

This phenomenon was by no means merely the working out of the natural processes of capitalist competition whereby the advantage generally accrues to those who are operating with the largest resources of capital, or who benefit from the development of new techniques or instruments of labor. Those favorably placed in the colony government used their legal authority to secure special advantages for themselves.[12] They were able to succeed each other in various high offices, including that of Governor; acting as the Colony Council, they determined the local laws and controlled the public stores of food, arms and gunpowder. They also commanded the special bodies of armed men who enforced "order," and they controlled the colony's relations with the mother country and with the Indians. Acting as the Virginia General Court, Colony Council members dispensed judgments as harsh as they pleased.[13] In these ways, the special difficulties of colonial life, coupled with the crass partiality of the Colony Council and the Virginia General Court, placed the tenants at an extreme disadvantage in contending with the bourgeois attack upon their rights and status.

"Renting Out" of Tenants

The operative principle for using the shortage of supplies, whether absolute or relative, to undermine the position of the tenants is perfectly exemplified by the cases of the one hundred tenants sent at the Company's expense on the *Bona Nova*, who arrived in Virginia on 4 November 1619 to work "under the Comand" of Captain Weldon and Lieutenant Whitaker. The terms under which these men had been engaged to come to Virginia as tenants were explicitly and emphatically published by the King's Council for Virginia:

Every man transported into Virginia, with intent there to inhabit, as Tenants to the Common land of the Company, or to the publike land, shall be freely landed there at the charge of the Company: And shall be furnished with provisions of victual for one whole year next after his arrival, as also of Cattle: And with apparell, weapons, tooles and implements, both of house and labour, for his necessary use. He shall enjoy the ratable moytie [half] of all the profits that shall be raised of the land on which he shall be Planted, as well Corne and Cattle, as other commodities whatsoever: the other halfe being due to the Owners of the land.[14]

But a week after their arrival in Virginia, the Governor and Colony Council wrote the authorities in London of a different arrangement that had been made:

It was thought expedient by the governor and Counsell to advise the said two gentlemen [Weldon and Whitaker] to rent out the greatest part of their people to some honest and sufficient men of the Colonie till Christmas Come twelve month for iij [three] barrels of Indian Corne and 55 [pounds] waight of tobacco a man.[15]

This manner of proceeding occasioned, as Weldon reported, "no small discontent among my whole Company [of tenants].[16] Not only did it involve the chattel-like transfer of tenants from one employer to another without the consent of the persons transferred, it also carried with it a drastic reduction of their prospective income from that which they had been promised as tenants-at-halves. According to contemporary authorities,[17] these tenants might normally be expected to produce by the end of that year of service from twelve to thirty-two barrels of corn and 250 to 1,000 pounds of tobacco, of which they would be entitled to a half-share. To be required to labor the full year for three barrels of corn and 55 pounds of tobacco was clearly oppressive.

As to who the lucky "sufficient men" were who were to have the services of these tenants assigned to them, there is no doubt that colony officials were prime beneficiaries of the policy, and of similar appropriations of tenants subsequently. John Rolfe, writing to England,[18] called attention to the

many complaints against the Governors, Captaines and Officers in Virginia: for buying and selling or to be set over from one to another for yearly rent, was held in England a thing most intolerable, or that tenants or servants should be put from their places, or abridged their Covenants, was so odious that the very report thereof brought a great scandall to the generall action.

The colony authorities justified the "renting out" of the tenants on the ground that they had come ill-provisioned, having only meal for food, and of that only enough for five and a half months, possibly less.[19] Captain Weldon defended his compliance with the arrangement on the same grounds, inadequate food supplies, and added that instead of the promised three suits of apparel for each of his tenants, there were only two, of which one was unserviceable for winter wear.[20] Furthermore, he said, there were only "5 iron pots & 1 small kettle for 50 men." Of "butter Cheese rice oatmeale or any other English victuall" there was none at all.

Yet, the record shows that there was no shortage of food in Virginia in that year. Colony Secretary John Pory wrote to Sir Dudley Carleton in September 1619 that Virginia was enjoying "a marvelous plenty, suche as hath not bene since our first coming into the land."[21] The ground was so fertile, he said, that with less cultivation than was required in Europe, "we shall produce miracles out of this earth." Cattle, hogs and goats, he said, grew larger in Virginia than in England, and they multiplied rapidly. He spoke of the general prosperity based on tobacco, noting that Governor Yeardley was the most prosperous person of all. The labor of the tenants, Pory said, was the most valuable asset of the colony, but he noted that the employer had to pay for the tenants' "armes, apparell, & bedding; and for their transportation, and casuall both at sea & for their first year comonly at lande also."

In an exchange of charge and countercharge with Captain Weldon two years later, the Virginia Company in London condemned the captain for his "renting out" of the tenants, and said that contrary to the claims of Weldon and the colony authorities, the *Bona Nova* invoices showed that the tenants had been supplied with one pound of meat a day for the first year.[22]

John Rolfe, who had preceded Pory as Colony Secretary, remained an active correspondent with persons in England specially interested in Virginia affairs. In January 1620 he reported to Edwin Sandys that toward the end of the previous August, Yeardley had exchanged victuals for "20 and odd" African laborers, men and women, who had been brought to Virginia in a "Dutch man of Warr."[23] The readiness to trade victuals for these workers, as Professor Morgan first pointed out, cannot be squared with the plea of a food shortage being advanced by the Governor and Colony Council, but it would be consistent with a policy of reducing labor costs by inducing an oversupply of laborers relative to the amount of food that would be available to them.[24]

Great significance attaches to the reaction of the Company to this "renting out" of its tenants, the violation of their contract rights, and their consequent impoverishment and deprivation of status. In order to appreciate that significance, it is helpful to contrast the Company's reaction in 1618 when Governor Argall expropriated Company tenants to his own private use, and committed other abuses of authority. The very violations of public trust for private gain that the company charged against Argall were practiced on a greatly expanded scale by the governors and Council of Virginia in the 1619–24 period. They included appropriating "the Indian trade to yourselfe";[25] using the Company boats and sailors to conduct private affairs; taking tenants from Company service, and using them for private plantations of colony officials.[26]

The message sent to Argall regarding his alleged peculations ended with the stern promise that he would be called to account: "either you must think highly of yourselfe or very meanely of us ... to do what you list [wish] ... without being called to account."[27] They then acted; they dispatched a special set of instructions to the Governor designate, Lord Delaware, then *en route* to Virginia, to "cause him [Argall] to be shipped home in this ship ... to satisfy the Adventurers by answering everything as shall be layde to his chardge."

Furthermore, to secure their interest in these proceedings, the Company instructed Delaware to "ceaze upon his [Argall's] goods, as Tobacko and Furrs, whereof it is reported he hath gotten together great stoare to the Colonies prejudice, and so sendinge them to us to be in deposite till all matters be satisfyed."[28]

The Company had the same authority to recall Governor Yeardley or his successor, Francis Wyatt, or any of the other "Captaines and Officers" denounced by Rolfe for violating tenants' contracts. The grounds for such action were certainly present. Captain Weldon, however, was merely reprimanded for his complicity in the matter. He continued his Virginia career, being granted a large land patent there in 1622.[29] Yeardley and the members of the Colony Council who had forced the transfer of the tenants were the recipients of no more rebuke than might be gleaned from the following paragraph in a letter from the Company to the Governor and Council, dated 25 July 1621:[30]

> We cannot conceale from youe, that it is heare reported that contrary to the public faith given, not the sicke but the ablest men are lett out to hire and theire provisions converted to private uses. And where it is pretended this planting them with old planters is for theire health, they are so unmercifully used that it is the greatest cause of our tennant's discontent; and though we hope this is not in all parts true, yet we cannot conceive such unwillingness to proceed in this worke should they not have some other grounds than is alledged: lett it therefore be your worke at the first general session of the Counsell to effect this business, and it shall be our care to provide for the well orderinge and furnishinge of them.

As that letter was being delivered to the Virginia colony, George Yeardley's term in office was coming to an end. As Governor, Yeardley had had one hundred tenants assigned to him. When his successor, Wyatt, counted the tenants turned over to him, he could find only forty-six. The Colony Council inquired about the other fifty-four. Yeardley coolly declined to supply the missing number.[31] To have done so would have required him either to return those he had taken or else to pay for the installation of a new supply from England. Seizure of Argall's property had been ordered in a similar situation, but now things were different. In reporting on the Yeardley matter in January 1622, the Colony Council showed no disposition to press the issue. "Sir George Yeardley denieth to make them good," it wrote to London, "[and] we have foreborne to Compell him thereunto, until we Receave your further directiones therein."[32] Apparently, these were not forthcoming. Yeardley remained a member of the Colony Council, restored no tenants to the Company, and continued to thrive in fortune and honors. Having come to the colony in 1610 with nothing but his sword, he lived sumptuously, and died in the second year of his second term as governor, possessed of a very large fortune.[33]

In the contrasting treatment of Argall and Yeardley, we can see measured the progress of the Company's conversion to the cause of tobacco monoculture, to the liquidation of its own productive enterprises in the colony, and to its own transmutation into merely a monopolist of English tobacco imports. It further reveals the essential concord that had been reached by the Anglo-American plantation bourgeoisie for the overthrow of the tenantry.

Another way of bringing pressure on the Company tenant was found in the restriction of tobacco planting. Although official policy was generally ineffective and pursued with steadily diminished vigor,[34] it none the less presented the employing class with opportunities for increasing the tenants' dependency and making tenants more vulnerable to degradation of their status.

When Captain Weldon informed his tenants, those remaining to him after the "renting out" of half their original number, that their tobacco planting was to be restricted, they denounced the policy. They well understood that, completely dependent upon supplies from England as they were, a lack of the medium of exchange, tobacco, would render them destitute. In a report to London, Captain Weldon described the angry mood of these tenants:

> [T]hey will with no patience endure to heare of it bitterly Complayninge that they have no other meanes to furnish themselves with aparell for the insuinge yeare but are likely as they say (and for ought I Cann see) to be starved if they be debarred of it.[35]

As a result of the tenants' strong resistance, the Governor consented to an easing of the restriction, although not to its outright and formal revocation.

When Yeardley was succeeded by Francis Wyatt as governor in 1621, the policy of restricting tobacco planting was officially continued, with output to be limited to 112 pounds per year per laboring hand.[36] To the extent that such a policy was effective, the burden fell with much greater impact upon the laboring tenants than upon the land-owning employer of a number of tenants; the tenant had only one half-share, but the employer would receive as many half-shares as he had tenants. The employer had an additional advantage since he, not the tenant, had the dividing of the product into the employer's and the tenant's shares.[37]

An altercation, involving corn not tobacco, occurred between tenant William Moch (variously spelled) and John Harvey, later to be governor, who was sent by the king and Privy Council to conduct an inquiry into Virginia affairs in 1624–25. Harvey summoned Moch and demanded to see his covenant papers, that is, the agreement under which Moch had been engaged as a tenant. The court minutes continue:

> To which he [Moch] replyed, first lett me see my Corne[.] Capt. Harvey told him he scorned to keep back his Corne, Mutch replyed againe he would have his corne before he should see them. Then Capt. Harvey told him he was an idle knave, and that he could find in his heart to Cudgell his Coate. To which Mutch answered scornefully, alas Sir it is not in you.[38]

Although according to testimony Harvey then struck Moch a blow across the head with a truncheon, Moch continued to "give other provoking speeches" to the king's appointed commissioner. Tenant Moch appears to have been a man of courage, and the record shows that he could have drawn strength from knowing that his stand represented the basic sentiments of the tenants generally.

The majority of the colonists were tenants, and, although they too were as hooked on tobacco as anyone else, they were determined to have their "moiety" of the crop, whatever the particular crop happened to be, and not to be "set over" from one landlord to another without their consent, nor to have their tenant status degraded to one of servitude. Like Captain Weldon's tenants they would "with no patience endure to hear of it." The tradition of Tyler and Ket was bred in their bones, and they had a deep sense of chartered "liberties, rights, and immunities" as their English birthright. Like tenant Moch in his retort to Commissioner Harvey, they could not believe that the landowners had the power to "cudgel the Coates" of the tenantry in a land where labor was destined to be in short supply for a long time to come.

Making One Crisis Serve Another

It was the external contradiction that precipitated the consummating crisis.[39] On 22 March 1622, the Indians of the Powhatan Confederacy mounted what was to be in relative terms the strongest effort ever made after the founding of Virginia to halt the Anglo-American occupation of Indian lands, with the possible exception of the Yamassee War of 1715 in South Carolina. Powhatan had died in 1618, on the eve of the period of accelerated English colonization.[40] His kinsman and successor Opechancanough watched the inpouring of immigrants – more in the next four years than had come during the four decades of Powhatan's time. Yet the Indian guests who had accompanied the ill-fated Pocahontas to England had found the natives too numerous to count.[41] Opechancanough saw them come and die like fish out of water; yet in greater numbers than ever they came, in ships carried by the winds. Tobacco had made them mad. They had guns and they took the land.

We cannot, of course, know the terms in which the discussion was carried on that united thirty-two tribes,[42] but clearly there was much discussion of

[T]he dayly feare that posseste them that in time (the English) by ... growing continually upon them, would dispossess them of this Country, as they had been formerly of the West Indies by the Spaniards.[43]

As Powhatan had succeeded in doing at Roanoke forty years before, and as O'Donnell and O'Neill had tried to do in the Tyrone War (1594–1603), Opechancanough and the Powhatan allies would strike to root out the English plantation.

The strategy against this enemy armed with guns and with cannon-bearing ships was to be that of the single massive blow and subsequent attrition. The English would later congratulate themselves on the partiality of their Divine Providence which, they said, stayed the hands of the Indian attackers;[44] but limited success may simply have been the most that Opechancanough or any other general could have achieved in the circumstances. Even his enemies' historians would concede that the attack was "planned by a master mind."[45] To hold together the alliance of thirty-two tribes for a long war against English firepower and the barrage of cheap commodities[46] was an improbable prospect. On the other hand, the obvious ineptitude of the English colonists gave reasonable grounds to expect that from the single catastrophe they might be moved to abandon the colony[47] and merge with the people of the country, as those of Roanoke had done, and a number of frequent defectors had done since the founding of the colony.[48]

The blow would be aimed at the colony's most vulnerable point, its food supply. It was the time for planting corn, not harvesting it. Even when they had planted corn, the colonists had begrudged each acre and day taken from "their darling tobacco."[49] Close observers perhaps saw the corn shortage as a particular, rather than a general, one, with the haves exploiting the have-nots by virtue of the haves' access to corn among the Indians.[50] If so, the situation presented an opportunity to take advantage of class divisions within the colony. Finally, the day chosen for the attack was, as English preachers and defectors had informed them, the most solemn moment of the Christian calendar, when perhaps their mountainous guilts would sit most heavily on their English souls – the day they called Good Friday.

Viewed from history's elevated ground, the strategy seems to have been foredoomed as far as the achievement of its maximum objective was concerned, even had the English not (as they claimed) received a last-minute warning from a Christianized Indian.[51] The difference in the level of development of productive forces would give the English the ultimate, fundamental advantage. It seems probable, too, that Opechancanough underestimated the persistence of the English promoters of colonization, who scrupled not at a 25 percent death rate if a 25 percent profit could be made in the process.[52] Whatever may have been the possibilities of strategic victory, the attack dealt the death blow to the Virginia Company, although the Company's charter was not formally revoked until 1624. More important was the fact that the attack struck to the very foundation of the life of the colony. It intensified to an extreme degree the uncertainties of existence that resulted from economic dislocation, epidemic disease, the heavy assignments of watching and warding, the dependence upon trans-ocean supplies, and the vulnerability of property and production relations.[53]

Four hundred English colonists died on that day, one-third of the total population.[54] All but a few of the settlements were abandoned, a major portion of the livestock was lost, and there was little prospect of growing corn in the colony during the remainder of the year. Only one-third of the survivors were men fit for work, and a large part of that potential labor was diverted to "watching and warding." The colony authorities forbade the planting of corn near dwellings on the grounds that it provided a lurking place for hostile Indians. They added that, even if corn were planted, it was liable to be cut down or harvested by Indians.[55] A similar problem was cited as a reason for forbidding individual colonists to hunt wild game in the woods; the hunter, it was claimed, would risk death or capture by Indians.[56] However, the colony officials were equally concerned with preventing hungry and overworked English laborers from fleeing the colony to join the Indians. In March 1623, George Sandys reported on a group of eleven Company tenants for whom the Company had no provisions. Seven were sold or relocated. Of the disposition of the other four, Sandys wrote: "two of these . . . ran away (I am afraide to the Indians) and no doubt the other two would have consorted with their companions if sickness had not fettered them."[57] Without food supplies from the outside, the colony would famish.[58] Widespread undernourishment rendered many colonists especially susceptible to the diseases brought from England by the eight hundred immigrants who came to Virginia in the year following the attack of 22 March 1622. According to the Company, six hundred of the emigrants themselves died in Virginia before the year was out.[59]

The dependence upon English supplies was made even more critical under these deprived circumstances. The record is filled with urgent, even anguished, appeals, public and private, for food to be sent from the Mother country. In their first letter to England after the Indian attack, the Virginia Governor and Colony Council asked for enough grain to sustain the colony for a year.[60] Lady Wyatt, wife of the Governor, despite her favored position was not above writing to her sister in England requesting a bit of butter, bacon, cheese and malt, explaining that "since we & the Indians fell out we dare not send a hunting but with so many men as it is not worth their labour."[61]

We may assume that the means and opportunity for writing letters to England describing the sufferings of the colonists, and appealing for assistance, were inversely proportional to the actual privations of the individual letter writers, and directly proportional to their prospects for special assistance from England. Letters by members of the laboring population of the colony are much more rare in the record than those written by members of the owning classes. The great majority of the laboring people could not write; and even if they could have written and had the means and opportunity to do so, they had no friends of substance in England to whom they might have appealed. Laboring people whose letters have been preserved seem to have been persons of "respectable" backgrounds, with significant connections in the middle class of the home country. Yet it is to these latter that we are indebted for what we have of an "inside" picture of the conditions of life as they pressed down on the laboring people of the colony. Frequent citations from these letters have given their authors a sort of immortality, which they doubtless would have traded for a little cheese had the choice been offered.

If the frequency of these letters in the record is indicative, the spring of 1623 was especially hard for the working people of the colony. Richard Frethorne was one of a group of men who arrived as laborers in Virginia about Christmas 1622.[62] Young Frethorne had been sent under an arrangement concluded between his father and Robert Bateman, London merchant, member of Parliament, and prominent member of the Virginia Company.[63]

What Richard Frethorne wished for more than anything else was just about what Opechancanough wanted for him – a swift return to England. Even an utterly incapacitated person, begging from door to door, was better off in England, said Frethorne, than a plantation laborer in Virginia. And this, he wrote, was the feeling of all his fellow workers. What with the Indians' hostility, the pervasive despondency, the scurvy and the "bloody fluxe," the population of Martin's Hundred, he said, had been reduced from 140 to only 22 in the past year. The surviving laborers were subsisting on one-third of a pint of meal per day.[64] It was only ten weeks after his arrival in Virginia, and he was writing to Bateman asking to "be freed out of this Egypt." Frethorne seemed to sense that his "right worshipfull" merchant sponsor might be unable to find it in his purse simply to pay for his immediate release from Virginia service and return passage to England. He sought, therefore, to appeal to Bateman's business instincts. In lieu of immediate deliverance, Frethorne would be satisfied, he said, if Bateman could send him some beef, cheese, butter or other victuals, which Frethorne could sell for a profit. Frethorne would send all the profit back to Bateman to cover the costs of termination of his contract and his return home. Frethorne suggested further that the people of his parish in England might be willing to contribute toward the cost.[65]

In his letter to Bateman, the young plantation worker discreetly refrained from complaints about the oppressive conditions of labor. But to his mother and father he spoke more freely. He had eaten more in a day in England than he had in Virginia in a week, he said. There were wild fowl in the woods, he wrote, but "We are not allowed to goe and get it, but must Worke hard both earlie and late for a messe of water gruell, and a mouthfull of bread and biefe." A part of his time was spent in hauling the employer's goods from ships anchored at Jamestown, ten miles from Martin's Hundred. On those occasions, he had to work until midnight, loading, rowing and unloading. He had had to sleep in an open boat, even on rainy nights, when on this duty, until a gunsmith named Jackson befriended him and built a cabin in which Richard could shelter when in Jamestown at night. There was only three weeks' supply of meal remaining on their plantation. Frethorne speculated with dread on the approaching day when: "My Master ... is not able to keepe us all, then wee shalbe turned up to the land and eat barkes of trees, or mouldes of the Ground." Richard Frethorne's last recorded words have become familiar by quotation: "I thought no head had been able to hold so much water as hath and doth dailie flow from my eyes."[66]

Another laboring man, Henry Brigg, wrote to his brother, a merchant at the Customs House in London, in that April of 1623, "to lett you understand how I live it is very miserable, for here we have but a wyne quart of Corne for a day and nothing else but Water, and worke hard from Sun rising to Sun sett at felling of Trees and we have not victuall not past xx [20] dayes."[67] He asked the London brother to send him provisions for a year, and a gun with ammunition "for I goe in danger of my life every day for lack of one."

Brigg also had a business proposition to make. If his brother would care to invest in a stock of trade goods, Henry would undertake to secure for him a clear profit of 100 percent. The list of items he thought might move well is especially interesting as evidence of the degree of dependence of the colonists upon English manufactured and processed supplies. Understandably, it was made up mainly of food and apparel: oatmeal, peas, butter, cheese, oil, vinegar, aquavita, linen or woolen cloth or apparel for men or women, shoes, stockings, metal-tipped laces, gloves, and garters. Knives and other metal utensils were also recommended.[68]

Thomas Nicolls wrote to England in March and April, saying that each laborer should be allowed "a pound of butter and a pound of cheese weekly, as there was no food in sickness or health but oatmeal and pease, and bread and water." Nineteen men had been captured by the Indians, he said, and conflict, disease and starvation had in the last eighteen months reduced the complement of men on one plantation from fifty-six to fourteen, and from ninety-seven to twenty on another.[69]

Perhaps nothing symbolized more clearly the colony's extreme dependence upon supplies of English commodities than did the waiting for the *Seaflower* in the spring and early summer of 1623. A ship of 140 tons,[70] the *Seaflower* left England around 1 January that year, Virginia-bound, with a cargo of meal and other provisions valued at £500 sterling,[71] to relieve the famine there, at the usual rate of 25 percent profit for the investors in the voyage.[72]

Governor Wyatt and chief councillor George Yeardley told the colonists "that except the Seaflower come in," or they could get corn from the Indians, more than half the colony would starve to death.[73] The people watched the sea, and wrote those letters; Colony Treasurer George Sandys, Colony Secretary Christopher Davison, plantation servant Richard Frethorne all prayed with small planter and silk-raiser Peter Arundell for "the speedie arrivall of the Seaflower."[74] Even as they prayed, the *Seaflower* lay at the bottom of a Bermuda harbor, sunk *en route* by the explosion of its powder magazine.[75] Two ships did come into Jamestown in April, but they lacked even adequate provisions for the people they brought with them.[76] It would be five months before the Company's next supply would arrive on the ninety-ton *Bonnie Bess* in September.[77]

The *Seaflower* sank, and the colonists starved, sickened and died. In self-defense against Company censure, George Sandys begged for understanding in England: "[W]ho is ignorant," he asked, "how the heavie hand of God hath suppressed us? The lyveying being hardlie able to bury the dead."[78] The annual March census was not sent to England, or, if sent, was concealed from public disclosure.[79]

Captain Nathaniel Butler had come from Bermuda and made an investigation of the conditions in Virginia in the winter of 1622–23. At the king's request, Butler wrote a report which came to be known popularly as "The

Unmasking of Virginia."[80] The dominion of death was so established in Virginia, he reported, that people "are not onely seen dying under hedges and in the woods, but beinge dead ly some of them for many dayes unregarded and unburied."[81] Not until 1625 would the population of the colony regain the level it had attained in March 1622.[82]

The difference in the suffering of the owning and the laboring classes apparent in Virginia at this time was, to a degree, normal for a society based on class exploitation. The same phenomenon was observable in England. But the special conditions of colony life presented unusual opportunities for profiteering by the merchant and planter bourgeoisie.

As I have noted, the Virginia Company of London expected investors to make a 25 percent profit on the food that was sent to the starving colony. Because of the continuing decline in the price of the overproduced tobacco,[83] this profit margin was a constant point of contention between the colony buyers and the Company, and in turn between the Company and the king in the tobacco contract negotiations. English colony tobacco, which had sold in England at from 3 to 4½ shillings, and more, the pound in 1619, was selling for 18 to 20 pence in March 1622/3.[84] A year later, it had fallen further to 18d. or less per pound.[85] In April 1624, a group representing "the poore Planters in Virginia" petitioned for a reduction of the combined 12d. per pound royal impost and import custom on tobacco. The price of tobacco in England was at that time so low, it was said, that such charges left insufficient return to continue production.[86] In January 1626, the Virginia Colony authorities reported that their efforts to maintain tobacco at 18d. had failed, and that it was then selling at less than 12d. per pound in the colony.[87]

Profit-making pressure on the colonists was intensified by the presence of the trading ships that anchored at Jamestown. They were laden with cargoes of delectable English commodities and they conducted their offshore business with colonists able and willing to give tobacco for wines, liquors, cider, salad oil, vinegar, butter, candies, cheese and Canadian fish.[88] Trading was so heavy, it was said, that almost the entire 60,000-pound crop of Virginia tobacco produced in 1622 was taken by these private traders.[89] Business was brisk despite the increasingly "excessive and unconscionable" rates of profit extorted by the merchants.[90]

The customers were people who had some tobacco above what they might have needed for purchasing corn. Undoubtedly, they were in the main the poor but free planters, such as constituted something less than half the population of the colony.[91] This aspect of profiteering must have impoverished many small planters and reduced some to proletarians. Certainly, after dealing with the trading ships they had little tobacco left for shipment to England for their own accounts. As the Company stated in March 1623:

[C]oncerning the poor Planters ... the quantitie of Tobacco brought home in right of their proprietie is for the most part verie smale it beinge expended in the Plantacons amongst the Marchantes trading thither with their several necessarie Commodities."[92]

Profiteering, official and otherwise, was coupled with outright expropriation, legal and illegal, on a grand scale, without any color of exchange. Given the special circumstances of colony existence, and given the continuing supply of laborers from England, this profiteering and expropriation were basic factors in the reduction of colony plantation laborers to chattels.

As the remark of Wyatt and Yeardley had indicated, the rulers of the colony had only one active policy for feeding the colony, namely to get corn from the Indians. Two general methods were employed to implement this policy. One was to make war against Opechancanough and his allies. The other was that of peaceful trade with the more distant, friendly Indians on the eastern shore of Chesapeake Bay.[93] But the main method seems to have been the former; when in doubt, or perhaps merely low on English trade goods,[94] the English would allege "treachery" against the Indians and attack them, taking corn without payment and destroying the growing corn of the Indians, a method of warfare that some of the English officers in Virginia had practiced under Mountjoy in Ireland.[95]

As noted above, shortly after the Indian attack of 22 March 1622 the colony authorities ordered drastic restrictions on the planting of corn, as a safeguard against lurking Indian enemies it was said.[96] Many colonists considered the "national defense" rationale for this policy to be spurious, and complained bitterly about it. Later they declared that if they had been allowed to plant corn as they wished, they could have provided for their own needs adequately,[97] even though little food, or none at all, was coming from England. The restriction on corn planting was also challenged in the meetings of the Court of the Virginia Company of London.[98] Nevertheless, the policy was enforced, although the temper of the colonists was so unruly by April 1623 that the governor asked London to institute martial law, as he said to terrorize the people.[99] The ban on hunting for food in the forests, and the abandonment of half the plantations and the withdrawal of the colony into a restricted perimeter, compounded the food supply problem.

It was a recipe for famine; but it was also a recipe for capitalist profiteering, by those equipped and opportunely positioned to exploit the situation. Captain Nathaniel Butler was only reporting, and in terms of understatement, what was an open scandal, when in the spring of 1623, regarding the hardship of the corn famines, he said:

> howsoever itt lay heavy uppon the shoulders of the Generallytie itt may be suspected not to be unaffected by some of the chiefe; for they onely haveing the means in these extremeties to Trade for Corn w[i]th the Natives doe hereby engrosse all into their hands and soe sell it att their owne prizes [prices].[100]

The means for trading for corn with the Indians were boats and small ships. Those who possessed or could secure the use of such vessels had a monopoly of the trade, since there was absolutely no other way of bringing corn into the colony from the Indians of the eastern shore of Chesapeake Bay. Having made it practically impossible for the people to trade simply and directly with their immediate Indian neighbors, the Colony Council and the Governor in the winter and spring of 1622–23 issued corn-trading licenses to owners and operators of cargo-carrying capital equipment. Not surprisingly, George Yeardley appears a foremost actor in this group. On 3 January, Governor Wyatt licensed Yeardley to send Captain William Tucker, an experienced officer and trader, on a corn-getting voyage, using "such shipps, pinnaces boates as hee the s[ai]d Sir George shall thinke fitt to appoint unto him & that doe in any way belong or are in service to him the said George."[101]

Tucker was authorized, on Yeardley's behalf, to "trade or take by force of Armes" in order to secure the Indians' corn. He was instructed to deliver the corn to Yeardley "by him to be disposed as hee in his best discretion shall thinke fitt."[102]

Seven corn-getting ventures were made in that same month, by George Sandys, Colony Secretary, and by a number of "Captains." Four of the six men engaged in these separate voyages in the privileged trade were members of the Colony Council.[103] Yeardley was the largest of the operators; of the four thousand bushels of corn brought into the colony by 20 March, Yeardley, in only one voyage, accounted for one-fourth of the total.[104] The oft-quoted old planter William Capps called Yeardley "[a] worthie statesman for his owne profit," who was willing to prolong the colony's distress in order to gain by it personally.[105] It is reasonable to infer, and it was so implied by Nathaniel Rich, that corn profiteering was the motive of the merchants in the Colony Council generally, when they advised the London authorities in January 1623 that they were "Confident there wilbe noe cause to intreat your helpe for supplie of corne or any other provisions," provided incoming colonists were accompanied by adequate food.[106]

Under ordinary conditions, the colony at its current size needed at least eleven thousand bushels of corn to get through to the next harvest from planting time.[107] The normal price of corn was 2½s. per bushel.[108] Under normal conditions, the five largest possessors of corn in the colony held 12 percent of the total supply.[109]

In March 1623, there were certainly less than four thousand bushels of corn on hand of that brought in during the previous three or four months. Very little corn had been harvested in 1622; the same would be true of 1623. At the same time a group of not more than a dozen of the colony elite held practically the entire corn supply of the colony. The supply was not distributed according to need; rather it was sold for the highest prices that could be extorted. The price of corn had risen to ten, and then fifteen, shillings a bushel in the winter of 1622. By the spring of 1623, the price was octupled, at twenty shillings per bushel.[110] And within a month after the *Seaflower* went down in Bermuda, Edward Hill was writing to his brother in England that the price of corn in Virginia had reached thirty shillings, and that the land faced "the greatest famine that ever was."[111] As the price of corn was rising to eight times its normal level, the price of tobacco was falling due to overproduction. We have already noted that the commodity-trading ships were said to have taken almost the entire sixty-thousand-pound tobacco crop of 1622.[112] While that estimate may have been exaggerated somewhat, the fact still contributed to the pressure of indebtedness bearing down on the people as a result of profiteering by the plantation bourgeois elite.

In 1623, the Governor and Colony Council sought to fix the exchange rate of tobacco in Virginia at 18*d.* per pound in order to discourage trade with the private ship-merchants.[113] This was only half the three-shilling rate that had been set before the crisis. If the price of corn rose eight times and the price of tobacco fell by half, then the four thousand pounds of corn secured in the winter of 1622–23 would, even at a price of fifteen shillings the bushel, be equal in exchange-value to forty thousand pounds of tobacco at 18*d.* per pound. If the total 1622 tobacco crop of sixty thousand pounds had nearly all been spent with the commodity-trading ships (see page 89), then the indicated indebtedness to the corn elite must have approached something like forty thousand pounds of tobacco. The crushing weight of such debt was enough to drive the tenants into long-term debt servitude. The same pressure was felt, perhaps only slightly less forcefully, by the freemen, the rank-and-file small landholders.

The uprooting of the inhabitants of many English settlements, combined with the extremely high death rate, simultaneously presented the plantation bourgeoisie with opportunities for direct capitalist expropriation of land and labor power in the furtherance of the alteration of labor relations to that of chattel-servitude.

In the aftermath of the 22 March 1622 attack, the boundaries of the colony were drawn back by deliberate decision to Jamestown and Newport-News and points on the north side of James River, and to a few plantation above and opposite Jamestown. In its report to London at the end of April, the Colony Council revealed that "halfe the people" had been uprooted and "enforced . . . to unite with" the other half, along with as much of their livestock as could be salvaged, within the confines of an area less than half that occupied by the colony before 22 March.[114] Two months later, the Colony Council advised London that "[w]e have been forced to quitt most of our habitations, so that many of our people are unsettled."[115]

One-third of the landholders had died in the attack of 22 March. Half of the surviving landholders were those who were displaced from the outlying settlements; and half of that number died within the ensuing year. Chaos in property relations was the result, especially in the common case in which there was no clearly entitled Virginia-dwelling heir-apparent. Three years after the attack, only twenty-eight of the seventy non-corporate landholders were still living of those who had been granted land patents in Charles City prior to 22 March 1622. Most revealing of the chaotic quality of the situation is the fact that sixteen of the seventy are listed as "probably" or "possibly" dead. It was difficult enough to straighten out the lines and portions of inheritance when the patent holder was known to be dead; it was impossible to do so where it was not certain that the original holder was dead. Still, the land "lived," and would yield tobacco for somebody, if "planted" with laborers. The corporate group that operated under the name Southampton Hundred was the holder of title to 100,000 acres in Charles City. In 1625, this land was still "virtually abandoned." In Henrico settlement, only nine of the pre-March 1622 patent holders remained alive in 1625; of these, only two were living in Henrico.[116]

It was a field rich with opportunity for land-grabbing.[117] Immediately after the March 1622 attack, the gentlemen of the Colony Council noted that in the straitened circumstances it would be necessary for colonists to be "contented with smale quantities of Land," and asked London for authority to assign planters "the place and proportions of Land" that the Council in Virginia should think proper.[118] Under cover of a reference to the settling of new planters, the Colony Council asked that the patent-granting authority be transferred from the Virginia Company Court in London to the Virginia Governor and Colony Council.

The Company's reply indicated that, in any case of divergence of interest among claimants, control should be unambiguously located in England. The Company categorically rejected the suggestion of the Virginia Colony council, immediately established a special committee of Londonders to receive claims of Virginia land heirs living in England, and enjoined the Virginia authorities to process these claims as they were forwarded, expeditiously and justly.[119] In November 1622, the Company's committee on Virginia land claims declared as follows:

> The Companie knoweth not what land is Due to men and every Day unjust and false claimes are put up especially upon pretences of beinge heires to persons [in Virginia].[120]

Aside from the individually held lands, around thirty thousand acres of Company lands reverted to the Crown in 1625,[121] to be distributed in time on its terms.

In consequence of this double process of death and displacement, one-third, at least,[122] of the surviving tenants, laborers and apprentices in the entire colony were left without employers or means of employing themselves. The moment had come to put into execution the proposal of Captain Nuce, which had been so ardently embraced by the Virginia Governor, Colony Council and House of Burgesses in January 1622 – to "turn the tenants into pencons."[123] The optimum conditions were conjoined for realizing the intention of the plantation bourgeoisie to reduce the general condition of the plantation laboring classes to that of unpaid bond-labor, working without wages, for board and lodging only.

As of the spring of 1622, there were five officially recognized social classes in Virginia Colony. Two of them were the owning classes: gentlemen (the bourgeoisie) and the freemen, small independent farmers and self-employed artisans (the petty bourgeoisie). The other three were the dependent laboring classes: the tenants-at-halves, the hired servants, and the apprentices.[124]

In the long crisis that followed the Indian attack of March 1622, however, the significant distinctions of status among the three laboring-class elements were deeply eroded by pervasive hunger and sickness, by economic dislocation, and by the general precariousness of existence.[125]

Theoretically, the average tenant could, under normal conditions, raise some five hundred or more pounds of tobacco in a year,[126] half of which was his, plus the corn, of which his share would supply him and his family (if he had a family in Virginia) for the year ahead. But the crisis had confronted the tenants with a far different reality. They were forced into debt by the restriction on tobacco planting, coupled with a fixed rate of rent. Forbidden to plant corn, they were compelled to pay extortionate prices for it from the corn-profiteering elite, and to the shipboard hucksters down at the river. Alderman Johnson, a critic of the Sandys administration in the Virginia Company, said in June 1623: "the planters, most of them being Tenants at halves ... for twelve moneths bread paye 2 years labor and for cloths and tooles he hath not wherewith to furnish himself.[127] Yet friends of the Sandys administration judged the proportion of the tenants' resources to be even less. In January the Virginia Colony Council had said that tenants could not feed themselves three months out of the year.[128] In March, Colony Secretary George Sandys would write that most tenants-at-halves "die of Melancholye, the rest running so farre in debt as keepes them still behind hand," and many too hungry to continue at their works or to wait for the harvest were hunting wild game to keep from starving.[129] And in April, those of Governor Wyatt's twenty-four tenants who still survived were sinking hopelessly into debt merely for corn to get them through the year, because their families would otherwise starve waiting for the year-end division of the crop. Eight of Wyatt's tenants were obliged to submit to being "rented out" to private planters, who paid Wyatt one hundred pounds of tobacco and three barrels of corns for each.[130]

In the case of the hired laborer, what did it matter that, even at the reduced official rate of 18d. per pound, his wage of a pound of tobacco per day was by the numbers equal to three times as much as the wages of a laborer in England? Corn, the basic food, cost four or five times as much in Virginia as grain in England.[131] Two-thirds of the possible employers of hired labor had died or been displaced from their lands in the space of a year. The opportunities for being hired were thus cut in half, while the number of hands available for hired labor was doubled by the displacement of half the tenants from their holdings. January letters from Jamestown described the laborer's situation in such terms as these:

> by occasion of the last massacre ... every man of meaner sort, who before lived well by their labour upon their owne land, being forced to foresake their houses (which were very farre scattered) & to join themselves to some great mans plantation; where having spent what before they had gotten, they are ready to perish for want of necessaries.[132]

The tendency to concentration of land ownership has been noted above. But the most significant index of wealth concentration in Virginia at that time was in numbers of laborers; as Secretary Pory had said, 'our principal wealth ... consisteth in servants.[133] Edmund S. Morgan lists the fifteen "winners" in the servant "sweepstakes," who by the winter of 1624–25 had accumulated a total of 302 "servants."[134] That was 60 percent of all those categorized as "servants" in the Colony.[135] Some significant portion of them had been forced by sheer want "to join ... great men's plantations." The individual holding of the grandees ranged from ten to thirty-nine "servants." Morgan emphasizes the extreme degree of concentration of this engrossment of the laborers in the hands of the colony elite by noting that contemporary Gloucestershire in England, with a labor force nearly forty times as great as that of Virginia Colony, had only slightly more employers of ten or more persons than Virginia's favored fifteen.[136] The concentration of "servants" in the colony was guaranteed for the future by the headright system of land acquisition and tenure; and the arrangement of political power based on it was certain to intensify the already apparent degree of concentration of land ownership in Virginia.

Now completely in the labor market were such ex-tenants as John Radish, one of the "rented-out" tenants-at-halves, who found himself so destitute late in 1622 that he was compelled by necessity to work for his master for food and clothing only, or die of starvation.[137] Such being the lot of the tenants-at-halves and the wage workers, what but despair would come to the apprentices, lacking a master, land and tools, unskilled in labor, possibly displaced from lodging, and three thousand miles from home? It need only be said that their situation was the most precarious of all, and to note that in April 1622 Edwin Sandys in England had come to the opinion that what Virginia needed most was "multitude of apprentices."[138]

A time came, in June 1623, when in labor-scarce Virginia food was proportionately even more scarce than laborers. Writing to his brother Edward in London, Virginia gentleman planter Robert Bennett acknowledged recent receipt of a shipment of "19 buttes of excelent good wyne, 700 jarse of oylle, 16 Barelles of Rysse, tooe halfe hoghedes of Allmonds, 3 half hoghedes of wheate ..., 18 hoghedes of Olives and some 5 ferkenes of butter and one Chesse."[139] Concerning general conditions in the colony, he added in a postscript: "Vittiles being scarce in the countrye noe man will tacke servantes."

Laboring People's Difficulty, Colony Elite's Opportunity

The extreme economic pressure on the laboring people created an opportunity for the abuse of their rights that was deliberately exploited by the official policy and actions of the Virginia Colony Council and General Court. Men on wages were sold after their employers died.[140] Poor planter William Tyler declared that "neither the Governor nor Counsell could or would doe any poor man right." Even if he were a man of means, Tyler said, he wouldn't be a member of the Colony Council, because as such he could not do right as his conscience would dictate, adding that the great men all hold together.[141] Laborer Elizabeth Abbot was whipped to death with 500 lashes, and Elyas Hinton was beaten to death with a rake by his employer, Mr Procter.[142] In the first recorded instance of the un-English practice of punishing a runaway laborer by adding years to his servitude, John Joyce was sentenced by the General Court to thirty lashes and a total of five and a half years' extra labor service.[143] Henry Carman, who had been shipped to Virginia as one of the "Duty boys" in 1619, was the first laborer sentenced to an added time (seven years) of unpaid labor for a criminal offense ("fornication").[144] Company tenants, who had been promised promotion to landowner upon completion of their contracts, were instead merely to serve again as tenants of the colony authorities for "terme of yeares." "Duty boys" who in 1626 completed their seven-year terms, were not promoted to tenants-at-halves, but were divided up among the Governor and members of the Colony Council, with whom they were to "make composition," that is, negotiate terms from their utterly dependent position.[145] Bruce's "explanation" of why the plantation bourgeoisie reneged on the conditions under which these laboring people were originally brought to Virginia seems cold-bloodedly true. If they had been granted land, he says, "the ability of the planters who had been their masters to secure laborers in place of them would have been diminished to a serious extent."[146]

For the laboring classes, it was as if Virginia had been visited with a combination of the plague of the fourteenth century – but without the chance to walk away to higher-paying employment – and the enclosures of the sixteenth century – but without a Pilgrimage of Grace of powerful allies, or their native Mousehold Heath to rally on. They could not escape from Virginia. Rebellion was, at that moment, practically impossible, even if the subjective element for revolt had been prepared. They were dependent upon the bourgeoisie for every peck of corn for their starved bellies. They were thus compelled to submit to the condition dictated by the plantation bourgeoisie: the status of unpaid labor, that is, bond-laborers.

Yet the tenants' desperate situation which had made it possible for the employing class to reduce labor costs to mere "vittles" would certainly end with new corn harvests,[147] although the price of tobacco was bound in shallows from which it would never return to its early high levels. How then would it be possible for the plantation bourgeoisie to make this momentary system of unpaid labor permanent, instead of being forced to return to "that absurd condition of tenants at halves,"[148] or to paying wages higher than those paid in England?[149]

6

Bricks without Straw: Bondage, but No Intermediate Stratum

Bond-labor was not new; in surplus-producing societies, in England and elsewhere, lifetime bondage had been the common condition of labor prior to capitalism. But the social structure of those times was based on production relationships in which each person was socially, occupationally and domestically fixed in place. Pre-capitalist bond-labor was tied by a two-way bond: the workers could not go away, but equally the master could not send them away. However, this relationship, which was essential to feudalism for instance, was inimical to capitalism. The historical mission of the bourgeoisie was to replace the two-way bondage of feudalism with the two-way freedom of the capitalist relation of production. The capitalist was free to fire the workers, and the workers were free to quit the job. The political corollary was that the bourgeoisie was the only propertied class ever to find advantage in proclaiming freedom as a human right.

Capitalism is a system whose normal operation is necessarily predicated upon the continuing presence of a mass of unattached labor-power of sufficient proportions that each capitalist can have access to exploitable labor-power, in season and out, in city or in countryside, and at a minimum labor cost. In newly settled territories, such a necessary reserve army of labor, though at first absent, would eventually be created[1] in the normal process of capitalist development, as a result of: immigration induced by higher wages caused by the shortage of wage labor; increased productivity of labor, resulting from the use of improved techniques and instruments of labor; the normal process of squeezing out the small or less efficient owners and making wage laborers of them by force of circumstance; and the natural increase of the dependent laboring population.[2]

But the situation in which the Anglo-American plantation bourgeoisie found itself in the 1620s, seeking to preserve its profitable tobacco monoculture in the face of the declining price of tobacco, did not permit – so far as its narrow class objectives were concerned – waiting for longer-term solutions.

Since the freedom of the capitalist to fire the workers is predicated on the freedom of the worker to leave the employer, the plantation bourgeoisie created a peculiar contradiction with respect to the free flow of capital within its system by reducing plantation laborers to bondage. The plantations, being capitalist enterprises, were subject to the normal crises of overproduction. As capitalist monocultural enterprises, they were furthermore subject in an extraordinary degree to the vagaries of the world market. Even in times of a generally satisfactory market, natural calamities, wars, or inimical governmental administration inevitably brought business failures and the abandonment or dissolution of individual enterprises in their wake. In the normal course of capitalist events, individual reverses of fortune require liquidation of enterprises, and the normal procedure in such circumstances is to "let the workers go," that is, to discharge them. But the very purpose of bond-servitude is to see to it that the workers are not "let go"; and a system of laws, courts, prosecutions, constabulary, punishments, etcetera, is instituted to enforce that principle. The plantation bourgeoisie dealt with this contradiction by establishing a one-way bondage, in which the laborer could not end the tie to the capitalist simply by his own volition; but the capitalist could end the tie with the worker. In the solution imposed by the plantation bourgeoisie, the unpaid aspect was designed to meet the need to lower labor costs, the long-term bondage was the surrogate for the nonexistent unemployed labor reserve, and the chattel aspect of the new system of labor relations made it operable by satisfying the functional necessity for the free flow of capital.

An Ominous New Word Appears – "Assign"

In attempting to fix the point in time at which the unambiguous commitment to chattelization began, it is helpful to take note of the first appearance of the term "assign" in relation to laborers. To "assign" means, in law, "to make over to another; to transfer a claim, right or property." The appearance of this term in relation to the change of a laborer from the service of one employer, or master, to another betokens the chattel status of the laborer. No longer is the contract for labor an agreement entered into between the laborer and the employer; it is rather a transacation between two employers, in which the laborer transferred, "assigned," has no more participation than would be had by an ear-cropped hog, or a hundredweight of tobacco, sold by one owner to another.

Between January and June 1622, the Virginia Company established a standard patent form.[3] The form carried a provision that the laborers transported under the patent could not be appropriated by the colony authorities for any purpose except the armed defense of the colony. What is significant in the context of the present discussion is that the Company guaranteed this protection not only to the original patentee but to his "heires and Assigns." Implicit here, and as would become explicit within less than four years, is the formal establishment of the legal right of masters to "assign" laborers, or to bequeath them. Already, of course, as early as 1616, a system had been established under which any private investor was entitled to fifty acres of Virginia land for himself for every worker whose transportation costs the investor paid.[4]

The case of Robert Coopy's indenture, dated September 1619, is the first recorded instance of a worker being obligated to work for a specified length of time without wages in order to pay off the cost of his transportation to Virginia.[5] Two years later, Miles Pricket, a skilled English tradesman, while still in England agreed with the Virginia Company to work at his salt-making trade in Virginia for one year "without any reward at all, which is here before paid him by his passage and apparell given him."[6] The one-year term was normal for England, but the worker's paying for his own passage was innovative. Prickett did come to Virginia, and in March 1625 was the holder of a 150-acre land patent in Elizabeth City.[7]

Retrospectively, these early incidents appear as preconditioning the reduction of laborers to chattels. But it was not until 1622 and 1623 that this portentous custom was established as the general condition for immigrant workers, formalizing their status as chattels. An analysis of a score of entries in the records of the time shows how the chattel aspect of bond-servitude was designed to adapt that contradictory form to capitalist categories of commodity exchange and free flow of capital.

Saving harmless the creditors of decedent. William Nuce, brother of Thomas Nuce and member of the Colony Council, died in late 1623. His estate was encumbered with debts, including one of £50 owed to George Sandys, and another of £30 to William Capps. Both debts were settled by the assignment of bond-laborers to the creditors.[8]

Disposal of unclaimed estate. William Nuce left eleven destitute laborers who had been in his charge as company employees, "some bound for 3 yeares, and few for 5, and most upon wages."[9] They were sold for two hundred pounds of tobacco each (not counting those four with whom George Sandys reported having such bad luck).[10]

Avoidance of bankruptcy. Mr Atkins, in order to relieve his straitened circumstances, sold all his bond-laborers.[11]

Option to buy. Thomas Flower was assigned to Henry Horner for three years. But it was stipulated by the Virginia General Court that if Horner decided to sell the man, John Procter would have first refusal.[12]

Capital market operations. In the prelude to the case cited immediately above, John Procter assured Henry Horner that he, Procter, would procure a servant for Horner, saying that "[H]ee [Procter] had daly Choice of men offered him." (Procter told Horner not to let the servant know he had been sold until they were embarked from England.)[13]

In January 1625, three servants of William Gauntlett were sold to Captain Tucker. The sale was recorded in the Minutes of the Virginia General Court.[14]

Velocity of circulation. Abraham Pelterre, sixteen-year-old apprentice, arrived in Virginia in 1624; within two years he had been sold hand to hand four times.[15]

Contract for delivery; penalty for failure to perform. Humphrey Rastill, merchant of London, contracted to deliver "one boye aged about fowerteene yeers ... To serve [Captain] Basse [in Virginia] or his assignes seaven Years," and bound himself "in the penaltye of forfeiture of five hundred pownd of Tobacco." On 3 January 1626, six weeks after the order had been due for delivery, on Basse's petition the Court ordered Rastill to make delivery by 31 January or pay the forfeit.[16]

Property loss: damages assessed. Thomas Savage, a young servant, was drowned in consequence of negligence on the part of a man who had use of him but was not his owner. The culprit was ordered to pay the owner three hundred pounds of tobacco as indemnity.[17]

Exploiting sudden entrepreneurial opportunities. John Robinson sailed from England in the winter of 1622–23, bringing bond-laborers with him, to settle in Virginia. He died *en route.* The ship's captain seized Robinson's property, including the bond-laborers, with the intention of selling all for his own account.[18]

The Privy Council in England in 1623 confirmed the gift to Governor Yeardley, of twenty tenants and twelve boys that had been left by the Company at its liquidation. Yeardley was authorized to "dispose of the said tenants and boys to his best advantage and benefit."[19]

The Colony Council in January 1627 divided up former Company tenants among the Council members themselves: eighteen to Yeardley; three each to five others; two to another; one to each of two others (including the Surveyor, Mr Claiborne, who was given William Joyce and two hundred pounds of tobacco).[20]

Liquidation of an estate. George Yeardley died in November 1627; at the time he was one of the richest men in the country, if not the very richest.[21] He left a will providing that, aside from his house and its contents, which was to go to his wife as it stood,

> the rest of my estate consisting of debts, servants [and African and African-American bond-laborers], cattle, or any other thing or things, commodities or profits whatsoever to me belonging or appertaining ... together with my plantation of one thousand acres of land at Warwicke River ... all and every part and parcell thereof [to be] sold to the best advantage for tobacco and the same to be transported as soon as may be ... into England, and there to be sold or turned into money.[22]

History's False Apologetics for Chattel Bond-servitude

The bourgeoisie, of whom the investors of capital in colonial schemes were a representative section,[23] could have had no more real hope of imposing in

England the kind of chattel bond-servitude they were to impose on English workers in Virginia than they had of finding the China Sea by sailing up the Potomac River.[24] The matter of labor relations was a settled question before the landing at Jamestown. But the Anglo-American plantation bourgeoisie seized on the devastation brought about by the Powhatan attack of 22 March 1622 to execute a plan for the chattelization of labor in Virginia Colony. There had been dark prophecy, indeed, in the London Company's response to the news of the 22 March assault on the colony. "[T]he shedding of this blood," the Company said, "wilbe the Seed of the Plantation," and it pledged "for the future ... instead of Tenants[,] sending you servants."[25] For from that seeding came the plantation of bondage, in the form known to history as "indentured servitude."

Early in Chapter 4, it was argued from authority that the monstrous social mutation in English class relations instituted in that tiny cell of Anglo-American society was a precondition for the subsequent variation of hereditary chattel bond-servitude imposed on African-Americans in Virginia.[26] Historical interpretations of the institution of "indentured servitude" in the Virginia Company period generally anticipate Winthrop D. Jordan's "unthinking decision" theory of the origin of racial slavery.[27] The initial imposition of chattel bond-servitude in continental Anglo-America is justified by its apologists using three propositions:

First proposition: There was a shortage of poor laborers in Virginia, and an abundance of them in England, so that between English laborers, who wanted employment, and plantation investors, who wanted to get rid of prohibitively costly tenantry and wage labor, a quid pro quo was agreed, according to which the employer paid the £6 cost of transportation from England and in exchange the worker agreed to be a chattel bond-laborer for a term of five years or so.[28]

Second proposition: This form of labor relations was not a sharp disjuncture, but was merely an unreflecting adaptation of some pre-existing form of master–servant relations prevailing in England.

Third proposition: Quid pro quo and English precedents aside, the imposition of chattel bond-servitude was "indispensable" for the "Colony's progress," a step opposed only by the "delicate-minded."[29]

The "quid pro quo" rationale

The argument for shifting the cost of immigrant transportation from the employer to the worker was in some ways analogous to the rationale advanced by the English ruling classes in the late fourteenth century.[30] Because of the plague-induced labor shortage, labor costs rose, and the ruling feudal class and the nascent bourgeoisie sought to recoup as much as possible of the increased cost by introducing a poll tax and increasing feudal dues exacted from the laboring people. Their rationale was that laborers "will not serve unless they receive excessive wages," and that as a result "[t]he wealth of the nation is in the hands of the workmen and labourers."[31] As rationales go, this was fully as valid as that advanced for indebting the laborers themselves for the cost of their delivery to Virginia. The English feudal lords in the fourteenth century used similar "logic" in trying to persuade "their people" of the impossibility of organizing production if the serf were freed. The great difference in the two cases was that the English laboring classes by the Great Rebellion of 1381 showed that the "impossible arrangement" was, after all, not impossible, while in Virgina rebellion, when it came, would fail.

Given the state of English economic and social development as it was at the beginning of the seventeenth century, under the Elizabethan Statute of Artificers (5 Eliz. 4), the "inevitable" thing would have been to employ free labor – tenants and wage laborers – in the continental colonies, not chattel bond-servitude. If the "inevitable" did not happen in Virginia Colony, it was because the ruling class was favored in the seventeenth-century Chesapeake tobacco colonies by a balance of class forces enabling them to promote their interests in a way they could not have done in England. And they could do so in spite of, rather than because of, the shortage of labor in the colonies. The "payment of passage" was simply a convenient excuse for a policy aimed at reducing labor costs and doing so in a way that was consistent with the free flow of capital. Incidentally, as Abbot Smith concluded, the "four or five years bondage was far more than they [the laborers] justly owed for the privilege of transport."[32] Indeed, producing at the average rate of around 712 pounds of tobacco a year, priced at 18d. per pound, even if the laborer survived only one year, he or she would have repaid more than seven times his or her £6 transportation cost.[33] The real consideration was therefore not the recovery by the employer of the cost of the laborer's transportation, but rather the fastening of a multi-year unpaid bondage on the worker by the fiction of the "debt" for passage.

The contrast of labor-supply situations in Holland and England has been discussed in Chapter 1. There appears to be an instructive corresponding contrast in the Dutch attitude toward binding immigrant workers to long periods of unpaid servitude for the cost of their transportation. On 10 July 1638, Hans Hansen Norman and Andreis Hudde entered into a partnership to raise tobacco "upon the flatland of the Island of Manhates" in New Amsterdam. Hudde was to return to Holland and from there to send to Hudde in New Amsterdam "six or eight persons with implements required" for their plantation. It was agreed that the partners would share the expense of "transportation and engaging them" and of providing them with dwellings and victuals.[34] Dutch ship's captain David Pieterzoon de Vries, who was engaged in the American trade at that same time, despised the bond-labor trade of the English, "a villainous people . . . [who] would sell their own fathers for servants in the Islands."[35]

Bond-servitude was not an adaptation of English practice

The imposition of chattel bondage cannot be regarded as an unreflecting adaptation of English precedents. The oppressiveness of the social and legal conditions of the English workers was outlined in Chapter 2 of this volume.[36] But laborers were not to be made unpaid chattels. Except for vagabonds, they had the legal presumption of liberty, a point they themselves had made by rebellion. Except for apprentices and the parish poor, workers were presumed to be self-supporting and bound by yearly contracts, with the provision for three months' notice of non-renewal. The contract was legally enforceable by civil sanctions, including the requirement of posting bond.[37]

Under the bond-labor system of Virginia Colony, the worker was presumed to be non-self-supporting; if taken up outside his or her owner's plantation without the owner's permission, the laborer, already bound to four or five years of unpaid bondage, was returned to that master and subjected to a further extension of his or her servitude. Above all, the Virginia labor system repudiated the English master–servant law by reducing laborers to chattels.

Nor can the origin of plantation chattel bond-servitude be explained by reference to English apprenticeship.[38] Confirmation on this point is to be found in a opinion (citing precedents) written in 1769 by George Mason as a member of the Virginia General Court: "[W]herever there was a trust it could not be transferred ... [as in] the case of an apprentice."[39] Under English law, "The binding was to the *man*, to learn *his* art, and serve *him*" and therefore the apprentice was not assignable to a third party, not even the executor of the will of a master who had died.[40]

Rather than being "a natural outgrowth"[41] of English tradition, chattel bond-servitude in Virginia Colony was as strange to the social order in England after the middle of the sixteenth century as *Nicotiniana tabacum* was to the soil of England before that time;[42] and as inimical to democratic development in continental Anglo-America as smoking tobacco is to the healthy human organism.

Was it inevitable? Was it progress?

Just as historians of the eighteenth century have chosen to see the hereditary chattel bondage of African-Americans as a paradoxical requisite for the emergence of the United States Constitutional liberties,[43] historians of seventeenth-century Virginia almost unanimously, so far as I have discovered, regard the "innovation" of "indentured servitude" as an indispensable condition for the progressive development of that first Anglo-American colony. It is most remarkable that of the interpreters of seventeenth-century Virginian history only one – Philip Alexander Bruce – has ever undertaken a systematic substantiation of that concept.

Here is a summary of Bruce's argument:[44]

The survival of the colony depended upon its being able to supply exports for the English market of sufficient value to pay for the colony's needs for English goods. The economy of the colony was necessarily shaped by its immediate economic interests. Tobacco alone would serve both of those purposes. Since maize – Indian corn – was not then appealing to the European palate, wheat was the nearest possible export rival to tobacco. But wheat required more land for the employment of a given amount of labor for the production of equal exchange-value in tobacco, and much more labor for clearing of the forested land for its profitable exploitation; furthermore, wheat in storage was much more vulnerable to rat and other infestation and required much larger ship tonnage for delivery than did tobacco of equal value.

In order to make profitable use of land acquired by multiple headrights or the equivalent by other means, the owner had to employ more labor than that of his immediate family. Tenantry was not adaptable for this purpose because landowners were not eager to rent out newly cleared land whose fertility would be exhausted in three years, and tenants were not willing to lease land that was already overworked when they could take out patents on land of their own at a nominal quit-rent of two shillings per hundred acres.[45] Labor being in short supply, wage laborers commanded such high wages that they too would have good prospects of acquiring land of their own, and thus of ceasing to be available for proletarian service.

Chattel bondage as the basic general form of production relations was therefore indispensable for the progress of the colony of Virginia.

It seems reasonable to believe that Bruce was aware that tenantry became a significant part of the agricultural economy in eighteenth-century Chesapeake. Allan Kulikoff's study indicates that in southern Maryland and the Northern Neck and Fairfax County in Virginia one-third to half of the land was occupied by tenants.[46] In Virginia, on new ground the first tenant was excused from paying rent for the first two years of the lease. This exemption for payment of fees and rent was "a most advantageous arrangement," writes Willard Bliss, so that, far from being unfeasible, "tenancy was a logical solution" to planters' problems.[47] The rise of tenancy that began in Virginia early in the eighteenth century, particularly in the Northern Neck, was a function of plantation capitalism, which was by then recruiting its main productive labor from African and African-American bond-laborers.[48] The most directly profitable exploitation of their labor was in the production of tobacco, not in clearing new ground, pulling stumps, ditching, fencing, etcetera. For that work, rent-paying tenants were to be employed.

In Maryland, English and other European laborers who survived their servitude were formally entitled to a fifty-acre headright, but to acquire the promised land was "simply impracticable."[49] They generally became tenants of landlords who needed to have their land cleared and otherwise improved for use as tobacco plantation land, or to build up their equity for speculative purposes.[50] In Prince George's County one-third of the householders were tenants by 1705.[51]

These facts would seem to cast doubt on Bruce's argument that the clearing of land could not have been done on the basis of tenancy. The key in both the seventeenth and eighteenth centuries was neither technical difficulty nor any economic impossibility of getting tenants to clear the land, but the owners' calculation of the rate of profit. In the seventeenth century the cheapest way to clear land was not by using tenants, but by using bond-laborers; in the eighteenth century, the cheapest way to clear land was not by using bond-laborers, but by using tenants. It was the work of Adam Smith's "invisible hand,"[52] and, in today's popular phrase, the logic of the "bottom line."

But what was the "bottom line" to the people on the bottom, who were being degraded from tenants and wage laborers to chattels? What good to them was an "invisible hand" systematically dealing from the bottom of the deck against the laboring class? Bruce answers with one word, "progress"; yet even as he does so, he concedes that after all bond-servitude was not inevitable, although he contends the alternative would have been undesirable. Without chattel bondage, he says:

> [t]he surface of the colony would have been covered with a succession of small estates, many of which would have fallen into a condition of absolute neglect as soon as their fertility had disappeared, their owners having sued out patents to virgin lands in other localities as likely to yield large returns to the cultivator. ... [The] Colony's progress would have been slow. Virginia without [chattel bond-] laborers from England and without slaves would have become a community of peasant proprietors, each clearing and working his ground with his own hands and with the aid of his immediate family.[53]

However unpalatable such an alternative may have seemed to Bruce, there were others who showed by word and deed over a span of two and a half centuries in Virginia that they would have assessed the matter differently, had they been given the choice between the life of peasant proprietors and that of unpaid chattel bond-laborers.[54] In New England an alternative practice was followed, as will be discussed in Chapter 9.

Francis Bacon's Alternative Vision: "Of Plantations"

Bruce takes note of Sir Francis Bacon's essay "Of Plantations," dated 1625, the year after the dissolution of the Virginia Company;[55] but while he does not attempt to discuss it in detail, he obviously does not find it persuasive.[56]

> Planting of countries is like planting of woods [wrote Sir Francis]; for you must take into account to lose almost twenty years profit, and expect your recompense in the end; for the principal thing that hath been the destruction of most plantations, has been the hasty drawing of profit in the first years. It is true, speedy profit is not to be neglected, as may stand with the good of the plantation, but not farther.

To this end, it was essential, Bacon said, to keep control out of the hands of the merchants, the most typical form of bourgeois life at that time, "for they look ever to the present gain."[57] The labor of the colonists should be first turned to the cultivation of native plants (among other things, Bacon mentions maize) in order to assure the colony's food supply. Bacon further advised, "Let the main part of the ground employed to gardens or corn be a common stock; and to be laid in and stored up, and then delivered out in proportions." Next, native products should be developed as commodities to be exchanged for goods that must be imported by the colony – but not, Bacon warned, "to the untimely prejudice of the main business; as it hath fared with tobacco in Virginia."[58]

Bacon's thesis seems to have anticipated Bruce's argument, and to refute in advance any attempt to justify the dominance of "immediate needs" and the plantation monocultural base of colonial development.

The record itself – the public and private correspondence, the Company and colony policy statements, laws and regulations, the court proceedings and decrees – presents much evidence of contradictory views within the ruling councils during the Company period. The Company and colony officials inveigh against the inordinate attention given to tobacco growing, while presiding over the ineradicable establishment of the tobacco monoculture, using tobacco for money, squabbling over its exchange-value, staking all on the "tobacco contract." The Company expresses concern over the abuse of the rights of servants while pressing helpless young people in England for service in the plantation. The Company in London continues to send boatloads of emigrants to Virginia without the proper complement of supplies to tide them over till their first crops can be harvested, while the Colony Council in Virginia demands that settlers not be sent without provisions. The colony officials complain that too many ill-provisioned laborers are being sent, and yet at the same time, they deplore the scarcity of "servants . . . our principal wealth," and the high wages due to that scarcity.

In puzzling out such apparent antinomies of sentiment, one must make due allowance for the effect of partisan conflicts within the Virginia Company. But as Craven points out, indictments of the treatment of laborers and tenants, or criticism of the tobacco contract with the king,[59] may have been to some extent inspired by factional interests, but that does not invalidate them.[60] When the dust had settled, the transformation of production relations by "changing tenants to servants" had developed from a proposal by the Virginia Colony Council into the prevailing policy of the Anglo-American plantation bourgeoisie as a whole, London "adventurers" as well as Virginia "planters." In all the documents involved in the transfer of the affairs of the colony to royal control, no trace remains of the urgent concern with registration of contracts, abuse of servants, etcetera, ideas that the worried friends and kindred of those gone to Virginia had pressed on the Company Court.

Some Knew It Was Wrong

Nevertheless, the substantial opposition within the Company to the chattelization of labor provides strong evidence that the options for monoculture and bond-servitude were not "unthinking decisions." The "quid pro quo" rationale for chattel bond-servitude was denounced as repugnant to English constitutional liberties and common law,[61] and to the explicit terms of the Royal Charter for the Virginia colony.[62] This concern was reflected in the "exceeding discontent and griefe [of] divers persons coming daylie from the farthest partes of England to enquire of friends and Kindred gonn to Virginia."[63] In October 1622, the Virginia Company established a Committee on Petitions, one of whose tasks was to consider wrongs done to "servants" sent to Virginia,[64]

> It beinge observed here that divers old Planters and others did allure and beguile divers younge persons and others (ignorant and unskillfull in such matters) to serve them upon intollerable and unchristianlike conditions upon promises of such rewardes and recompense, as they were in no wayes able to performe nor ever meant.

First among the "abuses in Carriing over of Servants into Virginia" was the following:[65]

> divers ungodly people that have onely respect of their owne profitt do allure and entice younge and simple people to be at the whole charge of transportinge themselves and yet for divers years to binde themselves Servants to them . . .

The remedy was not to be found at that time by strict regulation and control of emigration to Virginia, with a written contract for every worker of which a copy would be kept in Company files.[66] If, in those famine years, 1622–23, laborers had come to Virginia with a contract sealed with seven seals, they would still have surely starved if they could not pay twenty shillings for a bushel of corn, unless they were able to find a master who would *let* them work for mere corn diet and, perhaps, a place to sleep.

It was not the way it was supposed to be. Even those who had never heard of the Statute of Artificers knew as much. "Sold . . . like a damd slave!" raged Thomas Best, cursing his lot.[67] Henry Brigg had come to Virginia having Mr Atkins's promise that Brigg would never serve any other master. But now, in the spring of 1623, he wrote his brother, who had been witness to the promise, "my Master Atkins hath sold me & the rest of my Fellowes."[68]

Young Abraham Pelterre was favored to have a mother in England with some influence with her aldermen. They protested with some effect when they learned that Abraham was being sold from hand to hand in Virginia contrary to the proper conditions of apprenticeship.[69] They knew it was wrong.

Jane Dickinson knew that it was not a thing that could happen in England, and she asked the General Court to see it her way. She had come to Virginia in 1620 with her husband Ralph, a seven-year tenant-at-halves for Nicholas

Hide. Her husband was killed in the attack of 22 March 1622, and she was taken captive by the Indians. After ten months, she and a number of other captives were released for small ransoms. Jane's master had died in the meantime. Dr John Pott, who paid her ransom, two pounds of glass beads, demanded that she serve him as a bond-laborer for the unexpired time of her husband's engagement, saying that she was doubly bound to his service by the two pounds of glass laid out for her ransom. The only alternative, he told her, was to buy herself from him with 150 pounds of tobacco[70] (at the prevailing price of 18*d*. per pound, this would have been worth nearly twice the £6 cost of her transportation from England).

John Loyde knew that in England if a master died his apprentice was freed, or, perhaps, remained bound to the master's widow. After paying his master £30 to be taken on as an apprentice, and receiving his copy of the appropriate papers for the arrangement, Loyde embarked for Virginia with his master, taking with him the terms of his apprenticeship in writing. His master died *en route*, but the ship's captain had taken his papers that would have established his free status. Without them, Loyde was subject to being sold by the ship's captain into chattel bondage. Loyde sued in court to recover the papers.[71]

William Weston knew it was wrong. In November 1625, he was fined 250 pounds of good merchantable tobacco for failing to bring a servant into Virginia for Robert Thresher. The next month Weston was before the General Court again, and it was testified that, when again asked to bring servants to Virginia

> Mr Weston replied he would bring none, if he would give him a hundred pownde. Mr Newman [who wanted to place an order] asked him why. And Mr Weston replied that ... servants were sold here upp and down like horses, and therefore he held it not lawfull to carry any.[72]

John Joyce, bond-laborer, knew in his aching bones that it was not right; and in August 1626 he sought to reestablish by direct action the capitalist principle of two-way freedom of labor relations. He did not take his case to the General Court, however, preferring the mercy of the wilderness. (Captured by the colony authorities, as noted in Chapter 5, he had the distinction of being the first such fugitive bond-laborer who is recorded as being sentenced to an extension of his servitude time as punishment for his offense. He had six months added to his term with his master, and at the completion of that extended term he was to serve five years more as bond-servant to the colony authorities. It was all to begin with a brutal lashing of thirty stripes.)[73]

And so it came to pass that seventy-five years after the institution of the labor relations principles of the Statute of Artificers, when the good ship *Tristram and Jane* arrived in Virginia in 1637, all but two of its seventy-six passengers were bond-laborers to be offered for sale.[74] The following year, Colony Secretary Richard Kemp reported to the English government, "Of hundreds of people who arrive in the colony yearly, scarce any but are brought in as merchandize for sale."[75]

The Problem of Social Control Enters a New Context

There was another side to the coin of the option by the tobacco bourgeoisie for the anomalous system of bond-servitude as the basis of capitalist production in Virginia Colony. In the sixteenth century, as has been discussed, the English governing classes made a deliberate decision to preserve a section of the peasantry from dispossession by enclosures, in order to maintain the yeomanry as a major element in the intermediate social control stratum essential to a society without an expensive large standing army.[76] The military regime that the Virginia Company first installed under governors Gates and Dale, for all its severity, proved ultimately ineffective. That particular variant of social control had to be superseded because of defiance of the limitations on tobacco cultivation by laboring-class tenants – Rolfe's "Farmors" – who represented the potential yeoman-like recruits for an intermediate social control stratum for the colony.[77]

Following their instinct for "present profit," the plantation bourgeoisie on the Tobacco Coast forgot or disregarded the lesson taught by the history of the reign of Henry VII and the deliberate decision to preserve a forty-shilling freehold yeomanry.[78] Instead, convinced that the tenant class was an "absurdity"[79] from the standpoint of profit making in a declining tobacco market, the Adventurers and Planters decided to destroy the tenantry as a luxury they could not afford.

Perhaps there was special significance in the fact that it was a son of the yeoman class, Captain John Smith, who sounded the warning for those who were forsaking the wisdom of insuring the existence of an adequate yeomanry. Condemning the traders in bond-labor, he said, "it were better they were made such merchandize themselves, [than] suffered any longer to use that trade." That practice, said Smith prophetically, was a defect "sufficient to bring a well setled Common-wealth to misery, much more *Virginia*."[80]

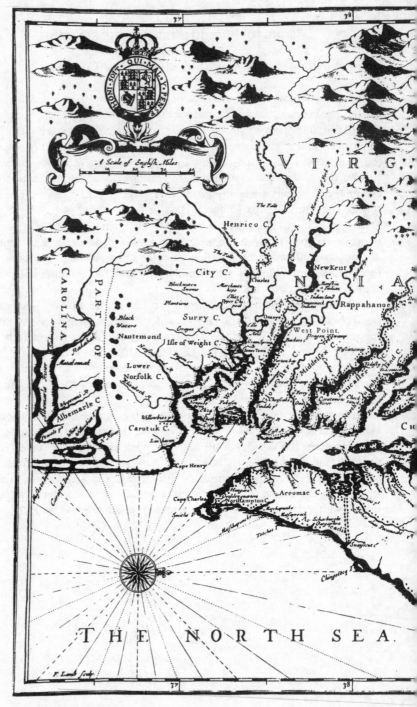

Figure 1 Map of the Chesapeake region, *circa* 1700

This map of Virginia and Maryland was graciously copied for me by the Map Division of the New Y
1629). This engraving of the map by Francis Lamb, although not dated, would seem to represent an "
abbreviated as "C."). Virginia was not divided into counties (first called "shires") until 1634. The New Y
formed in 1669, and does not mention any of the next three counties, which were formed in 1691, it se
parallel to the lines of almost all of the printed text), it shows details with great clarity. The Atlantic Oc
came to the Chesapeake by sailing north from the West Indies. I myself have labeled West Point, the reg
slavery" in 1676 (see Chapter 11).

 A MAP OF
VIRGINIA
AND
MARYLAND.

*Sold by Thomas Baffet in Fleetfreet
and Richard Chifwell in S.t Pauls
Church yard.*

MA

RY

Stafford C.

Brents

Mchqurin R

Patowmeck Falls

Nameffabmk

Pafcattaway

Maflerkont

betwene R

Wighcomanco

Anne Arundel

Horington

Minquaas

BAY

Sharpe I.

Oxford

Talbot C.

Indian Towns

Horn bay

Sassquahana
Ferre

Baltimore
Town

Baltimore M

Cecil fall

Sassquahana

Onsftego River

Konekotays

Tockwoghs

LAND.

Cæcil C.

Worlds end

Hatten

New
Castle

Chriftians c.

Martins pt

Minquaas

Delawar
Bay

Elfborgh

Narcait's pinck

Opland

Monymont

Hinlope

Kahanfink Indians

Sauwan

C. Maye

PART OF

NEW IARSY.

ıblic Library Research Libraries, whose map catalog identifies the cartographer as John Speed (1542–
ıted" version of Speed's work, to judge, for instance, from its identification of counties ("County" being
ıblic Library catalog tentatively assigns "1666?" to this version. But since it includes Middlesex County,
at this map should be dated sometime in the 1669–91 period. Despite its orientation (the North arrow is
here called "The North Sea," the designation presumably given to these waters by the English who first
which "four hundred English and Negroes in Armes" joined in the demand for "freedom from their

Figure 2 List of governors of Colonial Virginia

An attempt has been made to give as nearly as possible the dates of actual service of each of the men who acted as colonial governor in Virginia. The date of commission is usually much earlier.

President of the Council in Virginia

Edward-Maria Wingfield, May 14–September 10, 1607.
John Ratcliffe, September 10, 1607–September 10?, 1608.
John Smith, September 10, 1608–September 10?, 1609.
George Percy, September 10?, 1609–May 23, 1610.

The Virginia Company

Thomas West, Third Lord De La Warr, Governor. February 28, 1610–June 7, 1618.
Sir Thomas Gates, Lieutenant-Governor. May 23–June 10, 1610.
Thomas West, Lord De La Warr, Governor. June 10, 1610–March 28, 1611.
George Percy, Deputy-Governor. March 28–May 19, 1611.
Sir Thomas Dale, Deputy-Governor. May 19–August 2?, 1611.
Sir Thomas Gates, Lieutenant-Governor. August 2?, 1611–c. March 1, 1614.
Sir Thomas Dale, Deputy-Governor, c. March 1, 1614–April?, 1616.
George Yeardley, Deputy-Governor. April?, 1616–May 15, 1617.
Samuel Argall, *Present* Governor. May 15, 1617–c. April 10, 1619.
Nathaniel Powell, Deputy-Governor. c. April 10–18, 1619.
Sir George Yeardley, Governor. April 18, 1619–November 18, 1621.
Sir Francis Wyatt, Governor. November 18, 1621–c. May 17, 1626.

Royal Province

Sir George Yeardley. May?, 1626–November 13, 1627.
Francis West. November 14, 1627–c. March, 1629.
Doctor John Pott. March 5, 1629–March?, 1630.
Sir John Harvey. March?, 1630–April 28, 1635.
John West. May 7, 1635–January 18, 1637.
Sir John Harvey. January 18, 1637–November?, 1639.
Sir Francis Wyatt. November?, 1639–February, 1642.
Sir William Berkeley. February, 1642–March 12, 1652.
(Richard Kemp, Deputy-Governor. June, 1644–June 7, 1645.)

The Commonwealth

Richard Bennett. April 30, 1652–March 31, 1655.
Edward Digges. March 31, 1655–December, 1656.
Samuel Mathews. December, 1656–January, 1660.
Sir William Berkeley. March, 1660.

Royal Province

Sir William Berkeley. March, 1660–April 27, 1677.
(Francis Moryson, Deputy-Governor. April 30, 1661–November or December, 1662.)
Colonel Herbert Jeffreys, Lieutenant-Governor. April 27, 1677–December 17, 1678.
Thomas Lord Culpeper, Governor. July 20, 1677–August, 1683.

(Sir Henry Chicheley, Deputy-Governor. December 30, 1678–May 10, 1680; August 11, 1680–December 1, 1682.)

(Nicholas Spencer, Deputy-Governor. May 22, 1683–February 21, 1684.)

Francis, Lord Howard, Fifth Baron of Effingham, Governor. February 21, 1684–March 1, 1692.

(Nathaniel Bacon, Sr., Deputy-Governor. June 19–c. September, 1684; July 1,–c. September 1, 1687; February 27?, 1689–June 3, 1690.)

Francis Nicholson, Lieutenant-Governor. June 3, 1690–September 20, 1692.

Sir Edmund Andros, Governor. September 20, 1692–December 9?, 1698.

(Ralph Wormeley, Deputy-Governor. September 25–c. October 6, 1693.)

·Francis Nicholson, Governor. December 9, 1698–August 15, 1705.

(William Byrd, Deputy-Governor. September 4–October 24, 1700; April 26–June, 1703; August 9–September 12–28, 1704.)

Lord George Hamilton, Earl of Orkney, Governor. 1704–January 29, 1737.

Edward Nott, Lieutenant-Governor. August 15, 1705–August 23, 1706.

(Edmund Jenings, Deputy-Governor. August 27, 1706–June 23, 1710.)

(Robert Hunter was made Lieutenant-Governor April 22, 1707, but never took his office.)

Alexander Spotswood, Lieutenant-Governor. June 23, 1710–September 25?, 1722.

Hugh Drysdale, Lieutenant-Governor. September 25, 1722–July 22, 1726.

(Robert Carter, Deputy-Governor. July, 1726–September 11, 1727.)

William Gooch, Lieutenant-Governor. September 11, 1727–June 20, 1749.

(Reverend James Blair, Deputy-Governor. October 15, 1740–July?, 1741.)

William Anne Keppel, Second Earl of Albemarle, Governor. October 6, 1737–December 22, 1754.

(John Robinson, Sr., Deputy-Governor. June 20–September 5, 1749.)

(Thomas Lee, Deputy-Governor. September 5, 1749–November 14, 1750.)

(Lewis Burwell, Deputy-Governor. November 14, 1750–November 21, 1751.)

Robert Dinwiddie, Lieutenant-Governor. November 21, 1751–January 2–12, 1758.

(John Blair, Deputy-Governor. January–June 7, 1758.)

John Campbell, Fourth Earl of Loudoun, Governor. March 8, 1756–December 30, 1757.

Sir Jeffrey Amherst, Governor. September 25, 1759–1768.

Francis Fauquier, Lieutenant-Governor. June 7, 1758–March 3, 1768.

(John Blair, Acting-Governor. March 4–October 26, 1768.)

Norborne Berkeley, Baron de Botetourt, Governor. October 26, 1768–October 15, 1770.

(William Nelson, Acting-Governor. October 15, 1770–September 25, 1771.)

John Murray, Fourth Earl of Dunmore, Governor. September 25, 1771–May 6, 1776.

The State

Patrick Henry. July 5, 1776–June 1, 1779.

Thomas Jefferson. June 1, 1779–June 12, 1781.

Thomas Nelson. June 12, 1781–November 30, 1781.

Benjamin Harrison. November 30, 1781–November 30, 1784.

Source: William W. Abbot, *A Virginia Chronology, 1585–1783*, Richmond, 1957, pp. 74–6

Figure 3 Virginia counties, and dates of their formation

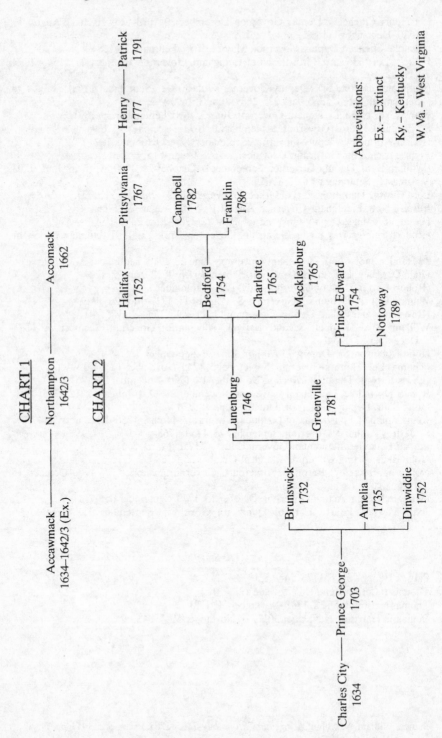

Abbreviations:

Ex. – Extinct

Ky. – Kentucky

W. Va. – West Virginia

CHART 1

Accawmack — Northampton — Accomack
1634–1642/3 (Ex.) 1642/3 1662

CHART 2

Patrick
1791

Henry
1777

Pittsylvania
1767

Campbell
1782

Franklin
1786

Halifax
1752

Bedford
1754

Charlotte
1765

Mecklenburg
1765

Prince Edward
1754

Nottoway
1789

Lunenburg
1746

Greenville
1781

Brunswick
1732

Amelia
1735

Dinwiddie
1752

Prince George
1703

Charles City
1634

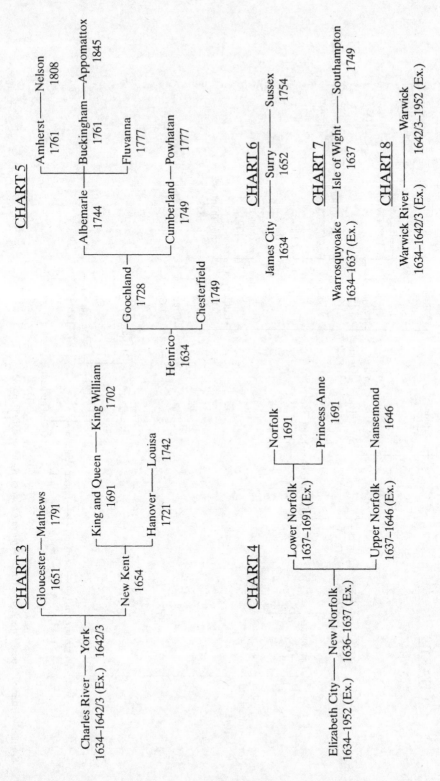

CHART 3

Charles River ——— York
1634–1642/3 (Ex.)   1642/3

Gloucester ——— Mathews
1651   1791

New Kent
1654

King and Queen ——— King William
1691   1702

Hanover ——— Louisa
1721   1742

CHART 4

Elizabeth City ——— New Norfolk
1634–1952 (Ex.)   1636–1637 (Ex.)

Lower Norfolk
1637–1691 (Ex.)

Upper Norfolk
1637–1646 (Ex.)

Norfolk
1691

Princess Anne
1691

Nansemond
1646

CHART 5

Henrico
1634

Goochland
1728

Chesterfield
1749

Albemarle
1744

Cumberland ——— Powhatan
1749   1777

Amherst ——— Nelson
1761   1808

Buckingham ——— Appomattox
1761   1845

Fluvanna
1777

CHART 6

James City ——— Surry ——— Sussex
1634   1652   1754

CHART 7

Warrosquyoake ——— Isle of Wight ——— Southampton
1634–1637 (Ex.)   1637   1749

CHART 8

Warwick River ——— Warwick
1634–1642/3 (Ex.)   1642/3–1952 (Ex.)

115

CHART 9

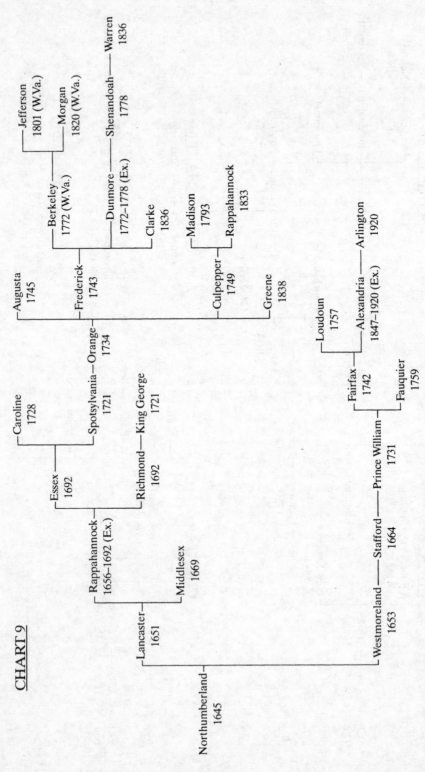

Source: Martha W. Hiden, *How Justice Grew: Virginia Counties*, Richmond, 1957, pp. 83–5

PART THREE
Road to Rebellion

7

Bond-labor: Enduring . . .

Together with the insubstantiality of the intermediate stratum, the oppressive conditions of the bond-laborers and their resistance to those conditions constitute the most significant social factors that contributed to that pivotal historic event called Bacon's Rebellion. That resistance was a challenge to the very economic basis of the society: the chattel bond-labor form of master–servant relations. Equally significant from the standpoint of the study of the origin of racial slavery is the fact that the record of this period of labor history shows no "white worker" component.

The "Servant Trade": a New Branch of Free Enterprise

The "servant trade," as it came to be called, that is, the export of chattel laborers from Europe, sprang up as a response to the profit-making needs of the tobacco business, and it soon became a special branch of commerce; these bond-laborers "provided a convenient cargo for ships going to the plantations to fetch tobacco, sugar, and the other raw products available,' writes A. E. Smith: "[T]he real stimulus to emigration was not the desire of servants to go to America, but the desire of merchants to secure them as cargo."[1] Investors found the trade attractive. In England, votaries of what today is euphemized as "market principles" sold English men and women for £2 per head (or even less, sometimes) if they had them already in captivity as convicts[2] or workhouse inmates.[3]

In all, some 92,000 European immigrants were brought to Virginia and Maryland between 1607 and 1682, the great majority being sent to Virginia. More than three-quarters of them were chattel bond-laborers, the great majority of them English.[4] In 1676, it was Governor Berkeley's estimate that about 1,500 European chattel bond-laborers were then arriving in Virginia yearly, "the majority English, with a few Scots and fewer Irish."[5] Others were brought to the Chesapeake after the defeat of the Catholic cause in 1689, and they were for a time especially worrisome to the colonial authorities for fear that they might "confederate with the Negroes," as Francis Nicholson warned when he was Governor of Maryland.[6]

Volunteer emigrant bond-laborers were those who boarded ship for America of their own conscious will, although in most cases that will was shaped by extreme hardship and defeat at home, or by self-delusion about the prospect of prospering in the new land. Of those who came thus voluntarily in the seventeenth century, some arrived with written contracts, called "indentures," setting forth the names of their owners, the duration of their periods of servitude, and perhaps some "consideration," or "freedom dues," that their owners were to give the laborers upon the completion of their terms. In some cases the indenture was between the worker and the particular plantation owner whom he or she was to serve in the colony. More frequently, the indenture was arranged with a merchant, ship's captain, or other middleman, who sold the laborer to the highest bidder and then signed over the indenture to the new owner.[7] As early as 1635 a standard indenture form was in use with blank spaces to be filled in with the names of the parties and witnesses.[8]

The involuntary immigrant bond-laborers who came from Europe may also be considered in two categories. There were those who came under sentence as convicted felons and political prisoners, including captives taken in civil war or rebellion in England, Scotland[9] and Ireland.[10] In 1664 a committee on plantation labor supply problems urged the Council for Trade and Plantations (subsequently to be known by various names, and ultimately as the Board of Trade) to have more systematic resort to this and other forms of recruitment of plantation bond-labor. Convicts should be sent to serve seven or fourteen years, said the Committee, according to the seriousness of their offenses. "Sturdy Beggers and Gipsies and other Wanderers" who could not be forced into a settled way of life should "be sent to the plantations for five years under the conditions of Servants." From among the unemployed poor of the towns, villages and parishes of England, some should be "invited or compelled" to emigrate to serve as unpaid bond-laborers "in Jamaica."[11]

The involuntary shipment of still others to the Anglo-Americans colonies, lacking even the color of law, depended on crimps and "Spirits" (so called because they "spirited" their victims away from their native places) who obtained their unwitting victims either by kidnapping or by gross and deliberate deception.[12] The latter and more common method was noted in an English pamphlet published in 1649:

> The usual way of getting servants, hath been by a sort of men nick-named Spirits, who take up all the idle, lazie, simple people they can intice ... who are persuaded by these Spirits, they shall goe into a place where food shall drop into their mouthes. ... The servants are taken up ... and by them [the Spirits] put in Cookes houses about Saint Katherines, where being once entered, [they] are kept as Prisoners until a Master fetches them off.[13]

The Council for Trade and Plantations report to which reference is made above acknowledged the leading part played by the "Spirits," who "receive a reward from the persons who employed them."[14] Like the beaver and deer skin trade that was proving so profitable in the colonies, the English bond-labor supply system in the seventeenth century had its subdivisions. William Haverland was a hunter and trapper, and was accounted a most aggressive one.[15] His role was that of initial seducer and captor of the laborer. Thomas Stone, one of Haverland's prey, told of the experience. One day late in November 1670, he was accosted in a London street by Haverland whom he did not know, but who represented himself to be a native of Stone's own county. By deceit coupled with brute force, Haverland delivered the besotted Thomas to a ship's captain to be taken and sold as a plantation laborer in America. [16]

John Steward and William Thiew, on the other hand, were traders. Since the late 1650s Steward had been buying from such men as Haverland such kidnap victims as Stone, at a price of twenty-five shillings a head. Thiew, another of Haverland's customers during this period, in just one year "spirited away" 840 persons.[17]

Besides the acquisition costs, there were other expenses, for storage, maintenance and transportation, which had to be borne by the entrepreneurs at various stages of the supply process. The cost of holding and maintaining a person for five or six weeks pending shipment came to £3.[18] Clothes provided for the prospective bond-laborer might cost £4, or possibly a little more.[19] But in 1649 this item was reckoned at £3 7s. 10d.;[20] and in 1631 the Essex overseers of the Poor "layd out in parill for two boys that were sent to Virginia, four pownde seven shillings three pence," which averages only £2 2s. 9½d. each.[21] In cases where the merchant and shipowner were one, the cost of transporting a bond-laborer came to about £3; otherwise, the owner of the laborer paid £5 or £6 for each worker's passage.[22]

The price per head of bond-labor delivered live in the plantation colonies varied considerably in response to fluctuations of supply and demand, but merchants could generally count on a profit of from 50 to 200 percent on the transaction.[23] Until 1683, captains of ships delivering European bond-laborers received an additional bonus, a fifty-acre head-right on each one, a claim that the shippers almost invariably sold rather than entering into the cultivation of tobacco themselves.[24] After that, the Virginia practice was followed, limiting such awards to those who used the bond-laborers to improve the land for which they had received patents within a limited period of time.[25]

Besides those regularly engaged in the servant trade, persons of means traveling to the colonies for any reason might be advised to take a few bond-laborers with them for use or sale, according to best advantage. The parents of young Thomas Verney, whom they were dispatching to Virginia, were assured by a supplier that such highly saleable human chattels could easily be secured. "If I were to send forty servants," he boasted, "I could have them here at a dayes warning." (Was he perhaps connected with such suppliers as the Essex Overseer of the Poor?) The cost would be £12 per head, presumably including the agent's own fee. If Verney decided not to stay in Virginia and use the head-rights to start up as a "planter," he could dispose of these chattels at a good profit to be applied against his own expenses.[26]

The shipment of convicts, as "His Majesty's passengers," to be plantation bond-laborers was an especially profitable branch of the trade since it was subsidized by the authorities in England. Although this practice proceeded systematically on a national scale under a law passed by Parliament in 1717, convicts were sent to the Chesapeake colonies in the seventeenth century. Those convicts who survived the voyage were sold by the ship's captain for his own or his employer's account. James Revel arrived in Virginia some time before 1680 at eighteen years of age, having been sentenced to fourteen years' bond-servitude. He later wrote recollections of his experiences, which began with the dockside marketing process. After a seven-week trip, the convicts were put ashore, where they were cleaned up to be made presentable to the prospective customers. The men and women were displayed separately, for "Examening like Horses."

> Some view'd our teeth, to see if they were good,
> Or fit to chew our hard and homely Food.
> If any like our look, our limbs, our trade,
> the Captain then good advantage made.[27]

As was sure to happen, the workings of "the invisible hand" of market forces led to the idea of further specialization. In 1683, Virginia capitalist William Fitzhugh proposed the establishment of a Virginia wholesale enterprise dealing in retailing ships' cargoes as a way of saving English shippers the loss of time and the expense of selling cargoes in the colony. Writing to business associates in London, Fitzhugh stressed the importance of the rate of turnover of capital in the formation of the annual rate of profit, saying, "a certain & sure Market, and easie charge & a quick Dispatch . . . is the life and profit of every trade."[28]

Domestic Sources of Bond-labor

Throughout the colonial period the maintenance of the plantation bond-labor supply was supplemented from domestic sources. For reasons already examined, the early notions of basing English colonial development on the labor of the Indians was short-lived.[29] Nevertheless, some Indians were employed on seventeenth-century tobacco plantations. In the early decades the Indian bond-laborers were mainly children, employed under rather strict limitations involving parental consent.[30] But beginning about 1660, Indian bond-laborers were drawn from the general population, although the Virginia Assembly decreed that they were not to serve "for any longer time than English of like ages should serve."[31] Their condition was worsened under a law passed in 1670 which required Indian bond-laborers to serve for twelve years, more than twice the term of English bond-laborers, and which required the Indian children to be bound until they reached the age of thirty, that is, six years longer than the usual servitude of underage English bond-laborers.[32] Early in

the period of Bacon's Rebellion, in June 1676, the Virginia Assembly authorized that "enemy Indians taken in war be held and accounted slaves dureing
life."[33] This policy was renewed the following year, after the defeat of the
rebellion, in order, it was said, to give the colonial soldiers "better encouragement to such service."[34] Six years later, planters were authorized to hold as
slaves for life Indians purchased from Indian tribes.[35]

For a brief period, Indian bond-laborers played "a considerable role" in the
economy of the tobacco colonies, but this was a phenomenon limited to the
eighth and ninth decades of the seventeenth century.[36] In 1691, the Virginia
Assembly passed a law that from that time forward "there be a free and open
trade for all persons at all times and at all places with all Indians whatsoever."[37]
This same law was re-enacted in 1705 and again in 1733.[38] But it was only after
more than a century of hereditary bondage of the descendants of Indian
women bond-laborers that Virginia courts suddenly discovered that this law,
which made no distinction between friendly and hostile Indians, as previous
laws had always done, and which made no exception as to social rank, was a
formal legal bar to enslavement of Indians in Virginia.[39]

Virginia-born African-Americans as a source of bond-labor

The main domestic source of bond-labor in the plantation colonies was by way
of the imposition of hereditary bond-servitude on African-Americans under
the system of racial slavery and white supremacy. Well before the end of the
colonial period the great majority of the bond-laborers in the plantation
colonies were American-born. In 1790, there were more than twice as many
African-American bond-laborers in the continental plantation colonies as had
come there from overseas in the entire colonial period.[40]

The plantation bourgeoisie had not achieved this condition, however, in the
seventeenth century; at that time most of the plantation laborers were limited-
term bond-laborers, a category composed in its great majority of European-
American immigrants. As far as the difference between limited-term and
lifetime bondage is concerned, that is a question that would have had no
practical significance in the early decades, when most of the bond-laborers did
not survive even their first year in Virginia.[41] Furthermore, the maintenance of
what some historians see fit to call a "dual [that is, black/white] labor
market,"[42] assuming it could have been done, would not have been (as the
phrase is) "cost-effective" in the early decades. One thing is certain: in the
census of 1624/25, taken at the end of the Company period, the colony's total
population of some 1,218 adults listed 507 "servants," of whom 23 were
"Negroes."[43]

Nevertheless, even before the yearning was made explicit in laws of the
early 1660s,[44] there was evidence of a desire on the part of some employers to
develop this source of added unpaid labor time by subjecting African-
Americans to lifetime hereditary bond-servitude. There were also early
instances of legislative and judicial inclinations in this direction.[45] After 1662

under Virginia law and after 1664 under Maryland law, the plantation bourgeoisie could begin to realize profits on the sale and exploitation of laborers born in the tobacco colonies.[46]

The production of a tobacco crop was a most labor-intensive process. Draft animals were not in general use during the seventeenth century.[47] At mid-seventeenth century, when the number of productive workers in Virginia was approaching 7,000,[48] there were no more than 150 plows in the colony.[49] The implements were the human hand[50] for sowing the seedbed and covering it, and for transplanting the seedling to the "hills," spaced at four-foot intervals, and dug with a long-bladed hilling hoe; the wide, sharp weeding hoe for keeping clear the ground between the plants; the tobacco knife for cutting off the top of the plant when the desired number of leaves had put forth; the human hand for pulling the horn worms from the plant, and for breaking the small shoots from the stalk to conserve the plant's energy and food uptake for the nine or so leaves that would mature; the tobacco knife for cutting the stalk at the appropriate time; the human back to bear the cut stalks to the tobacco barn; a knife to cut the pegs driven by hand-held tools into the stalks, before the stalks were hung aloft to allow the leaves to cure in the air for five or six weeks; the human hand again for stripping the cured leaves from the stalks, and removing the stems of the leaves, which had to be delicately handled to preserve their marketability; hand tools and the cooper's skill for the making of hogsheads to specifications to be fit to withstand the stresses of being rolled by workers down to the dock for shipment. The process began with seeding the beds in, say, mid-January, whence they were transplanted to the tobacco field early in May. Continuous attentive labor was required to bring the plant to perfection; in August the stalks were cut down. During the intervals between seeding and transplanting, during the five or six weeks of air curing, and in the months of November and December, there were other sometimes more laborious tasks to be done, such as clearing new fields, cutting down trees and pulling the stumps, burning brush, etcetera.[51] Due to the primitive technique of the process, in the fifty years between the dissolution of the Virginia Company and Bacon's Rebellion the capitalist plantation owners relied almost totally upon increased exertion by the laborers to more than double the annual tobacco output per laborer, from 712 to 1,653 pounds.[52]

Main Forms of the Oppression of Plantation Bond-laborers

The characteristic dependency of the proletarian under capitalism took the most extreme form in chattel bond-servitude. The ancient principle that "A man's home is his castle" had no meaning for the bond-laborers. The woman was denied whatever protection she might otherwise have had as a "feme covert." The limited-term bond-laborers were forbidden the comfort and release of sexual relationships, under heavy penalty. The owner was not only their employer, but their landlord and victualer as well. The extreme rural isolation of their situation, in colonies devoid of the civilizing influences of village and urban centers, limited to an extraordinary degree their ability to appeal their grievances to public conscience and legal remedy.

Edmund S. Morgan's study of colonial Virginia found little basis for the "kindly master" thesis. Nor is he so ready to place the blame for the bond-laborers' bad conditions on objective factors of climate and frontier, as some historians have done. Morgan largely blames capitalist cupidity for the hardships of bond-laborers' lives.[53] This impression is confirmed by the exhaustive studies of the record presented by Richard B. Morris's *Government and Labor in Early America*, and in the *Archives of Maryland* under the illustrious successive editorships of W. H. Browne, C. C. Hall, B. C. Steiner, J. H. Pleasants and Aubrey C. Land.

Most of the evidence of abuse of bond-laborers by their owners is taken from court proceedings wherein certain individual owners of bond-laborers are shown to have carried matters beyond what would seem to be the bounds of sound proprietorship. At the same time the depositions taken, decisions rendered, and orders issued in such cases also serve to illuminate the day-to-day life of the bond-laborers. That which in itself may have constituted a seemingly self-defeating excess of rigor in particular instances, served the general capitalist interest of stimulating the bond-laborers to be more diligent at their tasks, and to stifle their grievances. Such was the declared intention of Captain Bradnox, himself a Kent County Commissioner, who beat bond-laborer Sarah Taylor with extreme force, then reviewed the lesson, saying, "Now spoyle me a batch of bread again!"[54] Courts and legislatures occasionally found it expedient and proper to order some amelioration. Regardless of the degree to which the courts may have been moved by feelings of humanity in such instances, however, it seems certain that they had in mind the overriding interests of the plantation bourgeoisie as a whole in discouraging the wanton destruction of the labor force, and in minimizing the reductions in the labor supply resulting when accounts reached England of brutal treatment of bond-laborers.

The following brief sampling from the court records is not intended to improve on Professor Morris's presentation or to substitute for a reading in the *Archives of Maryland*, but merely to document the theme of social tension in the tobacco colonies arising out of the bond-labor relation of production.

Increasing the length of servitude

Given an adequate supply of labor power, the maximizing of capitalist profit, then as now, depended on raising the productivity of labor per unit of labor cost. In the tobacco colonies the owners did this by (1) extending the labor time of each worker, and (2) intensifying the effort of each worker.

A small minority of the bond-laborers arrived in the tobacco colonies with written indentures specifying the duration of their servitude. By far the greater number who arrived in Virginia in the seventeenth century came without indentures; the duration of their bondage was specified by law under the rubric "custom of the country." At first the custom of the country was set at four years for adult bond-laborers arriving in Virginia and Maryland; then, in 1661 and 1666, respectively, the colony Assemblies increased the custom of the country from four to five years, and made it applicable to all "christian" bond-laborers.[55] The Maryland Assembly in 1666 justified its action by criticizing the former law for

> providing but foure yeares service in which tyme itt is considered the Master and owners of such Servants cannot receive that reasonable satisfaction for the charges trouble & greate hazard which all masters and Owners of Servants are and must of necessity be att with their Servants.[56]

In that same year, the Virginia Assembly acted to eliminate what it saw as an "inequality" in the law, doing so in a way that turned the owner's possible loss into a gain. Under the old law, if a bond-laborer was under sixteen he or she was bound to serve until the age of twenty-four; but if sixteen or over, the term was to be five years. The Assembly, happily from the employers' point of view, raised the critical age to nineteen. Since all those under nineteen were now to serve until they were twenty-four, the masters by this law had claim to from one to three more years of unpaid bond-labor than before from those in the sixteen-to-eighteen-year range, while still retaining the service until twenty-four of those "never so little under sixteene" for whom they expressed such concern.[57]

Special opportunities for securing extra servitude

Besides such steps toward the general extension of the laborers' terms of servitude, the bond-labor relation of production afforded a number of legal opportunities for securing extended service in particular cases, in the form of penalties for a variety of infractions of the principles of the system. These were special opportunities available to the plantation bourgeoisie, which were not open to capitalists operating in England. There, under that normal capitalist labor system, the laborer who violated his or her contract could not be compelled to a specific performance, but could only be held liable for "pecuniary damages as in the case of a breach of any other contract."[58]

As already noted, the Virginia General Court, as early as 1626, imposed an extension of the term of bond-servitude upon a recaptured runaway bond-laborer.[59] Courts continued to apply this principle on a case-by-case basis[60] until it was given the form of legislative enactment that proportioned the extension of servitude to the length of the laborer's absence. In Virginia, the penalty was fixed at two days for every one day of absence.[61] For a repetition of the offense the runaway was to be branded on the shoulder with a hot-iron R. In Maryland in 1641, the death penalty was provided, but mercy and profit considerations coinciding, this penalty was made commutable to seven years' added servitude.[62] In 1649, the Maryland penalty was set at two days for each day of absence, but with the additional penalty of payment for all costs and damages, for which the employer might be compensated by a deduction from the freedom dues, and by a further extension of the time of servitude, or by a combination of the two.[63] In 1666, Maryland set the penalty at ten days' extension of servitude for each day of absence.[64] It is somehow not surprising that, with such an incentive, masters frequently sought to extend the period of servitude by alleging that the bond-laborer had been illegally asbent from service, a charge that the laborer was in a weak position to dispute before magistrates who were themselves actual or potential beneficiaries of that same law.[65]

Three cases from the record will illustrate how the employers were able to make such laws serve capital accumulation or, as the modern term has it, "economic growth."

George Beckwith owned Henry Everitt, who had been delivered to Maryland in 1666 at the age of thirteen.[66] Everitt, because of his age, was legally bound to serve nine years, that is, until he was twenty-two. The young worker proved to be a valuable piece of property, despite having at various times "failed to serve" for a total of six weeks. Beckwith, understandably reluctant to part with such an experienced laborer, made timely application to the Provincial Court, on the eve of what was to have been Everitt's last year of servitude, and secured an extension of Everitt's time by ten times six weeks beyond the end of the ninth year. The labor gained would bring Beckwith sufficient return to pay the freedom dues of three bond-laborers (who might perhaps prove more faithful than Everitt), or enough to pay three-fourths the cost of purchasing another thirteen-year-old bond-laborer.[67]

In April 1673, David Driver brought into court two men he owned, James Cade and Timothy Hummerstone, alleging that they had run away for thirty-six days. The court awarded Driver a year of the life and labor of each of the bond-laborers in compensation for the five weeks lost. For Driver this meant a net gain of almost one-fifth of the total labor time originally due him.[68]

On St Valentine's Day 1679, the court showed where its affections lay as between Thomas Doxey and Katherine Canneday:

> Came Thomas Doxey of St Maryes County & made Oath that his servant Katherine Canneday rann away & and unlawfully absented herselfe from his service att severall tymes One hundred and seven dayes, whereupon itt is ordered that shee the said Katherine serve the said Thomas for running away from him as aforesaid, tenn dayes for every one dayes absence according to Act of Assembly in that case made and provided, which amounts to One thousand and seventy dayes.[69]

The costs of recapture, prosecution and corporal punishment

Such proceedings involved costs, of course, as did subsequent execution of court judgments on bond-laborers. Among such costs were the fees paid to the "takers-up" of runaways.[70] Under a Maryland law of 1676, a payment of a matchcoat or the value thereof was provided for "any Indian or Indians which shall seize or take up any Runaway Servant & bring him before some magistrate of any County within this Province."[71] In the middle decades of the seventeenth century the legally established Virginia schedule of fees for sheriff and clerk services included the following items: for sheriffs, twenty pounds of tobacco for each arrest, pillorying and whipping;[72] for clerks, eight pounds of tobacco for writing or copying a court order; and for secretaries, fifteen pounds of tobacco for the same services.[73] In Maryland, sheriffs were paid fifty pounds of tobacco for whippings, and twenty pounds for each day a prisoner was held in jail. In both Maryland and Virginia such charges were at first paid by the county treasury, but in 1662 and 1670 respectively, the provincial assemblies acted to end the discerned gross inequities in such an arrangement. Not only did it make the public bear the costs of supporting criminals, said the lawmakers, it actually was "an encouragement to offendors" by rewarding their misdeeds with idleness and free room and board.[74] Whether such costs occasioned by the capture and public prosecution of bond-laborers were borne by the public treasury or by the individual owners, they were by law recoverable at the expense of the limited-term bond-laborer in terms of additional servitude.[75]

Denial of family life; women exposed to special oppression

For the purposes of quick capital turnover, the importation of unmarried laborers of working age was preferable: it provided the immediate prospect of full utilization of the maximum labor power of the workers; it was simpler in distribution than family-group bond-labor; and, in production, it maximized the employer's access to the laborer's time, unimpeded by the involvement of laborers in family connections and obligations. In short: marriage was fundamentally incompatible with chattel status.

In normal English capitalist conditions, the right to marry was exercised by persons regardless of social class, except that apprentices needed the permission of their masters. The family was the standard form of maintaining, perpetuating and reproducing the laboring classes in proportion to the requirements of capitalist commodity production at the lowest cost and with the highest returns for investors. The expenses of working-class weddings, births, child-rearing and funerals were provided in the wage costs of the employing classes no less essentially than the costs of the day-to-day maintenance of the economically productive population or of the instruments of production. In the seventeenth-century plantation colonies, however, the peculiar chattel bond-labor relation of production carried with it different implications for the lives of the bond-laborers. For almost the entire duration of the seventeenth century, the plantation bourgeoisie was able to secure a steady supply of bond-labor for which it was obliged to pay only the day-to-day subsistence and "operating" costs. All other charges were subsumed in the purchase price, which the laborer was bound to repay (many times over) by long periods of unpaid labor.

Since bond-laborers were wageless and propertyless (except for the few who brought personal items to America, which in the nature of the case would have been of little exchange-value), and since they had no rightful claim to any portion of the day's time for themselves, parenthood on the part of bond-laborers entailed direct and indirect deductions from capitalist revenues, for child-bearing and child-rearing, costs that the employers regarded as economically unjustifiable. The employing class, as a matter of sound business practice, outlawed family life among limited-term bond-laborers.[76] They were forbidden to marry without the express permission of their owners,[77] since, consistent with the principle of coverture, a woman was subject only to the husband.[78] Still, bond-laborers were granted no exemption from the laws against fornication.[79] While nominally laws against "bastardy" made human reproduction outside of legal wedlock a crime for free women, for them – in contrast to bond-laborers – marriage was an automatic defense against that charge;[80] "fornication" and "adulterie" were punishable by a fine for those who could pay it, or whipping or two or three months' imprisonment.[81]

In providing penalties for bond-laborers who violated the law in these respects, the bourgeoisie was typically underscoring its concern for the maintenance of social mores conforming to its own particular class character. But the peculiar nature of the chattel bondage form of labor relations permitted the plantation bourgeoisie to turn that concern to cash account in very specific and immediate ways, ways not available to employers in England.

When, in 1643, Virginia bond-laborers were first forbidden by law to marry, it was provided that the offending wife's term of servitude should be extended to double the time for which she was bound. The husband's term was to be prolonged only twelve months,[82] it being assumed that the anticipated distractions of child care would divert a minimum of his time from serving his employer. The makers of this law, however, did not find it necessary to mitigate the woman's punishment in cases where no child was born during her period of servitude. Twenty years later, the woman's legal punishment was made the same as the man's, one year of extended servitude just for marriage, childbirth and child-rearing penalties being separately provided.[83] At the same time, it was made a crime for a minister to perform the marriage of a bond-laborer without the owner's prior approval. Violators were subject to a fine of ten thousand pounds of tobacco, the equivalent of about five months of a minister's salary.[84] An important consequence of this new feature of the law was to make children of such marriages "illegitimate," as they would have been if no marriage had taken place.[85] Under the Virginia law of 1662, a free man marrying a woman bond-laborer without her owner's permission was obliged to pay a fine of 1,500 pounds of tobacco, or to serve as a bond-laborer for one year to the woman's owner.[86]

Under English law, fornication was punishable, certainly in the most commonly prosecuted cases, those in which pregnancy resulted.[87] In the plantation colonies, early laws were enacted to the same purpose, providing the penalty of a whipping or payment of a fine, as in this 1639 Maryland statute:[88]

> the offender or offenders shall be publicly whipped, or otherwise pay such fines to some publique use as the lieutenant general shall impose.

Free persons were subject to these laws no less than bond-laborers,[89] and "women and men were whipped indiscriminately, women on the bare back apparently as frequently as men."[90] In due course, laws were made that specified the number of lashes to be administered and the amount of the fine. Although the whipping and the fine were equally available forms of punishment under the law, the whipping was actually inflicted only in cases of non-payment of the fine.[91] But limited-term bond-laborers, as proletarians owning nothing of the goods their labor produced, were unable to pay fines. Owners were thus presented with an opportunity, which they routinely exercised, of establishing a claim to additional unpaid labor time by paying the bond-laborer's fine. The usual ratio was six months' extra service for the payment of a fine of five hundred pounds of tobacco.[92]

How "bastardy" laws compounded gender and class oppression

Under the English common law principle of "coverture," the husband was the legal father of children of his wife.[93] Coverture, as already noted, had no application to women bond-laborers, who by law were not allowed to have husbands; their children were by definition "bastards." In England the first specific mention of "illegitimate" children came in 1575–76, and it constituted the basic English "bastardy" law for at least three centuries. It fixed responsibility upon the parents for reimbursing the parish for the charges of keeping the child, by weekly or other periodic payments, on pain of being sent to jail for default.[94]

In the Anglo-American colonies, however, the employers were made direct beneficiaries of the "bastardy" laws as they applied to bond-laborers, with the labor of the mother accounting for the major share of those benefits. In both Virginia and Maryland in the middle of the seventeenth century, the mother was subject to extended servitude for the owner's "loss of service" on account of the distractions resulting from child-bearing and child-rearing. In 1662 the Virginia Assembly fixed the added period of unpaid labor at two years.[95] The Maryland Assembly enacted a similar law in the same year.[96] In addition to the obligation for "lost time," the mother was subject to be publicly whipped on her bare back. The Virginia statute of 1662 specified that the lashing continue only until the blood flowed,[97] but a Maryland court in 1658 called for it to be continued until the count reached thirty.[98]

If the owner felt it was not to his advantage to risk the incapacitation of his bond-laborer that might result from such punishment, he would typically pay the fine.[99] An equally, or even more, compelling motive to this humanitarian gesture was the reward it brought to the owner, as it did for example to the owner of Katherine Higgins, whose case was typical of hundreds. On 26 January 1685, Higgins was found guilty of having become a mother, and was sentenced to an added two and a half years of servitude to her owner, half a year for the fine that her owner paid to save her from whipping, and two years for his trouble and expense in saving the parish any expense for care of the newborn child.[100] Employers were thus able to turn an anticipated "loss of services" into a net profit.[101]

Examination of surviving seventeenth-century Virginia county court records[102] reveals some three hundred cases of such "bastardy" judgments against limited-term women bond-laborers. At a rate of 1,500 pounds of tobacco per year per worker, such of these women as worked in the field during their added 30 months' servitude would have produced tobacco worth more than three times the cost of their transportation to the colony,[103] that cost being the supposed debt for which they were relegated to a social status wherein they were denied the right to marry.[104]

Occasionally an employer was also able to gain some extra labor time from the father. If, as happened in a small number of cases, the identity of the father was established, he would be obliged to provide security to save the parish harmless, that is, to provide a guarantee that the cost of support of the infant would be repaid to the parish. If the father were a bond-laborer, the church wardens took charge of the child, paying the charges of the child's upkeep until it became of working age, or selling the child to a private individual as a bond-laborer-to-be. At the completion of the father's original term of servitude, he was obligated to make recompense for any charges outstanding for the cost of the child's early care. If he could not pay, he could be taken up by the sheriff to satisfy the debt by a period of bond-servitude.[105] But, unlike the mother, the father could not be made to serve extra time for the "loss of services" directly due to the pregnancy.

In a certain number of cases the owner himself was the father, suggesting the grossest form of sexual exploitation. The notorious Henry Smith of Accomack County fathered children by two of his bond-laborers in the late 1660s. Not long before November 1699, John Waugh of Stafford County sold Catherine Hambleton away across Chesapeake Bay, pregnant with his own child. The same sort of sale of his own progeny had been made by Nicholas Chapman of Norfolk County, in or shortly before 1677.[106] But unproven accusations were severely penalized. When, in March 1650, a "search of her body" led the court to disbelieve Sara Reinold's accusation that her owner had made her pregnant, she was sentenced to "thirty-five Lashes on the bare back."[107]

In Maryland, Lucy Stratton, bond-laborer, was brought before the Charles County, Maryland, Court in November 1671, charged with having borne a child. Stratton said that her owner was the father, but the court credited the denial of the owner, a wealthy planter named Turner. On the grounds of having made a false accusation against her owner, the woman was sentenced to and received thirty lashes at the public whipping post. But Turner was indeed the father, as he admitted shortly thereafter in offering to "make satisfaction by marrying" Stratton. Although it might mean an extended term of servitude to refuse, Stratton spurned the blessings of such a "coverture," calling her owner a "lustful man" whom she "could not love . . . much less make him her husband," adding that she "had suffered enough by him."[108] The Charles County, Maryland, Court, upon her petition, ordered Turner either to pay child maintenance or to take the child and raise it as his own. But on appeal to a higher court, Stratton's suit against Turner for support for the child was denied because she had refused the marriage offer.[109]

The social conscience of the plantation bourgeoisie – that is to say, the sense of the general interests of the ruling class as a whole – did exert some influence, even if it might possibly run counter to the desires and interests of some individual planters.[110] The supply of laborers was not so plentiful in the seventeenth-century plantation colonies, nor the number of women so great, nor social control so secure, that men of the owning classes could be allowed unrestricted indulgence of their sexual appetites at the expense of women bond-laborers, even if these owners might thereby gain a bonus of unpaid labor as a result. In their respective sixth decades, therefore, Virginia and Maryland adopted laws attempting to serve the general interests of the owning class, while safeguarding the individual owner against deprivation of his rights. In Virginia a woman in such a case was, by a law of 1662, obliged to complete her term of servitude, thus protecting the owner's right-by-purchase. On the other hand, it was provided that the owner should not have the benefit of the extra servitude which was to be imposed on the bond-laborer for her misconduct. Still, the lawmakers felt, it would be courting trouble to excuse the woman from punishment, as that might tempt others in a similar condition to make false allegations of paternity against their masters as a means of escaping their due in legal penalties. The Assembly found justice in a middle course by providing that upon completion of the mother's original term, she should be taken to the church wardens and sold to some new owner for a term of servitude. The purchase price went to the parish revenues, minus the costs of food and clothing for the child until the child was old enough to become a net producer for a private employer.[111]

In the context of these arrangements, occasional losses had to be accepted as a normal, indeed essential, part of the process as illuminators of possible operational limits of the system. Such appears to have been the case of Isabella Yansley, of Ann Arundell County, Maryland.[112] On 3 March 1671, as it was later charged, Yansley hid herself away, "without the company of any other women," gave birth to a boy, and caused him to die. The Provincial Court found her guilty of murder, and by its sentence she was hanged on 17 April. In England a woman facing motherhood unwed might have resorted to the same desperate course, and suffered the same fate for it. But, in a tobacco colony, where the child of a bond-laborer was to be a bond-laborer of the mother's owner until the child was over twenty years of age, such an outcome represented a loss of investment and possible future profit, negating the benefit of the special "fornication" and "illegitimacy" laws applied against bond-laborers.

The procedure for disposing of the potential and actual labor-power of the children of bond-servants in Anglo-America closely followed the pattern that had been established for dealing with indigent children in Tudor England. That system evolved under a series of laws beginning in 1536 and culminating in the fundamental English Poor Law of 1601.[113] First among the stated purposes of the 1601 law was that of "setting to work the children ... whose parents shall not be thought able to keep and maintain them."[114] In seventeenth-century Virginia and Maryland, under-age Europeans arriving without indentures were bound to serve according to the law. In 1666 in Virginia if they were under nineteen years of age, they were to serve until they were twenty-four. The Maryland law made a more particular differentiation of age levels, but merely to assure that children would serve at least seven years; those arriving at age twenty-two years old or older were bound for five years.[115]

But the peculiar character of the bond-labor relation of production gave these laws a greater practical scope than laws regarding "indigent" children in England. Since bond-laborers were by definition propertyless and unpaid, as parents they were, under 1666 laws, obliged to serve added time as recompense to the owner or the parish for the cost of maintenance of the child.[116] While the labor of indigent children was programmed for exploitation in both England and in the colonies, the profit to be gained therefrom by the exploiters was of relatively greater importance in the labor-scarce Chesapeake than in England. Perhaps it is significant that in 1632, when the per capita production of tobacco was some 700 pounds per year, two women bond-laborers who became pregnant on the voyage to Virginia were forthwith shipped back again;[117] but four decades later, by which time the output per worker had more than doubled,[118] the arrival of a woman in this predicament was more likely to be regarded as an opportunity to profit not only from the extension of the women's servitude, but also from the option on the labor of her child under the provisions of the 1662 law against "fornication."[119]

Nevertheless, despite the various expedients adopted for recapturing the owner's or the parish's expenses for support of the children of limited-term bond-laborers, those measures provided a relatively unprofitable way of recruiting plantation labor power in the seventeenth-century tobacco colonies.[120] The prospective period of unpaid bond-servitude to be had from such children, whether by their original owners or by other persons to whom they were assigned, was limited. The child might not survive until he reached the workable (tithable) age of sixteen.[121] The bond-laborer father, once his term was completed, could take possession of the child, making settlement with the parish or the owner for the care and maintenance of the child up until that time.[122] "Bastards" who remained with the mother's owner were bound to serve only until they were twenty-one if boys, or eighteen if girls. Bastards of European-American parents were bound out by their parents to other men, but they became free at the age of twenty-four if boys, at eighteen, if girls.[123]

If, however, the period of bastards' unpaid servitude could be increased sufficiently, the mating of bond-laborers might be made into a paying proposition for the owners. That was the principle behind the persistent pressure from the side of the plantation bourgeoisie to impose lifetime hereditary bondage on African-Americans. In 1662, the Virginia Assembly discarded English common law of descent through the father, and instituted the principle of *partus sequitur ventrem*, whereunder the child was declared "bond or free according to the condition of the mother."[124] That law was specifically aimed at giving the plantation bourgeoisie a predefined supply of self-perpetuating unpaid labor. Once the owners had this advantage, the courts no longer concerned themselves with prosecuting African-American bond-laborers for "fornication" or "bastardy." Supplementary sources of unpaid labor were tapped under a Virginia law passed in 1681, requiring a child of a European-American mother and an African-American father to serve until the age of thirty.[125] That was six years of extra unpaid labor beyond what would have been served by a child of two European-American bond-laborers. That extra labor should have yielded the owner 9,000 pounds of tobacco, more than enough to buy another limited-term bond-laborer.

Under a Maryland law in effect from 1664 to 1692, any "freeborne" woman who married an African-American lifetime bond-laborer was bound to serve "the master of such slave during the life or her husband." Presented with such an opportunity, many Maryland owners deliberately fostered marriages of European-American women and African-American men bond-laborers in order to get the benefit of the added unpaid labor time of their descendants.[126] The ruling class understood that the bond-laborers' sex drives were "as irresistible and ardent as those of others ... [and therefore t]here is no danger that the considering of their progeny's condition will stop propagation."[127]

In 1692, the Maryland penalty was modified to seven years' bond servitude. If the woman were a bond-laborer, the added seven years were to begin only after the completion of her original term.[128] The penalty for "fornication" and "bastardy" was especially severe (a double fine in Virginia in 1662) when an African-American/European-American couple was involved.[129] When the double penalty of the 1662 law proved generally ineffective, the Virginia Assembly in 1691 passed another, making any English woman in this circumstance, free or bond, subject to public sale by the churchwardens of the parish into bond-servitude for five years. For those who were bond-laborers, this added servitude was to be postponed until the completion of her current period of bondage.[130]

Why? That was the question implicit in the petition of European-American lifetime bond-laborer Mary Peters, who petitioned for manumission having already served eight years beyond the time she should otherwise have served if she had not "been drawn by her master and mistress into marrying a negro, and so being reckoned a slave."[131] Why, wondered Ann Wall, a free European-American woman who had borne two children of an African-American father, when she was sentenced by the Elizabeth County Court to five years' bond-servitude under "Mr Peter Hobson or his assigns" in Norfolk County, and forbidden ever to return to Elizabeth City County on pain of banishment to Barbados.[132] It was a matter that European-American bond-laborer Jane Salman could not understand; she fled from the jurisdiction of the Accomack County Court that had ordered her to be taken for sale by the church warden to another seven-year term of servitude.[133]

Why, indeed? An attempt will be made in Chapter 13 to suggest an answer to that question.

Exploiting the presumption of bondage

Enterprising employers frequently found it possible to retain laborers in bondage even though by law they were entitled to be free. As far as propertyless persons were concerned the presumption was bondage, as evidenced by the enactment of pass laws, in Virginia in 1643 and in 1663, and in Maryland in 1671.[134] In general, these laws made a laboring person subject to arrest as a fugitive, unless he or she had a pass signed by an owner or other officially designated authority.

Thus a laborer who had completed the full period of servitude still bore the burden of proof of his or her liberty. Without a certificate of freedom issued by the county court, the time-expired laborer was subject to arrest as a fugitive, and thereafter to additional servitude under laws provided in such cases. In order to secure the certificate of freedom, the laborer had to appear before the county court with the owner, or with a written deposition supplied by the owner, to establish the fact of the completion of the term of servitude.[135] If, instead of cooperating, the employer chose to attempt to keep the laborer in bondage, the laborer might well face a daunting prospect.[136] Aside from the many difficulties the laborer confronted in getting a petition for freedom before the court, there were commonly other problems. The bond-laborer who had come to Virginia or Maryland with a formal indenture obligating him or her to serve for a time less than that provided under the "custom of the country" had to produce in court the original paper to prove his or her case. To preserve such a document against destruction, loss or theft through several years of bond-labor was not always easy.[137] Yet without it the laborer would have to remain in bondage according to the "custom of the country." William Rogers came to Virginia under a three-year indenture to Anthony Gosse, who sold Rogers to John Stith, transmitting his half of the indenture paper to Stith. Stith, learning that Rogers had somehow left his half of the indenture contract in England, destroyed the paper Gosse had given him, and claimed Rogers for five years according to the custom of the country.[138]

The ordinary custom-of-the-country bond-laborers would perhaps be even more vulnerable to employers' attempts to extend their servitude beyond the legal limit.[139] If the laborer sought redress from the court, pending the court's decision he or she would remain under the absolute power of the owner, on a plantation from which it was a crime to depart without the owner's permission, a plantation moreover equipped with a whipping post or the equivalent for the administration of "moderate correction" by the master or his agent.[140] The owner thus had strong forces of persuasion at his disposal for inducing the bond-laborer to submit to an extension of unpaid servitude. The employer's chances of gains of this sort were perhaps enhanced where the bond-laborer had been sold from one employer to another, if the frequency of such cases in the court records is any indication.[141] Even if, as in the cases to be cited, the employer were not fully successful, he lost little by trying; he even stood to gain incidental benefits.

The Joseph Griphen and Daniel Ralston cases illustrate the denial of their right to a presumption of liberty in Maryland. In 1659, Joseph Griphen was bought by two Maryland merchants who shortly thereafter sold him to John Hatch. In November 1666, at the end of seven years of servitude, Griphen asserted his freedom by rowing downriver in a canoe. Hatch had him hunted by hue and cry, and brought back, alleging that Griphen had been bought for ten years, not seven.[142] Daniel Ralston came to Maryland in 1663 with a written indenture according to which he was bound for four years, at the end of which time he was to receive £10 sterling, plus a good suit and other clothes, and two hoes and an axe. Three years had passed when he ran away from his owner, Henry Robertson. After several weeks Ralston was recaptured and returned to his owner, and then he was sold again to another owner, David Johnson. After Ralston's indentured term was ended in July 1667, his new owner claimed added service at the rate of ten-to-one for every day that Ralston had run away from his former owner. Since Ralston took action in court before his new owner did, the owner's claim was not allowed, although the principle of the assignability of penalty time was not questioned. Though the decision of the jury favored the bond-laborer's claim, the owner was allowed to keep Ralston in servitude pending disposition of the appeal to the Provinical Court, and the freedom dues allowance was reduced to either £10 or the goods but not both, contrary to the terms of the original indenture.[143] In June 1678, John Hickes[?], identified in the record as a "Dutchman," was taken up as a runaway bond-laborer. Even though there was no "positive proof" of the charge, the court in the Virginia Eastern Shore county of Northampton ordered him to "goe along with Capt. Foxcroft" for thirty days while the court sent for information across the bay regarding Hickes's status. If during that time the man "absent[ed] himselfe" from Foxcroft, he was to be hunted "by Hue and Cry as a Runaway Servant."[144]

The removal of the owner from the scene might complicate the laborer's bondage predicament, as it did in the case that came before the Virginia Colony Council in 1675 on the petition of Phillip Corven, an African-American.[145] Originally, Corven had been an under-age bond-laborer of widow Annie Beazeley of James City County. When Mrs Beazeley died in 1664, she left a will assigning Corven to her cousin, Humphrey Stafford, for a term of eight years, until 1672, at which time Corven "should enjoy his freedom & be

paid three barrels of corn and as sute of clothes." Long before that day could
dawn, however, Stafford had sold Corven's time to Charles Lucas of Warwick
County. In his petition for freedom, Corven charged that he had been forced
to accompany Lucas to the Warwick County court and there to acknowledge
a formal "agreement" to remain a bond-laborer to Lucas, his heirs and assigns
for twenty years. Three years of this extra bond-servitude – beyond the original
eight years – were actually secured by Lucas in this way before Corven brought
his petition before the Colony Council. Corven's petition asked for his freedom
dues, and for compensation for the previous three years of unpaid labor. The
record of the final disposition of the case has not been preserved. But even if
Lucas lost on every point, he would still have been the gainer in all probability,
despite the very low price of tobacco in those years, if, as seems likely, Corven
was employed in tobacco and producing over 1,500 pounds of it per year; also
to be taken into account is the interest gained by Lucas by the delay of any
freedom dues.

It was no more than a normal risk of doing business that such aggressive
methods should occasionally miscarry, as in the case of William Whittacre.[146]
Whittacre bought an African-American bond-laborer named Manuel from
Thomas Bushrod, who himself had previously purchased the laborer from
Colonel William Smith. Somewhere along the line, whether by self or others
deceived, Whittacre came to believe that Manuel was a lifetime bond-laborer.
Thus believing, Whittacre paid £25 for the worker, twice what he would have
paid for a male limited-term bond-laborer. To Whittacre's utter dismay, the
Virginia Assembly subsequently adjudged Manuel to be "no slave but to serve
as other Christian servants do," and he was freed in September 1665. Whittacre
maintained his innocence in the affair and asked to be exempted from taxation
to compensate him for his loss. But the Assembly, "not knowing any reason
why the Public should be answerable for the inadvertency of the Buyer for a
Judgment given when justly grounded as that Order was," rejected Whittacre's
petition.

Cutting labor costs when no wages were paid

Although the employers of bond-laborers could not hope to increase profits
by reducing wages, they did have labor costs that they were always eager to
reduce – the cost of acquisition of the laborer (the purchase price); the cost of
maintenance during the period of servitude; and, finally, the cost of the
freedom dues to be paid to workers who survived to the end of their terms.
The first of these aspects, reduction of acquisition costs, has been discussed.
The owners were just as diligent in their efforts to reduce the costs of
maintenance and freedom dues.

In the seventeenth-century Chesapeake colonies no law was ever enacted to
provide a minimum level of food, clothing, drink, bedding, housing, or other
necessities.[147] The burden of legal remedy was entirely on the laborer. She or
he had to find the courage and means to present a magistrate (who himself

was certain to be an owner of bond-laborers) with a bill of particulars against her or his own master, citing evidence of insufficient diet, clothing, or shelter. Ordinarily, the worst that the owner might have to expect from such a proceeding was to be ordered to provide "sufficiently" for the laborer in the future. There was also the chance that the laborer might be sentenced to a lashing at the whipping post if the complaint were judged lacking in merit, as happened to William Evans for "saying that Mrs Stone starved her servants to death," and to Thomas Barnes who was judged to have "complained cause-lessly against his Master Mihill Ricketts."[148] From the standpoint of the employers, this manner of dealing with the question of the maintenance of laborers was preferable to any arrangement involving statutory "mandated expenditures" by legislation.

As for the day-to-day *costs* of maintenance of their workers, the employers of bond-labor were able to reduce that factor to zero. The cost of clothing and housing the bond-laborers was more than compensated by the accumulation of interest on the freedom dues, or even the avoidance of the payment of this terminal allowance in an assured percentage of cases.[149] But the most attractive part of the labor maintenance picture, as viewed by the employer, was the fact that the workers produced their own food. Of course, a portion of the laborers' time had to be given to the work, but that could not be considered a loss of labor, any more than waiting for a wet day to replant seedlings or for stripping the stalks could be considered a loss of tobacco. They were all necessary natural processes occurring in the cycle of reproduction and expansion of the owner's capital.

It was in the owner's interest, however, to reduce such "waiting time," and the expenses and risks incidental to it. This was done by forcing the laborers to subsist on Indian corn, even though the laborers desired the regular inclusion of meat and milk products in their diet.[150] The corn diet was cheaper. The same basic labor-training and the same hand implements were usable in cultivating corn as in cultivating tobacco. Corn was relatively easily stored, and it could be prepared and eaten in several forms.[151] The labor of producing and processing corn was easier to supervise than, for instance, that of rounding up cattle and hogs in the woods and thickets where they ranged, free as the bond-laborer wished to be. Finally, corn was not then a profitable export crop, whilst Virginia meats became increasingly so.[152] In England the prices of consumables rose generally throughout the seventeenth century;[153] but from the 1640s onward, food products in Virginia steadily declined in price.[154] As a result Virginia's exporters were able to secure a part of the trade to the sugar colonies in the West Indies. As early as 1657, oxen worth only £5 in Virginia were being exported to Barbados at a price of £25.[155] For all these reasons, the owners in the tobacco colonies found it sound business practice to feed their bond-laborers on corn, and correspondingly to reduce the amount of meat in the workers' diet.[156] By 1676, it was officially reported that in Virginia "the ordinary sort of people" had beef to eat only in the summer, and then only once or twice a week; in the winter they received "only the corn of the country, beat in a mortar and boiled ... [and] the bread [that] is made of the same corne, but with difficulty by reason of the scarcity of mills."[157] In 1679, two Dutch travelers in the northern Chesapeake tobacco country observed that "for their usual food, the servants have nothing but maize bread to eat and water to drink."[158]

Under normal capitalist conditions the employer makes payments to the employee daily, weekly, or semi-monthly. Under the system of limited-term bond-servitude, the only payment the employer was expected (it was not required by statute) to make to the laborer was in the form of the freedom dues paid upon satisfactory completion of the term of servitude, which usually lasted five years. This gave the employer of bond-labor a special advantage over the employer of wage labor. First, the wage-laborer has to advance his/her labor to the capitalist on credit, so to speak, for only a day, or at most a couple of weeks. But the bond-laborer was compelled to advance his/her labor to the capitalist for five years. The employer of wage labor has to pay out wages six or eight times before he gets his money (plus profit) back from the sale of the laborer's product. The employer of the limited-term bond-laborer, by contrast, was able to turn over his capital five times before the first penny of freedom dues had to be paid out. The original price paid to purchase the laborer was probably less than £12.[159] By the end of five years the bond-laborer could be expected to have brought the employer an income of nearly £40,[160] while the interest on the deferred freedom dues payment would cover the freedom dues cost, worth no more than £6.

Even at the minimum rate of a five-year return of £40 on the worker's labor, the owner would have recouped his purchase price perhaps within a year and a half. Since the £6 cost of freedom dues was equivalent to the product of about nine months' bond-labor, the last nine months of a bond-laborer's scheduled term might be one of diminishing returns for the employer. Ordinarily the owners were most vigilant to frustrate runaway attempts by their bond-laborers, but in this critical nine-month period it might actually be to the employer's advantage if the bond-laborer ran away, or died, since in such cases no freedom dues would have to be paid. At that point, masters possessing initiative and drive might seek to manage matters to that end, in a sort of timely "downsizing," as it might be called today. This practice was noted in the report submitted by George Larkin to the home government in 1701:

> When their time expired, according to custom they [the bond-laborers] are to have a certain allowance of corn and clothes, which in Maryland I think is to the value of £6, but in Virginia not so much, to save which a Planter about three months before the expiration of a servant's time will use him barbarously, and to gain a month's freedom the poor servant gladly quits his pretensions to that allowance.[161]

There is a normal rate of labor that can be continued by the laborer on a regular schedule without shortening his or her life span to less than what could be expected by an economically secure person in a non-competitive situation.

However, historical experience has shown that capitalist employers tend not to be satisfied by such a performance rate on the part of their workers. The wage-labor relation is specially adaptable to the needs of capital because it links wages to production; and it induces competition among the workers in performance of their tasks. To the extent that improved instruments of production are introduced into the labor process, the intensity of labor is more imposed than elicited because the rate of operations is removed from the workers' control. Under the bond-labor system, however, where the normal incentives to competition among workers was lacking, and where the implements of labor were limited to the human hand and the tools it held, the employers necessarily relied solely on close and constant supervision to secure higher labor productivity.[162] That was so whatever the crop, but such supervision was especially critical in making tobacco. Due to "the complete absence of machine processes, in the transplanting, topping, cutting, curing and sorting [of tobacco] . . . care must be supplied by detailed oversight," wrote Ulrich B. Phillips.[163] Joseph Clarke Robert, in his history of the North American tobacco industry, notes that "The best quality of tobacco was the fruit of only the most diligent supervision. To send to market a profitable 'parcel' required a sober crop master who kept a critical eye on the usual laborer."[164] In addressing his own question, "Why did productivity per worker increase?," Russell Menard concludes from his study of the colonial records that "the weight of the evidence suggests that the increased yield per worker was entirely due to the rise in the number of plants one man could handle."[165] George Fitzhugh was merely recording a bit of ancient bourgeois wisdom in noting that tobacco's profitability depended on the maintenance of a high ratio of supervisory force to laborers employed. "Six hands often make double as much money at tobacco as at cotton or sugar," he wrote, "but a crop of tobacco that employes sixty hands, always brings the farmer in debt."[166]

The monocultural economy added further importance to intense supervision. There was only one money, and its name was tobacco – the sole measure of value, standard of price, medium of exchange, and basis of credit. The one customary money function that tobacco, in consequence of its perishability, was unable to perform, was to serve as a means of hoarding.[167] Bruce cites a letter of William Fitzhugh, written in June 1690, complaining "that he had a large number of hogsheads [of tobacco] which it was impossible for him to export in consequence of the scarcity of shipping, their contents undergoing great damage by the delay, and in some cases falling into ruin."[168]

Although the bond-labor system held no positive incentives for increased effort on the part of the workers, it was peculiarly suitable for exerting "negative incentives." For a failure to perform satisfactorily, the laborer faced the threat of corporal punishment by the owner. To resist "correction" or to flee and be caught might entail even more severe treatment. While the bond-labor form inhibited the development of improved instruments of labor, still, the employer had at his disposal the entire twenty-four hours of the laborer's day, except on Sunday. The owner's power in the exercise of this authority was reinforced by the fact that he was not only the employer but also the laborer's landlord and victualer.

The laborers' "victuals" consisted mainly of hominy, which was prepared in a very laborious way. Shelled corn was placed in a mortar formed by hollowing out the end of a hardwood log cut to a suitable length. Then a laborer wielded a sizable stick, formed as a pestle, to pound the grains into hominy. The pestle might be attached to a low-hanging flexible tree branch by a cord, to even out the stress of the upward and downward motions of the pounder's arm. The pounded corn was then sometimes sifted through a cloth to free it of the inedible husks.[169] This was the one major aspect of plantation labor that perhaps presented the laborers with a positive incentive to produce, for whatever their corn allowance they were able to consume it only if the heavy chore of "pounding at the mortar" were regularly done. Having this incentive at his disposal, the owner of the bond-laborers found it the part of efficient management to reserve this task for the periphery of the work schedule, assigning it as a task to be performed after the day's work in the field or woods was done, or perhaps on Sunday, nominally the laborers' day of rest.

The owners' brutal pursuit of higher output per worker

Evidence of the earnestness with which the employers were able to press their advantage in order to raise output per worker is found throughout the colonial records. Frequently cited instances have by repetition come to constitute a body of esoteric lore among students of this aspect of American history.

Spurred on by the all-or-nothing nature of a monocultural economy, and subject to the vagaries of a generally glutted market, Virginia employers pushed matters to the limit to secure the highest possible return on their investment in laborers.[170] According to a mid-seventeenth-century account:

> the months of June, July, and August, being the very height of the Summer, the poore Servant goes daily through the rowes of Tobacco to worm it, and being over-heated, he is struck with a Calenture or Fever and so perisheth.[171]

Henry Smith of Accomack County Virginia strove to get the maximum effort from his bond-laborers; he tasked his workers heavily and punished them brutally for deficiencies in their performance. He was not disposed to make any allowances just because a worker was a woman fed on a meatless diet. Some of Smith's strongest men had weeded as many as three hundred and fifty cornhills in a day. Jane (at first mention the name is "Annie") Powell had been worked in the snow barefoot, and had got by on hominy and salt ever since coming to Virginia. But Henry Smith, perfectionist that he was, could not be moved by such considerations; one day in 1668, when Powell had weeded three hundred cornhills, Smith beat her severely with his whip fashioned from a bull's penis ("pizzle"), for the deficiency of her work performance.[172]

Increased labor intensity required greater time for rest if the laborer's physical condition were not to deteriorate. But nothing was to be permitted to interfere with the timely completion of the annual tobacco crop. According to the record, the owners often found it a profitable option to work their bond-laborers during time supposedly allowed for rest, even at the risk of some attrition of the labor force. Dankers and Sluyter, whose report on their visit to the northern Chesapeake in 1678–80 has been mentioned, found that the bond-laborers, though poorly maintained, were "compelled to work hard" with too little rest. Both African and European laborers, they wrote,

> after they have worn themselves down the whole day, and gone home to rest, have yet to grind the grain ... For their masters and all their families as well as themselves.[173]

When in 1657 bond-laborer William Ireland sought relief from being required to beat at the mortar at night after working all day in the field for his owner Captain Philip Morgan, the Maryland Provincial Court sided with the owner, although it said that such extra duty should be exacted only "at a Seasonable time in the yeare or in the case of Necessity."[174] The interpretation of these limitations, for practical purposes, was left to the owner. But when it was a matter of limiting bond-laborers' resting time, the law was specific. Despite the inclination of kind-hearted masters and English rural custom the government twenty years earlier had resolved that, "touching the resting of servants on Satturdaies in the afternoon . . . no such custom [is] to be allowed."[175]

Some employers had strong reservations as well about the value of "resting servants," even on Sundays, seeming to think that it was necessary and proper to keep the Sabbath day wholly occupied with bond-labor tasks. Such was the recollection of one disgruntled and literate former employee:

> We and the negroes both alike did fare,
> Of work and food we had an equal share;
> But in a piece of ground we called our own,
> The food we eat first by ourselves were sown.
> No other time to us they would allow,
> But on a Sunday we the same must do:
> Six days we slave for our master's good,
> The seventh day is to produce our food.[176]

The trials to which an employer might be put in attempting to raise per capita production may be seen in the case of John Little of Maryland. In the spring of 1657, no doubt a "Seasonable time" full of "necessity," Little commanded one of his bond-laborers, Henry Billsberry, to pound at the mortar on a Sunday. In close company with an Indian comrade, Billsberry fled out of bondage to Indian country. Possibly the youthful laborers were reacting to what they may have regarded as a compounding of injustice and hypocrisy by their owner. For, when sent for in their refuge, they returned reply that "they had rather live with the Pagans."[177]

Illness among bond-laborers was a frequent problem for employers in their constant pursuit of higher output per laborer. Besides the production loss, the cost of medical treatment for the laborer was likely to be too high, at least so high that, according to Bruce, "masters were tempted to suffer a servant to perish for want of proper advice and medicines rather than to submit to their [the physicians'] exactions."[178] Owners might be reluctant to excuse laborers from work on account of illness, as a former bond-laborer recalled:

> At length, it pleased God I sick did fall
> But I no favor could receive at all,
> For I was forced to work while I could stand,
> Or hold the hoe within my feeble hands.[179]

The temptation of masters to which Bruce referred was hard to resist, judging from the high death rate among bond-laborers in the Chesapeake in the seventeenth century.[180] One Maryland employer surrendered to it with such flawless ledger logic that diarists made special mention of it:

> a master having a sick servant ... and observing from his declining condition, he would finally die, and that there was no probability of his enjoying any more service from him, made him, sick and languishing as he was, dig his own grave, in which he was laid a few days afterwards, the others being too busy to dig it, having their hands full attending to the tobacco.[181]

It must be kept in mind that practically all the cases of physical abuse of bond-laborers by their owners are known to us only because the laborer risked bringing the matter to a magistrate, who as we have noted himself was necessarily an owner of many acres and numbers of bond-laborers. Benedict Talbot and William Walworth charged in court that their owner, Captain Hillary Stringer, had "occasioned the death" of their fellow bond-laborer Ellinor Conner. The Accomack County court finding the petition to be worse than groundless, a malicious concoction, ordered Talbot and Walworth to make satisfaction to their owner (presumably by added time of servitude) for all the expenses to which he had been put as a result of their accusation.[182] There were instances of courts ordering that a bond-laborer be sold away from an abusive master. But even on those extremely rare occasions, the owners were not penalized other than by being fined a relatively small amount of tobacco.[183]

There is no way of knowing how many bond-laborers died as a result of starvation, or overwork, or by physical abuse by their owners or on their owners' orders in seventeenth-century Virginia and Maryland. Morris catalogued descriptively half a dozen murders of bond-laborers by their owners.[184] The law passed by the Virginia Assembly in 1662 forbidding secret burials is clear evidence that such occurrences, glossed with suspect allegations of soul-damning "suicide," or other variations of blaming the victim, were of such frequency that they might interfere with the general overriding interest in maintaining the labor supply from the mother country. The law remarked that

[T]he private burial of servants & others give[s] occasion of much scandall against diverse persons, and sometimes not undeservedly so ... [and] servants are fearful to make discovery if murther were committed ... [all ending in] that barbarous custom of exposing the corps of the dead (by makeing their graves in comon and unfenced places) to the prey of hoggs and other vermine.[185]

Occasionally an owner's zeal for increased productivity verged on counter-productive pathology.[186] In Northampton County, Virginia, in the summer of 1640, Thomas Wood was whipped by two men with rope ends for objecting to being forced to beat at the mortar, an onerous chore from which he claimed his indenture exempted him. The next day he was found dead.[187] Early summer "was not the time of yeare for to be sick," said John Mutton to his bond-laborer Francis Burton, a "seasoned hand" who was complaining of a headache. Accusing Burton of "dissembling," Mutton struck and kicked Burton, who died within a few hours.[188]

In May 1657, John Dandy, a large planter, a smith, and owner of a water mill in Maryland, fractured the skull of his young lame bond-laborer Henry Gouge with an axe for reasons not given in the record. Gouge survived, although the wound did not heal. Dandy angrily rejected his wife's suggestion that he "look after" the matter. One day two months later, Dandy went to check on Gouge's performance of a task he had been assigned, and was disappointed at how little Gouge had accomplished. Fellow laborers nearby then heard Gouge cry out in pain as if he were being beaten. He was never seen alive again, but his body was recovered from Cole Kill a month later. Though Dandy denied guilt, the history of the life-threatening abuse he had dealt to Gouge, the two auditory witnesses, the record of his death sentence for killing a young Indian bond-laborer some ten years before (which had been commuted to seven years' service as the executioner of all corporal correction sentences handed down by the provincial courts), his attempt to flee to Virginia because he said Maryland authorities had treated him severely in the past, but above all the accusing blood from the corpse when he touched it – doomed him. He was convicted of murder and hanged.[189]

Late in August 1664, Ann Arundel County, Maryland, employer Joseph Fincher sought to secure a higher per capita output by increasing the size of the load of tobacco plants to be carried by a bond-laborer. When one of the bearers, Joseph Haggman, protested that the load was too great, Fincher tried to encourage him by threatening him with a beating worse than ever a dog was given. Haggman took up the burden, but he staggered under the weight of it. Fincher, apparently provoked beyond endurance, reacted by striking and kicking Haggman, perhaps by way of making an example of him for the edification of other bond-laborers. As it happened, Haggman died of this treatment. Fincher was found guilty of murder on 22 December 1664 and hanged for it.[190]

On 20 January 1665/6 Francis Carpenter, finding his bond-laborer Samuell Yeoungman to be dilatory about fetching firewood, broke a stick over the back of the worker's head as he bent to his task. Unable to recover,

Yeoungman died three weeks later. At trial, the jury found Carpenter guilty of manslaughter but granted him benefit of clergy.[191]

Henry Smith, whose brutality has already been noted, treated all his many bond-laborers with severity, but especially so John Butt, sixty years old and feeble. "Ould John," as Butt was known to all, could never seem to do his work to Smith's satisfaction, nor was he constituted to withstand the beatings that Smith regularly used in order to urge his workers on, even as he was starving them for food. Butt's condition steadily deteriorated, but he was forced to work, eventually in chains. Still somehow his performance could never come up to Smith's standard, and Smith would accuse Butt of shirking and call him a "dissembling rogue." As fellow bond-laborers testified, Smith "would very often Grievously beat the aforesaid Ould John with a Bulls pizzle because he being aged was unable to work." Finally bone weary, utterly broken in body and spirit, John Butt was left in isolation in the winter-idle tobacco house. It was then that he told his fellow bond-laborer Richard Chambers that "the blowes given by his master would be his death," and so they were; Butt died, cold and alone, on the floor of the tobacco house on 25 November 1666.[192] In the absence of further record it appears that Smith was never brought to court for this fatal mistreatment of bond-laborer Butt.

February was a time for clearing woodland that would soon be needed for new tobacco ground. Much of the work involved carrying logs. One Wednesday early in February 1681, James Lewis went to extreme lengths to impress upon his bond-laborers his determination to have the maximum individual effort from them. He became angered when certain of his laborers volunteered to help Joseph Robinson to carry a log which was too heavy for him to manage, even though, as was later revealed, he had nourished himself on a bit of meat stolen from the employer's closet. According to testimony presented to the Maryland Provincial Court, Lewis seized the feeble bond-laborer, "threw him down and Trampled Upon his Throat with such Violence that within Two hours the said Joseph dyed." Then Lewis threatened Mary Naines, another bond-laborer, "to serve her the Same and Swore Dam him he cared not a straw" for the consequences. The employer's careless attitude was not disappointed in the event; though eventually convicted of the murder, he was merely to be "burnt in the hand," a penalty that was more often a cold formality than an actual hot-branding of the fleshy base of the thumb.[193]

In a number of other horrifying cases the record does not link the brutality to supervisory concerns. In three cases now to be briefly noted, it seems that perhaps pure sadistic pleasure may have been the basic motive of the perpetrators. In the summer of 1660, bond-laborer Margarett Redfearne died after a severe beating by her mistress, Anne Nevell. Nevell was found "not Guylty" despite testimony of witnesses to the abuse, and Redfearne's deathbed accusation of Nevell.[194] That same year, bond-laborer Catherine Lake fell down and died within an hour of being kicked by her owner, Thomas Mertine (or Martine). After considering the evidence, including the failure of the corpse to exude blood when touched by the accused, in those times regarded as an accusation of the killer, the jury of twelve men exonerated Mertine.[195] The Maryland Provincial Court record of 27 October 1663 provides the graphic details of the merciless beatings administered by Pope Alvey to his bond-laborer Alice Sandford, which resulted in her death. Alvey was convicted of murder, but by pleading "benefit of clergy" he escaped punishment except for the ritualistic cold-iron "burning" of the flesh of his thumb.[196]

Some scholars who have examined the same documents that I have been citing in this chapter justify the chattel bond-labor system – despite occasional abuses by the owners – as a rational and on the whole benign adaptation to the colonial environment.[197] They are naturally appalled and horrified by the record left by Henry Smith, Pope Alvey, Joseph Fincher and their like. But they seem to ignore the essential relationship between the system of chattel bond-servitude and the documented brutality and hardship to which the chattels were subjected, whether in the extreme cases of murder and rape or in the routine cases of illicit extension of servitude and deprivation of food and clothing.

Psychopathic cruelty can be found in every historical era, and in the seventeenth-century Chesapeake court records there are occasional references to the mentally incompetent.[198] But in no case of murder or rape or other unspeakable brutality by owners of bond-laborers was it even suggested that the owner was acting irrationally. If Smith, Fincher, Alvey were psychopaths, which is the most generous allowance that may be made for them, one must ask why that defense was never invoked in such cases. The record does not tell us; perhaps it would have struck too closely to the irrationality of the same system that in England a century before had been rejected because of its "extremity."[199]

For, psychopaths aside, the records show that the employers of bond-labor were no more charitable toward their workers than were the "spirits", trepanners, "soul drivers", and run-of-the-mill merchants and ship captains in the "servant trade." Were not the "planters" driven by the same compulsion of their social character as accumulators of capital?[200] Who, then would be more likely to succeed in the tobacco-raising business: the owner who, whatever the climate, made lighter demands upon the "unadaptable" laborer, or the master who made heavier demands? And who could have been more vulnerable to those demands than the chattel bond-laborer?

Finally, of the general historians of the seventeenth-century Chesapeake whom I have encountered, with the exception of Allan Kulikoff, none give due attention to the special oppression of women bond-laborers. These workers were routinely sentenced to two and a half years' additional bond-servitude for becoming mothers. Then as now, patriarchy and male suprema-cism were in the ascendant. But the denial of the right to marriage and family, a unique feature of the Anglo-American bond-labor system, in the context of the plantation bond-labor system was not a social aberration; it was an indispensable condition for the preservation of that particular form of capitalist production and accumulation. The chattel bond-labor system of the continental

Anglo-American plantation colonies was incompatible with the status of "coverture" because "coverture" was an insurmountable barrier to the imposition of chattel status on the laborers. At the same time, by nullifying the "a-man's-home-is-his-castle" principle, it denied the plantation bourgeoisie the benefit of the patriarchy as a system of social control over the laboring people.

This is a matter of more than general humanitarian consideration. The family-barring oppression endured by the chattel bond-laborers contributed in a doubly fundamental way to the social tensions that finally rent the social fabric asunder in Bacon's Rebellion. Not only did it directly sharpen the class antagonism of proletariat and bourgeoisie; the very nature of the chattel bond-labor system made impossible the development of a buffer social control stratum normal to English society.

. . . and Resisting

W. E. B. DuBois, in his 1909 address to the American Historical Association on post-Civil War Reconstruction in the South, broke the silence regarding the role of bond-laborers as a self-activating social and political force in American history.[1] In time, thanks largely to the single-minded efforts of Carter G. Woodson, together with his associates in the publication of the *Journal of Negro Life and History*, and then later the studies of revolts of African-American bond-laborers, especially developed by Herbert Aptheker, the attention of a number of other scholars was directed to this aspect of our history. As a result of the consciousness-raising effects of the war against Nazism, and of the civil rights struggles of the 1950s and 1960s, there was an upsurge in interest in the study of the seventeenth-century origin of racial slavery, centering on issues that are noted in the Introduction in Volume One of the present work. That interest has focused on the colonial Chesapeake. But discussion of the bond-laborers as a self-activating social and political force has been almost completely neglected, with the exception of the excellent article by Timothy H. Breen, "A Changing Labor Force and Race Relations in Virginia 1660–1710."[2] Breen's argument is especially distinguished by its correction of the general tendency of historians to rely "too heavily upon statute law as opposed to social practice" in interpreting seventeenth-century Virginia history.[3] Breen was also exemplary in the consistency with which he noted the class character of the struggle of the African-American bond-laborers in the eighteenth century, and the overwhelming disadvantage to their cause "without the support of poorer whites and indentured servants."[4]

The present chapter documents instances of self-activation of bond-laborers as molders of their own fate. In keeping with the basic concern of this work, emphasis will be given to evidence of readiness of European-American bond-laborers to join with African-American bond-laborers in actions and plots of actions against their bondage, and to the readiness of free persons to support the struggles of the bond-laborers, both of which were inconsistent with racial slavery. It is to be hoped that this material will prepare the reader to appreciate the historical significance of the role of bond-laborers in the event called Bacon's Rebellion, and the relation of that event to the invention of the white race.

Where There Is Oppression, There Is Resistance

Where there is oppression, there is resistance, insufficient though it may be. When resistance is enough it becomes rebellion. Where the intermediate buffer social control stratum becomes dysfunctional, rebellion breaks through. So at least the records of the Anglo-American plantation colonies seem to show, particularly those of seventeenth-century Virginia.[5]

Denied a livable life, bond-laborers would commit suicide, hazarding hell's fire; alternatively, they might assault their owners. Starve them and they would steal from their owners, or kill hogs, wild or marked, for clandestine feasts, or on occasion they would rise in defiant mutiny. Bloody their backs with lashes "well laid on," add months or years to their servitude for "stealth of oneself," and they still would run away, singly or "in troops."[6] Double the penalty for European-Americans who ran away with African-Americans; they would do so anyway. Deny them the right to marry and the shield of coverture, lash women's backs; they would seek solace in "fornication," and be damned to ye! Double the penalty for European-American women who mated with African-American men; they would do so anyway. Attenuate the intermediate social control stratum; and at an opportune moment, they would join *en masse* in armed rebellion.

Suicide and assault

One day late in October 1656, a chattel bond-laborer known to the record only as "Thomas, an Irishman" and owned by John Custis, shortened his term of servitude by slashing his own throat and then throwing himself down a well.[7] There is no record of any note left or any notice he may have given for his last decision. Had he been an object in "the Irish slave trade" that thrived in the wake of the English conquest of his country?[8] Or was he perhaps brooding on news, conveyed by his owner, of the "custom-of-the-country" law requiring Irish bond-laborers to serve a year longer than English bond-laborers?[9]

At the height of the 1661 tobacco crop season, a bond-laborer, nameless in the record, "willfully Cast himselfe away" in a creek near his owner's Westmoreland County plantation. That was a year when tobacco prices were falling to their lowest level yet, so that each laborer would have to be made to produce twice as much as he/she had produced a couple of years before, just so the owner might stay even. Perhaps this circumstance added chagrin to the moral outrage of the court's order that this unfaithful worker be "buried at the next cross path . . . with a stake driven through the middle of him."[10] That same year, in York County, where tobacco prices were no higher, Walter Catford with spiteful disregard for the interests of his owner and "for want of Grace tooke a Grind stone and a Roape and tyed it around his Middle and Crosse his thighs and most barbarously went and drowned himselfe contrary to the Laws of the King and this Country."[11]

Bond-laborers of different temperament were disposed to turn their anger outward. They were likely to disappoint ruling-class expectations by individual displays of violence against owners or overseers, and by destruction of their owners' property, despite the whippings and extended bondage that the magistrates were certain to impose when such cases came before them, or even the death sentence that could be imposed by the General Court.

Around the end of 1658, Huntington Ayres, wielding a "lathing hammer," murdered his owner and his owner's wife as they slept.[12] No suggestion as to the particular motive for the murder is recorded; it seems to have been considered simply the extreme denouement of the general master–servant conflict. On 16 January 1671, on an Elke River, Maryland, plantation, owner John Hawkins was slain by axes wielded by a group of three of his bond-laborers – two European-Americans and one African-American – and one European-American former bond-laborer. As servants killing a master, they were charged with "petty treason," as if the motive were thereby sufficiently implied.[13]

The more common form of individual struggle was, in the words of a law passed by the Virginia Assembly in March 1662, "the audacious unruliness of many stubborne and incorridgible servants resisting their masters and over-seers."[14] That law prescribed an extra year of servitude for any bond-laborer who should "lay violent hands on his or her master, mistress or overseer."[15]

A hoe was the weapon of choice for Charles Rogers, Norfolk County bond-laborer, in his assault on his owner one August day in 1666.[16] It was the hoe too for bond-laborer William Page in 1671 in Lancaster County in September, a climactic period in the annual round of "making tobacco." Upon some disagreement with his owner, Page struck at him with a hoe and defied him to attempt to correct him. "God damn him," he was reported as saying, "if his master strock him he would beat out his braynes."[17]

A year later in Northampton County, Portuguese Nicholas Silvio apparently was sometimes absent without leave pursuing a love affair with Mary Gale, a bond-laborer on a nearby plantation, with whom he would soon have a child. When his owner, Captain John Savage, sought to call him to account, Silvio declined to respond, saying "hee was not intended to worke night & day too." Thereupon, Captain Savage made the mistake of kicking at Silvio, who then "flew att his master and struck him 4 blowes" and tore the Master's "good holland shirt very much."[18]

Provoked on some account one day in June 1765, bond-laborer Nicholas Paine (or Pane) threw "five or six bricks or brick batts" at his owner, Colonel Thomas Swann of Surry County, who saved himself by ducking behind a gate. A fellow bond-laborer wondered how Paine dared to do such a thing, and expressed awe at the sign of "the depression of three bricks in the gate." Paine's only comment was, "a plague take the damn gate[;] if it had not bin for that [I] would have hit him."[19]

Although John Bradley had served as a bond-laborer for eleven years – at a time when according to law no non-indentured bond-laborer was supposed to serve more than seven years[20] – the Norfolk County Court in November 1654 rejected Bradley's petition for freedom. Perhaps as a payback to the system for such abuse of his rights, Bradley set fire to a cornfield three times in less than a month.[21] A similar flaming farewell was tendered by bond-laborer John Parris before he ran away in the spring of 1687.[22]

Sometimes several bond-laborers would combine to confront the owner or overseer. In February 1648, the bond-laborers owned by John Wilkins told him in a menacing manner and in rudest terms that "they [would] not any longer bee his servants."[23]

In the matter of diet

In 1662 the penalty for hog-stealing was two years' added servitude for each hog, and a law passed in 1679 made the third offense punishable by death.[24] Yet there are many, many cases of bond-laborers, often acting in small groups, stealing and killing hogs to supplement their corn-and-water diet.[25] Several such group efforts were made by three European-Americans – John Fisher, Thomas Hartley, and Roger Crotofte (variously spelled) – and two African-American bond-laborers – Tony and one not named in the record – all the property of John West, who owned more bond-laborers than anyone else in Accomack County in that year, 1684. The five would more often than not dress and cook the stolen meat and feast on it in "the swamp," or other clandestine rendezvous. Usually they were able to make the food last for several days. When a fellow worker asked John Fisher about the possibility of being charged by a court, Fisher replied that in that circumstance he would run away and "send his master a very Loveing Letter that his sheep, his hogg & turkeys were very fatt."[26]

In other instances bond-laborers sought to improve their diet not by stealth, but by confrontation with the owning class. One Thursday in March 1663 in Calvert County, Maryland, Richard Preston's eight bond-laborers "peremptorily and positively refused to goe to their ordinary labour," saying that their diet of "Beanes and Bread" had made them too weak to "performe the imployments [Preston] putts us uppon." Preston asked the court's help, for fear that from the example of this unruly eight, "a worse evill . . . should ensue by encouraging other servants to do the like."[27] In 1670, bond-laborers owned by a Widow Hale got some alimentary relief when, upon their complaint, the Lancaster County Court ordered that Hale provide a milk cow for the use of the bond-laborers.[28]

In 1661, bond-laborers owned by Major Thomas Goodwin in York County had become "refractory" about their work because of their "hard usage" and being fed "nothing but Corne and water."[29] When magistrate Thomas Beale came to Goodwin's plantation to remonstrate with the workers there about their defiance of authority, he found 24-year-old freeman William Clutton, who well remembered his own sufferings as a bond-laborer. Indeed, he had declined to be Major Beale's overseer precisely because Beale fed his workers so poorly. Clutton told Beale in the presence of the aggrieved bond-laborers that they ought to be provided with meat three times a week and with cows for milking. The workers, taking encouragement from Clutton but realizing that their first idea, for sending a petition to the king in England, was not practicable, resolved to do battle for themselves not just for a better diet, but for an end to their bond-servitude. They would

> get a matter of Forty of them together & get Gunnes & . . . cry as they went along who would be for liberty and free from bondage & that there would be enough come to them & they would goe through the Countrey and Kill those that made any opposition that they would be either free or dye for it.[30]

The plot, frustrated by discovery, was investigated by Magistrate Beale. Seeing in the event a tendency to the "Disturbance of the peace of the Country & to the hazard of men's lives," Beale ordered "the Magistrates and Masters to looke into the practices & behaviour of their Servants." William Clutton was so widely respected that after he promised to cease his agitation of the workers, his good-behavior bond was returned to him.

Two years later the largest, most widespread insurrectionary plot of bond-laborers was discovered in Gloucester County, Virginia. Unfortunately, as a result of the total destruction of Gloucester County records in two fires, in 1821 and 1865, only a few scraps of the record remain concerning this event.[31]

The design was hatched by a number of Cromwellian veterans who had been sentenced to be transported to bond-servitude by the restored monarchy of Charles II. On the first weekend in September the plotters gathered in the house of Mr Knight (apparently a sympathetic free man) to discuss "a designe for their freedom"; each and all were pledged to secrecy on pain of death. The revolt was to be launched from their rendezvous at Poplar Spring at midnight on the following Sunday, 14 September. The core group, bringing with them "what Company, armes, and ammunicion [they] could gett," would assemble at Poplar Spring. Then, moving forth with the confidence of veterans, they would seize arms, ammunition and a drum from the militia's store. They would "goe from house to house to house" rallying bond-laborers to join in a grand march to Governor William Berkeley and demand their freedom. If the governor should refuse, they would "march out of the Country."

Their plan was betrayed to the authorities by a bond-laborer named Berkenhead,[32] so that the militia authorities were able to get to the Poplar Spring rendezvous ahead of the rebels and arrest them as they arrived. But word spread of the militia's trap, and only a few of the rebels were apprehended; of those, four were hanged.

The colony authorities were shaken by the revelation of the insurrectionary threat to the rule of the plantation bourgeoisie. The Virginia Assembly made the day of its discovery, 13 September, an annual holy day, and granted Berkenhead his immediate freedom and a reward of 5,000 pounds of tobacco.[33] Two other, more substantial, measures were taken in reaction to this event. One was the passage of a new law requiring owners of bond-laborers to prevent the workers from leaving the plantations to which they belonged without explicit permission, "on Sundayes or any other dayes."[34] The other, which will be further noted in Chapter 11 was a proposal to tax by landholding rather than by poll, thus disfranchising the landless poor.[35] While the record makes no mention of African-Americans in connection with the 1663 plot, it is of interest to the present study that there is no indication of any exclusionary tendency on the part of the plotters; rather, their depositions suggest that they intended to recruit every last bond-laborer to their freedom march.

Flight and "fornication"

Of the various ways that the bond-laborers found for defying and resisting their oppressors, the two most common forms were:[36] (1) continual attempts to free themselves by running away (a common theme of studies of the life and status of laborers in that period); and (2) sexual liaisons – criminalized under the term "fornication" – conducted in defiance of the ruling-class denial of the bond-laborer's right to be married (an aspect that, so far as I know, has not previously been even acknowledged as resistance to the owning class, except by Warren M. Billings and by Joseph Douglas Deal III).[37]

Running away

The official records regarding runaway bond-laborers, with few exceptions, concern cases in which recaptured fugitives are being arraigned or are listed in claims being made for payment to the "takers-up" of such fugitives. Occasionally there are grounds for believing that some of the runaways succeeded in avoiding recapture. Owners might refrain from bringing such cases to official attention because of the distance to be traveled to see the magistrate, or the inconvenient timing of court days, or the incidental fees that might have to be borne by the owner if the runaways were not caught; undoubtedly these factors together were responsible for many flights never being noted in the record.[38] For the great runaway year 1676–77, there is a general hiatus in the records in consequence of Bacon's Rebellion, which was fueled by the adherence to it of great numbers of "runaway" bond-laborers.[39]

In many instances bond-laborers sought to escape the jurisdiction of Virginia authorities by fleeing to the Indians, to Dutch colonial territory, to Pennsylvania, or to the more newly formed neighboring Maryland and North Carolina (known as Albemarle until 1691). Probably fewer than half the runaways traveled alone. Many were in groups of two or three, but there were instances of larger undertakings. In Gloucester County (whose records, as previously noted, have all been lost), the General Assembly noted in 1661 that "servants and other idlers [were] running away in troops."[40] I have tabulated a total of between 880 and 890 individual fugitives who were subject to the attention of the county courts. In addition, an indeterminate number were referred to by terms such as "several" and "groups," or simply as "servants" in the plural without enumeration.

With regard to the central concern of this work – the question of the origin of racial oppression – two facts of transcendent significance are presented by the record of runaways. First, considering the fact that no more than about one out of every four or five bond-laborers was an African-American even as late as the 1670s and 1680s,[41] there was a considerable degree of collaboration of African-Americans and European-Americans in a common endeavor to escape. In the records I have examined, such collaboration was noted in fifteen separate instances involving a total of some seventy or seventy-five persons.[42] Second, there was a readiness of free persons to assist bond-laborers in running away, as recorded in fifteen instances involving fifty-eight people. In this chapter, I accordingly cite principally instances that represent these two aspects of the runaway phenomenon. However, with respect to the subjective or ideological element, these cases do not differ in the least from any of the others; all represented a common front against the chattel bond-labor system, free of any evidence of social distinction or prejudice.

One form of resistance of women bond-laborers to their double yoke of gender and class oppression was to run away, usually in the company of men – bond-laborers or free sympathizers – but in some cases without male support. The generally greater vulnerability of women to the perils faced in leaving the plantation in this new strange country would seem obvious. Nevertheless, despite the fact that they were a relatively minor proportion in the population, among the runaways I have noted from the records there were sixty-nine women, including six African-Americans and two Indians.

By 1640, two years after Colony Secretary Kemp had reported on the predominance of human merchandise among Virginia immigrants, the Virginia General Court was receiving daily complaints about "servants that run away from their masters whereby much loss ... doth ensue to the masters." The problem had reached such proportion that the Colony Council made the recapture of runaway bond-laborers a public concern, and ordered that the expense of recovering fugitives be borne not by the owner, but by the public treasury of the counties involved.[43]

Early in June 1640, three Virginia bond-laborers, "Victor, a dutchman ... a Scotchman called James Gregory ... [and] a negro named John Punch," escaped together to Maryland. Unfortunately they were pursued and, at the insistence of the Virginia Colony Council, they were brought back to face the Virginia General Court.[44] That same month, the Virginia Colony Council and General Court commissioned a Charles City County posse to pursue "certain runaway negroes." The provision that the cost was to be shared by all the counties from which they had run away suggests that the phenomenon was extensive.[45] Since no further record seems to exist regarding this particular undertaking, perhaps these workers avoided recapture.

As if encouraged by such a possibility, seven bond-laborers – Andrew Noxe, Richard Hill, Richard Cookson, Christopher Miller, Peter Wilcocke (presumably English), an African-American, Emanuel, and John Williams ("a dutchman") – set off one Saturday night a month later in a stolen boat, with arms, powder and shot. They, however, were taken up before they could reach open water.[46]

In October of that same year, "a most dangerous conspiracy" was entered into by three free men – John Bradye, John Tomkinson, and Richard West – and six bond-laborers – Margaret Beard, John Winchester, William Wooton, William Drummer, Robert Rouse, and Robert Moseley – "to run out of the country" to "the Dutch plantation."[47] The plan was discovered before it could be executed. The punishments meted out by the authorities appear to reflect an increasing alarm that such escapes would reduce the pressure that employers might bring to bear on laborers in the course of their routine employments. In addition to the thirty-stripe whippings, extended periods of servitude, and the working in shackles imposed in the case of Noxe et al., a number of those charged with extensive conspiracies in this case were to be punished also by being branded on the cheek and the shoulder.[48]

In the fall of 1645, an African-American bond-laborer Phillip, owned by Captain Phillip Hawley, helped runaway European-American bond-laborer Sibble Ford hide from her pursuers for twenty days in a cave on Hawley's plantation. His collaborator was European-American Thomas Parks, who addressed the court defiantly when he was arraigned for going about "to intice and inveigle the mens Servants to runn away . . . out of their masters service."[49]

Two large-scale efforts to escape were made in Accomack County in the mid-1660s. In August 1663, some ten bond-laborers ran away together from Eastern Shore plantations. Making use of a horse named Tom Hall and a "good boat," they headed for points north – "the Dutch plantation," "the Manhatans," "New England." Although John Bloxam and Robert Hodge were retaken within a week, it was four years before Miles Grace was caught; but Thomas Hedrington and Robin Parker, and possibly others, were still free. John Tarr was captured, but as soon as he could he again escaped with three others; though Tarr was again caught, the others succeeded in eluding their pursuers.[50]

An elaborate plot was discovered in 1670 in Accomack County. It began with a group of some half-dozen bond-laborers inspired by the report of four others who had succeeded in escaping from another Eastern shore plantation at Pocomoke. A first attempt was made in October, that time being chosen because men of the local "power elite" would then be in Jamestown for a meeting of the General Assembly. However, because of a strong contrary northwest wind that blew on the night chosen for the escape, the men decided to stow the sails prepared for the escape craft and postpone the effort, although Mary Warren protested that "shee never saw such fooles in her life to loose such a opportunity." A second attempt was to be made, and on a grander scale. A score of bond-laborers from several Eastern Shore plantations, along with three to five free persons,[51] were eventually pledged to the enterprise. They were resolved to make good their purpose "by force against all that should oppose" them, according to one of their number, 25-year-old bond-laborer Renney Sadler. Depositions later given before the magistrate revealed that the runaways had planned to tie up one owner, Devorax Brown, and his wife,[52] disable the horse from pursuing, and carry off a large gun for installation on the small sailing vessel, a sloop, that would carry them to freedom. The sloop was to be well stocked with food prepared by a woman co-conspirator who had access to the necessary provisions. Their aim was to sail up Chesapeake Bay to "the dutch plantation" or "New England," with "black James," reputed "the best pylot in the land," at the helm.[53] Perhaps because the plan involved too many people and the preparation period was too long for the preservation of the necessary secrecy, their purpose was discovered in December and prevented.[54]

In February 1672, European-American bond-laborer William Richardson and an African-American bond-laborer, not named in the record, ran away together. How or why they became separated is not revealed, but only Richardson was recaptured and arraigned eight and a half years later; his partner was apparently never heard of again in those parts.[55] In the summer of 1679, three European-American bond-laborers, Mary Axton, Mary West and William Siller, together with African-American bond-laborer Thomas George, somehow managed to escape from the James River plantation belonging to their owner, Lieutenant-Colonel Thomas Milner, and row or sail across Chesapeake Bay to Hog's Neck on the Eastern Shore.[56] Later that same summer in Lancaster County, European-American bond-laborers William Adams, Robert Bull and John Stookley and an African-American bond-laborer, Tom, coordinated their efforts over three different plantations to run away in a boat belonging to a fourth plantation.[57] An African-American, whose name is not supplied in the record, and his fellow bond-laborer Hugh Callon in April 1683 collaborated in running away from the plantation of their owner, Colonel Thomas Brereton in Northumberland County.[58] European-American Thomas Callen [or Caller] and his African-American comrade William Powell "stole themselves" away from their owner, Aron Spring of Elizabeth River. They managed to get a boat in which they crossed Chesapeake Bay and reached Maggoty Bay in Northampton County; there they apparently became separated. Powell was taken up in May 1687, but a year later Callen still had not been recaptured.[59] Appropriating a boat and two sheep, three laborers, Anthony Jackson and Michael Connell, European-Americans, and Mingo, an African-American, ran away from their owner, Charles Egerton, some time before 5 August 1688.[60]

While it is not possible from the record to fit all the pieces together, there is no doubt that bond-laborers were resolved on escaping from Mr Ralph Wormeley, Esquire, their owner, of Middlesex County. In 1687 "John Nickson ... with divers other ill-disposed servants and others" were charged with having plotted "to procure Gunnes powder and Shott and other Armes and to Assemble themselves together with Design to withstand and Oppose all persons that should endeavour to Suppress them ... tending to the greate disturbance of his Majesties Peace and the terrours of his liege people."[61] Despite the discovery of the scheme, it appears that after a delay of some eighteen months the plotters succeeded to some extent; having taken guns and ammunition, a number of the rebels, including African-Americans Mingoe and Lawrence, and European-American Richard Wilkins, remained free for "a Considerable time," in Wilkins's case some twenty-eight months.[62]

The name of Richard Ayry's African-American friend is unknown to the court record; together they planned and, "in the height of the [1688] crop season," executed their escape from Captain Richard Kenner's plantation in Northumberland County.[63] African-American Thomas Roberts and Portuguese John Sherry, two bond-laborers belonging to William Wise, fled from York County, Virginia, on 18 August 1690 and stuck together all the way to Philadelphia.[64]

Free laboring people aid runaway bond-laborers
In the summer of 1669, the Widow Buckmaster and her son Henry Crow refused to enlist in the hue and cry after a runaway bond-laborer belonging to John Harris; instead, they harbored the fugitive in their own house.[65] Thomas Stephens, a skilled seaman, was arraigned in Lancaster County in March 1675 on the charge of devoting his expertise to being "the chiefe causer promoter and instrumenter" in the escape of three bond-laborers who had not been heard of since.[66] Late in 1675, freeman John Fennell accompanied bond-laborers William Beverly and his wife and Jane Getting in running away from their owner, William Carver.[67] At the June session of the Accomack County Court, freeman Thomas Lehay was found guilty of habitually assisting bond-laborers to run away. He was ordered to post £20 sterling for his future "good behaviour."[68]

Freeman Emanuell Rodriggus, an African-American, was brought before the February 1672 session of the Northampton County Court for having "unlawfully entertayned" two runaway European-American bond-laborers owned by Captain John Custis of Northampton County.[69] In mid-summer 1679, four African-Americans, including one child too young to work, ran away in the company of two free European-Americans, John Watkings and Agness Clerk.[70] In November 1690, freeman Edward Short was arraigned for "helping and assisting" European-American Roger Crotuff [Crotofte] and African-American bond-laborer John Johnson to break out of the Accomack county prison.[71] After Ann Redman, an African-American, took her child and ran away from the plantation of European-American Thomas Loyd in February 1696, she was sought by hue and cry. Some twenty months later Redman was seized from the home of European-American Edwin Thacker, where she had found refuge.[72]

In Henrico County early in 1696, two African-Americans, Betty and a man described only as being a "mulatto," ran away and were sheltered in the home of Henry Turner. Somehow constable Edward Tanner was able to arrest Betty and to confine her in his house. Betty broke out at night, however, and returned to Turner's place. Tanner, with two assistants, came to Turner's house and sought to seize and bind the African-American man (the "mulatto"), who naturally resisted, Tanner called upon Turner to help subdue the man, but Turner

> not only refused to assist [Constable Tanner], but forewarned[?] every body from meddling with the said malotto, and when [Tanner] with Edward Ward [his buddy] had gott the said Malloto fellow down and were going to binde him, Henry Turner caught hold of the Rope and plucket it from them, and threw it out of Doors, and taking up a hoe helve said that the fellow (meaning the mallatto that was seized) should not be tyed there for he [Turner] would defend him; which words so Encouraged the mallatto That he took up a pistoll that lay by him and Kockt it, but Tanner and [one of his helpers] layed hold of him and wrested the piston out of his hands, and again endeavoured to binde him; but Henry Turner catching hold of the pistoll that then was in [Tanner's helper's] hand said he would lay him in the face if he did not let goe; and the mallatto recovering his Gun and [standing] upon his Guard [Tanner along with his two buddies] who endeavoured to assist ... [were] forced to desist & goe their ways; all which [Constable Tanner] conceives to be a matter of Evill Consequence.[73]

Defiant solace

Deny them the right to marry and the shield of coverture; they would "fornicate" and be damned to ye. Double the penalty for European-American women who mated with African-American men; they would do so anyway.

As noted in Chapter 7, chattel bond-laborer status was incompatible with marriage. Furthermore, despite the various expedients adopted for recapturing the owner's or the parish's expenses for support of the children of limited-term bond-laborers, natural increase was a relatively unprofitable way of recruiting plantation labor-power in the seventeenth-century tobacco colonies. In these circumstances, it was simply good "bottom line" logic to outlaw sex by limited-term bond-laborers, calling it "fornication," for which cruel penalties were imposed. (See Chapter 7 pages 128–9.)

Male supremacism was a fundamental premise of Anglo-American colonial life as it was in England. The seventeenth-century records present depressing confirmation of that fact. Crimes against and abuse of women by men of all classes sometimes became the subject of judicial notice, in cases including uxoricide, rape, denial of access to food, eviction, sexual abuse, economic exploitation, and battery. Altogether I have noted 367 court cases relating to gender oppression. As has been argued in Chapter 7, chattel bond-servitude, which was the condition of the overwhelming majority of women arriving in the tobacco colonies, gave an added dimension to male supremacism, a distinctive blend of class and gender oppression that accounted for 304 of the cases characterized in the record as "fornication" and "bastardy." These more than three hundred court cases, in which the rigor of the law was visited upon women bond-laborer "fornicators," necessarily involved somewhere around twice that number of persons. If the figure of 850 listed runaway bond-laborers is indicative of widespread bond-laborer resistance to the system of chattel bond-servitude, so must the persistent and pervasive assertion by bond-laborers of the right to the solace of sexual relations be regarded as rejection of the enforced sexual abstinence imposed upon them as an essential characteristic of that very system.

In 140 of those 304 cases, the identity of the male partner is known.[74] In all, 17 were owners, 2 were overseers. Of the remaining 121, 67, including 2 African-Americans, were freemen, the great majority of whom had been bond-laborers.[75] Some 54 were bond-laborers – 31 European-Americans, 22 African-Americans, and 1 American Indian.[76]

Leaving aside the instances of sexual relations involving owners and overseers, in which the feelings of the bond-laborers hardly needed to be consulted, what do the general statistics and the particular case records suggest about the motivations of the bond-laborers in the other cases? The sex instinct of a bond-laborer was a power that the plantation bourgeoisie could only hope to curb by fear of legal retribution, glossed by preachments on the virtue of "abstinence." Abstinence, however, was one thing the bond-laborers had in plenty: "abstinence" from decent food, clothing, and shelter, from possessions, from receiving wages, from marriage and "coverture," from normal home life. At the same time, the record shows what one might assume, namely that sexually exploitative motives were common to persons of all social classes. In the male-supremacist environment, such motives accounted for the seduction, abandonment and sexual exploitation of many women, particularly those most vulnerable, the bond-laborers.

The predominance of freemen as partners in these cases may be significant. Anne Collins's interest in freeman Robert Pierce was particularly based on the hope to escape her bondage by alliance with him. "I should never have yielded to his desyres but hee told me he would free me from my Master, whatsoever it would cost him & that hee had Stocke Cattle Servants & a plantation [and] that I should ride his mare & then your [Collins's] Mistress will think much."[77] Despite the risks such bond-laborers ran in "yielding to the desyres" of freemen, it is reasonable to assume that Anne Collins's motivation was a common one for women bond-laborers. In such cases each woman bond-laborer was conducting her own individual strategy for throwing off chattel bondage, even though to do so risked subjection to a husband. Although liaisons between male bond-laborers and free women were rare, perhaps men in those cases were also motivated by a hope of gaining their freedom through such a connection. Yet truly felt and mutual love and sympathy in resistance to the bond-labor system might still have motivated sexual partners even in cases where those feelings were confused with hope for an improved social status.

We have noted that Lucy Stratton was one who did not invest herself in such confusion. In contrast to Anne Collins, Stratton spurned her owner's offer of marriage because she did not love him, and because his interest in her was mere lust.[78] In making the distinction between mere sexual male exploitation and love, she showed the normal desire to be truly loved and cherished, sexually and otherwise.

Being by law denied the right to dispose of property, as lovers bond-laborers[79] had little to offer each other but comfort and emotional support.[80] In 86 of the 140 male-partner-identified "fornication" cases brought against women bond-laborers, the men were free men, and thus property considerations and social mobility expectations might have been factors. Yet there were 50 instances of such charges against women bond-laborers where the man was a bond-laborer.[81]

One does not find many avowals of romantic love in seventeenth-century court records; love letters written by the bond-laborers and the free poor persons of that place and time must be extremely rare, if indeed any exist at all. But one can imagine the sense of love and fear, elation and despair, the passionate avowals and practical concerns they might have expressed regarding experiences described in court records. What love note could more adequately testify to their mutual devotion, for instance, than the decision of two lovers to risk together the perils and penalties of flight from chattel servitude?

What observations were exchanged on love and bondage between Penelope Sandford and Adam Robinson? In June 1666, for becoming parents, those two bond-laborers were sentenced to added servitude of two and a half years and two years respectively. Yet they persisted in their relationship, and a year later they were ordered to be whipped as "incorrigibble fornicators whom no goodness Mercy & admonition can reforme."[82] What might their diary have said about that day when they first decided that being together was worth the risk?

As the seasons changed in 1685, how did runaway bond-laborers William Lloyd and Mary Seymore cheer and advise each other in those nearly ten months before they were recaptured, still together?[83]

What would the journal of African-American bond-laborer Warner and Mrs Welch have told of adventures they experienced as they fled from Accomack County to Pennsylvania some time before September 1685? What opinions did they offer to each other on husbands and masters? Returned by order of a Pennsylvania justice of the peace, they were put in James City jail, and again escaped briefly, before they were retaken and assigned to be tried by a member of the Virginia Colony Council.[84] What might they have recalled for each other in all that time about their respective backgrounds, and of the universal language of love?

In Essex County, bond-laborer Robert Hughes and free woman Ellinor sought to sanctify their relationship by marriage in 1703. To their dismay, they were prosecuted under the law passed against bond-laborers marrying without their owners' prior consent.[85] Hughes was sentenced to an added year of bondage; Ellinor was ordered to pay Hughes's owner 1,500 pounds of tobacco or else she, too, would have to serve that owner for a full year as a bond-laborer.[86] What might the diary of one or the other disclose to us on the conquering power of love over bondage, and on the importance of defying the hypocrisy of the law?

Among the 54 identified male bond-laborer partners in the "fornication" cases examined, 22 were African-Americans involved with European-American women. This was a much higher percentage than the proportion of African-Americans in the bond-labor force. Although the record does not afford a reason for this disproportion, it is a fact that the plantation bourgeoisie came to regard the mating of European-Americans with African-Americans as a serious problem for themselves.[87] In any case, it appears to have been in keeping with the readiness of European-American and African-American bond-laborers to make common cause in the other respects described in this chapter.

No "White Race"

Through Acts of the General Assembly, the plantation bourgeoisie early on expressed its disposition to deny equal rights to African-Americans.[88] The evidence, however, clearly indicates that this purpose of the ruling class did not represent the desire or attitude of the European-American bond-laborers as a whole, or indeed of the common run of European-Americans in general. At the same time, however, it is not surprising that the explicitly anti-Negro tenor of these laws would find some echo in the attitude of ruled-over European-Americans, bond and free. I have found those instances to have been extremely few, however, in comparison to the record of solidarity of European-American and African-American bond-laborers, and in comparison to the readiness of free laboring-class European-Americans to make common cause with African-American fugitives from bond-labor. Here are the only such exceptional cases that I have turned up.

The General Assembly enacted a series of laws, beginning in 1662,[89] directed specifically against African-American women. In February 1669, bond-laborer Mary Hughes, appealing in vain against being raped by her owner, Henry Smith, said "he would make her worse than a Negroe by whoreing her."[90] In 1694, a deposition in a slander case told of mutual accusations between two European-American women of sexual misalliances with various European-American men, and claimed that one had said that the other was "such a whore that she would lye with a Negro."[91]

In Accomack County one day in 1677, when tavern-keeper George Boies refused credit to Indian bond-laborer James, James promptly invited Boies to "Kiss my Arse." Next, Boies and James exchanged the compliments of "Indian Dog" and "English Dogg." Boies attacked James; another patron, bond-laborer (or possibley former bond-laborer) Alexander Dun urged James to return the blows against Boies, and James did so.[92]

Some time prior to November 1681, European-American bond-laborer David Griffin, avowed in the course of an altercation with his overseer, an Indian named James Revell, that "it should never be said that he did yeild to an Indian Dog."[93]

On 5 November 1681, Frank, the African-American "servant" of Mr Vaulx, was sent by Vaulx to "speak with John Machart [or Macarty] about business." Machart and a friend he was with rebuffed Frank, saying "they were no company for Negroes." The following day at the Vaulx house, where some six or seven men were drinking, fighting occurred between Frank's friend Peter Wells and Machart, and then between Frank and Machart. It began with offense being taken by both Frank and Peter Wells at Machart's pretension of superiority. Just before the fighting began, Wells said to Frank, "God damn them he was as good a man as the best of them."[94]

In 1691, when Hannah Warwick was charged with refusing to do her work, the General Court made extenuation on the grounds that "she was overseen by a negro overseer."[95]

By contrast, in none of the hundreds of cases of the oppression of bond-laborers and the resistance by them have I found any instance in which European-American bond-laborers expressed a desire to dissociate their sufferings and struggle from those of the African-American bond-laborers, the case of Mary Hughes being the exception, and perhaps that of Hannah Warwick. It is to be noted that in three of these six exceptional incidents of hostility directed by non-ruling-class European-Americans at non-European-Americans, European-American bystanders were present; in two cases out of the three, the bystanders actively dissociated themselves from such chauvinism.

In general, as this chapter has illustrated, despite the six exceptions cited, the attitude of the laboring-class European-Americans stood in sharp contrast to the succession of enactments whereby the plantation bourgeoisie pressed for the lifetime, hereditary bond-servitude of African-American bond-laborers, and for the circumscription of the rights, and the ultimate practical proscription of free African-Americans.[96]

Two fair conclusions would seem to follow: First, "the white race" – supra-class unity of European-Americans in opposition to African-Americans – did not and could not have then existed. Second, the invention of the white race at the beginning of the eighteenth century can in no part be ascribed to demands by European-American laboring people for privileges *vis-à-vis* African-Americans.

9

The Insubstantiality of the
Intermediate Stratum

Virginia Colony evolved under the direct rule of a tiny elite which, in the fifteen years leading up to Bacon's Rebellion, included fewer than four hundred men, probably numbering no more than two hundred at any one time, owners of an average of 4,200 acres of land each.[1] The lowest-ranking members of this stratum were the county[2] commissioners, deliberately limited by Act of Assembly in 1661 to no more than eight per county,[3] who acted collectively as the county court, and served individually as magistrates, justices of the peace, in their respective districts. The members of the county courts, among whom the office of sheriff was rotated annually, were appointed from time to time by the Colony Council and Governor, upon the recommendation of the sitting members of the particular county court.[4] Next came the members of the Virginia House of Burgesses who were invariably elected from among the members of the county courts. Originally the vote was exercised by all freemen but as the ranks of propertyless former bond-laborers increased, in 1670 the General Assembly deliberately excluded these latter from the right to vote.[5] At the top were the Governor (appointed by Charles II, king of England during this period) and the Virginia Colony Council, made up of men appointed by the Governor with the formal approval of the General Assembly, the term used to describe the House of Burgesses and the Colony Council together. The Governor and the Colony Council constituted the General Court.[6]

County court and magistrate orders were enforced by the county sheriffs and constables, and through pursuit by hue and cry. But hue and cry after runaway bond-laborers was so generally neglected that in 1658 the General Assembly ordered the imposition of fines on householders and constables for such lapses in civic responsibility.[7] Two years later the General Assembly again faulted the constables for neglect of their duty to hunt down runaways.[8] In 1669, the General Assembly not only noted the plots made by bond-laborers to escape their owners but also charged that "some planters," instead of arresting the fugitives, "have given them assistance and directions how to escape."[9] The General Assembly then proceeded to provide a reward, not only to encourage constables but to enlist the general public in the capture of runaway bond-laborers, by offering to any person one thousand pounds of tobacco for each runaway recaptured. It was intended that when bond-laborers became aware of "soe many spies upon them," they would "keep within the bounds of their duty."[10] The general subject of runaways has been treated in Chapter 8; the point here is to emphasize the absence of an effective social control stratum.

Every man between the ages of sixteen and sixty was subject to service in the militia. Its organizational structure derived from the political structure of organization of the colony, the militia of each county being officered by local members of the colony elite. An establishing order issued by Governor Francis Moryson in June 1661 required each county to mobilize three militia companies, to be made up of "freemen and Servants of undoubted fidelity." Because the population was so widely dispersed that the entire county regiment could not be mobilized for sudden emergencies, a special unit called the "settled trayned band," was to be formed of one-eighth of the entire regiment and divided into three companies, selected because of the members' proximity to the plantation of the regiment's captain.[11] The Governor and Colony Council were obliged to confess the incompetence of the militia for sustained service, citing two factors: the impossibility of storing sufficient corn to sustain the militia on extended duty, because of the infestation of the grain by vermin; and the strenuous objections of the men against being diverted from making their tobacco crop.[12]

In summary, I quote Professor Morgan:

> There was no trained constabulary. The county commissioners, who annually chose the constables in each county, usually rotated the job among men of small means, who could not afford the fines for refusing to take it. There was no army except the militia, composed of men who would be as unlikely as the constables to make effective instruments for suppressing the insubordination of their own kind.[13]

There was, then, in Virginia no intermediate social control stratum based on a secure yeoman class such as had been preserved in England.

The Deference and Reverence Deficit

In well-ordered class societies, ancient traditions of pomp and circumstance play a vital part in instructing the masses in subservience to "their betters." "[R]everence," wrote Francis Bacon, "is that wherewith princes are girt from God."[14] But the claim to authority of the seventeenth-century planter elite rested on raw acquisitiveness, expressed first of all in their possession of mainly English bond-laborers, and in their large handholdings based not on ancient titles but on headrights purchased by import of human chattels.[15] There were no storied manors in Virginia to which they could say they had been born. Furthermore, the fact that the elite planters were necessarily as involved as the poorest of their neighbors in the cheek-by-jowl competition each for his share in the tobacco market was not calculated to promote a deferential attitude toward the same elite planters as the ruling circle.

Auxiliary institutions, particularly those of established religion, render indispensable service in preserving and protecting the awe in which ruling classes need to be held. But that great pillar of reverence for authority the established Church of England did not travel well to seventeenth-century Virginia, where it enjoyed the status of a mere subdivision of the London bishopric. Whereas in England the parish minister, upon recommendation of some eminent person or of a university, was appointed with life tenure, in Virginia, parish vestries made up of rich local planters had the nomination of the minister who was then formally chosen by the Governor rather than by a clerical authority. The result was that ministers, being no more than hired hands employed from year to year at the pleasure of the vestries, often lapsed into demoralization. In cataloguing the sad conditions prevailing in Virginia in the middle of the seventeenth century, an English clerical critic asserted that the colony's ministers were "for the most part, not only far short of those qualifications required in Ministers ... but men of opposite qualities and tempers ... by their loose lives, and un-Gospel becoming conversation."[16] Such a church "could not play its traditional role of fostering obedient habits" among the colonists.[17]

The Anglican church was enfeebled, and neither was the political climate favorable to Puritans. Quakers were outlawed in the seventeenth century; official hostility towards them did not slacken until early in the eighteenth century.[18] In any case, ministers were so few and far between that even if every one of them had been willing and able to play the social buffer role, they would have been an insufficient leaven for the colony's lump of irreverence. In a colony of forty or fifty thousand widely scattered people, there were only thirty-five Anglican priests in 1680.[19]

What is one to conclude, then, about the state of ruling-class social control in the decade before Bacon's Rebellion, when Colony Secretary Thomas Ludwell was fain to confess that Virginia's small landholders were restrained from rebellion only by "faith in the mercy of God, loyalty to the King, and affection for the Governor"?[20]

A Society Shaped by Monoculture

The basic cause of the failure of the plantation elite to establish a viable system of social control in the seventeenth century was, of course, the tobacco monocultural economy itself. Rainbolt stated the case most clearly:

> A colony where most men pursued the same occupation of tobacco planter seemed ill suited to the emergence of a heirarchical social system. A Province where most men lived in relative isolation on scattered plantations prevented that constant scrutiny of inferiors by their superiors deemed vital to the order of a society.[21]

After the margin of profit had been stabilized by the institution of the new chattel bond-labor relation of production in the 1620s, the farm price of Chesapeake tobacco averaged about 4*d*. per pound in the 1630s.[22] In the next two decades, however, the average price was reduced by almost half, to 2.2*d*. It is impossible to fix the year when the falling tendency of tobacco prices reached the critical level in regard to ruling-class social control, but the decline of tobacco to an average of 1.2*d*. per pound for the entire decade and a half beginning in 1660 was a basic condition for the eruption in 1676 of the social control crisis known to history as Bacon's Rebellion.[23]

Tobacco planters were trapped in a vicious spiral: efforts by each planter to make up in volume for the declining price forced all to do as each; as this drove the price even lower, the planters fell ever deeper into debt. In 1664 the planters of Virginia and Maryland went into debt of £50,000 on their shipments to England.[24] But the burden did not fall uniformly on the planters; indeed, it tended to enrich the planter elite.

Warren M. Billings has analyzed the year-to-year changes in the level of the indebtedness in six Virginia counties for the period 1660–75[25] by tabulating the amounts for which creditors sued for payment.[26] The total debt of all planters in cases decided in the courts of those six counties averaged 3,243,000 pounds of tobacco per year. In those counties, with a total population of several thousand,[27] the thirty or so members of the plantation elite accounted for 35.6 percent of the total credit, with the debts owed *to* members of the elite class amounting to twice as much as the amounts owed *by* them.[28] Social dissolution was especially portended by the fact that the indebtedness gap between the elite and the general run of planters tended to increase as time went on, by an average of 375,000 pounds of tobacco every year during the sixteen-year period.[29] The records suggest that the deteriorating conditions of the non-elite planters in these six counties were typical of Virginia as a whole.

This discrepancy between the elite and non-elite with respect to the debt burden would seem to be a reflection of a marked tendency toward concentration of land in the hands of the former (see Table 9.1). Morgan finds an extreme degree of land engrossment by headright for other counties: in 1658, thirty persons owned most of the land – 100,000 acres – on the south side of the Potomac; in 1664, 33,750 acres of headright land went to only thirteen persons in Accomack County, and 15,050 acres of Rappahannock land was claimed by only six persons. These nineteen patents accounted for 30 percent of all the headright acres patented in Virginia in that year, and averaged over 2,500 acres each; eight patents in Accomack, Isle of Wight and Rappahannock counties, averaging more than 4,300 acres each, accounted for 23 percent of all headright land patented in Virginia in 1666.[30] These figures from various counties appear consistent with and confirm the trend suggested by the comparison of figures for 1626 and 1704 shown in Table 9.1.[31]

The most significant indicator of increasing concentration of capital, however, is the number of laborers per plantation. Kevin P. Kelly's study of the records of Surry County, on the south side of the James River, revealed that

Table 9.1 Increase in concentration of landholdings in Virginia, 1626–1704

Holdings	1626	1704
100 acres or less		
(a) % of total acres	24.9%	4.9%
(b) % of all holdings	54.0%	24.0%
(c) no. of holdings	126	1,316
(d) acres	8,610	112,100
(e) average size	68	85
101 to 499 acres		
(a) % of total acres	41.4%	32.7%
(b) % of all holdings	36.9%	54.3%
(c) no. of holdings	42	2,971
(d) acres	13,140	742,000
(e) average size	313	250
500 to 999 acres		
(a) % of total acres	22.5%	22.3%
(b) % of all holdings	7.7%	13.5%
(c) no. of holdings	14	738
(d) acres	7,800	504,300
(e) average size	557	683
1,000 acres or more		
(a) % of total acres	10.2%	40.1%
(b) % of all holdings	1.6%	8.4%
(c) no. of holdings	3	461
(d) acres	3,582	907,900
(e) average size	1,284	1,969

Sources: John C. Hotten, *The Original Lists*, pp. 266–74, patented land in Virginia in 1626; 1704 Virginia Rent Rolls, printed in T. J. Wertenbaker, *The Planters of Colonial Virginia* (Princeton, 1922).

there, small households dominated throughout the seventeenth century, although "there was a growing divergence between the large planters controlling more than ten laborers, and the small, independent planter."[32] Wertenbaker found that the Surry County ratio of tithables to taxpayers in 1675 and 1685, considered together, was 18 to 10, but by 1704 the comparable ratio, of tithables to freeholders, was 39 to 10.[33] Edward Randolph, Royal Inspector of Customs, reported to the Lords of Trade and Plantations in 1696 that the "chief and only reason" for the retarded development of Virginia colony was that "Members of the Council and others ... have from time to time procured grants of very large Tracts of Land." By the use of headrights, he said, many of this elite group held "twenty or thirty thousand acres of land apiece" which were left unplanted yet unavailable to prospective planters.[34]

Reflecting the results of such egregious engrossment of headright land by importation of bond-laborers by the plantation bourgeoisie, 60 to 65 per cent of Virginia landholders, according to Wertenbaker's estimate, had no bond-laborers at all in the closing two or two and a half decades of the seventeenth century.[35] A corresponding pattern of differentiation is apparent in Russell R. Menard's comparison of estate inventories on the lower western Maryland shore of Chesapeake Bay, in the 1658–70 and 1700–1705 periods.[36] The proportion having bond-laborers declined by nearly one-tenth (49.4 to 45.2 percent). The proportion of the total bond-labor force represented by estates having only one or two bond-laborers was reduced by more than one-third (18.3 to 11.0 percent). At the other end of the scale, in 1700–1705 the proportion of estates with 21 or more bond-laborers was nearly six times what it had been in the 1658–70 period (rising from 1.1 percent to 6.2 percent of all estates), and their share of the total number of bond-laborers had increased to almost five times what it was in the earlier period (from 6.5 to 31.6 percent of all bond-laborers).

The Dutch Wars and Doubtful Loyalty

Threats of Dutch seaborne incursions during the Second and Third Anglo-Dutch Wars, in 1665–67 and 1672–74, served to underscore the weakness of the elite's social control of the colony. In 1667, a Dutch warship succeeded in entering the James River and capturing the Virginia tobacco fleet of twenty ships. That same year, the Dutch admiral de Ruyter audaciously sailed up the Thames and the Medway, and detroyed or captured some of the finest ships of the English navy. But there was a significant difference in the two situations, so far as the ruling class was concerned. England was in no danger of invasion and occupation by Dutch forces aided by the rank and file of the English people; in Virginia that prospect was perceived as real.

On 11 July 1673, during the Third Anglo-Dutch War, another Dutch naval force of nine ships conducted a raid up the James River, defeated the English in a three-hour battle, and captured eleven merchant ships laden with cargo.[37] Governor Berkeley and the Colony Council, writing to the King and Privy Council in England, asked that a large fort be constructed to command the entrance to the James and the Chesapeake Bay, or else that the home government provide regularly for a strong convoy for the Virginia tobacco fleet, the expense to be recovered through raised merchant freight charges. They based their appeal on the non-functional state of the Virginia militia.

But the social control question, which is a central concern of this work, is brought most starkly into focus by the following passage of their letter, which describes Virginia as

> intersected by Soe many vast Rivers as makes more Miles to Defend, then we have men of trust to Defend them, for by our neerest computacon wee leave at our backs as many Servants (besides Negroes) as there are freemen to defend the Shoare and on all our Frontiers the Indians. Both which gives men fearfull apprehentions of the dainger they Leave their Estates and Families in, Whilst they are drawne from their houses to defend the Borders. Of which number also at least one third are single freemen (whose labor Will hardly maintaine them), or men much in debt, both which

Wee may reasonably expect upon any small advantage the Enemy may gaine upon us, would revolt to them in hopes of bettering their Condicon.[38]

Fourteen such debt-ridden Surry County freemen attempted the following December and January to organize a mutiny against payment of the colony levy. Meeting first at Lawnes Creek Church and next in Devil's Field, they declared their determination to stand together come what might, "burn one, burn all." Their effort was thwarted; four were fined 1,000 pounds of tobacco, one 2,000 pounds, and all were put under bond for their future good behavior.[39]

Although the Lawnes Creek Mutiny was thwarted, it was both a validation of the fears of Berkeley and the Colony Council, and a portent of the general mutiny of 1676, Bacon's Rebellion. Objective "social and economic conditions" themselves "conspired against an effective control of the citizenry by the provincial leadership."[40]

Facing the Problem

Three means were available to the plantation bourgeoisie to combat the economic root of social instability: (1) regulate the production and shipment of tobacco to relieve the ruinous effect of the glut of the market; (2) diversify production in order to escape the desperate dependency on tobacco monoculture; or (3) find a way to lower the cost of labor per unit of output.

It was to be expected that contradictions would develop between English monarchy and mercantilism, on the one hand, and the colonial plantation bourgeoisie, on the other. These clashes of interest, which in time would find fullest expression as part of the American War of Independence, first emerged in the context of the long crisis of tobacco overproduction and low prices that began at the moment of the Stuart Restoration in 1660.

Throughout the seventeenth century, the Anglo-American plantation bourgeoisie preached the virtues of diversification of the Chesapeake economy, while reproducing decade after decade the economic morass of tobacco monoculture. Warnings were sounded by Virginia officials against basing Virginia's economy on tobacco alone; they urged that a variety of products be developed to meet a variety of English market demands. The longest-serving and most famous of Virginia colonial governors, Sir William Berkeley, was himself the most articulate denouncer of tobacco monoculture and the most enthusiastic advocate of diversification. "Our Governors," said Berkeley, in a treatise of the early 1660s, "by the corruption of the times they lived in, laid the Foundation of our wealth and industry on the vices of men ... [particularly] this vicious habit of taking Tobacco."[41] But, with encouragement and instruction from the home government, said Berkeley, Virginia within seven years could supply England with all its needs for "Silk, Flax, Hemp, Pitch, Tar, Iron, Masts, Timber and Pot-ashes," that were then of necessity being imported from other countries at great expense.

Over the years, various suggestions were made for reducing production – by limiting the number of leaves on the plant, or the number of plants, or by limiting the time allowed for transplanting seedlings – and for regulating the time of shipping the crop in order to maximize favorable seasonal factors. Repeated proposals were advanced for co-ordinating with Maryland and North Carolina in limiting tobacco production, but they came to naught. Merchant shipowners opposed this last idea because, as they said in 1662, it would seriously interfere with the shipment of bond-laborers and thus cause a burdensome increase in the number of unemployed in England.[42]

Other measures aimed at directly shoring up tobacco planters' profits by exemptions from export duties, by a measure of relief from the provisions of the Navigation Law, and by exempting Virginia-owned ships from export duties on their cargoes.

Topographical factors, involving the heavy costs of clearing away the ubiquitous forest, and the decentralizing influence of geography (Virginia being a series of peninsulas formed by navigable rivers), as well as clashes of various economic interests, hampered programs aimed at both diversification and the limiting of tobacco production.[43] With regard to diversification, furthermore, there was a lack of capital in Virginia for ventures into other lines of production, since the Virginia bourgeoisie was chronically in debt to English merchants. The three Dutch wars used up English resources that might theoretically have been available for investment in Virginia; later, the same drain of capital accompanied the first phase (1689–1713) of the Anglo-French wars of colonial rivalry. After the Restoration in 1660, the Crown itself was so desperate for funds that, far from wanting to embark on diversification experiments, it was determined to maximize the tobacco trade, which was its most lucrative source of income; integral with that, there was the interest of the English tax-and-customs "farmers," who contracted to collect the king's customs on tobacco imports. In 1671 the king's share from import customs collections on Virginia tobacco was estimated to be £80,000 per year; in 1682 the royal share of tobacco profits was calculated to be £7 per year for every plantation bond-laborer.[44] English merchants, who did have capital they might have invested, were not interested in taking unnecessary risks with it; and they were adamantly opposed to encouraging the rise of a set of competitive industries in Virginia.[45]

On general principles the English mercantilists were increasingly wary of deviations from the primacy of tobacco production, and especially of those deviations that might lead to the development of competition with goods produced in England and to the consequent economic independence of colonies. In April 1705 the Commissioners of Trade specifically instructed the Governors of Virginia and Maryland to "take care not to suffer the People employed in the making of Tobacco to be Deverted therefrom."[46] In the eyes of English manufacturers, such a development "would be of very ill consequence" to English woolen exports and tobacco shipping and imports, and would jeopardize the relation of dependence in which a colony should be kept.[47]

In 1707 Governor John Seymour warned the Board of Trade that credit-starved Maryland planters, rendered "almost starke naked" for lack of English-made clothing, were turning to making their own linen and woolen goods. He too worried about the "ill consequence to the Revenue arising on tobacco" if people in that colony generally laid aside tobacco-making in order to manufacture such goods as they customarily purchased from England.[48] Governor Gooch was confident that wages were so high in Virginia that Virginia-made linen would cost 20 percent more and woolen cloth 50 percent more than English textiles and therefore would be unable to compete with English-made goods as exports. But since they might reduce the market for British manufactures within the colony, such local industry should be discouraged. Acting on Gooch's information, the Board of Trade in London resolved to find a way to "divert their [the colonists'] thoughts from Undertakings of this nature."[49]

Diversification efforts were not aimed at supplanting the tobacco monoculture, but merely at protecting it. One premise was common to all parties – the Virginia ruling elite, the English Crown, English merchants, and rival provincial governments in Maryland and North Carolina. However much they differed over principles, such as those of the mercantilist Navigation Laws, or details regarding the regulation of production and shipment, or the number and location of centralizing port cities, they all held to one inviolable principle – the priority to be given to the maintenance and enhancement of profit on tobacco.[50] Consequently, schemes for limiting directly the supply of tobacco brought to the market were driven aground by the prevailing winds of competitive pressure for the quickest turnover of capital, coupled with the Crown's determination to resist any diminution of its tobacco revenues, which were based on physical volume rather than selling price.[51]

But even if, by a sudden rush of enlightened self-interest to the heads of all parties, some more than evanescent scheme for "economic reform" could have been instituted, it would have been foredoomed by the insubstantiality of the requisite buffer social control stratum. Virginia's "labor- and capital-scarce economy demanded efficient marshaling of effort and resources," requiring social discipline that could not be imposed by the plantation elite, having "large goals but small capacity to command," and "lacking strong supporting social and religious institutions."[52]

The Third Possibility: Reducing Labor Costs

The English bourgeoisie finally secured direct access to African labor at the end of the Second Dutch War, concluded in the Treaty of Breda in 1667.[53] Five years later, with the establishment of the Royal African Company, England embarked on a career that within less than forty years made English merchants the preeminent suppliers of African bond-labor to the Western Hemisphere. A rise in the demand for labor in England, and a corresponding rise in the wage level there (soon to be coupled with the great demand for cannon fodder for the far-flung battle lines of England's contest with France in Europe and in America), reduced the supply of persons available for bond-labor in the plantation colonies.[54]

As it had been when the source of supply had been in Europe, the African labor trade was a self-motivating capital interest. Virginia Governor Thomas Lord Culpeper was urged by King Charles II "to give all due encouragement and invitation to Merchants and others ... and in particular to the Royal African Company of England." Culpeper was further instructed to be on guard against any "interlopers" in that trade, which was intended to be a monopoly of the Royal African Company.[55] Replying a year later, Culpeper asserted that the king alone made at least £6 per year from the labor of each Negro bond-laborer in Virginia.[56]

Now, finally, the plantation bourgeoisie was brought within reach of the realization of the vision foreshadowed in a number of laws already enacted, of enrichment through the imposition of lifetime, hereditary bond-servitude of Africans and African-Americans. In seventeenth-century Virginia the buyer paid an average of £14 and £13 respectively for men and women five-year bond-laborers. The investment in "seasoned" hands depreciated, however, and at an increasing rate; at the end of three years its value would be only £7 for males and £4 for females. The buyer of an adult lifetime bond-laborer was making an average investment of £18 to £20, an amount that depreciated over the remaining years of the laborer's life. Thus the retained value of the investment at the end of three years would run in favor of the option for lifetime bond-labor. If that lifetime lasted ten years, the annual amortization on the investment would have been less than £2, about 30 percent less than on two five-year bond-laborers. There were ancillary benefits of investment in lifetime bond-labor since there was no outlay for freedom dues, and even at birth a child of a lifetime bond-laborer was of some capital value.[57] The anticipated reduction in labor costs would have been desirable for the employing class at any time, but as the end of the seventeenth century neared it appeared to offer the bourgeoisie both a way of evading the unresolvable contradictions between monoculture and diversity, and a significant easing of the contention between English and continental branches of the business with respect to profits from low-priced tobacco. Culpeper stressed this latter consideration in urging the Royal African Company to moderate its prices for the sale of lifetime bond-laborers in Virginia. "[I]n regard to the infinite profit that comes to the King by every Black (far beyond any other Plantation) ... and that Blacks can make [tobacco] cheaper than Whites, I conceive it is for his Majesty's Interest full as much as the Countrys, or rather much more, to have Blacks as cheap as possible in Virginia."[58]

But if a lack of "capacity to command" had made it impossible for the plantation bourgeoisie to impose the necessary social discipline on free and middle-rank tobacco farmers, what hope could there be for imposing social control on a society when masses of kidnapped Africans were added to the ranks of the disaffected bond-laborers already at the bottom of the heap?

A Reflective Postscript

With that question, the narrative portion of this chapter is complete, but a reflective postscript is in order. For the reader's indulgence, I appeal to the example of Philip Alexander Bruce's speculation on the possibility of an alternative path of development for the Old Dominion.[59]

Those historians who intend not only to record and interpret history, but also in so doing to affect its future course are impelled to offer judgments that for them seem to light the path ahead,[60] even though sooner or later other historians are sure to find the light misdirected or insufficient in one or more respects. Having studied the record of the travail of the common people of seventeenth-century Virginia, "The Ordeal of Colonial Virginia," as Professor Morgan has called it, I cannot but ponder if it was possible for history to have followed a different, happier course and, if so, what Virginia by such a course would have become. It is a speculation, but I hope not an idle one.

In 1625 Sir Francis Bacon cited Virginia as an example to be avoided in establishing plantations, arguing that "the base and hasty drawing of profit" from tobacco worked to "the untimely prejudice of the main business."[61] John Smith, son of the English yeomanry, soon warned that to base production on chattel bond-labor was a disastrous course.[62]

Received historiographical doctrine argues to the contrary as follows. Virginia colony could only survive by exports; tobacco was not only the most profitable prospect for that role, but the only practicable one. Because of the low price of tobacco and the high prevailing wages, chattel bond-servitude was indispensable. The alternative was "slow progress" as "a community of small peasant properitors." Such a course would (the thesis concludes) have been "utopian"; Virginia, indeed, was by nature designed to be "A commonwealth of tobacco plantations."[63]

Who is right? If the question were merely a historiographical one, it would be as well to let it rest with the dead past. But the issue is not dead; it is as vital today as it was those nearly four centuries ago. The equating of economic growth with the most rapid accumulation of capital, which led Virginia to misery just as John Smith predicted, has continued to this day to guide the ruling class of the USA, who subordinate to that principle all other interests, heedless of the misery that it may leave in its wake.

"Two roads diverged . . . And that made all the difference"

As Virginia was first getting high on tobacco, the Pilgrims landed at Plymouth Rock to begin in New England a form of internal economic organization that largely embodied the principles advanced by Francis Bacon in that respect.[64] In an appraisal of the condition of Virginia at the close of the seventeenth century, James Blair, the founder of William and Mary College lamented the fact that "No care was taken at the beginning to seat that Country [Virginia] in Townshipps, as in New England." The result, he continued, was that

Virginia was "deprived of the great Company of Citizens and Tradesmen that are in other Countryes."[65]

Although both colonies were products of bourgeois England, four sets of contrasting factors would determine their respective patterns of social development:

1. the domination of landholding by large plantations in Virginia versus the predominance of small farms in New England;

2. the Virginia monoculture, with its utter dependence upon export markets, versus the mainly non-market-centered, and definitely non-capitalist, basic New England economy;

3. the chattel bond-labor force of the Virginia Plantation system versus the non-bond-labor of the small New England farms;

4. the Virginia "family," which included all the persons belonging to one plantation even if most of them were not kin of each other, versus that typical New England family of a mother and father and their children.

The character of seventeenth-century Virginia society in these respects has been adequately described here; however, a brief elaboration of the New England case is in order. The statistics cited by Moller regarding contrasting seventeenth-century sex ratios in Anglo-American continental colonies[66] are explained in terms of the contrasting labor bases:

While in the New England immigration males outnumbered females three to two, the ratio was six to one in the Virginia immigration. The Puritans, broadly speaking, arrived by families ... The movement to Virginia, on the contrary, consisted predominantly of male workers [i.e., chattel bond-laborers].[67]

As we have seen, for every person brought into Virginia in the seventeenth century, a patent on fifty acres of land was bestowed on whomever had paid the cost of the immigrant's transportation. This custom, supplemented by special land grants to favored individuals, was the basis of the high degree of concentration of landownership in that colony. In the very earliest days in New England, the headright form of land grant was observed, but over the colonial period as a whole "by far the greater part of the land disposed of was granted to communities of settlers."[68] Thus was formed in New England the very "township" form of settlement whose absence in Virginia was so much lamented by Commissary Blair. Under the New England system of settlement by families, "Great pains were taken to guard against excessive grants and accumulation of large estates," writes Egleston. "Land, however abundant, was to be given by the community authorities to those who could use it."[69] New England settlement was in the form of communities initiated by a group of families securing, usually from the colony general court, an allotment of land not occupied by other settlers. These "proprietors" then distributed the land to colonists by plots of ground, proportioned to their payment for expenses of surveying, and other incidentals.[70] A tendency toward concentration of land ownership did occur in New England "[t]hrough purchase, marriage, inheritance, [and] proprietary rights ... with the result that later distributions of land, particularly those of the eighteenth century, showed more inequality;"[71] but it was relatively insignificant as compared to that in plantation Virginia.[72]

Schemes and hopes of diversification of the Virginia economy were frustrated, as has been noted, by a shortage of capital for investment. Caught as the planters were between a low-ranging elasticity of tobacco prices and the inelasticity of royal customs and shipping charges, they could not escape the discipline of the next year's indebted crop. Seventeenth-century New England settlers were not faced with that difficulty because "the household mode of production remained the dominant form of existence."[73] By the middle of the eighteenth century, when a degree of market development had occurred,[74] the New England farmer might profit from a cash crop, perhaps wheat. But where does a self-employed person, propertyless except for an ax, possibily a plow, two or three animals, and enough grain to get the family through to his first harvest – where, without credit resources, does such a self-employed person get the capital for clearing land, building shelter for the family and the animals, and storage sheds or barns, and cutting new road?

> [Such a] farmer may be compared to a business corporation which pursues a conservative dividend policy. Instead of paying out all of current income to stockholders, it puts a large share back into the business, thus increasing the value of his capital . . . [thus] literally ploughing in his profits.[75]

Such farmers made up the "communities of peasant proprietors" that Bruce argued were necessarily excluded from the march of "progress" in Virginia. Yet in New England they proved from their seventeenth-century beginnings to be perfectly viable and capable of eventual evolution from natural (subsistence) production to simple commodity production (the commodity beginning as the property of the producer) to capitalist production (wherein the product is never the property of the producer, but of the capitalist employer).[76]

Colonial Virginia has been assessed as "dynamic" and New England as the "least dynamic" of the continental colonies. By the eighteenth century, when Virginia and New England were about equal in population size, Virginia's exports and imports were six to ten times as large as New England's.[77] It is obvious that New England's climate and soil characteristics made the general employment of bond-labor impracticable, even if the land distribution system had formed plantations of a size suitable for profitable capitalist operation, and some staple had been struck upon that would not offend competitors in Old England. But it does not follow that Virginia's climate and soil could not have been settled on the basis of communities of small farmsteads. For New England it was not a matter of choice; for Virginia it was. So it was that New England, more than anywhere else in North America, re-created rural England, while the Virginia plantation bourgeoisie "cast away restraining ideologies and institutions [and] developed a labor process unknown in England."[78]

It was a conscious decision, not an unthinking one. In opting for the "dynamics" of monoculture and chattel bond-labor, the members of the

Virginia plantation bourgeoisie knew they were rejecting the counsel of perhaps the most illustrious member of the Virginia Company. "It is true," Bacon had said, "speedy profit is not to be neglected as far as it may stand with the good of the plantation, but no further."[79] It was simply what preacher Lionel Gatford warned them against in 1657 – the triumph of "Private Interest" over "Publick Good." Now fifty years after the fateful option was made, having ignored Sir Francis's precept and New England's example, the Virginia ruling elite found itself three thousand miles from home with no yeoman buffer between it and a people of whom "six parts of seaven at least, are Poore, Endebted, Discontented and Armed."[80]

10

The Status of African-Americans

For more than a century now, scholars have studied the records regarding the status of African-Americans in Virginia and Maryland in the seventeenth century.[1] Although I in turn have made my own independent study of these materials, persons familiar with the field will recognize the majority of my references to the records. What they and other readers will be challenged to do is to test my interpretation of the facts. Therefore, it seems appropriate at this point to review the basic definition of racial oppression and to enumerate the particular forms of that oppression as they were set forth in Volume One of this work.[2] The hallmark of racial oppression in its colonial origins and as it has persisted in subsequent historical contexts is the reduction of all members of the oppressed group to one undifferentiated social status, a status beneath that of any member of any social class within the oppressor group.[3] It is a system of rule designed to deny, disregard, delegitimate previous or potential social distinctions that may have existed or that might tend to emerge in the normal course of development of a class society.

In Chapter 8 and again in Chapter 9, I have argued inferentially that "the white race," and thus a system of racial oppression, did not exist and could not have existed in the seventeenth-century tobacco colonies. In Chapter 8 that conclusion was based on evidence of class solidarity of laboring-class European-Americans with African-Americans, and the consequent absence of an all-class coalition of European-Americans directed against African-Americans. In Chapter 9 the thesis was linked with the lack of a substantial intermediate buffer social control stratum. In the present chapter a third ply of the argument is to be developed primarily from the Virginia records, directly bearing on the actual social status of African-Americans in those decades. Since, so far as I know, this analytical approach to the study of racial oppression is different from that taken by other historians, I offer the following brief elaboration in justification of it.

Some scholars concerned with the problem of the origin of racial slavery have emphasized that the status of the African-Americans in the seventeenth-century Chesapeake cannot be fully determined because of a deficiency in the records for the early decades.[4] Others, by reference to Virginia statutes, assert that the differentiation of the status of African-Americans and European-

Americans can be determined as beginning only about 1660.[5] I would propose to dissolve this aspect of the debate over the origin of racial slavery by recognizing that the historical records of seventeenth-century Virginia compel the conclusion that the relative social status of African-Americans and European-Americans in that "Volatile Society" can be determined to have been indeterminate. It was indeterminate because it was being fought out:[6] fought out in the context of the great social stresses of high mortality, the vicissitudes of a monocultural economy, impoverishment, and an extremely high sex ratio – all of which were based on or derived from the abnormal system of chattel bond-servitude. The critical moment of that social struggle arrived with Bacon's Rebellion of 1676 which posed the question of who should rule. The answer, which would be contrived over the next several decades, would not only determine the status of African-Americans but would install the monorail of Anglo-American historical development, white supremacy.

The reduction of the almost totally English labor force from tenants and wage-laborers to chattel bond-servitude in Virginia in the 1620s was indeed a negation of previously existing laws and customs, but it was imposed by one set of colonists on another set of colonists. It was not, therefore, an act of racial oppression (no more than was the 1547 slave law in England[7]), but merely an extremely reactionary sort of class oppression. As for seeking to establish two distinct categories of servitude – limited-term and lifetime servitude – the death rate was so high for several decades[8] that there would have been no practical advantage for employers in such a distinction.[9]

In 1640, however, just such a distinction was anticipated when the Virginia General Court, in a singular instance, imposed lifetime bond-servitude on John Punch. Punch, an African-American, and two European-American fellow bond-laborers were arraigned for having run away.[10] But why did the appetite for profit not lead the court to sentence John Punch's European-American comrades to lifetime servitude also?[11]

Winthrop D. Jordan directs particular attention to this decree, and cites it as evidence for his belief that the enslavement of Negroes was the result of an "unthinking decision," arising out of a prejudice against Negroes.[12] It may be true that the court in this case was motivated by such feelings, although any such conclusion rests totally on inference; it is not a fact of the record. Other inferences are possible. Under English common law, Christians could not be enslaved by Christians; presumably, Scots and Dutchmen were Christians; but Africans were not. As a practical matter, England's relations with Scotland and Holland were critical to English interests, so that there might well have been a reluctance to offend those countries to whom English concerns were in hostage, whereas no such complication was likely to arise from imposing lifetime bondage on an African or African-American. The court members in all probability were aware of the project then under way to establish an English plantation colony, using African lifetime bond-laborers, on Providence

Island;[13] and they surely knew that some Africans were already being exploited elsewhere in the Americas on the same terms. They might have been influenced by such examples to pursue the same purpose in Virginia. They were also aware that the African-American bond-laborers arriving in Virginia from the West Indies (or Brazil via Dutch colonies to the north of Maryland[14]) did not come with English-style, term-limiting indentures; the members of the General Court may thus have felt encouraged to impose the ultimate term, a lifetime, in such cases. Whether the decision in this instance was a "thinking" or an "unthinking" one, the court by citing John Punch's "being a negro" in justification of his life sentence was resorting to mere bench law, devoid of reference to English or Virginia precedent.[15] What the record of this case does show, so far as the ideas in people's heads are concerned, is a disposition on the part of some, at least, of the plantation bourgeoisie to reduce African-Americans to lifetime servitude.

As the proportion of bond-laborers who were surviving their terms increased, some employers began to see an appeal in extending the bond-laborers' terms generally. The "custom of the country" for English bond-laborers in Virginia, which had been set at four years in 1658, was increased to five in 1662.[16] With the flourishing of the Irish slave trade in the wake of the Cromwellian conquest,[17] laws were enacted to make Irish bond-laborers (and, after 1658, "all aliens" in that status) serve six years.[18] That provision was eliminated, however, by the post-Cromwell law of 1660, in the interest of "peopling the country."[19]

The 1660 law equalized at five years the length of "the custom of the country" without distinction of "aliens," but that same law *for the first time* restricted term-limiting to those "of what christian nation soever" (the Anglican Church having been established in Ireland, Ireland now qualified as a "christian country"). Since the only "christian nations" were in Europe, this clause was most particularly, though not exclusively, aimed at persons of African origin or descent. This exclusion of African-Americans from the limitation on the length of servitude imposed on bond-laborers reflected and was intended to further the efforts made by some elements of the plantation bourgeoisie to reduce African-American bond-laborers to lifetime servitude. But even that, in and of itself, would have been no more than a form of class oppression of bond-laborers by owners, somewhat like the slavery of Scots miners and saltpan workers from the end of the sixteenth century to the eve of the nineteenth century, a form distinguished however by its categoric denial of social mobility to those in bondage.[20]

This was a long way from the establishment of a system of racial oppression; but its implicit denial to African-Americans of even the lowest range of social mobility, from bond-labor to freedom, contained a seed of a system of racial oppression, although that seed could not be fully developed without a strong intermediate social control stratum.

There are two sides to the coin of the General Court's order relating to John Punch; his sentence to lifetime servitude is equally proof that he was not a lifetime bond-laborer when he ran away. Indeed, by that act he was demonstrating his unwillingness to submit to even limited-term bond-servitude. The John Punch case thus epitomized the status of African-Americans in seventeenth-century Virginia. On the one hand, it showed the readiness of at least some of the plantation elite to equate "being a negro" with being a lifetime bond-laborer. On the other hand, development of social policy along this line was obstructed by several factors. First, there was what might be called institutional inertia presented by English common law, by the historic retreat from the slavery gambit of 1547 in the wake of Ket's Rebellion, and by the deep-rooted principles of Christian fellowship. Second, of course, there was the opposition of African-Americans,[21] both bond-laborers and non-bond-laborers, with the general support – certainly without the concerted opposition – of European-American bond-laborers and other free but poor laboring people, determined by a sense of common class interest.

For the period before 1676, the Virginia and Maryland records, particularly those of Virginia, are rich with examples of how the historically evolved legal, institutional and ideological superstructure of English society presented a countervailing logic to the General Court's equation regarding John Punch – examples of a recognition of normal social standing and mobility for African-Americans that was and is absolutely inconsistent with a system of racial oppression. Illustrative cases are found most frequently, though not exclusively, in the Northampton and Accomack county records.[22] In 1624, the Virginia Colony Court had occasion to consider an admiralty-type case, in the routine course of which the court considered the testimony of John Phillip, a mariner, identified as "a negro Christened in England 12 yeares since."[23] In a separate instance, a Negro named Brase and two companions, a Frenchman and a "Portugall," were brought of their own volition to Jamestown on 11 July 1625. Two months later, Brase was assigned to work for "Lady Yardley" for forty pounds of good merchantable tobacco "monthly for his wages for his service so long as he remayneth with her." In October, Brase was assigned to Governor Francis Wyatt as a "servant"; no particulars are recorded as to his terms of employment with his new employer. There was no suggesting that, "being a Negro," he was to be a lifetime bond-laborer.[24]

African-Americans who were not bond-laborers made contracts for work or for credit, and engaged in commercial as well as land transactions, with European-Americans, and in the related court proceedings they stood on the same footing as European-Americans. At the December 1663 sitting of the Accomack County Court, Richard Johnson and Mihill Bucklands disputed over the amount to be paid to Johnson for building a house for Bucklands. With the consent of both parties the issue was referred to two arbitrators.[25] The Northampton County Court gave conditional assent to the suit of John Gusall, but allowed debtor Gales Judd until the next court to make contrary proof, or pay Gusall "the summe & grant of fore hundred powndes of tobacco due per speciality with court charges."[26] Emannuel Rodriggus[27] arrived in Virginia before 1647, presumably without significant material assets, and was enlisted as a plantation bond-laborer.[28] Rodriggus became a dealer in livestock on the Eastern Shore (as the trans-Chesapeake Bay eastern peninsula of Virginia came to be known). As early as January 1652/3 there was recorded a bill of sale signed with his mark, assigning to merchant John Cornelys "one Cowe collered Blacke, aged about fowre yeares ... being my owne breed."[29] Thereafter, Rodriggus and other African-Americans frequently appear as buyers and sellers, and sometimes as donors, of livestock in court records that reflect the assumption of the right of African-Americans to accumulate and dispose of property, and that also assume the legal parity of buyer and seller.[30]

The Indian king Debeada of the Mussaugs gave to Jone, daughter of Anthony Johnson, 100 acres of land on the south side of Pungoteague Creek on 27 September 1657.[31] In 1657 Emannuell Cambow, "Negro," was granted ownership of fifty acres of land in James City County, part of a tract that had been escheated from the former grantee.[32] In 1669, Robert Jones (or Johns), a York County tailor, acting with the agreement of his wife Marah, "for divers good causes and considerations him thereunto moveing ... bargained & sold unto John Harris Negro all the estate rite [right] title & Inheritance ... in fiftie Acres of Land ... in New Kent County."[33] A series of land transactions – lease, sub-lease, and re-lease – was conducted by Manuell Rodriggus with three separate individuals over a ten-year period from June 1662.[34]

Marriage and Social Mobility

In the colonial Chesapeake in the seventeenth century, marriage might be a significant factor for social mobility. The prevailing high death rate and the high sex ratio resulted in a relative frequency of remarriages of widows in the records.[35] Whatever a widow might own generally became the property of the new husband. Phillip Mongum, though only recently free, had begun an ascent in the social scale that would eventually result in his becoming a relatively prosperous tenant farmer and livestock dealer (in 1672, he was a partner of two European-Americans in a joint lease of a plantation of three hundred acres[36]). When Mary Morris, a widow with children, and Phillip Mongum were contemplating marriage early in 1651, they entered into a prenuptial agreement regarding the property she then owned. Mongum agreed in writing that her property was not to be sold by him but was to remain the joint heritage of Mary and the children from her previous marriage(s): "one Cowe with a calfe by her side & all her increase that shall issue ever after of the said Cowe or calfe[,] moreover Towe featherbeds & what belongs unto them, one Iron Pott, one Kettle, one fryeing pan & towe gunnes & three breeding sowes with their increase." Mongum signed the agreement and bound himself to see to its faithful performance.[37]

Francis Payne's second wife Amy was a European-American. When Payne died late in the summer of 1673, his will made Amy his executrix and the sole heir of his "whole Estate real & personal moveables and immoveables."[38]

Within two years Amy married William Gray, a European-American, whose interest was to stop his own downward social mobility by looting Amy's inheritance from Francis Payne. In August 1675, Amy charged in court that Gray had not only beaten and otherwise abused her but had also "made away almost all her estate" and intended to complete the process and reduce her to being a public charge. The court did not attempt to challenge Gray's disposal of her inherited estate to satisfy his debts; but it did keep him in jail for a month until he satisfied the court that he would return a mare belonging to Amy and promised to support her enough to prevent her being thrown on the charity of the parish.[39] Some time in 1672, an African-American woman named Cocore married Francis Skipper (or Cooper), owner of a 200-acre plantation in Norfolk County. She had been lashed with thirty strokes the year before on the order of the court for having borne a child "out of wedlock." Perhaps there was a social mobility factor in her marrying Skipper. But they apparently lived together amiably for some five years until his death, an event which she survived by less than a year.[40]

Historical Significance of African-American Landholding

Landholding by African-Americans in the seventeenth century was significant both for the extent of it and because much of it, possibly the greater portion, was secured by headright. This particular fact establishes perhaps more forcefully than any other circumstance the normal social status accorded to African-Americans, a status that was practically as well as theoretically incompatible with a system of racial oppression. For the reader coming for the first time to the raw evidence in the Virginia Land Patent Books, or to the abstracts of them done by Nell Nugent, or to the digested accounts presented by historians of our own post-Montgomery boycott era – for such first-time readers the stories carry a stunning impact. Thanks particularly to the brief – but penetrating – emphasis on the subject by Lerone Bennett,[41] and to the special studies made by Deal and by Breen and Innes, the story of the Anthony Johnson family is readily available. Another African-American in this category, Benjamin Dole of Surry County, may yet find biographers. It is especially noteworthy that the persons for whose importation these particular patents were granted were mainly, if not all, bond-laborers brought from Europe.

Since considerable attention has been devoted to these African-Americans in the works referred to above, I will simply list them:

- Land patent granted to Anthony Johnson, on 250 acres for transport of five persons: Tho. Benrose, Peter Bughby, Antho. Cripps, John Gessorol[?], Richard Johnson (Virginia Land Patent Book No. 2, p. 326, 24 July 1651).

- Patent granted to John Johnson, son of Anthony Johnson, on 500 acres, on Great Nassawattocks Creek, adjacent to land granted to Anthony Johnson, for the transportation of eleven persons: John Edwards, Wm. Routh, Thos. Yowell, Fran. Maland, Wm. Price, John Owe, Dorothy Reely, Rich Hamstead, Law[rence] Barnes (Virginia Land Patent Book No. 3, p. 101, 10 May 1652).

- Patent on 100 acres bounded by lands owned by Anthony, Richard's father, and by brother John Johnson, granted by Governor Richard Bennett to Richard Johnson, "Negro," for the transportation of two bond-laborers: William Ames and William Vincent (Virginia Land Patent Book No. 3, p. 21, November 1654).

- Land patent dated 17 December 1656 granted to Benjamin Dole, "Negro," 300 acres in Surry County for the importation of six persons (Virginia Land Patent Book No. 4, p. 71, 17 December 1656).

It has been pointed out that headrights could be sold by the original importers to other persons, and that such a patent might therefore be granted to persons other than the original owners of the bond-laborers. There is no way of knowing whether the Johnsons and Benjamin Dole ever were in possession of the bond-laborers whose headrights they exercised, or whether they bought the headright from other persons. In any case, the point being made here is not affected. There was no suggestion that African-Americans were barred from the privilege of importing bond-laborers. Indeed, the enactment of such a ban in 1670 clearly implied that it was an accepted practice prior to that time.[42]

There is a case which for all of its uniqueness still sheds light on the question of the social mobility of African-Americans in seventeenth-century Virginia. Anthony Johnson acquired, presumably by purchase, a Negro bond-laborer named Casar. Casar stubbornly claimed he was entitled to be free, that he had come to Virginia around 1638, indentured for seven or eight years, but that Johnson was attempting to hold him as a lifetime bond-laborer. Under the threat of a lawsuit for unjustly detaining Casar, and persuaded by members of his family, in November 1653 Anthony Johnson agreed to abandon his claim and set Casar free. Four months later, in March 1654, Johnson, having thought more deeply, secured a court order returning Casar "into the service of his said master Anthony Johnson." Twenty years later the family had moved to Somerset County, Maryland, and Anthony Johnson had died there, but Casar was still living as a "servant" of Anthony's widow Mary.[43]

A Demonstrative Statistical Excursion

We know from the studies made by John H. Russell, Carter G. Woodson, Luther Porter Jackson and others that free Negroes in Virginia in the nineteenth century could acquire land by inheritance, gift, or purchase, and that they had the corresponding rights to dispose of it, although they lived under a system of racial oppression. Seventeenth-century data are not comprehensive.[44] The seventeenth-century Virginia Land Patent Books are available for the colony as a whole, but the preserved court records for Northampton and Accomack are more nearly comprehensive than those of the rest of the counties, and richer in detail than the records of the Virginia Colony Council and the House of Burgesses. The population of these two counties appears to have constituted between 7 and 8 percent of the population of the entire colony during the last third of the century.[45] These counties may not have been typical of the colony as a whole in respect to the prominence of African-Americans in matters that rose to the level of attention in the public records.[46] However, there is no evidence to indicate that other county courts or the central organs of government regarded proceedings in Accomack and Northampton counties as worthy of special notice. Nor have the works dealing with the Eastern Shore suggested that the attitudes of official society and the common run of European-Americans there differed qualitatively from those held in the rest of the colony.

The contrast in the ratios of landholding between African-Americans and European-Americans in Northampton County in 1666, and in Virginia as a whole in 1860, documents the difference between normal social class differentiation and a system of racial oppression. In Northampton County in 1666, 10.9 percent of the African-Americans and 17.6 percent of European-Americans were landholders. This disparity is no more than normal considering that 53.4 percent of the European-American landholders, but none of the African-Americans, came as free persons. The concentration of ownership is also normal, indeed an irresistible tendency of capitalist production. It is not surprising, therefore, to find that the ratio of farm ownership among European-Americans was 46 percent less in 1860 than was landholding in 1665. But the fact that the proportion of the African landholding population was 95 percent less in 1860 than it was in 1666 was the result not of normal capitalist economic development but of racial oppression. Let it be noted in passing that the proportion of European-Americans owning land in Virginia in 1860 was less than the proportion of African-American landowners in 1666. (See Table 10.1.)

If the proportion of landholding among African-Americans had declined, but only as much as the ratio of landholding among European-Americans, an indicated 30,000 landholdings would have been in the hands of the 53,000 free rural Virginia African-Americans in 1860. That would have represented an African-American landholding ratio nearly six times the actual ratio of European-American landholding in that year. The facts are even more dramatic when put in terms of family units, which averaged 5.6 persons per family in 1860. The operation of 30,000 African-American farms by some 5,400 families would have required a considerable degree of employment of European-American tenants and wage laborers. That would have been

Table 10.1 African-American and European-American landholding in the entire state of Virginia in 1860 and in Northampton County in 1666

	1666	1860
Landholders as percentage of:		
African-American rural population	10.93%	0.54%
European-American rural population	17.55%	9.53%
(tenants not included)		
Ratio of the frequency of landholding among African-Americans to that among European-Americans (tenants not included)	62.23%	5.6%

a. Virginia's population in 1860 was 1,595,906; African-Americans 548,607 (490,565 bond; 58,042 free); and 1,047,299 European-Americans. US Census Office, *Preliminary Report on the Eighth Census, 1860* [Washington, 1862], pp. 134–5. The state's population in 1860 was 91.5 percent rural. (Bureau of the Census, *Sixteenth Census of the United States, 1940*, Vol. I [Washington, 1942], Table 8, p. 23.) The rural/urban ratio is here assumed to be the same for the African-American and European-American populations. This assumption may tend to exaggerate the degree of landholding among African-Americans, since the rural proportion of the African-American population was higher than that of the European-American population. (See Richard Wade, *Slavery in the Cities* [New York, 1964], pp. 17–19.) A closer approximation, however, would only add force to the point that landholding by African-Americans was minimal in Virginia in 1860.

b. There were 92,605 farms in Virginia in 1860, of which 1,300 were owned by African-Americans. (Bureau of the Census, *Ninth Census of the United States, 1870. Statistics of Wealth and Industry*, Vol. 3 [Washington, 1872], p. 340. Luther Porter Jackson, *Free Negro Labor and Property Holding in Virginia in 1860* [New York, 1942], p.134.) The assumption is made here that each owned farm had a separate owner. Since multiple ownership was less frequent among African-Americans than among European-Americans, a stricter count, if it could be made, would lower the proportion of landholding among African-Americans less than it would the landholding ratio among European-Americans. However, the alteration could not significantly affect the argument of this table regarding the difference between the 1666 and 1860 ratios of landholding.

c. In Northampton County in 1666, seven of the 64 African-Americans were landholders, as were 145 of the 826 European-Americans. There were 422 tithables (54 African-Americans and 368 European-Americans), of whom 152 (7 African-Americans and 145 European-Americans) were landholders. (See the Northampton list of tithables for 1666, in Jennings Cropper Wise, *The Kingdom of Accawmacke, on the Eastern Shore of Virginia in the Seventeenth Century* [Richmond, 1911; Baltimore reprint, 1967], pp. 373–8. Edmund S. Morgan's figures vary slightly – 158 households, 434 tithables, and the African-American proportion of the total population a suggested 13.2 percent [*American Slavery, American Freedom*, New York, 1975, pp. 420, 425.])

My estimate of the total population (all rural, of course) of Northampton County in 1666 is based on the following assumptions: Children under sixteen years of age, the untithable portion of the African-American population, constituted 15 percent of all African-Americans, thus among African-Americans the ratio of total population to tithables would be 1.18. (Morgan uses this 15 percent figure, though he calls it a 'generous' estimate [pp. 421, and 422 n. 46.]. If this is indeed an overestimate of the untithable proportion of the African-American population, it will be on the safe, conservative, side of the argument being presented here concerning the greater dispersion of landholding in 1666 as compared to 1860.) The figure of 2.11 for the ratio of total population to tithables for Virginia is assumed to be true for Northampton County. This figure is an extrapolation based on Morgan's assumed linear rise in the ratio from 1.65 in 1640 to 2.69 in 1699; in 1666, the ratio would be 2.11 to 1. The statistical analysis is as follows: total population (2.11 x 422) 890; total African-American population (1.18 x 54) 64. The figures for the European-American population 368 tithable (men) multiplied by 2.11 makes a total of 826.

incompatible with the anomalies of social class relationships characteristic of a system of social control based on racial oppression.

The same point can be made in terms of social mobility, expressed as the ratio between the number of European-American tithables and those landholders who were former bond-laborers (identifiable through a search of the abstracts of land patents in Nugent's *Cavaliers and Pioneers*). Of the total 145 European-American landholders in Northampton in 1666, 58 are identifiable in these patents. Of these, 27, i.e., 47 percent, had come as bond-laborers. If this ratio is assumed to have been the same for the entire roster of 145 European-American landholders, then 68 were in that category. Since there were 209 European-American (tithable) bond-laborers, the social mobility ratio was 69 to 209, or 32.5 percent; for the African-American tithables the ratio was 7 to 44, or 15.9 percent.

The disparity of the two ratios seems understandable in terms of two main factors. Some of the European-American bond-laborers had family or other personal ties on one side of the Atlantic or the other that afforded them some support in getting started after the end of their terms of servitude. Such ties were less likely to be available to African-Americans, except possibly to those who came to the colony from England. Second, the disposition on the part of plantation owners to extend the bond-laborers' terms of servitude operated to extend the terms of limited-term African-American bond-laborers for periods longer than set by the custom of the country, thus reducing the relative number of African-Americans who survived to become socially mobile.

Yet even this relatively diminished rate of African-American social mobility of 1666 was such as would have been incompatible with a system of racial oppression. In 1860, the African-American proletarian population fifteen years of age and over in Virginia numbered around 330,000. The social mobility rate of 15.9 percent on that base would imply the existence of a class of African-American Virginia landholders of 52,740, a number nearly equal to the total number of free African-Americans (58,000) in Virginia in 1860. That would have meant a rate of landholding among free African-Americans nine or ten times the landholding ratio prevailing among European-Americans, a situation incompatible with the character of racial oppression and hence of racial slavery as a form of it. It may be concluded that the social mobility rate among African-Americans in Northampton County, Virginia, in 1666 was inconsistent with racial oppression.

African-American Owners of European-American Bond-laborers

In some cases, African-Americans became owners, buyers and sellers, of European-American bond-laborers. Francis Payne, when still a bond-laborer, was owned by Mrs Jane Eltonhead in right of her children from a previous marriage. In May 1649 the two signed an agreement in their own hands, according to which Payne was to have the usufruct of the land he was working for her for two crops, and then be free. The conditions were that Payne was to pay 1,500 pounds of tobacco and six barrels of corn out of the proceeds of the current crop.[47] Out of the second crop he was to supply Eltonhead with "three sufficient men servants between the age of fifteen & twenty fower & they shall serve for sixe yeares or seaven att the least." Mr Eltonhead made the search for the bond-laborers on behalf of Payne, and in March 1649/50 struck a bargain with "Mr Peter Walker merchant for Towe men Servants which is for the use of Francis Payne Negro towards his free-dome." In April, 1651, Eltonhead acknowledged receipt from "Francis Payne Negro the quantity of sixteen hundred & fifty pownds of Tobacco & two Servants (according Unto the Condition betwixt him & his mistris) also a Bill taken in of his mistris which she passed unto Mr. Edward Davis for a mayd servant Jeany."[48] In November 1656, Mrs Eltonhead, then living in Maryland presumably widowed a second time, acknowledged the receipt of 3,800 pounds of tobacco from Payne, and formally freed Payne and his wife and children "from all hindrance of servitude."[49]

On 28 April 1653 the Northampton County Court ordered John Gussall, "Negro," according to the terms of his contract with Montroze Evellyn, to pay 1,000 pounds of tobacco and "one sufficient able woman servant for four yeares time." If the woman bond-laborers were to die "in seasoning the first yeare," Gussal was to recompense Evellyn with 1,200 pounds of tobacco.[50]

Continuing Bourgeois Pressure for Unpaid Labor Time

All the while the pressure continued to reduce African-American bond-laborers to lifetime servitude. A law passed in March 1661 specifying punishment for runaway bond-laborers referred to "any negroes who are incapable of makeing satisfaction by addition of time."[51] In September 1668, free African-American women were declared tithable on the explicit grounds that "though permitted to enjoy their freedome ... [they] ought not in all respects be admitted to a full fruition of the exemptions and impunities of the English."[52] In October 1669, owners who killed their Negro or Indian lifetime bond-laborers under "correction" were "acquit from molestation" on the grounds that it would not be reasonable that an owner would destroy his own property with malice aforethought.[53] Three years later this immunity from prosecution was extended to any person who killed "any negroe, molatto, Indian slave, or servant for life" who became the object of hue and cry as a runaway.[54] All the laws were especially oppressive in their intentions regarding African-Americans, of course. Insofar as they made reference to African-Americans as lifetime bond-laborers, they were a denial of the possibility of achieving either any social distinction or the enjoyment of the legal rights of marriage and family formation. But it is the 1668 law directed at *free* African-American women that most explicitly anticipates racial oppression.

Contracts and last wills increasingly contemplated raising the number of African-Americans in the category of lifetime bond-laborers. As early as 1649, eleven African-American bond-laborers from Barbados were sold to Argoll Yardley "to have hold possess and quietly enjoy ... [by] him his heirs, or assigns for ever."[55] In 1653, Yardley contracted to provide John Machell "one Negro girle named Dennis Aged 12 yeares next November to serve him . . . his heyres or Assignes for her lifetime."[56] In his will, dated February 1656, Rowland Burnham bequeathed his English bond-laborers to members of his family for the limited terms they had been bought to serve; the African-American bond-laborers were to serve "forever" those to whom they were willed.[57]

At the same time there was a growing desire among owners of bond-laborers to make African-American servitude hereditary, an impulse that found expression in a depraved adaptation of the customary reference to property in animal stock. In September 1647, Stephen Charlton made a gift of a Mare colt, three Cows, and "A Negro girle named Sisley aged about fowre or five years . . . them and their increase both male and female Forever."[58] The settlement of the estate of Edmund Scarburgh in 1656 assigned to Charles Scarburgh "one Negro man called Tom & Masunke his wife with all their issue."[59] In his will dated 12 February 1656, Rowland Burnham distributed some seventeen bond-laborers to various beneficiaries, the ten English ones "for the full terms of tyme they have to serve"; "the negroes forever." Among the African-Americans given to his sons was a "woman called Joane with what Children she shall bear from this date to them and their heirs forever."[60] In December 1657 Captain Francis Pott sold Ann Driggus, nine or ten years old, "with all her increase forever" to John Panell.[61]

African-Americans Challenge Hereditary Bondage

As noted in Chapter 8, African-American bond-laborers joined in direct action with other bond-laborers in resisting their bondage by running away. They also were aware of the need to challenge aspects of the bond-servitude system that were or might be directly aimed against them in particular.

Phillip and Mingo, two African-American bond-laborers whom John Foster bought from Captain William Hawley in January 1649, were trouble from the moment the purchase was made. Concerned about the "fine print" of the Hawley–Foster contract, the workers engaged in what today would be called a "slow-down strike," making Foster "fearfull that [they] would run awaye from him" altogether. Upon their insistence, Captain Hawley was brought into the discussion. Acting as mediator, Hawley "went downe to the seaboard side, And made a wrighting to the Negros," specifying that at the end of four years, "they shalbe free from their servitude & bee free men; & labor for themselves." At some subsequent point the two workers were to pay Hawley 1,700 pounds of tobacco, or "one Man servant."[62]

Resistance might sometimes take the form of the buy-out. In May 1645, Emanuell Dregus (Rodrigues) arranged to purchase from his employer, Captain Francis Pott, the freedom of two children whom he had adopted, eight-year-old Elizabeth and one-year-old Jane, who were bound until the age of twenty-one and thirty respectively.[63] Rogrigues may well have been aware of the sentiment expressed by the General Court in the John Punch case, and of the disposition of some owners to keep Negroes in perpetual servitude, and he might, judging from his name, have had memories of such a regime in some Dutch or Portuguese colony. Although Pott appears to have been personally sympathetic to him, Rodrigues nevertheless preferred to have his children at his own disposal. Indeed, as noted above, the time would come when Pott himself would adopt the notion of hereditary bondage.

Perhaps the most frequent form of challenges to discriminatory terms of servitude in the court records were petitions for freedom presented by African-Americans. Some were submitted by persons who had come into Virginia as limited-term indentured bond-laborers, others were based on promises made by deceased owners' wills or otherwise. The story of the struggle of John Baptista, "a moore of Barbary,"[64] began in 1649, when he was sold by a Dutch merchant, Simon Overzee, to Major Thomas Lambert of Norfolk County, Virginia. But for how long? That was the matter that concerned John Baptista. There came a point at which Baptista refused to continue in servitude saying that "he would serve but fowre yeares" and that he intended to take the matter to the Governor. He did so and in March 1653/4 the General Court ruled that he had not been sold for his lifetime and ordered that Baptista serve Lambert for two more years and then be free. Alternatively Baptista was to buy back the two years by paying Lambert 2,000 pounds of tobacco. Baptista was free of Lambert in less than a year and had departed for Maryland with Overzee.[65]

Dego took his owner, Minor Doodes, to court in Lancaster County in March 1655/6. Apparently Doodes was intending to leave the area and wanted to sell Dego as a lifetime bond-laborer. A paper was presented signed by Doodes, providing that if he sold Dego, it was to be for no more than ten years.[66]

African-American John (or Jack) Kecotan arrived in Virginia as a bond-laborer in about 1635. Eighteen years later his owner, Rice Hoe Senior, promised Kecotan that if he lived a morally irreproachable life, he would be given his freedom – at the end of another eleven years! Sadly, Hoe Senior passed away before the time had elapsed, and the court ordered Kecotan to continue in servitude with Hoe's widow until her death. That mournful event occurred sometime before 10 November 1665, leaving Rice Hoe Junior in possession of the estate, including, he assumed, John Kecotan. But it being then thirty years since Kecotan had started his servitude under the elder Hoe, Kecotan petitioned the court for his freedom. When Junior Hoe opposed the petition on the grounds that some time during the elder Hoe's lifetime Kecotan had had child-producing liaisons with two or more English women, thus violating the good-conduct condition of the original promise of freedom, the Virginia General Court ordered that Kecotan be freed, unless Hoe could prove his charges at the next County Court. There five men, apparently all European-Americans, supported Jack Kecotan's petition with a signed testimonial to his character. Hoe produced two other witnesses for his side.

Apparently Jack Kecotan at some point secured his freedom, at least enough that he and his co-defendant, Robert Short, won a jury verdict in their favor in a suit brought against them by Richard Smith.[67]

In 1654 Anthony Longo was a hard-working farmer living in Northampton County with his wife Mary, two daughters and a son. He had long before demonstrated his mistrust of the intentions of European-American owners of bond-labor regarding the freedom of African-Americans. "For certain considerations" Longo had achieved freedom from his owner in 1635. Suddenly, five years later, in August 1640, two months after the General Court in the John Punch case sought to equate "being a negro" with lifetime bondage, Longo induced his former owner, Commander Nathaniel Littleton, to affirm Longo's freedom in the Northampton County Court record.[68] Longo had a contempt for government interference; and when he was served a warrant to appear in court to answer charges of obstructing a road by building a fence across it, he said he'd go to court when he had got his corn crop in and not before. He called the warrant server an "idle Rascall" adding, dismissively, "shitt of your warrant."[69] When, as mentioned above, in September 1668 the General Assembly made free African-American women liable to taxes, the Longo family was not one to submit quietly. Longo took his grievance directly to Governor Berkeley, petitioning "to be eased of his great charge of children."[70] As the eventual disposition of the petition shows, Longo's purpose was not to have his children taken away but to protest the discriminatory tax on African-American women such as those in his family. The County Court, in apparent retaliation for Longo's having "by his petition complained to the Honorable Governor," charged Longo with being a bad parent, and accordingly sought to deprive him of the children, cynically adding that Longo would be "discharged of publike taxes." The children were ordered bound out to two of Longo's richer neighbors until the children reached the age of twenty-four, the girls to learn "housewifery, knitting and such like;" the boy shoemaking.[71] Longo petitioned the court to be allowed to keep his children, and the order relating to the elder of the daughters was rescinded.[72]

Andrew Moore arrived in Virginia to serve as a limited-term bond-laborer. In October 1673 he petitioned the General Court for his freedom, contending that his owner, Mr George Light, was keeping him in bondage well past his proper time of service. He won a decision ordering Light to free him with the customary allowance of "Corn and Clothes," and to pay Moore 700 pounds of tobacco for his overtime.[73]

Thomas Hagleton, like Moore, came from England.[74] He arrived in Maryland in 1671 with signed indenture papers to serve for four years. In 1676, Hagleton petitioned the Maryland Provincial Court complaining that his owner, Major Thomas Truman, detained him from his freedom. The court, citing the presence of witnesses prepared to testify on Hagleton's behalf, granted Hagleton's request for a trial of the issue.[75]

European-American Nathaniel Bradford had become wary of such challenges. In April 1676 he purchased an African-American woman bond-laborer from Matthew Scarburgh for 3,000 pounds of tobacco, to be paid in two annual installments, presumably from the product of two years' labor. But the purchase agreement carried a protective clause requiring Scarburgh to post bond "to save [Bradford] harmless from ... any claime ... that she hath liv'd in England or Barbados" as a basis for suing for her freedom.[76]

Evangelical Questions and Objections

The obstructive effect of the institutional inertia of common-law principles and Christian religious scruples with respect to racial oppression found both implicit and explicit expression among the owning classes.[77] Three who explicitly addressed the issue were English ministers, Morgan Godwyn (fl. 1685), Richard Baxter (1615–91), and George Fox (1641–91). Godwyn, author of *The Negro's and Indians Advocate* and other works of the same tenor, was an Anglican minister who served in Virginia in Marston parish in the late 1660s.[78] Fox, the first Quaker, wrote and spoke on the subject of the treatment of African-Americans by Anglo-Americans, both before and after his journey to the British West Indies and the Chesapeake in 1671–74.[79] Richard Baxter, also a Puritan, wrote a scathing denunciation of the commerce in human commodities.[80] As they observed the extreme brutality and callousness of the actual practice of enslavement, their core theme of Christian equalitarianism led them to challenge aspects of slavery, the slave trade, the inhumanity of the treatment of the slaves, even to advocate replacing perpetual servitude by limited-term servitude.

The well-known authority Thomas E. Drake has said that these seventeenth-century preachers "sought the liberation of Negroes' souls, not their bodies."[81] They did not demand immediate general emancipation; rather, they preached to the slaves the sanctity of submissiveness. Nevertheless, the doctrine of a common humanity as children of God, and of Christ's blood as the universal solvent of sin, as well as the jubilee tradition of the people of the Book, limiting the time that even strangers might be held in bondage – all that was an obstacle that the plantation bourgeoisie knew it could not ignore.[82]

Such an ideology was unsuited to the superstructure of a colony founded on lifetime hereditary bond-servitude. "[W]e cannot serve Christ and Trade," said Godwyn, in warning to those who sought enrichment through denying the humanity of the plantation bond-laborers.[83] "From this fundamental idea of the brotherhood of men through the sacrifice of Christ," writes Drake, "Fox reasoned that the servitude of Negroes should end in freedom just as it did for whites"[84]; accordingly Fox urged Barbados Quakers to "deal mildly and gently with their negroes ... and that after certain years of servitude they would make them free."[85] These ideas if put into practice would negate the very purpose of lifelong bondage by shortening the period of servitude. Further-more, such a practice would reduce the supply of bond-labor in two ways. First, it would deprive the owners to some degree of property in newborn children. Second, the reduced profitability of bond-labor resulting from shortening the period of servitude, coupled with the moral crusade against the slave trade as "the worst kind of thievery" as Richard Baxter put it, would have reduced the profitability of that branch of free enterprise.[86]

Furthermore, these equalitarian implications were absolutely incompatible with racial oppression, which in Anglo-America would take the form of "white supremacy." Morgan Godwyn, for all his assurances about not prejudicing the interests of the owners of lifetime bond-laborers, justified his campaign for Christianizing African and African-American bond-laborers in terms that had quite different implications. Godwyn denounced plantation owners who opposed the admission of African-American bond-laborers to Christian fellowship by pretending "That the Negro's, though in their figure they carry some resemblance of Manhood, yet are indeed no Men." In terms of pure economic determinism, Godwyn ascribed this denial of the humanity of Africans and African-Americans to "the inducement and instigation of our Planters['] chief Diety, Profit."[87] Calling such ideas "strange to the People in England," Godwyn argued the case for a common humanity:

> How should they [Africans and African-Americans] otherwise be capable of Trades, and other no less Manly imployments, as also of Reading, and Writing; or show so much Discretion in management of Business; eminent in diverse of them; but wherein (we know) that many of our own People are deficient.[88]

The ruling elite in the plantation colonies found such notions so threatening that, despite Quaker disavowal of any intent to incite Negro insurrection, respective colony legislatures enacted stern measures against the sect. In Barbados, where Negroes were a majority of the population by the end of the third quarter of the seventeenth century, elaborate systems of repressive measures were instituted. Laws providing severe penalties were enacted against those who allowed the attendance of Negroes at Quaker meetings and schools.[89] In the Chesapeake, laws were enacted generally proscribing the Quakers, but without making any specific reference to African-Americans or bond-servitude.[90] Although throughout the seventeenth century a majority of the bond-laborers in the Chesapeake were European-Americans, the spread of such doctrines as Quakerism might threaten to unravel bond-servitude altogether, especially in light of the fact that, from its inception in the 1620s, it represented a violation of English master–servant principles. Of course, the equalitarian implications of Christian doctrine were not the invention of seventeenth-century Puritanism.[91] The rebels on Mousehold Heath in 1549 had based their argument against bondage on the grounds of an appeal to Christian fellowship.[92] Later in that same century, Thomas Smith had made the point in his *Republica Anglorum* – that Christians might not hold Christians in slavery, a principle drawn from ancient Hebrew tribal law.[93]

Elements of the Propertied Classes Oppose Racial Oppression

In Virginia in the period before Bacon's Rebellion, actions taken by some of the plantation owners implied a rejection on their part of the principle of racial oppression, although explicit references to English common law and Christian doctrine were omitted. Owners of African-American bond-laborers frequently encouraged them by allowing them to have livestock and small cultivable plots, not just for their subsistence but for disposal by sale. Such a practice was contrary to the conditions of chattel bond-servitude in general, since it implied the legal ability of the worker to make contracts for purchase and sale.[94] Indeed in the instances cited above of African-American cattle dealers, self-purchasers, plantation owners, and tobacco sellers, those persons first achieved social mobility through encouragement by their European-American owners. In other cases African-Americans were assured of places on the first rung of social mobility by the expiration of their limited terms of servitude, or under the terms of wills of owners who died, which frequently provided them with allowances of livestock. In order to resolve any doubts about the ownership of certain "Cattle, Hoggs & poultrey, with their increase" in the possession of African-Americans Emanual Driggs and Bashawe Farnando, two prominent planters, Francis Pott and Stephen Charlton, attested that those animals had been "Lawfully gotten, & purchased" from Pott when Driggs and Farnando were in Pott's employ, and that "they may freely dispose of them either in their life tyme or att their death."[95]

Aside from other cases mentioned incidentally in other parts of this chapter, here are half a dozen instances in which European-American employers acted on the assumption that African-American bond-laborers need not serve for life, nor hereditarily, but only for limited terms.

On 2 December 1648, Stephen Charlton made a legal record of his intention that "John Gemander his servant" was to serve a limited term of ten years, and then "the said Negro is to be a free man." On the same day, Charlton "assigned" Grace-Suzana, a "Negro childe," to serve Mr Richard Vaughan until the age of thirty and then "to be freed from further servitude."[96] On 16 April 1650 Richard Vaughan made a court record of his intention that when they reached the age of thirty, two Negro children owned by him, three-year-old Temperance and two-year-old James, should be free.[97] Stephen Charlton's will, probated on 29 January 1654/5, provided for freedom, on certain conditions, for Jack in four years, and for Bridgett if she paid his daughters 2,500 pounds of tobacco and cask, or otherwise at the end of three more years.[98] When Christopher Stafford died around the end of 1654 his will provided that Mihill Gowen was to be free after serving Stafford's uncle four more years. The executrix of the will, Stafford's sister, Amy Barnhouse, "for divers good causes" (and apparently a year ahead of time) freed Gowen and his baptized infant son William.[99] Francis Pott died before he had a chance to include in his will his intention to free "his Negroe Bashore." His widow and executrix married William Kendall, member of the County Court. On 30 May

1659 Kendall, in accordance with Pott's wishes, "set the said Bashore at Liberty and proclaim[ed] him to be free . . . for Ever."[100]

In the spring of 1660, Thomas Whitehead died; he was survived by two children, Mary Rogers, the elder, and James Rogers. Although Mary was still under age, Whitehead appointed her his chief heir and the executrix of his will. In a further provision he set free his African-American bond-laborer named John to "be his owne man from any person or persons whatsoever," and gave him a cow and a heifer, the house John lived in, and "ground to plant upon . . . and peaceably to injoy it his lifetime.' He also appointed John "to be Mary Rogers['] Guardyan & Overseer of hir & what I have given hir till she is of age." Finally, if Mary and his son James died before coming of age, the entire estate, which at that time included an unnamed boy bond-laborer with two years yet to serve, "shall returne to my Negro [John]." Whitehead correctly anticipated that the court might not accept John as Mary's guardian, and named one Andrew Rider to serve in John's stead. There are indications that Rider was negligent in the execution of the will. In September 1660, possibly on John's petition, the County Court "ordered that John Negro servant to Thomas Whitehead deceased be and hereby is declared Free & that hee have his Cattle & other things belonging to him delivered to him."[101]

One other will seems worth notice here, although it was not left by a member of the propertied classes. English seaman George Williams would never see home again. He died in October 1667 in Virginia, where he had been tended and comforted by Manuel Driggus in his last days. Like Joe Hill, he had little to divide, but that little he bequeathed to Driggus "for his care and trouble in tendinge mee in my sickness," namely, eleven months' back wages due for his service on his ship, *Loves Increase*, whatever tobacco he had laid by, his sea chest and its contents, and all else he owned in Northampton County. In keeping with the custom of the time, he made Driggus, his largest creditor, the executor of his will.[102]

The Case of Elizabeth Key

Elizabeth Key (the name is variously spelled) was born in Virginia around 1631. She was the daughter of Thomas Key, of Northumberland County, and of an African-American woman, not named in the record, but who was a bond-laborer owned by Key.[103] In 1636 the father, intending to return to England to stay, sold his plantation to Humphrey Higginson (the child's godfather and a member of the General Assembly), and bound Elizabeth to him for a term of nine years. Under the terms of this assignment, Higginson was "to use her more respectfully than a Comon servant or slave." Elizabeth was not to be sold to anyone else. If Higginson survived and stayed in Virginia until the end of the nine years, Elizabeth was then to be free. If Higginson were to return to England before that time, he was to take Elizabeth with him at his own expense and return her to her father there. If Higginson died in

Virginia before the end of the nine years, Elizabeth was then to be immediately free.

Thomas Key died before he could embark for England, and Higginson, too, died some time before Elizabeth's nine-year term was completed. Instead of achieving her freedom, however, she was held in servitude by the administrator of the Higginson estate, a planter named John Mottrom. Mottrom also died and in 1656 Elizabeth Key, with the assistance of William Greenstead as her attorney, brought suit for her freedom against those who were now in possession of Mottrom's estate. The grounds taken by the defense imparted a far-reaching significance to the case by claiming Key as a lifetime bond-laborer on the grounds that such had been the condition of her mother.

In January 1656 a jury of twelve men found Elizabeth Key to be rightfully entitled to her freedom. The overseers of the Mottrom estate appealed the decision to the Virginia General Court. The original record of the General Court for that period was destroyed by fire in 1865. But a transcript of it made prior to 1860 has the following entry under the date of 12 March 1656: "Mulatto held to be a slave and appeal taken." Historians may be correct in inferring that this is a reference to Elizabeth Key, and that it indicates that the General Court reversed the decision of the Northumberland County Court. That inference it strengthened by the fact that a week later the General Assembly, the normal court of appeal from General Court decisions at that time, took the case under its consideration. On 20 March a special committee of the General Assembly, chosen to make a determination of the matter, expressed the sense "of the Burgesses of the present Assembly," holding that Key was entitled to freedom on two legal grounds that are of critical importance for the present discussion of the origin of racial slavery as a particular form of racial oppression in continental Anglo-America. First, there was the ancient common law principle of *partus sequitur patrem*, according to which the condition of the child follows the condition of the father. Since Elizabeth was the daughter of John Key,[104] she should be free "by the Comon Law [that] the Child of a Woman slave begotten by a freeman ought to be free." Second, Key should be free based on the Christian principle against holding Christians as slaves. Elizabeth Key "hath bin long since Christened, Colonel Higginson being her God father." The Assembly ordered that the matter be returned for consideration, noting that Key should be given not only freedom dues, but also compensation "for the time shee hath served longer than shee ought to have done."

One of the Mottrom estate overseers, George Colclough, who was later to come into possession of one-third of the estate by marrying Mottrom's widow, appealed to Governor Berkeley. On 11 June the Governor ordered a suspension of further proceedings pending a rehearing of the case by the Fall term of the General Court. There is no record, however, of the General Court ever having taken further notice of the case. The last word in the litigation was had by the Northumberland County Court; in effect it ignored the Governor's order and instead implemented the sense of the General Assembly by ordering that Key be freed and compensated. The fact that the judgment of the General Assembly effectively prevailed is incontestably indicated by the following series of developments. The March sitting of the General Court ruled that, if a woman bond-laborer married a free man with the consent of her owner, she became free thereby. Key and Greenstead had developed a personal as well as a professional relationship. The banns of their marriage were proclaimed in the church, and since no one could "shew any Lawful cause whey they may not be joyned together," they were married. It is apparent that the administrators of the Mottrom estate were tacitly acknowledging that they had no legal grounds to prevent the marriage. The certificate of the marriage was recorded at the same July Northumberland Court that finally ordered Key freed. Lastly, when the Mottrom estate was finally divided the following January, it included one Irish, four English, and three African-American bond-laborers, but Elizabeth Key was not among them.

Lacking further legal recourse, the Mottromites finally let Elizabeth Key go, without, however, conceding the principle involved. Rather, they still asserted their right to "assign and transfer unto William Greenstead a maid servant formerly belonging to the estate of Col. Mottrom commonly called Elizabeth Key being nowe Wife unto the sad Greenstead." Thus the advocates of hereditary bondage covered their embarrassment with the principle of "the feme couvert," according to which the wife is not at her own disposal but at that of her husband, and thus is still not a free individual.

The Critical Importance of the Key Case

The case of Elizabeth Key presented a direct confrontation, played out on a colony-wide scale, between the desire among plantation owners to raise their rate of profit by imposing lifetime hereditary servitude on African-Americans, and an African-American's right to freedom on the basis of Christian principles and English common law.[105] The jury that heard the case and the General Assembly that reviewed it in 1656 acted on the traditional English principle in finding that Elizabeth Key's Christian baptism and rearing barred her from being held as a lifetime bond-laborer. At the same time, they took their stand on the common-law principle that the social status of the child followed that of the father.

If the principles affirmed in the findings of the Northumberland County jury and the special committee of the General Assembly had prevailed, the establishment of racial slavery would have been prevented. If African-Americans were to be reduced to lifetime hereditary bond-servitude and kept in that status, it was essential for the exploiters of bond-labor to establish the principle of descent through the mother. For, as an owner claimed when another woman sued for her freedom a century later: "If, in a case of a dispute about the property of negroes, it is not sufficient to prove the mother to be a slave, there will soon be an end to that kind of property."[106] What was involved here was not a mere matter of ancestry; it represented an attack on the patriarchy, though limited, of course, to the Negro family. In principle it was akin to the attack on the Catholic Irish family under the Penal Laws of the eighteenth century.[107] And, as in the case of that aspect of the Penal Laws, it was not associated with any equalitarian impulse on the part of the ruling class.

It was equally important, for purposes of maximizing profits by reducing labor costs, to cut the knot that tangled Christian baptism with freedom. Already a decade and a half earlier the organizers of the ill-fated English colony on Providence Island had said that only Negroes not yet converted to Christianity could be enslaved, but that those who had been converted could not.[108] The early response of Barbados planters to proposals to Christianize the Negroes there was that it would be the end of their system, because they could no longer be accounted as slaves.[109]

Notice has been taken of the quick reactions of the General Assembly to aspects of the runaway problem, and to the servants' plot of 1663, and of the timely changes in the terms of bond-servitude to be imposed on Irish bond-laborers, which reflected the alteration from the ascendancy of the Puritan Commonwealth to the restoration of the crypto-Catholic Stuarts in England. Each of these cases also involved considerations of labor costs, but they did not impinge on the sacred and constitutional principles of patriarchy and religious conversion, deep-running principles not to be disposed of quickly. It would be six years before the Virginia General Assembly in 1662 resolved "doubts that [had] arisen" about the status of children of English fathers and African-American women, by enacting that "all children borne in this country shalbe held bond or free according to the condition of the mother," establishing the principle of *partus sequitur ventrem*, directly contrary to the English common law principle of *partus sequitur patrem*, descent through the father.[110] In 1667, eleven years after Elizabeth Key had won her fight for freedom as a Christian, the General Assembly again was able to receive "doubts that [had] arisen" by decreeing that "the conferring of baptisme doth not alter the condition of the person as to his bondage"; thus, as it was said, "masters, freed from this doubt, may more carefully endeavour the propagation of christianity."[111]

A widened lens brings significant rough coincidences into focus. In January 1663, the year after the Virginia General Assembly enacted the legal principle of descent through the mother in order to make African-Americans subject to hereditary bond-servitude, the English government re-chartered the Company of Royal Adventurers to Africa, for the first time listing the trade in human chattels among its purposes.[112] In October the English bourgeoisie threw open a challenge to Dutch domination of that trade by sending a naval force to carry out extensive raids on Dutch posts on the coast of West Africa. The issue thus joined was to eventuate in the Second Anglo-Dutch War (1665–67); it ended with the Treaty of Breda which finally gave the Anglo-American plantation colonies secure direct access to African bond-laborers. In 1672, the Royal Adventurers, who had been bankrupted by the long struggle with the Dutch, were succeeded by the Royal African Company, which was granted a monopoly as the supplier of African laborers to Anglo-America.

The 1667 assurance given by the Virginia General Assembly to the plantation bourgeoisie at large that they need no longer fear the liberating effect of Christian baptism coincided with the signing of the Treaty of Breda. Three years later, in 1670, the General Assembly made it illegal for African-American planters to buy "christian" bond-laborers, limiting them to the purchase of persons "of their owne nation."[113] Although the reasoning that led to this enactment is not recorded, except that the issue "hath beene questioned," it was not intended as a way of promoting the sales of African bond-laborers. Rather, it was designed to promote the principle of racial oppression. The purchase price for Africans was half again as much as that for Europeans,[114] prohibitively high for poor planters such as African-American planters generally were. This restriction therefore was an effective bar to advancement to the employer class.

In 1672 the General Assembly enacted a law "for the apprehension and suppression of runawayes, negroes and slaves" because, it said,

> many negroes have lately beene and now are out in rebellion in sundry parts of this country, and ... noe means have yet beene found for the apprehension and suppression of them from whome many mischiefes of very dangerous consequence may arise to the country if either other negroes, Indians or servants should happen to fly forth and joyne with them.[115]

Into this Virginia in 1674 or 1675, some 250 bond-laborers were brought directly from West Africa in ships under contract to the Royal African Company.[116] The tobacco bourgeoisie generally certainly hoped to solve the problem of perennially low-priced tobacco by importing Africans as lifetime hereditary bond-laborers. The tobacco bourgeoisie was also strongly urged by the highest circles in the English government to patronize the African labor trade, "Blacks ... being the principall and most Usefull appurtenances of a plantation."[117]

But as the historian Bruce noted, "Those [bond-laborers] snatched directly from a state of freedom in Africa were doubtless in some measure difficult to manage."[118] If it came to that, who would do the "managing"? If the hopes of the rich planters and of the Royal African Company were to be realized in a rapid increase of the labor supply directly from Africa, how would the ruling elite cope with the attendant increase in problems of social control, of "negroes out in rebellion?" They could, of course, pass more stringent laws, but how effective would they be? Leaving aside the demonstrated moral and humane attitudes that ran counter to such denial of English rights to African-Americans, there were interests belonging to the field of political economy that were directly or indirectly inconsistent with devoted enforcement of repressive measures against African-Americans. In the years 1672 to 1674,

England was engaged in the last of the three Anglo-Dutch wars. Even some of the more prosperous Virginia planters, who might have been able to afford to buy lifetime bond-laborers at £18 to £20 each, were in a treasonous disposition, and were "saying openly, that they are in the nature of slaves" because they were being denied free trade with the Dutch. Their disaffection was so great, it was said, that Virginia was "in danger, with their consent, to fall into the enemy's hands."[119] Of course that war would end, but the English Navigation Acts directed against the Dutch trade would remain; still, these more prosperous planters might be expected to return to their allegiance and perhaps find common interest in acquiring lifetime bond-laborers from Royal African Company contractors. But, at the least, their priorities diverged from those of their government to a degree that was not for that moment propitious for effective administration of laws. The poor majority of the planters, and the landless freemen, could not afford to buy lifetime bond-laborers, who would be forced to compete with additional numbers of African lifetime bond-laborers; they had better things to do than to help the rich planters keep their newly arriving Africans. As for the bond-labor majority of the producing classes, they were so unreliable that of their number African-Americans and all but a few of the European-Americans were denied the right to bear arms even in face of the threat of a Dutch invasion.[120]

Given the English superstructural obstacles and the already marked resistance of African-Americans to lifetime hereditary bondage that have been described in this chapter, a rapid and large addition of African bond-laborers to the population would certainly tend to reduce the effectiveness of the already weak social control stratum in enforcing the laws for the "suppression of rebellious negroes." It might indeed lead to the appearance of *quilombos* in the Blue Ridge or the Allegheny Mountains rivaling in scope the Palmares settlement that withstood the assaults of Portuguese and Dutch colonialists for nearly a century.[121]

PART FOUR
Rebellion and Reaction

11

Rebellion – and Its Aftermath

In 1624, Captain John Smith had warned that basing the colony on chattel bond-servitude was bound to "bring ... [Virginia] to misery."[1] A half-century later, a revolt that had been brewing since about 1660, when the long period of very low tobacco prices began, fulfilled that prophecy.

No other event of Anglo-American colonial history has received so much attention from historians as Bacon's Rebellion, which convulsed the Virginia colony for nearly nine months beginning in May 1676.[2] Over a period of nearly three centuries, they have produced three main lines of interpretation of that event's historic significance. At first, Bacon's Rebellion was regarded as a bad thing because of its lawlessness; "rebel" was *ipso facto* a pejorative term, although extenuations were found by reference to errors of government policy, official corruption, and abuse of power. In the "Nationalist" period, between the American Revolution and the War against Great Britain of 1812, a new look in the light of new events led to a reinterpretation wherein Nathaniel Bacon himself was seen as "the torchbearer of the Revolution" and the rebellion was regarded as a dress rehearsal for the American Revolution; issues raised against George III by the Continental Congress were seen to vindicate Bacon's rebellion against Charles II's Governor, William Berkeley. One well-known variation on this theme eschews such hero worship and glorification of rebellion but nevertheless regards the events as the beginning of the shift in the locus of power from the royal provincial authorities to an aristocracy of the "county families" with a sense of a new Virginia identity that a century later they would assert by enlisting as "rebels."[3] To the extent that Bacon's Rebellion is seen as a reaction against the effects of the Navigation Act and exorbitant duties laid on tobacco sent to England, the parallel with the American Revolution has validity. But that analogy limps when it comes to Governor William Berkeley's role, for he, the villain of the piece, was the most articulate critic of the Navigation Laws. A more fundamental objection is that the comparison is limited to the matter of throwing off English domination and the establishment of an independent republic, and consequently ignores the factor of the extremes of economic inequality that resulted from the system of bond-labor.

When World War Two and then the modern civil rights movement brought the thesis of equal rights and anti-racism to the fore, Bacon's Rebellion was once again seen as a bad thing, but not because to "rebel" was unjustified, but because the rebellion was regarded as not a real rebellion at all, but merely a dramatic early event in the "frontier" phenomenon, whereby the path of white empire took its westward way completely disregardful of the rights of the American Indians. Wilcomb E. Washburn, author of the standard presentation of this point of view, concluded that the failure to take this "frontier aggressiveness" into account was due, at least in part, to "the white historian's immersion in his racial bias."[4]

All these various approaches, as well as that of the present work, share a common disregard of the admonition of the widely respected historian Wesley Frank Craven to avoid attempts to read any lasting significance into Bacon's Rebellion.[5]

My concern with the origin of racial oppression in continental Anglo-America stresses the class struggle dimension of colonial history. At the same time, it is consistently informed by an equalitarian motif.[6] I thus have a transient foot in both the second and the third of the three camps, but only in passing through to a still different interpretation. By the light of a consciousness raised by the modern civil rights movement, I have examined the records of the seventeenth and early eighteenth centuries, with which scholars have long been familiar, and it is on those records that my somewhat iconoclastic assessment of the historical significance of Bacon's Rebellion must stand or fall.[7]

Such being my focus, I have centered my attention on the second, civil war phase of Bacon's Rebellion – April 1676 to January 1677 – rather than the first, anti-Indian, phase – September 1675 to April 1676. In more explicit justification of this emphasis, I offer the following four considerations.

The first of these is that the details of the anti-Indian phase of the rebellion are all taken from accounts of the English; the Pamunkey, the Susquehannocks and the Occaneechee left no record of those events. Although the English accounts do acknowledge particular English faults in the conduct of the colony's relations with the Indians, they all presume that the English were licensed by divine providence, and/or the right of conquest (thinly disguised perhaps by "purchase" or "treaty"), to reduce them to subject, tributary status, and sooner or later to expropriate them.[8]

Second, despite the policy of enslaving Indian war captives, the basic Indian policy of the English ruling elite was motivated not primarily by consideration of social control over exploitable Indian bond-labor in Virginia, but rather by a desire to exclude the Indians from English-occupied territory. (To the English aggressors, the Indians were regarded much as were the "wild Irish", the "Irish enemy" outside the English Pale – the small portion of Ireland that was under English control – prior to the seventeenth century.)

Third, "white-race" identity was not the principle for which freemen were rallied for the anti-Indian phase of Bacon's Rebellion. The "not-white" and "redskin" classification of the Indian in Anglo-America would be the outcome of the invention of the white race, a transmogrification of the European-American that had not yet been accomplished in 1676.[9]

The fourth and final consideration is that Bacon's Rebellion was not primarily an anti-Indian war,[10] although that was the tenor of the first call to arms voiced by frontier plantation owners such as Nathaniel Bacon and William Byrd, capitalists recently arrived in Virginia.[11] An analogy is provided by the American Revolution which was not primarily an anti-Indian war, although Thomas Jefferson, the Virginian author of the Declaration of Independence, did indict George III for having "endeavoured to bring on the inhabitants of our frontiers, the merciless Indian savages" etcetera, etcetera, and Congress arranged for the "extinction" of Indian land claims in order to grant 9,500,000 acres to Revolutionary War veterans.[12]

The "lesson of history" to be drawn from the anti-Indian phase of Bacon's Rebellion is clear and retains its relevance today. The European occupation of Indian lands shows that, from Columbus to Custer, the bourgeois eye looks upon progress and genocide indifferently, as incidental aspects of the process of the accumulation of capital; the anti-Indian phase of Bacon's Rebellion was merely another example of that lesson. Its logic requires that the United States government that brought the American Indians to the verge of extinction make restitution in some form that will at least end the legacy of extreme poverty and discrimination that American white supremacy has imposed on them. The struggle for justice in this respect merges with the general struggle against white-supremacist racial oppression.

Departing from the "Great Men" Interpretation of the Rebellion

The civil war phase of Bacon's Rebellion offers relevant insights into the course of the history of Anglo-America in its colonial and in its regenerate United States form. The usual treatments of the rebellion describe it largely in terms of the contest between the Governor, William Berkeley, and the Rebel, Nathaniel Bacon, even though their differences are seen to involve policy questions of great interest to the free population generally. Bernard Bailyn's analysis avoids the heroic interpretation; he finds the significance of the rebellion in the struggle within the elite, but he ignores the bond-laborers and the poor farmers as well, except for the latter's opposition to unfair taxation and corruption and abuse of power by the Governor and his faction. I do not intend a narrative presentation, but rather merely to center attention on those elements of the rebellion that relate most meaningfully to the origin of racial oppression in continental Anglo-America.

Sir William Berkeley arrived in Virginia in 1642 as Governor and served in that office until January 1677, except for eight Cromwellian interregnum years, 1652 to 1659. To him, and to his appointed Colony Council, was assigned the custody of the imperial interest, and he was given great powers of patronage in establishing and maintaining the provincial bureaucracy for carrying out the appropriate official functions of that responsibility. Beginning in the mid-1640s, in the time of the English Revolution, and continuing during the first half-decade after the restoration of Charles II to the throne in 1660, a number of wealthy and well-connected newcomers reactivated claims descended from Company period "Adventurers". These claims, Bailyn says, were "the most important of a variety of forms of capital that might provide the basis for secure family fortunes."[13] These new planters became established as dominant families in the various counties. The political implications of this decentralization of power, through the ascendancy of the "county families," were at least potentially contradictory to English imperial interests, as represented by the Navigation Acts which required Virginia planters to ship their tobacco in English ships to England, so that the Crown and English merchants, respectively, could rake in the profit from the royal import duty on tobacco or from re-export sales from England mainly to continental Europe.[14]

This tension between the scattered county families and the imperial interest accounts for the English government's proposals for the establishment of a limited number of port towns as the sole authorized sites for shipping tobacco. These would facilitate enforcement of the Navigation Act and assure full collection of the 2s. export duty per hogshead of tobacco that supplied the Governor's salary and unaudited expenditures involved in the operation of the provincial government, including the work of collecting the royal quit-rents of 2s. per hundred acres of patented land. This divergence of interests was also expressed in the establishment in about 1663 of the elected House of Burgesses as a separate section of a bicameral Assembly and in the fact that for more than a decade the Governor did not call a single general election of burgesses. The result was the development of a political differentiation within the colony elite, between the county magnates, on the one hand, and the royally privileged inner circle around the Governor and the Colony Council that came to be called "the Green Spring" faction.[15] In 1676, that divergence would produce a breach in the ranks of the ruling elite through which would erupt profound social upheaval.

Bacon's Rebellion began in that year, not as a new bond-labor plot for flight or rebellion, nor as a mutiny of poor disfranchised freemen sinking hopelessly into debt and the regressive system of taxes by the poll,[16] but rather as a dispute within the ranks of the colony elite over "Indian policy". More specifically it was a dispute between Governor Berkeley and owners of "frontier" plantations where, beginning in June 1675, war had flared between settlers and mainly Susquehannock Indians.[17] Nathaniel Bacon (1647-76)[18] who had been appointed to the Colony Council by Berkeley in March 1675, just a year after Bacon's arrival in Virginia, was chosen by the "frontier" country planters the following April to lead their aggressive anti-Indian cause.[19]

The issue between Berkeley and Bacon was not whether Indians were to be displaced by the advance of English settlement – they were in fundamental agreement on that – but merely the priority to be given to it at a given time, and thus the rate at which it was to be done. There are those historians who feel bound to euphemize Berkeley's "Indian policy," and one of them presents Berkeley as a "champion of the right of the American Indians to hold undisturbed the land they occupied."[20] But such an assessment seems questionable in the light of the record. In October 1648, "upon the humble representation of the Burgesses to the Governour [Berkeley] and Council," it was enacted that, beginning in the following September, English colonists were authorized by the English colonial government to occupy land previously guaranteed to the Indians under the treaty of 1646 "upon the north side of Charles [later called the York] River and Rappahannock river." The justification for this displacement of the native inhabitants was that English planters needed those lands because their lands were overworked and their cattle needed more range.[21] In June 1666, Berkeley urged the Rappahannock militia to "destroy all those Northern Indians." He was particularly keen on the plan as being self-financing, because the militiamen would be paid by capturing "women & children." But, he slyly suggested, if the Rappahannock men did not think they could do the work alone, there were plenty of others from other counties who would be willing to serve in return for their "share of the Booty." The Rappahannock County court members (militia officers ex officio) hastened to reassure the Governor that they could do the job themselves, without outside help – that they needed only the "Incouradgement [of] the spoyles of our Enemies."[22] At the end of June 1676, Bacon led an onslaught on the friendly Pamunkey Indians, killed some of them and took others as captives to be sold as slaves of the English. According to a marginal note in one of the official documents, "The Indian prisoners were some of them sold by Bacon and the rest disposed of by Sir William Berkeley."[23] The tattered remnant of the Pamunkey people fled from the land that the England had assigned as their only legal place in the English scheme of settlement.[24] When requested to return to that "reservation," the Queen of the Pamunkey (a descendant of Opechancanough) replied that she and her people had fled for their lives, and that they would willingly return to their assigned place when the Governor could assure them of protection from murderous assault by the frontiersmen who made no distinction of friendly Indians. Berkeley's cold reply was that he was "resolved not to be soe answered but to reduce her and the other Indians" as soon as he had settled accounts with Bacon.[25]

For historians who have no investment in defending Berkeley's reputation, this aspect of the Governor's behavior should pose no difficult threat; rather it appears to be perfectly of a piece with his "Indian policy." Among the responsibilities of the Governor and the Colony Council was the formulation and maintenance of an "Indian policy" that would assure the minimum diversion from making tobacco. The essence of that policy was to maintain advantageous political and economic relations with the friendly neighbouring tribes, the Doegs, the Pamunkey, the Nottoway and the Meherrin, who were first subdued and then reduced to dependency as "tributary" subjects of the king of England. They were to serve as a two-way buffer, shielding the English from enemy tribes, and capturing and returning runaway bond-laborers who fled from servitude.[26] One such arrangement was designed to frustrate "all Loitering English as [blank in manuscript] which throughs [throws] themselves amongst" the Indians "for harbour or to be conveyed unto remote parts with intent to defraud their masters of their Time of Service." The "King and great men" were to bring any such runaway to the Rappahannock County magistrates and "be immediately payed five armes lenths of Roanoake or the value thereof."[27]

This agreement lends specificity to Governor Berkeley's general policy, which "alwayes and most prudently Indeavored to p[re]serve [the neighbor Indians] as being as necessarie for us as Doggs to hunt wolves."[28] Furthermore, in exchange for English firearms, powder and other goods, the tributary tribes supplied beaver and other pelts that were an easy source of profit for the plantation bourgeoisie, more particularly for those men who were expressly licensed by the colonial authorities to engage in the trade.[29]

Both aspects of this policy found opposition among the newer, "county family" types. Upon observing that much of the best tidewater land was already patented to earlier claimants, some of these new investors saw better prospects for exploiting bond-labor in opening up new areas to settlement. At the same time, the conduct of the fur trade monopoly was regarded as another instance of the use of provincial authority to line the pockets of the Governor and his faction. However, as Bailyn says, "These dissidents ... represented neither the downtrodden masses nor a principle of opposition to privilege as such. Their discontent stemmed to a large extent from their own exclusion from the privileges they sought."[30]

True, some planters were also only too eager to gain the bond-labor of Indian war captives when that opportunity presented itself.[31] Some, "rather than bee Tennants, seate upon the remote barren Land, whereby contentions arrise between them and the Indians."[32] But the fact that one out of every four of the freemen in Virginia were landless seems to indicate that the common run of the people did not see moving to the "frontier" as a viable option for achieving upward social mobility.[33] They indeed "thought it hard to be a Tennant on a Continent,"[34] but they saw that the most direct, preferable, sensible and the safest course out of their straitened circumstances lay not in "Indian policy" but in a change in Virginia land policy.[35] The remedy was, as stated in the proposal of James City County to the English government commissioners sent to investigate Bacon's Rebellion, to tax land, and tax it so heavily that the tidewater-land engrossers would find it prohibitively expensive to hold onto idle land, which would then become available to the land-hungry poor and dispossessed.[36] The validity of their view would be acknowledged many times by those reporting to the home government. William Sherwood deplored the activities of the "Land lopers, some [of whom] take up 2000 acres, some 3000 Acres, others ten thousand Acres, nay many [of whom] have taken up thirty thousand Acres of Land, and never cultivated any part of it."[37] Giles Bland, collector of the King's customs in Virginia, noted that "A poor man who has only his labour to maintain himself and his family, pays as much [taxes] as a man who has 20,000 acres." Bland proposed that "the richest sort" be taxed as a means of getting them to "lay down parte of their Land to bee taken up by such as will Employ it."[38]

This proposal for a land-tax incentive to induce a redistribution of the land represented the popular sense of the unfairness of the tax system. In the name of reducing costs of government, the Governor and Colony Council were authorized to impose annual levies, without consulting even the House of Burgesses.[39] The privilege of trading with the Indians was by law restricted to a few appointees of the Governor. In addition to the colony taxes, each tithable was subject to county and parish levies, and occasional additional levies for particular purposes. In 1673, during the Third Anglo-Dutch War, the Governor and Colony Council imposed a targeted levy for the construction of forts at points susceptible to Dutch shipborne incursions. In 1675, the Governor and Colony Council laid a special levy of 100 pounds of tobacco on each tithable, to be collected in two annual installments, to finance efforts to persuade King Charles to revoke two grants, made in 1669 and 1673, whereby some eight of his England-dwelling friends were endowed with the title to all the remaining unpatented "public" lands in Virginia, including the Eastern Shore.[40] The Governor and the Colony Council perceived these grants as prejudicial to their control over the acquisition of fee-simple land titles (held directly from the Crown) via the head-right system, or otherwise. The men sent to make the case before the government in England noted that the laying of this levy was intensifying the already existent "mutinous discontents" among the planters.[41]

The same class discrimination prevailed in relation to the fur trade with the Indians. Except for a few of the elite no colonists were allowed to have any interest in the fur trade.[42] In 1675, Nathaniel Bacon and William Byrd I, both of whom were Berkeley's cousins by marriage and members of the Colony Council, were given an exclusive license by Governor Berkeley, under terms requiring them to pay Governor Berkeley 800 beaver skins the first year and 600 every year thereafter.[43] Yet popular resentment over the fur monopoly was concentrated against Berkeley, as being a protector of Indians "for the lucre of the Beaver and otter trade &c."[44] The generality of the planters were excluded from this privilege; certainly the one-eighth or more of the adult male population who were freedmen just out of their time, and the half of the tithables who were bond-laborers, knew that they could not expect to become licensed in the fur trade. Richard Lee, a staunch supporter of the Governor and member of the House of Burgesses, was convinced that the zeal of the multitude in the rebellion was due to "hopes of levelling, otherwise all his [Bacon's] specious pretenses would not have persuaded them but that they believe to have equall advantages by success of their design."[45] Thomas Ludwell and Robert Smith advised the king that "the present disorders have their beginning ... from the poverty and uneasyness" of some of the "meanest" colonists.[46]

The quarrel that erupted between factions of the numerically small elite in 1676 over profit-making opportunities did not lead to new conquests of Indian territory for the expansion of English plantations.[47] Instead "the challengers were themselves challenged", says Bailyn, by "ordinary settlers [angered] at the local privileges of the same newly risen county magnates who assailed the privileges of the Green Spring faction."[48] The result was a complete breakdown of ruling-class social control, as the anti-Indian war was transformed into a popular rebellion against the plantation bourgeoisie.

In May 1676, Giles Bland, administrator of his father's plantation interests in Virginia, and collector of the King's customs there, informed Secretary of State Joseph Williamson in England that "Virginia is at this point of time under the greatest Destractions that it hath felt since the year 1622." A war with the Indians was impending; a force of five hundred volunteers had gone forth to war on Indians in general in defiance of the orders of the Governor; and tax collections were threatened with disruption. The main declared grievances of the rebels, however, were directed at unfair taxation and peculation in high places. Most serious of all, unlike the Lawnes Creek Parish mutiny of 1674, which had been "suppressed by a Proclamation, and the advice of some discreet persons," the present uprising was led by "Nathaniel Bacon lately sworne one of the Counsell and many other Gentlemen of good Condition." Bland worried that "the enemie," presumably some rival European power, would "take advantage of these Disorders."[49]

A new House of Burgesses was elected (it was the first election in fourteen years), a sort of official reconciliation was staged with Bacon, and legislation was passed for raising an anti-Indian army of 1,000 men and calling for the Governor to commission Bacon as the "general and commander-in-chief". When Berkeley temporized about signing the commission, several hundred armed men formed in combat array before the Assembly meeting house on 23 June, and by threatening the lives of the members forced Berkeley to sign the commission.[50] Thus, in effect, power had been conceded to the armed rebels, and the militia function had passed out of the hands of the nominal authorities, causing "the Indian design to recoil in a Civil War upon the colony."[51] This last fact was emphasized in July by the abject failure of the Governor's attempt to rally the Gloucester County militia to go against the rebels. Neither Governor nor king could control the situation sufficiently to prevent this extreme crisis.[52] So far from being in control was Colonel Joseph Brigder, chief of the colony militia, that "he could not ride safely on any road for fear of rebels," even six months after the supposed end of the rebellion.[53] So far from being in control was the Governor that from July 1676 to January 1677 "the only shelter for the Governor and his party" was Accomack, "separated Seaven Leagues distance."[54] Francis Moryson, one-time lieutenant governor of the colony and one of Virginia's representatives in England in October 1676, could only express his dismay that "Amongst so many thousand reputed honest men, there should not be one thousand" to fight against the rebellion.[55] Later Moryson and his fellow commissioner John Berry declared positively that of the fifteen thousand possible combatants in Virginia there were "not above five hundred persons untainted in this rebellion."[56]

The majority of the fifteen thousand were bond-laborers – six thousand European-Americans and two thousand African-Americans.[57] In view of the seventeenth-century Chesapeake record of resistance by the bond-laborers to the unconstitutional and oppressive conditions of their lives, how has it happened that, even in the course of invaluable and illuminating research, with very few exceptions,[58] historians have completely ignored this section of the population as a significant, self-activating shaper of history, and have instead relegated it to monographs on "white servitude,"[59] or to treatment as a mere economic category defined exclusively by market choices of the owning class?[60] Call it the bourgeois blindspot, that prevents them from seeing and accepting the capacity for historic self-activation in "people of no property."

My placement of the bond-laborers and the bond-labor relations of production at the center of the history of Bacon's Rebellion is not an exercise in self-indulgent revolutionary romanticism; rather, it proceeds directly from the record-based presentation of the history of Virginia Colony in the preceding chapters. Without bond-labor, there would have been no tobacco monoculture; without tobacco monoculture the economy would not have been dominated by an oligarchy of owners of large plantations gained by headrights on imported chattel bond-laborers.

Freedom for the bond-laborers would have revolutionized colonial Virginia from a plantation monoculture to a diversified smallholder economy.[61] The demand of the smallholders for a more equitable distribution of tidewater land if fully realized would have resulted in a predominance of family-sized farms without capital to import bond-laborers, and a more diversified economy. But, as the king's commissioners said in reply to county grievances, the oligarchy would never agree to that course of action. Indeed, that appears to have been the basis of the divide-and-conquer strategy proposed to the king by Virginia's representatives in England. The rebellion, they said, did not result from any desire of "the better or more industrious sort of people," and the best hope for ending the insurrection lay in "a speedy separation of the sound parts from the rabble."[62]

At the highest levels of government in Virginia and in England, the great question to which all others were secondary concerned the preservation of chattel bond-servitude. Five days after the Governor, Council and Burgesses capitulated to armed threat by Bacon's supporters and made him commander-in-chief of an army to go against the Indians, Philip Ludwell, Assistant Secretary of the colony and member of the Colony Council, wrote to Secretary of State Williamson confiding the possibility of a complete overthrow of the system fashioned by the tobacco bourgeoisie. For fear of having their throats cut by rebels, he said, the Assembly was granting Bacon's demands "as fast as they come." Ludwell also expressed concern about "the Indians on our

Borders." But his greatest fear was "our servants at home, who (if God prevent not their takeing hold of this Great advantage), must carry on beyond Remedy to destruc[ti]on."[63] That was the great danger for, in the words of Governor Berkeley himself, "The very being of the Collony doth consist in the Care and faithfulness, as well as in the number of our servants."[64] For those very reasons, it was the striving of the bond-laborers for freedom from chattel servitude that held the key to liberation of the colony from the misery that proceeded from oligarchic rule and a monocultural economy.

The prospect of freedom for the bond-laborers was more than a colonial concern; it bore heavily on domestic English politics. Charles II was in financial straits, but because he was at loggerheads with Parliament over other issues, he was unwilling to risk calling it into session to authorize revenue-raising measures. The collection of domestic excise taxes, income from Crown lands, and feudal dues, fell far short of the anticipated £1,200,000. In 1672, the government had been forced to repudiate its outstanding debt despite the secret subsidy of £200,000 a year supplied by Louis XIV of France.[65] In short, Charles found himself very much dependent on the £100,000 annual duties he collected on imports of tobacco from Virginia.[66] The losses caused by the Virginia rebellion, which completely disrupted the operation of the tobacco fleet of 140 ships, played a major part in compelling Charles to call for the election of a new parliament in 1678.[67] This domestic crisis no doubt added to the anxiety of the king and Privy Council as they prepared to send a military expedition to quell the rebellion; they wanted to know "[w]hether there be not more servants than Masters, and whether Bacon has not nor will not proclaim freedom to them?"[68]

Throughout Virginia in 1676 the county courts, where refractory bond-laborers were routinely sentenced to extensions of their servitude and lashes well laid on, were grossly disrupted by the rebellion. The same was true of the parishes in many of their functions, including their role in the execution of court orders regarding bond-laborers and their children. In Charles City County "the Courts of Justice [were] totally interrupted, hindered, and neglected" from the spring of 1676 until some time in 1677.[69] Social services (visiting the sick, burying the dead, performing marriages, caring for orphans and the indigent) normally performed by the minister, clerk and vestry of Middlesex County's Christ Church parish were suspended "by meanes and Armed Force of ill Desposed persons then in Rebellion."[70] Westmoreland County Court was adjourned begining in May 1676, and did not conduct business again until the following April or May.[71] The very circumstances that completely broke down the social control system also resulted in the main source of records regarding the day-to-day sufferings and struggles of the bond-laborers lapsing for much of 1676 and 1677. The editor of the colonial Virginia parish records concluded that, "in those parishes directly and fundamentally affected by Bacon's Rebellion it was found advisable the year following the Rebellion to destroy the existing parish records, or at least to render illegible some part of those records."[72]

However, it is not unreasonable to conjecture that bond-laborers in Charles City County would glory in the relaxation of social control.[73] At such a juncture of history, would not a person like Ann Berrey have been glad of her improved chance of a choice in the matter before being "gott with child" by her owner?[74] Might not one such as William Rogers have been tempted to validate his purloined indenture papers by simply walking away to seek better terms of employment, leaving half of his owner's tobacco seedlings untransplanted?[75] In the absence of a functioning Middlesex County Court to order him to "return to his Service," a bond-laborer would surely have gloried in the opportunity to defy Major Robert Smith, who sought to keep him in bondage by denying the validity of his "printed paper."[76] With the whole country in a state of social dissolution, who would have been there to capture a "Mulatto runaway boy" and return him to the parish minister who claimed him and on whose orders he was whipped to death?[77] There would have been no General Court or Charles City Council to order the pursuit of "certain runaway negroes," and nor would there have been any posse to carry that order out.[78] Perhaps among desperately unhappy bond-laborers the improved prospects for the outward expression of anger reduced the inclination to suicide.[79] A few names survive in the records of bond-laborers more disposed to turn their aggression outward. The Governor himself said that his own "servant," a carpenter named Page, had joined the rebellion and "for his violence used against the Royal Party [was] made a Colonel," and that another "servant," named Digby, was a rebel captain.[80] Bond-laborer James Wilson was apparently a rank-and-filer, as were William Baker, a "souldier ... by his own voluntary act," and John Thomas, who served in the rebellion for nearly six months.[82] Bond-laborer Mary Fletcher ran away to the rebel garrison that had taken over the house of Arthur Allen in Surry County.[82]

More significant than this random identification of individual bond-laborers is the fact that nameless-to-history bond-laborers intervened *en masse* in the rebellion for their own particular interest – freedom from chattel servitude. English poet and Parliament member Andrew Marvell reported on 14 November 1676 that a ship had recently arrived from Virginia with the news that Bacon had "proclam'd liberty to all Servants and Negro's."[83] A letter written from Virginia in October seemed to suggest that a class differentiation had occurred among the rebels: "Bacon's followers having deserted him he had proclaimed liberty to the servants and slaves which chiefly formed his army when he burnt James Town."[84] According to another ship's report, "most of the servants flock to [Bacon], and he makes their masters pay their wages."[85] The Virginia Assembly retrospectively declared that "many evill disposed servants in these late tymes of horrid rebellion taking advantage of the loosenes of the tymes, did depart from their service, and followed the rebells in rebellion."[86] The Royal Commissioners noted that "sundry servants and other persons of desperate fortunes in Virginia during the late rebellion deserted from their masters and ran into rebellion on the encouragement of liberty."[87]

Among the captains of merchant ships whom the king and Berkeley recruited for service against the rebellion, perhaps the most active, and certainly the most noteworthy, was Captain Thomas Grantham of the thirty-gun *Concord*. Grantham arrived in York River on 21 November.[88] Governor Berkeley came over from Accomack and, in a shipboard conference, agreed on a strategy whereby Grantham would attempt to go to the rebels and to persuade them to surrender and receive the Governor's pardon. The main concentration of some eight hundred men was around West Point, where the Pamunkey and the Mattaponi rivers meet to form the York. Laurence Ingram, who had assumed the rebel command after the death of Bacon on 26 October, was an old friend of Grantham, on whose ship Ingram had first arrived in Virginia.[89] Whatever the particulars of the conversation, an agreement was reached under the terms of which three hundred of the rebels marched with drums and colors down to Tindall's Point where the Governor was waiting aboard a ship. Through Ingram and the other rebel officers a ceasefire was agreed upon pending the arrival of "his Majesties Shipps." But such blind faith in the benevolence of His Majesty was not to be expected from the rebel rank-and-file; Ingram's arrangement with the Governor "was broke by the Rebells in three dayes time," and it became clear, in the words of one Virginia account, "the name of Authority had but litle power to [w]ring the Sword out of these Mad fellows hands." Authority failing, Grantham "resalved to acoste them with never to be performed promises" of pardon for the freemen and freedom for the bond-laborers, English and Negroes, such as had constituted the rebel army from the time of the burning of Jamestown.[90]

After a secret conference between Berkeley and Ingram and his lieutenant Gregory Walklett, three hundred of the rebels with only small arms at West Point did accept the terms.[91] But three miles further up the country, the chief garrison and magazine remained intact at Colonel West's house, armed with "five hundred Musketts and fowling pieces, and a Chest of Powder, and about a Thousand Weight of Bulletts and shott, and three great Guns." Not only were these rebels heavily armed, they were furious at Grantham for abusing the ceasefire to secure the absolute surrender of West Point. Grantham himself described the historic encounter:

> I went to Colonel West's house about three miles farther, which was their Cheife Garrison and Magazine; I there mett about foure hundred English and Negroes in Armes, who were much dissatisfied at the Surrender of the Point,[92] saying I had betray'd them, and thereupon some were for shooting mee, and others were for cutting mee in peeces: I told them I would willingly surrender myselfe to them, till they were satisfied from his Majestie, and did ingage to the Negroes and Servants, that they were all pardoned and freed from their Slavery: and with faire promises and Rundletts of Brandy, I pacified them, giving them severall Noates under my hand, that what I did was by the Order of His Majestie and the Governor ... Most of them I persuaded to goe to their Homes ... except about Eighty Negroes and Twenty English which would not deliver their Armes.[93]

Grantham's testament has a significance that is beyond exaggeration: in Virginia, 128 years before William Lloyd Garrison was born, laboring-class

African-Americans and European-Americans fought side by side for the abolition of slavery. In so doing they provided the supreme proof that the white race did not then exist.

Virginia was not Ireland, the Atlantic was not the Irish Sea. Reaction time from the burning of Jamestown to knowledge of it in England to the arrival of the royal expeditionary force in Virginia in late January and early February was four and a half months. In the meantime, the rebels having driven Berkeley into refuge on the Eastern Shore, they moved quickly to crush him. They commandeered a ship, installed cannon on it, and sent a force with it to capture Berkeley. If the plan had succeeded, the history of continental colonial America might have taken a much different path. The English expeditionary force of perhaps 1,350 soldiers, about one-third of them raw recruits,[94] might not have been able to win a timely victory. When interviewed by John Good (like Bacon a Henrico plantation owner), Bacon argued that "five hundred Virginians" could defeat 2,000 redcoats, by guerrilla strategy and tactics they had learned from the native fighters, "we having the same advantages against them that the Indians have against us."

> Are we not acquainted with the country, so that we can lay ambuscades?: Can we not hide behind trees so render their discipline of no avail? Are we not as good or better shots than they?

When John Good said that in the end the rebels would not be able to withstand being cut off from the supplies of necessities from the mother country, Bacon countered that the French or the Dutch would be willing to fill the trade vacuum. To Good's doubts on that score, Bacon countered with the prospect of extending the rebellion to North Carolina and Maryland.[95]

Bacon always had hope that if the king could be apprised of the actual state of affairs in Virginia, he would see justice in the rebel cause. Might not Charles II, mired in a state deficit and heavily engaged in his struggle with Parliament, have made a great effort to find some accommodation with the propertied element aligned with Bacon, so long as it could preserve the king's tobacco revenue? How would "Governor Bacon" have sounded, with Berkeley being treated in the same way that Charles's father had dealt with his close friend and advisor, Strafford?[96] Of course, Virginia's fundamental problems would have remained, but the rebel forces would have been divided beyond repair. No such deal would have been conceivable without the casting-off of the bond-laborers and the poor freedmen; their demands were incompatible with "all the principall Men in the Country," as Good termed them, and with the English Crown and merchants as well.

The initiative that the rebels held at the time of the Good interview was lost, however, with fatal consequences, when the attempt to invade Accomack miscarried and Bacon died of illness contracted by exposure to the elements. The Governor then enlisted armed merchantmen, whose strategy was based on the principle that "in this plentiful watered Country, the water commands the Land." The rebels' one bid for maritime strength having failed, the initiative swung to the side of the Governor and the king. By the middle of January, ten days before the first English soldiers arrived, these floating forts, by virtue of their mobility and the cannon they carried, had been decisive in reducing the half-dozen or more of the scattered garrisons.[97] The Royal Commissioners reported, "About the 16th of January [1676/7], the whole country had submitted to the Governor"; a week later he called a meeting of the General Assembly at his own house at Green Spring.[98]

In the Aftermath of Rebellion

By sitting as judges in ordering the death sentences of nine of the total of twenty-three rebels hanged,[99] the Royal Commissioners, Governor-designate Colonel Herbert Jeffreys, Major Francis Moryson,[100] and Captain Sir John Berry, gave countenance to Berkeley's defiance of the King's proclamation of 20 October 1676. That proclamation granted amnesty to rebels who took the oath of obedience within "the space of twenty days," but Berkeley dispatched these enemies without regard to the amnesty.[101] The Royal Commissioners were also at one with Berkeley with regard to repealing the measure, enacted by the "Bacon Assembly" the previous year, that had extended the vote to all freemen, propertied and propertyless. The new General Assembly withdrew the franchise from the propertyless "freemen."[102] But with regard to the most practical policy for capitalizing on their victory, controversy dominated the relations between Governor Berkeley and his most enthusiastic local supporters, on the one hand, and the Royal Commissioners, on the other.[103]

Berkeley was not willing to make any allowances for the rebellious disposition of the population of the colony, even though he himself had noted it and related it to the critical state of the tobacco monoculture economy. He regarded the rebellion as an intolerable repudiation of his stewardship, made the more infuriating by the king having so cavalierly, so to speak, handed him his hat courtesy of the meddling Royal Commissioners, and brought him home under a cloud of suspicion to render account for the breakdown of order in the colony. The Royal Commissioners and the entire English government, on the other hand, as Charles's proclamation suggests were less interested in vengeance than in the speediest revival of the tobacco trade.[104]

On 10 February 1676/7, commissioners Berry and Moryson addressed a letter to James, Duke of York. They were concerned to find that not one in thirty of the colonists was innocent of involvement in the rebellion. The populace was

> sullen and obstinate and unless they receive timely reddress it is to be feared that they will either abandon their plantations, discharging their servants and disposing of their stock, and go away to other parts, or else most of them will only make corn instead of tobacco, careless of their own estates and the King's customs.

They further warned that if the opportunity of a war presented itself, the people of Virginia "might throw off their yoke and subjugate themselves to a foreign power."[105]

Fundamental Destabilizing Factors Persisted

The social instability noted by the Royal Commissioners was rooted in five long-range fundamental factors.

1. The train of overproduction, mass impoverishment, and indebtedness produced by the tobacco monoculture, which continued to dominate the lives of the great majority of the population

Experienced observers consulted by the Lords of Trade in 1681 concurred in urging the continued presence of regular English troops in Virginia, noting that "Virginia is at present poorer and more populous than ever," and that "extreme poverty may cause the servants to plunder the stores and ships."[106] Colony Secretary Nicholas Spencer ascribed that danger to "the low price of tobacco [having] made them desperate," and he was fearful that mere plant-cutting "will not satiate their rebellious appetites."[107] In another letter on those riots, Spencer specifically alluded to the evil of monoculture: "Tobacco, the sole manufacture of the Country, [has] grown out of esteeme by its over great quantities yearely made."[108] In 1687, the price of tobacco was so low that potential creditors were rejecting it as collateral.[109] The following year Governor Culpeper, noting that everything else was being neglected in favor of tobacco growing, feared that "our great plenty will glutt the market again."[110] In March 1689, during the War of the League of Augsburg (King Billy's War) against the French, 1689–97, Spencer ironically suggested that "our poverty is our best defence, for where ther's noe Carcase, the Eagles will not resort."[111] In 1710, during the War of the Spanish Succession (Queen Anne's War), 1701–1713, the price of tobacco was so low that in Virginia the people were deeply in debt, yet there were few buyers for it.[112] A modern scholar declares that for thirty-five years, from 1680 to 1715, such conditions "recurred with appalling regularity."[113]

2. The plantation bourgeoisie's failure to diversify production, a subject treated in Chapter 9

In the House of Commons in 1671 it was estimated that £80,000 of the annual Crown revenues came from Virginia tobacco; ten years later Governor Culpeper asserted that the King's revenues from Virginia tobacco alone exceeded all the revenues from all the other colonies combined.[114] In 1690, when the price paid for tobacco in Virginia was less than a penny a pound, shipowners sold it in England for 7*d.*, of which 5*d.* was collected as the King's share.[115] Every additional pound sterling of royal tobacco import revenue was an argument for keeping Virginia engaged exclusively in making tobacco. Opposition to diversification was constantly voiced by English capitalists, who (a) were enriched by trading in Virginia tobacco and in bond-labor for the plantation colonies, and (b) were jealous of any colonial productive enterprise that might reduce colonial dependence on English export supplies. Finally it was impossible for chronically indebted Virginia to accumulate capital for the relatively long-term investment needed to develop new lines of production.[116]

3. The increase in the bond-labor population, eager as ever for "an end to their Slavery"

The numbers of bond-laborers grew despite the reduction of the exportable labor supply in England that resulted from the demands for ship crews and cannon fodder in two successive wars with France that lasted from 1689 to 1713 with only a four-year (1698–1702) interruption. It is impossible to construct a statistical table of the numbers of bond-laborers from year to year, but a reasonable estimate can be made for the period.[117]

As previously noted, three out of every four Europeans who came to the Chesapeake in the colonial period were imported as chattel bond-laborers.[118] In 1671, 8,000 of the 15,000 tithables in Virginia were bond-laborers according to Governor Berkeley, who put the total population of Virginia at 40,000.[119] Of the 30,000 Europeans who came to the Chesapeake region between 1680 and 1699,[120] we may assume that 24,000 were bond-laborers. In a roughly equivalent period, 1674–1700, around 6,000 African bond-laborers were imported.[121] In that same period, 1674–1700, the total number of Virginia and Maryland tithables (taxables) rose from about 21,000 to about 34,000,[122] a linear average of 1,600 per year. Europeans were arriving at an average rate of 1,500 per year, 1,125 of them bond-laborers, and Africans were arriving at the rate of 240 a year, presumably as bond-laborers, making an incoming total of 1,365, equal to 85 percent of the increase of the total tithables.[123] Not only was the number of bond-laborers increasing, it was increasing as a proportion of the number of tithables, and doubtless of the total population.[124]

The rebellion was over, but the rebelliousness of bond-laborers was not. In 1698, Francis Nicholas, then Governor of Maryland, reported to the Board of Trade the arrival of 326 "Negro" bond-laborers directly from Africa, and 70 more from Virginia and Pennsylvania. Pending an exact count soon to be made, he estimated that another 600 or 700 bond-laborers had arrived from Europe, "Chiefly Irish ..., most if not all, papists." If that trend were to continue, he said, the two groups might join forces in both Virginia and Maryland to make "great disturbances, if not a rebellion."[125] The following year, 1699, the Virginia House of Burgesses rejected the Board of Trade's idea of arming their "servants" against the possibility of a French invasion should war be renewed. With the signing of the Peace of Ryswick, a lull in the war with France had begun, but a by-product of the peace was that too many ungovernable Irish veterans were being shipped as bond-laborers to the Chesapeake. "If they were armed . . . we have just reason to fear they may rise upon us," said the Burgesses. Although of one mind with the Board of Trade on the possibility of a French invasion, the Burgesses feared the bond-laborers, "from the sake of their freedom and the difference of the religion, a great many of them (especially the Irish) and for other reasons . . . would rather be our enemies than contribute to our assistance."[126]

Apparently deciding to wait no longer for foreign invasion, African-American bond-laborers in two adjacent southside counties, Surry and James River, plotted an Easter rebellion in 1710 which was discovered just on the eve of R-Day.[127] In 1712, Virginia governor Alexander Spotswood declared that "insurrections" by African-American bond-laborers and invasion by Indians were dangers as serious as that of attack by sea had been during the height of the war with France.[128] At a new large plantation near the head of James River, the African-American bond-laborers looked not to rescue by sea, but to escape into the interior. They "formed a design to withdraw from their master and to fix themselves in the fastnesses of the neighboring mountains." They did indeed succeed in establishing briefly a settlement and began planting their crops, and defended it with arms against the militia.[129]

4. The continued lack of an effective intermediate buffer social control stratum

Berkeley's old Green Spring faction had been superseded by the hegemony of the county families, on terms that practically foreclosed the possibility of rebellion within the ruling class and led to a growing consensus against arbitrary administration by royal governors. But the attenuated state of the presumptive buffer stratum was demonstrated by the plant-cutting riots that occurred between May and August 1682, starting in Gloucester and then spreading to New Kent, Middlesex and York counties.

Narratives of the event are familiar fare to students of seventeenth-century Virginia history. The following brief description first published in 1705 has been appropriately cited by generations of historians:[130]

> ... despairing of succeeding in any Agreement with the Neighbouring Governments [to limit tobacco production, the rioters] resolved on a total Destruction of the Tobacco in that Country [Gloucester, New Kent, Middlesex, and York counties], especially of the Sweet-scented; because that was planted no where else. In pursuance of which Design, they contrived, that all Plants should be destroy'd while they were yet in their Beds, after it was too late to sow more.
>
> Accordingly the Ring-leaders in this Project began with, their own first, and then went to cut up the Plants of such of their Neighbours as were not willing to do it themselves.

The riots did succeed in reducing the glut of tobacco for that year by ten thousand hogsheads.[131] This, however, was not Bacon's Rebellion revisited; it was a spontaneous outburst of small planters[132] over a single issue, and rather than being directed at altering the government, it was merely a form of direct economic action for a season. Since the action was limited to the area specializing in sweet-scented tobacco, it did not become a colony-wide phenomenon. In consequence of that circumstance, indeed, the militias from remote areas were employed to suppress the riots.[133]

But this was no way to run a social control system in a civil society. Edmund S. Morgan makes the point concisely:[134]

> Although the plant-cutting rebellion had been successfully suppressed ... [it] is questionable how long Virginia could have continued on this course, keeping men in servitude for years and then turning them free to be frustrated by the engrossers of land, by the collectors of customs, by the county courts, by the king himself.

It is unfortunate, at least in my opinion, that Professor Morgan here introduces the idea that only desperate free men might rebel, implying what he subsequently states explicitly, namely that bond-laborers did not have rebellion in them.[135]

Virginia Governor Culpeper likened the tobacco-cutting riots to the anti-enclosure riots in sixteenth-century England.[136] Indeed, the high debts and the low price of tobacco were to the laboring-class free people of Virginia like the hedges and fences that had shut out the copyholders from their ancestral lands in England. But this "downsizing" of the poor planters in Virginia contemplated no purposeful and controlled "thinning" of a stand of social timber with the deliberate preservation of a proportion of yeomanry out of social control considerations.[137] The invisible hand of free market forces in seventeenth-century Virginia operated without such conscious allowances, and the devil take the hindmost. The English copyholder was competing with sheep for land; the laboring free poor in Virginia were forced to compete with unpaid chattel bond-labor. Sheep, however, do not rebel, bond-laborers did, and their freedom was a common class interest of the poor and landless free population such as had joined hands with bond-laborers in 1676.[138]

5. The practical unfeasibility of maintaining a system of social control in Virginia by means of the English army

First of all, there were the logistical problems. English government preparations for sending troops to Virginia to suppress Bacon's Rebellion were under way by the first week of October,[139] but the five companies of English troops that were despatched did not sail from England until around the end of November, and it was mid-February 1677 before the last of the troop-carrying merchant ships arrived at Jamestown,[140] a month after the end of the rebellion.

From the beginning the costs were a dominating consideration. The king was to bear the cost of the transportation and of victuals for the first three months. The colony government was supposed to provide quarters, but because Jamestown was in ruins the troops could not be disembarked promptly, and the king had to pay "demurrage" for quartering them on board ship until they could be put ashore. The troops were in the king's pay, but the colony had to pay for their victuals out of the quitrents assigned to them and from a special tax on wines and liquors enacted for that specific purpose.

Three months after the troops reached Virginia, the Lords of Trade and Plantations ordered Governor Jeffreys to send all but one hundred of them back to England as soon as possible. The cost factor was the primary consideration, as indicated by the proviso permitting those who so desired to stay in Virginia as "planters or servants."[141] Although Governor Culpeper wanted three 200-man companies of the king's troops to be kept in Virginia, the Lords of Trade and Plantations decided in August 1678 to allow him only two.[142] Three years later, in October 1681, Culpeper asked that two companies be kept permanently in Virginia, advancing the financial consideration that the presence of such a force in 1676 might have prevented the rebellion that "cost and lost the king above a hundred thousand pounds."[143] But the Privy Council ordered that the two remaining companies be disbanded by Christmas 1681, unless the colony paid the cost of maintaining them.[144] Subsequently the home government advanced money to pay the soldiers until April 1682. In May 1682, colony officials reported to England that the General Assembly, bitter because of the unremedied glut of tobacco, refused to do the one thing it was asked to do, namely to provide money for further maintenance of English soldiers. Because of the irregularity of their pay, some of the soldiers were reduced to selling themselves into servitude in order to survive. Consequently, just when they were expected to put down the plant-cutting riots in Gloucester, "the only time they [had] been needed since they came to Virginia," as Colony Secretary Spencer observed, they were "apter to mutiny than serve His Majestie."[145] The soldiers were finally paid off and disbanded in June 1682 even as the plant-cutting riots were still spreading.[146] In May 1683 the Virginia Colony Council unsuccessfully asked that the Crown pay for the maintenance of a garrison of sixty soldiers in Virginia.[147] In October of that year, however, the Privy Council did approve Governor Effingham's request for the stationing of a man-of-war in Virginia, as a guarantee to prevent "Disorder or Rebellion ... to grow to that head as it did in the year 1676," and to "cure the insolencies" of rioters in the future.[148] Whether such a guard ship was ever sent and, if sent, what role it might have played as a social control measure seems so far to be a blank page of Virginia history.

In January 1677 the Lieutenant Governor of Maryland, Thomas Notley, watching with understandable anxiety the unfolding events in Virginia, had sounded a warning. "There must be an alteration though not of the Government yet in the Government[;] new men should be put in power. The old men will never agree with the common people, and if that not be done, His Majestie will never find a well settled Government in that Colony."[149] Four months later, Notley again made the point in a letter to Lord Baltimore. If a new leader came forward ready to risk his life in the cause, he said, "the Commons of Virginia would Emmire themselves as deep in Rebellion as ever they did in Bacon's time." The plantation bourgeoisie must find a new strategy for social control, for

> if the ould Course be taken, and if Coll. Jeoffreys [Herbert Jeffreys, Berkeley's successor as Royal Governor of Virginia] build his proceedings upon the ould foundation its neither him nor all his Majesties Souldiers in Virginia will either satisfye or Rule those people.[150]

But what sort of "alteration in the Government" could be fashioned that would "agree with the common people" enough that it could rule them?

12

The Abortion of the "White Race" Social Control System in the Anglo-Caribbean

The English plantation bourgeoisie in the continental colonies and in the Caribbean opted to base their ventures on chattel bond-labor, at first European but – sooner in the Caribbean, later in the continental plantation colonies – mainly African bond-labor. Then, in both cases – sooner in the Caribbean, later in the continental plantation colonies – the ruling class sought to establish social control on the principle of racial oppression of non-Europeans.

In the very beginning, it was theorized that the ranks of European bond-laborers who survived their servitude might furnish the Anglo-American equivalent of the Ulster Scots or English-style yeomen as a middle class, with a vested property interest (as fee-simple smallholders or as secure tenants) and be the middle-class buffer between the plantation bourgeoisie and the bond-labor force. But circumstantial differences between the Ulster plantation and those in English colonies in America produced differences in the degree of dependence upon tenantry. In Ireland the English bourgeoisie was faced with the fact of the unassimilability of the Irish Catholic chieftains allied with Spain and the fact that English land claims were predicated on expropriation of those chieftains' tribal lands. In Anglo-America the plantation bourgeoisie was practically immune from successful native challenge to its continued possession of the land, and from an imminent overthrow by African bond-laborers "broken from their tribal stems." The denial of any degree of social mobility of Africans and African-Americans, the hallmark of racial oppression, was an option not rooted in geo-political considerations; rather it was driven simply and directly by the greater rate of profit to be had by the employment of lifetime hereditary bond-laborers – provided a cost-effective system of social control could be established.[1] The result was to give the term "plantation" a new meaning, implying monoculture and engrossment of the land by capitalist owners of bond-laborers. This meant that the early prospect for the establishment of an adequate intermediate stratum of European (and European-American), chiefly small freeholders or eviction-proof leaseholders was not to be realized. Consequently, different ways of maintaining ruling-class social control would be required. The class struggle would produce forms of social control in the Anglo-Caribbean colonies, however, that diverged in historically significant ways from that which was adopted in continental Anglo-America.

The Social Control Problem in the British West Indies[2]

In 1627, the English made Barbados a colony, using a labor force at first made up principally of bond-laborers brought from England, Ireland and Scotland.[3] The English also made efforts to reduce natives of the Caribbean to plantation bond-servitude; there are references to such workers in the record.[4] The class-undifferentiated Caribbean Indian tribes were not dominated by "casiques" possessing authority to deliver tribe members into European servitude.[5] Because of the Indians' warlike resistance, the English plans in this regard were by and large frustrated before they could be made operational. A pivotal point was reached in the mid-1660s. An English colony established on St Lucia in 1663 was wiped out by the native Indians by 1667. After retaking the island in March 1668, the English concluded an agreement with these Indians under which they were to be English subjects, but with the right to come and to depart at pleasure in the English islands.[6] "The Barbadians ... held Indian slaves," writes Richard S. Dunn, "but never very many."[7]

Regardless of their nativity, bond-laborers presented the owning class with serious problems of social control. When the *Ark*, bearing the first Maryland-bound colonists, stopped at Barbados on 3 January 1634, this fact of life was starkly dramatized for the voyagers:

> On the very day we arrived there we found the island all in arms, to the number of eight hundred men. The servants on the island had plotted to kill their masters and then handsomely take the first ship that came[,] and go to sea.[8]

After first being used primarily in tobacco cultivation, Barbados by the 1650s had been transformed into a sugar colony.[9] But the switch to sugar had done nothing to sweeten the disposition of the workers. On Barbados by 1648, when around one-fourth of the bond-laborers were Africans, it was reported that "many hundreds of Rebell negro slaves were in the woods."[10] The following year a plot was formed by European chattel bond-laborers to massacre their owners and seize control of the island. Some indication of the extent of the plot may perhaps be inferred from the fact that, after it was betrayed to the authorities, eighteen plotters were executed.[11] In 1655, Barbados received no less than 12,000 prisoners of the War of the Three Kingdoms, in addition to felons and vagabonds. Their numbers, combined with the draining away of artisans from Barbados to Jamaica, caused the authorities to be fearful of imminent mass rebellion by the bond-laborers.[12] Between 1675 and 1701, there were four major revolt plots in Barbados. In 1686, African and European rebel bond-laborers joined forces.[13] In 1692, a "Negro conspiracy" to seize the English fort at Bridgetown was discovered.[14]

Historican Richard S. Dunn identifies "seven separate slave revolts in the

English islands between 1640 and 1713, in which blacks and whites were killed."[15] "Rebellion, or the threat of it, was an almost permanent feature of Jamaican slave society," writes Orlando Patterson; he concludes that, "[W]ith the possible exception of Brazil, no other slave society in the New World experienced such continuous and intensive servile revolts" as Jamaica. Aside from the Second Maroon War (1795–96) Patterson mentions large-scale revolts, or discovered plots, in 1760, 1776, 1784, 1823 and 1824. "The last and most ambitious of all the slave rebellions of the island broke out two days after Christmas 1831," he writes; a roughly estimated 20,000 took part, with wide support, and 207 were killed; over 500 more were executed; 14 whites were killed, and property damage mounted to over £1.1 million; over £161,000 was spent in suppressing the revolt.[16]

The Jamaica maroons

When the Spanish abandoned Jamaica in 1655, some 1,500 Negroes escaped to the mountains. They became the Jamaica maroons who, from that time until 1796, maintained a separate set of independent communities.[17] In 1656 the main part of the maroons, under the leadership of Juan de Bolas, "surrendered to the English on terms of pardon and freedom." The others continued to be a thorn in the side of the English colony, so much so that they "intimidated the whites from venturing to any considerable distance from the coast." According to the account by the English historian of the West Indies, Bryan Edwards, the English governor offered, "full pardon, twenty acres of land, and freedom from all manner of slavery, to each of them who should surrender. But ... they were better pleased with the more ample range they possessed in the woods, where there [their] hunting grounds were not yet encroached upon by settlements." In 1663 the English sent a black regiment under Juan de Bolas, who was now their colonel, but he was killed and the general effort was a failure.

> In this way they continued to distress the island for upwards of forty years, during which time forty-four acts of Assembly were passed, and at least 240,000 *l*. expended for their suppression. In 1736, they were grown so formidable, under a very able general named Cudjoe, that it was found expedient to strengthen the colony against them by two regiments of regular troops, which were afterwards formed unto independent companies, and employed, with other hired parties, and the whole body of the militia, in their reduction.[18]

This struggle, known as the First Maroon War, 1725–40, was concluded under terms of a treaty signed at Trelawney Town on 1 March 1738/9. Under its terms, the maroons were guaranteed freedom, and possession of a region of 15,000 acres in which they might cultivate non-sugar crops and raise livestock, and the right to licenses to trade their products with people of the English colony.[19] The maroons, for their part, agreed "That if any negroes shall hereafter run away from their masters or owners, and fall into Captain

Cudjoe's hands, they shall immediately be sent back to the chief magistrate of the next parish where they are taken; and those that bring them are to be satisfied for their trouble, as the legislature shall appoint."[20] This latter provision is similar to previously mentioned agreements between the English colonial authorities in Virginia, Maryland and Carolina and various tributary Indian tribes, requiring the Indians to return runaway bond-laborers.

Objective Factors that Shaped Social Control Strategy

In relation to the question of social control and the invention of the white race, the British West Indies differed from the continental plantation colonies in five significant ways.[21] First, because of the narrow absolute limits of land area, and the relatively high capital costs of sugar production, the West Indies was especially inhospitable to non-capitalist farmers or tenants. Second, in the West Indies the attempt to establish a "white race" social control system was seriously and critically complicated by the substantial Irish presence. Third, the central role of the English military and naval forces regularly stationed in the West Indies constituted the most important guarantor of social control. Fourth, the predominance of persons of African descent in the population of the West Indies made it impossible to exclude them altogether from the intermediate stratum. Fifth, the reliance upon persons of African descent in the skilled trades and in the conduct of the internal economy of the West Indies colonies led to the emergence of the "free colored" as the predominant element in the middle class. The remainder of this chapter will be mainly an elaboration of these points.

1. Land area limits, capital costs

The plantation system, wherever it existed, was characterized by the engross-ment of the land by the bourgeoisie. But the effect of that engrossment on the prospective formation of an intermediate social control stratum was much greater in the island colonies than in continental plantation colonies. In the British West Indies, in addition to the typical economic and political difficulties facing the smallholder in a monocultural economy, the absolute limits of land area played a decisive part. In continental plantation colonies the barrier to the formation of a stable yeoman class was not an absolute scarcity of land, but merely the economic and political disadvantages of competing as non-capitalist entrepreneurs in a monocultural capitalist economy based on bond-labor. At the end of the seventeenth century, some 51,000 people, 88 percent of the total population of Virginia, lived in the Tidewater region, an area of 11,000 miles, representing a population density of 4.6 per square mile.[22] Virginia at large, including the transmontane region (not including Kentucky), had an area of some 64,000 miles. The total area of all patented land in Virginia in 1704 was equal to less than 40 percent of the area of the Tidewater region alone.[23] Even in the most heavily settled Tidewater area, the farms were so remote from each other as to hinder mustering the militia, and to make it difficult to assure effective collection of import and export duties.[24]

Barbados, the second-largest of England's Caribbean colonies, but with an area of only 166 square miles, was inhabited by 70,000 people in 1694 and had a population density of 423 per square mile.[25] By 1717, all but 6 percent of that island's total area was under cultivation; the great houses of the planter estates were not remote from their neighbors but were "within sight of each other."[26]

Jamaica was the exception; its 7,400 square miles made up more than half the land area of the British West Indies and had a population density of only 6.5 per square mile in 1698. Most of Jamaica was unoccupied, even in the early nineteenth century.[28] Only half its land was under patent, and only half of that was under cultivation.[29] At least until the end of the First Maroon War in 1739, the colony's frontiers were "no longer any Sort of Security [and] must be deserted."[30] But the main and sufficient reason for the limited number of smallholders in Jamaica was one that was common to the British West Indies generally – the relatively capital-intensive technology of the principal economic activity, the production of sugar and rum.

Excessive emigration of freemen
In the seventeenth-century Chesapeake, most of the limited-term bond-laborers never succeeded in completing their terms and becoming landowners. Those who did so needed only elementary individual hand-labor implements to engage in the common tobacco economy, poor and indebted though they most likely were destined to be. In the West Indies, the capital requirement for becoming a sugar planter – for buildings, mills, boiling pots, sugar pots, stills and, above all, for bond-labor – were beyond the means of the former bond-laborers.[31] The contrast in estate values in the late seventeenth century in Jamaica and Maryland is indicative. The average estate of the sugar planters of Jamaica in the last quarter of the seventeenth century was appraised at nearly £2,000, and the average value of all estates was £531, of which two-thirds to three-fourths might represent investment in bond-labor. In Maryland in the same period there were no estates appraised at as much as £2,000, and fewer than 4 percent of the estates had a value of more than £500.[32] Separate findings by highly regarded investigators suggest that in the late seventeenth century the prospect of a bond-laborer in Barbados surviving to become a landholder was only one-half as great as that of a bond-laborer in Virginia.[33]

From at least as early as the third quarter of the seventeeth century, many of those who survived their limited-term servitude in the English West Indies only to be confronted by this unpromising prospect were opting to leave their respective islands. Between 1660 and 1682, some 16,000 or 17,000 people emgrated from Barbados, most of them "landless freemen and small farm-ers."[34] In the last forty years of the seventeenth century the total population of Barbados is estimated to have doubled, from 40,000 to 80,000, but emigration was so great that the European population did not increase at all. Many of such emigrants chose initially to pursue their careers in nearby islands,[35] but it appears that nowhere in the British West Indies did such European migration reverse the long-range reduction of the European proportion of the population. Richard S. Dunn's table "Estimated Population of the English Sugar Islands, 1669–1713" shows a steady decade-to-decade decline in the European proportion of the populations of Barbados, Jamaica, and the Leeward Islands.[36]

Emigration became a major concern of the West Indies colonial authorities, not on account of the loss of labor-power it represented but because of the difficulty in maintaining the militias for defense against rival colonial powers, particularly the French, and for purposes of social control of the bond-laborers. The European population of Barbados in 1640 was around 25,000; of these more than one-third were proprietors and 10,000 were "servants," while the non-European bond-laborers, including a few Amerindians, numbered 6,400. By 1680, the total number of Europeans had fallen to 17,000, and because of the cost of capital and land requirements for sugar planting the number of "considerable proprietors" was less than 500, and the number of European bond-laborers in the island had shrunk to 2,000.[37] In the 1660s, Barbados had a fighting force of only 7,000 men, of whom only the large landholders were interested in the colony enough to be ready to defend it; the rest were concerned only with emigrating to find better prospects than they could have in Barbados.[38] Harlow's conclusion regarding Barbados was generally applicable to the British West Indies: it was "the concentration of land into large estates which was gradually depriving Barbados of her 'yeoman' class, and which eventually put an end to her development as a white community."

Social control was aimed at bond-laborers, whether of European or African descent. But the limited-term bond-laborers who, in the West Indies, were exclusively European, were prospective enlistees in the social control system as members of the militia, provided they survived their terms of servitude. This was a scheme for class collaboration of Europeans that required a new term of social distinction, namely "white," that would include not only laborer and capitalist but also bond-labor as well as free labor.[39] The alternative or redundant term "Christian," was sometimes applied to European bond-laborers, despite complications that arose regarding the Christian conversion of African bond-laborers;[40] or from the belief that some Europeans, namely the Irish, though Europeans had yet to be made Christians.[41] It became customary also to use the term "servants" for the European bond-laborers, potential militiamen, as distinct from African lifetime bond-laborers, called "slaves."[42]

A succession of proposals, schemes and laws were proposed, some of them adopted, that were explicitly aimed at increasing the proportion of the militia-producing European population in the English West Indies, or at least maintaining it. Compulsory measures were undertaken of which the most general type imposed fines on plantation owners who failed to keep in their employ a quota of one European, bond or free, for every so many African bond-laborers; these were the so-called "deficiency laws." The ratio varied from place to place and from time to time. Whatever the particular ratio, the home government constantly expressed its concern that it be met. In 1682 in Jamaica, the quota was one white bond-laborer to the first five lifetime bond-laborers, "for ten slaves two whites, and for every ten slaves over and above the said number one white . . . on penalty of £5 for every servant that shall be wanting."[43] In 1699, the Governor of the Leeward Islands was instructed "to use his utmost endeavor that each Planter keep such a number of white servants as the law directed."[44] The Nevis Assembly in 1701 passed "An Act for encouraging the Importation of white Servants, and that all Persons shall be obliged to keep one white Servant to every Twenty Negroes."[45] Other compulsory measures were designed to limit emigration. For example, English prisoners who had been sentenced to ten years' servitude in Barbados for the 1685 rebellion led by the Duke of Monmouth were ordered to be freed from bond-servitude, but they were forbidden to leave the island without royal permission.[46]

In the 1660s, the usual term of servitude in Barbados was reduced to encourage bond-laborers to come to the island.[47] In order to get and keep European craftsmen in Barbados, the island's Assembly prohibited the employment of Africans and Afro-Barbadians as coopers, smiths, carpenters, tailors, or boatmen.[48] In 1695, Governor Russell of Barbados remarked on the deplorable condition of the European former bond-laborers, who were "domineered over and used like dogs." Such treatment, he believed, would "drive away the commonalty of the white people." There were hundreds of such unfortunates, he declared, that never enjoyed fresh meat nor a dram of rum. That woeful lack could be made up, he suggested, by reducing the property qualification for voting at the annual elections in the expectation that candidates for the Assembly "would sometimes give the miserable creatures a little rum and fresh provisions and such things as would be of nourishment and make their lives more comfortable, in the hopes of getting their votes."[49] In 1709, a merchant trading to Jamaica proposed to the Commissioners of Trade and Plantations the settling of a colony of German Protestants in that island, because the European militia was reduced to 2,500 and there were 40,000 African bond-laborers to be repressed. These settlers were to "be free so soon as they set foot on shore in that island, and enjoy all privileges;" they were to be granted five or six acres of land in fee simple for every member of each family.[50] Six years later, the Lords of Trade and Plantations proposed that all Protestant European immigrants be extended those privileges on arrival in Jamaica.[51]

Suggestions were advanced that, voluntarily or otherwise, the great plantation owners should surrender title to a small portion of their lands to European ex-bond-laborers; but that notion came to naught because of a lack of sufficient support from the prospective donors.[52] Ultimately a compromise was reached; the land would remain in the ownership of the capitalist owners, but they would allow a few acres to be occupied by European tenants without any rent or other obligation except that of service in the militia. Properly called "military tenants," these men represented the ultimate stage in the evolution of "whiteness"; their contribution to the economic life of the colony was neglible to nonexistent, and there was no other rationale for their existence except the political one of serving as a ready reserve for social control over bond-laborers. For especially meritorious service in the war against external or internal enemies, some such men might be given ownership of an African bond-laborer. The result, however, was not an enhancement of their participation in the economic activity of the colony, but merely provided a means of making the "military tenants" more comfortable in their shiftless existence.[53]

In token of their acquired status as "whites," even European bond-laborers were by law protected against "excessive correction" by their owners, but by and large such encouragement failed to convince European laborers to come to and remain in the West Indies in the numbers that were necessary for the establishing of a civil regime of racial oppression.[54] In time the propertyless majority of the European population of the British West Indies would be assigned to a special category, socially and economically *marginalized* as "poor whites."[55]

2. The Irish complication

The policy designed by the plantation bourgeoisie to enlist laboring-class Europeans, as "whites," in a social control stratum against Africans occasionally encountered manifestations of the contrary normal tendency of European and African bond-laborers to make common cause against their owners. Such events were a challenge to the establishment of the new all-class, all-European "white" identity.[56] It was the behavior of many of the Irish bond-laborers that created the greatest breach in that concept.[57]

The Caribbean was a cockpit of European colonial rivalry. Over a period of eighty years from 1667 to 1748, the region was involved in four formal wars, in which England was aligned against one or more Catholic powers, primarily France, but also Spain.[58] This period coincided with much of the tragic English conquest of Ireland and Ireland's subjection under the most extreme period of the racial oppression under the "anti-Popery" Penal Laws.[59] In this period, Catholic Irish bond-laborers, who constituted a major proportion of the European bond-laborers in the British West Indies, were often disposed to ally their cause with any challenge to British authority, whether that challenge were made by African bond-laborers or by a rival colonial power.

In November 1655, following the Cromwellian conquest, when the "Irish slave trade" was at its fullest, the Barbados Colony Council was apprised that "there are several Irish servants and Negroes out in Rebellion in the Thicketts and thereabouts."[60] Two years later, the Barbados General Assembly warned that Irish men and women were wandering about the island pretending to be free, some of whom had "endeavoured to secure with Armes: and others now forth in Rebellion."[61]

During the War of Devolution in which the French captured and held St Kitts for two years, 1666–67, decisive roles were played by "French Negroes," who burned six strong English forts on the island's north coast, and by the Irish on the island, who "rose against the English planters and joined the French."[62] In 1667, Governor William Willoughby of Barbados wrote to King Charles II that of a possible fighting force of 4,000, "what with Blacks[,] Irish & servants, I cannot rely upon more then between 2 and 3000 men."[63]

In March 1668, it was reported that Barbados had contributed so many men to help retake the Leeward Islands from the French that it was "in an ill Condition, in regard to the multitude of Negros & Irish Servants, which is much superior to the rest of the Planters and Inhabitants."[64]

Citing five entries in the Great Britain *Calendar of State Papers, Colonial*, Gwynne documents Irish insurrections against the English in the battles for the Leeward Islands in 1689.[65] Although the law enacted on Nevis forbidding servants and slaves to "company" or to drink together did not specifically mention the Irish,[66] it is reasonable to believe they were among the usual suspects. In the 1692 plot to capture the Barbados fort, Irish bond-laborers undertook a special tactical role: by guile or by force, they were to open the doors of the fort to the Negro rebels.[67] Two laws were enacted by the Nevis Assembly on 21 December 1701: one "to prevent Papists, and reputed Papists, from Settling in the Island," and the second "for encouraging the Importation of white Servants."[68] As late as 1731, Governor Hunter of Jamaica was contesting an act of conciliation of the Irish Catholics, "of which our Servants and Lower Rank of People chiefly consists."[69]

Just as an eventual rapprochement was begun in Ireland between the Catholic bourgeoisie and the British rulers in the middle of the eighteenth century, so in the West Indies the spirit of Protestant Ascendancy and "anti-popery" directed against the Irish abated.[70] But by then it was irrelevant to the solution of the problem of ruling-class social control in the British West Indies. By the end of the seventeenth century "the old system of defence by white servants had broken down," writes military historian John W. Fortescue.[71] What he said with particular reference to defense applies also to the failure of the attempt to establish a system of social control in the Anglo-Caribbean by an English-style yeoman militia of European former bond-laborers.

3. "Sending an army to do it . . ." – English military and naval enforcement of social control

Contemplating the way in which control over the massive bond-labor population was achieved in the British West Indies, one is reminded of Sir John Davies's dictum that the conquest cannot be regarded as complete "if the jurisdiction of . . . ordinary Courts of justice doth not extend" to all parts of the territory ". . . unless he send an Army to do it."[72] Because of the breakdown the system of social control by European bond-laborers and former bond-laborers, a new concept and composition for an intermediate social control stratum that included persons of African ancestry was contrived. Nevertheless, social order depended on the constant presence of English military and naval forces. "[I]t was customary," writes our historian, "for British troops to police the slave population, in addition to fighting the soldiers of other colonial powers in the West Indies."[73]

In 1680, Port Royal, Jamaica, with four forts manned by two regular English army companies, was the most strongly fortified place in all of colonial Anglo-America. "Night and day," writes Dunn, "one of the Port Royal companies was always on duty, working twelve-hour shifts." Of the fort's 110 big guns, 16 were located to face any assault by land.[74] Throughout Queen Anne's War, 1701–13, Jamaica was "a garrison colony."[75] For most of the eighteenth century, at least two regular English army regiments were stationed in Jamaica.[76] During the First Maroon War two regiments sent from Gibraltar served effectively to deter bond-laborers from joining the revolt.[77] On its frequent calls in Jamaica ports, the British navy was counted on to assist in putting down revolts of African bond-laborers.[78] Although in 1788 the Jamaica militia of "whites" and "free Negroes and free persons of color" numbered about 7,000 or 8,000, 2,000 regular troops were maintained on the island – to assure control over one-quarter million Negro bond-laborers and 1,400 maroons.[79] A British observer writing in about 1774 believed that the inhabitants of Jamaica relied too much on the protection of the king's troops."[80] In the final Maroon War, 1796–1797, the number of regular British troops was increased to 3,000.[81] In 1793, at the beginning of Britain's war against revolutionary France, the dispatch of 700 soldiers, more than half the Jamaica garrison, "drained the island of troops that were to protect the inhabitants" just at the moment when the alarming news came that the French Assembly had proclaimed freedom for all slaves in French colonies.[82] At that time, "no fewer than nineteen British battalions – out of a total strength of eighty-one – were in the Caribbean or en route."[83]

A regiment of the king's troops was sent from England to protect St Kitts after the island's recapture from the French in 1697.[84] The President of the Council of Barbados in 1738 declared that the emigration from the island had been so great that that island would have to have a naval force to protect it.[85] There no doubt seemed to be good imperial reason for the stationing of a 1,200-man regiment on tiny Antigua, where a European population of 5,000 (not half what it had been forty years before), dwelt together with 45,000 "blacks, Mulattos, and mestees."[86]

4. Afro-Caribbean majorities in the British West Indies

When former bond-laborers in Virginia tried to start farming on their own, or small planters lost out to creditors, they did not embark for another country; they took their hoes and axes and headed for North Carolina or Maryland, or to the Piedmont, or even farther westward. Whatever the extent of migration may have been, the European-American population of every continental plantation colony, according to present best estimates, grew absolutely decade by decade, from a combined total of 71,847 in 1700 to 734,754 in 1780. Although the European-American proportion of the population of the plantation colonies declined from 84 percent to 59 percent, only in South Carolina had it been reduced to less than half, to 46 percent.[87]

In the British West Indies, on the other hand, Euro-Caribbeans were a minority population before the end of the seventeenth century. Barbados had a higher proportion of European-descent inhabitants than any other colony in British West Indies. Yet by 1713 in Barbados, and in the Leeward Islands as well, Europeans made up only one-fourth of the population; in Jamaica the ratio was only one in nine.[88]

In obvious acknowledgement of the absolute impossibility that the militia-providing former bond-laborers would ever become viable yeomen farmers, various laws were enacted to preserve other petit bourgeois opportunities for them, by excluding non-Europeans from engaging in skilled occupations or huckstering.[89] But in the end, the purpose of such measures, which were absolutely essential to the meaning of "white," were nullified by the economic advantage of the use of African bond-laborers in skilled and lower supervisory occupations on the plantations,[90] and by the valuable service to the internal market provided by African bond-laborers, particularly the women.[91]

In time, as a result of emancipation by self-purchase, by testaments of free owner-fathers, and in reward for special service, as well as by natural increase, a population of free persons of some degree of African descent developed throughout the West Indies. The same was true in the continental colonies. There was a critical difference, however, in the resulting proportion of the total free population constituted by persons of some degree of African ancestry. In the continental plantation colonies and in the Upper South and Lower South states of the United States in the period 1700–1860, free African-Americans never constituted as much as 5 percent of the free population. Their proportion reached its high point, 4.8 percent in 1830, but in the two ante-bellum decades it declined appreciably, to 3.1 percent.[92] By contrast in Jamaica, which had more than half the total population of the British West Indies, and of the total free population as well, free persons of color were 18 percent of all free persons in 1768, 36 percent in 1789, and 72 percent in 1834.[93] The proportion in Barbados was 5 percent in 1786, 12 percent in 1801, and 34 percent in 1833–34.[94] In the Leeward Islands toward the end of the eighteenth century, one-fourth of the free population was of some degree of African ancestry.[95]

By the late 1700s, freedmen throughout the West Indies were working in artisan trades. In Barbados the freedman usually began as a hired unskilled worker, but quickly sought skilled work for which there was greater demand, and which had a "higher prestige value."[96] Professor Sheppard notes that by late in the eighteenth century, European freemen in that colony were able to practice their trades only to a decreasing extent, and as hucksters "they faced severe competition, as in other spheres, from the free coloreds."[97] In Jamaica in the first decades of the nineteenth century, most of the freedmen were in skilled trades, as "carpenters, masons, wheelwrights, plumbers, and other artisans,"[98] while the freedwomen in Jamaica usually became shopkeepers and sellers of "provisions, millinery, confectionery, and preserves." In Barbados in 1830, writes Professor Handler, "the Sunday market was ... an institution of fundamental importance to all segments of Barbadian Society"; he cites the contemporary observation that most of the produce sellers were free colored people.[99]

5. Afro-Caribbeans as the middle class of the British West Indies

It seems to me that nothing could have prevented the development of a normal class differentiation within the African and Afro-Caribbean population of the British West Indies as the freedmen came to constitute a substantial proportion of the free population. That was not the original intention when the sugar planters for reasons of present profit began to recruit their skilled labor force from the ranks of African bond-laborers and, by land engrossment, made the flourishing of a European yeomanry impossible. Although from time to time they made legislative gestures toward reversing the trend, the need to make the highest possible rate of profit emptied such gestures of significance.

Just as the Irish Catholic bourgeoisie, disfranchised and barred from owning land, found entrepreneurial outlets for their acquisitive compulsion by becoming graziers and merchants,[100] so in the British West Indies freedman enterprise – both petit bourgeois and capitalist – sprouted through the cracks of "white" exclusionism despite the dogged opposition of the "white" diehards who, like the Orange Order in Britain, saw chaos in any concession to the oppressed majority.

In the British West Indies generally, the free coloreds included "shop-keepers, and ... owners of land and slaves." In the trade in non-sugar commodities with the North American colonies, many free colored merchants traded directly with captains of cargo vessels. In Barbados, the energy and initiative of freedmen hucksters in meeting bond-laborers on the way to market and ships just arriving in the harbor enabled them to control the supply of produce and livestock to the general public. They were likewise involved in supplying the sugar estates with essentials that could not be got from England. Indeed, this proved a route to sugar estate ownership by occasional foreclosure on a bankrupt creditor.[101] Three years after the repeal of the prohibition on freedmen acting as pilots, they had nearly monopolized Jamaica's coastal shipping.[102]

In 1721 the Jamaica Assembly took a positive view of such trends as it turned its attention to the problem of unsettled lands becoming "a receptacle for runaway and rebellious negroes." It occurred to them to establish a buffer zone between coastal sugar plantation regions and the mountainous (and maroon-infested) interior, by offering free homesteads to laboring-class settlers and their families. Among the beneficiaries were to be "every free mulatto, Indian or negro" who would take up the offer and remain on the land for seven years. Each was to have twenty acres of land for himself, and five acres more for each slave he brought with him.[103] Perhaps some of those homesteaders served in the "companies of free Negroes and mulattoes" who were employed effectively in the First Maroon War, ended with the 1739 Treaty of Trelawney Town binding the Maroons to capture and return runaway bond-laborers.[104] By the early 1830s, "free blacks and coloreds" owned 70,000 of the total of around 310,000 bond-laborers in Jamaica.[105]

When the militia system based on the European former bond-laborers proved a failure, the sugar bourgeoisie relied on the British army and navy to guarantee their control, while at the same time recruiting free persons, black and white, into the militias as an auxiliary. In Barbados, as in Jamaica, by the 1720s freedmen were required to serve in the militia, even though they were denied important civil rights.[106] The British army and navy, however, were subject to many demands because of the almost constant worldwide round of wars with France that would last for 127 years, from 1688 to 1815. In the decisive moment – the coming of the French Revolution and the Haitian Revolution – when all hung in the balance, more extreme measures were required, for then the British in the West Indies were confronted with "blacks inspired by the revolutionary doctrine of French republicanism" and were "forced to conduct operations against large numbers of rebellious slaves in the rugged and largely unknown interiors of their own islands" of Grenada, St Vincent and Jamaica.[107]

The internal and external dangers were so critical that the British supreme commander in the Caribbean was forced to conclude that "the army of Great Britain is inadequate to ... defend these colonies" without an army of black soldiers. Eight West India regiments were formed, composed in small part by freedmen, and partly of slaves purchased by the army from plantation owners; but more were acquired directly from Africa.[108] However, "[i]t was clear that the continued existence of the West India Regiments depended upon establishing the black soldier as a freedman"; indeed, in 1807 it was so declared by act of the British Parliament: the bond-laborers who entered the British army by that act became freedmen.[109] But the logic of the policy represented a major violation of the principle of denial of social mobility of the oppressed group.[110] Many of these soldiers when discharged settled on plantations as free persons.[111]

In the meantime, thoughtful observers had begun to advocate the advantages to be had from a positive attitude toward freedmen in general. Consider the advice put forward by four authoritative English writers: Edmund Burke, in 1758; Edward Long, in 1774; the Reverend James Ramsay, in 1784, and George Pinckard in 1803.

> Indubitably, [said Burke] the security ... of every nation consists principally in the number of low and middling men of a free condition, and that beautiful gradation from the highest to the lowest, where the transitions all the way are

almost imperceptible ... What if in our colonies we should go so far as to find some medium between liberty and absolute slavery, in which we might place all mulattoes ... and such blacks, who ... their masters ... should think proper in some degree to enfranchise. These might have land allotted to them, or where that could not be spared, some sort of fixed employment.... [T]he colony will be strengthened by the addition of so many men, who will have an interest of their own to fight for.[112]

[Mulattos, said Long,] ought to be held in some distinction [over the blacks]. They would then form the centre of connexion between the two extremes, producing a regular establishment of three ranks of men. [If mulatto children were obliged] to serve a regular apprenticeship to artificers and tradesmen [,that] would make them orderly subjects and defenders of the country.... But even if they were to set up for themselves, no disadvantage would probably accrue to the publick, but the contrary: they would oblidge the white artificers to work at more moderate rates.[113]

Reverend Ramsay, too, limited his proposal to mulattos. The girls should be declared free from their birth, or from the time the mother became free. Male mulattos should be placed out as apprentices "to such trade or business as may best agree with their inclination and the demands of the colony," and should be freed at the age of thirty. He was persuaded that, "By these means ... a new rank of citizens, placed between the Black and White races, would be established." They would be an intermediate buffer social control stratum since "they would naturally attach themselves to the White race ... and so become a barrier against the designs of the Black."[114]

George Pinckard had served several years as a surgeon in the British expeditionary forces in the Caribbean, and looked favorably on the prospect of gradual reform leading to abolition of slavery in the West Indies. What Pinckard suggested anticipated Charles James Fox's prescription for social control adaptation in Ireland from racial oppression to national oppression: "Make the besiegers part of the garrison."[115] Pinckard argued for the social promotion of a "considerable proportion of the *people of colour*, between the whites and negroes." The installation of such a middle class "would save Britain a great expenditure of life and treasure. This middle class would soon become possessed of stores and estates; and the garrison might be safely entrusted to them as the best defenders of their own property."[116]

In 1803, John Alleyne Beckles, Anglo-Barbadian member of the Barbados Council, denounced the limitations on property rights of freedmen. Such property ownership, he argued, "will keep them [the free colored] at a greater distance from the slaves, and will keep up that jealousy which seems naturally to exist between them and the slaves ..."

... it will tend to our security, for should the slaves at any time attempt a revolt, the free-coloured persons for their own safety and the security of their property, must join the whites and resist them. But if we reduce the free coloured people to a level with the slaves, they must unite with them, and will take every occasion of promoting and encouraging a revolt.[117]

Such ruling-class insights recognized the link between concessions to the freedmen and the maintenance of control over the bond-laborers, who in the late 1770s outnumbered the total free population of Barbados by nearly three and a half times, and outnumbered by nine times that of Jamaica.[118] As members of the militia that quelled the 1816 bond-laborer revolt in Barbados, "the free coloureds were reckoned to have conducted themselves 'slightly better' than the whites."[119] In Jamaica in the First and the Second Maroon Wars, the mulatto militia justified the expectation that they would be a "powerful counterpoise . . . of men dissimilar from [the Maroons] in complexion and manners, but equal in hardiness and vigour," capable of "scour[ing] the woods on all occasions; a service in which the [British Army] regulars are by no means equal to them."[120] As the struggle to end slavery entered its critical stage, there were freedmen who supported the cause of the bond-laborers, but they were the exceptional few.[121]

By the late 1770s, in Jamaica 36 percent of the free population was composed of persons of some degree of African ancestry; on the eve of emancipation, in 1833, they were a 72 percent majority. In Barbados in 1786, only 5 percent of free persons were persons of African ancestry; in 1833 they were 34 percent.[122] Although this increase in the freedmen population brought added forces to the intermediate social control stratum against the bond-laborers, it conversely became a major factor in the final crisis of the system of chattel bond-servitude, coming as it did in the larger context of the Haitian Revolution (in which the role of the free colored had been decisive) and the rise of the abolitionist movement in England. The "increasing wealth and numbers of the coloreds as well as their importance in the militia made it more difficult for the Assembly to deny them their rights."[123]

Of some 5,200 slaveowners in Barbados in 1822, around 3,600 owned no land; of these the majority were freedmen.[124] But due to "deficiency law" restrictions, the freedmen owners of bond-laborers for the most part exploited their bond-laborers in non-agricultural occupations. These same laws obstructed the employment of freedmen wage workers. In 1830, two persons of color were members of the Jamaican House of Assembly, but they were still barred from giving testimony in court unless they first produced proof of their baptism.

In 1816, a group of the "coloreds" petitioned for admission of all freemen to the "rights and privileges of white subjects."[125] This demand was the fulcrum by which the combined forces on the side of abolition of slavery – the Haitian example, the example of the West India regiments, the increasing rebelliousness of the plantation bond-laborers (expressed in revolts in Barbados in 1816 and Jamaica in 1831), English religious humanitarianism, and abolitionism – were able to leverage the abolition of slavery by act of Parliament in 1833. At the heart of the matter was the fact that every concession made to the freedmen to strengthen social control over the bond-laborers represented an erosion of the rationale of white supremacy upon which the system of plantation bond-servitude was based. Eventually, the essential politics of the

Haitian Revolution had its innings in Jamaica. The plantocracy's resistance to further concession to the "free coloreds" brought probably a majority of the freedmen to the support of abolition, especially when slaveowners among them were assured of being compensated by the British government for the loss of their human chattels.[126]

In continental Anglo-America, only the rivalry between the plantation bourgeoisie and the industrial bourgeoisie for national hegemony provided the civil war possibility of emancipation as a measure for preserving the Union. Emancipation in the West Indies, on the other hand, was forced by the struggle of the bond-laborers and by the demands of the "free colored" bourgeoisie and petty bourgeoisie for full citizenship rights in the wake of the Haitian Revolution.[127] The course of their struggles paralleled events that ended religio-racial oppression in Ireland. A century elapsed from the first recruitment of Irish Catholic soldiers for England's wars with the French for colonial primacy to the disestablishment of the Anglican Church of Ireland in 1869.[128] As in Ireland, so in the British West Indies, it was by no means a smooth steady evolution, but a procession by vicissitudes: from the recruitment of free Afro-Caribbeans into trades, commerce and professions countered by schemes for bestowing privileges on the "poor whites" to induce them to come and stay; from laws explicitly denying Afro-Caribbeans civil rights, and the obstruction of individual petitions for full rights by members of the Afro-Caribbean petty bourgeoisie and bourgeoisie, to the enactment of the "Brown Privilege Bill" in Barbados in 1831.[129] What most distinguishes the story of both the Irish and the Anglo-Caribbean histories, on the one hand, from that of continental Anglo-America, on the other, is that Catholic Emancipation in Ireland, and the admittance of "free colored" to full citizenship rights in the British West Indies were the culmination of the growing economic and political strength of the Catholic bourgeoisie in Ireland, in the one case, and of the "free colored" population of the British West indies, in the other. In the United States, on the other hand, free African-Americans were never acknowledged as a legitimate part of the body politic; quite the contrary, their very right to remain in the United States was officially and unofficially questioned, as, for instance, in the persistent demands for the forced exclusion of free African-Americans from the United States.

What is to explain the dramatic difference in the status achieved by free persons of African descent in the Anglo-Caribbean and in continental Anglo-America? And what larger historical significance is implied in that variation? That question brings us back to the Chesapeake and the problem that faced the plantation bourgeoisie there in the wake of Bacon's Rebellion.

13

The Invention of the White Race
– and the Ordeal of America

What Virginia's laboring-class people, free and bond, were fighting for in Bacon's Rebellion was not the overthrow of capitalism as such, but an end to the version of that system imposed by the plantation elite, based on chattel bond-servitude and engrossment of the land. Their idea regarding a proper social order was about the same as that which would be expressed by Edmund Burke some eighty years later: "the security ... of every nation consists principally in the number of low and middling men of a free condition, and that beautiful gradation from the highest to the lowest, where the transitions all the way are almost imperceptible." [1] If they had succeeded, the outcome of their struggle would have improved opportunities for social mobility within the colony. For the bond-laborers that would have meant an end to unpaid bond-servitude; for them and for the landless freemen, victory would have meant improved opportunity to become independent farmers. Most emphatically, they were not content to be "Tenants to the first Ingrossers, ... to be a Tennant on a Continent."[2]

However, just as the overthrow of the tenantry in the 1620s had cleared the ground for the institution of chattel bond-servitude, so the defeat of Bacon's Rebellion cleared the way for the establishment of the system of lifetime hereditary chattel bond-servitude. The relative position of the plantation elite became more dominant than ever not only because of the continuation of their large landholdings, but also because of their advantage in bidding for lifetime bond-labor.

Virginia's mystic transition from the era of "the volatile society," most dramatically represented in Bacon's Rebellion, to "the Golden Age of the Chesapeake" in the middle quarters of the eighteenth century is a much-studied phenomenon. It was during that period that the ruling plantocracy replaced "the ould foundation" that Governor Notley had warned them of, in order to "build their proceedings" on a new one. Central to this political process was, as John C. Rainbolt described it, "The Alteration in the Relationship between Leadership and Constituents in Virginia, 1660–1720."

In no other period or province did the relationship between rulers and ruled and the role of government alter so markedly as in Virginia between the departure of

Governor William Berkeley in 1676 and the administration of Alexander Spotswood from 1710 to 1722.[3]

The "art of ruling" so manifestly deficient during Bacon's Rebellion was retrieved; the ruling planter elite had learned "to improvise a style of leadership appropriate to the peculiar weakness of authority and the undisciplined and frustrated citizenry of Virginia."[4]

Edmund S. Morgan discusses the transition in a succession of chapters beginning "Toward" – "Toward Slavery," "Toward Racism," "Toward Populism," "Toward the Republic" – and concludes that the subordination of class by "race" at the beginning of the eighteenth century is the key to the emergence of the republic at the end of it.[5] Commentary directed specifically to the relationship of "race" and "class" is particularly relevant to the subject of the invention of the white race.[6] In a paper read before the Virginia Historical Society in December 1894, Lyon G. Tyler, son of President John Tyler, and seventeenth president of William and Mary College and editor of The *William and Mary Quarterly*, noted that "race, and not class, [was] the distinction in social life" in eighteenth-century Virginia.[7] The modern historian Gary B. Nash is more explicit: "In the late seventeenth century," he writes, "southern colonizers were able to forge a consensus among upper- and lower-class whites. . . . Race became the primary badge of status."[8]

Why was social transformation given this particular form; and *how* was it brought about? It will not do to say that this "race, not class" phenomenon was the result of the shift to Africa as the main labor supply source.[9] That same shift occurred in the British West Indies without the obliteration of class by "race". It will not do to ascribe it to the play of free market forces fashioning a "divided labor market" of skilled European-Americans and unskilled African-Americans.[10] The privileges and perquisites accorded to skilled workers do indeed express "free market economy" principles but "race" discrimination, in the form of the "deficiency laws" and prohibitions established in all English plantation colonies in the Americas against employing African workers in skilled occupations, did not. It will not do to say that persons arriving in the Americas already enchained were not good candidates for rebellion.[11] Consider the history of the maroons throughout the Americas, including British Jamaica.[12] Most important of all, it will not do to say that the "race, not class" phenomenon was the *result* of the reduction of African-Americans to lifetime hereditary bond-servitude.[13] One need only recall the solidarity of "the English and Negroes in Armes" in Bacon's Rebellion, at a time when the great majority of African-Americans were held as lifetime bond-laborers; or note the fact that 23 percent of the African bond-laborers in Jamaica on the eve of Emancipation were owned by persons of one degree or other of African ancestry.[14] Rather it was only because "race" consciousness superseded class-consciousness that the continental plantation bourgeoisie was able to achieve and maintain the degree of social control necessary for proceeding with capital accumulation on the basis of chattel bond-labor.

That the plantation bourgeoisie and those engaged in the labor supply trade favored the imposition of perpetual bondage on the plantation labor force can be seen as simply prudent business practice designed, in terms of current jargon, "to keep down inflationary labor costs in order to promote economic growth and to make Anglo-America competitive," by utilizing opportunities in Africa newly opened up by "the expanding global economy." At the same time, it was understood that, as always, success depended on establishing and maintaining an intermediate stratum for social control purposes. Why, then, were free Negroes and "mulattos" to be excluded from that stratum in the pattern-setting continental plantation colony of Virginia?

In September 1723 an African-American wrote from Virginia a letter of protest and appeal to Edmund Gibson, the Bishop of London, whose see included Virginia. On behalf of observant Christians of mixed Anglo-African descent, who were nevertheless bound by "a Law or act which keeps and makes them and there seed slaves forever," the letter asked for the bishop's help and that of the king "and the rest of the Rullers," in ending their cruel bondage.[15]

Aspects of discrimination against African-Americans also bothered British lawyer Richard West, the Attorney-General, who had the responsibility of advising the Lords of Trade and Plantations whether laws passed in colonial legislatures merited approval, or should be rejected in whole or in part as being prejudicial or contradictory to the laws of England.[16] In due course, West had occasion to examine a measure that was passed by the Virginia Assembly in May 1723, entitled "An Act directing the trial of Slaves, committing capital crimes; and for the more effectual punishing conspiracies and insurrections of them; and for the better government of Negros, Mulattos, and Indians, bond or free." Article 23 of that 24-article law provided that:

> . . . no free negro, mulatto, or indian whatsoever, shall have any vote at the election of burgesses, or any other election whatsoever.[17]

The Attorney-General made the following categoric objection:

> I cannot see why one freeman should be used worse than another, merely upon account of his complexion . . .; to vote at elections of officers, either for a county, or parish, &c. is incident to every freeman, who is possessed of a certain proportion of property, and, therefore, when several negroes have merited their freedom, and obtained it, and by their industry, have acquired that proportion of property, so that the above-mentioned incidental rights of liberty are actually vested in them, for my own part, I am persuaded, that it cannot be just, by a general law, without any allegation of crime, or other demerit whatsoever, to strip all free persons, of a black complexion (some of whom may, perhaps be of considerable substance,) from those rights, which are so justly valuable to every freeman.[18]

The Lords of Trade and Plantations "had Occasion to look into the said Act, and as it carrie[d] an Appearance of Hardship towards certain Freemen meerely upon Account of their Complection, who would otherwise enjoy every Priviledge belonging to Freemen [they wanted to know] what were the Reasons which induced the Assembly to pass this Act."[19]

Governor William Gooch, to whom the question was ultimately referred, declared that the Virginia Assembly had decided upon this curtailment of the franchise in order "to fix a perpetual Brand upon Free Negros & Mulattos."[20] Surely that was no "unthinking decision"! Rather, it was a deliberate act by the plantation bourgeoisie; it proceeded from a conscious decision in the process of establishing a system of racial oppression, even though it meant repealing an electoral principle that had existed in Virginia for more than a century.

But upon examination, Governor Gooch's explanation of the thinking that led to the decision seems grossly disingenuous. His response to the criticism comprised four points. (1) The immediate cause of the enactment of that law, he said, had been the discovery of a revolt plot among African-American bond-laborers in 1722, "wherein the Free Negros & Mulattos were much suspected to have been concerned (which will for ever be the case) . . . though there could be no legal proof" of it.[21] (2) Another reason, said Gooch approvingly, had been "to make the free Negros sensible that a distinction ought to be made between their offspring and the descendants of an English-man." As we might say today, Gooch felt threatened by "the Pride of a manumitted slave, who looks upon himself immediately on his acquiring his freedom to be as good a man as the best." (3) Gooch's perturbation was all the greater when the prideful offender was "descended from a white Father or Mother," these being mostly, he said, "the worst of our imported Servants and convicts." The law in question, he argued, served as a way of "discouraging that kind of copulation." (4) Anyway, he said, the number of persons disfranchised by the law was "so inconsiderable, that 'tis scarce worth while to take any notice of them in this particular."

Although Gooch's letter has been noticed before by our historians, it has never been subject to analysis. However that neglect is to be explained, let it end here: for such an examination gets to the heart of the motives of the Anglo-American continental plantation bourgeoisie in imposing not just a system of lifetime bond-servitude only on persons of African descent, but a system of *racial oppression*, by denying recognition of, refusing to acknowledge, delegitimizing, so far as African-Americans were concerned, the normal social distinctions characteristic of capitalist society. Consider the points of the Gooch thesis in that light.

(1) As noted in Chapter 12, in the Anglo-Caribbean societies the security of the social order based on lifetime bond-servitude of Africans and Afro-Caribbeans was deliberately linked to the making of such a social distinction among persons of African ancestry. In the early 1720s, at the same time that the Virginia Assembly was emphasizing the exclusion of free Negroes from any place in the intermediate social control stratum, in Barbados free Negroes and persons of color, like other free persons, were required to serve in the colony militia, and in Jamaica the Assembly offered free Negroes and persons

of color free homesteads. In both cases the policies were calculated to promote and maintain social control and the security of those colonies.[22] Far from undermining the slave system, the policy in the West Indies proved over and over again to be an effective counterweight to bond-labor revolt. It was correctly feared that to refuse to maintain such distinctions was to court disaster.[23] In Virginia there had been free African-Americans living as land-owners, owners of bond-laborers, livestock breeders, and hired laborers at least three-quarters of a century before Gooch ever left England. Although they sometimes helped bond-laborers to escape, that offense was more often committed by European-American free persons. Yet no proposal was made to reduce the latter to villeins by taking away their franchise.

(2) If poor free persons in England or in Anglo-America displayed delusions of social grandeur in such a degree as to discomfit their neighbors, hot ridicule and cold reality would likely soon disabuse them of the notion. The preser-vation of a civil society would not require the disfranchisement of a whole demographic category in order to preserve good order in such cases. The system of racial oppression is not characterized by the distinction maintained between one of the common run of laboring people and the "best of his neighbors," i.e., the gentlefolk of the leisure class. Rather, its hallmark is the insistence on the social distinction between the *poorest* member of the oppressor group and any member, however propertied, of the oppressed group.

(3) It is to be noted that when Gooch expressed his objection to sexual union between "whites" and African-Americans, he referred only to instances in which the former were "people of . . . mean condition." He passed over in silence the common practice of sexual exploitation of African-American bond-laborers by their owners and their owners' sons.[24]

Why this omission? There was a difference in the two cases so far as the purposes of racial oppression were concerned. In the second case, the mother being a lifetime bond-laborer, the child would also be bound for life. The father, as the owner or heir presumptive of the mother, would not find it in his interest, and very rarely in his heart, to acknowledge his child as his own. The mother and the child were, by the laws forbidding their testimony, incapable of making a claim against the owner. If the owner did acknowledge paternity, he was subject to the penalties for "fornication," which were doubled in cases of sexual congress between European-Americans and African-Americans. If, out of an elementary sense of human decency, he freed his own child, the child was bound by law to leave Virginia within a certain time or to be taken up and sold as a lifetime bond-laborer.[25]

According to Gooch, the majority of the parents of mulatto children were of the laboring class, and most were bond-laborers. Although only those whose mothers were African-Americans were to be bound for life, Gooch vents his hostility towards all mulattos, whether bond or free, whose mere presence presented a cognitive dissonance for the system of racial oppression. But his emphasis is on the laboring-class origin of those who, he says, made up the majority of the mulattos. Was that because he saw in it the seed of a revolutionary class solidarity such as had once been enacted in Virginia by "English and Negroes in Armes"? Whatever weight may be given to that speculation, it is clear that Gooch regarded bonds of mutual affection between African-Americans and European-American laborers as an affront to the "perpetual brand" of racial oppression.

(4) To dismiss the disfranchisement of African-Americans on the grounds that they included few persons who met the property qualifications was to reject the premise set in Attorney-General West's reference to the rights of "every free man." Furthermore, this argument seems inconsistent with Gooch's first point. If the number of substantial African-American propertyholders was so few that their disfranchisement was not worth noticing, then concern over the prospect of their involvement in the freedom-seeking exploits of bond-laborers would be correspondingly diminished.

I have given such prominence to the Gooch letter because it provides rare documentation of a discussion of the issue of white supremacy among the ruling classes in the eighteenth century in Virginia.[26] Although the Board of Trade acknowledged Governor Gooch's reply by saying that it would let the matter rest,[27] historians of the origin of racial oppression in Anglo-America should not be content. I have sought to show that Gooch's argument for "fixing a brand" on the free African-American is illogical, even in its own terms.

How, then, *is* this categoric rejection of the free Negro to be explained? The difference between the English plantation bourgeoisies in the British West Indies and in the continental plantation colonies cannot be ascribed to a difference of degrees of "white" consciousness. Down to the last moment, and past it, the sugar plantocracy resisted any attempt to undermine that consciousness, just as the ruling class did in the continental plantation colonies. The difference was rooted in the objective fact that in the West Indies there were *too few* laboring-class Europeans to embody an adequate petty bourgeoisie, while in the continental colonies there were *too many* to be accommodated in the ranks of that class.

The tobacco bourgeoisie assumed that bond-laborers would resist in every way they could, including marronage and revolt. Note has been made of the anxiety expressed in 1698 by Governor Francis Nicholson, then of Maryland, over the prospect of "great disturbances" in which he believed that the Irish bond-laborers would "confederate with the negroes."[28] In 1710 the Deputy Governor of Virginia reported to the Board of Trade the discovery of "an intended Insurrection of the negros which was to have been put in Execution in Surry and James City Countys on Easter Day." Two of the freedom plotters were hanged in the official hope that "their fate will strike such a Terror in the other Negros, as will keep them from forming such designs for the future."[29] Alexander Spotswood arrived in Virginia in 1710 to begin his ten-year tenure as Governor in June of that same year shortly after the discovery of the plot. Whatever reliance he intended to put upon terror, experience had shown, he said, that "we are not to depend on either their [the Negroes'] stupidity, or that babel of languages among 'em; freedom wears a cap which can, without a tongue, call together all those who long to shake of[f] the fetters of slavery."[30] Although the attempt of African bond-laborers to establish a free settlement at the head of James River in 1729 was defeated,[31] Governor William Gooch feared that "a very small number of negroes once settled in those parts, would very soon be encreased by the accession of other runaways," as had happened with "the negroes in the mountains of Jamaica."[32]

In 1736, William Byrd II, a member of the Virginia Colony Council, wrote to the Earl of Egmont, president of the Trustees of the Georgia colony which had been founded four years earlier on the principle of exclusion of slavery. Byrd expressed his approval of the new colony's policy, and his fear for Virginia's future in view of the rapidly increasing proportion of African-American bond-laborers. He too had Jamaica on his mind, worrying "lest they [the lifetime bond-laborers in Virginia] prove as troublesome and dangerous . . . as they have been lately in Jamaica. We have mountains, in Virginia, too, to which they may retire safely, and do as much mischief as they do in Jamaica." Open revolt might occur; there were already 10,000 African-American men capable of bearing arms in Virginia, he noted, and he warned that "in case there should arise a Man amongst us, exasperated by a desperate fortune he might with more advantage than Cataline kindle a Servile War."[33] In 1749, Virginia Council members Thomas Lee and William Fairfax favored discouraging the importation of English convicts as bond-laborers. They cited former Governor Spotswood's allusion to freedom's cap, and warned that increasing the number of convict bond-laborers in Virginia, "who are wicked enough to join our Slaves in any Mischief . . . in all Probability will bring sure and sudden Destruction on all His Majesty's good subjects of this colony."[34] Nothing could have been more apparent than that the small cohort of the ruling elite must have a substantial intermediate buffer social control stratum to stand between it and "great disturbances," or even another rebellion. Like the capitalist enclosers of the peasants' land in sixteenth-century England, the men for whom the plantation world was made needed an effective intermediate yeoman-type social control stratum.

Whilst I have made no special effort to check for occasions of the use of the term "yeoman" in the colonial Virginia and Maryland records, I do not recall having seen it there; nor have I seen it in citations from the records in secondary works. Thomas J. Wertenbaker transplanted it from the agrarian history of the mother country – where it meant the laboring-class "forty-shilling freeholder" – even though that designation had little practical significance to a society where freehold farmers paid their debts and taxes not in sterling money, but in pounds of tobacco.[35] Other historians have followed Wertenbaker's lead in synonymizing "yeoman" with "middle class." But that has not been of much help in arriving at a functional definition of either "yeoman" or "middle class."

Various standards of measurement have been used to draw the lines of class distinction in the colonial Chesapeake, such as land ownership, bond-labor ownership, the number of pounds of one's annual tobacco crop, tax lists, and estate inventories.[36] Even within one or the other of these particular parameter systems, one historian's "yeoman" can be another's "poor man." In the midst of the conceptual confusion, one does notice that the yeoman band is wider in the eyes of those who, on the whole, find that eighteenth-century Virginia was a democracy and not an aristocracy; on the other hand, the "yeoman" category tends to wash out in the studies of those who tend to be more sensitive to the prevalence of inequality in the Chesapeake tobacco colonies.

The present study is concerned with the question of ruling-class social control and the choice of a system of racial oppression in the Anglo-American plantation colonies. The concept of "yeoman" or "middle class" in this context is examined as an intermediate social control category. For that reason, I take as the first criterion the degree to which a "planter's" interest was benefited by the system of chattel bond-servitude. The lower boundary of the middle class by this standard would lie between those who owned lifetime bond-laborers (the number being augmented by incidental functionaries of the system, such as overseers, clerks, slave-traders), on the one hand, and those who did not own bond-laborers, on the other.[37]

In relation to the Chesapeake generally, Kulikoff states that by the 1730s the social power structure was dominated by the gentry, a leisure class comprising 5 percent of the Anglo-American men.[38] The "gentry" can be regarded as the ruling class, and it was composed of persons whose wealth, however gained, was such as to relieve them of any economic need to work. From their ranks came those who actually occupied the posts of political authority.[39] "About half the [European-American] men," says Kulikoff, "were yeomen, and many of them owned a slave or two, or hoped to someday."[40] Being dependent on the gentry for credit to tide them over rough spots or to expand their holdings, the yeomen reciprocated by going along with the system of rule by the gentry.[41]

Aubrey C. Land approached the study of class differentiation in the colonial Chesapeake by way of analysis of Maryland estate inventories,[42] which he grouped by a scale of hundreds of pounds sterling: £0–£100, £100–£200; £200–£300, etcetera. In the period 1690 to 1699, three-fourths of the planters were in the £0–£100 category. The typical annual crop of such a planter was from 1,200 to 3,000 pounds of tobacco. "Between investment and consumption he had no choice. . . . He could not invest from savings because he had none." For him to buy either a limited-term or a lifetime bond-laborer was "very difficult." Often, because of his debts, the heirs of such a person were left penniless.[43] More than one-third of the planters in this category were tenants on twenty-one-year or three-lives leases on wild lands.[44] It is interesting to note the contrast between the Scots tenant in Ulster, who retained property claim to the improvements he made on the leasehold,[45] and the Chesapeake tenant, who was obligated to clear the land and make improvements, the entire value of which was claimed by the landlord for expansion of a soil-exhausting monoculture based on bond-labor. Although the proportion of planters in £0–£100 group had declined by 1740, they still made up more than half the total.[46] Such a planter "was not the beneficiary of the planting society of the Chesapeake . . . [and] it would stretch the usual meaning of the term to call him a yeoman, particularly if he fell in the lower half of his group."[47]

The £100–£200 category presents a dramatic contrast, in that 80 percent of these estates included bond-labor.[48] Taking this category together with the others up to £500, representing 21.7 percent of all estates in the 1690–99 period, by 1740 their proportion had increased to 35.7 percent. Of this larger, £100–£500 band of estates, lifetime bond-labor accounted for between half and two-thirds of the total value of an estate. In this £100–£500 category, farms without bond-labor had crops of only from 1,200 to 3,000 pounds of tobacco. But with bond-labor the output increased in proportion to the number of laborers.[49]

In the interest of completeness of coverage, Jackson Turner Main based a study on the Virginia tax lists for 1787.[50] But by treating various regions, from east to west, as representative of successive historical stages of plantation development, as well as by drawing to some extent on historical regional data, Main concluded that the general tendency of social evolution in Virginia [within the white population] was toward "a larger landless class and a larger class, too, of those who had almost no property."[51] In conclusion, Main declared:

> . . . it is evident in the first place that landowners were in a minority. Excluding the Northern Neck, about 30 percent of the adult [white] males were laborers with very little property. About one tenth of the men had no land but had a fair amount of other property and had access to land owned by relatives. About one eighth were tenants. A little over one third of the men were small farmers with less than five hundred acres.[52]

To summarize, then, somewhat less than 50 percent of the total adult white male population were landowners. Of the total number of landowners, one-fifth were large landholders, those with 500 acres or more. Those with from 100 to 500 acres constituted two-thirds of the total. Of these, one-fourth worked their land without the employment of bond-labor. The one-tenth of the landowners having up to 100 acres were even more likely to do their own work. Thus while at least seven out of eight landowners were also owners of bond-laborers, around 60 percent of the adult white male population were not employers of bond-labor but, rather, were put in competition with employers of bond-labor.[53] Jackson T. Main's study suggests the presence of a "yeoman" or "middle" class in eighteenth-century Virginia of not more than 40 percent of the adult white male population. That seems compatible with Land's conclusions regarding Maryland estate evaluations.

Professor Kulikoff relates these relative class proportions in the population to the central concern of the present work, the question of ruling class social control, by concluding that, "Once the gentry class gained the assent of the yeomanry, it could safely ignore the rest of white society."[54] But, recalling the question raised by Attorney-General West, why should African-Americans "possessed of a certain proportion of property" have been effectively barred from the ranks of this "yeomanry"? I have great respect for Kulikoff's work, from which I have learned much, but I believe that this proscription of the free African-American can be explained best precisely by the fact that, despite its sway over the "yeomanry," the gentry could *not* "safely ignore the rest of white society" because their bond-labor system was antithetical to the interests not only of African-American bond-laborers, but also of all the rest of the population that did not own bond-laborers. In their solidarity with the African-American bond-laborers in Bacon's Rebellion, the laboring-class European-American bond-laborers had demonstrated their understanding of their interests, and bond-laborers had had the sympathy of the laboring poor and propertyless free population.

What was to be done? What was the "alteration in the government, but not of the government"[55] that would exorcise the ghost of Bacon's Rebellion? How was laboring-class solidarity to be undone? Back to first principles, never better enunciated by an English statesman than by Sir Francis Bacon.[56] "[I]t is a certain sign of wise government," Sir Francis advised, ". . . when it can hold men's hearts by hopes, when it cannot by satisfaction." And, with acknowledgment to Machiavelli, Bacon advocated "dividing and breaking of all factions and combinations that are adverse to the state, and setting them at distance, or at least distrust among themselves."[57]

In the world the slaveholders made, however, "hope" depended upon the prospect of social mobility into the ranks of owners of bond-labor, and as we have seen there was little opportunity for the non-owner of bond-labor to make that transition to the "yeoman" class. The cost of lifetime bond-laborers presented a threshold that few non-owners of bond-labor could reach. The monoculture tended to glut the market and leave the small producer who had no bond-labor in debt so that accumulation of the capital necessary for this path to "yeoman" status was drained away.

Instead of social mobility, European-Americans who did not own bond-laborers were to be asked to be satisfied simply with the presumption of liberty, the birthright of the poorest person in England; and with the right of adult males who owned sufficient property to vote for candidates for office who were almost invariably owners of bond-laborers. The prospects for stability of a system of capitalist agriculture based on lifetime hereditary bond-servitude depended on the ability of the ruling elite to induce the non-"yeoman" European-Americans to settle for this counterfeit of social mobility. The solution was to establish a new birthright not only for Anglos but for every Euro-American, the "white" identity that "set them at a distance," to use Sir Francis's phrase, from the laboring-class African-Americans, and enlisted them as active, or at least passive, supporters of lifetime bondage of African-Americans. Edmund S. Morgan introduces a catalogue of these white-skin privilege laws, with the assertion that "The answer to the problem [of preventing a replay of Bacon's Rebellion] ... was racism, to separate danger-ous free whites from dangerous slave blacks by a screen of racial contempt." In this way, he emphasizes, "the [Virginia] assembly deliberately did what it could to foster contempt of whites for blacks and Indians."[58] Bruce attests that "[t]oward the end of the seventeenth century" there occurred "a marked tendency to promote a pride of race among the members of every class of white people; to be white gave the distinction of color even to the agricultural [European-American bond-]servants, whose condition, in some respects, was not much removed from that of actual slavery; to be white and also to be free, combined the distinction of liberty."[59]

Here, then, is the true answer to the issue raised by the anonymous Virginian to the Bishop of London and by Attorney-General Richard West and the Board of Trade to Governor Gooch. The exclusion of free African-Americans from the intermediate stratum was a corollary of the establishment of "white" identity as a mark of social status. If the mere presumption of liberty was to serve as a mark of social status for masses of European-Americans without real prospects of upward social mobility, and yet induce them to abandon their opposition to the plantocracy and enlist them actively, or at least passively, in keeping down the Negro bond-laborer with whom they had made common cause in the course of Bacon's Rebellion, the presumption of liberty had to be denied to free African-Americans.

H. M. Henry, though writing about South Carolina, posed a question of general relevance.

The financial interests of the large planters are sufficient to explain why they sought to perpetuate such a system of labor [racial slavery]. But why should the non-slaveholders, who formed the majority of the white population, have assisted in upholding and maintaining the slavery status of the negro with its attendant inconveniences, such as patrol service, when they must have been aware in some measure at least that as an economic regime it was a hindrance to their progress?[60]

The Virginia General Assembly showed how it was to be done; it deliberately stuffed the "racial" distinction with anomalous privileges to make it look like the real thing, promotion to a higher social class. The distinction was even emphasized for European-American chattel bond-laborers, whose presump-tion of liberty was temporarily in suspension.

Any owner of an African-American, practically without hindrance, could legally use or abuse his African-American bond-laborers, or dispose of him or her by gift, bequest, sale, or rental as a matter of course, but by a law enacted in 1691, he was forbidden to set them free.[61] Examples of emancipation of African-Americans by final will and testament have been cited from the record in Chapter 10; never had such a will been challenged. But when in 1712, under the terms of the will of John Fulcher of Norfolk County, sixteen African-American bond-laborers were to be freed and given land in fee simple "to live upon as long as they Shall live or any of there Increase and not to be turned of[f] or not to be Disturbed," the Virginia Colony Council reacted by proposing to bar even this door to freedom.[62]

On the other hand, the revised Virginia code of 1705 took pains to specify unprecedented guarantees for the European "christian white" limited-term bond-laborers. Before, masters had merely been required not to "exceed the bounds of moderation" in beating or whipping or otherwise "correcting" the bond-laborer, it being provided that the victim, if one could get to the Justice of the Peace and then to the next county court, "shall have remedy for his grievances."[63] The new code forbade the master to "whip a christian white servant naked, without an order from the justice of the peace," the offending master to be fined forty shillings payable to the servant.[64] Upon a second offense by a master in treatment of "servants (not being slaves)," the courts could order that the servant be taken from that master and sold at outcry.[65]

Freedom dues for limited-term bond-laborers had never been specified in Virginia law, but were merely referred to in court orders by the loose term "corn and clothes." The 1705 code, however, noting that "nothing in that nature ever [had been] made certain," enumerated them with specificity: "to every male servant, ten bushels of corn, thirty shillings in money (or the equivalent in goods), a gun worth at least twenty shillings; and to every woman servant, fifteen bushels of corn, forty shillings in money (or the equivalent in goods)."[66] Lifetime bond-laborers were not to have freedom dues, of course, but they had been allowed to raise livestock on their own account, and to have them marked as their own. But in 1692, and again in 1705 with greater emphasis, livestock raised by African-American bond-laborers on their own account were ordered to be confiscated.[67]

The act of 1723 that was the subject of the correspondence between Governor Gooch and the Board of Trade was by no means the first evidence, in terms of the law, of ruling-class desire not only to impose lifetime hereditary bond-servitude on African-Americans, but to implement it by a system of *racial oppression*, expressed in laws against *free* African-Americans. Such were the laws (several of which have been previously noted) making free Negro women tithable;[68] forbidding non-Europeans, though baptized Christians, to be owners of "christian," that is, European, bond-laborers;[69] denying free African-Americans the right to hold any office of public trust;[70] barring any Negro from being a witness in any case against a "white" person;[71] making any free Negro subject to thirty lashes at the public whipping post for "lift[ing] his or her hand" against any European-American, (thus to a major extent denying Negroes the elementary right of self-defense);[72] excluding free African-Americans from the armed militia;[73] and forbidding free African-Americans from possessing "any gun, powder, shot, or any club, or any other weapon whatsoever, offensive or defensive."[74]

The denial of the right of self-defense would become a factor in the development of the peculiar American form of male supremacy, white-male supremacy, informed by the principle that any European-American male could assume familiarity with any African-American woman. That principle came to have the sanction of law. We have earlier cited the Maryland Provincial Court decision of 1767 that "a slave had no recourse against the violator of his bed."[75] "The law simply did not criminalize the rape of slave women," writes Philip Schwarz. "No Virginia judge heard [such] a case."[76] Free African-American women had practically no legal protection in this respect, in view of the general exclusion of African-Americans, free or bond, from giving testimony in court.[77]

The ruling class took special pains to be sure that the people they ruled were propagandized in the moral and legal ethos of white-supremacism. Provisions were included for that purpose in the 1705 "Act concerning Servants and Slaves" and in the Act of 1723 "directing the trial of Slaves ... and for the better government of Negros, Mulattos, and Indians, bond *or free*."[78] For consciousness-raising purposes (to prevent "pretense of ignorance"), the laws mandated that parish clerks or churchwardens, once each spring and fall at the close of Sunday service, should read ("publish") these laws in full to the congregants. Sheriffs were ordered to have the same done at the courthouse door at the June or July term of court. If we presume, in the absence of any contrary record, that this mandate was followed, we must conclude that the general public was regularly and systematically subjected to official white-supremacist agitation. It was to be drummed into the minds of the people that, for the first time, no free African-American was to dare to lift his or her hand against a "Christian, not being a negro, mulatto or Indian" (3:459); that African-American freeholders were no longer to be allowed to vote (4:133–34); that the provision of a previous enactment (3:87 [1691]) was being reinforced against the mating of English and Negroes as producing "abominable mixture" and "spurious issue" (3:453–4); that, as provided in the 1723 law for preventing freedom plots by African-American bond-laborers, "any white person ... found in company with any [illegally congregated] slaves" was to be fined (along with free African-Americans or Indians so offending) with a fine of fifteen shillings, or to "receive, on his, her, or their bare backs, for every such offense, twenty lashes well laid on." (4:129).

Thus was the "white race" invented as the social control formation whose distinguishing characteristic was not the participation of the slaveholding class, nor even of other elements of the propertied classes; that alone would have been merely a form of the "beautiful gradation" of class differentiation prescribed by Edmund Burke. What distinguished this system of social control, what made it "the white race", was the participation of the laboring classes: non-slaveholders, self-employed smallholders, tenants, and laborers. In time this "white race" social control system begun in Virginia and Maryland would serve as the model of social order to each succeeding plantation region of settlement.[79]

The effort bore fruit so far as danger from the European-American bond-laborers was concerned. "[t]he fear," writes Winthrop D. Jordan, "of white servants and Negroes uniting in servile rebellion, a prospect which made some sense in the 1660s and 70s ... vanished completely during the following half-century." He continues with a corollary: "Significantly, the only rebellions of white servants in the continental colonies came before the entrenchment of slavery."[80] But that is only half the story: the poor and propertyless European-Americans were the principal element in the day-to-day enforcement of racial oppression not only in the Chesapeake but wherever the plantation system was established. After 1700, according to Wertenbaker, "Every white man, no matter how degraded, could now find pride in his race.... Moreover, the immediate control of the negroes fell almost entirely into the hands of white men of humble means."[81] In 1727, special militia detachments known as "the patrol" were instituted "for dispersing all unusual concourse of negroes, or other slaves, and for preventing any dangerous combinations which may be made among them at such meetings."[82] A student of criminal laws in Virginia relating to bond-laborers states that "Patrollers were the ultimate means of preventing insurrection."[83] Historians who analyzed the Virginia militia records of 1757–58 have reported that "the muster rolls were apt to be filled mostly with the lower class." Many, they say, were "former indentured servants."[84] In colonial South Carolina, even the European-American bond-laborers were recruited into the militia and the "slave patrol," where "[their] role in defense against Negro insurrection was more important than as a defense against the enemy from without."[85] At the time of the American Revolution, a number of African-American bond-laborers were freed by their South Carolina Quaker owners. The law subsequently enacted to prevent further emancipations proved ineffective at first because only freeholders were authorized to collect rewards for reporting violations. But in 1788 effectiveness was achieved by extending this civic function to "any freeman." By this means, says our historian, "the State secured the co-operation of the landless whites who were usually strangely willing to have a fling at the slaves and who, no doubt, were anxious to get the reward offered for such information."[86]

In a mode often akin to modern-day "featherbedding," deficiency laws provided jobs for European-American workers simply for being "white." In 1712, the South Carolina Assembly, for example, passed a law stipulating that, at any plantation six miles or more remote from the owner's usual abode, for every "Six Negroes or other Slaves" employed, a quota of "One or more White Person" must be kept there. Ten years later the quota was one to ten, but that applied to the home plantation as well as to those far removed.[87] Job preference for "whites" was to be further guaranteed under a proposal of a committee of the South Carolina House of Assembly in 1750 "That no Handicrafts Man [other than the owner] shall hereafter teach a Negro his Trade."[88]

Georgia colony, founded by its trustees in 1732 on the no-slavery principle, was territory irresistible to the South Carolina plantation bourgeoisie anxious as its members were to "grow the economy," as it might be put today. They soon began to campaign for an end of this government interference with free enterprise. In the course of the controversy, a Savannah man objected that abandonment of the founding principle excluding slavery from Georgia "would take work from white men's hands and impoverish them, as in the case of

Charleston [South Carolina], where the tradesmen are all beggars by that means." The promoters of the slavery cause countered by saying that "the negroes should not be allowed to work at anything but producing rice . . . and in felling timber.[89] Accordingly, the 1750 act repealing the ban on slavery in Georgia included a "deficiency" provision requiring the employment of one "white man Servant" on each plantation for every four Negroes employed. It further barred the employment of Negroes except in cultivation and coopering.[90] Although this system of white-skin privileges had not been initiated by the European-American laboring classes but by the plantation bourgeoisie, the European-American workers were claiming them by the middle of the eighteenth century.[91] In South Carolina white workers were demanding the exclusion of Negroes from the skilled trades.[92] Richard B. Morris's monumental study of labor in the continental Anglo-American colonies found that "the effort of white artisans to keep free Negroes and slaves from entering the skilled trades" radiated from Charleston to "every sizeable town on the Atlantic coast."[93] In 1839, "white" mechanics in Culpeper and Petersburg, Virginia, demanded that Negroes be barred from apprenticeship, and from any trade without a "white" overseer. A decade later a similar petition from Norfolk showed a high degree of political sophistication. Barring Negroes from competing for employment, its sponsors said, would guarantee against "jealousy between slaveholders and non-slaveholders."[94] Within two decades slaveholding would end, but the appeal to "white race" solidarity would remain the country's most general form of class-collaborationism.

The White Race and Theories of American History

If the Virginia laws of 1705 represent ruling class manipulation of the rank-and-file, the inescapable implication seems to be that the social transformation that they expressed – to the system of racial slavery, racial oppression, white supremacy – must not have been in the real interests of the majority of the people, the smallholders, the tenants and laborers, those who did not own bond-laborers.

There have been many historians who would not accept this argument. Some would reject the premise, others the conclusion; still others would reject both the premise and the conclusion. There are those, the psycho-cultural cohort in the debate over the origin of racial slavery in continental Anglo-America, who see white supremacy as having been genetically or culturally foreordained before the English settlers sailed into James River.[95] Arguments made by others – based on considerations of demographics, blind market forces, Euro-Afro cultural dissonance, and the fact that only persons of African descent were held in lifetime servitude – along with my brief counterpoints are specified earlier in this chapter at page 240.

But a major theme shared by some who reject the premise and some who accept it concerns not the origin of racial oppression but the assessment of white-supremacism in relation to the foundation of the United States as a republic. That theme may properly be called the "paradox thesis" of American history. The essential element in this argument is that democracy and equality, as represented in the Declaration of Independence and the Constitution of 1789, were, by the logic of history, made possible by racial oppression. The lineage of this thesis goes back at least to 1758, when Edmund Burke argued that "whites" in the southern continental colonies were more "attached to liberty" than were colonists in the North because in the South freedom was a racial privilege.[96] Virginia scholar Thomas Roderick Dew contended that slavery made possible and actual "one common level" of equality "in regard to whites." "The menial and low offices being all performed by the blacks," he continued, "there is at once taken away the greatest cause for distinction and separation of the ranks of society."[97]

Special interest, however, attaches to Edmund S. Morgan's espousal of this rationale. His book *American Slavery, American Freedom* appeared in 1975 in the afterglow of the civil rights struggles, sacrifices and victories of the 1960s. Furthermore, his socio-economic approach to the origin of racial slavery supplied the most substantial response that had yet appeared to the "natural racism" thesis of Carl Degler and of Winthrop D. Jordan. Historian H. M. Henry had asked: "why should the non-slaveholders, who formed the majority of the white population have assisted in upholding and maintaining the slavery status of the negro . . .?" Sixty years later, Morgan posed essentially the same question. "How could patricians win in populist politics?" That question, Morgan says, "leads to the paradox . . . the union of freedom and slavery in Virginia and America."

The essence of Morgan's paradox, to the extent it is a true paradox, is a renewal of the same euphemism of the system of white-supremacism and lifetime hereditary bond-servitude that characterized the opinions of Burke and Dew. Unconsciously paraphrasing Edmund Burke, Morgan says, "Virginians may have had a special appreciation of the freedom dear to republicans, because they saw every day what life without it could be."[98] T. R. Dew and others are recognized in Morgan's approvingly quoted observation of Sir Augustus John Foster, an English diplomat who traveled in Virginia at the beginning of the nineteenth century: "Owners of slaves among themselves are all for keeping down every kind of superiority." It is pure Dew again when Morgan shares Foster's view that "whites" in Virginia, "can profess an unbounded love of liberty and democracy . . . [because] the mass of the people who in other countries might become mobs [in Virginia are] nearly altogether composed of their" African-American lifetime bond-laborers.[99]

The argument rests on the assumption that early in the eighteenth century "the mass of white Virginians were becoming landowners" and the small planters began to prosper, thus giving the large and small planters "a sense of common identity based on common interests."[100] This feeling, says Morgan, was sufficient basis for the small planters to put their trust in the ruling plantation bourgeoisie and thus cease to be a danger to social order.[101] Sources cited by me such as Jackson Turner Main, Gloria Main, T. J. Wertenbaker, Aubrey C. Land, Willard F. Bliss, Russell R. Menard, and Allan Kulikoff show that the economic assumption made here by Morgan is open to serious question. Morgan, in a passing reference to the growth of tenancy, devotes a reference note to Bliss and Jackson Main, but that is the limit of his concern with such studies, although they cast great doubt on his facile conclusion that of European-Americans "[t]here were too few free poor to matter,"[102] a conclusion without which his "paradox" unravels.

Morgan, in passages that I have previously cited with approval, declared that the answer to the problem of social control was a series of deliberate measures taken by the ruling class to "separate dangerous free whites from dangerous slave blacks."[103] But if, as the country moved "Toward the Republic" and after it got there, among "whites" there were "too few free poor to matter," why did the social order not revert to the normal class differentiation, Burke's "beautiful gradation" from rich to the less rich and so on through the scale, in which the free Negroes could take their individual places according to their social class? They could be expected, as James Madison said, to function properly in that social station.[104] The "white race," as a social control form-ation, would have been a redundancy. Instead, there was a general proscription of the free Negro, laws against emancipation, even by last will and testament, and banishment for those so freed. That, I submit, is unchallengeable evidence of the continued presence of poor whites who had "little but their complexion to console them for being born into a higher caste," yet served as an indispensable element of the "white race," the Peculiar Institution.[105]

Morgan's book was a trenchant contribution to the socio-economic and "deliberate-choice" explanation of the origin of racial slavery. In seeking to understand his adoption of the "paradox" thesis, it seems helpful to consider the following passage from his 1972 presidential address to the Organization of American Historians:

> The temptation is already apparent to argue that slavery and oppression were the dominant features of American history and that efforts to advance liberty and equality were the exception, indeed no more than a device to divert the masses while their chains were being fastened. To dismiss the rise of liberty and equality in American history as a mere sham is not only to ignore hard facts, it is also to evade the problem presented by those facts. The rise of liberty and equality in this country was accompanied by the rise of slavery. That two such contradictory developments were taking place simultaneously over a long period of our history, from the seventeenth century to the nineteenth, is the central paradox of American history.[106]

Morgan set out to meet the "challenge" of those who, in his opinion, overemphasize slavery and oppression in American history. Yet the effect of Morgan's "paradox" thesis seems no less an apology for white supremacy than the "natural racism" argument. At the end of it all, he writes, "Racism made it possible for white Virginians to develop a devotion to ... equality.... Racism became an essential ... ingredient of the republican ideology that enabled Virginians to lead the nation." Then, as if shying at his own conclusion, Morgan suggests the speculation that perhaps "the vision of a nation of equals [was] flawed at the source by contempt for both the poor and the black."[107] But what flaw? If racism was a flaw, then "the rise of liberty" would have been better off without it – a line of reasoning that negates the paradox. On the other hand, if racism made "the rise of liberty possible," as the paradox would have it, then racism was not a flaw of American bourgeois democracy, but its very special essence. Morgan's "paradox" therefore contains in itself the very challenge that he set out to refute. The "Ordeal of Colonial Virginia" was extended as the Ordeal of America, wherein racial oppression and white-supremacism have indeed been the dominant feature, the parametric constant, of United States history.

The white frontier

Being made to compete with unpaid bond-labor "practically destroyed the Virginia yeomanry," writes Wertenbaker. "Some it drove into exile, either to the remote frontiers or to other colonies; some it reduced to extreme poverty; ... some it caused to purchase slaves and so at one step to enter the exclusive class of those who had others to work for them. . . . The small freeholder was not destroyed, as was his prototype of ancient Rome, but he was subjected to a change which was by no means fortunate or wholesome."[108]

The tendency toward concentration of capital ownership is a prevailing attribute of capitalism. The social impact of that tendency is illustrated in Wertenbaker's comment on the Virginia colonial economy of the eighteenth century. But this was not the typical case of increased concentration of capital based on the introduction of new instruments of labor requiring increasing relative investments in fixed capital. It was caused by land engrossment in general, and by the diminished supply of good lands in the older, Tidewater area, but even more by the lower labor costs per unit of output of those planters who had means to invest in the high-priced lifetime bond-laborers. By the closing third of the eighteenth century this process had produced a situation in which at least 60 percent of the white adult men in Virginia were non-owners of bond-labor.[109]

Among that 60 percent were those encountered by the Marquis de Chastellux as he travelled through Virginia in spring 1782. For the first time in his three years in America, "in the midst of those rich plantations," he often saw "miserable huts . . . inhabited by whites, whose wan looks and ragged garments bespeak poverty." It seemed clear to him that the cause of this poverty was the engrossment of land by the plantation bourgeoisie.[110] The impoverished included those landless European-Americans previously noted who stayed in eastern Virginia but with "little but their complexion to console them."[111]

Wertenbaker asserts, however, that the number of such very poor was never large, because anyone with a little drive and ambition "could move to the frontier and start life on more equal terms."[112] Among those who moved and moved frequently were those who opted for being tenants,[113] some on leases but, says Kulikoff, more typically as tenants-at-will, working on shares with tools, buildings and marketing facilities furnished by the landlord. Share tenants moved on after a short tenure. Squatters left land where they could not afford the surveying and patent fees; two-thirds of the original settlers of Amelia County, formed in 1735 – mostly squatters – left the county between 1736 and 1749. In Lunenberg County, formed in 1746, only one-fifth of the laborers were able to establish households, whilst two out of five of the householders left the county between 1750 and 1764.[114] Others moved directly to "new" territories taking out patents as fee-simple owners.

The result was an increasing number of would-be planters moving to "the frontier," wherever that meant at a given time – the Piedmont, the south side of the James, North Carolina, the Shenandoah Valley, or beyond the Cumberland Gap – as tenants, as patentees of "new" land, or as unpatented squatters. Though the squeezing out of such a poor planter to the "frontier" negated the assumption of a common interest with the gentry, he was still "made to fold to his bosom the adder that stings him," the bondage of African-Americans.[115] Denied social mobility, these would-be planters were to have the white-skin privilege of lateral mobility – to the "frontier." By the same token they went as "whites"; resenting Negroes, not their slavery, indeed hating the free Negro most of all; ready now to take the land from the Indians in the name of "a white man's country."[116]

Turner's frontier-as-social-safety-valve theory

In 1893, Frederick Jackson Turner (1861–1932), one of the giants of American historiography, presented a theory, "a hypothesis," of American historical development. He likened it to the career of the ancient Greeks in the Mediterranean world, "breaking the bond of custom, offering new experiences, calling out new institutions and activities."[117]

> Up to our own day American history has been in a large degree the history of the colonization of the Great West. The existence of an area of free land, its continuous recession, and the advance of American settlement westward explain American development.[118]

Turner ended that essay with a portentous epitaph: "[T]he frontier is gone, and with its going has closed the first period of American history."[119] In 1910 he continued his theme: "The solitary backwoodsman wielding his axe at the edge of a measureless forest is replaced by companies capitalized at millions, operating railroads, sawmills, and all the enginery of modern machinery to harvest the remaining trees." He then formulated what came to be called the "safety-valve corollary" of the "frontier" thesis. "A new national development is before us," he said, "without the former safety valve of abundant resources open to him who would take." He delineated the consequent sharpening of class struggle between capital and anti-capital, between those who demand that there be no governmental interference with "the exploitation and the development of the country's wealth" on the one hand, and the reformers – from the Grangers to the Populists, to Bryan to Debs and Theodore Roosevelt – who emphasized "the need of governmental regulation . . . in the interest of the common man; [and] the checking of the power of those business Titans."[120] It is not surprising," he added later that year, "that socialism shows noteworthy gains as elections continue, that parties are forming on new lines. . . . They are efforts to find substitutes for the former safeguard of democracy, the disappearing lands. They are the sequence of the disappearing frontier."[121]

It is now more than a century since the disappearance of the "frontier", to which Turner ascribed a sharpening struggle between the "Titans" and "the common people." But his expectation of the emergence of a popular socialist movement of sufficient proportions to "substitute" for the end of the "freeland safety valve" was disappointed. Turner died in the midst of the Great Depression in 1932. Toward the end of his life, he felt "baffled by his contemporary world and [he] had no satisfying answer to the closed-frontier formula in which he found himself involved."[122]

The Great Social Safety Valve of American history

The white laboring people's prospect of lateral mobility to "free land", however unrealizable it was in actuality, did serve in diverting them from struggles with the bourgeoisie.[123] But that was merely one aspect of the Great Safety Valve, the system of racial privileges conferred on laboring-class European-Americans, rural and urban, poor and exploited though they themselves were. That has been the main historical guarantee of the rule of the "Titans," damping down anti-capitalist pressures by making "race, and not class, the distinction in social life." This, more than any other factor, has shaped the "contours of American history"[124] – from the Constitutional Convention of 1787 to the Civil War, to the overthrow of Reconstruction, to the Populist Revolt of the 1890s, to the Great Depression, to the civil rights struggle and "white backlash" of our own day. If Turner had taken note of the Southern Homestead Act and its repeal, and the heroic Negro Exodus of 1879, might he have given his "frontier" theory an added dimension? Would he have then taken into account the social safety-valve function of the two other broad general forms of lateral mobility in the nineteenth century – immigration into the United States and farm-to-factory migration – which like "free land" were also cast in the mold of "racial" preference for Europeans and European-Americans, as "whites"?[125]

The Civil Rights Legacy and the Impending Crisis

Properly interpreted, Turner's reference to the "safety valve" potential in anti-capitalist "reform" movements of his day had its innings in the Keynesian New

Deal which at least some of its supporters hoped might be a road to
"socialism," and some of its reactionary enemies regarded as the real thing.
The limitations of that line of reform, which had become evident by 1938,
were masked by the prosperity of the United States role as the "arsenal of
democracy" in World War Two, which ended with the United States being the
only industrial power left standing and the possessor of three-fourths of the
world's gold reserves. By 1953, other major powers had recovered to pre-war
levels; by 1957 the United States was beginning to experience a chronic
unfavorable balance of trade; in 1971 the United States formally abandoned
the gold standard for settlement of international balances of trade and the
"gold cover" for the domestic money supply. Finally, even the party of the
New Deal has cast all Keynesian pretense to the winds, proclaiming that "the
era of big government is over," and boasting of "ending welfare" in any
previously recognizable form.

Now, at the end of the twentieth century, the social gap between the Titans
and the common people is at perhaps its historic maximum, real wages have
trended downward for nearly two decades. "Entitlements" and "welfare," as
they relate to students, the poor and the elderly, have become obscenities in
the lexicon of official society. There is less of a "socialist" movement today in
the United States than there was in Turner's day, and anti-capitalist class-
consciousness is hesitant even to call its name. The bourgeoisie in one of its
parts mockingly dons "revolution" like a Halloween mask. "Class struggle" is
an epithet cast accusingly at the mildest defenders of social welfare reforms,
and the country is loud with the sound of one class struggling.

Yet, there are unmistakable signs of a maturing social conflict, such as that
noted by Turner a century ago, because of intensifying efforts to "balance the
budget" at the expense of the living standards of non-stockholders. But there
is a most significant variation. Unlike in Turner's time, the present-day United
States bears the indelible stamp of the African-American civil rights struggle
of the 1960s and after, a seal that the "white backlash" has by no means been
able to expunge from the nation's consciousness. Perhaps in the impending
renewal of the struggle of "the common people" and the "Titans," the Great
Safety Valve of white-skin privileges may finally come to be seen and rejected
by laboring-class European-Americans as the incubus that for three centuries
has paralyzed their will in defense of their class interests *vis-à-vis* those of the
ruling class.

Appendix II-A

(see Chapter 1, note 64)

"For more than four centuries, the communities formed by ... [African and African-American] runaways dotted the fringes of plantation America, from Brazil to the southeastern United States, from Peru to the American Southwest." Their existence "struck directly at the foundations of the plantation system, presenting military and economic threats that often taxed the colonists to their very limits."[1] Maroon communities, from Jamaica to Cuba, from Brazil to Mexico, were more successful where located in mountainous terrain, and continental mainland situations seem to have been of extra advantage, as in Panama, Colombia and Brazil, as compared to the more limited room of small insular colonies.

"The major concern of the colonial government of Cuba was the persecution of maroons and the destruction of *palenques*, even after the first half of the nineteenth century."[2]

"Mexico experienced its first widespread wave of slave insurrections in the period 1560–80. ... By the 1560s ... [T]he [Spanish colonial] bureaucracy and slave owners, outnumbered by slaves in the mining regions, were helpless in the face of such anarchy," which found Africans "allying with the Indians."[3] The main maroon settlement, in a mountain fastness located not far from Vera Cruz, was led by Yanga, an African reputedly of royal rank in his native Abrong kingdom. He was the first Mexican maroon, having fled to the mountains in about 1580. An expedition sent against the maroons' settlement failed in its search-and-destroy mission. Instead, the encounter resulted in a historically unique agreement, "The only known example of a fully successful attempt by slaves to secure their freedom en masse by revolt and negotiation, and to have it sanctioned and guaranteed in law."[4]

Another former African king, known to Cartagena (the Caribbean coastal region of Colombia) as Domingo Bioho, King Benkos, fled the Spanish plantations at the head of thirty men and women comrades and established a maroon settlement in a forest and marsh area of the interior, where these original maroons were soon being joined by individuals and small groups of runaways. After standing off a posse of slaveholders that came after them, the maroons finally established a *palenque* at a place to be known as San Basilio. The Spanish, after failing in two military expeditions against San Basilio, finally made a pattern-setting peace with the maroons in 1619, based on non-aggression principles.[5]

In the mid-1560s in the Darien province of Panama, maroons led by their elected king, Bayano, reputedly a former African king, secured a peace treaty with the Spanish colonial government.[6] These or such as these were those who allied with Sir Francis Drake against the Spanish as mentioned in *The Invention of the White Race*, Volume One.

As early as 1575 there was a maroon settlement near Bahia in Brazil; by 1597 it was reported that "the principal enemies" of the Portuguese colonists were such mountain-based groups of runaway African bond-laborers.[7] Hundreds of such settlements would come into existence in the seventeenth and eighteenth centuries. The greatest of these settlements, or group of settlements, was Palmares, founded some ninety miles from Pernambuco in northern Brazil, by Africans escaping from plantation slavery around the beginning of the seventeenth century.[8] Palmares was not merely a refuge, a *quilombo* (African word) from which to raid Portuguese and Dutch plantations, but a Negro republic in Brazil, with its own agrarian economy and elected ruler.[9] Despite repeated colonialist military assaults, Palmares grew until by the mid-1670s, by Portuguese report, it embraced some 99,000 square miles, an area about the size of Wyoming or Nevada, with a population of from 15,000 to 20,000 in ten major settlements.[10] The elected king of Palmares, called Ganga Zumba [Great Lord], and most of the ruling element were native Africans, although among the leaders named in a 1677 Portuguese report there was one, Arotirene, presumed to have been an Amerindian.[11] The Ganga Zumba in 1677 claimed to have been a king in Africa.[12] Having endured for almost a century, Palmares finally fell to the colonialist forces in 1694, after a siege of six weeks.[13]

Appendix II-B

(see Chapter 2, note 6)

By the beginning of the fourteenth century, expansion of agricultural production in England had led to a general decline of agricultural prices. The landowning class then sought advantage by demanding payment of rent in cash, rather than in a share of the product of the free tenant. In turn, these rent-paying tenants, if they wanted to expand production, were obliged to pay their workers wages, since the latter were under no feudal obligation to the peasant proprietor or tenant. Thus capitalist relations of production began to be introduced in English agriculture.

The bubonic plague that swept Europe between 1348 and 1351 struck England in August 1348, and within sixteen months it had wiped out one-third to half of the population.[1] Inconceivable horror though it was, the plague created such a shortage of labor that it became extremely difficult for landowners to continue to exact feudal labor dues from the villein, or to dictate the wages of labor: "The wages of labour were nearly doubled," writes Thorold Rogers, "and the profits of capitalist agriculture sank from 20 per cent to nearly zero."[2]

The ruling classes sought to reverse this trend by repressive measures, among the earliest of which was the Statute of Laborers of 1350, designed to impose compulsory labor at fixed wages under penalty of jail, hot branding irons, and outlawry. The wage-laborers and villeins struck back. The most common forms of resistance were those of combining for mutual strength and simple flight to other districts. Because this movement was so widespread, and escape so generally successful,[3] repressive measures were insufficient remedy for the landowners; they were forced to pay the higher wages and to reduce rents if they were to prevent their crops from rotting in the fields for lack of hands.

In 1381, the ruling classes sought to filch back part of their higher labor costs by the imposition of a one-shilling poll tax on every person above fifteen years of age (except clerics and licensed beggars). It quickly became apparent that they had misjudged the temper and mettle of the people. The result was the Great Rebellion of 1381, more popularly known as Wat Tyler's Rebellion, in honor of its leader.[4]

The revolt was national in scope. It lasted only one month, June, but in that time "half of England had been in flame."[5] The ranks of the rebels were composed about half of peasants and half of proletarians – rural wage-laborers, and journeymen and apprentices of London and other towns. Most chroniclers estimate their number at from forty to sixty thousand; but the only eyewitness account states that at Blackheath one hundred and ten thousand rebels assembled to confront the king with their demands. They were a disciplined force, and armed; in their ranks were thousands of longbow veterans of the Hundred Years' War, then in its forty-fifth year.

The lines of revolt converged on London, a metropolis with a population of some 23,000 (males of fifteen years of age and over). On 13 June a rebel army of ten thousand entered London through gates opened by the welcoming proletariat within; by that afternoon, "the rebels were in possession of London, without having had to strike a single blow."[6] Combining xenophobia with anti-feudalism, they killed a large number of the Flemish community of weavers whom the former king had imported and installed in London. Young King Richard II took refuge in the Tower of London with his armed guard and his advisers. His position was so desperate that "he was prepared to grant anything" the rebels were demanding.[7]

Through the voices of John Ball, the radical priest, and Wat Tyler, their commander-in-chief, the "commons of England" made their demands known: for an end to bondage of villeins and laborers, the revocation of the poll tax, and no more "outlawry" for resistance to forced labor. Tyler addressed the king as "Brother," and in the royal presence he declared, "there should be equality among all people," adding only courteously, "save the king."[8]

Even as the king parleyed with the rebels and agreed to their demands, he arranged for the assassination of Wat Tyler.[9] But he did not dare to revoke the promises he had made; not, that is, until the rebels had decamped from London and dispersed to their homes. Then the king did revoke his promises and sent forth his armed bands to wreak vengeance on the deceived and demobilized rebels, and to inaugurate a period of "pacification" and punishment.

Some commentators seem disposed to disparage the revolt as a factor in bringing feudalism to an end in England. It is true that there were a number of factors contributing to that end, but surely Wat Tyler's Rebellion was one of them. It barred the way to a raising of the rate of profit by means of feudal dues on the peasantry. Even a prime disparager conceded that in the following century "tenants did not find it impossible to resist pressure from their landlords."[10] Shorter-range goals achieved included the revocation of the attempt to force down wages to the old levels under the provisions of the Statute of Laborers of 1350. These ancient rebels would seem to merit the enthusiasm expressed by Thorold Rogers five centuries after their audacious rising: "The peasant of the fourteenth century struck a blow for freedom ... and he won."[11]

Appendix II-C

(*see Chapter 5, note 46*)

Perhaps the "cheap commodity" strategy for capitalist conquest of foreign countries was never more clearly outlined than by William Bullock in his *Virginia Impartially Examined*, which was published in London in 1649. Expressing the view that the Indians were too numerous and strong to be coerced, and too self-sufficient to be won to easy trust and dependence in their relations with the English, Bullock suggested a subtle strategy, which he defined and discussed as follows:

First, by making them sensible of their nakedness.

Secondly, by taking them off from their confidence upon nature, whereby they may take care for the future.

Thirdly, that they may desire commerce.

Fourthly, that they may be brought to depend. And for themselves, I shall propose that we gently steal through their nature, till we can come to pull off the scale from their eyes, that they may see their own nakednesse; which must be done in manner following.

Either by making them ambitious of Honour, or by making them ambitious of Riches ...

First, I shall advise that slight Jewells be made at the publique charge of thirty or fourty shillings price, and one better then [than] the rest, of some such toyes as they shall most affect, which fitted with Ribands to weare about their necks of their heads, as their custom amongst them is; shalbe sent from the Governour of the Plantation in his own, and also in the name of the People and the Governor to distinguish them by some pretty titles, which should always after be observed; as also to make some of them favourites, and to sollicite their preferment with their King, & this by degrees will kindle the fire of Ambition, which once in a flame must be fed, and then is the time to work.

For the second I shall advise, that their nature be observed what way it most poynts at, and then to fit them with what they most desire, and if by degrees you can bring some of them to weare slighte loose Garments in Summer, or to keep them warmed in the Winter; which if you can effect, the worke is halfe done ...

The author acknowledged that his plan would entail certain initial outlays by the English, but he assured his readers that even this cost would be recompensed by taking animal skins and provisions from the Indians in barter. Once having got that far, the English "need not fear the coming of the rest."

The poore Indian being cloathed, his sight is cleared, he sees himselfe naked, and you'le find him in the snare . . .

Bullock stressed that still the matter must be managed by stages, because "you shall finde that for themselves they will worke, but not for you." Therefore as the English bourgeoisie had done in their owne country, Bullock proposed a sort of contracting system of work to be done by the Indians in their own houses and villages. By steps then they could be introduced as laborers within the English colony. But they were not to be *fully* trusted "until you see them be so sensible of their poverty, that they come necessitated to worke." (*Virginia Impartially Observed*, [London, 1649], pp. 56–9.)

Appendix II-D

(*see Chapter 7, note 197*)

Some scholars are convinced that the bond-labor system, despite acknowledged abuses, represented an improvement for the laborers over the prospects they would have had in Europe. Bruce[1] and Ballagh[2] believe that, except for the axemen noted by Bruce, the work was easier than that of the English wage-laborer. McCormac, lowering his sights a few degrees, says merely that at any rate the lot of the limited-term bond-laborer was "better than languishing in a debtor's cell in England."[3]

Attention is also given to the condition of the European-American bond-laborers in the eighteenth century, when African-Americans came to constitute the majority of the plantation bond-labor force. Gray asserts that in the eighteenth century the conditions of the European bond-laborers were alleviated.[4] On the other hand, Richard B. Morris found that the increased employment of Africans did not bring "any material improvement in the treatment" of immigrant European bond-laborers.[5] McCormac seems to agree on this point with Morris, at least so far as Maryland was concerned. There, he says, the life of the European bond-laborer was better prior to the large-scale arrival of African laborers beginning at the end of the seventeenth century.[6] Despite the high mortality rate of the first years, and although the burdens of the poor were increased if they emigrated to the colonies as bond-laborers, still, says A. E. Smith, both masters and bond-laborers endured "the hardships of pioneer life," and in the end "America presented to the average man a far better chance of attaining decent independence than did Europe."[7] If the bond-laborers' plight was difficult, he declares, the difficulties should not be ascribed to bondage as such, nor to the evil disposition of the masters, but to the general difficulties of the earliest colonial years that made inevitable a harsh regime, in which little allowance could be made for "shiftless or weak servants." Within such limits, he found that the degree of oppressive treatment suffered by the bond-laborers depended largely upon the luck of the draw in the matter of masters to whom they were disposed. There were, Smith says, two basic sources of the sufferings of limited-term bond-laborers, and neither involved any disposition on the part of the plantation bourgeoisie to take advantage of the chattel bond-labor relation of production to exploit their workers in ways which they could not have done free tenants and wage laborers. These two fundamental causes of hardship were, he says: (1) the climate of the plantation colonies; and (2) the non-adaptability of non-farm laborers such as constituted a large part, if not the majority, of the bond-laborers drawn from England.[8] Russell R. Menard's study of early colonial Maryland led him to essentially the same conclusion as that drawn by Smith regarding the general state of master–servant relations. In the course of challenging Edmund S. Morgan's assertion that limited-term bond-servitude prepared the way for the lifetime bond-servitude eventually imposed on African-Americans, Menard is at pains to contrast the two cases. "Indentured servitude ... was not degrading," says Menard. True, their mortality rate was shockingly high, "nor were all servants well treated"; but Menard dismisses the notorious cases such as those of Henry Smith, John Dandy, and other monstrously cruel owners as "not typical." Menard stresses that "master–servant relationships were often friendly and sometimes affectionate and that servitude offered poor men a chance to gain entry into a society that offered great opportunities for advancement."[9]

These apologies for the chattel bond-labor system have not gone unchallenged. As for the contention that the life of the bond-laborers was better than it would have been if they had remained in England, that the work was not so hard in the tobacco plantations as that performed by agricultural laborers in England, there is more of assumption than substance in it. Edmund S. Morgan, on the basis of well-known English works on economic history, effectively maintains that the relatively easy regime of the farm worker in England utterly unsuited the English laborer for the unremitting round of heavy toil on the tobacco plantations.[10] Even McCormac's extreme analogy to the English debtors' prison loses much of its force when it is considered that the situation of the plantation bond-laborers was like a debtors' prison where the inmates of any age were regarded as minors, so far as their rights were concerned.

The more instructive comparison, that between the laborers in New England and those in the tobacco colonies in the seventeenth century, is almost totally ignored by apologists for the chattel bond-labor system.[11] But the late Richard B. Morris, in his exhaustively documented study *Government and Labor in Early America*, found that the treatment of bond-laborers was much more rigorous in the tobacco colonies than in New England. The contrast of the all-or-nothing dependence on the tobacco monoculture of the Chesapeake plantation economy, and the small independent farms of the varied, largely self-sufficient, New England economy was fundamental to the difference in day-to-day social relationships.[12] In the New England and Middle colonies, said Morris, the limited-term bond-laborers, who were relatively few in number, enjoyed close personal relationships with their masters, relationships that were normal to their occupations in crafts and household service; but in the plantation colonies, where the bond-laborers were "employed primarily in field work under the supervision of exacting overseers," master–servant relations were harsh.[13]

Without wanting to indict the entire planter class, Morris concluded: "Maltreatment of servants was most flagrant in the tobacco colonies." Not only did a large number of drunken and dissolute owners treat their bond-laborers with sadistic brutality, members of the Colony Council and county courts "set a poor example to their own communities in ruling with a rod of iron. . . . Such masters preferred to discipline their servants themselves rather than to bring them into court," says Morris. While only the most serious cases of maltreatment came to court, they serve to reveal the "fairly typical" life of the plantation bond laborer.[14]

My own study of the record affords more support to the views of Morris and Morgan cited here than to the apologists of the bond-labor system.

Appendix II-E

(*see Chapter 9, note 54*)

The population of England and Wales, which had grown by one-third in the first half of the seventeenth century, grew by only one-tenth in the second half.[1] In this last half of the century, the expansion of industrial production was based primarily on the increase in the mass of labor employed rather than on improved technology.[2] In consequence of the expansion of industrial employment, the "surplussed" agricultural workers found employment more easily than they had prior to the English Revolution.[3] The English military demand for manpower experienced two great surges at the end of the seventeenth and the beginning of the eighteenth centuries. England, traditionally a land without a large standing army, conscripted scores of thousands of men for military and naval duty in the War of the League of Augsburg (1689–97) and the War of the Spanish Succession (1702–13). Between 1698 and 1708, for instance, the number of English-speaking troops under arms was increased nearly fourfold, and the naval forces were nearly tripled.[4] Thus sectors of the population that had been a ready supply of plantation bond-laborers in England were needed elsewhere, as is made clear by Trevelyan's description of the methods employed to draft recruits for the continental armies of the Duke of Marlborough in the earliest years of the eighteenth century:

> ... armed raids of the press-gang [descended] on the folk of the port towns and neighboring villages. ... Criminal gangs were drafted wholesale; bounties sometime amounting to four pounds for each recruit tempted the needy to enlist. ... [Since] the country was prosperous and work abundant ... the naval press was abused for the purposes of the land service. ... Parish constables were to be given ten shillings for every person suitable for the press gang whom they produced before the authorities. Magistrates were instructed to hand over to recruiting officers persons who could show no means of supporting themselves.[5]

Already in 1667, a member of the House of Commons, Mr Garroway, had warned that emigration to Virginia would "in time drain us of people and will endanger our ruin."[6] In 1673, the author of *The Grand Concern of England*

Explained believed that the drain of emigrants from England had been made even more critical by the "two last great Plagues, the Civil War at Home, and the several wars with Holland, Spain and France [which] have destroyed several hundred thousands of men which lived among us."[7] Roger Coke argued that the drain of bond-laborers and other emigrant workers to the American plantations was seriously weakening England. His treatise, published in 1671, warned, "... we have opened a wide gap, and by all encouragement excited all the growing youth and industry of England which might preserve the trades we had herein, to betake them to those of the Plantations."[8] One of the most eminent voices cautioning against too much emigration of English labor was that of Sir William Petty. The "remote governments" of the American plantation colonies, according to Petty, "instead of being additions are really diminutions" of the national wealth of England. Far from favoring increased English emigration to America, Petty would have had the New England Pilgrims come home. "[A]s for the People of New England," he wrote, "I can but wish they were transplanted into *Old England* or Ireland."[9]

Appendix II-F

(*see Chapter 13, note 26*)

In April 1699, a joint committee of nine – three members of the Colony Council and six members of the House of Burgesses – was ordered to begin a complete revision of the Virginia laws.[1] Seven years later in June 1706, the new code was enacted into law on royal instruction. In the book of laws, however, the code is ascribed to October 1705, the date on which it was first passed by the Assembly.[2] It contains significant provisions relative to the establishment of racial oppression and the "white race," that are further noted in Chapter 13.

The instructions of the Commissioners of Trade and Plantations that first ordered the revision of the laws required that "if there bee anything in them, either in the matter or Stile which may bee fit to be retrenched or altered, you are to represent the same unto us, *with your opinion touching the said Laws.*"[3] Does a record of those opinions exist today? It seems reasonable to believe much light would be shed on that subject by the record of discussions and exchanges of dispatches and enclosures – the existence of which is a matter of record – that occurred within the committee, and in meetings of the Governor and Colony Council as well, and between the Virginia authorities and the government in England – if such records could be found. What was said by members of the Virginia committee or in the meetings held by the Commissioners of Trade and Plantations in England, or in the correspondence regarding those deliberations – some of which are specifically, but cryptically, alluded to in records that do exist?

This entire present work has been a rejection of the "unthinking decision" thesis coined by Winthrop D. Jordan. But where are the "thoughts" in this "revisall of the Lawes"? Somebody in the array of lawmakers and critics must have proposed that, after forty years, it was time to change the requirement that masters not "exceed the bounds of moderation in correcting" servants, and that if a servant were able to get to the justice of the peace and then to the next county court, "the servant shall have remedy for his grievances"; and, instead, to define "moderate correction" to mean that the master was not to "whip a christian white servant naked, without an order from the justice of the

272

peace," the offending master to be fined forty shillings payable to the servant.[4] Some "reviser" must have thought it necessary to provide that upon a second offense by a master in treatment of "servants (not being slaves)," the courts could order that the servant be taken from that master and sold at outcry.[5] Which member of the committee first took notice that in regard to freedom dues, "nothing in that nature ever [had been] made certain," and urged that they be enumerated specifically: "to every male servant, ten bushels of corn, thirty shillings in money (or the equivalent in goods), a gun worth at least twenty shillings; and to every woman servant, fifteen bushels of corn, forty shillings in money (or the equivalent in goods)"? In this case we do have evidence that the revisal was not an exercise in somnambulism. The Virginia Colony Council at the last minute proposed to amend the draft law, by providing a differentiation of the freedom dues to be paid to men and women bond-laborers.[6] But to whom did it occur to raise the question and by what argument? And, incidentally, who was it who successfully moved to strike out the words "at least" as proposed by the Colony Council, before the specification of the freedom dues to be required for women servants? What was the discussion that preceded the decision to include a totally new provision making any free Negro subject to a whipping of thirty lashes if he or she raised a hand against any "white" person?[7]

I shall not intrude here the details of my search for such substantive records, although I will gladly share that information with any scholar who might wish to join the hunt. A number of documents include references to meetings of the Lords of Trade and Plantations convened to consider the draft laws sent from Virginia for approval or disapproval. They note, among other relevant matters, the attendance of Virginia Colony Secretary Edmund Jennings, at their Lordships request, to explain and assist in the review of those proposed laws.[8] On 27 and 29 March 1704, Jennings did attend, and "presented to their Lordships his observations on the Collection of Laws."[9] Sir Sidney Godolphin (later Earl) Lord High Treasurer advised Virginia governor Nicholson on 12 December 1704 that over a period of several months, Jennings had diligently worked with the Lords of Trade and Plantations to complete the work of "Inspecting [and?] amending" the proposed revisions of the Virginia laws.[10] Reference is also found to communications with Virginia governors Andros,[11] Nicholson and Nott, but there are no particulars in those documents that might serve to reveal the thinking processes that produced the new set of laws. Sir Edward Northey first served as English Attorney-General from July 1701 to October 1707. Where are the opinions, if they exist at all, rendered by him regarding the proposed revisal of the Virginia laws? A sizable number of documents relating to the laws carry the notation "a Page inserted in the file to indicate that [the particular document]" had been "removed and filed elsewhere."[12] Where is "elsewhere"? Finally, do answers to some of these questions remain to be discovered in some family papers that my search at the Library of Congress did not turn up?

A collateral matter no less puzzling is this: Why has no historian I have studied even taken notice of this apparent gap in the records of that critical period of Virginia history?

The argument made in the present work – that the invention of the "white race" social control system was a deliberate course taken by the ruling plantation bourgeoisie – would, I suspect, be strengthened by the discovery of such records regarding the process of framing the new Virginia code. But the thesis does not depend upon such discovery.

Editor's Appendix G
A Guide to *The Invention of the White Race*, Volume II

Theodore W. Allen divides the thirteen chapters of *The Origin of Racial Oppression in Anglo-America* into four parts. Part One, "Labor Problems of the European Colonizing Powers," begins with an important chapter on "The Labor Supply Problem," in which Allen identifies the two common challenges faced by the European colonizing powers in the Americas on their path to what they perceived as "success": 1) securing an adequate supply of labor, and 2) establishing a system of social control. In both respects, the Anglo-American plantation bourgeoisie differed from other colonizing powers in ways that proved decisive for the invention of the "white race" (p. 3). Spain and Portugal had no surplus laboring population ready for export, but the population density in Peru and Mexico afforded them an adequate supply of labor. When Caribbean peoples were exterminated and the enslavement of the Indians of Brazil became problematic for the Spanish and the Portuguese, they turned to Africa (pp. 3–5). Engagé labor from France was used in St. Domingue as plantation labor at a very early stage, but this was high-wage labor of limited availability. Holland had no labor surplus for export; its main role was to supply plantation labor from Africa for existing plantation colonies. In contrast, England had a surplus of "necessitous poor" for export to the plantations that was cheaper than any alternative source accessible to English plantation enterprise prior to the 1670s (pp. 5–7).

Allen explains, "The conjunction of the matured colonizing impulse, the momentarily favorable geo-political constellation of powers, the English surplus of unemployed and underemployed labor, coupled with the particular native demographic and social factors as the English found them in Virginia, and the lack of direct English access to African labor sources, produced that most portentous and distinctive factor of English colonialism: *Of all the European colonizing powers in the Americas, only England used European workers as basic plantation workers.*" He also stresses that the uniqueness of labor in the Anglo-American plantation colonies came not from its chattel-labor form, nor from the fact that the supply of lifetime, hereditary bond-laborers was made up of non-Europeans – these were common throughout the plantation Americas. Rather, the peculiarity was in the way it was controlled. Specifically, in the social control system in continental Anglo-America: "1) all persons of any degree of non-European ancestry were excluded from the buffer social-control stratum; and 2) a major, indispensible, and decisive factor of the buffer social-control stratum maintained against the unfree proletarians was that it was made up of free proletarians and semi-proletarians" (pp. 12–13).

In Chapter 2, "English Background, with Anglo-American Variations Noted," Allen offers an instructive overview of the economic, social, and technological developments that propelled England toward colonization. He reviews the transition to capitalist agriculture; the economic slaughter of the leasehold and copyhold peasantry, despite their militant resistance; the transubstantiation of the laboring class from peasantry to proletariat; and the growth of a surplus population, which would become a cause for ruling-class concern and a theme for would-be colonialists. He discusses how, in England, a section of the freehold peasantry, the "yeomanry," was preserved to serve as the rank-and-file of the social control stratum – a status that carried privileges from which the propertyless, and poor people in general, were excluded – and he contrasts this with Anglo-America, where propertyless European-Americans were included in the social-control stratum and endowed with all its privileges (pp. 14–19).

In discussing "the labor question," Allen reviews the legislative attempt (1547–50) to reduce a portion of the propertyless class to slavery and the reasons for its failure including: 1) Ket's rebels' demand that "all bondmen be made free"; 2) the common-law principle against holding Christians in bondage; and 3) cost/benefit considerations, particularly the potential expense of administration and maintenance of a dual labor system in a period of labor surplus and falling wages. The balance was struck with the passage of the Statute of Artificers (1563), which remained the basic English labor law for more than two and a half centuries. The statute established that there would be no slavery, laborers would be paid wages, apprentices would be bound for seven years, and other workers would be bound by contract for one year at wages set by the magistrates. The problem presented by the massive indigent population was addressed by the Poor Law of 1601, which would remain in effect for more than three centuries. Overseers of the poor had to provide employment in parish workhouses for the "deserving" poor at piecework wages. The system was supported by the Poor Rate, a tax on persons of substance. The inmates were free to leave the workhouses for better oppor-tunities, including marriage. Allen emphasizes that, harsh as they were, the terms of these basic laws cannot be reconciled with the system of multi-year, unpaid chattel bondage imposed on English laborers in seventeenth-century colonial Anglo-America (pp. 19–26).

Regarding the oppression of women, Allen points out, "There was to be no reformation in the Reformation." Every man was still entitled to a subject wife, ruling-class men could still assume sexual privileges in relation to laboring-class women, women of the propertied classes were still hostages of their

property, and the wages of working women were set at about half that of
men. Allen again contrasts this with England's seventeenth-century Anglo-
American plantation colonies where the mass of the English laboring people
were denied even the right to marry and to form a traditional patriarchal family,
and where one sector of propertyless men was accorded sexual privileges over
all women of another sector of the propertyless population (pp. 27–9).

In Chapter 3, on "Euro-Indian Relations and the Problem of Social Control,"
Allen discusses various early attempts at European "social control" in Haiti
(Hispaniola), Cuba, Puerto Rico, Mexico, Peru, and Brazil, before turning to
Virginia. Of all the Iberio-American cases, Brazil most resembled the U.S.,
in that it was a continental colony (not an insular one), it exhibited little significant stratification, and it had a low population density. Any attempt of
the English plantation bourgeoisie to subjugate the Indians would face the
"Brazilian" problem, and in the early years the English simply did not have
the preponderance of military force required for this task. Allen writes, "With
regard to establishing social control, the Anglo-American continental bourgeoisie faced the 'Brazilian' problem: a continental people without a *cacique*
class" (pp. 31–4).

He details how the Powhatan population living in the vicinity of Jamestown
were well provisioned and even had enough supplies that they could share
with starving colonists in the early years of the Virginia Company. In the
first decade or two, the English in Jamestown also lacked the force that the
horse-riding conquistadors used in Mexico and Peru "against the indigenous
peoples upon whom they made war." Virginia, like Brazil, was inhabited by a
non-stratified society and presented similar difficulties for the European colonizing power: the native population could not be surrounded or exterminated
(as in the island colonies), and they could not be brought under the degree
of administrative control required for the normal pursuit of labor exploitation. Some eight or nine decades later, the English on the southern seaboard
were better armed and adequately supplied with horses and trade goods. By
then, however, other developments had foreclosed that option: the commitment to the soil-exhausting tobacco monoculture, which tended to destabilize
relations with Indian tribal society along the colony's expanding borders; the
development of profitable fur-trading relations with Indian tribes beyond the
frontier; and very importantly, the dependence upon neighboring Indian tribes
for the capture and return of runaway bond-laborers (pp. 35–6).

Allen points out that despite their early difficulties, "the English had a
fundamental potential advantage over the Indians from the beginning due
to the discrepancy in the development of productive forces and productivity of labor" (p. 36). Regarding Native Americans, Allen discusses three
important aspects of relations in this period: 1) resistance by the Indian bond-
laborers, principally by running away, a resistance which merged sometimes
with that of African and European bond-laborers; 2) the necessity to maintain
friendly, or "treaty," Indians in the buffer role, in the first instance between the
Anglo-American colonies and the more remote "hostile," or foreign-allied,

tribes; and in the second instance, against the escape of African-American bond-laborers beyond the Anglo-American "frontier"; and 3) with the institution of the "white race" system of social control, the key necessity of preserving "white-skin" privileges of laboring-class European-Americans *vis-à-vis* all non-European-Americans." (p. 41) After the historic transformation related to the invention of the white race and the plantation bourgeoisie's drawing of the color line, the "fate of the Indians under the principle of racial slavery and white supremacy" would be "controlled by twin parameters: non-enslavability and non-assimilability" (p. 45).

In Part Two, "The Plantation of Bondage," Allen opens with Chapter 4, "The Fateful Addiction to 'Present Profit,'" which discusses the "crucial significance" of the Virginia Company to the eventual development of chattel bond-servitude and, later, to racial slavery. He reviews the three periods of the Virginia Company, beginning with its original charter, which affirmed that all colonists "shall have ... all liberties, franchises and immunities of free denizens and natural subjects" of England (pp. 49–51). He also discusses the "starving time" (p. 52); the non-existence of chattel bond-servitude in the early years (p. 55); the turn to tobacco production, followed by the crisis of over-production (p. 56); the "first alleged instance of a worker being treated like chattel" (p. 58); intermediate forms of bond-servitude, as in the case of convicts, apprentices, "maids-for-wives," and the "Duty boys," in which neither the Company nor individual entrepreneurs had to pay wages (pp. 64–9); sex ratios and the impact of the chattelization of labor on family formation (pp. 69–70); the higher cost of labor in Virginia as compared to England (pp. 72–3); and Captain Thomas Nuce's plan "to chaunge the Conditione of Tenants into servants." Allen emphasizes, "The typical form of labor in Virginia at the beginning of 1622 was that of the tenant," most of whom were "Tenants at halves." But, by the spring of 1623, conditions had changed significantly and "Alderman Johnson would declare that the Colony officers had all desired to reduce their tenants to servants" (p. 74).

In Chapter 5, "The Massacre of the Tenantry," Allen begins by explaining the bourgeoisie's interest in lowering labor costs and how the first requisite for a successful offensive against the rights of the laboring classes was the maintenance of social control (p. 75). He then analyzes four special conditions that favored the aims of the colony elite: 1) the appallingly high death rate, 2) the Indians' resistance to aggressive English encroachment upon the land, 3) intensified economic pressure on the laboring people in England that predisposed more workers to consider emigration, and 4) the "complete and utter dependence of the colony upon England for supplies." He emphasizes that the dependence enhanced the power of the bourgeoisie, including the Governor and Council members, the plantation owners, the Cape Merchant, and the free-trading "magazine" captain (pp. 76–8).

In discussing the emergence of the colony elite, Allen explains how the "headright" principle, which promised compensation (often with a patent on 50 acres) "per head" for transporting, or agreeing to transport, people to Virginia, "tended to push the contradiction to the limit in terms of maximum profit for the capitalist and minimum provisions for the laborer." Concentration of land ownership also increased, and the elite used their positions in government for special advantage and to start "renting out" tenants (pp. 78–9).

In August 1619, the colony authorities exchanged "twenty-odd" African men and women for provisions for the Dutch ship on which these new arrivals had come. Their status was indeterminate as to conditions of employment. Allen points out that this was "consistent with a policy of reducing labor costs by inducing an oversupply of laborers relative to the amount of food that would be available to them" (p. 81). He also notes that it was only in September 1619 that a contract was signed which would have required a laborer to repay the cost of one's transportation from England to Virginia by an unpaid term of servitude and that person did not go (p. 99). By November 1619, the Colony Council caused more than fifty of the Company's tenants-at-halves to be "rented out," in violation of their contracts and over the tenants' objections (pp. 79–80).

Previously, the Governor of Virginia, Samuel Argall, had been accused by the Virginia Company of a criminal offense for "setting over" tenants to his own personal use without their consent. By 1621, however, the Virginia Colony Council endorsed and sent to London a proposal to reduce the status of tenants to "servants." The Company signified its concurrence with the proposal. Edwin Sandys, Treasurer and Chief Officer of the Virginia Company, called the tenants-at-halves status an absurdity and said that what Virginia needed was "a multitude of apprentices" (pp. 57–58, 81–82, 95).

On March 22, 1622, the Powhatan Indians under Opechancanough, fearing that the English "would dispossess them of this Country," mounted what was at the time "the strongest effort ever made ... to halt the Anglo-American occupation of Indian lands." On the first day alone, one third of the Anglo population of North America was killed. Within the next year, more would die from privation than died in the initial assault. Of the survivors, two-thirds were not fit for work (pp. 84–5).

In the aftermath of the attack, and concerned about additional attacks, the Colony authorities forbade game hunting and the planting of corn near dwellings. The settlement perimeter was constricted, inhabitants were uprooted, half the landholders were dead and could offer no places for tenants to stay nor wages for day-laborers. Corn supplies were limited and a monopoly on corn was established. The price of corn went up eight-fold in one year, while the price of tobacco, the colonists' only money, was cut in half. Tenants faced insupportable debt and reportedly could not feed themselves three months out of the year. For the employed wage-worker, a tobacco wage in real terms was two-thirds what it was in England (pp. 90–2).

The situation was different, however, for the Colony elite, particularly for those who had cornered the market in corn. They were the debt-holders of the impoverished tenants, and they embarked on a scheme whereby workers in general were reduced to unpaid, long-term bond-labor. The laboring classes were dependent on the bourgeoisie for corn, so they were "compelled to submit to the condition dictated by the plantation bourgeoise: the status of ... bond-laborers." By the spring of 1622, servants' contracts began to appear that contained a new unprecedented provision allowing the employer to dispose of the servant to the employers' "heirs and assigns," and by 1623, efforts to reduce tenants to servants were common (pp. 95–6).

In Chapter 6, "Bricks without Straw: Bondage, but No Intermediate Stratum," Allen makes the extremely important point that "Pre-capitalist bond-labor was tied by a two-way bond: the workers could not go away; but, equally, the master could not send them away." This two-way bondage was a "relationship, which was essential to feudalism" but "inimical to capitalism." In general, the bourgeoisie would seek "to replace the two-way bondage of feudalism with the two-way freedom of the capitalist relation of production" in which the "capitalist was free to fire the workers, and the workers were free to quit the job." In Virginia, however, the plantation bourgeoisie dealt with this contradiction by establishing a one-way bondage, in which the laborer could not sever the tie to the capitalist simply by his own volition, but the capitalist could sever the tie with the worker (pp. 97–8).

Between January and June 1622, the Virginia Company established a standard patent form regarding laborers transported by the colony authorities that guaranteed protection not only to the original patentee, but also to his "heires and Assigns." Within four years, the legal right of masters to "assign" or bequeath their laborers would be formally established. Allen discusses certain early incidents that in retrospect "appear as preconditioning for the reduction of laborers to chattels," and he finds that in 1622 and 1623 it was "established as the general condition for immigrant workers." An analysis of a score of entries in the records of that time shows how the chattel aspect of bond-servitude was designed to adapt that contradictory form to capitalist categories of commodity exchange and free flow of capital. Overall, as Allen points out earlier, "by far the greater number of European immigrants arriving in the southern colonies came as bond-laborers" (pp. 98–9).

Allen then describes how, despite the fact that "labor relations was a settled question before the landing at Jamestown," the "Anglo-American plantation bourgeoisie seized on the devastation brought about by the Powhatan attack of 22 March 1622, to execute a plan for the chattelization of labor in Virginia Colony" and how "from that seeding came the plantation of bondage" (pp. 100–1).

Allen also offers rebuttals to arguments that he refers to as "History's False Apologetic for Chattel Bond-Servitude," including the "*quid pro quo*" ratio-nale and the "unreflecting adaptation" argument. The first position suggests that there was a shortage of poor laborers in Virginia and an abundance of them in England, so that between English laborers who wanted employment and plantation investors who wanted to replace costly tenants and wage labor-ers a "*quid pro quo* was agreed, according to which the employer paid the £6 cost of transportation from England and in exchange the worker agreed to be a chattel bond-laborer for a term of five years or so." Allen responds that the "payment of passage" was "a convenient excuse for a policy aimed at reducing labor costs" in a manner "consistent with the free flow of capital." He cites the work of Abbot E. Smith, a specialist in this field, who concluded that the "four or five years bondage was far more than they [the laborers] justly owed for the privilege of transport," and he cites his own finding (based on available production rates and costs of tobacco) that a laborer in one year, "would have repaid more than seven times his or her £6 transportation cost." In response to the second position, that bond-servitude was an adaptation and was not very different from pre-existing forms of English labor relations such as apprenticeships, Allen points out that it was qualitatively different because it was a one-way bondage in which laborers were reduced to chattels (pp. 100–3).

By 1638, Virginia Colony Secretary Richard Kemp reported to London that "Of hundreds of people who arrive in this colony yearly, scarce any but are brought in as merchandize to make sale of" (p. 108).

In Part Three, "The Road to Rebellion," Allen begins Chapter 7, "Bond-labor: Enduring . . ." with a description of the pre–Bacon's Rebellion period and how "the insubstantiality of the intermediate stratum, the oppressive conditions of the bond-laborers and their resistance to those conditions constitute the most significant social factors that contributed to that pivotal historic event called Bacon's Rebellion." The resistance challenged the economic basis of society – "the chattel bond-labor form of master-servant relations" – and, significantly, "the record of this period of labor history shows no 'white-worker' component" (p. 119).

Of the 92,000 European immigrants brought to Virginia and Maryland between 1607 and 1682, more than three-fourths were chattel bond-laborers, the great majority of them English. In 1676, Governor William Berkeley estimated about 1,500 European chattel bond-laborers were arriving yearly, "the majority English, with a few Scots and fewer Irish." Allen discusses the coercive nature of most transcontinental labor recruitment and that few immigrants were whole-hearted volunteers, arriving with written contracts for their services. Many were kidnapped by a combination of deception and brute force, some were ordinary convicts, and still others were English, Irish, and Scots prisoners taken in rebellion and exiled, under pain of death, by whatever authority happened to rule in England at the time (pp. 119–20).

Allen also explains that plantation bond-labor pool was also supplemented from domestic sources. These included, beginning about 1660, Indian bond laborers who were drawn from the general population. For a brief time in the 1670s and 1680s, Indian bond-laborers played "a considerable role in the economy of the tobacco colonies" (pp. 122–3). The main domestic source of bond-labor in the plantation colonies was by the imposition of hereditary bond-servitude on African-Americans under the system of racial slavery and white supremacy.

However, in the seventeenth century, most of the plantation laborers were limited-term bond-laborers, a category composed mostly of European-American immigrants. Life expectancy of bond-servants was low, particularly in the early decades, when most didn't survive their first year. The census of 1624–25 showed a total colony population of some 1,218, which included 507 "servants," of whom 23 were "Negroes." In the early period, and increasingly so in the 1660s, there is evidence of a desire of some employers to develop this source of added unpaid labor time by subjecting African-Americans to lifetime hereditary bond-servitude. Overall, Allen points out that "the capitalist plantation owners relied almost totally upon increased exertion by the laborers to more than double the annual tobacco output" in the fifty years from the dissolution of the Virginia Company to the onset of Bacon's Rebellion (pp. 123–4).

Allen then spends twenty pages documenting the main forms of oppression of plantation bond-laborers. In this section, utilizing his command of primary sources, he draws special attention to the "hardship and brutality to which the chattels were subjected" and to "the special oppression of women bond-laborers." He treats such topics as: increasing the length of servitude; special opportunities for securing extra servitude; the costs of recapture, prosecution, and corporal punishment; denial of family life and women's exposure to special oppression; how "bastardy" laws compounded gender and class oppression; exploiting the presumption of bondage; cutting labor costs when no wages were paid; and the owner's brutal pursuit of higher output per worker (pp. 125–45). He also chastises historians who "justify the bond-labor system" as an "on the whole benign adaptation to the colonial environment" and calls attention to "the documented brutality and hardship to which the chattels were subjected" (p. 146).

In Chapter 8, "… and Resisting," Allen documents "instances of self-activation of bond-laborers as molders of their own fate." Again, he relies on his extraordinary familiarity with primary sources to discuss such forms of resistance as suicide and assault, stealth and insurrection in response to inadequate diet, and "defiant solace" in the form of fornication. He also discusses how "chattel bond-servitude, which was the condition of the overwhelming majority of women arriving in the tobacco colonies, gave an added dimension to male supremacism." It was a "distinctive blend of class and gender oppression." Allen takes note of 367 court cases related to gender oppression and offers some analysis of the 304 cases he found that involved "fornication" or "bastardy." He also discusses free laboring people assisting runaway bond-laborers. Of profound importance is Allen's finding that "there was a considerable degree of collaboration of African-Americans and European-Americans in a common endeavor to escape" (esp. pp. 148, 154, 158).

Allen describes how, early on, the plantation bourgeoisie expressed its disposition to deny equal rights to African-Americans through Acts of the General Assembly. Very importantly, however, he stresses, "The evidence … clearly indicates that this purpose of the ruling class did not represent the desire or attitude of the European-American bond-laborers as a whole, nor indeed of the common run of European-Americans in general." At the same time, however, he considers it "not surprising that the explicitly anti-Negro tenor of these laws would find some echo in the attitude of ruled-over European-Americans, bond and free." He found "those instances to have been extremely few, however, in comparison to the record of solidarity of European-American and African-American bond-laborers, and in comparison to the readiness of free laboring-class European-Americans to make common cause with African-American fugitives from bond-labor" (pp. 161–2).

Overall, Allen concludes that "the attitude of the laboring-class European-Americans stood in sharp contrast to the succession of enactments whereby the plantation bourgeoisie pressed for the lifetime hereditary bond-servitude of African-American bond-laborers; and for the circumscription of the rights, and the ultimate practical proscription of free African-Americans." He then draws two "fair" and extremely important conclusions:

> First, "the white race" – supra-class unity of European-Americans in opposition to African-Americans – did not and could not have then existed. Secondly, the invention of the white race at the beginning of the eighteenth century can in no part be ascribed to demands by European-American laboring people for privileges *vis-à-vis* African-Americans. (p. 162)

In Chapter 9, "The Insubstantiality of the Intermediate Stratum," Allen begins by discussing the fact that the Virginia colony evolved under the direct rule of a very tiny elite. In the fifteen years leading up to Bacon's Rebellion, it was "less than four hundred men, probably numbering no more than two hundred at any one time," who were owners of an average of 4,200 acres of land each. He describes the inadequacy of the militia for sustained service due to lack of corn and the strenuous objections of men to being drawn away from their tobacco crop. He also discusses how, even by 1680, there was no constabulary, no army except the inadequate militia, and only thirty-five Anglican priests amid a population of 40,000 to 50,000. His point, he writes, "is to emphasize the absence of an effective social control stratum" and that there was "in Virginia no intermediate social control stratum based on a secure yeoman class such as had been preserved in England" (pp. 163–4).

Allen sees a basic cause for the failure of the plantation elite to establish a viable system of social control in the seventeenth century in the workings of the tobacco monocultural economy. He then undertakes a statistical analysis that shows a "marked tendency toward the concentration of land," capital, and laborers on the plantations of the colonial elite (pp. 165–8).

He next discusses threats of Dutch seaborne incursions during the Second and Third Anglo-Dutch Wars (1665–67 and 1672–74), and explains how the English bourgeoisie finally secured direct access to African labor at the end of the Second Dutch War, concluded in the Treaty of Breda in 1667. Five years later, the Royal African Company was established, which, within less than forty years, made English merchants the pre-eminent suppliers of African bond-labor to the Western Hemisphere (pp. 168–9).

Allen writes, "Finally, the plantation bourgeoisie was brought within reach of the realization of the vision foreshadowed in a number of laws already enacted, of enrichment through the imposition of lifetime hereditary bond-servitude of Africans and African-Americans." The "anticipated reduction in labor costs would have been desirable for the employing class at any time, but as the end of the seventeenth century neared, it appeared to offer the bourgeoisie both a way of evading the unresolvable contradictions between monoculture and diversity, and a significant easing of the contention between English and continental branches of the business with respect to profits from low-priced tobacco." Virginia Governor Thomas Lord Culpeper would later stress this in a letter urging that the Royal African Company moderate its prices for the sale of lifetime bond-laborers in Virginia." "[I]n regard to the infinite profit that comes … I conceive it is for his Majesty's Interest full as much as the Countrys, or rather much more, to have Blacks as cheap as possible in Virginia" (p. 172).

Allen comments that it was "a conscious decision, not an unthinking one" by Virginia's plantation bourgeoisie to opt for monoculture and chattel bond-servitude. However, "a lack of capacity to command had made it impossible for the plantation bourgeoisie to impose the necessary social discipline on free and middle-rank tobacco farmers." In this setting, the Virginia ruling elite was considering using African labor when it found itself three thousand miles from home with no yeoman buffer between it and a people of whom, according to Governor William Berkeley in 1676, "six parts of seaven at least, are Poore, Endebted, Discontented and Armed" (pp. 175–6).

In Chapter 10, "The Status of African-Americans," Allen reviews his four-pronged definition of racial oppression and points out that, in Chapters 8 and 9, he had argued inferentially that "'the white race,' and thus a system of racial oppression, did not exist, and could not have existed, in the seventeenth-century tobacco colonies." In Chapter 8, that conclusion was based on evidence of class solidarity of laboring-class European-Americans with African-Americans, and the consequent absence of an all-class coalition of European-Americans directed against African-Americans. In Chapter 9, the thesis was linked up with the lack of a substantial intermediate buffer social-control stratum (p. 177).

In Chapter 10, he again utilizes Virginia records that directly bear "on the actual social status of African-Americans in those decades." Allen's position is that the records "compel the conclusion that the relative social status of African-Americans and European-Americans in that 'Volatile Society' can be determined to have been indeterminate." It was indeterminate because it was being fought out in the context of the great social stresses of high mortality, the monocultural economy, impoverishment, and an extremely unbalanced gender ratio – all of which were based on, or derived from, "the abnormal system of chattel bond-servitude." The critical moment of that social struggle arrived with Bacon's Rebellion of 1676–77, which posed the question of who should rule. The answer "would not only determine the status of

African-Americans," it would also "install the monorail of Anglo-American historical development, white supremacy" (p. 178).

Allen points out that "The reduction of the almost totally English labor force from tenants and wage-laborers to chattel bond-servitude in the 1620s was indeed a negation of previously existing laws and customs, but it was imposed by one set of colonists on another set of colonists," and it was not "an act of racial oppression." Other efforts were made at establishing two distinct categories of servitude, limited term and lifetime. Allen discusses one of the better-known such cases, that of John Punch. From his analysis of this case, he concludes that while "it showed a readiness of at least some of the plantation elite to equate 'being a negro' with being a lifetime bond-laborer," it also showed that the development of social policy along this line was obstructed by several factors. He cited "institutional inertia presented by English common law, by the historic retreat from the slavery gambit of 1547 in the wake of Ket's Rebellion, and by the deep-rooted principles of Christian fellowship." He also cited the opposition of "African-Americans, both bond-laborers and non-bond-laborers, with the general support – certainly without the concerted opposition – of European-American bond-laborers, and other free but poor laboring people, determined by a sense of common class interest" (pp. 178–80).

Regarding seventeenth-century African-Americans, he goes into great detail to examine how they exercised marriage rights, exhibited social mobility, held significant land-holdings, owned European-American bond-laborers, and manifested many forms of resistance. He also discusses Evangelical questions and objections, and opposition from members of the propertied class to racial oppression of African-Americans (pp. 181–94).

One of his most important treatments concerns the case of Elizabeth Key. The case "presented a direct confrontation between the desire among plantation owners to raise their rate of profit by imposing lifetime hereditary servitude on African-Americans, and an African-American's right to freedom on the basis of Christian principles and English common law." Elizabeth, the child of a European-American father and an African-American mother, was scheduled to complete her term of servitude when the estate to which she was bonded sought to impose lifetime bond-servitude status upon her on the grounds that this "was the condition of her mother." This argument contradicted the English common-law principle of *partus sequitur patrem* – the condition of the child follows the condition of the father. A jury found Elizabeth Key to be entitled to her freedom in 1656. That decision was also sustained on the traditional English principle that her Christian baptism and rearing barred her from being held as a lifetime bond-laborer. Allen points out that if those principles prevailed in all circumstances, they would have prevented the establishment of racial slavery. In 1662, the Virginia General Assembly took a different course and established the principle of *partus sequitur ventrem* (condition follows through the mother) (pp. 194–9).

Allen concludes, "Given the English superstructural obstacles and the already marked resistance of African-Americans to lifetime hereditary bondage, a rapid and large addition of African bond-laborers to the population in the 1670s would certainly tend to reduce the effectiveness of the already weak social-control stratum" (p. 199).

In Part Four, "Rebellion and Reaction," Chapter 11, "Rebellion – and Its Aftermath," Allen focuses on the later, civil-war phase of Bacon's Rebellion from April 1676 to January 1677. Bacon's Rebellion began as a dispute between the colonial elite, led by Governor William Berkeley, and the sub-elite, led by Nathaniel Bacon, over the rate of expropriation of Indian lands. Allen explains that it was not primarily an anti-Indian war, although that was the tenor of the first call to arms. But he shows that the "lesson of history" to be drawn from the anti-Indian phase of Bacon's Rebellion is clearly still relevant – the "bourgeois eye looks upon progress and genocide indifferently, as incidental aspects of the process of the accumulation of capital; the anti-Indian phase of Bacon's Rebellion was merely another example of that lesson." He adds that the U.S. government that subsequently brought the American Indians to the verge of extinction should "make restitution" and "the struggle for justice in this respect merges with the general struggle against white supremacist racial oppression" (pp. 204–5).

In his treatment of the civil-war stage of Bacon's Rebellion, Allen pays special attention to the bond-laborer component of the rebels and their demand for freedom from bondage. He highlights Captain Thomas Grantham's account of how he was confronted by "foure hundred English and Negroes in Armes who were much dissatisfied"; how "some were for shooting mee, and others were for cutting me in peeces"; and how, in the final stages of the struggle, he confronted "Eighty Negroes and Twenty English which would not deliver their Armes" (pp. 205–16, esp. 211, 214).

Allen writes that Grantham's testament has significance "beyond exaggeration." In Virginia, 128 years before William Lloyd Garrison was born, "laboring-class African-Americans and European-Americans had fought side by side for the abolition of slavery" and "provided the supreme proof that the white race did not then exist" (pp. 214–15).

In the wake of Bacon's Rebellion, major destabilizing factors persisted. Allen cited "the train of overproduction, mass impoverishment, and indebtedness produced by the tobacco monoculture," the plantation bourgeoisie's failure to diversify the economy, the increase in the bond-labor population, the continued lack of an effective intermediate buffer social-control stratum, and the "unfeasibility of maintaining social control in Virginia by means of the English army" (p. 217).

Allen's population analysis is of particular interest. He points out that in 1671 some 8,000 tithable individuals (roughly 6,000 European-American and 2,000 African-American) out of a total of 15,000 in Virginia were bond-laborers. The total population at that time was about 40,000. Approximately 30,000 European-Americans came to the Chesapeake region between 1680 and 1700, and Allen estimates that 24,000 were bond laborers. In "a roughly equivalent period, 1674–1700, around 6,000 African bond-laborers were imported." He emphasizes, "Not only was the number of bond laborers increasing, it was increasing as a total number of the tithables, and doubtless of the population" (pp. 217–22, esp. 218).

In Chapter 12, "The Abortion of the 'White Race' Social Control System in the Anglo-Caribbean," Allen explains that the English plantation bourgeoisie in the continental colonies and in the Caribbean "opted to base their ventures on chattel bond-labor, at first European, but – sooner in the Caribbean, later in the continental plantation colonies – mainly on African bond-labor." Then, in both cases, "the ruling class sought to establish social control on the principle of racial oppression of non-Europeans." He emphasizes that the decision to deny "any degree of social mobility" to Africans and African-Americans – the hallmark of racial oppression – "was driven simply and directly by the greater rate of profit to be had by the employment of lifetime hereditary bond-laborers – provided a cost-effective system of social control could be established." Ultimately, however, "different ways of maintaining ruling-class social control would be required" and the class struggle "would produce forms of social control in the Anglo-Caribbean colonies … that diverged in historically significant ways from that which was adopted in continental Anglo-America" (pp. 223–4).

Allen describes how in the British West Indies the English made efforts to reduce natives of the Caribbean to plantation bond-servitude, but the class-undifferentiated Caribbean tribes were not deminated by "casiques" and they responded with warlike resistance. The English occupied Barbados in 1625, and at first, it imitated Virginia as a tobacco colony using bond-laborers, mainly English and Scots. In the 1640s, with the aid of Dutch capital, techniques, and markets, and Dutch suppliers of African laborers, Barbados began its development as the prototype of the British West Indies sugar-plantation colony, of which Jamaica, captured from the Spanish in 1655, was to become the largest. However, even before the transition to sugar, there was rebellion. In 1634, the island was reportedly in a state of emergency over a bond-laborer revolt plot. Between 1675 and 1701, there were four major revolt plots, including a 1692 "negro conspiracy." There were at least seven separate slave revolts in the English islands between 1640 and 1713 in which Europeans and Africans were killed. Thousands of military prisoners were sent to Barbados as bond-laborers along with ordinary felons and vagabonds. In 1649, they devised a plot to take over the island. By that time, runaway African bond-laborers had established maroon settlements in outlying areas. In Jamaica, 1,500 African bond-laborers left behind in the Spanish evacuation of 1655 established themselves in the central mountains. These free, independent Jamaican maroons maintained a separate set of communities until 1796 (pp. 224–6).

Official notice was taken of the tendency of bond-laborers to make common cause regardless of ancestry, and this condition was general in the West Indies. Allen quotes military historian John W. Fortescue that by the end of the seventeenth century "the old system of defense by white servants had broken down." Allen adds, this "applies also to the failure of the attempt to establish a system of social control in the Anglo-Caribbean by an English-style yeoman militia of European former bond-laborers" (p. 231).

In "relation to the question of social control and invention of the white race," Allen explains, "the British West Indies differed from the continental plantation colonies in five significant ways." First, "because of the narrow absolute limits of land area, and the relatively high capital costs of sugar pro-duction, the West Indies was especially inhospitable to non-capitalist farmers or tenants" and the capital requirements for becoming a sugar planter were beyond the means of former bond-laborers. In time, "the propertyless major-ity of the European population of the British West Indies would be assigned to a special category, socially and economically *marginalized* as 'poor whites.'" Second, in the West Indies, the attempt to establish a "white race" social-control system was seriously complicated by a substantial Irish presence. Coming directly from the heightened racial oppression in Ireland, "the Irish bond-laborers in the British West Indies were often disposed to ally their cause with any challenge to British authority" including challenges "made by African bond-laborers." Third, the English military and naval forces were regularly stationed in the West Indies. Fourth, the predominance of persons of African descent in the population of the West Indies made it impossible to exclude them from the intermediate stratum. Euro-Caribbeans were a minor-ity in the Caribbean before the end of the seventeenth century. Fifth, the "reliance upon persons of African descent in the skilled trades and the inter-nal economy led to the emergence of the 'free colored' as the predominant element in the middle class" (p. 226). By the 1830s, "free blacks and color-eds" owned 70,000 of the approximately 310,000 bond-laborers in Jamaica (p. 235).

"What most distinguishes the story of both the Irish and the Anglo-Caribbean histories … from that of continental Anglo-America," Allen writes, "is that Catholic Emancipation in Ireland, and the admittance of 'free colored' to full citizenship rights in the British West Indies were the culmination of the growing economic and political strength of the Catholic bourgeoisie in Ireland, in the one case, and of the 'free colored' population of the British West Indies, in the other." In the United States, in contrast, "free African-Americans were never acknowledged as a legitimate part of the body politic," and "their very right to remain in the United States was officially and unof-ficially questioned" (p. 238).

He next seeks to offer an explanation for that dramatic difference and its "larger historical significance" (p. 238).

In Chapter 13, "The Invention of the White Race – and the Ordeal of America," Allen explains that Virginia's free and bond laborers were fight-ing in Bacon's Rebellion for "an end to the version [of capitalism] imposed by the plantation elite, based on chattel bond-servitude and engrossment of the land." They sought freedom from bondage and improved opportunities to become independent farmers.

However, just as the overthrow of the tenantry had cleared the ground for the institution of chattel bond-servitude in the 1620s, so did the defeat of the rebels in Bacon's Rebellion clear the way for the establishment of the system of life-time hereditary chattel bond-servitude. The relative power of the plantation elite increased because of the continuation of their large landholdings and their advantages in bidding for lifetime bond-laborers. (p. 239)

After Bacon's Rebellion, the ruling class turned to a system of control in which, according to historian Gary B. Nash, "among upper- and lower-class whites .... Race became the primary badge of status." Allen addresses why that happened (p. 240).

He contests the argument that this "was the *result* of the shift" to African labor as the main labor supply source and points out that the same shift occurred in the British West Indies with far different results. He contests the argument that it "was the *result* of the reduction of African-Americans to life-time hereditary bond-servitude" and cites the solidarity of "the English and Negroes in Armes" in Bacon's Rebellion "at a time when the great majority of African-Americans were held as lifetime bond-laborers." He notes that "23 percent of the African bond-laborers in Jamaica on the eve of Emancipation were owned by persons of one degree or other of African ancestry" (p. 240).

Allen counters that rather than this "white race" consciousness being the result, "it was only because 'race' consciousness superseded class-consciousness that the continental plantation bourgeoisie was able to achieve and maintain the degree of social control necessary for proceeding with capital accumulation on the basis of chattel bond-labor" (p. 240).

He recognizes that the "plantation bourgeoisie and those engaged in the labor supply trade favored the imposition of perpetual bondage on the plan-tation labor force ... as simply prudent business practice" designed to keep down labor costs and that it was also "understood that ... success depended on establishing and maintaining an intermediate stratum for social control pur-poses" (p. 241). But, he asks, "Why, then, were *free* Negroes and 'mulattos' to be excluded from that stratum in the pattern-setting continental plantation colony of Virginia?" (p. 241).

He notes how in May 1723 the Virginia Assembly passed "An Act directing the trial of Slaves ... and ... for the better government of Negroes, Mulattos, and Indian, bond or free," which provided that "no free negro, mulatto, or indian whatsoever, shall have any vote at the election." The reason for that act, according to Governor William Gooch, was "to fix a perpetual Brand upon Free Negros & Mulattos" (pp. 241–2).

Allen responds emphatically, "Surely that was no 'unthinking decision'! Rather, it was a deliberate act by the plantation bourgeoisie; it proceeded from a conscious decision in the process of establishing a system of racial oppres-sion, even though it meant repealing an electoral principle that had existed in Virginia for more than a century" (p. 242). Gooch's letter of explanation for the decision was "disingenuous" to Allen who then refutes it point by point. Allen emphasizes that the "difference between the English plantation bourgeoisie in the British West Indies and the continental plantation colonies with regard to the status of free persons of some degree of African ancestry ... was rooted in the objective fact that in the West Indies there were *too few* laboring-class Europeans to embody an adequate petit bourgeoisie, while in the continental colonies there were *too many* to be accommodated in the ranks of that class" (p. 244).

He further explains that the plantation bourgeoisie "assumed the bond-laborers would resist in every way they could, including maroonage and revolt," and they knew they needed "a substantial intermediate buffer social-control stratum." The ruling elite was a "small cohort" and needed "a substantial intermediate buffer social control stratum to stand between it and great disturbances, or even another rebellion" (p. 244).

Allen reviews historical research by Jackson Turner Main and Aubrey C. Land and finds that in eighteenth-century Virginia "somewhat less than 50 percent of the total adult white male population were landowners" and of these "one-fourth worked the land without the employment of bond-labor." Thus, "about 60 percent of the adult white male population were not owners of bond-laborers, but were put in competition with employers of bond-labor" (pp. 246–7).

Allen maintains that the reason for the "proscription of the free African-American can be explained ... by the fact that, despite its sway over the 'yeomanry,' the gentry could *not* 'safely ignore'" the laboring and non-bond-holding European-Americans "because their bond-labor system was antithetical to the interests, not only of African-American bond-laborers, but also of all the rest of the population that did not own bond-laborers." The laboring-class European-Americans had shown "their solidarity with the African-American bond-laborers in Bacon's Rebellion," "demonstrated their understanding of their interests," and had sympathy for their situation (p. 248). How was such "laboring class solidarity to be undone?"

The answer that the ruling class decided upon was clear. "Instead of social mobility, European-Americans who did not own bond-laborers were to be asked to be satisfied with simply the presumption of liberty, the birthright of the poorest person in England; and with the right of adult males who owned sufficient property to vote for candidates for office who were almost invariably owners of bond-laborers." The stability of the system of capital-ist agriculture based on lifetime hereditary bond-servitude "depended on the ability of the ruling elite to induce the non-'yeoman' European-Americans to settle for this counterfeit of social mobility" and on their ability "to establish a new birthright for not only Anglos but for every Euro-American, the 'white' identity" (p. 248).

Historians have detailed how, toward the end of the seventeenth century, there occurred "a marked tendency to promote a pride of race among the members of every class of white people." This was the real reason for the proscriptions against free African-Americans. "The exclusion of free

African-Americans from the intermediate stratum was a corollary of the establishment of 'white' identity as a mark of social status." If, as Allen explains,

> the mere presumption of liberty was to serve as a social status for masses of
> European-Americans without real prospects of upward social mobility, and yet
> induce them to abandon their opposition to the plantocracy and enlist them actively,
> or at least passively, in keeping down the Negro bond-laborer with whom they had
> made solidarity in the course of Bacon's Rebellion, the presumption of liberty had
> to be denied to free African-Americans. (p. 249)

The Virginia General Assembly showed how this was to be done. It "deliberately stuffed the 'racial' distinction with anomalous privileges to make it look
like the real thing, promotion to a higher social class." The distinction "was
even emphasized for European-American chattel bond-laborers." The owner
of an African-American bond-laborer "could legally use or abuse his African-
American bond-laborers, or dispose of them ... as a matter of course," but by
a 1691 law it "was forbidden to set them free." The revised Virginia code of
1705 "took pains to specify unprecedented guarantees for the European 'christian white' limited-term bond-laborers." Freedom dues were enumerated with
specificity and included "to every male servant, ten bushels of corn, thirty
shillings in money (or the equivalent in goods), a gun worth at least twenty
shillings; and to every woman servant, fifteen bushels of corn, forty shillings
in money (or the equivalent in goods)." In 1692 and in 1705, orders were
issued to confiscate livestock raised by African-American bond-laborers. The
act of 1723 not only imposed lifetime hereditary bond-servitude on African-
Americans, it also sought "to implement it by a system of *racial oppression*,
expressed in laws against *free* African-Americans," including laws

> making free Negro women tithable; forbidding non-Europeans, though baptized
> christians, to be owners of "christian," that is, European, bond-laborers; denying
> free African-Americans the right to hold any office of public trust; barring any
> Negro from being a witness in any case against a "white" person; making any free
> Negro subject to thirty lashes at the public whipping post for "lift[ing] his or her
> hand" against any European-American (thus to a major extent denying Negroes
> the elementary right of self-defense); excluding free African-Americans from the
> armed militia; and forbidding free African-Americans from possessing "any gun,
> powder, shot, or any club, or any other weapon whatsoever, offensive or defensive."

The denial of the right of self-defense would become a major factor "in the
development of the peculiar American form of male supremacy, white-male
supremacy, informed by the principle that any European-American male
could assume familiarity with any African-American woman" (pp. 249–51).

The ruling class also "took special pains to be sure that the people they ruled
were propagandized in ... white supremacism." Provisions were included for
that purpose in the "Act concerning Servants and Slaves" of 1705 and in
the Act of 1723 "directing the trial of Slaves ... and for the better government of Negros, Mulattos, and Indians, bond *or free*." To raise consciousness

and to prevent "pretense of ignorance," the laws "mandated that parish clerks or churchwardens … read ('publish') these laws in full to the congregants." Sheriffs "were ordered to have the same done at the courthouse door." The "general public was regularly and systematically subjected to official white supremacist agitation." It was to be "drummed into the minds of the people that, for the first time, no free African-American was to dare to lift his or her hand against a 'Christian, not being a negro, mulatto or Indian'"; that "African-American freeholders were no longer to be allowed to vote"; that "the provision of a previous enactment … was being reinforced against the mating of English and Negroes"; that,

> as provided in the 1723 law for preventing freedom plots by African-American bond-laborers, "any white person … found in company with any [illegally congregated] slaves," was to be fined (along with free African-Americans or Indians so offending) … or to "receive, on his, her, or their bare backs, for every such offense, twenty lashes well laid on." (p. 251)

"Thus," writes Allen, the "white race" was "invented as the social-control formation whose distinguishing characteristic was not the participation of the slaveholding class, nor even of other elements of the propertied classes; … What distinguished this system of social control, what made it 'the white race,' was the participation of the European-American laboring classes: non-slaveholders, self-employed smallholders, tenants, and laborers." In time, "this white-race social-control system begun in Virginia and Maryland would serve as the model of social order to each succeeding plantation region of settlement" (p. 251).

Not only would there no longer be African-American and European-American labor solidarity and rebellions, now "the poor and propertyless European-Americans were the principal element in the day-to-day enforcement of racial oppression." The "white" slave patrols were made up primarily of those from the "lower class." Although "this system of white-skin privileges had … been initiated by the European-American … plantation bourgeoisie, the European-American workers were claiming them by the middle of the eighteenth century" as when "white" workers in South Carolina demanded "the exclusion of Negroes from the skilled trades" (p. 252).

Allen writes, "If the Virginia laws of 1705 and others cited … represent ruling class manipulation of the rank-and-file, the inescapable implication seems to be that the social transformation that they expressed – to the system of racial slavery, racial oppression, white supremacy – must have been contrary to the real interests of the majority of the people, the small-holders, the tenants, and laborers, those who did not own bond-laborers" (p. 253).

He then reviews the work of historians who counter that conclusion with a different assessment of white supremacism in relation to the foundation of the United States as a republic. In particular, he discusses the "paradox thesis" of American history, which contends "that democracy and equality, as represented in the Declaration of Independence and the Constitution of

1789, were, by the logic of history, made possible by racial oppression." He focuses particularly on Edmund S. Morgan's espousal of this rationale, for the reason that his book, *American Slavery, American Freedom*, appeared in 1975 after the civil rights struggles and because his socio-economic approach to the origin of racial slavery supplied "the most substantial response that had yet appeared to the 'natural racism' thesis of Carl Degler and of Winthrop D. Jordan" (pp. 253–4).

Allen sees the "essence of Morgan's paradox" in his statement that "Virginians may have had a special appreciation of the freedom dear to republicans, because they saw every day what life without it could be." This argument, writes Allen, "rests on the assumption that, early in the eighteenth century, 'the mass of white Virginians were becoming landowners, and the small planters began to prosper, thus giving the large and small planters a sense of common identity based on common interests.'" Allen points out that the work of historians Willard F. Bliss and Jackson Main "cast great doubt on his [Morgan's] facile conclusion" that there "were too few free poor [white] to matter" (pp. 254–5).

"If … among 'whites' there were 'too few free poor to matter,'" asks Allen, "why did the social order not revert to the normal class differentiation … in which the free Negroes could take their individual places according to their social class?" In this context, the "'white race' as a social control formation would have been a redundancy." Instead, however, "there was a general proscription of the free Negro," a fact that Allen contends "is unchallengeable evidence of the continued presence of poor whites who … served as the indispensable element of the 'white race,' the Peculiar Institution" (p. 255).

Allen cites a passage from Morgan's 1972 presidential address to the Organization of American Historians in which he writes, "The rise of liberty and equality in this country was accompanied by the rise of slavery. That two such contradictory developments were taking place simultaneously over a long period of our history, from the seventeenth century to the nineteenth, is the central paradox of American history" (p. 255).

Allen contends that "the effect of Morgan's 'paradox' thesis seems no less an apology for white supremacy than the 'natural racism' argument." Morgan goes even further when he writes, "Racism made it possible for white Virginians to develop a devotion to … equality … Racism became an essential … ingredient of the republican ideology that enabled Virginians to lead the nation" (pp. 255–6).

Then, writes Allen, "as if shying at his own conclusion, Morgan suggests … that perhaps 'the vision of a nation of equals [was] flawed at the source by contempt for both the poor and the black.'" Allen responds, "What *flaw*? If racism was a flaw, then 'the rise of liberty' would have been better off without it – a line of reasoning that negates the paradox. On the other hand, if racism made 'the rise of liberty possible, as the paradox would have it, then racism was not a flaw of American bourgeois democracy, but its very special essence." Allen concludes, "The 'Ordeal of Colonial Virginia' was extended as the Ordeal of

America, wherein the racial oppression and white supremacism have indeed been the dominant feature, the parametric constant, of United States history" (p. 256).

Allen then reviews the work of Frederick Jackson Turner, famous for his theory that "the existence of an area of free land, its continuous recession, and the advance of American settlement westward explain Americans development." He also discusses Turner's subsequently articulated safety-valve corollary regarding the emergence of a popular socialist movement of sufficient proportions to "substitute" for the end of the "free-land safety valve" and work "in the interest of the common man" as a "safeguard of democracy" and how that expectation was disappointed (p. 257).

Allen comments, "The white laboring people's prospect of lateral mobility to 'free land,' however unrealizable it was in actuality, did serve in diverting them from struggles with the bourgeoisie." But that was only one aspect of "the Great Safety Valve, the system of racial privileges conferred on laboring-class European-Americans, rural and urban, poor and exploited" which "has been the main historical guarantee of the rule of the 'Titans,' damping down anti-capitalist pressures, by making 'race, and not class, the distinction in social life.' " He emphasizes, "This, more than any other factor, has shaped the 'contours of American history' – from the Constitutional Convention of 1787 to the Civil War, to the overthrow of Reconstruction, to the Populist Revolt of the 1890s, to the Great Depression, to the civil rights struggle and 'white backlash' of our own day" (p. 258).

He adds that Turner's reference to the "safety valve" potential in anti-capitalist "reform" had a successor in the Keynesian New Deal.

The limitations of that line of reform, which had become evident by 1938, were masked by the prosperity of the United States in its role as the "arsenal of democracy" in World War II, which ended with the United States as the only industrial power left standing and the possessor of three-fourths of the world's gold reserves. By 1953, other major powers had recovered to pre-war levels; by 1957, the U.S. balance of trade began to shift unfavorably; in 1971, the United States formally abandoned the gold standard for settlement of international balances of trade and the "gold cover" for the domestic money supply. Finally, even the party of the New Deal has cast all Keynesian pretense to the winds, proclaiming that "the era of big government is over," and boasting of "ending welfare in any previously recognizable form" (pp. 258–9).

Allen then describes the situation in 1997 at the time of publication of the second volume:

> Now at the end of the twentieth century, the social gap between the Titans and the common people is at perhaps its historic maximum, real wages have trended downward for nearly two decades. "Entitlements" and "welfare," as they relate to students, the poor, and the elderly, have become obscenities in the lexicon of official society. There is less of a "socialist" movement today in the United States than there was in Turner's day, and anti-capitalist class consciousness is hesitant even to call its name. ... "Class struggle" is an epithet cast accusingly at the mildest

defenders of social welfare, and the country is loud with the sound of one class struggling. (p. 259)

His next words, however, speak presciently to readers in the twenty-first century as he describes "unmistakable signs of a maturing social conflict … because of intensifying efforts to 'balance the budget' at the expense of the living standards of non-stockholders." He insightfully points out that "America bears the indelible stamp of the African-American civil rights struggle of the 1960s" and draws the strands of his historical research and analysis together, offering these final words:

Perhaps by virtue of that legacy, in the impending renewal of the struggle of the "common people" and "Titans," the Great Safety Valve of white-skin privileges may finally come to be seen and rejected by laboring-class European-Americans as the incubus that for three centuries has paralyzed their will in defense of their class interests *vis-à-vis* those of the ruling class. (p. 259)

Editor's Appendix H
Select Bibliography on
Theodore W. Allen

By Theodore W. Allen

Class Struggle and the Origin of Racial Slavery: The Invention of the White Race (Hoboken, N.J.: HEP, 1975). Reprinted with an Introduction by Jeffrey B. Perry (Stony Brook, NY: The Center for the Study of Working Class Life, SUNY, 2006).

"Contradictions in Keynesian Economics: *The Unstable Economy: Booms and Recessions in the U.S. Since 1945*," Review of Victor Perlo, *The Unstable Economy: Booms and Recessions in the United States* (New York: International Publishers, 1973), *Guardian*, April 11 & 18, 1973.

"Commentary on István Mészáros's *Beyond Capital*," *Cultural Logic* Vol. 8 (2005).

"In Defense of Affirmative Action in Employment Policy," *Cultural Logic* Vol. 1, No. 2 (Spring 1998).

Interview by Chad Pearson, May 13 and 20, 2004, available at http://www.albany.edu/talkinghistory/arch2004jan-june.html.

The Invention of the White Race Vol. 1: *Racial Oppression and Social Control* (New York: Verso, 1994).

The Invention of the White Race Vol. 2: *The Origin of Racial Oppression in Anglo-America* (New York: Verso, 1997).

"Nixon's Southern Strategy," Review of Kevin Phillips, *The Emerging Republican Majority*, *Guardian*, November 22, 1969.

"Notes on Base and Superstructure and the Socialist Perspective for a Panel Presentation by Theodore Allen on 'Base and Superstructure and the Socialist Perspective' at the Conference on 'How Class Works,' to be Held at New York State University at Stony Brook, June 10-12, 2004," *Socialism and Democracy* Vol. 21, No. 1 (March 2007).

"On Roediger's *Wages of Whiteness*," *Cultural Logic* Vol. 4, No. 2 (Spring 2001).

"'Race' and 'Ethnicity': History and the 2000 Census," *Cultural Logic* Vol. 3, No. 1.

"Slavery, Racism, and Democracy," Review of Edmund S. Morgan,

American Slavery, American Freedom: The Ordeal of Colonial Virginia (New York: W. W. Norton, 1974), *Monthly Review* 29, No. 10 (March 1978).

"Summary of the Argument of *The Invention of the White Race*," *Cultural Logic* Vol. 1, No. 2 (Spring 1998).

"' ... They would have destroyed me': Slavery and the Origins of Racism," *Radical America* Vol. 9, No. 3 (May-June 1975). Reprinted in *White Supremacy: A Collection* (Chicago: Sojourner Truth Organization, 1976).

"White Supremacy in U.S. History," A Speech Delivered at a *Guardian* Forum on the National Question, April 28, 1973. Reprinted in *White Supremacy: A Collection* (Chicago: Sojourner Truth Organization, 1976).

By Other Authors

Ignatiev, Noel, "Review of *The Invention of the White Race*, Vol. 1: *Racial Oppression and Social Control*, by Theodore W. Allen," *Journal of Social History* 2005.

Ignatin (Ignatiev), Noel and Ted (Theodore W.) Allen, *White Blindspot & Can White Workers Radicals Be Radicalized?* (Detroit: The Radical Education Project, 1969; and New York: NYC Revolutionary Youth Movement, 1969).

Perry, Jeffrey B., "In Memoriam: Theodore W. Allen," *Cultural Logic* Vol. 8 (2005).

Perry, Jeffrey B., "Theodore William Allen: Expert on Bacon's Rebellion," *History News Network*, October 11, 2005.

Perry, Jeffrey B., "Introduction," in Theodore W. Allen, *Class Struggle and the Origin of Racial Slavery: The Invention of the White Race* (Stony Brook, N.Y.: The Center for the Study of Working Class Life, SUNY, 2006).

Perry, Jeffrey B., "The Developing Conjuncture and Some Insights from Hubert Harrison and Theodore W. Allen On the Centrality of the Fight Against White Supremacy," *Cultural Logic* (2010).

Scott, Jonathan and Gregory Meyerson, "An Interview with Theodore W. Allen," *Cultural Logic* Vol. 1, No. 2 (Spring 1998) .

Winston, Stella, "The Invention of the White Race," video interview with Theodore W. Allen in two parts, available at youtube.com.

Notes

Abbreviations of Some Frequently Cited Sources

AHR	*American Historical Review*
Bacon, *Works*	*The Works of Francis Bacon*, edited by James Spedding, Robert Leslie Ellis and Douglas Denon Heath, 14 vols. (London, 1857–74).
Blathwayt Papers	Blathwayt Papers, ca. 1675–1715, 41 vols. on microfilm at Colonial Williamsburg.
CO	Great Britain Public Record Office, Colonial Office records.
County Grievances	"A Repertory of the General County Grievances of Virginia . . . with the humble opinion of His Majesties Commissioners annexed" (October 1677).
County Records	Virginia County Court Records (photocopies, microfilm and abstracts), available at the Virginia State Archives, Richmond.
Coventry Papers	[*Henry*] *Coventry Papers Relating to Virginia, Barbados and other Colonies*, microfilm prepared by the British Manuscripts Project of the American Council of Learned Societies and available at the Library of Congress (originals at the estate of the Marquis of Bath, Longleat House, Wiltshire, UK).
CSP. Col.	Great Britain Public Record Office, *Calendar of State Papers, Colonial Series: America and the West Indies,* 44 vols. (London, 1860–1969).
CTP	Commissioners of Trade and Plantations. Operated under various official designations: Committee (of the Privy Council) for Trade and Plantations (from 1660); Lords of Trade and Plantations (from 1675); and Board of Trade (from 1696).
Force Tracts	Peter Force, *Tracts and Other Papers, related principally to the Origin, Settlement and Progress of the Colonies in North America, from the discovery of*

	the country to the year 1776, 4 vols. (Washington, 1836).
Gwynne, *Analecta Hibernia*, No. 4	Irish Manuscripts Commission, *Analecta Hibernia*, No. 4 (October 1932), "Documents Relating to the Irish in the West Indies," Aubrey Gwynne SJ, collector, p. 266.
Hening	William Waller Hening, comp. and ed. *The Statutes-at-Large; being a Collection of all the Laws of Virginia, from the First Session of the Legislature in the year 1619,* 13 vols. (Richmond, 1799–1823; Charlottesville, 1969).
Hotten, *Original Lists*	John C. Hotten, *The Original Lists of Persons of Quality; Emigrants; Religious Exiles; Political Rebels; Serving Men Sold for a Term of Years; Apprentices; Children Stolen; Maidens Pressed and Others Who went from Great Britain to the American plantations, 1600–1700* (London, 1874).
Manchester Papers	In *Historical Manuscripts Commission, Eighth Report* (London 1881), Part 1, Appendix.
MCGC	*Minutes of the Council and General Court of Virginia,* edited by H. R. McIlwaine (Richmond, 1924).
Norfolk County Wills	*Volume 3 of Virginia Colonial Abstracts,* 34 vols., compiled by Beverley Fleet (Baltimore, 1961).
RVC	*Records of the Virginia Company of London,* 4 vols. edited by S. M. Kingsbury (Washington, DC, 1906–35).
Smith, *Travels and Works*	*Travels and Works of Captain John Smith, President of Virginia and Admiral of New England,* 2 vols., edited by Edward Arber and A. G. Bradley (Edinburgh, 1910).
VMHB	*Virginia Magazine of History and Biography.*
WMQ	*William and Mary Quarterly.*

1 The Labor Supply Problem: England a Special Case

1. See Klaus E. Knorr, *British Colonial Theories, 1570–1850* (Toronto, 1944), Part I, "Colonial Theories, 1570–1660."

2. As mentioned in Volume One of *The Invention of the White Race* (p. 8), in the early 1630s the English planted a colony on Providence Island, some 350 miles north of Panama and 135 miles from the eastern coast of present-day Nicaragua, but they were forced to abandon it in 1641.

3. E. E. Rich and C. H. Wilson, eds., *The Cambridge Economic History of Europe,* Vol. IV, *The Economy of Expanding Europe in the Sixteenth and Seventeenth Centuries* (New York, 1967), p. 304.

4. J. H. Elliott, *Europe Divided, 1559–98* (New York, 1968), pp. 24, 289.

5. Between 1503 and 1660, according to records kept at Seville, Spain received from America 16 million kilograms of silver and 185,000 kilograms of gold, of which the Spanish Crown's share was 40 percent. (J. H. Elliott, *Imperial Spain, 1469–1716* (New York, 1964), pp. 174–75.) This

treasure quickly passed from Spain to its creditors, most notably the Fugger family of Augsburg and Antwerp, as payments on imperial debts, however. (Immanuel Wallerstein, *The Modern World-System,* Vol. I, *The Modern World-System, Capitalist Agriculture and the Origins of the European World-Economy in the Sixteenth Century* [New York, 1974], pp. 178–85. See also Henri Pirenne, *A History of Europe, From the Invasion to the XVI Century* [New York, 1955], pp. 524–6.)

6. Vieira's *O Papel Forte* is here cited from Robert Southey, *History of Brazil,* 3 vols. (London, 1817); 2:225. "(I)t was men of which Portugal was in want," said Southey, "not extent of territory." (Ibid., p. 224.)

7. Charles R. Boxer, *The Portuguese Seaborne Empire, 1415–1825* (New York, 1969), p. 88.

8. Henry Raup Wagner, *The Life and Writings of Bartolomé de Las Casas* (Alburquerque, 1967), pp. 22, 38–43. Though Las Casas's plan for establishing a Spanish peasant colony in the Americas failed, his proposal for using Negro slaves would soon lead to the royal licensing of the wholesale shipment of African bond-laborers to the Americas, which would come to be known as the Asiento. Some thirty-five years later, Las Casas regretted his role in this development. Even though he felt he had made a well-intentioned mistake that was generally approved by his contemporaries, he feared the divine judgment that he had yet to face for his role in bringing such terrible injustice on the Africans. (Bartolomé de Las Casas, *História de las Indias,* 3 vols, edited by Augustin Millares [Mexico City, 1951]; 3:474 [Capitulo 129].)

9. Charles Edward Chapman, *Colonial Hispanic America* (New York, 1933), p. 109. Special permission of the king or other qualified official had to be obtained before anyone might go to the Indies.

10. In a comment that anticipated Adam Smith and Edmund Burke (See *The Invention of the White Race,* Vol. One, pp. 33 and 71), Las Casas decried the social anomaly of "rabble who had been scourged or clipped of their ears in Castile, lording it over the native chiefs." (Edward Gaylord Bourne, *Spain in America, 1450–1580* [New York, 1907], p. 208.)

11. Luis Ivens Ferraz, "The Creole of São Tomé," *African Studies,* 37:3–68 (1978), p. 16. Most of these survivors married men and women who were brought from the African mainland.

12. John Lynch, *The Hispanic World in Crisis and Change 1598–1700* (Oxford, 1992), p. 8; Elliott, *Imperial Spain,* pp. 300–301.

13. Elliott, *Imperial Spain,* pp. 300–301. Lynch, p. 8. In 1609, the *moriscos* constituted perhaps one-third of the population of Valencia, where they were chiefly agricultural laborers. (Elliott, p. 300.)

14. Ernest John Knapton, *Europe, 1450–1815* (New York, 1958), pp. 238–9.

15. Chapman, pp. 109–10. In an analogous situation, English governments, whether guided by Puritan or Anglican principles, were untroubled by sectarian scruples. Irish Catholics in significant numbers were sent to Anglo-American plantation colonies in the seventeenth century, where their substantial presence caused the plantation owners some anxiety. (See *The Invention of the White Race,* Volume One, p. 74, and chapter 12 and 13 below.)

16. James A. Rawley, *The Transatlantic Slave Trade: A History* (New York, 1981), p. 81.

17. Jan de Vries, *Dutch Rural Economy* (New Haven, 1974), pp. 87–8. Rich and Wilson give the proportion as three-fourths (*Economy of Expanding Europe,* pp. 46–7).

18. De Vries, pp. 120, 184 and 203–34. De Vries concludes this section of his discussion by speculating that the absense of a numerous displaced and unemployed agricultural population retarded Holland's industrial development.

19. Rawley, p. 80.

20. De Vries, pp. 120, 184 and 203–34.

21. Charles R. Boxer, *The Dutch Seaborne Empire: 1600–1800* (New York, 1965), p. 58.

22. Boxer, *Dutch Seaborne Empire,* p. 58.

23. Ibid., p. 218. Although in 1630 the Dutch seized from Portugal the northern region of Brazil and called it New Holland, they were driven out in 1654, in part because "they were never able to induce adequate numbers of Dutchmen to settle in the faraway colony to influence the ethnic makeup of the settlement." (Johannes M. Postma, *The Dutch in the Atlantic Slave Trade, 1600–1815* [Cambridge, 1990], p. 19.)

24. See *The Invention of the White Race,* Volume One, Appendix C, p. 207.

25. Boxer, *Dutch Seaborne Empire,* p. 219.

26. Jean Jacquart, "French Agriculture in the Seventeenth Century," translated by Judy Falkus, in Peter Earle, ed., *Essays in European Economic History, 1500–1800* (Oxford, 1974), pp. 165–84; 165, 177.

27. Ibid., p. 180.

28. The failure of one line of agricultural development is discussed in Sigmund Diamond, "An

Experiment in 'Feudalism': French-Canada in the Seventeenth Century," *WMQ*, series 3, 18:3–34 (1961).

29. W. J. Eccles, *France in America* (New York, 1972), pp. 76–7. Léon Vignols, "La Mise en Valeur du Canada à l'Époque Française,' *La Revue d'Histoire Économique et Sociale*, 16:720–95 (1928); p. 736.

30. Eccles, *France in America* p. 77. In 1680, Robert LaSalle, the noted French explorer, reported that in Canada more trade goods were being converted into beaver pelts than Indians were being converted into Christians. (Vignols, "La Mise en Valeur," p. 724.)

31. Hispaniola was the name first given by the Spanish to the island that the native people called Haiti. At the end of the seventeenth century, France took over the entire island and called it St Domingue. It reassumed the name Haiti when France lost possession as a result of the Haitian Revolution (1800–1804). Spain finally reasserted its claim to the eastern portion of the island in 1844. Since that time the island has remained divided: Haiti in the west, the Dominican Republic in the east.

32. Eccles, *France in America*, p. 148.

33. Ibid., p. 149.

34. For a further discussion of the French reasons for turning away from the idea of supplying plantation labor from among the French population, see W. J. Eccles, *Canada Under Louis XIV* (Toronto, 1964), especially pp. 52–8.

35. Eccles cites a 1681 finding that only one out of every twelve of the *engagé* laborers were surviving three years out of service, and another that in the eighteenth century only one out of every three African laborers were surviving as long as three years of labor in the French West Indies. (Eccles, *France in America*, pp. 149 and 151.)

For a more detailed treatment of the subject of *engagé* labor, see two articles by Léon Vignols: "Les Antilles Françaises sous l'Ancien Régime – aspects économiques et sociaux: l'institution des engagés, 1626–1774," *La Revue d'Histoire Économique et Sociale*, 16:12–45 (1928); and "Une Question mal posée: le travail manuel des blancs et des ésclaves aux Antilles (XVIIe–XVIIIe siècles)," *Revue Historique*, 175:308–15 (Jan.–June 1935); pp. 310–11.

36. Charles Woolsey Cole, *Colbert and a Century of French Mercantilism*, 2 vols. (New York, 1939), 2:19–20.

37. Eccles, *France in America*, pp. 76, 148. See also A. J. Sargent, *The Economic Policy of Colbert* (London, 1899; 1968 reprint), pp. 47–8; and Cole, pp. 21–2.

38. Elliott, *Imperial Spain*, pp. 174–5.

39. William M. Denevan, ed., *The Native Population of the Americas in 1492*, 2nd ed (Madison, 1992), xxiii–xvi, xxviii (Table 1); Noble David Cook, *Demographic Collapse: Indian Peru, 1520–1620* (Cambridge, 1981). Both Denevan (p. xxiii) and Cook (p. 2) note the irreconcilable extremes of the estimates of the 1492 population of Hispaniola, which range from sixty thousand to 8 million. Denevan, taking into account newly reported evidence of a devastating epidemic of swine flu in 1493, agrees with studies that fix the population at about 1 million. The 1514 figure is mid-range of a general consensus. (Cook, p. 2.)

40. In 1574 there remained in Hispaniola only two Indian villages, and in Cuba only nine, comprising 270 married Indian men. (Bourne, pp. 197–8.) Certain countervailing factors operated to limit the degree of destruction of the indigenous population of Puerto Rico in this period. (James L. Dietz, *Economic History of Puerto Rico: Institutional Change and Capitalist Development* [Princeton, 1986], p. 6; Salvador Brau, *Ensayos: Disquicisiones Sociológicas* [Rio Piedras, 1972], p. 15.) I am indebted to Bill Vila Andino for directing me to these sources relative to the history of Puerto Rico.

41. *Encomienda* was the assignment of a given number of Indian laborers to a Spanish employer. *Repartimiento* was the assignment of Indian laborers by an *encomendero* to another employer. Indentured servitude was an alternative form to the forced labor of the *repartimiento*. (See Charles Gibson, *Spain in America* [New York, 1966], pp. 144–7.)

Repartimiento involved movement to workplaces outside of one's village; however, it required twenty men to be travelling to and from the mines, to maintain a supply of ten working in the mine. (T. R. Fehrenbach, *Fire and Blood, A History of Mexico* [New York, 1973], p. 225.) The *repartimiento* miners were forced to labor at a wage one-fourth that of free laborers. (Lynch, pp. 306–7.)

Ultimately, the Indian agricultural laboring class in Mexico, though nominally free, was reduced to peonage, a form of practical bondage by debt to the owner of the *hacienda*. (Gibson, pp. 118–19, 147, 156).

42. Denevan, ed., Table 1, p. xxvii. Woodrow Borah and Sherburne F. Cook, *The Indian*

Population of Central Mexico, 1531–1610 (Berkeley, 1960), p. 48. Cf. Noble David Cook, *Demographic Collapse: Indian Peru, 1520–1620* (Cambridge, 1981), pp. 2–3.

The decline of the indigenous population of Mexico ended in the middle or late seventeenth century, but by the end of the eighteenth century their number was still less than it had been in 1492.

43. Markham, who spells the word *mitta*, identifies the term as a native Peruvian Quichua word meaning "time" or "turn." (Clement R. Markham, *A History of Peru* [1892; reprinted New York, 1968], p. 157.)

44. Cook, pp. 113–14, 246. Compare the slightly higher estimate of 11.7 million for the Indian population of the "Central Andes" at the time of the arrival of the Spanish. (Denevan, p. xxviii.)

45. Boxer, *Portuguese Seaborne Empire*, p. 88. Basic to the difficulties of the Portuguese in Brazil was the fact that the unstratified, non-sedentary, native social structure there – in contrast to the class-differentiated sedentary societies found by the Spanish in Mexico and Peru – did not present opportunities for co-optation of native social forms for colonialist purposes.

46. See Chapter 3 for further discussion of the Portuguese social control problems in Brazil.

47. The Belgian historian Charles Verlinden, a preeminent authority on slavery in medieval Europe, has contributed a series of studies showing the link between medieval European and Ibero-American colonial slavery, noting both parallels and divergences. He emphasizes the historical continuity that existed between slavery in medieval European societies, including the Portuguese plantation gambits in the Atlantic islands, on the one hand, and the labor supply system in colonial Ibero-America, on the other. See Charles Verlinden, *The Beginning of Modern Colonization: Eleven Essays with an Introduction*, translated by Yvonne Feccero (Ithaca, 1970), especially pp. 33–51, Chapter 2, "Medieval Slavery and Colonial Slavery in America."

48. African bondmen and bondwomen, nearly fifty thousand of whom were brought to Europe in the sixteenth century, worked mainly as domestic servants, artisans and farmers, and enjoyed a considerable degree of social mobility. (Verlinden, p. 47; Rawley, pp. 24–5.)

49. Verlinden, p. 38.

50. Basil Davidson, *The African Slave Trade, Precolonial History, 1450–1850* (Boston, 1961), pp. 33–4.

51. A. J. R. Russell-Wood, "Iberian Expansion and the Issue of Black Slavery: Changing Portuguese Attitudes, 1440–1770," *Journal of American History*, 83:16–42; 27.

52. Philip D. Curtin, *The Atlantic Slave Trade: A Census* (Madison, 1969), p. 116. See also Russell-Wood, p. 22; Boxer, *Portuguese Seaborne Empire*, pp. 88–9; Rawley, pp. 24–5.

53. Verlinden, p. 39. It is interesting to note that among these Africans brought to Portugal was the putative great-grandmother of Jesuit priest António Vieira (1608–1697), the famous royal adviser and advocate of sparing the Brazilian Indians of the Maranho region by substituting laborers bought and brought from Angola. ("Não custa a crer tivesse vindo a bisavó de Africa, trazida por escrava a Portugal.") (Lúcio de Azevedo, *História de António Vieira*, multi-volume [Lisbon, 1992–   ], 1:14. See also: the Inquisition documents, ibid., pp. 311–17; Mathias C. Kiemen, *The Indian Policy of Portugal in the Amazon Region, 1614–1693* [Washington, DC, 1954], p. 140.)

54. Verlinden, p. 40.

55. Wagner, p. 40. Chapman, p. 119. Rich Wilson, eds. p. 322.

56. Rawley, pp. 26–27. Postma, p. 31. George Scelle, "The Slave Trade in the Spanish Colonies of America: The Asiento," *American Journal of International Law*, 4:612–61 (1910), pp. 614, 618, 622.

57. Basil Williams, *The Whig Supremacy, 1714–1760*, revised 2nd ed. (Oxford 1962), pp. 265 n. 1, 315.

58. Estimates considered include: W. E. B. DuBois, 10 or 12 million (Herbert Aptheker, ed., *The Correspondence of W. E. B. DuBois*, Volume 1, *Selections, 1877–1934* [Amherst: University of Massachusetts Press], p. 124) and J. D. Fage, 11,360,000 (*A History of West Africa*, 3rd. edition [Cambridge, 1969], pp. 82–3, 225). David Brion Davis puts the number at a minimum of 15 million (*Slavery in Western Culture* [Ithaca, 1966], p. 9). Rawley estimates the number at 11,048,000 (Rawley, pp. 428–9). Philip D. Curtin concludes that more than 8 million and fewer than 10.5 million Africans survived the Middle Passage to arrive as bond-laborers in the Americas. (Curtin, p. 87). Fage bases his estimate on Curtin, adding a percentage for those who lost their lives during the voyage.

Discussing the overall impact of the Atlantic slave trade on Africa, Davidson writes: "it appears reasonable to suggest that one way or another, before and after embarkation, it cost Africa at least fifty million souls" (Davidson, pp. 80–81). See also Walter Rodney, *How Europe Underdeveloped Africa* (Washington, DC: Howard University Press, 1982), pp. 95–8. (This work was originally published in London and Dar es Salaam, 1972.) Compare Rawley, pp. 425–7.

59. Rawley, p. 428.

60. Rawley, p. 424. I hope that my remarks are not inconsistent with Rawley's intention.

61. Curtin, p. 87.

62. The concluding stanza of "We Have Fed You All for a Thousand Years," by "An Unknown Proletarian", in *IWW Songs, Songs of the Workers*, 27th edition (Chicago, 1939), p. 64. IWW stands for Industrial Workers of the World.

63. See "The Enslavement Process in the Portuguese Dominions of King Philip III of Spain in the Early Seventeenth Century" (1612), in Robert Edgar Conrad, *Children of God's Fire: A Documentary History of Black Slavery in Brazil* (Princeton, 1983), pp. 11–15.

English captain Thomas Phillips described the determined resistance of captive Africans being assembled for shipment to Barbados in 1693 in his ship the *Hannibal*. Though shackled two-by-two "to prevent their mutiny, or swimming ashore," "… they have often leap'd out of the canoes, boat, and ship, into the sea, and kept under water till they were drowned, to avoid being taken up by our boats, which pursued them; they have more dreadful apprehension of Barbadoes than we can have of hell. ("A Journal of a Voyage in the Hannibal of London, Ann. 1693, 1694 from England to Africa and so Forward to Barbadoes, by Thomas Phillips, Commander of the said Ship," in John and Awsham Churchill, comp., *A Collection of Voyages and Travels* [Churchill's Voyages], 6:171–239; 219.)

Compared with ships in Mediterranean or Baltic commerce, the slave ships required a higher crew-to-tonnage ratio to hold down their rebellious cargoes. (Kenneth L. Davies, *The Royal African Company*, [London, 1957], pp.193–4.) In this brutal commerce, writes Basil Davidson, "Every ship's captain feared revolt on board, and with good reason, for revolts were many." (Basil Davidson, *Africa in History* [New York, 1968], p. 187.) It was for fear of revolt that 120 Africans were suffocated below decks, in order that the remaining 380 could be delivered to New Spain (Mexico), on a Portuguese ship in about 1612. (Conrad, p. 15.) See, in the same work, pp. 39–40, Document 1.7, "A Slave Revolt at Sea and Brutal Reprisals [1845]".

64. See Appendix II-A.

65. "… the Moors, with their women and children were leaving their houses as fast as they could, for they had seen their enemies" (Document 1.1, "The Beginnings of the Portuguese-African Slave Trade in the Fifteenth Century, as Described by Chronicler Gomes Eannes de Azurata," in Conrad, pp. 5–11; p.6; the name of the chronicler is given as Gomes Eanes de Zurara in. biographical encyclopedias.)

66. In the nineteenth century, the liberation struggle tended to merge into the general abolitionist and anti-colonialist struggles, especially in Cuba, Venezuela, Mexico, Brazil and Uruguay. (In Richard Price, ed., *Maroon Societies: Rebel Slave Communities in the Americas* (New York, 1973), see: Jose L. Franco, "Maroons and Slave Rebellions in the Spanish Territories," p. 48; Miguel Acosta Saignes, "Life in a Venezuelan Cumbe," p.73; David M. Davidson, "Negro Slave Control and Resistance in Colonial Mexico," p. 99; Roger Bastide, "The Other [than Palmares] Palenques," p. 171. In Magnus Mörner, ed., *Race and Class in Latin America*, (New York, 1970), see: Carlos M. Rama, "The Passing of the Afro-Uruguayans From Caste Society into Class Society," pp. 21, 37–9; Richard Graham, "Action and Ideas in the Abolitionist Movement in Brazil," pp. 62–6.

The maroon settlements in the mountains in eastern Cuba "lasted till the beginning of the first War of Independence in 1868, when the maroons joined en masse the ranks of the Cuban Liberation Army." (Franco, p. 47.)

67. See: C. L. R. James, *Black Jacobins: Toussaint L'Ouverture and the San Domingo Revolution* (New York, 1963), p.411; Robin Blackburn, *The Overthrow of Colonial Slavery, 1776–1848* (London and New York, 1988), pp. 245–6.

68. Edward D. Neill, *History of the Virginia Company of London* (Albany, NY, 1869), p. 11. Wesley Frank Craven, *The Dissolution of the Virginia Company, the Failure of a Colonial Experiment* (New York, 1932), pp. 28–9. Philip Alexander Bruce, *Economic History of Virginia in the Seventeenth Century: An Inquiry into the Material Conditions of the People, based upon original records*, 2 vols. (New York, 1895; Peter Smith reprint, 1935), 1:10–19. Alexander Brown, *Genesis of the United States*, 2 vols. (Boston and New York, 1890), pp. 562–5.

69. Las Casas denounced his Christian fellow countrymen on this account. Spanish *encomenderos*, given Indians of Hispaniola into their care to teach them the Catholic faith, merely "took care," said Las Casas, to "send the men into the mines, to make them drain them out gold." (Bartolomé de Las Casas, *Brevisima Relación de la Destruicion de las Indias Occidentales*, written in 1539; first printed in 1552, excerpted in George Sanderlin, trans. and ed., *Bartolomé de Las Casas: A Selection of his Writings* (New York, 1971), p. 84.) The Indian *cacique* Hathuey, who had

fled from Hispaniola to Cuba in about 1511, explained to the people what he had learned of the Spanish religion. Pointing to a small chest of gold and jewels, he said: "Behold here the God of the Spaniards." (Ibid., p. 87.)

Francis Bacon, the famous English essayist and statesman and member of the Virginia Company, generalized as follows: "It cannot be affirmed (if one speak ingenuously) that it was the propagation of the Christian faith that was the adamant of that discovery, entry and plantation [of America]; but gold and silver and temporal profit and glory." (Bacon, *Works*, 7:20–21, "An Advertisement Touching An Holy War.")

70. Robert Brenner, "Agrarian Class Structure and Economic Development in Pre-industrial Europe," *Past and Present*, no. 70, pp. 31–73 (February 1976); p. 69. R. H. Tawney, *The Agrarian Problem in the Sixteenth Century* (New York, 1912), p. 195. George M. Trevelyan, *A Shortened History of England* (New York, 1942), pp. 206–8.

71. "This fortress built by Nature for herself/ Against infection and the hand of war ... / ... set in the silver sea, / Which serves it in the office of a wall" (Shakespeare, *Richard II*, Act 2, Scene 1). This sentiment perhaps was even more appropriate to Shakespeare's time than in the reign of Richard II (1377–99).

72. J. D. Mackie, *The Earlier Tudors* (Oxford, 1952), p. 450. Tawney, p. 195–6. Eric Kerridge, *Agrarian Problems in the Sixteenth Century* (London, 1969), pp. 120–21, 126–8, 132–3, 201.

73. Mackie, pp. 374–5.

74. See Tawney's discussion of the stimulating effect of the confiscation and redistribution of monastic lands on the pace of the conversion of arable to pasture land (Tawney pp. 379–84).

75. C. S. L. Davies believes that the turbulence of the following couple of years may have been worsened by the tardiness of their reabsorption into civilian life. ("Slavery and the Protector Somerset: the Vagrancy Act of 1547," *Economic History Review*, 2nd series, 19:533–49 (1936); p. 538.)

This retreat from France marked the withdrawal from the alliance with Charles V, as whose ally the English had invaded France in September 1544. It was the beginning of the Tudor "island policy," which relied on the build-up of the Royal Navy rather than on military campaigns in Europe to protect the English position. (Trevelyan, p. 216.)

76. C. G. Cruickshank, *Elizabeth's Armies*, 2nd edition (Oxford, 1966), pp. 14–16. For the number of English soldiers in the Tyrone War (1594–1603), see *The Invention of the White Race*, Volume One, Chapter 5.

77. Demographers' corrected figures, based on London bills of mortality for seven plague years in the period 1563–1665 (three in the sixteenth century and four in the seventeenth century), totalled 292,598, only one-fifth of them in the sixteenth century. (E. A. Wrigley and R. S. Schofield, *The Population History of England, 1541–1871: A Reconstruction* [Cambridge, Mass., 1981], pp. 81–2 [Table 3.9].)

78. Wrigley and Schofield, pp. 531–5 (Table A3.3). The annual rate of natural increase of the English population in the last six decades of the sixteenth century averaged 0.76 percent contrasted with 0.36 and 0.57 percent for the ten decades of the seventeenth and the eighteenth centuries respectively. (Ibid., p. 183 [Table 6.10].)

79. Lawrence Stone, taking issue with Tawney, asserts that, "It was relentless demographic growth ... rather than the enclosing activities of monopolistic landlords which ... was responsible for the rise of a landless labourer class, of a semi-employed squatter population eking out a living in cabins in the wastes and heaths, and of a small but conscious body of unemployed vagrants." (Lawrence Stone, Introduction to the 1967 edition of Tawney's *The Agrarian Problem in the Sixteenth Century*.)

80. Joan Thirsk and J. P. Cooper, eds., *Seventeenth-century Economic Documents* (Oxford, 1972), p. 200.

81. Sir John Clapham, *A Concise History of Britain from the Earliest Times to 1750* (Cambridge, 1949; Princeton, 1963), pp. 251–2.

82. Thirsk and Cooper, eds., p. 1 (House of Commons, 26 February 1621).

83. *Journals of the [English] House of Commons*, I:711.

84. E. M. Leonard, *The Early History of English Poor Relief* (Cambridge, 1900), p. 266.

85. John Eastcott Manahan, "The Cavalier Remounted: A Study of the Origins of Virginia's Population, 1607–1700," PhD Dissertation, University of Virginia, 1946; p. 28.

86. Leo Francis Stock, ed., *Proceedings and Debates of the British Parliaments Respecting North America*, 5 vols. (Washington, DC, 1924), 1:64, "Petition of the Virginia Company" (26 April 1624).

87. "A Letter of Advice Written to the Duke of Buckingham" (1616), in Bacon, *Works*, 13: 13–24, 21. Richard Hakluyt, *A Discourse of Western Planting* (1584), in *Collections of the Maine*

Historical Society, 2nd ser., 2:37 (1877). R. I. (Richard Johnson), *Nova Britannia* (1609), p. 19. The original sources are given here, but these quotations, along with twice as many more to the same point, are found in Knorr, pp. 42–4.

The opposing minority did not challenge the colony-makers on the fact of the surplus of common labor. Instead, they argued mainly from the following three principles: (1) that a large population was essential to the strength of the realm; (2) that colonies, once established, might become unwelcome competitors in the markets supplied from England; and (3) that emigration might seriously reduce the home supply of skilled workers.

88. "A Consideration of the Cause in Question before the Lords touching Depopulation," British Museum Mss., Cottonian Mss., Titus F, iv, ff. 322–3 (5 July 1607). Reprinted in Kerridge, pp. 200–203.

89. See *The Invention of the White Race*, Volume One, pp. 8–11, for my criticism of Winthrop Jordan's use of the term "unthinking decision" in his psycho-cultural explanation of the origin of racial slavery.

2 English Background, with Anglo-American Variations Noted

1. The religious issue in England, which culminated in the overthrow of the Catholic King James II, and which paralleled the establishment of the racial oppression of Catholics in Ireland, had its echoes in Maryland, which was founded as a proprietary colony of Catholic convert George Calvert (c. 1580–1632). A number of Protestant rebellions, interlinked with class conflict, were launched in the province, with varying degrees of success, against a succession of Lords Baltimore, until 1715 when the third Lord, Charles Calvert, converted with his family to the Protestant religion. The difference between the fate of Catholics in Maryland and of those in Ireland is betokened by the fact that the land holdings of Maryland Catholics remained intact, even in the 1691–1715 period when the Calvert proprietorship of the colony was revoked on religious grounds. In Ireland, as has been discussed in Volume One, the Catholic landowning class was systematically expropriated by Protestants under the Protestant Ascendancy regime of racial oppression. Irish Catholics brought to Maryland as chattel bond-laborers did become the occasion for expressions of ruling-class alarm, principally because of the worry that they would join the African-American bond-laborers in class solidarity.

2. See Part Two below.

3. Adam Smith, *An Inquiry into the Nature and Causes of the Wealth of Nations* (London: Ward, Lock & Co., n.d.), Book III, Chapter IV, p. 329.

Karl Marx, Thorold Rodgers, R. H. Tawney and Rodney Hilton present a more sober view. Tawney's concluding eloquence on this point should not be missed. (R. H. Tawney, *The Agrarian Problem in the Sixteenth Century* [New York, 1912] pp. 406–8.)

Eric Kerridge (*Agrarian Problems in the Sixteenth Century* [London, 1969], Introduction), however, thinks that Tawney sacrificed scholarship to the social dogma to which Tawney supposedly adhered as a member of the Fabian Society and the Labour Party. By portraying capital as relentless and remorseless, as the violator of common-law rights of peasants, and as the perpetrator of giant exploitation of man by man. Tawney – as Kerridge sees it – led "whole generations of history students into grievous error."

For a sharp counter-criticism of Kerridge, see Lawrence Stone in the *Times Literary Supplement*, 2 October 1970, pp. 1135–6.

4. A paraphrase of Tawney, p. 264.

5. Estimates range from 20 percent mortality (Josiah Cox Russell, "Demographic Patterns in History" *Population Studies*, no. 1, 1948) to possibly half (J. H. Clapham and Eileen Power, eds., *The Agrarian Life of the Middle Ages* [Cambridge, UK, 1944], Volume I of *Cambridge Economic History of Europe*, p. 512).

The preamble of the 1349 Statute of Labourers posed the feudal lords' problem more adequately than the remainder of the law served to assuage it: "Because a great part of the people, and especially workmen and servants, late died of the pestilence, many seeing the necessity of masters and the great scarcity of servants, will not serve unless they may receive excessive wages." (23 Edw. III, *The Statutes at Large from Magna Charta to the forty-first year of the reign of King George, the Third, inclusive* [London, 1786–1800].)

6. See Appendix II-B, on Wat Tyler's Rebellion. Historians such as Charles Dobson (*The*

Peasant Revolt of 1381 [London, 1970], p. 30) question the importance of the revolt as a factor in bringing an end to feudalism in England. Yet Dobson concedes that in the following century "tenants did not find it impossible to resist pressure from their landlords."

Thorold Rogers, on the other hand, declares that, "the gradual emancipation of the serfs [dates] unquestionably from the great Insurrection [of 1381] .... The peasant of the fourteenth century struck a blow for freedom ... and he won." (Thorold Rogers, *Economic Interpretation of History* [London, 1889] pp. 31 and 82.) Rodney Hilton's *Bond Men Made Free: Medieval Peasant Movements and the English Rising of 1381* (London, 1973) presents an equally sympathetic discussion of the revolt, but takes note of fateful shortfalls in its accomplishments.

7. Rogers coined the term (p. 82).

8. W. H. R. Curtler, *The Enclosure and Redistribution of Our Land* (Oxford, 1920), p. 117.

9. "It is not easy to discover any economic reason why the cheap wool required for the development of the cloth manufacturing industry should not have been supplied by the very peasants in whose cottages it was carded and spun and woven" (Tawney, p. 407).

10. The peasants in Ket's Rebellion put forward a program which, had they won, would have given a severe check to the ascendancy of the bourgeoisie. (See S. T. Bindoff, *Ket's Rebellion, 1549* [London, 1949], Historical Association, General Series G. 12.)

11. Tawney, p. 318.

12. Ibid., p. 333.

13. For the most comprehensive treatment of this event, see Madeleine Hope Dodds and Ruth Dodds, *The Pilgrimage of Grace, 1536–1537 and the Exeter Conspiracy, 1538* (Cambridge 1915), 2 vols.

14. J. D. Mackie, *The Earlier Tudors* (Oxford: Clarendon Press, 1952), p. 385.

15. Dodds and Dodds, 1:220 and 2:225–6. Tawney, pp. 334–35.

16. Tawney, p. 11.

17. Gilbert Bernet, *History of the Reformation* (originally published in 1679–81 and 1714; republished Oxford: Clarendon Press, 1865; 3 vols., cited in George L. Craig and Charles Macfarlane, *The Pictorial History of England, being a History of the People as well as a History of the Kingdom*, 4 vols. (New York, 1843), 2:464. Edwin F. Gay, "The Midland Revolt and the Inquisition of Depopulation of 1607," *Transactions of the Royal Historical Society*, Vol. 18 (1904): 195–214; p. 203 n. 2. John Hales, *The Discourse of the Common Weal*, edited by E. Almond (circa 1549) (London, 1893), p. viii. [Raphael] Holinshed, *Chronicles of England, Scotland and Ireland* (originally published 1577; London, 1808; AMES Reprint [New York, n.d.]), 3:963–85 (Holinshed's account of Ket's Rebellion).

18. Tawney, pp. 335–7. Bindoff, *Ket's Rebellion*, p. 9. The quotation is from Bindoff. (Although "privatizing" is my own anachronism, it seems appropriate for this earlier process of "the rich stealing the property of the poor.")

The government did make a notable concession in response to the demands of the rebels, although it proved to be a time-limited and fundamentally ineffectual one. Two years after Ket's Rebellion, Parliament enacted a law (5 & 6 Edw. VI 5) requiring that as much land be established in tillage as was in tillage in the first reign of Henry VIII (1509). This law was repealed a decade later by 5 Eliz. 2. (E. M. Leonard, "The Enclosure of Common Fields in the Seventeenth Century," in E. M. Carus-Wilson, ed., *Essays in Economic History* 3 vols. (New York, 1966), 2:227–56; p. 242 n. 65.)

19. Edwin F. Gay, "The Midland Revolt and the Inquisitions of Depopulations of 1607," *Transactions of the Royal Historical Society*, 18:195–244 (1904); pp. 212, 216 n. 3, and 240.

An interesting example of how in formulating a deliberate policy of social control, ruling-class concessions were weighed against the danger of encouraging rising expectations, is to be noted in a House of Lords commentary following the Midlands anti-enclosure revolt of 1607. If indeed "depopulation" was to be adjudged the cause of the revolt, the House of Lords wondered "Whether time may be fit to give remedy, when such encouragement may move the people to seek redress by the like outrage, and therefore in Edward the sixth his time was not pursued until two years after the rebellion of Kett." (Kerridge, pp. 200–203; p. 200, Document No. 27 [British Museum, Cottonian Manuscripts, Titus F. iv, ff. 322–3, "A Consideration of the Cause in Question before the Lords touching Depopulation," July 6, 1607].)

20. Curtler, p. 117.

21. Robert Brenner, "Agrarian Class Structure and Economic Development in Pre-industrial Europe,' *Past and Present*, 70(1976):31–73; 63 n. 80.

22. D. C. Coleman, "Labour in the English Economy of the Seventeenth Century," in Carus-Wilson, ed., 2:291–308; 295 (originally published in *Economic History Review*, 2nd ser., 8(1956),

no. 3). Sir John Clapham, *A Concise History of Britain from the Earliest Times to 1750* (Cambridge, 1949; Princeton, 1963), pp. 212–13. "By no means the least burden of complaint," writes Kerridge (p. 132), "was that family farmers were deprived of their livings and replaced by wage workers."

23. E. H. Phelps-Brown and Sheila V. Hopkins, "Seven Centuries of Building Wages," in Carus-Wilson, ed. 2:168–78; pp. 177–8 (originally published in *Economica*, vol. 22 [1955]). E. H. Phelps-Brown and Sheila V. Hopkins, "Seven Centuries of the Prices of Consumables compared with Builders' Wage-Rates" in Carus-Wilson, ed., 2:178–96; pp. 194–6. (originally published in *Economica*, vol. 23 [1956]).

24. Peter Laslett, *The World We Have Lost* (New York, 1965), pp. 14–15.

25. Francis Bacon, *The History of the Reign of King Henry Seventh*, in *Works*, 6:124. Laslett, pp. 14–15. Coleman, 2:295.

In 1688, Gregory King estimated that of the total English population of 5,500,000, nearly one-fourth, or 1,300,000, were just such "cottagers and paupers" (Gregory King, "A Scheme of the Income and Expense of the several Families of England calculated for the year 1688," in Jan Thirsk and J. P. Cooper, eds., *Seventeenth-century Economic Documents* [Oxford, 1972], pp. 780–81).

26. Phelps-Brown and Hopkins ("Wage-Rates and Prices: Evidence for Population Pressure in the Sixteenth Century," *Economica*, 24(1957): 289–306) relate this question specifically to the wage earners, but I have taken the liberty of giving it more general reference. The term "upheaval" is not precise, although the peasant revolts of 1536, 1549 and 1607 certainly qualify for that term. But an "upheaval" sufficient to check the ascendance of the bourgeoisie and its heedless and heartless expropriation and impoverishment of the laboring people did not occur. It is in this broader sense that I wish the matter to be understood in the discussion that follows concerning the establishment of bourgeois social control.

Rodney Hilton, a historian who identifies emotionally with the peasant rebels, traces their defeat in the sixteenth century to the fourteenth-century "failure of the rebels [behind John Ball and Wat Tyler in 1381] to end villeinage and to extend the rights of free tenure [as against mere manorial copyhold rights] to all tenants." Such a thorough sweep, he maintains, "would have meant the end of manorial jurisdiction ... [and] it would have involved the removal of all cases about land to the common law courts. ... At one stroke the material basis for deference and the respect for the hierarchy which had dogged the English rural masses for centuries would have been removed." (Hilton, pp. 232 and 224).

The "long" sixteenth century might be taken to mean roughly 1500–1640. For a discussion of this concept, see I. W. Wallerstein, *The Modern World-System: Capitalist Agriculture and the Origins of the European World-Economy in the Sixteenth Century* (New York, 1974), pp. 67–9.

27. These gradations related to the degree of security of the tenant's claim to the land. See Tawney, Chapter III; Kerridge, Chapter 2; and Mildred Campbell, *The English Yeoman Under Elizabeth and the Early Stuarts* (New Haven, 1942), Chapter IV.

28. The term "forty-shilling freeholder" was first defined by Thomas Littleton, in his treatise on *Tenures*, near the end of the fifteenth century. Strictly interpreted, it would mean a person free of personal labor obligations to any lord, and holding a hereditary lease on lands yielding at least forty shillings' annual income. While the land-income qualification remained constant, the term came to be not so strictly applied in other respects.

29. See Tawney, pp. 340–44. "It was an essential feature of Tudor policy to foster the prosperity of the yeomanry, from whose ranks were recruited the defenders of the realm" (Ephraim Lipson, *The Economic History of England*, 3 vols. [London, 1926, 1931, 1931]; 1:141).

30. Francis Bacon, *History of the Reign of King Henry VII*, in Francis Bacon, *Works*, 6:28–245; pp. 93–5.

31. Ibid., 6:95.

32. Though the producer "intends only his own security ... [and] only his own gain, ... he is ... led by an invisible hand to promote an end which was no part of his intention" (Smith, *The Wealth of Nations*, Book IV Chapter 2, p. 354). But where does one's self-interest lie? In this yeoman-preserving policy, the English ruling class was drawing a distinction between the self-interest of the individual exploiter and the overriding self-interest of the exploiting class as a whole.

33. Bacon, *History of the Reign of King Henry VII*, in *Works*, 6:94.

34. Ibid., p. 219.

35. Campbell. Chapter IX, "For the Common Weal," is the general basis for this paragraph on the public functions of the yeomen.

36. Thomas Smith, *De Republica Anglorum, Discourse on the Commonwealth of England* (1583; 1906, edited by L. N. Alston; reprint New York, 1974), pp. 43–4.

37. Bindoff, p. 216. Joseph Clayton, *Robert Kett and the Norfolk Rising* (London, 1912), p. 217.

38. Gay, p. 216.

39. The Statute of Artificers, in *The Statutes at Large from Magna Charta to the forty-first Year of the Reign of King Goerge, the Third, inclusive* (London, 1786–1800).

40. The wage level, whether high or low, operates as an essential mechanism of social stability. The limits of its fluctuation, however, are set by the premises of the bourgeois social order itself. The formulation of this basic principle has not been improved upon since Sir Bernard de Mandeville first set it down in his *Fable of the Bees, or, Private Vices, Publick Benefits. With an Essay on Charity and Charity-Schools, and A Search into the Nature of Society*, 6th edition (London, 1732), pp. 193–4: "[T]hose that get their Living by their daily Labour . . . have nothing to stir them up to be serviceable but their Wants, which it is Prudence to relieve but Folly to cure. The only thing then that can render [them] industrious, is a moderate quantity of Money; for as too little will . . . either dispirit or make [them] Desperate, so too much will make [them] Insolent and Lazy.'

41. 25. Edw. III, Stat. 1, c. 1 (1351); 37 Edw. III, c. 6 (1363); 12 Richard II, c. 3–9 (1388); 13 Richard II, Stat. 1, c. 8 (1390); 6 Henry VI, c. 3 (1427); 8 Henry VI, c. 8 (1429); 23 Henry VI, c. 12 (1445); and 11 Henry VII, c. 72 (1495). In *The Statutes at Large from Magna Charta to the forty-first year of the Reign of King George, the Third, inclusive* (London, 1786–1800). See also W. E. Minchinton, ed. *Wage Regulation in Pre-Industrial England* (republished, New York: Barnes and Noble, 1972). This collection comprises works by R. H. Tawnet originally published in *Vierteljahrschrift fur Sozial- und Wirtschaftsgeschichte*, XI (1914), pp. 307–37 and 533–64; R. Keith Kelsall, "Wage Regulation under the Statute of Artificers" R. Keith Kensall, and, "A Century of Wage Assessment in Hertfordshire, 1662–1772," originally published in *English Historical Review*, vol. 57 (1942):115–19.

42. Phelps-Brown and Hopkins, in Carus-Wilson, ed., pp. 171, 177, and 194.

43. Rodney Hilton, ed., *The Transition from Feudalism to Capitalism* (London, 1978), p. 27.

44. 1 Edw. VI, 3. In *The Statutes at Large from Magna Charta to the forty-first year of the Reign of King George, the Third, inclusive.*

45. C. S. L. Davies, "Slavery and the Protector Somerset: the Vagrancy Act of 1547," *Economic History Review*, 2nd ser., 19:533–49 (1966); 535–6. "The 1547 act," says Davies, "was aimed at a wider target than those bands of wandering beggars which terrorized the Tudor countryside. The latter were a useful excuse to make palatable a policy of enforced employment, and, by implication at least, to reduce still further the worker's limited ability to bargain" (p. 536).

46. 1 Edw. VI, 3, *Statutes at Large from Magna Charta to the forty-first Year of the Reign of King George, the Third.*

47. 3 & 4 Edw. VI, 16, *Statutes at Large from Magna Charta to the forty-first year of the Reign of King George, the Third.*

48. Cited in Lipson, 1:149.

49. Cited in ibid.

50. Davies, pp. 547–8.

51. Tawney, p. 11.

52. John Cheke, "The Hurt of Sedition" (1549; republished, 1569), in Holinshed, 3:987–1011.

53. Davies, p. 546.

54. F. W. Russell, *Kett's Rebellion in Norfolk* (1859), p. 48; cited in Tawney, p. 337.

55. Bindoff, while calling it "the only resounding denunciation of villeinage ever heard in Tudor England," still thinks that it had no reference to the slavery provided by the 1547 law; he considered this rebel programmatic point as merely high-flown symbolic verbiage borrowed from the German peasant uprising of 1512 (*Bindoff*, pp. 12–13).

Diarmuid MacCullogh rejects Bindoff's speculation. He believes that the anti-bondage demand was narrowly directed against Thomas Howard, late Duke of Norfolk, who was much disliked for mistreatment of and refusal to manumit bondmen (villeins) on his East Anglia estates (Diarmuid MacCullogh, "Kett's Rebellion in Context," *Past and Present*, 84(1979):36–59; p. 55).

56. Davies, p. 547. The original voice was that of one Fitzherbert, *Description of England*, which Davies cites from E. R. Cheyney, "The Disappearance of English Serfdom," *Economic History Review*, vol. 15:20–37 (1900); 24.

57. Davies, p. 548.

58. Davies is here citing Charles Lyell, *A Second Visit to the United States*, 2 vols. (New York, 1849), 2:72. Davies's reference is by way of the citation in Kenneth Stampp, *The Peculiar Institution: Slavery in the Ante-bellum South* (New York, 1956), p. 399. I cannot explain why Stampp's page reference differs from mine.

59. Davies, p. 544, citing ms. *Cecil Papers*, 152/96. But a century after the repeal of the 1547 law, it yet provided the model for the first Barbadian slave code. (Rev. George Wilson Bridges, *The*

Annals of Jamaica, 2 vols. [London, 1827], 1:507. Cited by Lewis Cecil Gray, assisted by Esther Katherine Thompson, *History of Agriculture in the Southern United States to 1860*, 2 vols. [Washington, DC, 1932], 1:347.)

60. R. H. Tawney, "The Assessment of Wages in England by the Justices of the Peace," in Minchinton, ed., *Wage Regulation in Pre-Industrial England*, pp. 47–53.

61. 5 Eliz. 4, "An Act touching the divers Orders for Artificers, Labourers, Servants of Husbandry and Apprentices." Good modern discussions of this statute are to be found in Minchinton, ed. and in S. T. Bindoff, "The Making of the Statute of Artificers," in S. T. Bindoff, J. Hurstfield, and C. H. Williams, eds., *Elizabethan Government and Society* (London, 1961), pp. 56–94.

62. Bindoff, "Making of the Statute of Artificers," p. 72.

63. The studies made by Phelps-Brown and Hopkins would indicate that the statute did not affect the trend in nominal or real wages. (See Carus-Wilson, ed., 2:168–96, especially pp. 177–78 and 193–96.) But Tawney's study of magistrates' records led him to believe that "it is probable that the practice of assessing wages tended to keep them low by setting up a standard to which the master could appeal, [but, he adds] it is also probable that it was evaded without much difficulty by the exceptionally competent journeyman, or by the master who was in difficulties through a shortage of labor" (Tawney, "Assessment of Wages," pp. 92–3).

64. 53 Geo. 3, c. 40, *Statutes of the United Kingdom*, p. 191, "Act to Repeal the Statute of Artificers." Reprinted in Joel H. Wiener, ed., *Great Britain, The Lion at Home, A Documentary History of Domestic Policy, 1689–1973*, 4 vols. (New York: Chelsea House Publishers in association with R. R. Bowker Company, 1974), 1:913.

65. The testimony of Sir Thomas Smith, who had himself been a major architect of the Statute of Artificers (see Davies, pp. 542–3), provides a catalog of degrees of servitude and freedom of labor as they had evolved in the sixteenth century: "Thus necessitie and want of bondmen hath made men to use free men as bondmen to all servile services: but yet more liberally and freely, and with more equalitie and moderation, than . . . slaves and bondemen were wont to be used. This first [apprenticeship] and Latter [wage-labor] fashion of temporall [limited-term] servitude, and upon paction [mutual agreement of employer and employee] is used in all such countryes, as have left off the old accustomed man[n]er of servaunts, slaves, bondemen and bondwomen, which was in use before they received the Christian faith." (*De Republica Anglorum*, p. 139 [lib. 3, ch. 9].)

66. For instance Rogers (p. 38); Tawney ("Assessment of Wages," p. 49), and Marxists such as A. L. Morton (*A People's History of England*, 2nd edition [London, 1948], p. 173).

67. Matthew Bacon, *A New Abridgement of the Law*, 5 vols., 5th edition (Dublin 1786), p. 359, paragraphs 46–8. The remedy, "when any Man covenants to do a Thing, . . . and that cannot be, then [he is] to render Damages for not doing of it."

68. Michael Dalton, *The Country Justice* (1619); edited, with an appendix, by William Nelson, London, 1727), p. 179.

69. Under certain unusual circumstances – such as the death of a master or the removal of his master to another place – the apprentice, if he were willing, might be put with another master, but the apprentice could not be compelled to accept the assignment against his will. (Dalton, pp. 222, 245; John Strange, *Reports of Adjudged Cases in the Courts of Chancery, King's Bench, Common Pleas and Exchequer*, second edition, 2 vols. [London, 1782], 2:266–7.)

70. In 1648 a promotional pamphlet for colonizing in Virginia was written by Beauchamp Plantagenet entitled, *Description of the Province of New Albion*. It was printed in Peter Force, ed., *Tracts and Other Papers Relating Principally to the Origin, Settlement, and Progress of the Colonies of North America from the Discovery of the Country to the Year 1776*, 4 vols. (Washington, DC, 1836–46); vol. 2, no. 7.

71. A number of modern historians, such as Edwin F. Gay, W. H. R. Curtler, and Eric Kerridge, stoutly maintain that the actual extent of the economic dislocation occasioned by the Agrarian Revolution was exaggerated in the original accounts, and subsequently by uncritical historians. To the present writer these objections seem narrowly based. However that may be, the fact remains that real wages declined from decade to decade throughout the sixteenth century and into the first decade of the seventeenth, when they were only 44 percent of what they had been in the first decade of the sixteenth century (Phelps-Brown and Hopkins, ". . . Prices of Consumables," 2:194–5). It is impossible to believe that such a catastrophic decline in real wages could have occurred without massive unemployment.

72. Tawney, p. 273, citing Historical Manuscripts Commission, *Marquis of Salisbury*, Part VII (November 1597, "Notes for the present Parliament").

73. These laws included 14 Eliz. 5 (1572) and 39 Eliz. 4, 5 and 17.

74. Preamble to 14 Eliz. 5 (1572), cited in George Nicholls, *A history of the Country and Condition of the People*, 3 vols. (supplementary volume by Thomas Mackay) (1898; 1904; Augustus M. Kelley reprint, 1967), 1:157.

75. Nicholls, 1:178, citing John Stow, *Survey of London and Westminster* (1598), book V, chapter 30.

76. Richard Hakluyt, *A Discourse of Western Planting* (1584), in *Collections of the Maine Historical Society*, 2nd ser., 2:37 (1877).

77. Nicholls, 1:178.

78. Sir Henry Knyvet, *The Defense of the Realme* (1596; Oxford, 1906), p. 11. Cited in Klaus E. Knorr, *British Colonial Theories 1570–1850* (Toronto, 1944), p. 43.

79. Nicholls, 1:188.

80. It was repealed by the National Assistance Act of 1948, Geo. 6, c. 29, Public General Statutes (1948), declaring that "The existing poor law shall cease to exist." Reprinted in Wiener, ed., 4:3553–9.

81. Nicholls, I:189–92.

82. E. M. Leonard, 255–6, citing *State Papers, Domestic*, Vol. 185, No. 86.

83. Tawney, pp. 275–6 and 280.

84. I cite but two examples: First, A Virginia law passed in April 1662 provided that "all horses, cattle, and hoggs" belonging to any African-American or other lifetime bond-laborer were, in default of the claim of the bond-laborer's owner, to be "forfeited to the use of the poore of the parish" through the good offices of the churchwardens. (Hening, 3:103.)

Second, under the provisions of a Maryland law of 1717, any free African-American who married a European-American, or any European-American marrying a free African-American, was to be taken and sold by the county court into a seven-year term of servitude, the proceeds of the sale to be "applied to a [whites only] Public School." (Thomas Bacon, comp., *Laws of Maryland at Large* [Annapolis, 1765], Chapter XIII, Section V.)

85. Male domination – the practice and the doctrine – is a social institution of such immemorial origin that both the makers and the recorders of history may have mistaken it for a natural condition, and thus outside the scope of their concerns. Except for those investigators specifically committed to exposing and abolishing the wrongs that women, as women, have been forced to bear, our historians have generally ignored the function of male supremacy as a basic element of ruling-class social control.

86. The unmarried adult woman ("feme sole") of the propertied classes was a partial exception, she having some limited individual rights with regard to property. But even so, because of the generally subordinate social status of women she would find her position extremely vulnerable if she attempted to capitalize on her property independently.

87. Of the 216 persons executed for treason for participating in the Pilgrimage of Grace, only one, Margaret Cheyne, Lady Bulmer, was burned at the stake. Many women had been involved in the ill-fated rebellion, and some of them more directly and deeply than Cheyne. But Henry VIII preferred to make examples rather than to carry through large-scale executions, and Lady Bulmer was vulnerable. She and her husband were true lovers; some of their children were born before she and John were married; and they remained faithful to each other to the end. According to the Dodds, Henry's aim was "an object lesson to husbands, which should teach them [women] to dread their husband's confidence" (Dodds and Dodds, 2:214 and 226).

Anne Boleyn, convicted of treason on charges instigated by her husband, Henry VIII, in 1636, after she had twice miscarried in an attempt to bear him his much-desired male heir, was treated with greater mercy than that shown to Margaret Cheyne a year later. Instead of being burned alive, Anne Boleyn was beheaded. A specially skilled executioner with his special French sword was brought from Calais for the occasion. Anne Boleyn privately insisted on her innocence to the end, but she abstained from doing so publicly for fear of bringing down the wrath of her husband on her daughter, Elizabeth, the future queen. (William Douglas Hamilton, ed., *A Chronicle of England During the Reign of the Tudors from AD 1485 to 1559, by Charles Wriothesley* [hereafter referred to as *Wriothesley's Chronicle*] 2 vols. [London: Camden Society, 1875 and 1877]).

But Henry's purpose was constant. When Anne Seymour, whom he married the day after Anne Boleyn's execution, pleaded with him to desist from his expropriation of church abbeys, a course that had brought on the beginnings of the Pilgrimage of Grace, Henry warned her against meddling in "his" affairs, and cowed her into silence by a direct reference to the fate of her predecessor (Dodds and Dodds, 1:108).

88. Unless otherwise noted, the comments made here on social relationships under feudalism in England are based on the following readings: (1) Paul Vinogradoff, *Villainage in England* (London,

1927), especially Chapter II, "Rights and Disabilities of the Villain," and Chapter V, "The Servile Peasantry and Manorial Records"; (2) idem, *The Growth of the Manor*, 2nd. edition (London, 1911), especially Book III, Chapter III, "Social Classes"; (3) H. S. Bennett, *Life on the English Manor* (London, 1948), especially pp. 240–44; (4) a legal discussion of the status of the serf *vis-à-vis* that of the lifetime bond-laborer in continental Anglo-America, set forth in a decision by Judge Daniel Dulany, of the Maryland Provincial Court, 16 December 1767; printed in Thomas Harris and John McHenry, *Maryland Reports, being a Series of the Most Important Cases argued and determined in the Provincial Court and the Court of Appeals of the then Province of Maryland from the year 1700 down to the American Revolution* (New York, 1809), 1:559–64, especially 560–61.

89. Once, during the days of the final paroxysms of English feudalism, an agent of the Duke of Norfolk (in order to promote a prosecution of interest to the Duke) entreated a certain widow whose testimony was to be required "to be my Lord's wewe [a form of the Anglo-Saxon word "widewe' (widow)] by the space of an whole year next following, and thereto he made her to be bound in an obligation." ("R. L. to John Paston," 21 October 1471, in John Warrington, ed., *The Paston Letters*, 2 vols. (London: Everyman, 1956), pp. 118–19. The editor notes that, "The widow of a feudal tenant was called the lord's widow."

In Roman times, the Latin term "nativus" was applied to the personally unfree, the born slave. In feudal England, its etymologically evolved form "naif" was reserved for the serf woman, thus emphasizing her doubly servile role, by virtue of class and gender. A man of the laboring classes, whether free or serf, was simply termed "villein."

90. At one point during the Pilgrimage of Grace, in 1536, non-gentlemen rebels sought to put this sort of upper-class concern to their own purposes, but in a way was equally informed with callous and cruel male supremacism. Having the Earl of Cumberland besieged in Skipton Castle in Yorkshire, these rebels threatened to use the Earl's two daughters and his daughter-in-law as shields in assaulting the castle; and if they failed in that, they said, they would "violate and enforce them with knaves unto my Lord's great discomfort" (Dodds and Dodds, 1:210, citing James Gairdner, ed., *Letters and Papers of Henry VIII*, [London, 1888], vol. XII [1], 1186).

91. Henry VIII justified it as a necessity for the "purity of the succession," when he had his second and fifth wives charged with "adultery," and executed. (*Wriothesley's Chronicle*, 1:xxxviii [Hamilton's introduction]). This was but a royal example; the same basic principles applied (though not with the same latitude of remedy) wherever women and inheritable property were present in conjunction.

92. Lawrence Stone, *The Crisis of the Aristocracy, 1558–1641* (London: Oxford University Press, 1967), pp. 200–205.

93. 1 Edw. VI, 3, *The Statutes at Large from Magna Charta to the forty-first year of the Reign of King George, the Third.* See also Davies, p. 534.

94. Documents relating to the assessment of wages for the East Riding of Yorkshire in 1593, Lancaster in 1595, and Rutland in 1610. (James E. Thorold Rogers, *A History of Agriculture and Prices*, 7 vols. in 8 [London, 1886–1902], 6:686–93.

95. Francis Bacon, "The Case of the Post Nati of Scotland" (1608), in *Works*, 7:641–79; pp. 644–6.

96. In "An Advertisement Touching An Holy War," an uncompleted dialogue written about 1618, Bacon has one of his characters pose a case which in his view would justify holy war: "Now let me put a feigned case (and yet antiquity makes it doubtful whether it were fiction or history) of a land of Amazons, where the whole government public and private, yea the militia itself, was in the hands of women. I demand, is not such a preposterous government (against the first order of nature, for women to rule over men) in itself void, and to be suppressed?" The speaker then goes on to link such a government with two others whose very existence would justify holy war for their destruction: "... for those cases, of women to govern men, sons the fathers, slaves freemen, are much in the same degree, all being perversions of the laws of nature and nations." (*Works*, 7:33).

Bacon understood: "And therefore Lycurgus [the great Spartan state-builder], when one councelled him to dissolve the kingdom, and to establish another form of estate, answered, 'Sir, begin to do that which you advise first at home in your own house;' noting, that the chief of a family is as a king; and that those that can least endure kings abroad, can be content to be kings at home" ("Case of the Post Nati of Scotland," *Works*, 7:633–4).

97. Dodds and Dodds, 2:216.

98. J. C. Jeafferson, ed., *Middlesex County Records*, 4 vols. (London, 1886–92), 1:lii–liii. Wynstone's social station is inferred from the fact that he is not accorded any distinguishing term of address.

99. I must not commit the error for which I have criticized Jordan and Degler, by making

sweeping assertions about the "English mind." All I mean here is that I have not come across records of any contemporaries of Bacon and Wynstone repudiating male privileges.

100. Virginia laws imposed a year of extra servitude for a male bond-laborer and two years for a woman bond-laborer for marrying without the consent of the owner, and laid a heavy fine on any minister who performed such a marriage. (Hening, 1:252–3 [1643]; 2:114 [1662].)

A Maryland man, together with his wife, was forced by impoverishment to enter into a seven-year term of bond-servitude. One day in 1748 when his wife was bound up to undergo a whipping by her overseer, the husband endeavored to loosen her bonds, avowing that he would untie her "If it cost me my life . . . for she is my lawfull Wife." He himself was severely beaten and the whipping proceeded. When he appealed to the county court for redress, his appeal was rejected. (Prince George's County Court Records, Book HH, 165–8, CR 34717, Maryland Hall of Records.)

101. In a previously mentioned decision (see *The Invention of the White Race*, Volume One, pp. 89, 90) handed down by the Maryland Provincial Court in 1767, Judge Dulany made this point clear in differentiating between the status of the English villein and the lifetime hereditary bond-laborer in Anglo-America. "If a neif married a freeman," he said, "she became free, it being the necessary consequence of her marriage, which placed her in the power of her husband [even though this] without doubt was an injury to the lord." But "slaves are incapable of marriage . . .," he said, and consequently "we do not consider them as the objects of such laws as relate to the commerce between the sexes. A slave has never maintained an action against the violator of his bed." (1 Harris and McHenry, Appendix, pp. 560, 561, 563.)

"To debauch a Negro woman they do not think fornication . . . they still have the feeling that the blacks at large belong to the whites at large." (Statement of Colonel Samuel Thomas, Assistant Commissioner, Bureau of Refugees, Freedmen, and Abandoned Lands for Mississippi, appended to the Report of Major General Carl Schurz to President Andrew Johnson, 27 July 1865, on "Conditions of the South," 39th Congress, 1st Session (1865–66), *Senate Executive Documents*, Vol. 1, p. 81.

As noted in *The Invention of the White Race*, Volume One (p. 148), a major motive of the Negro Exodus of 1879 was the necessity to escape the gross imposition of the white male privilege against black women in the South. See 46th Congress, 2nd Session (1879–80), Senate Report 693, *Report and Testimony of the Select Committee of the US Senate to Investigate the Causes of the Removal of the Negroes from the Southern States to the Northern States*; Part II, pp. 177–8; part III, pp. 382–3.

3 Euro-Indian Relations and the Problem of Social Control

1. Of sixty-eight mentioned by name, thirty-eight were "Council Members," and "Gentlemen" (*Travels and Works of Captain John Smith, President of Virginia and Admiral of New England*, 2 vols., edited by Edward Arber and A. G. Bradley [Edinburgh, 1910], 1:93–4. In subsequent references, this work will be abbreviated Smith, *Travels and Works*.)

2. "I came to get gold, not to till soil like a peasant!" Cortés replied when it was first suggested that he might receive a large grant of land in Cuba. (William H. Prescott, *History of the Conquest of Mexico and History of the Conquest of Peru* [New York: Modern Library, n. d.], p. 130.)

3. "Until 1622 each side [Virginia colonists and Powhatan Indians] tried to gain control over the other one." (Christian F. Feest, "Virginia Algonquians," in Bruce G. Trigger, ed., *Northeast*, Volume 15 of *Handbook of North American Indians*, William C. Sturdevant, General Editor, 20 vols. (Washington, DC: Smithsonian Institution, 1978–), 15:256.)

Waterhouse, Martin and Smith were speaking in the immediate aftermath of the massive attack made by the Powhatan Indians on the English settlement on 22 March 1622. (See Chapter 5.)

4. Edward Waterhouse, "A Declaration of the State of the Colony . . ." [1622], in Susan Myra Kingsbury, ed., *Records of the Virginia Company of London*, 4 vols. (Washington, DC, 1906–35); 3:541–79; 562–3 (hereafter abbreviated *RVC*). Waterhouse appears to have been right about the decline of Spanish silver and gold. The peak of receipts of bullion at Seville was reached in the early 1590s. (See J. H. Elliott, *Imperial Spain, 1469–1716* [New York, 1964], p. 175.)

5. See Gonzalo Aquirre Beltrán, "The Integration of the Negro into the National Society of Mexico," in Magnus Mörner, ed., *Race and Class in Latin America* (New York, 1970), p. 18.

6. *RVC*, 3:558–9.

7. John Martin, "The manner howe to bringe the Indians into subjection without makinge an utter exterpation of them . . ." [1622], in *RVC*, 3:704–7; 706.

8. Smith, *Travels and Works*, 2:579 (1622). A decade before he got to Virginia, Smith had been captured in battle against the Turks in Hungary and served in Turkey as a slave, eventually escaping through Russia. (Ibid., 1:360.)

9. Smith, *Travels and Works*, 2:955–6.

10. Anthropologist William M. Denevan remarks that he and other scholars in that field "more and more find a causal relationship between size of population and cultural change and evolution." (William M. Denevan, ed., *The Native Population of the Americas in 1492*, 2nd edition [New York, 1992], p. 235.) Though I am not an anthropologist, it seems to me that comparisons such as that between Portugal and Hispaniola suggest a more indirect relationship between population density and complexity of social structure; that both increasing population density and class differentiation are functions of the development of the productivity of labor. *If* the productivity of labor is such as to provide a storable surplus, population density may be higher *and*, moreover, a possibility of the seizure of power may exist through control of the surplus product by a segment of the society; then, and only then, is a basis for class differentiation present. Without the wheel and domesticated animals, the level of disposable surplus in Portugal would have made it as impossible as it was in contemporary Haiti for a parasitic leisure class to emerge. This is not meant to be the basis for a wider comparison; Noble David Cook points out that intensive agriculture with terracing and irrigation, like that of ancient Peru and in some places in the modern Far East, makes possible a higher level of labor productivity (generally expressed in calories per unit of cultivated area) than that achieved in some other places cultivated with domesticated animals and wheeled equipment.

11. Bartolomé de Las Casas, *Brevisima relación de la Destrución de las Indias* (written in 1539; first printed in Spain in 1552), edited by André Saint-Lu (Madrid, 1982), p. 72.

12. Las Casas commented sarcastically, that the Spanish *encomenderos*, who were supposed to care for the souls of the island natives, merely took "care … to send the men into the mines, to make them drain out golde" (ibid., p. 84).

13. Charles Gibson, *Spain in America* (New York, 1966), pp. 51–2.

14. Las Casas, pp. 81–2.

15. Salvador Brau, *La Colonizacion de Puerto Rico, Desde el descumbrimiento de la Isla hasta la reversión a la corona española de los privilegios de Colón*, 4th edition (San Juan de Puerto Rico, 1969), pp. 142–63, 259.

16. Salvador Brau, *Ensayos: Disquicisiones Sociológicas* (Rio Piedras, 1972), p. 15. Dietz, *Economic History of Puerto Rico*, p. 6. Las Casas reported that the natives of Hispaniola also resisted the Spanish by inter-island flight (Las Casas, p. 83).

17. Comprising the present-day Mexican states of Vera Cruz, Oaxaca, Guerrero, Puebla, Tlaxcala, Morelos, Mexico, Hidalgo, Distrito Federal, Michoacán, Jalisco, Colima, and Nayarit, plus small portions of Zacatecas, Querétaro, and San Luis Potosi (William T. Sanders, "The Population of the Central Mexican Region, the Basin of Mexico, and the Teotihuacán Valley in the Sixteenth Century," in Denevan, p. 87.

18. Denevan, p. xxviii, Table 1.

19. "The Central Mexican Symbiotic Region," as it was termed by demographer William T. Sanders, comprises the present-day Distrito Federal and the states of Mexico and Morelos, plus southern Hidalgo, southwestern Tlaxcala, and the western third of Puebla (Sanders, in Denevan ed., p. 87). For population and population density figures, see ibid., pp. 130–31, Table 4.9. To convert square kilometers to square miles, divide by 2.59.

20. Woodrow Borah and S. F. Cook, *The Population of Central Mexico in 1548*, p. 7. The Aztec Empire was an alliance of three city states in the Valley of Mexico, composed of Tenochtitlan (Mexico City), Tezcoco, and Tlacopan.

21. Borah and Cook, pp. 57, 66–67.

22. Gibson, p. 149. In another work, Gibson's glossary defines *cacique* as an Aztec "Indian chief or local ruler." (Charles Gibson, *The Aztecs under Spanish Rule: A History of the Indians of the Valley of Mexico, 1519–1810* [Stanford, California, 1964], p. 600). According to the dictionary, *cacique* originated as a Haitian word. Clement R. Markham, writing of the *caciques* of Peru, tends to this view, but he allows the possibility that it derived from the Arabic term for chieftain, *sheikh*, which the Spanish adapted for Hispaniola. (Clement R. Markham, *A History of Peru* [1892; reprinted, New York, 1968], p. 156.)

Socially subordinate to the Aztec *caciques*, but still free, were the commoners, the land-owning but tribute-paying *macegual* class. The social attributes of this class – their relatively substantial numbers, their wide distribution, and their direct contact with the serf-like *mayeques* – were characteristics typical of a buffer social control stratum. But I do not know whether they actually functioned as such. (See Borah and Cook, pp. 8, 60.)

23. Gibson, *Aztecs Under Spanish Rule*, pp. 78–80.

24. Gibson, *Spain in America*, p. 149.

25. Ibid., p. 149.

26. Ibid., pp. 150–51.

27. Markham, p. 156.

28. See ibid., p. 157; Lynch, *The Hispanic World in Crisis and Change*, pp. 330–31.

29. James Lockhart, *Spanish Peru, 1532–1560: A Colonial Society* (Madison, 1968), p. 210.

30. Markham, pp. 145–6, 152. At the ceremonial banquet in Lima, Sayri Tupac fingered the richly fringed table covering, saying, "All this cloth and fringe were mine, and now they give me a thread of it for my sustenance and that of all my house." Returning to his own ancient capital, Cuzco, he languished in melancholy and died not long after. (Ibid., p. 146.)

31. The sheer population decline eventually diminished the importance of these executors of the colonial labor supply system. Between 1650 and 1680, say Borah and Cook, "much of the Indian nobility [in Mexico] ... vanished into the general mass of commoners which had become too small for supporting an upper [Indian] stratum." (*The Population of Central Mexico in 1548*, p. 65.) I do not intend to pursue the matter of the history of the replacement of this Indian *cacique* class as the intermediate stratum, beyond referring to the finding of T. R. Fehrenbach that in Mexico this role came to be played by descendants of European fathers and non-European mothers. (T. R. Fehrenbach, *Fire and Blood: A History of Mexico* [New York, 1973], pp. 238, 240.)

32. Borah and Cook, pp. 59–60; Lynch, p. 305. One would hope that Fehrenbach intended to allow room for an ironic interpretation of his characterization of the Chichimec resistance as "merely the savage struggles ... against advancing civilization." (Fehrenbach, p. 217.)

33. Markham, pp. 93–6.

34. After the defeat of the rising, the Spanish beheaded the young Tupac Amaru on 4 October 1571, after instructing him in the Christian religion and baptizing him. (Markham, pp. 152–3.)

35. Five years after Bacon's Rebellion, Virginia Governor Thomas Culpeper made that point in his appeal to the English government for the continued maintenance of two companies of soldiers in Virginia to prevent a renewal of rebellion. "There is a vast difference [he wrote] between Virginia and Jamaica, Barbados and all other Island Plantations, by its situation on the Terra Firma. They have little to fear whilst England is Master of the Sea ... [In island colonies] there is no shelter or hopes for Rebels to escape long unpunished." (Culpeper to the Lords of Trade and Plantations, 25 October 1681. In Great Britain Public Record Office, Colonial Papers, CO 5/1355, pp. 407–9; 407.)

36. Charles R. Boxer, *The Portuguese Seaborne Empire 1415–1825* (New York, 1969), p. 86.

37. Richard Graham, *The Jesuit Antonio Vieira and his Plans for the Economic Rehabilitation of Seventeenth-century Portugal* (São Paulo, 1978), p. 29.

38. Mathias C. Kieman, *The Indian Policy of Portugal in the Amazon Region, 1614–1693* (Washington, DC, 1954), p. 181.

39. Graham, p. 30. Justification was found for holding still other Indians captured in "just wars" (ibid.).

40. Boxer, p. 88.

41. Kieman, p. 184.

42. See ibid., pp. 181–6.

43. A similar effort was made, but ultimately failed, in Spanish Florida, where, writes Robert L. Gold, "the [Franciscan] mission rather than the *encomienda* became the institutional structure upon which colonial power rested." "The indigenous peoples, and territories of Florida," he continues, "were integrated within a system of missions which offered the Spaniards the typical opportunities of expansion, exploitation and proselytization." Robert L. Gold, *Borderline Empires in Transition: The Triple-Nation Transfer of Florida* [Carbondale and Edwardsville, Illinois, 1969(?)], pp. 6–7.

44. António José Saraiva, *História e Utopia, Estudos sobre Vieira* (Lisbon, 1992), pp. 56–7.

45. See Stuart B. Schwartz, "Indian Labor and New World Plantations: European Demands and Indian Responses in North-eastern Brazil," *Journal of American History*, 83:43–79 (1978); 45–7. It was a society characterized by "[a] communal or reciprocal attitude toward production and consumption, a domestic mode of production, a society on [in?] which status was not derived from economic ability" (p. 47).

46. In the following argument, I have relied upon the analysis by Helen C. Rountree and the criteria she has adapted from Mary R. Haas defining strong rulership (Helen C. Rountree, *Powhatan Indians of Virginia: Their Traditional Culture* [Norman, Oklahoma, 1989], especially Chapter 6, "Social Distinctions"); upon Feest, in *Handbook of North American Indians*, 15:256–62;

and upon Philip Alexander Bruce, *Economic History of Virginia in the Seventeenth Century*, 2 vols. (New York, 1895; reprinted 1935), 1:149, 157, 168, 175, 178.

47. This thesis is anticipated in *The Invention of The White Race*, Volume One, pp. 12–13, 23–4, 69–70, and Appendix G. It must be understood that the distinction made here – between societies with and without the intermediate stratum – is different from that between kinship and non-kinship societies. Kinship societies may in some cases be class-stratified, even though the two patterns of social division – kinship and class – are contradictory to each other. (See the discussion of Irish tribal society in Volume One.)

48. Maurice A. Mook, "The Aboriginal Population of Tidewater Virginia," *American Anthropologist*, 46:193–208 (1944); pp. 206–7. Mook considers valid John Smith's estimate that the indigenous population numbered 5,000 within a sixty-mile radius of Jamestown. (Smith, *Travels and Works*, 1:360.) This was the most densely populated area of the "South Atlantic Slope" region, wherein the total Powhatan Confederacy numbered some 8,000, in an area of 0.89 inhabitants per square mile, compared with 0.43 per square mile for the entire region. Other scholars present somewhat different estimates, on the basis of different population numbers and territorial extent, ranging as high as just over two persons per square mile. (Rountree, p. 143 and Feest, in *Handbook of North American Indians*, 15:256.) The most important primary sources in this regard are John Smith, *Map and Description of Virginia* (1612) and William Strachey, *Historie of Travaile into Virginia Britannia* (c. 1616), in Smith, *Travels and Works*.

It should be noted that, from the vantage of a consciousness raised by the civil rights struggles of the 1960s, anthropologists and historians have critically reexamined the scholarly European-American estimates of the population north of the Rio Grande prior to the contact with the exotic diseases of the Europeans. They have persuasively argued that the actual numbers were some ten times greater than those given by earlier authorities. For examples of the earlier ethnography see: James Mooney, "The Powhatan Confederacy, Past and Present," *American Anthropologist*, 9:128–30; idem, "The Aboriginal Population North of Mexico," in *Smithsonian Miscellaneous Collections, LXXX, No. 7* (1928), edited by J. R. Swanton, pp. 1–40; and A. L. Kroeber, *Cultural and Natural Areas of Native North America*, University of California Publications in American Archaeology and Ethnology, XXXVIII (Berkeley and Los Angeles, 1939). For examples of recent critical examinations of the subject, see: Francis Jennings, *The Invasion of America: Indians, Colonialism and the Cant of Conquest* (Chapel Hill, 1975); Sherburne F. Cook, "The Significance of Disease in the Extinctions of the New England Indians," *Human Biology*, 45:485–506 (1973); and Henry F. Dobyns, "Estimating Aboriginal American Population: An Appraisal of Techniques with a New Hampshire Estimate," *Current Anthropology*, 7:395–416 (1966).

49. "It pleased God, after a while to send those people which were our mortall enemies to releeve us with victuals, as Bread, Corne, Fish, and Flesh in great plentie ... otherwise wee had all perished. Also wee were frequented by diverse Kings in the Countrie, bringing us store of provision to our great comfort." (George Percy's *Discourse* [1608?], in Philip L. Barbour, *The Jamestown Voyages Under the First Charter, 1606–1609*, 2 vols. [Cambridge, 1969], 1:145.)

50. Rountree, p. 143.

51. The possibility of a Mexican-style *encomienda* and *hacienda* form of sedentary labor reserve never arose. But if it had, it would surely have proved unsuitable for the constant westward-rolling cycle of clearing and transplanting characteristic of the tobacco monoculture to which the Chesapeake colonies were committed almost from the moment, around 1618, when the bourgeoisie got the first whiff of its profitable possibilities. Of Mexico and Peru, Gibson says: "Native agriculture was little affected by European techniques or crop innovations ..." (*Spain in America*, p. 142.)

52. Though veteran soldiers were important in the Company period of Virginian history which ended in 1624, the colony was by no means primarily a military force. They certainly had no cavalry. When Hernado Cortes sailed from Cuba to invade Mexico, his forces included 110 mariners and 553 soldiers (including 32 crossbowmen and 13 men with firearms) plus 200 Cuban Indian auxiliaries. The force brought 10 heavy guns, four lighter pieces, well furnished with ammunition, and sixteen cavalry horses. (Prescott, pp. 145, 157.)

53. Wesley Frank Craven, *The Dissolution of the Virginia Company, the Failure of a Colonial Experiment* (New York, 1932), pp. 167–8.

"The argument of technological superiority at that time was a weak one; despite guns and large ships, the Europeans could not wrest a living from a terrain which, by English standards, supported an exceptionally large population." (Nancy Oestreich Lurie, "Indian Cultural Adjustment to European Civilization," in James Morton Smith, ed., *Seventeenth-Century America, Essays in Colonial History* [Chapel Hill, 1959] pp. 33–60; 39.)

54. "The appearance of the English was probably far less alarming [to the Indians] than 350 years of hindsight indicate it ought to have been" (Lurie, p. 36).

55. "There was never any real chance of holding the English back after 1646 ..." (Helen C. Rountree, *Pocahontas's People: The Powhatan Indians of Virginia through Four Centuries* [Norman, Oklahoma, 1990], p. 89.)

56. "Treaty of Peace with Necotowance, king of the Indians," 5 October 1646 (Hening, 1:323–6).

57. See *The Invention of The White Race*, Volume One, pp. 36–8.

58. Ibid., pp. 52–3.

59. Hening, 2:15–16 (11 October 1660).

60. Hening, 2:346, 404, 440; Hening, 4:10, 102.

61. Almon Wheeler Lauber, *Indian Slavery in Colonial Times within the Present Limits of the United States* (New York, 1913), pp. 108–9, 123–5.

62. See tabulations of peltry exports from Carolina and Virginia and the prices of various trade goods in the early eighteenth century in Verner W. Crane, *The Southern Frontier, 1670–1732* (Durham, North Carolina, 1928), Appendices A and B.

63. "The native tribes were encouraged [by South Carolina traders] to make war on one another and to sell their prisoners to the colonists." (Lewis C. Gray, assisted by Esther K. Thompson, *History of Agriculture in the Southern United States to 1860* [Washington, DC, 1932; 1958 reprint]. p. 361.) See also: Lauber, pp. 170–71; 183–4; 184 n. 1; 286; Gary B. Nash, *Red, White and Black: The Peoples of Early America* (Englewood Cliffs, New Jersey, 1974), pp. 116–17; Chapman James Milling, *Red Carolinians* (Chapel Hill. 1940), p. 87.

64. A section of the Cherokee Indians complained in 1715 that if they complied with English Yamassee War policy by ceasing to make war on the Creek tribe, "they should have no way in getting Slaves to buy ammunition and Clothing" (Crane, p. 182).

65. Nash, p. 152.

66. See note 61.

67. Ibid., pp. 283–9.

68. No separate comment on the second thesis is attempted; it will be briefly noted in the context of the discussion of the third thesis. (See note 122.) Lauber's fourth thesis seems consistent with the argument I am presenting.

69. Stuart B. Schwartz, "Indian Labor and New World Plantations: European Demands and Indian Responses in Northeastern Brazil," *Journal of American History*, 83:43–79 (1978); pp. 76–8.

70. Kiemen, p. 183. See also Graham, pp. 28–31, 34–35; the quoted phrase, used in a letter written by Vieira to Portugal's King John in May 1653, is at page 28. Charles Edward Chapman, *Colonial Hispanic America: A History* (New York, 1933), p. 80.

71. Lauber, pp. 173–4.

72. The preamble of the first (1712) South Carolina slave law justifies its enactment on the ground of the "barbarous, wild, savage natures" of Negroes and Indians. Richard Hildreth, *The History of the United States of America from the Discovery of the Continent to the Organization of Government under the Federal Constitution, 1497–1789*, 3 vols. (New York, 1848), 2:271–2.

Alexander Stephens, who became the Vice-President of the slaveholders' Confederacy, declared that the Confederacy was founded on "the great truth, that the negro is not equal to the white man; that slavery – subordination to the superior race – is his natural and normal condition." (Savannah Georgia speech, 21 March 1861, quoted in Michael P. Johnson, *Toward a Patriarchal Republic: The Secession of Georgia* [Baton Rouge, 1977] p. 125.) See Volume One of *The Invention of the White Race*, p. 287 n. 15, for other examples.

73. William C. Sturtevant, "Creeks into Seminoles," in Eleanor Burke Leacock and Nancy Oestreich Lurie, eds., *North American Indians in Historical Perspective* (New York, 1971), p. 101. Nash, p. 117.

74. Lauber, p. 171.

75. Ibid., pp. 169, 174.

76. Ibid., pp. 126–7.

77. Bruce, 2:385, 386; Nash, p. 112.

78. Bruce, 1:572–3.

79. Lauber, pp. 108, 187. Governor Berkeley reported that there were 2,000 "black slaves" in Virginia in 1671. (Samuel Wiseman's Book of Record, 1676–77, Magdalene College, Cambridge, Pepysian Library, document 2582.) He did not offer an estimate of the number of Indian slaves. Lauber does not seem to be justified in implying that Berkeley included Indian slaves in the 2,000 figure. (Lauber, p. 108.)

80. Indeed, Lauber says, "it would seem that the supply was sufficient to nourish the system of

Indian slavery indefinitely ..."; he adds, however, that the Indian tribes were "generally remote from the English settlements." (Ibid., p. 283.)

81. Ibid., pp. 124–7.

82. The total population was 9,580, of whom only 41 percent were free persons (1,360 men, 900 women and 1,700 children). In addition to Indians, the bond-labor force included 4,100 Negroes (1,800 men, 1,100 women and 1,200 children), 43 percent of the total population, and 120 "whites", 60 men and 60 women. (Governor and Council of South Carolina to the Commissioners of Trade and Plantations, 17 September 1709. *CSP, Col.*, 24:466–9.)

83. Lauber, p. 106. Crane, pp. 112–13. I have not sought to check their respective sources to account for the substantial discrepancy between Lauber and Crane regarding the number of African-Americans (Lauber 4,100; Crane: 2,900).

84. Lauber, pp. 124–7.

85. Ibid., p. 106. Lauber in this instance was referring to South Carolina but, as has been noted, the same policy was followed in other colonies.

86. Ibid., pp. 169, 174. Crane, p. 113.

87. Crane, p. 113. Lauber, 245.

88. Nash, p. 155.

89. There is at least one record referring to Carolina chiefs as "cassiques" (Crane, p. 137). The cited sources are (1) CO 5/288, p. 100, *Report of the Committee, Appointed to examine into the Proceedings of the People of Georgia* [1737], and (2) Collections of the South Carolina Historical Society, 5:456, n. But in terms of the colonial power social control function, there was a fundamental difference between the Carolina chiefs and the Mexican and Peruvian *caciques*; the Carolina chiefs were in no position to recruit from their own tribes bond-laborers for the colonizing power.

90. The space advantage could be limited in special circumstances, as in the case of the Apalachees and, later, the Seminoles, on the Florida peninsula; and that of the Wampanoags cut off by the English-allied Mohocans of New York in the 1675–76 Metacom War. See Nash, p. 127; and Sturtevant, p. 75.

91. Milling, p. 86. The Delaware were by then under the hegemony of the Iroquois. (Ibid.) See also Nash, p. 118.

92. The Creeks moved away from the English in 1717. (Sturtevant, p. 101.) The Tuscarora plan to migrate to Pennsylvania failed in 1711 because they were not able to get timely approval from the Quakers there. (Nash, p. 147.)

93. A portion of the Wampanoags merged into the Mohicans after defeat in the Metacom War, 1675–76; and the Delaware tribe was formed by a number of remnants of other tribes. (T. J. C. Brasser, "The Coastal Algonkians," in Leacock and Lurie, eds., p. 75; The Natchez, after defeat by the French in the Lower Mississippi in 1730, "in small bands sought refuge with other southeastern tribes." (Nash, p. 109.)

94. The phrase was used by Ulrich Bonnell Phillips in contrasting the situations of Indians and Africans *vis-à-vis* the Anglo-American plantation colonists. (Ulrich Bonnell Phillips, *Life and Labor in the Old South* [Boston, 1929], p. 160)

95. Crane, p. 113.

96. William S. Willis, "Divide and Rule: Red, White and Black in the Southeast," *Journal of Negro History*, 48:157–76 (1963); p. 162.

97. Ibid., p. 161.

98. Ibid.

99. Ibid., p. 162.

100. Lauber, pp. 172, 172 n. 1. Kenneth Wiggins Porter, "Negroes on the Southern Frontier," *Journal of Negro History*, 33:53–18 (1948) pp. 59–62. Sturtevant, pp. 100, 101. Crane, pp. 255–6, 274. Willis, p. 159.

101. Crane, pp. 247–8.

102. Porter, pp. 67–8.

103. Crane, pp. 162–5.

104. Willis, p. 158.

105. For a highly informative dissertation on "Indian policy" of the English colonial governors and legislatures of New York and Maryland, and the involvement of Indian tribes in the rivalries of England, France, Holland and Sweden in the seventeenth century, see Francis Jennings, "Glory, Death, and Transfiguration: The Susquehannock Indians in the Seventeenth Century," *Proceedings of the American Philosophical Society*, 102:5–53 (1968).

106. Crane, pp. 254, 272–3, 275. "[I]t certainly is of the Highest Consequence that they [the Cherokees] should be engaged in Your Majesty's Interest, for should they once take another party,

not only Carolina, but Virginia likewise would be exposed to their invasion" (Commissioners of Trade and Plantations to King George I, 8 September 1721 [CO 324/10, pp. 367-8]).

The thesis that history repeats itself finds expression in the pithy colloquialism "What goes around comes around." History's cruel revisit to the Cherokees, the most "English" of all tribes, is briefly noted in *The Invention of the White Race*, Volume One, pp. 33-4, 37, and 243 n. 44.

107. CO 324/10, pp. 367-8. (8 September 1621).

108. Bruce, 2:115-16. Porter, pp. 59, 63. Willis, p. 169. Sandford Winston, "Indian Slavery in the Carolina Region," *Journal of Negro History*, 19:430-40 (1934); p. 439.

109. Nash, p. 294. He goes on to say, however, that the bounties offered "often evoked little response on the part of the Indians" (ibid.).

110. Willis, p. 163. See also Winston, p. 439.

111. Hening 1:325-6; a similar "agreement" was imposed in South Carolina following the 1711-12 Tuscarora War. (Winston, p. 439.)

An April 1700 treaty between the English colony of Maryland and the Piscataway Indians provided that "[i]n case any servants or slaves run away from their masters to any Indian towne in Oquotomaquah's territory, the Indians shall be bound to apprehend them and bring them to the next English Plantation; any Indian who assists fugitives shall make their masters such compensation as an Englishman ought to do in the like case." (*CSP, Col*, 18:150-52; 9 April 1700 Minutes of the Maryland Colony Council, a treaty between the Governor of Maryland and Oquotomaquah, Emperor of Piscataway.)

112. *CSP, Col.*, 18:150-52.

113. The critical significance of "nearness" informed an order issued by the South Carolina Proprietors in 1680, purposing to prohibit colonists from engaging in the Indian slave trade within 200 miles of Charles Town; two years later the exclusion zone was widened to 400 miles (Crane, pp. 138-9). The settlers on the ground, for whom at that time the Indian slave trade was the principal source of income, were able to evade and nullify such formal restrictions. But their disregard of the "nearness" principle would eventually become a major consideration in the ending of Anglo-American enslavement of Indians.

114. Milling, pp. 86-7.

115. In the extremity of its situation, the South Carolina Provincial government sent emissaries to Virginia to appeal for three hundred "white" volunteers. These recruits were to be paid 22s. 6d. per month. In addition, for each volunteer who came, the South Carolina Provincial government undertook to send one African-American woman to Virginia. (Milling, pp. 144, 146-7, 149.)

South Carolina Governor Charles Craven reported to the English government that he had enlisted about two hundred Afro-American men, "who with a party of white men and Indians are marching toward the enemy," the Yamassees. (*CSP, Col*, 28:228 [23 May 1715].) Noting the irony of the situation, Kenneth Porter commented on its uniqueness: "So far as I can discover, in no other part of the British colonies in North America were slaves so employed." (Porter, p. 55.)

116. Crane, p. 138.

117. *CSP, Col.*, 13: 331-2, Proprietors of Carolina to Governor Colleton, 18 October 1690.

118. Indian employees within the colony played an important part in the surprise Indian attack of Good Friday 1622. At the same time, the English credited an Indian employee with giving the English warning of the attack (*RVC*, 3:555).

119. "Colonial Papers," folder 30, item 29 (27 October 1709), Virginia State Archives, Richmond.

120. Hening 4:78. Morgan Poitiaux Robinson, *Virginia Counties, Those Arising from Virginia Legislation* (Richmond, 1916), p. 95.

121. William Byrd II of Westover to Mr Ochs, ca. 1735. *Virginia Magazine of History and Biography*, 9:225-8 (1902); 226. This periodical will hereafter be abbreviated *VMHB*.

122. Lauber's second thesis regarding the decline of Indian slavery involves not a reduction in the number of slaves but rather an official ethnic reclassification. Upon the birth of a child of an Indian bond-laborer whose other parent was an African-American, the Indian identity ended. Any such child was classified as a Negro, or "mustee," a corruption of the Spanish term *mestizo*. Lauber considers this erasure of the Indian identity simply a matter of the dominance of African genetic traits. (Lauber, p. 287.)

Lauber might better have considered the cases of African-American male bond-laborers who escaped to Indians beyond the boundaries of the colonies, and who "in most cases ... seemed to have disappeared into Indian society where they took Indian wives [and] produced children of mixed blood" (Nash p. 296). Two "disappearances," but in one case the "Indian" identity disappears; in the other, the Negro identity disappears. The disappearance of the Negro identity is by the normal assimilation of the immigrant. But the disappearance of the Indian identity does not involve immigration from one people to another. Rather, the official stripping-away of the Indian identity may be better understood in relation to the following three social control considerations: (1) it was a way of breaking the children from the Indian tribal stems, with the enhanced propensity for running away that such ties entailed; (2) it was a cheap way of formally accommodating the policy of discontinuance of the enslavement of Indians without losing any bond-laborers; and (3) it served to preserve and strengthen the system of white-skin privileges of the European-American colonists, first of all the presumption of liberty.

4   The Fateful Addiction to "Present Profit"

1. The periodicity is noted in Wesley Frank Craven, *The Dissolution of the Virginia Company* (New York, 1932) p. 47; Philip Alexander Bruce, *Institutional History of Virginia*, 2 vols. (New York and London, 1910), 2:229; Philip Alexander Brown, *The First Republic in America* (Boston and New York, 1898), Table of contents; and by others.

2. *RVC*, 3:98–99 (Virginia Company. Instructions to George Yeardley, 18 November 1618, *RVC*, 3:98–109). The document is also available in Jamestown 350th Anniversary Booklet, No. 4, *The Three Charters of the Virginia Company of London, 1606–1624*, with introduction by Samuel M. Bemiss, pp. 95–109, and in *Virginia Magazine of History and Biography*, 2:154–65 (July 1894). The title of this journal will hereafter be abbreviated *VMHB*. See also: Brown, p. 309; Lyman G. Tyler, *Narratives of Early Virginia, 1606–1625* (New York, 1907), "Proceedings of the Virginia Assembly, 1619," pp. 249–78; Craven pp. 52–54.

3. The well-known facts in this introductory paragraph are conveniently presented in William W. Abbot, *A Virginia Chronology, 1585–1783*, Jamestown 350th Anniversary Historical Booklet No. 4 (Williamsburg, 1957), pp. 1–11.

4. Brown, pp. 332 and 650. See also 2:633–6.

5. A corollary of the "germ" theory is found in the idea sometimes advanced that the history of the Company period offers a vindication of the "free enterprise" economic system as against the supposed "collectivism" of the efforts made during the first two phases of the Company period, namely up to 1618. A. E. Smith is one who subscribes to this view. In his standard general work in the field of "white servitude," as it is called, Smith sees the failure of the early efforts of the Virginia Company as due to a "kind of collective farming" approach: "The colony was saved because private individuals took over the activities formerly reserved for the company, and made the profits of the free planters themselves the basis of the settlement's life". (Abbot E. Smith, *Colonists in Bondage: White Servitude and Convict Labor in America, 1607–1776*, [Chapel Hill, 1947; New York, 1971] p. 14.)

Considering the dearth of material on the origin of chattel bondage during the Company period, however, Smith's brief discussion of it (pp. 6–16) is still valuable.

6. Philip A. Bruce, *Economic History of Virginia in the Seventeenth Century*, 2 vols. (New York, 1895), 1:586–7.

7. James C. Ballagh, *A History of Slavery in Virginia* (Baltimore, 1902), pp. 31–2.

8. Eric E. Williams, *Capitalism and Slavery* (Chapel Hill, 1944), p. 19.

9. Lerone Bennett Jr, *The Shaping of Black America* (Chicago, 1975), pp. 40–41.

10. For example: Charles M. Andrews, *The Colonial Period in American History*, 4 vols. (New Haven, 1914–1938); Wesley Frank Craven, *The Southern Colonies in the Seventeenth Century, 1607–1689* (Baton Rouge, 1949); idem, *Colonies in Transition, 1660–1713* (New York, 1967); and idem, *White, Red and Black, The Seventeenth-Century Virginian*; Carl N. Degler, *Out of Our Past* (New York, 1959 and 1970); Winthrop D. Jordan, *White Over Black, American Attitudes Toward the Negro, 1550–1812*, (Chapel Hill, 1968); Richard L. Morton, *Colonial Virginia*, 2 vols. (Chapel Hill, 1960); Edward D. Neill, *Virginia Carolorum* (Albany, NY, 1886); Herbert L. Osgood, *American Colonies in the Seventeenth Century*, 3 vols. (New York, 1904–1907); Thomas J. Wertenbaker *Patrician and Plebeian in Virginia* (Charlottesville, 1910); idem, *Virginia under the Stuarts* (Princeton, 1914); and idem, *The Planters of Colonial Virginia*, (Princeton, 1922).

11. By Russell R. Menard, in his works *Economy and Society in Early Colonial Maryland* (New York, 1985), especially pp. 191–201, 234–5, 268–9, 286, and "From Servants to Slaves: The Transformation of the Chesapeake Labor System," *Southern Studies*, 16:355–90 (1977); and by David W. Galenson in his "White Servitude and the Growth of Black Slavery in Colonial America," *Journal of Economic History*, 41: 39–47 (1981), in his *White Servitude in Colonial America: An*

Economic Analysis (New York, 1981), and in *Traders, Planters and Slaves: Market Behavior in Early English America* (New York, 1986).

As historians, Menard and Galenson are economists rather than political economists. The class struggle between laborers and employers does not enter at all into their discussions; indeed Menard spends a lot of time establishing the absence of class struggle, especially between poor and rich, bond-laborer and owner among European–Americans. They seem to presume that all the employer had to do was to decide that a given category of laborers was more advantageous to employers' interests, and that all else automatically followed. On this basis Menard challenges Edmund S. Morgan's attempt to suggest that racial oppression of the Negro was a deliberate decision by the ruling class. Menard and Galenson offer their presumption under the rubric of "the divided labor market." Job discrimination in early colonial times is rationalized by Menard and Galenson as a function of the common language of the English master and servant and the skills that the English workers brought with them to America. This discrimination was undergirded, Menard says, by "cultural barriers and the depth of racial prejudice." (*Economy and Society*, p. 270).

Menard and Galenson appear not to be disposed to look at the "white" identity objectively.

12. Cited here from Hening, 1:64; 95. This work will hereafter be cited as "Hening, [vol. no.]: [page no.]." See also: Jamestown 350th Anniversary Booklet, No. 4, *The Three Charters of the Virginia Company of London, 1606–1624*, with an introduction by Samuel M. Bemiss; and Brown.

13. Hening, 1:103.

14. See Table 5.1.

15. Charles E. Hatch Jr, *The First Seventeen Years, Virginia, 1607–1624*, Jamestown 350th Anniversary Booklet, No. 6 (Williamsburg, 1957), p. 10.

16. Brown, pp. 126–7.

17. "Coppie of A Letter from Virginia, Dated 22nd of June, 1607. The Councell there to the Councell here in England;" printed in Alexander Brown, *The Genesis of the United States* (Boston, 1890) 1:106–8; 107.

18. Bruce, *Economic History*, 1:588 n. 1.

19. Answers to a 1624 Royal Commission on "the reformation of Virginia" (Smith, *Travels and Works*, pp. 615–20; pp. 616, 618).

20. Brown, *First Republic* ("John Rolfe's Relation," [1616]), pp. 135, 144. Evarts B. Greene and V. D. Harrington, *American Population before the Federal Census of 1790* (New York, 1932), p. 135.

21. See Thomas Niccolls's complaint, p. 68.

22. Referring to the 1609 charter, Alexander Brown says: "this charter, it seems, was drafted by Sir Edwin Sandys, possibly assisted by Lord [Francis] Bacon" *Genesis*, 1:207.

23. Sir Fernando Gorges (1566–1647), an early venturer in American colonization schemes, took note of the predisposition of English mercenaries displaced by the (1603–24) peace with Spain to find employment of their talents in Virginia. The Spanish spy Molina reported from Virginia in 1613 rather disparagingly on the quality of the English soldiers there, while noting "the great assistance they have rendered in Flanders in favor of Holland, where some of them have companies [of soldiers] and castles" (Brown, *Genesis*, 2:649). From 1607 to 1627, from Captain Edward Maria Wingfield to Sir George Yeardley (second term), every head of the Virginia colony government, except Francis Wyatt (a kinsman by marriage of the Sandys clan), was a veteran of mercenary service in the Netherlands. They were, as was said of Yeardley, "truly bred in that university of Warre, and Lowe countries" (Brown, *Genesis*, 2:1065). Some also served against the Turks, and others against the Irish in the brutal plantation of Ulster. (See Brown, *Genesis* vol. 2, "Brief Biographies" of Delaware, Thomas Dale, Thomas Gates, George Percy, John Ratcliffe, John Smith, Winfield and Yeardley.) Gates and Dale each served in Holland, both before and after their terms as governor in Virginia. When Gates went to Virginia, he brought his company from the Netherlands to Virginia (by way of England) under the command of George Yeardley (Brown, *Genesis*, 2:895). Such references leave no doubt that such men constituted the chief supply source for the "Governors and Captaines for peace and war" which the Company was sending to Virginia in this period. (The quoted phrase is from "Briefe Declaration of the State of Things in Virginia," by the King's Council for Virginia [1616] [Brown, *Genesis*, 2:775–9; 775]. As "governors" they would oversee the laboring people; as "captains" they would organize war against the Indians or against Spanish or other European intruders. It would seem that their role corresponded to that of the "Servitors" in the plantation of Ulster. (See *The Invention of the White Race*, Volume One, pp. 118–19.) See especially Darrett B. Rutman, "The Virginia Company and Its Military Regime," in Darrett B. Rutman, ed., *The Old Dominion: Essays for Thomas Perkins Abernathy* (Charlottesville, 1964), pp. 1–20. Sir Richard Moryson, whose participation in the conquest of Ireland by starvation in the Tyrone War (1594–1603) has been noted in Volume One, urged "using Irish

veterans in Virginia." Indeed three veterans of the Tyrone War (see Volume One) did serve successively as governors of Virginia in the 1610–16 period, namely, Acting Governor Sir Thomas Gates (promulgator of the "Laws Divine, Moral, and Martial," a draconian set of laws derived from European military codes in which he was well versed), Governor Lord De La Warre (Delaware) and Acting Governor Sir Thomas Dale. (See: *A Memorial Volume at Virginia Historical Portraiture*, Alexander Willbourne Weddell, ed., [Richmond, 1930], pp. 66, 68, 79, 80; Darrett B. Rutman, "Virginia Company" pp. 6–7; idem, *A Militant New World, 1607–1640* [New York, 1970, a reprint of the author's PhD dissertation, University of Virginia, 1959], pp. 134–9.)

24. "[T]obacco not militarism was to prove the 'sovereign remedy' for Virginia's ills," writes Rutman (*Militant New World*, p. 231).

25. Craven, *Dissolution of the Virginia Company*, p. 33.

26. Ibid., p. 34.

27. "Nova Britannia: Offering Most Excellent fruits by Planting in Virginia. Exciting all such as be well affected to further the same," By R. I. (Robert Johnson probably, London alderman, rich merchant, and Deputy Treasurer of the Virginia Company from 1616 to 1619), London, 1609; printed in *Force Tracts*, Vol. I, No. 6, p. 23.

28. "A Letter from the Councill and Company of the honourable Plantation in Virginia to the Lord Mayor, Aldermen and Companies of London," London, 1609; printed in Brown, *Genesis*, 1:252–3. The term "inmate," as used here, simply means "inhabitant."

In their crusade to "end welfare as we know it," our modern-day conservatives will doubtless find reassurance in this ancient expression of bourgeois "traditional values".

29. See Bruce's comment on the laborers of Charles Hundred: "The probability is that the emancipated laborers of Charles Hundred became tenants" (*Economic History* 1:220).

30. Ralph Hamor, *A True Discourse of the Present Estate of Virginia* (London, 1615); cited in Brown, *First Republic* pp. 205–11; p. 205.

31. Bruce, *Economic History* 1:213–15, 219–20. Bruce says: "It is impossible to give the proportion between those who received and those who did not receive this privilege" (p. 214 n. 2).

32. Deputy-Governor Sir Thomas Dale promulgated this code in mid-1611. It was published in London in 1612. See William Strachey, comp., *For the Colony of Virginian Britannia, Lawes Divine, Morall, and Martiall*, edited by David H. Flaherty (Charlottesville, 1969). See Tyler; H. R. McIlwaine, *Minutes of the Council and General Court of Virginia* pp. 14, 62, 85, 93, 117, 163–64 (hereafter abbreviated *MCGC*; Rutman, *Militant New World*, p. 135.

33. John Rolfe, *Relation of Virginia* (London, 1616), reprinted in part in Brown, *First Republic*, pp. 226–9; p. 227. The bracketed emendations are Brown's. The term "familie," as used here and generally in documents cited in this present work, includes the household of persons, and not merely the blood and marriage kin.

As late as 1622, the official catalogue of social statuses comprised "Gentlemen," "Freemen," "Tenants," "Hired Servants," and "Apprentices" (*RVC*, 3:658 [Governor Francis Wyatt's proclamation against drunkenness, 21 June 1622]). The absence of an "indentured servant" category presumably reflects the fact that the plantation bourgeoisie's option for chattel-bond servitude was just then being made.

34. Speaking specifically of laborers in this middle period, L. D. Scisco states: "they were really hired employees and were treated as such. [P]rivate property in labor was absent." ("The Plantation Type of Colony," *American Historical Review*, Vol. VIII, No. 2 [January 1903], 260–70; pp. 261.) This periodical will hereafter be abbreviated *AHR*.

35. "Newes from Virginia," by Robert Rich (London, 1610), in Brown, *Genesis*, 1:420–26; pp. 425–6. The author of "Newes from Virginia" was an interested party and an enthusiast, of course; but so was the author of another promotional pamphlet, titled "Leah and Rachel," published to the glory of Virginia and Maryland half a century later. In the later tract, however, there is no promise of "day wages for the laborer," but rather the prospect of long-term, unpaid, chattel bond-servitude, at the end of which the worker would find that the right to land was but "an old delusion." ("Leah and Rachel, or, the Two Fruitfull Sisters Virginia and Maryland: Their Present Condition, Impartially Stated and Related," by John Hammond [London 1656]; printed in *Force Tracts*, III, No. 3, esp. pp. 10–11.)

36. Rolfe, p. 229.

37. Bruce, *Economic History*, 1:220.

38. Edwin Sandys, Report to the June 1620 Court of the Virginia Company of London, in Edward D. Neill, *History of the Virginia Company of London* (Albany, NY, 1869), p. 180.

39. Bruce, *Economic History*, 1:221, 227–8.

40. Native Virginia tobacco could not complete with the product of the Spanish colonies in the

world market. John Rolfe induced a friendly ship captain to smuggle Trinidad and Venezuela tobacco seeds into Virginia. When planted in Virginia they produced the "sweet-scented" product that tobacco users found as appealing as the Spanish-American product. The first shipment to England was made in 1615–16. George Arent, "The Seed from which Virginia Grew," *WMQ* second series, 19:123–9 [1939], pp. 125–6.

41. Bruce, *Economic History* 2:566. Here Bruce was assuming the indefeasibility of the capitalist principle of the "bottom line," as it might be called today. When that assumption was brought into question by social upheaval later in the seventeenth century, class struggle was revealed as an even more fundamental determinant of Virginia's fate. However, when considered simply in terms of the historical impact of innovations in capitalist production techniques in Anglo-America, the "discovery" of tobacco as a profitable Virginia crop in 1616 can only be compared with the invention of the cotton gin in 1793 (see *The Invention of the White Race*, Volume One, pp. 160–61).

42. Bruce, *Economic History*, 1:226.

43. Ibid., 1:222–3.

44. Craven, *Dissolution of the Virginia Company*, pp. 33–4.

45. Brown, *Genesis*, 2:776, 777–9.

46. Bruce, *Economic History*, 1:225–6. Bruce comments: "Beginning his control of the affairs of Virginia with the strict enforcement of the regulation that every cultivator of the ground should plant four acres in grain, he [Argall] ended with this regulation in entire abeyance."

47. Brown, *First Republic*, p. 254. A year later Argall was trying to get the price of tobacco raised *vis-à-vis* the magazine supplies (ibid., p. 279).

48. Ibid., p. 278.

49. Ibid., p. 279.

50. Neill, *History of the Virginia Company*, p. 117.

51. Brown, *Genesis*, 2:550–51.

52. Ibid., 2:939; "William Lovelace" biographical note. Argall came to Virginia the possessor of a new patent for 400 acres as the transporter of eight tenants.

53. "Letter of the Virginia Company to Deputy Governor Argall, 22 August 1618"; in Neill, *History of the Virginia Company*, pp. 114–19; p. 115. Argall was liable to criminal prosecution for his acts. In a letter to Lord Delaware regarding Argall, the Company said, "the adventurers . . . are hardly restrayned . . . [,] the Kings Court in progress[,] from going to the Court to make there complaynte and to procure his Majesty's command to fetch him [Argall] home" (ibid, p. 119).

54. Ibid., p. 115.

55. Recent historians have seemed more inclined to suspend judgment regarding Argall's actions. For examples of the earlier condemnatory view, see Brown, *First Republic*, and Bruce, *Economic History*; for the revised view, see Craven, *Dissolution of the Virginia Company*, and Morton.

56. "The Trades Increase," by R. I. (Robert Johnson) (London, 1615); extract in Brown, *Genesis*, 2:766. "Briefe Declaration of the present state of things in Virginia, and of a Division now made of some part of those Lands in our Actuall possession, as well to all such as have adventured their moneyes there, as also to those that are Planters there" (London, 1616) (ibid., 2:775–9).

57. My use of "headright" here is anachronistic, since that laconic term was not in vogue until some time later than 1616.

58. Brown, *Genesis*, 2:779.

59. Events were to show that absentee landlordism was not practicable. Rutman notes that these so-called "'particular plantations' were soon to disappear altogether from Virginia, their owners having first lost money in their undertakings then lost interest" (Rutman, *Militant New World*, pp. 307–8).

60. *RVC*, 2:350 (Virginia Company. A Delcaration of the State of Virginia. 12 April 1623). In the four years 1619 to 1622, the number of "adventurers," London investors in Virginia plantations, increased by ten times the previous number, and each of the ventures involved at least 100 men (ibid.).

61. Bruce, *Economic History*, 1:507–9. The patents lapsed, however, for failure to settle the lands with the required numbers of tenants (ibid., 1:505–6).

62. Minutes of the Quarterly meeting of the General Court of the Virginia Company of London, 2 February 1619; reprinted in Neill, *History of the Virginia Company*, pp. 129–30.

63. "Newes from Virginia," in Brown, *Genesis*, 1:420–26; p. 426.

64. See Table 5.1.

65. Pocahontas's actual native name was Matoaka. She was christened by the English "Rebecca." She and Rolfe were married around the middle of April 1614. Their Virginia-born son was named Thomas. (Brown, *First Republic*, pp. 203, 204, 225).

66. Rolfe, p. 226.

67. The three southern plantation colonies of the seventeenth century were Virginia, founded in 1607; Maryland, founded in 1634; and South Carolina, founded in 1670. Virginia was first also in the volume of exports. Tobacco was first in time and importance, and it held the leading place throughout the colonial period. The commercial cultivation of rice in South Carolina did not begin until the end of the seventeenth century. (Lewis C. Gray, assisted by Esther K. Thompson, *History of Agriculture in the Southern United States to 1860*, 2 vols. [Washington, DC, 1932] 1:57–8.) As in substance, so in form: Virginia was the pattern-setter for the institution of racial slavery in the southern colonies and in the development of the social and legal structure of white supremacy to reinforce the institution. "The discovery of the great resource for profit in raising tobacco," writes Ulrich B. Phillips, "gave the spur to Virginia's large-scale industry and her territorial expansion ... [and] brought about the methods of life which controlled the history of Virginia through the following centuries and of the many colonies and states which borrowed her plantation system" (in Ulrich Bonnell Phillips, *The Slave Economy of the Old South: Selected Essays in Economic and Social History*, edited by Eugene D. Genovese [Baton Rouge, 1968], p. 8). Emphasizing the pattern-setting role of Virginia in legal institutions of white supremacy and racial slavery, Phillips says: "the legislation of Virginia was copied with more or less modification by all the governments from Delaware to Mississippi and Arkansas" (ibid., pp. 26–7).

Maryland was a proprietary colony of the Catholic Calverts, with "manorial" land ownership, where – in contrast to Virginia – the "headright" principle of land acquisition never applied to the importation of African laborers. These circumstances appear to have been the cause of the "large proportion" of limited-term bond-laborers held by small planters there. (Menard, pp. 129, 189.)

South Carolina was different in that the rice plantation economy did not emerge there until after the pattern of racial slavery (including the system of white-skin privileges of European-American workers) had been firmly established in Virginia and Maryland. The general employment of European-American bond-laborers in plantation field labor in South Carolina came late, was relatively less important than it was in the other two early plantation colonies, and was short-lived.

Unless one accepts the "natural racism" theory of the "psycho-cultural" school, these Maryland and South Carolina distinctions *vis-à-vis* Virginia have no contrary implications for the thesis being developed in the present work, namely that the chattelization of English plantation labor constituted an essential precondition of the emergence of the subsequent lifetime chattel bond-servitude imposed upon African-American laborers in continental Anglo-America under the system of white supremacy and racial slavery.

68. Craven, *Dissolution of the Virginia Company*, pp. 44–6.

69. Ibid., pp. 47–57.

70. Neill, *History of the Virginia Company*, p. 180.

71. Morgan, "The First American Boom," *WMQ* 28:169–98 (1971).

72. For deriving these ratios the following sources were used: export figures from Gray pp. 21–2; population figures from Brown, *First Republic*, pp. 226, 309, 464.

73. Craven, *Dissolution of the Virginia Company*, p. 59. *RVC*, 2:350.

74. Craven, *Dissolution of the Virginia Company* pp. 176–9, 301.

75. Ibid., p. 178. In 1619, the Virginia Assembly was established as the first elected legislative body in Anglo-America. At its first meeting, the Assembly decreed tobacco to be the money of the colony, making it clear in the following order to the Cape Merchant of the Colony: "you are bound to accept the Tobacco of the Colony, either for commodities or upon letters, at three shillings the beste and the second sort at 18d the pund, and this shallbe your sufficient discharge." Tyler, p. 260.

76. Craven, *Dissolution of the Virginia Company*, p. 190 n. 33, 301. See also Table 4.1.

77. *VMHB*, 2:154–65 (1894); pp. 155, 159. *RVC*, 3:99, 104 ("Instructions to Yeardley," *RVC*, 98–109 18 November 1618).

78. Smith, *Travels and Works*, 2:571.

79. *RVC*, 3:584 (Virginia Colony Council letter to Virginia Company in London, January 1621/22).

80. *RVC*, 3:479 (Virginia Company of London Instructions to Virginia Colony Governor and Council, 24 July 1621, 3:468–84); 3:489 (Treasurer and Company in London to Virginia Colony Council, 25 July 1621, 3:485–90).

81. Craven, *Dissolution of the Virginia Company*, pp. 149–50.

82. Ibid., p. 184.

83. *RVC*, 3:98–108.

84. "A Briefe Declaration" (by the Virginia Company), Brown, *Genesis* 2:774–9.

85. *Force Tracts*, III, no. 5, pp. 14–15. Cf. Craven, *Dissolution of the Virginia Company*, p. 56; Bruce, *Economic History*, 1:231.

86. "Instructions to Yeardley," *RVC*, 3:108.

87. Craven, *Dissolution of the Virginia Company*, pp. 100–102, 191.

88. Ibid., p. 189.

89. Gray, 1:259.

90. Craven, *Dissolution of the Virginia Company*, pp, 230–32. "Sandys had accepted the Company's dependence on tobacco" (ibid., p. 178).

91. At a meeting of the Virginia Company Court in July 1621, Samuel Wrote, member of the King's Council for Virginia, called attention to the unreality of the high official price of tobacco in Virginia, and deplored the fact that "It hath not been possible hitherto to awaken out of this straunge dream." (Virginia Company of London, *Court Book* I, cited in Gray, 1:260.)

92. The king got one-third of the crop and that transported to England free of charge, plus a duty of half a shilling on the other two-thirds. Furthermore, at a time when the Virginia crop sent to England would reach just 60,000 pounds the Company was required to agree to the English import of not less than 80,000 pounds of Spanish-produced tobacco, an amount approximatley equal to the crops being sent from Virginia at that time. (Craven, *Dissolution of the Virginia Company*, pp. 233–4. Bruce, *Economic History*, 1:269–70. See Gray, 1:22, for the 1622 Virginia tobacco export figure.)

93. See, for example: King James I, *Counter Blast* (1610); Gray, 1:25, 180–81, 231. "It was easier to decide upon such limitations [on tobacco-growing] than to make them efffective in Virginia." (Craven, *Dissolution of the Virginia Company*, p. 176.)

94. *CSP, Col.*, l:117, Governor John Harvey's Report to the Privy Council, 29 May 1630. The price recovered to 6 pence a pound in 1635, but from then to 1660 the price averaged no more than 2¼ pence. A major crisis of overproduction in 1638 brought prices down to extremely low levels, says Gray, and even with recovery prices ranged between 1½ pence per pound until the mid-1660s. (Gray, 1:26.) See also Russell R. Menard's tabulations of prices paid for tobacco in the Chesapeake (*Economy and Society in Early Colonial Maryland*, pp. 444–50, Tables A-5 and A-6).

In London in 1634, "Virginia tobacco was so low in price that it would no longer bear the old duty of twelve pence a pound; nor even the nine pence to which the duty had been reduced in 1623." (*Aspinwall Papers*, Massachusetts Historical Society Collections, Series 4, IX [Boston, 1871], p. 71.)

95. Brown, *First Republic*, pp. 562–3. See also Bruce, *Economic History*, 1:255.

96. Gray, Vol. 1, Chapter XII. See Chapter 9 of this volume for further treatment of the diversification of the Virginia economy.

97. This is another insight to be had from the frequently quoted comment of the Secretary of the Virginia Colony, John Pory, in 1619: "Our principall wealth consisteth of servants" (Pory to Sir Dudley Carleton, 30 September 1619 [*RVC*, 2:219–22; 221]). In 1618 a method was suggested of airing tobacco leaves by hanging them on strings rather than laying them on loose hay. When they could get the needed string from England, the colonists used this method which, by preserving tobacco, raised the productivity of labor. Aside from this innovation, however, there was to be but little technological advance in tobacco raising, and that would come slowly. (Brown, *First Republic*, p. 260. Craven, *Dissolution of the Virginia Company*, p. 181. See "Pounds of Tobacco Per Laborer, 1619–1699," Menard, *Economy and Society in Early Colonial Maryland*, p. 462.)

98. Brown, *First Republic*, pp. 248–9.

99. Ibid., p. 348.

100. Minutes of the meeting of the Virginia Company Court, 17 November 1619 (*RVC*, 2:271). See *The Invention of the White Race*, Volume One, p. 118, for the shipment into exile of mainly Ulster Irish rebels in 1610. George Hill notes the 1619 proposal of the English Lord Lieutenant of Ireland for shipping away Irish "woodkernes." (George Hill, *An Historical Account of the plantation in Ulster at the Commencement of the Seventeenth Century, 1608–1620* [Belfast 1877], p. iii, n. 2.)

101. They were forbidden to return except by express permission of the Privy Council as provided in a General Order of 24 March 1617. *Acts of the Privy Council of England, Colonial Series*, Vol. I, 1618–1638 (London, 1908), pp. 12–13, 19, 22, 52, 55, 56. See also Bruce, *Economic History* 1:603–4: "At this time, there were three hundred crimes in the calendar from which capital punishment was inflicted. It seemed to be too harsh a punishment to impose deaths for the smallest offense. Transportation was a compromise on the part of the English judges with the more humane feelings of their nature."

102. This man was put to death in Virginia in 1623 for the theft of a cow worth £3 sterling. The cow was the property of the once and future governor Yeardley who himself had stolen with impunity fifty-four men from the Virginia Company, his employer, two years previously. (*MCGC*, 4, 5.)

103. Brown, *First Republic*, pp. 273–4.

104. *RVC*, 2:270–71 (General Court of the Virginia Company of London meeting, 17 November 1619).

105. *RVC*, 2:271.

106. Acts of the Privy Council, Colonial, 1:28–9 (31 January 1619/20). Prior to 1750, the legal year began on 25 March. Therefore dates falling between 1 January and 24 March inclusive appear in the records in the form shown here. Where one year only is indicated, it is to be understood according to the modern calendar.

107. Brown, *First Republic*, p. 375.

108. *RVC*, 2:271.

109. Gray, 1:366. Bruce, *Economic History*, 1:629–30.

110. This is the average of estimates in the record as made by: John Rolfe, in 1619, 250 pounds (Smith, *Travels and Works*, 2:541); John Pory, in 1619, two "rare cases" averaging about 1,054 pounds according the 1619 price of 42*d.* in London (*RVC*, 3:221); William Spencer, recalling his experience in 1620, which works out to an average of 538 pounds (*RVC*, 1:256, 268); William Capps, in 1623, 500 pounds (*RVC*, 4.38); and Richard Brewster, also in 1623, 700 pounds (*RVC*, 2:524). Russell Menard's estimate of 712 pounds per worker for the period 1619–29 appears to be based on his figures for this same five-year 1619–23 period. (Menard, *Economy and Society in Early Colonial Maryland*, pp. 460, 462.) Although my average figure of 712 per pounds per worker is exactly the same as Menard's, they were not derived altogether from the same sources.

111. Menard, *Economy and Society in Early Colonial Maryland*, p. 444, Table A-5, "Chesapeake Tobacco Prices. 1618–1658." The average is calculated from fourteen citations (all but two being for 1619 and 1620) mainly from the *Records of the Virginia Company*; I did not count those tagged as "overstatements." Averaging by the year, the price paid in Virginia for the 1619–23 period was 20*d.* (Ibid. p. 448, Table A-6.)

112. Ibid. This is the average of fifteen instances of London wholesale prices.

113. *RVC*, 3:264 (William Weldon, letter to Sir Edwin Sandys, 6 March 1619/20).

114. Ibid.

115. See discussion and notation in Chapter 6, under the heading "Bond-servitude was not an adaptation of English practice."

116. Records of Magistrate's Court, Netherstone, Somerset, England, 19 October and 13 November 1618, *Correspondence, Domestic, James I*, vol. 103, Nos. 42, 42, I, 87 and 87 I; reprinted in *VMHB*, vi (1898–99), pp. 228–30.

117. Neill, *History of the Virginia Company*, p. 121. Brown, *First Republic*, p. 292.

118. Brown, *First Republic*, p. 376. The late Professor Richard L. Morton made the erroneous statement that "the women who were sent to be wives" in Virginia were not sold like merchandise, and that the enterprisers did not intend to make a profit on the transaction. (*Colonial Virginia*, 1:71.)

119. Virginia Company Court, 22 June 1620, *RVC*, 3:115. See also David Ransome, "Wives for Virginia," *WMQ* 48:3–18 (1991).

120. *RVC*, 3:313.

121. Brown, *First Republic*, pp. 459, 461. Actually a few of these women arrived in January on the pinnace *Tiger*.

122. Craven, *Dissolution of the Virginia Colony*, pp. 191–2. Of these five subsidiary joint-stocks launched in 1621, only the matrimonial business returned a profit (*RVC*, 2:15).

123. Virginia Company in London to the Virginia Colony Council in Virginia, 12 April 1621; in Neill, *History of the Virginia Company*, pp. 233–9; 234–5.

124. Ibid., pp. 241–50.

125. Ibid., p. 235.

126. *MCGC*, p. 54.

127. Neill, *History of the Virginia Company*, p. 235.

128. Ibid.

129. Manchester Papers, in *Historical Manuscripts Commision, Eighth Report* (London, 1881), Part I, Appendix, p. 41 (hereafter referred to as *Manchester Papers*).

130. Ibid.

131. *MCGC*, pp. 154–5 (11 October 1627).

132. Brown, *First Republic*, p. 627.

133. *MCGC*, pp. 117, 142 (11 October 1626 and 4 April 1627).

134. Herbert Moller, "Sex Composition and Correlated Culture: Patterns of Colonia America,"

WMQ 3d ser., 2:113–53 (1945), p. 114. *Historical Statistics of the United States, Colonial Times to 1970* (Washington, DC, 1975), Series Z-121–131 (p. 1171).

135. Moller, p. 115, citing J. A. Goodman, *The Pilgrim Republic* (Boston and New York, 1920), pp. 182–4.

136. Rutman, *Militant New World*, p. 355.

137. Moller, pp. 116–17. John C. Hotten, *The Original Lists of Persons of Quality, Emigrants; Religious Exiles; Political Rebels; Serving Men Sold for a Term of Years; Apprentices; Children Stolen; Maidens Pressed and Others Who went from Great Britain to the American plantations, 1600–1700* (London, 1874), pp. 35–138. Hereafter noted as Hotten, *Original Lists*.

138. Menard, *Economy and Society in Early Colonial Maryland*, p. 145.

139. "The Puritans, broadly speaking, arrived by families, although they had a considerable surplus of men. The movement to Virginia, on the other hand, consisted predominantly of male workers" (Moller, p. 118).

140. Allan Kulikoff, *Tobacco and Slaves: The Development of Southern Cultures in the Chesapeake, 1680–1800* (Chapel Hill, 1986), p. 34.

141. Bruce, *Economic History*, 1:538–89; Morgan, p. 176; A. E. Smith, pp. 14–16.

142. Craven, *Dissolution of the Virginia Colony*, p. 311.

143. John Smyth of Nibley Papers, documents in the New York Public Library, calendared in the New York Public Library *Bulletin*, 1:68–72 (1897), and 3:276–95 (1899).

144. "A Lyste of the men nowe sent for plantacon under Captayne Woodleefe ..." (September 1619), *RVC*, 3:197–8.

145. Ibid. See also "Capt Woodleefes Bill, Setpember, 1619," New York Public Library *Bulletin*, 3:221 (1899), p. 221.

146. "Berkeley, Thorpe, Tracy, and Smith. Agreement with Richard Smyth and Wife and Others" (1 September 1620), *RVC*, 3:393–4.

147. A. E. Smith, p. 14.

148. *RVC*, 3:210–11 (Indenture between the Four Adventurers of Berkeley Hundred and Robert Coopy of North Nibley, 7 September 1619). Among thirteen other men engaged for Berkeley Hundred in that same month, there were two other Coopys – Thomas and Samuell – but I do not know whether they were kin.

149. *RVC*, 3:210–11.

150. A. E. Smith, *Colonists in Bondage*, p. 15.

151. Part of "Drafts of a Statement touching the miserable condition of Virginia [May and June, 1623] by Alderman Robert Johnson" (*RVC*, 4:174). This was the opening blast of the campaign that was to end in the following year in the revocation of the Virginia Company charter. Johnson was a rich London merchant, who had over the years held positions of great authority in both the East India Company and the Virginia Company. See note 27.

152. Broadside published by the Virginia Company in 1622, prior to the receipt of the news of the Indian attack aof 22 March of that year; in Brown, *First Republic*, p. 486.

153. Ibid.

154. Virginia Governor and Council to Virginia Company of London (January 1621/22), *RVC*, 3:585–8; 586.

155. Thomas Nuce to Edwin Sandys, 27 May 1621 (*RVC*, 3:457).

156. *RVC*, 3:588. The actual enclosure seems not to have survived in the records, but the essential substance is clear from references to it in documents that have been preserved. It is curious that historians have chosen to ignore Nuce's proposal, while at the same time noting (Craven, *Dissolution of the Virginia Colony*, p. 173, Morgan, "First American Boom," p. 172) a letter written seven months earlier in which he states that his tenants are depressed by the prospect of a seven-year term of service, "which course, I am of opinion you should alter" (Nuce to Edwin Sandys, 27 May 1621 [*RVC*, 3:456–7]). The facts are that the conditions of the tenants were altered – to those of chattel bond-labor; that Nuce specifically recommended that tenants be replaced by "servants"; and that he was unwilling to pay the wages of free wage workers. Therefore, the imputation of benign motives to Nuce should not divert attention from his apparent role in promoting the change in the conditions of labor that took place in the 1620s in Virginia.

157. Virginia Company of London to the Virginia Governor and Council, 10 June 1622; (*RVC*, 3:646–52; 647).

158. Virginia Company of London to the Virginia Governor and Council, 7 October 1622 (*RVC* 3:683–90; 684).

159. Idem, 20 January 1622/23 (*RVC*, 4:9–17; 16).

160. *RVC* 4:178. The word used in this instance was, "pencons." This word is nowhere else to be

found in the records, but it seems to suggest a servant who lives with the employer, or at least one whose meals are provided by the employer. Indeed, references to this proposed change from tenantry all translate the term as "servant." Although the term "servant" has various applications in the records of the time, it is not necessary to explore that matter here; it is clear that the purpose was to reduce the cost of labor, and to levels below the wages then current in Virginia.

5 The Massacre of the Tenantry

1. See pp. 56, 61.

2. Back projection of the average annual crude death rate, 1619–1625, inclusive of a 4.16 percent spike for 1625. (E. A. Wrigley and R. S. Schofield, *The Population History of England, 1541–1871: A Reconstruction* [Cambridge, Massachusetts, 1981], p. 352.) This modern study confirms the reliability of the estimate of 2.5 percent made by Sir William Petty more than three centuries ago in his *An Essay concerning the Multiplication of Mankind together with another Essay in Political Arithmetick concerning the Growth of the City of London . . .* (London 1686), reprinted in part in Joan Thirsk and J. P. Cooper, eds., *Seventeenth-century Economic Documents*, (Oxford, 1972), pp. 761–4.

3. Edmund S. Morgan, *American Slavery, American Freedom: the Ordeal of Colonial Virginia* (New York, 1975), p. 120. Idem, "First American boom: Virginia 1618 to 1630," *WMQ*, 28: 169–198 (1971), p. 185.

4. "The answere of the Generall Assembly in Virginia to a Declaration of the state of the Colonie in the 12 years of Sir Thomas Smiths Government, exhibited by Alderman Johnson and others" (*RVC*, 4:458, 20 February 1623/40). Edward D. Neill, *History of the Virginia Company of London* (Albany, NY, 1869), pp. 407–11.

5. *RVC*, 3:74.

6. See Chapter 1, pp. 10–11.

7. [House of] Commons Journals, I, p. 711.

8. "Instructions to Yeardley," *VMHB*, 2:154–65.

9. Wesley Frank Craven, *The Dissolution of the Virginia Company* (New York, 1932), p. 60.

10. Alexander Brown, *The First Republic in America* (Boston and New York, 1898), p. 427.

11. This conclusion is based on an analysis of the following two documents: the Virginia Muster of 1624/25 in Annie Lash Jester and Martha Woodruff Hiden, eds., *Adventurers of Purse and Person: Virginia, 1607–1625* (Princeton, 1956); and "The Virginia Rent Rolls of 1704;" in T. J. Wertenbaker, *Planters of Colonial Virginia*. See further in Chapter 9, Table 9.1.

12. See McIlwaine, *MCGC*, pp. 72–3, 83, 136–7, 154.

13. Neill, p. 408.

14. *RVC*, 3:307–40; 313–14 ("A Declaration of the State of the Colony and Affaires of Virginia. By his Majesties Counsell for Virginia," 22 June 1620).

15. *RVC*, 3:226–7 (Virginia Colony Council, 11 November 1619, "The putting out of the Tenants that came over in the B. N. [*Bona Nova*], with other orders of the Councell").

16. Letter of William Weldon to Sir Edwin Sandys, 6 March 1619–20 (*RVC*, 3:262–5; p. 263).

17. See Smith, *Travels and Works*, p. 541. *RVC*, 3:586 and 4:38.

18. Smith, *Travels and Works*, 2:542.

19. *RVC*, 3:226 (The Governor and Council in Virginia "The putting out of the Tenantes that came over in the B. N. [*Bona Nova*] . . .," 11 November 1619).

20. *RVC*, 3:263 (William Weldon. Letter to Edwin Sandys, 6 March 1619/20).

21. *RVC*, 219–22; 220–21 (Letter of Colony Secretary John Pory in Virginia to Sir Dudley Carleton in England, 30 September 1619).

22. *RVC*, 1:584–604 (Record of the Meeting of the Virginia Company of London Court, 30 January 1621/22).

23. *RVC*, 3:241–8; 243 (Letter of John Rolfe to Sir Edwin Sandys, January 1619/20). Rolfe does not describe these new arrivals as "Africans" but as "Negroes." The fact that some of these new workers bore Christian names (Maria and Antonio, for example) and the fact that the ship on which they arrived came to Virginia from the West Indies, suggests that at least some had spent time in the Caribbean, or might even have been born there.

24. Those who read Edmund S. Morgan's "First American Boom" and Chapter 4 of his *American Slavery, American Freedom*, may realize how much I am indebted to his insights. Credit

must go to Morgan for opening the way to a reexamination of the history of the Company period, particularly the critical years 1619–24, from the standpoint of the consideration of the internal contradictions of the colony, those between the few rich and the common run of the people. After a year-by-year review and analysis of colony's food supply situation, Morgan concludes: "Yeardley's complaints, his purchase of the Negroes, and his disposal of the men from the Bona Nova at a time when the colony was reporting an unprecedented abundance, suggest that the problem was not altogether one of whether supplies existed, it was a question of who had them and who could pay for them. In a year of plenty the governor and Council were unable or unwilling to make use of fifty men without supplies when other Virginians were able and willing to do so. The great shortage of supplies, to which we attribute the failure of the Sandys program, was not an absolute shortage in which all Virginians shared and suffered alike. It was a shortage that severely afflicted the Company and its dependants, but it furnished large opportunities for private entrepreneurs and larger ones for Company officials who knew how to turn public distress to private profit." ("First American Boom," p. 175).

25. *RVC*, 2:375; *RVC*, 4:186; 234. Morgan, "First American Boom," p. 182.

26. Smith, *Travels and Works*, 2:571. *RVC*, 3:581–7; 584 (Virginia Colony Council to Virginia Company of London, January 1621/22).

27. Virginia Company of London to Deputy Governor Argall, 22 August 1618 (Neill, *History to the Virginia Company*, pp. 114–17; p. 115).

28. Virginia Company of London to Lord Delaware, 22 August 1618 (Neill, *History of the Virginia Company* pp. 117–29; p. 119). Delaware died *en route* to Virginia. Argall returned to England aboard a ship specially sent by his patron, the Earl of Warwick, not waiting for instruction or permission from the London authorities.

29. *RVC*, 1:601 (13 February 1622). *RVC*, 1:579 (30 January 1622). The Virginia Company Court granted Weldon a patent for the transportation of one hundred persons which, at the allowance of fifty acres each, implied for him a private plantation of five thousand acres.

30. *RVC*, 3:485–9; 489. Virginia Company of London to the Governor and Council in Virginia, 25 July 1621 (Neill, *History of the Virginia Company*, pp. 223–33; p. 230).

31. *RVC*, 3:584–5 (Virginia Colony Council to Virginia Company of London, January 1621/22).

32. *RVC*, 3:219–23; 221 (John Pory to Sir Dudley Carleton, 30 September 1619): "the Governor here [Yeardley], who at his first coming, besides a great deale of worth in his person, brought onely his sworde w[i]th him, was at his late being in London, together with his lady, out of his meer gettings here, able to disburse Very near three thousand pounds to furnish himselfe for his [return] voiage."

33. An incomplete indication of Yeardley's success at self-enrichment is to be found in his Last Will, dated 12 October 1627 (*New England Historical and Genealogical Register*, 28: 69 [1884], p. 69). Yeardley's estate, "consisting of goods debts, servants 'negars,' cattle ..." and including his thousand-acre plantation on Warwicke River, was valued at six thousand pounds by his uncle in a petition to the Privy Council in 1629.

34. Craven, *Dissolution of the Virginia Company*. pp. 176–8.

35. Weldon to Sandys (*RVC*, 3:263).

36. *RVC*, 3:581–8; 586 (Council in Virginia to Virginia Company of London, January 1621/22).

37. In 1622, tenants who had been brought to Bermuda by Captain Nathaniel Butler included in a letter of grievances the charge that they had been "forced to send all their tobacco into England unto their undertakers [employers], undivided," in spite of the fact that their contracts provided that they were to "divide their yearly tobacco" and "to be accountable for the moiety [half] only" (*Manchester Papers*, p. 38).

38. *MCGC*, p. 46 (Last day of January 1624/25).

39. "It was the Powhatan Uprising that both unleashed the company's self-destructive urges and accelerated Virginia's evolution" (J. Frederick Fausz, "The Powhatan Uprising of 1622: A Historical Study of Ethnocentrism and Cultural Conflict," Ph.D Dissertation, College of William and Mary, 1977, p. 547).

40. Alexander Brown, *The Genesis of the United States* (Boston, 1890), 2:971.

41. Neill, *History of the Virginia Company*, pp. 96–105. Philip Barbour, *Pocahontas and Her World: A Chronicle of America's First Settlement in which is Related the Story of the Indians and the Englishmen – Particularly Captain John Smith, Captain Samuel Argall, and Master John Rolfe* (Boston, 1970), pp. 169–70.

42. Richard L. Morton, *Colonial Virginia* 2 vols. (Chapel Hill, 1960), 1:74.

43. *RVC*, 3:556 ("A Declaration of the State of the Colony and ... a Relation of the Barbarous Massacre," after April 1622, 3:541–80).

George Yeardley was accused in England of having provoked the Indian attack of 22 March by treacherously attacking an assembly of the friendly Chickhominy Indians with whom he had asked to parley. Thirty to forty of the Indians were killed. "The perfidious act made them all fly out & seek revenge, they joined with Opichankano" (*RVC*, 4:118 [Sir Nathaniel Rich's Draft of Instruction to the commissioners to investigate Virginia affairs, 4:6–8]).

44. *RVC*, 3:555 (Edward Waterhouse "A Declaration of the state of the Colony and ... a Relation of the Barbarous Massacre, 1622).

45. Brown, *First Republic*, p. 467 n.1.

46. See Appendix II-C.

47. *RVC* 3:613; 4:11–12. In the summer of 1622 the Virginia Governor and Council did contemplate moving out, but to just across the Chesapeake Bay. The Company in London strenuously condemned the notion, and by the following January the Governor and Council were disowning the idea. *RVC*: 3:613 (Virginia Colony Council to Virginia Council in London, 3:609–15, 13 April 1622). *RVC*: 3:366–7 (Treasurer and Council for Virginia to Governor and Colony Council of Virginia, 3:366–73, 1 August 1622). *RVC*, 4:11–12 (Virginia Colony Council to Council for Virginia, 4:9–17, 20 January 1622/23).

48. The first English colony was established in 1587 on Roanoke Island on the North Carolina coast by an expedition organized by Sir Walter Raleigh (a second attempt). When the first relief ship returned to the spot in 1591, there was no trace to be found of the colony, except the eternally mystifying scrawl "Croatan." It is assumed that the colonists were adopted into an Indian tribe of the region. (See Hamilton MacMillan of Robeson County, North Carolina, "Sir Walter Raleigh's Lost Colony, with the traditions of an Indian Tribe in North Carolina indicating the fate of the Colony" (1888), cited in Brown, *Genesis*, 1:189–90. During a military trial in 1864, according to MacMillan, an Indian named John Lowrie asserted he was descended from this merger, and complained that nevertheless "white men have treated us as negroes."

49. *RVC*, 3:146 (Treasurer and Council in Virginia to George Yeardley, 3:146–8, 21 June 1619). *RVC* 3:496 (Virginia Company in London to Virginia Colony Council, 3:492–8, 12 August 1621).

50. See Morgan, "First American Boom," pp. 172–3, 175.

51. *RVC*, 3:555.

52. At the end of October 1618, the Company, in order to reduce overcharging for goods at the colony's supply store (called the "magazine"), forbade any mark-up on goods beyond "the allowance of 25 in the hundred proffitt" (*RVC*, 3:167).

53. The precariousness of property claims in the conditions of epidemic death prevailing at that time in Virginia, and the danger of fraud in disposition of property of deceased persons there is to be seen in the letter addressed by the Company to the Colony Governor and Council, 7 October 1622, in which they noted "greevances for wrongs by unjust factors and partners in Virginia, and of claymes to lands and foods by the late death of friends" (*RVC*, 3:689 [Virginia Company to the Governor and Council of Virginia, 3:683–9]).

54. *RVC*, 3:537 gives the population as 1,240 (Notes from Lists showing Total Number of Emigrants to Virginia [1622]). See also Brown, *First Republic*, pp. 467, 624.

Regarding the number of lives lost in the colony, Brown writes, "The exact number may not be certainly known ... [at first] the company published a list of 347; but it was almost necessary to make the list as small as possible at that time.... The Company afterwards placed the number at 'about 400,' and Edward Hill put it at '400 and odd.'" Hill was a Virginia planter living in Elizabeth City. (Brown, *First Republic*, 467, 624; and Philip A. Bruce, *Economic History of Virginia in the Seventeenth Century*, 2 vols. [New York, 1895] 2:71.)

55. *RVC*, 3:611–15 (Virginia Colony Council to Virginia Company of London, April (after 20) 1622). *RVC*, 4:13 (Virginia Colony Council to Virginia of London, 4:9–17, 20 January 1622/23).

56. *RVC*, 4:58 (Richard Frethorne letters, 4:58–62, Spring 1623).

57. *RVC*, 4:22 (George Sandys to Mr Ferarr).

58. *RVC*, 3:613.

59. *RVC*, 4:525 (Virginia Company of London, Discourse ... April (?) 1625).

60. *RVC*, 3:614

61. *RVC*, 4:233 (Letters arriving in England on the *Abigail*, 4:228–29, 19 June 1623).

62. *RVC*, 4:61 (Richard Frethorne letters to his father and mother, 20 March and 2 and 3 April, 1623, *RVC*, 4:58–63).

63. *RVC*, 4:41, 59. Brown, *Genesis*, 2:802–3, 826.

64. *RVC*, 4:58.

65. *RVC*, 4:41 (Frethorne to Bateman, 5 March 1622/23).

66. *RVC*, 4:62.

67. *RVC*, 4:236.

68. Ibid.

69. *RVC*, 4:231–2. Great Britain Historical Manuscripts Commission Eighth Report and Appendix (London, 1881), Part I; Appendix (Duke of Manchester Papers), p. 41.

70. *RVC*, 3:639.

71. *RVC*, 4:525 (Virginia Company "Discourse of the Old Company," April 1625, 4:519–61).

72. This is an inference drawn from the rate of profit specified to be secured on the supplies subsequently sent on the relief ships the *George*, the *Hopewell*, and the *Marmaduke* (*RVC*, 4:263–4).

73. *RVC*, 4:61–2.

74. *RVC*, 4:107, 116, 230.

75. *RVC*, 4:120 (Letter from Captain Kendall in Somers Islands to Sir Edwin Sandys, 14 April 1623).

76. *RVC*, 4:105 (Sir Francis Wyatt to John Ferrar, 7 April 1623).

77. Brown, *First Republic*, p. 559.

78. *RVC*, 3:639 (28 March 1623).

79. *RVC*, 4:215–16 (Draft for a Report on the Condition of the Colony, June or July 1623).

80. Butler was a leading opponent of the Edwin Sandys headship of the Virginia Company, and might therefore be expected to be biased. But Alexander Brown, an early and staunch historiographical supporter of Sandys, believes that Butler's report was on the whole factual (*First Republic*, p. 506).

81. In seeking to counter this point in Butler's report, Sandys's supporters conceded that such public dying might occur in Virginia. But they were confident that it did not take place under hedges, because, they asserted, "there is no hedge in Virginia" (*RVC*, 2:382). Next case!

82. Brown, *First Republic*, pp. 444, 506, 627. Professor Morgan revises the total population figures upward from those given by the records for 1623–24 and 1624–25, by 20 percent and 10 percent respectively. He does not suggest any revision of the 1622 figure. (*American Slavery, American Freedom*, pp. 101, 404.)

83. Besides the specific references to the record for the period up to 1626 in this paragraph, see Chapter 4, note 94.

84. *RVC*, 4:46 (17 March 1622/23).

85. *RVC*, 2:523. Brown, *First Republic*, p. 563.

86. *RVC*, 2:519–20 (Virginia Company of London Court, 21 April 1624).

87. *RVC*, 4:453 (30 January 1623/24); 4:570 (4 January 1625/26).

88. *RVC*, 4:271–2. ("A proclamation touching the rates of Comodities," 31 August 1623.)

89. *RVC*, 4:14.

90. *RVC*, 4:271.

91. The census of Virginia Colony for 1624–25 (March 1625) showed 432 male adults who were free in a total population of 1,227. Of the non-free adults, 298 were in the service of an elite bourgeois group of fifteen employers. (Hotten, *Original Lists*, pp. 261–5.) See also Morgan's analysis and tabulation in "First American Boom," pp. 188–9.

92. *RVC*, 2:339 (Virginia Company of London Court, 24 March 1622/23).

93. *RVC*, 3:614. Brown, *First Republic*, pp. 474–5.

94. It seems not unlikely that there was a shortage of English trade goods, since the production of glass beads had been halted at this time in the colony for lack of suitable sand (*RVC*, 4:108).

95. RVC, 4:9–10 (Virginia Colony Council to the Virginia Company of London, 20 January 1622/23). For references to Mountjoy's strategy of starvation in the Tyrone War, see Volume One of *The Invention of the White Race*.

96. RVC, 3:614.

97. *RVC*, 4:186 ("Rough Notes in Support of the Preceding Charges of Mismanagement of the Virginia Company, May [after May 9] or June, 1623," 4:183–7); 4:234 (letter of Edward Hill to his brother Mr Jo. Will, 14 April 1623).

98. *RVC*, 4:186.

99. *RVC*, 4:105. Brown, *First Republic*, p. 513.

100. *RVC*, 2:375 ("The Unmasked face of our Colony in Virginia as it was in the Winter of the yeare 1622," 2:374–6).

101. *RVC*, 4:6–7.

102. Ibid.

103. *RVC*, 4:9–10. These Colony Council members were Yeardley, Tucker, George Sandys and Hamor.

104. Ibid.

105. *RVC*, 4:37 (Letter of William Capps to Dr John Wynston, March or April, 1623).

106. *RVC*, 4:14.

107. Brown (*First Republic*, p. 627) says that 11,185 bushels was regarded as a minimum supply in March 1625.

108. Smith, *Travels and Works*, 2:615.

109. Brown, *First Republic*, pp. 625–6, 627.

110. *RVC*, 4:89, 92, 231.

111. *RVC*, 4:234.

112. *RVC*, 4:14.

113. *RVC*, 4:453.

114. *RVC*, 3:612 (Virginia Colony Council to Virginia Company of London, April [after 20 April] 1622, 3:611–15).

115. *RVC*, 3:656 (Sir Francis Wyatt, A commission to Sir George Yeardley, 6 June 1622).

116. Brown, *First Republic*, pp. 617–20.

117. See Morgan, "First American Boom," pp. 189.2.

118. *RVC*, 3:613.

119. *RVC*, 2:94–5 (Virginia Company of London Court, 17 July 1622). *RVC*, 3:689 (Virginia Company of London to Governor and Council in Virginia, 3:683–90, 7 October 1622).

120. *RVC*, 2:124 (Virginia Company of London Preparative Court, 18 November 1622, 2:124–31).

121. Brown, *First Republic*, pp. 617, 618, 620, 623, 627. Brown adds, however, that he does not know the particulars of the disposition of the large corporate holdings such as Southampton Hundred. John C. Rainbolt argues that English heirs of Virginia Company land claims "parlayed [these holdings] into estates of several thousand acres" in the third quarter of the century. ("An Alteration in the Relationship between Leadership and Constitutents in Virginia, 1660–1720," *WMQ*, 27:411–34 [1970]; 413). Bernard Bailyn, in his essay on the evolution of the Virginia social structure, provides the details, showing that mid-seventeenth century claims on Company period inheritances constituted "the most important, of a variety of forms of capital" that provided the fortunes on which were based the oligarchy of slaveholding families of Virginia of the eighteenth century (Bernard Bailyn, "Politics and Social Structure," in James Morton Smith, *Seventeenth-century America, Essays in Colonial History* [Chapel Hill, 1959], p. 99).

122. I have assumed that the death rate was at least as high among workers as among employers.

123. *RVC*, 4:185 (May or June [after 9 May] 1623).

124. *RVC*, 3:658 (Proclamation of Governor Sir Francis Wyatt for the suppression of drunkenness, 21 June 1622). The quintuplex of social classes set forth in this Virginia order perfectly mirrored the categories as established in England at that time: noblemen, freemen, yeomen, artisans, and farm laborers. See Sir Thomas Wilson, *The State of England, Anno Dom. 1600*, Publications of the Camden Society, 3rd ser., Vol. 52, *Camden Miscellany*, Vol. 16 edited by F. J. Fisher (London, 1936), p. 17.

125. See Morgan, "First American Boom," pp. 171–75. The use by Professor Morgan of the "mining camp", boom-town metaphor seems somewhat questionable on the grounds of one-sidedness. Lewis C. Gray used the same argument (see Gray, assisted by Esther K. Thompson, in the *History of Agriculture in the Southern United States to 1860* [Washington, DC, 1932; reprinted 1958], 1:256). I am no student of that aspect of social history, but was it characteristic of the gold and oil boom towns in the American West and in Alaska, for example, to have two-thirds of the people die of starvation and starvation-related disease in a one- or two-year period? In a boom town, do not wages rise, even though the lucky, grasping few may fare better? In Virginia in the 1620s, the position of the laboring people deteriorated not only relatively but absolutely.

126. *RVC*, 4:37–8 (William Capps, Letter to Doctor Thomas Wynston. March or April 1623). But that same April, Governor Wyatt said that on the best ground a pair of tenants could make 2,500 pounds, and that because of guard duty his sixteen tenants produced only 1,000 pounds per capita. (*RVC*, 4:104–6 [Wyatt to John Ferrar, 7 April 1623].)

127. *RVC*, 4:175 ("Alderman Johnson(?), Parts of Drafts of a Statement Touching the Miserable Condition of Virginia," 4:174–87, May or June [after 9 May] 1623).

128. *RVC*, 4:13 (Virginia Colony Council to the Virginia Company of London, 4:9–17).

129. *RVC*, 4:74 (George Sandys to Sir Samuel Sandys, 30 March 1623, 3:73–5).

130. *RVC* 3:105 (Sir Francis Wyatt to John Ferrar, 7 April 1623, 4:104–6).

131. "From 1606 to 1624, the average value of wheat in England was only five shillings a bushel" (Bruce, 1:256). As noted above (page 91), the price of corn in Virginia was twenty shillings per bushel in 1623.

132. *VMHB*, 71:410 (1963), citing Harleian Ms. 389, f. 309, unsigned letter to Joseph Mead, 4 April 1623.

133. *RVC*, 3:221 (John Pory to Sir Dudley Carlton and Edwin Sandys, 30 September 1619).

134. Morgan, *American Slavery, American Freedom*, p. 119.

135. See *Historical Statistics of the United States, Colonial Times to 1970* US Department of Commerce, Bureau of the Census (Washington, DC, 1975), series Z-125-128.

136. Morgan, *American Slavery, American Freedom*, p. 119 n. 50. Morgan refers to A. J. and R. H. Tawney, "An Occupational Census of the Seventeenth Century," *Economic History Review*, 5:25–64 (1934–35). Although Morgan omits page references, his comment seems to be supported by the Gloucestershire figures showing 19,402 men between the ages of twelve and sixty (p. 31), and, in agricultural and domestic occupation, only sixteen employers with ten or more employees (tables VI and VII, pp. 52 and 53).

137. *VMHB*, 71:409 (1963). See also *RVC*, 4:104.

138. *RVC*, 3:618 (Edwin Sandys Letter to John Ferrar, 30 April, 1622 [before news of the 22 March Indian attack had arrived in England]). Historians (Craven, *Dissolution of the Virginia Company*, pp. 152–3, and Morgan, "First American Boom," pp. 171 and 183, for example) have considered it a "blunder" on Edwin Sandys's part to have persisted in the policy of sending thousands of ill-provisioned emigrants to Virginia. If so, it was a blunder that flowed from flawless bourgeois logic: an oversupply of dependent and ill-supplied laborers was an objective necessity for securing a general reduction of labor costs and thus keeping tobacco profitable enough to attract capital investment.

139. *RVC*, 4:220–22 (9 June 1623).

140. Colony Secretary George Sandys was one of the purchasers (*Manchester Papers*, p. 39 Letter from "G. S." [George Sandys?] to "Mr Ferrer" [Ferrar]).

141. *MCGC*, pp. 19–20 (16 August 1623). Tyler's opinions are from testimony against him in the General Court.

142. *MCGC*, pp. 22–4 (10 October 1624).

143. *MCGC*, p. 105 (7 and 8 August 1626).

144. *MCGC*, p. 117 (11 October 1626). For her part, servant Alice Chambers was ordered to receive unspecified "worthy punishment."

145. *MCGC*, pp. 135–7 (13 January 1626/7). "The Order by which the [thirty-six] Tenants of the Company are distributed to the Governor & [8 other members of the] Councill" shows eighteen assigned to Governor George Yeardley, and three to most of the others. The Colony Council order regarding the "Duty boys" was issued on 10 October 1627 (p. 154).

146. Bruce, 2:43.

147. By the end of 1624, the Virginia Colony Council was reporting to the Virginia Company that there was much corn in the colony, but that they were short of laborers (*RVC*, 4:507–8, 2 December 1624).

148. So characterized by George Sandys in a letter to his brother Samuel in England, 30 March 1623 (*Manchester Papers*, p. 39).

149. *RVC*, 4:106 (George Sandys to John Ferrar in England, 8 April 1623). See also Bruce, 1:47–8.

6 Bricks without Straw: Bondage, but No Intermediate Stratum

1. See Oliver Ellsworth's comment cited in *The Invention of the White Race*, Volume One, p. 286 n. 3.

2. Labor might also have been recruited from among the native population if terms were made sufficiently attractive, or as a result of the destruction of the original native population's economy of the area by the bombardment of cheap commodities, or by the expropriation of the lands and resources. But this alternative and reasons for its ineffectiveness were discussed in Chapter 3.

3. *RVC*, 3:592–8 (Virginia Company, The Form of a Patent, 30 January 1621/22); 3:629–34 (Virginia Company, The Form of a Patent for a Planter Only, 22 May 1622).

4. This principle of granting land patents at the rate of fifty acres for each person brought into Virginia would later be known as the "headright" system. See Chapter 4, pp. 58–9.

5. See p. 72.

6. *RVC*, 3:507.

7. *RVC*, 3:586; 4:558.

8. *RVC*, 2:105, 3:699, 4:14 (7 October and 2 November 1622; 20 January 1622/23).

9. *RVC*, 4:22 (March 1622/23).

10. See p. 86.

11. *RVC*, 4:235 (12 April 1623).

12. *RVC*, 4:466–7. *MCGC*, p. 12 (9 March 1623).

13. *RVC*, 4:467 (9 March 1622/23).

14. *MCGC*, p. 40 (3 January 1624/25).

15. *MCGC*, p. 109 (28 August 1626). Hotten, *Original Lists*, p. 237.

16. *MCGC*, p. 90 (20 January 1625/26).

17. *MCGC*, pp. 131–2 (20 January 1626/27).

18. *RVC*, 4:5–6 (between January and April 1622/23).

19. *MCGC*, p. 83 (19 December 1625).

20. *MCGC*, pp. 136–7 (13 January 1626/27).

21. Alexander Brown, *The First Republic in America*, (Boston and New York, 1898), p. 627.

22. *New England Historical and Genealogical Register*, 38:69 (January 1884).

23. See Theodore K. Rabb, *Enterprise and Empire* (Cambridge, Massachusetts, 1967).

24. "The liberties of Englishmen – the privileges and immunities of the free-born English subject ... [include] personal liberty ... signifying the freedom to dispose of one's person and powers of body and mind, without control by others who are not representatives of the ultimate supreme authority."(John Codman Hurd, *The Law of Freedom and Bondage in the United States*, 2 vols. [Boston, 1858; Negro Universities Press reprint, 1968] 1:140.)

25. *RVC*, 3:683–4 ("Virginia Company. A Letter to the Governor and the Council in Virginia, October 7, 1622," *RVC*, 3:683–90).

26. In the Gloucestershire occupational census of 1606, the only such existing record for seventeenth-century England, tabulations of employers and their servants in agriculture or domestic employment show that servants constituted 27 percent of the total; 4 percent were of the leisure classes, 11 percent were yeomen, and 58 percent were husbandmen (A. J. Tawney and R. H. Tawney, "An Occupational Census of the Seventeenth Century," *Economic History Review*, 5:25–64 [1934–35]; see Tables VI and VII, pp. 52 and 53). In Virginia in the era that followed the economic massacre of the tenantry, the great majority of the laboring population were to be not even husbandmen, but chattel bond-laborers.

27. The reader is referred particularly to my Introduction to *The Invention of the White Race*, in Volume One.

28. With the honorable exception of Edmund S. Morgan, those historians who have concerned themselves with the origin of chattel bond-labor of European-Americans have repeated this rationale as an article of faith.

See, for example, Marcus W. Jernegan, *Laboring and Dependent Classes in Colonial America* (New York, 1931), p. 46; Lewis C. Gray, assisted by Esther K. Thompson, *History of Agriculture in the Southern United States to 1860* (Washington, DC, 1932; reprinted 1958), 1:342; Philip A. Bruce, *Economic History of Virginia in the Seventeenth Century: An Inquiry into the Material Conditions of the People, based upon original records*, 2 vols. (New York, 1895; reprinted 1935), 1:587. Winthrop D. Jordan is content to say "it was indentured servitude that best met the requirements for settling in America" (*White Over Black: American Attitudes Toward the Negro, 1550–1812* [Chapel Hill, 1968], p. 52].).

29. Abbot E. Smith, *Colonists in Bondage: White Servitude and Convict Labor in America, 1607–1776* (Chapel Hill, 1947; New York, 1971), pp. 8–9. Bruce, *Economic History*, 1:262.

30. It is also analogous to the argument advanced by coalmine owners in the twentieth century, with the support of even United Mine Workers officials in McDowell County, West Virginia in 1940–41. Resolutions passed by several United Mine Workers locals demanding portal-to-portal pay were dismissed as utopian. "What!" opponents cried. "Do you think the coal operators are going to pay you for just sitting in the man-trip?" But in that case the general relationship of class forces was such that after Pearl Harbor we miners got our just due in this matter.

31. *(English) Statutes at Large*, 23 Ed. III (1349).

32. A. E. Smith, p. 305. Smith was here generalizing about the entire history of "white servitude."

33. See pp. 65–6.

34. *Documents relating to the History of the Early Colonial Settlements, principally on Long Island, with a Map of its Western Part, made in 1666, translated and compiled from this Historical Records by B. Fernow* (Albany, 1883).

35. *Voyages from Holland to America, AD 1632–1644*, Collections of the New York Historical

Society, 2nd ser., vol. III, part 1, translated and edited by Henry Murphy (New York, 1857). There is no indication of de Vries's feelings regarding the buying and selling of African bond-laborers in which the Dutch were then principal merchants.

36. See especially pp. 22–4.

37. Under English common and statute law, the failure of a servant to fulfill his or her contract could be remedied by pecuniary damages only, not by "compelling a specific performance." (Hurd, 1:138). The English courts resolved as follows. By 27 Henry VIII, legal compulsion to performance of a contract was ended; failure to perform as contracted could only be remedied by the recovery of damages from the party failing to meet the contractual obligation. (Matthew Bacon, *A New Abridgement of the Law*, 5th edition, 5 vols. [Dublin, 1786], 5:359, "Covenants to stand seized to Uses," paragraphs 46–48).

The distinction between the penalty of adding time to the bond-laborer's term of servitude in colonial Virginia and the provision of English law is underscored in a Virginia manumission agreement requiring a to-be-freed laborer to pay to his emancipator 6,000 pounds of tobacco over a three-year period, but with the proviso that the worker could "not bee restrained of his liberty for default of payment, but is left to the course of the Law as all other free subjects are in case of debt." (*Northampton County Records, 1668–80*, pp. 158–9 [1678]).

38. Paul H. Douglas begins by equating plantation bond-servitude and apprenticeship. But he then honestly presents "the chief differences" until, in spite of his intentions, his premise is in tatters (Paul H. Douglas, *American Apprenticeship and Industrial Education* [New York, 1921], pp. 28–9).

Louis P. Hennighausen says that though "white servitude" was sometimes called "apprentice-ship," it was slavery (Louis P. Hennighausen, *The Redemptioners and the German Society of Maryland* [Baltimore, 1888], p. 1. Cheesman Herrick found that in Pennsylvania, "What ordinarily passes as the apprenticeship system differs from that now under discussion . . ." (Cheesman Herrick, *White Servitude in Pennsylvania* [Philadelphia, 1926; Negro Universities Press reprint, 1969], p. 108). There is no reason to think the conditions and status of bond-laborers were more favourable in Virginia in the seventeenth century than they were in Maryland in the eighteenth and nineteenth centuries.

39. Thomas Jefferson, *Reports of Cases Determined in the General Court of Virginia, from 1730 to 1740; and from 1768 to 1772* (Charlottesville, 1829); Gwinn *v.* Bugg, p. 89.

40. John Strange, *Reports of Adjudged Cases in the Courts of Chancery, King's Bench, Common Pleas and Exchequer*, 2 vols. (London, 1782); 2:1266–7. See also: William Salkeld, *Report of Cases Adjudged in the Court of King's Bench . . .*, (Philadelphia, 1822) 6th edition, 3 vols., 1:67–8; and Michael Dalton, *The Country Justice* (1619; edited with an appendix, by William Nelson London, 1727), p. 191. (I am grateful to Director Frederic Baum and the staff of the Library of the Association of the Bar of the City of New York for making these old books available to me.) In a marginal note, Dalton says that by London custom (allowance for which appears to be made in the Statute of Artificers [5 Eliz. 4] section 40 – T.W.A.) an apprentice "may be turned over to another." But the consent of the apprentice was presumably still required. With regard to such transfers of an apprentice to another master, according to Lipson, only rare exceptions were made, and these involved extraordinary and particular review and agreement by the wardens of the trade (Ephraim Lipson, *Economic History of England*, 3 vols. (London, 1926), 1:285).

The distinction between assignability and non-assignability, between chattel and non-chattel indenture to bond-servitude, was explicitly instanced in an order of the Charles County Maryland Court of 28 January 1661. The court approved an agreement between widow Ane Ges binding out her step-daughter (called "daughter-in-law" in those times) to one man for six years, and her three-year-old son, for fifteen years, to another man, specifying in each case that the child was bound to the man, "his heirs, Executors, administrators but not Assignes"(*Archives of Maryland*, 52:182–3). For Virginia examples of such specific provisions, see: *Rappahannock County Records, 1656–64*, pp. 275–6 (1683); *Northumberland County Records, 1678–1698*, pp. 250, 826 (1685; 1698).

41. This characterization is given by Gray in his *History of Agriculture in the Southern United States to 1860* (1:344), in concluding his discussion of the origin of "indentured servitude" (1:342–4). On this point, Gray appears to have misappropriated the authority whose title he cites but does not quote. Indeed, that authority seems to contradict Gray's assertion most directly, as follows: "[T]he relation of master and servant in indented servitude was unknown to that [English apprenticeship] law, and could neither be derived from nor regulated by its principles. it had to depend entirely for its sanction on special statutes, or on the action of tribunals which had no precedents before them." (James Curtis Ballagh, *White Servitude in the Colony of Virginia: A Study of the System of Indentured Labor in the American Colonies* [Baltimore, 1895; 1969 reprint], p. 46).

Awareness of the distinction between colonial indentured chattel servitude and terms of employment in the home country is revealed in the exceptional indentures that were conditioned upon non-assignability. See, for example, Virginia County Records, *Rappahannock County Records, 1656–64*, pp. 275–6 (18 February 1662/3; *Lancaster County Records, 1660–80*, p. 353 (8 March 1675/6); *Northumberland County Records, 1678–98*, pp. 250, 826 (1 January 1684/5 and 15 June 1698).

42. Tobacco seeds were first planted in England in 1565 (*Encyclopedia Britannica*, 15th edition (Chicago, 1997), 11:812, "Tobacco."). The short-lived 1547 slave law (1 Edw. VI, 3) was repealed in 1550.

43. See *The Invention of the White Race*, Volume One, p. 19, and p. 239 n. 96, for the names of half a dozen champions of the "paradox" thesis.

44. Bruce, *Economic History* 1:52–69; 238–9; 254–62; 411–12; 585–6; 2:43, 48–51, 415–17.

45. The patentee's first seven years in possession were free of quit-rent (Hening, 1:228).

46. Allan Kulikoff, *Tobacco and Slaves: The Development of Southern Cultures in the Chesapeake, 1680–1800* (Chapel Hill 1986), pp. 132–4. Authorities agree that elsewhere in Virginia tenancy was much less practiced, although the tax records provide no category for tenants. (Ibid., p. 134; Jackson Turner Main, "The Distribution of Property in Post-Revolutionary Virginia," *Mississippi Valley Historical Review*, 41:241–58 (1954–55); pp. 245 n. 12; 248 n. 21. The name of this publication was later changed to *Journal of American History*.)

47. Willard F. Bliss, "The Rise of Tenancy in Virginia," *VMHB*, 58:427–41 (1950), p. 429.

48. Ibid., p. 427. Cf. Carville V. Earle, *The Evolution of a Tidewater Settlement System: All Hallow's Parish, Maryland, 1650–1783*, University of Chicago Department of Geography Research Paper No. 170, 1975. "Slaves did not cause tenancy and the decline of the yeomen," says Earle (p. 226).

49. Russell R. Menard, *Economy and Society in Early Colonial Maryland* (New York, 1985), p. 72.

50. Ibid., p. 76; Kulikoff, p. 133; Gregory A. Stiverson, *Poverty in a Land of Plenty: Tenancy in Eighteenth-century Maryland* (Baltimore, 1977), p. 10.

51. Kulikoff, p. 133.

52. Adam Smith, *An Inquiry into the Nature and Causes of the Wealth of Nations* (1812 reprint of 3 vols. in 1 by Ward Lock, & Co., London, n.d. [19th century]), p. 354.

53. Bruce, 1:586. A. E. Smith likewise rejects the possibility of any alternative to chattel bond-servitude, seeing it as being "too expensive," for purposes of colonization "without rearranging society in some utopian fashion" (*Colonists in Bondage*, p. 305). Craven describes the bond-labor system as merely a part of Virginia's being "allowed to follow what was perhaps her most natural development as a commonwealth of tobacco plantations" (Wesley Frank Craven, *The Dissolution of the Virginia Company; the Failure of a Colonial Experiment* (New York, 1932), p. 334).

54. Incidentally, while it is true enough to say, as Bruce does, the "The system of large estates was the result of tobacco culture alone," large estates are by no means necessary for the raising of tobacco. Indeed, tobacco is especially suitable for cultivation on small farms. (Fernando Ortiz, *Contrapunteo Cubano del Tabaco y Azucar* [Havana, 1940], pp. 82–3, 466; Eric Bates, "The 'Tobacco Dividend': Farmers Who are Kicking the Habit," *The Nation*, 13 February 1995, pp. 195–8. Bates quotes a "farm activist" as saying that, "If it weren't for tobacco, we wouldn't have small farms" [p. 196]).

55. Francis Bacon, *Works*, 6:93–5.

John C. Rainbolt (*From Prescription to Persuasion, Manipulation of Eighteenth Century Virginia Economy* [Port Washington, NY, 1974]) examines circumstantial factors that frustrated efforts at diversification of the Virginia economy. Although the title refers to the eighteenth century, Rainbolt's main attention is directed to the 1650–1710 period, well after the commitment to tobacco had become a settled question in practical terms, and the guiding principle of colonial Virginia government had been firmly established: to secure the highest quickest profit for the Virginia planters, shippers, servant-trade merchants, English Crown interests, tax-and-customs farmers.

56. Bruce, *Economic Histroy*, 1:51–2.

57. Being of the aristocracy himself, Bacon favored control by "noblemen and gentlemen." But this would seem to lapse from Bacon's wonted attachment to empirical data. The Earl of Warwick, a prominent member of the Virginia and Bermuda companies, was so passionate for present gain that he directed his main adventurers to piracy (Wesley Frank Craven, "The Earl of Warwick – A Speculator in Piracy," *Hispanic American Historical Review*, 10:457–79 [1930]). And by 1622 the arch-aristocrat King James I had come to a view of the matter quite opposite to that held by Bacon. Said the king: "Merchants were the fittest for the government of that Plantation [Virginia]" (*RVC*, 2:35).

58. In regard to the rate of expansion of the colony's population and the colony's relations with the native population, Bacon's words seem like good advice wasted: "Cram not in people, by sending too fast company after company; but hearken how they waste, and send supplies proportionably; but so as the number may live well in the plantation, and not by surcharge [excess population] be in penury." Then, in logical corollary to this doctrine of slow and controlled population expansion, Bacon urged that: "If you plant where savages are, do not only entertain them with trifles and jingles; but use them justly and graciously, with sufficient guard nevertheless: and do not win their favor by helping them to invade their enemies, but for their defense it is not amiss."

Bacon was successively Solicitor-General, Attorney-General, Lord Keeper of the Seal, and Chancellor during the period of the completion of the plantation of Ulster by the English. In that light, it is especially interesting to find Bacon saying in this essay: "I like a plantation in a pure soil; that is, where people are not displanted to the end to plant in others. For else it is an extirpation than a plantation."

59. James and Charles, father-and-son Stuart kings of England, decreed the encouragement of the sale of Virginia tobacco in England at the expense of English-grown tobacco (royal Proclamations of 29 September 1624 and 9 May 1625: reprinted in Ebenezer Hazard, *Historical Collections*, 1:198ff, 203ff). This act brought a net gain to the English balance of trade, in which English-grown tobacco was a negligible factor.

60. See Craven's comment on Nathaniel Butler's "Unmasking of Virginia" (*Dissolution of the Virginia Company*, p. 255).

61. "The practice was loudly condemned in England and bitterly resented on the part of the servants, but the planters found their justification in the exigencies of the occasion ...' (Ballagh, p. 43).

62. See p. 51.

63. *RVC*, 2:125.

64. *RVC*, 2:110–13.

65. *RVC*, 2:129.

66. *RVC*, 2:124–5, 128–31 (Report of the Committee on Registering of Contracts between men of the Company and their Servants, 18 November 1622).

67. *RVC*, 4:235 (12 April 1623).

68. *RVC*, 4:235 (12 April 1623). Atkins was also the employer who sold Thomas Best.

69. *MCGC*, p. 109 (28 August 1626).

70. *RVC*, 4:437 (30 March 1624).

71. *RVC*, 4:128–9 (26 April and 3 May 1623).

72. *MCGC*, pp. 75–6, 82.

73. *MCGC*, p. 105 (7 and 8 August 1626).

74. Martha W. Hiden, "Accompts of the Tristram and Jane," *VMHB*, 62:427–47 (1954); p. 437.

75. Richard Kemp, Secretary of Virginia colony to Francis Windebank, English Secretary of State, 6 April 1638; in *CSP*, Col., Vol. 18). Hurd, 1:136, n. 4.

76. See pp. 17–19.

77. See pp. 55–6.

78. See pp. 17–18.

79. See p. 96.

80. Smith, *Travels and Works*, 2:618 (Reply to the questions of the royal commission for inquiring into the state of conditions in Virginia in 1624), emphasis in original. Looking back two and a half centuries later, Scharf, a most eminent historian of his state, seemed to confirm Smith's prediction of "misery" and its root cause: "Unquestionably, tobacco made Maryland a slave State, and much poorer than she would otherwise be" (J. Thomas Scharf, *History of Maryland from the Earliest Period to the Present Day*, 3. vols. [Baltimore, 1879; 1967 reprint], 2:48).

7 Bond-labor: Enduring ...

1. Abbot E. Smith, *Colonists in Bondage: White Servitude and Convict Labor in America, 1607–1776* (Chapel Hill, 1947), p. 39. Smith makes this generalization for the entire period 1607 to 1776.

2. Smith, pp. 99, 102, and 103.

3. Essex [County, England] Overseers of the Poor, 1631 accounts (extract), Broadside, "Transportation of the Poor to Virginia, 1631," courtesy of Francis L. Berkeley, Manuscripts Division, Alderman Library Manuscripts Division, University of Virginia, Charlottesville.

4. Wesley Frank Craven, *White, Red, and Black: the Seventeenth-century Virginian* (Charlottesville, 1971; New York, 1977), pp. 5, 14–16, 85–86. Craven's count of some 66,000 head-rights granted in Virginia between 1625 and 1682, plus his estimated 6,000 free immigrants for the period prior to 1625, minus some 1,400 head-rights granted for persons of African ancestry, gives a European immigration total for Virginia of between 70,000 and 71,000. A. E. Smith, working with head-right records for Maryland, estimated the European emigrants to that colony in the period 1633 to 1680 at 21,000, practically all of them bond-laborers (*Colonists in Bondage*, pp. 323–4). See also: Russell R. Menard, "Immigration to the Chesapeake Colonies in the Seventeenth Century," *Maryland Historical Magazine*, 68:323–7 (1973); idem, *Economy and Society in Early Colonial Maryland* (New York, 1985), pp. 117, 128; Eugene I. McCormac, *White Servitude in Maryland 1634–1824* (Baltimore, 1904) p. 30; James Horn, "Servant Emigration in the Seventeenth Century," in Thad Tate and David L. Ammerman, eds., *The Chesapeake in the Seventeenth Century: Essays in Anglo-American Society and Politics* (Chapel Hill, 1979), pp. 51–95; p. 54.

5. Governor William Berkeley's answers to questions submitted by the Lords of Trade and Plantations: Hening, 2:511–17; 515 (1671). The same questions, together with answers stated in the third person plural, appear in Peypsian ms. 2582, Magdalene College, England, *Samuel Wiseman's Book of Record, 1676–1677* (available on microfilm of the Virginia Colonial Records Project, survey report 578, pp. 108–11, microfilm reel 6618). They are signed by John Hartwell as being "a true copy." The date of the answers in the Hartwell copy is not given. Since Samuel Wiseman was the Secretary of the Royal Commissioners who arrived in Virginia in January and February 1677 to investigate the causes of Bacon's Rebellion and to propose remedies in its wake, it would appear that the answers were sufficiently current for the Royal Commissioners' purposes.

6. CO 5/714, Nicholson letter to the Lords of Trade and Plantations, 20 August 1698.

7. Robert Powis, a minister of the Church, lost out in the bidding for Eleanor Clure. But "in a drinking merriment," in order to frustrate the high bidder, he married Clure to a third party, Edward Cooper. Months later, by way of penalty against Powis for his abuse of office, the court deducted 300 pounds of tobacco from a judgment of a debt of 3,200 pounds owed him by Cooper. It appears that Clure herself was not asked to testify. (Norfolk County Records, 1656–1666, pp. 125, 151 [16 February 1657/8; 15 June 1658].) As a general note on the marketing process, see also Smith pp. 17–18.

8. *A Relation of Maryland* (London, 1635), Ann Arbor University Microfilms, Inc., March of America Facsimile Series, 22; p. 53.

9. The military force dispatched from England in October 1651 to reduce Virginia to obedience to the Cromwellian Commonwealth also brought "one hundred and fifty Scotch prisoners, taken in the recent battle of Worcester, and sent over to be sold as servants" (John Thomas Scharf, *History of Maryland from the Earliest Period to the Present Day*, 3 vols. [Baltimore, 1879; 1967 reprint], 1:209).

10. Of the total of some 250,000 limited-term bond-laborers that came to the continental colonies from 1607 to 1783, 35,000 to 50,000 were convicts; most of them, however, were sent following passage of a law (4 Geo. I 11) in 1717 "for the further preventing robbery, burglary, and other felonies, and for the more effectual transportation of felons and unlawful exporters of wool," and at the same time supplying the "great want of servants who by their labor and industry might be the means of improving and making more useful the said colonies." By that time the term "servants" was reserved for European-Americans bond-laborers.

A Council of State of the Commonwealth in 1653 authorized Richard Netherway of Bristol "to export one hundred Irish tories who were to be sold as slaves in Virginia." (Philip Alexander Bruce, *Economic History of Virginia in the Seventeenth Century: An Inquiry into the Material Conditions of the People, based upon original records*, 2 vols. (New York, 1895; reprinted 1935), 1:609, citing *Interregnum Entry Book*, vol. 98, p. 405.) Perhaps the order was interpreted to include potential "tories": in October 1654, two Maryland investors bought eight Irish boys, four of whom were so little that it was suggested that the buyers should have "brought cradles to rock them in." (*Archives of Maryland*, 41:478). See also *The Invention of the White Race*, Volume One, p. 74, for reference to "the Irish slave trade." See also John W. Blake, "Transportation from Ireland to America, 1653–60," *Irish Historical Studies*, 3:267–81 (1942–43), especially pp. 271, 273, 280 in relation to Virginia.

11. "Certain propositions for the better accommodating Forreigne Plantations with servants," CO 324/1, ff. 275–83; f. 275.

12. The number of kidnapped British laborers in the entire colonial period has been estimated at between ten thousand and twenty thousand. (Albert Hart Blumenthal, *Brides from Bridewell, Female Felons Sent to Colonial America* [Rutland, Vermont, 1962], p. 76.)

13. William Bullock, *Virginia Impartially Examined* (London, 1649), pp. 14, 47.

14. CO 324/1. "A much larger portion of our colonial population than is generally supposed found itself on American soil because of the wheedlings, deceptions, misrepresentations and other devices of the 'spirits.'" (Smith, p. 86.)

15. CO 389/2, items "I," "J," and "K." These were affidavits taken in proceedings before Justice William Morton in England in January 1671. Haverland's aggressiveness is noted in the testimony given by Thomas Stone and by Mary Collins who, it seems, was also a spirit. According to her, Haverland was reckless and disdainful of the law in the practice of his profession. He replied to hints of possible trouble with the authorities in unrestrained language: "... He did not care a turd for my Lord Chief Justice nor his warrant and that he would wipe his arse with the Warrant." Speaking of a Dorsetshire Justice of the Peace who was said to be seeking Haverland, Haverland "swore God damn him ... He would have the life of ... [the Justice of the Peace] Mr Thomas or hee should have the life of him [Haverland], and shooke his sword and Swore God damn him, his sword should be both Judge and justice for him" (CO 389/2, item "I").

16. CO 389/2, items "I," "J," and "K."

17. CO 389/2, item "K," Haverland affidavit, 30 January 1670/1.

18. Bullock, p. 47.

19. Smith, p. 36.

20. Bullock, pp. 35–6.

21. Francis L. Berkeley (see note 3) cites that entry as evidence that "persons dependent on the parish were transported to the colonies."

22. Smith. In 1668, sixty-nine bond-laborers were shipped from England to Thomas Cooper, Maryland merchant or planter, at a charge of about £3 10s. each.

23. Ibid., p. 36.

24. Ibid., pp. 41–2.

25. The principle was reinforced by Royal Instructions, as in Queen Anne's directions to Francis Nicholson, who was then Governor of Virginia: "[N]one shall acquire a [head] Right meerly by importing or buying servants." The patentee was required to employ the bond-laborers in work on the headright land within three years. (CO 5/1360, p. 268. 16 October 1702.)

26. Apparently young Verney opted for the latter course; he was back in England in less than a year. *Verney Papers*, Camden Society Publications, 56:160–63 (1853).

27. James Revel, 'The Poor Unhappy Transported Felon's Sorrowful Account of His Fourteen Years of Transportation at Virginia in America (circa 1680)," cited by John M. Jennings, *VMHB*, 56:189–94 (1948). There is no way of tracing the lineage of this poem to an actual identifiable author; its first publication was in the form of a chapbook, or popular pamphlet, sold by street peddlers in London in the middle of the eighteenth century. Its authenticity is indicated by certain place names, topographical references and travel routes, that were not familiar in England. Jennings refers to authorities such as Jernegan, Ballagh, and Bruce in concluding that, in any event, the work "presents a realistic picture of conditions in Virginia in the middle of the seventeenth century." Jennings is able to deduce that the author would have had to have come to Virginia somewhere between 1656 and 1671. I would further hazard that, since the poem does not allude to Bacon's Rebellion, Revel would have completed his term of servitude before that unignorable event. That fact would seem to fix the date of his arrival in the colony between 1656 and 1662. The poem is reprinted in Warren M. Billings, ed., *The Old Dominion in the Seventeenth Century, A Documentary History of Virginia, 1606–1689* (Chapel Hill, 1975), pp. 137–42. This particular passage is found there at pp. 138–9.

28. Richard Beale Davis, ed., *William Fitzhugh and his Chesapeake World, 1676–1701* (Chapel Hill, 1963), pp. 128–9.

29. See Chapter 3, especially pp. 40–45.

30. Hening, 1:396 (1656); 1:410 (1655); 1:455–6 (1658); 1:481–2 (1658); 1:546 (1660).

31. Hening, 2:143 (1662).

32. Hening, 2:283.

33. Hening, 2:346.

34. Hening, 2:404 (February 1677).

35. Hening, 2:492–3. This 1682 law resulted in the "importation of many more Indian slaves than has usually been recognized." (Edmund S. Morgan, *American Slavery, American Freedom: The Ordeal of Colonial Virginia* [New York, 1975], p. 330.)

36. Bruce, 2:129. *Economic History*. James C. Ballagh, *A History of Slavery in Virginia* (Baltimore, 1902), pp. 35-6.

37. Hening, 3:69.

38. Hening, 3: 69 n.

39. William W. Hening and William Munford, *Reports of Cases, Relating Chiefly to Points of Practice, Decided by the Supreme Court of Chancery for the Richmond District*, 2nd edn., "Hudgins v. Wrights," (1806), 1:133-43; p. 137. But the court refused to extend the presumption of liberty to African-Americans as Judge George Wythe had urged. That privilege, the court stated, "relates to white persons and native American Indians" but not "to native Africans and their descendants" (pp. 134, 143).

40. Lewis C. Gray, assisted by Esther K. Thompson, *History of Agriculture in the Southern United States to 1860* (Washington, DC, 1932; reprinted 1958), 2:1025; Table 39 gives the number of African-American bond-laborers for four colonies/states (Virginia, Maryland, North Carolina, South Carolina, and Georgia) as 632,000. Philip D. Curtin, *The Atlantic Slave Trade: A Census* (Madison, 1969), p. 72, estimates the number of African bond-laborers brought into the thirteen original colonies to have been around 275,000.

41. Replying to an inquiry about the mortality rate made by the Commissioners for Foreign Plantations in 1676, Governor William Berkeley said that, "whereas previously not one in five escaped the first year," the situation had so improved that "not one in ten unseasoned hands die now." *Samuel Wiseman's Book of Record*, pp. 108-11. Cf. Hening, 2:515.)

The average annual death rate in England in the 1670s was less than 3 percent. (E. A. Wrigley and R. S. Schofield, *The Population History of England, 1541-1871: A Reconstruction* [Cambridge, Mass., 1981], p. 532.)

42. Russell R. Menard: *Economy and Society in Early Colonial Maryland* (New York, 1985), pp. 254, 268-9; idem., "From Servants to Slaves: The Transformation of the Chesapeake Labor System," *Southern Studies*, 16: 355-90 (1977); David W. Galenson, "White Servitude and the Growth of Black Slavery in Colonial America," *Journal of Economic History*, 41:39-47 (1981); idem, *White Servitude in Colonial America: An Economic Analysis* (New York, 1981); idem, *Traders, Planters and Slaves: Market Behavior in Early English America* (New York, 1986), pp. 162-6.

43. Annie Lash Jester, comp. and ed., *Adventurers of Purse and Person: Virginia, 1607-25* (Princeton, 1956; 2nd edition, 1964), pp. 1-70. The discussion of the muster by Irene W. D. Hecht, "The Virginia Muster of 1624/25 as a Source for Demographic History" (*WMO*, 30:65-92), is of invaluable help to students of that period. Her use of the phrase "Negro servants or slaves" in the "or slaves" part does not reflect the record that she has produced and discussed.

44. Hening, 2:170 (1662). *Archives of Maryland*, 1:533 (1663-64). See further in Chapter 10.

45. *MCGC*, p. 466 (June 1640). Hening, 2:26 (1661). Helen Tuncliff Catterall, ed., *Judicial Cases Concerning Emerican Slavery and the Negro*, 5 vols. (Washington, DC, 1926-37 Octagon reprint, 1968), 4:189.

46. Hening, 2:170 (1662). *Archives of Maryland*, 1:533 (1663-64). See also: Whittington B. Johnson, "The Origin and Nature of African Slavery in Seventeenth Century Maryland," *Maryland Historical Magazine*, 73:236-45 (1978); p. 237.

47. Gray, 1:203.

48. Morgan, p. 404.

49. "A Perfect Description of Virginia," in *Force Tracts*, Vol. 2, No. 8, p. 14. A study of twenty-two estate inventories recorded in Surry County, Virginia in the years 1686 to 1688, found not one plow listed. (Kevin P. Kelly, "Economic and Social Development of Seventeenth-century Surry County, Virginia," PhD Dissertation, University of Washington, 1972; p. 138.)

50. Tobacco historian Robert says that in order to remove buds more efficiently in order to limit the number of tobacco leaves drawing on the plant's nutrition, "Some of the yeomen who worked their own crops allowed their thumb nails to grow long and then hardened these nails in the flame of a candle." (Joseph Clarke Robert, *The Story of Tobacco in America* [New York, 1940], p. 14 n. 3.) I have not seen any evidence of this practice among bond-laborers; perhaps they did not see any advantage for themselves in such an improvement in "the instruments of production."

51. Gray, 1:215-17. Bruce, 1:439-43. Joseph Clark Robert, *The Tobacco Kingdom: The Plantation, Market, and Factory in Virginia and North Carolina (1800-1860)* (Durham, North Carolina, 1938), pp. 34-55. Ulrich Bonnell Phillips, *Life and Labor in the Old South* (Boston, 1929; 3rd edn., 1967), pp. 112-15.

52. Russell R. Menard, *Economy and Society in Early Colonial Maryland* (New York, 1985), p. 462. Menard's summary of extensive data that he presents on the previous two pages for the

period 1619 to 1698 cites mainly, but not exclusively, Maryland data only from 1635 on. There is no significant discrepancy between the increase of product per worker in Virginia and Maryland. See also Gray, 1:218–19.

53. Morgan, pp. 126–9, 281–2. Morgan also attaches much importance to the "unadaptability" of English laborers for colonial labor. (He seems to imply that Africans were better suited by their previous labor experience.) But whereas Smith attributes the inability to adapt to those who had not been agricultural laborers in England, Morgan finds the typical rural English worker to have been unsuited for plantation labor. He even gives this typical emigrant worker a sobriquet, "The Lazy Englishman," linking his unsuitability for plantation labor to that of "The Idle Indian" (Ibid., Chapter 3, especially, pp. 50–65).

54. *Archives of Maryland*, 54:234.

55. Hening, 1:257; 2:113. *Archives of Maryland*, 2:147–8. I have used the term "adult bond-laborers" to cover the various cases in which the non-youth ages range from sixteen for Irish and "aliens," in 1643 and 1658, respectively, and then for all bond-laborers in 1662 in Virginia, to twenty-two in Maryland in 1666.

56. *Archives of Maryland*, 2:147–48.

57. Hening, 2:240.

58. John Codman Hurd, *The Law of Freedom and Bondage in the United States*, 2 vols. (Boston, 1858; Negro Universities Press reprint, 1968), 1:138–9. Under the Statute of Artificers of 1562, a laborer who failed to fulfill the terms of a contract for a particular job might also be put in jail for one month. (See pp. 22–3.)

59. *MCGC*, p. 105.

60. *MCGC*, pp. 466–8.

61. Hening, 1:440. (1658).

62. *Archives of Maryland*, 1:107–8.

63. McCormac, p. 52.

64. *Archives of Maryland*, 2:524; "Runaway servants were usually rewarded with a severe whipping by their masters . . ." (*Proceedings of the County Court of Charles County, 1658–1666, and Manor Court of St Clement's Manor, 1659–72, Archives of Maryland*, 53:xxxiii (editorial comment).

65. *Proceedings of the County Court of Charles County, 1666–1674, Archives of Maryland*, 60:xxxv–xxxvi (editorial comment).

66. Ibid., 2:149; 65:xxxiii.

67. At that time the average product per worker was 1,553 pounds of tobacco per year, and the price of tobacco was exceptionally low at 0.9*d.* per pound. The price of male bond-laborers with four years or more to serve was then 2,100 pounds of tobacco. (Menard, *Economy and Society in Early Colonial Maryland*, pp. 249 (Table VII–2); 448 (Table A–7); 462 (Table A–14). The product of sixty-two weeks of labor would equate to nearly 1,800 pounds of tobacco.

68. *Archives of Maryland*, 65:92

69. *Archives of Maryland*, 69:154–5.

70. For Virginia laws, see Hening, 2:273–4 (1663), 277–8, (1669) and 283 (1672). See also *Archives of Maryland*, 54:502, 527, 524, for examples of court awards to captors of runaway bond-laborers.

71. *Archives of Maryland*, 2:523–8.

72. In authorizing the expenditure of 1,000 pounds of tobacco for construction of the apparatuses for these forms of punishment, the Northumberland County Court gave most particular specifications: "The said pillory is to be supplied with two Locust posts, the plank of which it is made to be white oake two inches and a halfe thick [not recommended for the short-necked], Eight foot in Length, and at least Seaven foot and a halfe high from the holes [for the hands and the head of the victim] in the pillory to the Ground, with a bench of Convenient height to stand upon[.] The stocks to be made of white oake ten foot long and three inches and halfe thick with a bench to sitt upon[.] The whip[p]ing post to be of Sound Locust at least Eight foot above the ground and three foot and halfe within the ground, to be eight-square [octagonal] and at least eight inches in Diameter" (*Northumberland County Records, 1678–98*, p. 424 [15 February 1687/8]).

73. Hening, 1:265–7, 463–5; 2:143–6.

74. Raphael Semmes, *Crime and Punishment in Early Maryland* (Baltimore, 1938), pp. 37–8. Semmes comments: "A man must indeed have been in wretched circumstances if life in one of the jails seemed attractive." See also Hening, 2:278–9.

75. Hening, 2:278–9 (1670). *Archives of Maryland*, 10:292.

76. Good surveys of this aspect of the status of bond-laborers are to be found in: Smith

pp. 270–274; Bruce, 2:35–9; *Economic History* (Baltimore, 1895) and James C. Ballagh, *White Servitude in the Colony of Virginia*, pp. 50–51.

Smith generalizes: "Legal marriage without the consent of the masters was always forbidden" (p. 271). Bruce appears to empathize with the owners: "Secret marriages among the servants of the colony seem to have been a common source of serious loss to masters" (2:37).

77. If a master consented to the marriage of a woman bond-laborer belonging to him, the woman was freed from him (*MCGC*, p. 504 [12 March 1655/56]).

78. The record seems to reflect the fact that defiance of this law was more likely where the bond-laborer was attempting to marry a free person, since it almost necessarily involved absconding from the owner's plantation. In 1656, the Lancaster County Virginia Court judged the marriage of a bond-laborer John Smith to be "no marriage" and ordered him to be returned constable-to-constable to his owner (*Lancaster County Records, 1652–57*, p. 285). The following year, the fine for ministers conducting such marriages was by law increased from 1,000 pounds of tobacco to 10,000 pounds (Hening, 1:332, 433). For other examples of such illegal marriages, see: *Norfolk County Records, 1637–46*, p. 51 (1640); *Norfolk County Records, 1646–51*, ff. 147–147a (1650); and *Essex County Records, 1703–1708*, p. 3 (1703).

79. Hening, 1:252–3 (1643). *Archives of Maryland*, 1:97 (1640). See also John Leeds Bozman, *The History of Maryland from Its First Settlement in 1633 to the Restoration in 1660*, 2 vols. (Baltimore, 1837), 2:135.

80. Forlorn bond-laborer Sarah Hedges was unsuccessful in her invocation of this defense because the man she said was her husband, a seaman, did not return with "the next shipping." (*Norfolk County Records, 1656–66*, f. 423 [17 April 1665]; *Norfolk County Orders, 1666–75*, f. 2 [10 May 1666].) For successful invocations of this immunity, see: *Accomack County Records, 1690–97*, pp. 173–173a (21 November 1695). See Also *Northampton County records, 1657–64*, ff. 163, 166 (23 March 1662/3; 28 April 1663).

81. See Hening, 3:74, 139, 361.

82. Ibid., 1:253.

83. Ibid. 2:114–15.

84. A minister's salary was £80 by law (ibid., 2:45 [1662]). Ten thousand pounds of tobacco would have equated officially to £34 (ibid., 2:55).

85. When the English takeover of New Netherlands began in 1664, the so-called "Laws of the Duke of York" were promulgated for the former Dutch territories. These were compiled from those already in effect in earlier Anglo-American colonies. One paragraph of these laws declared that marriages of bond-laborers done without owner consent "shall be proceeded against as for Adultery or fornication." Children of such unions were to be "reputed as Bastards." (Cheesman A. Herrick, *White Servitude in Pennsylvania Indentured and Pennsylvania Labor in Colony and Commonwealth* [Philadelphia, 1926. Negro Universities reprint, 1969], pp. 28, 287.)

86. Hening, 2:114–15.

87. Bozman, 2:135n.

88. Ibid.

89. The Maryland Provinical Court in 1657 sentenced a free woman and free man to twenty lashes each for "having lived in a notorious and Scandalous Course of life tending to Adultery and Fornication." The man's punishment was remitted upon the payment of a fine of five hundred pounds of tobacco. (*Archives of Maryland*, 1:508–9, 588.)

In April 1649, in an instance that apparently involved no physical punishment, a Virginia county court ordered that "William Watts & Mary, Captain Cornwallis's Negro Woman . . . each of them doe penance by standing in a white sheet with a white Rodd in their hands in the Chapell of Elizabeth Rivers in the face of the congregation on the next Sabbath day that the minister shall reade divine service and the said Watts to pay the court charges." (*Norfolk Wills and Deeds, 1646–51*, p. 113a.) I have noted half a dozen early Norfolk County cases in which this "white sheet, white rod" penance was imposed on fornicators.

90. *Archives of Maryland*, Vol. LIII, *Proceedings of the County Court of Charles County, 1658–66*; editor's comment, p. xxx.

91. Bozman, 2:135n.

92. Hening, 2:115 (1662); 3:139 (1696).

93. For Virginia instances in which the "coverture" defense was used (once unsuccessfully and once successfully) see *Henrico County Record Book No. 1, 1677–92*, p. 164 (1 August 1684); and *Accomack County Records, 1690–97*, f. 153 (18 June 1695).

On the other hand, the Virginia Assembly in 1662 ordered the erection of a ducking-stool for punishment of women whose utterances might make "their poore husbands" subject to law suits under the "coverture" principle. But it appears that there were reasons for which unmarried women as well could be subjected to this sometimes fatal treatment. In 1663, Elizabeth Leveritt, a husbandless bond-laborer, was sentenced to endure the ordeal of watery suffocation for being "impudent" to her owner. In an order that was unique so far as my study of the seventeenth-century Chesapeake records goes, the same court ordered that her owner be similarly tortured for failing to maintain a proper discipline over Leveritt. (*Accomack County Records, 1663–1666*, f. 26.)

94. 18 Eliz. I, c. 3. George Nicholls, *A History of the English Poor Law in Connection with the state of the country and Condition of the People*, 3 vols.; (supplementary volume by Thomas Mackay), (1898; 1904; Augustus M. Kelley reprint, 1967), 1:165–6.

95. Hening, 2:115, 167. In 1691, the added time was reduced to one year when the parents were European-Americans (Hening, 3:139–40).

96. *Archives of Maryland*, 1:373–4.

97. Hening, 2:115. Bruce, 2:35–6.

98. *Archives of Maryland*, 58:28. The editors of this volume (*Proceedings of the County Court of Charles County, 1658–1666 and Manor Court of St Clement's Manor, 1659–1672*) state that "Both men and women were whipped indiscriminately, women on the bare back apparently as frequently as men" (p. xxx).

99. Ballagh, *White Servitude in the Colony of Virginia*, p. 48. Smith, p. 271.

100. *York County Deeds, Orders, Wills Etc., 1684–87*, f. 7 (26 January 1685).

101. Commenting on the common occurrence of sentences of two or three years for mothers in such cases, A. E. Smith notes that the actual time off for child-bearing rarely lasted for more than a month or six weeks. "[I]t is plain that the maidservant generally served far more extra time than she can possibly have lost through her misdeeds [let that judgementalism pass]; sentences of two and even three years are quite common, though childbirth can rarely have incapacitated a woman for more than a month or six weeks." (Smith, p. 271.)

102. See Chapter 8, note 37, regarding the extent of these records.

103. Rating tobacco at 10s. per hundred pounds, and the cost of transportation of European-American bond-laborers at £6 each.

104. Output per worker in pounds of tobacco increased in every decade from 1619 to 1699, and it is estimated to have been more than 1,500 pounds in the 1660s. (Menard, *Economy and Society in Early Colonial Maryland*, p. 426, Table A–14.) Though the price of Chesapeake tobacco fluctuated, it was officially rated at about ten shillings a hundred pounds, 1.2d. per pound, during the last four decades of the seventeenth century. (See Morgan, p. 204 n. 29.)

105. Smith, p. 271. Hening, 2:168.

106. *Accomack County Records, 1666–70*, f. 176, 3 February 1669/70. *Accomack County Records, 1697–1703*, f. 78, 17 November 1699. *Norfolk County Records, 1675–86*, p. 44, 22 November 1677.

107. *Norfolk County Records, 1646–51*, f. 140, 26 March 1650.

108. *Archives of Maryland,*, 53:xxviii–xxix, pp. 28–30.

109. Ibid., 53:xxix, p. 37.

110. For instances of this aspect of gender-class oppression, see: *Norfolk County Records, 1651–1656*, ff. 35 and 46 (1653); *Lancaster County Records, 1655–1666*, p. 82 (1659); *Charles City County Records, 1655–1665*, p. 523 (1664); *Norfolk County Records, 1666–1675 (part 2)*, f. 74a (1671); *Norfolk County Records, 1675–1686*, ff. 44 and 99 (1677, 1679); *Accomack County Records, 1697–1703*, ff. 78–78a, and 129a–130 (1699, 1702); *Surry County Records, 1671–91*, pp. 454–55 (1684). In four of these cases, the owner sold away his own child in the womb of the pregnant bond-laborer.

These acts were treated as "fornication," which entailed a fine of 500 pounds of tobacco on each party. If the woman bond-laborer was unable to pay her fine, she was to suffer 20 or 30 lashes at the whipping post "on her naked back," or alternatively, if the owner paid her fine, she was bound to serve six months for that, and two years more for the expense her pregnancy and the child would be to the master (Hening, 2:115; 3:74, 159). In Virginia after 1662, as is noted below, the extra two years was to be served under a different master, to whom she was to be sold by the churchwardens (Hening, 2:167).

111. Hening, 2:167. In Maryland in 1694 a woman in this situation was required to swear "in her pains of Travaille" that the owner was the father. This oath, which the bond-laborer could swear falsely only at the peril of hell's eternal fire, would be taken as proof only if it seemed to the male judges to be consistent with all other evidence and testimony. (*Archives of Maryland*, 19:47.)

112. *Archives of Maryland*, 60:xxxvi, 9–11. The court record identifies Yansley as a "Spinster," most likely a reference to her occupation, not to her unmarried status. The editor of this volume of the *Archives of Maryland*, says that Yansley was "presumably" a bond-laborer.

113. George Nicholls, 1:114–19, 121–5, 189. The laws were 22 Henry VIII c. 10, 27 Henry VIII c. 25, and 43 Eliz. c. 2.

114. Nicholls, 1:189.

115. Hening, 2:240. *Archives of Maryland*, 2:147–8. See also Semmes, pp. 85–7.

116. Hening, 2:115, 168.

117. Hening, 1:552.

118. Menard, *Economy and Society in Early Colonial Maryland*, pp. 460–61, 462. It is to be noted that European-American women were not tithable unless they were "working in the ground"; but the records indicate that many, perhaps most, were engaged directly in the cultivation of tobacco fields.

119. See the cases of Bridgett (last name omitted in the record) and Wilking (?) Jones: *Norfolk County Records (part 2, Orders), 1666–75*, pp. 94, 101 (June and August 1673); *Norfolk County Order Book, 1675–86*, p. 108 (2 March 1679/80). For the 1662 law, see Hening, 2:114–15.

120. When the plantation bourgeoisie was able to reduce its labor force to mainly lifetime, hereditary servitude, in the eighteenth century, the birth of the children did become "cost-effective," as the bourgeois term is.

121. Hening, 1:361 (1649); 3:256. Under a law passed in 1680, *imported* children of African origin were not to be tithable until they were twelve years of age, those coming from Europe not until they were fourteen years old (Hening, 2:479–80).

122. Hening, 2:168 (1662).

123. Ibid., 2:298 (1672).

124. Ibid., 2:170.

125. Hening, 3:87.

126. In the opinion of Whittington B. Johnson, "This course of action was probably forced upon slaveowners because there were so few African females in the colony"; it brought the owner "potential monetary gain" (Johnson, p. 242.)

127. This calculation was propounded in an opinion delivered by Judge Daniel Dulany, himself a slaveholder, in a historical appendix delivered by him on behalf of the Maryland Provincial Court on 16 December 1767. (Thomas Harris Jr and John McHenry, *Maryland Reports, being a Series of the Most Important Cases argued and determined in the Provincial Court and the Court of Appeals of the then province of Maryland from the Year 1700 down to the American Revolution* [New York, 1809], 2 vols., 1:559–64; 563.)

128. *Archives of Maryland*, 1:533 (1662); 13:546–9 (1692).

129. Hening, 2:170. Ballagh, *History of Slavery in Virginia*, p. 57.

130. Hening, 3:87.

131. *CSP, Col.*, 13:644 (Minutes of the General Assembly of Maryland, 21 May 1692).

132. *Elizabeth City County Records, 1684–99* (transcript), p. 83 (30 December 1695).

133. *Accomack County Records, 1703–9*, ff. 107–a, 118 (3 February and 2 June 1708).

134. Hening, 1:153–4; 2:195; 273. *Archives of Maryland*, 2:523–4. For some Virginia cases arising under such laws, see *Norfolk County Records, 1665–75*, p. 42 (1670), and ibid., *1675–86*; *Middlesex County Records, 1673–80*, f. 135 (1678); and *Accomack County Records, 1678–82*, p. 173 (1680).

135. Hening, 2:115–16 (1662).

136. The situation reported by an emissary of the London government in 1701 surely was not of recent origin. "A great many," he said, "choose to sit down loosers rather than go to the Law." (Report of George Larkin to the Lords of Trade and Plantations, CO 5/1312, 22 December 1701.)

137. Richard B. Morris, *Government and Labor in Early America* (New York, 1946), pp. 312–13.

138. *Charles City County Court Orders, 1655–1658*, in Beverley Fleet, comp., *Virginia Colonial Abstracts*, 34 vols., (Baltimore, 1961), vol. 10, p. 441 (8 February 1663/64).

139. McCormac, p. 44.

140. Ibid., p. 66. Ballagh, *White Servitude in the Colony of Virginia*, p. 59. Hening, 2:268 (1668).

141. *Archives of Maryland*, Vol. 60, *Proceedings of the County Court of Charles County, 1666–1674*, pp. xxxv–xxxvi.

142. Ibid., pp. 45–47. The matter is presented in fuller detail in the record.

143. Ibid., pp. 108–9.

144. *Northampton County [Wills] Order Book*, No. 10, 1674–1679, p. 270.

145. *Calendar of Virginia State Papers and Other Manuscripts ... Preserved in the Capitol at Richmond, 1652–1859* edited by W. P. Palmer, S. McRae, H. W. Flourney, et al., 11 vols. (Richmond, 1875–1893); 1:9–10.

146. *Journals of the House of Burgesses of Virginia*, H. R. McIlwaine, ed., 13 vols. (Richmond, 1915); 2:34–5. Library of Congress, Jefferson Papers, Series 8, Vol. 7 (Miscellaneous Documents), p. 232 (24 October 1666).

147. Smith, pp. 237-8. This was not so in Barbados in the late decades of the seventeenth century, where by law the European bond-laborers were guaranteed five pounds of meat a week and four pairs of shoes every year, along with corresponding quantities of other items of wearing apparel (Smith, p.237). This contrast is rooted in the relative difficulty of keeping European bond-laborers in the West Indies as compared with the continental plantation colonies. (See Chapter 12.)

148. *Accomack County Order Book I, 1632-1640*, p. 68 (1 February 1635/36); *Accomack County Deeds & Wills [Orders], 1666-1670*, p. 48 (17 February 1667/8). See also Smith, p. 250.

149. Gray, 1:366. Smith, p. 250.

150. For the customary diet in England, see E. H. Phelps-Brown and Sheila V. Hopkins, "Seven Centuries of the Prices of Consumables compared with Builders' Wage-rates," *Economica*, 23:296-307 (1956). Although the tabulation skips from the sixteenth to the eighteenth century, it indicates a trend of increase in the importance of meat and dairy products in the English diet. While the grains-and-peas proportion declined slightly, beef replaced herring in the diet, and by 1725, out of every 100 pence [the equivalent of less than ten days builders' wages] spent on "consumables" (food, drink, fuel and light, and textiles), the meat and dairy products portions accounted for 37½ pence and included 33 pounds of beef, 10 pounds of butter, and 10 pounds of cheese. (See ibid., Tables 1 and 2.) How nearly this approximated the wage worker's diet is not revealed, however.

See pp. 151-2 for bond-laborers' struggles over diet.

151. Aubrey C. Land, "The Planters of Colonial Maryland," *Maryland Historical Magazine*, 67:109-28 (1972); p. 124.

152. Bruce, 1:486. Gray, 1:209.

153. E. H. Phelps-Brown and Sheila V. Hopkins, "Wage-rates and Prices: Evidence for Population Pressure in the Sixteenth Century," *Economica*, 24:289-306 (1957); table 4, "England" column 1.

154. Bruce, 2:205-11.

155. Gray, 1:209.

156. Cf. Bruce, 2:8. Bruce cites York County records for 1657-1662 to argue that in 1661 bond-laborers were given meat three times a week. But he seems unable to find grounds for his speculation that, "It could not have been many years before this allowance was extended to each day in consequence of the enormous increase in the heads of hogs and horned cattle." Perhaps he might have cited from the same volume of York County records the rebellious complaint of bond-laborers that they were dieted on only corn and water, whereas they were supposed to get meat three times a week. (York County *Deeds, Orders, Wills, Etc*, f. 149 [6 January 1661/2]. Besides the folio number given here, there is page number 297 inscribed by the Virginia State Library, and a typescript page 384 of the same record. Bruce cites "p. 384." Could he have been using the typescript; and did he mean 1662 instead of 1661?) See references to this bond-laborers' plot in Chapter 8.

157. "Questions proposed by his Majestie and Councell for which I return this humble plain and true answer." [Henry] In *Coventry Papers Relating to Virginia, Barbados and other Colonies*, microfilm prepared by the British Manuscripts Project of the American Council of Learned Societies and available at the Library of Congress (originals at the estate of the Marquis of Bath, Longleat House, Wiltshire, England, hereafter to be cited as *Coventry Papers*.) The present citation is Vol. 77, f. 332. The report is not dated, but was obviously written in the fall of 1676. Henry Coventry was a Secretary of State with primary responsibility for the colonies.

158. Jasper Dankers and Peter Sluyter, *Journal of a Voyage to New York and a Tour in Several of the American Colonies in 1679-80*, translated and edited by Henry C. Murphy, Long Island Historical society Memoirs I (Brooklyn, 1867), p. 191.

The report of George Larkin to the Lords of trade and Plantations in December 1701 revealed that in Virginia and Maryland the owners still held to the principle of getting pennies by saving them at the expense of the bond-laborers' food allowance: ". . . a man had really better be hanged than come a servant into the Plantations, most of his food being homene and water. . . . I have been told by some of them that they have not tasted flesh meat in three months." (CO, 5/1312).

159. Gray, 1:365-6.

160. Using Menard's tabulations for the period 1660-79 inclusive for Maryland, the average output per worker was 1,603 pounds of tobacco, and the average price was 1.18*d*. In five years the labor of each bond-laborer would thus have brought to the owner an income of £39 8*s*. (See Menard, *Economy and Society in Early Colonial Maryland*, pp. 449 and 462.) In Virginia before 1660, according to Thomas J. Wertenbaker, "the average annual income from the labor of one able worker ... was not less than £12" (*The Planters of Colonial Virginia* [Princeton, 1922], p. 71). Morgan says that Virginia tobacco prices were "probably somewhat higher" than those in Maryland,

and he notes that in official transactions in Virginia in the last four decades of the seventeenth century, tobacco was rated at 10s per hundred pounds (1.2d per pound). (Morgan, p. 204 n. 20.) See also L. C. Gray's discussion of tobacco prices, 1:262–8.

Semmes states that an owner made an annual profit of "about fifty pounds sterling," citing, among other facts, the claim by a member of the Maryland Colony council that on average the bond-laborer "would produce to his master, at least fifty pounds sterling clear profit into purse, most commonly far more." (Semmes p. 80; the quoted phrase is cited from "Letters of Robert Wintour", unpublished manuscript in the collection of Dr Hugh H. Young, of Baltimore, Maryland.)

161. CO 5/1312. See notes 136 and 158 above. A quarter of a century before, the Virginia Assembly noted the practice among owners of pressuring bond-laborers who were nearing the end of their terms to agree to extend their servitude. (Hening 2:388–9.)

162. '... The observed increase in productivity probably resulted from making servants work harder" (Joseph Douglas Deal, *Race and Class in Colonial Virginia: Indians, Englishmen, and Africans on the Eastern Shore during the Seventeenth Century* (New York, 1993), p. 115).

163. Phillips, p. 126.

164. Robert, *Tobacco Kingdom*, p. 18.

165. Menard, *Economy and Society in Early Colonial Maryland*, p. 239.

166. George Fitzhugh in *De Bow's Review*, 30:89 (January 1861), cited in Phillips, p. 126.

167. Consequently, early in the season, when ready tobacco might not be available, exchanges were sometimes made completely or partially by direct barter, as in the following cases found in the Maryland court records. In April 1663, Elizabeth Holbrooke, a bond-laborer belonging to John Williams with four years to serve, was exchanged for "One yearling heyfer, with her encrease." In March 1667, John Godshall acquired a parcel of land called "Hogge Quarter" for "a Servant named Thomas Porch in hand paid." When Thomas King the following year bought five hundred acres of land on the north side of Nangemy Creek from Thomas and John Stone, he paid "Seven Thousand Pounds of Tobacco and Caske and two Servants" (*Archives of Maryland*, 49:7 [1663]; 60:147, 168–9 [1668]). The Lancaster County Virginia records for that same month reveal that Thomas Williamson had taken out a "mortgage" on a male bond-laborer, one Samuel Pen[?], on whom the mortgage holder, Thomas Williamson, was seeking foreclosure. (*Lancaster Orders, Etc., 1666–1680*, p. 34 [13 March 1666/7].)

168. Bruce, 1:447.

169. Land, p. 124.

170. Referring particularly to the 1660–80 period, when tobacco prices were much lower than in previous decades, Edmund S. Morgan writes that the small self-employed farmer was apt to be debt-ruined in times of especially low tobacco prices, but "a man with capital or credit to deal on a large scale" could thrive through it all by prudent market operations, and "by working his men [and women] a little harder" (Morgan, p. 191).

171. Bullock, p. 11. See also *A Perfect Description of Virginia, Being a Full and True Relation of the Present State of the Plantation, Their Health, Peace, and Plenty ...* (London, 1649) in *Force Tracts*, II, No. 8, p. 6.

A century later the much-quoted William Eddis found that in Maryland, as a general rule, European bond-laborers were "strained to their uttermost to perform their allotted labor" under the watchful eye of the "rigid planter [who] exercises inflexible severity in matters of supervision."

172. *Accomack Court Orders, 1666–1670*, ff. 60–62 (16 June 1668). The name of this entrepreneur is notorious to the fellowship of scholars of the seventeenth-century Chesapeake.

173. Dankers and Sluyter, p. 216.

174. *Archives of Maryland*, 10:521 (22 September 1657).

175. *Archives of Maryland*, 1:21.

176. James Revel, "The Poor Unhappy Transported Felon's Sorrowful Account ...," *VMHB*, 56:189–94 (1948). Reprinted in Billings, p. 140.

177. *Archives of Maryland*, 10:484–5 (10 March 1656/7).

178. Bruce, 2:33.

179. Revel, p. 140.

180. According to the author of *A Description of the Province of New Albion, And a Direction for Adventurers with small stock to get two for one, and good land freely*, written in 1649, only one out of nine Virginia immigrants was dying in the first critical year in the colony, but in the first three decades, five out of six died in the first year of bondage, called the "seasoning" time. (*Force Tracts*, II, No. 7, p. 5.) Governor Berkeley reported to the Lords of Trade and Plantations in 1671 that the bond-laborers then generally survived the first "seasoning" year, but that "heretofore not one of five escaped the first year" (CO 1/26, f. 198. Hening 2:515).

The Virginia records led Thomas J. Wertenbaker to conclude in 1922 that in the 1635–60 period one-third or more of the bond-laborers died in the first year of their servitude, but that conditions improved so much that by 1671 the proportion was only one out of five (Wertenbaker, pp. 40, 80). Abbot E. Smith, in 1947, without giving specific dates, wrote thus of the bond-servitude of European immigrants: "kill them it usually did; at least in the first years, when fifty over seventy-five of every hundred … died without ever having a decent chance at survival" (Smith, p.304). Walter Hart Blumenthal, in 1962, believed that of the bond-laborers coming to the tobacco colonies between 1620 and 1680, 35 percent of the women and 50 percent of the men died within five years after landing. (Blumenthal, p. 23). Wesley Frank Craven, in 1971, noted the high death rate among the earliest Virginia immigrants, but believed that subsequently the "first year … was usually not fatal" (Craven, p. 26).

The odds against a chattel bond-laborer surviving the first year are indicated by the fact that a new laborer with five years to serve was commonly sold for less than a seasoned hand who had only three or four years to serve (Morgan, pp. 175–6). Russell Menard believes that the inflow of immigrant laborers did not rise steadily after 1644 as Morgan (p. 180) argues, but that it rose and fell in response to the rise or fall of tobacco prices (*Economy and Society in Early Colonial Maryland*, pp. 119–26). But, he says, "the mortality rate among new arrivals must have been frightening" (ibid;, p.191; see also Table IV–4, p. 137).

Both Morgan and Menard call attention to the disparity between the mortality rates of New England and those in the tobacco colonies. That disparity explains why New England's population growth in the seventeenth century did not depend upon immigration, while in Maryland and Virginia population growth did. Among the factors making for the difference was that while some 80 percent of the immigrants to the Chesapeake were chattel bond-laborers, only a small percentage of New England immigrants were in that category. (Morgan, p. 180; Menard, pp. 129–30, 140, and Tables IV–3 and IV–5, pp. 135 and 141.)

181. Dankers and Sluyter, p. 217.

182. *Accomack County Wills, Deeds, & Orders, 1678–1682*, p. 260 (18 August 1681).

183. *Accomack County Order Book I (Orders, Deeds, Etc., No. 1), 1632–1640*, p. 104 (3 July 1637). *Norfolk County Wills & Deeds B, 1646–1651*, p. 117a (19 April and 31 July 1649). In 1692 the Provincial Assembly of Maryland enacted a law providing that owners who grossly abused "any English Servant or Slave," or denied them provisions, or forced them to work beyond their strength, for the first and second offense were to be. fined, and if the offense were then repeated, the bond-laborers were to be "free from their servitude.'.' Accordingly, Thomas Courtney, who "most barbarously dismembered and cutt off both the Ears" of a "Molattoe girl," a limited-term bond-laborer, was merely ordered to set her free. There was no further "recompense" to the girl. Furthermore, that did not mean she was to be freed from servitude, but merely from servitude to Courtney. (*Archives of Maryland*, 13:451–7 [4 June 1692]).

184. Morris, pp. 485–7.

185. Hening, 2:53.

186. Although I am working directly with the colonial records as cited, almost all, or nearly all, of the cases mentioned here are also mentioned in Morris, pp. 485–8 and 491–96 (the Henry Smith case).

187. *Northampton County Orders, Deeds, Wills, Etc., No. 2, 1640–1645* (3 August 1640). I have had to interpolate somewhat in describing the indenture, because of damage to the manuscript.

188. But the inquest jury said, 'how hee came by his death wee know not." (*Northampton County Order Book, 1654–1664*, pp. 21–2 [29 June 1658].) Burton may have had no reason to feign a headache. In a subsequent autopsy, a physician found that Burton's "heart [had been] very defective and … his Lungs imperfect blacke and putrefied." (Ibid., p. 25 [same date].) For other examples, see: *Charles City County Records, 1655–1665*, p. 357 (3 February 1662/3; bond-laborer found starved to death, his body showing stripes from a whipping administered by the wife of his owner). *Northampton County Order Book, 1657–1564*, pp. 140, 142 (10 July and 24 August, 1662; owner posts "good behaviour" bond, which is returned' to him three months later). *Lancaster County Orders, Etc., 1666–1680*, f. 10. (2 September 1666; bond-laborer dies "very shortly after" being "switched" by owner for "feigning" illness; court finds owner "innocent.") *Northampton County Order Book, 1664–1674*, p. 130. (28 June 1672; owner's agent kicks, a young African-American boy to death, depositions are taken from fellow bond-laborers but no further court action is recorded.) See also: *Surry County Records, 1671–91*, p.219. (12 September 1678; inquest finds owner to have caused the death of his woman bond-laborer; the court nullifies that finding.) *Middlesex County Order Book, 1694–1705*, pp. 234–42, 300, 458. (1 August and 2 October 1699; account of the whipping to death of a "Mulatto runaway boy" at the specific orders of his owner, Samuel Gray, a

minister; there is no record of any penalties.) The minister remained "one of the boys" of the county elite; he served as a member of the first Board of Visitors and of the Board of trustees of the College of William and Mary. (Richard L. Morton, *Colonial Virginia*, 2 vols. [Chapel Hill, 1960], 1:346 n. 15.)

189. *Archives of Maryland*, 3:146, 187–8; 10:522, 534–45. Seven years later, a member of the indicting grand jury, John Grammer, killed one of his bond-labors with a hundred lashes, but the grand jury declined to indict him. *Archives of Maryland*, 49:307–12.

190. Proceedings of the Provincial Court, 1663–1666 *Archives of Maryland*, 49:290, 304–7, 311–14. Fincher's last words before sentence of death was pronounced are a curiosity; after three months in jail he displayed none of the choler he had shown when in authority: "If I deserve it I must die" (p. 313).

191. *Archives of Maryland*, 54:390–91; 57:60–65. To be granted "benefit of clergy," a person found guilty was merely shown a bible and asked if he could read it "as a cleric." If the answer was "yes," the defendant was let go with a formalistic branding of the base of the thumb. This routine was a vestigial relic of medieval times when only persons of clerical status were able to read the Bible and when priests were to be tried only in ecclesiastical courts. Carpenter was assessed 2,998 pounds of tobacco for sheriff's fees, and 1,000 for the surgeon who "opened the skull" of the victim at inquest. (Ibid., 54:410.)

192. Smith appears in the record as a successful planter and as a thoroughgoing pathological brute. He scorned his wife, and beat her until she finally had to return to England to save her life. He sexually assaulted two of his women bond-laborers, so that they ran away. (Retaken, they were ordered to serve additional time double the days of their absence from Smith.) Another bond-laborer, mother of a child by him, charged that Smith had killed it. *Accomack County Orders, 1666–1670*, pp. 67 (December 1668); 112 (4 February 1668/9); 129, 131–7 (17 March and 2 April 1668/9); 168 (25 January 1669/70); 176–9 (3 February 1669/70). *MCGC*, p. 217 (1668–70), cited by Morris, p. 496 n. 145.

193. *Archives of Maryland*, 69:xvi–xvii, 413. Morris, p. 486.

194. *Archives of Maryland*, 41:478–80.

195. Ibid., p. 385.

196. Ibid., 49:166–8, 230, 233–5.

197. See Appendix II-D.

198. For cases in which special judicial consideration was given to psychopathic persons accused of crime, see Hening, 2:39 (1661) and *Northumberland County Records, 1678–98* (1 November 1683).

199. See p. 22, above.

200. "You may be a model citizen, perhaps a member of the Society for the Prevention of Cruelty to Animals, and in the odor of sanctity to boot; but the thing that you represent face to face with me has no heart in its breast. That which seems to throb there is my own heart-beating." Thus spake Marx's wage-worker in 1869. It was just as true for the relations of labor and capital in the plantation bond-labor system. (See Karl Marx, *Capital*, Vol. I, Chapter X, "The Working Day," Section 1.)

8 ... and Resisting

1. W. E. B. Du Bois, in *Annual Report of the American Historical Association for the Year 1909* (1911), a forerunner of his *Black Reconstruction*, published in 1935.

2. Timothy H. Breen, "A Changing Labor Force and Race Relations in Virginia 1660–1710," *Journal of Social History*, Fall 1973, pp. 3–25.

3. Ibid., p. 7.

4. Ibid., p. 17. It will be apparent that this chapter draws on many of the same records cited by Breen. However, as I have indicated briefly in the Introduction of this work (*The Invention of the White Race*, Volume One, p. 20), I question Breen's attribution of the disappearance of solidarity of European-American and African-American laborers against the plantation bourgeoisie after 1676 to exclusively objective factors (such as tobacco prices and the arrival of non-English-speaking laborers directly from Africa). I also object to certain assertions requiring the reader to share his undocumented speculations about the attitudes of the European-American workers (he called them "whites") (pp. 7, 17). Finally, I attempt in this work to give some attention to the role of male supremacy and the resistance to it in the. history of the period embraced in the title of Breen's article. This aspect appears to have been ignored, but not only by Breen.

5. "Servants responded to their lot in different ways. Some ran off at the first opportunity; other stole from their owners or attacked them; still others found momentary solace in drink or casual sexual liaisons. Planters viewed such behavior as a clear and constant danger to an orderly society and to their own economic well being. And why not? As a group the servile population accounted for half of Virginia's settlers." (Warren M. Billings, "The Law of Servants and Slaves in Seventeenth-Century Virginia," *Virginia Magazine of History and Biography*, 99:45–62 [January 1991]; p. 50.)

6. In the words of the Virginia Assembly in 1661 (Hening, 2:35).

7. *Northampton County Records, 1655–57*, p. 26. This first John Custis was the great-grand-father of Daniel Parke Custis, whose widow, Martha Dandridge Custis, married George Washington. (Edward Duffield Neill, *Virginia Carolorum, the Colony under the Rule of Charles the First and Second, AD 1625–1685* [Albany, NY, 1886], p. 209.)

8. See *The Invention of the White Race*, Volume One, p. 74, and Chapter 7, note 10 of this volume.

9. Hening, 1:411 (March 1655). After the restoration of the crypto-Catholic Charles II to the throne in England, the distinction was repealed in 1662, but the new law was not retroactive (Hening 2:113–14).

10. *Westmoreland County Records, 1661–62*, p. 52.

11. *York County Records, 1657–62*, f. 122. For other cases of bond-laborer suicide, see: *Archives of Maryland*, 53:501–2; *Northampton County Records*, p. 106 (1651); *York County Records, 1657–62*, f. 67. (1659); *York County Records, 1665–72*, p. 115 (1666); *Accomack County Records, 1676–78*, p. 29 (1677); *Accomack County Records, 1676–90*, f. 122 (1678).

Perhaps there was a class predisposition to "want of Grace"; I have found no seventeenth-century record of a suicide by a Chesapeake owner of bond-laborers.

12. *York County Records, 1657–62*, f. 46.

13. *Archives of Maryland*, 65:2–8. A second African-American bond-laborer was among the group of those originally charged, but the jury found him not guilty. Nevertheless, he was ordered to act as hangman of the other four.

The editorial definition of "petty treason" is "the killing of a master by his servants, of a husband by his wife, or of a high ecclesiastic by one of his inferiors" (p. xvii).

14. Hening, 2:118.

15. For a number of such Virginia "violent hands" cases, besides those detailed here, see: *Accomack County Records, 1666–70*, pp. 14, 38 (1666, 1667); *York County Records, 1665–72*, f. 52 (1666); *Northampton County Records, 1664–74*, pp. 69–70 (1669); *Northumberland County Records, 1666–78*, f. 93 (1670); *Lancaster County Records, 1666–80*, p. 200 (1671); *Middlesex County Records, 1673–80*, f. 6 (1674); *Northumberland County Records, 1666–78*, f. 197 (1674); *Accomack County Records, 1676–78*, pp. 20–21 (1676).

16. *Norfolk County Records, 1666–75*, p. 7 (1666).

17. *Lancaster County Records, 1666–80*, pp. 200–201.

18. *Northampton County Records, 1664–74*, pp. 133, 134, 137–8, 219, (1672, 1673).

19. *Surry County Records, 1671–84*, ff. 82, 97. You had to be there!

20. Hening 1:257 (March 1643).

21. *Norfolk County Records, 1651–56*, pp. 101, 105, 114. No reference is made to Bradley's age. The next law on this subject (Hening, 1:441–2) required non-indentured, "custom-of-the-country" bond-laborers who were under fifteen years old at the time of their arrival to serve until they were twenty-one. But that law was not enacted until 1658.

22. *Northumberland County Records, 1678–98*, p. 389.

23. *Northampton County Records, 1645–51*, ff. 132–3.

24. Hening, 1:244 (1643), 350 (1647); 2:129 (1662), 441 (1679). To kill a marked hog would logically make one subject to prosecution; but why did the ruling class insist on these severe penalties for killing and eating wild hogs? Was it a way of emphasizing to bond-laborers their general dependence on their owners for their "diet"? Was it aimed at discouraging runaways who might hope to maintain themselves on wild pork? Governor Francis Nicholson articulated that concern: the "stock of cattle and hogs" running "in the woods and about the frontiers," he said, "would supply them [runaways] with victuals." (*CSP, Col.*, 16:391, Nicholson to Commissioners of Trade and Plantations, 20 August 1698.)

25. For typical examples, see: *Northumberland County Records, 1652–65*, f. 351; ibid., *1666–78*, f. 151; ibid., *1678–98*, p. 6; *Lancaster County Records, 1666–80*, ff. 142, 215, 230, 352; *Middlesex County Records, 1673–80*, f. 36; ibid., *1680–94*, pp. 5, 31; ibid., *1694–1705*, p. 98, 289–90.

26. *Accomack County Records, 1676–90*, pp. 389–90 (7 November 1684).

27. *Archives of Maryland*, 49:8–10 (31 March 1663). The sentence of the court was that six suffer 30-lash whippings, to be administered by the other two.

28. *Lancaster County Records, 1666–80*, f. 158 (13 July 1670).

29. In regard to the components of the English diet at that time see page 321, n. 150.

30. *York County Records, 1657–62*, ff. 85 (24 July 1660); 143 (24 January 1661/2); 149 (25 January 1661/2); 150 (10 March 1661/2). A part of this record is printed in *VMHB*. 11:34–6 (1902–1903).

31. Library of Congress, Virginia (Colony) Collection microfilm, reel 4, depositions taken 13 September 1663. These materials have been printed in *VMHB*, 15:38–43 (1907–8). See also Robert Beverly, *History and Present State of Virginia* (1705); John Burk, *The History of Virginia from its First Settlement to the Commencement of the Revolution*, 3 vols. (Petersburg, Virginia, 1822), 1:135–7; and Charles Campbell, *History of the Colony and Ancient Dominion of Virginia* (Philadelphia, 1860).

32. Perhaps this was the Birkenhead mentioned in the Interregnum Record Book for 28 June 1653, who was scheduled to speak with a committee "concerning matters of importance" and to "give in names of such other persons as to be summoned before the Committee" (Great Britain Public Record Office, *Calendar of State Papers, Domestic*, 37:445).

33. Hening, 2:204 (16 September 1663).

34. Hening, 2:195.

35. Hening, 2:204.

36. A great portion, quite possibly half, of the seventeenth-century Virginia court records no longer exist. Of the lost seventeenth-century county records, a major part was destroyed by fires set when Robert E. Lee's Confederate army retreated from Richmond in the first days of April 1865. However, says an archival specialist, "an awful lot of [the] dates of destruction have nothing at all to do with the Civil War," many of the records having been lost in other wars, and in floods and non-wartime fires. Some few seem not to be accounted for at all. (Robert Clay, of the Virginia State Library Archives, in *The Callaway Family Association Journal, 1979*, pp. 48–56; see p. 51 for a list of Burned Record Counties.) This is simply a limitation to which historians must be reconciled, aware as they must ever be of the risks of attempting to generalize on the basis of incomplete information.

Of the approximately 1,675 total of all the years of existence of all the 27 Virginia counties that at some time existed in Virginia between 1634 (the beginning of county formation) to 1710, county court records of varying extents are available in photocopy and on microfilm as well as in abstracts from the records, at the Virginia State Archives in Richmond, comprising some 1,275 county-years. In the preparation of this study, I have examined the records covering some 885 of these county-years, including some made in four counties that were extinguished during that period: Accawmacke, Charles River, and Warrosquoake in 1643; Rappahannock in 1693. (See Martha W. Hiden, *How Justice Grew, Virginia Counties: An Abstract of Their Formation*, Jamestown 350th Anniversary Historical Booklet No. 19 [Richmond, 1957], especially charts 1–9, pp. 83–5.)

37. Billings, p. 50, J. Douglas Deal, *Race and Class in Colonial Virginia: Indians, Englishmen, and Africans on the Eastern Shore During the Seventeenth Century* (New York, 1993), p. 126.

38. There were paradoxical cases, as noted in Chapter 7, when the owners might find it to their advantage to "encourage" flight of bond-laborers in the last month or so of their bondage to avoid payment of the customary "corn and clothes" due at the end of their terms.

39. Due to "the late unhappy rebellion," the Assembly said in amending the statute of limitations in October 1677, "all judiciary proceedings were impeded and hindred for the greatest part of the last year." (Hening, 2:419–20). The records of the Provincial Court of Maryland tell of the flight of eight African-American bond-laborers from that province to Virginia during the time of Bacon's Rebellion. (*Archives of Maryland*, 49:355–6.)

40. Hening, 2:35.

41. Governor Berkeley to Lords of Trade and Plantations (Hening, 2:515): according to Berkeley there were bond-laborers in Virginia. 6,000 European-American and 2,000 African-American. Governor Culpeper's estimate, 12 December 1681, put the numbers at "fifteen thousand servants," of whom 3,000 were African-Americans (*CSP, Col.*, 11:157).

42. When "takers-up" of runaways applied to be certified by the General Assembly for compensation, the list of the captives gave no indication of whether two or more had acted in concert.

43. *MCGC*, p. 467 (17 October 1640). In the end the costs were to be repaid by extensions of the servitude of bond-laborers recaptured.

44. *MCGC*, p. 466. The owner would have preferred to dispose of them in Maryland.

45. *MCGC*, p. 468.

46. *MCGC*, p. 467 (22 July 1640).

47. *MCGC*, p. 467 (13 October 1640). By "The Dutch Plantation" they may have meant present-day Delaware.

48. Ibid.

49. *Northampton County Records, 1645–51*, f. 2 (11 November 1645). In this and subsequent notes, the dates given are those of the court proceedings; where the dates of the events described are significantly different from the date of the court record, those dates will be given.

50. *Accomack County Records, 1666–70*, ff. 31–3. Although the depositions in this case were taken in August 1663, they were not entered in the record until 16 July 1667.

51. Two, and possibly three, of the women were married, from which fact I infer that they were probably not chattel bond-laborers. By the same reasoning, I conclude that the conspirator husbands of two of them were not chattels. In all probability they were former bond-laborers.

52. They were, respectively, the son-in-law and daughter of Colonel Scarburgh (Deal, p. 119).

53. "Black James," was associated in the accounts with "Cornelius a dutchman's wife." James is not further identified. It is worth noting, however, that among the tithables of Lieutenant Colonel William Kendall in 1668 in neighbouring Northampton County were "Cornelius Arreale" and "James Negro." (*Northampton County Records, 1664–74*, p. 55.)

54. *Accomack County Records, 1671–73*, pp. 93–7. Although the depositions were taken in December 1670, they are entered in the record on 23 April 1672, more than two years later. Possibly they were used in evidence against one of the plotters, Isack Medcalfe, who at the later date was appealing for leniency in the matter of the extension of his time of servitude.

55. *Middlesex County Records, 1673–80*, f. 226 (4 October 1680).

56. *Accomack County Records, 1678–72*, p. 95 (16 July 1679).

57. *Lancaster County Records, 1666–80*, ff. 487–8 (10 September 1679).

58. *Northumberland County Records, 1678–98*, p. 176 (18 April 1683).

59. *Accomack County Records, 1682–97*, p. 131 (2 April 1688).

60. *Norfolk County Records, 1686–95*, p. 108 (17 February 1688).

61. *Middlesex County Records, 1680–94*, pp. 309–10 (14 October 1687).

62 *Middlesex County Records, 1680–94*, pp. 526–7 (9 October 1691); 535 (23 November 1691); 539 (4 January 1691/2. See also *Rappahannock County Orders, 1686–92*, p. 335 (3 February 1691/2).

63. *Northumberland County Records, 1678–98*, p. 443 (17 October 1688).

64. *York County Records, 1687–91*, p. 527 (26 January 1690/91; the date of their flight was 18 August 1690). One might speculate that these men had hoped for a better lot in Quaker country.

65. *Norfolk County Records, 1666–75*, f. 37 (18 August 1669).

66. *Lancaster County Records, 1666–80*, ff. 211–18 (10 March 1674/75).

67. *Norfolk County Orders, 1675–86*, f. 10 (15 December 1675). The Beverleys apparently represented the exceptional case of a bond-labor marriage.

68. *Accomack County Records, 1697–1703*, f. 67 (24 June 1699).

69. *Northampton County Records, 1664–74*, p. 123 (28 February 1671/2). A previous entry of the same date, concerning Rodriggus's wife, indicates that Rodriggus was employed by planter Mr John Eyre (or Eyres), though not as a bond-laborer.

70. *Norfolk County Orders, 1675–86*, p. 99 (16 August 1679).

71. *Northampton County Records, 1690–97*, p. 4 (19 November 1690), Presumably this is the same Crotofte of the clandestine feasts (see p. 151). Has he survived as a bond-laborer after all these six years? But who is this John Johnson? Presumably he is neither the son nor the grandson of Anthony Johnson, the patriarch of Pungoteague Creek. And what were the respective offenses for which they were in jail?

72. *Richmond County Records*, 1694–99 (4 August 1697). When Loyd sued Thacker for the long loss of Redman's services, Thacker, citing the 1662 Virginia law of descent through the mother, successfully contended that Redman was a free person, the child of an African-American father and a European-American woman.

73. *Henrico County Records, 1694–1701*, pp. 100–101 (1 April 1696).

74. In view of the fact that the woman was legally obligated to reveal the name of the father of the child, and in some instances was jailed until she complied, it is a mystery that the majority of the court records of such cases do not provide the name of the child's father. Does that mean that the owner was being protected? The person who paid the bond-laborer's "fornication" fine generally claimed the six months of servitude due from her on that account. Sometimes that claim

was not explicitly asserted in the record. Although it might be surmised that in some such cases the fine-payer was the father, I have left them out of account.

In some of these 140 cases where the identity has been given *only* as "a negro," the social status is assumed to be that of a bond-laborer. For the rest, when a person is not explicitly identified as a bond-laborer, it is assumed that he/she is a free person, because bond-laborers were identified as servants of an owner. It is possible to identify the male partner's social status in fewer than half the "fornication" case records; no conclusions can be drawn as to the free-to-bond proportions among the male partners in the other cases.

75. This inference is based on two facts. The overwhelming proportion of the seventeenth-century male inhabitants of the Chesapeake arrived as bond-laborers. Second, of these 121 men, only one is termed "Mr," the lowest order of honorific address.

76. Four of the women – three Europeans and one African-American – were free persons involved with male bond-laborers. Of the total of 139 women (one was involved with two different bond-laborers), eight were African-Americans, the rest were European-Americans.

77. *York County Records, 1657–62*, f. 148 (25 [?] January 1661/2).

78. See p. 131.

79. Two Middlesex County Court decisions applied this principle in declaring invalid two separate contracts executed by bond-laborers Rebecca Muns and of Martha Carroll (*Middlesex County Records, 1673–80*, ff. 54, 83 [10 April 1676, 19 November 1677]).

80. Friedrich Engels dwells on this subject in relation to the proletariat, arguing that true monogamous relationships are best achieved where property considerations are absent (Friedrich Engels, *The Origin of the Family, Private Property and the State* [New York, n.d.], p. 59]).

81. Four of the women, including one African-American, were free persons.

82. *Accomack County Records, 1666–67*, pp. 59, 150.

83. *York County Records, 1677–84*, p. 535.

84. *Accomack County Records, 1682–97*, pp. 70, 95 (1 and 7 September 1685).

85. Hening, 2:114 (1662).

86. *Essex County Records, 1703–1708*, pp. 3, 10 (August and September 1703).

87. This point will be elaborated on in the discussion of Governor Gooch's letter to the Commissioners of Trade and Plantations of 1736, in Chapter 13.

88. The general subject of the status of African-Americans in the Chesapeake colonies will be treated in Chapter 10.

89. Hening, 2:84 (March 1662); 170 (December 1662); 267 (September 1668).

90. *Accomack County Records, 1666–70*, p. 112 (4 February 1668/69).

91. *York County Records, 1694–97*, pp. 9–13.

92. *Accomack County Records, 1676–78*, pp. 54–5. (18 June 1677). Dun is identified as a bond-laborer of John David in the 1675 list of tithables.

93. *Accomack County Records, 1678–82*, pp. 271, 295–6. How much was Griffin's attitude different from that of two bond-laborers who nearly beat to death a James "a Scotchman" whom their owner had appointed to be their overseer? *Northampton County Records, 1664–74*, p. 61 (1 March 1668/9).

94. *York County Records, 1677–84*, pp. 360, 362–4 (2 December 1681). It is not absolutely clear whether the "he" in Wells's remark referred to himself or to Frank. What is not in doubt is that Wells and Frank were on the same side in the affair. All the persons mentioned in this account were European-Americans, except Frank.

95. Conway Robinson, "Notes from the Council and General Court Records, 1641–1672," p. 279, April 1669, in *VMHB*, 8:243 (1900–01).

96. "If, as Winthrop Jordan has remarked, the language of the laws against miscegenation was 'dripping with distaste and indignation,' it was the language of the most politically active of the planter class. We have no evidence that during most of the seventeenth century, most whites shared it. . . . The ideology of racism may have been present in the culture of the elite as early as 1600, but nonslaveowning whites in the Chesapeake seem to have absorbed it only gradually, with the growth of slave society in the late seventeenth and early eighteenth centuries" (Deal, p. 181.)

9 The Insubstantiality of the Intermediate Stratum

1. Warren M. Billings, "'Virginia's Deploured Condition,' 1660–1676: The Coming of Bacon's Rebellion," PhD thesis, University of Northern Illinois, June 1968, p. 128.

2. The county (originally "shire") form was adopted in August 1634 (Hening, 1:224). Martha W. Hiden, *How Justice Grew, Virginia Counties: An Abstract of Their Formation*, Jamestown 350th Anniversary Booklet No. 19 (Richmond, 1957).

3. Hening, 2:21 (March 1661).

4. Hening, 1:402 (March 1665/6). The county courts were courts of origin for all civil cases involving damages and costs amounting to less than 1,600 pounds of tobacco, and for all criminal cases except those in which the penalties included dismemberment or death (Hening, 2:66).

5. Hening, 2:280. The right of all freemen to vote had had its legislative ins and outs. In 1658, the last law on the matter (Hening, 1:475) enacted before that of 1670 had restored the right that had been taken away in 1655 (Hening, 1:411–12).

6. Hening, 2:59.

7. Hening, 1:483.

8. Hening, 2:21. As encouragement to the constables, they were to be rewarded by the owner of each runaway recaptured and returned.

9. Hening, 2:273–4.

10. Ibid. A year later the General Assembly, upon reflection on the prospective cost of the law and its susceptibility to local collusion, reduced the amount of the reward to 200 pounds of tobacco, payable for fugitives taken up more than ten miles from their owner (Hening, 2:277). See also Hening, 2:283–4, regarding fraudulent claims.

11. *Charles City County Records, 1655–65*, pp. 279–81, 284–8.

12. CO 1/30, pp. 114–15 (16 July 1673). This document may also be read in *VMHB*, 20:134–40 (1912).

13. Edmund S. Morgan, *American Slavery, American Freedom: The Ordeal of Colonial Virginia* (New York, 1975), pp. 247–8.

14. Sir Francis Bacon, Essay No. 15, "Of Seditions and Troubles" (1625) in *Works*, 6:406–12; p. 407. Bacon draws this reference from Isaiah, 45:1.

15. In the period 1660–76, seven out of ten of the colony elite had been in the country for no more than twelve years (*Billings*, p. 130).

16. Lionel Gatford, *Publick Good Without Private Interest* (London, 1657), p. 3.

17. John C. Rainbolt, *From Prescription to Persuasion: Manipulation of Eighteenth-century Virginia Economy* (Port Washington, NY, 1974), pp. 19–20. William S. Perry, ed., *Collections Relating to the American Colonial Church* (Hartford, 1870), 1:11, 15; Philip Alexander Bruce, *Institutional History of Virginia in the Seventeenth Century*, 2 vols. (New York and London, 1910), 1:131, 194–207; George M. Brydon, *Virginia's Mother Church and the Political Conditions under Which it Grew* (Richmond, 1947–52), 1:passim.

Apparently disregarding the mammonistic implication of the observation, one doctoral student commented in a footnote that "tobacco was to prove almost the coalescing factor in Virginia that religious fanaticism was to prove in New England" (Darrett B. Rutman, "The Virginia Company and Its Military Regime," in Darrett B. Rutman, ed., *The Old Dominion: Essays for Thomas Perkins Abernathy* [Charlottesville, 1964; Arno Press, 1979], p. 231). In justice to Rutman, it must be noted that the book and the author had "grown very far apart" in the interval between its writing and its publication (see the author's prefatory "Apologia," dated 1978).

18. Hening, 2:48, 180–83, 198; 3:298.

19. Rainbolt, p. 19. *Historical Statistics of the United States from Colonial Times to 1970*, p. 1168.

Yet in 1692, when Commissary James Blair, head of the Anglican Church in Virginia, requested funds to found a college in order to train up soul-savers for gospel-starved Virginia, English Attorney-General Hedges expostulated, "Damn your souls! Make tobacco!" (Charles Campbell, *History of the Colony and Ancient Dominion of Virginia* [Philadelphia, 1860], p. 346; Campbell cites "Franklin's correspondence"). This was reminiscent of the comment of a Barbadian slaveholder about 1680, that sugar planters "went not to those parts to save Souls, or propagate Religion, but to get money" (Morgan Godwyn, *The Negro's and Indians Advocate* [London, 1680], p. 39 marginal note). Godwyn repeated the observation five years later in his *Trade Preferr'd before Religion and Christ made to give place to Mammon* (London, 1685), p. 11. Nevertheless Blair's proposal for a college was given financial support by the English government, and when it opened its doors in 1697, it was named after the then reigning English monarchs, William and Mary.

20. Thomas Ludwell to John Lord Berkeley (Sir William Berkeley's brother), 24 June 1667 (Cited in Philip A. Bruce, *Economic History of Virginia in the Seventeenth Century*, 2 vols. [New York, 1895], 1:394.)

21. Rainbolt, p. 6. Rainbolt examines circumstantial factors that frustrated efforts at diversification of the Virginia economy. Although the title of his book (*From Prescription to Persuasion:*

Manipulation of Eighteenth Century Virginia Economy) refers to the eighteenth century, Rainbolt's main attention is directed to the 1650–1710 period, yet well after the commitment to tobacco had become a settled question in practical terms, and the guiding principle of colonial Virginia government had been firmly established: to secure the highest quickest profit for the Virginia planters, shippers, servant-trade merchants, English Crown interest, tax-and-customs farmers.

22. I fully accept the conclusion reached by Edmund S. Morgan, in a general note on tobacco prices, that "no reliable or regular series of annual prices current can be constructed for seventeenth-century Virginia" (Morgan, pp. 135–6, n. 7). Morgan refers to Russell R. Menard's work in assembling the available data. I have chosen to draw upon Menard's figures for present purposes, referring particularly to his summary of Chesapeake farm prices (Russell R. Menard, *Economy and Society in Early Colonial Maryland* [New York, 1985], pp. 448–9). I feel justified in this course because I have found much of the same data by my own research, and because Menard's picture of decade-to-decade trends is supported by other economic historians, such as Philip Alexander Bruce and Lewis C. Gray, and by Morgan himself.

23. Wilcomb E. Washburn is a dissenter from this generally accepted view. Washburn acknowledges the prevalence of desperate poverty among the people and their "unwillingness to accept their fate passively," but at the same time he considers poor planters' mutinies as insignificant (Wilcomb E. Washburn, *The Governor and the Rebel: A History of Bacon's Rebellion in Virginia* [New York, 1957], pp. 31, 187 n. 63). Moreover, Washburn denies that Bacon's Rebellion can be ascribed to the existence of class conflict within the colony. Rather, he regards the rebellion as merely a manifestation of "frontier" hostility to Indians (ibid., p. 235 n. 3).

Readers of Volume One of *The Invention of the White Race* will know how much I appreciate Dr Washburn's research and argument regarding the white-supremacist treachery toward, and repression of, American Indians under Anglo-American and United States "Indian policy." But his sensitivity to "racism" seems curiously limited in the dismissive terms with which he treats the participation by African-Americans in Bacon's Rebellion. As bond-laborers they were not motivated by anti-Indian interests, but by a determination to be freed form their bondage. (Ibid., p. 88. See Chapter 11.)

24. Bruce, *Economic History*, 1:391.

25. Accomack (for all the years except 1660, 1661, and 1662), Lancaster, Lower Norfolk, Northampton, Northumberland, and York (all years except 1663 and 1664). (Billings, pp. 168–73.)

26. Ibid., p. 159.

27. Edmund S. Morgan shows a total population of 3,628 in these six counties in 1674. (Morgan, pp. 412–13.)

28. The total of all debts was 51,870,000 pounds of tobacco; those owed *to* the elite amounted to 12,225,000 pounds; those owed *by* the elite totalled 6,227,000 pounds.

29. In three years the amount owed by the elite exceeded the amount owed to them, in the amount of 585,000 pounds; in the other thirteen years, the account stood the other way by 6,596,000 pounds.

30. Edmund S. Morgan, "Headrights and Head Counts," *VMHB*, 80:361–71 (1972); p. 366. The same information is largely recapitulated in Morgan, *American Slavery, American Freedom*, pp. 221–2.

31. Although Menard did not find a similar pattern of concentration of land ownership in three Maryland counties in the 1659–1706 period, he does not regard those findings as adequate for drawing a general conclusion regarding the matter. He comments on the rise in tenancy in this period, noting that an increasing number of people were falling into a landless status, a condition that would eliminate them from land ownership statistics altogether (Menard, pp. 309–12).

32. Kevin P. Kelly, "Economic and Social Development of Seventeenth-century Surry County, Virginia," PhD thesis, University of Washington, 1972, p. 137.

33. Thomas J. Wertenbaker, *The Planters of Colonial Virginia* (Princeton, 1922), p. 58.

34. CO 5/1539, pp. 20–22 (margin date, 6 October 1696). By way of remedy, Randolph recommended a strict collection of the one shilling per fifty acre quit-rent and the limiting of future land patents to 500 acres.

35. Wertenbaker, p. 59.

36. Menard, p. 316.

37. CO 1/30, pp. 114–15 (16 July 1673). This document may also be read in *VMHB*, 20:134–40 (1912).

38. Ibid.

39. *Surry County Records, 1671–84*, pp. 40–43 (3 and 20 January 1673/4); *1671–91*, pp. 41–2 (6 January 1673/4). Extensive excerpts from the record are printed in Warren M. Billings, ed., *The*

Old Dominion in the Seventeenth Century, A Documentary History of Virginia, 1606–1689 (Chapel Hill, 1975), pp. 263–7.

The proportion of propertyless freemen remained high. An exchange between the Surry County Court and Governor Effingham provides a rare example of precision regarding this economic differentiation among the free population. Surry County submitted the names of a total of 314 men for the militia at the end of 1687. Effingham returned the list and asked that the names of those who were "Free men [but] not free holders, or Housekeepers ... be struck out." As a result, the roll was reduced by 114, or 36 percent, presumably propertyless freemen. (*Surry County Records, 1671–91*, pp. 597–601; 619–23.)

40. Rainbolt, p. 12.

41. Sir William Berkeley, *A Discourse and View of Virginia* (London, 1663), p. 5.

42. Rainbolt, p. 46.

43. Historians have frequently taken note of the recurring enthusiams for diversification of the Virginia economy and of efforts to curtail tobacco production; the most thorough study of the subject is John C. Rainbolt's *From Prescription to Persuasion* (see note 17, and note 21 on the period mainly covered).

See also the special study of the subject by Sister Joan de Lourdes Leonard, "Operation Checkmate: The Birth and Death of a Virginia Blueprint for Progress," *WMQ*. ser. 3, 24:44–74 (1967).

44. Leo Francis Stock, ed., *Proceedings and Debates of the British Parliaments Respecting North America*, 5 vols., (Washington, DC, 1924); 1:374. House of Commons, 7 March 1671. *CSP, Col.*, 11:318. Petition of sundry merchants possessing estates in America to the Lords of Trade and Plantations, received 7 November 1682.

45. Rainbolt, pp. 154, 155, 159.

46. CO 324/9.

47. *Calendar of Virginia State Papers and Other Manuscripts, Vol I, 1651–1781* (Richmond, 1875), edited by William P. Palmer; pp. 137–8.

48. *Archives of Maryland*, 25:266–7.

49. "Representation of the Board of Trade relating to the Laws made, Manufactures set up, and Trade Carried on in His Majesty's Plantations in America," 1734; manuscript in the Rare Book Room of the New York Public Library, Research Libraries.

50. See, for example, the justification of "An Act for Ports" as a design to stop the "import or export [of] goods and merchandises, without entering or paying the duties and customes due thereupon." (Hening, 3:53–4 [1691]. In the end, the consequences of the prolonged struggle to achieve a diversified economy were thoroughly incongruous with the initial motives behind the effort. Designed as a solution to the economic ills of the tobacco economy, the various schemes often only disrupted the economy still more (Rainbolt, p. 171).

51. Eighteenth-century developments lie largely beyond the scope of the present work, but in the context of this discussion of diversification, brief mention is required of the increase in the relative importance of grain cultivations in the Chesapeake beginning in about 1740. This shift was not the result of any general diminution of demand for tobacco exports; indeed, tobacco exports to Britain, including that portion destined for re-export, followed a generally rising trend between 1740 and the War of Independence. (*Historical Statistics of the United States: Colonial Times to 1970* [Washington, DC, 1976], Series Z-441, Z-442, Z-449.) Rather, it resulted from two principal causes. The exhaustion of the soil under tobacco cultivation was such that under the custom of field rotation, twenty acres per hand was required to maintain tobacco production on three acres. That compelled either the acquisition and clearing of new land or a reduction of the size of the labor force, both of which tended to reduce the rate of profit. Second, there was a rise in demand for grains, particularly wheat, in Europe, as well as in northern colonies and the West Indies. This shift hardly qualified, however, as significant diversification of the economy of the region. Despite the limited increase in the value of grains in total exports, tobacco still accounted for three times as much as wheat and corn together in the period 1768–72 (Klingaman, "Significance of Grain", pp. 274–5, cited in full below); and the profits of the Chesapeake bourgeoisie remained absolutely dependent on exports of one major and one or two minor crops. (This paragraph is based on the following sources: Lewis Cecil Gray, assisted by Esther K. Thompson, *History of Agriculture in the Southern United States to 1860*, 2 vols., [Washington, DC, 1932], pp. 166–9; David Klingaman, "The Development of the Coastwise Trade of Virginia in the Late Colonial Period," *VMHB*, 77:26–45 [1969], especially pp. 30–31; idem, "The Significance of Grain in the Development of the Tobacco Colonies," *Journal of Economic History*, 29:268–78 [1969] especially pp. 270–75; Allan Kulikoff,

"The Economic Growth of the Eighteenth-century Chesapeake Colonies," *Journal of Economic History*, 39:275–88 [1979], especially pp. 284–6.)

Yet instead of promoting the rise of a domestic market by investing in developing improved instruments of production and raising the productivity of labor, the plantation bourgeoisie spent their revenues "to increase their standard of living, improve their land, and expand the size of their labor force" (Allan Kulikoff, *Tobacco and Slaves: The Development of Southern Cultures in the Chesapeake, 1680–1800* [Chapel Hill, 1986], p. 118).

The capitalist exploiters of bond-labor seemed to sense their dilemma before Marx and Engels made it manifest: "The bourgeoisie cannot exist without constantly revolutionizing the instruments of production and thereby the relations of production . . ." In 1690, Dalby Thomas pointed out that diversification of production in the colonies would lead the plantation bourgeoisie to "part with their black slaves" (Dalby Thomas, *An Historical Account. Rise and Growth of the West Indies Colonies and great Advantages they are to England in Respect to Trade* [London, 1690], in Harleian Miscellany, 12 vols., 9:432.) Obversely, among reasons cited by General James Oglethorpe in the eighteenth century for excluding slavery from the projected colony of Georgia was his conviction that it would result in a market-glutting monocultural economy rather than a diversified one (*Diary of the Earl of Egmont*, entry for 17 January 1739, cited in Elizabeth Donnan, *Documents Illustrative of the History of the Slave Trade* [Washington, DC, 1931], 4 vols; 4:592.)

52. Rainbolt, p. 169.

53. In 1663, the English seized a number of labor-exporting locations in West Africa. The Dutch made a generally successful counterattack later that year, but the English did manage to maintain their hold on one major fort there, at Cape Corso, or Cape Coast Castle, and their position there was confirmed by the Treaty of Breda. (Sir George Clark, *The Later Stuarts, 1660–1714*, 2nd edn. [Oxford, 1956], p. 332.) Those disposed to deal with the almost arcane diplomatic language of the relevant documents may read them in Frances Gardiner Davenport, ed., *European Treaties bearing on the History of the United States*, 5 vols. (Washington, DC, 1929; volume 2, documents 53 and 57.

54. See Appendix II-E.

55. CO 5/1356, p. 47 (King in Council to Culpeper, 27 January 1681/82). The Royal African Company was headed by the Duke of York, Charles's brother, who reigned as James II from 1685 to 1688. But a number of the leading shareholders had a dual interest as employers of plantation bond-labor. (Kenneth L. Davies, *The Royal African Company* [London, 1957], pp. 64–6.)

56. CO 5/1356, p. 138 (Culpeper to the Lords of Trade and Plantations, 20 September 1683).

57. See Gray, 1:369–71. I apologize for the tone of these lines, but that is how the bourgeoisie weighs investment choices. The Royal African Company in 1672 posted a price of £18 each for bond-laborers to be delivered in Virginia (Davies, p. 294).

58. CO 5/1356, p. 138. In the years 1680 to 1688, capitalists in both commerce and agriculture were naturally concerned that nearly one-fourth (23.5 percent) of their investment was lost in the Middle Passage. A half-century later they could congratulate themselves that these losses were down to 10 percent. (Davies, p. 292.)

59. Reference has been made in Chapter 6 to Bruce's exposition of the question, and to his conclusion that the Virginia colony was destined by nature for tobacco monoculture.

60. Sir Francis Bacon advised historians to leave observations and conclusions to others (*Advancement of Learning*, Book II, in *Works*, 3:339), but he himself could not forgo the opportunity, as when he interpreted the events of the reign of Henry VII.

61. Bacon, Essay Number 33, "Of Plantations," in *Works*, 6:457–9; p. 458.

62. See p. 109.

63. Philip Alexander Bruce, A. E. Smith and Wesley Frank Craven are among those who propound this thesis. See Chapter 6, pp. 103–6, and p. 312 note 53 for full citations.

64. New England's genocidal policy with regard to the native population, however, was far from that advocated by Bacon in his essay.

65. Michael G. Kammen, ed., "Virginia at the Close of the Seventeenth Century: An Appraisal by James Blair and John Locke," *VMHB*, 74:141–69 (1966); p. 155. Kammen says that while the opening lines were written by John Locke, the most influential member of the Commission of Trade and Plantation and a strong support of Blair, this work "has to be Blair's composition" (p. 147).

66. See p. 69.

67. Herbert Moller, "Sex Composition and Correlated Culture: Patterns of Colonial America," *WMQ*, 3d ser., 2:113–53 (1945) p. 118.

68. Melville Egleston, *The Land System of the New England Colonies*, Johns Hopkins University Studies in History and Political Science, Vol. 4 (Baltimore, 1886), pp. 15, 21–2, 26.

This practice was the basis of the six-mile square "township" form of allotment of "public" land established by the Continental Congress in 1785 that prevailed in states formed out of the Northwest Territory. It is relevant to note that, "The southern members ... did not believe in the township system of settlement." (Payson Jackson Treat, "Origin of the National Land System under the Confederation," in Vernon Carstensen, ed., *The Public Lands; Studies in the History of the Public Domain* [Madison, Wisconsin, 1968], pp. 11–12.)

69. Egleston, pp. 44–5.

70. Percy Wells Bidwell and John L. Falconer, *History of Agriculture in the Northern United States, 1620–1860* (Washington, 1925; 1941 reprint), pp. 49–50.

71. Ibid., p. 54.

72. In the first three decades of the Massachusetts colony, before individual royal land grants were discontinued in favor of community land grants, just over one hundred individual land grants were made. Six were extremely large, ranging from 2,000 to 3,200 acres each; the rest averaged less than 400 acres each. But the greatest part of New England land distribution throughout the colonial period was made out of community land grants by the communities themselves. (Egleston, pp. 19–20.)

73. Gary B. Nash, "Colonial Development," in Jack P. Greene and J. R. Pole, *Colonial British America: Essays in the New History of the Modern Era* (Baltimore, 1984), p. 238. An economic historian, referring to "the northern colonies" generally throughout the colonial period, writes: "In the absence of a market strong enough to enforce specialization and necessitate acquiring anything by purchase, people produced for themselves." (Robert E. Mutch, "Yeoman and Merchant in Pre-industrial America: Eighteenth-century Massachusetts as a Case Study," *Societas*, 7:279–302; 282.

74. Recent academic discussions of the subject of "the transition to capitalism" in continental Anglo-America have directly and indirectly shed important light upon this aspect of the question. The discussion centers on the extent to which households in non-plantation areas were engaged in exchange of products, even to the extent of interregional exchanges. The time period that gets most attention begins about the middle of the eighteenth century. Regardless of how one may view the controversies that arise in this regard, for our present purpose all of these studies serve to show that communities of family households, largely independent of export/import exchanges, were characteristic of these areas. For a bibliography on this discussion see Allan Kulikoff, "The Transition to Capitalism in Rural America," *WMQ* 46:120–144 (1989).

This debate seems to have been induced by the long-running debate on the transition from feudalism to capitalism as it occurred in Europe. I find discussion conducted under this heading useful for drawing conclusions regarding the degree of dependence on, or independence of, the New England colonial economy with respect to the export/import trade. But as Kulikoff points out (pp. 126–7), there is a fundamentally different significance to be attached to the class struggle interpretation of the revolutionary transition from feudalism to capitalism in Europe, on the one hand, and the evolution from subsistence farming to capitalist production (neither the producer nor the consumer being the owner) in non-plantation areas of rural continental Anglo-America.

75. Bidwell and Falconer, pp. 82–3.

76. One informative narrative of this transition is Hannah Josephson, *The Golden Threads: New England's Mill Girls and Magnates* (New York, 1949).

77. Gary B. Nash, "Social Development," in Greene and Pole, eds., pp. 236, 243.

78. Ibid., pp. 236, 247.

79. Francis Bacon, "Of Plantations."

80. Governor William Berkeley to Thomas Ludwell, 1 July 1676. In *Coventry Papers*, microfilm reel no. 63.

The outbreak of Bacon's Rebellion, says Thomas J. Wertenbaker, was the outcome of policies that "practically eliminated the middle class" (Thomas J. Wertenbaker, *Bacon's Rebellion, 1676*, Jamestown 350th Anniversary Historical Booklet No. 8 [Williamsburg, 1957], p. 55. Cf. Charles M. Andrews, *Narratives of the Insurrections, 1675–1690* [New York, 1915], pp. 11–12.)

10 The Status of African-Americans

1. Works particularly concerned with this aspect of seventeenth-century Chesapeake history include: Philip Alexander Bruce, *Economic History of Virginia in the Seventeenth Century*, 2 vols. (New York, 1895), especially 2:121–9; James Curtis Ballagh, *A History of Slavery in Virginia*

(Baltimore, 1920; reprinted 1968); John H. Russell, *The Free Negro in Virginia, 1619–1865* (Baltimore, 1913); Susie M. Ames, *Studies of the Virginia Eastern Shore in the Seventeenth Century* (New York, 1940); James H. Brewer, "Negro Property Owners in Seventeenth Century Virginia," *WMQ*, vol. 12 (1955); Ross M. Kimmel, "Free Blacks in Seventeenth-century Maryland," *Maryland Historical Magazine*, 71:19–25 (1976); Whittington B. Johnson, "The Origin and Nature of African Slavery in Seventeenth Century Maryland," *Maryland Historical Magazine*, 73:236–45 (1978); Tomothy H. Breen and Stephen Innes, *"Myne Owne Ground": Race and Freedom on Virginia's Eastern Shore in the Seventeenth Century* (New York, 1980); Douglas Deal, "A Constricted World: Free Blacks on Virginia's Eastern Shore," in Lois Greene Carr, Philip D. Morgan and Jean B. Russo, *Colonial Chesapeake Society* (Chapel Hill, 1988); Joseph Douglas Deal, *Race and Class in Colonial Virginia: Indians, Englishmen, and Africans on the Eastern Shore During the Seventeenth Century* (New York, 1993).

2. See pp. 32 and 34 of *The Invention of the White Race*, Volume One.

3. "[E]xcluded from many civil privileges which the humblest white man enjoyes" – that was the contemptuous description of free Negroes as expressed by a meeting of white men in Northampton County, Virginia, in December 1831. (Luther Porter Jackson, *Free Negro Labor and Property Holding in Virginia, 1830–1860* [New York, 1942] p. 13.)

4. Winthrop D. Jordan, *White over Black: American Attitudes Toward the Negro, 1550–1812* (Chapel, Hill, 1968), p. 44.

5. Oscar Handlin and Mary F. Handlin, "Origins of the Southern Labor System," *WMQ*, 3d series, No. 7:199–222 (1950), pp. 211–12.

6. "Freedom, like slavery, acquired social meaning not through statute law or intellectual treatises, but through countless human transactions that first defined and then redefined the limits of that [the African-American condition]." (Breen and Innes, pp. 31–2.) I merely wish to stress that the essential character of those "human transactions" was the struggle between the contending social classes.

7. See pp. 19–22.

8. See Edmund S. Morgan, *American Slavery, American Freedom: The Ordeal of Colonial Virginia* (New York, 1975) Chapter 8, "Living With Death," especially pp. 158–63.

9. ". . . it was easier to incorporate the negroes in [the existing] system than to put them in a class apart." (Helen Tunncliff Catterall, ed., *Judicial Cases Concerning Slavery and the Negro*, 5 vols. [Washington, DC, 1926–37], 1:55.)

10. See p. 154.

11. Each of the three was to receive a whipping of thirty lashes. The terms of servitude of each of the two European-Americans were to be extended by four years.

12. Jordan, p. 75. For a criticism of Jordan's views, see the Introduction to Volume One of *The Invention of the White Race*.

13. See *The Invention of the White Race*, Volume One, pp. 80, 346 n. 34. But as pointed out, there was a sharp difference among the officers of the Providence Island venture regarding the enslavability or non-enslavability of Christians by Christians.

14. Breen and Innes, pp. 70–72.

15. The first Negroes who arrived in Virginia, says Phillips, "were . . . not fully slaves in the hands of their Virginia buyers, for there was neither law or custom establishing the institution of slavery" (Ulrich Bonnell Phillips, *American Negro Slavery: A Slavery of the Supply, Employment and Control of Negro Labor as Determined by the Plantation Regime* [New York, 1918], p. 75.)

16. Hening, 1:257; 2:113.

17. See *The Invention of the White Race*, Volume One, pp. 73–5. Recall Sir William Petty's assessment made in 1672 of the values of human chattels: Irish men and Negro men at £15 each. *Economic Writings of Sir William Petty*, 2 vols. (London, 1691; Augustus Kelley reprint; New York, 1963); 1:152.

In 1653 a license was granted to one Richard Netherway of Bristol, England, to export one hundred Irish men to be sold as slaves in Virginia. (Great Britain. Public Record Office. Calendar of State Papers, Domestic, vol. IV; Interregnum Entry Book, Vol. 98, p. 405. Cited by Bruce, 1:609.)

18. Hening, 1:411. Although this law was enacted in 1655, its provisions were made to apply to such surviving Irish bond-laborers as had arrived since the beginning of 1653. Recaptured runaway bond-laborer Walter Hind was ordered, "according to the act for Irish servants," to "serve continue and complete the term of six yeares from the time of arriveall, and make good the time neglected." (*Charles City County Deeds, Wills, Orders, Etc., 1655–1665*, p. 223. [3 February 1659/60].)

19. Hening 1:538–9.

20. See *The Invention of the White Race*, Volume One, Appendix H.

21. The one brief, wavering exception was Anthony Johnson, as is noted below, p. 183.

22. The Accomack and Northampton records have been treated in great detail by other historians, most recently by Breen and Innes, and by Joseph Douglas Deal (*Race and Class in Colonial Virginia*). For that reason I shall select only a few individual cases recorded in those two counties for brief elaboration; I will attempt to cover the rest by suitable generalizations accompanied by full footnote references for the convenience of those who may desire to study the records directly.

23. *MCGC*, p. 33.

24. *MCGC*, pp. 66–8, 71–2, 73.

25. *Accomack County Records, 1663–66*, p. 54. The Northampton County Court found for Francis Payne in a suit arising out of his contract to build a house for Richard Haney. (*Northampton Country Records, 1657–64*, p. 173, 28 August 1663.)

26. *Northampton County Records, 1651–54*, p. 215 (3 January 1653/4). "Speciality" meant a bond or a contract. In August 1647, Mr Stephen Charlton was awarded a judgment for a debt against Tony Longo, to be paid out of the next crop. (*Northampton County Records, 1645–51*, p. 111.)

27. The name (variously rendered in the records as Manuel and Rodriguez, Rodriggus, Drigges, Drigs, etcetera) suggests a personal history with the Iberians or with the Dutch leaving Brazil.

28. Susie M. Ames, *Studies of the Virginia Eastern Shore in the Seventeenth Century* (Richmond, 1940), p. 97.

29. *Northampton County Records, 1651–54*, p. 148; court record dated 12 September 1653.

30. Since all the entries listed in this note are from *Northampton County Records*, the volume years will serve to locate the citations. *1645–51*, p. 26: sale of calf by John Pott to John Johnson, 6 May 1647. Ibid., p. 38: sale of a heifer by Francis Payne to slow-paying Marylander Jospeh Edlowe, 28 July 1651. *1651–54*, p. 133: 8 February 1652/3. *1657–66*, p. 30: sale of a cow and a heifer by John Johnson to Edward Marten, 30 May 1659. Ibid., pp. 49–50: gift of a heifer by Emanuel Driggs to Sande, son of a bond-laborer, 28 May 1659. Ibid., p. 47: signing over by Anthony Johnson of five calves to his son John, 30 May 1659. Ibid., p. 62: sale of a mare colt by Francis Payne (the name is variously spelled) to Anthony Johnson, 31 January 1659/60. Ibid., p. 88: sale by Emanuell Dridges of a gray colt to Alexander Wilson, 15 May 1661. Ibid., pp. 137–8: sale of a mare by Manuel Rodrigues to Willim Kendall, 11 March 1661/62, *1664–1674*, p. 146: dispute in court between John Francisco and John Alworth over the sale of a filly, 19 September 1672.

31. The gift was recorded January 1657/8. *Northampton County Records, 1657–64*, pp. 2, 7.

32. Nell Nugent, *Cavaliers and Pioneers; Abstracts of Virginia Land Patents and Grants, 1623–1666*, 2nd edn. (Baltimore, 1963), 2:11 18 April 1667.

33. *York County Records, 1665–72*, p. 237–8 (28 August 1669); the court record is dated 12 April 1670.

34. *Northampton County Records, 1657–66*, p. 116, 236 (4 June 1662, 28 December 1665); and *Northampton County Records, 1668–80*, pp. 3, 34 (4 December 1668; 28 December 1672).

35. See Morgan's discussion in *American Slavery, American Freedom*, pp. 166–72.

36. Mongum first appears in the record in July 1650 when he and two other men – Demigo Matthews[?] and a European-American plantation overseer, Robert Berry – are said to have reported a plot of the Nanticoke Indians to attack the Eastern Shore settlements (*Northampton County Records, 1645–51*, f. 217). See also *Northampton County Order Book, 1674–79*, p. 273. For the joint tenancy, see Ralph T. Whitelaw, *Virginia's Eastern Shore*, 2 vols. (Richmond, 1951), 1:228; 2:216. The name is variously spelled; I have decided to use the "Mongum" form throughout, except when direct quotations have an alternate spelling.

37. *Northampton Country Records, 1651–54*, pp. 32–3. The agreement was witnessed by Thomas Gilbert and Richard Buckland on 5 March 1650/1; it was entered in the court record on 22 December 1651. Joseph Douglas Deal reads the name as "Merris" and notes that she does not again appear in the records. She is not to be confused with the African-American named Mary, a second[?] wife of Mongum, who is listed in available Northampton tithable records beginning in 1665 and on through 1674. It seems that Breen and Innes confuse the two "Marys." (see Breen and Innes, p. 83.)

Another such disclaimer in contemplation of marriage was subscribed by parish minister Francis Doughty of Northampton County Court before his marriage to Ann Eaton, whereby he did "disowne and discharge all right, to her estate and to her children." (Richard Duffield Neill, *Virginia Carolorum: The Colony under the Rule of Charles the First and Second, AD 1625–1685* [Albany, NY, 1986], p. 407.)

38. *Northampton County Records, 1664–74*, pp. 220–21. The will was dated 9 May 1673 and probated 29 September 1673.

39. *Northampton County Records, 1674–79*, p. 59 (29 August 1675). See also ibid., pp. 58, 70, 72.

40. The couple came to the notice of the court when Skipper (Cooper) was ordered to pay "levies tythes for his wife (shee being a negro)"; and again when they were suspected of shielding the father of her child from the hue and cry. (*Norfolk County Wills and Deeds "E" 1665–75, Part 2, Orders*, ff, 75, 76–7.) See *Norfolk County Deed Book, No. 4, 1675–86*, pp. 14 and 30, regarding the times of their deaths. See Nugent, 2:232, for the landholding of Skipper (Cooper).

With regard to other intermarriages of African-Americans and European-Americans, it is to be inferred that the Mary Longo who married John Goldsmith in Hungars parish on 13 October 1660 was an African-American, since the only Longos found in Northampton County records at that time were African-Americans; and that Emannuel Driggus's first wife, Elizabeth, the mother of the father of Thomas Driggus, was a European-American. (See Stratton Nottingham, *Accomack*, p.452; and ibid., cited by Deal, *Race and Class in Colonial Virginia*, pp. 271, 284.) See also the marriage of Elizabeth Key and William Greenstead, below.

41. Lerone Bennett Jr, *The Shaping of Black America* (Chicago, 1975), pp. 14–16, 24–7.

42. Breen and Innes make this point in relation to Anthony Johnson's patent, saying that none of the names, except Richard Johnson, appear on subsequent Northampton tithables lists. They identify this Richard Johnson as the same Richard Johnson who later appears as Anthony Johnson's son. But how could Anthony's son, presumably born in Virginia, qualify for a headright? Was Richard Johnson, Negro, Anthony's biological son, or possibly a Negro from England whom Anthony adopted?

43. *Northampton County Records, 1651–54*, f. 226; 8 March 1653/4. Some doubt remains, however, about Johnson's final decision, since his original signed agreement to free Casar was entered in the record of 26 September 1654. (Ibid., *1654–1655/6*, f.35-b) *Archives of Maryland*, 54:760–61. See also Clayton Torrence, *Old Somerset on the Eastern Shore* (Richmond, 1935), pp. 75–7.)

In 1638, George Menefie, a member of the Virginia Colony Council, laid claim to 3,000 acres of land for the importation of sixty bond-laborers, including twenty-three unnamed "Negroes I brought out of England with me." (Virginia Land Patent Book, No. 1, 1623–34, abstracted in Nugent, 1:118.) Possibly Casar was one of that number.

44. See p. 326, note 36.

45. See Morgan, pp. 412–13, Table 3, "Population Growth by County."

46. Deal is one who emphasizes that "a larger proportion of Eastern Shore blacks were free than was probably the case elsewhere in Virginia" (*Race and Class in Colonial Virginia*, p. xi).

47. *Northampton County Records, 1651–54*, ff. 118–19, 174–5 (13 May 1649). Court record date 30 December 1652. Estimates of tobacco production per capita in the Chesapeake at mid-century range between 1,500 and 2,000 pounds. See: *A Perfect [or New] Description of Virginia*, in *Force Tracts*, II, No. 8, p.4, "two thousand waight a year'; William Bullock, *Virginia Impartially Examined*, (London, 1649), p. 9; Russell R. Menard, "From Servant to Freeholder: Status Mobility and Property Accumulation in Seventeenth-century Maryland," *WMQ*, 30:37–64 (1973); p. 51.

48. *Northampton County Records, 1651–54*, ff. 118–19, 174–5. Note that Payne and the Elton-heads were all literate. Breen and Innes appear to have misread the year of the deal with Walker (Breen and Innes, p. 74).

49. *Northampton County Records, 1654–55/6*, p. 100-b. *Northampton County Orders, No. 7, 1655–57*, p. 19. A bond of £200 was pledged by Mrs Eltonhead to insure the Payne family against any challenge that might be made to their free status. At the current price of about 2*d.*, this would be the equivalent of 24,000 pounds of tobacco.

50. *Northampton County Records, 1651–54*, f. 178.

51. Hening 2:26. The same phrase was used in a law on runaways passed a year later. (Hening 2:116–17).

52. Hening, 2:267.

53. Hening, 2:270.

54. Hening, 2:239.

55. *Norfolk County Records, 1646–51*, pp. 115–16. A year earlier the term "forever" was used in referring to the "conveyance" of three bond-laborers from the widow of George Menefie to Stephen Charlton. But since the phrase "heirs and assigns" is missing, the term may merely refer to the conveyor's relinquishment "forever" of all claims to these workers. (*Northampton County Records, 1651–54*, p. 28.)

Argoll was the son of Francis Yeardley, the Governor of Virginia mentioned in Chapters 4 and 5.

56. *Northampton County Records, 1651–54*, pp. 165–6.

57. *Lancaster County Records, 1654–1702*, pp. 46–9.

58. *Northampton County Records, 1645–51*, p. 120.

59. *Northampton County Records, 1655–57*, p. 8.

60. *Lancaster County Records, 1654–1702*, pp. 46–9.

61. *Northampton County Records, 1655–57*, f. 78. At his death three years later, Pannell bequeathed Ann Driggus "and her increase" to his daughter. (Ibid., *1657–66*, pp. 82–4.) Ann Driggus was the daughter of Emannuel Driggus (see note 27).

62. *Northampton County Records, 1654–1655/6*. ff. 25-b, 54-a. Some time before 29 August 1654, Phillip and Mingo did pay off the 1,700 pound obligation. (Ibid., f. 27-a.) For an earlier event involving Phillip, see p. 155.

63. *Northampton County Records, 1645–51*, p. 82.

64. He was so described at the Virginia General Court on 10 March 1653/4, the record of which is preserved apparently only in the record of the Baptista case as it was continued before the Maryland Provincial Court in 1661. (*Archives of Maryland*, 41:499.)

65. *Norfolk County Records, 1651–56*, ff. 8, 68, 75, 137, *Archives of Maryland*, 41:499. For further information on Baptista's involvement with courts see: *Norfolk County Records, 1656–66*, pp. 226–7, 233, 244; *Archives of Maryland*, 41:460, 485, 499–500; and Beverley Fleet, *Virginia Colonial Abstracts, No. 31, Lower Norfolk County, 1651–54*, pp. 12–13.

66. *Lancaster County Records, 1655–66*, f. 370.

67. *Charles City County Records, 1655–65*, pp. 601–5, 617–18. Beverley Fleet, *Virginia Colonial Abstracts*, 34 vols. (Baltimore, 1961; originally published in 1942); 13:54–7, 65–6.

68. *Northampton County Records, 1640–45*, p. 16 (3 August 1640). Littleton himself was a member of the court.

69. *Northampton County Records, 1654–55/6*, ff. 60b–61a (1 November 1654.)

70. *Accomack County Records, 1666–67*, p. 151.

71. Ibid.

72. Ibid. p. 154 (26 August 1669).

73. *Robinson Transcripts, Virginia (Colony) General Court Records*, Virginia Historical Society, Mss. No. 4/v 81935/a 2, p. 161. Printed in *MCGC*, p. 354.

74. In 1658 John Bland, a rich London merchant, recruited bond-laborers for his Virginia plantation from among inmates of Chelsea College jail; "two mulattoes offered to go rather than remain eternally in prison." (Neill, p. 365 n. 1.)

75. *Archives of Maryland*, 66:294.

76. But it was apparently assumed that the Virginia law of 1662 (see p. 197) was sufficient guarantee that no claim could be made on the grounds of having been baptized a Christian, and that therefore Scarburgh did not need to post any bond against that contingency. (*Accomack County Records, 1676–78*, p. 7.)

77. Winthrop D. Jordan's chapter titled "The Souls of Men: The Negro's Spiritual Nature" is a mine of informative bibliographic references on the relation between Christian principles and racial oppression, as revealed in the opinion of English and Anglo-American preachers and theologians during the colonial period. The works cited are with three or four exceptions products of the eighteenth century. (Jordan, pp. 179–215.) The chapter is made an integral part of his history of "American attitudes," which, as is noted in the Introduction to the present work, is anchored in Jordan's presumption of a psychological need for Anglo-Americans to know they were "white." (Jordan, p. xiv. The page citation in *The Invention of the White Race*, Volume One, p. 236 n. 41, was erroneously given as p. ix.)

78. Morgan Godwyn, *The Negro's and Indians Advocate, Suing for their Admission into the Church, or a Persuasive to the Instructing and Baptizing of the Negro's and Indians in our Plantations, That as the Compliance therewith can prejudice no Mans just Interest, So the wilful Neglecting and Opposing of it, is no less than a manifest Apostacy from the Christian Faith. To which is added, A brief Account of Religion in Virginia* (London, 1680); idem, *A Supplement to The Negro's and Indians Advocate: or, Some Further Considerations and Proposals for the Effectual amd Speedy Carrying on of the Negro's Christianity in Our Plantations (Notwithstanding the Late Pretended Impossibilities) without any Prejudice to their Owners* (London, 1681); idem, *Trade preffer'd before Religion, and Christ made to give place to Mammon: Represented in a Sermon Relating to the Plantations. First Preached at Westminster Abby, And afterwards in divers Churches in London* (London, 1681). For Godwyn in Virginia, see Neill, pp. 342–5.

79. George Fox, *Gospel of Family-Order, Being a Short Discourse Concerning the Ordering of Families, Both of White, Blacks and Indians* (London, 1676); idem, *A Journal or Historical Account of the Life, Travels, Sufferings, Christian Experiences, and Labour of Love in the Work of the Ministry of that ancient, Eminent and Faithful servant of Jesus Christ*, 2 vols. (London, 1694).

80. Richard Baxter, *A Christian Directory, or, a Summ of Practical Theologie and Cases of Conscience* (London, 1673).

81. Thomas E. Drake, *Quakers and Slavery in America* (New Haven, 1950), p. 3.

82. It is not my intention to undertake a treatment of this historical phenomenon, but merely to point to it as one of the elements of the institutional inertia that obstructed the imposition of lifetime hereditary bondage on Africans and African-Americans. It seems only fair to note that Quaker slaveholders late in the eighteenth century finally acceded to the logic of their doctrine and stopped owning or dealing in lifetime bond-laborers. (See Drake, pp. 68–84. In this way they were following the leadership of the Mennonites who had refused to engage in such traffic and exploitation from the beginning of their settlement in the colonies.

83. Godwyn, *Trade preferr's before Religion*, p. 11.

84. Drake, *Quakers and Slavery*, p. 6

85. George Fox, *Journal*, 2:131. Cf. Drake, *Quakers and Slavery*, p. 6.

86. A century later, English enemies of the African slave trade such as James Ramsay and William Wilberforce were pointing to the possibility that ending that inhuman traffic would be of benefit to the bond-laborer already at work in the West Indies. (Elsa V. Goveia, *Slave Society in the British Leeward Islands* [New Haven, 1965], p. 25.)

87. Godwyn, *The Negro's and Indians Advocate*, pp. 3, 12.

88. Ibid., pp. 13–14.

89. Joseph Bess, *A Collection of the Sufferings of the People Called Quakers for the Testimony of a Good Conscience . . .*, 2 vols. (London, 1753); see the section on Barbados, especially pp. 305–8.

90. Hening, 2:48 (1662), 180–83 (1663). Under the terms of the 1663 law, Quaker Meeting was outlawed altogether, and violators were to be fined 200 pounds of tobacco for the first offense and 500 for the second offense, to be satisfied by seizure and sale of the offender's assets, with the Quaker community made collectively responsible for any unsatisfied amount. For the third offense, the penalty was to be banishment from the colony to a place chosen by the Governor and Colony Council. Other provisions were aimed at preventing Quaker preachers from coming into Virginia by imposing a fine of 5,000 pounds of tobacco upon householders who hosted those preachers.

91. ". . . the freedom and equality of man [was] involved in the true profession of Christ." (Ballagh, p. 46.)

92. See p. 21.

93. See Chapter 2, n. 65; Leviticus, 25:8–10.

94. The Virginia General Court ruled in 1772 that Indians were free by virtue of the 1691 "Act for a free trade with Indians." (Hening 3:69.) The court, relying on ancient English legal precedent, held that allowing the right of free trade carried with it "all incidents necessary to the exercise of that right, as protection of their persons, properties, &c, and consequently takes from every other the right of making them slaves." (Thomas Jefferson, *Reports of Cases Determined in the General Court of Virginia, From 1730 to 1740, and from 1668–1772* [Charlottesville, 1829].) The ruling was made in relation to Robin, an Indian being held as a slave, who sued for his freedom. The opinion was written by George Mason.

95. *Northampton County Records, 1651–54*, f. 114 (12 January 1652/3). The clerk noted in the margin that the statement, which was dated two weeks earlier, had been signed by Pott but not Charlton.

96. *Northampton Country Records, 1645–51*, ff. 150–51. "Hardly rejecting slavery outright," notes Douglas Deal, "Charlton nevertheless displayed some uneasiness about the custom of owning and selling Africans for life." (Deal, *Race and Class in Colonial Virginia*, p. 254.)

97. *Northampton County Records, 1645–51*, f. 205. Richard Vaughan, Stephen Charlton's brother-in-law, "seems to have been wholeheartedly opposed to owning Africans and slaves for life." (Deal, *Race and Class in Colonial Virginia*, p. 254.)

98. *Northampton County Records, 1654–55/6*, f. 54-b. Yet as noted above (p. 188), Charlton specified hereditary bondage for Sisley in a transaction in 1647.

99. *York County Records, 1657–62*, f. 16.

100. *Northampton County Records, 1657–66*, f. 47.

101. *York County Records, 1657–62*, ff. 82, 85, 89.

102. *Northampton County Records, Deeds and Wills, No. 8 (1666–68)*, p. 17. Although the fact is

not noted in this document, Driggus is elsewhere identified as a "Negro"; whether Williams may have been one of England's Negro seamen is not indicated.

103. The facts presented here regarding the Key case are drawn from *Northumberland County Court Records, 1652–58,* ff. 66–7, 85, 87 and 124–5; *1652–65,* ff. 40, 41, 46, 49; *1658–66,* f. 28; and from *MCGC,* p. 504. Credit for bringing this case into the discussion on the origin of racial slavery is due to Warren M. Billings for "The Cases of Fernando and Elizabeth Key: A Note on the Status of Blacks in the Seventeenth Century," *WMQ,* 30:467–74 (1973), and for his presentation of material from the record of the Key case in his edited work *The Old Dominion in the Seventeenth Century: A Documentary History of Virginia, 1606–1698* (Chapel Hill, 1975); pp. 165–9. All the documents cited here by me, except one, are to be found in the latter work, though with certain errors of transcription. In Anthony Lenton's deposition (p. 146), a passage is made unintelligible by the inadvertent omission of fifteen words, and the name "Mottrom" is given where it should have been "Key." On the same page, a June and a July record entry are presented as if they were one entry and for a single day.

Regrettable as these editor's errors may be, they do not detract from the force of the evidence he presents, evidence that led him to challenge Winthrop D. Jordan's argument that racial slavery was the result of an "unthinking decision." To the contrary, says Billings in "The Cases of Fernando and Elizabeth Keys," the laws passed by the Virginia Assembly in 1662 and 1667 (for descent through the mother, and uncoupling freedom from Christian conversion – see p. 197) "were deliberately calculated to undercut the meager rights of black laborers" (*WMQ,* 30:473–4).

However, his concluding allusion to "white alarm" as the motive for the course of events that ended in racial slavery seems too facile, and not based on his evidence. Furthermore, it would seem to undermine his own challenge to Jordan's entire thesis, which is based on the presumption of an immemorial "white alarm."

104. As indicated by the fact that he had paid the fine for "getting her Mother with Child."

105. "The planters," writes Billings, "were beginning to look upon slavery as a viable alternative to indentured servitude." (Billings, "The Cases of Fernando and Elizabeth Key," 30:471.) I belong with Billings in favoring the economic interpretation of history. But his phrase "the planters" suggests a unanimity among the plantation owners, whereas the great significance of the Elizabeth Key case is precisely that at that moment some "planters" had basic reservations that, had they prevailed, would have prevented the eventual imposition of racial oppression in Anglo-America.

106. From the brief of the appellant in the case of Eleanor Toogood v. Dr Upton Scott, held in October 1782 in the Maryland Provincial Court. (Thomas Harris Jr and John McHenry, *Maryland Reports, being a series of the Most Important Cases argued and determined in the Provincial Court and the Court of Appeals of the then Province of Maryland from the Year 1700 down to the American Revolution* [New York, 1809, 1812] vol. 2; 26–38; p. 37.) One shrinks from the callousness of this language, but it proceeded in the circumstances of the time from the same "market principles" that still, today, leave "no other nexus between man and man than naked self-interest, than callous 'cash payment.'" (Marx and Engels, *The Communist Manifesto,* in Karl Marx and Frederick Engels, *Selected Works in Two Volumes* (Moscow, 1955), 1:36.

107. See *The Invention of the White Race,* Volume One, pp. 86–7.

108. See ibid., pp. 8, 80, 236, n. 34.

109. See ibid., p. 80, 81.

110. Hening, 2:170.

111. Hening, 2:260.

112. Kenneth G. Davies, *The Royal African Company* (London, 1957), p. 41.

113. Hening, 2:280–81.

114. See p. 172.

115. Hening, 2:299.

116. Susan Westbury, "Slaves of Colonial Virginia: Where They Came From," *WMQ,,* 42:228–48 (1985); pp. 229–30. In the absence of further records, Westbury makes this conjecture based on bills of exchange and the price prevailing at that time. These workers may be among those referred to in the following record: "A List of Ships freighted by the Royal African Company Since January 1673/4." The account shows a total of 5,200 persons taken from Africa, of whom 300 on the *Swallow* and 350 on the *Prosperous* were supposed to be being sent to Virginia, the others being destined for Jamaica, Barbados and Nevis. (CO 1/31, f. 32.)

117. CO 324/1. "Certain Instructions and Additional Instructions to Colonial Governors, Comissions and Orders in Council." The date is between 1662 and 1774, according to Charles. M. Andrews, *Guide to the Materials for American History to 1783, in the Public Record Office of Great Britain,* 2 vols. (Washington, DC, 1912–14); 1:226.

118. Bruce, 2:59. This comment, however, was made in the context of Bruce's opinion that in general African-American bond-laborers were not defiant or rebellious.

119. Sir John Knight to the Earl of Shaftesbury, 29 October 1673 (*CSP, Col.*, 7:530).

120. Sir Henry Chicheley to Sir Thomas Chicheley, 16 July 1673 (*CSP, Col.*, 7:508).

121. See Appendix 2-A. That was precisely the prospect that concerned William Byrd II "of Westover." Byrd noted that "On the back of the British Colonys on the Continent of America about 250 miles from the ocean, runs a chain of High Mountains." He urged that steps be taken to "prevent the Negroes taking Refuge there as they do in the mountains of Jamaica" and making allies with the French against the English as did many of the Indian Tribes. (William Byrd II of Westover to Mr Ochs, ca. 1735, *VMHB*, 9:225–8 [1902]; 226.)

11 Rebellion – and Its Aftermath

1. See Chapter 6, note 80.

2. The reader is referred to: (1) the excellent bibliographic essay done by the late Jane Carson for the Jamestown Foundation, *Bacon's Rebellion, 1676–1976* (Jamestown, Virginia, 1976); (2) John B. Frantz, ed., *Bacon's Rebellion: Prologue to the Revolution?* (Lexington, Massachusetts, 1969), a volume of extensive excerpts from source documents, supplemented by selections from the writings of ten of the principal historians of the colonial period, analyzing the causes and assessing the significance of the rebellion; (3) the entries for Nathaniel Bacon, the rebel, and Bacon's Rebellion in *The Virginia Historical Index*, compiled by Earl G. Swem, an exhaustive bibliography compiled of materials published in the *Calendar of Virginia State Papers*, Hening's *Virginia Statutes*, and five principal historical magazines published between 1809 and 1930. Finally, an indispensable guide to primary source materials is John Davenport Neville, *Bacon's Rebellion: Abstracts of Materials in the Colonial Records Project* (Jamestown, 1976).

3. See Bernard Bailyn, "Politics and Social Structure in Virginia," in James Morton Smith, ed., *Seventeenth-century America, Essays in Colonial History* (Chapel Hill, 1959).

4. Wilcomb E. Washburn, *The Governor and the Rebel* (Chapel Hill, 1957). The quoted phrase is at p. 162.

Washburn's challenge to the uncritical glorification of Bacon's Rebellion supplied an overdue corrective to the white-chauvinist "frontier democracy" myth, but he made the case in the form of an uncritical assessment of Governor Berkeley. As a result, there seems to be no room in Washburn's account for the mass of poor freemen, freedmen and bond-laborers, relief of whose sufferings was of no more concern to Berkeley than it was to his peers, despite his invocation of those sufferings to pursue easement of the rigors of the Navigation Act. So far as any self-activation on their part is concerned, Washburn sees only "frontier aggression." It is regrettable that Washburn, in his laudable purpose of exposing the counterfeit of "frontier democracy," did not so much as look at the Virginia County Records. If he had done so, he might not have canonized Berkeley as he did, and he might not have so completely ignored the bond-laborers and their own independent cue and motive for rebellion unrelated to "Indian policy." He particularly failed to give any historical significance to the bond-laborers' participation in the rebellion. He mentions Negroes being among the rebels, for which he deserves credit; but he attaches no thematic significance to the fact. (See ibid., pp. 80–81; 88; 209 n. 23.) Francis Jennings's research into the records regarding the Indians of the eastern section of the continent and his forceful, sympathetic treatment of them are a truly seminal contribution. (See particularly his *The Invasion of America: Indians, Colonialism, and the Cant of Conquest* [Chapel Hill, 1975].) In an earlier article, Jennings defended Washburn's *The Governor and the Rebel* as the best work on Bacon's Rebellion, free of the common fault of relying on Virginians' "self-serving depositions." Apparently he, too, did not interest himself in a study of the Virginia County Records and he certainly takes no account of the bond-laborers; he is content to characterize the rebellion as nothing other than an action of "militant back settlers" led by a demagogue for the sole purpose of seizing "attractive real estate" from Indians. (Francis Jennings, "Glory, Death and Transfiguration: The Susquehannock Indians in the Seventeenth Century," *Proceedings of the American Philosophical Society*, 102:15–53 [1968]; pp. 34–5.)

5. Craven believes it is an anachronistic error to interpret that event in terms of democratic principles that are standards of a much later time: "Bacon's Rebellion belongs to the seventeenth century . . .," he writes, and historians should leave it there (Wesley Frank Craven, *The Colonies in Transition, 1660–1713* [New York, 1968], p. 142).

6. John B. Fiske, writing in the populist era at the end of the nineteenth century, presented a class-struggle interpretation of Bacon's Rebellion, but one short on equalitarianism. He draws the line at the "rabble ... who [had] little or nothing to lose, ... [and who] entertained communistic notions" typical of the "socialist tomfoolery" of such times. His single reference to the bond-laborers is as "servile labor," without any political personality of their own. (John B. Fiske, *Old Virginia and Her Neighbors*, 2 vols. [Boston and New York, 1900], 106.)

7. I am, of course, indebted to Edmund S. Morgan, Timothy H. Breen, and Lerone Bennett Jr, who before me ventured somewhat along this line. See my Introduction to Volume One of *The Invention of the White Race*, pp. 16–21.

8. Those who are interested in the details as they are presented by English and Anglo-American chroniclers will want to follow the bibliographies and sources as listed in note 1. Among works noted there, a good selection for the reader with a critical eye would surely include: the section on Bacon's Rebellion in Charles M. Andrews, *Narratives of the Insurrections, 1675–1690* (New York, 1915) pp. 16–28, 47–59; Richard L. Morton, *Colonial Virginia*, 2 vols. (Chapel Hill, 1960) particularly Chapter 13 of Volume One, "Indian War – The Background of Rebellion"; and Washburn, particularly Chapter 2, "Background to Rebellion," and Chapter 3, "The Occaneechee Campaign."

9. Alden T. Vaughan writes: "[C]olor prejudice ... happened to Indians ... though not until two centuries of culture contact had altered Anglo-American perceptions ... The perceptual shift from Indians as white men to Indians as tawnies or redskins was neither sudden not universally accepted" until the eighteenth century. (Alden T. Vaughan, "From White Man to Redskin: Changing Anglo-American Perceptions of the American Indian," *American Historical Review*. 87:917–53 (October 1982); pp. 918, 930.)

10. In July 1676 a petition apparently initiated by the local Gloucester County elite and asking Governor Berkeley for protection against Bacon, invoked the specter of "their wives & Children being exposed to the cruelty of the mercyless Indians." (Sherwood, *Virginia's Deploured Condition, Or an Impartiall Narrative of the Murders comitted by the Indians there, and of the Sufferings of his Majesties Loyall Subjects under the Rebellious outrages of Mr Nathaniell Bacon Junior*, dated August 1676, Massachusetts Historical Society *Collections* 4th ser. 9:162–76 (Boston, 1871); p. 173. The text of the petition and Berkeley's reply are printed in the same volume, pp. 181–4.)

11. Andrews, p. 110–11.

12. Jerry A. O'Callaghan, "The War Veteran and the Public Lands," in Vernon Carstensen, *The Public Lands: Studies in the History of the Public Domain* (Madison, Wisconsin, 1968), p. 112.
A similar analogy is presented by the English Revolution which began in a fury at the massacre of Protestants in an uprising of the Irish in the fall of 1641, but ended with the overthrow of the monarchy in England. (Brian Manning, "The Outbreak of the English Civil War," in R. H. Parry, ed., *The English Civil War and after, 1642–1658* [Berkeley, 1970], p. 4.)

13. Bailyn, p. 99. In this paragraph I have followed Bailyn's impressive treatment of the etiology of the division in the ranks of the Virginia colony elite.

14. As already mentioned (see note 4), however, that the Navigation Act was not an issue as such in Bacon's Rebellion, although Nathaniel Bacon did speak of the Dutch trade as an alternative to dependence on England. (Dialogue with John Good, around 2 September 1676, CO 5/1371, ff. 121vo–122. It appears at this location on reel 32 of the microfilm prepared by the Virginia Colonial Records Project. Thomas J. Wertenbaker [*The Planters of Colonial Virginia* (Princeton, 1922) p. 17, n. 22] and Washburn [*Governor and the Rebel*, p. 235 n. 22] both cite CO 5/1371, pp. 233–40. I cannot account for this confusion of page or folio numbers. In the *Coventry Papers*, I found it at 77:347–8, as did Washburn. The text is printed in Fiske, 82–6. Ever since 1663, Governor Berkeley had complained of the unfairness of the Navigation Act under which "40,000 people [were] impoverished to enrich little more than 40 [English] merchants, who being the whole buyers of our tobacco, give us what they please for it." (Sir William Berkeley, *A Discourse and View of Virginia* (London, 1663), p. 6. Berkeley to the Lords of Trade and Plantations, 1671, CO 1/26, f. 77, cited in Wertenbaker, pp. 95–6.)

15. So called after the name of Berkeley's home plantation.

16. In 1645, the Virginia General Assembly declared that taxation exclusively by the poll, or head, had "become insupportable for the poorer sort to bear," and enacted that all levies were to be paid on "visible estates," in which the poll tax was to constitute only 30 percent of a composite list of such taxable properties (Hening, 1:305–6). Meeting as a committee of the whole, the General Assembly adopted a resolution favoring the enactment of legislation providing for taxation on landholdings rather than by the poll (Hening, 2:204). Though this sentiment was regularly expressed, taxation continued to be by the poll throughout the seventeenth century.

In 1656, on the no-taxation-without-representation principle, all freemen, propertyless as well as propertied, were given the right to vote (Hening, 1:403), but in 1670 the Assembly repealed the 1656 provision and restricted the suffrage to landholders or "householders" because former bond-laborers were judged not to have "interest enough to tye them to endeavour of the public good" (Hening, 2:280). In 1661 and 1662, in the name of reducing the costs of government, the Governor and Colony Council were authorized for a period of three years to impose annual levies without consulting the House of Burgesses (Hening, 2:24, 85).

17. These "frontier" plantation owners were the vanguard of the emerging "county family" faction. The flare-up was in the context of English aggression and Indian defensive response. The particular incident, according to English accounts, was the result of a barter between an English planter named Mathews and some Doeg Indians, residents of Maryland on the other side of the Potomac. The Indians fulfilled their end of the bargain on time but Mathews did not, and the Indians acted to settle the account by taking some of Mathews's hogs, The Susquehannock Indians (who had moved from Pennsylvania to Maryland on Maryland's invitation, or else because of pressure from the Iroquois Seneca) became involved when five of their chieftains were murdered while parleying with the English under a flag of truce, an act of treachery that was condemned formally even by the Maryland and Virginia officials. (Andrews, pp. 16–19, 47–8, 105–6. Jennings, "Glory, Death, and Transfiguration," pp. 27, 34.)

18. Bacon is sometimes called Nathaniel Bacon Junior to distinguish him from his older cousin of the same name who was also a member of the Colony Council. The birth year of Bacon the rebel, 1697, is inferred from the date of the death of his mother, Elizabeth. (*New England Historical and Genealogical Register*, 37:191 [1883].) Wertenbaker so interprets the record (Thomas J. Wertenbaker, *The Torchbearer of the Revolution: The Story of Bacon's Rebellion and Its Leader* [Princeton, 1940] p.215). June Carson apparently accepts 1647 also, since she says Bacon was twenty-seven when he arrived in Virginia in 1674. Carson; p. 24.

19. Bacon arrived in Virginia in the spring of 1674; he was appointed to the Colony Council on 3 March 1675; and he assumed the role of leader of the anti-Indian campaign in April 1676, and was for the first time declared a rebel by Governor Berkeley. (Jane Carson, *Bacon's Rebellion, 1676–1976* [Jamestown, 1976], "Chronology," pp. 4, 6.)

20. Wilcomb E. Washburn, "Governor Berkeley and King Philip's War," *New England Quarterly*, 30:363–77 (1957); p. 377. But Washburn cites Berkeley's assertion that the English who were driving the Indians out of their land had "this privilege by his Majesties Grant." (Ibid., p. 375, Berkeley to Secretary Joseph Williamson, 1 April 1676.)

21. Hening, 1:323–4, 353–4.

22. *Rappahannock County Records, 1663–68*, pp. 57–8. When Berkeley himself came into possession of a thirteen-year-old Indian girl as an item of booty from the estate of a Bacon rebel, he gave her "to the Master of a ship who bath caryed her for England." (CO 5/1371, f. 243.) Cf. Warren M. Billings, "Sir William Berkeley – Portrait By Fischer: A Critique," *WMO*, 3d ser., 48:598–607 (1991), p. 602; and "David Hackett Fischer's Rejoinder," ibid., 608–11; p. 610.

23. "… all but five which were restored to the Queen by Ingram who was Bacon's Generall." (Andrews, p. 127.) Andrews. cites CO 5/1371, "A True Narrative of the Rise, Progress, and Cessation of the Late Rebellion in Virginia, Most Humbly and Impartially Reported by His Majestyes Commissioners appointed to Enquire into the Affaires of the Said Colony" (July 1677).

24. Andrews, pp. 123–7.

25. Sherwood, p. 168.

26. See also p. 43.

27. *Rappahannock County Records, 1656–64*, p. 13. The date of the agreement is missing, but by interpolation it appears to have been in 1656 or 1657. Roanoake (or Wampompeake) was a medium of exchange made by the Indians. It was made of polished shell beads strung or woven together, and was sometimes exchanged as the equivalent of English money at the rate of five shillings per six feet (*Encyclopedia Britannica*, "Wampum or Wampum-Peage"). See also Hening 1:397.

28. Assistant Colony Secretary Philip Ludwell to Secretary of State Williamson, 28 June 1676, *VMHB* 1:180 (1893).

29. Hening, 2:20, 114, 140. See also p. 60.

30. Bailyn, p. 103.

31. County Grievances, CO 5/1371, ff. 149–9. Sixteen counties and one parish submitted a total of 204 grievances. Only two counties called for the enslavement of Indian war captives. Surry County requested "that the Indians taken in the late Warr may be made Slaves" (f. 156), and James

City County asked that "Indian slaves that were taken in the late Indian Warr ... be disposed to a Publick use and Profitt" (f. 150vo).

The names of the authors of the "grievances" are not supplied. It is certain that none of them were bond-laborers.

32. Sherwood, p. 164.

33. Thomas Ludwell and Robert Smith, Virginia representatives in England, writing to the king, 18 June 1676, *Coventry Papers*, 77:128. Cited in Edmund S. Morgan, *American Slavery, American Freedom: The Ordeal of Colonial Virginia* (New York, 1975), p. 221.

"Few of the indentured servants, coming over after 1660," writes Wertenbaker, "succeeded in establishing themselves in the Virginia yeomanry." "[P]robably less than fifty per cent [of the bond-laborers] could hope even in the most favorable times [i.e. prior to 1650] to become freeholders," he concludes, and by the time of Bacon's Rebellion, the probability was reduced to about one out of twenty. (Wertenbaker, *Planters of Colonial Virginia*, pp. 80–83, 97–98.) Menard finds a parallel experience in Maryland where "Opportunities declined after 1660," when, the indications are, only 22 to 29 percent of the freemen became landowners. (Russell R. Menard, "From Servant to Freeholder: Status Mobility and Property Accumulation in Seventeenth-Century Maryland," *WMO*, 30:374 [1973]; pp. 57, 62–3.)

34. County Grievances, CO 5/1371, ff. 150vo–151. James City County grievance number 10.

35. The grievances of three counties (Lancaster, Isle of Wight, and Nansemond) expressed a desire for a general anti-Indian war. Every list of grievances included at least one complaint about taxes, the amount, the manner of their imposition, and their misappropriation, and the exemptions granted to some favored few. James City, Warwick and Isle of Wight wanted land taxes be imposed instead of poll taxes. The request by Rappahannock County and Cittenborne Parish that landholders be forced to pay their quitrents was, in terms of logic, linked with the desire for a break-up of the large landholdings. (CO 5/1371, County Grievances, ff. 150vo–151, 151vo, 153, 156vo, 157, 161vo.)

36. Ibid. In replying to each separate proposal of this tenor, the commissioners acknowledged that the "unlimited liberty of taking up such vast tracts of Lande is an apparent cause of many mischiefs," and that the proposed remedy was desirable. But, they said that such a radical step was impractical because of the certain opposition of the great landholders. They proposed a more modest revision, whereby the poll tax would be retained but for every 100 acres over a thousand the owner would pay an added levy equal to that for one tithable. (CO 5/1371, ff. 150vo–151, 160, 161vo.)

37. Sherwood, p. 164.

38. CO 1/36. Received in England in June 1676 by English Secretary of State Joseph Williamson. See note 49.

39. Hening, 2:85. See also note 15.

40. Morgan, pp. 244–5. Hening, 2:518–43, 569–83. The second of these two grants, covering all of Virginia south of the Rappahannock, was limited to thirty-one years. (Hening, 2:571–2.) In 1684, Thomas Lord Culpeper sold his rights back to the king. (Ibid., 2:521.)

41. Noted by Francis Moryson and Thomas Ludwell in their urgent appeals to the king for a revocation of the massive grants he had made to his friends. (Hening, 2:539.)

42. From 1661 until the declaration of war against the Indians in March 1676, the Governor had the licensing of traders dealing with the Indians, authority that Berkeley could exploit for his own enrichment. Then all those licenses were revoked, and each of the counties was authorized to designate five or fewer traders, with the provision that no powder, shot, or arms might be sold to Indians. Under a law passed in 1677, all restrictions on trade with Indians were removed. (Hening, 2:20, 124, 140, 336–8, 402.)

43. Washburn, *Governor and the Rebel*, p. 29, citing *Coventry papers*, Vol. 77, ff. 6, 8.

44. Sir John Berry, Francis Moryson and Herbert Jeffreys, *A True Narrative of the Rise, Progress, and Cessation of the Late Rebellion in Virginia, Most Humbly and Impartially Reported by His Majesty's Commissioners Appointed to Inquire into the Affaires of the Said Colony* (October 1677), *VMHB*, 4:117–54 (1896); p. 121.

This suspicion was voiced in popular irony: "Bullets would never pierce Bever Skins." (Thomas Mathew, *The Beginning, Progress and Conclusion of Bacon's Rebellion in Virginia in the Years 1675 and 1676*, in Andrews, p. 20.)

45. Lee to Secretary Coventry, 4 August 1676 (*Coventry Papers*, 77:161).

46. *VMHB*, 1:433 (1893).

47. I take the formation of new counties as a rough index of colony expansion. Counties were first established in Virginia in 1634. In the nineteen-year period 1651 to 1669, ten new counties

were formed. It was twenty-two years before the next county, King and Queen, was formed in 1691. (Martha W. Hiden, *How Justice Grew – Virginia Counties: An Abstract of Their Formation*, Jamestown 350th Anniversary Historical Booklet No. 19, [Richmond, 1957], pp. 83–5.)

48. Bailyn, p. 105.

49. CO 1/36, ff. 111–12. The only date recorded is that of the receipt of the letter, June 1676; the time of transatlantic transmittal was usually over a month.

50. Major Isaac Allerton, one of the coerced burgesses, to Secretary Coventry 4 August 1676 (*Coventry Papers* 77:160–61). Hening, 2:380.

51. "A Review, Breviary and Conclusion drawn from the narrative of the Rebellion in Virginia" by Royal Commissioners John Berry and Francis Moryson, 20 July 1677, in Samuel Wiseman's Book of Record, 1676–1677 Pepysian Library ms. no. 2582. In Neville, pp. 318–24. Wiseman was the clerk to the Royal Commission sent to investigate the rebellion and to suggest remedies.

52. Wilcomb E. Washburn, "The Effect of Bacon's Rebellion on Government in England and Virginia," United States National Museum *Bulletin* 225 (1962), pp. 137–40; p. 139.

53. Samuel Wiseman's Book of Record, p. 107 (16 July 1677). In Neville, p. 332.

54. CO 5/1371, Proceedings and Reports of the Commissioners for Enquiring Into Virginian Affairs and Settling the Virginian Grievances, f. 180 (15 October 1677).

55. Moryson to Secretary of State William Jones, October 1676 (CO 5/1371, ff. 8vo–13vo). Francis Moryson was a royalist veteran of the English Civil War and the son of Richard Moryson and nephew of Fynes Moryson who were engaged in the Tyrone War under Mountjoy in Ireland. (See *The Invention of the White Race*, Volume One, especially pp. 61–5 and Appendix F.)

56. Berry and Morsyon to Thomas Watkins, Secretary to the Duke of York, 10 February 1676/7. Samuel Wiseman's Book of Record. See Virginia Colonial Records Project, Survey Report 6618, for microfilm number. The letter is also printed in *Coventry Papers*, 77:389.

57. Hening, 2:515. In Virginia in 1676, at age sixteen or over, all men, African-American women, and Indian women bond-laborers were tithable. There seems to have been no intersection of the two sets – all possible combatants and tithables – in which bond-laborers were not the majority.

58. Eric Williams stressed the bond-laborers' struggle as the key factor in the general history of the British West Indies. (Eric Williams, *Capitalism and Slavery* [Chapel Hill, 1944], pp. 201–2.) C. L. R. James does the same in *Black Jacobins*, his full-blown history of the Haitian Revolution. Morgan, in his main work on colonial Virginia, does not ignore the bond-laborers, but in effect disparages their aptitude for rebellion, especially so far as African-Americans are concerned. (*American Slavery, American Freedom*, pp. 296–7, 309.) Breen alone has, in passing, noted the bond-laborers' role in Bacon's Rebellion. (Timothy H. Breen, "A Changing Labor Force and Race Relations in Virginia, 1660–1710," *Journal of Social History*, Fall 1973, pp. 10–12, 17.) See the fuller discussion of this aspect in *The Invention of the White Race*, Volume One, pp. 15–21.

59. See, for example, the pioneering works done for Johns Hopkins University on "white servitude" in continental Anglo-America, including: James C. Ballagh, *White Servitude in the Colony of Virginia* (Baltimore, 1895); and Eugene Irving McCormac, *White Servitude in Maryland, 1634–1824* (Baltimore, 1904).

60. See, for example, Russell R. Menard, *Economy and Society in Early Colonial Maryland* (New York, 1985) and David Galenson, *White Servitude in Colonial America: An Economic Analysis* (New York, 1981).

61. In the Royal Commissioners' report, the Lancaster County Grievances nos. 11 and 12 call for laws for "the encouragement of servants." However, no particulars are supplied and the Royal Commissioners simply say the petitioners should seek remedy by the Assembly. (CO 5/1371, f. 156vo.)

62. CO 1/3, ff. 35–62/8/6 (October 1676), "Proposals most humbly offered to his most sacred Majestie by Thomas Ludwell and Robert Smith for Reducing the Rebells in Virginia to their obedience." Printed in *VMHB* 1:433–5.

63. CO 1/37, f. 37 (Ludwell to Williamson, 28 June 1676).

64. *Northampton County Records, 1168–80*, p. 11, in a proclamation concerning the apprehension of runaway bond-laborers dated 30 December 1669.

65. G. N. Clarke, *The Later Stuarts, 1660–1714* (Oxford, 1934), pp. 5–8, 82–3. David Ogg, *England Under the Reign of Charles II*, 2 vols. (Oxford, 1934), 1:74–5; 2:342, 346, 446, 449.

66. CO 1/34, f. 200 (Petition of Virginia's representatives to the King, June [?] 1675). CO 1/36, ff. 111–12 (letter from the collector of customs, Giles Bland, in Virginia to Secretary of State Sir Joseph Williamson, received in England in June 1676).

Besides the loss of tobacco revenues, the government spent £80,000 in quelling the rebellion.

(Governor Alexander Spotswood to the Board of Trade, 4 June 1715, referring to "Journals of this Colony in 1676" [*CSP, Col.*, pp. 199–201].)

67. So one might conclude from a letter from Mr William Harbord to the Earl of Essex, dated 17 December 1676, in which reference is made to revenue losses due to both Bacon's Rebellion and King Philip's War in New England: "[I]ll news from Virginia and New England doth not only alarm us but extreamly abates the customs so that notwithstanding all the shifts Treasurer can make this Parliament or another must sitt." (Clements Edwards Pike, ed., *Selections from the Correspondence of Arthur Capel, Earl of Essex, 1675–1677*, Camden Society Publications, 3rd ser. [London, 1913], p. 87. My attention was directed to this letter by Washburn's citation of it in *Governor and the Rebel*, p. 214, n. 5.) This crisis, to which the rebellion in Virginia so materially contributed, marked the beginning of party politics that was to lead to the so-called Glorious Revolution and the end of the Stuart monarchy. For the tobacco fleet number, see Ogg, 1:75.

68. *Coventry Papers*, 77:332. The document, which was apparently addressed to Secretary of State Williamson, is not dated, but it was probably written in October 1676 during preparations for sending troops to Virginia.

69. *Charles City Records (Order Book) 1677–79*, 9 August 1677.

70. *The Vestry Book of Christ Church Parish, 1663–1767* (in Middlesex County), edited by C. G. Chambelayne (Richmond, 1927), p. 25.

71. *Westmoreland County Records, 1675–89*, p. 68.

72. *Petsworth Parish Vestry Book, 1677-1795* (Gloucester County), edited by C. G. Chamberlayne (Richmond, 1933), p. 17. Chamberlayne suggestively noted that Nathaniel Bacon's death occurred at the home of Thomas Pate, the churchwarden of Petsworth Parish.

73. Such conjecture would not suit John Finley, apparently. He steadfastly refused to be freed from servitude by the rebels, preferring to remain their close prisoner for the space of twelve weeks. That's what he said, in support of his owner's action for trespass against a rebel officer. His faithfulness presumably exempted him from the added year of servitude imposed on bond-laborers absent from their owners during the rebellion. (*Charles City Order Book, 1677–79*, pp. 179–80 [13 September 1677].)

74. *Charles City County Records, 1655–66*, p. 5234 (18 October 1664).

75. See p. 135.

76. *Middlesex County Records, 1673–80*, f. 135 (2 September 1678).

77. *Middlesex County Order Book, 1694–1705*, pp. 234–42 (1 August and 2 October 1699).

78. See p. 154.

79. See p. 149.

80. "The Names and short Characters of those that have bin executed for Rebellion" submitted by Berkeley to the Royal Commissioners, in Samuel Wiseman's Book of Record. (See Neville, pp. 274–75.)

81. Neill identifies Wilson as a "servant," and says the death sentence was passed on him on 11 January. (Richard Duffield Neill, *Virginia Carolorum: The Colony under the Rule of Charles the First and Second, AD 1625–1685* [Albany, NY, 1886] pp. 373, 377.) *York County Records, 1677–84*, f. 88 (24 April 1679). *Accomack County Records 1678–82*, p. 158 (17 March 1679/80).

82. Fletcher was in court on four occasions between 17 February and 9 July 1677, and it appears that the beatings and kicking she suffered from her owner(s) followed her return from several months as a rebel. Even though she was sentenced on 4 July to two added years for bearing a child, and another five months for the time she was with the rebels, she embarked on a campaign of "wearying" her owner until he should sell her to someone else. As part of this wearying process, she resisted a whipping in the following manner, "when (her owner) began to strike her shee layd hold of him and flung him downe." (*Surry County Records, 1671–84*, ff. 121, 131; ibid., *1671–91*, 133, 152.)

83. Manscript of a letter from Andrew Marvell, poet and member of Parliament, to his friend Henry Thompson, 14 November 1676. I am grateful to the Henry E. Huntington Library and Art Gallery, San Marino, California, for supplying me with a photocopy of the letter.

84. New York Public Library, George Chalmers Collection, I, folio 49. The Bacon forces burned Jamestown on 19 September 1676. The letter was dated 19 October.

Why would Bacon want to free bond-laborers? Of 25 condemned rebels whose estates were inventoried, 14 were listed as owners of bond-laborers. The largest individual holding was that of Bacon's own 11 bond-laborers – 1 Irishman, 2 African-American men, 1 African-American woman and her one-year-old "mulatto" daughter, and 5 Indians, ranging in age from four to sixteen years of age. (CO 5/1371, f. 219vo-246ro; Bacon's list, 227vo-230vo.) Neither Bacon nor anyone else has left a record concerning his motives in this respect. One obvious reason is that he was fighting for his life – it was indeed victory, or death by drawing and quartering – that he needed the bond-laborers on his side, and that they would not go along without a promise of freedom.

85. Thomas Holden(?) to Secretary Joseph Williamson, 1 February 1677, at the end of a three-month return voyage from Virginia. (*CSP, Dom.*, 18:530.)

86. Hening 2:395 (February 1677).

87. Samuel Wiseman's Book of Record, entry for 11 March 1676/7. For an abstract of this document see Neville, p. 328; or Virginia Colonial Records Project Survey Report 6618 (old designation C-7) at Virginia State Archives.

By royal proclamation dated 26 October 1676 regarding the bond-laborers of rebel owners who failed to accept the king's offer of pardon and surrender by the middle of November, those bond-laborers, if they enlisted in Berkeley's forces, were to be freed from "the Said offenders." (*Coventry Papers*, 77:263.) Berkeley's offer was limited and did not promise liberty, but only liberty from Baconite owners.

88. *Coventry Papers*, 77:301–2. Unless otherwise explicitly noted my section on Grantham's encounters with the rebels is based on this document.

89. *CSP, Dom*, 19:115.

90. "This History of Bacon's and Ingram's Rebellion," Massachusetts Historical Society *Proceedings*, 9 (1867), pp. 299–342. Reprinted in Andrews, pp. 47–104; pp. 93.4.

91. Berkeley wrote a letter to Walklett on 1 January thanking him for his "letters . . . so full and discreet and your Actings so judicious," urging Walkett to go further and try to capture another rebel leader especially hated by Berkeley. He closed by saying that "Mr Ingram and Capt. Langston are with mee and wee shall dine togther within this quarter of an hour, where wee will drinke your health and happy success." (*Coventry Papers*, 78:177.) Walklett and Langston had been commanders of horse troops under Bacon. (Andrews, pp. 34–5, 87.) Herbert Jeffreys, one of the Royal Commission to Virginia and successor to Berkeley as Governor there, declared that the rebels would not have been "so easily reduced had not the said Walklett and one Ingram then general, surrendred their armes to Sir William Berkeley and disbanded their forces whereby the country came to a speedy settlement." (*Coventry Papers*, 78:175.)

92. Their bitterness was no doubt particularly caused by loss of West Point as a strategic location almost impregnable to heavily armed merchantmen or English naval attack by virtue of "the difficulty of the Channell and the Shoaliness of the water [that would] prevent any Great Shipps from pursuing . . . and where alsoe the Narrowness of the River and Commodiousness of the place Contribute soe much to our Advantage that we may with the Greatest facility given an effectuall Repulse to all the force that can their [there] Attack us." Such was the assessment submitted by experts whose opinions were sought by the Virginia Governor and Colony Council regarding defense against a possible French invasion in 1706. I have assumed that at the time of Bacon's Rebellion thirty years earlier both the rebels and Grantham similarly appreciated its strategic advantage. (See "Colonial Papers," Virginia State Archives, Richmond, folder 17, item 29.) "Bacon, with the instinct of the true strategist, had already selected West Point . . . as his headquarters and his main point of concentration." (Wertenbaker, *Torchbearer of the Revolution*, p. 184.)

93. Grantham said that most of these four hundred rebels accepted his terms, "except about eighty Negroes and twenty English which would not deliver their Armes." Grantham tricked these one hundred men on board a sloop with the promise of taking them to a rebel fort a few miles down the York River. Instead, towing them behind his own sloop, he brought them under the guns of another ship and thus forced their surrender, although "they yielded with a great deal of discontent, saying had they known my resolution, they would have destroyed me."

94. CO 1/38, f. 31. Andrews gives the number as "more than 1,100 officers and men." (Andrews, p. 102.)

95. CO 5/1371, ff. 119vo–a23. Report submitted to Governor Berkeley, ca. 30 January 1676/7, by John Good, a Henrico plantation owner on or about 2 September 1676. See note 14.

96. Thomas Wentworth, Earl of Strafford, sentenced for treason and beheaded 12 May 1641.

97. Aside from the garrison at West Point, and two others near West Point (the Brick House at King's Creek, under William Drummond and Richard Lawrence, chief co-leaders of the Bacon movement, and the four hundred at the chief garrison at Colonel West's house, scene of Grantham's most historic encounter, three miles north from West Point), they were located at: Green Spring (now Williamsburg), on the north side of the James River; Arthur Allen's expropriated house (since known as Bacon's Castle), further down and on the south shore of the James, about twenty-five miles northeast of the scene of Nat Turner's Rebellion in 1831; the expropriated house of Bacon's cousin, a Berkeley adherent, at King's Creek on York River; and further down at the place later made famous as Yorktown, scene of Cornwallis's surrender; and two other locations

expropriated from prominent Berkeleyites, one in Gloucester County and another in Westmore-land. (Locations as given in Wertenbaker, *Torchbearer of the Revolution*, pp. 184–6). The total number in all those places is not known; it appears that the one thousand in and around West Point comprised the majority of the rebel troops.

98. Andrews, p. 140. The Royal Commissioners' narrative was dated 20 July 1677. (Neville, p. 220). The cessation of fighting on one river is noted laconically in the 29 January entry in the journal of the *Young Prince*: "Blowing, 'thick weather.' Wind at SW. The cundry being reduced so went about our owne businesse as per the Governor['s] Proclamation." (CO 1/37.)

99. Neill, pp. 373, 374. CO 5/1371, ff. 219vo–246ro. CO 1/39, ff. 64–5. Two other condemned rebels cheated the gallows by dying in prison before they could be executed.

100. Francis Moryson was the son of Sir Richard Moryson and the nephew of the chronicler Fynes Moryson. The uncle and the father are mentioned in Volume One in connection with the Mountjoy conquest of Ireland. (See *The Invention of the White Race* Volume One, pp. 62–5 and Appendix F.) However, the view taken there differs from that of Charles M. Andrews, who unreflectingly credits Sir Richard with "a long and honorable career in Ireland." (Andrews, p. 102.)

101. *Coventry Papers*, 77:263. This proclamation is also to be found at Hening, 2:423–4, where the date is given as 10 October. But the defeated rebels were given no chance to swear such an oath.

102. Hening, 2:280 (1670), 356 (1676), 380 (February 1676/7). The "Bacon Assembly's extension of suffrage to freemen was strongly condemned by the Royal Commissioners in response to a Grievance of Rappahannock County and by the Colony officials in Maryland" (5/1371, f. 152vo; "Remonstrance by the Governor and Council of Maryland," *Maryland Archives*, 15:137–8).

103. For a defense of Berkeley in his quarrels with the Royal Commissioners, see Washburn, *Governor and the Rebel*, Chapter 8.

Excepting Washburn, historians have customarily characterized Berkeley's demeanor as simple vindictive fury linked with the spoils-to-the-victors program. Some of them add references to the old Governor's notorious irascibility, and to a possible sensibility about the great age disparity between Berkeley and Lady Frances, his wife. Paradoxical though it may seem, perhaps his attitude is better understood as foreshadowing the ultimately ascendant colony-centered, rather than "empire-centered," position on which the Virginia ruling elite eventually united.

104. Charles II is reported to have reacted to news of Berkeley's vendetta by noting that "that old fool has hanged more men in that naked country than I did for the Murther of my father." (Andrews, p. 40.) The same point was made by Royal Commissioners Berry and Moryson. Letter to Mr Watkins, 10 February 1676/7, abstracted in Neville, p. 246.

The reliability of the attribution is not established, but the accuracy of the observation is. Charles II hanged a total of thirteen, not counting Cromwell and Ireton, whose dead bodies were exhumed for hanging. ("Regicide," *Encyclopedia Britannica*, 15th edition, [Chicago, 1997], 26:1035.

105. Samuel Wiseman's Record Book, abstracted in Neville, pp. 245–6.

106. *CSP, Col.*, 11:134 (31 October 1681).

107. CO 5/1356, f. 71, Spenser to Sir Leolin Jenkins, 8 May 1682.

108. Blathwayt Papers, ca. 1675–1715, 41 vols. on microfilm at Colonial Williamsburg; vol. 15, Spencer to Blathwayt, 29 May 1682. William Blathwayt was Secretary to the Lords of Trade and Plantations. I am indebted to the New York Historical Society Manuscripts Library for the use of its microfilm set of the Blathwayt Papers.

109. *VMHB*, 2:16, 136–7, 141, 142 cited in Morton 1:327.

110. Culpeper to Blathwayt, 20 March 1682/3 (Blathwayt Papers, Vol. 17).

111. Spencer to Blathwayt, 1 March 1688/9 (Blathwayt Papers, Vol. 15).

112. Dudley Digges to Blathwayt, 23 October 1710 Blathwayt Papers, Vol. 18.

113. Allan Kulikoff, *Tobacco and Slaves: The Development of Southern Cultures in the Chesa-peake, 1680–1800* (Chapel Hill and London, 1986), p. 79.

114. *CSP Col.*, 11:130 (Culpeper to the Lords of Trade and Plantations, 25 October 1681).

115. Dalby Thomas, *An Historical Account, Rise and Growth of the West Indies Colonies and great Advantages they are to England in Respect to Trade* (London, 1690), in Harleian Miscellany, 12 vols.; 9:425.

116. "It was evident," says Professor Richard L. Morton, "that diversification of industry as a remedy for overproduction of tobacco would take years ... But a remedy was needed at once" (Morton, p. 300). But I would respectfully suggest that, of all the Anglo-American colonies, none had had more time than Virginia; time was not the problem, but rather the plantation system based on bond-labor.

117. In 1708, Virginia Colony Secretary Edmund Jennings said that of a total of 30,000 tithables,

there were slightly more than 12,000 bond-laborers, although the number of European-American bond-laborers was "inconsiderable" because "so few have been imported since the beginning of the war" (*CSP Col.*, 24:156). But the Virginia and Maryland laws and official records show that in subsequent years their presence was anything but "inconsiderable."

118. See p.119.

119. Hening, 2:515.

120. Kulikoff (p. 39.)

121. Ibid., p. 40.

122. Menard, *Economy and Society in Early Colonial Maryland*, p. 433.

123. Kulikoff, p. 42, Menard, *Economy and Society in Early Colonial Maryland* Appendix II.

124. In Virginia in 1699 there were 21,888 tithables in a total population of 57,339, a ratio of 1:2.62, or 38 percent (*CSP, Col.*, 19:635–6; Cf. Morgan p.414). In Maryland in 1712 the total population was 46,073. Of that number, European-American men werre 11,025, and the number of "Negroes" was 8,830, making a total of 19,855, On that basis, the ratio of tithables to total population in Maryland would be 1:2.42, or 43.1 percent. An uncertain number of European-American women in Maryland worked in the crop and were therefore tithable. (See CO 5/717 [15 July 1712] and 5/716, Governor Seymour to Board of Trade, 21 August 1706). These total population figures from the records correspond closely with the figures for 1700 and 1710 for Virginia and Maryland respectively as presented in *Historical Statistics of the United States, Colonial Period to 1970*, series Z 13, 14.

125. *CSP, Col.*, 16:390–91 (20 August 1698).

126. *CSP, Col.*, 17:liv, 261.

127. *CSP, Col.*, 25:83 (24 April 1710).

128. *CSP, Col.*, 27:70 (15 October 1715).

129. *CSP, Col.*, 36:414–15 (29 June 1729).

130. Louis B. Wright, ed., *The History and Present State of Virginia*, (Chapel Hill, 1947), p. 92. This edited work is a revised edition of the 1705 work, published in 1722.

131. "Culpeper Report on Virginia in 1683," *VMHB* 3:222–38; p.222. A hogshead at this time probably contained 475 to 500 pounds of tobacco. Cutting as many plants in an hour "as well would have imployed twenty men a Summers tendance to have perfected," in Gloucester alone these plant-cutting rioters destroyed 200 plantations in the first week of their campaign. (CO 5/1356, p. 70, Colony Secretary Spencer to Secretary Leoline Jenkins, 8 May 1682.)

132. Perhaps Governor Culpeper was exaggerating somewhat in saying, "scarce one of them was worth a Farthing" ("Report on Virginia in 1683," *VMHB*, 3:231).

133. Morgan, p. 286, citing CO 1/48, ff. 261, 263, 275, and CO 1/49, f. 56.

134. Morgan, pp. 291–2.

135. Ibid., pp.308–9. See also my comment on Morgan's book in the Introduction to Volume One of the present work.

136. *VMHB*, 3:222–38; p. 230.

137. See the discussion of Sir Francis Bacon's essay on the history of the reign of Henry VII in Vol. I, Chapter 2, pp. 17–18.

138. The Colony Council had roughly estimated that one-third of free men in 1673 were either unable to make a living or were else mired in debt (see pp. 168–9).

139. Samuel Pepys, Secretary to the Admiralty, to Secretary of State Henry Coventry, 7 October 1676 (*Coventry Papers*, 77:233–4).

140. Admiralty Papers, 51/134, Log of HMS *Bristol*, entry for 15 February 1676/7.

141. CO 389/6, p. 200.

142. CO 5/1355. Culpeper's request, 13 December 1677; Lords of Trade and Plantations reply, August 1678.

143. CO 5/1355, p. 408, Culpeper to the Lords of Trade and Plantations, 25 October 1681.

144. CO 5/1356, ff. 2–3, 22 November 1681.

145. CO 5/1356, 8 May 1682.

146. *CSP, Col*, 11:498.

147. CO 5/1356, pp. 183–4.

148. CO 5/1356, pp. 247–8.

149. *Archives Maryland*, 5:152–4. *Proceedings of the Council 1671–1681*. Governor Notley to [name not given in the record], 22 January 1676/77.

150. CO 1/40, f. 186, Notley to Charles Calvert, Lord Baltimore, Proprietary of the Province of Maryland, 22 May 1677. It appears from the copy of this document made by the Virginia Colonial Records Project that this folio once was numbered "88," by which number Wertenbaker refers to

it. (Thomas J. Wertenbaker, *Virginia Under the Stuarts* [Princeton, 1914], p. 137, n. 58.) I thank Cecily J. Peeples for last-minute checking of the records relating to this and half a dozen other facts at the Virginia State Archives.

12 The Abortion of the "White Race" Social Control System in The Anglo-Caribbean

1. Speaking of those forms of the bourgeoisie whom he had studied most closely, Professor Dunn renders this documented judgement: "The sugar planters were always businessmen first and foremost, and from a business standpoint it was more efficient to import new slaves of prime working age from Africa than to breed up a creole generation of Negroes in the Caribbean.... Some of the slave masters found it hard to resist the temptation to get rid of the young and old by systematic neglect and underfeeding." (Richard S. Dunn, *Sugar and Slaves: The Rise of the Planter Class in the English West Indies, 1624–1712* [Chapel Hill, 1972; W. W. Norton reprint, 1973] p. 321.

2. Strictly speaking, it is only after the formation of Great Britain by the Act of Union of England and Scotland in 1707 that the Anglo-Caribbean islands are referred to as the British West Indies. But aside from the effect of the opening of trade between Scotland and the English islands, this is a distinction that may generally be ignored in the present discussion.

The British West Indies comprised a dozen island colonies, annexed over a period of 178 years: from Barbados (1625) to St Lucia (1803); from the Bahamas (1718[?], 1729[?]; see Michael Craton, *A History of the Bahamas* [London, 1962], p. 120) in the northwest to Trinidad (1797) in the southeast; from formerly Spanish Jamaica captured by the English (1655) with its 4,470 square miles, to Nevis (1628), with 50 square miles. Some were captured from Britain one or more times by the French: for example, Nevis, St Kitts (St Christopher), Antigua, Montserrat, Grenada, and Dominica. Though I generalize regarding certain common characteristics of these colonies, I am aware that each has its own distinctive history and traditions. At the same time I believe that the Anglo-Caribbean colonies were characterized by a common history of a ruling-class social control policy that led to the establishment of a tripartite social structure that included persons of some degree of African ancestry in the intermediate buffer social control stratum, a social structure that differed fundamentally from that established in continental Anglo-America at the beginning of the eighteenth century.

3. Almost simultaneously, English colonies were begun on St Kitts (St Christopher), St Eustatius, Tobago, Antigua, and Montserrat. In 1655 the English began settling in Jamaica, which they had captured from Spain. All were essentially monocultural enterprises; the principal product was sugar; minor products were tobacco, cotton, aloes and indigo. The main labor force was made up of chattel bond-laborers.

4. *Coventry Papers*, 85:11 cited in Dunn, p. 74. See the testimony of Captain Henry Powell regarding his efforts to employ Indians in his Barbados plantation. "Papers relating to the early History of Barbados," *Timehri*, new ser., 5:53–5 (1891) (cited in Dunn, p. 227). *The Laws of Jamaica, Comprehending all the Acts in Force Passed between the Thirty Second Year of the Reign of Charles the Second and the Thirty-third Year of the Reign of King George the Third ... Published under the Direction of Commissioners appointed for that Purpose*, 2 vols. (St Jago de la Vega, Jamaica, 1792), pp. 129–30. 8 Geo. I, c. 1 (1721), "An Act to encourage the settling the north-east part of this island," refers to "every free mulatto, Indian or negro."

5. When Dunn says p. 74 that "Indians could not be turned into acceptable agricultural laborers" I take him to mean *bond*-laborers. Dunn himself cites the record of Guiana Indians who in 1627 voluntarily came to Barbados with Captain Henry Powell to cultivate land as "free people" there and to help to promote trade with the mainland. (Ibid., p. 227.) Twenty years later, Powell returned to Barbados and found that those Indians and their families had been involuntarily integrated into the chattel bond-labor system. He petitioned the Barbados Assembly "to set these poor people free that have been kept thus long in bondage." (*Timehri* [1891], 5:53–5.)

6. Historical Manuscripts Commission, Vol. xiv, part 2, Portland Manuscripts, III, p. 268; and CO 1/22, no. 55. (cited in Vincent T. Harlow, *A History of Barbados 1625–1685*, [Oxford, 1926; Negro Universities Press reprint, 1969] pp. 152, 192).

7. Dunn, p. 74.

8. "A Briefe Relation of the Voyage Unto Maryland," in the *Calvert Papers*, Number Three (Baltimore, 1899) p. 32. This account, of which there are two slightly differing versions, one in

Latin, the other in English, is credited to Father Andrew White. A translation of the Latin version is found in Peter Force, *Tracts and Other Papers Relating Principally to the Origin, Settlement and Progress of the Colonies in North America From the Discovery of the Country to the Year 1776* (Washington, 1836, 1947 reprint), vol. 4, no. XII (referred to throughout as *Force Tracts*). The *Force Tracts* version uses the word "slaves" instead of "servants."

9. The Dutch invaded Brazil in 1624, and by 1637 had seized half of the Portuguese administrative areas of settlement (*capteaneos*) there. Dutch-held Pernambuco alone accounted for one-third of Brazil's plantation and sugar mill enterprises, and imported more than half the African bond-laborers brought to Brazil. A rebellion of Portuguese, in which free Afro-Brazilians played a major part, succeeded in finally ousting the Dutch in 1654. Already for the better part of a decade before that final evacuation, Dutch plantation owners had been liquidating their Brazilian operations and leaving the country. A significant number of them settled in Barbados with their capital and technology, and with access to credit and markets in Holland. (Johannes M. Postma, *The Dutch in the Atlantic Slave Trade, 1600–1815*, [Cambridge, 1990] pp. 14, 16, 17, 19–20. R. K. Kent, "Palmares, An African State in Brazil," in Richard Price, ed., *Maroon Societies: Rebel Slave Communities in the Americas*, pp. 170, 171, 174. E. E. Rich and C. H. Wilson, eds., *The Economy of Expanding Europe in the Sixteenth and Seventeenth Centuries* [Cambridge, 1967], [Volume IV of the *Cambridge Economic History of Europe*], p. 334. Harlow, p. 84.)

10. Harlow, p. 325.

11. Ibid., p. 305.

12. Barbados governor Daniel Searle to John Thurloe, Secretary of the Council of State, 18 September 1655 (*A Collection of the State Papers of John Thurloe . . .*, 7 vols. [London, 1742], 4:39–40.)

13. *CSP, Col.*, 12:155 (Minutes of the Barbados Colony Council, 16 February 1686).

14. *CSP, Col.*, 13:733–4 (Barbados Governor Kendall to the Lords of Trade and Plantations, 3 November 1692). The investigation found that "the ringleaders" were mainly "overseers, artisans and domestic servants," who could exploit their relatively greater freedom of movement for organizing the revolt.

15. Dunn, p. 256.

16. Orlando Patterson, *The Sociology of Slavery: An Analysis of the Origins, Development and Structure of Negro Slave Society* (London, 1967), pp. 266, 271–3.

17. R. C. Dallas, *History of the Maroons*, 2 vols. (London, 1803), pp. 23–4.

18. Bryan Edwards, *The History, Civil and Commercial, of the British Colonies in the West Indies* 3 vols. (West Indies, 4th edition, 3 vols. London 1807) 1:522–35, and 537–45 reprinted in Price, ed., pp. 230–32.

19. Dallas (*History of the Maroons* p. 60) says "fifteen hundred" acres, less than two and a half square miles, but such an area would seem absurdly small to provide farming land sufficient for even the one section of the maroons signing this particular treaty. I have substituted the figure given by Patterson: 15,000 acres. (Patterson, pp. 279–71, citing the Jamaica *Journal of the House of Assembly*, 3:458.)

20. Dallas, pp. 58–65.

21. The basic economic, demographic and sociological facts on which the following five points of differentiation rely are long established and are well known to every student of the history of the West Indies. The original colonial-period sources are familiar to all, and the vast bibliography of secondary works, although they differ in interpretation and emphasis, presents a general consensus regarding those facts.

22. I have used Morgan's estimate of the total population, but excluded Henrico County (partially above the Fall Line) and the Eastern Shore counties of Northampton and Accomack. (See Edmund S. Morgan, *American Slavery, American Freedom: The Ordeal of Colonial Virginia* (New York, 1975), Table 3, pp. 412–13.) The Tidewater area is given in standard encyclopedias.

23. The 11,000 squares miles of the Tidewater area is equal to 7,040,000 acres. The quitrent rolls for Virginia's twenty counties in 1704 show an area of some 2,780,000 acres. (Thomas J. Wertenbaker, *The Planters of Colonial Virginia* [New York 1922], Appendix, "Rent Rolls of Virginia 1704–1705.")

24. See pp. 164, 170. See also Virginia laws (Hening, 2:53–69 (1691), and 404–19 (1705), aimed at centralizing customs collections in specific port locations because otherwise royal "customes and revenues [were] impossible to be secured" (2:53). See also John C. Rainbolt, *From Prescription to Persuasion* (Port Washington, NY, 1974), pp. 6, 113.

25. For seventeenth-century Barbados population figures, see Harlow, p. 338; and Sheppard, p. 33. I have used Harlow's figure here. I have made no attempt to investigate the decline of the

total Barbados population suggested by the estimate of only 62,324 in 1748 contained in Jerome S. Handler and Arnold A. Sio, "Barbados," in David W. Cohen and Jack P. Greene, eds., *Neither Slave Nor Free: The Freedman of African Descent in the Slave Societies of the New World* (Baltimore, 1972), p. 338.

26. Hilary Beckles, *Black Rebellion in Barbados: The Struggle Against Slavery, 1627–1838* (Bridgetown, Barbados, 1984), p. 62.

27. The 1698 population of Jamaica is given as 47,400 in Cohen and Greene, eds., p. 338.

28. Philip D. Curtin, *Two Jamaicas: The Role of Ideas in a Tropical Country* (Cambridge, Massachusetts, 1955), p. 69. "Unlike Barbados and the Leewards, where all the land suitable for sugar cane was soon taken up and overproduction exhausted the soil, Jamaica was never quite fully exploited before sugar and slavery declined." (Michael Craton, *Sinews of Empire: A Short History of British Slavery* [Garden City, New York, 1974] p. 46.)

29. Dallas, p. 1xix. Dallas's proportion of unused land is consistent with Curtin's, but his absolute number of acres exceeds the area of Jamaica by some 40 percent.

30. Patterson, p. 270 (citing CO 137/18).

31. Dunn, pp. 170–71, 197, 266–7. Hilary Beckles, *White Servitude and Black Slavery in Barbados, 1627–1715*, pp. 157–58.

32. Dunn, pp. 171 (Table 18), 197, 266 (Table 24), 267 (Table 25).

33. According to Beckles, it was less than 3 percent in Barbados. Wertenbaker puts the Virginia proportion at between 5 and 6 percent. (Beckles, *White Servitude and Black Slavery*, p. 158; Wertenbaker, p. 98.)

34. Sheppard, p. 33.

35. "Lacking means of sustenance, 30,000 Europeans streamed out of Barbados alone during the latter half of the seventeenth century . . . but the majority remained in the Caribbean relocating over and over again in Jamaica, Guiana, the Windwards, and Trinidad." (David Lowenthal, *West Indian Societies* [London, 1972], pp. 29–30.)

In February 1679, however, only a minority appeared to have chosen other West Indies islands. Of 593 persons granted leave to depart Barbados in 1679, 233 were going to North America, 205 to England, 154 to other Caribbean islands, and 1 to Holland. It appears that somewhat over half of these were former bond-laborers. (Dunn, pp. 110–11.)

36. Dunn, p. 312.

37. Craton, p. 44.

38. Harlow, 174–5.

39. The novelty of this form of social identity is to be noted in the comments of George Fox and Morgan Godwyn. During a visit to Barbados in 1671, Fox, founder of the Quaker religion, addressed some members of a Barbados audience as "you that are called white." (George Fox, *Gospel of Family-Order . . .* [London, 1675], p. 38.) About the same time, Godwyn found it necessary to explain to his readers that in Barbados "white" was "the general name for Europeans." (*The Negro's and Indians Advocate . . .* [London, 1680], p. 83.) Even a century later a historian, writing in Jamaica for readers in Britain, felt it necessary to supply a parenthetical clarification: "white people (as they are called here)." (Edward Long, *The History of Jamaica, or, General Survey of the Antient and Modern State of the Island, with Reflections on its Situation, Settlements, Inhabitants, Climate, Products, Commerce, Laws, and Government*, 3 vols. [London, 1774], 2:289.)

40. See *The Invention of the White Race*, Volume One, p. 80.

41. In ordering the forced exile of 1,500 to 2,000 Irish boys to Jamaica to serve as bond-laborers, Henry Cromwell, Oliver's son and deputy in Ireland, wrote to Secretary Johne Thurloe, "who knows, but that it may be a measure to make them Englishmen, I meane rather, Christians." (H. Cromwell to John Thurloe, Secretary of the Council of State, 11 and 18 September 1655. *Papers of John Thurloe* 4:23–4, 40.)

The free persons of color in Barbados made known their determination that "Christian" should not be regarded as a mere euphemism for "white." When the "slave consolidation act" of 1826 was passed making it a crime for a slave to assault "any white person," the free persons of color protested that it deprived them of a protection that they had had as Christians since 1688. (Jerome S. Handler, *The Unappropriated People: Freedmen in the Slave Society of Barbados* [Baltimore, 1974], p. 98.)

42. English Attorney-General Edward Northey, in the normal course of his duty of reviewing laws passed in the colonies, objected to a Nevis Assembly enactment providing for punishment by death or dismemberment for slaves who attempted to escape their bondage. In particular he argued that "white slaves" who had been kidnapped and sent to bondage in the West Indies, should not be so treated merely for trying to regain the freedom of which they had been unjustly deprived. Joseph

Jory, representative of Nevis in London, clarified matters by saying that "white servants are not to be taken as slaves." Whereupon Northey withdrew his objection (though he did say that the application of such penalties against Africans should be approved for only a limited time, and then be subject to review as to their effects.) (*CSP, Col.*, 23:126 [1 May 1706].)

43. A reminder given by the Commissioners of Trade and Plantations in 1709. (*CSP Col.*, 24:454.)

44. *CSP, Col.*, 17:423.

45. *Acts of Assembly Passed in the Island of Nevis from 1664, to 1739, inclusive* ([London?], 1740) pp. 37–9. Alan Burns (*History of the British West Indies* [London, 1954], p. 217) says that the general rule was one European man to every ten Africans.

46. *CSP, Col.*, 13:348 (Lords of Trade and Plantations to Barbaros governor Kendall, 20 November 1690). This provision apparently was designed to prevent a repetition of the exodus of pardoned rebels from Jamaica that had been followed by a rebellion of five hundred African bond-laborers there on 29 July 1690. (*CSP Col.*, 13:315–17 [31 August 1690].)

47. Harlow says that after 1660 in Barbados the former five-to-seven years of servitude required of English bond-laborers was reduced to three or four years. The motive was the plantation owners' fear of "the slave menace." (Harlow, p. 301.) Representatives of the Barbados plantation bourgeoisie asked the king to allow one or two thousand English bond-laborers, "though but for 2 yeares service for the charge of their passage." (Irish Manuscripts Commission, *Analecta Hibernia*, No. 4 [October 1932], "Documents Relating to the Irish in the West Indies," Aubrey Gwynne SJ, collector, p. 266 [16 September 1667]. Hereafter these materials will be referred to as "Gwynne, *Analecta Hibernia*, No. 4.")

48. Dunn, p. 242, citing CO 30/2/114–25 (Barbados MSS Laws, 1645–82).

49. *CSP, Col.*, 14:446–7.

50. *Journal of the Commissioners of Trade and Plantations*, 2:63–4 (17 August 1709). *CSP, Col.*, 24:450–52 (24 August 1709).

51. *CSP, Col.*, 28:154–5.

52. Sheppard, p. 38. Philip Rowell of Christ Church Parish in Barbados was an exception; sometime around 1680 he gave five of his time-expired bond-laborers six acres of land and two lifetime bond-laborers each in order that they might avoid the common fate of beggary or dependency on parish charity. (Beckles, *White Servitude and Black Slavery*, p. 159.)

53. Sheppard, pp. 38–9, 44, 63. This unique slim volume is indispensable for the study of the subject of "race" in Anglo-America. In Barbados, where the "poor whites" were the majority of the European population, the story of the "military tenants" epitomized the marginalization of that entire class in the system of social control. If our American sociologists were to examine this phenomenon, they might find a new application for their term "underclass." An order of the Jamaica Colony Council Assembly provided that a European bond-laborer disabled in military service "shall have an able negro delivered to him forever, for his maintenance." (*CSP, Col.*, 7:474 21 March 1673.)

54. See *The Invention of the White Race*, Volume One, points 1 and 2 of "operative principles of social control in a stable civil society constituted on the basis of racial oppression," pp. 134–5.

55. Europeans made up a higher proportion of the population in Barbados than in any other British West Indies colony. For the specific reference to the majority being "poor whites" in 1680 and a century and a half later, see Sheppard, pp. 31, 63, 68. Follow the declining social career of the "poor white" majority through Sheppard's Chapter 4, "From Indentured Servants to Poor Whites (1704–1839)"; Chapter 5, "Disbandment of the Military Tenants (1839)"; and Chapter 6, "The Problems of Degeneration." Beckles's study of Barbados parishes found that "From the mid-1680s on [through 1715, the terminal year of his study] the majority of freemen were categorized by vestries as 'very poore'." (Beckles, *White Servitude and Black Slavery*, p. 159.)

Concluding her study of the "Redlegs" of Barbados, Professor Sheppard supplies a comment that may yet prove to have a wider application: "As soon also as poor whites were forced, through the removal of any special status, to mix on equal terms with their black peers, then much of their former arrogance began, albeit slowly, to disappear." (Sheppard, p. 120.)

56. The Nevis Assembly showed sensitivity to this challenge. In 1675 it made it a crime for "servants and slaves to company or drink together." (*CSP, Col.*, 9:236. Also cited by C. S. Higham, *The Development of the Leeward Islands Under the Restoration, 1660–1688: A Study of the Foundations of the Old Colonial System* [Cambridge, 1921], pp. 174–5.) Another Nevis law, passed in 1700, made it a crime for "any white Person to converse or keep Company with" "Negroes or other slaves." (*Acts of Assembly Passed in the Island of Nevis from 1664 to 1739, inclusive* [London, 1740], p. 28.) A marginal note here says "Obsolete, but re-enacted in 1717."

57. The Barbados Colony Council felt this Irish "whiteness gap" so keenly that in 1690, while urgently asking for "white servants," they excluded "Irish rebels . . .; for we want not labourers of that Colour to work for us; but men in whom we may confide, to strengthen us." (*CSP, Col.*, Vol. 13, Item 1108, cited in Sheppard, p. 35.) Perhaps they meant green.

58. The War of Devolution, 1667–68; the War of the League of Augsburg (known in England as King Billy's War), 1689–1697; the War of the Spanish Succession (known in England as Queen Anne's War), 1701–1713; and the War of the Austrian succession, 1740–48, for which England's War of Jenkin's Ear, against Spain, was a prelude.

59. See *The Invention of the White Race*, Volume One.

60. Gwynne, *Analecta Hibernia*, No. 4, p. 233.

61. Ibid., pp. 236–7.

62. Ibid., pp. 243, 245. According to an English eyewitness, during one engagement on St Kitts, the Irish in the rear of the English forces fired into the ranks of the English ahead of them. (Ibid., p. 244.) Compare this with Mountjoy's policy of putting the Irish allies in the front ranks. (*The Invention of the White Race*, 1:64.)

63. Gwynne, *Analecta Hibernia*, pp. 265–6.

64. Ibid., p. 267.

65. Ibid., pp. 278–9.

66. *CSP, Col.*, 9:236 (26 May 1675). See note 56.

67. *CSP, Col.*, 13:733 (Governor Kendal to the Lords of Trade and Plantations, 3 November 1692).

68. *Acts of Assembly Passed in the Island of Nevis from 1664, to 1739 inclusive*, pp. 35–9.

69. Gwynne, *Analecta Hibernia*, No. 4, p. 282.

70. See ibid., pp. 282–5.

71. See Fortescue's Preface to *CSP, Col.*, Sol. 16 (27 October 1697 31 December 1698), p. viii.

72. Sir John Davies, *A Discovery of the True Causes why Ireland was never entirely Subdued nor brought under Obedience of the Crowne of England, Until the Beginning of his Majesties happie Reign* (London, 1612), pp. 6–7. Cited in *The Invention of the White Race*, Volume One, p. 65.

73. Roger Norman Buckley, *Slaves in Redcoats: The British West India Regiments, 1795–1815* (New Haven, 1979), p. 124, citing Great Britain Public Record Office, WO [War Office] 1/95, Brigadier General Thomas Hislop, "Remarks" enclosed to the Duke of York, 22 July 1804.

74. Dunn, p. 181.

75. Ibid., p. 4.

76. Patterson, p. 49.

77. Ibid., p. 282, citing CO 137/19, Governor Hunter to the Board of Trade.

78. Ibid., citing CO 137/20, ff. 165, 184, 192–3.

79. Dallas pp. 9–10.

80. Long, 1:147−8.

81. Dallas, 1:1xvii.

82. Ibid., 1:19–20. Buckley, p. 9 (citing C. L. R. James, *Black Jacobins Toussaint L'Ouverture and the San Domingo Revolution*, [New York, 1963] pp. 128–9, 139–142; and Thomas O. Ott, *The Haitian Revolution, 1789–1804* [Knoxville, Tennessee, 1973], pp. 65–72, 82–3).

83. Buckley, p. 8.

84. *CSP, Col.*, 16:vii–viii.

85. Sheppard, p. 42.

86. John Luffman, *A Brief Account of Antiqua, together with the Customs and Manners of its Inhabitants, as well White as Black* (London, 1789), pp. 15, 87, 172. This work is a series of letters addressed by Luffman in Antigua to a correspondent in London during the period 1786–88.

87. The 1700 total is for Virginia, Maryland, South Carolina, and North Carolina; the 1780 total includes Georgia, which was founded as a colony in 1732. Taking the continental plantation colonies/states as a whole, from 1700 to 1860 European-Americans were never less than 60 percent of the total population. (*Historical Statistics of the United States, Colonial Times to 1970* US Department of Commerce, Bureau of the Census [Washington, DC, 1975], p. 1168, Series Z 1–19. Cohen and Greene, eds., p. 339, Table A-9 "United States, Upper and Lower South, 1790–1860.")

88. Dunn, p. 312 (Table 26). In Barbados by 1768 they were fewer than one out of six. (Sheppard, p. 43.)

89. *CSP, Col.*, 7:141 (Barbados planters in London, 14 December 1670). p. 71.

90. Dunn, pp. 198, 319. On Barbados sugar estates already in 1667, an English observer noted that skilled Negro bond-laborers were being substituted for European tradesmen, while European

workers were toiling at field work. (Harlow, *History of Barbados, 1625–1685*, p. 309, citing CO 1/21, No. 170.)

91. Douglas Hall, "Jamaica," in Cohen and Greene, eds., pp. 202–3. Hilary Beckles devotes an entire absorbing chapter to Afro-Barbadian women bond-laborers in retail trade, "Marketeers: The Right to Trade." Again and again laws were enacted designed to deny these women trading rights, but the laws proved ineffective. (Hilary McD. Beckles, *Natural Rebels: A Social History of Enslaved Black Women in Barbados* [New Brunswick, 1989] Recurring references to the ineffectiveness of the prohibitory laws are found at pp. 77, 79, 84, 86–7.) For the same activity by black women bond-laborers in Antigua, see Luffman pp. 138–41, Letter XXII, 28 March 1788.

92. Cohen and Greene, p. 339.

93. Gad J. Heuman, *Between Black and White: Race, Politics and the Free Coloreds in Jamaica, 1792–1865* (Westport, Connecticut, 1981). p. 7.

94. Handler and Sio, pp. 218–19.

95. Elsa V. Goveia, *Slave Society in the British Leeward Islands at the End of the Eighteenth Century* (New Haven, 1965), p. 312.

96. Handler and Sio, pp. 240–41. In the West Indies, the terms "freedman" or "freedwoman" strictly speaking implied that the person had once been a bond-laborer. "Free black," or Negro, was reserved for persons of presumed undiluted African descent. "Free colored," or sometimes "mulatto," was used to describe a person of mixed African and European ancestry. Such terminological differences implied important social distinctions in the West Indies. In continental Anglo-America they were not important. Except where the context requires a distinction, or where a quotation must be preserved intact, I shall feel free to use the term "freeman" or "freedwoman" to mean any non-bond-laborer in the West Indies who is of one degree or another of African ancestry.

97. Sheppard, p. 44. In continental Anglo-American colonies, by contrast, free African-Americans were excluded from trades by "white" workers, but they could do little to discourage the employers from employing African-American bond-laborers in skilled occupations. See Charles H. Wesley, *Negro Labor in the United States* (New York, 1927), pp. 69–73. See also Frederick Douglass's eloquent analysis of this peculiarity. (Frederick Douglass, *Life and Times of Frederick Douglass* [1892; New York, 1962], pp. 179–80.)

98. Heuman, p. 9. The quoted phrase is intended to apply to the British West Indies generally. (Hall, p. 202.)

99. Handler, pp. 129–30. George Pinckard, *Notes on the West Indies: Written during the Expeditions under the Command of the late General Sir Ralph Abercromby*, 3 vols., 2nd ed (London, 1803), 1:369–70.

100. See *The Invention of the White Race*, Volume One, pp. 93, 260 n. 52, and the references there to Lecky and Sullivan.

101. Hall, pp. 202–3. Handler, 126–7.

102. Heuman, p. 28.

103. There was a discrimination in favor of "whites," who were offered thirty acres. *Laws of Jamaica* (8 Geo. I, c. 1, 1:129–30.) This combination of concession and discrimination parallels the Bogland Act of 1772 in Ireland granting Catholics expanded rights to lease, but not to purchase land; and the Southern Homestead Act of 1866 in the United States allowing African-Americans only half the 160 acres allowed to whites under the Homestead Law of 1862. (See *The Invention of the White Race*, Volume One, pp. 93, 140–41.)

104. Burns, *History of the British West Indies*, p. 441.

105. Heuman, p. 84. For the total number of slaves, see Hall, p. 194.

106. Handler, pp. 68–72.

107. Buckley, pp. 11, 17–18.

108. Buckley, pp. 13, 53–5. Between 1795 and 1808 the British army in the West Indies purchased 13,400 Africans for military service, of whom 8,924 were purchased in Africa.

109. Buckley, pp. 13, 30–31, 41, 127.

110. In 1673, the Barbados authorities had tried to have the best of both possibilities. While increasing the exploitation of the African bond-laborers unrelentingly, even as they reduced their rations, the authorities sought to strengthen the militia by recruiting and arming militiamen from among these same bond-laborers. But that proved a prelude to a plot for a general African rebellion in 1675. (Dunn, pp. 257–8. Sheppard, p. 34.)

111. Buckley, p. 124. Of the African-born soldiers, who generally did not want to return to Africa, some were settled in Trinidad and Honduras, the others, willingly or otherwise, were sent

to Sierra Leone. Those who had been inducted from the West Indies, along with the youngest of those brought from Africa, remained in the West Indies. (Ibid., p. 35, citing CO 318/55.)

112. Edmund Burke, *An Account of European Settlements in America*, 2 vols. (London, 1758), 2:118, 130–31.

113. Long, 2:333–4.

114. James Ramsay, *An Essay on the Treatment and Conversion of Slaves in the British Sugar Colonies* (London, 1784), pp. 288–9. Ramsay (1733–89) served as an Episcopal priest in the West Indies on two separate occasions, but his espousal of Christian charity toward the bond-laborers earned the hostility of the planters. On his final return to England he published the *Essay*, and became associated with the abolitionist movement. (*Dictionary of National Biography*.)

115. See *The Invention of the White Race*, Volume one, p. 112.

116. Pinckard, 2:532 (emphasis in original). Pinckard's design seem to have worked out very satisfactorily for the British ruling class, at least as late as the second decade of the twentieth century. Sir Sidney Olivier, after serving as Governor of Jamaica from 1907 to 1913, was convinced that "this [mulatto] class as it at present exists is a valuable and indispensable part of any West Indies community, and that a colony of black, coloured, and whites has a far more organic efficiency and far more promise in it than a colony of black and white alone.... The graded mixed class in Jamaica helps to make an organic whole of the community and saves it from this distinct cleavage." (Sir Sidney Olivier, *White Capital and Coloured Labour* new edition, rewritten and revised [London, 1928], pp. 65–6.)

117. Beckles, *Black Rebellion in Barbados*, p. 83, citing Minutes of the Council, 1 November 1803, Barbados Archives.

118. Handler and Sio, pp. 218–19. Table 7–1. Heuman, p. 7.

119. Sheppard, p. 61.

120. Long, 2:335. See also A. E. Furness, "The Maroon War of 1795" *Jamaican Historical Review*, 5:30–45 (1965).

121. Handler, p. 205. Handler was writing about Barbados.

122. The Jamaica figures are from Heuman, p. 7. Handler and Sio, pp. 218–19, Table 7–1.

123. Heuman, p. 30.

124. Handler, pp. 148, 150. These were not merely normal "owners" of members of their own families, as might be the case in the United States. See Carter G. Woodson, *Free Negro Owners of Slaves in the United States in 1830* (Washington, 1935); Luther Porter Jackson, *Free Negro Labor and Property-Holding in Virginia, 1830–1860* (New York, 1942), p. 22.

125. Heuman, p. 29.

126. See Robin Blackburn, *The Overthrow of Colonial Slavery* (London, 1988), Chapter XI, "The Struggle for British Slave Emancipation, 1823–38,," especially pp. 421–8, 432–7, 439, 447–8, 451–2, and 454–9.

127. Hall, "Jamaica," pp. 207–8.

128. See *The Invention of the White Race*, Volume One, Chapter 4.

129. Handler and Sio, p. 238. "The event that tipped the scales in favor of ameliorative legislation was a slave revolt which broke out on the night of April 14, 1816." (Ibid., p. 234.)

"In the late eighteenth and early nineteenth centuries the Jamaican legislature passed hundreds of bills granting well-educated and well-to-do coloured individuals the perquisites of whites." (Foreword by Philip Mason to David Lowenthal, *West Indies Societies* [London, 1972], p. vi.)

13 The Invention of the White Race – and the Ordeal of America

1. Edmund Burke, *An Account of European Settlements in America*, 2 vols. (London, 1758); 2:118.

2. CO 5/1371, 150vo–151 (James City County Grievance No. 10).

3. John C. Rainbolt, "The Alteration in the Relationship between Leadership and Constitutents in Virginia, 1660–1720," *WMQ*, 27:411–34 (October 1970); p. 412.

4. John C. Rainbolt, *From Prescription to Persuasion* (Port Washington, NY, 1974), p. 97.

5. Edmund S. Morgan, *American Slavery, American Freedom: The Ordeal of Colonial Virginia* (New York, 1975), chapters 15–18, the closing section of the book.

6. "... social peace gradually arrived, according to several studies, as race, not class, separated the privileged from the unprivileged." (A. Roger Ekirch, "Exiles in the Promised Land: Convict

Labor in the Eighteenth Century Chesapeake," *Maryland Historical Magazine*, 82:95–122 [Summer 1987]; p. 96).

7. Lyon G. Tyler, "Virginians Voting in the Colonial Period," *WMQ*, ser. 1, 6:7–8 (1897–98). Tyler may also have been the author of a piece by "Lafayette," "No Feudalism in the South," in which it is stated that, "The great distinction in Virginia was color not class." *Tyler's Quarterly Historical and Genealogical Magazine*, 10:73–5, p. 74.

8. Gary B. Nash, "Colonial Development," in Jack P. Greene and J. R. Pole, eds., *Colonial British America: Essays in the New History of the Modern Era (London, 1984), pp. 244–5*.

9. Nash says that this all-class "white" unity was the result of the plantation bourgeoisie "relocating their reservoir of servile labor from . . . England and Ireland to . . . West Africa." (Nash, p. 244).

10. Russel R. Menard, *Economy and Society in Early Colonial Maryland* (New York, 1985) and David W. Galenson, *White Servitude in Colonial America: An Economic Analysis* (New York, 1981) are of particular interest in this regard. Neither seems to have taken into account the "racial quotas," deficiency laws, and laws passed in the plantation colonies to bar Negroes from skilled trades – enactments that had nothing to do with a "free market" search for skilled workers, but everything to do with maintaining "the southern labor system." See Galenson's generalization of the argument (pp. 166–8). Menard combines the assertion that "African slaves could not compete with indentured servants for the few good jobs that did exist," with a reference to "cultural barriers and the depth of racial prejudice" (p. 269). This seems at best redundant to the argument that the skilled labor shortage was the determinant of the transformation of "the labor system"; or tautological, if it is meant to explain racial discrimination in employment by reference to racially discriminatory ideas in employers' heads; and at worst it is a reversion to the "natural racism" rationale for racial slavery. A very recent review by Menard, however, seems to indicate a readiness to take a new look at the "white race." (Menard's comments appeared in *Journal of American Ethnic History*, spring 1996, pp. 57–8.) Incidentally, while my point of view and interpretation differ from those of Menard regarding historical subjects of common interest, I have never presumed to characterize his work as "tendentious,"; and I am at a loss to know why Menard thinks I have done so.

11. "Slaves . . . had none of the rising expectations that have often prompted rebellions in human history." (Morgan, p. 309.)

12. Orlando Patterson finds that the newly arriving Africans, who had been born free, were especially difficult to control. Though displaced from their native lands, their tribal stems retained a marked degree of vitality. In Jamaica in the last quarter of the seventeenth century, it was precisely they who were the most resistant, as shown in insurrections mounted by them in 1673, 1682, 1685 and 1690. Orlando Patterson, "Slavery and Slave Revolts: A Historical Analysis of the First Maroon War, 1665–1740," *Social and Economic Studies*, 19:289–325 [1970], reprinted in Richard Price, ed., *Maroon Societies: Rebel Slave Communities in the Americas* [Garden City, NY, 1973], pp. 246–92; 255–8.)

13. Thomas Roderick Dew (1802–46), Professor of History and Political Law at William and Mary College and the thirteenth president of that institution, set forth this inversion of the cause and effect of "white solidarity" and racial slavery. Because of the imposition of lifetime hereditary bondage on African-Americans, he said, "there is at once taken away the greatest cause for distinction and separation of the ranks of ["white"] society." (Thomas Roderick Dew, *The Pro-Slavery Argument* [Charleston, South Carolina, 1852; Negro Universities reprint, 1968], p. 461.)

14. See p. 235.

15. Thomas N. Ingersoll, ed., "'Releese us out of this Cruell Bondegg': An appeal from Virginia in 1723," *WMQ*, 3d ser., 51:777–82. The author of this letter did not reveal his or her name for fear of being put to death if identified. There is some reason to believe, as Ingersoll points out, that the letter was a collective effort. The date of the letter is 8 September 1723, but there are indications that it may have been composed over a period of days.

16. West served as counsel to the Board of Trade from 1718 to 1725. Soon thereafter he assumed the office of Chancellor of Ireland, but survived there only a year. George Chalmers, comp. and ed., *Opinions of Eminent Lawyers on Various Points of English Jurisprudence chiefly concerning the Colonies, Fisheries, and Commerce*, 2 vols. (London, 1814; Burt Franklin Reprint, 1971, from the original edition in the Brooklyn Public Library), p. xxxiii.

17. Hening, 4: 133–4.

18. Chalmers, 2:113–14.

19. Alured Popple, Secretary to the Board of Trade, to Governor William Gooch of Virginia, 18 December 1735 (CO 5/1366, pp. 134–5). Although West made his report in January 1724, it was

eleven years later that the objection came to the attention of the Board of Trade, who then instructed Popple to ask for an explanartion from Gooch. There is as yet no accounting for the board's long delay in taking up the matter with the Virginia government. (See Emory G. Evans, ed., "A Question of Complexion," *VMHB*, 71:411–13 [1963].) Is it possible that Bishop Edmund Gibson played some part in getting particular attention paid to the question after receiving the African-American appeal for freedom sent from Virginia in 1723? (See p. 241, n. 15).

20. CO 5/1324, ff. 19, 22. The Gooch quotations in the following paragraph are from this same document.

21. Along with Catholics who refused to conform to the Protestant way, "and others not being Christians," Negroes were "incapable of in law, to be witnesses in any cases whatsoever" under terms of the Virginia code of 1795 (Hening, 3:298). It may be speculated that Gooch's choice of words here implicitly referred to that law. But Gooch must have been aware that in 1723, and again in 1732, this loophole was closed by making it possible for African-Americans to give evidence in trials of other African-Americans for rebellion or other capital offenses. (Hening, 4:127 [1723], 327 [1732]).

22. The contrast between the denial of middle-class status to persons of any degree of African descent and the middle-class role of mulattos and free blacks in the Caribbean was occasionally dramatized in the Virginia courts. In 1688, on the cusp of King Billy's War, John Servele (the name is variously spelled), a "molatto" born in St Kitts of a French father and a free Negro mother and duly baptized there, through a series of misadventures was sold into Virginia where he was claimed as a lifetime bond-laborer by a succession of owners. In consideration of testimonials from the Governor of St Kitts and a Jesuit priest there, and the fact that Servele had already served more than seven years, the Governor and Council ordered that Servele be released and given his "corn and cloathes" freedom dues. (*Norfolk County Records, 1686–95, (Orders),* pp. 107, 115, 17 September and 15 November 1688.) Another man, Michael Roderigo, a native of St Domingue, likewise a victim of misadventures that ended with him being sold as a lifetime bond-laborer in Virginia, took advantage of a lull in the Anglo-French warring to petition the Virginia Colony Council for his freedom. In support of his claim as "a Christian and a free subject of France," he proposed to call as a witness a Virginia plantation owner "who hath bought slaves" from him in Petit Guaves, St Domingue. (Virginia Colony Council proceedings, 22 February 1699/1700. Library of Congress, Virginia [Colony] Collection, 80–75775.)

23. It would be another half-century before James Madison, speaking as a member of the Virginia Council of State, would propose, though unpersuasively, that freedmen were readily absorbed into the system of control over bond-laborers. Replying to the idea of inducing "whites" to join the "fight for freedom" by giving each one an African-American lifetime bond-laborer, Madison suggested a more direct approach to recruitment: "would it not be as well," he said, "to liberate and make soldiers at once of [those] blacks themselves as to make them instruments for enlisting white Soldiers?" He reassured doubters that this course would constitute no danger to the institution of slavery, "experience having shown that a freedman immediately loses all attachment & sympathy for his former fellow slaves." (William T. Hutchinson and William M. E. Rachle, eds., *The Papers of James Madison,* 9 vols. [Chicago, 1962]; 2:198–201, 209–11; the cited passage is at page 209 [Correspondence with Joseph Jones, 24 and 28 November 1780]. See also *Journal of the [Virginia] House of Delegates, 1777–1780* [Richmond, 1827], pp. 56, 64, 65, 67, 98, 100, 105, 113, 116, 119, cited by Robert E. Brown and B. Katherine Brown, *Virginia 1705–1786, Democracy or Aristocracy?* [East Lansing, 1964], p. 68).

24. "Instead of creating problems, the union of a white man and a Negro woman was sometimes considered a judicious mingling of business with pleasure." (Brown and Brown, p. 68). Thomas Jefferson's considered opinion on the subject of "breeding women" was that "a child raised every 2 years is of more profit than the crop of the best laboring man." "What [such a] mother produces," he wrote, "is an addition to capital, while his labors disappear in mere consumption." (Jefferson, letters to William Yancey, 17 January 1819, and to W. Eppes, 30 June 1820; cited in William Cohen, "Thomas Jefferson and the Problem of Slavery," *Journal of American History,* 16:518 [1969].)

25. Hening, 3:87–8 (1691).

26. See Appendix II-F.

27. "In regard to the Reasons you have offered in behalf of the Act we shall let that Act lie by." (Board of Trade to Gooch, 15 October 1736 CO 5/1366, p. 137.)

28. *CSP, Col.,* 16:390–91.

29. CO 5/1363 Jennings to Commissioners for Trade and Plantations, 24 April 1710. See also Virginia State Archives, "Colonial Papers' collection, folder 20, items 11, 13, 14.

30. *Journals of the House of Burgesses of Virginia, 1619–1777,* edited by H. R. McIlwaine and J.

P. Kennedy, 13 vols. (Richmond, 1905–15); volume for 1702 to 1712, p. 240. Cited by Brown and Brown, p. 70.

31. See p. 219.

32. *CSP, Col.* 36:114, Gooch to the Board of Trade, 29 June 1729.

33. *American Historical Review*, 1:88–90 (1895, "Documents" [No.1]). Byrd to Lord Egmont. One may speculate that his reference to a man of "desperate fortune" was in memory of Nathaniel Bacon, whose rebellion Byrd's father had first urged on, and then abandoned when the English and Negro bond-laborers enlisted in it.

34. *Legislative Journal of the Council of Colonial Virginia*, 3 vols., edited by H. R. McIlwaine (Richmond, 1918), 2:1034–35 (11 April 1749). An estimated 30,000 convict bond-laborers were sent to America in 190 shiploads between 1717 and 1772. Of these cargoes, 100 went to the Chesapeake, 53 to Maryland and 47 to Virginia. (Arthur Price Middleton, *Tobacco Coast: A Maritime History of Chesapeake Bay in the Colonial Era* [Newport News, 1953], p. 152.)

35. Thomas J. Wertenbaker, *Patrician and Plebeian in Virginia, or the Origin and Development of the Social Classes of the Old Dominion* (New York, 1910, 1958, 1959). Idem, *The Planters of Colonial Virginia* (Princeton, 1922; New York, 1959). The "Middle Class," to whom Wertenbaker devotes Part Two of the former work, is called "the Virginia yeomanry" in the latter (pp. 137, 160).

See Chapter 2 above for a discussion of the "forty-shilling freeholder."

36. One historian drew the line between those who inherited any wealth at all and those who inherited none: "Herein lay the contrast between the two classes often but erroneously confused, the "poor whites" and the yeomen." (Ulrich Bonnell Phillips, *Life and Labor in the Old South* (Boston, 1929), p. 346). Another, Edmund S. Morgan, states that a man qualified as a yeoman if he owned land, (Morgan, p. 377.)

37. Robert E. and B. Katherine Brown reject such a definition of interests. After observing unselfconsciously that, "Slavery was profitable, it enabled a man to live with a minimum of physical labor," they conclude with the self-standing assertion that: "Protection of slave property was of constant and vital concern to all classes of the white population…. [Slavery] definitely set off the white man as the master in society, and it did create a lower class – which could be exploited by the master race." (Brown and Brown, p. 77).

38. Allan Kulikoff, *Tobacco and Slaves: The Development of Southern Cultures in the Chesapeake, 1680–1800* (Chapel Hill, 1986), p.262. Taking estates in personalty as the index, Aubrey Land says that the "great planters … never formed more than a fraction of the total community of planters, something like 2.5 percent in the decade 1690–1699 and about 6.5 percent half a century later." (Aubrey C. Land, "Economic Behavior in a Planting Society: The Eighteenth-century Chesapeake," *Journal of Southern History*, 33:469–85; pp. 472–3.)

39. These latter constituted the self-perpetuating ruling bourgeois elite. "The wealthiest planters and planter-merchants," writes Kulikoff, "dominated local [County Court) benches and provincial legislatures from the 1650s to the Revolution…. By 1705, three-fifths of Virginians who owned two thousand or more acres of land were justices or burgesses." (Kulikoff, p.268.)

In Virginia over the period 1720 to 1776, 630 men held seats in the House of Burgesses. Of this number, 110 dominated the proceedings of the House by virtue of their committee positions in that body. Of that 110, three out of four each owned more than 10,000 acres of land. With regard to the extent of their holdings of lifetime bond-laborers, eleven held more than 300 each; 25 held from 50 to 300; 25 held from 50 to 300 each; and 22 others held more than ten. (Jack P. Greene, "Foundations of Political Power in the Virginia House of Burgesses," *WMQ*, ser. 3, 16:485–506; pp. 485–8.) A tabulation of the population and the voting in seven Virginia counties in the period 1783–90 shows a total population of 80,893, including 45,111 "whites". Free "white" males sixteen years of age and over numbered 11,084, of whom 4,242 were owners of the 25 acres required of qualified voters. (Charles S. Sydnor, *Gentlemen Freeholders: Political Practices in Washington's Virginia*, Chapel Hill, 1952, pp. 141–3.)

40. Kulikoff, p. 268, While this definition of "yeoman" is more elastic than my standard for "middle class", and Kulikoff's "above half" may be on the high side of the estimates by Land and Main given below, it has the virtue of being related to ownership of lifetime bond-laborers.

41. Ibid., p.262. See also the half-dozen authorities cited by Kulikoff there. With regard to the yeomen's credit dependency on the gentry, see ibid., pp. 288–9.

42. Aubrey C. Land, "Economic Base and Social Structure; The Northern Chesapeake in the Eighteenth Century," *Journal of Economic History*, 25:639–54 (1965); p. 641. Although this study is limited to Maryland, Land believes that "differences between the areas [of the Chesapeake] are not very great" in respect to the thesis he presents.

43. Ibid., pp. 642–3.

44. Ibid., p. 648. See also my comments on eighteenth-century tenancy on pp. 104–5.

45. See *The Invention of the White Race*, Volume One, pp. 122–3.

46. Land, "Economic Base and Social Structure," p. 653.

47. Ibid., pp. 643–4.

48. Ibid., p. 644.

49. Ibid., pp. 644, 654.

50. Jackson Turner Main, "The Distribution of Property in Post-Revolutionary Virginia," *Mississippi Valley Historical Review*, 41:241–58 (1954–55). (The name of this publication was later changed to *The Journal of American History*.) See also Jackson T. Main, *The Social Structure of Revolutionary America* (Princeton, 1965), esp Chapter II, "The Economic Class Structure of the South."

51. Main, "Distribution of Property," p. 258.

52. Jackson Turner Main, "Distribution of Property," pp. 241, 242–3, 248. The "Northern Neck," the area between the Potomac and the Rappahannock rivers, had double the proportion of landless, and of these most were laborers, not tenants. (Ibid., p. 248.) See also Gloria L. Main's study of probate records of Virginia and Maryland, "Inequality in Early America: The Evidence from Probate Records of Massachusetts and Maryland," *Journal of Interdisciplinary History*, 7:559–81; 570–2, 580.

Brown and Brown, p. 31 n. 142, refer to the contrast between their view and that of Jackson T. Main with regard to laboring-class expectations. However, they do not make any effort to challenge Main's thesis. But also compare D. Alan Williams, "The Small Farmer in Eighteenth-century Virginia Politics," *Agricultural History*, 43:91–101 (1969).

53. Not more than 49 percent of the total adult white male population were landowners. The large-owner one-fifth, plus three-fourths of the middle-size landowners' two-thirds share of the total number of landowners, would make up a total of 70 percent as the approximate proportion of landowners who were also owners of lifetime bond-laborers, and that would represent less than 35 percent of the total adult white male population. Main does not even suggest any statistically significant employment of bond-labor by owners of one hundred acres or less. Taking into account Main's mention of the ownership of bond-laborers by non-landowners, I have attempted to make a generous discount for that factor in setting the proportion of non-owners of bond-labor at around 60 percent of the total adult white male population.

54. Kulikoff, p. 262.

55. Governor Notley's words of advice. See pp. 221–2.

56. The coincidence of names is not accidental. This Nathaniel Bacon and Sir Francis had a common ancestor; Nathaniel's great-grandfather and Sir Francis were first cousins. It is also interesting to note that Nathaniel Bacon's grandfather, also named Nathaniel, was an artist and a republican writer during the time of Cromwell. ("The Bacons of Virginia," *New England Historical and Genealogical Register*, 37:189–98 [1883]; p. 197.)

57. Francis Bacon, Essay No. 15, "Of Seditions and Troubles," in *Works*, 6:406–12. The slavocracy's most eminent "theoretician" well understood the premise of that strategy. "The dominant party," he said, "can only be overturned by concert and harmony among the subject party." (Thomas Roderick Dew, *An Essay on Slavery* [Richmond, 1849], p. 103.)

58. Morgan, p. 328. Ira Berlin appears to endorse Morgan on this point. "Chesapeake planters," he writes, "consolidated their class position by asserting white racial unity." (Ira Berlin, "Time, Space, and the Evolution of Afro-American Society on British Mainland North America," *American Historical Review*, 85:44–78 [1980]; p. 72.

59. Philip Alexander Bruce, *Social Life in Virginia in the Seventeenth Century, An Inquiry into the Origin of the Higher Plantation Class, Together with an Account of the Habits, Customs and Diversions of the People* (Richmond, 1902), pp. 137–8.

60. H. M. Henry, *Police Control in South Carolina* (Emory, 1914), pp. 190–91. Henry asks rhetorically whether the poor whites cooperated with the slaveholders because they perceived that a threat was posed by African-Americans to "their personal security and that of their families." (Ibid.) He does not attempt to sustain this speculation. If they were worried on that score why would they encourage the expansion of the system by providing security for the large planters?

61. Hening 3:87–8. In such cases the emancipator was required to pay for the exiling of the freed person within six months, or else to pay a £10 fine which would be used to pay for the freed person's transportation out of Virginia as arranged by the church wardens of the parish.

62. *Norfolk County Wills*, p. 26. *Executive Journals of the Council of Colonial Virginia*, edited by H. R. McIlwaine (Richmond, 1928), 3:332. The Colony Council justified this unprecedented

infringement of testamentary rights on the grounds that the increase in the number of free Negroes would "endanger the peace of this Colony" by encouraging the freedom aspirations of others held in bondage.

63. Hening, 2:117–18 (1662). In Maryland, also in 1705, laws were passed to guarantee "white" servants against abuse and against being detained in servitude beyond their time, and declaring that "Negroes [were] Slaves during their Naturall Lives nor freed by Baptisme." (CO 7/15, pp. 14, 15. Report of Governor John Seymour, 3 July 1705, to the Board of Trade on laws passed in Maryland that year.) Bond-laborer Margaret Godfrey sought in vain to claim the protection of her "white" status by defiantly telling her overseer, "If you whip me it will be worse for you for I am not a Slave." The overseer, with the express leave of the mistress, cut Godfrey's clothes from her body and beat her severely two successive times. Her offense had been to plead for humane treatment for her severely injured husband. The Godfreys' petition for relief was rejected by the Court. (*St George's County Records*, HH, pp. 165–8 [June 1748]. Maryland State Archives, Annapolis.)

64. Hening, 3:448 (1705).

65. Hening, 3:449

66. Hening, 4:351.

67. Hening, 3:103, 459–60. As noted in Chapter 12, throughout the British West Indies it was customary for even bond-laborers to earn money by marketing goods produced on plots of land allowed them whereby they might buy themselves out of bondage. Hilliard d'Auberville proposed, among other measures to control the bond-laborers of St Domingue, "to give them wives, encourage them to raise cattle, hold them with ties of property." (Hilliard d'Auberville, *Considérations sur l'état présent de la colonie française de St Domingue*, 2 vols. [Paris, 1776–77]; 2:59–62. Cited in Gwen Midlo Hall, *Social Control in Slave Plantation Societies: A Comparison of St Domingue and Cuba*, [Baltimore, 1971], p. 83.)

68. Hening, 2:267 (1668).

69. Hening, 2:280–81 (1670).

70. Hening, 3:251 (1705).

71. Hening, 3:298 (1705); 4:327 (1732).

72. Hening, 3:459 (1705).

73. Hening, 4:119 (1723).

74. Hening, 4:130 (1723). A provision was made for free African-American "householders", and any free African-American who lived on a "frontier plantation" and was able to secure a license from a justice of the peace, to keep one gun and the powder and shot needed for it.

75. See *The Invention of the White Race*, Volume One, p. 89. "The white man's pursuit of black women frequently destroyed any possibility that comely black girls could remain chaste for long," writes Blassingame. According to autobiographies of former bond-laborers, the home of a bond-laborer was "considered by many white men ... as a house of ill-fame." (John W. Blassingame, *Plantation Life in the Ante-Bellum South* [New York, 1972], p. 82.)

76. Philip J. Schwarz, *Twice Condemned: Slaves and the Criminal Laws of Virginia, 1705–1865* (Baton Rouge, 1988), p. 159.

77. "A white man may go to the house of a free black, maltreat and abuse him, and commit any outrage upon his family, for all of which the law cannot reach him, unless some white person saw the act committed." Thus observed Mr Wilson of Perquimon County, speaking at the 1835 North Carolina State Constitutional Convention of 1835. (John S. Bassett, *Slavery in the State of North Carolina* [Baltimore, 1899], bound as one of a number of studies in Bassett, *Slavery in the United States, Selected Essays* [New York: Negro Universities Press, 1969], p. 42.)

78. Hening, 3:447–62, 4:126–34 (emphasis added). The citations of these laws that follow are from Hening.

79. Ulrich Bonnell Phillips spoke of "the methods of life which controlled the history of Virginia through the following centuries and of the many colonies and states which borrowed her plantation system." This was "Dixie," where, he said, "the white folk [are] a people with a common resolve indomitably maintained – that it shall be and remain a white man's country." (Ulrich Bonnell Phillips, *The Slave Economy of the Old South: Selected Essays in Economic and Social History*, edited by Eugene D. Genovese [Baton Rouge, 1968], pp. 8, 274. The dates of these pronouncements were 1910–11 and 1918, respectively.)

80. Winthrop D. Jordan, *White Over Black: American Attitudes Toward the Negro, 1550–1812* (Chapel Hill, 1968), p. 123. I find Jordan's observation accurate and very pertinent, but I have appropriated it for an argument that he does not support. His "unthinking decision" approach to the origin of racial slavery rejects Morgan's (and my) attribution of deliberate ruling-class manipulation for social control purposes.

81. Wertenbaker, *Patrician and Plebeian*, p. 212.

82. Hening, 4:202.

83. Schwarz, p. 13.

84. Brown and Brown, p. 48.

85. Warren B. Smith, *White Servitude in the Colony of South Carolina* (Columbia, 1961), p. 30. The American Revolution wrought no difference in this respect. Seventy-five years later "[p]oor white men habitually kept their eyes open for strange Negroes without passes, for the apprehension of a fugitive was a financial windfall … [W]hite workingmen on the Baltimore and Susquehanna Railroad caught several Maryland bondsmen who had escaped to within five miles of the Pennsylvania border. The workingmen returned them to their owners and collected the reward." (Kenneth M. Stampp, *The Peculiar Institution: Slavery in the Ante-Bellum South* [New York, 1956], p.153.)

86. Basset, *Slavery in the State of North Carolina*, pp. 29–30.

87. Smith, pp. 30–31. Other variations of the same quota principle were enacted.

88. Ibid., p. 35.

89. Elizabeth Dorman, ed., *Documents Illustrative of the Slave Trade to America*, 4 vols. (Washington, DC, 1935), 4:595 (1739), 605 (1742).

90. Ibid., 4:610. See also Klaus G. Loewald, Beverley Starika and Paul S. Taylor, eds., "Johann Martin Bolzius Answers a Questionnaire on Carolina and Georgia," *WMQ*, ser. 3, 14:218–261 (1957); pp. 227, 242.

91. "Irish-Americans [arriving in the United States in the ante-bellum period] were not the originators of white supremacy; they adapted to and were adopted into an already existing 'white' American social order." (*The Invention of the White Race*, Volume One, p. 199.)

92. Ulrich Bonnell Phillips, "The Slave Labor Problem in the Charleston District," *Political Science Quarterly*, 22:416–39 (1907); reprinted in Phillips, *Slave Economy of the Old South*, p. 198.

93. Richard B. Morris, *Government and Labor in Early America* (New York, 1946), p. 182.

94. James Hugo Johnston, *Race Relations in Virginia and Miscegenation in the South, 1776–1860* (Amherst, Massachusetts, 1970), p. 58, citing *Archives of Virginia, Legislative Papers*, petitions: 9789, Culpeper, 9 December 1831; 9860, Dinwiddie, 20 December 1831; 177707, Norfolk, 12 November 1851). It would seem relevant to note that the first two of these petitions were submitted in the wake of Nat Turner's Rebellion and during the Virginia House of Delegates' debate on slavery. (See Theodore William Allen, "'… They Would Have. Destroyed Me': Slavery and the Origins of Racism," *Radical America*, 9:41–63 (1975); pp. 58–9.)

95. For this aspect of the question, see the Introduction in Volume One of *The Invention of the White Race*, pp. 4–14, "The Psycho-cultural Argument."'

96. Edmund Burke, *Writings and Speeches*, 12 vols. (London, 1803). 2:123–4.

97. Dew, *Essay on Slavery*, p. 99.

98. Morgan, p. 376. The general term "Virginians" is used by Morgan to mean "white" people in Virginia. In the concluding Chapter 18 the term appears some twenty-two times, but only twice is it modified by "white". Morgan's imposition of this "white" assumption on the reader, objectionable in itself, more importantly conforms with his treatment of the African-Americans as mere background to the rise of "liberty and equality."

99. Ibid., p. 380.

100. Ibid., p. 364.

101. Ibid., pp. 366, 369.

102. Ibid., p. 386.

103. See page 240.

104. Hutchinson and Rachel, eds., *The Papers of James Madison*, 2:209.

105. Letter from "Civis," an eastern Virginia slaveholder, in the *Richmond Enquirer*, 4 May 1832.

106. Edmund S. Morgan, "Slavery and Freedom, The American Paradox," *Journal of American History*, June 1972, pp. 5–6.

107. Morgan, *American Slavery, American Freedom*, pp. 386, 387.

108. Wertenbaker, *Planters of Colonial Virginia*, p.160.

109. See pp. 245–7, particularly the summary on p. 247.

110. Marquis de Chastellux, *Travels in North-America in the Years 1780, 1781, and 1782*, translated by an English gentleman who resided in America at that period, 2 vols., 2nd edn. (London 1787; 1968 reprint), 2:190.

111. See p. 255.

112. Wertenbaker, *Patrician and Plebeian*, p. 211.

113. "[T]here existed a numerous supply of potential tenants … from that group of small planters

who, in consequence of the trifling quantity of poor tobacco produced on their overworked land in the east, could not successfully compete with a large amount of excellent tobacco grown on the fresh land of the great planters. Faced with impoverishment they looked to the more fertile lands of the Piedmont and Valley as a means of bettering their condition." (Willard F. Bliss, "The Rise of Tenancy in Virginia,"*VMHB* 58:427–442 (1950).

114. Kulikoff, pp. 150, 152, 153, 296, 297–8. See also pp. 104–5.

115. George W. Summers of Kanawha County, speaking in the Virginia House of Delegates, during the debate on slavery, following Nat Turner's Rebellion (*Richmond Enquirer*, 2 February 1832).

116. "[T]he 'warlike Christian men' recruited by Virginia to defend its borders in 1701 were the direct ancestors of the dragoons whose Colts and Winchesters subdued the Sioux of the Great Plains a century and a half later." (Ray Allen Billington, *America's Frontier Heritage* [New York, 1966], p. 40.) The interior quotation is from an Act passed by the Virginia Assembly in August 1701, designed to encourage English frontier settlers (Hening, 3:207).

117. Frederick Jackson Turner, *The Frontier in American History* (New York, 1920; 1947), p. 38.

118. Ibid., p. 1. A century has passed since that first essay, and Turner's frontier thesis continues to be meat and drink for historiographical evaluation and disputation. But a marked tendency has been apparent to limit the "frontier" concept, reducing it to a Western regional subject, which of course risks "abandonment of the cross-regional and national emphasis he [Turner] sought to establish for the field" (William Cronon, cited in John Mack Farragher, "The Frontier Trail: Rethinking Turner and Reimagining the American West," *American Historical Review*, 98:106–17 [1993], p. 117). Since the 1960s, critics have shown a welcome sensitivity to Turner's neglect of Indians, Mexicans and Chinese or, worse, his chauvinistic attitude toward them. Finally, in 1995, a reference was made to Turner's pervasive "whiteness," the significant fact that "his own racial identity was a completely foreign concept to him" (Patricia Nelson Limerick, "Turnerians All: The Dream of a Helpful History in an Intelligible World," *American Historical Review*, 100:697–716 [1995], p. 715).

119. Turner, p. 38.

120. Ibid., pp. 280–81.

121. Ibid., p. 321.

122. James C. Malin, *Essays on Historiography* (Lawrence, Kansas, 1946, p. 38, cited in Harry Nash Smith, *Virgin Land* (Cambridge, 1950), p. 302.

123. The free-land "safety valve" theory at one time was the subject of extensive debate among economic, labor and land historians. Its limitations, even in its own white-blind terms, as an explanation of the low level of proletarian class-consciousness were forcefully pointed out decades ago by such historians as Carter Goodrich, Sol Davison, Murray Kane, and Fred A. Shannon, whose names are prominent in the extensive bibliography of the "safety valve" controversy. Subsequently it could only be defended in a greatly watered-down form of the original Turner formulation. See Ray Allen Billington, *The American Frontier Thesis: Attack and Defense* (Washington, DC, 1971, pp. 20–25, and idem, *America's Frontier Heritage*, pp. 31–8, 292–3.

124. I borrow here the title of a well-known work of William Appleman Williams, *The Contours of American History* (New York, 1988; originally published in 1966).

125. See *The Invention of the White Race*, Volume One, pp. 145–7, 152–7, 184–6, 195–7, 198–9.

Appendix II-A

1. Richard Price, ed., *Maroon Societies: Rebel Slave Communities in the Americas* (New York, 1973), pp. 1, 3.

2. Jose L. Franco, "Maroons and Slave Rebellions in the Spanish Territories," in Price, ed., p. 47, 48.

3. David M. Davidson, "Negro Slave Control and Resistance in Colonial Mexico, 1519–1659," in Price, ed., p. 91.

4. Ibid., pp. 96–7.

5. Aquiles Escalante, "Palenques in Colombia," in Price, ed., pp. 77–9.

6. Price, ed., pp. 20, 33; Franco, p. 41.

7. Roger Bastide, "The Other Quilombos," in Price, ed., pp. 191–2.

8. R. K. Kent, "Palmares: An African State in Brazil," in Price, ed., p. 172.

9. Ibid., pp. 179, 185, 187.
10. Ibid., pp. 177, 178–80, 183, 185.
11. Ibid., pp. 180–81.
12. Price, ed., "Introduction," p. 20.
13. Kent, p. 172.

Appendix II-B

1. No one, then or since, could know within any great degree of exactitude the proportion of the English population destroyed by the plague. The lowest estimate seems to be 20 percent. (Josiah Cox Russell, "Demographic Patterns in History," Population Studies, No. 1, 1948; cited in Cambridge Economic History of Europe, 4:612.) The same economic historians say the toll was one-third to half of the population. James E. Rogers, in The Economic Interpretation of History (London, 1889), says it was one-third (p. 263). George M. Trevelyan says three-eighths of the people perished (A Shortened History of England [New York, 1942] p. 192).
2. Rogers, p. 22.
3. H. S. Bennett says that, even before 1348, "once the serf made up his mind to run away, it was difficult to restrain him." (H. S. Bennett, Life on the English Manor [London, 1948], p. 306.) See also Charles Oman, The Great Revolt of 1381 (Oxford, 1906), pp. 8–9.
4. This discussion of the revolt of 1381 is based mainly on Oman, The Great Revolt and R. B. Dobson, The Peasants Revolt of 1381 (London, 1970).
5. Oman, p. 1.
6. Ibid., p. 56.
7. Ibid., p. 64.
8. "Anonimal Chronical"; cited by Oman, pp. 200–201.
9. Dobson, p. 25.
10. Ibid., p. 30.
11. Rogers, p. 82.

Appendix II-D

1. Philip A. Bruce, Economic History of Virginia in the Seventeenth Century, 2 vols. (New York, 1895; reprint, 1935), 2:15.
2. James C. Ballagh, White Servitude in the Colony of Virginia, A Study of the System of Indentured Labor in the American Colonies (Baltimore, 1895; 1969 reprint), pp. 75–6.
3. Eugene I. McCormac, White Servitude in Maryland, 1634–1824 (Baltimore, 1904) p. 75.
4. Lewis C. Gray, assisted by Esther K. Thompson, History of Agriculture in the Southern United States to 1860, 2 vols. (Washington, DC, 1932) 1:506.
5. Richard B. Morris, Government and Labor in Early America, (New York, 1946), p. 484.
6. McCormac, pp. 61, 72–5.
7. A. E. Smith, Colonists in Bondage: White Servitude and Convict Labor in America, 1607–1776, p. 204. In considering Smith's conclusions cited here, one must keep in mind that his book dealt with bond-servitude in all Anglo-American colonies during the entire colonial period of the seventeenth and eighteenth centuries, whereas the present work is concerned with bond-servitude in the continental colonies, and particularly the seventeenth-century tobacco colonies, Virginia and Maryland.
8. Ibid., pp. 254, 258–60.
9. Russel R. Menard, Economy and Society in Early Colonial Maryland (New York, 1985), pp. 190–91. David W. Galenson, a University of Chicago economics professor, brings "bottom-line" logic to bear: "it would be surprising if severe physical abuse had been very common, for it would have interfered with the servants' work capacity, to the detriment of their masters' profits." "The Rise and Fall of Indentured Servitude in the Americas: An Economic Analysis," Journal of Economic History, 44:1–126 [1984]; p. 8. Galenson's argument on this point is essentially the same as that made by South Carolina governor Hammond and by George Fitzhugh in justification of slavery in the ante-bellum period. (See Volume One, p. 163.)

10. Edmund S. Morgan, *American Slavery, American Freedom: The Ordeal of Colonial Virginia* (New York, 1975) pp. 63–8.

11. Russell R. Menard, commenting on his own finding of a wide gap between life expectancy of immigrant Marylanders and men born in New England in the seventeenth century, does suggest that "This wide regional variation in mortality might prove a useful reference point for scholars concerned with differences in the social history of New England and the Chesapeake colonies." (*Economy and Society in Early Colonial Maryland*, p. 140.)

See Chapter 9 for further discussion of the New England contrast.

12. See Gloria L. Main, "Inequality in Early America: The Evidence from Probate Records of Massachusetts and Maryland, *"Journal of Interdisciplinary History*, 7:559–81 (1977),

13. Morris, pp. 282–3.

14. Ibid., p. 482.

Appendix II-E

1. Leslie A. Clarkson, *The Pre-industrial Economy of England, 1500*, New York, 1972, pp. 26–7.

2. Eleanora Mary Carus-Wilson, ed., *Essays in Economic History*, 3 vols. (London, 1962), 2:299.

3. Clarkson, pp. 26–7.

4. George M. Trevelyan, *Blenheim*, pp. 113, 216, 218.

5. Ibid., pp. 216–18.

6. Leo Francis Stock, ed., *Proceedings and Debates of the British Parliaments Respecting North America*, 5 vols. (Washington, DC, 1924), 1:343, n.

7. Cited in Klaus E. Knorr, *British Colonial Theories, 1570–1850* (Toronto, 1944), p. 72.

8. Roger Coke, *A Treatise Wherein is demonstrated that the Church and State of England are in equal danger with the trade of it,* p. 16. Cited in C. H. Hull, ed., *The Economic Writings of Sir William Petty* (London, 1899; 1963 reprint), 1:242, n.

9. William Petty, *Political Arithmetick,* in Hull, ed., pp. 293, 301–2.

Appendix II-F

1. Hening, 3:181.

2. Hening, 3:229–481.

3. CO 5/1356 (emphasis added). These instructions were addressed to Governor Effingham in 1684.

4. Hening, 2:117–18 (1662); 3:448 (1705).

5. Hening, 3:449.

6. Virginia State Archives, "Colonial Papers," folder 17, item 13. "Amendments proposed by the Council to the Bill entituled and concerning Servants and Slaves." [17 May 1706].

7. Hening, 3:459.

8. CO 391/16, f. 357, 1–2 March 1703/4.

9. CO 391/8.

10. Virginia State Archives, "Colonial Papers," folder 15, item 17. See also CO 5/1361, f. 46, 28 November 1704.

11. CO 391/7.

12. See CO 5/1312, Part 1, ff. 303, 305–11; and part 2, ff. 1–4, 202, 205–6, 228; and CO 5/1313, ff. 83, 249–55.

Index

Abbot, Elizabeth 96
Abolition 237, 253, 303n66
absentee landlords 322nn59–61
Accomack County 157, 161, 166, 180, 350n22: plot 155, 350n51
"Act concerning Servants and Slaves" (1705) 250–1: and establishment of racial oppression and "white race" 272–4; as ruling class manipulation 253
Act "directing the trial of Slaves … and for the better government of Negroes, Mulattos, and Indians bond or free" (1723) as deliberate act of racial oppression 241–2, 250–51
Act for Trade with Indians (1691) 361n94
Act of Assembly (1661) 163
Act of Union of England and Scotland (1707) 372n2
act repealing ban on slavery in Georgia (1750) 253
adultery 129, 311n91, 341n85, 341n89
Adventurers 53–4, 63–4, 109, 206, 322n60
African-American bond-laborers: abuse of 141, 346n183, 346n188; barter by 345n167; bastardy laws and 134; joint struggle with European-American bond-laborers against bondage 148–62, 188, for freedom in Bacon's Rebellion 211, 248, 369n93; denied right to bear arms 199; Elizabeth Key case 194–9; evangelical issues 191–2; John Punch case 178–80; livestock confiscated 250; marriage 134, 341n77, 343n126; not motivated by anti-Indian interests 205, 353n23; number of 123–4, 211, 339n40; owners prohibited from setting free 249, 382n61; plots 219, 242; rebelliousness of 363n118, 223; reduction to lifetime bond-servitude: preceded by chattel bond-servitude of European-Americans 323n67, pressure to reduce to 123–4, 187–8, challenged 180, 188–91, 193; in skilled positions 377n97; threat of alliance with French 363n121, with Indians 42;

Virginia-born 123–4; Washburn ignores 363n4; "white identity" and keeping down 249
African-Americans: arrival in Virginia 81, 327n23, 327n24, 357n15; barred from bearing witness 250; buyers and sellers 181; in center of economic history of hemisphere 9; challenge hereditary bondage 188–91; class character of 148; in contracts and wills 180–81, 187–8; in court 180; denial of rights 249–51, 339n39, 382–3n62; and social mobility 179; excluded from militia 250; excluded from trades 377n97; exclusion of, as corollary of "white" identity 249; forbidden from owning: Christians 250, "horses, cattle, and hoggs" 310n84; free 233, 250, 359n46, 372n2, women declared tithable 187, 190, 250, 359n40; and gun licenses 250, 383n74; and intermarriage 310n84, 359n40; and importation of bond-laborers 183; laborers' rights undercut 362n103; landholding, historical significance of 182–6; law against free female "anticipates racial oppression" 187; loss of voting rights 242; not motivated by anti-Indian sentiment 205, 353n23; opposition to racial oppression of, by elements of propertied class 193–6; as owners of European-American bond-laborers 186–7; prohibited from buying Christian bond-laborers 198; racial oppression of, in laws against free 250; and social control 168–9; social mobility of, incompatible with racial oppression 181–2, 186, 279; social status: normal 182, relative "indeterminate" 178; in trades 377n97; Virginia seeks "to fix a perpetual brand on Free Negros & Mulattos" 241–2, 250–51; women, union with white men 380n24. *See also* African-American bond-laborers; African bond-laborers; Africans; Afro-Caribbeans; Bacon's Rebellion; free African-Americans; free

Colored; racial oppression; racial slavery; social control in Anglo-American plantation colonies

African bond-laborers: eighteenth-century English preeminent suppliers of 171; in the Americas 178–9, 302n58; Asiento 4, 300n8; attempt at free settlement in Virginia 245; in British West Indies 38–9; discrimination against, in skilled occupations 240; Dutch principal merchants buying and selling (1630s) 333–4n35; Europe 302n48; number of 8, 198–9, 218, 302n48, 302n58; and prospect of escape 363n121; rebellions of 218, 224–5, 240, 375n46, 362n116; and social control 198–9, 224–5, 228–9; status of 177–90

African laborers: prohibitions against, in skilled occupations 229, 240; shift to, as main supply 240; trade in 172; from West Africa 8,198, 300n11, 355n53, 379n9

Africans: allying with Indians 261; ancestry and headrights 337n4; British army purchase for military service 377n108; children, tithable 343n121; and intermediate stratum 226, 228; rebelliousness of 379n12; resistance 9, 303n63

Afro-Brazilians 34, 261–2

Afro-Caribbeans: Emancipation struggle and parallels with Irish 238; excluded from skilled occupations at first 233; "free blacks and coloreds" as majorities in British West Indies promoted as intermediate buffer social control stratum 232–4, 236–7; different status than African-Americans 238; as slave owners, shopkeepers, and recipients of free homesteads in Jamaica 234–5; traded for enslaved Indians 41

Allen, Theodore W.: egalitarian motif 1, 38, 204; origin of racial oppression 204; records research 273, 349n36. *See also The Invention of the White Race*

Amaru, Tupac 33

American Revolution 169, 203, 205

Andros, Governor 273

Anglican Church 165, 238, 352n19

Anglo-American plantation bourgeoisie: decides on attack on laborers and tenants 64, 77, 79–96 *passim*; and on plantation of bondage 101; base venture on chattel bond-labor and social control on racial oppression 223; and capitalism based on chattel bond-servitude and engrossment of land 239; choose monocultural economy 62, and perpetual bondage 240; costs 127–8, 352n8, 352n10; decide to tenants and laborers 64, 109, and plantation of bondage 101; desire to extend servitude 179, 357n13; desire to impose lifetime servitude on African-Americans 179, 186, 196; develop South Carolina after pattern of racial slavery established

323n67; elite, 166, 239, 353nn28–9, 381n39; enrichment of 166; free Negroes and "mulattos" excluded from intermediate social control stratum 241; and general interests of ruling class 132; impose bond-labor status 96, 101; indebtedness of 166, 353nn28–9; sought extreme dependency of laborers 75; "white race" social control policy 17–19

Anglo-American plantation colonies: "too many" laboring class Europeans in continental colonies to be in petty bourgeoisie, too few in West Indies 244; social structure differs fundamentally from Anglo-Caribbean 372n2

Anglo-Caribbean plantation colonies 38–9, 40–1, 223–38, 240, 242–4; ruling class social control with people of African descent in intermediate buffer social control stratum 372n2

Anglo-Dutch wars 168–70, 199, 209

Anglo-French wars 170, 271

Angolans, enslavement of 34

Antigua 232, 372nn2–3, 377n91

Apalachees 40, 317n90: as slaves of Creeks 4

apprentices 22–3, 70, 93, 309n69: chattel bond-servitude distinct from 103, 334n38; could not be sold 66; Duty Boys 64–6; issues of transfer and non-assignability 334n40, 336n41

Argall, Governor Samuel 56, 322n46, 328n28: accused of diverting tenants to private use 57–8, 61, 322n53, 322n55, 322nn81–2

army 16, 231–2, 235, 270

Asiento de negras 8, 300n8

assigns 61, 98–100, 334n40

Atlantic slave trade 8–9

Azores 40

Aztecs 32

Bacon Assembly 216, 370n102

Bacon, Sir Francis 311n96, 311–12n99, 335n57, 352n14, 355n60, 355n64: dividing and breaking combinations 248; monarchy and male domination 28–9; "Of Plantations," an alternate vision 105–6; rate of expansion of colony's population and relations with native peoples 336n58; relationship to Nathaniel 382n6; reverence 164; role of profit and glory in Virginia 304n69; role of "yeomanry" 16–18; slavocracy's "theoretician" 382n7; Virginia example to be avoided 173; Virginia Company member 304n69

Bacon, Nathaniel 203, 364n10, 364n14, 369nn91–92, 381n33: advocates guerrilla tactics 215; background of 340n2, 365n18, 365n19, 368n72, 382n56; and onslaught on Pamunkey, sells prisoners 206; proclaims liberty "to all Servants and Negro's" 213,

368–9n84; and rebellion 205–10, demands of 211

Bacon's Rebellion (1676–7): African-American/European-American collaboration in 211, 239–240, 248, 353n23, 369n93, 381n33; aftermath 26–7, 178, 217–21; analogy to American Revolution 205, to English Revolution 364n12; anti-Indian phase 204–7, 209–210, 353n23, 366n35; basic English ruling elite policy to exclude Indians from territory rather than enslave war captives 204; begins as dispute within ruling elite over "Indian policy" 206–7; bibliography on 363n2, 364n8; bond-laborers in 205, 368–9n83, 369n87, 381n33, number in 211, 369–70n97, intervene *en masse* in 213; captured rebels 370n99, 370n103; civil war phase 204–5, 210; colonists involvement in 216; "common run of the people" sought change in land policy, not "Indian policy" 205, 208, and call to tax land 208, 366n35; Craven on 363n5; destabilizing factors of 217–22; declaration of war 366n42; defeat in, clears way for lifetime hereditary chattel bond-servitude 239; and domestic crisis 212; and elimination of middle class 356n80; elite factions in 206–10; fears of overthrow of system 212, of involvement of other forces 217, 369n92, 369–70n97, of servants 212; Fiske on 364n6; and freedom from bondage 368–9n84, 369n87; grievances of rebels in 210; and king's amnesty proclamation 216, 370n101; Navigation Acts not an issue in 364n14; outbreak of 356n80; post-Rebellion destabilizing factors in 217–21; reaction time of expeditionary force in 215; revenue losses in 368n67; and runaways 153, 349n39; social factors contributing to 119; Virginia Assembly law enslaving Indian war captives for life 37, 123; Washburn on 363n4; Wertenbaker on 356n80

Bahamas 372n2

Bahia 262

Bailyn, Bernard 205–6, 208, 210, 331n121, 363n13

Ball, John 264, 307n26

Ballagh, James C. 50, 267, 338n27

Baltimore, Lord 221, 371–2n150

Baptism: and freedom 197; no basis for freedom 360n76

Barbados: African bond-laborers in 224, recruitment into militia of 377n110; African-American bond-laborers from 187; Afro-Barbadians in trades 229, women in retail trades 377n91; Afro-Caribbean majorities 233–4; attempts to reduce natives to bond-servitude in 223; banishment to 135; Brown Privilege Bill 238; and Colony Council 230, 376n57; Dutch in 373n9; early settlement of 3; emigration: from 232, of Europeans 374n35, of freemen 227–9; estate size in 227; European bond-laborers 223–4, 344n147, join forces with African bond-laborers 224; fear of "slave menace" 375n47, little to fear from rebels on an island 314n35; free coloreds 226, 234–5, 237–8, 374n41, in intermediate buffer social control stratum 242–3; free persons of African ancestry 237; free Negroes required to serve in militia 242; freedmen 234–7, 375n53; General Assembly warns of Irish 230, Indians 372nn4–5; Irish bond-laborers 224, rebels excluded 376n57; landholding 227, 374n33; "military tenants" 375n53; Negro bond-laborers substituted for European tradesmen 376–7n90; planters' opposition to baptism of Negroes 197; plantation owners in 375n47; plots by bond-laborers in 224; population of 38, 373–4n25, 374n28, density 227; prisoners 229, 375n46, of war 224; Quakers and Christianity in 165, 191–2, 197; rebellions in 229–30, 375n46; "Redlegs" 375n55; repressive measures 192, 361n90; revolt (1816) 237, 378n129; ruling class social control by including people of African descent 372n2; Scottish bond-laborers in 224; slave law in England as model for slave code of 308–9n59; slaveowners in 237, 378n124, desire to get money 352n19; and Sunday markets 234; transformed into sugar plantation economy 63; unfitness rationale 38–40; vagabonds 224; "whites" in 374n39, 374n41, 376n57, 377n91, 377n97, "poor whites" 375n53, 375n55

bastards 24, 341n85: bastardy laws 129–35

Bayano 262

Beckles, Hilary 374n33, 375n53, 377n91

Beckles, John Allayne 236

benefit: "of clergy" 347n191; of planters 246; of ending the "slave" trade, for West Indian bond-laborers 361n86; majority of Virginia planters do not 247

Bennett, Lerone, Jr. 50–51, 182, 364n7

Berkeley, Governor William: and Bacon's Rebellion 203, 205–10, 212–15, 369n91, aftermath 216, 218; complains about Navigation Acts 364n14; defiance of king's proclamation 216; denouncer of monoculture 169; departure (1676) 240; and Elizabeth Key case 95; flees Jamestown 210; gives Indian girl to shipmaster 365n22; hangings by 370n104; historians on 370n103; and "Indian policy" to "destroy" Northern Indians and maintain relations with neighboring tribes 207; licenses Indian trade 366n42; on mortality rate 339n41, 345–6n180; on number of bond-laborers 119, 349n41, less than one-fifth of English chattel laborers survive "indentures" 38;

offers freedom to bond-laborers of Baconite owners 369n87; rebels plan to demand freedom from 152; on threat of insurrection 168–9

Berkeley Hundred 70–71, 78, 326n148

Bermuda 3, 40, 49, 66, 88

Berry, Sir John 211, 216, 370n103

Billings, Warren M. 153, 166, 362n103, 362n105

Blair, James 173–4, 352n19, 355n65

Bland, Giles 201, 209–210

Board of Trade 120, 171, 218–19, 244: and Gooch case 249–50, 379–80n19

Bolas, Juan de 225

Bolívar, Simón 10, 210

Bona Nova 79–81, 327–8n24

bond-labor: acquisition costs of 121, 137; African 178, 223; Afro-Barbadian women 377n91; assault by 149–50; "assign" 98–100; attempts to reduce Caribbean natives to 223; bastardy laws and 129–35, 341n80, chattel form 119; chattelization of European-Americans essential precondition for lifetime bond-servitude 268, 323n67; Chesapeake, majority European-American in seventeenth century 192; common class interest with poor and landless free 220; common in surplus producing societies 97; denied arms 199, 218; domestic sources 37, 122–4; Dutch and 102, 333–4n35; employment of European-Americans in South Carolina came later and was short-lived 323n67; ending "slave" trade would benefit West Indian bond-laborers 361n86; "enduring" 97–114 *passim*; English 223; European 223; European-American, abandon opposition to plantocracy 249; feudal pre-capitalist, was two-way bondage 97; Fiske on 364n6; freedom: Bacon's Assembly extends to 370n102, implications of 211, in West Indies if enter British army (after 1807) 235; general conditions of 267–9; historians ignore 211; illness among 142–3; increase of 218; Indian 36–45, 122–3, no "transportation charges" 44, war captives 207; inevitability argument 103–5; Irish 218, 223, "confederate with the negroes" 244, boys forced exile to Jamaica 374n41; kidnapping for use as 120–1, 172, 338n2; lifetime of 177–8, 310n74, 312n101; and "loss of services" 130–1, 342n95, 342n101; majority of planters and landless freemen could not afford 199; majority of "white" adult males not owners of 247, 256; marriage of exceptional 350n67; murder by owners 143–6, 345–6n188, 346n189, 347n192; "negative incentives" imposed on 140; number of 69, 211, 217–8; opposition to 107–8; oppression of 119, 124–47; owners of African ancestry 240;

owners' profit on 344–5n160; percent becoming landholders 374n33; positive incentive to produce 141; "*quid pro quo*" rationale 101–3, 107; rebelliousness of 218; "resisting" 119–47 *passim*; Scottish 223; "seasoning" time 345–6n180; as self-activating shapers of history 211; servant trade 119–22, merchants stimulate 119; social control problem 109; struggle, key to history of West Indies 367n58; tithable 367n57; tobacco plantations and 335n54; unpaid, to meet bourgeoisie's desire to lower labor costs 98, as surrogate for unemployed labor reserve 98. *See also* chattel bond-servitude

bond-labor, lifetime hereditary 134, 196, 198–9, 223, 254, 312n101: African-Americans challenge 188–91; and Christianity 361n82; economics of 172; path cleared by defeat in Bacon's Rebellion 239; not cause of "race not class" 240; plantation owners desire to raise profit by imposing on African-Americans 188, 196. *See also* hereditary bond-labor

bond-labor, limited-term 77, 123–4, 139, 177–9, 250, 267–8: extension of 345n161, 354n37, 357n18; indistinct from lifetime bond-labor 123, 357n9; large proportion held by small planters in Maryland 323n67; outlaw sex for 158

bond-labor system: antithetical to interests of African-Americans 248; basis of extreme inequality 203; and bond-servitude 8, 344n38, 386n7; chattelization to meet bourgeoisie's desire for free flow of capital 98–100; costs: maintenance 137–8, of workers 121, prosecution and punishment 127–8, recapture 349n42, 352n8, 352n10, transportation 71–2, 99, and repayment by extension of servitude 349n43; historians on 267–9; inhibits family formation 70; and interest of planters 132, 246; and monoculturul economy 226

bond-laborers (colonial Anglo-America): abuse of 141–7, 269, 346–7n188, 347nn191–2; acquittal of killers of Negro or Indian lifetime 186; adult 340n55; armed rebellion 149; Bacon's Rebellion 205, 368–9n83, 349n87, 381n33, number in 211, 213, 369–70n97; Berkeley estimates less than one-fifth of English, survive "indentures" 38; children of 132–3, 343n120; Christian 192, 250; commodity in barter 345n167; convicts 120, 338n27, 381n34, transportation costs 121, 338n22, 342n104; English in Maryland 324n94, 325nn110–1, 339–40n52, 355–6n180; European 370–1n117; European-American 186, 267–9, solidarity with African-American 153, 161–2, 177, 240, 243–4; extended length of

service 108, 179, 357n18; importation of, by
African-Americans 183; Irish 244, 367n18;
main forms of oppression of bond-laborers
124–47; majority of population 351n75;
missing in Washburn 363n4; mortality
rate of 345–6n180, 346n183; murder by
masters 143–6; number of 210, 337n4,
337n10, 345–6n180, 370–1n117; plots of
155–6, 344n156; self-activation of 148;
social control strategy and free Negroes
and "mulattos" 240, 242–3; and social
mobility 366n33; striving for freedom 211;
supervision of 345n171; tobacco bourgeoisie
assumes resistance of 244
bondmen: Duty Boys 65–6; intermediate bond-
servitude forms 64–9; "maids-for-wives" 64,
66–9; "that all bondmen be made free" 21
Borinqueños 31
bourgeoisie: and accumulation of capital 63,
205; and African bond-labor 223; blindspot
of 211; chooses chattel bond-labor 223;
deliberately fosters middle class 17; English,
uniqueness of 10, repression by 17; eye 205;
Marx on 374–5n51; and social control 3,
222, 307n26; and two-fold problem of labor
supply and social control 3
bourgeoisie (Anglo-American plantation)
354–5n51, 379n9: and birth of children
343n120; desire to use African-Americans
as lifetime hereditary bond-laborers 179–80,
198; draws color line 45; elite 381n39;
establishes one-way bondage 98; failure to
diversify 217–18; fear of resistance 244–5;
initiates white-skin privilege system 253;
logic, and oversupply of laborers 332n138;
power enhanced by dependence of colonists
78; pressure for unpaid labor time 187;
and racial oppression 223; seeks to create
extreme dependence of laborers 75, 95
branding 20, 126
Brazil 303n66: African labor in 7–8; Dutch in 7,
300n23, 373n9; Indian labor: non-enslavable
34, forced 39; indigenous society of 314n45;
Portuguese in 7–8, 33–4; runaways and the
Quilombo of Palmares 261–2; social control
in a continental colony issue similar to
Virginia 33–5
Breen, Timothy H. 182, 358n22, 358n36,
364n7: class character and self-activation of
African-American bond-laborers' struggle
148, 367n58; use of term "whites" and
attribution of lost solidarity to exclusively
objective factors 347n4
Brigder, Colonel Joseph 210
British West Indies: African bond-laborers in
38–9; contrast with continental colonies
224–6, 314n35; emancipation 10, freed
by serving in army 235; involvement in
England's wars with Catholic powers
230, British army and Africans 377n108,

377–8n111; markets of 383n67; Negro
population of 39; ruling class social control
policy 372n2
Brown, Alexander 49–50, 71, 329n54, 330n80,
331n121
Brown Privilege Bill 238
Bruce, Philip Alexander 143, 267, 322n46,
338n27, 344n156: on African and African-
American bond-laborers 198, 363n118; on
chattel bond-servitude and "progress" 50,
103–6, 267, 335n53, 355n59, 355n63; on
promoting "pride of race" among "white
people" 249; on possible alternative path
173; on tobacco: cultivation 335n54, in
Virginia history 56, 175, 322n41, 355n59,
perishing 140, prices 353n22
"buffer" role 43–4, 149
buffer social control stratum (Anglo-America):
absent until Bacon's Rebellion 164, 219–20;
English plantation variation is in recruitment
to and exclusions from 12–13; Indians in
Virginia serve as two-way buffer 41, 43,
208, subsequently excluded from "white
race" system of social control 41; peculiarity
of system established was in "control"
aspect 12–13
buffer social control stratum (Anglo-Caribbean):
ruling class policy puts people of African
descent in intermediate stratum 372n2
buffer social control stratum (Spanish colonies):
exterminates Indians and lacks intermediate
stratum in Hispaniola, Cuba, and Puerto
Rico, uses socially demoted caciques in
Mexico and Peru 32
Bullock, William 265–6
Burke, Edmund 235, 239, 251, 254
Butler, Nathaniel 88–9, 330nn80–1
Byrd, William, I 205, 209
Byrd, William, II 245, 363n121, 381n33

Cabot, John 3
caciques 31–4, 224, 303–4n69, 314n31,
317n89; absence of 36, 39, 41; definitions
of 313n22; socially demoted by Spanish to
buffer social control stratum 32
Canaobo, Chief 31
Cape Corso 355n53
capital: accumulation 10, 205, and misery 173,
social control necessary for 240; "breeding
women" (Jefferson) as addition to 380n24;
costs 226–30; concentration of 166, 256;
drain of 170–71; interest and African labor
trade 172; relation to labor 347n200; venture
66–9
capitalism: ascendant 25; based on chattel
bond-servitude and engrossment of the
land 239; development in Europe 263–4; in
England 10–11, 14–25; predicated on need
for unattached labor-power 97; and tenantry
104; transition to 14–24, 356n74

capitalist: bond-labor owner as 223; and crisis of overproduction 62–3, 324n94; as exploiters of bond-labor 354–5n51; plantation owners reliance on increased exertion by laborers 124; plantation bourgeoisie establish a one-way bondage between labor and capitalist 98; plantations as capitalist enterprises 97; production 175, 356n74; relations of production in England 263–4; society, social distinctions in 242

Caribbean Indians 224

Catholics 35, 197, 305n1

Charles I, King of Spain 3, 8, 336–7n41

Charles II, King of England 209, 231, 348n9: and Bacon's Rebellion 203, 215–16; on Berkeley 370n104; brother heads Royal African Company 355n55; financial difficulties 212; profit from African and African-American lifetime bond-laborers 172

Charles V 304n75

Charlton, Stephen 188, 193, 358n26, 359n55, 361nn95–8

chattel bond-laborers: common throughout plantation Americas 12: as percent of European immigrants 119; number of 119, 210; unpaid bought and sold 24. See also bond-laborers

chattel bond-servitude 321n35: absent in England 100–101, condemned 336n61; capitalism and plantation elite 239; extreme form of proletarian dependence under capitalism 124; history's false apologetics for 100–105; inimical to democratic development 103; not an unreflecting adaptation of English precedents, repudiates master-servant relationship 103, distinct from 334–5n41; overthrow of tenantry clears way for 239, tenants reduced to 72–4, 326n156; resented by servants 336n61; resistance to 148–62; Smith on origin of 319n5; and social control 240; in Virginia 174. See also bond-labor

chattelization: commitment to, begins 98; of English plantation labor, a precondition for lifetime 323n67; plantation bourgeoisie plan for 101; transfer to another without consent 80

"cheap commodity" strategy 265–6

Cherokees 35, 316n64, 317–8n106: buffer role 43–4

Chesapeake: class distinction 246–7; convicts 120, 122; European immigrants 119; forms of oppression 133, 137, 139, 142, 146, racial oppression 252; "Golden Age" 239; marriage and social mobility 181; master-servant relationships 268; monoculture 166; Quakers 192; resistance 211; ruling class favored by balance of forces 102; social instability 218–19; status of African-Americans 177; tenantry 104. See also Virginia

Chichimecs, relatively class-undifferentiated 33

Chickasaws 35

Chickhominy Indians 328–9n43

Christians: baptism 196–8, 228; fellowship 180; freedom, uncoupled from 362n103; Las Casas concerned with genocidal exploitation by 4; nations 179; principle against holding as slaves 192, 195, 357n13; and racial oppression 360n77; religious orders 34; servants 137; warlike 385n116

Christians (term): equated with Englishmen 374n41; euphemism for "white" 374n41, used for European bond-laborers 228

civil rights struggle 148, 203–204: and impending crisis 258–9

class: analysis 246–8; antagonism 147; conflict and resolution 19–24, 353n23; collaboration 228; consciousness 240; differentiation 313n10; distinction 62, 85, 184, 209, 245–8, 251; exploitation and suffering 89; family denial and sharpening of antagonism of 147; five officially recognized classes in spring of 1622 93–4; forces, general relationship of 333n30; solidarity 177; and special conditions for profiteering 89; stratification 315n47; struggle 9, 15–6, 34, 204, 223, 233–4, 257, 259, 319–20n11, 322n41, interpretation 356n74, 357n6, 364n6; "transitions" 14–16; and wage payment in England 22–4; yeomanry 17–19; English bourgeoisie foster a lower middle-class stratum 17–19

class oppression: compounded by "bastardy laws" 130–35; lifetime servitude as 179; and oppression of women 26–9; and Poor Law 24–6, 133; reduction of almost totally English labor force to chattel bond-servitude in 1620s an extremely reactionary form of 178–9; resistance to 148–62 passim; slavery of Scots miners as 179

cloth industry 10

Colbert, Jean Baptiste 7

"color, not class" 379n7

Columbus, Christopher 205

Commissioners of Trade and Plantations 43, 170–71, 229, 272, 355n65

commodity production, simple 175, 356n73, 356n74

"common people" 173, 259

Company of Royal Adventurers to Africa 197

conscious decision: to opt for monoculture and chattel bond-labor 175

Constitution of 1789 254

convicts 5, 70, 245: include captives taken in civil war or rebellion 120; thirty-five to fifty thousand brought to continental colonies as bond-servants 337n10, thirty thousand brought (1717–72) 381n34, Privy

Council orders to transport as "servants" 64–5; profitability in shipment as bond-laborers 122; in Virginia 70; Spanish and Portuguese 5

Coopy, Robert E. 72, 99, 326n148

corn 83, 90–92, 138, 332n147, 354–5n51

Cortés, Hernán 312n2, 314n52

cotton gin 322n41

"counterfeit of social mobility," "white" identity as 248–9

Craven, Wesley Frank 106, 335n53, 337n4, 355n63: on Bacon's Rebellion 204, 363n5; on death rate 345–6n180; on Sandys sending ill-provisioned laborers to Virginia 332n138

Creek Indians 35, 317n92

crimps 120

crisis: following attack (1622) 93–4; making one, serve another 84–95; of overproduction 62–3, 169

Cromwell, Oliver 230, 337n9, 370n104

Cuba 7, 10, 301n40, 303n66, 314n52: in need of social-control stratum 31–2

Cudjoe, Captain 225–6

Culpepper, Governor Thomas Lord 172, 217, 220–21, 314n35, 349n41

"cultural barriers" 319–20n11

Curtin, Philip D. 339n40

"custom of the country" 126, 135, 149, 179, 348n21: unpaid chattel status as 24

Dale, Governor Thomas 54, 109, 320–1n23

Davies, C.S.L. 21, 304n75, 308n45

Davies, Sir John 231

Deal, Joseph Douglas III 182, 358n22, 358n37, 361n96: on growth of racism 351n96; "larger percentage of Eastern shore blacks were free" 359n43; on sexual liaisons as resistance 153

death penalty 126, 144, 324n100, 370n103

death rate 181, 327n2, 331n122: one-sixth of new immigrants alive (in 1625) 76; one-third of colonists die in one day (1622) 85; "dominion of death" (1622) 89, 93, 329nn53–4; two-thirds die in one- to two-year period 331n125

Debeada 181

Declaration of Independence 254

defiant solace 158–61

"deficiency laws": for social control in West Indies 228–30, 237, 240; in South Carolina and Georgia 252–3

Delaware tribe 317n90, 317n93

deliberate ruling-class social control policy: conferring of privileges 248–50, 319–20n11; English governing classes' sixteenth-century decision to preserve section of peasantry as intermediate social control stratum 109; House of Lords and 306n19; laws "deliberately calculated to undercut … black laborers" (Billings) 362n103;

Morgan on 248–9, 255, 319–20n11; "to fix a perpetual brand on" (Gooch) and to establish system of racial oppression 242; Virginia Assembly's decision to promote "racial contempt" and establish "anomalous privileges" 249; "white race" as 274

Dew, Thomas Roderick 254, 379n13

diet: Bruce on 344n156; in England 344n150; of European bond-laborers in Barbados 344n147; bond-laborers' corn 138; and hog-killing penalties 348n24; in Virginia 151–3

disease 32, 34, 37, 40, 77: impact of epidemic European 7, 315n48

diversification 169–71, 175, 370n116, opposition to 217–18

"divided labor market" 240, 319–20n11

Doegs 207, 365n17

Drake, Sir Francis 262

Drummond, William 369–70n97

Du Bois, W.E.B. 148, 347n1

"ducking stool" 341–2n93

Dunn, Richard S. 224–5, 228, 232, 372n1

Dutch 168–70, 178, 198–9, 215, 300n23: East and West Indies 5; invasion of Brazil 373n9; plantation owners in Barbados 373n9; posts in West Africa 197; trade 364n14; Virginia susceptible to incursions by 209

Duty Boys 65–6, 96

economic interpretation of history 362n105

Edward VI. See English monarchs

Effingham, Governor 221

Eighty Years' War (1568–1648) 5

emancipation struggles 9–10, 193–6, 238, 249–50, 255

emigration 4–5, 60–1, 76, 227–30, 270–1

encomenderos 39, 303n69, 313n12

encomienda 7, 33, 301n41, 314n43, 314n51

engagés 6–7, 301n35: survival rate 38

Engels, Friedrich 351n80

England: army, unfeasibility of maintaining in Virginia 220–21; civil war 3–4, 19; contest with France 171; cloth-making industry as transformer of economic life to capitalist basis 10; differs from other colonizing powers and venting of surplus "necessitous people" 3, 11–12, 304–5n87; enclosures 21; English Expeditionary Force 215; English Revolution 206, 270, 364n12; expropriation of peasants 18; feudal ruling class 101, social relations under 310–11n88; industrial production expansion 270–71; kidnapped laborers 338n12; "Master of the Sea" 314n35; mercantilism 169–70; military and naval presence 226, 231–2; monarchy 10, 169; Parliament 235; servile labor from 379n9; tobacco revenues 217–18

English common law: actions against racial oppression without reference to 193;

African-American bond-laborers and 134; and bond-servitude 103, 167, 178–9, 191, 334n37; fornication penalties 129–30, 243; non-assignability 103, 334n40, 334–5n41; *partus sequitur patrem* 195, 197; *partus sequitur ventrem* 134

English people: immunities of 333n24; "would sell their own fathers" 102

English monarchs: Edward VI (1547–53) 21; Henry VII (1485–1509) 3, 18, 109, 355n60; Henry VIII (1509–47) 11, 15, 28, 310n87, 311n91, 334n37; James I (VI of Scotland) (1603–25) 3, 11, 49, 62, 282, 335n57, 336n59; James II (1685–89) 216, 305n1, 355n55; George III (1760–1820) 203, 205

European-American bond-laborers: collaboration with African-American bond-laborers in Bacon's Rebellion 211, 248, 369n93; collaborative actions against their bondage 148–62, readiness for 161; in contracts and wills 187–8; costs of 121, 139; most did not survive terms 44; number of 211, 370–1n117; owned by African-Americans 186–7; voluntary and involuntary 120. *See also* bond-laborers

European-Americans: Chesapeake 192; collaboration with African-Americans 148–50, 162, 248; and disappearance of labor solidarity 347n4; and "divided labor market" explanation for "race not class" challenged 240; elements opposed to racial oppression 193–6; evangelical questions and objections 191–2; fleeing to Indians 77; intermarriage 359n40; laborers had no desire for privileges vis-à-vis African-Americans 162; landholding 184–6, increasing concentration of 166, 174; opposition to lifetime bond servitude 193; owned by African-Americans 186–7; owners of African-Americans 190, 193; population 232–3, 376n87; right to bear arms 199; sexual liaisons with African-Americans 160–61, 243–4, 250–51; status reduction from tenants and wage-laborers to chattel bond-servitude 178; transmogrification into the "white race" 204–5; treatment of 267–9, disparate 342n95

Europeans: colonizing powers and colonial labor supply 3–13; emigrants 374n35; fathers, non-European mothers 314n30; and Medieval slavery 8; number of immigrants in Virginia and Maryland 119; occupation of Indian lands 205; in West Indies propertyless marginalized as "poor whites" 230

Fairfax County 104

family: barring oppression 147; formation inhibiting bond-labor system 70, in Virginia and Maryland 174; life, denial of 128–30, 340–1n76

farm-to-factory migration 258

felons 120, 338n27

feudalism: bourgeoisie replaces two-way bondage of, with two-way freedom 97; end of 264, 305–6n6, 310–11n87, 311n89; lines drawn by 15

"to fix a perpetual brand" (Gooch) 242

Florida 40, 42, 314n43, 317n90

food scarcity: and dependence on Indians 90, on English 77–8, 85–8

fornication: African-Americans involved with European-Americans 161; Dutch laws in New Netherlands 341n85; extra time for 96; as form of resistance 149, 153, 158–61; cases involving "a negro" 350–1n74; as gender and class oppression 342n110; and Maryland laws 341n89

Fortescue, John W. 231

forty-shilling freeholders 17–19, 307n28, 381n35

Foster, Sir Augustus John 254

"foure hundred English and Negroes in Armes" 214

Fox, Charles James 236

Fox, George 191: "you that are called white" 374n39

France: colonization efforts different from England 11; plantation colonies 6–8, 301n31; wars with 172, 218, 230, 235

Francis I, king of France 3

"free colored" (or "free black" or mulatto): in British West Indies as majorities, shopkeepers, and slave-owners 232–4; contrast roles in British West Indies and Virginia 238, 380n22; definitions of (in West Indies) 377n96; demands for full citizenship after Haitian Revolution 238; in Jamaica own 70,000 of 310,000 bond-laborers and offered free homesteads 234–5, 240; number in Barbados and Jamaica 237; plots (1722) 242

"free enterprise" 319n5

free laborers, solidarity with bond-laborers 148, 150–52

"free land": diverts from struggles with the bourgeoisie 258; "safety valve" theory 385n123

"free market economy" principles 240

freedmen and freedwomen: in British West Indies 232–8; definitions of 377n96; and social control 235–7

freedom: and class struggle 357n6; dues 137, 250, 273

freemen: definitions of (in West Indies) 377n96; excessive emigration of 227–30; and social control 168–9; and voting rights 352n5, 364–5n16

French 215, 317n93: possible invasion by 369n92

"French Negroes" 231

Frethorne, Richard 86–8
frontier 204, 353n23, 365n17: "frontier democracy," white chauvinism of 363n4; as-social-safety-valve theory (Turner) 257–9, 385n118
Fugger family 300n5
fur trade 209, 366n42

Gates, Governor Thomas 51, 109, 320–1n23
gender oppression 69, 345n183: number of cases 158; and class oppression 130–5, 154, 158–61, 342n110. See also male supremacy; women
genocide 33, 205
"gentry" 246
George III. See English monarchs
Georgia colony: act repealing ban on slavery (1750) included "deficiency" provision 253; founded on no-slavery principle 245, 252, 354–5n51
"germ theory" 319n5
Gibson, Charles 32
Gibson, Edmund 241, 379–80n19
Gloucester County: elite 364n10; militia 210; plot 152–3; records 152; riot 219, 371n131
Godolphin, Sir Sidney273
Godwyn, Morgan 191–2, 352n19, 374n39
gold 7, 30, 39, 259, 312n3
Golden Age 15, 239
Gooch, Governor William: exclusion of free African-Americans from intermediate social control buffer corollary of establishment of "white race" 249; "fix a perpetual Brand upon Free Negroes & Mulattos" letter 242–5, background to 250, 379–80n19; on Virginia linen 171
Grantham, Captain Thomas 214, 369nn92–3, 369n97
Gray, Lewis C.: on bond-servitude 267, 334–5n41; and Morgan's "boom" 331n125; number of African bond-laborers brought to the thirteen colonies 339n40; and tobacco prices 353n22
Great Charter (1618) 49–50, 53
Great Rebellion (1381) 15, 19, 102, 263–4
Green Spring faction 206, 210, 219
Grenada 235, 372n2
Guayabana 31

Haiti (Hispaniola) 7, 31–2, 301n31
Haitian Revolution 9–10, 237–8: James on 367n58
Hakluyt, Richard 12, 25
Handler, Jerome S. 234
hanging 144, 370n103
Harlow, V. T. 228, 375n47
Harvey, John 83–4, 324n94
Hathuey 303–4n69
headrights: basis of high concentration of

land-ownership 78, 166–7, 174; captains of ships and 121; could be sold 183; Governor and Colony Council seek to protect 209; and importation of bond-laborers 104, 167; increased class differentiation 62; in Maryland did not apply to importation of African laborers 323n67; number of 337n4; principle of 58–60, 322n57, 332n4, 338n25
Henrico 93, 157
Henry VII. See English monarchs
Henry VIII. See English monarchs
Henry, H. M. 249, 254, 382n60
Holland 5–6, 8, 11, 102, 178, 320–1n23
homesteads 234–5, 242–3, 258, 377n103
Honduras 377–8n111
"household mode of production" 175
Humacao 31
Hunter, Governor 231

identity: stripping of Indians' and African-Americans' 318–9n122; "white," established 248–9; exclusion of free African-Americans as corollary 249; "white race" as new all-class, all-European social 228–30, 374n39
immigration 77, 97–8, 102, 258, 345–6n180
Incas 33
incubus of "white-skin" privileges paralyzed will of European-American laborers 259
indebtedness: and deteriorating conditions of non-elite planters 66; a cause of Bacon's Rebellion 217; Virginia's chronic 218
indentures 72, 120, 326n148, 336–7n41
Indian labor: abandonment of as plantation bond-labor 36–45, 122–3; invention of the white race and non-enslavability and non-assimilability of 44–5; retrospective thoughts by colonists on 30; and social control 40–41
Indian policy: Act of 1723 for "better government of ... Indians" 241–2, 250–51; in the Americas 30–45; apprehension of runaway slaves 318n111; buffer role of 208; encouraged to make war on one another 224, 316nn63–4; English buying and selling of 36–7; enslavement of captives 37, 204; "frontier aggressiveness" and 204; genocidal policy toward 33, 205, 355n64; Jennings on 317n105; motivated at first not by desire to maintain social control over exploitable Indian bond-labor but to exclude from territory 204; laws authorizing enslavement of 123, 316n72, 316–17n122, 337n75; legal bar to enslavement of 123; need for friendly Indians in buffer role 41; non-enslavability and non-assimilability 45; presumption of liberty extended to 339n39; shipping out of colony 41; and social control 30–31, 40–41; treaties (1646) 36, 43, 207–8; as tributary subjects 208; under Berkeley 206–7
Indians: alleged "treachery" of 90; allies

with French 363n121; attacks 36–7, 224;
(1622) 36, 84, 90, 93, 312n3, 318n118,
328n39, 328–9n43; as bond-labor 122–3,
161; Brazil 314n45, non-enslavability in
34; in Canada 6; captives, English buying
and selling of 36–7; Caribbean 223–4; in
center of economic history of hemisphere 9;
in Central Andes 302n44; colonists fear of
unity with African-Americans 42; colonists
adapted into tribe 329n48; "completely
broken from their tribal stems" (Philips)
42, 317n94; "control" aspect rather than
"supply" aspect decisive for decline of
enslavement 41; Cuba 301n40, 314n52,
deaths in 84, 328–9n43, 329n54; (1644)
36; declared free in Virginia 361n94;
depopulation of 37, 40–41; displacement
of 207; as employees within Virginia
colony 318n118; English fomenting war on
37; enslaved in Barbados 224, in Europe
8, in Virginia 316n79, 365–6n31; and
European rivalries 317n105; extermination
of 30–31; flight to 77, 153; free 234–5;
hostile 123; identity stripping and social
control 318–9n122; inter-tribal rivalries 41;
insurrection of 364n12; Jennings on 327n4;
as labor source 7–8; lands, occupation of
by Europeans 205; in Maryland 317n105;
massacre of 364n12; in Mexico 301n41;
in New York 317n105; non-enslavability
in Brazil 34; "not white" and "redskin"
classification as outcome of the invention
of the white race 204–5, 364n9; parallel
with Irish 204; peace made with more
distant, friendly 90, 123; population in
Tidewater Virginia 315n48; presumption of
liberty 339n39; provide corn to colonists
90, 315n49; in Puerto Rico 301n40; rebels
shipped into exile 324n100; resistance of
41–3, 77; runaways 154, return of 127–8;
St. Lucia 224; trade with 40–41, 366n42;
as chief means of securing Indian bond-
laborers 37; "Trail of Tears" 35; treaties
(1646) 36, 43, 207, (1700) 43; Turner's
"whiteness" and neglect of 385n118;
uprising (1622) 84–6, 90, 92–4, 318n118;
Vaughan on 364n9; Washburn on 353n23.
See also Amaru, Tupac; Apalachees;
Arotirene; Aztecs; bond-labor; Borinqueños;
caciques; Canaobo; Caribbean Indians;
Carolinas; Cherokees; Chichimecs;
Chickasaws; Chickhominy Indians; Creek
Indians; Debeada; Delaware tribe; Florida
Indians; Guayabana; Huacao; Inca; Inca
Manco; Maguana people; Matoaka;
Meherrin; Metacom; Nanticoke Indians;
Narragansetts; Natchez; Occaneechee;
Pamunkey; Piscataway Indians; Powhatans
of Virginia; Pungoteague Creek; Roanoake;
Robin; runaways; Sioux; Susquehannock;

Titu Yupanqui; Tuscaroras; Wampanoags;
Yamassees
Ingram, Laurence 214, 365n23, 369n91
institutions 80, 171, 180, 361n82
insurrections: Barbados 224–5, 229, 231, 237;
intended, "of the negroes" in Virginia 244;
Brazil 225; Irish in the Caribbean 231; in
Jamaica 225, 232, 237, 375n46, 379n12;
Leeward Islands 237; Mexico 261; St. Kitts
231, St. Lucia 224. See also rebellion
intermediate stratum: absence of 97–109,
163–4, 171, 177; normal to English society
not possible under chattel bond-labor system
147; difference between societies with and
without 315n47; early prospects for 223;
free Negroes and "mulattos" excluded
from 240, 242–3, included in 242–3;
insubstantiality of 119, 163–76
invention of the white race 148, 204–5, 240,
239–59 passim
The Invention of the White Race (Allen) on:
attitudes of European-American workers
347n4; Bennett 364n7; bond-laborers'
struggles 367n58; Breen 347n4, 364n7;
champions of the "paradox" thesis 335n43;
criticism of Jordan 357n12; difference
between societies with and without
intermediate stratum 315n47; difference
between status of English villein and
lifetime bond-laborer in Anglo-America
312n101; European-American and African-
American solidarity 347n4; "Irish slave
trade" 337n10; male supremacy 347n4;
Morgan 364n7; Oliver Ellsworth 332n1;
"operative principles of social control in a
stable civil society constituted on the basis
of racial oppression" 375n54; shipment of
Irish rebels 324n100; study origin of racial
slavery 148; social safety valve of American
history 385n125; treatment of Cherokees
318–9n106
Ireland 215, 223, 379n9: and end of religio-
racial oppression parallels 238
Irish: Irish-Americans not originators of white
supremacy, were adopted into it 384n91;
bond-laborers 179, 197, 228, 230–31; boys
to Jamaica as bond-laborers 374n41; in
British West Indies 226, 230–31; Catholic
chieftains 223; Catholics right to lease not
purchase in Ireland 377n103; "confederate
with the negroes" 244; extended length of
service for 357n18; insurrections 231; "Irish
slave trade" 149, 179, 337n10; men to be
sold as slaves in Virginia 357n17; rebels
shipped away 324n100; troops and English
376n62; ungovernable veterans shipped to
Virginia as bond-laborers 218–19
Iroquois Seneca 365n17
Isle of Wight County 166, 366n35

Jamaica: Assembly 234; authorities fearful of rebellion 224; black regiments in 225; coloreds 237, and "perquisites of whites" 378n129; English begin settlement using chattel bond-laborers 372n3; European immigrants from Barbados 374n35; Europeans population decline 227–8, 233; exodus of pardoned rebels followed by rebellion of African bond-laborers 375n46; "free blacks and coloreds" ownership of bond-laborers in 235, 240; population of free people of color in 237; freedmen into trades and freedwomen shopkeeping in 234; garrison colony 232; German Protestants and 229; Gooch fears runaways as in 245; and Haitian Revolution 238; homesteads free to "every free mulatto, Indian, or negro" 234–5, 242–3; insurrections plots revolts and rebellions 225, 232, 237, 375n46, 379n12, Port Royal 232; Irish in 231; island colony different from Virginia in controlling rebels 314n35; land not fully exploited in 374n28; landholding 227; maroons 225–6, 240, 261–2, 363n121; militia 232; mulatto in 378n116; "perquisites of whites" for "coloured" 378n129; population density of 227; proposal for unemployed in England, Scotland, and Ireland to serve as chattel bond-laborers in 120; ruling class social control policy with persons of African ancestry in intermediate social control stratum 372n2; "whites," discrimination in favor of 377n103

James I (VI of Scotland). *See* English monarchs

James II. *See* English monarchs

James, C. L. R. 367n58

Jamestown 30, 92, 315n48: burning 213–15; founders 14; settlement 3

Jefferson, Thomas: "breeding women" for "profit" 380n24; on "merciless Indian savages" 205

Jeffreys, Governor Herbert 216, 221–2, 369n91

Jennings, Edmund 273, 370–1n117

Jesuits 34

John IV, king of Portugal 4

Johnson, Alderman Robert 72, 74, 94, 326n151

Johnson, Anthony 181–3, 350n71, 358n30, 359nn42–3

Johnson, Richard 12, 180, 182–3, 359n42

Jordan, Winthrop D.: author's criticism of 272, 357n12, 360n77, 362n103; Deal on 351n96; on indentured servitude 333n28; John Punch case 178; "natural racism thesis" 254; presumption of an immemorial "white alarm" 362n103; "unthinking decision" 101, 178, 383n80; on "white servants and Negroes" and rebellion 251–2

Kelly, Kevin P. 166–7

Kemp, Richard 108, 154

Ket's Rebellion 16, 21, 84, 180, 306n6, 306n10, 306n18, 306n19

Key, Elizabeth, case of: deliberately calculated to undercut rights of black laborers 362n103; history and critical importance of 194–9; significance is some planters had "reservations" that would have prevented imposition of racial oppression 362n105

Keynes, J. M. 258–9

king's share from customs on tobacco 170: profit on each Negro bond-laborer 172

kinship society 315n47

Kulikoff, Allan: casts doubt on Morgan's economic assumption 255; on class proportions 246–7, 381n39; and special oppression of women 146; on tenants in southern Maryland and Northern Neck Virginia 104; on yeomanry 248, 381nn40–41

labor: African 8; in Brazil 7–8; chattelization of 99–100; colonial supply 3–13, and England's uniqueness 10–13; costs 137, 171–2, 197; in Cuba 7; demand for 171; England and 10–13, 102; English plantation variation in recruitment to and exclusions from social control buffer 12–13; France and 6–8; Haitian Revolution and 7, 9–10; in Hispaniola 7; Holland and 5–6, 8, 102; "labor question" conflict and revolution 19–24; laws, negation of 178; in Mexico 7; in Peru 7; Powhatan and 35; regulation 19; relation to capital 347n200; shortages 101, 171, 263, plague-induced 101, 263; and Spain and Portugal 3–5, 7–10; supply problems 3–13, 101–2, 171, 263; surplus 19, 75, 332n138; tenant decisive element in cost of 73; time, unpaid 187–8; Virginia plantation bourgeoisie create a labor process unknown in England 175

labor productivity: average production of tobacco laborers 129, 131, 133; increase in 345n162; increasing population density and class differentiation as functions of 313n10; intense supervision and 140; in Maryland and Virginia 339–40n52; owners pursuit of higher 141–7; statistics on 325n110, 340n67, 342n104, 344–5n160; tenants 331n126

laborers: African 3; British, kidnapping of 338n12; European-American no desire for privileges vis-à-vis African-Americans 162; conditions of (c. 1622) 70–2; desire to reduce tenants to servants 74; deterioration of position of 331n125; in Goucestershire 332n136: economic pressure on, deliberately exploited by Colony Council and General Court 95–6; growing dependency of 75, 86; hired 321n33–4; jailing of 340n58; letters of 86–8; majority chattel bond-servants 333n26; in Mexico 278–41; non-proletarian reduced to proletarians 75; Nuce's plan

for getting "hands at Cheaper rates" 72–3; peonage 301n41; plantation 3, 166; primarily tenants 70–1; suffering of (in 1622) 89; unemployed 11–12, 24–5, 309n71, obliged to work 22–3; unpaid 8; white 258
Lamb, Francis 110
land: area limits 226–30; engrossment 166; grabbing 93; grants 209, 356n72; ownership 54, 94; reclamation 60; tax 208–9, 366n35; tenure 61; titles 58
Land, Aubrey C. 125, 246–7, 255, 381n38, 381n42
land tenure principles (1618) 61
landholding: African-American, historical significance of 182–6; concentration of 79, 94, 166–7, 174; desire to break up 366n35; landholders with and without bond-laborers 167–8; taxation on 153, 364–5n16, 366nn35–6
landless: disfranchising of 153, one-fourth of freemen 208
landlords, absentee 322nn59–61
landownership: African-American 184–6; concentration 94, 174; elite 163; by less than 50 percent of white males 247, 382n53; manorial 323n67; Virginia Company inducement to poor in England 54
Las Casas, Bartolomé de 4, 9, 31, 33, 300n10; proposal for using Negro slaves 303n69, 313n12, 313n16; role in development of Asiento 300n8
Lauber, Almon Wheeler 37–40, 316n68, 316–7n80, 318n122
Lawes Divine, Morall, and Martiall 55, 75
Lawnes Creek Mutiny 169, 210
laws: against African-Americans 187–8, against African-American women 161; against marriage 341n85; against miscegenation 351n96; against mating of English and Negroes 251; allow Virginia and Maryland to profit on sale and exploitation of laborers 124; bastardy 129–35, 341n80; deficiency 228–30, 240, 252–3, 379n10; deliberately calculated to undercut rights of black workers 362n103; descent through the mother 134, 350n72; Dutch 338n85; for apprehension of runaways 198; foreshadowing lifetime hereditary bond-servitude 172, negation of 178; Gooch on 242, 249–50, 379–80n19; Maryland 341n89; Pass laws (1643 and 1663) 135; Penal 197, 230; prohibiting gross abuse of "English Servant or Slave" 346n183; racial oppression in laws against free African-Americans 250; reduction of tenants and wage-laborers to chattel bond-servants negating previous 178; related to sex 312n101; revision of Virginia's 272–4; requiring owners to prevent bond-laborers

from leaving 152–3; slave 316n72. *See also* Statute of Artificers
leaseholders, eviction proof 223
Leeward Islands 228–9, 231, 233, 374n28
"liberties, franchises, and immunities"/ "liberties, rights, and immunities" 51, 84, 333n24
liberty: "and equality" 384n98; presumption of 248
Logan, Rayford W. 38
London Common Council 65
Long, Edward 235–6
"long sixteenth century" 307n26
Lords of Trade and Plantations 221, 241, 273
Louis IV, king of France 7, 212
Louisiana 42
Ludwell, Philip 211–12
Ludwell, Thomas 165, 209–10, 366n41
Lunenberg County 257

McCormac, E. I. 267–8
Machiavelli, N. 248
Madison, James 255, 380n23
Maguana people 31
"maids-for-wives" 66–70, 325n118, 325n121
Main, Gloria 255
Main, Jackson Turner 247, 255, 382nn52–3
male supremacy: cases related to "defiant solace" 158–61, to "fornication" and denial of right of self-defense 250–51, 312n101; fundamental premise of Anglo-American colonial life as in England 158; as instrument of ruling-class social control 29, 310n85; and male privilege 311–12n99; and rape 146–51, 312n101; resistance to 347n4; special oppression of women 146–7. *See also* gender oppression
Mao Tse-tung 39
maroons 261–2, 303n66: in Jamaica 225–7, 232, 235, 237, 261
marriage: of bond-laborers 350n67; as defense against bastardy 29, 341n80; denial of 24, 128–30, 340–1n76; difference between villein and lifetime hereditary bond-laborer in Virginia regarding 312n101; intermarriage 129, 134, 343n126, 359n40, penalty for 310n84; laws against 341n85; "maids-for-wives" 64, 66–9; if master consents woman bond-laborer freed by 341n77; relative frequency of 181; "slaves incapable of" 289; and social mobility 181–2
Marvell, Andrew 213
Marx, Karl 347n200: and Engels "bourgeoisie … revolutionizing the instruments of production and thereby the relations of production" 354–5n51; "market principles" and "naked self-interest," 362n106
Maryland: analysis of estate inventories 227, 246–7; Archives of 125; Bacon suggests

extending Rebellion to 215; bond-servitude in 267–8; class differentiation in 246, 381n42; debt 166; early settlement 3; estate size 227; European immigrants 119; forms of oppression in 127–8, 131–4, 136, 143; governor 170; Indians and runaways 153–4, 318n111; involuntary laborers brought to 120, 337n10; law allows profit on sale and exploitation of laborers 124; law prohibiting gross abuse of "English Servant or Slave" 346n183; mortality rates 345–6n180, 387n11; Negroes slaves for life in 383n63; pass law (1671) 135; productivity 325n110, 339–40n52; population of 371n124; Provincial Court 190, 251; rebellion 153; and runaways 226; social control system 242–3, 251; status of African-Americans in 177–99, 177, 179, 3718n24; statute of 1639 130; tenants in 104; tithables 371n124; tobacco prices 324n94, 325n111, fall of 69, 171; "white" servant guarantees 383n63; women 371n124

Massachusetts 37, 41, 356n72

Menard, Russell R.: apology for bond-labor system 268; bond-laborer statistics 168; doesn't take into account "racial quotas" and "deficiency laws" 356n10; farm prices 353n22; inflow of immigrant laborers 346n180; life expectancy gap between immigrant Marylanders and New England-born 346n180, 387n11; questions Morgan's assumptions 255; sex ratios 69; tobacco prices 324n94, 325n111, 353n22; tobacco worker productivity rates 140, 325n110, 339–40n52

Mennonites 361n82

mercantilists 170–71

mercenaries: former English, employed in Virginia 75, 320–1n23; Spanish 4

Mestizos 318n122

Metacom ("King Philip") 40; Metacom's War 317n90, 317n93

Mexicans 385n118

Mexico: Aztec Empire 313n20; Basin 32, 313n17; *caciques* 313n22, 317n89, as principle social control buffer in 33; class-differentiated sedentary society 302n45; *encomienda* and *repartimiento* 7, 39, 301n41, *encomienda* and *hacienda* forms of labor never arose in Chesapeake 314n51; liberation struggles in 303n66; maroons in 261; population of 313n19, reduction of 7, 39; social control in 32–3; Spanish in 7, 30; slave insurrections in 261

middle class 246, 381n35, 381n40: fostered by English bourgeoisie 17

Middle Passage 355n58

Middlesex County110–13, 219

migration 9, 42, 258. *See also* emigration; immigration

military: anti-Indian army 210; dictatorship 75; English, in British West Indies 231–2, 235; first ineffective in Virginia 109; regime 32, 36; "tenants" 229–30

militia: free African-Americans excluded from in Virginia 250; freedmen: included in Barbados 242, required to serve in Jamaica 235; in British West Indies 228–9; European, in Jamaica 229; incompetent, in Virginia 164; "military tenants" and acquired status as "whites" 229–30; special detachments known as "slave patrol" 252

ministers 165, 337n7, 341n78, 341n84

missions 314n43

mita laborers 7, 33, 39, 302n43

Mohicans 317n90, 317n93

monasteries, dissolution of 11

Monmouth rebellion (1685) 229

monoculture: barriers to development of yeomanry 226; and dependence upon export markets 174; and diversification 354–5n51, economy based on 178; and engrossment of land 223; and intense supervision 140; and lack of viable social control 165; society shaped by 165–8. *See also* tobacco

Moors 5, 8

moradores 34, 39

Morgan, Edmund S.: author indebted to 327–8n24, 364n7; blames capitalists for hardships 125; finds "boom" metaphor questionable 331n125; challenges *"quid pro quo"* rationale of chattel bond-servitude for transportation 101, 333n28; concentration of engrossment of laborers by plantation elite 95, 332n136; contradictions between few rich and common people 327–8n24; deliberate ruling-class manipulation for social control 248–9, 382n58, 383n80; disparages bond-laborers aptitude for rebellion 220, 367n58; on lack of intermediate social control stratum 164; "Lazy Englishman" of 340n53; limited-term bond-servitude prepared way for lifetime bond-servitude 268; on monocultural economy 345n170; mortality rate among new arrivals 345–6n180; "Ordeal of Colonial Virginia" 173; "paradox thesis" 254–6, rests on assumption that "the mass of white Virginians were becoming landowners" and small planters prospered giving "sense of common identity based on common interest" 254, critique of 254–5; population figures 166, 185, 330n82, 353n27; trade of victuals for first African workers inconsistent with food shortage, consistent with reducing labor costs by oversupply of laborers 81; on Sandys sending ill-provisioned laborers to Virginia 332n138; tobacco prices 353n22; Virginia's transformation 240, and criticism of 240–41;

yeoman 381n36; "white" assumption of 384n98
moriscos 5
Morris, Richard B. 125, 143, 253, 267–9, 346n186
mortality rate: engagés 301n35; England 304n75, 305n5, 339n41; Maryland 345–6n180, 387n11; Mexico and Peru 39; New England 387n11; St. Domingue 3, 7; Virginia 38, 76, 178, 339n41, 345–6n180
Moryson, Francis 164, 366n41, 370n100: on hanging of Bacon's rebels 216, 370n104; on number of rebels 210–11
Mousehold Heath (1549) 96, 192
mulattoes: abuse of 346n183; 234–5, 346–7n188; act concerning 241–2, 250–1; contrasting role in Caribbean and Virginia 238, 380n22; in English jail recruited for bondage in Virginia 360n74

"nadir" 38
naïf 311n89
Nanticoke Indians plot 358n36
Narragansetts 35
Nash, Gary B. 37, 43, 240, 379n9
Nat Turner's Rebellion 369–70n97, 384n94
Natchez 317n93
"nativus" 311n89
"natural racism" thesis 254, 323n67, 379n10
Navigation Acts 169–71, 199, 203, 206, 364n14
Negro Exodus of 1879 258, 312n101
"Negroes." See African; African-Americans; Afro-Caribbeans
Nevis 231, 372n2, 374–5n42; Assembly (1701) 229, 374–5n42, 375n56
New Deal 258–9
New England 17, 40, 105, 174–6, 268, 354n72: comparison with Virginia 69–70, 173–6, 345–6n180, 356n72; Indians 35, 36, genocidal policy toward 355n64
New Kent County 219
Niccolls, Thomas 68, 88
Nicholas, Francis 218
Nicholls, George 25
Nicholson, Governor Francis 119, 244, 273, 338n25, 348n24
North Carolina (former Albemarle) 37, 153, 170–71, 215
Northampton County 144, 157, 180, 184, 358n22
Northern Neck 104, 382n52
Northey, Sir Edward 273, 374–5n42
Northumberland County Court 195–6
Notley, Governor Thomas 221–2, 239
Nott, Governor 273
Nuce, Captain Thomas 70, 72–4, 93, 99, 326n156
Nugent, Nell 182, 186

Occaneechee 204

Oglethorpe, General 42, 354–5n51
Opechancanough 36, 84–5, 87, 90–91, 206
origin of racial oppression 153, 195, 204, 253
origin of racial slavery debate 148, 177
Overseers of the Poor 18, 19, 24–6; "white" 253

palenques 261–2
Palmares 199, 262
Pamunkey 204, 206
Panama 261–2
paradox thesis 254–6, 335n43
"particular plantations" 58–9
partus sequitur patrem 195, 197
partus sequitur ventrem 134, 197, 350n72
pass laws 135
passage: cost of 101–2; fiction of "debt" for 102
patents 78, 121, 174, 335n45, 338n25: and African-American landholding 182–3; and extreme land engrossment 166; mentions "heires and Assigns" 98
patriarchy 146–7, 197. See also male supremacy
patrols 252, 384n85
paupers 24–6, 307n25
"peculiar institution": peculiarity of system in "control" aspect 12–13; white racial oppression and racial slavery as 3
Penal Laws 197, 230
Penalties 57, 69, 334n37
"pencons" 93, 326n160–61
peonage 301n41
Pequots 35; Pequot War (1636–7) 37
Pernambuco 262, 373n9
Peru 7, 30, 32–4, 39, 302n45, 313n10, 314n30, 314n51, 317n89
Pétion, Alexandre 10
Petty, Sir William 271, 327n2, 357n17
"petty treason" 150
Phillips, Ulrich Bonnell 140, 317n94, 323n67, 383n79
Pilgrimage of Grace (1536) 15, 28, 96, 310n87, 311n90
Pinckard, George 235–6, 378n116
Piscataway Indians 318n111
plague 15, 263, 271, 386n1
plantation bourgeoisie: English 223–4; French 6–7; resistance to concessions to "free coloreds" 238; Spain and Portugal 3–5. See also Anglo-American plantation bourgeoisie
plantation labor: in the Americas 3–4, 6–13. See also African bond-laborers; African-American bond-laborers; bond-labor; European-American bond-laborers
Plantation of Ulster: 336n58
plantations: company selling lands for 60; large 174; non-company 60; large 174; "plantation" given new meaning 223–4; three southern system 323n67
Planters 53–4
plots: Accomack County 155, 350n51;

African-American and European-American 154–7, 242, (1722) African-American bond-laborers 29, 244, and "Free Negros & Mulattos" 242; bond-laborers 148–62,155–6, 224, 344n156; Gloucester County 152–3, 219, 358n36, 371n31; in Jamaica 225, 232, 237, 375n46, 379n12; Nanticoke 358n36; Poplar Spring 152; in 1663 197

Plymouth 3, 41

Pocahontas 59, 84, 322n65

poll tax 101, 364–5n16, 366nn35–6

Poor Law (1601) 24–6, 133

Poor Relief 25–6

population: African in Europe 8; Americas 8–9; Barbados 38, 228–9; British West Indies 38–9; Central Andes, 302n44; Cuba, 7; density in Barbados, Jamaica, and Virginia 226–7; European in the Americas 232–3, 376n87; England 11, 270–1, 304nn77–9, 307n25; Hispaniola 7, 313n10; Holland 5; Indian 7, 315n48; Mexico 7, 302n42, 313n19, 314n31; Peru 7; Portugal 313n10; South Carolina 317n82; Spain 5; Virginia 76, 88–9, 218, 330n82, 330n91, 353n23, 373n22, 381n39, in 1622 85, 329n54, 332n136; Wales 270; "white" 381n39

Portugal: capitalists 39; colonization differs from England 11; comparison with Hispaniola 313n10; interest in Africa 4; labor-supply problem 3–5; looked to native laborers 7; plantation owners in Brazil 34; received captive Indian bond-laborers 40; turn to African labor 8

Pory, John 81, 95, 324n97, 325n110

Powhatans 35–6, 84, 312n3: uprising 101, 328n39

prices: bond-laborers 121, 338n22, 355n57, 357n17, 359n43; corn 331n131; food 138; grain 10; Irish men 357n17; laborers 138, 340n67; lifetime bond-laborers 172, 199; Negro men 357n17; tobacco 63–4, 89, 92, 173, 203, 217–18, 325n112, 340n67, 344–5n160, 345n170, 353n22, 359n55; trade goods 316n62; wheat 331n125; wool 10

Prince George's County 105

prisoners: English former, in Barbados 229, 375n46; Irish 64; mulatto 360n74; political 120; Scotch 337n9; shipped into exile 324n101; transported to Virginia 64–5, 120, 360n74

"privatizing" 306n18

privileges: anomalous 249; "brown" 238; male, as indispensible element of bourgeois social control 29; yeoman 19, 24. See also racial privileges; "white-skin privileges"

Privy Council 64–5, 100, 221

production: capitalist 175; costs 63; forces 77; instruments of 354–5n51; relations of 53–5, 58, 69, 166, 354–5n51, transformation of 106; simple commodity 175, 356nn73–4;

tobacco 124, 133, 325nn110–11, 354–5n51, 359n47; transformation of 51, 106

profit: addiction to 49–74 passim; blind drive for 19; in bond-servant trade 121; bourgeois class and tendency of rate to fall 63; of Chesapeake bourgeoisie 352–3n21, 354–5n51; expected 89; and intermediate bond-servitude forms 64–9; inviolable principle 171; profit-making pressure 89; and overproduction crisis 62–3; plantation owners desire for and lifetime hereditary servitude 196; rate of 223, 354–5n51; sex ratio and economic base 69–70; tenantry and wage labor 70–4; tendency of the rate of, to fall 63; tobacco 323n67, 352–3n21

proletarians 11, 13, 75–6, 96, 124

Providence Island 178–9, 197, 299n2, 299n67, 357n13

Puerto Rico 31–2, 301n40

Punch, John 154, 178–80, 189–90

Pungoteague Creek 181

punishment: of African-American runaways 186; cut off ears 346n183; "ducking stool" 341–2n93; imposed by plantation bourgeoisie on bond servants 96, 125–47 passim; lashes 341n89; of owner 341–2n93; psychopathic cruelty never invoked 146–7, 347n198; structures 340n72; Virginia laws indicates not an "unthinking decision" 272–4; in West Indies 374–5n42; "white sheet, white rod" 341n89. See also bond-labor; bond-laborers; whipping

Puritans 165, 174, 191–2, 326n139

Quakers 191–2, 232, 317n92, 361n82

"quid pro quo" rationale 101–2, 333n28, 333n30

guilombo 34, 199, 262

quit-rent 335n45

quotas 228–30, 237, 240, 252–3, 379n10

"race, not class," explanations for 240, 258, 378–9n6

"race" consciousness 240

racial oppression: in Anglo-America 14; and Christian principles 360n77; deliberate act by plantation bourgeoisie 242, 274; definition of 177; denial of social mobility of African-Americans 179; did not exist in seventeenth-century tobacco colonies 177; differences in labor supply and control bearing on 3; dominant feature of United States history 256; England's use of European labor and 12; exclusion of free Negroes and "mulattos" from intermediate stratum 241–2, 244, 249; from, to national oppression 236; hallmark of 177, 223, 243; intermediate social control stratum needed 179; in Ireland 14; and landholding 184–6; law directed at African-American women anticipates 187; law prohibiting African-Americans from purchasing Christian bond-servants to promote 198; made to look like promotion to a higher social class 249; Morgan suggest that, was a deliberate decision of ruling class 319–20n11; not in real interest of majority of the people 253; opposed by some elements of propertied classes 193–6; Protestant Ascendancy and 305n1; racial slavery as 195; revision of Virginia laws (1705) and establishment of the "white race" and 272; social mobility rate incompatible with 186; struggle against white-supremacist racial oppression 205; system in Anglo-American continental colonies was a choice 246; white supremacy as 192

racial slavery: fate of Indians under 45; inversion of cause and effect of "white solidarity" and 379n13; labor supply and control and 3; not in interest of majority of people 253; origin 148, 177, "origins" debate 362n103; reduction to chattel status and 99–100, 178; Virginia as pattern-setter 323n67

"racism" 249, 255–6, 351n96

Rainbolt, John C. 331n121, 335n55, 352–3n21, 354n43: on failure of plantation elite to establish social control in seventeenth century 165–6; ruling elite improvises new style of leadership 239–40

Ramsay, Reverend James 235–6, 361n86, 378n114

rape 251, 312n101

Rappahannock (County) 160, 208: militia 207, 366n35

Ratcliffe, John 320–1n23

rebellion: by African-American bond-laborers and descendants 9; Anglo-Caribbean 224–5; different opportunities on "Terra Firma" and "Island Plantations" 314n35; Dutch Wars and doubtful loyalty 168; and dysfunctional social control 149; English bourgeoisie meet, with armed repression 17; fear of, from Barbados to Jamaica 224; Great Rebellion (1381) 15, 19, 102, 263–4; Hispaniola 31; Indians 36; Ket's Rebellion (1549) 16; Lawnes Creek Mutiny 169; Mexico 261; Midland (1607) 16; peasants 15–16, 21, 75, 305–6n6, 307n26; poor planters mutinees 353n23; Monmouth (1685) 229; Nat Turner's 369–70n97, 384n94; Pilgrimage of Grace (1536) 15, 28, 96, 310n87, 311n90; Peru 33; Portuguese in Brazil 373n9; prisoners in 229, 375n46; Puerto Rico 31; revolts 242–3, 307n26; Tupac Amaru as symbol for 33, 314n34; Wat Tyler's 15, 102, 263–4, 386n4. See also Bacon's Rebellion; Barbados; insurrections; Jamaica

repartimiento 7, 39, 301n41

resistance: African-Americans 188; attention given to 9; Indians: in Canada 6, in Hispaniola 313n16, Nanticoke plot 358n36; harboring runaways 157–8; self-activation of bond-laborers 41–3, 148; to poor diet 151–3; runaways and sexual liaisons as 153–7; sexual relations and "defiant solace" as 158–61; suicide and assault as 149–51; throughout Americas 39. See also bond-laborers; insurrections; rebellion

Rogers, James E. Thorold 73, 263–4, 305–6n6

Rolfe, John 56, 59, 109, 321–2n40, 322n65: describes new arrivals as "Negroes," not as "Africans" 304n23; on many complaints against "buying and selling" of tenants 80; on production relations in Virginia (1614–16) 55

Royal Adventurers 198

Royal African Company 171–2, 198–9, 355n55, 355n57

Royal Charter 107

Royal Commissioners 216–17, 370n98, 370n103

royal decree on rootless people (1593) 25

ruling class: contradictory views 106; general interest 132; gentry as 246; and rapid accumulation of capital 173; and social control 372n2

runaways: communities formed by African and African-American communities 261–2; African-Americans 153–8, 349n39, 361–2; special penalty for 187; assistance of free persons 153, former bond-laborers 350n51, planters 163; captors of 340n70, 349n42, 352n8, 352n10, 384n85; Caribbean 235; collaboration between African-American and European-American bond-laborers 153–8; destinations 153, 155; extended length of service for captured 96, 136, 357n18; failure to hunt 163; fear of 245; and Indians 127–8, 153–4, 157–8, 226, 318n11, two-way buffer role under Berkeley 207–8; Jamaica maroons and 226, 261–2; number of cases 153, 158–9; problem 197; and resistance to oppression 149; rewards involving 163–4, 226, 352n8, 352n10; serf 386n3; servant 348n5; Virginia law "for the apprehension of runaways …" 198; women 154–7, 350n51

Russell, John H. 183–4

social safety valve 257–9

St. Christopher 63

St. Domingue 38, 301n31, 380n22, 383n67

St. Eustatius 372n3

St. Kitts (St. Christopher) 231–2, 372nn2–3, 376n62, 380n22

St. Lucia 224, 372n2

St. Vincent 235

San Basilio 262

Sandys, Edwin: on "absurd condition of tenants at halves" 96, 332n148; Alderman Johnson critic of 94; and basis for rise of elite 78; and Butler's report 330nn80–1; and first African-Americans 81, 327n23, 327–8n24; and intermediate bond-servitude forms 64–5, 67, 95; instructions (the "Great Charter") by 49; and need for "apprentices" 95; policy creates oversupply of dependent laborers 332n138; Virginia Company executive 11, 60; and Virginia Company bankruptcy 62

Sandys, George 88, 91, 332n140: accepted payment of bond-labor assignment for debt owed 99, 332n140; and colonists for whom Company had no provisions 86; corn-getting from Indian ventures 91, 330n103

São Tomé 5, 300n11

Sayri, Tupac 33, 314n30

Scots 178–9, 246

self-defense, denial of right of 250–51, 312n101

Seminoles 317nn90–91

serfs 305–6n6

"servants": concentration of, and headright system 95; difference in penalties for failure to fulfill contract in England and Virginia 334n37; encouragement of 367n61; extra servitude 108, 125–7, 150; hired 93; killing a master 150, 348n13; Bacon "proclam'd liberty to" 213; as "merchandize for sale" 108; "our principall wealth consisteth of" (Pory) 324n97; over half of Virginia's settlers 348n5; plot (1663) 197; Royal Instructions on 338n25; "Servant Trade" 119–22; as term for Europeans and European-Americans 228, 337n10; "were sold here upp and down like horses" (Weston) 108

servitors 320–1n23

sex ratios 52, 69–70, 174, 178, 181

sexual relations: assault 347n192; between European-Americans and African-Americans 160–61, 243–4, 351n76; denial of 147, 158–61; exploitation 243; liaisons 153–7, 348n5, 351n76

Seymour, John 171

Sherwood, William 208–9

Sioux (Great Plains) 385n116

"six parts of seven at least, are Poore, Endebted, Discontented, and Armed" (Berkeley) 176

skilled trades, Negroes barred from 379n10

Slav: as word for "slave" 8

slavery: absent in early Virginia 357n15; and class struggle 357n6; consolidation act 374n41; ending trade would benefit bond-laborers 361n86; Georgia exclusion 354–5n51; Medieval European 8, 302n47; patrol 252. See also chattel bond-servitude; laws

"slaves": became customary to call African lifetime bond-laborers 228; for life 383n63; lack of rights regarding sex 312n101; revolts 224–5, fear of 303n63; "Sold ... like a damd slave" (Best) 107; used against Indians 318n115

Smith, Abbot Emerson 338n22, 342n101: on bond-servitude in all Anglo-American colonies 267, 386n7; "first ... indenture" 72; "four or five years bondage was more than they justly owed for ... transport" 102, 333n32; and "germ" theory 319n5; stimulus for bond servant trade not desire to emigrate but profit-making needs of tobacco business 119, 336n1; survey of outlawing of family life among bond-servants 340–1n76; thesis on chattel bond-servitude 173, 335n53, 355n63

Smith, Adam 105

Smith, Captain John 31, 52, 203, 312n3, 300–1n23: denounced buying and selling of workers 109, 173; prediction of "misery" 173, 336n80; as a slave in Turkey 313n8

Smith, John (bond-laborer) 173, 341n78

Smith, Henry 131, 141, 145–6, 161, 347n192

Smith, Robert 209–10

Smith, Thomas 192, 304

social classes: five in 1622 in Virginia 93, as in England 331n124; Gloucestershire contrasted with Virginia after massacre of tenantry 333n26

social control: deliberately fostering a lower-middle-class stratum 18; differences between Anglo-Caribbean and Anglo-America 223–4; operative principles for stable civil society based on racial oppression 375n54; problem enters new context 109; rejection of England's pattern in sixteenth century 14; where intermediate buffer social control stratum becomes dysfunctional rebellion breaks through 149

social control in the Americas 30–32, 36, 39–45, 313n10

social control in Anglo-American plantation colonies: absence of 163–76, 219–20; buffer, intermediate stratum 32; class struggle and resistance to 9; conditions favorable to maintenance of, in interest of tobacco bourgeoisie 16–17, 76–8, 169; continental-vs.-insular factor 314n35; "control" aspect rather than "supply" aspect decisive for decline of Indian enslavement 41; crisis of and Bacon's Rebellion 166; deference and reverence deficit 164–5; differences with Anglo-Caribbean 223–4, 238, 372n2; different from England 14, 109; Dutch Wars and insurrection 168–9, 171, 197, 199; failure to establish under tobacco monocultural economy 165–6; free Negroes and "mulattos" excluded from 240–3, included in 242–3; invention of the "white race" social control formation a deliberate course taken by ruling plantation bourgeoisie 236, 251, 255, 274; lack of "capacity to command" 172; male privilege and 29; military regime in early Virginia 109; need to maintain 3, 75; "peculiarity" of 12, 14; plantation bourgeoisie's deliberate decision to destroy tenants 109, achieved social control necessary for capital accumulation based on chattel bond-servitude 3, 75, 198, 240, disregarded forty-shilling freehold yeomanry concept 109; problems 109, 198; "race consciousness" supersedes class consciousness as key 240; ruling class social control and choice of system of racial oppression 165, 231, 246; social distinctions and 242–3, denial of 177; social gap and 259; social instability, means to combat 169–73; social mobility and 181–2, 185–6, 248–9, 258, 366n33, vs. counterfeit of 248–9; unfeasibility of use of English army 220–2; in Virginia 168–9; white-skin privileges "incubus" that paralyzed will of European-American laborers and 259

social control in the Anglo-Caribbean: abortion of "white race" system in 223–38 *passim*; Afro-Caribbean majorities 232–4, as middle class 234–8; factors shaping 226–38, 372n2, 373n21; free Negroes and "mulattos" role in 242–3; Irish bond-laborers and complications 230–31; Jamaican maroons 225–6; land area limits and capital costs 226–30; military and naval enforcement 231–2; problem in British West Indies 224–6; social contact prohibited 375n56

social control in England: armed repression 17; balance of class policy and drive for maximum immediate profit 19–24; defeat of rebel forces 307n26; deliberate ruling class decision to preserve portion of peasants as petit bourgeois yeomanry ("forty-shilling freeholder") 17–19, 109; male domination and 26–9; mercenaries used absent standing army 17; Poor Law as 24–6; propertyless classes and 19, 29; slavery law (1547) exceeded grasp as system of social control 21–2; yeoman and 19, 109

social control and Euro-Indian relations: Brazil 33–4, 314n45; "buffer" stratum absent 164, ambivalence of 43–4; English buying and selling Indian captives 36–7; Haiti, Cuba, and Puerto Rico 31–2; Mexico and Peru 32–3; native sources of plantation bond-labor, abandonment of 37–44; Powhatans of Virginia 35–6; resistance to enslavement 40–43; "unfitness" sour-grapes rationale 38–40; white supremacy and 44–5

social status: African-Americans 177–99 *passim*, indeterminate 178; normal in seventeenth century 182; exclusion of free African-Americans from intermediate stratum corollary of "white" identity as mark of 249; 1622 320n233

social structure: difference between Anglo-Caribbean and continental Anglo-America 372n2; stratified, class differentiated 301n45, 313n10; importance of claims on Company-period inheritances to 331n121; tripartite 372n2; unstratified 301n45

solidarity disappearance of 347n4, in Bacon's Rebellion 240

South Carolina: absence of *cassique* class in 44, 317n89; Assembly depends on Indian buffer tribes 43; European-American bond-laborers recruited into militia and "slave patrol" 252; and Georgia 232; Indian bond-laborers and enslavement 36–7, 39–40, 42–4, 317n89; population of 317n82; preamble to slave law 316n72; "white" volunteers from Virginia 318n115; and why non-slaveholders support racial slavery 249; white workers demand exclusion of African-Americans from trades 253

Southampton, Earl of 67

Southampton Hundred 93, 331n121

Southern Homestead Act 258, 377n103

Spain: colonization differs from England's 11; emigration policy: laborers not going to America 4–5, *moriscos* ineligible 5, special permission required 300n9; England aligned against 230; expulsion of Moors 5; King Charles I begins *Asiento* (1518) 8; population decline 5; use of foreign mercenaries 4

Spanish colonial rule: access to gold and silver 4, declines, turn to agriculture 30; accessibility of some natives and genocidal labor policy 7; beheading of Tupac Amaru 314n34; Bolivar seeks to break from 10, 299n5, 312n3; imposed forced labor on Indians 31, 39; inaccessibility to some natives due to resistance 8; Indian captives from Anglo-America bond-laborers in West Indies 40; social control Hispaniola, Cuba, and Puerto Rico no intermediate social stratum 31–2; social control Mexico and Peru adapt pre-existing structure and preserve buffer function for *caciques* 31–2; tobacco from, sent to England 324n92

Speed, John 111

Spencer, Nicholas 217, 221

"Spirits" 120–21, 338nn14–15

Spotswood, Alexander 219, 240, 244–5

squatters 257

St. Domingue 9, 38, 301n31

starvation 143, 149, 331n125, 345–6n188

Statute of Artificers 1563 (5 Eliz. 4, 1563) 28, 107–8, 338n58: basic English master-servant law for over 250 years 22–4; in direction

of tenantry and wage laborer 102; had to be
overthrown for lifetime hereditary chattel
bondage 51; unmarried, unpropertied
women lowest labor status under 28
Statute of Laborers (1350) 263–4, 305n5,
309n61, 309n63, 309n65
Stephens, Alexander 316n72
stratification: Anglo-American continental
bourgeoisie faced "Brazilian" problem of
continental people without *cacique* class
35–6; 315n47
sugar 9, 224, 226–7, 372n1
suicide 149–51, 348n11
Summers, George W.: "fold to his bosom the
adder that stings" 385n115
supplies: dependence of colonies on England for
77–8, 86; shortage of 327–8n24
Surry County 150, 167, 182–3, 339n49,
365–6n31; plots 164, 169, 219, 244
Susquehannock 204, 365n17

Tawney, R. H. 15, 304n74, 305n3
technological advance 324n97: superiority
314n52
tenants: brought to Bermuda 328n37; Captain
Nuce's plan to reduce to servants 70–74;
in Chesapeake 246–7, 256–7, 384–5n11;
clearing land cheaper with in eighteenth
century, cheaper with bond-laborers in
seventeenth century 105; decision to destroy
109; definition of and terms of service
(1618) 61; differences of dependence on in
Ulster and in English colonies in America
223; and laborers majority of English
in Virginia (1616) 56; lateral mobility
to "frontier" 256–7; massacre of 75–96,
109, 239, 333n26; military 230; number
of 84, 104, 334n46, majority of colony
56; overthrow of 239; productivity of 94,
331n125; and poor whites 255; reduced
to chattel bond-servants 74–5, 93, 178,
326n156; renting out of 79–84; Scots in
Ulster (seventeenth century) 246; "slaves"
did not cause decline of yeomen 335n48;
tenant class rejected from standpoint of
making profit 109; tenants-at-halves typical
72, 93; tenants-at-will 257; terms of 61,
70–71, 79–80; transfer of 80; without
work 93
testamentary rights 249, 382–3n62
testimony, denial of and loophole 380n21
textiles 10–11
"they would have destroyed me …" (Grantham)
369m93
tithables: bond-laborers included 367n57;
European-American women excluded
343n118; free African-American women
included 187, 190, 359n40, 367n57; Indian
women included 367n57; number of 185,
218, 370–1n117, 371n124

Titu Yupanqui 33
"to fix a perpetual brand on Free Negros &
Mulattos" (Gooch) 242, 244
"too few free poor to matter" (Morgan) 255
"too few" laboring class Europeans in West
Indies, "too many" in continental colonies
244
tobacco: addiction 63–4; "Boom" 60, 331n125;
capitalist profiteering on 345n170; contract
62; crisis of overproduction 62–3, 169,
217, 324n94, 374n28; cultivation 335n54;
discovery of 322n41; diversification 169,
175, 324n94, 354n43, 354nn50–1, frustrated
335n55, 352–3n21, 354–5n51; duties
collected in England 212; first shipment
321–2n40; historical importance 56, 140;
intense supervision 140; king gets one-third
of crop 324n91; limitations on 324n93,
354–5n51; Maryland 323n67; and "misery"
336n80; as money 323n67; monoculture
61, 171, 175, 178, 355n59, Berkeley critic
of 169, Chesapeake colonies committed
to 315n51; shapes society 165–8; party
62; plantations and bond-labor 335n53;
planter elite enrichment and planters' debt
166; price of 60, 169, 324nn91–2, 324n94,
342nn103–4, 166, declining prices of 97,
217, 345n170; production 60, 133, 170,
324n97, 338n50, 354–5n51; restriction of
planting 83; revenue, loss of 367–8n66;
riots, tobacco-cutting (1682) 219–21; and
small farms 335n54; South Carolina 323n67;
Spanish-produced 324n91; stringing
324n97; Virginia 321–2n40, 323n67, 336n59
transportation: costs of laborers 99, 101–2, 121,
342n103; of indigent prohibited by Louis
XIV 7
Treaty of Breda (1667) 171, 197–8, 355n53
Trelawney Town treaty (1738–39) 225, 235
Trevelyan, G.M. 270
Trinidad 321–2n40, 372n2, 374n35, 377–8n111
Tucker, Captain William 91, 99, 330n103
Tupac Amaru 23, 314n34
Turner, Frederick Jackson 257–9, 385n118,
385n123
Turner, Nat, 385n115
Tuscaroras 35, 317n92, 318n11
Twain, Mark 39
Tyler, Lyon G. 240
Tyrone War (1594–1603) 14, 84, 364n75,
320–1n23, 330n95

Ulster/America analogies: plantation 64, 223;
Scots 223
"unthinking decision" 12, 175, 242, 305n89:
Jordan and 101, 178, 362n103, 383n80

Vagrancy Act of 1547: anti-"vagabond"
enslavement of unemployed laborers 20–24;
model for Barbadian slave code 308–6n45;

not racial oppression 178; resistance to 21, 308n55; retreat from 180; repeal 25; special disability on women 27–9

vagrancy/vagabonds 11, 20–21, 23–5, 65

"venting" surplus of "necessitous people" 11

Verlinden, Charles 302n47

"villein" 311n89, 312n101

Virginia Assembly: Captain Nuce's plan to 72–4; denial of equal rights to African-Americans 161; deliberate conferring of privileges 248–50; discards English common law of descent through the father 134; domestic source of bond-labor 122–3; established under "Great Charter" (1618) 53; forms of oppression 126, 130, 134, 143; free African-Americans denied role in intermediate social control stratum 242–3; percent bond-laborers to landholders 374n33; mark-up on goods from England 63; population of 371n124, 373n22; and rebellion 150, 152, 213; tithables 371n124; and Elizabeth Key case 195; voting 241–2

Virginia Colony: abuse of rights 95; at least 60 percent of adult white men non-owners of bond-labor 256; authorized to impose levies 364–5n16; Bacon's Rebellion (1676) and 206–7, 209–10, 314n34; breech in ranks of ruling elite 206; buying and selling of Indians 36–7; and Captain Nuce's proposal 93; colonists abandonment of plantations 90; colonists lack preponderance of military force 35, 315n53, 316nn53–54; colony-centered position 370n102; colony elite: description of 163–4, 364n13, desire for capitalism based on chattel bond-servitude and 239, emergence of 78–9, 352n15, 206, division in ranks of 364n12, 94–5, engrossment of land by 226, extreme economic pressure on laborers deliberately exploited by 95–6, factions 206, 210, number of 163, small capacity to command 171–2; comparison with Maryland and South Carolina 323n67; comparison with New England 173–6, sex ratio comparison 69–70; as continental colony 35; contract tenants 70–71; contradiction between few rich and common people 327–8n24; contrast with Caribbean 238, 314n35, 380n22; corn planting restriction 90–91; counties 114–15, 353n25, 365–6n31, 366n33, 366–7n47; county courts 163, 349n36, 352n4; debts in 353n28; decentralization of power 206; dependence on England for supplies 77–8, 86; dependent upon trade with Indians 35; desperate poverty 353n23; division of former tenants 100; emancipation by Quakers 252, by will 250; emigrants to 70–71, 332n138; English: immigrants 69, laborers 339n53, capitalists oppose diversification in 217, settlement in 3,

227; establishment 30, 51, 312n1, 323n67; exploitation of presumption of bondage 135–7; fears of 169; "featherbedding" 252; five chieftains murdered 365n17; flight to Indians 77; forms of oppression 136–7; general conditions 171, 174, 338n27, that shaped social control policy 226–8; governors of 112–13, 320–1n23; grain production in 354–5n51; historical resources 182, 184, 275–6, 338n43, 349n26, 363n2, 363n4; hunting ban 90; and ill-provisioned laborers 106; impoverishment 178, 217; intermarriage 359n40; Irish men to be sold as slaves in 357n17; labor conforming to English system 52; laboring people's difficulty 95–6, 106; laborers, shortage of 332n147; lack of effective intermediate buffer social control stratum 219–20, 245; land allocation 93; laws against mating of English and Negroes 251; Maroon potential in 363n121; master-servant relationships 269; militia 164; and Navigation Acts 206; non-free adults 330n91; officers 78–9; as pattern-setter for institution of racial slavery 323n67; poor majority unable to buy bond-laborers 199; population density 226–7; preachers prevented from coming to Virginia 361n90; procure large tracts of land 167; proposal on "changing tenants to servants" 106; punishment 272–3; renting out tenants 81–2, 95; similarity to Brazil 35; Sioux of Great Plains subdued by descendants of 385n116; social control problem 221; survival in 38; tenants 94–6; threat of Dutch invasion and insurrection 168–9; Tidewater 226–7; tobacco as money in 92, 323n67; wealthy newcomers 206; "white" volunteers for South Carolina 318n115. See also Chesapeake

Virginia Colony Council 49, 63, 75, 205, 359n43: divides up former Company tenants among themselves 100; and Governor consider moving across Chesapeake (1622) 328n47; members participate in revising law (of 1705) with provisions relative to establishment of racial oppression and "white race" 272; proposal from, for "changing tenants to servants" develops into prevailing policy of Anglo-American plantation bourgeoisie 106

Virginia Company: to "assign" 98–100, no provision for 71; bankruptcy of 62; a capitalist failure 60; Charters (1606) 49, 51, (1609) 49–51, 53, 59, (1612) 49–51, 57–8; Committee on Petitions 107; competition with plantations for labor and capital 61; condemned "renting out of tenants" 81; contradictory views 106; corn planting restriction 90–91; contrasting treatment of Argall and Yeardley 82–3; end of 63,

326n151; expects investors to make 25 percent profit 89; Francis Bacon member of 176; labor relationships (1616) under 55; reports much corn, but shortage of laborers (1624) 332n147; future in commodity production 30; and Governor Argall 57–8, 82; homeless boys and girls 65; Indian captives 41; Indian uprising as death blow to 85; intermediate bond-servitude forms 64–6, 67–8; internal factional disputes 50; investors 30; laborers 56; landholding 226–7; laws, revision of 272–4; liquidation 100; military force 314n52, regime 109; officers: diverting tenants to private use 61, Company land apportioned among 78–9; opposed to chattelization 107; periods of 51–63, 319n1, 319n3, 328–9n24: First (1607–10) 51–2, Second (1610–18) 53–60; Third (1619–24) 60–63; pledge to send servants instead of tenants as seed of "plantation of bondage" 101; quest for settlers 54; statuses of bond-laborer, apprentice, and "white servitude" 324n38; tenants 83, 94; transport of emigrants 70

Virginia General Assembly 49, 75, 163, 352n10, 364n16: authorizes apprehending and selling Indians 36–7; disposition to deny equal rights to African-Americans 161; Elizabeth Key case 195–8, withdraws franchise from propertyless "freemen" 216

Virginia General Court: abuse of rights of laboring people exploited by 95; authorizes option to buy bond-laborer 99; chattel bond-servitude not outgrowth of apprenticeship, Court member Mason explains apprentice not assignable 103; crass partiality of, put tenants at extreme disadvantage 79; Elizabeth Key case 195–8; extreme economic pressure on laborers deliberately exploited by 95–6; imposes extended time on runaways 108, 126; John Punch case 178–80, 189; part of governance of colony 75, 163; and runaways 154; says Indians were free 361n94; woman brought to be wife became servant of former fiancé 68

Virginia Governor 163–4, 206, 329n47, 329n53, 364n16: instructed not to have laborers diverted from tobacco (1705) 170; embraced Captain Nuce's proposal 93; privilege of trading with Indians restricted to appointees of 209

Virginia House of Burgesses 93, 163, 206–7, 364–5n16, 381n39: members involved in revising law (of 1705) relative to establishment of racial oppression and "white race" 272; and Bacon's Rebellion 209–10; legislation for anti-Indian army 210; and social instability 218–19; and status of African-Americans 184

"volatile society" 239

voting: denial of 244, 251; property qualifications 229; rights 242, 248, 352n5, 364–5n16

wage-labor 22–4, 70–74: wage-laborers 6–7, 263, 307n26

wages: absence of 99; comparative 73; decline in real 309n71; downward trend of real 259; high 173; of labor 22–4, 70–74, 263; levels 171, 308n40; right to be paid under Poor Law 26

Wampanoags 35, 40, 317n93

War of Devolution (1666–7) 231

War of the League of Augsburg 217, 270, 376n58, 380n22

Warre, Governor de la 52, 320–1n23

Warwick 67

Washburn, Wilcomb E. 204, 368n67: defends Berkeley 370n102; denies class conflict role and emphasizes hostility to Indians; 353n23; ignores bond-laborers 363n4, 365n17

water suffocation 341–2n93

Waterhouse, Edward 30, 312n3

Wat Tyler's Rebellion (1381): historians on 305–6n6, 307n26; laboring classes and 102; peasant "struck a blow for freedom …" (Thorold Rogers) 263–4, 282–3n6; role in ending feudal order 15; tradition of 84

wealth "consisteth of servants" 95, 324n97; indexes 94–5

Weldon, Captain 79–84, 328n29

Wertenbaker, Thomas J. 67–8: equates yeoman with "middle class" though term originally referred to laboring class in England 245, 356n80, 381n35; competition with unpaid bond-labor "practically destroyed the Virginia yeomanry" 256, 345–6n180, 353n80; findings challenges Morgan's assumption 255; immediate "control of the negroes" put into "the hands of white men of humbler means" (after 1700) 252; prospect of bond-laborer becoming landholder in Virginia at 5 to 6 percent 366n33, 374n33

West, Richard, Attorney-General 240, 244, 248–9, 379n16, 378–80n19

West Indies 354–5n51: Africans purchased by British Army in 377n108, 377–8n111; mulatto in 378n116; rise in demand for wheat 354–5n51; terms "freedman," "freedwoman," "Free black," Negro, "Free colored" and "mulatto" in 377n96; West Indian Regiment 235. *See also* Anglo-Caribbean; British West Indies

West Point 110, 214, 369n92, 369–70n97

Westmoreland County 212

Westo War (1708) 43

whipping 126, 138, 149–50: to death 96, 345–6n188; in England 23, 25; examples of 144, 346–7n188, 347n189; men and women 342n98; resistance to 368n82; for refusing to go to work 349n27; for runaways in John Punch case 357n11; Virginia code (1705) prohibits whipping "a Christian white servant naked" 250; of women 141, 182, for fornication 129–30

"white": assumption 384n98; Christians as 374n41; "consciousness" 244; exclusionism 234, 249; a new term 228; "historian's" bias 204; identity, established 248–9, exclusion of free African-Americans as corollary of 249; "man" and abuse of free black family 383n77, and pursuit of black women 383n75, union with Negro woman 380n24; "man's country" 383n79; "people" 384n98; poor 230, contrast with yeomen 381n35; not looked at objectively 319–20n11; presumption of liberty extended to "white persons and native American Indians" not to African-Americans 339n39; "servitude" 319n5, 333n32, 334n38, 367n59; 60 percent of males in Virginia non-owners of bond-labor 256; "slaves" 374–5n42; "solidarity" and inversion of cause and effect of and racial slavery 379n13; supremacism 255, propagandized in 251; unity, all-class 379n9; "Virginians" as 384n98; volunteers 318n115

"white sheet, white rod" 341n89

"white-skin privileges" 41, 248–9: incubus of 259, system of initiated by plantation bourgeoisie 253

"white race": new all-class, all-European social identity 228–30, 374n39; did not exist and could not have existed in seventeenth-century tobacco colonies 161–2, 177, 215; deliberate course by ruling plantation bourgeoisie 274; identity 204, and exclusion of free Negro 249; Indian labor and 44–5; invention of, and social control 41, 44–5, 226, 274; and presumption of liberty 339n39; privileges 41, 258; and racial oppression in 1705 Act and revisals of Virginia law with provisions relative to establishment of 272–4; social control system 41, 255, and abortion of in West Indies 223–38 passim; solidarity 253; and theories of American History 253–8

white supremacy: civil rights and impending crisis 258–9; deficiency laws 228–30, 240, 252–3, 379n10; development of social and legal structure of 323n67; emancipation of African-Americans 249–50; fate of Indians under 45; frontier-as-social-safety-valve-theory (Turner) and 257–8; and landowners 244; and male supremacy 250–51; mechanics 253; monorail of U.S. history 178; not in real interest of majority of people 253; and paradox thesis 254–6; as racial oppression 192; sexual union between "Whites" and African-Americans

243–4; social control formation 251; social distinction 242–3; social mobility and 223, 248–9; social order and 242–3; and tenancy 256–7; Virginia as pattern-setter 323n67; white frontier 256–7; yeomanry 245–8; "white man's company" 257

"white worker": demand exclusion of Negroes from skilled trades 253; record of period shows no "white worker" component 119

"whiteness," certificates of 230

"whites": acquired status as 230; Christians as 374n41; denied social mobility 257; in Jamaica 232; "perquisites of" 378n129

Williams, Eric E. 50, 368n58

Willoughby, Governor William 231

wives 70: buying of, as "property" inhibited free flow of capital 69; coverture 28, 130, 132, 146–7, 196, 341–2n93; intermarriage 359n40; "maids-for-wives" 66–9

women: European-American not tithable unless "working in the ground" 343n118, 371n124; "feme covert" 28, 196; "feme sole" 310n86; feudal naïf doubly oppressed by class and gender 311n89; hanged 310n87; Jefferson on "breeding women" 380n24; of laboring class compelled to work 24; "maids-for-wives" 66–70, 325n118, 325n121; oppression of 24, 26–9, 128–30, 146–7; on white man and Negro woman 380n24, 383n75, 383n77

women bond-laborers: African-Americans tithable 187, 190, 359n40; denied right to marry 24, 130, 340–1n76, 341n78; double penalty for mating with African-American 158; extra servitude for marrying 311–12n99; freedom for, if allowed to marry 341n77; importation of 69; Maryland European-American crop workers tithable 371n124; mortality rate of 345–6n180; and oaths 342n111; in Pilgrimage of Grace 310n87; sexual liaisons 158–61; shipping of 62; special oppression of 128–30; 35 percent die within five years of landing 345–6n180; in 1624/5 Virginia census 68–9; whipping of 141, 182, 342n98, for fornication 129–30, resistance to whipping 368n82

Woodson, Carter G. 148, 183–4

Worcester, Battle of 337n9

Wyatt, Governor Francis 88, 90–91, 320–1n23, 331n126: "Negro named Brase" assigned to as a "servant" 180; on tenant productivity 331n126; tenants starving, some "rented out" 94; Yeardley's tenants turned over to him 82–3

Yamassees 35, 40, 316n64, 318n115

Yamassee War (1715) 42–4, 84

Yeardley, George 100, 246, 330n103: accused of appropriating tenants for private use 61, 82, 324n102, of having provoked 1622 Indian attack 328–9n43; exchanged victuals for

"20 and odd" African laborers (1619) 81, 327–8n24; and food scarcity 82, 88, 90–91, 95; purchase of "Negroes" 327–8n24; as governor (1619–21) 49–50, 60, 83; and rise of Colony elite 78–9; tenants of Virginia Company assigned to 332n145; mercenary service in Netherlands 320–1n23; violation of tenants' contracts 82; wealth of 328nn32–3, most prosperous person 81

"yeoman": African-Americans barred from ranks of 248; in Anglo-America plantation colonies different than Ulster Scots or English-style 223; category 246; competition with unpaid bond-labor "practically destroyed" in Virginia 256, 345–6n180; deliberately fostered lower-middle-class stratum 17; few former bond-servants 366n33; historians on 381nn35–6, 381nn40–41; Main suggest "yeoman" or "middle" class of 40 percent of adult white male population 246; non-owners of bond-laborers 246; non-yeoman, ruling class induces to settle for counterfeit of social mobility of "white" identity 248–9; privileges 19; as social control stratum missing in Virginia 164, 245; state makes political decision for social control to preserve proportion of peasants to serve in militia and police functions 17–19, 307n29, 307n35; term not found in colonial Virginia and Maryland records 245; understood as intermediate social control category 246; Wertenbaker equates with "middle class" though term originally referred to laboring class in England 245, 381n35

York County 219